THE NEW DICTIONARY OF CATHOLIC SOCIAL THOUGHT

The New Dictionary of Catholic Social Thought

Judith A. Dwyer
Editor

Elizabeth L. Montgomery
Production Editor

A Michael Glazier Book
THE LITURGICAL PRESS
Collegeville, Minnesota

To the memory of my father,
James P. Dwyer

A Michael Glazier Book published by The Liturgical Press.

Cover design by David Manahan, O.S.B. Typography by Graphic Sciences Corporation, Cedar Rapids, Iowa.

1 2 3 4 5 6 7 8 9

Library of Congress Cataloging-in-Publication Data

The New dictionary of Catholic social thought / Judith Dwyer, originating editor.
p. cm.
"A Michael Glazier book."
Includes bibliographical references and index.
ISBN 0-8146-5526-2
1. Sociology, Christian (Catholic)—Encyclopedias. 2. Church and social problems—Catholic Church—Encyclopedias. 3. Catholic Church—Doctrines—Encyclopedias. I. Dwyer, Judith A.
BX1753.N497 1994
261.8'08'822—dc20 94-4264
CIP

CONTENTS

INTRODUCTION

Vatican II's *Pastoral Constitution on the Church in the Modern World* (*Gaudium et spes*) opens with a concept that best captures the dynamic nature of Catholic social thought: "The joy and hope, the grief and anguish of the people of our time, especially of those who are poor or afflicted in any way, are the joy and the hope, the grief and anguish of the followers of Christ as well. Nothing that is genuinely human fails to find an echo in their hearts."

The New Dictionary of Catholic Social Thought, testifying to this deep solidarity that Christians experience with the human race and its history, seeks to present and analyze the major modern social encyclicals, from Leo XIII's *Rerum novarum* to John Paul II's *Centesimus annus*, as well as to inspect central movements, figures, and themes that have been the hallmark of Catholic social thought for over one hundred years.

The New Dictionary of Catholic Social Thought also attempts to indicate the manifold social dimensions of the various moral issues that confront the human community. The dictionary, therefore, addresses such topics as abortion, homosexuality, birth control, and euthanasia, in order to emphasize that no issue is purely "sexual," or "biomedical"; all ethical problems contain social ramifications that must be a vital part of any critical evaluation.

The New Dictionary of Catholic Social Thought has had the support of many people, and without that support the project could not have come to fruition. As editor, I had the privilege of communicating with contributors from throughout the world. Their scholarship and dedication are inspiring, and I am grateful to each one of them for their commitment to this endeavor.

I wish to thank the administration, faculty, and students of Weston School of Theology, Cambridge, Massachusetts, who encouraged this idea from the very beginning. The administration of Villanova University has also been supportive of my attempt to balance my own administrative duties with the completion of this project.

I am deeply grateful to Elizabeth L. Montgomery for copyediting the manuscripts, for directing the elaborate proofing process involved in this project, and for creating the index. Further, I am grateful to Frances Hart, S.S.J., who aided with the preparation of the manuscripts. Finally, I thank Colleen Stiller, production manager of The Liturgical Press, and the staff of The Liturgical Press for their diligent and professional work on this dictionary.

It is my hope that *The New Dictionary of Catholic Social Thought* will serve as a valuable resource for anyone involved in social outreach or connected with the field of ethics. The essays contained in the dictionary testify to the richness of the Catholic heritage. May they engender an enlivened hope for the future, as human hands and hearts and minds struggle to shape a more just and peaceful world.

JUDITH A. DWYER

The New Dictionary of Catholic Social Thought takes its place as a companion volume to *The New Dictionary of Theology*, published in 1987 by Michael Glazier, Inc., and *The New Dictionary of Sacramental Worship* and *The New Dictionary of Catholic Spirituality*, published by The Liturgical Press: Michael Glazier Books in 1990 and 1993 respectively. Also in the series are *The Concise Dictionary of Early Christianity* by Joseph F. Kelly (1992) and *The Liturgical Dictionary of Eastern Christianity* by Peter D. Day (1993), both published by The Liturgical Press: Michael Glazier Books.

E.L.M.

CONTRIBUTORS

Kay Aitchison, Christian Family Movement, Ames, Iowa
Christian Family Movement

Michael E. Allsopp, Creighton University, Omaha, Nebraska
Subsidiarity, Principle of

Frank D. Almade, Incarnation of the Lord Parish, Pittsburgh, Pennsylvania
Just Wage

George M. Anderson, S.J., St. Aloysius Church, Washington, D.C.
Homelessness

Oscar Cole Arnal, Waterloo Lutheran Seminary, Waterloo, Ontario, Canada
Confédération des Travailleurs Catholiques du Canada (1921–1960); Sangnier, Marc (and Sillon); Worker Priests

Steven M. Avella, Marquette University, Milwaukee, Wisconsin
Pius XII

Marcello de C. Azevedo, S.J., Catholic University of Rio de Janerio, Brazil
Base Communities

Robert Barry, O.P., University of Illinois, Champaign-Urbana, Illinois
Thomas Aquinas, Contribution of

Ernest Bartell, C.S.C., Kellogg Institute for International Studies, University of Notre Dame, Notre Dame, Indiana
Goods, Access to; Goods, Distribution of; Greed

Anthony Battaglia, California State University, Long Beach, California
Agnosticism; Atheism; Enlightenment, The (Influence of); Existentialism

Gregory Baum, McGill University, Montreal, Quebec, Canada
Action Libérale Nationale; Laborem Exercens; Politisés Chrétiens

Joseph Cardinal Bernardin, Archdiocese of Chicago, Chicago, Illinois
Arms Race

Vivian Boland, O.P., Dominican House of Studies, Tallaght, Ireland, and Milltown Institute, Dublin, Ireland
Mater et Magistra

Philip Boyle, The Hastings Center, Briarcliff Manor, New York
Mental Health, Ethical Issues in

Frank Brennan, S.J., Xavier House, Yarraluma, Australia
Land Rights; Rights and Duties

James F. Bresnahan, Northwestern University Medical School, Chicago, Illinois
Civil Law, Function of

Neil Brown, Catholic Institute of Sydney, New South Wales, Australia
Humanism

Walter J. Burghardt, S.J., Senior Fellow, Woodstock Theological Library, Washington, D.C.
Preaching, Role of

Jeffrey M. Burns, The Archdiocese of San Francisco Chancery Archives, Menlo Park, California
Kerby, William Joseph; Knights of Labor; Ozanam, Frédéric; Ryan, John Augustine; Settlement Houses

Vincent M. Burns, S.J., Fairfield University, Fairfield, Connecticut
Business Ethics

Curt Cadorette, M.M., Maryknoll School of Theology, Maryknoll, New York
Medellín; Profit; Puebla; Recession; Tariffs; Transnational Corporations

Lisa Sowle Cahill, Boston College, Chestnut Hill, Massachusetts
Marriage

Jean-Yves Calvez, S.J., ETUDES Review, Paris, France
Sollicitudo Rei Socialis

Patrick Carroll, O.S.M., Milltown Institute of Theology and Philosophy, Dublin, Ireland
Debt; Exploitation; Marginal Persons

Stephen J. Casey, University of Scranton, Scranton, Pennsylvania
Aggression; Force

Sheila Cassidy, The Plymouth Department of Palliative Care, Derriford Hospital, Plymouth, England
Torture

Philip J. Chmielewski, S.J., Loyola University, Chicago, Illinois
Affirmative Action; Collectivism; Community Organization; Cooperative Associations; Copartnership; Nell-Breuning, Oswald von

Drew Christiansen, S.J., Department of Social Development and World Peace, United States Catholic Conference, Washington, D.C.
Aged, Care of

Edward Cardinal Clancy, Archdiocese of Sydney, Sydney, Australia
National Conference of Catholic Bishops, Australia

Gerald Coleman, S.S., St. Patrick's Seminary, Menlo Park, California
Stewardship; Values

John A. Coleman, S.J., The Jesuit School of Theology, Berkeley, California
British Distributists

Robert J. Coll, Interfaith Hunger Appeal, New York, New York
Hunger

Mary Collins, O.S.B., The Catholic University of America, Washington, D.C.
Liturgical Movements, Social Influence of; Michel, Virgil

M. Shawn Copeland, Yale University Divinity School, New Haven, Connecticut
Black Theology; Minorities

James A. Coriden, Washington Theological Union, Silver Spring, Maryland
Due Process

John C. Cort, Writer, Boston, Massachusetts
Association of Catholic Trade Unionists

Michael H. Crosby, O.F.M.Cap., St. Benedict Friary, Milwaukee, Wisconsin
Sacred and Secular, Relationship of; Spirituality

Charles E. Curran, Southern Methodist University, Dallas, Texas
Anthropology; Taxes

Frederick J. Cwiekowski, S.S., St. Patrick's Seminary, Menlo Park, California
Vatican Council II

Mary Rose D'Angelo, University of Notre Dame, Notre Dame, Indiana
Beatitudes

Allan Figueroa Deck, S.J., Loyola Marymount University, Los Angeles, California
Culture

Jack Dominian, One Plus One (a marriage research organization), England
Divorce

James A. Donahue, Georgetown University, Washington, D.C.
Conglomerates

Donal Dorr, Irish Missionary Union, Maynooth, Ireland
Poor, Preferential Option for

James E. Dougherty, St. Joseph's University, Philadelphia, Pennsylvania
Communism

Avery Dulles, S.J., Fordham University, Bronx, New York
Synod of Bishops

François-Xavier Dumortier, S.J., Institut Supérieur de Theologie et de Philosophie de la Compagnie de Jésus, Paris, France
Totalitarianism

John C. Dwyer, St. Bernard's Institute, Diocesan Pastoral Center, Albany, New York
Person, Dignity of

John J. Egan, DePaul University, Chicago, Illinois
Catholic Committee on Urban Ministry

Jean Bethke Elshtain, Vanderbilt University, Nashville, Tennessee
Public and Private, Relationship of

Bernard F. Evans, St. John's University, Collegeville, Minnesota
Campaign for Human Development; Octogesima Adveniens

Margaret A. Farley, Yale University Divinity School, New Haven, Connecticut
Family

Daniel Rush Finn, St. John's University, Collegeville, Minnesota
Economic Order

Francis Schüssler Fiorenza, Harvard Divinity School, Cambridge, Massachusetts
Church, Social Mission of

Michael Fleet, Marquette University, Milwaukee, Wisconsin
Christian Democracy

Gerald P. Fogarty, S.J., University of Virginia, Charlottesville, Virginia
Americanism; Leo XIII

George L. Frear, Jr., St. Lawrence University, Canton, New York
Animals, Rights of

Josef Fuchs, S.J., Pontifical Università Gregoriana, Rome, Italy
Natural Law; Reason, Role of

James Gaffney, Loyola University, New Orleans, Louisiana
Freedom

Vincent J. Genovesi, S.J., St. Joseph's University, Philadelphia, Pennsylvania
Homosexuality, Social Implications of; Hope

Marie J. Giblin, Maryknoll School of Theology, Maryknoll, New York
Corporatism; Quadragesimo Anno

John W. Glaser, Center for Healthcare Ethics, Orange, California
Health Care

Fred Glennon, Le Moyne College, Syracuse, New York
Social Security; Welfare/Welfare State

Michael Graham, S.J., Xavier University, Cincinnati, Ohio
LaFarge, John

Joseph Gremillion, University of Notre Dame, Notre Dame, Indiana
Pastoral Care

Christine E. Gudorf, Florida International University, Miami, Florida
Children, Rights of; Mutuality; Sexism

Gustavo Gutiérrez, Pontifical Catholic University of Peru, Lima, Peru
Liberation Theology

Roger Haight, S.J., Weston School of Theology, Cambridge, Massachusetts
Praxis

Kenneth P. J. Hallahan, LaSalle University, Philadelphia, Pennsylvania
Aid; Pacem in Terris

Cyril T. Hally, S.S.C., Pacific Mission Institute, Sydney, Australia
Secularism; Secularization

Ronald Hamel, The Park Ridge Center, Program in Clinical Ethics and Medical Humanities, Park Ridge, Illinois
Justice in the World

James P. Hanigan, Duquesne University, Pittsburgh, Pennsylvania
Birth Control; Demographics; Population

Daniel Harrington, Weston School of Theology, Cambridge, Massachusetts
Kingdom of God

Zachary Hayes, O.F.M., Catholic Theological Union, Chicago, Illinois
Eschatology

Charles C. Hefling, Jr., Boston College, Chestnut Hill, Massachusetts
Creation

Eustás Ó. Héideáin, O.P., University College, Galway, Ireland
Socialization; Society

Alfred T. Hennelly, S.J., Fordham University, Bronx, New York
Colonialism; Populorum Progressio

James Hennesey, S.J., Canisius College, Buffalo, New York
Pius XI

Theodore M. Hesburgh, C.S.C., University of Notre Dame, Notre Dame, Indiana
Education, Role of

Kenneth R. Himes, O.F.M., Washington Theological Union, Silver Spring, Maryland
Pacifism; War

Barbara Hogan, LaSalle University, Philadelphia, Pennsylvania
Economic Planning, Social Importance of; Feminism and Catholic Social Thought

David Hollenbach, S.J., Boston College, Chestnut Hill, Massachusetts
Common Good

J. Leon Hooper, S.J., Woodstock Theological Center, Georgetown University, Washington, D.C.
Dignitatis Humanae; Religious Freedom

Leslie J. Hoppe, O.F.M., Catholic Theological Union, Chicago, Illinois
Decalogue

Thomas Hoppe, Institut für Theologie u. Frieden, Barsbüttel, Germany
Human Rights

Gerard J. Hughes, S.J., Heythrop College, University of London, London, England
Authority, Political

Brian V. Johnstone, C.SS.R., Accademia Alfonsiana, Rome, Italy
Methodology, Moral

John Francis Kavanaugh, S.J., St. Louis University, St. Louis, Missouri
Advertising

Philip S. Keane, S.S., St. Mary's Seminary and University, Baltimore, Maryland
Imagination, Role of

James F. Keenan, S.J., Weston School of Theology, Cambridge, Massachusetts
Cooperation, Principle of; Double Effect, Principle of; Privacy, Right to; Toleration, Principle of

Marjorie Keenan, R.S.H.M., Pontificium Consilium de Iustitia et Pace, Vatican City
Pontifical Council for Justice and Peace

David F. Kelly, Duquesne University, Pittsburgh, Pennsylvania
Euthanasia, Social Implications of

James R. Kelly, Fordham University, Bronx, New York
Right-to-Life Groups

John S. Knight, Pontifical Council Cor Unum, Vatican City
Cor Unum

Werner Kroh, Universities of Hildesheim, Hannover, and Lüneburg, Lower Saxony, Germany
Political Theology

Matthew L. Lamb, Boston College, Chestnut Hill, Massachusetts
Solidarity

Stephen E. Lammers, Lafayette College, Easton, Pennsylvania
Peace

John Langan, S.J., Georgetown University, Washington, D.C.
Political Philosophy

Hans Langendörfer, S.J., Foyer der Jesuiten, Bonn, Germany
Disarmament; John XXIII

Lois Ann Lorentzen, University of San Francisco, San Francisco, California
Gaudium et Spes; Suffrage Movement

Vincent MacNamara, St. Patrick's Missionary Society, Dublin, Ireland
Moral Life, Christian

Daniel C. Maguire, Marquette University, Milwaukee, Wisconsin
Disabilities, Persons with

Peter J. Matheson, Australian Catholic University, Mercy Campus, Melbourne, Australia
Aborigines, Australian

William E. May, John Paul II Institute for Studies on Marriage and Family, Washington, D.C.
Work, Theology of

Dennis P. McCann, DePaul University, Chicago, Illinois
Call to Action Conference; Laity, Role of; "Signs of the Times"

Jeremiah J. McCarthy, St. John's Seminary, Camarillo, California
Capital Punishment; Killing

James J. McCartney, O.S.A., Villanova University, Villanova, Pennsylvania
Abortion, Social Implications of

Patrick T. McCormick, St. John's University, Jamaica, New York
Centesimus Annus

Brian O. McDermott, S.J., Weston School of Theology, Cambridge, Massachusetts
Grace

Robert W. McElroy, St. Patrick's Seminary, Menlo Park, California
Murray, John Courtney

Arthur F. McGovern, S.J., University of Detroit, Detroit, Michigan
Class; Class Struggle; Marxism

Ralph McInerny, Jacques Maritain Center, University of Notre Dame, Notre Dame, Indiana
Maritain, Jacques

Martin McLaughlin, Consultant to United States Catholic Conference, Arlington, Virginia
Agriculture

Joseph M. McShane, S.J., Fordham University, Bronx, New York
Bishops' Program of Social Reconstruction of 1919

Francis X. Meehan, SS. Simon and Jude Church, West Chester, Pennsylvania
Conscientious Objection; Pax Christi

Gerhard Meier, Caritas Internationalis, Vatican City
Caritas Internationalis

Kenneth R. Melchin, St. Paul University, Ottawa, Canada
National Conference of Catholic Bishops, Canada

Judith A. Merkle, S.N.D.deN., Xavier University, Cincinnati, Ohio
Personalism; Sin

Amata Miller, I.H.M., NETWORK, Washington, D.C.
Banks and Banking; Competition; Corporations; Inflation; Insurance

Richard B. Miller, Indiana University, Bloomington, Indiana
Deterrence

Paul Misner, Marquette University, Milwaukee, Wisconsin
Associationism; Credit Union; Ketteler, Wilhelm Emmanuel von; Modernism; Opera Dei Congressi; Paternalism; Volksverein

Sandra Yocum Mize, University of Dayton, Dayton, Ohio
Dietz, Peter E.; Mutual Benefit Societies; National Conference of Catholic Bishops, United States

Christopher F. Mooney, S.J., Fairfield University, Fairfield, Connecticut
Church-State Relations in the United States

Franz H. Mueller, University of St. Thomas, St. Paul, Minnesota
Pesch, Heinrich; Solidarism

Philip J. Murnion, National Pastoral Life Center, New York, New York
Catholic Committee on Urban Ministry

Michael Novak, American Enterprise Institute, Washington, D.C.
Enterprise; Neoconservatives

John O'Brien, C.S.Sp., Holy Ghost College, Dublin, Ireland, and Catholic Church, Rahim Yar Khan, Pakistan
Poverty

William V. O'Brien, Georgetown University, Washington, D.C.
Terrorism

June O'Connor, University of California Riverside, Riverside, California
Catholic Worker, The

Mark O'Keefe, O.S.B., St. Meinrad School of Theology, St. Meinrad, Indiana
Energy; Land; Natural Resources; Ownership; Partnership

William R. O'Neill, S.J., The Jesuit School of Theology, Berkeley, California
Private Property

Ladislas Örsy, S.J., The Catholic University of America, Washington, D.C.
Canon Law, Function of; Episcopal Conferences, Concept of; Episcopal Letters, Function of

Normand Paulhus, Wheeling Jesuit College, Wheeling, West Virginia
Fribourg Union

John T. Pawlikowski, O.S.M., Catholic Theological Union, Chicago, Illinois
Anti-Semitism; Genocide; Holocaust, The

Lawrence A. Pezzullo, Catholic Relief Services, Baltimore, Maryland
Catholic Relief Services

Peter Phan, The Catholic University of America, Washington, D.C.
Augustine, Influence of; Fathers of the Church, Influence of

Michael D. Place, Archdiocese of Chicago, Chicago, Illinois
AIDS

John F. Pollard, Anglia Polytechnic University, Cambridge, England
Fascism

Stephen J. Pope, Boston College, Chestnut Hill, Massachusetts
Rerum Novarum

John R. Popiden, Loyola Marymount University, Los Angeles, California
Paul VI

Gerard F. Powers, Department of Social Development and World Peace, United States Catholic Conference, Washington, D.C.
Peace and Justice Commissions

Lucien Richard, O.M.I., Weston School of Theology, Cambridge, Massachusetts
Inculturation; Revelation

Norbert J. Rigali, S.J., University of San Diego, San Diego, California
Magisterium; Pluralism

Maria Riley, O.P., Center of Concern, Washington, D.C.
Alienation; Women

Peggy Roach, DePaul University, Chicago, Illinois
Catholic Committee on Urban Ministry

Richard R. Roach, S.J., Marquette University, Milwaukee, Wisconsin
Income; Industrialization; Industry; Manual Labor

Philip J. Rossi, S.J., Marquette University, Milwaukee, Wisconsin
Community

Thomas Ryan, S.M., Marist Centre, Toongabbie, New South Wales, Australia
Ecology

John R. Sachs, S.J., Weston School of Theology, Cambridge, Massachusetts
God, Images of

Robert Schreiter, C.Pp.S., Catholic Theological Union, Chicago, Illinois
Evangelii Nuntiandi; Evangelization

Thomas L. Schubeck, S.J., John Carroll University, Cleveland, Ohio
Prison

Michael J. Schuck, Loyola University, Chicago, Illinois
Modern Catholic Social Thought

Thomas A. Shannon, Worcester Polytechnic Institute, Worcester, Massachusetts
Reproductive Technologies, Social Aspects of

Paul E. Sigmund, Princeton University, Princeton, New Jersey
Democracy

Anne Simpson, Freelance Writer
Catholic Charities USA

Mary Hembrow Snyder, Mercyhurst College, Erie, Pennsylvania
Development

Richard Sparks, C.S.P., Paulist Press, Mahwah, New Jersey
Almsgiving

William C. Spohn, S.J., Santa Clara University, Santa Clara, California
Scripture, Use of in Catholic Social Ethics

John M. Staudenmaier, S.J., University of Detroit, Detroit, Michigan
Computerization; Technology

Maryanne Stevens, R.S.M., Creighton University, Omaha, Nebraska
Redemptor Hominis; Strike, Right to

Carroll Stuhlmueller, C.P., Catholic Theological Union, Chicago, Illinois
Covenant

Edward Collins Vacek, S.J., Weston School of Theology, Cambridge, Massachusetts
Charity; Love

Neil Vaney, S.M., St. Margaret's College, Dunedin, New Zealand
Evil, Social

James J. Walter, Loyola University, Chicago, Illinois
Discipleship

William Werpehowski, Villanova University, Villanova, Pennsylvania
Labor and Capital in Catholic Social Thought

Michael D. Whitty, University of Detroit, Detroit, Michigan
Keynesianism

Charles K. Wilber, University of Notre Dame, Notre Dame, Indiana
Credit; Employment and Unemployment; Investment; Monopoly; Trusts

Elizabeth Willems, S.S.N.D., Notre Dame Seminary, New Orleans, Louisiana
Censorship; Prostitution

Oliver F. Williams, C.S.C., University of Notre Dame, Notre Dame, Indiana
Capitalism

Walter J. Woods, St. John's Seminary, Brighton, Massachusetts
Conscience

LIST OF ENTRIES

An asterisk (*) indicates that the topic is treated under the cross-references for that entry.

The numbers refer to the pages on which the entries are found.

ABBREVIATIONS

AA	*Apostolicam acuositatem* (Vatican Council II, Decree on the Apostolate of Lay People)
AAS	*Acta apostolicae sedis* (Vatican City: Vatican Polygot Press, 1909–)
AG	*Ad gentes* (Vatican Council II, Decree on the Church's Missionary Activity)
CA	*Centesimus annus* (John Paul II, *On the Hundredth Anniversary of Rerum Novarum*)
CC	*Casti connubii* (Pius XI, *On Christian Marriage*)
CD	*Christus Dominus* (Vatican Council II, Decree on the Pastoral Office of Bishops in the Church)
CEBs	*Communicades eclesiales de base* (basic ecclesial communities)
CFM	Christian Family Movement
CCUM	Catholic Committee on Urban Ministry
CHD	Campaign for Human Development
CELAM	*Conferencia Episcopal Latinoamericana* (Latin American Episcopal Conference)
CCJP	Catholic Commission for Justice and Peace
CM	*Catholic Mind*
CRS	Catholic Relief Services
CP	*The Challenge of Peace: God's Promise and Our Response* (National Conference of Catholic Bishops, United States)
DH	*Dignitatis humanae* (Vatican Council II, Declaration on Religious Liberty)

DR	*Divini Redemptoris* (Pius XI, *On Atheistic Communism*)
DS	Denzinger-Schönmetzer (H. Denzinger and A. Schönmetzer, *Enchiridion symbolorum*)
EJA	*Economic Justice for All: Catholic Social Teaching and the U.S. Economy* (National Conference of Catholic Bishops, United States)
EN	*Evangelii nuntiandi* (Paul VI, *On Evangelization in the Modern World*)
ES	*Ecclesiam suam* (Paul VI, *On the Church*)
ECPC	*Ethical Choices and Political Challenges* (Canadian Conference of Catholic Bishops)
FC	*Familiaris consortio* (John Paul II, *On the Family*)
HG	*Humani generis* (Pius XII, *Warning Against Attempts to Distort Catholic Truth*)
HV	*Humanae vitae* (Paul VI, *On the Regulation of Births*)
ID	*Immortale Dei* (Leo XIII, *On the Christian Constitution of States*)
JM	*Justitia in mundo* (Synod of Bishops' Second General Assembly, *Justice in the World*)
LE	*Laborem exercens* (John Paul II, *On Human Work*)
LG	*Lumen gentium* (Vatican Council II, Dogmatic Constitution on the Church)
MbS	*Mit brennender Sorge* (Pius XI, *The Place of the Catholic Church in the German Reich*)
MD	*Mediator Dei* (Pius XII, *On the Sacred Liturgy*)
MM	*Mater et magistra* (John XXIII, *On Christianity and Social Progress*)
NCCB	National Conference of Catholic Bishops
NT	New Testament
NCWC	National Catholic Welfare Conference
OA	*Octogesima adveniens* (Paul VI, *On the Eightieth Anniversary of Rerum Novarum: Call to Action*)
OR	*Osservatore Romano*
OT	Old Testament

PC	*Perfectae caritatis* (Vatican Council II, Decree on the Up-to-Date Renewal of Religious Life)
PG	*Patrologia Graeca* (J.-P. Migne, ed.)
PL	*Patrologia Latina* (J.-P. Migne, ed.)
PP	*Populorum progressio* (Paul VI, *On the Development of Peoples*)
PT	*Pacem in terris* (John XXIII, *Peace on Earth*)
QS	Qumran Scrolls
QA	*Quadragesimo anno* (Pius XI, *On Reconstructing the Social Order*)
QAM	*Quod apostolici muneris* (Leo XIII, *On the Socialists*)
RH	*Redemptor hominis* (John Paul II, *On Redemption and the Dignity of the Human Race*)
RN	*Rerum novarum* (Leo XIII, *On the Condition of Workers*)
RP	*Reconciliatio et paenitentia* (John Paul II, *On Reconciliation and Penance*)
SR	*Social Reconstruction* (Bishops' Program of Social Reconstruction of 1919)
SRS	*Sollicitudo rei socialis* (John Paul II, *On Social Concern*)
ST	*Summa theologiae* (Thomas Aquinas)
Syl	*Syllabus of Errors* (Pius IX)
TS	*Theological Studies*
TT	*Theology Today*
USCC	United States Catholic Conference

A

ABORIGINES, AUSTRALIAN

Archaeologists suggest that aborigines have been present on the island continent of Australia about forty thousand years, although recent discoveries could push that estimate much further back into history. Among the many clans and races of people on earth, their story goes back the furthest. Their survival, however, was severely threatened by the arrival of Europeans in the latter part of the 18th century. Estimates of population figures at the time of European arrival vary from as few as 300,000 to as many as 1.4 million or more, but within one hundred years their numbers had been depleted to fewer than 100,000. The 1986 Australian census indicates a total of 227,645 people who call themselves aboriginal.

The *Annual Report (1987–88)* of the Australian government's Department of Aboriginal Affairs indicates the nature and effects of basic injustices. The *Report* states that "many of the original inhabitants were dispossessed and dispersed, their culture disrupted and threatened and, today, their descendants are the most disadvantaged people in Australian society" (p. 1). The *Report* outlines the threats and disadvantages: average life expectancy of an aborigine is fifteen to twenty years less than that of other Australians; infant mortality is nearly three times nonaboriginal infant mortality; unemployment is six times the national average; earnings average half that of other Australians; and imprisonment rates are fourteen times higher than rates for other Australians. The problems are immense. Dispossession of lands has brought with it dispossession of identity. This article can only touch on some of the many dimensions of the human-rights questions vis-à-vis the Australian aborigines and on the part played by the Catholic church.

English colonization in Australia began when the First Fleet, under the command of Captain Arthur Phillip, arrived at Sydney Cove on the east coast in January 1788. When Phillip raised the flag and uttered a particular formula, aborigines across the continent, at least from the 135th degree of longitude eastward (the eastern half of Australia), became subjects of King George III. Australia thereby became British Crown land, and the traditional rights of aborigines to the land were extinguished.

The aboriginal capacity for self-determination as a people, their dignity and identity as a people, their culture, and their spirit were all related to the land. The English did not realize that they were dealing with groups of people who had occupied and marked out this continent to the extent that they could have told the English invaders to within some twenty meters where their own land ended and another clan's began. From being tribal nomadic people, many have scattered—some to urban centers, some to the fringes of urban centers, some to reserves, and some to pastoral leases. In the 1981 census 58 percent of aborigines were identified as urban dwellers. In recent times there have been attempts through the homelands movement for an aboriginal return to traditional lands and traditional languages, but the movement has met limited success so far.

The Catholic church's interest in the aboriginal question was first noted two years after the arrival of the first Catholic vicar-general, William Ullathorne. His assessment of the colony was damning. Transportation (of convicts) had made it a "cesspool," and the aborigine, "the naked savage, who wanders through these endless forests, knew nothing monstrous in crime, except cannibalism, until England schooled him in horrors through her prisoners" (O'Farrell, p. 1). This statement was uttered in 1835, forty-seven years after the arrival of the First Fleet. John Bede Polding arrived in Sydney in September of that year as the first Catholic bishop of Australia. Like Ullathorne, he was Benedictine and English. Ten years later, as archbishop, Polding pursued a possible land-rights law for aborigines. A parliamentary committee was established to report on the condition of the aborigines, and Polding was one of the people interviewed by the committee. His empathy with and concern for the aboriginal situation, which is evident in the 1845 report, was remarkable, given the general sectarian ecclesiastical focus at that time. Polding's sensitivity to this issue was to continue and was evident twenty-four years later in the 1869 pastoral letter of the archbishop and the bishops of the province, obviously occasioned by a reminder in the previous year from Pope Pius IX concerning the Australian bishops' duty to the aborigines. The pope had become aware of the aboriginal situation during a Roman audience with Dom Salvado, bishop of New Norcia in Western Australia, who had worked among the aborigines in that mission for fifty years.

Polding died in 1877 and was succeeded by his coadjutor, Roger Vaughan, who, although only forty-three at the time, was not to live long. In September 1884 Patrick Moran arrived in Sydney as its third archbishop and the first non-English and non-Benedictine bishop. One of his first major activities was to organize the first plenary council of the Australian church, which took place in Sydney in November 1885. There were thirty-two decrees promulgated by that council, one of which was *De propaganda fide inter aboriginales.* The particular principles for this propagation of the faith involved instruction in the "first elements of civilization" and "segregation from white colonies." In addition, aboriginal missions were to be provided with sufficient tracts of land from which whites were to be excluded. The plenary council also called upon the government not to relax its effort to end atrocities perpetrated against aborigines.

The government, on its part, established reserves for aborigines toward the end of the 1890s and into this century, but on lands not wanted by white settlers. The reserves were considered a temporary expedient, as the aborigines were expected sooner or later to die out. These lands were to be policed and controlled by either government or mission administrators, while title to the lands remained with the government. But the aborigines survived, and in the 1940s "assimilation" became the general government policy. In 1963 the government described the policy as ensuring that "all aborigines and part-aborigines will attain the same manner of living as other Australians and live as members of a single Australian community enjoying the same rights and privileges, accepting the same responsibilities, observing the same customs and influenced by the same beliefs, hopes and loyalties as other Australians" (Roberts, p. 28). Assimilation had only a short-lived respectability, however.

The inherent idea was that whites had nothing to learn from the black culture and religion. But more than this, it meant cultural genocide. Aboriginal poet Kath Walker put it concisely: "Pour your pitcher of wine into the wide river / And where is your wine? There is only the river. / Must the genius of an old race die / That the race may live?" (Walker, p. 22).

The question of land rights for aborigines, so strongly advocated by Polding in 1845, reemerged strongly in the late 1960s. In Catholic terms the beginning of this new movement could be linked to the Australian bishop's formation in 1968 of the Catholic Commission for Justice and Peace (CCJP). In secular terms the beginning could be linked to the federal referendum of the previous year, when Australians had voted an overwhelming yes to giving full citizenship status to aborigines. The referendum also gave the commonwealth power to legislate with respect to aborigines (Brennan, p. 6). Following the referendum, aborigines slowly began to take pride in their identity.

In 1970 the Aboriginal and Islander Catholic Council began as a national movement, but survived strongly only in the northern state of Queensland. The federal government, however, had become more deeply conscious of the land-rights claims of the aboriginal people and in 1973 set up the Aboriginal Land Rights Commission to inquire into and report on various matters related to the recognition and establishment of the traditional rights and interests of the aborigines in relation to land. The most recent specific history of the land-rights debate began with the enactment of the Aboriginal Land Rights (Northern Territory) Act by the Commonwealth government in 1976. It was not long before that act was under immense pressure in the Northern Territory from powerful mining interests, in particular the Australian Mining Industry Council (AMIC), who foresaw their own economic interests thwarted by the veto of aboriginal landholders. Under Australian law minerals are usually owned by the Crown, not the landowner. But the landowner's consent to the mining is respected, as are the realities of compensation and royalties. The AMIC contends that aboriginal land legislation means total loss of government initiative and control over exploration and mining.

Aboriginal land-rights legislation in both federal and state governments has had a complicated history. Since the late 1960s and early 1970s most governments have followed a policy of returning aboriginal reserve lands to the ownership and control of local aboriginal communities in the form of land trusts. Most reserve land was not needed for economic development; hence the changeover has not significantly affected other citizens. In more recent developments different states and the Northern Territory have made large tracts of unalienated Crown land (land not part of the reserves) available for claim by aboriginal land councils on the basis of traditional ownership, historical association, and/or specific need (Brennan et al., p. 21f.). Figures issued by the Department of Aboriginal Affairs in *Aboriginal Statistics 1986* indicate that 8.37 percent of Australia's land mass was granted to aborigines as freehold land and 1.16 percent as leasehold land; a further 2.71 percent was aboriginal reserve or mission land (p. 4). The states and territories where most resistance has been encountered have been the three largest states and territories, where most land is open to claim, namely Western Australia, Queensland, and the Northern Territory.

A major channel of action employed by the bishops was the CCJP, although the relationship between this commission and some of the bishops was sometimes fraught with tension. The CCJP, which had sponsored an annual social-justice statement since 1973, issued a statement in 1978 entitled *Aborigines—A Statement of Concern,* which strongly raised the question of land rights. Because of the nature of the relationship between aboriginal people and the land they occupied, the taking of the land from them, both in itself and because of the violence with which it was done, was noted in that document as being the root cause of the destruction of aboriginal society. The statement was widely acclaimed as a protest against injustices done to the aborigines. Some bishops, however, felt it expressed only one range of facts and was therefore weakened by imbalance. Consequently several declined to actively support the statement.

In December 1983 the federal labor minister for aboriginal affairs outlined the government's plan to recognize the rights of aborigines to land according to five basic principles: (1) aboriginal land to be held under inalienable freehold title, (2) protection of aboriginal sites, (3) aboriginal control in relation to mining on aboriginal land, (4) access to mining royalty equivalents, and (5) compensation for lost land to be negotiated. The plan unfortunately was never brought to a debate or a vote in Parliament. In May 1987 the CCJP was replaced with the Australian Catholic Social Justice Council (ACSJC). That council, together with the Australian National Committee for Australian Catholic Relief, advises the new Bishops' Committee for Justice, Development, and Peace. With the formal appointment in the same month of Frank Brennan, S.J., a qualified civil lawyer, as adviser on aboriginal affairs to the AEC, there were definite signs of growing unanimity among the bishops on various justice issues relating to aborigines. At the suggestion of various church leaders and following Brennan's active negotiation, the federal Parliament passed a motion on August 23, 1988, recognizing Australia's aboriginal prehistory, the first item of business in the new Parliament House in Canberra. The motion was passed by the Labor majority in both houses of Parliament.

Besides the statements of the AEC, issued on their behalf by the CCJP and more recently by the ACSJC, there have been the efforts of individual state conferences of bishops concerning aboriginal rights. In addition, Paul VI (in Sydney, 1970) and John Paul II (in Alice Springs, 1986) have spoken out boldly for the aborigines. The rights of aboriginal claim to land has been strongly argued by many people over a long period of time, and the church's current contribution to this argument largely focuses on four points: (1) first occupancy of the land by the aboriginal people and their particular gentle working of the land together with their right to use material goods gained therefrom for sustenance (see Pius XI, *Quadragesimo anno,* 1931; John XXIII, *Mater et magistra,* 1961); (2) their needs and rights for identity as human persons stemming from the link between their aboriginality and the land—that is, they do not own the land, the land owns them; (3) their right to self-determination as a people, which involves their right to retain and develop their own culture, so intimately connected to the land; and (4) their right to religious freedom, stemming from the fact that they have many sacred sites, or places of the Dreaming, which are intimately linked with the land (see Brennan et al. for full argumentation).

No matter how strongly the church and others put forward arguments for land rights, it is ultimately the federal government that has responsibility for successfully achieving a just settlement for the descendants of those aborigines dispossessed by the 1788 annexation of Australia to the British Crown. It has not been easy, and the backdown by the Labor government with regard to different aspects of the 1983 Land Rights Plan reflects the continuing difficulty. There is discontent still in government circles and the general electorate as well as in the powerful mining lobby. The struggle to find appropriate structures and recompense moves slowly. There are continuing discussions about a treaty with the aborigines mooted in 1988, during the Bicentennial Year. More recently the minister of aboriginal affairs proposed a dramatic Aboriginal and Torres Strait Islander Commission, which would give the aborigines both the economic right and the political responsibility to run their own affairs, along with a budget of more than $400 million. The proposal went before Parliament in April 1989 and met with amendments and opposition. By the middle of 1990 it seems to have disappeared from the agenda.

A further important initiative by the government was the establishment in October 1987 of a royal commission to investigate aboriginal deaths in custody for the period beginning January 1, 1980. There were 103 cases of deaths in custody between January 1980 and November 1988, with 22 deaths occurring in 1987 alone, more than half by hanging. An *Interim Report* by the commissioner was published in December 1988 in which fifty-six recommendations were made. The *Report* notes that "the deaths, the over-representation of Aborigines in our prisons and lockups are a consequence of history, of appalling neglect, of ignorance, and of traditional perceptions of 'the Aboriginal problems' and the way they should be coped with. . . . It will be unfortunate if the work of this commission is impeded by narrow, selfish or political considerations" (p. 65). In the eighteen months following the publication of this *Report* the governments of Australia had tackled very few of those fifty-six recommendations. There is obviously much still to be done.

See also COLONIALISM; EVIL, SOCIAL; HUMAN RIGHTS; LAND RIGHTS; MARGINAL PERSONS; PERSON, DIGNITY OF; POOR, PREFERENTIAL OPTION FOR.

Bibliography: F. Brennan, et al., *Finding Common Ground: An Assessment of the Basis of Aboriginal Land Rights,* 2nd ed. (Melbourne: Collins Dove, 1986). R. Bowden and B. Bunbury, *Being Aboriginal* (Crow's Nest, New South Wales: An ABC Book, 1990). CCJP, *Issues No. 4, Aboriginal Land Rights* (1985). M. Howe, *Aborigines and Christians: An Introduction to Some of the Issues Involved* (Queensland: The Foundation of Aboriginal and Islander Research Action, 1977). P. O'Farrell, *The Catholic Church and Community in Australia* (West Melbourne: Nelson, 1977). J. Roberts, *Massacres to Mining* (Blackburn, Victoria: Dove Communications, 1981). K. Walker, *My People* (Milton, Queensland: Jacaranda, 1988). M. Wilson, *Ministry Among Aboriginal People* (Melbourne: Collins Dove, 1988).

PETER J. MATHESON

ABORTION, SOCIAL IMPLICATIONS OF

A decision to terminate a pregnancy has many ramifications. In addition to the obvious religious and ethical quandaries and the debates over when personhood begins, an intention to abort has significant social implications that are often passed over or ignored. Additionally, the issue of abortion can be analyzed and debated from the perspectives of the various social theories of ethics and law that compete for the hearts and minds of people today. In this article some social implications of abortion will be presented, after which an analysis of some of the values and operating assumptions of Catholic social teaching will be undertaken, which might help to illuminate and broaden our understanding of this vexed issue today.

Abortion as a Social Issue

It is truly ironic that the U.S. Supreme Court in *Roe* v. *Wade,* which made it possible for states if they so choose to legalize abortion on demand until birth, did so on the grounds of protecting personal privacy (the privacy of the relationship between the woman and her doctor). Given the web of relationships and responsibilities the pregnant woman has with her unborn offspring, with the father of the child, with her family, with her peers, and with her education and career, as well as with her doctor, it would seem that the decision whether or not to terminate a pregnancy, however it is resolved ethically, is an inherently social decision and hardly "private" at all. Thus it is true, but trivial, that the choice to abort or not is the pregnant woman's to make, since the rationale for that choice ought not be grounded on individualistic whim (privacy in a narrow sense) but on a mature consideration of the social relationships and demands that situate each human life in its concrete specificity and context.

Robert N. Bellah and his coauthors have masterfully shown in *Habits of the Heart* that this tendency to individualize inherently social decisions is a characteristic of American culture. And Larry R. Churchill in *Rationing Health Care in America* has demonstrated how the negative ramifications of this one-dimensional individualism continues to influence contemporary attitudes toward health care in the United States. Our modern emphasis on individualism and privacy has pushed to the background of awareness our relatedness and responsibility to others and theirs to us, and has thus led to a diminished sense of the "common good." Nowhere is this emphasis on extreme individualism more rampant than in the rhetoric of those who are "pro choice" on the issue of abortion, who are not willing to consider any restrictions of that choice no matter what social good may be accomplished by reasonable procedures and limits. This American emphasis on the rights of decontextualized individuals in abortion and divorce law has been accurately portrayed by Mary Ann Glendon in her important study, *Abortion and Divorce in Western Law.*

This overemphasis on privacy and the subsequent downplaying of the social implications of the abortion decision has been acknowledged by the United States Supreme Court. In its decision in *Planned Parenthood of Southeastern Pennsylvania* v. *Casey,* the Court, although retaining and once again reaffirming what it understands to be the essential holding of *Roe* v. *Wade* that a woman has a constitutionally protected right to choose to have an abortion before viability and to obtain it without undue interference from the state, does so because it believes that "the ability of women to participate equally in the economic and social life of the nation has been facilitated by their ability to control their reproductive lives." This is surely a social reason, but one that moves the Court away from *Roe*'s emphasis on privacy and leads the plurality, sensitive to other social dimensions of the decision to terminate a pregnancy, to assert what is implied in the *Roe* holding that "the state has legitimate interests from the outset of the pregnancy in protecting the health of the woman and the life of the fetus that may become a child." In a later section of this decision, the justices emphasize that this part of the *Roe* holding "has been given too little acknowledgment and implementation by the Court in its subsequent cases." This can be interpreted as the Court's acknowledgment that some negative social dimensions of abortion should properly and constitutionally be regulated by statutory law.

Polls have shown that Americans, although agreeing that a woman has the right to procure an abortion, are comfortable with some restrictions of this right because of the social implications of the abortion decision. For example, a great majority of people are opposed to the use of abortion as a means of sex selection or career enhancement, even though many of these same people would support a termination of pregnancy in other situations. Many are also comfortable with parental notification laws for minors and laws providing a time and a context for truly informed decision making to take place. Some are opposed to public funding of abortion because they believe that the government should have other spending priorities, and there are those who are opposed to using public facilities or those who work in them for the procurement of abortions because of the state's legitimate interest in the protection of fetal life. Others, of course, would be opposed to almost all abortions because of what our casual acceptance of the termination of pregnancy says of our attitude as a society about the dignity of human life. All of these critiques are based primarily on a value-weighted analysis of the social implications of abortion and not primarily or exclusively on the moral judgment that the murder of an innocent person is taking place.

One very specific area where the social implications of abortion are raising profound conceptual questions is in the field of medicine itself. The involvement of physicians in the abortion procedure can at least be understood, even if not justified, when the life or health of the pregnant woman is in question. However, eugenic or other nontherapeutic abortions are a different matter altogether. Traditional canons of medical professionalism have required physicians to use their skills to alleviate suffering, prolong life, and restore health, not to kill their patients or to do anything at all requested by patients unless what patients want has some reasonable relationship to these aforementioned medical goals. Eugenic abortions, however, are performed precisely because it is decided by the mother, the physician, or both, that the life of the child is a life not worth living or that society would be excessively burdened if this child were allowed to go to term. While alleviation of suffering might be claimed in this situation, first it must be determined who exactly is the patient in this situation, the mother or the child. If the mother is considered the patient, it is hard to see how the alleviation of the child's suffering by terminating the pregnancy is relevant, or even how the alleviation of the mother's suffering by killing the unborn child can be justified. If the unborn child is considered the patient, then the doctor acts directly against traditional canons of medical professionalism by killing the patient in order to prevent the patient's suffering. Only if the physician sees himself or herself as an agent of social beneficence and not as a helper and healer of vulnerable patients can these types of interventions be allowed. But social beneficence was precisely the justification used by the Nazi doctors in their infamous genetic and hypothermic experiments conducted half a century ago.

Other types of nontherapeutic abortions, for example, abortions for career enhancement, convenience, or gender selection can only be performed by physicians who adopt the "Dr. Feelgood" model of medicine, a model that emphasizes that free people can enter into any kind of contractual relationship they please as long as there is no coercion on either side. This extreme form of individualism in medicine runs counter to centuries of accumulated wisdom that demands the public use of the physician's skills in meeting the basic needs and goods of sick and vulnerable people. One logical consequence of this contractual model is the contemporary reality of physicians who will not enter into healing relationships with persons solely because they have infectious diseases, usually AIDS, or who will not treat those suffering because they do not have the ability to pay.

Attitudes toward physician involvement in abortion along with other contemporary health-care issues will help determine and shape what kind of doctors and nurses there will be in the future. In the light of history and contemporary experience, society should be very concerned if physicians and health-care professionals focus too much on either social beneficence or individual contract. As can be seen, the social implications of abortion are far-reaching and will probably affect the quality of future health-care practitioners.

Catholic Social Teaching and Abortion

In the last hundred years Catholic theology and the church's magisterium have made significant contributions to the development of a profoundly Christian social theory, as many other articles in this dictionary will readily attest. In this article, some values or operating assumptions characteristic of Catholic social thought will be analyzed and applied to the abortion debate. This is not done in order to ground the ethical analysis of abortion exclusively within the limits of social theory but to use the richness of Catholic social teaching to provide a more full moral perspective for the consideration of the decision to terminate a pregnancy.

The first value Catholic social teaching has consistently emphasized is the dignity of the human individual. Human dignity is rooted in the biblical belief that humans are created in God's image and that personal life, since it reflects the spirit of God in its own spirituality, is intrinsically valuable and to be considered as an end in itself and not merely as a means to some other end. However, this stress on the dignity of the individual ought not be misinterpreted as focusing on individual autonomy; rather, human persons are understood in the Catholic tradition as essentially social beings whose personhood has both a private and a relational dimension insofar as our concrete actions influence both the world of persons around us and the subjects we ourselves are continuing to become. In his book *The Acting Person* Pope John Paul II describes these phenomena as the transitive and intransitive (reflexive) dimensions of human actions.

The church's emphasis on the dignity of the person, especially the personhood of the unborn, is what has motivated its opposition to almost all abortions. However, it is becoming increasingly clear that the social, gender, and economic injustices that often force women to an abortion decision are also significant affronts to human dignity. This reality has led many church leaders to emphasize what is called a "seamless garment" approach to life issues, which holds that an emphasis on human dignity demands that human life at all its stages and in every context be protected and that its quality be enhanced and improved. In fact, many "pro-life" organizations take a holistic approach and are trying to change some of the injustices that motivate decisions to terminate pregnancies. They also provide realistic alternatives for women who believe they must make this decision, and are establishing "Project Rachel" programs to provide support and counseling for women who have already procured abortions.

The interpersonal dimension of human dignity is the basis for Catholic social teaching's continuing emphasis on the notion of the common good. This operating assumption is empirically grounded, since experience demonstrates that we are not isolated individuals but are profoundly related to one another in many dimensions of our lives. Indeed, as the world itself continues to shrink through improvements in telecommunications and travel, this coming millennium promises to be the most interconnected in the history of humankind. While grounded in empirical observation, Catholic social thought also emphasizes the value and obligation of societal responsibility. This responsibility is valuable insofar as it benefits, at least indirectly, the individual person himself or herself; it is an obligation insofar as individuals cannot exist or flourish without belonging to at least one community of shared values and goals. Human solidarity, as understood by Pope John Paul II, is the virtue that motivates us to transform the existential fact of human interrelatedness into collaborative and purposeful social activity.

Although its conclusions can and will be contested, it was just such a "common good" motivation that prompted the plurality in the *Planned Parenthood* decision of the United States Supreme Court to uphold the basic provisions of the *Roe* holding as described above. These justices worried that if they were to overturn *Roe,* reliance on the stability of law and the societal benefits this provides would be radically undermined and possibly destroyed. Thus they decided that the common good demanded that *Roe* be upheld, even though as individuals some of them are opposed to abortion. Perhaps the "common good" would be more emphatically protected and enhanced if the Court were to take a "seamless garment" approach to life issues, providing the constitutional right to life to the unborn, outlawing capital punishment and euthanasia, and providing constitutional grounds for the improvement of access to affordable housing and to quality education and health care.

Seeking to imitate Jesus of Nazareth whose teaching it proclaims, the church in its social teaching emphasizes that Christians must have a fundamental commitment to improving the lot of the poor and marginalized just as Jesus himself did. Actualization of this commitment, of course, can take many forms, but Catholic social teaching, whether supporting the rights of workers to organize, condemning racism and sexism, or decrying the structural injustices of Third World nations and institutions, has had as one of its central values the empowerment of the disenfranchised and dispossessed.

This concern for biblical justice has special relevance to the abortion debate. Unborn persons are radically marginalized in our society, and for this reason alone the church must constantly be holding up their plight before our eyes. Not only are unborn persons vulnerable, but many people of color are convinced that abortion is being promoted in order to bring about genocide for reasons of race and ethnicity under the guise of concern about population control. Others who have been marginalized in decisions to terminate pregnancy include the father of the unborn child, the family of the pregnant woman, and sometimes even the pregnant woman herself. Sometimes even well-intentioned ecclesial sanctions (e.g., excommunication) have had the unintended side effect of alienating and spiritually dispossessing the very people the church should be most concerned about helping. These penalties should be reconsidered in the light of the church's fundamental commitment to the marginalized, something many bishops have already begun to do.

It should be clear that there are many social implications of abortion, which are only beginning to be adequately conceived and considered. Using the values and operating assumptions of the church's rich social teaching tradition may help to illumine and contextualize an issue that remains increasingly contentious and vexed.

See also COMMON GOOD; DIGNITATIS HUMANAE; HEALTH CARE; HUMAN RIGHTS; MARGINAL PERSONS; MODERN CATHOLIC SOCIAL THOUGHT; PERSON, DIGNITY OF; RIGHT-TO-LIFE GROUPS.

Bibliography: M. Glendon, *Abortion and Divorce in Western Law* (Cambridge: Harvard, 1987). S. Nicholson, *Abortion and the Roman Catholic Church,* JRE Studies in Religious Ethics 2 (Knoxville, Tenn.: Religious Ethics, 1978). J. McCartney, *Unborn Persons: Pope John Paul II and the Abortion Debate* (New York: Peter Lang, 1987). J. Noonan, Jr., ed., *The Morality of Abortion: Legal and Historical Perspectives* (Cambridge: Harvard, 1970). W. Bondeson et al., eds., *Abortion and the Status of the Fetus,* Philosophy and Medicine 13 (Boston: D. Reidel, 1983).

JAMES J. McCARTNEY, O.S.A.

ACTION LIBERALE NATIONALE

Action libérale nationale (ALN) was a short-lived political party (1934–36) in Quebec, the largely Catholic and French-speaking province of Canada, which responded to the misery produced by the Depression with an economic reform program drawn from Catholic social teaching.

When in 1932 the decision was made in Western Canada to found the Cooperative Commonwealth Federation (CCF), a radical farmer-worker party following the pattern of British socialism, the Quebec clergy became nervous. A meeting of thirteen priests organized by the École sociale populaire on March 9, 1933, rejected the CCF program as coming too close to the socialism condemned by Pius XI, and as the Catholic answer to the CCF, they formulated an economic reform program, Pour la restauration sociale au Canada, in keeping with the passages of the 1931 encyclical of Pius XI *Quadragesimo anno* critical of the abuses of capitalism, particularly monopoly capitalism. The program outlined the necessary reforms: new forms of associations, insurance plans, bold labor laws to protect farmers and workers, and new powers of the Quebec government to nationalize industrial monopolies and promote the national economy. This promotion was to take place through a corporatist organization of production and the creation of an economic council that would represent the corporations and, together with the government, plan the national economy. In line with the antimodern nationalism of the École sociale populaire, the program envisaged a largely agricultural Quebec with small industries distributed among the small towns of the different regions.

The group of thirteen priests decided to hand the reform program to a group of sympathetic laymen, recommending that they rework the proposal and make it the platform of a political party. The laymen replaced the corporatist recommendations with a demand for the creation of a national ministry to foster economic development, underlining the program's nationalist orientation. Since the monopoly industries in Quebec were owned by "foreigners"—British, American, and Anglo-Canadian—nationalist sentiment could be harnessed to unite farmers, workers, small producers, and businessmen in a political movement for bold economic reconstruction. In Quebec, the oppression of "a class" was in fact the oppression of "a people."

When in April 1934 Paul Gouin and several other politicians left the Liberal party in protest over its lack of action and decided to form a new political party, the ALN, they adopted the reworked proposal of the group of thirteen as the official party program. The new party hoped that it could unite the different classes in Quebec, especially proletariat and petite bourgeoisie, to struggle against the remnants of the colonial system, bring about greater economic independence, and create a society attached to Catholic values—a largely rural society with small-scale industries scattered across the country and owned and run by French Canadians.

The reform program of the ALN was received in Quebec with great enthusiasm. Under the leadership of Paul Gouin, the party reached out to the public through a new publication, *La province,* and meetings were organized all over the province. The ALN received the support of the well-known nationalist intellectuals. In the election of 1935, the party gained twenty-six seats in the National Assembly and seriously weakened the Liberal government.

But the party was not to last long. Because of its success, the ALN was wooed by the newly elected leader of the Conservative party in Quebec, Maurice Duplessis, who, realizing that his party could not unseat the Liberal government, persuaded his own party to accept the reform program of the ALN. He then negotiated an agreement with the leaders of the ALN to merge the two political organizations into a single new party, the Union nationale, which would have a good chance to form the government at the next election. At the election in August 1936 the Union nationale was swept into power. Maurice Duplessis, the new premier, betrayed the leaders of the ALN, disregarded the reform program, and adopted economic policies in support of monopoly capitalism.

See also CORPORATISM.

Bibliography: G. Baum, *Catholics and Canadian Socialism* (Toronto: Lorimer, 1980). H. Quinn, *Union Nationale: A Study in Quebec Nationalism* (Toronto: Univ. of Toronto Press, 1963). S. Trofimenkoff, *The Dream of a Nation* (Toronto: Gagé, 1983).

GREGORY BAUM

ADVERTISING

John Paul II in his first encyclical letter, *Redemptor hominis* (1979), warned that the institutions of our social world could be instrumental in the loss of our own identity and purpose as persons. In this remarkable document, which is offered as a

Christology, the central passages are surprisingly given to the problem of human alienation. The social forces of political organization, the productive (economic) system, and the means of social communication have been invested with the power to enslave men and women to the production process and to products themselves.

In advanced industrial societies, these social forces come to a confluence in the world of advertising, the matrix of productive, political, and media life.

By the late 1980s worldwide advertising expenditures had leaped beyond $250 billion, more than the gross national product of Denmark, Finland, Ireland, Israel, and Kenya combined—a growth so astounding that projections are given for world expenditures by the year 2000 at $1 trillion. In the context of the United States, the chair of the Federal Trade Commission has characterized American advertising as having the "largest information budget in the world," $118 billion by 1989.

An almost universally agreed-upon principle of human behavior is that appetite, desire, attitude, and choice all follow from and are based upon cognition and information. Information is formation: formation of choice and formation of persons. This principle is operative in all education, politics, therapy, propaganda, and thought control. Whoever controls the information of a society controls the formation of that society and the range of its choices. Thus advertising, as having the "largest information budget in the world," is a strategic phenomenon in understanding social life and social reality.

Proponents of advertising range from those who acknowledge its cardinal contribution to capitalism and the free market, through those who laud its diversity of information, to those who see it as central to social and political freedoms. These advocates point out that advertising has its own self-corrective dynamisms in the free market and in product-quality demand as well as in the self-policing mechanisms of internal regulation.

Those critical of advertising, however, focus upon the hidden social, psychological, and interpersonal costs of an information industry that is based frequently on illusion and entirely upon the principle that possession of goods and services delivers human satisfaction.

The preponderance of advertising—especially in a society already glutted with a diversity of products—is oriented toward the identification of products with powerful human values and relational experiences. While it is true that personification and valorization of objects is characteristic of almost all literature, the continual highly sophisticated association of products and possessions with profoundly personal fulfillments raises pressing questions for a consumer society.

What happens to the personal self, to interpersonal relations, and to social solidarity in a culture where the dominant information and formation system constantly offers data that purchasable commodities alone ensure personal identity, compensate for lost intimacy, and displace civic or social responsibility?

Whether one agrees or disagrees with the claim that the preeminence of advertising as an information system generates a society of narcissistic individualism whose members paradoxically seem incapable of love for self or others, it is indubitable from the arguments of both sides that advertising has a profound impact upon moral consciousness, social cohesion, personal identity, and even the most fundamental epistemological and metaphysical categories of what is "real" and "true" in the human world.

See also CAPITALISM; ECONOMIC ORDER; GREED.

Bibliography: *Advertising Age* (Crain: Chicago). E. Clark, *The Want Makers: The World of Advertising: How They Make You Buy* (New York: Viking, 1988). S. Ewen, *All Consuming Images* (New York: Basic Books, 1988). I. Mitroff and W. Bennis, *The Unreality Indus-*

try (New York: Birch Lane, 1989). D. Ogilvy, *Ogilvy on Advertising* (New York: Pan, 1983). M. Schudson, *Advertising, The Uneasy Persuasion* (New York: Basic Books, 1984).

JOHN FRANCIS KAVANAUGH, S.J.

AFFIRMATIVE ACTION

The discussion of affirmative action involves (1) a program in the United States on the federal level, the goal of which is intergroup justice in the face of previous discrimination, most notably but not exclusively across racial and gender lines; and (2) the controversy concerning the propriety and extent of the elements of this program. In addition, the treatment of affirmative action must handle the dissemination of the program's values throughout the society and the difficulties this education in public values meets.

Affirmative action is a program to diminish the present effects of past discrimination and to prevent its future occurrence. "Discrimination" here means differentiation in treatment that is arbitrary or invidious. Invidious discrimination treats persons differently solely on the basis of race, sex, or age for no purpose justifiable in terms of the rights and considered desires of the individuals affected. This clarification of the sense in which "discrimination" is used empties the term "reverse discrimination" of vital content.

Racism can occur within and through social structures; affirmative action is a legislated, judicial, and administrative mechanism for addressing such system-inherent tendencies that carry out discrimination. Insofar as the discrimination has effectively reached its targets and proceeds from a depersonalizing prejudice, it renders its objects dispensable and insignificant in social decisions and allocations; the dispensable persons become removed, separated, and forgotten. Affirmative action is set against a serious and deep-seated evil; the gravity of this wrong contributes to the justification for the use of the method and explains both the incomprehension on the part of many and the explicit resistance by some. Affirmative action enables persons previously discriminated against to have open to them certain ranges of choice connected with income, decision, and recognition. The goal of affirmative action, finally, is to bring certain minority populations and women into the social institutions that shape and contribute to the common life.

The program derives from the Civil Rights Act of 1964, especially Title VII. Executive Order 11246 (EO) of 1965 was a particularly effective force for bringing about the implementation of affirmative action in the workplace. The Rehabilitation Act of 1973 was another step in establishing the range of the program. *Johnson* v. *Transportation Agency of Santa Clara County* (1987) confirmed its direction against gender bias.

The goal of the program advances beyond nondiscrimination in order to reach integration in the sense of solidarity, that is, a situation where diverse persons reflexively share a common fate in a complex society and join in achieving a common good. Affirmative action is also a step beyond equal-opportunity plans. Affirmative action presupposes that merit and rights have not only a personal value but also a social meaning. They secure specified goods for persons within a given society, and the society itself also derives benefit from this protection of the fair and broad distribution of merit and the universal guarantee of rights. The redistribution of social opportunities specifies the field of the practical results sought by means of the actual policies and programs of affirmative action. In the readjustment, affirmative action utilizes certain markers: social origin or gender are used as highly probable indices of previous discrimination.

Two Supreme Court cases in particular have stimulated and focused public discussion: *Regents of the University of California* v. *Bakke* (1978) and *Kaiser Aluminum and United Steel Workers* v. *Weber* (1979). The reaction to affirmative action that centered around and continues subsequent to the cases in broad sections of society is, minimally, sharp distaste for the program. An examination of the sources of this aversion (or worse) can be instructive for an ethical evaluation of the program. Citizens fail to understand the law or misinterpret it. When they fail to grasp the law as it has been written, they may not see it as an articulation of central values that they hold in common with other citizens. When they believe their own voice is not being heard, persons even more tenaciously attempt to defend their interests and future opportunities.

Ordinary citizens also perceive federal law as heteronomous or imposed. They may identify the law as an intrusion by the state into the sphere of the society or even of the family. Indeed, insofar as the state may enter these spheres, they perceive affirmative action as a gratuitous aggravation, for if it reaches for its goal in the areas of jobs and professional training, so much else that is required, as common sense indicates, for the elimination of discrimination goes untouched, for example, housing, education, and the administration of justice.

Even if citizens clearly understand that retribution is not the basis of affirmative action, the current understanding of rights, whether of personal inviolability or of civil/political involvement, may hinder the person from grasping that the social support that affirmative action essays is secured to a person on the basis of attention to his or her unfolding dignity in those circumstances in which the usual treatment for a person in this category has been inequitable. Seldom, too, is the understanding of social-historical process such that it includes a collective, future-directed responsibility without personal fault, yet at possible present individual cost. Because the beneficiaries of the program, minorities and women, may be either near or visible—near in the sense that there is a perceived indirect benefit to a person because of an advantage that accrues to another, visible in the sense that this other is a peer—but not both, the complaints and anger of many concerning the program arise.

Some reactions to the program fail to distinguish the legal circumstances in which procedures are imposed. Title VII 706g indicates that a court may impose affirmative action. Distinct from this situation (approved in *Kaiser Aluminum and United Steel Workers* v. *Weber*) is an affirmative-action program established through an agreement of a company and a union. Then too, a company involved in a federal contract may set up a program in compliance with the executive order. These instances are different from the suspect compulsion of ad hoc "affirmative action" decisions.

Further, in the heat surrounding the issue, many persons fail to pay proper attention to the clear constraints toward fairness that the courts and federal agencies attempt to secure. The court outlined a pattern for such guidelines in *Weber*. The majority noted that there was an underrepresentation in training programs and that the affirmative-action program was voluntary. There was no absolute bar to entry for members of the majority population; there was no dismissal of those already in the training program or already employed, and the program was temporary. It provided a clear target appropriate to the local population pattern. An affirmative-action program in a given firm is a temporary construct. It holds until the partners to the agreement or the subjects of a court decision reach a certain goal, which is not arbitrary but rather a step in these particular circumstances toward a larger social good.

Some of the provisions of EO 11246 indicate key ethical elements in the program, which may have become ignored in the practice or in the reception. The executive order links affirmative action as a means to the end of eliminating discrimination. It is a tool to an end that is a social good, that is, through it the body politic attempts to realize a value that it holds in common. It requires contractors to submit an array of information. Although the point of this is to secure fairness and to achieve national tabulation, this may be perceived only as red tape. The executive order requires the contracting party to indicate its nondiscriminatory policy in all advertising and to notify every union with which it negotiates. Also it must add an equal-opportunity clause in each subcontract. Here the means do not attain the implied, significant goal. Granted, a practical policy heading toward the elimination of discrimination must educate and disseminate, but these specified requirements are minimal. Without further education, such emblems are merely counters of legal reckoning rather than marks of shared values.

Civil-rights legislation—school integration, equal employment opportunities, fair housing programs, voter registration, equal access to public accommodations—attempts to end discriminating practices. As approximate models of the ideal they can mediate advanced values to the members of society. If this educational intention is at disparity with core values held by particular persons or if these persons do not understand the reasoning behind the legislation and programs, attitudes remain unchanged while programs affect spheres close to these persons (home, school, job); then anger and resentment well up. If justice is to take place through participation and not merely in accord with procedures, then citizens must attain the goals of affirmative action by means of extensive communication and education.

Then again, in the public discourse that shapes our common values, no community readily presses the value of affirmative action as an element of its central concerns, for it is (1) an instrumental value only, and (2) it is a value that rests uneasily in a constellation of "liberal" values, values more like faceless rules than group-inherent goals or characteristics.

Part of the rationale for affirmative action is that a program connected with the classification by some external mark that had previously led to a person's being set at disadvantage will now remedy the previously observed and currently still-impending negative effects. In this way such a plan will prevent the recurrence of bias. Two difficulties emerge in connection with this rationale. Some of those who were not marked in such a way may be ignorant of the effects that this bias has on those who have been designated as different. Even if the program does contribute toward blocking anticipated discrimination, this is difficult for many to grasp, for it requires that they must admit that they themselves are those very persons who are capable of discriminating in the future.

The use of external markers as indices of previous discrimination, no matter how probable the connection, leaves two gaps in the trajectory toward social goals. Some who have been discriminated against are not clearly marked externally. This accounts for some discontent on the part of minorities who are not recognized as within the purview of the program. Others, who are marked, have no need of the remedy.

Roman Catholic ethics develops its position toward affirmative action on the basis of the church's condemnation of racism (*Sublimis Deus* [1537]; *In plurimis* [1888]; *Mit brennender Sorge* [1937]; *Gaudium et spes* 29; *Nostra aetate* 5; *Ad gentes* 15) and of discrimination (GS 29.2, 29.3; *Pacem in terris* 44).

Common fatherhood and being brothers and sisters of the one Son are central theological tenets that support this ethical position. That the Spirit brings us to Pentecost through and beyond cultural differences and that the church itself is universal are further articles (see "The Church and Racism" 21–22) that enjoin activity in order to bring about the kingdom.

Although brute greed or understandable self-interest or commendable concern for one's near and dear may be factors that impel someone to resist affirmative-action programs, a type of atheism may be at the root, one that denies the other a relationship to the Lord equivalent to one's own (see GS 19).

The Justice and Peace Commission makes clear that taking unfair advantage of persons in particular segments of the work force because of their imputed inferiority is a type of racism ("The Church and Racism," sec. 13). A related degradation takes place when persons are unable to enter the work force or are unable to locate adequate programs of education because of their alleged inferiority.

Some Catholics find it difficult to accept affirmative action even if they firmly accept the just-considered theological bases for equal human dignity because many believers have not yet grasped that the issues and events in secular society are one field where they are to seek, discover, and collaborate in God's will. Affirmative action, insofar as the efforts to secure civil rights and economic justice are dimensions of that field, is one way of attempting to live out the gospel (GS 66; "Brothers and Sisters to Us," p. 387). To urge citizens to assume their responsibility for institutional racism may at first confuse them. Those who are Christians must come to comprehend how the life of faith facilitates the uncovering of evils in the day-to-day patterns and how faith-based, collaborative freedom can alter these patterns.

Likewise, the danger of those approaches reacting against affirmative action that urge "color blind" treatment of persons is that such approaches are incapable of taking the historical and cultural characteristics of persons and their groups into account. This means that the color-blind evaluation will filter out positive, uniquely developed personal habits and collective traits before they can contribute to the common good and that this constraint prohibits those responsible for guiding our collective social efforts from examining the negative results that are part of the deposit of the years, for example, the results of discrimination in education.

The arguments for affirmative action do not present it as an adequate model for social coordination; its proponents advance it in a context of the current unavailability of alternative means for attaining the goal, of profound prejudice and discrimination that are systemic (that is, widespread, institutionalized, and viscous), of a lack of options for escape out of disadvantage on the part of the individuals discriminated against (Maguire, p. 129).

The church's emphasis on the historical dimension of human persons and their groups is also a prudent caution concerning any sudden reform. "In the apprenticeship to difference, everything cannot be expected all at once, but the possibilities for new ways of living together and even of actual enrichment must be considered" ("The Church and Racism," sec. 29). This prudence is, however, a necessary means toward the required society, one that is more complete, just, and peaceful.

Some of the groups whose members have been discriminated against are those whose traditions can offer the predominant social groups ways of recovering the interrelation of freedom and justice so that more persons may readily grasp affirmative action's special concern for the victims of discrimination and adopt still other (and perhaps more adequate) means for maintaining vigilance against discrimination. Two such sources are the experience and reflection of the black churches and the articulations of concerned scholars in the feminist movement.

See also CIVIL LAW, FUNCTION OF; COMMON GOOD; EMPLOYMENT AND UNEMPLOYMENT; EVIL, SOCIAL; GOODS, ACCESS TO; MINORITIES; PERSON, DIGNITY OF.

Bibliography: R. Dworkin, "How to Read the Civil Rights Act," in *A Matter of Principle,* pp. 316–31 (Cambridge: Harvard Univ. Press, 1985). D. Maguire, *A New American Justice* (Minneapolis: Winston, 1980). C. Mooney, *Inequality and the American Conscience: Justice Through the Judicial System* (New York: Paulist, 1982). NCCB, "Brothers and Sisters to Us," *Origins* 9 (November 29, 1979) 381–89. Pontifical Justice and Peace Commission, "The Church and Racism," *Origins* 18 (February 23, 1989) 613–26. G. Ezorsky, *Racism and Justice: The Case for Affirmative Action* (Ithaca: N.Y.: Cornell Univ. Press, 1991).

PHILIP J. CHMIELEWSKI, S.J.

AGED, CARE OF

Eldercare as a Natural Duty

Care for those who are aged is a primal natural duty widely shared across cultures. Though it is a traditional value with ascriptive role responsibilities, eldercare retains its practical salience even in industrial democracies, with up to 90 percent of support for infirm old people in the United States coming from the so-called informal sector, mostly from spouses, adult children, and other close family members (Lewis). At the same time, governments have increasingly regarded eldercare as a responsibility of the welfare state, with the public providing old-age insurance and medical services for the elderly population (Wolfe). In the 1980s, however, changing demographics and costly advances in medicine have raised difficult questions about the financial burdens medical care of the aged will place on the public and the personal costs it will place on younger family members. These anticipated difficulties have led in turn to controversial proposals about rationing health care to men and women in old age (Callahan, 1987, 1989; Wolfe).

A Basic Obligation

Filial responsibility. The Hebrew and Christian traditions regard filial responsibility to elderly parents as a basic duty for all human beings. The Decalogue lists the fourth commandment, "Honor your father and your mother" (Exod 20:12), as the first duty to members of the human community immediately following duties to God, thus showing its importance. For centuries a mistaken rabbinic and patristic interpretation of this text applied the command to the obedience and reverence of young children for their elders, but the injunction actually fell upon adult children and required them to support their parents in old age (Collins) and to defend their honor when they became feeble or senile (Sir 3; Harrelson). Furthermore, Jewish piety regarded support of widows (and orphans) as paradigmatic of the justice of the pious Jew (Harris).

Christianity maintained and expanded the Jewish concern for care of elders. The Gospels record Jesus rebuking the Pharisees for legal subterfuges that allowed people to avoid contributing to the financial support of parents (Mt 15:1-9, parr.), and John's Gospel depicts Jesus entrusting his mother to the Beloved Disciple's care (19:25-27). The Letter of James, in continuity with the Jewish tradition, taught that pure, unspoiled religion consisted in coming to the help of orphans and widows (1:27). In keeping with this tradition, the early Christian community organized support for widows who had no male relative to support them, and the Jerusalem community instituted the office of deacon to oversee the distribution of bread to them (1 Tm 5:3-16; Acts 6:1-6; Laporte).

At the same time, the NT contains antifamilial strains that modulated the absoluteness of intergenerational bonds as they existed in ancient Israel. True disciples transferred their allegiance from their human families to God's family, from parents and children to the person of Jesus (Mt 12:46-50, parr.; 10:37-39, parr.). Thus the early Christians expected that the gospel would divide family members from one another (Mt 10:35-36). Exegetes explain these texts both as accurate representations of the kind of familial divisions prompted by acceptance of the gospel and as entailments of an "interim ethic" prompted by belief in imminence of the end-time. Some explain the dominical saying "Unless one hates father and mother" (see Lk 14:26-27) as Semitic hyperbole and contend that Jesus is demanding a preferential love for himself and God's kingdom rather than a complete rejection of family ties. In any case, the antifamilial themes in the Gospels established a biblical foundation for celibacy in service of God and the church.

The antifamily texts notwithstanding, from the patristic period onward the church has taught that care for elderly people is an obligation under the natural law and has interpreted the eschatological ethic as "counsels of perfection." On this reading, religious, for example, might be considered free of the ordinary obligation to care for their parents by reason of their professed poverty and other special commitments. In the *Summa theologiae*, however, Thomas Aquinas held that insofar as it is in their power, religious ought to care for their elderly parents (2a IIae, q. 101). In sum, caregiving to those who are elderly is a basic obligation even in the Christian dispensation, and only especially grave circumstances (e.g., family's opposition to the gospel, missioning to preach the gospel) exempts an individual from undertaking eldercare. Contemporary Catholic social teaching, moreover, makes eldercare an element of the common good, which the several units of society (family, local community, public authority) ought to supply according to the principle of subsidiarity (Curran).

The content of the obligation. The duty to honor father and mother consists in three offices: support, care, and respect. *Support* involves financial assistance to preserve the elder from hardship and poverty as well as provision of services that the impairments of age prevent elders from carrying out on their own (e.g., shopping, seasonal yard work, coping with bureaucracies). *Care* refers to the more intimate work of bathing, grooming, and nursing the enfeebled or chronically ill old person. Care, in other words, is associated with basic nursing tasks, including supervising medication and assisting with basic therapies. Finally, *respect,* what Aquinas refers to as "cultus," involves those deeds that contribute to the elder's well-being and self-respect. These include visiting, gift giving, and other expressions of esteem and affection. But the basic elements of caregiving, that is, support and care, also contribute to reverence for elders in that such services preserve them from neglect and establish a ring of privacy that shelters enfeebled and senile persons from the public derision that attends isolated living (or abandonment).

In a Christian context a special form of respect for elders may be found in spiritual friendship between elder and caregivers or between elder and adult children (Christiansen, forthcoming). Housebound or bedfast, having outlived many of their contemporaries, men and women in late old age sometimes desire companionship even more than physical care. The life-tasks of late old age include (1) integrating life experiences, (2) coping with disengagement and loss, and (3) facing finitude, diminishment, and death. By listening to their stories, sharing their feelings, and praying with them, family members and other caregivers can assist frail and sick old people in meeting these psychological and spiritual needs, thus enriching their last years together. Because the physical and psychological strains of caregiving are often so great, both family caregivers and institutional providers need to make conscious efforts to care for these deep personal needs.

Distributing responsibility. The advent of the welfare state saw a decline in the legal requirements that adult children support parents in their old age, but in the 1980s escalating public expenditures induced several U.S. states either to enforce the provisions of older poor-laws or to draw up new legislation mandating filial assistance to impoverished parents (Wolfe; Curran). Even the Scandinavian welfare states have found it necessary to reevaluate programs for the aged population. Any honest assessment must acknowledge that support for elders is a responsibility shouldered by a number of parties, beginning with elders themselves and including family members, voluntary organizations, and government at all levels.

Seniors are a major source of aid to one another. Elderly spouses, for example, form the largest block of caregivers, and widows form networks of support for one another. Furthermore, Social Security and other old-age insurance plans have made it possible for a large portion of the aged population to remain financially independent. Indigency among this group is far less common than it was thirty years ago. Old age by itself is seldom any longer a cause for poverty. Insofar as these social insurance plans are contributory, elders are self-supporting. With life expectancy growing and the ratio of old to young changing, however, the relative contribution of the older generation to its own support has shrunk, and the financial independence of retirees from younger family members rests more and more on public funding. Similarly, through health-care programs like Medicare, the public sector bears the brunt of the financial cost for eldercare.

Family Caregiving

While the financial support offered by family members is limited, their involvement in primary care of elderly relatives is significant and growing. In the 1980s the proportion of caregiving to infirm old people provided by family members grew from 65 percent to 90 percent of the total. The contribution of family members comes largely through direct services: household chores, shared living accommodations, companionship, cooking, grooming, and nursing.

Familial justice. Typically the primary caregiver to elderly relatives is a woman, and with increased participation of women in the work force, the strains of caregiving on middle-aged women has grown. Likewise, the rapid growth of the very old (eighty-five years or more) has increased burdens for those in middle and early old age who themselves are beginning to be impaired. On the whole, U.S. public policy, with a bias for helping only needy individuals, has been reluctant to acknowledge the costly contribution made by family members to care of elders. But some states and voluntary organizations have begun to assist caregivers with experimental respite programs, adult day health-care facilities, and counseling to caregivers.

Whatever public or voluntary assistance can be offered family caregivers, greater burden sharing within families has become a necessity. Justice requires that siblings provide help and relief for the primary caregiver and her (or his) household. Similarly, spouses and adult and teenage children ought to carry some share of responsibility for eldercare and exercise care for the primary caregiver.

Familial dependence: is it paternalism? In its early development, contemporary bioethics placed a great deal of emphasis on the principle of autonomy and so questioned relationships in which adults might be dependent on others. While familial dependence offers occasions for abuse of elderly family members, on the whole the risks of paternalism are slight compared to the dangers of isolation, neglect, or abandonment in late old age. Thus elders rationally choose dependence on family members over isolation or premature institutionalization (Halper). Moreover, in most situations caregivers and caregiving families surrender a measure of freedom when they commit themselves to support an elder over the long term (Christiansen, 1982). Finally, in most circumstances family care extends the effective freedom of the elder in ways that neither isolation nor institutionalization would permit.

In social terms dependency is a normal developmental condition in the life of the mature intergenerational family, and autonomy is an appropriate controlling principle for only limited periods of life (early adulthood and middle age). Still, physically impaired elders maintain a critical interest in making fundamental choices about their lives. Under ordinary conditions they retain the right to make key decisions about living conditions, long-term care, and terminal medical treatment.

A Right to Eldercare

In liberal democratic societies the traditional concept of filial obligation has to a considerable extent been replaced by the notion of a right to care in old age. Even contemporary biblical treatments of the fourth commandment reformulate elders' interest in moral practices that assure welfare in old age as a basic human right (Harrelson). Official Catholic social teaching, particularly Pope John XXIII's *Mater et magistra* (1961) and *Pacem in terris* (1963), affirms the right of all persons to social security and health-care services in old age (Curran). While rights language strengthens the hand of elders in satisfying their needs, it creates social tensions in liberal democracies (Wolfe). Because liberal societies identify rights with specific entitlements, it becomes politically difficult to alter particular patterns of services offered to seniors in order to meet other needs, whether of seniors or of other needy groups. In addition, because the Anglo-American tradition regards rights as unconditional or absolute, people think it objectionable to weight the rights of elders against those of other dependent groups (e.g., persons with disabilities or children) or against the burdens such groups place on the rest of society.

The Roman Catholic rights tradition represents an alternative model that obviates some of these difficulties. Alternative policy packages are understood to be instrumental to satisfying the right, and only core rights, in this case the general right to care and support in old age, are absolute (Hollenbach). Thus society must find some way to meet old people's needs, but no one way to do so is prescribed. In addition, contemporary Catholic social teaching affirms that people ought to sacrifice their rights when continued enjoyment of rights would make them privileged at the expense of other groups (Christiansen, 1989). Elderly persons would be no exception in this regard. When their entitlements make them an advantaged group, the common good requires that they support policies that sacrifice their advantages so that the disenfranchised may share in a better quality of life. A counterexample to this principle was the resistance of affluent U.S. seniors to a tax surcharge required by the 1988 Catastrophic Health Care Act, which prompted Congress to repeal this vital legislation the following year. In the absence of willingness to sacrifice for the sake of the common good, the expanding costs of eldercare may force public examination of rationing health care for old people.

Intergenerational Justice

Elder support and the common good. In his 1987 book, *Setting Limits,* Daniel Callahan proposed that skyrocketing health-care costs could be brought into line by restricting treatment of elderly persons, defined as those eighty years or older, to chronic and palliative care. Old people would be systematically denied acute care and expensive new technological interventions.

Callahan's argument went this way. An individual ethic of compassion has combined with a pattern of medical innovation to produce enormous inequities in public expenditure. The symbol for this gross imbalance in fiscal priorities is that the preponderance of the health-care dollar is spent on the last year of life. Callahan reasoned that since a person should have reasonably fulfilled his or her expectations in a natural life span of fourscore years, it would be fair to restrict life-extending treatment of octogenarians. Motivated by a concern for justice in the health-care system and in society at large, Callahan conditioned his proposal on the politically difficult condition of just distribution of the savings to society's have-nots, especially poor children.

In a comprehensive 1989 study of justice in health care, *What Kind of Life: The Limits of Medical Progress,* Callahan has elaborated on his position. Aside from preventative care and public health, he argues, the public has no obligation to offer medical treatment to individuals. He continues to adhere to the proposal that age be a standard for rationing health care and that elderly people be excluded from acute treatment. Furthermore, appealing to the natural priority of caring over curing he argues that caregiving ought to be the basis of any public health-care policy, thereby setting a limit to the exploding costs of inappropriate curative medicine. Such a limited health-care program, Callahan contends, would better attain the common good by providing equal care for all and restricting the escalation of health-care costs so that other public needs (e.g., education and child welfare) could also be served.

Insofar as the Callahan proposal aims at greater equity, broader distribution of health-care benefits across the generations, and greater justice between groups, it promotes the common good as understood by Catholic social teaching. Since that teaching requires, moreover, that privileged groups such as middle-class senior citizens yield their especially advantaged status for the sake of allowing marginal groups like poor children to share in a common quality of life, rationing acute medical treatment to the very old and terminally ill is not unreasonable. Because it refocuses public policy on the essential role of caring in health care, the Callahan proposal also fits the realities of eldercare far better than programs centered on medical treatment. A care-centered public policy may better satisfy the needs of frail old people and offer more useful assistance to their caregivers than present cure-centered policies. But to the extent that it permanently excludes old people from the improving quality shared by the society at large, it departs from the standard of relative equality in social conditions repeatedly affirmed by contemporary Catholic social teaching. For the foreseeable future, limits may have to be set on the explosion of health-care costs for aged people; however, these people ought not be unalterably banned from sharing in the advances of modern medicine.

Caregiving and Christian Virtue

The intimate, demanding, and ever-changing conditions in which both families and health-care professionals care for the old people are an invitation to practice specifically Christian virtues and to experience the workings of grace in the moral life (Christiansen, forthcoming). Caregiving, especially to frail and chronically infirm old persons, is a humble service. The intimate tasks of bathing, grooming, feeding, and so on that caregivers carry out are menial by nature. The sacrifice of career opportunities and social involvement for the sake of care narrows the caregiver's life and results in a loss of status. The indeterminateness of the span of the caregiving relationship, the increasing needs of the elder, and the frequent isolation of the caregiver produce psychic and physical strain. Thus, in attending to the needs of the elder the caregiver experiences a Christlike self-emptying and humiliation (Phil 2:3-8). At the same time, caregiving requires Christlike virtues of gentleness, patience, and forgiveness. These special qualities distinguish Christian love, especially as a preferential option for those who, like men and women in old age, live in need at the margins of society. The presence and growth of such virtues under the protracted pressures of caregiving confirms the virtues of caregiving as "fruits of the Spirit" (Christiansen, forthcoming).

See also AUTHORITY, POLITICAL; COMMON GOOD; DECALOGUE; FAMILY; HEALTH CARE; NATURAL LAW; RIGHTS AND DUTIES.

Bibliography: D. Callahan, *Setting Limits: Medical Goals in an Aging Society* (New York: Simon & Schuster, 1987). D. Callahan, *What Kind of Life: The Limits of Medical Progress* (1989). A. Christiansen, "Autonomy and Dependence in Old Age: An Ethical Analysis" (Ph.D. diss., Yale Univ., 1982). D. Christiansen, "The Common Good and the Politics of Self-Interest," in Donald Gelpi, ed., *Beyond Individualism* (Notre Dame: Univ. of Notre Dame Press, 1989). D. Christiansen, *When My Strength Is Spent: A Theological Ethics of Caregiving to the Elderly* (forthcoming). R. Collins, "The Fourth Commandment: For Children or Adults," in *Christian Morality: Biblical Foundations* (Notre Dame: Univ. of Notre Dame Press, 1986). C. Curran, "Filial Responsibility for an Elderly Parent," *Social Thought* 11:2 (Summer, 1985) 40–52. D. Halper, "Paternalism and the Elderly," in Stuart Spicker et al., eds., *Aging and the Elderly: Humanistic Perspectives in Gerontology* (Atlantic Highlands, N.J.: Humanities Press, 1978). W. Harrelson, *The Ten Commandments and Human Rights* (Philadelphia: Fortress, 1980). J. Harris, *Biblical Perspectives on Aging: God and the Elderly* (Philadelphia: Fortress, 1987). D. Hollenbach, *Claims in Conflict: Retrieving and Renewing the Catholic Rights Tradition* (New York: Paulist, 1979). J. Laporte, "The Elderly in the Life and Thought of the Early Church," in W. Clements, ed., *Ministry with the Aging* (San Francisco: Harper & Row, 1981). M. Lewis, "The Parish and the Elderly," *Church* 4:2 (Summer, 1988) 18–22. A. Wolfe, *Whose Keeper? Social Science and Moral Obligation* (Berkeley: Univ. of California Press, 1989).

DREW CHRISTIANSEN, S.J.

AGGRESSION

The term "aggression" has two separate and largely unrelated histories. The older is the use of the term in international affairs and the moral analysis of warfare. The second concerns the use of the term in the social sciences and ethics.

In international politics "aggression" refers to offensive military incursions; the term suggests action that is not warranted and thus is immoral. In traditional just-war theory a nation should resort to war only when a set of criteria is met (*jus ad bellum*). Traditionally, three reasons (defense, avenging evil, restoring violated rights) made this resort to war moral. Pius XII narrowed the three to one, defense. Repelling aggression (defending against an unjust attack) is quite central to just-war reasoning. Despite this, Catholic thinkers after World War II have noted critically the destructive nature of modern weapons, which often fail to meet the moral standards of reason and faith. The Second Vatican Council reasserted the right of a nation-state to self-defense in the absence of adequate transnational structures, legal or political, to protect the populace of a nation against aggression (*Gaudium et spes,* pt. 2, chap. 5). Subsequent church teaching emphasizes the reduction of injustice as a means to reduce aggression.

A review of the social-science literature on aggression reveals voluminous but confusing reports of observations, laboratory research, and theory. In a generic sense aggression refers to belligerent and uncontrolled behavior, conflictual behavior leading to violence, or behavior aimed at domination of others. In most cases aggression is viewed negatively, but being "aggressive" in the pursuit of goals (as diverse as profit, efficiency, and justice) is often lauded as good.

Social scientists differ on the definition of the term "aggression" and on what is studied; their terminology often differs widely from common usage. As a result, it is often difficult to evaluate conclusions from such studies. It is easiest to characterize schools of thought on this subject by examining their theories of causation.

The social environment is often seen as the locus of aggression; from this perspective aggression is viewed as a learned response to social situations or a response to stimuli in the environment. Beginning in the work of Dollard et al. (*Frustration and Aggression,* 1939), the cause of aggression was identified as frustration. Critics saw this explanation as circular and simplistic.

Advances in the methodology of the social sciences and the social unrest of the 1960s prompted more sophisticated theory incorporating social-learning theory and reinforcement (Leonard Berkowitz, *Aggression,* 1962). Reports submitted to the national commissions created to examine the causes of violence and civil disorders late in the decade modified the frustration/aggression theory by adding the idea that relative deprivation causes frustration. Reformist in intent, these reports were built on the postulate that reducing discrimination would decrease relative deprivation; the latter caused aggression and, consequently, violence. Social reform would engender greater peace. The *Report of the National Commission on Civil Disorders* (1969), called the "Kerner Commission Report," is an example of this type of literature.

A second theoretical school attributes aggression to an innate drive or instinct. Thinkers in this school include Konrad Lorenz (*On Aggression,* 1966) and E. O. Wilson (*Sociobiology,* 1975; *On Human Nature,* 1978). One can assume a buildup of explosive internal forces or genetically coded adaptive behavior as the basis of aggression, but within this school the fundamental presuppositions are the immutability of human nature and the inescapable traits of aggression and self-interest. To raise questions about the human ability to modify, limit, or control aggressive behavior is to raise the issue of what type of anthropology one holds; can one dismiss the question of human freedom? Theories proceeding from reductionistic and deterministic postulates, if accepted, negate the very basis of Christian ethics, as human freedom is a precondition for its existence.

Those authors who favor environmental causation suggest that while it is difficult to accurately predict aggressive behavior, this behavior correlates well with such factors as substance abuse, age, sex, and socioeconomic status. Research reveals that control of behavior has been more effective when contingency management measures were used than when psychotherapy was employed. Such information is useful for those evaluating aggression in light of Christian ethics. Theories proceeding from the presupposition of innate causes are suspect on both theoretical and ethical grounds. Theories postulating environmental causes have potential in both areas. However, a review of the social-science *Abstracts* over an extended period reveals that less than 1 percent of aggression studies have been designed with an explicit connection with ethics. Thus this literature is best seen as tangential to the formation of a Catholic social ethic. It can be useful in defining the problem and providing empirical assessment of parameters, but it cannot provide the core of moral assessment. Moral assessment will flow from a Catholic tradition of realism about human nature; it will avoid extremes of Manichaean pessimism and Pelagian optimism. A sense of sin is appropriate when assessing the social world, but a vision of redemption is necessary if we are to avoid an abject acquiescence to the "natural" condition of aggression. While we are unlikely to see an end to aggression (as we are not likely to abolish concupiscence), we can suggest a reduction of and limit to aggression. When formulating an attitude toward aggression we must consider nonviolence as a gospel imperative and a viable practical option.

See also CONSCIENCE; FREEDOM; GAUDIUM ET SPES; METHODOLOGY, MORAL; WAR.

Bibliography: J. Hehir, "The Just-War Ethic and Catholic Theology: Dynamics of Change and Continuity," in *In the Name of Peace: Collective Statements of the United States Bishops on War and Peace, 1919–1980* (Washington: USCC, 1983). A. Caplin, *The Sociobiology Debate* (New York: Harper & Row, 1978). A. Dulles, "Catholicity from Below: The Aspiration of Nature," in *Catholicity of the Church* (New York: Oxford Univ. Press, 1985). M. Neal, "The Future of Altruism," in *The Just Demands of the Poor* (New York: Paulist, 1987).

STEPHEN J. CASEY

AGNOSTICISM

Originally the assertion that we can neither know nor deny with certainty that God exists, the word "agnostic" was coined by British philosopher Thomas Huxley in 1869 and was intended to contrast with atheism, a much older notion. While the latter was the belief or conviction that God did not exist, agnosticism indicated a lack of knowledge whether God existed or not. At one time the etymological roots of the word were disputed, but the likeliest derivation is in the negation (*a-*) of knowledge (*gnosis*) about God. In its origins "agnosticism" can best be understood as a reaction to the same forces to which Vatican Council I responded the following year, producing the Roman Catholic assertion of confidence in human reason's ability to know God by natural means. The word has taken on a life of its own in subsequent years.

More broadly, "agnosticism" can be distinguished into several positions. The first, original meaning asserts the inability of human beings to know God by natural or rational means. Reason would thus have no choice but agnosticism, and belief in God could only be achieved through a "leap of faith." This meaning is the one denied by Vatican Council I, with its insistence that God is knowable by "the natural light of reason." A second possible use of the term asserts the absolute incomprehensibility of God and can be said to be widespread among Christian theologians and mystics like Thomas Aquinas and John of the Cross who emphasize the *via negativa.* The word "agnosticism" is applied to their position only retrospectively and academically.

At the time the term was coined, reason and proof were understood in a specific way. Made explicit, this version of agnosticism assumes a separate, third identity, one that asserts human inability to prove God's existence according to the understanding of proof commonly accepted as scientific in much of the 19th and 20th centuries. The opposite of such an agnosticism, an insistence on the efficacy of reason in an equally narrow sense—for example, the ability to prove that God exists—became de facto the official Catholic position through much of the 20th century. Confidence in human reason thus came to mean insistence that truths of faith such as God's existence could be proved according to the same understanding of proof and reason then common among scientistic agnostics. The same kind of certainty could be reached by reason with regard to the truths of faith, it was held, as scientific truths could be reached by science. Such an understanding of the reasonableness of faith was given offical sanction by Pius X during the Modernist crisis and became a part of the anti-Modernist oath. It was presupposed in documents such as Pius XII's *Humani generis* (1950) and was common in Catholic theology until Vatican II, when it became less acceptable. (At the same time, it should be noted, the acceptability of this idea of rational proof has also diminished—in fact, is all but disappearing—among philosophers of science.)

More recently Karl Rahner and others have insisted on God's unknowability and otherness (related to agnosticism in the second sense above) in a way that undermines the certainty of the traditional proofs and indeed casts serious doubt on their usefulness at all. Reason is here understood more broadly than in the anti-Modernist oath. Knowledge of God is distinguished from the ability to prove God's existence. Thus this position denies that God's existence can be proved but not that God can be known by human reason. It is not agnostic but asserts the naturalness of human knowledge of God according to a different, less deductive understanding of reason. Though the insistence on scientific proofs for God's existence has declined, the assertion of the reasonableness of faith has not changed. There has thus been a return to the doctrine of Vatican I, away from that of the anti-Modernist oath.

Although the term "agnosticism" continues to be used, it can be said that interest in agnosticism has shifted from theoretical to practical concerns. Without an emphasis on proving God's existence, agnosticism in the strict sense has declined as a topic of official church discourse. Its place has been taken by concern for the marginalization of religion common in advanced industrial societies. It has become identified with secularization and/or the privatization of religion in modern pluralistic societies. In recent Catholic discussion agnosticism is rarely referred to alone but is usually linked with secularism or atheism. In a 1986 statement in Colombia, John Paul II seems to have been referring to agnosticism when he spoke of one kind of materialism as "the practical attitude of those who live as if God did not exist." This would be agnosticism in a practical rather than a theoretical sense, a fourth meaning of the term.

See also ATHEISM; MODERNISM; PLURALISM; REASON, ROLE OF; SECULARISM; THOMAS AQUINAS, CONTRIBUTION OF.

Bibliography: K. Rahner, *Foundations of the Christian Faith* (London, 1978). H. Küng, *Does God Exist?* (Garden City, N.Y.: 1980).

ANTHONY BATTAGLIA

AGRICULTURE

Agriculture, the central economic contribution of the Neolithic age (ca. 10,000 B.C.) to the progress of civilization, was developed primarily by women as a deliberate way to use the resources of nature to supplement the product of hunting and fishing. All prehistory and early history—of the Sumerians, the Egyptians, the Persians, the Chinese—testify to its centrality and describe its traditional but constantly improving methods. The OT abounds in references to, descriptions of, and prescriptions about agriculture and how it should be organized. For example, the land was to lie fallow in the seventh year, and all land was to return to its owners in the 49th year. Throughout the Hebrew and Christian Scriptures there is an underlying assumption that the farmer, tilling the soil and producing crops, is closest to God in the act of creation.

Just as agriculture was the basis of economics, it was also the basis of politics. Towns and cities, the locus of politics, developed from original markets and trading posts. Armies traveled on their stomachs in ancient times, as today. The Romans developed a relatively sophisticated commercial agriculture, which declined after the collapse of the empire in the West. It is generally recognized that no nation has grown and remained powerful or developed a modern industrial economy without a sound and productive agricultural sector. Agriculture was the foundation of the strength and growth of modern France, England, Germany, and the United States; its weakness or failure brought about the decline of many earlier civilizations (the succession of empires in Mesopotamia, the Moghuls in India, the Mayans in Central America) and was the major obstacle to economic progress in the former Soviet Union.

The early church was mainly urban and had little immediate impact on the agricultural sector of society. From the 4th century on, however, the practice fostered by the Benedictines of monks working in the fields with peasants grew and sustained agricultural development. In the 10th and 11th centuries the Cistercians stimulated international agricultural trade and the growth of market towns. But in the 14th century, after the Crusades and the Black Death had weakened both the nobility and the feudal society, primitiveness returned to agriculture.

Modern agricultural development, beginning four centuries later, coincided with the Industrial Revolution, the enclosure movement, and other social changes, all of which reduced the peasantry and increased the urban labor force in societies where religion was no longer central. While Jethrow Tull in England in the 18th century was changing the face of agriculture forever by substituting row tillage for broadcast sowing and Johann Liebig in Germany in the 19th was perfecting chemical fertilizers, theologians were wrestling with less mundane matters.

Today, however, several trends have stimulated an interest in developing a systematic approach to the ethics and, perhaps, the moral theology of agriculture: (1) the sharp contrast between the steady and sometimes dramatic industrialization of agriculture in the modern surplus-producing nations and its stagnation in the many countries that remain poor and hungry; (2) the new emphasis on the multiple dangers to the physical environment, many of which arise in the agricultural sector; and (3) the remarkable breakthroughs in genetic research and biotechnology, which both promise and threaten.

Parables about the sower, the likening of the Resurrection to the gestation of seed, and other concepts from the Christian tradition were not intended to represent a theology of agriculture. Nor do St. Gregory the Great's letters to Peter, the subdeacon of Sicily, which provide interesting insights into grain-pricing policies and agricultural and tax practices on Vatican land, constitute a systematic approach. Relations between the monasteries and the landed aristocracy in the Middle Ages and during the Renaissance do not yield such an approach either, and they raise several other social and political questions not directly related to agriculture.

Nevertheless, "theology of land" conferences have become increasingly frequent in recent years, and religious lobbyists on social policy constantly seek a logical intellectual structure to support what they advocate in agriculture as in other fields. At the same time, the environmental movement and creation theology have provided added motivation in this direction, partly because of the clear contribution of many agricultural practices to the deterioration of the physical environment.

Although scattered references to agriculture will be found in the early church fathers (e.g., St. John Chrysostom and those letters of St. Gregory), in the *Summa* writers of the Middle Ages (e.g., St. Thomas Aquinas), and in early social encyclicals, the first extended treatments appear in Pope Pius XII's addresses in the 1950s and in Pope John XXIII's encyclical *Mater et magistra,* written in 1961 for the 70th anniversary of Pope Leo XIII's *Rerum novarum.*

Any systematic approach to the overall problem of food and agriculture broadly conceived must discuss both sides of the fundamental economic equation: the supply side (how food is produced) and the demand side (how it is distributed). Agriculture itself is basically concerned with production and supply. Essentially it is farming the sun via the natural process of photosynthesis: plants convert solar energy into food, which sustains human energy. In order to effect this conversion there must be land (now roughly one acre per person worldwide); water (more essential, in the end, than land—much of it supplied by irrigation); energy (some of it human or animal, some of it mechanical, some of it fossil-fuel-powered technology); seeds (some natural, but an increasing amount laboratory generated); technology (tools, tractors, combines, irrigation systems, etc.); research in all these areas; money to pay for all of them; and in the end the weather—the direct contribution of Divine Providence.

Demand-side elements include population (the people who consume, increasing by about 100 million per year); consumption patterns (very different in both quality and quantity for rich and poor); and social and political structures affecting production and distribution. The main thrust of post–World War II papal statements in this area has been on this demand side of the equation—expressing concern about the social injustice represented by malnutrition, famine, and chronic hunger amid bountiful harvests.

When Catholic social teaching has focused on the supply side, however, that is, on agriculture itself, it has tended to concentrate on four themes: equity in the land tenure system (ownership or the security of leases); the threat to rural life and rural communities posed by the accelerating industrialization of agriculture; the rights of farm workers; and, most recently, the increasingly dangerous degradation of the environment. These themes have been repeated many times by the popes, partly because the presence in Rome of the main international food and agriculture organizations, especially the United Nations Food and Agriculture Organization (FAO), has provided frequent occasions for papal addresses.

In several such talks to diplomats and to the successive annual conferences of the FAO, Pope Pius XII commended "the depth of vision which prompted the United Nations to set up an institution especially to deal with food and agriculture problems. . . . By working to increase and balance out the production and distribution of all food and agricultural products . . . you are contributing towards freeing nations from the miseries of poverty. . . . It is only right to concentrate on bettering the living conditions of rural peoples. By their labor these have been the diligent providers to and even the agents of the entire community" (*Pio XII,* vol. 9, March 2, 1947).

On several occasions Pope Pius expressed his concern about those who lack access to food, that is, who are not part of *effective* demand (ability to pay); but he clearly understood the supply side as well: "It is much more urgent to provide for the increased productivity of those very places where famine is felt. For that, you want first to reduce the sometimes considerable losses due to the inexperience of the growers, and due to epidemics; then to raise yields by improvement of the methods of cultivation, by the use of fertilizers, by the choice of plant species; and finally you are looking toward bringing into use areas still uncultivated, especially by means of irrigation" (*Pio XII,* vol. 14, March 2, 1953).

The social context of the production side did not go unnoticed either: "It is useless in effect to put in place experts to teach new methods and to perfect the mechanical equipment, if the human conditions in which man moves prevent him from obtaining from his effort the fruit he has the right to expect from it. . . . Thus, your economic work doubles itself with a social value that is not less decisive" (ibid.). Pope Pius also demonstrated a farsighted understanding of what we would now call the broader dimensions of the problem, "among other things, the rigidity of productive structures and the difficulty they have in responding adequately to the demand; the stagnation of world commerce in agricultural products; and the inadequate level of farm income compared with other activities" (AAS 48:53–57).

Pope John XXIII continued these themes in his annual addresses to the FAO conference. However, in *Mater et magistra,* having presented his initial description of the economic situation, he turned his systematic analysis first to agriculture as the primary sector. Dealing with what he termed new aspects of the social question, he noted that although the overall number of rural dwellers had not changed significantly, "many farmers have abandoned their rural birthplace, and seek out either the more populous centers or the cities themselves." While much of this exodus was attributed to visions of a more comfortable life, Pope John had no doubt that "rural dwellers leave the fields because nearly everywhere they see their affairs in a state of depression, both as regards labor productivity and the level of living of farm populations" (MM 123–24).

He proceeded to ask three questions arising out of "this grave matter," which are still very current today: (1) "What is to be done to prevent so great imbalances between agriculture, industry, and the services in the matter of productive efficiency?" (2) "What can be done to minimize differences between the rural standard of living and that of city dwellers?" (3) "How can it be brought about that those engaged in agricultural pursuits no longer regard themselves as inferior to others?" (125). It was clear to Pope John that "where . . . requirements for a dignified farm life are lacking to rural dwellers, economic and social progress does not occur at all, or else very slowly" (127). The encyclical went on to speak of equity in taxes, insurance, social security, credit, price protection, and income.

Rural workers received special attention and commendation; Pope John did not distinguish between owners and wage laborers—all were operators: "In rural affairs, the principal agents and protagonists of economic improvement, of cultural betterment, or of social advance, should be the men personally involved, namely, the farmers themselves. . . . Their work is most noble, because it is undertaken, as it were, in the majestic temple of creation; because it often concerns the life of plants and animals, a life inexhaustible in its expression, inflexible in its laws, rich in allusions to God, Creator and Provider. . . . Work of this kind, moreover, possesses a special nobility because it requires farmers to understand well the course of the seasons and to adapt themselves. . . . Since everything that makes for man's dignity, perfection, and development seems to be invoked in agricultural labor, it is proper that man regard such work as an assignment from God with a sublime purpose" (144–45, 149).

Pope Paul VI maintained the tradition of addressing the annual FAO conferences beginning with the Young World Assembly in 1965, which celebrated FAO's 20th anniversary. While continuing the emphasis on the scandal of hunger and other demand-side problems, he looked at agriculture more in the context of his first encyclical, *Populorum progressio,* which concentrates on development, understood as improvement of the quality of life of poor people. He also expressed an optimistic view of the contribution technology could make. He addressed the young people as "fortunate enough to live in a world in which technology is continually placing novel and wonderful instruments in the hands of human beings." "It rests with you," he said, "to see that these instruments really be used in the service of all mankind, so that the world of tomorrow may be different from that of today, a world where all may be brothers and sisters and at peace with one another" (AAS 57:995–97).

Pope Paul's central interest in development led him, like his immediate predecessors, to pay the greatest attention to the socioeconomic context of agricultural development: "We are . . . up against radical transformations that are causing upheavals in the life of the world. Rural civilization, which was formerly that of the majority of men and ensured their legitimate development, is now attacked on all sides by the rise of an urban, mechanical civilization that provides multiple objects intended to make men's lives more comfortable. Frequently isolated in remote country areas, are not the young often losing hope in their future as human beings? . . . Young rural people wish to live like other young people today, to exercise a well defined profession, to have a clearly marked social status, a house equipped with a minimum of comfort with surroundings worthy of the name. . . . In short, it is no longer sufficient to check the growing discrepancy of the situation of the rural populations in the modern world. It is a question of giving them a full place in it" (AAS 63:875–79).

Nevertheless, what Pope Paul esteemed the FAO for was its "tenacious efforts against hunger . . . this united work of research, comparison, forecast, organization, mutual help." He urged FAO to "specify the trends of international policy in the field of agriculture and food." At the same time, continuing in the vein of his encyclical, he deplored the diminution of the rich countries' contribution to development. Anticipating his successor, Pope John Paul II, he asserted that "the moment has come to strengthen and widen the movement of *solidarity* between the peoples of the world" (AAS 65:656–59).

During Pope Paul's pontificate the United Nations' World Food Conference convened in Rome in November 1974 in a sober atmosphere of global food shortages and famines. In his speech to that conference he addressed supply-side considerations in the vocabulary of *Populorum progressio:* "One of the most evident causes of the present disorder is the increased price of foodstuffs and of materials needed for producing them: Think, for example, of fertilizer, the scarcity and high price of which are threatening to reduce the beneficial effects that were rightly expected from the green revolution. But are not scarcity and high prices connected with fluctuations in a production that is regulated with a view to profit rather than to meeting the needs of mankind? The decrease in stocks of food . . . is at least partially due to commercial decisions that lead to our having no reserves." "Our real need, therefore," he continued, "is for courageous reforms to eliminate obstacles and imbalances deriving in part from outmoded structures that perpetuate unbearable injustices or hinder production and the effort to assure the adequate flow of vital goods" (AAS 66:644–52).

Returning to the recurring theme of his predecessors, Pope Paul insisted that "even the most generous international aid, a more intense research into and application of agrarian technology, and a very careful planning of food production will be almost useless unless we quickly repair a serious defect in our technological civilization. The worldwide food crisis cannot be overcome without the help of the farmers. That help will not be fully and effectively given unless we radically change the attitude of the contemporary world which attaches little importance to agriculture. . . . However valuable the technological means available, nothing will be accomplished without the true reform represented by the rehabilitation of agriculture and the reversal of present attitudes towards it" (ibid.). Farmers themselves, of course, would have to change as well: "Farmers must esteem and be faithful to the way of life they have chosen; they must implement the programs for crop improvement that are indispensable if farming is to escape its age-old sameness and narrowly empirical basis, and to adopt new working methods, new machines and new approaches" (*Osservatore Romano,* November 1966, pp. 14–15).

Pope John Paul II kept up the tradition of FAO addresses, added to it an annual World Food Day (October 16) message, and emphasized the role of agriculture in the characteristically disciplined intellectual and doctrinal articulations of both *Laborem exercens* (1981) and *Sollicitudo rei socialis* (1987). In the former he wrote that "in many situations radical and urgent changes are . . . needed in order to restore to agriculture—and to rural people—their just value as the basis for a healthy economy, within the social community's development as a whole" (LE 21). In the latter he called attention to "the production and distribution of foodstuffs" as the first of those sectors characterized by the gap between the abundance available in the industrialized North and the chronic hunger of the impoverished South (SRS 14).

Pope John Paul II has addressed peasants and farmers in every country he has visited, including the United States. In Mexico in 1979 he told the Indians of Cuilapan: "The depressed rural world, the worker who with his sweat waters also his affliction, cannot wait any longer for full and effective recognition of his dignity, which is not inferior to that of any other social being. He has the right to be respected and not deprived with maneuvers which are sometimes tantamount to real spoliation of the little that he has. He has the right not to be impeded in his aspirations, to share directly in his own advancement. He has the right to be rid of the barriers of exploitation, often made up of intolerable selfishness, against which his best efforts of advancement are shattered. He has the right to real help—which is not charity or crumbs of justice—in order that he may have access to the development that his dignity as a person and as a child of God deserves" (AAS 71:209).

A decade later he told farmers and others in Monterey, California, that "we must use the land to sustain every human being in life and dignity." Noting that "the productivity of American agriculture is a major success story," he commended growers, workers, processors, distributors, and consumers, whose interaction was responsible for this success (September 20, 1987).

One of Pope John Paul's most cogent contributions to the teaching on agriculture is his concept of the "social mortgage" on private property, which he first stated at the Third General Conference of the Latin American bishops (Puebla, January 28, 1979) and then applied expressly to agriculture in his address to the World Conference on Agrarian Reform and Rural Development in Rome on July 14 of that year. "Your Conference in Rome," he said, "is dealing with a subject of extreme importance for the destiny of the human family, and one of lively interest for the Church, which by virtue of her mission feels a commitment to making an impartial contribution, corresponding to her nature, to the human uplifting of those who live and work on the land. . . . With conditions as they are within individual countries, one foresees a land reform involving a reorganization of land holdings and the stable and direct assigning of productive areas to agricultural workers, together with the elimination of forms and structures that are unproductive and damaging to the community" (AAS 71:1343–48).

It was Pope John Paul's World Day of Peace message of January 1, 1990, that provided the latest breakthrough toward a theology of agriculture. By concentrating on the problems of the environment, it moved beyond the specific emphases of his predecessors and brought a further dimension to Catholic social teaching in this area. He had already begun this emphasis years before, reminding his American audience in Monterey, for example, that "we cannot say we love the land and then take steps to destroy it for use by future generations."

In the 1990 World Peace Day message Pope John Paul wasted no time getting to the point: "In our day, there is a growing awareness that world peace is threatened not only by the arms race, regional conflicts and continued injustices among peoples and nations, but also by a lack of due respect for nature, by the plundering of natural resources and by a progressive decline in the quality of life." The pope was not satisfied with the response of "better management or a more rational use of the earth's resources, as important as these may be." He insisted on viewing this crisis in the light of creation and human dignity, excusing no area of society from responsibility.

Turning specifically to agriculture, he decried "unrestricted deforestation" and the use of "certain herbicides" and noted that "delicate ecological balances are upset by the uncontrolled destruction of animal and plant life or by a reckless exploitation of natural resources." "We are not yet in a position," he continued, "to assess the biological disturbance that could result from indiscriminate genetic manipulation and from the unscrupulous development of new forms of plant and animal life."

To be effective, he asserted, any program to halt and reverse environmental degradation must not only be international and informed by the virtue of solidarity but must also address both the supply and the demand aspects. "Rural poverty and unjust land distribution in many countries, for example, have led to subsistence farming and to the exhaustion of the soil. Once their land yields no more, many farmers move on to clear new land, thus accelerating uncontrolled deforestation, or they settle in urban centers which lack the infrastructure to receive them. Likewise, some heavily indebted countries are destroying their natural heritage, at the price of irreparable ecological imbalances, in order to develop new products for export. . . . The poor, to whom the earth is entrusted no less than to others, must be enabled to find a way out of their poverty."

Church leaders in most countries with modern agricultural systems have become involved in public policy questions; many Catholics are farmers or live in rural areas, and many are involved in agro-industry. For example, after the publication of their 1986 pastoral letter on the U.S. economy, *Economic Justice for All,* the bishops, who had discussed agriculture as one of four specific economic issues in that letter, established an ad hoc task force on food and agriculture to take a deeper look at that sector in the United States. Noting that the then current farm crisis reflected "the changing structure of ownership, greater concentration and control of food production and distribution and of the agricultural resource base, and the deteriorating condition of land, water and air," the task force asked five basic questions: (1) "Who effectively controls the system?" (2) "Who makes the crucial decisions?" (3) "Who benefits from the system?" (4) "Does it enable people to participate effectively in it?" (5) "Are the major actors . . . responsive to the needs of society?"

The task force's report focused on land ownership, food security, rural poverty, food trade, and the stewardship of natural resources. It made recommendations for the church's rural ministry and proposed that the bishops publish an official statement on food and agricultural policy. That statement, *Food Policy in a Hungry World,* was adopted by the full body of bishops on November 8, 1989. The statement noted that it was not the first time that the bishops or Catholic agencies had spoken out on these issues, and it grounded itself specifically in the scriptural and encyclical tradition:

"First, at the core of Catholic social teaching is the sacredness of the human person. Each one of us is created in the image of God. . . . Second, understanding human dignity leads to a commitment to the rights of the human person—the base line against which the justice of a society can be measured. One such right is the right to food to sustain life. . . . Third, the human person is not only sacred but social. . . . Fourth, the Scriptures and our tradition express a special concern—a preferential option—for the poor. . . . Fifth, by acknowledging that the earth is the Lord's and that God is present in all of creation, we show respect for God's creation" (6–9 passim).

It should be clear from the foregoing that Catholic social teaching, particularly in the 20th century, has been far from silent on the problems of agriculture, even though that subject itself has rarely been the identifiable thrust of a particular document. And while there is a designated patron saint of farmers, St. Isidore (May 15), there appears to be no definitive treatise *de agricola.*

Contrasts between Catholic social teaching and the directions agriculture is actually taking are notable. Much emphasis, for example, has been laid on the family farm as the preferred organization of agriculture; but family farms are inexorably disappearing all over the world. In the poorer developing countries displaced farmers swell the populations of urban slums; in the industrialized world they become contractors growing crops or raising animals for a vertically integrated agro-industry.

A particular uniqueness has been ascribed to agriculture because of its closeness to creation and because its main product, food, is so essential to human survival, yet agro-industry has proven itself capable of producing enormous quantities of food without the small farm unit. These harvests are achieved through heavy use of sophisticated machinery that degrades the soil and depletes the groundwater, as well as of chemicals that damage the environment and harm both the people who use them and those who consume the products.

Agriculture is generally considered to have as its purpose the production of food and fiber, with any surplus production to be exchanged in the market; but modern agriculture clearly subordinates production to marketing, that is, farming is undertaken to produce profit rather than to feed people. Catholic social teaching on food and agriculture, however, insists on viewing the marketing component not simply as one economic sector producing for profit but as an element in both a proximately larger system (that of food and agriculture) and a more remotely larger one (the international systems of finance, trade, politics, and social development as a whole). It has also focused repeatedly on the question of urban-rural equity, the personal worth of farmers and rural people, and the requirement of stewardship of God's creation. In short, Catholic social teaching regards the problems of agriculture in the context of social justice based on human dignity rather than as mere economic activity.

The contrasts outlined above pose new and formidable challenges to the church. Without questioning the soundness of the now-traditional approach to this set of issues, it seems clear that a moral theology dealing with agriculture will have both to treat it in the larger context and to deal with powerful trends, which, although they are unlikely to be reversed, can and must be arrested.

See also DEVELOPMENT; ECOLOGY; ECONOMIC ORDER; HUNGER; LAND; NATIONAL CONFERENCE OF CATHOLIC BISHOPS, UNITED STATES; SOLIDARITY; TECHNOLOGY.

MARTIN M. McLAUGHLIN

AID

Aid is assistance extended from one individual or group to another motivated by charity (*Gaudium et spes* 69) that is Christian (*Populorum progressio* 67) or universal (PP 43); by social or distributive justice (GS 69; PP 43); by the "right to have a share of earthly goods sufficient for oneself and one's family" (GS 69); by the duty incumbent upon wealthy nations (*Sollicitudo rei socialis* 7); or by the common good (*Mater et magistra* 80).

The biblical passages most often used to justify the demand for aid are the story of the rich man and Lazarus (John Paul II, homily at Yankee Stadium 7; *Economic Justice for All* 48) and the Last Judgment scene from Mt 25 (EJA 44). Regarding the first John Paul II pointed out that the rich man was not condemned for being rich but "because he did not pay attention to the other man."

Aid is given to the weak (PP 45), the young (MM 183), the needy (Paul VI's call for the Holy Year 37), the economically underdeveloped (SRS 39), the developing countries (GS 86), and refugees (John Paul II, Mexico City, January 1979).

Rerum novarum (1891) emphasized charity from wealthy individuals to poor ones or from the wealthy class to the poor class (RN 68). Even as late as *Mater et magistra* (1961) aid was seen as a transaction from the advanced to the less privileged countries (MM 160). During the pontificate of Paul VI (1963–78), however, official teaching placed much more emphasis on structural change. John Paul II acknowledges the need for structural change but often mentions the responsibility of individuals.

Since John XXIII official documents have spoken of reciprocal relations between donor and recipient, noting the dignity of the recipients of aid (Paul VI's U.N. speech and his address to the church of Africa 21) and urging that developing nations cultivate "their own talents and traditions" (GS 86) and "contribute to the common good with their treasures of humanity and culture" (SRS 39) and that donors respect the "moral heritage and ethnic characteristics" of recipients (*Pacem in terris* 125). More recent documents couch their discussion of aid in the context of solidarity, participation, cooperation, and mutual respect.

There are frequent exhortations that recipients of aid should feel responsible for their own destiny (MM 151), should "become the principal architects of their own economic and social development" (*Justitia in mundo* 71), and should always be treated as equals (JM 71). Likewise, donors should not give aid in order to establish their own political control over the recipients (MM 171), which would amount to neocolonialism (Paul VI to peoples of Africa 21). And foreign specialists, when they give aid, "should not behave as overlords but as helpers and fellow-workers" (GS 85).

The kinds of aid mentioned include emergency assistance (MM 161) as well as long-term or structural aid for agriculture (156), education (GS 85), technological development, and economic development. Vehicles of assistance can include grants, bilateral agreements (PP 52), regional cooperation (SRS 45), multilateral channels (JM 69), international organizations (PP 51), and worldwide collaboration (52). A more recent actor, which complicates the matrix of which aid is a part, is the transnational corporation (EJA 255).

The goals of aid are not simply to provide for the needy but also to minimize imbalances within countries and among countries (MM 150–52), to restore human relations among peoples (PT 163), and to assure "to each man a life conformed to his dignity" (Paul VI at U.N., October 4, 1965). The hope is that such aid will increase feelings of brotherhood among peoples (MM 155), a brotherhood that will last long after the need for aid disappears (PP 73).

Difficulties with foreign aid include lack of willingness to distribute goods (Paul VI to World Food Congress 4); failure of wealthy nations to recognize their duty to help poorer countries (SRS 16), including the United States, which gives the lowest amount of development assistance of any of the industrialized nations (EJA 266); and structural defects that prevent the facing of complex problems (PT 134–35). The U.S. Catholic bishops acknowledged the complexity of the issue of aid by setting it in the context of a fourfold system of transfer of resources: aid, trade, finances, and investment (EJA 281).

The most frequently cited obstacle to adequate aid is the excessive amount that is earmarked for military aid (PP 51), including military aid to oppressive regimes that use the weaponry against their own citizens. American foreign aid has been largely reduced to "selective assistance based on an East-West assessment of North-South problems, at the expense of basic human needs and economic development. Such a view makes national security the central policy principle. . . . This tendency must be resisted" (EJA 262).

The church's role includes providing aid (GS 88); helping the "advancement of civil institutions" (MM 179); sharing in "the responsibility in the construction of a new world order" (John Paul II, Monterrey, Mexico, January 1979); nurturing "aspirations for justice and peace" (John Paul II, Brazil, July 1979); and "assisting the birth of . . . liberation" from "famine, chronic disease, illiteracy, poverty, injustices in international relations and especially in commercial exchanges, situations of economic and cultural neo-colonialism" (*Evangelii nuntiandi* 30). Sometimes, the church is even required to sell its "expensive furnishings" to help the poor (SRS 31).

The tenor of the official documents has shifted in the three decades following the accession of John XXIII. The documents of the 1960s are marked by optimism, those of the 1970s by disillusionment, and those of the 1980s by a recognition of the immense complexity of the issues. Aid regarding food and agriculture offers a good illustration. John XXIII praised the United Nations Food and Agriculture Organization in 1961 (MM 156). Paul VI lamented the "notoriously insufficient" agricultural aid in his speech to the World Food Congress in 1975. The U.S. bishops in 1986 noted the complexity of the "international food system" in which "resource transfer channels . . . intersect and overlap" more clearly than in any other area of the global economy, involving huge amounts of assistance, trade, international financing, and private investment (EJA 281; see also *Octogesima adveniens* 43).

The teachings on aid have been met with criticism and praise. Milton Friedman, an economist who emphasizes the freedom of entrepreneurs criticizes *Economic Justice for All* as placing too much emphasis on aid to foreign governments, which are often tyrannical and which run the country "in the interest of the governing class and not of the people" (Gannon, p. 104). Donal Dorr, on the contrary, sees the recommendations about aid as part of a balanced program of both economic and political reforms (pp. 149–50).

See also ALMSGIVING; DEVELOPMENT; GOODS, DISTRIBUTION OF; TRANSNATIONAL CORPORATIONS.

Bibliography: Donal Dorr, *Option for the Poor* (Maryknoll, N.Y.: Orbis, 1983). T. Gannon, *The Catholic Challenge to the American Economy* (New York: MacMillan, 1987).

KENNETH P. J. HALLAHAN

AIDS

The gains of medicine in controlling and eliminating disease has been one of the success stories of Western society. In fact, by the early 1980s it appeared as if it were the beginning of the end for infectious diseases in the United States. However, in the spring of 1981 health-care professionals became aware that some young men were dying from an unknown cause that was attacking their immune systems.

In time, the disease came to be known as AIDS (acquired immunodeficiency syndrome), and its cause was identified as the human immunodeficiency virus (HIV). As of June 30, 1990, the Centers for Disease Control reported that 139,765 cases of AIDS had been reported in the United States and 85,430 persons with AIDS had died. Currently (all figures given in this article represent 1990 statistics and estimates), the United States Public Health Service estimates that about one million persons are infected with the virus. The Public Health Service projects that the cumulative number of AIDS cases by the end of 1993 will be between 390,000 and 480,000 with the cumulative deaths between 285,000 and 340,000.

Of those who have died of the disease in the United States, the largest number are homosexual and bisexual males (82,304) with the second largest category being male intravenous drug users (22,798). This is different from Africa, where the disease has primarily impacted heterosexuals. It is estimated that on the international level 700,000 people either have the disease or have died of it, while about 8 million people are infected with the virus. In the United States it is estimated that under 1 percent of the population is infected. Though some studies suggest a slowing of the rate of increase of new infections in some major metropolitan areas, it is evident that minority groups are disproportionately represented, that women of childbearing age and their infants are increasingly becoming infected, and that adolescents are more and more at risk. It is possible that in time AIDS in the United States no longer will be identified primarily with those who are homosexual.

The properties of HIV are such that it is quite resistant to treatment or elimination. First of all, it is a retrovirus, that is, it is a virus that is reverse-transcribed into the basic cell formulation pattern (DNA) of a person. Because the virus is able to become permanently incorporated into human genetic material it is able to reproduce itself rapidly and, therefore, to create large numbers of infectious viral particles. Once this retroviral integration has occurred, it is not possible to eliminate the "viral blueprint" by therapeutic means. Based on current scientific information, it would appear that any postinfection treatment of the uninfected cells would, therefore, have to continue for the rest of the life of the patient until such time as a way is found to alter the DNA.

Second, because the virus is intranuclear, the usual process by which the body fights off infection, namely the production of antibodies, is not effective. The result is that the virus is able to follow a course that includes the gradual loss of T4 cells and immune deficiency with the eventual onset of one or the other of those diseases considered by the Centers for Disease Control to be part of the immunodeficiency syndrome. These opportunistic infections include pneumocystis carinii pneumonia, tuberculosis, and forms of cancer such as Kaposi's sarcoma. This feature of the virus has two consequences: it will be more difficult to develop a vaccine to prevent infection, and those already infected, whether showing signs of illness or not, are able to infect others.

The complex nature of the virus and its course of development have led many in the scientific community to suggest that the term "AIDS" is obsolete and that it should be replaced by the term "HIV infection." This is because the HIV infection is a continuum of conditions ranging from the initial mononucleosis-like syndrome that usually is associated with a person's conversion to seropositive (carrying the virus), to a period of being asymptomatic (carrying the virus but showing no signs of illness), to showing symptoms of HIV infection, and finally to AIDS. Such a change in approach highlights several points: the asymptomatic period can vary in length from person to person, but the potential for spreading the infection remains; the need is for early diagnosis because it is possible that drugs will be developed either to prolong the life of persons with AIDS, for example, the drug zidovudine (AZT), or to halt or slow the progression of the disease in infected but asymptomatic persons; finally, it is not clear how many persons infected with the virus will progress to full-blown AIDS. Current data would suggest that without effective therapy the great majority of those infected by the virus will progress to AIDS and eventually death.

One of the more controverted questions related to the HIV infection is the way it is transmitted. All existing studies support the conclusion that the infection is not transmitted by casual contact or bug bites. Rather, it is limited to sexual contact in which there is an exchange of body fluids, sharing of contaminated needles or syringes, exposure to infected blood or blood products, transplantation of infected organs or tissues, and transmission from mother to child either in utero or during delivery.

It is in light of the above information that pastors and theologians of the church have addressed the ethical issues that surround the HIV infection. In the United States the discussion of some of the ethical issues was focused by the publication in December 1988 of a statement on AIDS by the Administrative Committee of the National Conference of Catholic Bishops/ United States Catholic Conference entitled *The Many Faces of AIDS: A Gospel Response.* Many considered the document to be moderate in nature. It addressed three issues: how should Christians relate to persons with AIDS or who have been exposed to the virus; what social responsibilities do we have for their care and support; and what can be done to prevent the spread of the disease.

In response to the first question the bishops indirectly rejected the position held by some that the HIV infection is the result of divine retribution for immoral behavior. Instead, it spoke of a God of compassion and forgiveness who revealed in Jesus the redemptive meaning of human suffering and pain. In this context the document called on believers to relate to those with the HIV infection in a gospel manner. (It should be noted that Pope John Paul II, in the remarks made during his 1987 visit to the United States and in subsequent addresses, has spoken in a similar fashion.)

As regards the social responsibilities of the church and society, the bishops addressed several specific public policy questions, two of which concerned testing for HIV antibodies and insurance. In essence the bishops argued that at the present time there was no need for widespread mandatory testing and spoke to the need for adequate health care for those who are infected.

Finally, the bishops spoke of the prevention of the disease. Recognizing the limited means available to treat the disease and the absence of any cure, they affirmed the importance of education as the one vehicle that could limit the spread of the disease and stressed that such education must be in the context of a fully integrated understanding of human sexuality. In such an understanding "human sexuality . . . is to be genitally expressed only in a monogamous heterosexual relationship of lasting fidelity in marriage . . . [and] is essentially related to permanent commitment in love and openness to new life." Any solution to AIDS, educational or otherwise, that is not in accord with this vision of human sexuality "will be merely short-term, ultimately ineffective and will contribute to the trivialization of human sexuality."

Within this context of clearly affirming church teaching on the meaning of human sexuality, the bishops then addressed two topics that became the source of much controversy: public education programs and education programs or counseling for those who are at risk or who have the virus. The bishops on the Administrative Committee argued that traditional Catholic moral reasoning would support a discussion about the use of condoms to prevent the spread of AIDS in public education programs *if* such programs presented such information in the context of the moral vision outlined above and *if* they indicated that such usage was neither medically sure nor morally correct. Turning to the question of public education programs for those at risk of being infected or who are already infected, the bishops argued in a more tentative fashion that the same traditional ethical wisdom *might* provide guidance for how such public education programs could be developed. In the appendix of the document, the bishops addressed the question of private counseling of persons at risk or who are infected and who are going to engage in activity that could endanger others. The bishops reasoned that the person providing such counseling, first of all, has the obligation to present authentic Catholic teaching, that is, to propose chaste living. The text then says: "If it is obvious that the person will not act without bringing harm to others, then the traditional Catholic wisdom with regard to one's responsibility to avoid inflicting greater harm may be appropriately applied."

In the days and weeks following the publication of *The Many Faces of AIDS* these three positions were debated vigorously. In an unusual development some bishops publicly disavowed parts of the statement while others supported it. Theologians and Roman officials spoke directly and indirectly to the issues under discussion. In retrospect it is evident that part of the controversy was fueled by a misunderstanding of what the bishops had said. But much of the discussion did center on one of the most pastorally sensitive areas of Catholic moral reasoning—its discussion of toleration of evil and cooperation in evil. At issue in the evolving discussion was the nature of these principles, their application to the specific issues mentioned above, and how closely the church as a social reality, as distinguished from its more "private" or personal pastoral action, can be involved in the application of these principles.

After months of discussion the full conference of bishops addressed the question and came to the decision that *The Many Faces of AIDS* would "remain in possession" as a statement of the bishops of the Administrative Committee and that the full conference would issue its own comprehensive statement on AIDS. That statement was approved by the full conference in November 1989. In many ways it affirmed the previous text. It also addressed some new questions. What it did not do was address the three areas of controversy.

In addition to the ethical issues noted above, several other ethical issues related to the HIV infection are of importance:

The treatment of HIV-infected persons. Whether from latent or overt homophobia or from fear of being exposed to the virus, some in the medical and dental professions have refused to treat people who are HIV positive. Involved in the discussion of whether there is an obligation to treat is the much broader question of how one should understand the nature of medicine and dentistry. Are they services ordered to the good of the human family, or are they business occupations like any other? If the self-interest that is most often associated with business were to dominate patient care, then self-exemption would be more easily justified. If, however, patient care is dominated by the notion of service, then one would reason with Pope John Paul II, who, in his September 1987 address to the Catholic Health Association in Phoenix spoke of "your moral obligation and social responsibility to help those who suffer" from the HIV infection.

The screening of persons for HIV infection. A debate continues over whether there ought to be mandatory screening for hospital patients, prison inmates, persons applying for marriage licenses, immigrants, and other groups of persons who might carry the disease and potentially place others at risk. The traditional entry into an ethical discussion of this question begins with the principle that one ought to have respect for persons. Such respect involves the observing of certain rules with regard to liberty, privacy, and confidentiality. These rules are not absolute rules; however, departure from them requires justification.

Dr. James Childress, in *AIDS and Public Policy* (Winter, 1987), proposes four conditions that must be met if these rules are to be violated. These conditions provide a matrix for determining whether mandatory screening is ethically appropriate: (1) such screening would have to be effective in protecting public health and the benefits outweigh costs and burdens; (2) there is no feasible alternative to this type of screening; (3) such screening should be done in such a fashion as to infringe as little as possible on personal liberty, privacy, and confidentiality; (4) other necessary conditions, when appropriate, must be fulfilled. In light of these conditions, most ethicists would argue that universal mandatory screening cannot be justified. At the present, screening of marriage license applicants and general workplace screening also are rejected. Screening where blood, semen, and organ donation are involved is justified.

Confidentiality of test results. Distinct from the question of mandatory testing is the matter of how one addresses the issue of a person who has tested positive but will not inform the spouse or any other person who might be at risk of becoming infected.

Often the discussion of this issue is contextualized by the recognition that the revelation of such information could lead to loss of employment, eviction from housing, termination of health insurance, and social isolation. Further, fear of revelation could keep those in need of testing from being tested and thus from the possibility of being treated. As one tracks the discussion of this question, it seems that the ethical choice is between giving priority either to the social benefit of almost absolute confidentiality or to the justice of equal treatment. Many in the Catholic tradition would argue that it does not seem responsible for social benefit to override the life of an innocent person.

Other health-care issues. How does one allocate health care—for example, in public urban hospitals where large numbers of AIDS patients at the end stage of their disease could potentially consume existing resources? What is the measure of "adequate" care for a person with AIDS when there is no hope for cure? Who makes health-care decisions for HIV-infected persons no longer considered competent to make such decisions? How are such decisions made?

Can persons with HIV infection enter into a sacramental marriage? This question has both canonical and moral implications. The moral issues are (1) the positive obligation not to bring harm to another, which would argue that an HIV-positive person should not engage in intercourse; and (2) the nature of marriage as a communion of life and love. In analyzing these issues some have argued that since the HIV infection is potentially fatal there is a natural-law prohibition against such a marriage. At the same time, they would say that it would be possible for the church to witness the marriage of a person with AIDS when in danger of death. Others would argue in a more nuanced fashion that if the couple cannot freely commit themselves to abstain from marital intercourse and if in such a situation they cannot sustain a community of life and love, then they should not marry. The general conclusion to be drawn from this discussion is that it is unlikely, other than in the case of imminent death, that an HIV-infected person should attempt to celebrate a sacramental marriage.

Can a condom be used in marital intercourse when one of the partners becomes infected during the course of the marriage? In a sense, this question involves many of the issues discussed with regard to *The Many Faces of AIDS.* Some would argue that while such an action would not be contraceptive, it would violate the nuptial meaning of marital intercourse and would be morally illicit. Others would say that just as medication ordinarily prescribed for contraceptive purposes can be morally licit when used for medical reasons, so too the condom can be morally licit in marriage when used to prevent the spread of disease.

Obviously, HIV infection is a reality that confronts society with the medical challenges associated with a pandemic as well as with significant moral issues.

See also COOPERATION, PRINCIPLE OF; DOUBLE EFFECT, PRINCIPLE OF; HEALTH CARE; HOMOSEXUALITY, SOCIAL IMPLICATIONS OF; NATIONAL CONFERENCE OF CATHOLIC BISHOPS, UNITED STATES; NATURAL LAW; PASTORAL CARE; TOLERATION, PRINCIPLE OF.

Bibliography: Institute of Medicine and National Academy of Science, *Confronting AIDS, Update 1988* (Washington: National Academy Press, 1988). M. Place, "The Ethical Response to AIDS," *America* 158:6 (February 13, 1988). W. Spohn, "The Moral Dimensions of AIDS," *Theological Studies* 49 (1988) 89–109. J. Keenan, "Prophylactics, Toleration, and Cooperation: Contemporary Problems and Traditional Principles," *International Philosophical Quarterly* 29 (1989) 205–20. G. Coleman, "Can a Person with AIDS Marry in the Catholic Church?" *Jurist* 49 (1989) 258–66.

MICHAEL D. PLACE

ALIENATION

Alienation is both a physical and a spiritual state. Its root in the word "alien" establishes its basic meaning of foreign in origin, allegiance, nature, or character: a stranger. "Alienation" develops the idea of the stranger to the concept of estranged, to be cut off, and applies it to feelings and affections as well as to property, the taking or diversion of anything from its owner or original purpose.

Karl Marx adopted the idea of alienation as estrangement and developed it as the moral foundation for his critique of the capitalistic system. He identified the wage worker in the capitalistic system as being in a state of alienation. She/he is alienated from the product of her/his labor because that product is owned and controlled by others. The worker is also alienated from the process of production because she/he has no control over the workplace. Workers are alienated and isolated from one another both through the productive process and through the competition that capitalism breeds. According to Marx, this state of alienation seriously impedes the workers' self-realization as human persons and the full flowering of their potential as creative, productive citizens in the society.

Socialist feminists extend the meaning of Marxist alienation beyond work into the social context of patriarchy, identifying women as living not only in an alienated work environment but also in an alienated social environment. Through the process of socialization and education women are schooled to view themselves as sexual functionaries for men and nurturing functionaries for children. Femininity as the cultural norm alienates women from themselves as strong, autonomous adults. Socialist feminists use this expanded concept of alienation as the theoretical framework for understanding women's consciousness and their place in the social structures. Although the theory has been articulated by socialist feminists, the feminist movement as a whole has applied its insights to describe women's alienation from their bodies, from themselves, and from other women, who are possible competitors for the affection of men, the other half of the social system built on patriarchy.

See also CLASS STRUGGLE; CULTURE; FEMINISM AND CATHOLIC SOCIAL THOUGHT; MARXISM; PERSON, DIGNITY OF; SEXISM; WOMEN.

MARIA RILEY, O.P.

ALMSGIVING

Almsgiving is any act of helping those in need, motivated both by human compassion and by love of God. While alms usually refer to corporal sustenance, they may also involve social and spiritual succor. The corporal works of mercy traditionally number seven, six taken from the Last Judgment story (Mt 25:31-46) and the seventh from Tob 1:20. These are (1) to feed the hungry, (2) to quench the thirsty, (3) to clothe the naked, (4) to shelter the homeless, (5) to visit the sick, (6) to ransom the captive, (7) to bury the dead. The spiritual works of mercy likewise number seven, though their origin is less clear: (1) to instruct the ignorant, (2) to counsel the doubtful, (3) to comfort the sorrowing, (4) to reprove sinners, (5) to forgive injuries, (6) to bear wrongs patiently, (7) to pray for the living and the dead.

Donations motivated by pride or other forms of selfishness, while still materially helpful to the recipients, do not constitute genuine almsgiving in the Judeo-Christian sense (1 Cor 13:3). Rooted in the experience of gratitude for God's mercy and benevolence, the proper motivating force for almsgiving is a spirit of love or charity (*caritas*), love of the neighbor as well as love of God. This is not meant to imply a dichotomy between the virtue of charity and that of justice. Love exceeds but does not negate the work of justice.

Throughout the OT almsgiving—manifested in care for the widow, the orphan, and the stranger—was seen as a constitutive element in Israel's covenant fidelity to Yahweh. The Torah mandated that the gleanings of the harvest should be left for the poor (Lev 19:9-10; 23:22). The faithful were admonished to hear and respond to the cry of the poor, because the Lord would surely hear them (Sir 4:1-6). Alms given generously could serve as sin-offerings, expiating one's own guilt (Tob 12:9; Dan 4:24).

Likewise the NT admonished disciples to be generous toward those in need. Jesus' public ministry embodied both the corporal and spiritual works of mercy. Luke's Gospel focuses particular attention on the value of giving alms, even to the point of renouncing all material possessions (3:11; 6:33-35; 11:41; 12:13-21; 33-34; 14:28-33; 16:19-31; 18:24-27; 19:1-10; 21:1-4). In the Acts of the Apostles one finds the early Christians sharing all material goods in common (2:44-47; 4:32) and the institution of a diaconate to ensure that the needs of the poor be addressed (6:1-6).

The Fathers focused on the necessity of almsgiving both for the benefactor and the recipient. Cyprian suggested that in feeding the poor one nourishes Christ himself (*De Opere et Eleemosynis*). Clement of Alexandria in his classic treatise *What Rich Man Shall Be Saved?* asserted that the just use of wealth can contribute to one's own salvation. Basil went so far as to declare that to withhold bread, a cloak, shoes, or money from the truly needy constituted an injustice, a form of stealing from the poor (*Homilia super Luc.* 12.18).

Thomas Aquinas, the Scholastic era in general, and the manuals that followed focused on the origin and degree of the obligation imposed by almsgiving. All agreed that there was a universal obligation to give alms to the needy, an obligation rooted in justice and the command to love one's neighbor. The degree of the obligation hinges on two factors: (1) the availability of "surplus" means on the part of the benefactor, and (2) a determination of the gravity of the need of the supplicant. If a person has sufficient means to provide the necessities of life for oneself and one's dependents, then that person ought to make available to those in need some measure of the superfluous goods that remain. If the needy person is in extremis, as in the case of potential starvation or life-threatening illness, then the obligation on the donor is grave. If, however, the need is real but not essential, then the obligation to meet it is less grave, though meritorious (ST IIa, IIae 32).

The attempt to delineate precisely the degree of obligation to give alms found some approbation in modern Catholic social thought in Leo XIII's giving a certain primacy to the right to private property (*Rerum novarum* 4, 5, 9, 10, 35). Over the subsequent century there has been a shift toward greater emphasis on the common good, the inherent dignity of all people, a preferential option for the poor, and the rights of people not only to the bare necessities of life but also to full participation in the corporal and spiritual goods of the earth. In more recent Catholic social teaching, as in various theologies of liberation, less emphasis is given to discussions of almsgiving, and a greater focus is placed on personal responsibility, social justice, and the need, in some situations, for systemic change.

See also CATHOLIC CHARITIES USA; CATHOLIC RELIEF SERVICES; CHARITY; CHURCH, SOCIAL MISSION OF; COMMON GOOD; GOODS, ACCESS TO/DISTRIBUTION OF; MODERN CATHOLIC SOCIAL THOUGHT; POOR, PREFERENTIAL OPTION FOR.

Bibliography: T. Aquinas, *Summa theologiae,* IIa, IIae, qq. 30–32. B. Häring, *The Law of Christ,* vol. 2 (Westminster, Md.: Newman, 1963) pp. 389–406. W. Levi, *From Alms to Liberation: The Catholic Church, Theologians, Poverty, and Politics* (New York: Praeger, 1989).

RICHARD SPARKS, C.S.P.

AMERICANISM

The Americanism controversy developed in the 1890s from four major issues. First, the spirituality of Isaac Hecker (1819–88), founder of the Congregation of St. Paul the Apostle (the Paulists), emphasized the indwelling of the Holy Spirit within each person. Members of his congregation were to be so responsive to the Spirit that they did not need to take the traditional vows of religious orders. Not well trained in Scholastic theology, however, Hecker loosely used terms like "natural" and "active" virtue in a way subject to misunderstanding to the Thomism of that time. An optimist about the American experience, he argued that if Catholic doctrine were to be presented in a positive light, American Protestants would convert. Second, American Catholics had from the time of their first bishop, John Carroll, praised the American separation of church and state and attributed to it the progress of the American church. In 1887 James Cardinal Gibbons (1834–1921), archbishop of Baltimore, then in Rome to receive his red hat, praised the freedom that resulted from that separation in an address. A third issue was the social question. While in Rome, Gibbons had successfully defended the Knights of Labor, an early union, and argued against a condemnation of Henry George, a social reformer. He did this just as Archbishop Michael A. Corrigan of New York (1829–1902) was moving to excommunicate Fr. Edward McGlynn, a George supporter.

The hierarchy, already divided over the social question, was further fragmented by the fourth issue—Americanization. John Ireland (1838–1918), archbishop of St. Paul, called for the Americanization of immigrants, praised public schools, and even negotiated for two public school boards to lease his parochial schools during school hours and supervise the education given. He eulogized the American republic at the same time that European republics and liberal states were denying the church its rights in areas such as education. Gibbons consistently sided with Ireland's programs, especially Americanization, but seldom took the initiative in the movement. Bishop John Keane (1839–1918), first rector of The Catholic University of America, was deeply influenced by Hecker's spirituality and saw the university as the cutting edge of a new Catholic intellectual insertion into American society. In Rome, Msgr. Denis J. O'Connell (1849–1927), rector of the North American College, aided the movement and articulated it to Europe.

The Americanizers aroused strong opposition within the hierarchy. Corrigan of New York saw Ireland's accommodation with the public schools as surrendering the church's rights. Frederick Katzer (1844–1903), archbishop of Milwaukee, shared this view and interpreted it in light of the Kulturkampf (1872–87). With other German-Americans, he considered the Americanizing program detrimental to the preservation of the faith of German-American children. The domestic dispute in the United States church crossed the Atlantic to Rome, where Ireland's controversial school plan was upheld by the Congregation of Propaganda in 1892. As one result, however, the Holy See decided to appoint Archbishop Francesco Satolli the first apostolic delegate to the American hierarchy in 1893.

Other issues soon drew the attention of Roman officials, notably the participation of Ireland, Gibbons, and Keane in the World Parliament of Religions, a pioneering ecumenical endeavor held in Chicago in 1893. In his apostolic letter to the church in the United States, *Longinqua* (1895), Leo XIII warned against making the American separation of church and state an ideal to be exported and argued that the church in the United States would flourish still more if it enjoyed some favor of the law. But he did not condemn the American separation of church and state. Other actions followed. In the summer of 1895, Gibbons, again in Rome, failed to gain approval for Catholic membership in certain secret societies and learned that the pope had demanded O'Connell's resignation as rector of the North American College because of his partisanship. In 1896 Keane also had to resign from the Catholic

University and moved to Rome as a consultor to the Congregation of Propaganda.

In the meantime Ireland's speeches and sermons had been translated into French as a guide for French Catholics to rally to the Third French Republic, the policy Leo XIII had initiated in 1892 at the instigation of Mariano Cardinal Rampolla, his secretary of state, who sought French assistance in ending the Roman Question. Americanism, properly so-called, however, resulted from the French translation in 1897 of *The Life of Father Hecker* by Walter Elliott, C.S.P. The controversy arose not so much because the translation was poor as because it was impossible to translate the American experience into European culture, which had a different understanding of such American practices as the separation of church and state and religious liberty. Charles Maignen, writing under the pseudonym "Martel," wrote a series of articles in *La vérité* attacking Hecker for denying the need for external authority in the church, for denigrating religious vows, and for praising the separation of church and state, which, he said, was clearly condemned by the *Syllabus of Errors*.

While this controversy was raging, O'Connell delivered an address at the Fourth International Catholic Scientific Congress at Fribourg, Switzerland, in August 1897. It became the definition of what Americans meant by "Americanism." He distinguished between political and ecclesiastical Americanism. The former he defined as the "order of ideas" flowing from the Declaration of Independence that asserted that all "are created equal and are endowed by their creator with certain unalienable rights." Such ideas were expressions of the British and American common law, O'Connell argued, and were more in keeping with the dignity conferred in baptism than was the Roman law, in which subjects had only those rights the state gave them. Ecclesiastical Americanism he described as the separation of church and state in the United States. Here, he considered—erroneously—the Catholic theory of "thesis" to be a union of church and state and the "hypothesis" whatever was tolerable where the thesis could not be realized. He concluded that the "American hypothesis" worked more to the advantage of the church in carrying out its spiritual mission than various forms of European union.

O'Connell's strategy was to internationalize the Americanist movement and gain European support for it. Hermann Schell, professor of theology at Würzburg, Germany, wrote approvingly of Ireland's progressive ideas. Encouraging this internationalization, Ireland delivered an address stating he had never opposed Germans or German-Americans, but only those who resisted what he saw as his interpretation of Leo XIII's progressive program. In Italy his speeches and sermons were translated and adapted from the American republic to the kingdom of Italy to provide a program for ending the Roman Question.

As Americanism gained European supporters, Maignen widened his focus to include O'Connell, Ireland, Gibbons, and Keane. Ireland, he said, would be deposed and Gibbons would be assigned a coadjutor. O'Connell, he thought, used a peculiar type of Anglo-Saxon logic that praised the theory of church-state union but argued for the superiority of the hypothesis. Maignen now decided to publish his articles as a book under the title *Le Père Hecker: c'est il un saint?* Refused an imprimatur by Cardinal Richard in Paris, he obtained one from Alberto Lepidi, O.P., Master of the Sacred Palace in Rome. The Americanist prelates protested in vain that the imprimatur implied the pope's own approbation.

In the summer of 1898 Leo XIII appointed a commission to investigate Americanism. Clouding the decision of this commission was the victory of the United States in the Spanish-American War, which presented the specter that Americanist ideas might prevail by force of arms. Other commissions, moreover, were investigating historical criticism of Scripture and evolution. On January 22, 1899, Leo issued *Testem benevolentiae* condemning certain aspects of Americanism. While he praised Hecker's devotion to the Holy Spirit—he specifically noted that the Second Council of Orange (529) had stated that the first movement toward faith began with the Holy Spirit—he went on to challenge Hecker's assertion that that was an age of a greater outpouring of the Spirit. Having alluded to the semi-Pelagianism condemned at Orange, the pope chastised those who spoke of "natural" virtues as though nature without grace was superior to nature with grace. Among the other errors the pope attributed to Americanism were the denigration of religious vows, the rejection of the need for external authority, and the watering down of doctrine to gain converts.

Since the pope did not state that anyone actually held any of the condemned notions, a new controversy now arose over the interpretation of the papal letter. Gibbons, Ireland, and Keane flatly denied that anyone in the American church held such notions. Corrigan and Katzer, however, thanked the pope for exercising his infallible office in preventing the spread of the heresy. The division in the hierarchy over Americanism mirrored the division in the earlier disputes. The condemnation ushered in a period of intellectual slumber for American Catholicism and was a harbinger of the anti-Modernist movement at the beginning of the 20th century.

See also GRACE; KNIGHTS OF LABOR; LEO XIII; RERUM NOVARUM.

Bibliography: T. McAvoy, *The Great Crisis in American Catholic History, 1895–1900* (Chicago: Regnery, 1957). G. Fogarty, *The Vatican and the American Hierarchy from 1870 to 1965* (Wilmington, Del.: Glazier, 1985).

GERALD P. FOGARTY, S.J.

ANIMALS, RIGHTS OF

The human animal, according to Catholic teaching, has rights, but many hold that neither Christianity in general nor Catholicism in particular (Gaffney, pp. 149–54, 159–61) has defended the intrinsic value of other animals. Still, the tradition has possibilities.

First, the Scriptures place a high value on animals. Animals share in the good, indeed very good, creation, work of the Divine Word and Spirit (Gen 1; Ps 104; Wis 11:24; Jn 1:1; 1 Cor 8:6); they share in the vicissitudes of the historical drama of the Bible (Exod 12:12, 29; Josh 6:21; Jdt 4:10; Hos 4:3; Jonah 3:7-8; 4:11; Mk 5:1-20; etc.); and they are part of the universal drawing together of all things in Christ's peace-bringing redemption (1 Cor 15:28; Eph 1:10; Col 1:15-20; Heb 1:2; Mk 1:13). The Bible celebrates wild animals (Job 38:39–41:26; Mt 6:26; 10:29-30; Lk 12:6-7, 24; etc.). In biblical psalmody animals join other beings in praising God (Pss 96:11-12; 98:7; 103:22; 148:7, 10; 150:6; Dan 3:79-81; Rev 5:13).

The moral teachings of the Bible regarding animals appear to be twofold. On the one hand, its visions of a peace in a creation where humans and even all animals are vegetarian (Gen 1:29-30; 2:16) and where "dominion" (Gen 1:26, 28) involves no killing or eating or scaring of animals (cf. Gen 9:2) and its corresponding visions of the final peaceable kingdom, where wolf and lamb, lion and ox, child and poisonous snake, will live together without harm (Isa 11:6-9; 65:25; Hos 2:20 [18]; Rev 22:1-2), supplemented by St. Paul's evoking of the travail of the whole creation as it stretches out toward liberation from corruption (Rom 8:19-22), suggest that ultimately every animal is, like every human, a primal and sacred being. We cannot, of course, bring about a world utterly free from harm and death, but some may live in a way that witnesses to it, and all can see ambiguity and sacrifice in our appropriation of animal life.

On the other hand, in the imperfect world between beginning and end, when animals are handed over to humans (Gen 9:3; Sir 17:3-4), the Bible countenances a moderate use of them. Humans may eat animals if they do so with reverence. Their blood is sacrosanct (Gen 9:4; Lev 17:10-14; Deut 12:23-24; Acts 15:20, 29; 21:25). In the NT the verb *thyein,* which means "to sacrifice," is the regular word for "to kill" an animal, even where no ritual is implied (Mt 22:4; Lk 15:23, 27, 30; Jn 10:10; Acts 10:13; 11:7). This seems to suggest that every killing of an animal has the aura of sacrifice.

Some passages express affection for domestic animals (Num 22:21-33; Tob 6:2; 11:4; Isa 1:3). Especially, love for sheep (2 Sam 12:1-6; Mt 18:12-14; Lk 15:3-7) makes meaningful the picture of the model shepherd who lays down his life for his sheep (Jn 10:1-18, 26-28). The Mosaic Torah provides for food and rest for domestic animals and respect for the different species (Exod 20:10; 23:4-5, 12; Lev 19:19; Deut 5:14; 22:1-4, 10; 25:4), provisions echoed in Proverbs (12:10) and the Gospels (Mt 12:11; Lk 14:5. But cf. 1 Cor 9:9-10; 1 Tm 5:18). A special respect is enjoined for animal mother and child (Exod 22:29 [30]; Lev 22:27-28; Deut 22:6-7, and the threefold repetition of Exod 23:19; 34:26; Deut 14:21). Animals may eat from the fallow fields of the Sabbath Year (Exod 23:10-11; Lev 25:1-7).

This biblical outlook should lead to a love of creation and the animals within it and at least to a moderate ethic of care for animals: the avoidance of cruelty in husbandry and experimentation that the Humane Society of the United States advocates (McDaniel, p. 70). A brief but suggestive expression of such an outlook is the 1990 papal New Year's message, "Peace with God the Creator, Peace with All Creation," a text rich in biblical allusions. The pope calls on Christians to respect the integrity of creation and appeals to the inspiration of St. Francis, who manifested a sense of "fraternity" for all created things (John Paul II, p. 468; see also *Sollicitudo rei socialis* 34 and *Centesimus annus* 37–38).

If Catholic teaching has not on the whole, however, espoused the integrity of animals, the cause is probably not biblical texts about the image of God in humanity (Gen 1:26-27; 5:3; 9:6) or about human dominion (Gen 1:26, 28; cf. Ps 8:7 [6]). The human capacity for foresight and control is, after all, a fact; defenders of animal rights appeal to it. Humans in the image of God might exercise their dominion "with wisdom and love" (John Paul II, p. 465). The more likely cause is the traditional dualistic interpretation of human nature with its sharp distinction between material body and rational soul. According to such doctrine, only in the bodily realm do humans have kinship with animals. For the human body may have evolved from living matter; the human soul, however, was immediately created by God (DS 3896). When animals are understood simply as "living matter," as "brutes," as "irrational," it is natural to place them at our free disposal (cf. ST II-II, q. 64, a. 1).

Thus every modern movement toward reinterpretation of humanity as a body-soul unity contains the possibility of according a high place to animals. Every tendency to see the universe as a single process of nature and history, every understanding of the biblical drama as a single story of creation and redemption, every account of human reality that stresses other aspects than rationality, as in our valuing of those who cannot yet or can no longer think (Gaffney, pp. 161–69), are so many moves in this direction. At a minimum they should lead to a "chastened anthropocentrism" with a "consciousness of belonging to the whole" or "being members of one another," even as we "manipulate" nature (Häring, pp. 180–81). But they might go further. They might complicate but also enrich our pursuit of justice and peace on earth by inducing us to take into full account the integrity, the pains, and the desires of our fellow creatures: the other animals.

See also CREATION; ECOLOGY; ESCHATOLOGY; STEWARDSHIP.

Bibliography: J. Gaffney, "The Relevance of Animal Experimentation to Roman Catholic Ethical Methodology," in T. Regan, ed., *Animal Sacrifices: Religious Perspectives on the Use of Animals in Science* (Philadelphia: Temple Univ. Press, 1986). John Paul II, "Peace with God the Creator, Peace with All Creation," *Origins* 19, no. 28 (December 14, 1989) 465–68. B. Häring, *Free and Faithful in Christ,* vol. 3, *Light to the World* (New York: Crossroad, 1981). J. McDaniel, *Of God and Pelicans: A Theology of Reverence for Life* (Louisville: Westminster/John Knox, 1989 [includes a very useful bibliography]).

GEORGE L. FREAR, JR.

ANTHROPOLOGY

Catholic moral teaching and theology have consistently emphasized the importance of anthropology. An often-repeated axiom insists that human action is based on human being (*agere sequitur esse*). The human person as agent expresses self in actions and as subject constitutes self by actions. This article discusses the central and crucial role anthropology plays in hierarchical Catholic social teaching and in Catholic social thought in general.

Catholic anthropology has traditionally seen the human being as an image of God, which grounds both the dignity and responsibility of the person. According to Thomas Aquinas, the leading figure in the history of Catholic theology, the human being is an image of God precisely because, like God, the human being has intellect, free will, and power of self-determination. Theological language in the later hierarchical documents of Catholic social teaching speaks about the vocation of human beings to use responsibly the gifts that God has given them.

From a theological perspective the Catholic emphasis on image and mediation sees the connection between the call and gift of God on the one hand and human fulfillment on the other. The glory of God is the human person come alive. The will of God is that human beings should come to their perfection. Catholic anthropology at its best thus says yes both to God and to the human being but sees God's call mediated in and through the gifts of God to human beings.

Catholic anthropology generally strives for an integral approach that recognizes and respects all aspects of the human. The economic and political are important aspects of the human and cannot be neglected. However, the human being cannot be reduced only to the economic and the material. There was and is a tendency in hierarchical Catholic social teaching to order these aspects with the more spiritual values of love, friendship, prayer, and contemplation being higher (*Populorum progressio* 20). Catholic anthropology has recognized the social aspects of the human person and has tried to steer a middle course between the two extremes of individualism and collectivism. Catholic social teaching and Catholic social thought well illustrate this anthropological approach.

Within this general anthropological framework, there have been some changes and developments in the anthropology found in the modern hierarchical Catholic social teaching, which began in 1891 with the encyclical *Rerum novarum* of Pope Leo XIII. This article will discuss in greater detail the following aspects of the anthropology of Catholic hierarchical social teaching: the theological aspects of anthropology, the social and communitarian dimension, the shift toward a greater appreciation of the subject, and the move toward greater historical consciousness.

Theological aspects. Pacem in terris in 1963 is the last document of official Catholic social teaching to employ a consistent and almost inclusive natural-law approach to anthropology. From the theological perspective the natural law insists on a human nature that remains the same in all the different possible states of salvation. The doctrine of creation grounds the fact that human reason can know human nature and thus discover the plan of God for human action. Such an anthropology prescinds from scriptural insights, grace, and Christology in its consideration of concrete human actions, and in practice the human person often appears to exist in a separate realm of the natural as distinguished from the supernatural.

The Second Vatican Council (1962–65) in general and its Pastoral Constitution on the Church in the Modern World in particular attempted to overcome the split between faith or the gospel and daily life by proposing an anthropology nourished by scriptural reflection and ultimately connected with grace and Christology. Within such a perspective the human person in the world is not living merely in the realm of the natural. The social action and involvement of the Christian person become an important and integral part of the spiritual life itself. In the words of *Justitia in mundo,* the document of the 1971 synod of bishops: "Action on behalf of justice and participation in the transformation of the world fully appear to us as a constitutive dimension of the preaching of the gospel, or, in other words, of the church's mission for the redemption of the human race and its liberation from every oppressive situation."

This anthropological shift opened the door for the development of liberation theology, which originally occurred in the Latin American context. The gospel message of freedom is a call for freedom from sin, which also includes the social and political structures of sin. The liberation of the Jewish people in the Exodus serves as a model and stimulus for the liberation of oppressed people today. The special concern of the Bible and its God for the poor must mark the attitudes and lifestyle of Christians and of the Christian Church today.

The more distinctively Christian anthropology has also raised important issues for Catholic social thought and ethics. How precisely should the Scriptures be used in developing an anthropology and an ethics? What is the difference between the Christian person and others? Are Christians called to act differently from others in bringing about a more just society?

The distinctively Christian anthropology first developed at Vatican II tended to be overly optimistic. In its attempt to relate the gospel, Christ, and grace to daily life the pastoral constitution did not give enough importance to sin and to the fact that the fullness of the reign of God lies beyond history. The older natural-law anthropology also had downplayed the role of sin and in its own way could be accused of natural-law optimism. Traditionally, Roman Catholicism has always disagreed with a highly negative and pessimistic anthropology. Pope John Paul II in *Sollicitudo rei socialis* (1987) employs a moderately optimistic anthropology. The pope recognizes the sad experience of recent years and the many complex and troublesome problems facing humankind, but he has confidence in human beings. Yes, sin exists, but there is a fundamental goodness in human beings, who are images of the Creator, redeemed by Christ, and under the influence of the Holy Spirit (47).

Social and communitarian dimension. Catholic social teaching and ethics have consistently emphasized the social and communitarian dimensions of anthropology. The earlier hierarchical social teaching was based on neo-Thomistic and Scholastic philosophy, which accepted the Aristotelian principle that the human being is by nature social and political. The state, or political society, is therefore natural for human beings who come together as a society, thereby overcoming their own insufficiencies and becoming better able to achieve their own good and the good of others. Such an anthropology grounds the concept of the common good as the end or goal of the political order, which ultimately redounds not only to the good of society and the good of others but also to the good of the individual persons involved. This optimistic and communitarian anthropology involves a moderately positive view of the role and function of the state. The state or government is not seen as something negative or evil that is primarily coercive.

The communitarian anthropology of papal social teaching is opposed both to individualism and to collectivism. Historically, different emphases have appeared at different times. In the 19th century Catholic thought strongly opposed individualistic liberalism (understood in the classical sense of the term), insisting very much on the communitarian dimension of reality. However, as the 20th century developed and totalitarianism emerged Catholic social teaching began to emphasize the dignity, freedom, and rights of the person. Despite strong opposition to communism in the 1940s and 1950s, Catholic social teaching since the 1960s has opened the door to dialogue with Marxism and has even been willing to see some aspects of the Marxist sociological analysis as legitimate for some Christians (*Octogesima adveniens* 31–34). To this day Catholic social teaching continues to criticize the evils of both individualism and collectivism, as illustrated in *Sollicitudo rei socialis* and in the 1986 pastoral letter of the United States Catholic bishops on the economy.

In the light of a more biblical approach, recent hierarchical documents emphasize the concept of solidarity (SRS 39ff.). Peace is truly the fruit of solidarity, which is based on the recognition of the common parenthood of God and the fact that we are all sisters and brothers. This biblically based solidarity includes a special place for those who are poor, marginalized, and victimized.

The shift toward the subject. Within the hundred-year span of hierarchical Catholic social teaching there has been a distinct shift toward the subject with a greater emphasis on the freedom, equality, and participation of all concerned. The historical circumstances of an uneducated people, the fear that freedom and individualism were being absolutized in Continental liberalism, and the historic Catholic concern about freedom being the freedom to do the true and the good all influenced the position of Leo XIII, who had a paternalistic and authoritarian understanding of society and condemned the modern liberties, including religious freedom. However, even Pope Leo in *Rerum novarum* gave some emphasis to the rights of workers and to the need for workers to participate in defending their own rights. Within one hundred years Catholic hierarchical social teaching became a strong defender of freedom, participation, and human rights. What happened?

As the 20th century developed, the primary problem for Catholicism was no longer individualistic liberalism but totalitarianism of the Right and especially totalitarianism of the Left. Pope Pius XI in the 1930s condemned Nazism, fascism, and communism. Throughout the 1940s and 1950s Catholic social teaching strongly opposed communism. As a result, this teaching began to defend the dignity, freedom, rights, and participation of the person. Only in *Pacem in terris* in 1963 did such official documents develop the theory of human rights. Catholic teaching previously avoided the concept of human rights because of the danger of individualism and insisted rather on duties. To its credit, *Pacem in terris* recognizes duties and rights and also insists not only on the political and civil rights associated with the Enlightenment but also on social and economic rights such as the rights to food, clothing, shelter, medical care, and security in cases of inability to work, unemployment, and old age (PT 9–34). Today church pronouncements often use a human-rights anthropology to criticize existing social and economic systems. The biggest hurdle for official Catholic social teaching was the acceptance of religious freedom, which finally took place with the Declaration on Religious Freedom of the Second Vatican Council in 1965.

In *Octogesima adveniens* (1971) Pope Paul VI highlighted the growing importance and centrality of aspirations to equality and participation, two forms of human dignity and freedom (22). Pope John Paul II has fully subscribed to this turn to the subject, as exemplified in his insistence in *Laborem exercens* (1981) on the priority of labor and of the subject over what is produced (13).

The move toward historical consciousness. The documents of hierarchical Catholic social teaching also show an important anthropological shift from classicism to historical consciousness, which has occurred in much of contemporary Catholic theology. Classicism sees the human person in terms of an immutable, eternal, and unchanging human nature. Historical consciousness gives more importance to the particular, the individual, and the contingent without falling into a sheer existentialism. Classicism has employed a more deductive methodology, whereas historical consciousness uses a more inductive approach.

The earlier documents of the modern hierarchical social teaching employed a classicist anthropology, stressing the immutable nature of human beings. Pope Pius XI in *Quadragesimo anno* (1931) proposed a rather specific plan (solidarism), which was to be followed everywhere in the world. *Pacem in terris* introduced the concept of "the signs of the times" at the end of its four chapters. The Pastoral Constitution on the Church in the Modern World of the Second Vatican Council began its discussion of particular topics with the signs of the times—the contemporary historical realities. Paul VI in *Octogesima adveniens* recognized the diversity of situations throughout the world, because of which it is neither the ambition nor the mission of the pope to put forward a solution that has universal validity (4). Pope John Paul II has not been as strong in insisting on historical consciousness. The emphasis on experience and praxis in contemporary liberation theologies well illustrates the anthropological shift to historical consciousness.

The movements toward the subject and toward historical consciousness have also raised the anthropological question of the nature and role of women. Leo XIII saw women as inferior and dependent upon men. John XXIII in *Pacem in terris* recognized as one of the signs of the times the participation of women in public life (41). More recent documents stress the dignity and equality of women, but they also propose a dual human nature. Women are different from men and therefore have different roles and functions (OA 13). Feminists continue to rightly criticize such an anthropology.

Anthropological concerns have been and will continue to be a central and important aspect of hierarchical Catholic social teaching and of Catholic social thought in general.

See also DISCIPLESHIP; FREEDOM; HUMAN RIGHTS; LIBERATION THEOLOGY; MARGINAL PERSONS; PERSON, DIGNITY OF; POOR, PREFERENTIAL OPTION FOR; SOLIDARITY; WOMEN.

Bibliography: G. Baum, *Theology and Society* (New York: Paulist, 1987). C. Curran, *Directions in Catholic Social Ethics* (Notre Dame, Ind.: Univ. of Notre Dame Press, 1985). D. Hollenbach, *Justice, Peace, and Human Rights* (New York: Crossroad, 1988). M. Riley, *Transforming Feminism* (Kansas City, Mo.: Sheed & Ward, 1989). J. Segundo, *Jesus of Nazareth Yesterday and Today,* 5 vols. (Maryknoll, N.Y.: Orbis, 1984–88). O. Williams and J. Houck, eds., *The Common Good and U.S. Capitalism* (Lanham, Md.: Univ. Press of America, 1987).

CHARLES E. CURRAN

ANTI-SEMITISM

Anti-Semitism is a modern term, coined only in the 19th century, but it is rooted in the reality of suspicion, contempt, hostility, and hatred toward Jews that goes back to ancient times. Jews were disliked in pre-Christian Greece and Rome for their general unwillingness to adapt to the prevailing social mores. Antipathy toward Jews arose fairly quickly in the early days of Christianity. Part of it was no doubt inherited from the Greco-Roman world. Part of it was due to the widespread ignorance about Jews and Judaism among the Gentile converts to the church, who quickly overwhelmed the Jewish Christians in numbers, as well as to the desire of these new Christians to distance themselves from the Jews after the disastrous Jewish revolt against Roman authority, which saw the destruction of the Jerusalem Temple. Part of it may be rooted in the NT itself, though that is a question still being debated by biblical scholars. Clearly Christians in subsequent centuries used NT texts as a basis for anti-Semitism. On this question, there is little disagreement. But whether this is a proper interpretation of these texts or whether the so-called anti-Jewish texts of the NT should be seen primarily as inter-Jewish critique in the tradition of the prophetic writings and the Talmud remains under discussion. Some scholars would maintain at the minimum that certain texts in the Gospel of John that identify Jews with darkness and even with the devil must be seen as anti-Semitic.

After the formal expulsion of Christians from the synagogue in the latter part of the 1st century and particularly following Constantine's conversion to Christianity in A.D. 313, Christian contempt for Jews intensified. The church fathers played a major role in this escalation, bringing the church to the point where Jews were viewed as inherently opposed to Christ and the church. A theological construct of the Jew was created that by the 4th century had lost many of its human features. Part of this prevalent *adversos Judaeos* tradition, the "left hand of Christology," as Rosemary Ruether has termed it, included what came to be known as the perpetual-wandering notion of Jewish existence. In this perspective Jews were destined to roam the world as a destitute people without a homeland of their own as a perpetual punishment for murdering the Messiah and as an ongoing reminder of what can happen to those who abandon Christ and his teachings. Some contemporary Jewish and Christian scholars detect traces of this tradition in the way certain Christian church leaders have approached the question of Zionism and the modern state of Israel.

The zenith of anti-Semitism was surely reached in the brutal annihilation of six million Jews by Nazi Germany. In some ways Nazi anti-Semitism was a distinctly new phenomenon. It was based on the fundamental racial inferiority of Jews, who, along with certain other groups (Gypsies, homosexuals, Poles, mentally or physically impaired), had to be eliminated or subjugated in the process of creating a new, advanced race of humans. Yet it has to be said that real ties exist between this new Nazi form of anti-Semitism and its classical Christian predecessor, even though there is no simple straight line between the two. The reason why the Nazis looked upon Jews as the worst of all the "subhuman" groups had everything to do with the denigration of Jews throughout the centuries of Christian civilization. And the Nazis would never have secured the popular support for their "final solution" of the Jewish question, which they did, were it not for the continuing influence of traditional Christian anti-Semitism on the masses of baptized believers in Europe.

Another form of anti-Semitism that arose during the Nazi period was rooted in the notion of the Jews as alien, in this case alien to the drives for nationalistic identity, often religiously based, that were spreading throughout Eastern and Western Europe at the time. The typical attitude of many Christians was that while what Hitler was doing to the Jews was horrible and tragic, it was helping Christians build more cohesive nations; it was solving their "Jewish problem."

Contemporary scholars, in trying to explain the origins of anti-Semitism, have generally focused on one of three explanations. The first is the sociological or "scapegoat" theory, which sees anti-Semitism as a convenient escape from pervasive social and economic difficulties. The second is the theologically oriented explanation referred to previously. The third is the psychopathological approach, which views anti-Semitism as an inherent mental disease, especially in Western culture, whatever its root cause. The first and second are the more common explanations.

See also CHURCH-STATE RELATIONS IN THE UNITED STATES; DECALOGUE; FASCISM; GENOCIDE; HOLOCAUST, THE; HUMAN RIGHTS; JOHN XXIII; PIUS XII.

Bibliography: R. Ruether, *Faith and Fratricide: The Theological Roots of Anti-Semitism* (New York: Seabury, 1974). E. Flannery, *The Anguish of the Jews: Twenty-Three Centuries of Anti-Semitism* (New York: Macmillan, 1965, rev. ed., Mahwah, N.J.: Paulist, 1985). M. Curtis, ed., *Antisemitism in the Contemporary World* (Boulder/London: Westview, 1986).

JOHN T. PAWLIKOWSKI, O.S.M.

ARMS RACE

Since the end of World War II the world has experienced an arms race unprecedented in human history. Governments have spent enormous sums of money, literally trillions of dollars, on weapons and other military expenditures. In 1988 alone military spending exceeded $1 trillion a year for the first time. The arms race is at once the result of global insecurity and the cause of continuing mistrust among nations.

The United States and the former Soviet Union played the dominant roles in shaping the arms race after the Second World War. Their competition took place on several levels. Most prominent has been the stockpiling of nuclear arms. They also led the world in military expenditures, incurring almost two-thirds of global military spending, and have been the two major suppliers of weapons to other nations. The scope of the arms race can be demonstrated by reference to the separate but related issues of nuclear and conventional forces.

The two superpowers engaged in a *nuclear* arms race that led to the development of a massive stockpile of increasingly sophisticated weapons. According to 1989 estimates these two nations had amassed over fifty-five thousand nuclear warheads and bombs, 98 percent of the world's total. Although only a very small number of nations now have nuclear capacity, the proliferation of nations with nuclear capability in the near future looms as a political and moral issue of great importance. Moreover, because the destructive potential of these weapons dwarfs any historical precedent, all nations have a stake in the determination of this dimension of the arms race. Pope John Paul II captured this fact well when he said in Hiroshima: "In the past it was possible to destroy a town, a region, even a country. Now it is the whole planet that has come under threat."

Conventional arms and military expenditures are a major factor in the national budgets of virtually every country in the world. Developed nations account for most of this spending, but developing nations have allocated an unconscionable percentage of their national budgets for military purposes despite the daunting social needs of their people. Foreign-aid programs have also been increasingly skewed toward military rather than economic purposes.

Chemical and *biological* weapons have played a lesser role in the arms race. However, church teaching has treated them, like nuclear arms, as weapons of indiscriminate destruction. International agreements have officially outlawed these weapons, although without complete success.

The multidimensional arms race confronts the world with complex dilemmas. Nuclear arsenals possess destructive potential inconceivable to previous generations. The vast sums spent on military expenditures usurp resources of the earth that could be reallocated to serve the pressing human needs of the world's poor. In responding to the issues pertaining to the arms race, Catholic social teaching does not presume to offer technical solutions to the complex questions the arms race compels the international community to address. Rather, church teaching addresses the moral dimension of these issues and offers direction on how to respond to them in an ethically responsible way.

Three particular effects of the arms race have led the Catholic church to speak prophetically against it. First, the qualitative and quantitative development of nuclear weapons has raised the specter of cataclysmic war. The menacing threat of such development cannot be countenanced. Second, conventional weapons used in the approximately 150 armed conflicts since World War II have become increasingly more sophisticated and deadly. More than twenty-one million people have died in these conflicts. These wars have occurred almost exclusively in the developing countries, and by the end of the 1980s, civilians accounted for almost 75 percent of the deaths, a tragic rise from about 50 percent in the 1950s. Third, the allocation of resources for military purposes has prevented the nations of the world from dealing with the profound and tragic social problems afflicting so many of the world's people. The human cost attendant to this third effect is impossible to calculate. Nonetheless, it is clear in the church's teaching that there is a moral imperative calling upon the nations of the world to redirect resources away from military purposes and toward human development.

The church addresses the arms race in several ways, but three are of particular importance: a prophetic denunciation of the misdirected priorities of the costly arms race, participation in the shaping of public policies, and articulation of a vision of peace for the future drawn from the church's rich tradition.

Papal and conciliar documents have employed the first approach with a consistent and strong repudiation of the arms race. In his 1963 encyclical, *Pacem in terris,* Pope John XXIII wrote, "Justice, right reason and humanity . . . urgently demand that the arms race should cease" (112). Blending its critique of the arms race with a plea on behalf of the world's poor, the Second Vatican Council declared, "the arms race is an utterly treacherous trap for humanity, and one which injures the poor to an intolerable degree" (*Gaudium et spes* 81). Pope Paul VI echoed the council's judgment in his 1967 encyclical, *Populorum progressio.* Pointing to the variety of unmet social needs, he said, "All public or private squandering of wealth, all expenditure prompted by motives of national or personal ostentation, every exhausting armaments race, becomes an intolerable scandal" (53). Pope John Paul II has made this issue a major social concern of his pontificate. In *Sollicitudo rei socialis* (1987) he asked, "How can one justify the fact that huge sums of money, which could and should be used for increasing the development of peoples, are instead utilized for the enrichment of individuals or groups, or assigned to the increase of stockpiles of weapons?" He added, "If 'development is the new name for peace,' war and military preparations are the major enemy of the integral development of peoples" (10).

This brief summary of papal and conciliar statements reflects the consistency of the teaching. The prophetic denunciations emanate from the conviction that the massive and complex arms race is taking the human family on a path to destruction. The dignity of the human person, the bedrock of Catholic social teaching, is violated directly when weapons are used indiscriminately in battle and indirectly when resources go toward preparations for war instead of human development.

Reversing the arms race, consequently, is a moral imperative for the global community. This is the point of departure for the second approach. The moral dimension of reversing the arms race is intimately joined to the more expansive problem of building and maintaining a just peace in the nuclear age. By definition, such a peace would preserve the freedom of nations, promote their right to development, and protect the human rights of all peoples. In exercising its public responsibility, the church helps provide a framework for the consideration of the moral dimension of public policy decisions.

In addressing questions of arms control and disarmament, church teaching takes into account political realities that must be carefully weighed when concrete proposals are made. The teaching is cautious and carefully drawn when it moves from principles to practice. The Holy See avoids evaluating specific national policies. However, national bishops' conferences have offered prudential judgments that apply the principles of the church's tradition to the concrete policies of their nations.

The 1983 U.S. Catholic bishops' pastoral letter, *The Challenge of Peace,* is an example of a systematic treatment of United States nuclear policy. It abides by criteria set forth in papal teaching that disarmament be gradual, controlled, guaranteed, and multilateral.

The moral analysis of a nation's nuclear strategy is one of the church's important tasks today. It provides a significant contribution to the public debate on matters of profound moral urgency. In the midst of an altered global context the church must continue to apply the principles found in Catholic social teaching to the questions raised by the perpetuation of the arms race.

The church's third approach to the global arms race is the creation of a vision for the future. Beginning with Pope Pius XII, the popes of the nuclear age have taught that the world needs an international order that mirrors the growing interdependence characterizing the world today. The arms race signals the failure of the current system to address the material and security needs of all the nations of the world. For this reason, *The Challenge of Peace* stresses that "mutual security and survival require a new vision of the world as one interdependent planet" (244).

Moving toward the realization of this new vision of the world order will help reverse the arms race. This vision embodies a comprehensive understanding of peace that can only be constructed on the foundation of truth, justice, freedom, and love. Working to realize this vision while being mindful of the reality of sin in the world is essential for the church, which is called to peacemaking by our Lord Jesus Christ.

See also DETERRENCE; DISARMAMENT; PACEM IN TERRIS; POPULORUM PROGRESSIO; SOLLICITUDO REI SOCIALIS; WAR.

JOSEPH CARDINAL BERNARDIN

ASSOCIATION OF CATHOLIC TRADE UNIONISTS

In February 1937 eleven men gathered around the kitchen table at 115 Mott Street, the New York headquarters of the Catholic Worker, and founded the Association of Catholic Trade Unionists (ACTU). The country was still in the grip of the Great Depression. The Catholic Worker breadline was sufficient evidence of that. But the New Deal reforms of President Franklin Roosevelt had given the workers new hope and some protection for the right to organize their own unions, an opportunity quickly seized by John L. Lewis and the newly organized Congress of Industrial Organizations (CIO).

Four of the eleven men who founded ACTU were from such CIO unions. One was from the Teamsters, one of the more corrupt American Federation of Labor (AFL) unions. Of the CIO unions, one was the Utility Workers from the vast New York Edison system, a small union struggling against bitter opposition from management and at the same time concerned with a threat of communist infiltration in its own leadership.

These two unions, the Teamsters and the Utility Workers, symbolized three major concerns of the ACTU throughout its lifetime, which ended about 1970.

The first concern was the desperate need of unorganized American workers for strong, independent unions of their own choosing and included the effort, led by the formidable Lewis, to provide such unions. The ACTU became a major factor in rallying Catholic workers and the Catholic clergy in support of this drive. A second concern was the necessity to purge some of the older AFL unions of the racketeer influence that had perverted their basically sound purposes. This was a perilous business, because the racketeers frequently used violence to achieve their goals. A third concern was the effort of the communists, often competent and zealous organizers, to take over leadership of the CIO unions.

While the ACTU was not solely or even mainly responsible for the ouster of a dozen Stalinist-led unions from the CIO in 1949, it was a significant factor in such centers of CIO strength as New York, Detroit, and Pittsburgh. This has given rise to a myth created by Stalinist sympathizers that anticommunism was the *only* ACTU activity. On the contrary, ACTU's major activity over the years was the defense of the rights of American workers, as in the Woolworth strike in New York and the Chrysler strike in Detroit.

In New York, the saleswomen at Woolworth's had gone on strike shortly after that founding meeting of the ACTU. Heywood Broun, columnist, Catholic convert, and president of one of the new CIO unions, the Newspaper Guild, had written a column for the *New York World* calling attention to the wages at Woolworth's—for some, less than $10 a week for six days of work—and, by contrast, the vast fortune of Barbara ("Babs") Hutton, glamorous Woolworth heiress. A society columnist had responded to Broun and defended Hutton on the ground that she had given $11 million to various charities. Nevertheless, an ACTU membership meeting voted to support the strike, and a group went to the big store on Fourteenth Street with crudely lettered signs, one of which read, BABS GAVE $11,000,000 TO CHARITY, BUT "THE WORKER IS NOT TO RECEIVE AS ALMS WHAT IS HIS DUE IN JUSTICE"—POPE PIUS XI.

In Detroit, on Sunday, November 11, 1939, famous radio priest Fr. Charles Coughlin devoted his talk on a national network to supporting an extraordinary effort to break the strike that the United Auto Workers (UAW) had called at Chrysler. The ACTU already had a vigorous chapter in Detroit led by a brilliant newspaperman, Paul Weber; Paul St. Marie, president of the Ford local; and Tom Doherty, secretary of a large Chrysler local. It also had the support of Archbishop Edward F. Mooney and its own network of forty labor schools, which were turning out trained Catholic unionists. At a UAW rally in Cadillac Square attended by forty thousand auto workers, Msgr. John Mies, an ACTU priest, took issue with Father Coughlin and urged the crowd to stick by their union. That same night, the Detroit ACTU sponsored a radio talk by one of its chaplains, Fr. Raymond Clancy, who refuted Father Coughlin's arguments point by point. The back-to-work movement failed, and the strike went on to a successful conclusion.

By the early 1940s there were 14 ACTU chapters around the country in most of the major cities, and approximately 150 labor schools were turning out close to 5,000 graduates every year. Allied with the ACTU schools in this effort of education was another network, the Jesuit labor schools. One of the first and best was Xavier Labor School in New York, headed by Fr. Philip Carey. His assistant, Fr. John

Corridan, became especially active on the waterfront, where the corrupt Longshoremen's union (ILA) had become a haven for homicidal gangsters. George Donahue, an early leader of the New York ACTU, had been threatened by them and driven off the docks but came back to help lead an AFL drive to organize a rival union after the ILA had been ousted from the AFL.

Support of rank-and-file efforts to reform corrupt and undemocratic unions remained a prominent activity of the ACTU, especially in New York, but this also gave rise to opposition and controversy and was probably one reason for ACTU's decline during the 1960s. Some chapters disaffiliated and did good work under other names, such as the Catholic Labor Alliance of Chicago, led by Ed Marciniak and Bob Senser; and the Catholic Labor Guild of Boston, now simply the Labor Guild, under successive directors, Frs. Frank McDonnell, Mort Gavin, and Ed Boyle. A secular organization, the Association for Union Democracy, now carries on the ACTU's campaign against corrupt and undemocratic elements. One of its attorneys, John Harold, along with John Sheehan and Edward Scully, were for years a mainstay of an ACTU subsidiary, the Catholic Labor Defense League.

The ACTU program was hammered out in early meetings in New York and was mainly the work of Martin Wersing, president of the Utility Workers local, and John Cort, the first executive secretary. It was based on the labor encyclicals of Leo XIII and Pius XI and the writings of Msgr. John A. Ryan. The ACTU program argued that workers have a right to (1) job security, (2) sufficient income to support self and family in reasonable comfort, (3) collective bargaining through union representatives freely chosen, (4) a share in the profits after just wage and return to capital have been made, (5) strike and picket peacefully for just cause, (6) a just price for the goods they buy, (7) decent working hours, and (8) decent working conditions. At the same time, workers have a duty to (1) perform an honest day's work for an honest day's pay, (2) join a bona fide union, (3) strike only for just cause and after all other legitimate means have been exhausted, (4) refrain from violence, (5) respect property rights, (6) abide by just agreements freely made, (7) enforce strict honesty and democracy inside the union, and (8) cooperate with employers who respect rights to bring about a peaceful solution to industrial war by establishing industry councils for the self-regulation of industry, and producer cooperatives in which workers share as partners in the ownership, management, and profits of the business in which they work.

With its record of strong support for honest, democratic trade unionism, the ACTU was in a good position to challenge the Stalinists after World War II. In their largest union, the United Electrical Radio & Machine Workers (UE), the anticommunist opposition first organized itself in New York, while in Pittsburgh, Msgr. Charles Owen Rice worked to pull together opposition in the same union. In an even more crucial situation, the struggle for control of the UAW, the Detroit ACTU was a critical factor. With its excellent weekly, *The Wage Earner,* the ACTU was a major element in the coalition that finally elected Walter Reuther and his supporters and defeated officers who were either committed to or more tolerant toward communist policies. Finally, in New York the ACTU was not only effective in the UE but also in helping to oust from office the Stalinist leadership in the Transport Workers union and the New York local of the Newspaper Guild, which had 6,000 members and was for years considered one of the top prizes in the possession of the Communist party.

The removal of the communist threat to the CIO and some improvement in the racketeer presence in the AFL as the result of federal legislation and of activity by the AFL itself plus the partially successful organization of unorganized workers all contributed to the decline of the ACTU in the 1950s and 1960s. Another factor may have been the failure to do more in the area of spiritual formation, as some of its leaders maintained throughout its history. Nevertheless, its record overall has to be evaluated as positive—as an active champion of honest, independent trade unions, as an educational force through its labor schools and newspapers, and in its successful campaign to ally the Catholic church on the side of workers.

See also CATHOLIC WORKER, THE; COMMUNISM; JUST WAGE; LABOR AND CAPITAL IN CATHOLIC SOCIAL THOUGHT; QUADRAGESIMO ANNO; RIGHTS AND DUTIES; STRIKE, RIGHT TO; WORK, THEOLOGY OF.

Bibliography: *The Labor Leader* (National ACTU newspaper) and *The Wage Earner* (Detroit ACTU newspaper). Microfilm files available in New York and Boston public libraries.

JOHN C. CORT

ASSOCIATIONISM

The principle of association was invoked long before the 19th century in various contexts and variations. But it was after the upheaval of the American and French revolutions and under the impact of the rise of the bourgeoisie as a new class concurrent with the beginnings of the Industrial Revolution that "association" solidified into a formula, almost a panacea, appealed to in the face of all signs of social disintegration or atomization. For present purposes it may be most useful to see associationism, or anti-individualism, as that general outlook on social practice that occupied a middle ground between feudalism and doctrinaire liberalism. On the one hand, associationism's proponents were too aware of the shortcomings of feudal ways to wish to go back to the ancien régime; feudal survivals had been subjected, after all, to an amalgamation with early modern absolutism to mostly perverse effect. On the other, they were too repelled by the harshness of modern individualism to uncritically accept "Manchester" or laissez-faire liberalism and hence domination by a moneyed elite, the Third Estate. The associationism of the 19th century is thus a very broad phenomenon, capable of being found across the whole spectrum of that era's conservatism and liberalism. It may be seen as the matrix from which a whole series of social movements arose: the early socialisms and cooperativist movements, other movements harking back to a more communitarian mode of life such as the Shakers and the Brook Farm experiment, various types of Social Catholicism, and self-help movements of liberal social reformers as well.

It may also be seen as part of the awakening of the people that eventually led to democracy; but "government of the people, for the people, and by the people" was not yet seen as a distinct, positive possibility in most early 19th-century associationism, except perhaps in the United States. A main difference between the broad middle band of associationism and its extremes was that the former accepted the new economic class structure of modern nations as a fact of life and attempted to mitigate its harsh effects. On their part, the extremes met in holding that an individualistic Enlightenment or "liberal" basis for society was self-contradictory and had to be rejected. The extreme Right resorted to authoritarianism to impose an associative society of unequals from the top down. The Left appealed to the egalitarianism ingredient in Enlightenment anthropology to insist on the empowerment of the masses. But this easily turned into a regimented majoritarian or even totalitarian collectivist view (communism) unless the human dignity of individuals and minorities was respected.

As a last general observation, the analogy may be noted between associationism and the traditional Christian notion of "the communion of saints." Both are broad, not highly determinate concepts. Their coherence lies mainly in a tendency to oppose the isolation of the human individual. Both lend themselves to a variety of uses and applications.

1. A particular movement with which the name "associationism" was conspicuously connected was that of the Fourierist socialists in the 1830s and 1840s (cf. Jean Bruhat, in Droz 1:349–58). Charles Fourier (1772–1837), in the wake of Henri de Saint-Simon (1760–1825), propagated an associationism by which to organize people into pleasant, self-supporting communities called "phalansteries." After all, people's "passions" conflicted with conventional social and economic structures; the problem lay, however, not with the passions, which were God-given, but with the structures. Fourier claimed to have discovered the shape of society that would accommodate the passions in freedom and social harmony. After his death, Victor Considérant (1808–93) tried to winnow the wheat of Fourier's associationism from the chaff, giving it a Christian baptism (Cort, pp. 125–29; cf. Delano, pp. 16–25).

2. In the 1848 revolution in Paris, another Catholic associationist, or "Christian socialist," came into prominence, one who had long been proposing an associationist critique of the political economy. The name of Philippe Buchez (1796–1865) is also connected with the historiography of the French Revolution and with the origins of cooperativism. Indeed, Cole (1:179) considers Buchez to be the key link between Robert Owen and Fourier on the one hand and the Christian socialists J. M. Ludlow and F. D. Maurice in England after 1848 on the other. His insight into the new class system, by which proletarians were forced into a dependency on property owners more brutal than in the past, led him to propose and help found a cooperative of production. In it all workers were partners, from the manager to the hod carriers. The change rung here on the theme of association was the workers' "association," or sharing in the profits of their labor, otherwise skimmed off to an undue degree by the providers of capital and management. On this reading the principle of association called for a rejoining of all the factors that had been pitted against one another by recent economic developments: of property owners with the labor force, of workers with the materials and tools with which they worked (through shared ownership), of workers with the profits earned by their labors. The antagonism between the different economic classes, he thought, "can only disappear if equality in interests comes about, in other words, if their mutual association is established. In our view, this is the end purpose of Christianity" (Duroselle, p. 89). For Buchez, association was not only the goal, it was also the way to the goal.

In his "worker associations" (artisanal producer cooperatives, of which perhaps just one or two ever operated under Buchez's direct influence) every effort was made to avoid pitting capital and labor against each other (Cort, p. 119). Corporate earnings that exceeded wages and other costs would not simply be distributed among the partners, for instance, but would be added to the common and inalienable capital for reinvestment in the enterprise and for social needs (like a self-funded insurance and pension plan). So that class divisions would not arise in the heart of the cooperative, every worker in an enterprise had to be a full participant: there could be no category of mere hired help subject to exploitation by the owners, that is, by the "full partners." In 1848 a commission was set up to make government credit available to worker associations; several Buchezians were members. It struggled with Buchez's criteria, which presupposed a high level of (religiously motivated) selflessness and an unusual sense of solidarity in the leading figures of such shops. However, it ended up extending credit to conventional private entrepreneurs thinly disguised as heads of worker associations.

3. Associationism may also refer to the proliferation of organizations that assumed such an important role in church and civil life since the passing of the ancien régime (cf. Heinz Hürten, "Katholizismus," *Staatslexikon,* 7th ed., 3:373–78). To replace the many communal and occupational associations of prerevolutionary Europe, voluntary organizations (German, Vereine; French, *associations* or *oeuvres*) were more and more allowed in increasingly liberal regimes. Associations of many types, typically springing from lay initiative, accordingly became an important pillar of pastoral work (see, e.g., the paradigmatic Irish Catholic Association of Daniel O'Connell [1775–1847]; or, in the latter part of the century, the Oeuvre des cercles catholiques d'ouvriers in France with its periodical, *l'Association catholique;* the Italian Opera dei Congressi; the German Volksverein—but consider also the Society for the Propagation of the Faith, the St. Vincent de Paul conferences, the Kolping journeymen's association, and the Catholic press, to name just a few lay movements that emerged in the 19th century alongside numerous congregations of religious, especially women religious). They were often grafted onto the existing network of Tridentine parishes and were the source of a vigorous church life that resulted from bringing laity and clergy closer together, before "Catholic Action" was even ideated.

What the above types of associationism have in common historically is that they all constituted attempts to fill the modern individualistic void left by the emancipatory upheavals in European society since the late 18th century. As far as the Catholic church was concerned, the void was all the more noticeable, since it meant the end of church-state relations established for centuries in a "Christendom" mode. As hollowed out as that arrangement had become by the Enlightenment, it was the main institutional framework within which the church had been able to exercise influence on the societies in which it lived and worked. The 19th century called for its replacement by other means, and mostly lay associations, including political parties in some cases, sprang up to fill the gap.

See also CHRISTIAN DEMOCRACY; COMMUNITY; CO-OPERATION, PRINCIPLE OF; ENLIGHTENMENT, THE (INFLUENCE OF); FREEDOM; OPERA DEI CONGRESSI; SOLIDARITY; TOTALITARIANISM; VOLKSVEREIN.

Bibliography: J. Beecher, *Charles Fourier: The Visionary and His World* (Berkeley: Univ. of California Press, 1986). G. Cole, *A History of Socialist Thought* (New York: St. Martin's Press, 1953–58). J. Cort, *Christian Socialism: An Informal History* (Maryknoll, N.Y.: Orbis, 1988). R. Van Davidson, *Did We Think Victory Great? The Life and Ideas of Victor Considerant* (Lanham, Md.: Univ. Press of America, 1988). S. Delano, The Harbinger *and New England Transcendentalism: A Portrait of Associationism in America* (Cranbury, N.J.: Associated Univ. Presses, 1983). J. Droz, ed., *Histoire génerale du socialisme* (Paris: Presses universitaires de France, 1972–78). J. Duroselle, *Les débuts du catholicisme social en France (1822–1870)* (Paris: Presses universitaires de France, 1951). J. Komonchak, "The Enlightenment and the Construction of Roman Catholicism," *CCICA Annual* (1985) 31–59. P. Misner, *Social Catholicism in Europe* (New York: Crossroad, 1991).

PAUL MISNER

ATHEISM

Atheism is the assertion or belief that God does not exist. Scarcely mentioned in the Bible, it became in the Enlightenment a major preoccupation of European intellectuals outside the boundaries of official church life. Reconciling God's existence with modern science was a major preoccupation of 17th-century figures such as Descartes and Pascal, who struggled to reaffirm more-or-less traditional ideas. In the 18th century widespread systematic questioning led to the emergence of a special field called the "philosophy of religion." In response, a kind of natural theology emerged, which emphasized that God's existence could be demonstrated by proofs such as the argument from causality, insisted on the logicalness of faith in God, and attempted to prove basic tenets of the Christian religion.

Nicholas Lash persuasively argues that 18th-century interest in atheism was paralleled by a compatible understanding of what God must be like, one that made God much too much a part of our ordinary knowledge. He identifies this latter position as "theism" and asserts that though atheism and theism define each other, the outcome of the argument between them does not have as much to do with the Christian faith as the arguers might think. In Christian understanding God is much less comprehensible, and Christians ought not identify God according to the wishes of thinkers who narrowed their options regarding the mystery of God in this unnecessary way.

Historically, however, the past two centuries have seen an increase in the numbers of those turning to belief in reason or in science as substitute for belief in God or, more recently, dismissing the issue of God's existence as superfluous. In reaction to this trend, modern atheism has been the object of considerable attention in official church documents, for example, *Humani generis.* Aside from its obvious importance in systematic theology and its epistemological and philosophical importance in itself, atheism was often named in contexts of social teaching rather sweepingly, for example, as the cause of such difficulties of the church in the modern world as the separation of church and state (*Syllabus of Errors*), in connection with modernistic agnosticism (*Pascendi*), and especially with Marxist communism (*Rerum novarum*). Up to the recent past, materialistic communism has continued to be the context in which official documents most often raise the issue of atheism, but this situation seems likely to change.

Since Vatican II atheism has been increasingly understood as a much more complicated matter. In *Gaudium et spes* a pastoral attitude is taken. In origin atheism is not to be understood as a spontaneous development of human beings but rather one that arises from a variety of causes, some of which would be removed if the doctrines espoused and the morality practiced by believers were more appropriate to their belief. An understandable error that sometimes gives rise to atheism is a sincere but misguided desire to attend to the needs of the world. The council's characterization of modern forms of atheism includes an affirmation that atheism is sometimes a denial of a particular idea of God rather than of all possible ideas of God. In addition, atheism is said to arise sometimes from an alternative source of human values, and this alternative may be said to have a status similar to God. Implicitly, then, many issues of atheism increasingly seem to be better described as idolatry.

In later documents Paul VI has called atheism "the most serious problem of our times" while at the same time acknowledging that modern atheism has many forms (*Ecclesiam suam* 99). Vatican II had avoided narrowing the focus of atheism to materialistic communism; Paul VI in 1971 went further and was careful to distinguish the atheistic elements of communism from communism as such (*Octogesima adveniens*). Atheism continues to be the object of condemnation and concern, but the tendency to blanket whole movements with this title has all but disappeared. John Paul II says that "it is not possible to speak of atheism in a univocal way" but identifies "a true and profound materialism" as atheistic (*Dominum et vivificantem*). In some very recent versions, atheism is less than explicit and may take the form of a lack of interest in the question of God or a conviction that the idea of God is one that need not arise at all. Accordingly, John Paul II has characterized such an "agnostic or atheistic view" as "one of the 'signs of the times' of our age" (World Peace Message, January 1, 1988).

See also ENLIGHTENMENT, THE (INFLUENCE OF); GAUDIUM ET SPES; MARXISM; OCTOGESIMA ADVENIENS; PAUL VI; REASON, ROLE OF; "SIGNS OF THE TIMES."

Bibliography: M. Buckley, *At the Origins of Modern Atheism* (New Haven: Yale Univ. Press, 1987). N. Lash, *Easter in Ordinary* (Charlottesville, Va.: Univ. Press of Virginia, 1988). K. Rahner, *Foundations of Christian Faith* (London: Darton, Longman & Todd, 1978).

ANTHONY BATTAGLIA

AUGUSTINE, INFLUENCE OF

It is an eloquent testimony to Augustine's greatness and influence that soon after his death he was proclaimed "the teacher of all the churches after the apostles" (*post apostolos omnium ecclesiarum magister*), a title already attributed by Jerome to Origen. Pope Celestine I, hardly nine months after Augustine's demise, in his condemnation of semi-Pelagianism declared that "the life and merits of Augustine of holy memory have always kept him in our communion; never has there been any least suspicion about him. We remember him as a man of so great a learning that our predecessors have always counted him among the best teachers (*inter magistros optimos*)" (*Letter* 21).

Augustine's General Influence

To appreciate the influence of Augustine's sociopolitical thought it is necessary to recall here very briefly other aspects of Augustine's theology in which he has exercised a profound impact on Western culture. One may single out his Trinitarian theology (the so-called psychological theory), in particular his doctrines of divine relations and *Filioque;* his doctrine of grace, for which he is called *doctor gratiae;* his theology of the church and the sacraments; his emphasis on charity as the heart of moral life (his celebrated *ama et fac quod vis*); his views on sexuality and marriage; his ascetical teaching and his introduction of monastic life into the West (the famous Rule of St. Augustine, even though he may not be its author); his philosophical insights, in particular his illumination theory, his metaphysics of evil, and his views on the relationship between reason and faith (his double formula *crede ut intelligas* and *intellige ut credas*); his teaching on the ecstatic nature of human beings (his oft-quoted "*fecisti nos ad te, et inquietum est cor nostrum, donec requiescat in te*").

This is but a mere sample, of course, and other influential teachings of Augustine can easily be adduced. An alternative way of gauging his influence is to glance at the theologians themselves. They all have either accepted or modified or rejected Augustine, but none has disputed his place as the uncontested master of Catholic thought. Among his ardent admirers one can count Fulgentius of Ruspe (whose nickname is "Augustinus abbreviatus"), Isidore of Seville, Caesarius of Arles, Pope Gregory the Great, Anselm, Abelard, Bernard, the Victorine theologians, Bonaventure, and Duns Scotus. Those who followed him, but more selectively, are Thomas Aquinas, Giles of Rome, and Erasmus, among many others. Some claimed to be his disciples but have misinterpreted him so grievously as to have fallen into error: Gottschalk, Gregory of Rimini, Thomas Bradwardine, Luther, Calvin, Michael Baius, Cornelius Jansen and his followers of Port-Royal. Others combated Augustine bitterly, from Julian of Eclanum to Cassian to some contemporary feminists who regard him as the worst perpetrator of sexism in the West.

Church councils, too, have accepted Augustine, especially the councils of Carthage, Orange, Trent, and Vatican II, which quoted him copiously. An inscription on the oldest effigy of St. Augustine in the Lateran basilica sums up best: "*Diversi diversa Patres, sed hic omnia dicit Romano eloquio mystica sensa tonans*" (Different Fathers have said different things, but only he has said everything in Latin, explaining the mysteries with his thunderous voice).

Augustine's Influence in Social Thought

In social ethics Augustine has been no less influential. In our discussion of his impact in this area we will leave aside doctrines he inherited from the Greco-Roman and Judeo-Christian traditions, even though he has put a personal stamp upon them. These include ideas concerning the origin, nature, and foundation of power; the object, nature, and kinds of laws; the source, tasks, and purpose of justice. We will direct our attention only to those aspects of Augustine's social thought that are strictly his own and have had an indisputable influence in the formation of sociopolitical theories in the Middle Ages and beyond.

A word of caution is in order here. Augustinism is not the same as Augustine's own thought. The former is a development of the latter, at times faithful to it and at times extending it beyond recognizable limits. Two examples will suffice. What H.-X. Arquillière has called medieval "political Augustinism"—the tendency to absorb natural law into supernatural justice, the law of the state into that of the church, as it was gradually elaborated from Gelasius I through Gregory the Great, Isidore of Seville, Gregory VII, and Innocent III to Boniface VIII—can indeed claim some legitimate parentage in Augustine's conception of the good of the church as a prime political principle (see *City of God* 5.25–26), but this theory certainly fails to preserve his important contribution to political theory, namely his political realism based upon the concept of the state as secular. Similarly, the use of coercive power by the state to repress heresies and to maintain ecclesiastical communion can be traced back to Augustine's reactions against militant Donatists (see his *Contra epistulam Parmeniani* 2 and *Retractationes* 5); nevertheless, one can hardly appeal to his authority to warrant imposition of the death penalty and persecution of the Jews.

It is important therefore to distinguish what F. Cayré calls "essential or historical Augustinism" (the particular teachings of Augustine on sundry aspects of the Christian faith) from "partial Augustinisms" (more-or-less faithful developments of his thought) and the "great Augustinism" (the basic philosophical and theological principles of his thought). In what follows we will examine the influence of Augustine's social thought in the issues of the relationship between church and state, the duties of secular authority, the use of coercive power and religious freedom, and the morality of war.

Church and State

One of the central concerns of the medieval papacy was the relationship between church and state. Recall Gregory I's appointing governors to Italian cities and providing war materials, Gregory VII's struggle against Henry IV and lay investiture, Innocent III's attempt to establish feudal overlordship, and Boniface VIII's quarrels with Philip the Fair. In the cauldron of these conflicts was forged the so-called two-sword theory, most sharply formulated in Boniface VIII's bull *Unam sanctam* (1302). According to it both swords, the spiritual and the temporal, are in the power of the church, but the latter is to be used *for* the church, the former *by* the church, "the former by the priest, the latter by kings and captains but at the will and by the permission of the priest." In Innocent III's earlier words, the pontifical power and the royal power are like the sun and the moon, the latter deriving its light from the former and inferior to it both in size and in quality.

As has been pointed out, the seeds of this tendency to absorb secular power into ecclesiastical and papal power were already sown in Augustine's writings. While affirming the distinction, independence, and collaboration between church and state, Augustine insists that the church, by virtue of its nature and end, enjoys a certain legal primacy over the state. Further, from the religious and moral points of view, kings are, as any other citizen, under the authority of the church, and therefore must, not only as human persons but also as kings, serve, promote, and defend morality and religion (*City of God* 5.24; *Letter* 185.19; *Against Cresconium* 3.56). This teaching, which in itself leaves the rights of the state intact in the strictly political sphere, became the common doctrine in the Middle Ages. Isidore of Seville states: "Secular princes sometimes occupy the highest positions in the church in order to protect ecclesiastical discipline with their power. Indeed, in the church such positions would not be necessary if they did not impose by the fear of discipline what the priests are incapable of enforcing by the persuasion of their teaching" (*Sententiae* 3.48.7).

Unfortunately, in the struggles between popes and emperors, the primacy of the church was gradually transformed into supremacy, and in the end spiritual power swallowed secular power. Thus Gregory VII excommunicated and deposed Henry IV on the basis of the principle that "if kings are to be judged for their sins, by whom are they more justly judged than by the Roman Pontiff?" (*Letters* 4.2; 8.21). Hugh of St. Victor declares that "first the priesthood was instituted by God, and only afterward, through the priesthood, at God's behest, the royal power" (*De sacramentis* 2.c4). John of Salisbury affirms: "The prince receives the sword from the hand of the church. The sword, however, belongs to the church and the church uses it through the hand of the prince" (*Policraticus* 4.3). For Innocent III the appointment of an emperor came within the sphere of papal authority *principaliter* (since the transfer of the empire from the Greeks to the Romans took place through the pope) and *finaliter* (because the blessing, coronation, and investiture of the emperor lay with the pope). For Boniface VIII, the Holy See possesses *plenitudo potestatis.* His declaration in *Unam sanctam* is well known: "We declare, state, define and pronounce that it is altogether necessary to salvation for every human creature to be subject to the Roman pontiff."

Such doctrine of papal *plenitudo potestatis* is found in Henry of Cremona, Giles of Rome, James of Viterbo, and Tolomeo of Lucca. Henry makes use of Augustine's commentary in "Render to Caesar" to conclude that Christ had the fullness of political power and transmitted it to Peter in his saying "Whatever you bind on earth . . . ." Giles, whose *De summi pontificis potestate* was the foundation of Boniface VIII's bull *Unam sanctam,* argues on the basis of the *City of God* 17.19, that temporal power comes from God but through spiritual power (*De Ecclesiastica potestate*). James declares that there is only one power with two areas of exercise, temporal and spiritual, and this power belongs to the church: "It should not be understood as though there were two distinct and different powers; rather the church oversees the temporal and the spiritual spheres by its own unique power" (*De regimine Christiano* 2.8.7). Tolomeo advocates ecclesiastical theocracy on the basis of the *City of God* 5.21: "As the body exists through the soul, so the temporal power of princes derives its force and operations from the spiritual power of Peter and his successors" (*De regimine principum* 3.7).

Fortunately, in these controversies between church and state, there were theologians who succeeded in maintaining Augustine's more balanced teaching: the two powers are, each in its own sphere, autonomous, even though the church, by reason of its nature and end, possesses its proper excellence and is permitted to exercise, in collaboration with the state, a moral primacy and a spiritual direction. Though having written that "the secular power is subject to the spiritual, even as the body is subject to the soul" (*Summa theologiae,* II[a] I[ae], q. 60, a. 6, ad 3), and that excommunication leads to forfeiture of power (*ibid.,* q. 12, a. 2), Thomas nevertheless affirms that the church must limit itself to "spiritual arms" (*ibid.*, q. 40, a. 2, ad 1). In II *Sentences,* dist. XLIV, q. 2, a. 2, Thomas says that secular power is subject to spiritual power in those things that pertain to the salvation of the soul, but in those things that pertain to the political well being one must obey secular power rather than spiritual power ("*in his autem quae ad bonum civile pertinent, est magis obediendum potestati saeculari quam spirituali*").

John of Paris, in the midst of the struggle between Boniface VIII and Philip the Fair, arguing against Giles of Rome and James of Viterbo, writes: "There are two distinct powers that should not be reduced one to the other: just as spiritual power is immediately from God, so is secular power. Thus the empire is from God alone. . . . The pope does not receive the sword from the emperor nor does the emperor receive the sword from the pope. . . . God decreed that these powers be distinct in substance and in subjects . . . so that love and charity of the members of the church may be served through mutual need and collaboration . . . insofar as the prince needs the priest in spiritual matters, and conversely the priest needs the prince in temporal matters" (*De potentate regia et papali* 10). It is Augustine's teaching, almost word for word. It is this teaching that has become the common doctrine of the church.

The Duties of the State

In the *City of God* 5.24, Augustine draws the picture of a "happy" emperor and outlines the duties of a Christian ruler. These are grouped into three categories: the duty of governing (*officium imperandi*), the duty of providing (*officium providendi*), and the duty of advising (*officium consulendi*). Rulers are charged to command and govern, to care for the needs of their subjects so as to secure justice and peace, and to do so not in the manner of kings and masters (*reges aut domini*) but of advisors (*consules*), so that "those who advise, govern" (*imperant qui consulunt*) (*City of God* 5.19).

Such ideas find echo in *Letter* 10.51 of Gregory the Great: "The kings of nations are masters of slaves, but he who governs Romans must be masters of free people. Whatever you do, Emperor, safeguard first of all the rights of justice, then respect those of freedom. Give to those who are subjected to you the same freedom that is given to yourself." Isidore of Seville reproduces the very words of Augustine: "The special duty of the king is to govern his people with equity and justice. He must be the defender of the church, of the servants of God, of widows and orphans, of the poor, and of all those deprived of support. As far as he can, he must employ his zeal to prevent injustice, and if it is committed, to remove it. Thus, he who is the judge of judges must attend to the cries of the poor, lest those whom he appoints as his representatives oppress the little ones by their negligence and iniquity" (PL 73:718–25).

With Charlemagne, the emperor's role as "defender of the church" became predominant. Charlemagne, who often had the *City of God* read at meals, conceived his first duty as "to defend everywhere from the outside, by means of arms, the holy church of Christ against the incursions of pagans and the destruction by infidels, and from the inside to strengthen the church by the knowledge of the Catholic faith" (*Epistol. Carol.* 10). It is a more priestly than political conception of the kingly office. The common political good is confused with the practice of Christian virtues. The strong notion of the state, developed by the Romans on the basis of natural law, was being diluted and absorbed by the high religious function exercised by Charlemagne. The old notion of the state as independent and distinct from the church was gradually lost, and it was but a short step from here to claim that since the pope is the highest religious authority, he exercises authority over the emperor.

The Use of Coercive Power

Augustine teaches that it is better to convert heretics by persuasion than by force. But he recognizes that should persuasion fail, the state has the right to use coercive power. However, he places three conditions on the exercise of the secular arm: (1) that the severity of the judge be tempered by the mercy of the bishop; (2) that punishments be limited to flagellation, fines, and exile; and (3) that torture and death be proscribed.

In view of later abuses of coercive power, it is important to emphasize that Augustine's basic stance was in favor of religious freedom; that it was only with great reluctance, in the struggle against the violent Donatists, that he changed his position toward constraint; that for him constraint was the last resort to be used only after all other means of persuasion have failed; and that coercive power must aim at delivering the heretics from their errors and securing their eternal salvation.

Unfortunately, during the hostilities against the Albigensians, Augustine's teaching was severely distorted. After the Fourth Lateran Council (1215) Emperor Frederick II decreed the death penalty against obstinate Albigensians and, ironically, borrowed the title of his constitution, *Inconsutilem tunicam,* from Augustine's letter (66.2). Furthermore, he not only decreed that culprits be punished but also that those suspect of heresies be sought out with care ("*Inquirendi sunt*"). Augustine's authority was invoked to justify all sorts of physical punishments. Whereas Augustine allowed flagellation, which was but a common and somewhat benign form of punishment adopted in families, schools, and monasteries of his times, medieval canonists and theologians were willing to include torture with wooden horse, rack, iron heel, and other cruelties.

It would be much more difficult to appeal to Augustine for a death penalty, but there was no lack of trying. Even Thomas Aquinas, unable to find in him a text in favor of capital penalty for heretics, quoted Augustine's *Letter 185 to Boniface,* but in a truncated fashion so as to make Augustine say that he accepted without sorrow the death of certain heretics (ST II^{a}–II^{ae}, q. 10, a. 8, ad 4).

The Morality of War

Almost the only source for medieval discussions of the morality of war was Augustine. In all his writings Augustine evinces a deep horror for war and a fervent desire for peace. At the same time he rejects the pacifism and antimilitarism of church fathers such as Origen, Tertullian, and Lactantius. With pain and realism he recognizes that wars are inevitable as long as humans and their societies are moved by avarice, greed, and lust for power. And to restrain their destructive forces he seeks to determine the conditions under which wars can be tolerated as just. Medieval authors have followed Augustine's teachings closely in this regard. Ivo of Chartres in his *Decretum* and *Panormia* and Gratian in his *Decretum* carefully collect Augustine's statements on war; Thomas Aquinas, in his *Summa theologiae* (II^{a}–II^{ae}, q. 40) quotes Augustine copiously, as do Francisco de Vitoria in his *Relectiones, De Indis,* and *De jure belli* and Francisco de Suarez in his *De caritate, De fide,* and *De virtute et statu religionis.*

Thomas, Vitoria, and Suarez agree with Augustine that the fundamental condition for a just war is a violation of a right. They quote his definition: "*Justa bella definiri solent quae ulciscuntur injurias.*" Forbidden, therefore, are wars for pillage, for conquest, wars out of ambition and desire for military glory, and personal revenge. They also accept Augustine's description of the rights the violation of which justifies war. Suarez develops Augustine's thought: "Three kinds of wrong may justify a war: the taking by a prince of the goods of another and refusing to restitute them; the refusal, without reasonable motives, of the common rights of nations such as passage and commerce; the grave injury to the honor and reputation of another" (*De caritate* 13.4.3).

The three theologians are unanimous in requiring that the war, to be just, must be declared by legitimate authority. Vitoria adds that the prince must consult not only his council of advisers but also enlightened people so that his decision be that of the majority and even of the whole nation (*De jure belli* 21). Suarez speaks of a higher authority than princes, namely the pope, who can judge the rightness of a war (*De caritate* 13.2.5).

Augustine affirms that a just person when fighting for a sacrilegious king has the right to obey his orders if these are not contrary to divine laws. Vitoria adds that if a soldier has doubt about the justice of a war he must, "according to the teaching of Augustine, obey his prince" (*De jure belli* 23). For Augustine the aim of war is to reestablish order in the world by repairing the damage caused by the enemy. The three theologians also follow this teaching.

In conducting the war one must, says Augustine, remain true to the conventions agreed upon with one's allies or the enemy. Thomas and Vitoria fully concur. Suarez concurs with two restrictions: "Unless the enemy does not keep the agreement or if external circumstances have changed" (*De virtute et statu religionis* tract. 2, bk. 2, chap. 28.8.9). Augustine allows deceit and ambushes, Thomas follows suit (ST II^{a}–II^{ae}, q. 40, a. 3). Augustine allows the killing only of combatants and demands that the lives of prisoners be respected. Thomas, strangely enough, omits the distinction between combatants and noncombatants. Vitoria fills this lacuna by declaring that "it is never allowed intentionally to kill the innocent" (*De jure belli* 38), though it is not immoral to kill them without intending to do so, in a siege, for instance.

From this brief survey, it is clear that Augustine's social thought has had an extensive and lasting influence. Many of his ideas on authority, law, war, the relationship between church and state, coercive power, and justice have become the common teaching of the church, from the Middle Ages to recent social encyclicals of popes to the U.S. bishops' letter *The Challenge of Peace* (1983). In times of conflict, Augustine's teachings added fuel to the polemics; all sides claimed his authority and at times exaggerated and deformed his thought. But there can be no doubt that the Bishop of Hippo, through his teachings in philosophy, dogmatics, moral and mystical theology, ecclesiastical policy, and public jurisprudence is the master craftsman of Western culture.

See also ALMSGIVING; COMMON GOOD; FATHERS OF THE CHURCH, INFLUENCE OF; GOODS, ACCESS TO; GOODS, DISTRIBUTION OF; RERUM NOVARUM; STEWARDSHIP; WAR.

Bibliography: G. Combès, *La doctrine politique de Saint Augustin* (Paris: Librairie Plon, 1927). H. Deane, *The Political and Social Ideas of St. Augustine* (New York/London: Columbia Univ. Press, 1963). H. Arquillière, *L'Augustinisme politique: Essai sur la formation des théories politiques du moyen-âge* (Paris: Librairie philosophique: J. Vrin, 1955). J. O'Meara, *Charter of Christendom: The Significance of the "City of God"* (New York: Macmillan, 1961). H. Marrou, *St. Augustine and His Influence Through the Ages,* trans. P. Hepburne-Scott, texts of St. Augustine trans. by E. Hill (New York: Harper Torchbooks, 1957). V. Giorgianni, *Il concetto del Diritto e dello Stato in S. Agostino* (Padova: Cedam, 1951). P. Phan, *Social Thought,* Message of the Fathers of the Church 20 (Wilmington, Del.: Glazier, 1984).

PETER PHAN

AUTHORITY, POLITICAL

The notion of authority occurs in two principal contexts in social ethics: (1) the source and limits of the authority of the state and (2) the relationship between the authority of the state and the authority of the church. Official Catholic teaching has undergone a notable shift on both these points, a process that has been partly one of development and partly one of change. It is convenient to consider three periods: from the pontificate of Leo XIII until the First World War; from the end of the First

World War until 1950; and from the years leading up to the pontificate of John XXIII and Vatican II until the present.

1870–1914

At the end of the 19th century Leo XIII was faced with what he took to be the extreme threat of socialism, especially in France and Italy. In his view socialist concerns about the plight of the industrialized masses, liberal theories of political authority, and revolutionary activism were all aligned in principle with anticlericalism and with the desire of secularized states to control and indeed to hamper the ministry of the church. His encyclical letters on social teaching reflect these concerns without much attempt to discriminate between matters of principle and the particular political circumstances of the time. In *On the Socialists* (1878) he castigates "that sect of men who, under various and almost barbarous names, are called 'Socialists, Communists, or Nihilists' . . . bound together by the closest ties in a wicked conspiracy" of refusing "obedience to those higher powers to whom, according to the admonition of the Apostle, every soul ought to be subject, and who in turn derive the right of governing from God; and they proclaim the absolute equality of all men in rights and duties" (*Quod apostolici muneris* 1). He goes on to develop the several positions that were to characterize his social teaching throughout his pontificate. Private property may not be seized under the guise of caring for the needy (3), and the inequality of rights and power is the will of God, to be peaceably endured rather than combated by insurrection (5–7, 11). Similarly, in *On Civil Government* (1881) he argues that political power is ordained by God for the common good and not conferred on rulers by the will of the people. The people may designate those persons who exercise political power, but the power itself is conferred by God and hence subject to God's authority. No other political theory can guarantee stability in the common good, which it is the end of the state to promote (*Diuturnum* 3–8). The early Christians are commended for their submission and refusal to resort to sedition even when harrassed in a most unjust and cruel way by pagan emperors (14–16).

Leo XIII's most important social encyclical, *On The Condition of Workers* (1891), elaborates this position without any notable change. The authority of the state over individual citizens is strictly limited. Both the individual and the family as a social unit are prior to the existence of the state, which therefore has no right to interfere with their own efforts to provide decent living conditions by working and acquiring private property (*Rerum novarum* 6–11). The state may intervene only if individuals or families have irretrievably failed to provide for themselves, in the interests of desperate need or severe injustice. Socialist theories about the community of goods are rejected as totally unjust (RN 12) as are their efforts to iron out all social inequalities (14). In 1903 Pius X discouraged the Italian Christian Democrats from speaking of claims of justice when what was in question was charity alone, presumably because he thought that such language served only to encourage socialists to resort to the forcible redistribution of wealth. Such expropriation exceeds the authority of the state.

In *On the Christian Constitution of States* (1885) Leo XIII also insists that the church and the state each has divinely given authority over citizens, the church in all matters related to salvation (which include many matters of personal and social morality), the state over temporal affairs (*Immortale Dei* 5–8). Ideally, these work in perfect harmony with each other. He harks back to the ideal Christian states of medieval Europe (ID 9), contrasting them with the godless modern states, which, totally secular in inspiration, pay no heed to the law of God or the position or authority of the church. In particular he castigates the view that the state should itself profess no religion, should grant equal rights to every creed, and should allow citizens to practice whatever faith they choose to (10–15). "To exclude the Church, founded by God Himself from the business of life, from the power of making laws, from the training of youth, from domestic society, is a grave and fatal error." A secular state can never be well regulated, since only the church is the true teacher of morals (17). He therefore objects to the cancellation of concordats between the Vatican and the states of Europe. Groups of Catholics who engaged in political activities of which the Vatican disapproved were suppressed under Pius X (Vidler, pp. 137–38, 157).

1914–50

In *On Reconstructing the Social Order* (1931) Pius XI, while claiming to reiterate the principles outlined by his predecessors, in fact changes the emphasis considerably. He explicitly rejects the interpretation of *On The Condition of Workers,* according to which the state has no right to interfere in the free play of the capitalist market, as quite contrary to Leo's intentions (*Quadragesimo anno* 41–58). He rejects the view that the task of charity is "to make amends for the open violation of justice" (QA 4) and is much more explicit in his insistence on the right and duty of the state to intervene to secure the requirements of justice and the common good. Whereas Leo XIII was primarily concerned to combat the encroachment by socialist states on individual liberties, Pius XI sees a more urgent problem in the laissez faire individualism of a totally free capitalist economic system and is correspondingly more insistent on the proper exercise of state power to emancipate the proletariat. The state has the right to own property for the common good (QA 45–46) and to "direct, watch, stimulate and restrain, as circumstances suggest and necessity demands" (80), provided only that it respects the competence of smaller social units. Still, in *On Atheistic Communism* (1937) he repeats Leo's rejection of radical egalitarianism as a social goal and his claim that the rights and duties of states and individuals are complementary (*Divini Redemptoris* 44–45).

While he continues to say that socialism in the true sense is incompatible with Catholic belief, *On Reconstructing the Social Order* does perhaps leave room for maneuver in that it admits that some socialists may perhaps no longer be socialists in the objectionable sense (QA 113–20). More generally, Pius XI still holds the position of Leo XIII that the Catholic church lays down clear moral principles of social government and it is the duty of the state to take whatever technical steps are needed to apply them. Not merely has the church the right to religious freedom, it ought, ideally, to be a recognized partner with the state in maintaining a just social order (DR 53). Such a Christian social order, authoratively proclaimed by Christ's one true church, is the only middle way between socialism or communism and the rampant capitalism whose fruits were to be seen in the economic deprivation of the Great Depression.

1950–80

The 19th- and early 20th-century papal pronouncements on the relations between church and state had always proved an embarassment in those countries that had never, or had not for centuries, been officially Catholic. Nowhere was this more true than in the United States, especially after the suppression under the title of "Americanism" of the attempts of United States Catholics to develop a national church, which could take its place among the institutions of a state in which there was no establishment of religion. In the years between 1945 and Vatican II, enormous credit must go to John Courtney Murray, S.J., who articulated a fully developed theology and philosophy of religious freedom and a correspondingly nuanced account of the authority of the church. The fruits of his work are to be seen in the encyclical letters of John XXIII and in the documents of Vatican II, especially the Pastoral Constitution on the Church in the Modern World and the Declaration on Religious Liberty. In his 1961 encyclical, *On Christianity and Social Progress,* John XXIII speaks of the mutual tolerance required of Christians who hold differing views on the application of Catholic social teaching (*Mater et magistra* 238); and, while repeating the right of the church to teach with authority on social questions, he points out that Catholics must cooperate with those who do not share their view of life. In the Pastoral Constitution on the Church in the Modern World there is explicit recognition of the sincerity of many atheists and of the claim that states that make a distinction between believers and unbelievers thereby violate fundamental human rights. In context, this probably refers to the denial of the right to worship as a Christian, but the Declaration on Religious Liberty makes it clear that the principle is of universal application. The state has no right to insist that parents should send their children to particular schools, nor to insist on the profession or repudiation of any religion *(Dignitatis humanae* 6).

Similar dramatic developments are to be found in the social teaching of the period. John XXIII's encyclicals start from the assertion of fundamental human rights, rights that can be claimed against any state authority (*Pacem in terris* 1–27). The authority of the state comes from God and must therefore not be used in a way that coerces its citizens or violates their rights, but this teaching is compatible with any democratically chosen form of government (PT 46–48). These documents also endorse a much more explicitly interventionist view of the duties of the state in regulating the social and economic conditions in which such rights can alone be safeguarded: in the areas of health, education, economic regulation, recreation, and the media. All of these are in principle welcomed (MM 59–67). The state needs authority not merely to arbitrate between economic liberalism and totalitarianism but to regulate the economic system in such a way as to mitigate the injurious effects of changes in the social and economic structures of society and to achieve a reasonable balance between various sectors of the economy.

The Pastoral Constitution on the Church in the Modern World, while still reiterating the basic principles articulated by Leo XIII, shows a marked difference in emphasis: all human beings are fundamentally equal with the same basic rights (*Gaudium et spes* 29), which place limits on the exercise of public authority; the state has a duty and therefore a right to intervene to remove economic and other inequalities, provided that basic human rights are not infringed, and to regulate the economy; private property has a social dimension, and reforms must be instituted to ensure that this social dimension is respected. Paul VI, in *On the Development of Peoples,* states explicitly that the right to private ownership is not an unrestricted or absolute right and that the state might have a duty to expropriate privately owned land that is not being used in such a way as to contribute to the common good (*Populorum progressio* 23–24).

Especially in the Pastoral Constitution on the Church in the Modern World, the authoritarian tone of many of the earlier documents is almost entirely lacking. The church is there presented as contributing to a dialogue in which it can learn from other churches and other institutions (GS 42–44). Its own message is best communicated not by seeking ecclesiastical domination but by the practice of faith and charity (ibid.), and in so doing it must respect the political freedom and responsibilities of citizens. It is better on occasion to renounce civil privileges given to the church when these might actually impede the effectiveness of its witness (76).

In short, the social thought in the official teaching of the church has changed considerably since the time of Leo XIII. The constant principles have been comparatively general: the authority of the state derives from God as a consequence of the nature of human beings and not from any arbitrary human decision; its proper exercise is therefore limited by the demands of the common good; the church has an important role to play in promoting the values of the gospel in society and has the right to do so freely. But the application has changed enormously because of the different political preoccupations of the Vatican at different times and because of the rapid change in economic and social circumstances over the period, which has led to very different perceptions of the main threats to social well-being. That the state has the authority to intervene in the working of the economy was admitted only with much reservation by Leo XIII, while it is regarded as essential by popes and the council since 1960. To own private property is still seen as a basic right, but the state has on occasion the authority to seize private property in the interests of the common good. The church no longer demands and in some circumstances would actually reject any legally enshrined position in the state. The state has no authority to interfere in the religious beliefs or (with some safeguards) practices of its citizens. The church recognizes that its members, clerical and lay, have not always been faithful to the gospel and that its own teachings can be formulated only by using the help and experience of others (GS 43).

The application of these teachings in the context of Latin America and, in particular, the views that violent revolution may be the only path to social justice and that the church must use its authority on the side of the poor are still the subject of controversy. The Medellín Conference (1968) and the Puebla Conference (1979) of the Latin American bishops are illustrative of the difficult political and moral decisions that must be faced.

Authority and Hermeneutics

It is obvious that contemporary church documents, at any rate in the field of social ethics, claim to teach authoritatively only on issues of comparatively general principles. The detailed application of these principles is left to be worked out by experts in economics or sociology, and the legitimacy of divergent views is recognized. There is a growing awareness from the time of Pius XI on that the specific conclusions of earlier papal documents were much conditioned by the perceived political and social conditions of the time.

Behind the particular problems of the extent of the authority of the state over its citizens and of the relationship between the authority of the state and the authority of the church, there lies a much more fundamental problem about the authoritativeness of the teaching of the church generally. Since the Enlightenment the respective claims of reason and revelation in interpreting the human condition have been perceived as to some extent conflicting. Within the church itself, besides theological discussions about the precise status to be accorded particular expressions of belief and the kind of assent appropriate in each case on the part of Catholics, there have been major differences in the assumptions underlying these more superficial disputes. What are the criteria by which any interpretation of the gospel in a particular milieu can be regarded as in any degree authoritative?

The philosophical assumptions of the earlier documents of this period were largely those of Scholasticism as it was interpreted in the neo-Scholastic revival. The emphasis is on the natural law, a fundamentally rationalist position whose arguments are in principle available to any thinking person. Appeals to biblical texts are used to confirm these arguments, for the most part, rather than to go beyond them. More recently, in the light of criticisms of that entire philosophical approach, it has been claimed that only the official church can authentically interpret the natural law. This view is seen by some as a proper statement of the church's divine authority, by others as almost a contradiction in terms and not obviously consonant with the much less dogmatic stance of the Pastoral Constitution on the Church in the Modern World.

Most recently, there has been the suggestion that the test of an authentic and therefore authoritative interpretation of the gospel for our times is to be sought in the effects of putting such an interpretation into practice, and especially in the effects on those who are most deprived or underprivileged. This emphasis has been characteristic of some liberation theologians in Latin America. Gustavo Gutiérrez has written, for instance, that "the praxis that transforms history is not a moment in the feeble incarnation of a limpid, well-articulated theory, but the matrix of authentic knowledge, and the test of the validity of that knowledge" (p. 59).

No generally accepted solution to the hermeneutical issues raised by these disputes is in sight. It must be recognized that Catholic social teaching in the last century has not always been careful to distinguish unchanging truths from politically, culturally, and socially conditioned responses to particular pressures. It is perhaps also helpful to remember that Thomas Aquinas taught, as the more recent popes and Vatican II have explicitly recognized in their social teaching, that the more specific the issue the less clear are the arguments of natural law. It ought to be common ground that fundamentalism, whether with regard to the biblical literature or with regard to the later documents of Christian tradition, is rationally indefensible. And while pragmatic tests for truth are indeed essential, since it is by their fruits that you shall know them, the assessment of those fruits is itself just as liable to be conditioned by the hopes and expectations of limited human beings as it is to be informed by the faith and charity of the gospel. The Pastoral Constitution on the Church in the Modern World frequently speaks of dialogue and of the need for Catholics to learn from one another, from other Christians, and from the experience and expertise of nonbelievers. While such an approach does not propose clear criteria for authoritative truth, it does properly emphasize the method by which, under God, such truth is most likely to be attained.

See individual popes and encyclicals under their Latin names. *Also see* AMERICANISM; HUMAN RIGHTS; LIBERATION THEOLOGY; MEDELLÍN; MURRAY, JOHN COURTNEY; POLITICAL PHILOSOPHY; POLITICAL THEOLOGY; PUEBLA.

Bibliography: Leo XIII, *On the Socialists* (*Quod apostolici muneris*) (1878); *On Civil Government* (*Diuturnum*) (1881); *On the Christian Constitution of States* (*Immortale Dei*) (1885); *On the Condition of Workers* (*Rerum novarum*) (1891). Pius XI, *On Reconstructing the Social Order* (*Quadragesimo anno*) (1931). John XXIII, *On Christianity and Social Progress* (*Mater et magistra*) (1961); *Peace on Earth* (*Pacem in terris*) (1963). Vatican Council II, Pastoral Constitution on the Church in the Modern World (*Gaudium et spes*) (1965); Declaration on Religious Liberty (*Dignitatis humanae*) (1965). A. Vidler, *A Century of Social Catholicism* (London: SPCK, 1964). J. Murray, *We Hold These Truths* (London: Sheed & Ward, 1961). D. Forrester, *Theology and Politics* (Oxford: Basil Blackwell, 1988). G. Gutiérrez, *The Power of the Poor in History* (London: SCM, 1983). D. Hollenbach, ed., *Justice, Peace, and Human Rights* (New York: Crossroad, 1988).

GERARD J. HUGHES, S.J.

B

BANKS AND BANKING

The name "bank" is a general and somewhat vague term applied to many different kinds of institutions that carry on one or more of the following functions: (1) accepting deposits; (2) lending and investing; and (3) issuing money (in the form of accounts from which individuals and businesses can spend). Other financial institutions not designated as banks also carry on one or more of these functions.

A banking system is a group of financial institutions that exist to foster the flows of credit and money so as to facilitate economic transactions and growth. Early banking systems were mainly places of safekeeping for funds, but modern banking systems see the creation of credit as their primary purpose.

The words "bank" and "banking" are almost nonexistent in the documents of modern Catholic social teaching. Perhaps it is because the medieval teaching was never formally retracted that money was unproductive and moneylending at interest was therefore immoral, yet the church itself became an active investor (Maritain). Perhaps it is because economists define money as a medium of exchange and distinguish between money value and "real" value of goods and services, while moral teachers focus on the real. Or perhaps it is because the church was so deeply involved in financial affairs at the highest levels that it was in no position to criticize.

There are, however, some themes in modern Catholic social teaching related to financial institutions and their activities: the degree of control exerted by financial managers over the economic life of a nation, the value of savings banks, the special credit needs of farmers, the responsibilities of bankers as trustees, the role bankers can play in local and regional self-help efforts, and the key role of international financial institutions in the problems of poor countries.

Degree of Control by Financiers

Pius XI in *Quadragesimo anno* (1931), aware of the excesses of financial capitalism, deplored the "economic dictatorship" resulting from the concentration of wealth in the hands of a few. Without using the word "banker," he described this dictatorship as "being most forcibly exercised by those who, since they hold the money and completely control it, control credit also and rule the lending of money. Hence they regulate the flow . . . of the lifeblood whereby the entire economic system lives, and have so firmly in their grasp the soul, as it were, of economic life that no one can breathe against their will" (QA 105–7).

In their 1933 statement, "Present Crisis," the U.S. bishops reiterated Pius XI's concerns about the concentration of control in the hands of "hard, cruel and relentless . . . financial magnates" ("Present Crisis," no. 45, in Byers, ed., p. 406). They commended New Deal legislative efforts, but cautioned that they would be ineffective unless the Christian concept of "justice and fair dealing" prevailed among the people at large and in business, banking, and labor relations (42). They praised the spirit of thrift and the self-reliance of the population, citing the existence of savings banks and building and loan societies as evidence (44).

In their 1937 "Statement on Social Problems" the U.S. bishops cited Pius XI's description of the power of "those who hold and control money." They added their concern that responsibility was divorced from ownership, since the control was being exercised by those who were not real owners of the wealth but merely the trustees and administrators of the invested funds. They called for further study of "the whole intricate problem of money and credit," citing concern over both the increased volume of debt relative to total wealth and the effect of this on prices ("Statement on Social Problems," nos. 13–14, in Byers, ed., *Justice in the Marketplace,* p. 423).

This same theme was revisited in the documents of the 1970s and 1980s as the debt crisis of the poor nations developed and intensified.

Special Credit Needs of Farmers

John XXIII in *Mater et magistra* (1961), recognizing that investors found it more profitable to invest elsewhere, called on public authorities to make special provisions for agricultural financing, establishing "banks that provide capital to farmers at reasonable rates of interest" (MM 134).

This same special concern for agricultural credit needs was voiced by the U.S. bishops in their 1986 pastoral, when they called for "emergency credit, reduced rates of interest and programs of debt restructuring" for farmers and access to temporary assistance for rural lending institutions suffering because of nonpayment of loans (*Economic Justice for All* 242).

Stewardship Responsibility of Managers of Finances

Gaudium et spes (1965) directed individuals, groups, and public authorities who make decisions about the distribution of goods and money to "be careful not to do harm to their own country or to any other" in financial transactions (GS 70).

In their 1986 pastoral the U.S. bishops treated the ethical responsibilities of owners and managers in detail (EJA 110–18). They stressed that the freedom of business and finance should be protected, "but the accountability of this freedom to the common good and the norms of justice must be assured" (110). "No one can ever own capital resources absolutely or control their use without regard for others and society as a whole" (112).

The bishops recognized the power of large financial institutions to shape institutions within the United States and internationally and called for the exercise of social responsibility in the use of that power (111, 116, 92). They stressed that the moral imperative of addressing the basic needs of the poor challenges policies that invest heavily in luxury production and military technology while failing to supply capital to sectors that provide basic goods and services (92).

The bishops were explicit about accountability of owners and managers of capital to the local communities in which they exist. "They are accountable to these workers and communities when making decisions" (113). They called on local and regional financial institutions to cooperate with other community institutions and groups to help develop job opportunities in cities and regions plagued by lack of financial resources and other problems (307–10).

International Financial Relations

In *Mater et magistra* John XXIII praised international banks along with private citizens and nations that make loans to help increase production in poor nations (MM 165). In *Populorum progressio* (1967) Paul VI called for the establishment of "a great World Fund" to be made up of part of the money spent on arms to address the needs of the world's poor. He saw it counteracting neocolonialist tendencies and providing preferential rates of interest and terms to poor nations and guarantees to lenders pp. 51–54). This call for a multilateral development fund was reiterated by the 1971 synod of bishops in *Justice in the World* (chap. 3).

Reflecting the same concern for the effects on the poor nations, popes and bishops have been increasingly critical of the international financial system itself. Paul VI in 1972 called for the revision of the relationships between nations, explicitly mentioning the monetary system, in the light of the "prior call of international duty" (*Octogesima adveniens* 43).

In 1979 in his first encyclical, John Paul II raised a theme that he would continue to develop: the inability of current systems—"financial, monetary, production and commercial"—to address unjust social situations inherited from the past or the urgent challenges of the present (*Redemptor hominis* 16).

In *Sollicitudo rei socialis* (1987) he referred to causal "structures of sin" (SRS 36) and called specifically for the reform of the world monetary and financial system, which harms poor nations by excessive fluctuations of exchange rates and interest rates (43). He also called for regional monetary and financial cooperation among the developing nations (45).

The Canadian bishops in 1983 identified as a cause of harmful structural change in Canada the role of transnational banks and corporations in moving capital to take advantage of cheaper labor conditions, lower taxes, and easier environmental standards (ECPC 2).

John Paul II addressed the debt crisis of poor nations in *Sollicitudo rei socialis*, saying that international loans to poor nations, though originally recommended as a way to aid development, have "turned into a counterproductive mechanism" (SRS 19).

In their 1986 pastoral the U.S. bishops identified the role of commercial banks in causing the crisis (EJA 272) and cited the inability of the "global system of finance" (the World Bank, the International Monetary Fund, and the General Agreement on Tariffs and Trade) to help debtor nations deal with the debt situation (273–76). They recommended specific ways to meet the immediate emergency (274) and called for systemic change to provide immediate relief and prevent recurrence (277). They applied John XXIII's judgment that current structures of authority are "inadequate to promote the universal common good" (*Pacem in terris* 135) to these international financial institutions (EJA 323), and they called on the people of the United States to work to increase effectiveness of international agencies (EJA 324).

See individual popes and encyclicals. *Also see* CREDIT; DEBT; DEVELOPMENT; ECONOMIC ORDER; ECONOMIC PLANNING, SOCIAL IMPORTANCE OF; INVESTMENT.

Bibliography: D. Byers, ed., *Justice in the Marketplace: Collected Statements of the Vatican and the United States Catholic Bishops on Economic Policy, 1891–1984* (Washington: USCC, 1985). J. Maritain, "A Society Without Money," *Review of Social Economy* 43 (April 1985) 75–83. A. MacEwen, *Debt & Disorder: International Economic Instability & U.S. Imperial Decline* (New York: Monthly Review Press, 1989). N. Coulbeck, *The Multinational Banking Industry* (New York: New York Univ. Press, 1984).

AMATA MILLER, I.H.M.

BASE COMMUNITIES

Semantics

Base communities emerged with this name in Europe in the late 1950s and through the 1960s. Especially in France and Italy the communities emphasized their critical and alternative character to the institutional and hierarchical church. During this same period in the United

States, features analogous to European groups can be identified in what was then called the "underground church" rather than "base communities," as in Europe.

After Vatican II and especially after the General Assembly of Latin American bishops in Medellín, Colombia, in 1968, the so-called Christian base communities and base ecclesial communities were becoming consolidated. This latter name, abbreviated as "CEBs," took hold during the ten years between the Medellín assembly and the Third General Assembly of Latin American bishops in Puebla de los Angeles, Mexico, in 1979 and remains to this day. The CEBs are most developed in the Latin American continent, though the style differs in the various regions, for example, in Brazil and in Central American countries. There are also CEBs in the Philippines with characteristics similar to those in Latin America, as well as in some African countries such as Zaire and Mozambique, although these avoid the form and name of CEBs.

Recently, CEBs were established in Italy with this name, but with significant adaptations in format and style. During the 1970s and 1980s in the United States there was a sense of urgency to build Christian communities inside or outside of the parish context. Initiatives such as RENEW and "Intentional Communities" were made at the national level, small church communities or actual base Christian communities and basic ecclesial communities at the local level, and even *comunidades eclesiales de base* among Hispanics, especially in southern California, Texas, and New Mexico.

It will not be possible here to work with such a broad spectrum of meanings and models of base communities. These communities are distinct from one another not only because of superficial nuances but also because of their diverse theological and sociological concepts, which originate in various types of pastoral praxis. There exists, however, a common denominator among all of these forms that allows us to examine them according to their ecclesiological affinity. They express, in fact, a specific paradigm, a way to be church.

While keeping in mind the existence of these multiple forms of small Christian ecclesial communities in various parts of the world, this article will reflect on one concrete reference, the CEBs in Brazil in the context of the Roman Catholic church. This is an epistemological and methodological option. This option renders viable both semantic rigor and an adequate treatment of the theme without intending to grasp in a generic and undifferentiated way all of the meanings of CEBs or analogous groups. One cannot speak or write seriously about base communities in general. One must necessarily be specific.

Admittedly, the first CEBs surfaced in Brazil. There, more than in any other country, the CEBs had not only the greatest development and continuity but also the most extensive presence among the people of God, official acceptance by the hierarchy, and a broad and competent process of original theological reflection with corresponding bibliographic coverage translated into various languages. Keeping this referential in mind will help to keep clear the concept as well as the realization of this way of being church, which characterizes the actual base communities and will help establish relations of approximation and differentiation with other models of communities in other regions of the world and in other religious denominations.

From the mid-1960s and during the 1970s and 1980s the CEBs multiplied throughout Brazil—groups of twenty-five to fifty persons, more adults than youths or children, and with a marked female presence. The CEBs were established as a church initiative, especially sensitive, however, to the real social-cultural situation of its members. The CEBs, estimated in Brazil today between seventy and eighty thousand, have become a significant ecclesiological constituency from a theological, pastoral, and institutional point of view.

The vast bibliography on base communities of varying quality can be classified in three categories: *phenomenological,* which describes the base community's way of living and operating; *methodological,* which focuses on the internal dynamics of relationships, personal training, and the presence of prayer and action both within and outside the church; and *theological,* which deals with the community as a faith community and as an evangelizing-liberating locale in the pastoral context of the local churches. The ecclesial conscience of the CEBs brings them to understand themselves neither as a movement nor as an association but as a new way of being church, of living and acting as church. In this sense the CEBs have a comprehensive reach that is not merely functional or sectorial in relation to the life of their members.

In spite of the above-mentioned diversity and multiple typologies of CEBs (even when they are analyzed in only one country), one can also find in Brazil a common foundation in the reality of the CEBs. They are *communities.* They want to recover the Judeo-Christian tradition of living faith in community and not only individually; of living faith in a public way, not a privatized way; of defying, through solidarity, the individualist and competitive character imposed by the contemporary culture; of transcending the privatistic spirituality centered solely on the individual person that has prevailed for the past five centuries. The CEBs insist on translating the binomial of Puebla, communion and participation, into their daily lives, on trying to live fully the breadth of a *koinonia* lest it be a mere physical or institutional juxtaposition of persons. Therefore, they seek to improve both the quality of interpersonal relationships among their members as well as their co-responsibility in making decisions of a communitarian or social nature.

The CEBs are also *ecclesial.* In contrast with the European base communities of the 1960s, the CEBs give importance to their ecclesiality. This is evident in the oneness of faith and in faith and by the visible belonging to the institutional church—at the same time *ekklesia* and *kahal*—articulating their dependence on the Catholic hierarchy with a healthy ecumenical opening in relation to the base communities of other Christian denominations. Hence the CEBs understand themselves not only as isolated actors in the reign of God in history but also as participants in an ecclesial mission and subjects of pastoral action.

Finally, the CEBs are *of the base.* They are of the base from an ecclesial point of view because they are above all groups of laypersons conscious of their specific lay vocation with all its consequences, both inside and outside the church. They are of the base from a sociological point of view because, in the Third World in general and in Brazil in particular, the CEBs are predominantly groups of poor persons. As laypersons and as poor persons, being of the base brings them to a faith that is not only listening to and knowing the Christian message, nor only a liturgical translation of the word, nor merely a sacramental or devotional practice. Faith guides them to draw ethical consequences along the lines of the construction of justice and consequently leads them to concrete and transforming actions at the individual and communitarian level, the ecclesial and sociocultural level, and the economic and political level. Thus they express the dimension of service, an ecclesial expression of a specific *diakonia* essential to the CEBs. This corresponds directly to the community's lay vocation as much as to its aspiration as a community of poor persons to social transformation. This particular connotation of being of the base in Third World CEBs contrasts with a certain resistance to this same qualification in First World communities. They attempt small ecclesial communities there but without insisting on the exclusive or predominant sociological characteristic of being of the base either as laypersons or as poor persons.

Looking at the semantic elements of the CEBs, one sees that they are situated in three principal realms that pervade their three fundamental dimensions in being a community that is ecclesial and of the base: the psychosocial, the ecclesial, and the political realms.

Historical Context of the Emergence of the CEBs

Three factors were inspiring and decisive in the emergence of the CEBs in the Brazilian context. The first was Vatican II, not just as a singular event but especially insofar as it was the result of a theological-ecclesiological process that was in gestation from the beginning of the 20th century. Many of the central elements of the CEBs—the biblical dimension, the consciousness of the lay vocation, a social perspective of the Christian life, and the importance of community—came directly from conciliar theology and ecclesiology. During the 1940s and 1950s Brazil's Catholic Action, especially among workers and university people, helped prepare for the acceptance and fruitfulness of the council.

Second, the diversified consciousness of the local churches and the contextualized reading of the council at Medellín and Puebla focused specific attention on reality as theological locus. A third, decisive factor was the social-cultural and economic-political context of the Latin American countries, especially in Brazil, due to the military dictatorship (1964–1985) and the historical arrangement that preceded it. This was marked and always aggravated by the stratification of society, the discriminatory concentration of political and economic power, the cultural and political dependence of the country in the international context, and by the church's own participation in this process since colonization and the first evangelization. These factors interacted in a unique way in the Latin American context and are at the root of the CEBs' very configuration in Latin America and, concretely, in Brazil.

While the first two factors are common to every church, the third is more specific to the Third World. Hence there is in principle a latent potential for the formation of CEBs as a way of being church everywhere, with some common characteristics and some specific ones, starting from the same presuppositions indicated above.

Origin and Formation

As an ecclesial phenomenon, the CEBs appeared in Brazil even before Medellín, in the first half of the 1960s. The idea of the CEBs first came from the internal life of the church, concretely at the sociological level of decentralizing and animating parishes, which were territorially large and demographically dense. Thus they were accepted and appreciated at Medellín and considered basic cells of Christian life. This need to dynamize the parish persists in various countries today as one of the principal sociological reasons for the rise of the CEBs, especially where clerics are scarce or quickly disappearing.

Since the territorial parish is still the basic jurisdictional unit in the Catholic church, the CEBs are still linked in some way to their respective parishes, even when they come about in other ways. There are some cases of dioceses that functionally and pastorally reorganized themselves around the CEBs without extinguishing the parishes juridically, as happened in Vitória and Sao Mateus in the state of Espírito Santo, Brazil.

Within a parish context the CEBs have generally emerged from Bible groups and/or prayer groups on the one hand and from the reshaping of traditional, preexisting organizations and associations on the other. Groups of people that gather together to read, reflect, and pray with the Sacred Scriptures progressively discover the need to relate them to their concrete lives, with the problems they find in their own contexts. Inversely, there are people that experience dramatic situations in their own reality and then search the Bible or communal prayer for a way to position themselves in relation to this reality. This linking of faith and life, prayer and life, Word of God and life, celebration of faith and of life, is a fundamental feature of the CEBs and one of the biblical-theological sources of their emergence even when they remain temporarily at the mere individual and familial level of religious practice without any social or political scope.

There is, nevertheless, a third and important factor that gave birth to the CEBs. This one qualifies the two preceding sources—the parish and associations or Bible and prayer groups. It has to do with the sensitivity of these groups to the shared situation of poverty and injustice, violence and oppression, in which they live. The perception of this situation in the light of the gospel as contrary to the human condition and to God's plan and, consequently, as a perversion of society and a sinful structure has a mobilizing effect that gives rise to the formation of communities. The social and religious dimensions are integrated in such a way that they are today seen as inseparable in an authentic CEB. This is not only a religious movement animating parish life. Nor is it merely a popular movement engaged in the transformation of society. A CEB articulates both sides of the same coin. It lives faith starting from reality, and at the same time it perceives and analyzes, interprets and transforms, reality in the light of faith, impelled by the urgency of faith's ethical consequences.

In this sense the CEBs in Brazil are the most conclusive and effective substantiation of the solidarity, prophetic vision, and preferential option for the poor that carved the very countenance of ecclesial identity and pastoral praxis of many local churches in the Latin American context. This in turn shapes the ecclesial-ecclesiological identity of the CEBs concerning their sociological and biblical-theological presuppositions.

Though these three main sources shaping the CEBs had their local flavor in Latin America, it is easy to verify that they can be reproduced in other parts of the world with their own connotations. In any time or latitude Christian life is confronted with dynamization of the parish, the collective and not only individual linking of faith and life, and the articulation of faith with its ethical demands at the level of questioning and transforming social structures and cultural presuppositions. Potentially, then, the CEBs can be substantiated as a new way of being church even when conditions for their realization are diverse. New ecclesiological and pastoral perspectives are implicit in this process.

Evangelizing Dynamic

The CEBs present a new paradigm of evangelization in relation to the previous model of evangelization that marked the past five centuries of apostolic action in Brazil and beyond.

The *former model,* which prevailed from the 16th century until shortly before Vatican II, was centered in the person and authority of the ordained minister, the parish and its various chapels, occasional sacramentalization, the individual person, and salvation of the soul. The main consequences of these characteristics were the hegemonic presence of the cleric, the small or null conscience and vocational initiative of the laity, the priority of the individual in the nearly total lack of communal perspective, the secondary importance of the Word and of access to the Bible in the process of evangelization and catechesis, and an emphasis on a sacramental practice that was more ritualistic and disciplinary than properly "theologal" (inspired and nourished by faith, hope, and love) and theological.

In large part, this model was inspired during the process of evangelization and ecclesial organization drawn up by the

Council of Trent and was coincident with the discovery and colonization of new continents and new lands by the Europeans from the 14th century forward. While their lacunae are evident one cannot deny their positive fruits. Among others, the Latin American peoples' profound popular religiosity and identification with Catholic faith in spite of no former education or elaboration of this faith; the consciousness of sociological-religious belonging to a church in spite of the chronic lack of priests and true theological-ecclesial consciousness; the association of the religious dimension with the cycle of life (birth, adolescence, marriage, death); and the great missionary courage and vitality of the evangelizers and pastoral agents, clerics and laity, who faced all kinds of difficulties to evangelize the populace and consolidate the church in unknown and hostile regions and situations.

The *CEB model* of evangelization is centered in the diversity of vocations, each with a specific scope and meaning, within a communal ecclesial setting. The lay vocation is emphasized in the community, in the Word, in salvation understood as integral liberation (immanent and transcendent) of the total human person (body and soul), in the individual and social level, and in the diversification of ministries understood not as mere substitutes for the diminishing or absent cleric but as an adequate response to the community needs.

The principal consequences of this model are (1) the co-responsibility of all members in the life of the faith community, which makes the community members subjects of the evangelizing process and not only its receivers; (2) the appreciation of the layperson within a subsidiary and complementary understanding of the various vocations; (3) the deepening of the Word of God and a greater familiarity with the biblical text; (4) creativity in the process of faith education; (5) participation in the effective preparation of community members for sacramental life (baptism, confirmation, etc.), stressing the ecclesial and social meaning of the sacraments more and their ritual or disciplinary role less; and (6) the emergence of new forms of "ministry" in a process of decentralization of apostolic action.

An important limit on the concrete situation of these communities, which are in fact lacking priests, is the impossibility given the regulations of the church of fulfilling the Eucharist as a sacrifice and sacrament in their own communities. This absence is felt more deeply today because of a parallel growth in the understanding of the social range of the Eucharist and in the awareness of its theological importance for the unity and nourishment of an ecclesial faith community.

This change in the evangelizing paradigm is not something that is confined exclusively to Latin America. On the contrary, many of these elements are present today in various other regions of the world and in other ecclesial contexts and have given inspiration to the Brazilian CEBs as well as to CEBs in other parts of the world.

Theological and Ecclesiological Roots

The theological perspective of Vatican II is the root of the inspiration and emergence of the CEBs. The concept of church as the people of God and as community; the emphasis on the Word of God as a source of inspiration and nourishment for the church; the church's interactive relationship with the world in which the church dwells; the appreciation of local churches and the prominence given to the lay vocation and role; the respectful opening to other ways of encountering, praising, and reverencing God; and so many other central elements of conciliar and post-conciliar theology were, on a small scale, assimilated and reinterpreted by this new form of being church, to which the CEBs aspired. The CEBs especially developed the biblical roots of this conciliar theology.

In Latin America and concretely in Brazil the CEBs chronologically preceded the first thematization of liberation theology and were of great worth and inspiration in its development. However, beginning in the 1970s the CEBs became tributary to this contextualized theological reflection, which matured between Medellín and Puebla. The CEBs agree with some basic principles and the very framework of the various liberation theologies: feminist theology, black theology, theology of the poor, and theology of repressed and oppressed cultures.

Concretely, Latin American liberation theologies distinguish themselves for the historical attention they give to faith, the importance of the liberating action of God in history, the incarnational dimension of the mystery of Jesus Christ, the active participation of the human being in the construction of history, and for that very reason, the centrality of reality as the theological locus. Hence reality is taken as the starting point from which one shapes a reading of the sources—Scripture and tradition—and from which proceeds theological reflection in the ecclesial context. However, this same perception, analysis and interpretation of reality, is in turn conditioned by the social perspective from which it is approached. This social perspective is not a sociological category—a position someone occupies on a social scale—but an epistemological category: a way of perceiving and knowing.

In the reality of Latin America, the dominant fact is an experience of a poverty that is not episodic but structural; that is, it is produced and reproduced by the very organization of society and its cultural assumptions. Hence the experience of the poor is a central element in theological reflection, which is done from the social perspective of the poor. The reality of the poor recapitulates on the one hand the foundational experience of God and the people of Israel (in the Exodus and in the fulfillment of the covenant alongside the history of the chosen people) and on the other hand the fundamental experience of Jesus Christ in relation to the poor of his time (sick, publicans, women, children, sinners, foreigners). In both testaments, poverty is seen as a result of injustice, discrimination, and marginalization and for that very reason as a form of oppression, a structure of sin.

There is in this perspective, therefore, a consciousness of individual sin but also of social sin and of the intimate relationship between them, which is made explicit in this situation of radical poverty—the negation of liberty and disrespect for human dignity. All of this contradicts the basic principles and the internal structure of salvation history made manifest in the pedagogy of God, which culminated in the mystery of Jesus Christ.

This theological substratum conditions the stance of the CEBs, be it in their propensity for critical analysis of such reality, in their prophetic positioning before the life situation of the majority of these populations, or in their awareness of the need for integral liberation, which embraces redemption from individual and social sin as well as transformation of the structures that produce sin. The exclusive and irreplaceable action of God who saves is thus integrated with the mutual responsibility of those who believe in this God of Jesus Christ and are, through him, partners in the construction of a society based in the values of the reign—love and truth, liberty and justice.

Political Dimension

This far-reaching theological understanding of faith does not diminish the importance of the Christian mystery and the relation of the human being to the transcendent. But this transcendent is seen in its relation with the immanent. The integral understanding of the human being at both the social and individual level as well as the understanding of the historical and incarnational rootedness of the mystery of Jesus Christ makes the CEBs aware of the importance of the political dimension. They find this inscribed in the very nature of Christian faith as well as in the church's apostolic mission and in the building of the reign of God. Christian faith establishes a deep relationship between the historical project and the eschatological destiny of individual and social human life. Consequently, the political is a necessary part of human endeavor to shape social-cultural reality according to gospel values.

In a pluralist and conflictive society political praxis, through which one reveals the inherently political dimension of faith, constitutes one of the most difficult problems for the CEBs. This is aggravated by the precariousness of the organization and the configuration of partisan mediations (political parties and trade unions) so typical in Third World countries. The problematic relationship between the political and the ecclesial was always a serious problem in the history of the church. It will be no less a problem in this new way of being church that the CEBs embody. It is precisely in relation to this political dimension that one sees the distinct evolution of the CEBs in the diverse contexts of various Third World countries and, concretely, of Latin America. The combination of urgency and political viability was certainly very different in Brazil, Chile, Nicaragua, and El Salvador. In each of these places a distinct relationship between the political and religious dimension was established. Each of these countries gave birth to a specific identity of ecclesial reality and therefore to the actual profile of their CEBs.

Possible Limits and Risks

In *Evangelii nuntiandi* (58) Paul VI summarized some conditions to help the CEBs respond to the hopes placed in them. The document also points to some possible limits and eventual risks that have in fact been verified to a greater or lesser degree in the life of the CEBs. The pope encouraged the communities to stay linked to the local church and the universal church without isolating themselves as the only authentic way to be the Church of Christ. The church is incarnated in many other ways, therefore the faithful should show themselves to be open and not sectarian. They must strive to develop the missionary ideal and zeal, never looking on themselves as the only recipients or agents of evangelization, and they must avoid the temptation of systematic or hypercritical criticism under the pretext of authenticity. Finally, Paul warned against becoming embroiled in political polarization or ideologies that try to exploit human potential.

The lived experience of the CEBs indicates yet other areas of risk. Sometimes in reading the Bible, so central for the CEBs, there is a selective, reductive, and even ideological instrumentalization of the Word of God. In their sensitivity to the urgency of social liberation and transformation they can minimize or even lose sight of the necessary integration of the eschatological and transcendent orientation of humanity and its opening to God who saves in and through Jesus Christ. This salvation-liberation is not restricted to the immanent historical reality of the social-cultural and economic-political structures but opens itself in history to the eschatological-transcendent perspective of human destiny. Furthermore, when discerning political action and grass roots, labor, or partisan activism consistent with the lay vocation, the CEBs should be sensitive to the theologal unity of the community and adopt a dialogic and dialectic attitude to deal with and overcome conflicts in a way that results in neither radical polarizations nor alienating and untenable neutralities.

Conclusion

The importance, meaning, and range of the CEBs for the Brazilian church derive from some significant breakthroughs that have occurred in them. One notes among them:

1. The passage from the ecclesiastic hegemony of the cleric to the ecclesial and active presence and significance of the laity as well (concretely, women religious) in the

apostolic and evangelizing process of the church.

2. The passage from a purely spiritual focus on the human person to a consideration of the human's total reality: material and spiritual, body and soul, individual and community, society and culture, historical and eschatological, immanent and transcendent. All should be evangelized.

3. The passage from the Christian faithful who are the recipients of the evangelizing process to the Christian faithful who are subjects of their own evangelization and the spreading of their faith in the world.

4. The passage from the idea of a hierarchical and institutional church primordially oriented to protect and maintain, defend and conserve, a concrete historical model to a church that is open to being creatively transformed at the level of persons and structures.

5. The passage from the primacy of theoretical elaboration as a previous condition for evangelization, catechesis, and Christian living to an attentiveness to the contribution of lived experience as a fertile referent for the enrichment of reflection and knowledge and for the transmission of theological, liberating, transforming praxis, which leads to the building of the reign of God.

All of these breakthroughs, which have occurred in the Brazilian CEBs, are not exclusive to the CEBs of the Third World. They can also be found in any part of the world where the universal unity of faith and church is lived in the diverse plurality of small, conscious groups that are authentic ecclesial communities.

Bibliography: M. Azevedo, *Basic Ecclesial Communities in Brazil: The Challenge of a New Way of Being Church* (Washington: Georgetown Univ. Press, 1987). R. Banks, *Paul's Idea of Community: The Early House Churches in Their Historical Setting* (Grand Rapids: Eerdmans, 1980). L. Boff, *Ecclesiogenesis: The Base Communities Reinvent the Church* (Maryknoll, N.Y.: Orbis, 1986). S. Clark, *Building Christian Communities: Strategy for Renewing the Church* (Notre Dame, Ind.: Ave Maria, 1972). D. Clark, *Basic Communities: Towards an Alternative Society* (London: SPCK, 1977). R. Collins, "Small Groups: An Experience of Church," *Louvain Studies* 13 (Summer, 1988) 109–36. G. Cook, *The Expectation of the Poor: Latin American Basic Ecclesial Communities in a Protestant Perspective* (Maryknoll, N.Y.: Orbis, 1985). M. Crosby, *House of Disciples: Church Economics and Justice in Matthew* (Maryknoll, N.Y.: Orbis, 1988). *The Church at the Crossroads: From Medellín to Puebla (1968–1979)* (Rome: IDOC, 1978). John Paul II, "Message for Base Christian Communities," *Origins* 10 (1980) pp. 140–41. J. Marins, "Basic Ecclesial Communities in Latin America," *International Review of Mission* 68/271 (July 1979) 235–42. C. Mesters, "The Use of the Bible in Christian Communities of the Common People," in S. Torres and J. Eagleson, eds., *The Challenge of Basic Christian Communities* (Maryknoll, N.Y.: Orbis, 1982). P. Palmer, *The Company of Strangers* (New York: Crossroad, 1981). Paul VI, *Evangelii nuntiandi,* AAS 68 (1976) 7–76. L. Rhodes, *Co-creating: A Feminist Vision of Ministry* (Philadelphia: Westminster, 1987). S. Torres and J. Eagleson, eds., *The Challenges of Basic Christian Communities* (Maryknoll, N.Y.: Orbis, 1982).

MARCELLO de C. AZEVEDO, S.J.

See also CHURCH, SOCIAL MISSION OF; CULTURE; EVANGELII NUNTIANDI; EVANGELIZATION; INCULTURATION; LIBERATION THEOLOGY; MEDELLÍN; POOR, PREFERENTIAL OPTION FOR; PUEBLA.

BEATITUDES

The beatitudes have inspired both the search for an evangelical life and the demand for justice and liberation in Catholic spirituality and theology. This article will suggest that these uses are in harmony with "the beatitudes" function in the social teaching of the gospels of Matthew and Luke. It will attempt to look behind the texts to the question of how they functioned in Q, the hypothetical common source of Matthew and Luke, and in the teaching of Jesus.

Beatitudes appear throughout the gospels of Matthew and Luke as individual sayings, but here, as in common use, "the beatitudes" refers to the two collections of sayings that introduce the Sermon on the Mount in Matthew and the Sermon on the Plain in Luke (Mt 5:2-11; Lk 6:20-26). Matthew and Luke have only three beatitudes in common: the blessings on the poor, the hungry, and the persecuted. These three beatitudes also appear in the

Coptic *Gospel of Thomas* (*logia* 54 and 68–69). A fourth blessing, on weepers, in Luke is closely related to the blessing on mourners in Matthew. It is likely that both Matthew's and Luke's beatitudes derive from a similar composition of four beatitudes in Q.

The Formal Character of the Beatitudes

Beatitudes are gnomic or wisdom sayings that begin with the word "blessed" or "happy" and describe a person in terms of an exemplary characteristic or behavior; some also announce the reward of this behavior. They functioned in Jewish wisdom traditions as a form of ethical teaching. In keeping with the close relations of wisdom and apocalypticism in 300 B.C.E.–200 C.E., beatitudes played a role in apocalyptic literature not only as moral teaching but also as prophetic sayings, frequently with a strong eschatological focus (Dan 12:12; Rev 1:3; 14:13; 16:15; 19:9; 20:6; 22:7, 14). Most beatitudes occur as isolated sayings, but there are some compositions that resemble the series in Mt 5:2-11 and Lk 6:20-26 (Sir 25:7-11; *2 Enoch* 42:6-14; 52:1-15). In Mt 5:1-11 and Lk 6:20-23 each saying is composed of a blessing followed by a second clause promising or announcing an eschatological reward.

Matthew's Beatitudes

The beatitudes play a unique role in the Gospel of Matthew, where they are an introduction not only to the Sermon on the Mount but also to all the teaching of Jesus and in fact to his entire career. Preceded by Jesus' entry into Galilee, the call of the disciples, and a brief miracle summary (4:12-25), the sermon is the opening programmatic word and deed of Jesus in Matthew. In contrast to Mark, for whom the authority of Jesus' teaching is displayed in power to command the demons (1:21-28), Matthew finds Jesus' words themselves endowed with life-giving power and wisdom—at least for those who *do* as well as hear (7:24-29). As the opening words of Jesus in both sermon and Gospel, the beatitudes complete the call of the disciples and extend it to the reader or hearer of the Gospel. They describe the blessed or happy life that is the goal both of the Greek philosopher and of the Jewish sage. Matthew and Matthew's community encounter Jesus primarily as a teacher always present in their midst (18:18-20; 23:10; 28:16-20), a teacher of wisdom who is also Wisdom's self (11:25-30). In this Gospel "disciple" has the literal meaning of "learner" or "student," and the call to discipleship is "learn of me" (11:28-30).

Matthew seems to have amplified the four beatitudes of Q in a highly deliberate and structured way, doubling or more than doubling them to form two sets of four beatitudes, all in the third person plural, followed by a ninth beatitude in the second person plural. Each of the two sets concludes by blessing those committed to righteousness/justice. The first and last of the eight parallel beatitudes proclaim "of them [the poor, the persecuted] is the heavens' [i.e., God's] reign." The words "of them" should probably be understood not as a possessive but as a partitive: "heavens' reign is *made up of* them." Thus "heavens' reign" is a community, and the beatitudes describe those who enter it. The ninth beatitude predicts the fate that will fall upon the newly called disciples who listen to the sermon and the later disciples of Matthew's community who read or hear it.

On the basis of Matthew's version of the first beatitude, these sayings are often characterized as "spiritual" over against Luke's, which are seen as more "literal." This is an inappropriate characterization of Matthew's beatitudes if it implies that the poverty that is blessed is a disposition of heart and not literal. A significant portion of the sermon is devoted to poverty as a pious practice (6:19-34), and while this poverty does indeed require a disposition of the heart, the insistence that one cannot serve God and Mammon (6:24) and the call to sell what you have and follow

(19:16–20:16) seem to be taken with absolute literalness. A better translation of the first beatitude might be "Blessed are the voluntarily poor." This translation helps to convey the true focus of Matthew's beatitudes: they are concerned with *practice*. The eschatology embodied in them is at least partly realized; their promises are for this world also. This is the case not only with the announcement that the poor make up the kingdom but also with the promise that those who hunger and thirst for justice will be satisfied. The counsel to forgo anxiety for food and drink and seek first heavens' (God's) reign and justice also promises that "all these things will be added to you" (6:33).

The concern with practice that is manifest in the beatitudes also informs the rest of the introduction to the sermon: the good deeds of the disciples enlighten and preserve the world; their righteousness must be greater than that of the scribes and Pharisees. This greater righteousness consists in doing the commandments of the Law as strictly as possible and teaching others to do likewise (5:12-20). The body of the sermon presents Jesus' interpretation of righteousness; this interpretation consists in instruction not only in doing the Law (5:21-48) but also in performing the practices of piety (6:1–7:12). The closing of the sermon requires the hearer to choose between two ways, the wise way of hearing these words and doing them and the foolish way of hearing these words and not doing them (7:13-27).

Matthew's amplifications of the beatitudes come primarily from the Scriptures. The third beatitude is virtually identical with Ps 37:11; the sixth is strongly reminiscent of Ps 24:4; the second seems to draw upon Sir 7:34, 48:24, and Isa 61:1, perhaps also Ps 126:5 and Isa 57:15. The fourth resembles Sir 24:21. Thus the beatitudes invite the hearer or reader to learn a wise and just way by which the disciples of Jesus join the poor of the earth and the sages and saints of the Bible.

The rest of the first set, or stanza, of Matthew's beatitudes consists of blessings on mourners, the meek, and those who are hungry and thirsty for righteousness. The fourth, which blesses those who hunger and thirst after righteousness, seems to draw upon wisdom traditions like the ones articulated in the proclamation of Wisdom in Sir 24:20: "Those who eat of me will hunger still, those who drink of me will thirst for more." The righteousness Jesus teaches in the sermon is equated with the teaching of Wisdom herself, God dwelling with us in Jesus. The blessing on the meek invokes the messianic example of Jesus: Mt 12:15-20 uses Isa 42:1-4 to transform Mark's messianic secret into an exemplary practice of humility and meekness on Jesus' part. The disciple who is burdened by the demands of justice can find refreshment by learning of Jesus, who is meek and lowly of heart (Mt 11:28-30). Mourning, too, appears in wisdom contexts as a practice of compassion and virtue (see Sir 7:34; 48:24; 51:19; see also Rom 12:15).

The second stanza blesses the merciful, clean of heart, peacemakers, and those persecuted for the sake of righteousness. The exact practice associated with them is difficult to specify; these blessings seem not to envision practitioners who are distinct from one another or from the poor in spirit, meek, mourners, or those who hunger and thirst for righteousness. Rather, they elaborate their righteousness. Mercy evokes almsgiving; it comes from the same word. But it also suggests forgiveness and compassion. The blessing of the clean of heart may reflect a growing interest in the practice of sexual asceticism. But it could also refer to those whose hearts and hands are clean of violence, as do the blessings on peacemakers and on those persecuted for righteousness. The details of practice are spelled out in the interpretation of individual commandments of the Law by the rejection of anger, nonretaliation, forswearing lust and divorce, refusing of oaths, requiring undiscriminating love of neighbors and enemies.

Matthew's context is a complex one. The Gospel's audience is clearly Greek-speaking, and the Gospel's emphasis on the commission to teach all the Gentiles strongly suggests that the community included Gentiles. But the Gospel also shows close acquaintance with the Judaism of land as it was regrouping from the Jewish war in the late 1st century. The radicalization of the commandments so commonly remarked in Mt 5:21-48 is paralleled in Jewish sectarian groups. The *Community Rule of Qumran* prohibits anger (1QS 5.25-26), and Josephus relates that the Essenes banned oaths (Josephus *Jewish War* 2.135; *Antiquities of the Jews* 15.371). Like the *Community Rule of Qumran* and the *Damascus Document,* Matthew's beatitudes and sermon do not provide a complete morality or legal code; rather they supply examples of interpretations of the Law. For Matthew's community as for the covenanters of the *Community Rule* and the *Damascus Document,* a few examples suffice, for these communities are convinced that they are the chosen congregation of the last times, endowed with the authority of the prophetic spirit to interpret the Law. But there is something more in Matthew; it is the continuing presence of Jesus that guarantees the power to bind and loose, which resides in the community, indeed in every two or three of these little ones whose one teacher is the Christ.

Luke: The Beatitudes and Woes

Luke's beatitudes have a less prominent place in the literary structure of the Gospel but are equally central to Luke's thought. They, too, introduce a sermon of Jesus, the much shorter Sermon on the Plain (Lk 6:12–7:1). Functioning less as ethical teaching than as prophetic words of judgment, they serve to characterize the Jesus who speaks them as the "prophet mighty in word and work before God and the people" (24:19), who "went about doing good to all who were downtrodden by the devil" (Acts 10:38). Like Matthew, Luke seems to have doubled an original four beatitudes, but this time by adding four woes. These woes, which occur only in Luke, provide simple reversals of the four beatitudes.

Luke's lengthy setting places the Sermon on the Plain in the context of the election of the Twelve (Lk 6:12-19). The fourth beatitude and woe clearly predict their future in a special way. The "you" of the other beatitudes and woes must include the Twelve but is not limited to them or even to believers. Rather these sayings underline the deep-seated and absolute demand for economic justice that characterizes Luke's Gospel. The first three beatitudes seem to be virtually synonymous: the poor, the hungry, those who weep, are differing descriptions of the same population. It is for them that Jesus' opening, programmatic sermon in Luke proclaims an acceptable year, a year of release (4:18-22). But the import of the blessings extends beyond that year. The third beatitude manifests their eschatological character as prophetic sayings that announce God's judgment: those who weep now will have the last laugh. In Luke, in contrast to most of early Christianity, this judgment seems not to be postponed to the final day of reckoning but to fall at the end of every human life (16:16-30; 12:16-21).

Luke's beatitudes and woes are best illustrated by the parable of the rich man and the poor man (16:16-30). In it, the ultimate fates of the rich man who feasted every day and the poor man who longed to be filled from the scraps that fell from his table are reversed. The same reversal is announced in the *Magnificat:* God has "filled the hungry with good things and sent the rich away empty" (1:53). For Luke, the warning of the beatitudes and woes is the message not only of Jesus but also of the Law and the Prophets; the rich who have not listened to the Law and the Prophets will not listen to one who is risen from the dead. This is not to say that Luke cannot envision a rich man who will be saved: Zacchaeus, who gives half his goods to the poor is one example (19:1-10). Significantly, he also volunteers to restore fourfold anything he has defrauded. While tax collectors in particular are liable to defraud, Zacchaeus' promise may well derive from Luke's evaluation of wealth in the context of a "limited good economy" and may reflect a conviction on Luke's part that property is theft.

The threat expressed in the parables of the rich man and the poor man and of the man who laid up wealth is to some extent distanced from the readers by being addressed to the "money loving" Pharisees, as the example of Zacchaeus is distanced by his singularly objectionable profession. But Luke also warns Christian readers who "have eaten and drunk in the presence of" Jesus that if they feast without regard for the poor, they too will hear: "Depart from me, all you workers of iniquity" (13:27).

Unlike Matthew, Luke envisions an audience beyond a single, closely knit community. In keeping with the author's conviction that "these things were not done in a corner" (Acts 26:26) but on and for the stage of world history, Luke-Acts manifests the beginnings of an apologetic appeal to the empire. In Acts, Luke's concern to show the attraction of wealthy and respectable people to the early Christian community produces tensions with the prophetic demand for radical economic justice voiced by Jesus in Luke's Gospel. Acts presents an ideal resolution of the problem of wealth and justice among Christians by depicting the Jerusalem church as embodying the antique ideal of community of property. While for the Greek philosophical schools sharing of goods is the means of detachment or of equality and friendship, and for the Jewish community of Qumran it signifies incorporation in the covenant, Luke's concern is with supplying the needs of the poor. The rest of Acts addresses the issue by the less ambitious means of an emphasis on the ministry of charity.

Q

"Q" is the designation of a Greek document postulated by a substantial number of scholars as the source of material common to Matthew and Luke that is not from Mark. It consists almost entirely of the words of Jesus and seems to have derived from a community that continued to live as preachers of God's reign, as prophets, and as sages.

Evidence from the *Gospel of Thomas* indicates that the beatitudes did not originate as a unit, and were probably brought together by the author of Q. Comparison of Matthew and Luke suggests that a version of the four beatitudes in Luke introduced a sermon very like Lk 6:20-49 (the Sermon on the Plain), and that this sermon was the inaugural teaching of Jesus in Q, preceded only by the preaching of John and the testing of Jesus. Thus the beatitudes, originally separate sayings, seem to have been drawn together by the author of Q to form the opening proclamation of God's reign. In view of Q's sapiential character and the focus on prophecy that emerges in some sayings, they are likely to have functioned both as wise teaching and as prophetic words of judgment, evoking the community's itinerant following of Jesus.

Jesus

Did the beatitudes form part of the teaching of Jesus, and what did they mean to his context? Conclusions about Jesus must remain still more tentative than conclusions about Q. But an increasing number of scholars see Jesus as an "apocalyptic revolutionary," like other prophetic figures and movements in 1st-century Judaism who responded to the increased pressure of Roman imperial domination by an urgent call for renewal and intense expectation of a second redemption of Israel. Jesus' movement seems to have been composed of men and women who chose an itinerant, prophetic life of wandering and preaching God's reign as an alternative to the oppressive Roman rule. Some version of the beatitudes found in the *Gospel of Thomas* and in Luke accords well with this picture. Circulating separately, these sayings of wisdom and prophecy would have articulated the identity and the program of the reign-of-God movement.

Summary

As social teaching, Matthew's beatitudes are the expression of a community that chose a life of practicing wisdom that joined them to the poor of the world. Luke's beatitudes and woes together announce the grounds on which God's judgment is made. In Q the beatitudes appear to function as the proclamation of God's reign. If the beatitudes indeed originated with Jesus and his companions, they are likely to have expressed the hopes and the self-understanding of the reign-of-God movement.

See also DISARMAMENT; DISCIPLESHIP; GOODS, ACCESS TO; GOODS, DISTRIBUTION OF; KINGDOM OF GOD; PEACE; POOR, PREFERENTIAL OPTION FOR.

Bibliography: W. Davies, *The Setting of the Sermon on the Mount* (Cambridge: Cambridge Univ. Press, 1964). J. Kloppenborg, *The Formation of Q*, Studies in Antiquity and Christianity (Philadelphia: Fortress, 1987). W. Meeks, *The Moral World of the First Christians*, Library of Early Christianity 6 (Philadelphia: Westminster, 1986). H. Moxnes, *The Economy of the Kingdom: Social Conflict and Economic Relations in Luke's Gospel*, Overtures to Biblical Theology (Philadelphia: Fortress, 1988).

MARY ROSE D'ANGELO

BIRTH CONTROL

The term "birth control" was coined by Margaret Sanger in 1914 and has come to connote all methods of preventing conception, whether used by the male or the female. As commonly used, the term now includes all methods of fertility control, including abortion and sterilization. The related term "family planning" came into common use in the 1930s followed by the notion of "planned parenthood." Because of these associations birth control took on an essentially negative connotation in Catholic social thought. As a result both the Second Vatican Council (*Gaudium et spes* 51) and Pope Paul VI (*Humanae vitae* 10) preferred to speak of responsible parenthood when they addressed the issue of the legitimate control of human fertility.

The human effort to control fertility has been evident in all cultures at all times. The earliest written evidence on suggested medical methods to control fertility dates back to an Egyptian papyrus around 1850 B.C. Since that time birth control methods have had a place in medical practice, usually reserved for royalty and the wealthy, though numerous folk methods for preventing conception or inducing miscarriages are also part of the historical record. The OT betrays knowledge of at least one method for preventing conception, withdrawal of the penis from the vagina before ejaculation (Gen 38:9).

The historical record also indicates that for most of human history birth control was a personal or familial concern rather than a public concern. What made a pregnancy unwanted was something that touched directly on the perceived physical, emotional, economic, or social well-being of an individual or a family. Public policy tended to favor the birth of children, since social and political well-being were generally thought to be related to increased population. It has only been since the time of Thomas Malthus at the close of the 18th century that birth control came to be associated with the control and limitation of national populations as essential to their social and economic improvement.

At least five major historical developments are responsible for the present shape of the birth-control question. (1) The Industrial Revolution and the accompanying social process of urbanization had the effect of separating work from home life and of rendering children an economic burden rather than a benefit for most families, thus providing large numbers of people with social and economic motives for family limitation. (2) Developments in medical science and technology not only led to a better understanding of human and animal reproductive processes but also to more effective and less dangerous chemical and mechanical contraceptive devices. (3) Increased affluence and longer life expectancies made necessary and possible a new understanding of the place of sex in human life. Sex came to be understood primarily as a vehicle of interpersonal communication and fulfillment and only secondarily, and by choice, as a means of procreation. (4) The growing awareness of the rapid growth in human population and the resulting strain on the environment and on economic and social development provided whole societies and their governments with an urgency to limit population. (5) The rise of the feminist movement along with the general, increased emphasis on human rights led to a search for a way to ensure women's rights, including the right to control their own bodies and their procreative choices.

As a consequence of these five developments both individuals and whole societies have been provided with strong motives for birth control. Effective artificial means of birth control have become readily and widely available. The physical and psychological separation of sexual behavior from procreation has been effected for heterosexual partners. And motherhood has ceased to be the dominant and defining aspect of female identity.

These consequences, and the birth control movement as a whole, were strongly resisted by almost all the Christian churches until well into the 20th century. Their opposition focused publicly upon the dissemination of birth-control information and devices and morally upon the practice of birth control or deliberate contraceptive intercourse. The first significant break in that opposition came from the Anglican church at the Lambeth Conference in 1930. The Anglicans were quickly followed by most Protestant denominations (Noonan, p. 490), but Catholic teaching on the subject reacted by insisting on the immoral nature of all forms of artificial contraception (*Casti connubii* 82) even while accepting in a qualified way the use of the so-called rhythm method (CC 85). The Catholic church, in its official pronouncements at least, continues today to affirm that natural family planning and sexual abstinence are the only morally acceptable means of controlling births.

Catholic social teaching, however, did not escape the influence of the historical developments mentioned above. For one thing, it has clearly affirmed the obligation of responsible parenthood, recognizing that a variety of reasons and circumstances make limitation of family size a basic human responsibility (GS 50; HV 10). For another thing, it has acknowledged the interpersonal significance of sexual intercourse for the promotion of stable marriages and family well-being and has affirmed both the nobility of marital sexual love even when procreation is not possible and the possible conflict between the so-called unitive and procreative goods of marriage (GS 50; HV 2; *Familiaris consortio* 14). For a third, it has somewhat mildly affirmed the rights of women to full social and political participation in the societies to which they belong (*Pacem in terris* 41). What has become the key issue for Catholic thought in the matter of birth control, therefore, is not the intended ends sought by proponents of artificial birth control but the morally legitimate means to the admittedly good ends that birth-control advocates claim to seek and the human values that will be lost or distorted in using morally illegitimate means.

There seem to be several major concerns behind the continued opposition of Catholic social teaching to the practice of artificial means of birth control, be those means mechanical (condoms, IUDs, diaphragms, cervical caps), chemical (spermicidal agents, the "pill"), or surgical (sterilization, abortion). Those concerns focus on the dignity of men and women, the well-being of children and families, and God's role in the creation of new life. More cynical or suspicious views of Catholic social teaching would also see a fear and contempt for sex on the part of celibate clerics and a desire by these same celibates to maintain their power in the church and their control over the laity. Whatever merit such suspicious views may have, they are not necessary to account for the continued opposition of the official teachers of the Roman Catholic church to artificial contraception.

At the heart of the faith tradition of both Jews and Christians is a God who is the author and giver of life, who creates human life out of the superabundance of divine love, and who endows human creatures with the capacity to transmit that life to new human beings. In such a perspective human procreative powers enable humans to become co-creators with God in the fashioning of new human life. Children are seen to be a gift and a blessing of God and a sign of God's continued covenant fidelity throughout history, ensuring a human future. The human willingness to cooperate with God in conceiving, bearing, and rearing children is both a testimony to and an essential demand of a couple's faith, hope, and love. The human refusal to accept the link between the unitive and procreative goods of human sexuality is, therefore, understood to be a rejection of a divine calling and a violation of the dignity with which God has endowed human beings.

The likely consequences for human dignity, as well as for marriage and family life, resulting from the separation of the unitive and procreative goods of sex were articulated most clearly by Paul VI. Among those consequences the pope saw an increase in marital infidelity, increased sexual promiscuity especially among the young, and a further loss of respect for the personal dignity of women "to the point of considering her as a mere instrument of selfish enjoyment, and no longer as his respected and beloved companion" (HV 17). Most worrisome, however, would be the intervention of public authority, the state, into the sacred domain of conjugal intimacy, imposing upon people whatever methods of contraception the government judged to be necessary and effective. Such usurpation of personal responsibility strikes directly at the dignity of men and women.

Endowed with the capacity to procreate new life, human beings are responsible for the exercise of that capacity, and out of this generic sense of responsibility there developed a code of sexual and parental ethics. In the Christian faith tradition procreation was seen as the primary purpose of human sexual love, and parents were held responsible not only for procreating children but also for their physical nurture, social education, and spiritual formation. This social responsibility was a grave one and became central to Catholic social teaching about sexuality, marriage, and the family. As the Second Vatican Council would express this basic tenet of Roman Catholic thought, "the family is the foundation of society. In it the various generations come together and help one another to grow and to harmonize personal rights with the other requirements of social life" (GS 52).

It is in the family that human beings first learn the meaning and practices of love and so develop the virtues essential to personal and social life, including respect for human differences and special concern for the weakest and most needy family members. It is in the family that faith is first handed on and lived and conscience receives its first formation. It is in the family that one first learns that human dignity and worth are gifts intrinsic to one's being and are to be respected as such, not achievements to be realized or rewards to be earned. Of course such a view of the family may be called idealistic. Catholic social thought calls it normative, for it recognizes that there is simply no substitute for the family, no other social setting in which these lessons can be equally learned.

Catholic social thought has also come to recognize that what it calls responsible parenthood is an essential aspect of family life. But it is insistent that the responsibility for control of births belongs only to the parents. Vatican II expressed the matter strongly: "For in view of the inalienable right to marry and beget children, the question of how many children should be born belongs to the honest judgment of parents. The question can in no way be committed to the decision of government" (GS 87). Pope Paul VI repeated this teaching, expanding on the factors that parents should take into account. "Finally, it is for parents to decide, with full knowledge of the matter, on the number of their children, taking into account their responsibilities toward God, themselves, and the children they have already brought into the world, and the community to which they belong. In all this they must follow the demands of their own conscience enlightened by God's law authentically interpreted, and sustained by confidence in Him" (*Populorum progressio* 37).

The third concern that seems to infuse Catholic teaching on birth control is the relationship of the couple to God in the creation of new life. Marital love is said to have its supreme origin in God. Marriage is "the wise institution of the Creator," through which the divine purpose of love is realized among humankind (HV 8) and in which human beings are called to collaborate with God in the generation and education of new lives. Hence the couple, as well as having duties toward themselves, their children, and society, primarily have duties toward God. In entering marriage the couple express the willingness and accept the responsibility of being co-creators with God in raising up new life. The practice of artificial contraception, it is claimed, negates this willingness and so fails in this responsibility.

The widespread and unprecedented dissent to the church's teaching on birth control by numerous theologians and ordinary Catholics alike did not quarrel with the general view of marriage and family expressed in the official teaching. It focused, rather, on the papal insistence that "each and every marriage act must remain open to the transmission of life" (HV 11). At a deeper level the dissent spoke to the kind of dominion over life that God had entrusted to human beings and the extent to which human agency had authority to interfere with or alter natural, biological processes. Paul VI had expressly limited human dominion in this regard, asserting that "just as man does not have unlimited dominion over his body in general, so also, with particular reason, he has no such dominion over his generative faculties as such, because of their intrinsic ordination towards raising up life, of which God is the principle" (HV 13).

The significance of the argument over human authority to alter nature has reached beyond the birth control issue itself to include issues of reproductive technology, of ordinary and extraordinary life-sustaining procedures, of alternative, nonmarital sexual lifestyles, and finally of the relationship of church teaching and practice to the political and social institutions of society. This last issue has become reflected most clearly in the public debates about abortion.

At present birth control remains a matter of controversy within the church, though no official voices have been raised in support of the dissenting view. Polls repeatedly indicate that over 75 percent of Catholics disagree with the official teaching and actually employ various methods of artificial contraception. Considerable effort is being expended by various local church agencies to explain the very real benefits of natural family planning and to teach its practice. These efforts usually center on the cervical-mucus, basal-body-temperature method of birth control, a method claimed to be theoretically 98 percent effective and, when practiced by knowledgeable, motivated persons, 90–93 percent effective. Since the method requires careful instruction and high motivation, its usefulness for social policy has been seriously questioned.

See also DEMOGRAPHICS; FAMILY; GENOCIDE; HUMAN RIGHTS; MARRIAGE; PAUL VI; PERSON, DIGNITY OF; REPRODUCTIVE TECHNOLOGIES, SOCIAL ASPECTS OF.

Bibliography: J. Connery, *Abortion: The Development of the Roman Catholic Perspective* (Chicago: Loyola Univ. Press, 1977). J. Hanigan, *What Are They Saying About Sexual Morality?* (New York/New Jersey: Paulist, 1982). J. Noonan, Jr., *Contraception: A History of Its Treatment by the Catholic Theologians and Canonists* (Cambridge: Harvard Univ. Press, 1965, enlarged ed. 1986). Karol Wojtyla, *Love and Responsibility,* trans. H. Willetts (New York: Farrar/Straus/Giroux, 1981).

JAMES P. HANIGAN

BISHOPS' PROGRAM OF SOCIAL RECONSTRUCTION OF 1919

Although it was published over the signatures of the members of the Administrative Committee of the National Catholic War Council (NCWC), the Bishops' Program of 1919 (formally known as *Social Reconstruction: A General Review of the Problems and Survey of Remedies*) was really the work of one man, Msgr. John A. Ryan (1869–1945). Therefore it was understandably influenced by his intellectual formation and reflected his apostolic dreams.

Brought up in rural Minnesota and educated at St. Paul Seminary and The Catholic University of America, by the time he had completed his doctoral studies Ryan had been exposed to both the Populist and Progressive strains of the American reform tradition and to the thought of Leo XIII. Struck by the similar natural-law thinking that undergirded both bodies of thought, he dedicated himself to the task of trying to forge an alliance between the church and the American reform camps active at the turn of the century. This task, however, was complicated by two factors: first, American Catholics were either completely ignorant of the contents of *Rerum novarum* or chose to construe its message in an exclusively antisocialist way; and second, the church both feared and distrusted the Progressives, whose rhetoric was sometimes tainted by nativist overtones and whose calls for state intervention to advance the cause of social justice sounded suspiciously socialist to conservative Catholic ears.

Ryan was undeterred by these obstacles. He spent the early part of his career as a professor at Catholic University and as the editor of the *Catholic Charities Review* trying both to give American Catholics a more balanced view of *Rerum novarum* and to demonstrate the similarities that existed between the American and Catholic traditions of social thought.

In spite of his best efforts, however, by 1914 the American church still interpreted and applied *Rerum novarum* in a rather narrow-minded fashion, and it continued to view Progressivism with suspicion. The circumstances surrounding the church's involvement in World War I, however, made it possible for Ryan to make considerable headway in his crusade.

In challenging the nation to rally to the war effort, Woodrow Wilson used Progressive rhetoric and spoke of "making the world safe for democracy." The church rushed to respond to his call to arms. In fact, in order more effectively to discharge its patriotic duties, the church formed the National Catholic War Council, an agency charged with coordinating all Catholic war-related activities. Moreover, in an effort to win recognition for its endeavors in the course of the war, the NCWC hired the public-relations firm of Larkin Mead and entrusted to him the task of spotlighting the contributions that the church was making to the war effort. In the process, the Catholic community adopted the Progressive-inspired rhetoric of the war crusade and thus found itself in the same camp with the very reformers it had previously viewed with such suspicion.

Following the armistice the Progressives turned their attention to a new arena in which the war "to make the world safe for democracy" was to be fought: the sphere of domestic industrial relations. Linking this war with the European war and using successful wartime experiments to justify their proposals, they presented a vast array of programs for building a more just and humane social order based on the ideal of "industrial democracy." Fearful that they would lose the public-relations momentum they had built up during the war (and pressured by their publicist to come up with a story that would grab headlines in the postwar era), in the closing days of the war the NCWC formed a committee on reconstruction and asked it to produce a program on postwar social reconstruction that would compare favorably with hundreds of similar programs already before the public.

In desperation, John O'Grady, chair of the committee, turned to Ryan for help in formulating a statement before the deadlines imposed on him by the bishops and their publicist had passed. Although he initially begged off the assignment, Ryan later reversed himself and gave O'Grady a hastily revised speech on reconstruction that he had prepared for delivery at a Knights of Columbus convention. As time went on, he realized that the bishops' request was the opportunity of a lifetime, for it gave him the chance to produce a document that wedded Leonine Catholic social thought with American Progressivism. In addition, due to the fact that it was published under the bishops' names, it gave him the unparalleled opportunity to present a unified and Progressive Catholic social program to the entire church.

Published on February 12, 1919, the document was divided into three unequal parts, all of which were interspersed with a commentary that mixed Leonine and Progressive justifications for its positions: a brief introductory essay; a survey of other reconstruction proposals, both foreign and domestic; and a series of proposals that Ryan hoped would be implemented during the postwar era. The proposals themselves were divided into two categories: short-term proposals, most of which were standard Progressive fare and which were justified (in typically Progressive fashion) by appeals to the success that similar measures had produced in wartime; and two long-term proposals that were more radical in their implications. Into the former category fell calls for minimum-wage legislation, social insurance (to protect workers in cases of industrial accidents and unemployment), child-labor laws, the recognition of labor's rights to organize and bargain collectively, the continuation of the National War Labor Board to mediate labor disputes, public housing for the urban poor, the creation of a national employment service, progressive taxation, the regulation of monopolies, government control of utilities, a land colonization program for returning soldiers, and the retirement of women from the industrial jobs they had assumed during the war emergency. The more radical long-range proposals called for the formation of workers' cooperatives and the realignment of industry in such a way as to foster co-partnership in industry. Under the terms of the latter plank Ryan suggested that workers be given a say in determining their wages and working conditions and, indeed, in the management of the entire industrial enterprise.

As a result of the shrewd and ambitious campaign mounted by the NCWC's publicist, the publication of the program caused quite a sensation, a fact that had both positive and negative results for the church. Liberals (both Progressives and social gospelers) and labor greeted it with incredulous delight. Conservatives (both Catholic and non-Catholic) and the business community, however, were quite hostile. Moreover, in spite of Ryan's comments in his introductory essay and throughout the text that the program's proposals were both traditional and conservative (by which he meant that they were rooted in the thought of Leo XIII), in reacting to the program both friends and foes alike said that it seemed to be rather innovative and radical for a group of Catholic bishops. In addition, one group of Catholic critics sought to undermine its binding authority by calling attention to the anomalous canonical standing of the NCWC, a body that had no clearly defined magisterial position within the church.

The wide coverage accorded the program in the press and the sometimes bitter debates it sparked within the church highlighted its importance. Furthermore, the charges of radicalism and novelty leveled against it obliquely testified to the fact that nearly thirty years after its publication most American Catholics still did not understand *Rerum novarum.* The confused and hostile reaction given the document, however, was strangely fortuitous. Faced with Catholic ignorance of the Leonine tradition of social criticism, both Ryan and his colleagues at the NCWC embarked on an educational program to make Leo's thought more widely known in the American church. This educational task turned out to have two components, both of which proved to be quite important: a short-term defense of the Bishops' Program and its proposals and a more long-range plan to provide the church with a permanent agency for social analysis, social criticism and advocacy, and legislative lobbying.

The short-term task of defending the program fell largely on the shoulders of Ryan and a cadre of like-minded social theorists and activists at Catholic University and in the National Conference of Catholic Charities. In addressing the program's critics, Ryan was forced to make the Leonine justification for his Progressive proposals more explicit than he had in his original presentation. Some proposals could be squared with Leo's positions quite easily. Since, for instance, Leo had clearly defended the laborer's right to a living wage in *Rerum novarum,* Ryan was able to show that the program's plank calling for minimum-wage legislation was clearly Leonine in inspiration. Some proposals, like that dealing with a national employment service, however, required considerable mental sleight of hand to square with Leo's thought. Ryan was more than equal to the challenge. Arguing that the right to a living wage was obviously dependent on a worker's ability to land a job in the first place, he declared that the idea of a national employment service was implied in the idea of a living wage. Thus as a result of a free and creative adaptation of Leo's thought Ryan was able to declare that the entire program was inspired by Leo XIII and rooted in *Rerum novarum.*

In order to deal with the more long-range task of educating Catholics in the social thought of the church, in 1919 the NCWC issued a pastoral letter that reaffirmed the positions stated in the program and formed the Social Action Department, which was charged with the threefold task of producing educational programs in Catholic social thought for the members of the church, engaging in ongoing analysis of social conditions in America, and trying to bring Catholic influence to bear on social legislation before Congress. Initially under the direction of Ryan, the Social Action Department understandably continued to highlight the points contained in the Bishops' Program. Therefore, it was especially vocal in its support of both the rights of labor and the use of state intervention to advance the cause of social justice.

On balance, then, it could be said that the Bishops' Program of 1919 played a significant threefold role in the development of American Catholic social thought. First, it represented a step forward in the attempts to retrieve the full critical potential of *Rerum novarum* and to apply its central insights to concrete local circumstances. Second, on the basis of a perception of a shared natural-law basis, it sought to effect a reconciliation between the American and

Catholic traditions of social criticism. Finally, in that it gave impetus to the founding of the Social Action Department, it marked the beginning of the church's institutionalized and ongoing ministry of social criticism in the United States, a ministry that continues to the present day.

See also ECONOMIC PLANNING, SOCIAL IMPORTANCE OF; JUST WAGE; LABOR AND CAPITAL IN CATHOLIC SOCIAL THOUGHT; NATIONAL CONFERENCE OF CATHOLIC BISHOPS, UNITED STATES; NATURAL LAW; RERUM NOVARUM; RYAN, JOHN AUGUSTINE.

Bibliography: A. Abell, *American Catholicism and Social Action: A Search for Social Justice, 1865–1950* (Garden City, N.Y.: Hanover, 1960). F. Broderick, *Right Reverend New Dealer: John A. Ryan* (New York: Macmillan, 1963). J. McShane, *"Sufficiently Radical": Catholicism, Progressivism, and the Bishops' Program of 1919* (Washington: The Catholic Univ. of America Press, 1986).

JOSEPH M. McSHANE, S.J.

BLACK THEOLOGY

Black theology is a global theology thematized primarily in the United States and South Africa but to some extent in the Caribbean, in South America, and in Africa. This essay focuses on black theology in the United States (BTUSA) and black theology in South Africa (BTSA). Like all Christian theology, black theology strives to discern, to understand, to interpret, and to impart the word of God and its meaning in various cultural and social (i.e., political, economic, technological) matrices. However, black theology explicitly addresses the historical, cultural, and structural subordination of black peoples within social contexts dominated by white supremacist rule. Black theology explicitly contests the heretical use of the Hebrew and Christian Scriptures, Christian doctrine, and theology to justify that subordination. So while it breaks with forms of Christian theology that overlook the particularities of historical social context and social praxis, black theology does not sever its relation to the Christian tradition. Through critical biblical and doctrinal interpretation black theology has recovered the liberating dimension of key Christian notions: God's abiding and profound love of black humanity (the Christian doctrine of the person); God's liberating activity in history on behalf of the poor, oppressed women and men, the "wretched of the earth"; the intimate connection between divine eschatological reality and the historical struggles of suffering women and men against the powers and principalities of domination; the radical social character of Christian worship, work, and witness.

The Origin of the Term

While no precise account of its coinage can be determined, the term "black theology" emerged in the mid to late 1960s in the United States in the ferment churned by the political and cultural movement of black consciousness. The term seems to have surfaced in the preparation of a 1968 report by the Theological Commission of the National Conference of Black Churchmen (NCBC), a predominantly Protestant group then known as the National Committee of Negro Churchmen. It is quite likely that a member of the NCBC, Albert Cleage, Jr., who was teaching a controversial black Christian nationalism, was the first to articulate and introduce the expression "black theology." However, no writer or theologian has claimed to have used the term before the publication of James H. Cone's *Black Theology and Black Power.*

In the expression "black theology," theology does not denote a finished system in which all the major Christian doctrines are interrelated; although black theologians attend to common themes and questions, these men and women do not compose a "school." In fact, since black theology focuses on the dialectical relation of Christian meanings and values to the oppressive situations of black peoples and their struggles to realize personal, communal, and social change in society and history, it is quite appropriate to speak of "black theologies."

Phases of Development

Although the 20th-century formal and self-conscious articulation of black theology is the starting point in this essay, the religious and political resistance of black women and men in the 18th and 19th centuries to white supremacist rule stands as its hermeneutical antecedent. Four phases may be distinguished in the development of BTUSA and three in the development of BTSA; this division extends the interpretations of Gayraud S. Wilmore and Mokgethi Motlhabi.

Development in the United States

The *first phase* of BTUSA runs roughly from about 1960 to 1969 and coincides with the civil rights movement and the rise of the black power movement; it concludes with the publication of James Cone's work. Under the charismatic leadership of Dr. Martin Luther King, Jr., the civil rights movement confronted the ethos and structures of racial segregation with a doctrine of suffering love and nonviolent protest. But Stokley Carmichael's call for "black power" disavowed this strategy and splintered the precarious harmony blacks and whites had achieved under King's leadership. Rather than denounce the rejection of the absolute commitment to peaceful protest, black clergy issued the "Black Power Statement" in the *New York Times,* July 31, 1966. Their affirmation of black power was a benchmark in the development of black theology: inaugurating a radical religious movement among black Christians and preparing the conceptual, psychological, and theological ground for the appearance of *Black Theology and Black Power.* Cone's intent in the first of seven books was to demonstrate that the politics of black power was a bold and precise interpretation of the gospel of Jesus and addressed to the United States of 20th-century America.

BTUSA in its *second phase,* 1970 to 1976, may be described as a "turn to the academy." A small group of seminary and university professors, black and white, explored the meaning and import of black theology in monographs and articles, organized conferences, and seminars. The most provocative black theologians of this phase include Cecil Cone, Vincent Harding, Major Jones, William Jones, C. Eric Lincoln, Charles Long, J. Deotis Roberts, and Gayraud Wilmore. During this period the Society for the Study of Black Religion was established and, under the direction of Shelby Rooks, resumed the dialogue begun in the 1960s by the NCBC with African theologians under the aegis of the All Africa Conference of Churches. From 1969 through 1977 black theologians from the United States and Africa met in six formal conferences.

In its *third phase,* 1977 to 1989, BTUSA was shaped by intensified contact with the theologies of liberation irrupting around the globe, by the work of black philosopher Cornel West, and by the critiques of black women theologians and church leaders.

In August of 1977 the Black Theology Project (BTP) sponsored the first national consultation on black theology. BTP was associated with the organization Theology in the Americas, which was led by exiled Chilean priest Sergio Torres. At his initiative liberation theologians from Africa, Asia, Latin America, and the United States established formal dialogues that led to the formation of the Ecumenical Association of Third World Theologians (EATWOT). The ecumenical BTP consultation, "The Black Church and the Black Community," was held in August 1977 in Atlanta. Participants included not only pastors, priests, Roman Catholic sisters, church executives, and bishops but also the men and women in the pews and representatives of progressive political groups. Moreover, the consultation was less preoccupied with the criticisms and questions coming from the white churches and the academy. In the keynote address to the assembly James Cone called black theology to address itself to the cry for justice from the "two-thirds world." Black theology must assume a global perspective—analyzing the black struggle for justice within the United States in structural relation to the demands of the poor and exploited around the globe. Having come under the influence of black philosopher Cornel West, Cone proposed a reappraisal and nuanced application of a Marxist analysis of U.S. capitalism in framing black theology's political praxis. West confronted not only the political but the intellectual foundations of BTUSA. In *Prophesy Deliverance!* West sketched out the revolutionary potential of an alliance between prophetic Christianity and progressive Marxism, borrowing Antonio Gramsci's notion of hegemony as a framework for the reinterpretation of the dynamic relations among religion, Celtic-, Anglo-, European-American culture, and black culture on the one hand and economic and political power in a radicalized society on the other.

Finally, during this period black women theologians (some of whom had been Cone's students) began to comment on the sexist bias of black theology. Katie Cannon, Jacquelyn Grant, and Delores Williams along with sociologist of religion Cheryl Gilkes began to chart a course that took seriously black women's religious, cultural, and social experiences as data for theological reflection. They named this enterprise "womanist theology" in order to differentiate black women's theology from that of black male theologians and white liberal feminist theologians. Both groups had taken the presence and physical labor of black women (labor that often made it possible for these men and women to theologize) for granted, ignoring black women and their intellectual work, silencing their distinctive perspective.

The *fourth phase,* 1990 to the present, coincides with the egregious cultural and social conditions of the masses of black people in the United States at the close of the 20th century. The future of BTUSA lies in addressing this situation, in meeting the challenges of earlier stages: to articulate an explanatory analysis of the cultural and social matrix that comes to terms with the interaction between racism, sexism, class exploitation, and imperialism; to develop a differentiated understanding of economic and political decline on local, regional, and global scales; to respond to pressing psychological and spiritual needs, which are related so intimately to the suffering and despair engendered by dominative biased social interpersonal relationships and structures; to support the black church in its concrete ministerial practice.

Development in South Africa

In South Africa, the *first phase* of BTSA can be dated from about 1970 to 1977. Motlhabi has described this phase as "polemic and definitional." Although its origin is disputed, black theology seems to have been introduced in South Africa in the early 1970s by the Black Theology Project of the multiracial University Christian Movement (UCM). Nonetheless, this new theological work struck a responsive chord.

At that time, black (and some white) Christians and political activists were straining under the repressive atmosphere that followed the Sharpeville Massacre. On March 21, 1960, police, unprovoked, fired into a crowd of peaceful demonstrators, killing 67 and wounding 187. Widespread public protest was met by a state of emergency decree, massive arrests, and the ban of both the Pan African Congress (PAC) and the African National Congress (ANC). Leaders who eluded arrest were forced either underground or into exile. The absence of coherent internal leadership brought active resistance to a halt and left a gaping void. It is in this charged environment, under the leadership of Steve Biko, that the Black Consciousness Movement (BCM) was born. BCM advocated black solidarity through a notion of group power and called for the eradication and correction of the false and negative images that blacks held of themselves. For Biko, the heart of black consciousness was the realization by the blacks that the most potent weapon in the hands of the oppressor is the mind of the oppressed. Black consciousness advocated a profound renewal of culture, education, religion, and economics in light of the African genius. The stage was set for the reception and substantive, creative appropriation of black theology in South Africa.

Sabelo Ntwasa, then a seminary intern, organized and directed the first seminar on black theology in 1970. The papers read and debated there were compiled and edited by Mokgethi Motlhabi as *Essays on Black Theology,* which was immediately banned in South Africa for "security reasons." The book was subsequently published abroad, the U.S. edition edited by white theologian Basil Moore and entitled *The Challenge of Black Theology in South Africa.* The only academic theologian among the clergy associated with BCM was Manas Buthelezi, now Lutheran bishop of Johannesburg. Buthelezi wrote more than a dozen articles probing the meaning of living Christian faith under apartheid and a stenciled booklet, *The Relevance of Black Theology.*

A second conference was sponsored by the Black Theology Project in 1975 in Lesotho and coordinated by Smangaliso Mkhatshwa. But the attempt to sustain an ongoing consultation floundered under financial and political pressures stemming from the government ban of leaders of black student and political organizations and harassment of the UCM and other groups sympathetic to developing black theology.

Although the project dissolved, individuals continued to publish occasional essays in church periodicals and journals; however, the first full-length scholarly discussion of black theology in South Africa did not appear until 1977, Allan Boesak's *Farewell to Innocence: A Socio-Ethical Study on Black Theology and Black Power.* Not surprisingly, BTSA provoked suspicion and rejection among blacks and whites. Some critics charged that BTSA was simply a conflation of black power and black consciousness and was guilty of fomenting revolution; others accused BTSA of reducing the gospel to a program for social and political liberation; yet others acknowledged that BTSA had exposed the grave and sinful failure of Christianity in its collusion with apartheid.

The *second phase* of black theology in South Africa extends from about 1978 to 1989; it is a fertile period marked by growth and consolidation. Black theologians including Frank Chikane, Sigibo Dwane, Bonganjalo Goba, Simon Maimela, Itumeleng Mosala, and Takatso Mofokeng generated a sizable and rigorous corpus of literature. The following are among the most striking themes in their work: the interrogation of the role of traditional religious and cultural practices (African theology); the interjection of Marxist analysis; the critical reinterpretation of township violence in the light of the structural violence of apartheid; attentiveness to the black poor and workers; and the call for ongoing self-criticism. During this period BTSA also benefited from increased dialogue with black theologians from the United States as well as liberation theologians from other countries under the auspices of EATWOT.

Collective theological dialogue and critique among black theologians has taken the form of the Institute for Contextual Theology (ITC), and Chikane served as the first general secretary. Under the auspices of the ITC, in 1985 Christians—black and white, lay and ordained—gathered to respond to the state of emergency. The *Kairos Document* was their theological commentary on the condition of the church and theology in South Africa. This document defined two types of church-state relations and the resulting theologies and promoted an altogether new theological consideration. The relation between the Dutch Reformed church and the Afrikaner government spawned a perverted "state theology," which used Sacred Scripture to justify white supremacist oppression of black people. The equivocating liberal rhetoric of the white English--speaking churches bred a "church theology," which admitted only superficial reconciliation, ignoring the difficult work of justice and urging nonviolence on victims of apartheid's institutionalized violence. The theological shift advanced by the *Kairos Document* was called "prophetic theology." This theology was to be a biblically rooted, action-oriented theology of oppressed people; a prophetic theology would contest both external (white) and internal (black) oppressions and employ critical social analysis to comprehend the totality of racial-political-economic capitalism.

Like its North American counterpart, BTSA has practiced sexism. The tool of black people's liberation has not been applied to the situation of black women. In 1984 the Institute for Contextual Theology sponsored a conference on feminist theology that dealt with a range of issues including the male image of God projected by theologians and the church in its practice, cultural and social practices that exploit women, educational discrimination against women, and oppression of women by women. Black women theologians Bernadette Mosala and Bonita Bennett have argued that the condition of black women in South Africa is structured by a fourfold oppression. Women are discriminated against and oppressed as black people (race), as workers (class), as women (gender), and by one another as women both as individuals and a group. Mosala insists than an authentic black theology has the "moral imperative" to eradicate the oppression of women in church and society.

In 1990 South Africa itself embarked on a new phase. The government's release of Nelson Mandela from prison, the lifting of the ban against the ANC, its leaders and members, as well as other activists has generated a thoroughly and radically distinctive political opportunity. Given the seriousness with which it regards the political situation, BTSA has been catapulted into a *third and current phase.* While many petty strictures of apartheid have been eliminated, blacks remain educationally, economically, and politically marginalized and disenfranchised. The future of black theology in South Africa lies in its ability to incarnate a prophetic political theology of liberation: a biblically rooted, action-oriented theology of oppressed people—healing the deep wounds against black humanity and nourishing black culture; employing social analysis to fight the oppressions of race, gender, and class; and promoting a vision of a just society that yields only to the reign of God.

See also JUSTICE IN THE WORLD; POLITICAL THEOLOGY; PRAXIS; SEXISM; SOCIETY.

Bibliography: *Black theology in the United States:* K. Cannon, *Womanist Ethics* (Atlanta: Scholars, 1988). A. Cleage, *The Black Messiah* (New York: Sheed & Ward, 1969). J. Cone, *Black Theology and Black Power* (New York: Seabury, 1969). J. Cone, *God of the Oppressed* (New York: Seabury, 1975). J. Cone, *Martin and Malcolm: The Dream or the Nightmare* (Maryknoll, N.Y.: Orbis, 1990). J. Evans, *Black Theology: A Critical Assessment and Annotated Bibliography* (Westport, Conn.: Greenwood, 1987). J. Grant, *White Women's Christ and Black Women's Jesus: Feminist Christology and Womanist Response* (Atlanta: Scholars, 1989). D. Hopkins, *Black Theology USA and South Africa: Politics, Culture, and Liberation* (Maryknoll, N.Y.: Orbis, 1989). D. Hopkins and G. Cummings, *Cut Loose Your Stammering Tongue: Black Theology in the Slave Narratives* (Maryknoll, N.Y.: Orbis, 1991). W. Jones, *Is God a White Racist? A Preamble to Black Theology* (New York: Anchor/Doubleday, 1973). P. Paris, *The Social Teachings of the Black Churches* (Philadelphia: Fortress, 1985). J. Roberts, *Black Theology in Dialogue* (Philadelphia: Westminster, 1987). G. Wilmore, *Black Religion and Black Radicalism: An Interpretation of the Religious History of the Afro-American People,* 2nd ed. (Maryknoll, N.Y.: Orbis, 1983). G. Wilmore, *African American Religious Studies* (Durham, N.C.: Duke Univ. Press, 1989). G. Wilmore and J. Cone, *Black Theology: A Documentary History, 1966–1979* (Maryknoll, N.Y.: Orbis, 1979). J.

Young, *Black and African Theologies: Siblings or Distant Cousins?* (Maryknoll, N.Y.: Orbis, 1986).

Black theology in South Africa: A. Boesak, *Farewell to Innocence* (Maryknoll, N.Y.: Orbis, 1977). A. Boesak, *Black and Reformed* (Maryknoll, N.Y.: Orbis, 1984). B. Goba, *An Agenda for Black Theology in South Africa: Hermeneutics for Social Change* (Johannesburg: Skotaville, 1988). Kairos Theologians, *The Kairos Document: A Theological Comment on the Political Crisis in South Africa,* 2nd. rev. ed., *Challenge to the Church* (Johannesburg: Skotaville, 1986). S. Maimela, *God's Creativity Through the Law* (Pretoria: UNISA, 1984). T. Mofokeng, *The Crucified Among the Crossbearers: Towards a Black Christology* (Uitgeversmaatschappij: J. J. Kok, 1983). I. Mosala, *Biblical Hermeneutics and Black Theology in South Africa* (Grand Rapids: Eerdmans, 1989). I. Mosala and B. Tlhagale, *The Unquestionable Right to Be Free* (Maryknoll, N.Y.: Orbis, 1986).

M. SHAWN COPELAND

BRITISH DISTRIBUTISTS

The British distributists, narrowly defined, represented the readers and followers of an English social Catholic journal, *The Distributist,* which was published from 1934 to 1937 as the organ of The League for the Restoration of Liberty and the Distribution of Property, with chapters in Birmingham, Bradford, Bristol, Cardiff, Clydesdale, Glasgow, London, Manchester, Norwich, and York. Besides the journal, the Distributist League (as it came to be known) published, from 1928 on, a series of pamphlets on such issues as trade unions, small crafts, and the press monopoly, including the very nuanced, sophisticated, and influential *Distributist Program* (1934). At the height of the movement the league numbered around twelve thousand members. Its program encouraged cooperatives, land settlement schemes, credit unions, and syndicalism and laid great stress on the particular, the local, the small. Equally as anticapitalist as it was antisocialist (indeed, stressing that socialism, though mistaken, made more sense than capitalism), the distributists sought a wide and equitable distribution of ownership of property and, following John Ruskin, saw wealth as "that which serves human life."

Writing in *The Distributist* in September 1934, V. N. Lukas summed up the program: "If Distributism stands for anything, it stands for decentralization of control and for the majority as independent owners of the means of production. . . . Thus, distributism looks to a guild of masters while the trade unions [look] to a guild of employees." The distributist watchword came from *Rerum novarum*'s famous passage: "Private ownership must be held sacred and inviolable. The law, therefore, should favor ownership and its policy should be to induce as many as possible of the humble class to become owners." Again, following *Quadragesimo anno,* the distributists decried monopoly practices in capitalism and approved of the nationalization of essential industries if necessary for the common good.

The origin and impact of distributism are broader and more important than the meager numbers would suggest. The term was coined by Hilaire Belloc in his famous book *The Servile State* (1913), and the themes set in that work were taken up from that time until the 1930s by G. K. Chesterton, Eric Gill, Vincent McNabb, O.P., and Hilary Peppler in many books and in the pages of Chesterton's journals, *The Eye-Witness, The New Witness,* and *G. K's Weekly.*

Populist and often muckraking in style, Belloc and Chesterton saw both socialism and capitalism as examples of the servile state: without widespread property there could be no political liberty. In their view "industrial capitalism was a half-pagan thing." Belloc in a series of books postulated social Catholicism as the only viable alternative to communism. He argued that "socialism and capitalism are twin successive products of the same false philosophy." Both negate economic freedom and property (the one by placing all property in the hands of monopoly capitalism, the other by placing it in the hands of a bureaucracy that ran the state), and their own quarrel was over which of the two might produce goods more efficiently. Belloc saw that "property, as widely distributed as possible, but sacred as a principle, is an inevitable social accompaniment of Catholicism." For his part Chesterton in his usual epigrammatic way claimed, "It is the negation of property that the Duke of Sutherland should have all the farms in one estate; just as it would be the negation of marriage if he had all our wives in one harem." For Chesterton "the shortest way of defining what we are always denouncing as abnormal in this country and century is to say that only the capitalists have any capital." He liked to deride the capitalists by taunting that they did not really believe in private property but in monopoly.

Despite G. B. Shaw's famous conflation of the two figures into one Chesterbelloc, there are important differences between Chesterton's consistent Populism and localism (illustrated in his novel *The Napoleon of Notting Hill*) and his sympathetic evocation of the indigenous English craft resistance to industrial capitalism (in his book *William Cobbett*) and Belloc's greater nostalgia for a genuine aristocracy and his anti-Semitic crudeness in equating monopoly capitalism with Jewish bankers (in his 1904 novel, *Emmanual Burden, Merchant,* and his somewhat scurrilous 1927 book, *The Jews*).

Like Chesterton, the sculptor and printer Eric Gill linked distributism not only to papal encyclicals but to an indigenous British anticapitalism found in Ruskin, William Morris, and William Cobbett. Gill founded communes at Ditchling and later at Capel-y-fin in Wales, which became pilgrimage sites for those seeking models of simplicity of life, craft skills, and farming. Gill, a marked influence on Dorothy Day and the Catholic Worker movement in the United States and himself a contributor to *The Catholic Worker,* wrote prolifically about work and property, work and leisure, money and morals, and pacifism. He saw his communes as an effort "to make a cell of good living in the chaos of our world." Anticipating many of the themes of work found in John Paul II's *Laborem exercens* as central to the understanding of human being in this world, Gill claimed that "the Industrial Revolution degraded both the thing made and, especially, the makers of things." Industrialism in his view divorced the idea of work from the idea of art. Workers should see themselves as artisans, makers of good objects. Gill, who had read Emmanuel Mounier, wrote to *The Catholic Worker* in 1937: "The first thing to be done (first in the sense of most important) is for the workers to recapture the control of industry." He championed worker co-ownership and co-management of industry.

The fourth major writer in this group, Vincent McNabb, O.P., was also something of a saint. He went about London and frequented Hyde Park's speakers' corner in a worn habit woven at Gill's commune in Ditchling and handmade boots. He espoused "the principles of true communism" in social Catholicism. McNabb, for twenty-five years a preacher for the Catholic Evidence Guild and a former prison chaplain and organizer of a Belgian relief fund during World War I, preached land reform, cooperatives, and forms of pacifism, and he attacked the church's concordats with Franco and Mussolini. If Belloc represented a more right-wing and *resentiment*-fueled wing of the distributists and Chesterton the radical democratic option of Populism, Gill and especially McNabb were closer to a radical Catholicism akin to the evangelical radicalism of *The Catholic Worker.* The distributists' writings had great impact not only in the United Kingdom and Ireland (McNabb was Irish-born) but in Canada, where they influenced the Antogonish movement, and Australia, where they fostered social Catholicism.

In the United States, Belloc and Chesterton enjoyed enormous followings among Catholics (Chesterton taught at the University of Notre Dame in the 1930s), and the voluminous writings of Gill and McNabb were devoured not only by *The Catholic Worker* but in non-Catholic circles as well. The Southern agrarians, ranged around John Crowe Ransom and *The American Review,* claimed inspiration from the distributists, and Msgr. Luigi Ligutti also claimed to have received inspiration for the National Catholic Rural Conference from the distributist program.

For the history of Social Catholicism, however, the importance of distributist thought and movement lies in its wedding of Social Catholicism's radical economic thought with Anglo-Saxon notions of civil and political liberties. Both Belloc and Chesterton (subject to libel suits in the 1920s for exposing government corruption during the Marconi scandal) wrote eloquently of the necessity of a free press and free speech. In his 1918 book, *The Free Press,* Belloc linked the rise of a free press sympathetically with the religious dissenters. Importantly, also, the distributists linked their encyclical-inspired social Catholicism with native reformist groups in England, with Cobbett, Morris, and Ruskin. It did not seem a foreign graft on the English shoot.

By linking a leftist, indeed, radical reform vision to the family, Vincent McNabb could debate leading socialists in England and fault the Left for neglecting the family; while Gill, in addressing the link between art and social justice, similarly excoriated the Left (with whom he remained sympathetic) for not showing how art and social justice went together. He gave an interview to *The Daily Worker* and in 1934 exhibited some of his sculptures with Artists' International. Some distributists degenerated into antimachine nostalgics who sought "three acres and a cow" as the solution to the industrial problem. But the *Distributist Program* of 1934 (in which Belloc and Chesterton had a hand) remains a nuanced exposition of the best of Social Catholicism.

See also AGRICULTURE; ANTI-SEMITISM; CATHOLIC WORKER, THE; COMPETITION; COPARTNERSHIP; GOODS, DISTRIBUTION OF; PRIVATE PROPERTY; WORK, THEOLOGY OF.

Bibliography: H. Belloc, *The Servile State* (London: Constable, 1927). H. Belloc, *An Essay on the Restoration of Property* (London: The Distributist League, 1936). G. K. Chesterton, *The Outline of Sanity* (London: Methuen, 1926). G. K. Chesterton, *William Cobbett* (London: Hodder & Stoughton, 1925). E. Gill, *Work and Property* (London: J. M. Dent, 1937). V. McNabb, *Nazareth or Social Chaos* (London: Burns, Oates & Washbourne, 1933).

JOHN A. COLEMAN, S.J.

BUSINESS ETHICS

Many of the issues such as the just price and the just wage, false advertising, disclosure of substantial defects, usury, property rights, discussed in what is now called "business ethics," were treated by the great moral theologians of the 16th and 17th centuries—De Lugo, Lessius, Molina, and others—and were passed on in the manuals of moral theology that persisted in the seminary training of confessors until the Second Vatican Council. The great social encyclicals, *Rerum novarum, Quadragesimo anno, Mater et magistra,* and *Populorum progressio,* responding to the rapid growth of capitalism and the modern industrial world, championed new and important issues of social justice, for example, the rights of labor, the just distribution of wealth, and the use of economic power and sparked Catholic interest in issues that were to develop into the discipline now called business ethics. However, the term "business ethics" itself as well as the discipline is relatively new. It has been the focus of burgeoning interest and significant growth in the last thirty or forty years. This development of the ethics-in-business movement is perceived as a necessary response to the modern event of the evolution of democratic capitalism.

The traditional locus for dealing with issues of business ethics in Catholic moral theology was the treatises of special ethics concerned with the exercise of the virtues, particularly prudence, justice, and charity, in the "states of life." The scope of ethics or morality was the conformity of human conduct to the divine law so that this conduct might be ordered to the total good of humankind. Thus from the general principles of ethics, one more-or-less readily deduces rules applicable to the organization, management, and all the complex relationships of business.

From this point of view "business ethics" is defined as "a study of how these moral standards apply to the conduct of individuals involved in these organizations through which modern societies produce and distribute goods and services . . . in other words, a form of applied ethics . . . [that] includes not only the analysis of principles and norms, but also attempts to apply the conclusions of this analysis to particular kinds of behavior: the behavior of people in business institutions" (Velasquez, p. 17) and as emphasizing the "development of guiding principles that can be used to form consciences able to cope with situations arising in the business world . . . [and] developing and maintaining sufficient motivation to acquire the habits of acting in conformity with our principles" (Wirtenberger, p. 12).

These definitions tend to focus on the individual's moral agency and derive from the confessional tradition of guiding the individual conscience according to a natural-law morality that finds religious or theological reference in its ultimate rather than proximate intentionality. Ultimate intentionality would include the social common good and the transcendental response to the vocation of God, which eludes proximate intentionality.

A different strain in Catholic thinking offers a Scripture-based approach that considers the task of business ethics as not merely to solve problems within an established system but also to challenge institutions and lifestyles in light of the biblical way of life. This approach seeks to identify essentially Christian values, "power as service," for example, and then proceeds to develop rules and principles to protect and promote these values in business life, thus creating ways to help persons develop their humanity in the business world (Williams and Houck, p. 44). Akin to this is the notion of doing business as one's vocation and evolving life-roles into personal moral character. Along similar lines, many are suggesting the possibility of constructing a foundation for business ethics in terms of the central concepts that ground ethical expectations in the noble professions of law and medicine.

Problem Areas

Business ethics usually focuses on fairly well-defined problem areas: the employee, marketing, pricing and competition, the environment, the power of the corporation. Once one gets beyond the preliminary questions of the proper virtues and principles to apply to cases, discussions of the moral meaning of commerce, and the discovery of an ethic responsive to the central activity of business, the issues that present perennial practical problems are fairly constant in the literature. An important preliminary is the conflict of market theories, which impinge on ethics because of their influence on the attitudes and intentionality of business with regard to labor, consumers, society, and government. The classical or laissez faire ideology emphasizes the free market and unrestrained competition, while the managerial ideology favors social cooperation with government and labor unions as well as concern for the employee in the workplace.

The Employee

The duties of the employer to the employee revolve around several major ethical issues. The problems of discrimination in hiring, promotion, and firing and inequity in wage payments are primary. Under this rubric are subsumed equal-opportunity obligations, affirmative action, reverse discrimination, due process. Safety in the workplace, important with regard to the health and well-being of employees, has been complicated lately by the question of discrimination against women of childbearing age whose fetuses might be damaged by exposure to lead and other toxic and/or oncogenic processing materials.

Job satisfaction and the right to meaningful work are perceived as necessary for the human dignity of employees. The same may be said of freedom from invasion of privacy in personal and family matters, in polygraph testing and in the use of electronic surveillance and data-collection devices, in access to and use of personal information, and in extra-workplace associations. Whistle-blowing, understood as calling the attention of outside agencies to dangerous or defective products, dishonest, illegal, or fraudulent practices, or other injustices that constitute serious harm to society, generally is protected as a means of safeguarding the employee's freedom of conscience from undue pressures. The right of employees to organize for purposes of collective bargaining has long been recognized. The movement toward organizational democracy, the participation of workers in major policy decisions, however, has not made much headway in the United States. The impact, beneficent or otherwise, of labor-management teams on both sides is hotly disputed.

The obligations of the employee vis-à-vis the company is another source of ethical importance. The basic duty of the employee to promote the best interests of the firm is threatened essentially by actual or potential conflicts of personal with company interests; by illicit appropriation of the company's assets, whether on a large scale or relatively petty expense-account padding; by extortion and bribery in the conduct of commerce; by the unfair use of insider information; by commercial espionage; and by accepting gifts that may bias judgment.

Marketing

The moral obligations of manufacturers and vendors cluster for the most part around product safety and reliability and advertising. There is particular concern with liability for dangerous and defective products, warranties, recalls, just pricing, misrepresentation, coercion, and, lately, the irresponsible offering of products to foreign markets (infant formula, tobacco). The multiple problems located here are addressed by three different theories of manufacturer-consumer relations: (1) the specific performance of contractual duties, "caveat emptor" (let the buyer beware); (2) the duty of reasonable care in production, a weak version of "caveat vendor" (let the seller beware); (3) strict liability, or the social-costs theory, which has the manufacturer assume responsibility even for unforeseen risks, a strong version of "caveat vendor" (Velasquez, p. 224). The proper and truthful communication of information to consumers is the basic focus of advertising ethics. This issue, often complicated by the distance between the advertiser's intentions and the consumer's response, is too often reduced simplistically to the obligation not to deceive. More serious problems seem to be found in the areas of undue persuasion, harmful manipulation, and the creation of irrational or even dangerous needs.

Pricing and Competition

The question of the just price has always been central in assessing the ethics of seller-buyer relations. In the perfectly free market supply and demand would balance in a price range that would generate a model of fairness covering production costs and guaranteeing a reasonable return on investment. The ideally free competitive market is rarely approximated in the real world, which normally abounds in the less competitive markets known as "oligopolies" with a small number of firms that can limit supply in a variety of ways and thus affect pricing. Price-fixing is the best known of the collusive attacks on the basic justice of the free market. Very similar is price leadership, or the administered price, whereby prices are set by one firm to which the others tacitly conform. Price discrimination is the selling of identical goods at different prices to different customers, often with the intention of harming competitors. Other unethical practices include price maintenance by the retailer, exclusive dealing arrangements, and tying the availability of one item to the purchase of other items.

Environmental Issues

The last part of the 20th century has witnessed significant growth in concern for the present and future well-being of human and nonhuman elements of the ecology. At issue is the industrial pollution of water and air by acid rain, nuclear waste, and other toxic materials as well as the depletion of natural resources, the loss of species—mammals, birds, plant life, and forests—as industry and technology multiply geometrically. An ecological ethic has developed that insists that business must respect the rights of the various ecosystems in the world. It is argued that property rights are subordinate to the right of all to a livable environment. An equitable balancing of these rights is very difficult given the practical impossibility of measuring the social costs of pollution over against private and societal benefits.

Incidental to this discussion are the issues of the rights of animals and the value of nonhuman life in general. Humanity's stewardship of creation is now perceived as restricted to development rather than as the exploitation of the nonhuman universe. An extremely thorny ethical issue is that of the rights of future generations, not yet existing, to limited, nonrenewable resources that are rapidly being depleted. A rather vague general principle seems to have wide acceptance, namely, the obligation of conserving resources in such a way that our immediate descendants receive from us a planet not substantially worse than what previous generations left to us.

Corporations

Modern business is dominated by large corporations, and the most serious issues of business ethics center around them. How best society can provide for the public interests over against the immense power possessed by the monopolies or oligopolies in our society is a question hotly debated. Various groups propose various solutions for various problems: government regulation, strict antitrust policies, public ownership, the natural balance of countervailing forces in society such as labor, the buying public, competition between large corporations.

The effectiveness of government regulation seems to be undisputed when it deals legally with consumer safety, product liability, workplace safety, price-fixing, some serious environmental problems, and blatantly corrupt foreign practices. But it is clear that the law provides only minimal standards inadequate for the social control of business. The notion of the social responsibility of the corporation becomes crucial at this juncture: what is it precisely, what is its locus, and how far does it extend? Conjoint with this is the vociferously debated question of corporate responsibility: can the corporation be held morally responsible as a moral agent, or is the morality of the corporation's acts deduced from the moral analysis of the decisions of individual agents? Ownership hardly furnishes a locus of responsibility, since it tends to be atomized among thousands of anonymous shareholders who have invested in a variety of unrelated portfolios. Boards of directors and professional managers are the primary persons within the corporation who effectively make the free decisions that entail moral responsibility. The contemporary trend is to focus on managerial ethics. But given the complexity of the organization and its bureaucratic structures, the task of discerning accountability is often practically impossible. Thus institutional structure itself becomes an ethical issue insofar as collective activity ought to be responsible, even if only by somehow incorporating the purposes of individuals.

Recent studies suggest that ethical behavior in business depends as much upon the "ethical climate" in which the corporation operates as upon individual virtue. "The values of corporations are not simply the sum of the values of individuals in the corporation. . . . Social structures come to embody a distinctive character with dominant images and a hierarchy of values. . . . Each . . . has its own characteristic flavor which shapes and forms all who join" (Williams and Houck, p. 44). This ethical climate is created by the corporate leaders who are sensitive to their social obligations, the first of which is the duty of enhancing the welfare of both employees and consumers by means of efficient production. This responsibility of purpose is filled out in the context of responsibility to various constituencies (shareholders, owners, employees, society), honesty in communication, reliability (fidelity, competence), fairness, integrity, respect for the individual and the property of others, especially the public's (Woodstock). Social responsibility embraces ethical analysis in such matters as plant closings for the advantage of stockholders in the face of economic devastation for a given community and labor force, and the recent hostile takeover frenzy in which the interests of shareholders are maximized in the process of short-term capital relocation that may be seriously detrimental to employees and communities and the future of business.

The immense economic and even political power of the great corporations unrestricted by national borders poses a very serious challenge to an effective ethic of social responsibility. In the years since the end of World War II the movement of corporations to do business in several different countries has caused several new problems to surface in business ethics with respect to the employee, the consumer, and the common good. The basic question is which ethical tradition, that of the home or of the foreign country, should prevail when conflict arises in such matters as the conditions of employment, hiring and firing, promotion, salary norms, workplace safety, and the exploitation of workers. Likewise at issue is the determination of which culture's standards should be dominant in matters of product safety, acceptable risks to users, advertising and marketing, obligations to warn of potential dangers, and the duty not to market items not acceptable in the home country. Here arises also the ethical question of investing in corporations that do business in societies that repress basic human rights. Again, the variations in governmental regulations and traditions between countries can make it difficult to determine, beyond the bare minimum set by the Federal Corrupt Practices Act, whether certain gratuities or practices constitute a normal way of doing business or ought to be perceived as unacceptable forms of bribery and extortion that violate justice and risk harm to the public interest.

Conclusion

Despite the proliferation of courses and programs and treatises, as yet there does not seem to have developed an unequivocal general understanding of what the discipline of business ethics essentially is or should be. According to Goodpaster (p. 2) there are three levels on which ethical analysis can be applied to business: (1) personal behavior and character, (2) organizational policy and culture, and (3) the systemic values that define capitalism itself. Many approaches to business ethics are limited to the first level, the proper behavior of individuals by educating individual consciences, and to the second, with codes of ethics and lists of virtues. Such are obviously inadequate. But even the approach that includes the third level in terms of finance, production, and international business conduct will fail to the extent that it neglects to assess how the core activity of business affects human flourishing—in individuality, creativity, and freedom—as this is perceived in the Christian understanding of the nature of human existence in both personal and social dimensions, which in origin, meaning, and destiny transcends the loftiest purposes of the business world.

See also ADVERTISING; CONGLOMERATES; EMPLOYMENT AND UNEMPLOYMENT; GREED; NATURAL RESOURCES; PROFIT; STRIKE, RIGHT TO; TRANSNATIONAL CORPORATIONS.

Bibliography: T. Beauchamp and N. Bowie, eds., *Ethical Theory and Business* (Englewood Cliffs, N.J.: Prentice Hall, 1979). T. Garrett, *Business Ethics* (New York: Appleton-Century-Crofts, 1966). K. Goodpaster, *Ethics in Management* (Cambridge: Harvard Business School, 1984). D. Jones, ed., *Business, Religion, and Ethics: Inquiry and Encounter* (Cambridge, Mass.: Oelgeschlager, Gunn & Hann, 1982). W. Manley, *Critical Issues in Business: Legal, Ethical, and Social Issues for the 1990's* (Westport, Conn.: Quorum, 1990). C. McCoy, *Management of Values* (Boston: Pitman, 1985). A. Muller, *La Morale et La Vie des Affaires* (Tournai-Paris: Casterman, 1951). M. Velasquez, *Business Ethics* (Englewood Cliffs, N.J.: Prentice-Hall, 1982). O. Williams and J. Houck, *Full Value: Cases in Christian Business Ethics* (New York: Harper & Row, 1978). H. Wirtenberger, *Morality and Business* (Chicago: Loyola Univ. Press, 1962). Woodstock Theological Center, *Creating and Maintaining an Ethical Corporate Climate* (Washington: Georgetown Univ. Press, 1990).

VINCENT M. BURNS, S.J.

C

CALL TO ACTION CONFERENCE

The Call to Action conference that assembled for three days in Detroit's Cobo Hall in October 1976 was meant to be the centerpiece of the church's celebration of the bicentennial of the American Revolution. Three years earlier preparations began with the expectation that Call to Action would advise the National Conference of Catholic Bishops (NCCB) on how to implement the 1971 synod of bishops' statement, *Justice in the World* (*Justitia in mundo*). Planners hoped that it would provide counterpoint to any "uncritical consecration of the American system," the all-too-predictable outcome of the ensemble of secular bicentennial events. But if Call to Action was intended as an American Catholic model of critical patriotism, its enduring legacy seems to be in the area of practical ecclesiology.

John Cardinal Dearden of Detroit opened the conference by saluting the delegates for "beginning a new way of doing the work of the church in America." These were not empty words, for the conference was merely the culmination of an unprecedented consultative process involving over 800,000 people representing over a hundred dioceses. The organization of the hearings, workshops, and delegate training-sessions preparatory to the conference may have raised expectations too high that the church was about to practice what it preaches about social justice and participation. At any rate, once assembled at Cobo Hall the delegates apparently considered themselves empowered to promote a radical breakthrough in Catholic social teaching. After rather intense but slapdash discussion in various committees and subcommittees, the delegates debated and voted in plenary session to accept some 30 resolutions containing over 180 recommendations. The vast majority of these accomplished what the USCC planners had envisioned, namely, an outline for implementing the church's social teachings more effectively. But some pivotal resolutions tried to break new ground, particularly with reference to birth control, homosexuality, clerical celibacy, women's ordination, and the nature of the church's own internal accountability structures.

So Call to Action provoked an unusually high degree of postconference controversy. The issues raised, of course, are predictable: to what extent is the NCCB bound by the findings of the consultative processes that it has commissioned; how representative are such processes; and how representative should they be. On a more theoretical plane, however, these questions helped define the contours of the problem of social power and ideological conflict within a church tentatively exploring its new commitment to open dialogue and shared responsibility. Neither the admirers nor the critics of Call to Action were about to deny that the delegates and their concerns accurately reflected the increasingly liberal views of "middle management," particularly, lay leadership within the church. But should this organized and articulate minority—whose indispensable role in actually doing "the work of the church" cannot be denied—be allowed to create the impression that it speaks for the whole of the laity, if not for the NCCB itself? Observers not in sympathy with the delegates' aspirations noted that the Call to Action conference, mesmerized by the ideals of participatory democracy, had fallen into the worst excesses of interest-group politics.

The history of American Catholicism is littered with abortive attempts to recognize formally the role of lay leadership in a local church that, contrary to its inherited European traditions, must operate as a private, voluntary organization. The ultimate verdict on Call to Action will have to be read as part of a recitation that includes battles over lay trusteeship at the dawn of the 19th century and the lay congresses that marked its close. This same story in the 20th century includes the formation of the National Catholic Welfare Council, the United States Catholic Conference, and the countless lay apostolates they have helped to organize. Given the distinctive set of opportunities and constraints represented by American culture in the late 20th century, Call to Action seems to have established two benchmarks within that story: (1) lay Catholics must be consulted not just in the implementation of Catholic social teaching but even as it is formulated in the first place; and (2) the church's prophetic witness to the demands of social justice in the world will tend to be ignored, especially by American Catholic laity, so long as these are not matched by equally prophetic attempts to achieve justice within the church itself.

See also AMERICANISM; EPISCOPAL CONFERENCES, CONCEPT OF; NATIONAL CONFERENCE OF CATHOLIC BISHOPS, UNITED STATES; "SIGNS OF THE TIMES"; WOMEN.

Bibliography: "Marking the 10th Anniversary: A Call to Action: An Unfinished Experiment," a symposium with contributions by D. O'Brien, J. Cardinal Dearden, F. Butler, D. Curran, J. Finn, D. McCann, K. Briggs, and J. Ellis, *Commonweal,* vol. 113, no. 22 (December 26, 1986) 697–712. J. Dolan, *The American Catholic Experience: A History from Colonial Times to the Present* (Garden City, N.Y.: Doubleday, 1985). D. McCann, *New Experiment in Democracy: The Challenge for American Catholicism* (Kansas City, Mo.: Sheed & Ward, 1987). D. O'Brien, *Public Catholicism,* The Bicentennial History of the Catholic Church in America Authorized by the National Conference of Catholic Bishops (New York: Macmillan, 1989). J. Varacalli, *Toward the Establishment of Liberal Catholicism in America* (Lanham, Md.: Univ. Press of America, 1983).

DENNIS P. McCANN

CAMPAIGN FOR HUMAN DEVELOPMENT

In November of 1969 the National Conference of Catholic Bishops of the United States (NCCB) passed a resolution establishing the National Catholic Crusade Against Poverty. The bishops envisioned that the goal of the Campaign for Human Development (CHD), as it came to be called, would be "self-sufficiency and the development of people caught within the cycle of poverty and dependence." This effort would quickly become one of the clearest practical expressions of the church's social teaching regarding participation and social change. Noting that "there is an evident need for funds designated to be used for organized groups of white and minority poor to develop economic strength and political power within their own communities," the 1969 resolution also called for an educational effort to promote "a greater spirit of solidarity among those who have acquired some share of the nation's goods, and those still trapped in poverty" (NCCB, 1969).

The two programmatic areas within CHD, allocations and education, reflect the goals of its founding resolution. The allocations program provides grants to projects that "empower organized groups of poor and low-income people to influence decisions that affect their lives" (CHD, 1988). Annually around $7 million are distributed in grants to projects throughout the United States that aim to change institutions—public policies, social attitudes, and economic structures—that perpetuate poverty. Since it was launched CHD has become the largest funder of its type in the nation.

On the educational side, CHD through its TARGET program provides on-site consultations for diocesan directors and their staffs to assist them in their efforts to educate Catholic parishioners about the conditions and causes of poverty. In addition, educational materials dealing with justice issues are provided for parishes and schools, diocesan conferences, regional meetings, and national convenings. A major resource is the experiences of people working in the funded projects to change unjust structures. These become the real-life case studies for educating the nonpoor about injustice and social change.

The Campaign for Human Development is directed by the national CHD Committee, a standing committee of the United States Catholic Conference chaired by a bishop elected by his peers. A national staff manages the day-to-day operation of CHD's programs and activities, which include allocations, education, and promotion. Diocesan directors manage all CHD activities on the diocesan level; the national Advisory Committee recommends to the national CHD Committee the projects most qualified for funding; and the TARGET Advisory Committee advises national staff on programs and direction of CHD's education efforts.

Pope John Paul II's 1987 encyclical, *Sollicitudo rei socialis,* stated, "By virtue of her own evangelical duty the church feels called to take her stand beside the poor" (SRS 39). The Campaign for Human Development is a concrete expression of the church exercising this preferential option for the poor. In addition, the U.S. Catholic bishops recognized CHD's realization of the principle of participation and its effectiveness: "Our experience with CHD confirms our judgment about the validity of self-help and empowerment of the poor" (*Economic Justice for All* 357). This relationship between CHD and the broader field of Catholic social thought finds articulation in the words of Bishop Joseph Fiorenza, chair of the national CHD Committee: "What the Campaign is, at its heart, is a Campaign for Human Development of poor and marginalized people: human development, self-respect, human dignity, personal integrity. The Campaign makes real the church's call for a preferential option for the poor" (Fiorenza, 1988).

See also CHURCH, SOCIAL MISSION OF; COMMUNITY ORGANIZATION; DEVELOPMENT; POOR, PREFERENTIAL OPTION FOR; POVERTY.

Bibliography: NCCB, "Preamble to the Resolution on the National Catholic Crusade against Poverty" (later to be called the Campaign for Human Development). Minutes of the General Meeting of the National Conference of Catholic Bishops (Washington, November 1969). NCCB, "Resolution on the Campaign for Human Development," adopted by the National Conference of Catholic Bishops (Washington, November 1970). Campaign for Human Development, *Annual Report* (Washington: USCC, 1988).

BERNARD EVANS

CANON LAW, FUNCTION OF

The focus of this article is the function of canon law in the Roman Catholic church; all our statements and conclusions, therefore, refer primarily to that institution. Yet other Christian churches or communities, such as the Orthodox, Anglican, Lutheran, and Presbyterian, operate also with a system of laws. Much of what follows, therefore, should apply to their situation as well.

The classical and generic definition of "law" in the Aristotelian-Thomistic tradition is "ordination of reason [order or command based on reason] issued by the one who is in charge of the community, for the sake of the common good, duly promulgated." In the case of canon law, however, some elements in this definition take on a special meaning not found in any secular law. Canon law is more than an order based on reason: it is rooted in faith, hope, and charity, since it is intended for a community brought together and held in unity by the Spirit. Further, the overall purpose of canon law reaches beyond any visible common good: it is in the service of divine redemption.

The insertion, however, of a legal system into the mystery of revelation and salvation does not take away its human character. Although in its texts it may include norms taken from the Scriptures, canon law strictly speaking (called also "ecclesiastical law") is of human creation, and under many aspects it reflects our human condition. It can display various degrees of learning, wisdom, and balance. Its role, therefore, must be a subordinate one in the church of God. The Holy Spirit gathers the faithful, the Word of God gives them a common mind, and the sacraments provide the opportunity for their frequent encounters with God. The function of the law in such extraordinary community is to provide norms for necessary structures and orderly activities.

Most of the "statutes" (a medieval expression) of the church are contained in the Code of Canon Law, second of its kind in history. It was promulgated by John Paul II in 1983 after extensive consultation with the worldwide episcopate, academic institutions, and professional societies. (The first was promulgated in 1917 by Benedict XVI.)

The new code divides the operations of the law according to the threefold mission that the church has received from Christ: to govern, to teach, and to sanctify God's people. (This approach is inspired by the symbolic description, favored by Vatican Council II, of the ministry of Christ: he was king, prophet, and priest.)

The function of canon law in matters concerning government is to give practical effect to the belief that the church is a "hierarchical communion" (*Lumen gentium* 21, 22). The principal accent is on communion: the mutual rights and duties of the faithful (which includes everyone from the bishops down to the last member of the laity) must be constitutionally defined and protected. This communion, however, has a hierarchical structure: some are called to serve the others by presiding over their assemblies; they are the bishops. It is for the law to give precise scope to their sacramentally given authority. In this whole process faith gives a basic direction, but human ingenuity contributes the rules that make a broad vision into everyday reality; a postulate of divine origin becomes embodied in a system of norms of human construction. What is divine must always remain; its human expression is subject to change. For instance, the primacy of the successor of Peter is of divine law for Catholics, but the manner of its exercise is a matter of human law to a high degree (see Book One, "General Norms," and Two, "The People of God," in the *Code of Canon Law*).

The role of the law in the matters of teaching and preaching is twofold: to protect the integrity of the Word of God and to assure that the Word is proclaimed. This includes the creation of procedures for determining where the truth lies in case of disputes concerning orthodoxy: the college of bishops (whether gathered in council or dispersed over the world) or the pope are the authentic judges. It includes also extensive determinations as to how the Word should be spread: through catechesis, educational institutions, media of communication, and so forth (see Book Three, "The Teaching Office of the Church").

In the matter of sanctification the purpose of the law is to create the best support for those encounters with God that are the sacraments. The law must promote them and should not impose any undue restrictions on their availability. The recent policy of making what once was called "extreme unction" much more widely available to those who are seriously ill is a good example of the right use of the law. The law can do much also to assure the dignity and beauty of the celebration of the sacramental encounters (see Book Four, "The Office of Sanctifying in the Church").

In the matter of the ownership and administration of church property, a twofold goal must be achieved by rules and regulations: on the one hand the church must be prevented from such an accumulation of wealth that would destroy its credibility; on the other hand the church must be helped to possess enough material assets to carry out its spiritual mission. History shows that to find the right balance between those two demands has never been easy; in our past, excessive trends in either direction can be found (see Book Five, "The Temporal Goods of the Church").

No religious community can maintain its identity if there is not a substantial unity among the members concerning their beliefs and their aspirations and actions. Whenever there is a breach of this unity, the question arises how to handle it, even more, how to handle the person who causes it and persists in causing it. The answer of the law (as a kind of last resource) is in imposing certain sanctions, which may vary in proportion to the gravity of the misdeed from a light correction to the denial of communion. The aim is to find the right balance between the respect and compassion for an individual person and the needed protection of the community (see Book Six, "Sanctions in the Church").

Finally, to protect the church itself from the "rule of man" (as that ancient expression goes, meaning the arbitrary rule of an individual person) and let the "rule of law" prevail, firmly planted procedural norms are necessary even in a community of "saints"—a Pauline expression. In such matters canon law can learn a great deal from well-tried secular systems; after all, the purpose is to protect the just from the unjust or to safeguard the community against the vagaries of our human nature (see Book Seven, "Processes").

The above description of the function of the law shows an ideal that always must be aimed for but can hardly ever be achieved. Human laws, including ecclesiastical laws, in their functioning are marked by our imperfections. For this reason they are always subject to revision, no less than the church is subject to an ongoing reform (see *Unitatis redintegratio* 6).

The last major revision of our canon law took place in the years after Vatican Council II and was concluded with the promulgation of the presently valid code. The main purpose of this reform was to translate the vision of Vatican Council II into legislative norms. The effort brought good results on a number of issues; for example, the fundamental rights of the faithful are now clearly defined, the apostolic call of the laity on the strength of their baptism is recognized, there are less restrictive measures on the administration of the sacraments, both the law of sanctions and of procedure are much simpler and more humane. In some other matters, however, the new canons provide little support for the vision of the council; for example, there are no speedy and effective procedures for redress in the case of violation of fundamental rights, no constitutional channels for the faithful to represent their concerns to the hierarchy, there is more than the necessary emphasis on the "sacred power" conferred through episcopal ordination and less than necessary on the power given through baptism, there are no adequate structures for the episcopal college to exercise their collegial power; also, there are provisions that allow an excessive centralization that leaves little room for the particular churches to develop.

This complex character of the presently valid code should be of no surprise to anyone who is familiar with the somewhat turbulent history of the church after Vatican Council II. Catholics differed widely in the interpretation of the council, and such divisions were not conducive to a uniformly harmonious legislation. In fact, the new

Code of Canon Law reflects faithfully the conditions of the church during the years of its drafting. It reflects the existing differences and often attempts to resolve them in the only way the law can: through compromises where norms inherited from past ages and made for other circumstances coexist uneasily with others born from new insights and responding to modern needs. It is reasonable to expect that in the coming decades experience will show more clearly what is still needed to have a "law of Vatican Council II," and that eventually the church will produce norms that will in an uncompromising fashion represent the doctrine of the council.

The question What is the function of canon law in the church? can be answered briefly: it is to create a favorable environment for the use of all energies, divine and human, present in the church. Canon law cannot produce those energies: if they are divine, they come from God; if they are human, they come from the human spirit sanctified by grace. Canon law, however, can do much to provide a framework in which those energies can operate freely and in an orderly way to the benefit of all.

See also CIVIL LAW, FUNCTION OF; DUE PROCESS; HUMAN RIGHTS; NATURAL LAW; RIGHTS AND DUTIES; SUBSIDIARITY, PRINCIPLE OF; VATICAN COUNCIL II.

Bibliography: A good survey of the history and content of canon law of Christian churches can be found in "Canon Law," *Encyclopaedia Britannica* (1973) Macropaedia 3:773–80. For Catholic canon law see J. Coriden et al., eds., *The Code of Canon Law: A Text and Commentary* (New York: Paulist, 1985).

LADISLAS ÖRSY, S.J.

CAPITAL PUNISHMENT

The authority of the state to administer a death penalty for heinous crimes against the common good of persons and society has traditionally enjoyed support from biblical and theological resources in the Christian community. Such support is not without criticism, and contemporary ecclesial reflection on this question raises important moral issues. This entry will review the warrants for the death penalty, the arguments against its endorsement, and will conclude with summary reflections.

Support for the practice of capital punishment has been sought from biblical sources. In the Hebrew Scriptures Gen 9:6 recognizes the Noachic covenant and the divine admonition, "If anyone sheds the blood of man, by man shall his blood be shed; for in the image of God has man been made." In the Law of Moses fifteen different crimes were singled out for the death penalty. Rabbinic reflections on these sanctions compiled in the Talmud, however, reveal restraint in the exercise of capital punishment. For example, an accused murderer could only be convicted on the testimony of two witnesses, no circumstantial evidence was allowed in a criminal case, and prior warning was to be given to the accused concerning the consequences of the crime. While it is clear that the Hebrew Scriptures condemn with utmost severity any violation of human life, recourse to the death penalty to assure this protection of life decreased in frequency in later centuries.

In the NT Rom 13 is invoked as recognizing the authority of the state to administer a capital penalty. Subsequent Christian reflection, however, reveals further qualification of the death penalty. In Mt 9:13 Jesus states that it "is mercy I desire and not sacrifice." In the Sermon on the Mount Jesus instructs his disciples to seek no revenge for wrongdoing. The admonition to love even one's enemies emerges as a profound trajectory within the NT. Jesus' own life and his endorsement of suffering love unto the cross further accentuate a heightened awareness of the dignity of human life.

Nonetheless, the theological tradition has provided support for the administration of the death penalty. The arguments take the following forms:

1. The authoritative power of the state is affirmed in the NT (Rom 13), and the sovereign is empowered to act on behalf of the common good of the society. When the common good is threatened, particularly when human life is directly assaulted, the sovereign must take appropriate measures to defend the lives of innocent citizens. Such protection may require the execution of the lawless. The endorsement of the death penalty is seen as an appropriate application of the principle of justice in which the life of the criminal is forfeited commensurate with the gravity of the crime of murder.

2. The death penalty serves as a deterrent and contributes to the preservation of public order.

3. The death penalty is an exercise in judgment and not hatred. To quote Pope Innocent III: "We assert concerning the power of the state that it is able to exercise a judgment of blood, without mortal sin, provided it proceed to inflict the punishment not in hate, but in judgment; not incautiously, but after consideration" (*Anti-Waldensian Profession*, DS, no. 795).

Contemporary theological reflection, however, argues for the elimination of the death penalty. Among the arguments proffered are the following:

1. The death penalty is useless and unnecessary. The incidence of violent crime does not appear to be appreciably lessened by the retention of capital punishment. An alternative is to deter the offender by means of lengthy incarceration.

2. The death penalty dehumanizes society by legitimating violence as a strategy to deal with human wrongdoing. The genuine lack of social justice and solidarity promotes the climate of violence, which remains unaddressed by recourse to capital punishment as a means to deter crime.

3. The death penalty does not reflect the consistent biblical trajectory of forgiveness, hope, and redemption. Even the law of the talion is an exercise in restraining violence as a means of adjudicating human conflict. The forgiveness preached by Jesus is at variance with a perceived need to administer capital punishment.

The theological discussion of capital punishment is frequently intertwined with the question of torture. Francesco Compagnoni argues, however, that the tradition reveals a distinct bias against torture and capital punishment and includes condemnation of these practices in the writings of Lactantius, Tertullian, and Augustine. In the November 1980 statement of the U.S. bishops opposing the death penalty the authority of Aquinas is cited as providing some criteria for the administration of punishment: "In this life, however, penalties are not sought for their own sake, because this is not the era of retribution; rather, they are meant to be corrective by being conducive either to the reform of the sinner or to the good of society, which becomes more peaceful through the punishment of sinners."

The reconsideration of the death penalty has undergone searching analysis by numerous episcopal conferences. In the statements prepared by the bishops of California, Pennsylvania, Florida, and Ohio several themes are accentuated in acknowledging a "new moment" in ecclesial consciousness.

First, abolition of the death penalty communicates an awareness that the cycle of violence can be broken. Alternative forms of punishment are encouraged, including compassionate efforts to provide correction rather than vindictive judgment for the criminal. It should be noted that there is clear acknowledgment of the rights of victims and a forthright recognition of the need for lifetime incarceration for those who are incorrigible and a genuine danger to society.

Second, the argument for abolition supports a life-affirming ethic coherent with the church's position on abortion, euthanasia, and the defense of innocent human life. The affirmation of human dignity is an important value to be strengthened lest the death penalty further erode respect for the sanctity of human life.

Third, abolition promotes the awareness that God is life's sovereign. Such a recognition provides an important check on human power to take life.

Fourth, the bishops appeal to the example of Jesus as being more clearly delineated by rejecting capital punishment. His example of unceasing forgiveness is also supported by the gesture of forgiveness extended by Pope John Paul II to Mehmet Ali Ağca, who attempted to assassinate the pontiff in 1980.

Various statements also dwell on the potential for mistakenly applying the death penalty, the legal complications in terms of delays, and the real danger of discriminatory use of capital punishment. Rather than accept capital punishment as an acceptable option, the bishops argue for reform of the penal system, for the administration of appropriate incarceration as a penalty, and for due care for the innocent victims of violent assaults. Related to this set of concerns are penumbral issues such as the deleterious glorifying of violence in public media, the ready access to guns and other weapons, and the conditions of poverty and injustice, which are the seedbed of systemic violence in the contemporary world.

In summary, while the Roman Catholic theological tradition has provided a rationale justifying the qualified administration of the death penalty, contemporary theological assessment questions the necessity for this form of punishment and challenges the theological assumptions that have heretofore governed its exercise.

See also CIVIL LAW, FUNCTION OF; COMMON GOOD; COVENANT; DECALOGUE; DETERRENCE; DUE PROCESS; KILLING; TORTURE.

Bibliography: F. Compagnoni, in F. Bockle and J. Pohier, *The Death Penalty and Torture* (New York: Seabury, 1979). Selected episcopal statements of the United States hierarchy: U.S. bishops, *Origins* 10 (November 27, 1980) 373–77; California bishops, *Origins* 15 (October 17, 1985) 301–3; Ohio bishops, *Origins* 16 (March 26, 1987) 726–28; Pennsylvania bishops, *Origins* 16 (January 22, 1987) 579–80; Tennessee bishops, *Origins* 14 (June 14, 1985) 65–72.

JEREMIAH J. McCARTHY

CAPITALISM

Capitalism has been aptly described as a moving target. That is to say, the economic system that people call capitalism has evolved with time and circumstances, and even today there are a number of kinds of capitalism in various nations throughout the world. The key characteristic of a capitalist economy is that it relies on a *market* system to solve the fundamental economic problem: what should be produced, who should produce it, how should it be produced, and for what people. Referred to as the "free market" system, it requires a private-property system (property and contract laws) and a voluntary exchange system (the legal freedom to come together and buy and sell goods).

The dynamics of the free-market system are evident all around us. Entrepreneurs or privately owned firms, seeking to make a profit, decide what they will produce and how they will produce it. The products are then sold at the highest price feasible given the competition. The price level serves as the signal regulating production. A highly profitable product that is in demand will encourage more entrepreneurs to produce the goods even more efficiently and enter the market, while a low-profit item will discourage new investors and hence additional production. Typically a market system is contrasted with the other major way of solving the fundamental economic problem, a *command* system. When a command system governs an economy there is no diffusion of power. Rather, a single authority or group makes all the decisions, as, for example, the central planning system of the former Soviet Union. Unlike capitalism, in this command system the government owns the means of production.

This article will offer a brief history of the notion of capitalism, a discussion of the rationale for church involvement in economic issues, and an outline of some highlights of church teaching. It will conclude with some discussion of the U.S. bishops' response to the American economy.

The Development of Capitalism

While capitalism as we know it only emerged in the last two centuries, some of the developments of capitalism like trade and moneylending were present in the life of the ancient Greeks and Romans. Lewis Mumford in *Techniques and Civilizations* (1934) has suggested that the Benedictine monks of the 6th century might well be considered the founders of capitalism. Life in the monasteries was organized with the central conviction that through the common life of work, prayer, and recreation the monks grew closer to God. To ensure ample time for prayer and meditation the monks were ever alert to develop labor-saving devices. They also standardized the tasks of the monastery so that they might easily be interchanged among the brothers. Because the monastic style of life was so simple and frugal, monasteries began to accrue wealth, which was then used to build more efficient equipment. Thus Mumford sees in this pattern the rationale for calling the monks the first capitalists.

A key characteristic of a market system is the type of motivation or incentives involved. Arnold Toynbee in *A Study of History* (1947) notes a significant parallel between monasticism and capitalism in that they both rely on an inner-directed motivation: "The Benedictine Rule achieved what has never been achieved by the Gracchan agrarian laws or the Imperial alimenta, because it worked, not, as state action works, from above downwards, but from below upwards, by evoking the individual's initiative through enlisting his religious enthusiasm." From the positive attitude toward work on the part of the monks, there was a growing acceptance throughout the Middle Ages that dignity and self-respect could be found in labor and doing work well, for "to labor is to pray."

Adam Smith

The thinker who is perhaps most responsible for helping people understand the dynamics of what today is called a market system is the moral philosopher Adam Smith (1723–90). Smith asked a very simple but ingenious question: Why are some nations noticeably wealthier than their neighbors? In his famous work, *An Inquiry into the Nature and Causes of the Wealth of Nations* (1776), Smith related his observations. Some nations were wealthier because they used an effective division of labor in making products and because they utilized the free competitive market. His notion of the market mechanism continues to underpin what have become known as capitalist economies: "In civilized society he stands at all times in need of the cooperation and assistance of great multitudes, while his whole life is scarce sufficient to gain the friendship of a few persons. . . . Man has almost constant occasion for the help of his brethren, and it is in vain for him to expect it from their benevolence only. He will be more likely to prevail if he can interest their self-love in his favour, and show them that it is for their own advantage to do for him what he requires of them. Whoever offers to another a bargain of any kind proposes to do this. . . . It is not from the benevolence of the butcher, the brewer, or the baker, that we expect our dinner, but from their regard to their own interest" (p. 18).

When each person pursues his or her own self-interest, the common good is enhanced. The baker bakes the very best bread possible and sells it at the lowest price feasible so that the proceeds of the sale can be used to buy what he or she wants. Although motivated by self-interest, the net result is that the community has quality products at a reasonable cost. What Smith did was to show how economic action based on self-interest could be beneficial for the community. This was indeed a remarkable turn of events, for economic self-interest was heretofore not thought to be respectable.

Reflecting on the commerce of his time, Smith concluded that goods would be produced more efficiently and cheaply for all if each person strove to maximize his or her self-interest in the marketplace. Producing attractive goods at competitive prices would be in the self-interest of the producer and in the best interest of the public. Smith spoke of "an invisible hand," which guided self-interested behavior to be of benefit to the whole society. His hope was that if governments would understand the real source of the wealth of nations, they would forgo all tariffs and other measures that provide protection to the producers and advocate a free market.

The prevailing mercantile view looked to the quantity of precious metals to measure wealth. Smith rejected this understanding, for he saw that real wealth was a nation's productivity, "the value of the annual produce of its land and labour." Increased productivity (wealth) was not an *end* in itself but a *means* to increase the quality of life of people. Smith accepted the Judeo-Christian vision that portrayed a land where all might enjoy the good things of creation. His insight was that this vision, while far from realized in any nation, was gradually becoming a reality in those places that utilized incentives, economic action based on self-interest (profit motive), and a market economy. Smith assumed that the *self* that was self-interested would be shaped by moral forces in the community so that economic self-interest would not degenerate into a crass selfishness. His vision was one of a market economy enabling a humane community.

Max Weber

The causes of the full flowering of industrial capitalism in the 18th century from its tiny seeds in the small-scale commercial capitalism of previous centuries have been the subject of much scholarly speculation. Most find merit in the thesis advanced by Max Weber in the early 20th century. In *The Protestant Ethic and the Spirit of Capitalism* Weber argued that two central doctrines of the Protestant Reformers provided the motivation and legitimation for the birth of modern capitalism: Martin Luther's doctrine of vocation and John Calvin's teaching on predestination.

What made capitalism unique, according to Weber, was the pursuit of profit by means of systematic and rational behavior. He cited rational bookkeeping as a key characteristic of this entity called capitalism. Why was it that capitalism was able to marshal such enormous amounts of human energy for the cause of economic growth? Why was it that characteristic pre-Reformation Christian attitudes that extolled the virtue of poverty, encouraged withdrawal from the world, and honored the intellectual life over commerce were suddenly transformed into attitudes that fostered the development of business—attitudes of austerity, industry, thrift, frugality, and so on? The answer to these questions, according to Weber, lay in the theological teachings of Luther and Calvin and the way in which these teachings were passed along to the people by Reformed pastors. It is worth noting that R. H. Tawney and other scholars modified Weber's theory. For example, Tawney included the influence of the bankers of Venice and Florence, and hence of Catholic ideas, in the ethos that spawned capitalism. In any event, it is instructive to consider the original Weberian thesis.

Luther brought a fresh perspective to the notion of Christian vocation. He taught that one's occupation in the world was not to be taken lightly, for doing the task well was the way to serve God and to give thanks for divine justification. This conviction provided motivation for high performance in one's station in life, whether as a scholar, craftsperson, or laborer. Yet Weber argued that the life-pattern of systematic and rational activity that characterized capitalism was not sufficiently explained by Luther's doctrine of calling or vocation. He also examined Calvin's doctrine of predestination. In Calvin's theology God elects some to be saved and others to be damned, and one is powerless to affect the outcome of God's sovereign will. In the face of the great uncertainty over salvation, there were many in these communities who suffered great anxiety. Weber suggested that one look to the advice given by Reformed pastors who were ministering to this salvation-anxiety problem in order to find the significant motive power for economic growth.

In order to calm consciences, the pastors were saying that there were *signs* of election and that these signs were material success in one's business. While one could not attain salvation by prudent management of a business enterprise, one could have some assurance that salvation was in line for one if material prosperity prevailed. Thus everyone struggled to ensure that businesses were profitable, and this produced the driven quality in the "Protestant ethic." Although the pastors encouraged people to live frugally, to be austere, they were also counseling industriousness and persistence. This combination of advice enabled people to overcome their anxiety and also to accrue wealth. Since Calvinism taught that wealth would be an obstacle to holiness in that it led to pride and sensuality, this posed a problem. It was not long, therefore, before a new teaching emerged to account for the new condition. The doctrine of stewardship was developed; it taught that wealth was a trust and was to be used for the common good.

The crucial point in Weber's analysis is that making profit became a value in its own right. Since anxiety over possible damnation is calmed if one is materially successful, it made sense to be almost single-mindedly focused on material success. Thus the Protestant ethic changed history, for heretofore ethical values had always discouraged such a single-minded quest for profits.

Weber went on to show how the Protestant ethic eventually lost its religious roots and yet still maintained its vitality with a secular vision. Benjamin Franklin epitomizes this secular vision. Reading Franklin's works, one is struck by the fact that all the values of the spirit of Christian asceticism are present, although the religious basis of these values has died. What remains is what Weber called a "fundamental element of the spirit of modern capitalism: Rational conduct on the basis of the idea of calling." Weber quotes Franklin: "Remember that money is of the prolific, generating nature. Money can beget money, and its offspring can beget more, and so on. Five shillings turned is six, turned again it is seven and threepence, and so on, till it becomes a hundred pounds. The more there is of it, the more it produces every turning, so that the profits rise quicker and quicker. He that kills a breeding-sow destroys all her offering to the thousandth generation. He that murders a crown, destroys all that it might have produced, even scores of pounds" (p. 49). The writings of Benjamin Franklin exhort the reader to the practice of austerity, honesty, frugality, thrift, industry, and so on—all the virtues of the Puritan ethic—not for the sake of the signs of salvation but rather in order to accrue wealth and to live as a moral athlete. This was the best way to live, according to Franklin.

Why the Church is Involved in Economic Issues

The church statements that reflect on and offer guidance to capitalist economies are attempts to restore the religious vision and to be the moral force assumed by

Adam Smith ensuring that a market economy does not so blind a people that it becomes an acquisitive society. The goal is growth with equity, and the perennial target of condemnation by Catholic social teaching is materialism. Church teaching has never seen fit to condemn capitalism as intrinsically evil, although some theologians have, but rather has aimed its guidance at the reform of institutions, structures, and personal life involved with the free-market economy.

To understand Catholic social teaching on economic life it is necessary to see it in the context of a religious view of earthly existence. The overarching Catholic vision was stated in systematic form by Thomas Aquinas (1225–74), and this perspective continues to guide the church today. Aquinas, drawing on biblical teaching and the writings of the church fathers, wove an enduring tapestry with an Aristotelian and Neoplatonic philosophic framework. All of creation flows from God and finally will return to God. The goal of life on this earth is to become the sort of person who will finally enjoy the vision of God in the next world. "Man's ultimate happiness consists solely in the contemplation of God" (*Summa contra Gentiles* 3.37).

Becoming the sort of person who might enjoy this vision, becoming virtuous, is only thought to be possible because of a gift of God (a supernatural gift of grace). Appropriating the virtues over a lifetime is the *means* to the *end* of human life. Then one is oriented properly to God and may see God in the next life. For Aquinas, however, all creation is fundamentally good, and being properly oriented to God entails as well the appropriate orientation toward the natural good. Aquinas highlighted the key biblical virtues (faith, hope, and charity), but he also stressed the need to form character in Aristotle's four cardinal virtues (wisdom, justice, temperance, and fortitude).

For Aquinas, then, moral and spiritual nourishment was crucial, for this was the way one prepared for life in the next world. The focus was on personal morality, and in this context the medieval theologians wrote much about just prices, trade, and usury. The efforts of the moralists were largely directed to individual Christians and were designed to ensure that each kept faithful to a path of personal virtue.

While the churches have never forsaken their role of shaping the character of individual Christians through preaching, teaching, and liturgy, there has been a new realization that the Christian mission also entails criticizing unjust social structures and transforming the world. Aquinas lived in an era when it was generally assumed that society was static. People most often remained in the socioeconomic group into which they were born, as lord, peasant, craftsperson, or merchant. "Justice" was understood to mean that each person was entitled to whatever his or her particular role in society required. Thus, in "justice," a lord had considerably more material goods than a peasant. Viewing the world in terms of the analogy of the human body, each class of society was seen to have a different role to perform in society, but all were united in an organic unity.

How is it that transforming the world and hence being involved in social and political issues have come to be understood in the church as an integral part of its mission, as a "constitutive dimension of the preaching of the Gospel" (*Justice in the World,* 1971)? On one level, it could be argued that in the United States only in recent years have Catholics assumed positions of power in business, government, and the wider society. It would have made little sense to speak of changing social structures to the immigrant parents or grandparents of the current generation of American Catholics. As a result of education and the upward mobility of their parents, present-day Catholics are often very influential in the United States.

In 1891 Pope Leo XIII issued *Rerum novarum,* published in face of the impact of the Industrial Revolution and the church's growing concern over severe working conditions and the exploitation of workers. American Catholics were largely blue-collar people, and *Rerum novarum* championed their cause—political and economic rights. Today the descendants of those poor workers probably do not need to hear a comforting word but rather a challenging one—a call to continue to fashion a world that is more humane for the poor and the powerless!

The church has had much to say in the last century in the area of economic ethics. While it is true that the skill of producing wealth is a relatively new one in the history of the human race and that this skill has the potential to create a more humane life, thus advancing the kingdom of God, the church insists that wealth production always be carried out in the context of the end of life on this earth, which is the formation of virtuous persons. Economic activity is only a means, and it must be guided by reference to the moral ends. This is the heart of the teaching of Thomas Aquinas, and it continues to form the basis of church documents. The Second Vatican Council's Pastoral Constitution on the Church in the Modern World (*Gaudium et spes*) restates the point clearly: "Economic activity is to be carried out according to its own methods and laws but within the limits of morality so that God's plan for mankind can be realized" (GS 64).

Catholic Social Teaching and Capitalism

The basis of all Catholic social teaching on economic matters is the dignity and inalienable rights of the human person. The heart of the church's criticism of capitalism is summed up well by Pope John Paul II: "What was mainly seen was the possibility of vastly increasing material wealth, means, while the end, that is to say man, who should be served by the means, was ignored" (*Laborem exercens* 13). It may be helpful to review some of the major attempts by the church to shape a capitalism more in service of humankind.

In 1891 Pope Leo XIII in *Rerum novarum* put the church squarely on the side of the workers in the struggle for recognition of trade unions. Since workers have a right to a living wage, they have the additional right to join labor unions in order to secure this right. *Rerum novarum* also indicated that the state has the right and duty to ensure that this right and others are promoted and protected by legislation.

Msgr. John A. Ryan was most influential in U.S. Catholic circles, writing *A Living Wage* (1906) and *Distributive Justice* (1916). Ryan drafted a crucial document of the National Catholic Welfare Conference (the predecessor of the United States Catholic Conference), which was issued in 1919 by the U.S. bishops and often cited as the forerunner of some of Franklin Roosevelt's New Deal policies. Titled *Social Reconstruction: A General Review of the Problems and Survey of Remedies,* Ryan's document offered a moral perspective on the economy and made suggestions for such reforms as minimum-wage laws, child-labor laws, the right of labor to organize, and unemployment and health insurance. For the most part, Ryan's suggestions have become public policy in the United States.

In 1931 Pope Pius XI issued *Quadragesimo anno.* While its proposed alternative model of society is of dubious value today, the role of the church as an agent of change in the sociopolitical order was clearly established. Three principles enunciated in the document have been dominant in all subsequent Catholic social theory: the need to protect the dignity of the person; the concern that organizations be no larger than necessary (subsidiarity); and the focus on the necessity for mediating structures (family, professional associations, church, etc.) between the person and the state.

Quadragesimo anno outlined a vision of society and its relationship to the state that has continued to develop in Catholic social thought. Society comprises all the various groupings that people find necessary or helpful: families, churches, unions, professional associations, business corporations, social clubs, neighborhood associations, and so on. The role of the state is to be *in the service of* society; that is, its role is primarily to facilitate the cooperation and well-being of all these groupings, or "mediating structures," as they are often called today. The encyclical uses the verbs "direct," "watch," "urge," and "restrain" "as occasion requires and necessity demands" when describing the role of the state (QA 80). The 1961 encyclical of Pope John XXIII, *Mater et magistra,* employs similar terms: the role of the state is to "encourage, stimulate, regulate, supplement and complement" (MM 53).

Catholic social thought is ever vigilant against collectivist tendencies that tend to obliterate legitimate mediating structures. This defense of personal rights is clearly evident in the 1981 encyclical, *Laborem exercens,* in which Pope John Paul II vigorously defends the solidarity of workers and their right to come together in organizations to defend common interests. Eschewing the model of interest-group pluralism, which tends to view the world exclusively through the prism of one set of interests, Catholic social thought repeatedly returns to the notion of the common good as the appropriate context in which to consider one's own interests. John Paul II emphasizes this point in *Laborem exercens:* "Just efforts to secure the rights of workers who are united by the same profession should always take into account the limitations imposed by the general economic situation of the country. Union demands cannot be turned into a kind of group or class 'egoism,' although they can and should also aim at correcting—with a view to the common good of the whole society—everything defective in the system of ownership of the means of production or in the way these are managed" (LE 20).

Society is often *identified with* the state in socialist theory and practices. Thus, the state has control of all aspects of life—the arts, sciences, politics, economics, and so on. Some would argue that in time the appropriate social structures will transform persons so that state control will be unnecessary. People will be almost selfless. Catholic social theory could never accept this perspective. Assuming that human nature is flawed, one of the roles of the state, according to this religious perspective, is to facilitate the growth of desirable character traits and mute those that are less noble. Yet there is a confidence in the goodness, the cooperative dimension, of the person, so that the social constraints of the state are designed to enhance human freedom and curtail selfishness for the common good.

This confidence in the fundamental goodness of the person underlies the church's basic strategy of appealing to the consciences of those who control wealth and power in order to bring about basic changes in society designed to alleviate the plight of the poor. Pope Paul VI in *Populorum progressio* argues for a new international economic order, but he appeals for strategies of negotiation and consensus rather than any violent means. His *Octogesima adveniens* (1971) echoes a similar theme. Pope John Paul II in his address in Oaxaca, Mexico, also makes this point: "It is not just, it is not human, it is not Christian to continue certain situations that are clearly unjust. You must implement real, effective measures on the local, national, and international levels, following the broad line marked out by the encyclical *Mater et magistra* [Part 3]. And it is clear that those who can do the most are the ones most obligated to collaborate in this effort" (address to the Indians of Eaxaca and Chiapas, January 29, 1979). Again, speaking in Brazil, John Paul says: "So the church of the poor speaks like this: You, particularly the ones who in decision making have power, you, on whom the world situation depends, do everything so that the life of each man in your country may become more human, more worthy of man. Do everything so that at least gradually the abyss that divides the few excessively rich from the great multitudes of poor, those who live in want, may disappear" (*remarks at Favela Vidigal, July 2, 1980*).

"A Preferential but Not Exclusive Option for the Poor"

In 1968 at the Second General Conference of Latin American bishops at Medellín, Colombia, the assembled pastors took a bold step in publicly stating their intention of focusing the church's efforts to do all that is necessary to help the poor organize and overcome injustices. In 1971, Paul VI in *Octogesima adveniens* spoke of the "preferential respect due to the poor." To be sure, this focus on the poor is not a new idea for Christianity. Jesus began his ministry by reading a text from Isaiah that summarized his central concerns: "He has sent me to bring good news to the poor, to proclaim liberty to captives and to the blind new sight, to set the downtrodden free, to proclaim the Lord's year of favor" (Lk 4:18). The Hebrew Scriptures tell of how God and all God's people ought to regard the poor: "He will free the poor man who calls to him, and those who need help, he will have pity on the poor and feeble, and save the lives of those in need" (Ps 71:12-13). What is significant about this "option for the poor" is that it signals a commitment by the bishops to promote social justice in the economic and political arenas.

In January 1979 the third General Conference of Latin American bishops was held at Puebla, Mexico, and was attended by Pope John Paul II. The document from this assembly has a chapter entitled "A Preferential Option for the Poor," which not only stresses the need for a change in people's minds and hearts but also for a change in those structures of society that impede the progress of the poor (*Evangelization in Latin America: Present and Future*). Pope John Paul, speaking at Puebla, encouraged the bishops to speak out against injustice, but he also warned against any movement that would present Christ as a political revolutionary. A year later, in Brazil, John Paul spoke of "a preferential but not exclusive option for the poor" (*remarks at Favela Vidigal, July 2, 1980*).

John Paul throughout his writings is trying to steer a course between simply supporting the status quo, which may be unjust, and unabashedly encouraging violent revolution. To the rich and the powerful, he counsels concern for the poor and the environment that nurtures them. To the poor, he preaches solidarity, that is, taking a stand and collectively reacting to exploitative situations and systems.

The sort of society envisioned by Catholic social teaching is one in which private property is respected. Following the medieval scholar Thomas Aquinas, the church assumes that private property enables the human development intended by the Creator. Yet the teaching has always insisted that private property has a social dimension that requires that owners consider the common good in the use of property (ST II–II, 66, 2). This vision of society assumes that some persons will have more material goods than others but that the affluent will provide for the less fortunate, either through the channels of public policy or other appropriate groups of society. The emphasis is always on respect for the human dignity of the poor, even in their unfortunate situation. The ideal is to structure society so that all those who are able might provide for themselves and their families by freely employing their talents.

The insight of Catholic social teaching, applied in various circumstances throughout the last century, is that capitalism without a context in a humane community seems inevitably to shape people into greedy and insensitive human beings. Thus church teaching accepts the market economy but with a key qualification: that the state intervene where essential to promote and protect human dignity. A good summary statement of the teaching in this area was provided by Pope John XXIII: "At the outset it should be affirmed that in economic affairs first place is to be given to the private initiative of individual men who, either working by themselves, or with others in one fashion or another, pursue their common interests. But in this matter . . . it is necessary that public authorities take active interest, the better to increase output of goods and to further social progress for the benefit of all citizens" (MM 52).

This framework underpins all the economic teaching of the church. While accepting the value of a market economy, religious social thought argues that one must have a conscious concern for the common good of all and not depend on unconscious workings of the market, the "hidden hand," to solve all problems. Some disciples of Adam Smith believed in God's providence working to ensure the common good, a self-regulating economy. Religious social thought says in effect that we must make God's work our own, that we must have a conscious care for the common good. This sometimes requires government regulation of the market. To be sure, regulation is tricky business, and the good consequences sought are often elusive. A failure in a particular regulation is no argument against regulation, however, but rather one for better regulation. The continual refrain of Catholic social teaching is that all efforts must be made to promote and protect human dignity.

Church social teaching recognizes that participation in market economy can be a great aid toward developing character. The habits and virtues required to participate in the market—honesty, industriousness, patience, deferred gratification, for example—are ones extolled by the church. *Laborem exercens* reiterates this point: "The church's teaching has always expressed the strong and deep conviction that man's work concerns not only the economy but also, and especially, personal values. The economic system itself and the production process benefit precisely when these personal values are fully respected. In the mind of St. Thomas Aquinas, this is the principal reason in favor of private ownership of the means of production" (LE 15).

The 1986 Pastoral Letter of the U.S. Bishops

On November 13, 1986, the more than three hundred Roman Catholic bishops of the United States, assembled at their annual meeting in Washington, D.C., culminated a six-year process by voting approval of a landmark document on the moral dimensions of the U.S. economy. Entitled *Economic Justice for All: Catholic Social Teaching and the U.S. Economy,* the pastoral invited U.S. Catholics to reflect on the human and ethical dimensions of economic life and to fashion a more just society for the poor and the powerless.

The bishops intended the letter not only to provide guidance for Roman Catholics but also to help shape new public policy for the United States. The hope was that the document would foster a "renewed public moral vision." It is significant that the bishops decided not to write their document on capitalism but rather to focus on the actual mixed economy currently in place in the United States. They did this because after a number of hearings it became clear that there is no one theoretical position on capitalism, and in any event their real concern was the United States economy and its global effect, not some construct called "capitalism."

The point of the bishops' statement was to remind people that the U.S. economy is still far from where it might be. There are too many able-bodied people who cannot find work, and a disproportionate number of those are minorities and women. There are too many who slip through the safety net, going without adequate food, housing, and medical care. The plight of people in developing countries is also a central concern. So many in the United States live so well that it is easy to forget about those who are barely getting along.

The bishops decided in November 1980, following the counsel of papal teaching, to write a pastoral letter on the economy that would bring Catholic social teaching into dialogue with the particular situation of the United States (*Economic Justice for All* 26). After listening to theologians, major religious leaders of all faiths, economists, business and government leaders, and a host of others, and after receiving critical comments on three drafts of the document, the bishops finally issued the fourth and final version in November 1986.

The bishops' letter formulated a vision from biblical and theological grounds and was rooted in "its vision of the transcendent worth—the sacredness—of human beings" (EJA 28). Recognizing that human dignity can only flourish in community, the pastoral draws on a rich biblical tradition to elaborate the essential social dimension of the person. In fidelity to Scripture, the poor and the powerless are never to be forgotten. "The dignity of the human person, realized in community with others, is the criterion against which all aspects of economic life must be measured" (28). "The fundamental moral criterion for all economic decisions, policies and institutions is this: They must be at the service of all people, especially the poor" (24). This vision is developed with the biblical motifs of creation, covenant, and community.

By exploring these three biblical motifs, the document reminds Christians of the sort of people they ought to become and of the sort of communities they ought to form. For Christians, the Bible ought to have a decisive influence on their overall vision of life, their attitudes, convictions, and intentions. Creation stories remind us of the gift-like character of life and the mandate to be faithful stewards of God's world. Using human talents and ingenuity, people are indeed called to continue God's creative work by building a more humane world. "Men and women are also to share in the creative activity of God. . . . They can justly consider that by their labor they are unfolding the Creator's work" (32).

As the ancient Hebrews fleeing Egypt came together in solidarity during the Exodus and finally formalized their community in the covenant, so too, those living today under the new covenant should be known for their community and solidarity. Because of this bond, the Christian community ought to be a model of concern for those who are less fortunate.

In the biblical vision, the justice of a community is demonstrated by its treatment of the powerless in society—the widow, the orphan, the poor, and the stranger. The poor in early Christianity were seen as the special concern of God. Following the 1979 statement at Puebla by the assembled Latin American bishops and the speeches of John Paul II, the pastoral focused on "the preferential option for the poor." The document details some specific challenges that follow from this option for the poor.

Economic Rights

Underpinning the pastoral letter is the idea that today the notion of the rights of an individual must be expanded to include not only civil and political rights but also economic rights.

The concept of a right is embedded in the very founding of the United States. The Declaration of Independence and the Bill of Rights enumerate a long list of entitlements, or rights. These legal rights of U.S. citizens, such as life, liberty, and the pursuit of happiness, are correlated with a duty others have toward the individual. For example, to the framers of the Declaration of Independence the right to life meant that a person had the right not to be killed and that the government had the duty to protect this entitlement. In the

18th century the concept of a right was understood to circumscribe an area in which others had a duty *not* to interfere. The role of government was to ensure that a person's free speech, privacy, property, and other rights were protected from undue interference. Today these civil rights are discussed in the philosophic literature as "negative rights"; that is, they point to the duty another has of *not* interfering. Although it is surely a significant accomplishment that a whole range of negative rights are guaranteed for so many today, a body of literature has developed in the 20th century arguing for "positive rights." Positive rights are taken to be those entitlements a person has by virtue of being human. It is these rights that were championed by the bishops in their pastoral on the economy.

The concept of a positive right implies that someone or some institution in society has the positive duty to provide for whatever is necessary to pursue the interest in question. For example, today when one speaks of the "right to life," in contrast with the 18th-century understanding of the right not to be killed what is generally meant is that a person has a right to the minimum necessities of life. The United Nations 1948 "Universal Declaration of Human Rights" lists a whole array of positive rights that are taken to be entitlements for all by virtue of being a person: the right to work, to just and favorable conditions of work, to protection against unemployment, to rest and leisure, including reasonable limitation of working hours and periodic holidays with pay, and so on.

The pastoral letter reminded the reader that Pope John XXIII, in the encyclical *Pacem in terris,* enumerated the rights that are the minimal conditions for a just economy: such things as the right to food, clothing, shelter, jobs, basic education, and medical care, as well as the right to security in the event of sickness and the rights of property ownership. However, the bishops recognized that there was no consensus in the United States that all of these really *are* rights that ought to be guaranteed, nor was there agreement as to how one might actually guarantee them. To help form this consensus was one of the major purposes of the pastoral. It must begin with the formation of a new cultural consensus that *all people really do have rights in the economic sphere* and that society has a moral obligation to take the necessary steps to ensure that no one among us is hungry, homeless, unemployed, or otherwise denied what is necessary for living with dignity.

Four principles to guide policies in all economic institutions are suggested in the document: (1) the fulfillment of the basic needs of the poor is of the highest priority; (2) increasing active participation in economic life by those who are presently excluded or vulnerable is a high social priority; (3) the investment of wealth, talent, and human energy should be especially directed to benefit those who are poor or economically insecure; (4) economic and social policies as well as the organization of the work world should be continually evaluated in light of their impact on the strength and stability of family life (EJA 90–93).

Chapter 3 of the pastoral letter focuses on four economic issues in the light of the religious vision and ethical principles discussed in the first two chapters. The issues—employment, poverty, food and agriculture, and the U.S. role in the global economy—are not intended to exhaust the concerns of Catholic social teaching, but they do lend themselves to specific applications of Catholic moral principles. Thus new policies are advocated for reaching full employment, for eradicating poverty, for preserving family farms and discouraging agribusiness from dominating agricultural resources, and for aiding developing nations. Chapter 3 comprises 167 paragraphs, more than 45 percent of the document.

Chapter 4 moves beyond particular policy recommendations and offers "a long-term and more fundamental response" to the challenge of achieving economic justice for all. It suggested new forms of cooperation and partnership to replace the adversarial relationships that so often dominate the major actors in society. Four areas are considered: cooperation within firms and industries, local and regional cooperation, partnership in the development of national policies, and cooperation at the international level.

Chapter 5 concludes the letter with reflections on the church as a model of economic justice and on the importance of the notion of vocation in the world today. "Through their competency and by their activity, lay men and women have the vocation to bring the light of the Gospel to economic affairs so that the world may be filled with the spirit of Christ and may more effectively attain its destiny in justice, in love and in peace" (332). The letter is hopeful that together people can fashion a world that is both more humane and more virtuous.

The response to the bishops' pastoral letter was mixed. A group of Catholic laypersons under the leadership of theologian Michael Novak argued that the letter focused too much on distributing wealth and too little on producing it. Such an emphasis, they argued, would end up hurting the poor more than helping them. Because the Catholic social teaching on capitalism is reformist and does not engage in a critique of the system as intrinsically exploitative (Karl Marx), many Latin American liberation theologians and some North American theologians such as Rosemary Reuther would find it deficient. A number of theologians have argued that socialism is the more just economic system from the Christian perspective. For example, Gregory Baum finds the bishops' letter lacking in prophetic challenge.

Recent statements on the church and the economy, particularly *Economic Justice For All,* have played a major role by raising the level of discussion in the wider society of the moral dimension of economic decisions. Whether one agrees with the policy recommendations or not, what becomes clear in the ensuing debates is that trade-offs are inevitable. While no one doubts that a society must continue to produce wealth, there is always a concern in church teaching for some equity or fairness in how wealth is distributed. There is also concern for the quality of life and the fear that an inordinate focus on material prosperity overshadows these broader considerations. Concern for the environment and fairness in distribution as well as the general quality of human relations are all recognized as proper issues for public policy. Just where to draw the line on harnessing the free market through regulation to promote rights and justice in the mixed economy of a society is no easy task and is often solved best by trial and error. The debate goes on! What is certain is that because of these debates in the past, the capitalism of late 20th-century America is far more humane than that of the turn of the century. The capitalism of the future promises to be even more humane if the church continues to champion the cause of human dignity realized in community.

See also BISHOPS' PROGRAM OF SOCIAL RECONSTRUCTION OF 1919; CHURCH, SOCIAL MISSION OF; COMMON GOOD; DEVELOPMENT; ENTERPRISE; GOODS, DISTRIBUTION OF; PRIVATE PROPERTY; TRANSNATIONAL CORPORATIONS.

Bibliography: O. Williams, in J. Houck and O. Williams, eds., *Catholic Social Teaching and the U.S. Economy: Working Papers for a Bishops' Pastoral* (Washington: Univ. Press of America, 1984). O. Williams and J. Houck, eds., *The Judeo-Christian Vision and the Modern Corporation* (Notre Dame, Ind.: Univ. of Notre Dame Press, 1982). O. Williams, in G. Steiner and J. Steiner, eds., *Business, Government, and Society,* 5th ed. (New York: McGraw-Hill, 1988). R. Benne, *The Ethic of Democratic Capitalism* (Philadelphia: Fortress, 1981). R. Heilbroner, *The Economic Problem,* 3rd ed. (Englewood Cliffs, N.J.: Prentice Hall, 1972). C. Lindblom *Politics and Markets* (New York: Basic, 1977). P. Samuelson, *Economics,* 9th ed. (New York: McGraw-Hill, 1973). J. Schumpeter, *Capitalism, Socialism, and Democracy,* 3rd ed. (New York:

Harper & Brothers, 1950). A. Smith, *An Inquiry into the Nature and Causes of the Wealth of Nations,* E. Cannan, ed. (Chicago: Univ. of Chicago Press, 1976). R. Tawney, *Religion and the Rise of Capitalism* (New York: New American Library, 1958). M. Weber, *The Protestant Ethic and the Spirit of Capitalism,* trans. T. Parsons (New York: Charles Scribner's, 1958).

OLIVER F. WILLIAMS, C.S.C.

CARITAS INTERNATIONALIS

Caritas Internationalis, founded in 1950, is a confederation of national Catholic social-welfare and development organizations. There are currently 125 member organizations; these are designated by the respective episcopal conference or hierarchy of the country. Each member organization is autonomous; Caritas organizations often extend to both diocesan and parochial levels. The president, regional vice-presidents, and treasurer are elected by the member organizations every four years at a general assembly, at which time the confederation also formulates a work plan, which includes planned actions in response to the major social problems and issues of the period.

The general secretariat of Caritas Internationalis is located at Palazzo San Calisto, Vatican City. It performs the following functions: (1) animation and conscientization of member organizations and other church leaders with regard to major social problems and needed action; (2) coordination of church-based international disaster relief and development action in various parts of the world with a special view toward safeguarding the initiative and autonomy of the local church; and (3) representation of the confederation at the United Nations and other intergovernmental bodies and in various international social-welfare forums.

See also CHARITY; CHURCH, SOCIAL MISSION OF; DEVELOPMENT; POVERTY; SOLIDARITY.

GERHARD MEIER

CATHOLIC ACTION

See ASSOCIATIONISM; CHURCH, SOCIAL MISSION OF; LAITY, ROLE OF; MODERN CATHOLIC SOCIAL THOUGHT; PIUS XI; QUADRAGESIMO ANNO.

CATHOLIC CHARITIES USA

Catholic Charities USA, a nationwide network of 630 agencies and institutions, is the largest nongovernmental provider of diverse social services in the United States. The national headquarters in Washington, D.C., works for humanitarian laws and policies at the federal government level and serves as an administrative, communications, and activities base for local Catholic Charities throughout the United States.

Organized in 1910 as the National Conference of Catholic Charities, Catholic Charities USA member agencies annually serve nine million individuals and families regardless of creed, race, sex, or age through community-based social programs. Funding for agency programs and services comes from a combination of sources including government grants and contracts for services, program fees, church support, the United Way, and grants and other donations.

History

By the beginning of the 20th century industrialization, urbanization, and immigration caused upheaval and strife in the United States. At the time, more than eight hundred Catholic institutions provided care to children, elderly people, and those who were ill. Most operated through parishes supported by local chapters of Catholic women's charities and the Society of St. Vincent de Paul.

In 1910 church social-service leaders decided to establish a national link among these caregivers and to incorporate social work's expanding scholarly and professional developments in church social-service practices. A convening at The Catholic University of America in Washington, D.C., yielded the National Conference of Catholic Charities to serve as clearinghouse for mutual aid and discussion. The movement soon attracted the membership of many existing charities and worked to educate clergy and lay Catholics regarding their role in social issues.

The first president of Catholic Charities, Bishop Thomas J. Shahan, invoked the Christian obligation toward humanitarian service when he wrote that "the Magna Charta of Catholic charity was written on Mount Olivet, when Jesus Christ said to his disciples: 'For I was hungry, and you gave me to eat; I was thirsty, and you gave me to drink.'" But Shahan stressed the overriding importance of preventive charity, that is, social change to avert the causes of human distress.

Accordingly, the history of the contribution of Catholic Charities USA includes not only direct service to the anguished and impoverished but intervention and advocacy to prevent the need for emergency aid. Examples of such work include Catholic Charities' initiation of and assistance in preparing the Social Security Act of 1935, public-works programs for the unemployed, the National Public Housing Conference, national housing legislation, health insurance for wage earners, federal funding of specialized care for disabled children, and the first White House Conference on Families.

National Office

Catholic Charities USA recognizes that preventive charity offers a twofold benefit: for the individual, who attains a better life, and for society, which gains a more productive participant. This point pervades Catholic Charities USA's advocacy on public policy issues, one of the major functions of its national headquarters.

The office, under the direction of a twenty-member board of trustees, represents Catholic social philosophy to government and private agencies, convenes forums to address human needs and injustices, and directs the Catholic church's response to natural and human-made catastrophes. In addition, it educates the membership in governmental relations, parish social ministry, and upcoming issues in public social policy matters. Among its publications are *Charities USA* and *Social Thought,* an annual survey of the services and structures of its member agencies, and many documents and videos on specific subjects.

Local Offices

In each of the nation's 170 dioceses Catholic Charities agencies work to protect human dignity through services such as adolescent pregnancy and substance-abuse counseling, refugee resettlement, child care, adoption, marriage counseling, day care, respite care, health, nutrition and shelter, and care for frail elderly people and children at risk.

Through its direct service the Catholic Charities USA membership gains insight into the causes and consequences of social and economic problems that affect communities. It uses this information in its advocacy work with federal and state policymakers and in its efforts as "attorney for the poor." Agencies strive to involve parishes and communities in their work and attract more than 150,000 volunteers annually.

See also AID; CHARITY; CHURCH, SOCIAL MISSION OF; HUMAN RIGHTS; PERSON, DIGNITY OF; POOR, PREFERENTIAL OPTION FOR; SOCIAL SECURITY.

Bibliography: D. Gavin, *The National Conference of Catholic Charities: 1910–1960* (Milwaukee: Bruce/Catholic Life, 1962). J. O'Grady, *Catholic Charities in the United States* (Washington: National Conference of Catholic Charities, 1930).

ANNE SIMPSON

CATHOLIC COMMITTEE ON URBAN MINISTRY

The Catholic Committee on Urban Ministry (CCUM) was a national network of priests, sisters, brothers, and laypersons, all of whom were involved in one or another aspect of social and pastoral ministry. CCUM's goal was to give support and encouragement for these members by providing a forum for the exchange of ideas in programming and training.

Several factors played important roles in CCUM's formation. These include (1) the establishment of offices of urban affairs or social action with Catholic diocesan structures during the late 1950s; (2) the development of camaraderie among priests and other religious leaders working the area of social action; (3) community organization activity that was taking place in the larger society, particularly in relation to the civil rights movement and the war on poverty; (4) the existence of other groups within the church that provided support and resources for CCUM; (5) the development of a "tradition" around the role of fostering communication among persons involved in social ministry; (6) the development of a staff structure; and (7) pressures for activity arising from persons and offices in various regions of the country. Each of these factors contributed in some way to the creation and institutionalization of CCUM between 1967 and 1977.

Though informally begun in 1967, the history of CCUM really began almost ten years earlier with the establishment of offices of urban affairs or social action within Catholic diocesan structures, a comparatively new development in the Roman Catholic church. And though new, diocesan urban affairs offices merely extended the strong social action development that had taken place in other areas of Catholic life in previous years. Earlier social action movements included the Catholic Interracial Councils, the "labor priests," the Catholic Worker, the Catholic Rural Life Movement, Catholic Charities, the Christian Family Movement, and the Young Christian Workers and Students, to name a few. All these groups were consonant with the emerging social teaching of the Catholic church, especially found in the encyclicals of popes Leo XIII and Pius XI.

The Chicago archdiocese was the first to establish an Office of Urban Affairs in 1958, with Msgr. John Egan named as director; rapidly, other dioceses followed Chicago's example as the church attempted to relate its work to the fast-moving contemporary social scene.

As various community organizations sprouted up in the 1960s, church offices were deluged with requests for funds from these organizations. In 1967, in an effort to assess the need for funds and monitor their use, church and synagogue leaders met to form an intermediate structure—the Interreligious Foundation for Community Organization (IFCO)—whose responsibility would be the channeling of denominational funds to community organizations and evaluating their efforts. In order to join the Protestant and Jewish representatives on the IFCO board, Monsignor Egan called together sixteen diocesan priests active in urban work in eleven cities in the spring of 1967. This group formed the Catholic Committee on Community Organization (forerunner of CCUM) and sought representation on the IFCO Board. Meeting again in the summer of 1967 in conjunction with the National Catholic Conference for Interracial Justice held in Kansas City, the group changed its name to CCUM in order to reflect more accurately their concerns.

Through the years, CCUM developed a pattern of service for persons engaged in social ministry, reaching a variety of areas of involvement and levels of experience. Activities included an annual national conference held at the University of Notre Dame, a four-week Pastoral Institute for Social Ministry, a newsletter, *Connector,* and regional training programs. All CCUM programs attempted to uphold the conviction that excellent theology must be presented as the foundation for all effective pastoral and social work.

After 1976, several events occurred that altered CCUM's growth and development. These include changing leadership roles and organizational structures within CCUM, the formation of a Protestant Committee on Urban Ministry, an organization with which CCUM interacted heavily, and, finally, the 1976 Call to Action Conference in Detroit, a conference to which CCUM members actively contributed.

CCUM, for a variety of reasons, ceased to exist as an organization in 1980. Today numerous parish, diocesan, regional, and national organizations follow CCUM's organizational leadership in the areas of social and pastoral ministry.

See also CALL TO ACTION CONFERENCE; CHURCH, SOCIAL MISSION OF; COMMUNITY ORGANIZATION.

JOHN J. EGAN
PEGGY ROACH
PHILIP J. MURNION

CATHOLIC RELIEF SERVICES

Catholic Relief Services/United States Catholic Conference (CRS), administered by a board of fifteen bishops selected by the United States Catholic Conference, is the official overseas aid and development agency of the United States Catholic community. Set up in 1943 as War Relief Services/National Catholic Welfare Conference, it was to be, under the direction first of Msgr. Bryan J. McEntegart and then of Msgr. Patrick A. O'Boyle, a compassionate response to the human devastation created by World War II. With the adjustments to peacetime, CRS executive director Bishop Edward E. Swanstrom recalled that true Christian responsibility for one's neighbor is not limited to one's own homeland but literally stretches around the globe. So CRS reshaped its program to provide immediate relief for victims of disasters, for unemployable or disabled persons, and for sponsorship of long-range efforts to help eliminate the causes of hunger, poverty, and disease. Because of its mandate it has always remained nonpartisan and has offered assistance based on need, not creed, race, or nationality. The name change to Catholic Relief Services took place in 1954.

Program Phases

CRS has had operations in more than one hundred countries on all continents. On average it has conducted programs annually in seventy countries. The following brief summary outlines the program activities without detailing the sweeping vision of the planners, the dedicated commitment of the staff, the unprecedented generosity of financial supporters, and the hope experienced by those served.

1943–47: War and Postwar Relief

CRS wartime programs included assistance programs for various groups: (1) German refugees in the United States, Polish refugees in twenty-three countries, Italian and stateless refugees in Spain and Portugal; (2) war-stricken civilian populations in England, Malta, North Africa, China, and Egypt; (3) victims of concentration camps, seamen, prisoners of war, students.

Even before the end of the war, CRS with other voluntary organizations and the U.S. government rushed assistance to the peoples of the war-torn lands of countries being liberated from Axis control. At the end of the war large relief programs were undertaken in former enemy territories such as Austria, Germany, Hungary, and Japan.

1948–65: Services to Refugees

Since millions of persons displaced from their homelands by the war were in need of special help, a Resettlement Division of CRS was established with headquarters in New York. CRS, with other Catholic organizations, undertook advocacy in Congress to allow the admission of refugees to the United States, and the first such legislation, the Displaced Persons Act, was passed in 1948. From 1945 to 1965 CRS assisted with the resettlement of 243, 571 refugees in the United States; and from 1961 to 1965, through its Cuban Refugee Office in Miami, it assisted with the relocation of 53,241 Cuban refugees to other parts of the United States. In addition, many tens of thousands of refugees were processed by CRS overseas offices with the help of church and government agencies in Canada, Australia, and South America.

1966–90: Program Directions

At the close of 1965 the focus of CRS service to refugees became food and medicine programs in Africa, the Middle East, Afghanistan, Indochina, and Central America. A major effort was inaugurated during 1979 and 1980 in the refugee camps along the border between Thailand and Cambodia. On average about 6 percent of the annual budget has been allotted for this work. The CRS Resettlement Divison was phased out and its work turned over to the United States Catholic Conference Division for Migration and Refugees Services. In 1966 CRS overseas resettlement activities were transferred to the International Catholic Migration Commission in Geneva.

With the resolution of many of the postwar overseas relief and reconstruction needs, CRS initiated strategies targeting endemic problems that were reducing the quality of life among the masses of poverty-stricken peoples of the developing countries. Three basic types can be identified: emergency and disaster aid, food and nutrition, and development.

Emergency and disaster aid. CRS gained worldwide recognition for prompt and effective action in responding to the needs of victims of natural and human-made disasters. Disaster and emergency relief consume on average about 16 percent of the annual budget. Examples of such programs were its participation in the mercy airlift into Biafra from 1969 to 1970 during the Nigerian civil war; the Peru earthquake of mid-1970; assistance to Pakistani refugees during the Bangladesh crisis of 1971 and 1972; the earthquakes in Nicaragua in 1972, in Mexico in 1973, and in Italy in 1980; the hurricane in the Caribbean in 1989; monsoons in Bangladesh and the Philippines during the 1980s; and famine, the result of years of drought, which the peoples of the African Sahel have experienced almost without interruption since the 1970s. In these emergencies, CRS supplied hundreds of thousands of tons of food, medicines, housing materials, agricultural and livestock replacements. Outstanding even among these human tragedies of gigantic proportions was the largest food-relief operation in history in Ethiopia from 1984 to 1986, an ecumenical partnership project forged by CRS.

Food and nutrition. One of the principal CRS activities since 1950 has been the food-distribution programs in Africa, Asia, and Latin America. The U.S. government has donated the food and paid the ocean freight on shipments to countries unable to assume these expenses. Governments of the receiving countries permit duty-free entry and in most instances pay the cost of the inland freight and warehousing of the food. Distribution of the foodstuffs takes place in the receiving countries through local counterparts under the supervision of CRS or other agencies.

In addition to the foodstuffs supplied during disasters and emergencies, CRS has sponsored three types of food-distribution programs with a self-help dimension: *Food-for-Work* projects, in which foodstuffs make up all or part of the payment for labor on community betterment projects; *Maternal/Child Health,* in which infants, children under five, and their mothers are reached through an extensive network of health and nutrition clinics where monthly food rations are given to the mothers as their children are examined by trained medical personnel and height/age/weight growth charts are monitored; *School Feedings,* which provide basic nutritional needs to children in participating school distribution programs.

Development. Paul VI's insightful comment that "development is the new name for peace" became the CRS motto. Development has accounted for about 66 percent of the annual budget. Without neglecting emergencies, disasters, and food shortages, CRS aims to eliminate the causes of need with long-range socioeconomic programs. Priority has been given to community development, nutrition education, agricultural cooperatives, credit structures, irrigation and well drilling, road building, and leadership training. To serve these development programs, CRS has maintained regional offices in Africa, the Middle East, Southeast Asia, India, and Central and South America, where staff specialists assist development projects. The emphasis has been on the strengthening of local infrastructures, that is, on institution building. Where a counterpart agency demonstrates the capacity to administer projects, CRS supervises the people of a program country and the organizations that represent them so that they gain control of their own future. Lawrence Pezzullo, CRS executive director, has said: "Our social programs should increasingly seek responses to the problems of the poor that empower them materially to support and care for themselves. . . . [We] need to promote the skills and values that will reclaim the poor into the wider society."

Support for CRS Programs

As stated in the annual reports, support for CRS programs usually totals about $230 million and comes from individuals of many faiths, governments, community organizations, foundations, corporations, and student groups. Basic to its support is an annual collection taken up in over eighteen thousand parishes and a special Lenten program of prayer, fasting, and almsgiving known as Operation Rice Bowl. As a result, CRS has enjoyed one of the lowest overhead costs of any agency providing overseas relief and development.

Conclusion

The fundamental motivating force in all CRS activities has been the gospel of Jesus Christ as it pertains to the alleviation of human suffering, the development of peoples, and the fostering of charity and justice throughout the world. The policies and programs of the agency witness to the Catholic church, whose social teaching the agency has aimed to translate into action. In its brief history CRS has consistently offered its resources, skills, time, and energy to poor people and has focused on economic opportunity as a way of improving their lives. This single-minded "option for the poor" has enabled the United States Catholic community, so graciously endowed with the blessings of this earth, to be in solidarity with its brothers and sisters all over the world. Such a grass-roots approach has been a major attribute of CRS activity. Pope John Paul II has said: "In the case of Catholic Relief Services, the American bishops conceived and constituted a whole ecclesial program on the basis of the principles of interdependence, solidarity and collaboration, to be carried out with keen human sensitivity and the full power of Christian charity. The supreme motivation for solidarity—for the church and all her institutions—will remain the love that God has in Christ for all humanity: 'God so loved the world that he gave his only son.' "

See also ALMSGIVING; CHURCH, SOCIAL MISSION OF; DEVELOPMENT; HUNGER; JUSTICE IN THE WORLD; NATIONAL CONFERENCE OF CATHOLIC BISHOPS, UNITED STATES; POOR, PREFERENTIAL OPTION FOR; POVERTY.

LAWRENCE A. PEZZULLO

CATHOLIC WORKER, THE

The Catholic Worker is a newspaper and a community of people who follow a program of action intended to improve the social order. The newspaper was established in New York City in 1933 by journalist Dorothy Day (1897–1980), a convert to Catholicism who became influenced by the French itinerant Christian intellectual Peter Maurin (1877–1949). Maurin proposed a social and religious program of action designed to improve the social order and create a society in which it would be easier for people to be good. An advocacy publication established to create news and not merely to report news, *The Catholic Worker* exemplifies the first of Maurin's four-point program: (1) distribution of a labor newspaper for workers and the unemployed, (2) the establishment of houses of hospitality for people who are hungry and homeless, (3) round-table discussions for clarification of thought about questions pertaining to the social order, and (4) the establishment of farming communes to employ the unemployed and provide food for the houses of hospitality.

The paper carries articles and editorials about work, poverty, the need for food and employment for people who are destitute, war and conscription, pacifism, civil disobedience, conscientious objection, capital punishment, and related social, ethical, and religious issues. Articles on the philosophy and theology of personalism, the social encyclicals and social mission of the churches, prayer, retreats, and God are also featured, as well as letters of appeal, diary-like entries by Day, essays by Maurin, and announcements of lectures and discussions. Circulation of the paper has varied from 2,500 copies for the first issue (May 1, 1933) to 120,000 in 1940 and nearly 104,000 in 1983 (Roberts, pp. 179–82).

As a social movement the Catholic Worker comprises communities of workers who are committed to practicing the works of mercy: feeding the hungry, clothing and sheltering the homeless, visiting the sick, freeing the prisoner, burying the dead, instructing the ignorant, counseling the doubtful, correcting the sinner, bearing wrongs patiently, forgiving injuries, and praying. In addition to staffing houses of hospitality to assist poor people, workers engage in direct and public actions to arouse the consciences of others and to resist the militarist state and materialist society. These actions have included refusal to cooperate with compulsory air-raid drills, refusal to be conscripted into the armed services, the burning of draft cards, the returning of interest on properties, participation in demonstrations for social justice on behalf of laborers, support for civil-rights causes and for those resisting American foreign policy (for example, Vietnam, Central America), and the advocating of nonpayment of income taxes because these support the purposes of warfare. Many workers have served time in prison for these and similar activities such as protesting at the Nevada nuclear test site. Dorothy Day herself "did time" on numerous occasions, having engaged in a wide variety of civil-disobedience activities, which she hoped would communicate her values and arouse the conscience of others.

An organization without much organization (no constitutions or bylaws, no elected officers, no legal standing such as incorporation, no official membership lists), the Catholic Worker is rooted in the philosophy of anarchism, placing the accent on individual initiative and personal responsibility rather than on institutional structures. The personalism of Emmanuel Mounier, Jacques Maritain, Nicholas Berdyaev, together with the anarchism of Peter Kropotkin and the writings of Fyodor Dostoevsky, Leo Tolstoy, Francis of Assisi, Thérèse of Lisieux, and others, inform the Catholic Worker vision of life. Dorothy Day's anarchist sympathies were evident in her refusal to vote; she regularly criticized government for being implicated in the commercial and political gains of the arms race. Christian communitarianism, cast in the imagery of the mystical body of Christ wherein all are members of one another, establishes a context for understanding the personalist and anarchist emphases. Catholic Worker cofounders Day and Maurin believed that people are responsible for one another and must work for the common good. Voluntary poverty serves as an undergirding Catholic Worker principle, enabling workers to empathize with those they serve, to free themselves from needs and desires, and to share what they do have with others.

Structurally the Catholic Worker has been likened to a wide variety of forms: the army, a Trappist monastery, an Israeli *kibbutzim,* an Indian *ashram,* a Tolstoyan commune, a benevolent dictatorship. Dorothy Day regarded a "revolutionary headquarters" to be the most accurate description (Day, *Loaves and Fishes,* viii), for she and Maurin sought to carry on a personal revolution aimed at conversion of heart and spirit. They envisaged a world in which people would take seriously their responsibilities for improving the social order and creating a society in which it would be easier to be good. Day believed that the good life should not require heroic virtue and that God intended life to be much easier than people have made it.

Catholic Workers who have moved into other spheres of influence include Eugene McCarthy, John Cogley, John Cort, Jim Forest, Michael Harrington, Ammon Hennacy, Gordon Zahn, Edward Marciniak, and Marc Ellis. St. Joseph's, the original house of hospitality in New York, has served as a model for others throughout the United States and in Canada and Australia: Boston, Chicago, Los Angeles, Las Vegas, Milwaukee, Baltimore; Montreal and Toronto, Canada; Victoria and Queensland, Australia. Many of these communities publish their own newspapers. Farming communes include those established at Tivoli, New York; Easton, Pennsylvania; Avon, Ohio; Detroit, Michigan; and Sheep Ranch, California.

The Catholic Worker newspaper and movement exemplify American Catholic radicalism and lay leadership. Dorothy Day often remarked that she did not seek permission to establish either the paper or the houses of hospitality. She simply recognized human needs and met these through personal and nonviolent direct action and urged others to do likewise. Catholic Worker communities (which vary annually in size, number, and location) appropriate, adjust, and transform this vision according to regional needs and resources.

See also CALL TO ACTION CONFERENCE; CHURCH, SOCIAL MISSION OF; COMMON GOOD; MORAL LIFE, CHRISTIAN; PACIFISM; PERSONALISM; POVERTY; SOCIETY.

Bibliography: R. Coles, *A Spectacle unto the World: The Catholic Worker Movement* (New York: Viking, 1973). D. Day, *Loaves and Fishes* (New York: Harper & Row, 1952). D. Day, *The Long Loneliness,* part 3 (New York: Harper & Row, 1963). M. Ellis, *A Year at the Catholic Worker* (New York: Paulist, 1978). P. Maurin, *Easy Essays* (Chicago: Franciscan Herald, 1984). W. Miller, *A Harsh and Dreadful Love: Dorothy Day and the Catholic Worker Movement* (New York: Liveright, 1973). M. Piehl, *Breaking Bread: The Catholic Worker and the Origin of Catholic Radicalism in America* (Philadelphia: Temple Univ. Press, 1982). N. Roberts, *Dorothy Day and the Catholic Worker* (Albany, N.Y.: State Univ. of New York, 1984). J. O'Connor, *The Moral Vision of Dorothy Day: A Feminist Perspective* (New York: Crossroad, 1991).

JUNE O'CONNOR

CENSORSHIP

Civil Restraints

Censorship is the act of prohibiting the use of media that reveals religiously, morally, or socially offensive information. The content is frequently of a sexual nature, but it can also deal with dissident teachings and prejudice of a religious, racist, sexist, political, nationalist, and ageist nature. In the past censorship referred primarily to the print media, but more recently the legal community has expanded censorship norms to include audio and visual materials such as music, paintings, videos, and advertising materials. Types of censorship can be proscriptive or restrictive. Prosciptive censorship forbids the reading of certain kinds of books, while restrictive censorship aims to control the circulation of books to certain classes of people, for example, minors.

Ethical concerns include moral formation of the young, freedom of expression and diversity of views, constitutional right to freedom of speech, and moral guidance from the church. The formation of character in the young is the responsibility of adults, particularly parents and teachers. Censorship aims to impart moral values to the young by restricting access to materials contrary to the values and beliefs of the community. Among the diverse opinions on moral formation, censorship is held by some to be one method of safeguarding the young from a deviant formation. Others maintain that a more successful method is the use of rational persuasion rather than reliance on bribes, threats, and coercion by supervising restricted materials. These methods could serve to stimulate unwanted curiosity in the forbidden subject matter and thereby make it more appealing. A more successful approach would be censorship that makes offensive materials unavailable to minors. Those concerned with freedom of speech and expression hold that limiting access to books in a school should be a last resort, since this would obstruct the basic principle of democracy, something students need to learn through guidance and responsibility. Students should be exposed to a variety of ideas presented with sensitivity to their ability to absorb and criticize ideas. Rather than advocating censorship, most feminists believe that energies should be put into positive programs promoting respect for women and equality of sexes.

In democratic and pluralistic societies, diversity is allowed and respected as an expression of freedom. Many would argue that it is better in a democracy to allow pornography, even if it is degrading and has potentially damaging effects (unless such effects are clearly demonstrated), than to risk the loss of free expression. The moralist would argue that tolerance in a democracy can suggest that all ideas are equal and are a matter of taste, since there is no common philosophical, moral, or religious heritage. However, no one believes all ideas are equal, and studies indicate that pornography will bring negative effects. One must then speak of obligations of citizens to each other rather than rights. Rights tend to be individualistic and to set up spheres of influence where one's rights are sovereign. Censorship would safeguard the common good by protecting people from violence and sexual crimes, would protect personal dignity, and would shield the young from developing detrimental attitudes.

Freedom of speech and expression is a right of citizens in the United States protected under the First Amendment to the Constitution. In upholding this right, the U.S. Supreme Court has often declared that obscenity is not protected by the free-speech clause of the First Amendment, for example, *Roth* v. *United States* (1957). In the *Miller* v. *California* case (1973), Supreme Court Chief Justice Warren Burger stated: "This much has been categorically settled by the court, that obscene material is unprotected by the First Amendment." Consequently, the law of the land is clear, but local communities show reluctance to enforce it because of local pressures from business and political groups. The American Civil Liberties Union argues that censorship is an attempt to impose religious values on society, and since censorship cannot be enforced, it demeans the law.

Ecclesial Censorship

The church guides its members through censorship of publications. With the decree *Ecclesiae pastorum* (1975) the church established a new discipline on censorship of books (*cf. Gaudium et spes 62*) that placed the rules for the imprimatur into Book 3 of the 1983 Code of Canon Law (cann. 822–32). In the revised code a structure is provided for censorship of matter contrary to church teaching on faith and morals. Responsibility of censorship lies mainly with the bishop, who is to compile a list of censors to aid both him and the diocesan curia in judging the content of a proposed text. The bishop can entrust the judging of books to his appointed censor rather than submit it to outside sources. In making a judgment, the censor considers only the teachings of the church concerning faith and morals as proposed by ecclesiastical magisterium. The censor is to submit an opinion in writing: if favorable, permission will be granted to publish the text; if unfavorable, no permission will be granted, and reasons are to be communicated by the ordinary to the author. The imprimatur is necessary only for those books considered most official and whose need for accuracy calls for special screening. These include "whatever pertains to religious or moral disciplines" and "anything of special religious or moral interest." This reduces the books requiring an imprimatur to biblical and liturgical texts, prayer books, catechisms, school textbooks dealing with religious or moral matters, and religious literature sold or given away in churches. All other theological and religious writings are exempted.

Censorship reflects the religious and social values of a body of people through its teaching, legislation, and practice. While censorship is a controverted approach to the formation of moral values and the protection of people, it continues to be a civil and religious practice.

See also EDUCATION, ROLE OF; EVIL, SOCIAL; FREEDOM; HUMAN RIGHTS; PUBLIC AND PRIVATE, RELATIONSHIP OF; RIGHTS AND DUTIES.

ELIZABETH WILLEMS, S.S.N.D.

CENTESIMUS ANNUS

Published on the first of May, 1991, John Paul II's third social encyclical celebrates the centenary of Leo XIII's *Rerum novarum* and, by implication, the developing tradition and corpus of official Catholic social teaching. Continuing a practice reaching back to Pius XI's *Quadragesimo anno,* the pope intends here a twofold purpose: seeking both to honor the rich and vital heritage of an earlier encyclical and to apply the teachings of that document to contemporary issues. Characteristically, this approach of John Paul II and his predecessors has also often included the nuancing, reworking, and enriching of significant elements in earlier documents, thereby contributing to the ongoing development of the church's social doctrine. This text is no different.

Written against the backdrop of Leo XIII's *Rerum novarum, Centesimus annus* turns the light of its attention upon the events that prepared for and culminated in the transformations sweeping Eastern Europe and other parts of the globe in 1989. The encyclical seeks to offer an analysis of the changes in and around this pivotal year, changes that include a double movement: economic and political. On the one hand, there are the obvious and important steps toward the deconstruction of the Soviet bloc and the concomitant shift toward market economies in Eastern Europe. On the other hand, while this economic movement seems at first glance to draw center stage in the encyclical, a parallel shift in the political arena is also being noted and scrutinized. For the recent changes (or efforts to change) in Eastern Europe and elsewhere include as well a move away from totalitarian and/or dictatorial regimes and toward more limited, participatory, and democratic forms of governance.

In response to these economic and political shifts, John Paul II's *Centesimus annus* offers a moral and theological reflection upon the character of the two paradigms being selected (capitalism and democracy) and their failed competitors (socialism and totalitarianism) as well as upon the proper role of the economy and the authority of the state. Consistent with earlier encyclicals, the pope does not see it as the magisterium's task to baptize any particular form of economic or political structure but rather to submit every such system and structure to a critique grounded in the centrality, dignity, and true social character of the human person. This vision he finds in the Christian anthropology informing *Rerum novarum* and the social teaching of the church.

While the direct object of *Centesimus annus'* attention seems focused upon the collapse of "Real Socialism" and numerous totalitarian or dictatorial regimes, making way for the supposed ultimate victory of capitalism and democracy, there is at the same time another theme running the length of the encyclical's fabric and informing its tone and color. This subtext, often rising to the surface, deals with the nature of competition, struggle, and conflict. Repeating a theme found often in earlier encyclicals, *Centesimus annus* seeks to formulate a Christian analysis of and guidelines for a just struggle, pointing out the error, roots, and devastating consequences of unrestrained conflict.

From Rerum Novarum to Centesimus Annus

Since *Quadragesimo anno* every papal social encyclical has been explicitly conscious of its place in the ongoing tradition of official Catholic social teaching. Usually published on the anniversary of an earlier encyclical, each found in the tradition that preceded it the authority, fundamental operating principles, and vital font of its fresh analysis. In this way each successive encyclical operates from and is characterized by a specific grasp of the tradition from which it springs.

In *Centesimus annus,* John Paul II's reflections upon *Rerum novarum* (and through it, on Catholic social teaching) reveal a strong sense of the centrality, continuity (linear), development, and dynamic character of the church's social magisterium. At the same time, while the magisterial voice of official Catholic social teaching indicates the authority and importance of its vision and principles, its concrete application and fulfillment are seen to depend upon the critical judgment and expertise of all the baptized and upon a willingness to enter into dialogue and collaboration with the larger human community.

Like the social encyclicals that preceded it, *Centesimus annus* claims for the magisterium a pastoral authority and a responsibility to address social concerns. This important duty pertains not only to in-house conversations but also to the church's obligation to speak the social message of the gospel to the larger world. In this document John Paul II reiterates his conviction regarding the centrality of this social magisterium, arguing that "in effect, to teach and spread her social doctrine pertains to the Church's evangelizing mission and is an essential part of the Christian message" (CA 5). Not simply a valid contribution to socioeconomic analysis, Catholic social teaching is part of the evangelizing task of the church and belongs to the field of theology and particularly of moral theology (see CA 54; *Sollicitudo rei socialis* 41). Indeed, the tenor of this and other encyclicals makes it clear that persuasive and effective social teaching witnessing to the dignity of the human person is a sign of the church's religious and transcendent mission on behalf of humankind.

As in *Laborem exercens* (6), this encyclical's introduction turns to Matthew's metaphor of the scribe who brings out both the new and the old as an apt description of the continuity of Catholic social teaching. In *Centesimus annus* the pope intends a rereading of *Rerum novarum* that confirms "the permanent value of such teaching" and "builds upon the foundation laid by our fathers in the faith" (CA 3). While the pontiff clearly intends more than a mere application of *Rerum novarum* to a contemporary setting, aiming specifically at an enrichment of and a building upon the accumulated tradition of the social magisterium, there is nonetheless a strong sense that he understands this development as a more linear sort of growth from the seminal roots of Leo XIII.

Within *Centesimus annus* the pope offers numerous indications of this continuity and linear development. The enduring value of Leo's analysis and principles is revealed in the abiding validity of his judgment regarding (1) the injustice behind the workers' problem; (2) the errors of socialism (noticed by Leo XIII even before it took the form of a state); (3) the grounds for and demands of a just wage; and (4) the various rights of workers. Furthermore, John Paul II finds in the writings of Leo XIII the origins or springboard for much that characterizes contemporary Catholic social teaching, including (1) a balanced grasp of the natural right to private property and its relation to the universal destination of all material goods; (2) a developed understanding of and support for the principle of religious freedom (as found in Vatican II's *Dignitatis humanae,* the United Nations' Universal Declaration of Human Rights, and other statements by John Paul II); (3) the right of labor to organize and struggle for the rights of workers vis-à-vis employers; (4) the recognition of a constitutional government balancing the legislative, executive, and judicial branches; (5) the key notions of solidarity and preferential option for the poor; and (6) the dignity of the human person as the key to Catholic social teaching.

And yet there is more discontinuity between *Rerum novarum* and *Centesimus annus* than the pope has adverted to. His own position on the purpose of unions, the justification of strikes, and the nationalization of property as well as his understanding of the priority of the universal destination of goods over the limited natural right of private ownership reflects more of a shift and nuancing than a simple unpacking of seminal notions found in Leo XIII. Even if *Rerum novarum* mentioned or discussed many of the same (or similar) concepts found in contemporary Catholic social teaching, the present emphases or interpretations of the limited role of the state, religious liberty, human rights, and democracies, to name a few, indicate some significant shifts in the social magisterium. The sense of continuity and theory of coherence espoused by the pope in this encyclical falls short of a critical historical realism.

Within *Centesimus annus* John Paul II argues to the dynamic character of Catholic social teaching, aiming as it does to move beyond words to the powerful and transformative witness of action. He notes that "as far as the Church is concerned, the social message of the Gospel must not be considered a theory, but above all else a basis and a motivation for action." As a result of this, "today more than ever, the Church is aware that her social message will gain credibility more immediately from the *witness of actions* than as a result of its internal logic and consistency" (CA 57). Thus the social magisterium calls Christians to a charity that demands the promotion of justice through more than the sharing of surplus goods. Instead, as he had indicated in *Sollicitudo rei socialis* (31), the church and Christians must make sacrifices from their very necessities, altering lifestyles and transforming sinful social structures on the national and international level into systems that serve the needs of the poor.

Finally, given its dynamic character, it is clear that the activity of the laity constitutes a distinct and essential part of the tradition of Catholic social teaching, having a task that "does not fall *per se* within the Magisterium's specific domain" (CA 3). Through the exercise of their critical judgment and expertise, the community of the baptized, as individuals, members of associations and organizations, and responsible citizens participating in the implementation of social reform, contribute to the application and realization of this vital body of Catholic teaching (43, 56). Furthermore, the actualization of Catholic social principles depends upon the ability of the church to enter into and learn from a fruitful dialogue with those trained in the modern and social sciences and upon its willingness to collaborate actively with other Christians and believers, and indeed with all men and women of good will committed to working for social justice and human dignity (60).

Capitalism and the Fall of "Real Socialism"

Certainly the most controversial and interesting question to surface within and in response to *Centesimus annus* has been whether this encyclical represents an endorsement of capitalism and thereby a significant shift in Catholic social analysis. "Can it perhaps be said that, after the failure of Communism, capitalism is the victorious social system, and that capitalism should be the goal of countries now making efforts to rebuild their economy and society? Is this the model which ought to be proposed to countries of the Third World which are searching for the path to true economic and civil progress?" (42).

"The answer," as the pope goes on to note, "is obviously complex," and any attempt to adequately understand the encyclical's response to this question requires an examination of the context of the argument, the document, and the issue. First, it is necessary to review the pope's analysis of the character, errors, and collapse of "Real Socialism," including his assessment of the causes and implications of this failure. Second, the reflections of *Centesimus annus* need to be located within the developing tradition of Catholic social teaching, particularly John Paul II's two previous social encyclicals, *Laborem exercens* and *Sollicitudo rei socialis*. For while the pope clearly intends "to contribute to the development of Christian social doctrine" in this encyclical, he bases his current analysis on the work he did in these earlier documents (CA 22, 30). Third, any judgment regarding the replacement for "Real Socialism" will need to sift through capitalism's various forms, examining its strengths, limits, and historical weaknesses from the critical perspective of Catholic social teaching.

"Real Socialism" and Its Demise

The error of socialism. John Paul II cites the perspicacity of Leo XIII's *Rerum novarum* "in recognizing the evil of a solution which, by appearing to reverse the positions of the poor and the rich, was in reality detrimental to the very people it meant to help" (CA 12). According to *Centesimus annus* the events of 1989 and 1990 confirmed both the earlier pope's judgment of the malice of the socialist solution and his prognosis of its ultimate failure.

In his own analysis, John Paul II understands "the fundamental error of socialism" as being "anthropological in nature." At its heart socialism considers the person merely as an unthinking cog in the larger machinery of the society. Failing to grasp the moral freedom of the individual or the autonomous integrity of various intermediate groups, the socialist state "reduces the person to a series of social relationships," eliminating the "subjectivity" of the individual and society and "hindering the progress towards the building up of an authentic human community" (CA 13).

This inadequate anthropology is rooted ultimately in atheism, which, in denying God's existence, "deprives the person of his foundation," and leads to a "social order without reference to the person's dignity and responsibility." As a result, freedom is cut loose from its moorings to the full, moral, and transcendent truth of humanity, leading to a denial of the need for the divine, a failure to respect the rights of the other, and an increasingly inordinate worship of the self. Not surprisingly, this atheism is also the root of socialism's class struggle, an often violent conflict unrestrained by any concern for the moral order or rights of others.

The reasons for its failure. Echoing the predictions of Leo XIII, John Paul II argues that the collapse of "Real Socialism" in Eastern Europe was due primarily to this system's violation of the rights of those very persons it claimed to protect: the workers. Beginning with the solidarity movement in Poland, the difficult and oppressive experience of workers throughout the Eastern bloc led to the rejection of a system that had violated their rights "to private initiative, to ownership of property and to freedom in the economic sector" (CA 24). *Centesimus annus* goes on to note that these violations in turn produced an inefficient economic system, further contributing to the crisis that precipitated "Real Socialism's" downfall. Finally, the atheism undergirding socialism failed to uproot the need for God from the human heart. Instead, the spiritual void created by Marxism often stimulated a resurgence of religious belief and a dissatisfaction with the inadequacy of the socialist worldview.

The implications of its failure. Centesimus annus sees in the collapse of "Real Socialism" major transformations having significant implications not only for Eastern Europe but also for the Western powers and the nations of the Third World. While the largely peaceful fashion in which these changes occurred has implications to be addressed later, the fact of the deconstruction of this system has created opportunities and challenges for the altered world it leaves behind.

Itself a response to the excesses and injustices of liberalism, the growth of socialism from an ideology into a state and then a bloc altered the face of the globe, provoking a variety of reactions on the national and international level. Individual nations responded to the threat of communist revolutions with efforts to construct (1) just democratic societies with humane and morally restrained market economies, (2) rigid "national security" states whose dictatorial control fought Marxist infiltration in ways that undercut the dignity and rights of its citizenry, and (3) affluent consumerist societies outproducing materialist socialism while ignoring the fuller development of person and culture. On the international level the competition with "Real Socialism" and the "logic of the power blocs" polarized the globe along two axes, creating a cold war between East and West and a chasm of inequality and dependence between North and South. Third World countries suffered greatly from this hostile competition between the blocs; they were drawn into the increasing global militarization, disenfranchised through the diversion of planetary resources, and forced to choose between inadequate models of development. As a result, numerous countries tried with mixed success to forge alternative economic models incorporating a variety of borrowed and indigenous elements.

In the vacuum left by the failure of "Real Socialism" the logic of many of the above responses has evaporated, leaving sometimes disoriented nations with new opportunities and dangers. Faced with a postwar economic recovery delayed by forty-five years, Eastern Europe confronts the challenge of constructing an authentic model of human and economic development while avoiding a relapse into "old forms of totalitarianism and authoritarianism" or a resurgence of regional conflicts and ethnic violence. While much of the work must be done by these nations themselves, their Western neighbors will need to help. Urged on by a concern for justice and a commitment to the common good of Europe, such nations must collaborate in the establishment of international structures providing arbitration and negotiated settlements for regional conflicts as well as assistance in achieving long-delayed economic stability and development.

At the same time, this commitment to assisting in the development of Eastern Europe "must not lead to a slackening of efforts to sustain and assist the countries of the Third World, which often suffer even more serious conditions of poverty and want" (CA 28). *Centesimus annus* argues that resources for this broader developmental task may be found through "redefining the priorities and hierarchies of values on the basis of which economic and political choices are made." Specifically, disarming the "huge military machines constructed for the conflict between East and West" and taking steps to control the international arms trade, particularly in the Third World, would release abundant resources for supporting global economic recovery and development.

According to *Centesimus annus,* this failure of "Real Socialism" is "proving to be important also for the countries of the Third World, which are searching for their own path to development." While "this crisis of Marxism has not rid the world of the situations of injustice and oppression which Marxism itself exploited," John Paul II argues that recent events further illustrate the futility of any compromise between Marxism and Christianity, pointing instead to the need for a fresh and authentic theory and praxis of liberation, one grounded in the social doctrine and Christian anthropology of the church (26).

Indeed, according to *Centesimus annus,* "the first consequence" of the events taking place in Eastern and Central Europe in 1989 "was an encounter in some countries between the Church and the workers' movement, which came about as a result of an ethical and explicitly Christian reaction against a widespread situation of injustice" (26). John Paul II sees in the recent collapse of "Real Socialism" the deliverance of the worker movement from its Marxist tutelage and a rapprochement with Catholicism and the church's social doctrine. In light of this shift and the church's own commitment to offer searching Third World nations "an authentic theology of integral human liberation," the original question returns: will the church recommend capitalism "as the path to true economic and civil progress"?

Capitalism and Catholic Social Teaching: A Sustained Critique

Situating the analysis of Centesimus annus. Given John Paul II's emphasis upon the continuity and seminal development of Catholic social teaching, it seems evident that *Centesimus annus* needs to be seen as part of the sustained critical dialogue that this tradition has had with the various forms of an evolving capitalism. Of particular interest here is the way in which this encyclical's analysis relates to and is filled out by the pope's two previous social documents, *Laborem exercens* and *Sollicitudo rei socialis.*

The text of *Centesimus annus* reflects John Paul II's intent to distinguish among the various forms that capitalism has taken over the past century or more. Referring at different points to "primitive" or "new" capitalism, "liberalism," and finally to "business economy," "market economy," or "free economy," the pope's language traces both the historical evolution of this economic system and the church's own critical conversation with it, a conversation quick to point out errors and excesses at each step in its development.

In *Centesimus annus* (4) John Paul II echoes the judgment of *Laborem exercens* (30) that primitive capitalism fundamentally and erroneously reversed the priority of labor over capital, rendering the worker a mere commodity. This violence to the human person was at the heart of the injustice of the workers' problem critiqued by Leo XIII's *Rerum novarum* and was wrongly supported by a liberalism grounded in an incomplete grasp of human freedom. Indeed, John Paul II sees this same "freedom" as the root of both liberalism and socialism. He further criticizes this "unbridled capitalism" for its denial of the universal destination of material goods, its laissez faire attitude regarding the role of the state in economic matters, and its violation of the rights of workers to a just wage capable of supporting their families, noting that such excesses and positions continue to produce devastating effects in some contemporary Western societies (SRS 42; CA 6–10).

The movement of capitalism into the international scene is critiqued in Paul VI's *Populorum progressio* and later in John Paul II's own *Sollicitudo rei socialis.* Echoing and deepening his predecessor's analysis, the pope challenges some of the basic assumptions of the Western model of development, arguing that it is in need of a "radical correction" (SRS 21). Too often the capitalist approach has ignored the broader issues of distributive justice and moral development as well as the subjectivity of the person or society (SRS 17, 33). In a similar vein, *Centesimus annus* argues for a more profound grasp of human and social development in the economic recovery of Eastern Europe and criticizes the contemporary disenfranchisement of Third World nations from the global free-market economy, cut off as they are from the new "capital" of information and technology (27–28, 33).

As capitalism's competition with socialism evolved into a struggle between superpowers, John XXIII's *Pacem in terris* raised serious questions about the international arms race and the trade it sprouted, a practice threatening global peace and harming the poorer nations. John Paul II's *Sollicitudo rei socialis* saw this "logic of the blocs" as the primary threat to global development and peace and an exercise of imperialism by both sides, a position he does not retreat from in *Centesimus annus* in spite of accusations of "moral equivalency."

Finally, the present encyclical continues the pope's sustained criticism of consumerist tendencies in modern capitalist societies. *Centesimus annus* argues that such tendencies, flowing from an inadequate anthropology focused on "human-havings" instead of "human-beings," reveal themselves in a "demand for quality" that produces and consumes goods and services that meet the lowest and most superficial levels of human needs. Failing to attend to either the higher and spiritual goods of the individual or the common good of the community, consumerism cheapens the person, harms the society, and ultimately poisons the planet (36–37).

Capitalism's strengths and weaknesses. At the present critical juncture, however, *Centesimus annus* does find itself examining the capitalist system with a certain freshness. This is due in part to the collapse of "Real Socialism" in the Eastern bloc, the concomitant presumption by many that this leaves capitalism as the natural victor, and John Paul II's recognition of the evolving form of capitalist economies.

Distinguishing his subject from the "unbridled" or "primitive" capitalism of the past as well as from a "radical capitalistic ideology" that might sweep into the vacuum left by Marxism's crisis, the pope finds a number of strengths in what he would prefer to call a "business economy" (42). Such an economy, grounded in human freedom, recognizes the legitimate right of persons to private ownership while encouraging them to utilize their resources (both the subjective and objective elements of work) in a collaborative and creative initiative that responds with foresight and accuracy to the needs of others, thus increasing the wealth of the society. "Important virtues are involved in this process, such as diligence, industriousness, prudence in undertaking reasonable risks, reliability and fidelity in interpersonal relationships, as well as courage in carrying out decisions which are difficult and painful but necessary" (32). Furthermore, "it would appear that, on the level of individual nations and international relations, the free market is the most efficient instrument for utilizing resources and effectively responding to needs" (34).

At the same time John Paul II offers a number of caveats. The serious historical excesses and errors of various forms of capitalism are rooted in the deeper failure to put the economy and economic freedom in the service of the greater good and truth of the human person. The malice of "unbridled" or "radical" capitalism is found in its inability to attend to deeper social and human values and in the unwillingness of persons and societies to make it do so. The elevation of an economic tool to an ideology that seeks to adequately explain and govern the totality of human experience has led to countless abuses and injustices (39).

Further, according to *Centesimus annus,* many of the concrete wrongs of capitalist societies—including the violation of workers' rights, twofold alienation of consumer and laborer, idolatry of profitability, harms to the environment, and the increasing relative impoverishment of the Third World—stem from the failure to recognize the limits of a market economy. The efficiency and profitability of this paradigm notwithstanding, it lacks the wherewithal to notice, attend to, or give priority to deeper human and moral values (34–36).

Therefore, the sort of "business economy" John Paul II envisions and affirms is a system wherein economic freedom is "circumscribed within a strong judicial framework which places it at the service of human freedom in its totality, and which sees it as a particular aspect of that freedom, the core of which is ethical and religious" (42). Applying the principles of subsidiarity and solidarity, the pope affirms the necessary and active roles of the state, society, and various groupings in setting the moral boundaries of a just economy: supporting judicial restraint, state intervention, and committed struggle in response to injustice (15–16, 40, 48). He notes that a just society will protect not only the rights to freedom of religion, private ownership, and economic initiative but also the rights to "a sufficient wage for the support of the family, social insurance for old age and unemployment, and adequate protection for the conditions of employment" (34). Finally, a moral international economy will provide for the "subjectivity" of the person and society, ensuring to both the right to real participation and economic initiative in a just and open market.

Not a "third way." Ultimately, *Centesimus annus* is not intended either as a baptism of capitalism as "the only model of economic organization" or as an unveiling of a "third way" proposed by Catholic social teaching. Reiterating *Laborem exercens* (15), the pope argues that it is not the role of the church to offer economic models, deferring here to "those who responsibly confront concrete problems in all their social, economic, political and cultural aspects, as these interact with each other" (CA 43). Instead, the social doctrine of the church is offered "as an indispensable and ideal orientation," a critique grounded in an authentic Christian anthropology flowing from the gospel and applied unflinchingly to every system and structure. While many have found in the tone of *Centesimus annus* a more positive and nuanced presentation of capitalism, including a discussion of its various positive aspects and an affirmation, even recommendation, of one sort of capitalism as the path of economic development and recovery; the hopefulness of recent events should not overshadow the document's discussion of the serious harms and dangers in this system. Refusing to collapse into the dualistic thinking of the "logic of the blocs" even after the failure of "Real Socialism," John Paul II's encyclical continues its critical conversation with capitalism; attending to both its strengths and its weaknesses while offering a criteria and perspective challenging modern societies to construct ever more just economic systems.

The State and Democracy

The other major characteristic of the changes of 1989 has been political, a move from closed totalitarian regimes to those characterized by a more limited role for the authority of the state as well as a higher degree of participation and freedom on the part of all citizens, that is, constitutional democracies. Further, this shift impacts upon the geopolitical situation so recently dominated by the "logic of the blocs" and the cold war. Both of these need to be attended to. In chapter 5, "State and Culture," *Centesimus annus* reflects upon this shift, offering an analysis of both totalitarian and democratic regimes and ultimately of the nature, responsibilities, and rights of the state in its relation to the citizen, to other groups, and to the international order.

Centesimus annus traces a historical process culminating in certain key 19th-century political changes that generated "a *new conception of society and of the State,* and consequently *of authority itself.* A traditional society was passing away and another was beginning to be formed—one which brought the hope of new freedoms but also the threat of new forms of injustice and servitude" (4). This promise was to be found in the increased levels of responsible freedom and participation available in democratic societies. The danger came from an unconnected concept of freedom that would in turn undercut the rights of free moral persons and associations, rendering both mere parts of a totalitarian state. Again, at root here for John Paul II is an adequate understanding of human freedom, one grounded in the deeper truth of the person's transcendence and social character and supportive of a true "subjectivity" of the individual and society.

Centesimus annus offers an extended critique of the basic error and harmful consequences of a totalitarian theory of the state. Failing to recognize the transcendent and objective truth regarding persons and society, the totalitarian regime takes unto itself the uncontested right and unlimited authority to define reality in theory and praxis. Claiming a special insight into the deeper truth of the social order, such regimes are unfettered by the limits of an objective morality, the rights of persons and societies, or the "rule of law" (44). As a result, persons and associations are subsumed into a homogenous body politic where rights and dissent cease to exist. In fact, the arrogance of such systems is usually revealed in their willingness to engage in deception, violence, and the abuse of rights in order to maintain this "perfect" political society.

In opposition to this, John Paul II argues for a theory of the state where the exercise of authority is limited by an adherence to the objective, abiding, and transcendent truth about the human person, as well as a recognition of the imperfection of this or any other political system. In the concrete such a limit would include, among other things, a constitutional government following the "rule of law" and protecting the civil and economic rights of persons. Such a state, constructed with adequate internal checks and balances, would carry out its limited aims and responsibilities in harmony with the efforts of "other spheres of responsibility" and associations, thus preserving both the rights of all and the common good. This is particularly evident in the encyclical's discussion of the real but limited role of the state in providing for justice in the economic sector. Seeking a via media between the laissez faire approach of radical capitalism and the excesses he finds in the "Social Assistance State," the pope relies upon the principles of solidarity and subsidiarity in an attempt to sharpen the parameters of the government's responsibility to support, restrain, or intervene in the economic processes of a society (10, 15, 48). Finally, *Centesimus annus* contextualizes the rights and duties of the state by adverting to the interdependence of all nations and the need to construct a moral world order that recognizes and respects that relationality, working for the common good in ways that respect the "subjectivity" and rights of every nation.

In its preference for a democratic form of governance *Centesimus annus* continues a shift in Catholic social teaching begun by Pius XII but solidified in John XXIII's *Pacem in terris* (PT 67–76). "The Church values the democratic system inasmuch as it ensures the participation of citizens in making political choices, guarantees to the governed the possibility both of electing and holding accountable those who govern them, and of replacing them through peaceful means when appropriate" (CA 46). Indeed, given the tradition's increasing focus upon the dignity and rights of the human person, particularly the right to participate as a subject within society, it would be difficult to imagine Catholic social teaching not offering such support for the democratic state and for the "legitimate autonomy of the democratic order" (CA 47).

At the same time *Centesimus annus* offers some distinctions and cautions regarding its understanding of the theory and praxis of democracy. According to the church's social doctrine the ultimate authority or rightness of any democratic decision does not flow from the mere will of the majority, nor should a democracy be grounded in "agnosticism or skeptical relativism." Instead, "authentic democracy is possible only in a State ruled by law, and on the basis of a correct conception of the human person" (46). John Paul II's criticism here is that when democratic states lose sight of this "correct conception" the majority sometimes ignores or overrides the legitimate and inviolable rights of the minority, those very human rights upon which the democratic model is based. This is true in their relation to their own citizens as well as in their response to other nation-states in the international realm.

Class Struggle and Nonviolence

One of the most interesting chords running through *Centesimus annus* concerns the pope's analysis of conflict. Scattered throughout his discussion of economic and political transformations, John Paul II sketches out a Christian reflection on the roots, character, and consequences of unrestrained conflict. His aim here is both to distinguish such violence from a justifiable and sometimes necessary struggle for justice and to offer a gospel solution to this problem.

In his discussion of *Rerum novarum* John Paul II takes exception to the notion that Leo XIII's encyclical rejected "every form of social conflict"; the earlier pontiff recognizing as he did the inevitability of conflicts between the interests of different groups and the occasional necessity of the church to take a decisive stand in such disagreements (CA 14). Having himself articulated in *Laborem exercens* "the positive role of conflict when it takes the form of a 'struggle for justice,'" John Paul II argues that Leo XIII's opposition was to the unrestrained and violent notion of class conflict recommended by the socialists of his day.

The class struggle that Leo XIII condemned in *Rerum novarum* is described by John Paul II as "a conflict which set man against man, almost as if they were 'wolves' . . . a conflict all the more harsh and inhumane because it knew no rule or regulation" (CA 5). It is this unrestrained character that both popes oppose, for such conflict is not mitigated by the rights of others or the rule of law or reason. Instead, such unrestrained violence, which intends the complete destruction of the adversary without any attention to moral limits, denies the very dignity of the self, the neighbor, and the covenantal relationship with God.

From this theory blossom forth the malice of total warfare as well as the arrogance of militarism, imperialism, totalitarianism, and all kinds of terrorism. For class conflict becomes an instrument that, for the sake of the cause, "justifies" every sort of immoral means and all types of violations of ethical behavior and human rights. The atheistic vision from which it sprouts prevents such a theory from recognizing the transcendent dignity of the human person or the sanctity of the individual's conscience (CA 14). This is, according to *Centesimus annus,* in direct opposition to the Christian truth, which must always respect the deeper freedom of the person (46).

Repeating his analysis from *Laborem exercens,* John Paul II admits that there will be adversarial relationships, that groups will need to come together to defend their interests vis-à-vis other parties, and even that there are justifications for struggle against economic and political systems (CA 23, 35). However, for the Christian (or indeed any just person) the response to such crises and injustices cannot be unrestrained conflict. Instead there must be a two-pronged approach addressing the "real and serious grievances" that lead to such violence while relying upon negotiation, arbitration, and compromise to arrive at just and peaceful resolutions of such crises.

As a concrete example John Paul II points to the nonviolent character of the revolutionary changes in the Eastern bloc, something all the more amazing when one considers that common wisdom of both the East and West had believed such political and economic changes could only be brought about through another major war (23). Relying instead upon the "weapons of truth and justice . . . the protests which led to the collapse of Marxism tenaciously insisted on trying every avenue of negotiation, dialogue, and witness to the truth, appealing to the conscience of the adversary and seeking to reawaken in him a sense of shared human dignity." The just struggle does not gloss over wrongs but confronts sinful structures and systems in a spirit of solidarity with the marginalized and with respect for the truth and the adversary.

A similar moral commitment and restraint will be necessary to deal with the impending threat of racial, ethnic, and national violence surfacing now in the disintegrating Eastern bloc (27). It will also be needed to confront the threats and rumors of war around the globe, violence born of political and economic injustices and fueled by militarization and the arms trade. But if this moral stance of solidarity and nonviolence is to bear fruit it must be matched with a twofold institutional transformation on the international level. Those economic and political structures of sin that oppress and alienate peoples and nations must be replaced by viable and effective systems protecting the full spectrum of personal and national rights, particularly the rights to development and full participation in a new world order. Second, nations must cooperate in the construction of international structures and channels of arbitration and negotiation, offering a real alternative and counterweight to the use of force or war. For John Paul II the continued reliance upon war as a means for resolving conflicts becomes progressively more senseless given the increasing interdependence and militarization of the globe (51–52).

Conclusion

A first reading of this document may tend to focus exclusively on the encyclical's treatment of capitalism, finding here a groundbreaking baptism of that economic system. A deeper study locates this document in the larger context and conversations of social encyclicals, discovering John Paul II's intent to celebrate the centenary of *Rerum novarum* with a creative "re-reading" of Leo XIII's encyclical in light of current events and a century's development of Catholic social doctrine. In a critical reflection upon capitalism, democracy, and conflict, John Paul II offers a probing analysis of what he believes lies at the root of much that ails modern society: an atheistic vision that sees human freedom as severed from the larger truths of the human condition. The response to this moral and social malaise is to be found in a Catholic social doctrine grounded in an authentic Christian anthropology, one that takes seriously the transcendent and social character of the person. And so the social teaching of the church is not only a prophetic stand against injustice but expresses a theological vision and is an essential part of its evangelical mission.

See also CAPITALISM; COMMUNISM; LABOREM EXERCENS; LEO XIII; MARXISM; MODERN CATHOLIC SOCIAL THOUGHT; RERUM NOVARUM; SOLLICITUDO REI SOCIALIS.

Bibliography: J. Coleman, ed., *One Hundred Years of Catholic Social Thought: Celebration and Challenge* (Maryknoll, N.Y.: Orbis, 1991). Congregation for Catholic Education, *Guidelines for the Study of the Church's Social Doctrine in the Formation of Priests* (Rome: Vatican Polyglot Press, 1988). D. Dorr, *The Social Justice Agenda: Justice, Ecology, Power, and the Church* (Maryknoll, N.Y.: Orbis, 1991). D. Dorr, *Option for the Poor* (Maryknoll, N.Y.: Orbis, 1983). J. Gremillion, ed., *The Gospel of Peace and Justice: Catholic Social Teaching Since Pope John* (Maryknoll, N.Y.: Orbis, 1976). J. Houck and O. Williams, eds., *Co-Creation and Capitalism: John Paul II's* Laborem Exercens (Washington: University Press of America, 1983). F. Kammer, *Doing Faithjustice: An Introduction to Catholic Social Thought* (Mahwah, N.J.: Paulist, 1991). M. Schuck, *That They Be One: The Social Teachings of the Papal Encyclicals, 1740–1989* (Washington: Georgetown Univ. Press, 1991). M. Schultheis, E. DeBerri, and P. Henriot, *Catholic Social Teaching: Our Best Kept Secret* (Maryknoll, N.Y.: Orbis, 1988).

PATRICK T. McCORMICK

CHARITY

In contemporary usage, the word "charity" is ambivalently used. For example, it refers to society's condescension toward those who cannot afford to help themselves; it refers to money Christians are asked to provide; it refers to good deeds done for those whom we do not like. In what follows we consider charity as a specific form of Christian love.

The NT is filled with references to the familial and friendship relations we have with God and with one another. We are adopted daughters and sons of the God who is the *Abba* of Jesus Christ, and we are sisters and brothers of one another. Charity is this set of relations. Aquinas calls it an "intimate living with." God makes a difference in our lives, and we make a difference to God. It is a mutual love in which we participate in varying ways and degrees. While preserving our distinct natures and identities, we come to know and will and love as God does. In so doing we are transformed, made a "new creation."

The basic structure of charity is this: we are loved by God; we accept this love; we love God in response; we form a community with God; and we cooperate with God's love, which is directed to God, to ourselves, and to the rest of creation. In this endlessly evolving relation is found the inner unity of the two great love commandments. Because we share a love relation with God, we cooperate with the work that God's Spirit wants to achieve in and through us. This cooperation occurs within the church, but it extends beyond, especially to those who are poor and marginalized. In brief, charity is the life of grace.

See also ALMSGIVING; CATHOLIC CHARITIES USA; COMMUNITY; FAMILY; GRACE; LOVE; MUTUALITY.

EDWARD COLLINS VACEK, S.J.

CHILDREN, RIGHTS OF

Catholic social teaching has not used rights language, in particular the term "rights of children," until very recently, for a number of reasons. Rights language emerged from liberal democracy, which the church combated during the 19th and into the 20th century. Even John XXIII, Vatican Council II, and Paul VI, in their introduction of rights language, were careful to define and link rights and responsibilities and to recognize the limits of proclamations and laws about rights in improving human welfare (*Mater et magistra* 82–84; *Pacem in terris* 8–38; *Gaudium et spes* 29–31; *Populorum progressio* 22–24; *Octogesima adveniens* 24, 35). Their caution emerged from long-standing papal suspicion that liberal democratic capitalism, in proclaiming universal equality and basic human rights, introduced a mechanistic and potentially conflictual model of society in which the former moral obligations of the rich and powerful to paternalistically care for the weak and poor were removed, without any augmentation of the ability of these groups to protect their own interests (OA 23). This suspicion of rights language can be assumed to be especially strong in the case of children's rights due to the greater powerlessness of children to care for themselves.

In addition, social teaching tended to treat children indirectly, through a focus on families. After the ascent to power of anticlerical democratic movements in Europe in the mid-19th century, when the church could no longer maintain its claim to control marriage and education, the church turned to the defense of the rights of the family: to sacramental marriage and to education of their choice. Thus the defense of the rights of the family became institutionalized in social teaching, which continues in *Familiaris consortio* (46). Children's interests were understood to be protected and promoted through defense of the rights of the family.

A third reason for the lack of developed treatment of the rights of children is a result of the model of the family assumed in social teaching. Through the papacy of John XXIII, social teaching insisted on the family as a hierarchically ordered social unit under the headship of the husband with children subordinate to parents, a model in which the rights of husband over wife and children, and wife over children, were exercised with a love that assumed the welfare of the subordinate members (Pius XI, *Casti Connubii,* pp. 543–50; Pius XII, *The Christian Wife,* p. 68; John XXIII, *Ad Petri cathedram,* pp. 509–10). Where such love and authority worked for the welfare of children, asserting the rights of children was not only unnecessary but potentially conflicted with the right order maintained by the authority of fathers/parents.

As social teaching shifted to examine more and more social problems in ever greater depth, especially within the broad topic of Third World development, the plight of children drew more and more attention. Yet even when John Paul II referred to the rights of children in *Familiaris consortio* (26), he never named any specific rights of children but instead spoke of "concern for the child," "developing profound esteem for their personal dignity," and the obligation of Christians to render "acceptance, love, esteem, many-sided and united material, emotional, educational and spiritual concern for every child that comes into this world."

Despite the lack of developed treatment of the rights of children in social teaching, it is possible to compose a sketch from a variety of documents of the rights of children recognized in social teaching:

1. *Right of the unborn to life.* First and most consistently argued for is the right of the unborn to life. This right to protection against direct attack is understood to be without exception, taking precedence over all competing claims (*Humanae vitae* 14; FC 30).

2. *Right to full-time care by mothers.* Children are understood, especially when young, to have a right to the full-time care by mothers, upon whom their education and personal development depend (GS 52; John Paul II, *E'giunto al termine,* p. 182). This right of children is the basis for the demand that mothers of young children not work and that adequate economic and social support be provided to mothers in the home (*Laborem exercens* 19; FC 23). The presence of fathers in the home is regarded as in the best interests of the child (GS 52; FC 25), but it is not regarded as necessary, and there is no attempt in social teaching to restructure men's work or society in general in order to involve men more fully in child care.

3. *Right to adequate material support and protection.* In social teaching the just wage is consistently presented (Pius XII,

La solennità, p. 202; PT 20; GS 67; LE 19) as a wage that enables a parent to support spouse and children adequately with food, clothing, shelter, education, and basic medical care. Nevertheless, social teaching has never demanded the family wage (proportional to the size of one's family) for fear this would lead to discrimination against parents of large families, who would be more expensive to hire. Children without parents are understood to have rights to compensatory care (John Paul II, *Charter of Rights of the Family* 4f.) by Christian families (FC 41). All children have a right to legal and institutional protection from harmful drugs, pornography, alcoholism, and the like (FC 46).

4. *Right to education.* Children have a right to education, which prepares them for responsible adulthood. This is understood in two senses, both in terms of secular education, which includes literacy and job skills (Paul VI, *Development in Africa* 20, 38; FC 46), and in terms of education by parents in living the gospel, in sex education, and in basic values (FC 36–39).

5. *Right to culture.* Children have a right to be raised in their indigenous culture. Their education should not be merely technical but should prepare them to appreciate and participate in the cultural life of their societies, to experience continuity with their heritage (GS 61, 31; PP 68; Paul VI, *Development in Africa* 37–38; FC 46).

All of these rights of children are presented as morally binding on the state, though it is unclear how states with insufficient resources to meet all their obligations are to rank the rights of children among their other priorities. Do children come before or after the rights of people who are elderly, sick or handicapped, poor, and refugees? It is curious that the church has focused more on rights of children that are binding on the state or on society as a whole than on rights that are binding on parents, who are the most closely connected with and have primary responsibility for children.

Among the rights of children, the church seems to place priority on the right of the unborn to life, inserting the defense of this particular right into many documents. Yet the right of the unborn to life is only absolute against direct attempts on fetal life. Conditions such as pesticide spraying, long work hours for pregnant women, and inadequate food, shelter, and prenatal care, all of which produce spontaneous abortions and high infant mortality, are not covered by the ban on abortion. Aside from direct attack by the mother or her assistants, the rights of fetal life occupy the same social status as the rights of all other groups: the right to compete against other asserted rights for the available resources of any given society. Yet within the family, fetal freedom from direct abortion takes priority over all other rights of children as well as those of the parents.

Today the greatest obstacle to the further development of social teaching around the rights of children is the romanticism that masks the refusal of the magisterium to analyze its model of the family. That model assumes that the marital bond not only produces and nurtures children but is oriented to offspring as a primary purpose; that men and women were created to be complementary, with inherent traits that fit men to be breadwinners and heads of families and women to be supportive spouses with a primary vocation to motherhood and child nurture (*Casti connubii*, pp. 543–50; Pius XII, *The Christian Wife* 67). While Paul VI hinted at a need to examine this traditional model, he never developed this thought (PP 36; OA 13).

A phenomenological approach to family produces a great deal more ambiguity. There are, particularly in developed countries, fewer couples who marry in order to have children (even if they do have them), fewer research-supported arguments for sexual complementarity being inherent rather than a product of socialization, and a growing rejection of the division of men's and women's roles into breadwinner and child nurturer/home maintenance, not to mention increasing rejection of male headship in the family. Perhaps even more challenging to the traditional model of family is the evidence that adherence to the traditional model can put the welfare of children at risk.

There is rapidly accumulating evidence that romanticization of the hierarchically ordered family masks a great deal of mental and physical abuse of children. In the United States alone 20 to 25 percent of girls and 10 to 11 percent of boys experience sexual abuse; over 90 percent of sexual abuse of children occurs in the home with men as primary offenders. Around 15 to 25 percent of families experience domestic battering; over 90 percent of the offenders are husbands/fathers. Among the hundreds of thousands of child runaways, sexual abuse for girls and physical abuse for boys are given as the chief reasons for flight. Thousands of children are yearly removed from their parents by child-protective agencies for neglect and abuse (1985 report by Margaret Heckler, U.S. Secretary of Health and Health Services). Focus in social teaching on the romantic image of families, as centered on the loving authority of parents and the need for trusting obedience from children, works not only to discourage any critical attention to the needs of children in potentially abusive homes but denies children support for recognizing abusive behavior as wrong and resisting it.

Social teaching cannot cure or prevent every abuse of children merely by addressing it or by expanding the rights it claims for children. Parents who abandon or sell their children of five or six under the pressure of culture or extreme poverty are not likely to refrain merely because the church explicitly condemns such practices. But this is no excuse for the church's failure to address the worst abuses of children. Child sexual abuse, for example, is not noticeably related to the pressures of poverty: in the United States the typical child sexual abuser is middle class, married, and with more than moderate religious involvement.

Women are increasingly abandoning the role of exclusive full-time child-care provider in the home. The reasons for this vary from the sheer economic necessity of single mothers or of families in which the primary salary is insufficient to provide food, shelter, and clothing, through parental desire to provide "extras" such as a college education or travel for children, to the desire of women to develop careers and personal fulfillment outside the home. Social teaching has failed to deal adequately with this trend; it has defended the right of women to equality in employment and responsible involvement in cultural life (GS 60) while simultaneously teaching that women who have children, which is every woman's vocation (John Paul II, *E'giunto al termine,* p. 182), are absolutely necessary to their young children on a full-time basis. Social teaching only touches on the conflict between the needs of children and the desires/needs of women with regard to those women who work for sheer economic necessity, as when John Paul II insists that societies find ways to support families so that mothers of the young are not compelled to work. Absent is any treatment of women who work for reasons other than economic necessity and any recognition that child rearing could, much less should, be a joint task of both parents.

Interestingly enough, the conjunction of the breadwinner and headship roles in the husband/father within the magisterium's model of family is never criticized in the light of broader social teaching. Whether intended or not, the conjunction of these two roles is experienced by children as evidence that authority is based on economic power—a conclusion the church has been at pains to denounce elsewhere in social teaching. Both common family dynamics and laws regarding children reinforce the father's (or in the absence of fathers, the mother's) right to announce that "so long as you live in my home, and I support you, you do what I say." The absence of any teaching that elaborates the meaning of the dignity of children or the limits of parental authority allows such interpretations of parental authority to pass from generation to generation in the same way that authority of industrialists and estate owners over their workers was formerly justified on the grounds of the economic dependency of workers. By contrast with church teaching on the rights of these other weak groups to share in decision making (OA 47), social teaching has not granted children rights to participate in any family decisions affecting their welfare.

If the worst abuses of children have been ignored by social teaching due to romanticization of the family, the more general issues of children's dignity and justice have not been raised due to a failure to recognize children as capable of participating in responsible decision making. This is interesting in the light of the treatment of children within the sacramental framework of the church. Children are normally regarded as having reached the age of reason by age seven, of being capable of recognizing, committing, and being responsible for serious sin and are therefore initiated into the sacrament of reconciliation. Confirmation is conferred after age twelve and initiates the child into the church as an adult. Yet despite these sacramental recognitions of responsibility, there is no affirmation in social teaching of children's right to participate in family decision making.

It is interesting that for as often as social teaching invokes the household codes found in the NT (e.g., Eph 5:21–6:9; Col 3:18–4:1), including the command that children obey parents, we virtually never find explanations of the reciprocal command: "Fathers, do not provoke your children, lest they become discouraged" (Col 3:21) and "Fathers, do not provoke your children to anger, but bring them up in the discipline and instruction of the Lord" (Eph 6:4). The most basic shift in all of Catholic social teaching in the 20th century has been away from paternalistic understandings of justice and charity toward the recognition that the dignity of all persons demands participation in decision making. Social justice is best created not through merely attempting to persuade the powerful to take into consideration the needs of the powerless but through structural change that empowers the weak to recognize their own legitimate needs and to interact with others in order to meet them. This shift to participatory models of society began with treatment of industrial workers and has been expanded to cover ethnic and racial groups, agricultural workers, and the poor nations of the world. The time has come to recognize that if the family is, as social teaching insists, the basic unit of society, then it, too, must be approached not with rose-colored glasses through which parents seem always wise, caring, and protective of children's best interests but as human and therefore sometimes selfish, neglectful and even abusive, and often blind to the needs and aspirations of children. To empower children to have a voice in the family—a voice that must be nurtured to grow stronger, clearer, and more responsible with years—can only contribute to the welfare of the entire family unit. To the extent that children come to have a voice in the affairs of a family, parents will be inclined to take the perspective of children more seriously and to give more serious attention to them. Children who are allowed to participate in decision making in the family are better prepared for adulthood and for responsible parenthood themselves and do not experience the abrupt shift from dependency to independence that so disturbs many young people today.

See also ABORTION, SOCIAL IMPLICATIONS OF; CHRISTIAN FAMILY MOVEMENT; FAMILY; HUMAN RIGHTS; JUST WAGE; LABOREM EXERCENS; OCTOGESIMA ADVENIENS; POPULORUM PROGRESSIO; REASON, ROLE OF.

Bibliography: John XXIII, *Ad petri cathedram,* AAS 51 (1959); *The Pope Speaks* 5:4. *Mater et magistra,* AAS 53 (1961); *The Pope Speaks* 7:4. *Pacem in terris,* AAS 55 (1963); *The Pope Speaks* 9:1.

John Paul II, *Considerando che (Charter of Rights of the Family); The Pope Speaks* 29:1. *E'giunto al termine, The Pope Speaks* 24:2. *Familiaris consortio,* AAS 73 (1981); *Origins* 11:28, 29. *Laborem exercens,* AAS 73 (1981); *Origins* 11:15.

Paul VI, *Development in Africa,* AAS 59 (1967); *The Pope Speaks* 13:1. *Humanae vitae,* AAS 60 (1968); *The Pope Speaks* 13:4. *Populorum progressio,* AAS 59 (1967); *The Pope Speaks* 12:2. *Octagesima adveniens,* AAS 63 (1971); *The Pope Speaks* 16:2.

Pius XI, *Casti connubii,* AAS 22 (1930); *Papal Teachings: Matrimony,* trans. M. Byrnes (Boston: Daughters of St. Paul, 1963).

Pius XII, *The Christian Wife. Discorsi e Radiomessaggi de Su Santita Pio XII* 3:191; *Papal Teachings: Woman in the Modern World* (Boston: Daughters of St. Paul, 1959). *La solennità,* AAS 33 (1941).

Vatican II, *Gaudium et spes: Pastoral Constitution on the Church in the Modern World,* AAS 58 (1966); *The Gospel of Peace and Justice,* ed., J. Gremillion (Maryknoll, N.Y.: Orbis, 1976).

CHRISTINE E. GUDORF

CHRISTIAN DEMOCRACY

Christian Democracy is an influential political tendency in Europe and Latin America. Encouraged initially by Pope Leo XIII in the late 19th century and later embraced by lay Catholic philosophers and political activists, it offered a progressive alternative to the socioeconomic and political conservatism with which Roman Catholicism had been identified since the Middle Ages. It sought to foster lay Catholic participation in social and political life and to incorporate elements of democracy, liberalism, and reform without endorsing the individualistic and philosophically skeptical bases with which these values had been associated historically.

The values and institutions of liberal democracy first emerged in Protestant and, more specifically, Puritan cultures, in which reformers demanded the separation of church and state. Although they were not secularists themselves, the reformers and their values were viewed with alarm by Catholic authorities (Egon-Lonne). They were seen as part of a larger secularization movement that threatened Catholic values, legitimate church prerogatives, and the socioeconomic and political elites with whom the church was traditionally aligned.

Accordingly, when lay Catholics became active in social and civic organizations during the 1930s and 1940s they were closely monitored by anxious church authorities. Tensions arose and persisted over the proper degree of lay involvement in politics, collaboration with non-Catholic and leftist groups, the need and appropriate means for defending church interests from anticlerical attack, lay independence from episcopal authority generally, democratization of internal church structures, and other issues. (Leo XIII had initially embraced and promoted the notion of Christian Democracy in *Rerum novarum* [1891] but then narrowly redefined and practically abandoned it in *Graves de communi re* [1901].)

Following World War II, specifically Christian Democratic parties emerged, initially in Europe and subsequently in Latin America. They did so on the initiative of lay Catholics who had been affiliated with one or another Catholic social organization and were generally more reformist, more comfortable with pluralism and liberal democracy, and more determined to build bridges to working- and middle-class groups than most Catholic bishops at the time.

Over the years, their relations with the institutional church have varied in accord with episcopal attitudes, the extent of a country's secularization, and the resulting cultural and political influence of church authorities. The tone and content of party positions have also varied from country to country. Although all parties embrace the institutions and practices of liberal democracy, all advocate an enlightened or reformed capitalism that provides for basic needs and calls for some worker participation in company decision making, and most seek the support of business interests, middle-class elements, and workers.

In Europe the most successful Christian Democratic parties have been those in countries (West Germany, Italy, and the Netherlands) in which traditional right-wing forces had been discredited and where there was thus room for an "enlightened" alternative to the secular Left. In the process, however, these Christian Democratic parties have been pushed to the right and center right of the political spectrum and have defended and sustained a prosperous, if less than ideally just, status quo.

In Latin America the conditions of underdevelopment, the poor historical record of capitalist development strategies, and the enduring strength of traditional socioeconomic and political elites combined to push Christian Democracy in an initially progressive direction. In those countries where Christian Democrats have been in power (Chile, Venezuela, El Salvador, and Ecuador), however, tensions later developed between reformist and accommodationist wings and were generally resolved in the latter's favor.

In Europe, the center-right orientation of most Christian Democratic parties and governments has been opposed by some of their intellectuals and trade unionists. However, these groups have remained part of minority left wings within such parties, while in Latin America similar elements have abandoned party ranks to form separate Catholic leftist parties (as in Chile) or to join erstwhile leftist adversaries (as in El Salvador and Venezuela) in a single, united leftist party.

The tensions and divisions experienced by most Christian Democratic parties during the 1960s, 1970s, and early 1980s were partly a result of their failure to develop a common sociological perspective. This prevented them from analyzing social reality and developments in a consistent manner and left their common social Christian principles susceptible to varied interpretation and application. In countries (Germany and Italy) where sustained economic growth and prosperity provided additional margin for error, such divisions caused little or no political damage. In most other instances (Chile, El Salvador, and Peru), however, economic decline further polarized social and political forces, forced parties to choose between Right and Left, and led to the alienation of important constituencies.

During the late 1980s, Christian Democratic movements and parties were political and electoral beneficiaries of the breakdown of Marxist economies and political systems in Eastern Europe. In Latin America, Christian Democracy has enjoyed a renaissance of sorts as well, thanks to a new willingness on the part of Marxists and other leftists to form alliances with "democratic" centrists and rightists as an alternative to continued military rule, with the breakdown of some of the experiments in neoliberal economic development favored by private banks and international financial institutions.

Christian Democratic parties coordinate with one another internationally through loosely structured mechanisms such as the International Union of Christian Democratic Parties, the (Latin) American Christian Democratic Organization, and a Christian Democratic caucus within the European Parliament.

See also DEMOCRACY; ECONOMIC ORDER; MARITAIN, JACQUES; MODERN CATHOLIC SOCIAL THOUGHT; NELL-BREUNING, OSWALD VON; PERSONALISM.

Bibliography: K. Egon-Lonne, "The Origins of Christian Democratic Parties in Germany, Italy, and France, 1943–1945," in G. Baum and J. Coleman, eds., *The Church and Christian Democracy* (Edinburgh, T. & T. Clark, 1987).

MICHAEL FLEET

CHRISTIAN FAMILY MOVEMENT

The Christian Family Movement (CFM) had its beginnings in middle America and combined Catholic Action and the Family Life movement. The seeds for CFM were sown in several places in the 1940s.

One of these seedbeds was the first men's Catholic Action group in Chicago. In February 1943 six professional men, all married, and a priest began meeting weekly. They struggled to find a direction for their meetings and eventually adopted the Jocist methodology of Belgium canon Joseph Cardijn, in which each individual observes and gathers facts on a particular problem, the problem is judged in light of the Gospels, and an action is taken. They eventually applied their methodology to the field of husband-wife relationships. This achieved the distinctive characteristic that was to mark CFM: the social-inquiry technique applied to family life.

Several of these men's wives later organized Catholic Action groups for women, and by the late 1940s some men's and women's groups merged to form couples' groups. This was a new development, as church groups had traditionally been separated by gender. Almost simultaneously, Catholic Action groups for married couples sprang up in other parts of the country. These first groups developed in New York, South Bend, Indiana, and among married students at Notre Dame University.

In August of 1948 Pat and Patty Crowley, leaders in the Chicago groups, met Burnie and Helene Bauer of South Bend, where the Bauers had formed young married couples' groups. They applied the observe-judge-act inquiry technique to the common problems of family life, with the assistance of their group chaplain, Fr. Louis Putz, C.S.C., who had worked first-hand with the Jocist movement in France prior to World War II.

The national Christian Family Movement was born in June 1949, when fifty-nine delegates representing movements in eleven cities met at Childerly, Illinois, to lay the foundation. Pat and Patty Crowley were elected as secretary couple and served as CFM national leaders for twenty-five years. A national office was established and remained in the Chicago area until 1981, when it was moved to Ames, Iowa. The movement spread to more than forty countries in the 1950s and 1960s. In 1967, the International Confederation of Christian Family Movements was established.

The Chicago groups published the first basic inquiry program, *For Happier Families,* in 1949, which became the magnet that drew Catholic family-action groups across the country together. This program helped couples to see the Gospels as a call to action. In the early 1950s CFM began publication of an annual inquiry to follow the basic inquiry program. These inquiries focused on issues of significance to families. In recent years annual programs have dealt with the U.S. Catholic bishops' peace and economic pastorals, the domestic church, and the spiritual and corporal works of mercy.

CFM programming provides a format and a methodology for participants to apply the gospel to their everyday life. In so doing, CFM explores four key relationships: husband-wife, parent-child, family-church, and family-community. The movement also provides benefits to families, parishes, and communities. Because CFM members are formed through their actions, CFM helps to strengthen marriages, enrich families, deepen faith, develop leaders, raise social consciousness, and build community.

CFM is a unique network of small faith-sharing groups. Its membership now includes single-parent families, two-parent families, blended families, interfaith families, Catholic families, clergy, and religious.

Mission Statement

To improve the quality of family life by reaching out: (1) providing a framework within which families can support and affirm one another; (2) promoting Christian attitudes, values, and actions in individuals as they interact within their family, with friends, neighbors, and co-workers, and with institutions affecting the family.

Goals

(1) to develop a consciousness (both a family and a social consciousness) based on Christian principles and examples; (2) to develop responsible, concerned, and happy families that are part of a supportive and affirming network of families within every community who will individually and collectively reach out to others in need; (3) to offer opportunities for families to grow in their personal relationships with one another as well as their friends, neighbors, and co-workers; (4) to develop a caring society that not only recognizes but actively supports family life; (5) to initiate and encourage research that impacts on the actual needs of families; (6) to continue to foster the international spirit of the Christian Family Movement.

See also BASE COMMUNITIES; FAMILY; JUSTICE IN THE WORLD; MARRIAGE; VALUES.

Bibliography: *ACT,* vols. 1–3 (Chicago: The Christian Family Movement, 1946–48). P. Goulding, M. Goulding, et al., *This Is CFM: Christians in the World* (Chicago: The Christian Family Movement, 1965). J. Kotre, *Simple Gifts* (New York: Andrews & McMeel, 1987). R. Lucey, *Roots and Wings* (San Jose, Calif.: Resource Publications, 1987).

KAY AITCHISON

CHURCH, SOCIAL MISSION OF

The term "mission" is a broad term. Dictionaries usually give several meanings. Mission is an assignment one is sent to carry out, or it is a diplomatic office in a foreign country, or it is inner conviction of a goal to be pursued. The term "mission of the church" has the same diversity. Mission can refer to a specific task of the church; then mission is like an assignment that one carries out. In its plural, "missions," the term refers to missionary work in foreign countries. In addition, "mission of the church" also refers to the goal or purpose of the church itself. The term "social mission" of the church contains a similar diversity and, therefore, raises questions: Does "social mission of the church" refer to a social task or to one of many tasks that the church performs? Is the social mission of the church somehow a task in which the church moves into areas that are foreign to the church's religious mission? Or does social mission of the church mean that the social task is the very goal and purpose of the church itself?

Today, the meaning of the church's social mission has become increasingly debated. Some argue that the social mission is not simply one of the church's many tasks but is at the center of the church's identity. Others argue that the church has become too involved in social issues so that it has neglected its primary religious task. These debates, revolving around the mission of the church, concern the purpose and function of the church. They involve the interrelation between the religious and social mission and how the church fulfills its mission in contemporary society.

To clarify the meaning of the church's social mission, this article will first examine the reasons why the mission of the church in general and the social mission in particular have become such central issues. Second, it will examine how changes in the understanding of the social mission of the church relate to changes in the understanding of the church's mission in general, through a survey of diverse theories of the mission of the church itself. Third, a sketch of diverse conceptions of the social mission of the church will show that in contemporary theological reflection the social mission of the church has become more directly related to the church's identity and purpose. Fourth, recent church statements in the post–Vatican II period dealing with the meaning of the church's social mission reflect these significant shifts within contemporary theology. Fifth, the final section of this article will sketch elements of a theology of the church's social mission.

Centrality of the Social Mission

The Christian community has from its very beginning been involved in social issues. It has cared for the poor, sick, and needy. Its criticisms of social and political injustices extend from the critique of the Roman Empire tax policies to the critique of capitalistic exploitation of poor countries. Nevertheless, theological discussion of the church's social mission as such is a relatively late phenomenon. The church's mission itself and the social mission of the church have only recently become an explicit and controversial topic within theology. A complex host of factors intersecting with one another have led to this development.

Religious Reality of the Church

During the last decades theological reflection on the church has increasingly shifted its focus from the institutional structures to the religious nature and purpose of the church. In previous centuries the controversies with Protestantism led to an apologetic approach to the church. Roman Catholic theologians defended those institutional structures and offices that Protestant theologians denied. A sea change took place in the 20th century. The Second Vatican Council placed the theological and pastoral treatment of the church at the forefront. It accentuated the religious nature of the church by employing images of the church as the people of God, the body of Christ, and the sacrament of salvation.

This shift from an institutional to a theological view of the church has significant consequences for understanding the social mission of the church. When the church is seen in its religious nature and understood with sacramental categories rather than simply in its institutional structure as a hierarchical organization, then the church's social mission acquires a new meaning. The social mission is no longer one of the specific tasks that the institution of the church performs. Instead, the social mission becomes a symbol and sacrament of the religious nature of the church as such. It is the church in action, expressing and symbolizing itself in practice. The social mission of the church, as an integral and essential action of the church, constitutes the very being of the church.

Changing Nature of Society

The increased awareness of the changing nature of society is the second significant factor that has accentuated the social mission of the church. Modernity had led not only to the political revolutions within society and the emergence of liberal democratic thought but also to an accelerated rate of change within societies. Consequently, modernity has transformed consciousness about the nature of society and an increasing awareness of the contingency of societies and historicity of its structures. The structures of society, social status, and occupational roles are no longer divinely ordered. Instead societies are now seen as historically conditioned, subject to change, and open to transformation.

This awareness of the mutability of societal structures makes the social mission of the church much more central and meaningful. It is not just individuals or leaders who can be changed but societies as well. Therefore the church exercises its social mission in a way that can be critical and transformative of the structures of society. The church is not limited to the conversion of individuals but seeks also to transform societies. The church not only condemns individual sin and personal moral failures; it also denounces unjust structures and exploitive practices. Its social mission concerns not only the dispositions of individuals but also the ideologies of nations.

Increased Awareness of Social Injustice

A third factor is the growing awareness of social injustice within the world today. Poverty and hunger have existed throughout history. Pestilences and famines have continually devastated humankind. Yet what is distinctive today is the increased gap between the wealthy and the poor nations. While some nations and people have access to health care, food, and shelter, other nations and people do not. During the 20th century this disparity has not lessened but has increased. In many cases nations and persons that are well off have to no small extent benefited from the exploitation of the cheap labor of those who are poor. Moreover, much of the hunger and disease could be lessened if structural changes were made such as increased sharing of wealth, less military expenditures, restructuring of international debt, more equitable forms of taxation. This awareness of the political and social causes of hunger, poverty, and disease makes clear that the church's social mission is much more than engaging in works of mercy but involves a mission to social, political, and economic life.

Relation Between Theory and Practice

A fourth factor contributing to the increased centrality of the social mission of the church is a new understanding of the relation between theory and practice. Previously theory related to practice as knowledge to application. One first acquired knowledge, then one applied this knowledge to practice. Practice was the skill or technique of putting knowledge into practice. Ministry, practical theology, and the mission of the church were considered merely matters of skill or application. The new understanding of the theory-practice relation gives to practice a new status and higher priority. Practice is no longer merely the aftermath of theory so that practice reflexively flows from theory. Instead practice is a source of experience that affects theory and influences how we interpret the world and our tradition. Practice is, therefore, not simply the acquired skill in applying knowledge to concrete practice. Instead practice is a way of life, a source of knowledge by which we come to new insights. In such a view of praxis, the praxis of the church and its social mission is not the application of knowledge already acquired but is a source of knowledge and insight.

Social Ethics to Ecclesiology

The development of Roman Catholic social teaching during the 19th century took place in the wake of modern political revolutions and the resulting separation of church and state. Political sovereignty became increasingly secularized and society became more pluralistic. To deal with this situation, Roman Catholicism sought to explicate its social teaching primarily on the basis of natural law. A social teaching based on a natural-law ethic could deal with pluralism and secularism because, as it was argued, natural law was in principle open to rational discussion with persons of diverse beliefs. To the extent that Roman Catholic theologians grounded social teaching in natural law, they did not seek so much to explicate a distinctively Christian gospel message or a specific doctrinal vision but sought, instead, to explicate a social and political ethics for the public realm.

With the focus in Vatican II on the church as a sacrament of the salvation of all, a transformation took place not just in ecclesiology but also within social ethics. The question arose about the distinctively Christian contribution to social and political life. This accent on the distinctively Christian contribution led in turn to a further concentration on the social mission of the church as heralding the distinctive contribution of the Christian gospel and practice to social and political reality.

The Change of Modern Social Welfare

A fifth factor is the development of social welfare within modern societies. Social welfare has become increasingly taken over by the state. Many institutions of care that were previously run almost exclusively by the churches, for example, hospitals, orphanages, and schools, are now run by the state. To the extent that social welfare, care of the sick, and education become matters of civic and political management, questions emerge about the specific role of the churches. What becomes of the social mission of the church in these areas? Is there something distinctive about a Catholic hospital in contrast with a public hospital or a nonreligious private hospital? Is there a relation between the churches and the social legislation of the states? All these questions focus attention on the meaning of the social mission of the church.

Voices of the Third World

Finally, new voices, especially the voices of those in the Third World countries, have raised criticisms of the church's foreign missionary activity as well as of its previous practice and conception of the social mission. These criticisms have led to a new reflection on the social mission of the church, for these criticisms have emphasized that missionary activity often took place in cooperation with, if not in support of, European colonialism, imperialism, and paternalism toward the missionized people and cultures. This colonialism exploited the people, took advantage of their natural riches, capitalized on their labor, and undermined their native religious beliefs. It subordinated their native culture to European culture. Many in the Third World argue that the Christian churches are not guiltless but are implicated in the very injustices of colonialization.

These criticisms have led many to reflect critically on the nature of the church's mission and missionary activity. Missiologists began to reflect on how to conceive of the mission of the church in a way that avoided colonial imperialism and paternalism. Moreover, since the global disparity between rich and poor nations is due in part to the very imperialism of colonialism, the church needs to understand its social mission not only regionally but also globally.

Mission of the Church in Modern Theology

The notion of the social mission of the church should be understood within the context of the understanding of the church and the church's mission. Such an obvious statement has to deal with the fact that explicit reflection on the nature of the church, as such, is a relatively late development. Within the history of Christianity and Christian theology, the topic of the church emerged as a separate treatise only in the post-Reformation times. Neither Peter Lombard's *Sentences* nor Thomas Aquinas' *Summa* contains such a separate treatise. The theological center was God as the creator and goal of human life. Christ and the sacraments were studied as part of God's economy of salvation, but not the church as such. Only in the post-Reformation period was ecclesiology developed as a separate treatise. This treatise concentrated on the controversial issues with Protestantism, especially the hierarchical structure of the church. It is within this context that explicit reflection on the mission of the church begins. Only in the last hundred years has the discipline of missiology become a distinct discipline and specific theories of the mission of the church emerged.

Mission as Conversion

The first institute in missiology was established at the University of Münster in 1914. Its director, Joseph Schmidlin, developed a theory of mission that came to be called the conversion theory, which was associated with the Münster Institute. Schmidlin argued that the mission of the church primarily is to convert individuals to Roman Catholicism (*Catholic Mission Theory,* Techny, Ill.: Missions Press, 1931). The church's mission was primarily to spread faith through conversion. Since the institutional Roman Catholic church was the objective institution of salvation, the church's task was to proclaim the gospel for the sake of an inner conversion that would become an external conversion to the church and lead to baptism. This view of the church's mission considered the church's social mission primarily as a preparation or a foundation for conversion. The social mission prepared a material basis as well as an intellectual and ethical horizon for the reception of the Christian faith. This approach was Eurocentric insofar as it viewed this basis as European in culture and civilization.

Mission as Spread of Institution

Pierre Charles at the University of Louvain developed a contrasting position (*Les dossiers de l'action missionaire: Manuel de missiologie,* Louvain and Brussels: Desclee, 1939). Charles argued that conversion does not provide an adequate foundation for mission. For as long as the church does not co-exist with humankind, one has then still not fulfilled the missionary mandate that Jesus gave his disciples. The church's mission has the primary purpose of spreading the church and of establishing the visible church in all countries where it is not yet present. The formal object of missionary activity is therefore to establish a local and native church. This establishment of local churches was called the "planting of churches," and so this approach was called the "plantation theory" of the Louvain school.

Conversion was not the mission of the church, for then the church would only be a means to conversion. Instead, the spread of the church was the church's goal. Since this identified the church with the kingdom of God, it considered the planting of local churches in foreign soil to be the planting of the seeds of the kingdom of God. The church was in its missionary activity fulfilling its very mandate to increase the growth of God's kingdom. The planting of churches in other countries was so that they would grow into independent native churches. Therefore, this approach did not advocate the conversion to European civilization as a presupposition of conversion as the conversion mission theory did.

Mission as Evangelization

A third approach to mission underscores that evangelization is the primary purpose of the church's mission. The church does not so much preach itself as it proclaims God's Word and God's reign. In this respect the notion of mission as evangelization rather than as the planting of churches rests on a different understanding of the kingdom of God. Whereas the plantation theory tended to identify the Roman Catholic church with the kingdom of God, the evangelization theory centers on the kingdom of God as transcending the church. The emphasis on evangelization de-centers the mission of the church away from the spread of the church itself and turns mission toward the spread of the gospel message, which is greater than the church and provides the goal of its mission. This conception of mission as evangelization became widespread within Roman Catholic missiology since the 1950s. Its popularity was in part due to the influence of neo-orthodox Protestant theology, especially Karl Barth's theology of the Word, upon Roman Catholic and Protestant missiology.

However, a certain lack of preciseness still remains when the mission of the church is equated with evangelization. Usually, one defines evangelization as the proclamation and explanation of the gospel through preaching, catechesis, and homiletics. Such a definition leaves open the content of evangelization, for it leaves undecided whether evangelization essentially includes a social mission or whether the social mission is only a precondition or a consequence of evangelization. The same questions about the meaning of the church's mission arise regarding the meaning of evangelization.

Mission as Inner Mission

A significant discussion of mission took place in France in the 1950s and 1960s. Several theologians and sociologists observed that in many respects France was no longer a Christian country. In a newly renamed journal, *Parole et Mission,* J. Dunas criticized previous conceptions of mission as too juridical, institutional, and too narrowly focused on the conversion of souls or the spread of the church. Moreover, he argued, the traditional missiological distinction between inner and outer mission was inadequate, for it viewed the mission of the church primarily in terms of "foreign missions." Sociologically and empirically, mission should not relate to the geographical limits of Christianity whereby Christians from predominantly Christian countries missionize non-Christians in non-Christian countries. Instead the church's mission needs to focus on France and other traditionally Catholic countries. Dunas and others associated with the journal, known as the "Paris school," emphasized this mission to the so-called Christian countries that were increasingly "de-Christianized." The church therefore needs to engage in an "inner mission" in view of the widespread disbelief within these countries.

This emphasis on inner mission called for a "sociological implantation" of Christian faith—one that would entail a fermentative Christianization of the social environment within traditionally Christian countries. By attacking the dichotomy between a mission oriented to the "outside," that is, to foreign countries, and one to the inside, this approach did not assume that the church had one specific missionary task to deal with unbelievers and another task to deal with Christians. This approach, thereby, reconceptualized mission: mission was not simply one of the tasks of the church; mission was the activity of the church itself, an activity embracing the church's very own attempt to socialize its culture with freedom for Christian and non-Christian. This rethinking of the notion of mission came to have enormous influence in the following decades and upon contemporary theology.

Mission as the Continuation of Salvation History

The more one refrained from limiting the term "mission" to the foreign missions, the more one refocused the concept of mission and explicitly identified it with the purpose of the church in general. This trend was further advanced by the theological interpretation of the church as a sacrament within the context of Christology and salvation history. For now the mission of the church was more than to convert souls or to plant local churches; it was to continue to make present in history God's salvation in Jesus Christ. The church continued the function of Christ. Jesus is a "real symbol" of God's presence in the world insofar as Jesus is not only a sign of God's presence but is, as a sacrament of God, a real presence of God in the world. As a sacrament, the church is likewise both a sign and a presence. Therefore the church through its nature as a sign and a symbol continues the function of Christ to express and to be a symbol of God's presence in the world.

This sacramental view of Christ as a real symbol of God's presence in the world and of the church as the continuation of this sacramental/symbolic presence of God has a profound effect upon the understanding of the mission of the church. It inseparably links the mission and being of the church. The mission of the church is not simply one task of the church but is its symbolic/sacramental function: to symbolize and make present God's reality and grace within the world. The mission of the church is the reality of the church itself in very sacramental and symbolic nature. This view of the church and its mission, most explicitly and comprehensively developed by Karl Rahner, has had enormous influence on contemporary theology. Karl Rahner has himself applied this conception of the mission of the church to the understanding of practical theology as the church in action (*Handbuch der Pastoraltheologie: Praktische Theologie der Kirche in ihrer Gegenwart,* vol. 2, Freiburg: Herder, 1966). Josef Amstutz, following Rahner's conception, has further developed a theology of mission based on the church as an explicit symbol of salvation history (*Kirche der Völker: Skizze einer Theorie der Mission,* Freiburg: Herder, 1972). Leonardo Boff's doctoral dissertation has drawn out the implications of this salvation-historical conception for a liberation-theological view of the church's social and political mission (*Die Kirche als Sakrament im Horizont der Welterfahrung,* Paderborn: Schoningh, 1974).

Mission as a Task of Eschatological Promise

The theology of mission based upon hope and promise takes issue with the previous theologies of mission, even the most recent salvation-historical approach. It argues that these theologies start out from revelation, salvation history, and the institution of the church as acts or events of the past. They do not sufficiently consider that biblical revelation is not so much an "unveiling" of something existing and hidden as it is a revelation of a promise and hope for the future. This failure leads them to neglect the church's orientation to the promised future in their understanding of the church's mission.

The eschatological promise is taken as the basis not only for understanding mission but also church and world. The basis as well as the goal of mission is the universal promise of God for the world. The world is not the background or presupposition of God's salvation. Instead the world is viewed as based upon God's promise and hope. Consequently, the world is historical and the world is a world created to God's promised future. This has been developed especially by taking up the ideas of Moltmann and Metz, L. Rütti, *Zur Theologie der Mission: Kritische Analysen und neue Orientierungen* (Mainz: Matthias-Grünewald, 1972).

Models of Social Mission

These diverse understandings of the church's mission in general provide the background and context for the more explicit reflections on the relation between the church's mission in general and the social mission in particular. A development has taken place from understanding the social mission of the church as a preparation for or consequence of its religious mission to an understanding that makes the social mission more integral to its religious mission.

Social Mission as Preparation for Evangelization

Within the conceptions of missionary activity as the conversion of souls or as the implantation of the church, it was these missionary activities that were primary. The social mission was important but secondary to this primary role of conversion or ecclesial implantation. These approaches acknowledged that insofar as the spread of Christian beliefs and churches presupposed certain conditions, both material and cultural, it was necessary to be concerned with these. The hungry could not hear the Word of God. Certain cultural presuppositions were necessary for the ample reception and implantation of Christian belief. The churches did indeed have a social mission, and this mission was concerned with these material and cultural preconditions. Within this conception, especially in the conversion theory, the social mission of the church was often equated with the bringing to colonial countries Eurocentric values and Western attitudes along with certain material goods. This mission, however, was not only distinct but was subordinate to the religious mission of conversion.

Social Mission as Social Teaching and Lay Apostolate

Another view of the social mission locates the social mission of the church primarily in relation to the application to society of the church's teachings, especially its social teachings. These social teachings were elaborated over the centuries and especially explicated within the 19th and 20th centuries in the papal documents. This social teaching pointed to the errors of specific social and economic systems, for example, communistic socialism, liberal individualism, or the unrestricted free market of capitalism. The Roman Catholic social teaching incorporated specific values consonant with Christian values, for example, the family or living wage. Through its social teaching, the church engaged in the social mission. Its social teachings were primarily based upon social ethics, especially the natural law, so that they were in principle accessible to the public realm and even to those not sharing the Christian faith.

The church's actual engagement in the world and in politics takes place, however, primarily through the laity or the lay apostolate. The movement, known as Catholic Action, presupposed this view of the church's social mission. Its members sought to put Roman Catholic social teaching, especially the papal encyclicals, into practice within the social and political realms. Its lay apostolate consisted not simply in laypersons as individuals engaging in social action or political action but in the forming of Catholic associations, societies, and groups. A principle of subsidiarity was at work insofar as the Catholic Action movement encouraged the formation of mediating institutions to take care of specific social tasks. These lay groups and societies, under the supervision of the Roman Catholic hierarchy, represented a Catholic communal life and purpose. They thereby carried out the social mission of the church.

Social Mission as Consequence of Evangelization

The emphasis that the primary purpose of the church is evangelization over against any secondary mission does not exclude a social mission. Instead the social mission receives its significance in relation to evangelization. It is at the same time both subordinate to evangelization and required by evangelization. Evangelization includes moral and religious values, and these have implications and consequences for social and political life. The emphasis on evangelization provides a specific view of the social mission, since it attempts to differentiate the church's religious message from a specific political vision. It does so when it values the social mission as less than the religious mission through characterization of evangelization as primary versus social as secondary, or characterization of evangelization as essential (that is belonging to the essence of the church's mission) versus social as integral (belonging to the completeness or fullness of the church's mission). It thereby seeks to curb a political activism or integralism. For this reason the next two approaches, the political and liberation theological, have criticized some views of evangelization.

Social Mission as Inculturation

Aware of the close relationship between culture and beliefs, this approach underscores that the mission of the church is not simply a consequence of evangelization but of inculturation. It is not so much a question of a translation of the gospel message into diverse languages as it is a question of the integration of the gospel into the culture. The result should be a complex system of belief, values, and life-praxis in which the gospel message is, together with the culture, generative and creative.

The understanding of the social mission as inculturation is the result of considerable reflection. At first the more generic conception of "incarnational" approach was used, especially in the 1940s and 1950s. One saw the church's social mission as the vitalization of the culture through the integration of Christian values within a culture. This incarnation of the Christian message was what produced an effective social mission. For it was through the cultural vitalization that flowed from that inculturation that the church influenced the social and political structures of society. In European countries, especially in the post–World War II period, the formation of Christian Democratic parties was seen as part of this inculturation and was an attempt to realize in practice this conception of the relationship between church and society. In the 1970s, the term "inculturation" was used to describe a specific approach that went beyond both the previous incarnational and the much earlier accommodational or acculturation approach. The inculturation approach stressed the contextuality and cultural penetration of the gospel much more strongly than the more generic notion of incarnation or accommodation. It paid specific attention to the dynamics of the culture, and it was primarily through its effect upon the culture—understood as reciprocal—that the church realized its mission within a particular societal and cultural context.

Social Mission as Prophetic Critique: Political Theology

During the 1960s Johann Baptist Metz and Jürgen Moltmann advocated a political theology. Aware of the terrible effects of nazism and World War II, they emphasized the political mission of the church. Through their reinterpretation of Christian eschatology, they argued that the church's social mission entailed a political mission. Their arguments involved both a diagnosis of modern society and a critique of modern theology. They described modern society as secularized and as a market society that reduced religion to the private sphere. Religion was now primarily a matter of private individual choice just as other consumer goods were. These political theologians criticized existential theology (Rudolf Bultmann) and transcendental theology (Karl Rahner), influential in the 1950s and 1960s, for failing to confront this privatization—an accusation that others have challenged. These political theologians argued that existential theology adapted religion to the private role to which a consumer-oriented society had relegated it because it had made religion primarily a matter of existential decision. Moreover, the existential interpretation of the kingdom of God went contrary to the very social language and political images of biblical eschatology.

Political theology used the biblical categories of promise and prophetic critique to explain the significance of biblical eschatology for political society. The category of promise was inclusive, for it did not separate church and world or spirit and nature into false dichotomies. The category of prophetic critique enabled political theology to suggest that the churches could have a political mission and at the same time not seek a return to a kind of Constantinian integralism between church and state. For example, influenced by the Frankfurt school's understanding of negative dialectic, Metz argued that if the churches brought an eschatological proviso as a critique to political practice, they could obtain a greater consensus, even among those with different belief systems, than if the churches advocated concrete political programs. By taking such a critical political stance, the churches could express a solidarity with the poor, hungry, and homeless within society without identifying with a particular party or a particular social program. The reign of justice and peace that the churches proclaim is an eschatological reign that stands in critical contrast to every concrete political arrangement.

Social Mission as Concretization of Salvation: Liberation Theology

Latin American liberation theology contrasts with political theology in its understanding of the church's social mission because it interprets differently the contemporary situation, responds to a dissimilar theological background, and develops a quite different interpretation of Christian eschatology. Latin American liberation theologians argue that it is not so much secularization and privatization of religion that characterizes the European and North American situation as it is exploitation, extreme poverty, and relations of dependency. On a political and economic level liberation theology criticizes economic developmental theories that overlook these relations of dependency. On a theological level it criticizes those conceptions of the church's social mission that link the church to political practice primarily through a social or political ethic and through the role of lay organizations in society. Such conceptions downplay the relevancy of the gospel message itself for political practice, and they split the church into two levels: the hierarchy (episcopacy and clergy) is responsible for the church; whereas the laity is for the world. Instead, this responsibility belongs to the whole church as a sacrament of God's saving grace.

Latin American liberation theology develops the social mission of the church in terms of the concrete sacramentality of God's grace and kingdom. Its explanation and application of eschatology to the mission of the church differs from that of political theology. Latin American liberation theology underscores that every act of love and justice is already a concrete realization of God's eschatological kingdom of love and justice on earth. Though this realization is incomplete and fragmentary, it is nevertheless a concrete manifestation of God's reign. Love and justice on earth do not relate to the love and justice of God's kingdom as shadow or image to reality but rather as the incomplete and imperfect realization in the historical concrete to perfect and completed reality. This view of eschatology has significant consequences for the understanding of the church's social and political mission. Political theology emphasizes that eschatology provides a transcendent reservation or proviso over against every political position and program. Hence it emphasizes that the church exercises its political mission through negative critique rather than through identification with concrete political programs. Insofar as liberation theology appeals to the realization of the eschatological kingdom in concrete conditions of love and justice, it appeals to eschatology not as a critical contrast image but rather as an impetus for the concrete formation of peace and justice on earth in both ecclesial and political communities.

Recent Church Documents

Since Vatican II many official church documents on the social mission of the church have been issued. The various constitutions of the council have made a distinctive contribution to the Roman Catholic understanding of the social mission of the church. In the wake of the council significant documents have been issued by the various popes, by the universal synod of bishops, and by episcopal conferences of diverse countries and regions. These have all sought to implement Vatican II by drawing out the implications of the council for the concrete realization and understanding of the church's social mission within the contemporary world.

Important differences exist between the papal social encyclicals prior to Vatican II and those documents at the council and afterwards. *Rerum novarum* (1891) and *Quadragesimo anno* (1931) focus on the problems of industrial society, especially the conflict between capital and labor and the contrast between liberalism and socialism. These issues are still being treated; however, since Vatican II there is an additional focus on the problems of human rights, the world economic order, and the imbalances of economic development within the world. The former encyclicals dealt with a European political and economic situation and with the vision of Catholic or Christian political parties in contrast to liberalism or socialism. The later encyclicals deal with the global situation, the extreme contrasts of wealth and poverty, the basic possibility of human existence, and the importance of human rights. In addition the former documents are framed primarily in the language of a neo-Scholastic natural-law ethic, whereas Vatican II and the ensuing documents seek to elaborate the biblical, Christological, ecclesial, and eschatological bases of the church's social mission.

Vatican II

Vatican II (1962–65) has contributed to the understanding of the social mission of the church through various documents, especially the Dogmatic Constitution on the Church *(Lumen gentium)*, the Pastoral Constitution on the Church in the Modern World (*Gaudium et spes*), and the Decree on the Church's Missionary Activity (*Ad gentes*). Vatican II explicates the social mission of the church through its treatment of the church as a sacrament, its exposition of the relation between the mission of the church itself and the contemporary world, and its vision of the church as both local and international.

Vatican II's Dogmatic Constitution on the Church defines the church as the people of God and elaborates the understanding of the church as a sacrament. Its fundamental statement about the church is: "By her relationship with Christ, the church is a kind of sacrament of intimate union with God, and of the unity of all humankind, that is, the church is a sign and instrument of such union and unity. For this reason . . . , this Council wishes to set forth more precisely to the faithful and to the entire world the nature and encompassing mission of the church" (LG 1). This statement underscores that the sacramental nature of the church is the basis of its mission precisely insofar as the church is a sacrament of unity. The church is a sacrament not merely of the unity with God, nor simply of the unity of humankind, but rather of the double unity that exists between the unity with God and the unity of the whole human race.

Within the plurality of nations and diversity of peoples, the church is to be sign to the world of unity with God and among people. The council speaks of the church as sign of unity in a threefold manner: as mystery, as sacrament of unity, and as sacrament of universal salvation. Mystery is intended, as the word was used by the Greek fathers of the church, to express the mission of the church within God's plan and economy of salvation for the world. The church as a sacrament of unity and the church as a sacrament of salvation express a similar truth but with a different accent. "Sacrament of unity" refers to the church as an instrument of unity within the plurality of humankind and in relation to God. "Sacrament of salvation" refers to the necessity of the church. What these descriptions signify is that mission and being are not distinct, that it is the very nature of the church to exercise its salvific mission.

The social mission of the church as an expression of the church's salvific mission is elucidated by Vatican II in the first three chapters of the Pastoral Constitution on the Church in the Modern World. The church exercises its social mission in elevating and upholding human dignity, in fostering the bonds of unity in society, and in explicating the profound meaning of human activity. These chapters make concrete the dogmatic statements of the church as a sacrament of unity and of universal salvation. In elaborating this social mission the council makes a decisive shift insofar as it incorporates into its vision of modern society three traditions that many in the church had previously contested: the tradition of human and civil rights, the tradition of a constitutional state, and the tradition of modern democracy.

In addition, Vatican II's Decree on the Church's Missionary Activity discusses missionary work and reaffirms the centrality of mission: "The whole Church is missionary, and the work of evangelization is a basic duty of the People of God" (AG 35). It gives a Trinitarian foundation of the church's mission. The sending of God's son should establish "peace and community" among all humans. The mission of the church continues this mission and is the responsibility of the whole people of God.

Vatican II represents a milestone in Roman Catholic official teaching. It locates the social mission of the church in relation to the church's nature as sacrament, its task to continue the mission of Christ, and its evangelization of the kingdom of God. In many ways its affirmations seek to integrate many diverse theological opinions into an integral vision of the church and its social mission.

Roman Episcopal Synods

In addition to emphasizing that the church does not exist for itself but has a mission to the world, Vatican II stressed both the importance of local churches and the episcopal collegiality of the universal church to implement Vatican II within the modern world. In seeking to implement the teaching of Vatican II, several episcopal synods of the whole church have, in elaborating the missionary responsibility of the church in the contemporary world, given special emphasis to the church's social mission.

Justitia in mundo, issued in 1971, asserted that the mission of the church to create more justice in the world was integral to the church's proclamation of the gospel. The church should engage itself with justice and the transformation of the world, for its mission concerns the redemption of humanity and its freedom from every condition of oppression (JM 6). The first section deals with justice on a worldwide level. It describes the injustices in the economic order, the lack of basic human rights for many, the influence of international power systems, and the structural hindrances to justice. Dealing with the relation between the gospel message and the mission of the church, the second section shows the significance of that message for justice by underscoring the indissoluble unity between the relation of human persons to God and the relation of human persons to their fellow human persons. The love of neighbor requires justice because of the dignity and rights of humans.

Important is the synod's teaching that justice is a constitutive dimension of the church. "Action on behalf of justice and participation in the transformation of the world fully appear to us as a constitutive dimension of the preaching of the gospel, or, in other words, of the church's mission for the redemption of the human race and its liberation from every oppressive situation" (36). The Latin term used, *ratio constitutiva,* has led to some controversy. Some argue that it too strongly links evangelization and justice, whereas others see such a link as the proper understanding of evangelization.

De evangelizatione, issued in 1974, dealt with the problems that evangelization faces within the contemporary world: secularization, atheism, and prohibitions of religious freedom as well as cultural obstacles. The document deals with the issue of the relation between evangelization and human liberation and salvation. It emphasizes the solidarity of the faithful with all humans and the message of salvation for the whole human race. Salvation in the world is an anticipation of the total salvation of humans. The synod thereby advances reflection on the relation between the church's religious and social mission when it affirms that the church, in carrying out the work of evangelization, already initiates the total salvation and total liberation of humanity.

Ad populum Dei nuntius (1977) deals with catechesis, its significance for ecclesial practice, and its part within the missionary function of the church. Catechesis is viewed in relation to the problem of inculturation. Therefore catechesis cannot abstract from the social mission of the church but must be related to social issues.

From the perspective of justice, evangelization, and catechesis, each of these three synods deals with the church's social mission. The episcopal synods are innovative primarily insofar as they incorporate new forms of ecclesial collegiality and reflection. They apply Vatican II's teaching to concrete issues as they elaborate the integrity of the church's social mission to its very nature and mission. The church's mission is concerned with the proclamation of the gospel. This proclamation, however, extends to all humans, attends to their situation, and involves their total salvation.

Paul VI

On the eightieth anniversary of *Rerum novarum* in 1971, Pope Paul VI in his encyclical *Octogesima adveniens* gave a new accent to Roman Catholic social teaching and to the church's social mission by underscoring that many social and economic ills have their roots and causes in political issues. What is needed is a change in the models of economic growth both within rich nations and in the relation of these nations to poor nations. New forms of democracy are required so that more persons can be informed and can exercise shared responsibility. It is evident in this encyclical that the church's mission as social mission involves a political mission: one concerned with political and economic decisions as these have both internal and international social effects. The political is integral to the social and economic.

In 1975, on the tenth anniversary of Vatican II, Pope Paul VI issued an apostolic exhortation, *On Evangelization in the Modern World (Evangelii nuntiandi).* Defining evangelization as the proper call of the church and its most profound identity (14), Pope Paul VI uses the term "liberation" as well as "integral" to characterize the meaning of this evangelization in order to underscore a holistic conception of liberation and salvation. This holism means that salvation includes the social and political, but it also goes against any politicization that reduces the religious message to a particular political program or social agenda. This description of evangelization places the church's social mission at the center of evangelization. It thereby contrasts with those theories of mission that view the social mission only as a precondition or consequence of evangelization. At the same time, Paul VI wants to make sure that in making the social mission integral to evangelization, one does not lose sight of the primacy of the religious dimension of evangelization.

John Paul II

Pope John Paul II has dealt with the social mission of the church in his various encyclicals, sermons, and addresses. The encyclicals especially dealing with the social mission of the church include his first encyclical, *On Redemption and the Dignity of the Human Race (Redemptor hominis),* in 1979; *On Human Work (Laborem exercens)* in 1981; *On Social Concern (Sollicitudo rei socialis)* in 1987; and *On the Mission of the Redeemer (Missionis Redemptoris)* and *On the Hundredth Anniversary of* Rerum Novarum *(Centesimus annus)* in 1991. John Paul II's description of the church's social mission displays two emphases. On the one hand, he acknowledges the systemic and structural causes of social injustice within the world. For example, in his encyclical *On Social Concern,* Pope John Paul II underlines the increased gap between the North and South and views the conflict between the societies' development. On the other hand, he stresses the personal involvement within the church of the works of mercy. The mission of the church primarily relates to the personal level, to transforming the hearts and minds of individuals. Through such personal transformation, John Paul II argues, the church contributes to overcoming structural injustice. The church's social mission is to elaborate ethical principles and to convert persons. Such action expresses the church's distinctive and religious nature. Its social mission does not consist in advocating a particular economic or political order—a "third way" between liberal capitalism and socialism—as it proclaims moral principles and calls for the conversion of hearts.

This double perspective helps to profile Pope John Paul II's approach in relation to Latin American liberation theology. Both denounce the social, economic, and political causes of injustice. Both point out the structural deformations of international economic arrangements; however, Latin American liberation theology advocates a much more direct political and social engagement of the church in social and political reform. Identifying structural injustice as a form of structural or social "sin," liberation theology envisions the church's mission to be much more directly related to the change and transformation of these structures, while John Paul II approaches the social mission with a much stronger emphasis on personalism—much more so than Pope Paul VI. Hence he stresses that the sin of personal egoism is at the root of structural injustice, and he gives a primacy to the church's role in combating that egoism of personal sin. Moreover, he cautiously wants to avoid a too-explicit involvement of the churches, especially the hierarchy and clergy, within political life.

Regional Episcopal Conferences

In the wake of Vatican II many regional and national episcopal conferences have contributed to the understanding of the church's social mission in various ways. On one level, they have contributed to the social mission through an actual exercise of that mission by addressing specific social problems and issues. Such a concrete exercise of social mission is exemplified by the pastoral letters of the U.S. National Conference of Catholic Bishops *The Challenge of Peace* and *Economic Justice for All* and by the Canadian Conference of Catholic Bishops with their statement *Ethical Reflections on the Economic Crisis*. Likewise, Mexican bishops took up the recommendation of *Justice in the World* to apply its principles and issue their own document *Justice in Mexico* (1971) to analyze the situation in Mexico. Later episcopal conferences in 1986 and 1987 explicitly take up the concrete issue of foreign debt and its effects upon Mexico's social and economic poverty.

On another level, some of the regional conferences have contributed to the social mission of the church through their reformation of the understanding of the church's mission, in Latin America, for example, at Medellín and Puebla. That explicit formulation of the church's social mission in relation to liberation, preferential option for the poor, solidarity, and signs of the times has become influential in other documents throughout Christianity. From a different perspective, the Thirty-second General Conference of the Jesuits has elaborated the relation between faith and justice in its attempt to reflect theologically on the social mission of the Jesuit order. Theologically and historically, faith and justice are reciprocally and inseparably related.

Toward a Theology of Social Mission

A theological interpretation of the church's social mission has to consider the nature of the church and its mission in relation to its confession of Jesus as the presence and revelation of God in history. Such an interpretation has to take into account the tradition of the church's attempt—through diverse changing social conditions and changing background assumptions about the nature of society—to interpret faithfully and to apply constructively the Christian meaning of God for social and political life. Consequently such an interpretation, while faithful to the tradition, is not static but is based upon the learning experiences of Christian communities, both past and present, in its attempt to articulate the meaning of the social mission for the contemporary situation.

The Theological Basis of the Social Mission

Just as the understanding of the social mission of the church is linked with the understanding of the church, so too is the understanding of the church linked with the understanding of Jesus. The Christian community is a configuration of religious belief and praxis originating with the life and praxis of Jesus. Classical Christianity developed many categories for the interpretation of Jesus. The category of Logos, as a model for understanding God's act and presence in Jesus, affirmed Jesus to be God's Word, the concrete embodiment of God's creative Word and meaning. The category of Logos, which interpreted Jesus as the incarnation of God's Logos, became the dominant model in classical Christology.

This central Christian affirmation can be further illumined by the term "praxis." This term, which is prevalent in current theological and philosophical literature, goes back to Aristotle's distinction in his *Nicomachean Ethics* between *poiesis* as a technical skill involved in making something and *praxis* as a basic way of life. Theologians use the term "praxis" to emphasize a configuration of meaning and action. The Christian belief in Jesus affirms Jesus as a configuration of God's meaning and action. This view of the presence and action of God in Christ as a specific configuration, or praxis, hinders the reduction of meaning of God's incarnation in Jesus to a specific teaching or a particular idea—as if Jesus' role were only to preach and to teach. This view inseparably links the reality and meaning of Jesus with the praxis of his life. Jesus does not so much bring a new knowledge (*gnosis*) as he expresses the reality of God in a concrete life-praxis.

Church as a Community of Discipleship

The disciples of Jesus formed communities after Easter. They saw their discipleship and their belief in God's presence in Jesus' life and praxis as confirmed by God in the resurrection of Jesus. The Christian community that emerged in the post-Easter situation sought to reflect and live out the meaning and praxis of Jesus. The community understood that to be Christian was not merely to adhere to a certain configuration of beliefs, nor was it simply to affirm God's presence in Jesus; but to be Christian was to receive creatively, that is, to carry forward and to continue, the meaning and praxis of Jesus. The gospel traditions contain strong affirmations of this continuation of the praxis of Jesus as constitutive of discipleship. The parable of the last judgment in Mt 25 makes such a praxis constitutive of discipleship. The inauguration of Jesus' public ministry as described in Lk 4 underscores the holistic nature of the praxis of Jesus' ministry. As configurations of meaning and praxis of Jesus and his ministry, they paradigmatically illustrate the meaning of the discipleship of the Christian community.

The Relation Between Social and Religious Mission

A theological interpretation of the social mission of the church has to raise and to resolve the question of the relationship between the social and religious mission of the church. Is the social mission just a precondition or consequence of the religious mission as some propose, or is the social mission integral (belonging to the completeness) or constitutive (belonging to the essence) of the religious dimension? This theological issue is prior and basic to any consideration of the proper form or appropriate role of the church's social mission within contemporary society. Some theological responses distort the possible answer when they look for an exclusive and specific difference or a singular essence rather than a much more comprehensive approach that seeks to take into account the complex intersection between religious and social mission.

Inadequate approaches. One inadequate approach to the relation between the religious and social mission of the church asks what is the specific difference in an exclusive rather than inclusive manner. This approach defines the essence of the social mission precisely in its difference. An example from the interpretation of human nature can easily illustrate the flaw in this approach. If in asking what is distinctively human, one answers by specifying the difference between animals and humans as rationality and by defining humans exclusively in terms of rationality, then one has distorted what is human. The answer has downplayed the significance of emotions and corporeality to human nature. In defining what is distinctively human, one needs to point to the overlap and intersection between rationality and animality within humans. The same is true of the church's social mission. The interpretation of the church's social mission has to define the religious not exclusively but in a way that shows how the religious dimension crisscrosses and links with the social and political dimension. Exclusive definitions of the religious and social missions necessarily distort each.

A second inadequate approach is to look for the distinctive essence of the church in an "essentialist" manner that posits one essential contribution or role of the church. The philosopher Wittgenstein has used the example of a game to illustrate the weakness of a one-dimensional essentialist approach. What is the essence of a game? Playing with others, think of solitaire; amusing, think of chess; skill, think of ring-around-a-rosy; competition, think of bouncing a ball off a wall. In short, there is no single, essential definition of a game but only a cluster of overlapping characteristics; some are present sometimes; others, other times. This cluster of crisscrossing characteristics is what Wittgenstein calls a "family resemblance" rather than an essence. What is true for the phenomenon of a game is even more true for the complex phenomenon of a church and its mission. The religious and social mission of the church relate to each other not in a singular or essential manner but with overlapping and crisscrossing characteristics.

A dialectical relation—both constitutive and critical. The affirmation of ultimacy in religious belief entails both a constitutive and a critical dimension. These dimensions do not simply complement each other but relate to each other dialectically. On the one hand the constitutive is the basis for the critical. On the other hand the constitutive contrasts with the critical. It is the appropriate application of the dialectic that an adequate exercise of the church's social mission requires. If the religious is related to the social and political primarily as critical, as political theologians do in their appeal to eschatology primarily for prophetic critique, then the church fails to support positive historical initiatives and programs for social justice. If the religious is related to the political primarily as constitutive, as in an integralist appeal to religion to justify and confirm a particular social order, then the church may be reduced to an ideological justification of the status quo. Instead the dialectic of the relation between the religious and the social-political requires an appropriate and prudential judgment.

Religious belief involves a center of value and ultimacy. The constitutive is involved when religion points to the transcendent, ultimate, and sacred value present within reality. This is, for example, the case when human dignity and rights are viewed as sacred in relation to the belief that all humans are creatures of God, made in God's image and sharing in the co-humanity of Christ. The Christian vision of God's presence in all humans entails an intensification and an ultimacy of human values and rights, and the Christian affirms them with a religious ultimacy that makes them sacred. To use humans as a means to some end and thereby functionalize and instrumentalize them is a moral imperative that has its historical roots in a religious vision of human nature. Such a religious vision makes the social mission not simply integral but constitutive of the church's mission. The Christian vision crisscrosses with the building up of society, with the affirmation of human values, with the humanization of society. Such a humanization is not simply a social task; it is a sacred task for a vision of the world and humanity, as created and redeemed by God in an eschatological hope and promise.

Yet the Christian vision is also critical. The belief in God as transcendent and as paradigmatically configured in the biblical images of the life-praxis of Jesus represents a vision critical of ideologies, be they political or religious. The church symbolizes its vision of divine transcendence and its image of a paradigmatic praxis in and through its social and political mission—a vision and praxis that often demands a prophetic critique of society and politics. The transcendence affirmed in the Christian vision is therefore not only a transcendence that underscores the ultimacy of human values; it is also a transcendence that points to the limitations, finitude, and failures of human endeavors.

The understanding of the social mission of the church in terms of a dialectic, both constitutive and critical, avoids reducing the social mission to a specific difference or to a singular essence. Instead it points to a pattern in which judgments of appropriateness are central. Such a pattern of discriminating judgments is evident within the biblical tradition and the distinction between true and false prophecy. This distinction did not rest on a single definition of prophecy but on the appropriateness of the prophetic address. Depending upon the historical circumstance, the authentic prophetic voice either sought to constitute Israel in its identity or sought to critique idolatrous practices. True prophecy did not differ from false prophecy in emphasizing one aspect over the other but in the correct interplay between the constitutive and critical dimension. A similar dialectic is present in the early Christian community articulating both its identity and its critical stance within its historical environment.

Theological Vision: Relation Between Solidarity and Justice

The concrete integrity of the religious and human in Jesus' life and praxis as well as the dialectical relation between the constitutive and the critical provides a general guideline for the social and political mission of the church. Some argue that the church has a specific social mission because it has a mission of love or compassion. Moreover, this love and compassion characterizes the social and political mission of the church in contrast to other social institutions of society. These operate with rules of justice based on consensus about rational principles, whereas the church operates out of love and compassion based on the gospel message.

Such a view overlooks the interrelation between solidarity and justice. It thereby misconstrues the church's social mission. First of all, justice is not independent of love and solidarity, for solidarity and love determine what kind of justice one envisions. Our principles of justice depend upon our conceptions of society and of the human person, just as our conceptions of these influence the determination of justice. For example, a considerable debate exists within contemporary political and ethical theory as well as within political policy and practice about two diverse conceptions of justice. One conception emphasizes the maximizing of equal opportunity, whereas the other conception stresses entitlement rights. Robert Nozick's notion of justice stresses that individuals are entitled to what they have earned, and he therefore criticizes governmental regulations that distribute wealth or greatly support social welfare (*Anarchy, State, and Utopia,* New York: Basic Books, 1974). John Rawls' conception of justice emphasizes both the principle of freedom and the difference principle (*A Theory of Justice,* Cambridge: Harvard Univ. Press, 1971). The difference principle underscores that the most disadvantaged in society should receive more help so as to provide them with equal opportunity. Likewise, international relations between rich and poor nations can be seen in terms of a theory of justice that stresses entitlements or one that underscores the distribution of wealth and resources so that the poor and disadvantaged can be given opportunities.

These issues of justice within society and among nations are not just issues of rational argumentation. They also rest on different visions of society and human personhood. These visions affect how one assesses the relations of persons to one another—individually and politically—and of the relation between society and nature. The Christian vision of solidarity and love does not provide simply a complementary vision to one of justice but provides a vision and practice that determines one's conception of justice among nations and people, among rich and poor. The Christian tradition of solidarity with the poor, which recent papal teaching and liberation theology has so strongly articulated, incorporates the meaning of both justice and love.

Second, justice is a form of love and solidarity. The love of others and the solidarity with them requires that we respect and acknowledge their dignity and worth. When justice requires that all possess basic rights and that all have a right to an adequate share in the goods of the world so that they can live their human lives with dignity and respect, it not only expresses that these rights and goods are justly owed them but it also expresses a genuine love and solidarity with them. To deny persons their rights and just share of the earth's goods is to refuse them love and solidarity. Love requires that we acknowledge that humans have such value that can place obligations upon us and our possessions—obligations of justice. If persons are homeless and hungry, then one loves them not simply by handing out doles but by acknowledging that they have a right not to be homeless and hungry and by structuring social and political life to ensure them that just right.

Moreover, often the wealth of some individuals, groups, and nations is due not solely to their own efforts and achievements so that it can be viewed solely as an entitlement, but is also in part due to exploitation and excessive profit. Consequently, when one associates love and generosity with beneficence and compassion rather than with justice, then one not only disregards the dignity and rights but one also distorts the relationship between the rich and poor and disregards the connection between prosperity and pauperization. The option for the poor is therefore not an option of love alone but one of justice.

Social Context of the Church's Social Mission

Any theological interpretation of the social mission of the church needs to consider the role and form of this mission. The nature of modern society and the specific North American context set parameters for the exercise of the social mission.

Modern Evolution of Society

Modern societies have evolved in that their economic, social, and political structures have become increasingly complex. These economic structures have, moreover, become much more interrelated with those of other nations. In addition, the economic and political administrative systems increasingly differentiate themselves from the life-world of people, but they also increasingly influence it through internationalization, bureaucratization, and monetarization. These tendencies affect the church's social mission in several ways.

One tendency is the increasing bureaucratization and socialization of social welfare. Much of the social welfare that previously belonged almost exclusively to the provenance of the churches now belongs to the provenance of the state and its bureaucratic administration. This shift has consequences for the church's social mission. The churches still have responsibilities in these areas—though lessened. If, however, they are to be faithful to their traditional mission they also have a responsibility that relates to the state's organization of social welfare, that is, its adequacy and its form. There is the problem of the adequacy and equity of social-welfare programs in covering all groups, especially minority groups lacking political voice or power. Moreover, the churches have responsibility toward individuals who may fall through the administrative system and who are not covered by its care. In addition, the monetarization of social welfare affects the nature of social welfare. The state provides monetary payments to indigent persons with which they obtain social assistance. Health, disability, and unemployment insurance as well as social security provide for social services by providing persons with money. Yet money alone does not take care of the many personal needs associated with these, for example, the loneliness of illness, the need for self-respect for disabled persons, and the fear of not finding jobs for those who are unemployed. It becomes important for smaller communities within society—and the church comprises such communities—to provide persons within such a monetarized social-welfare system with the personal community and with the personal interaction and holistic care that they might lack.

Complex societies also have an increased interrelation between economic and political systems as well as the internationalization of the economical systems. The interrelation between economic and political systems is evident in the connection between development of the economy and government's priorities regarding spending. Budgetary priorities, spending for military or for health, education, and welfare not only affect social welfare but also affect the economy itself. The internationalization of economic systems means that the social question has become much more complex than the conflict between capital and labor. The social problem has become an international contrast based not only on capital but also on technology, communication systems, knowledge, and military power. The social problem has become more complex because it runs up against the limits of progress and of the earth's resources. A progressive view of history no longer exists. Science and technology are not simply the answer to the elimination of social ills. These changes have consequences for the social mission of the church, which must now deal with more than the conflict between capital and labor; it must face the contrast between poor nations and those nations with wealth, technology, knowledge, and the power to exploit limited natural resources. The task of the church's social mission then involves focusing the consciousness of those areas and countries on this disparity in wealth, technology, and power. It involves coming to clarity about the extent to which these are often used to exploit others. As society becomes international, the solidarity with the poor is no longer simply a solidarity with the least of the brethren within the local religious or political community; rather, it becomes a solidarity with others within the global community of humankind.

Pluralism and the North American Context

Theological reflection on the church's social mission needs to consider the specifics of the situation in which the theological reflection is taking place. Within the United States it is necessary for the churches to take into account the religious pluralism, religious ideology, and international political role of the United States.

A tradition of religious pluralism exists in the United States. This religious pluralism with its history of voluntary church membership and its interpretation of religious freedom as the separation of church and state has implications for the church's exercise of its social mission to public and social policy. Church statements have to take some form of discourse and pronouncement that takes into account the pluralism in moral, religious, and political issues. This pluralism requires what could be called a communicative conception of the social mission. Within a society with pluralistic conceptions of the good, the churches are communities of praxis and interpretation. Through their social praxis they become symbols of solidarity and justice. Through their interpretation of the moral and social force of their religious traditions they communicate the significance of their tradition for public and social values, for the public discourse of a democratic society. Both their social ministry and the interpretation serves to form through symbol and discourse the quality of moral reflection and praxis within the social and public realm.

This religious pluralism and separation of church and state is often interpreted as a secularization of society. However, such an interpretation overlooks certain underlying religious convictions that shape the cohesiveness and form the mentality of public consciousness. The conviction of being a chosen people, so predominant in the settlement of the colonies, continues as a quasi ideology of national righteousness. The history of the United States as the land of unlimited opportunity for all feeds the ideology that all—even the poor and victims of discrimination—have equal access to opportunity and need only to be industrious to realize fully this opportunity. The religious voluntarism and privatism, often positively associated with freedom of religion, also fosters a negative individualism that undercuts a sense of accountability to community as well as a social responsibility. In this respect the public-private distinction does not take into account the politicalization of the private. A religious ideology of national righteousness when combined with individualism and privatism presents a particular challenge to a nation whose dominance is due to its military, economic, and political power.

The church's mission to represent symbolically and discursively on earth God's transcendence as paradigmatically present in the life and praxis of Jesus has as its social and political task to take a stance of solidarity with the disadvantaged and one of critique for corruptions of power and religious righteousness. This social and political mission is constitutive of the church as the disciples of Jesus within the contemporary world.

See also ECONOMIC PLANNING, SOCIAL IMPORTANCE OF; EVANGELII NUNTIANDI; EVANGELIZATION; GAUDIUM ET SPES; HUMAN RIGHTS; JUSTICE IN THE WORLD; LIBERATION THEOLOGY; POLITICAL THEOLOGY; VATICAN COUNCIL II.

Bibliography: G. Anderson and T. Stanksy, *Mission Trends,* 5 vols. (New York/Toronto: Paulist, Grand Rapids: Erdmanns, 1974–1981). R. Bassham, *Mission Theology: 1948–1975* (Pasadena: William Carey Library, 1979). W. Buhlmann, *The Coming of the Third Church: An Analysis of the Present and Future of the Church* (Maryknoll, N.Y.: Orbis, 1977). G. Collet, *Das Missionsverständnis der Kirche in der gegenwärtigen Diskussion* (Mainz: Matthias Grünewald, 1984). P. Cotterell, *Mission and Meaninglessness: The Good News in a World of Suffering and Disorder* (London:

SPCK, 1990). D. Dorr, *Option for the Poor: A Hundred Years of Vatican Social Teaching* (Maryknoll, N.Y.: Orbis, 1984). F. Fiorenza, *Foundational Theology: Jesus and the Church* (New York: Crossroads, 1984). M. Hobgood, *Catholic Social Teaching and Economic Theory* (Philadelphia: Temple Univ. Press, 1991). L. Lutzbetak, *The Church and Cultures: New Perspectives in Missiological Anthropology* (Maryknoll, N.Y.: Orbis, 1988). J. Provost, *The Church as Mission*, Permanent Seminar Studies, no. 2 (Washington: Canon Law Society of America, 1984). L. Rütti, *Zur Theologie der Mission: Kritische Analysen und neue Orientierungen* (Mainz: Matthias Grünewald, 1972). F. Eigo, ed., *The Works of Mercy: New Perspectives on Ministry* (Villanova: Villanova Univ. Press, 1992).

FRANCIS SCHÜSSLER FIORENZA

CHURCH-STATE RELATIONS IN THE UNITED STATES

When they first became law in 1791, the establishment and free-exercise clauses of the First Amendment to the Constitution constituted a relationship between the churches and government that was unique in the world of that time. It was an achievement of political intelligence that was truly revolutionary: a reversal of that momentous event of the 4th century when the church first changed from a voluntary society to a society conceived as necessarily co-extensive with the civil community.

This reversal had been carefully scrutinized and discussed in America long before it was codified into law. Initially it was thought of as an experiment with a very important structure of civil society: institutional religion. As such it involved risk, for a religion mediates the values and ideals of a society just as effectively as do institutions that are political, economic, or educational. This risk continues today and involves a threefold commitment: to religious pluralism, to religious freedom, and to government neutrality. What follows is a summary of these three commitments.

Religious Pluralism

Religious pluralism was a fact in America long before it became an object of belief. The reason there was at the same time so much religious freedom in the colonies was chiefly due to the openness and sparsely settled nature of the country: the nonconformist simply moved away into that vast space where deviance immediately became orthodoxy. Groups holding divergent and incompatible views on religious questions thus gradually came to co-exist in different parts of the country.

This de facto pluralism meant that none of the dominant churches was in a position to press for religious uniformity. Indeed, there was a practical necessity for all of them to connive at religious variety: because no single church could make a successful bid for national establishment it was to the self-interest of each to be tolerant of all in order to guarantee such toleration for itself. Since so many sects holding very different beliefs were able to co-exist in peace, it followed that uniformity of religious practice was obviously not essential to the public welfare, something hitherto for centuries assumed to be true by all the countries of Western Europe. It was this last realization, that religious solidarity was not needed to stabilize the social order, that paved the way for the establishment and free-exercise clauses of the First Amendment.

"Congress shall make no law respecting an establishment of religion, or prohibiting the free exercise thereof." These clauses did not create a new idea but were rather the legal recognition of an actual state of things that had come to be seen as practically unavoidable. The Founders wanted to formulate a principle that would guarantee the participation of all churches in the common social unity of the republic while at the same time not compromising those distinctive modes of worship and belief proper to each. The religion clauses were therefore conceived to be an experiment in the political realm, a rejection of coercion in favor of voluntarism and persuasion, and an effort to strengthen the new nation by excluding from federal government concern all religious differences among its people.

Religious Freedom

The second commitment, to religious freedom, has to be seen as an extension of the commitment to religious pluralism. The First Amendment was an emphatic reaffirmation of the distinction between the religious and political orders, a distinction quite common in medieval Christendom but almost completely lost to Europe through the rise of national monarchies and the development of royal absolutism. This distinction meant so much to those who wrote the Bill of Rights because of its power to allay the fears of statesmen like James Madison and Thomas Jefferson that too much church would corrupt the state, and the fears of ministers like Roger Williams that too much state would corrupt the church. Such fears made both groups eager to establish freedom in this area as the rule. They therefore pressed the distinction between spiritual and temporal—to an exaggerated degree perhaps, but everyone then and since has agreed that exaggerating the distinction is a danger much to be preferred to its abolition.

Nevertheless, for over a century and a half religious and political values continued to be inextricably connected in the public mind, even though the establishment clause had severed all institutional bonds between churches and the federal government. Christian citizens were educated for civic responsibility in a nation they believed to have a destiny under God. This unusual historical situation was made possible because none of the original amendments to the Constitution had any application to the states; they were limitations on the national government only. This did not mean that the states were any less committed to religious freedom. Rather, what it meant was that state and local governments tended to accommodate religion. There was everywhere an official encouragement of ethical and spiritual beliefs symbolized most strikingly by a strong church presence in all public schools. Until the mid-20th century such local cultural meshings of the civil and the religious raised no legal problems at all in the context of the First Amendment.

In the 1940s, however, the United States Supreme Court nationalized the religion clauses, making them applicable to every state and local government through the due-process clause of the Fourteenth Amendment, which specifically obligates states, not Congress. This absorption of the First into the Fourteenth Amendment meant the elimination of all regional diversity in dealing legally with how government might accommodate religion. Disputes previously settled in state and local courts were now governed by constitutional law and could be brought into federal courts. When combined with the expansion of federal government power by mid-20th century, this nationalization process was clearly a moving of the earth under the traditional legal and religious landscapes. Litigation mushroomed in the federal courts. A fundamental transformation began to take place in regard to how religious groups and interests should be treated. The relationships between government and religion, culturally stabilized for over a century and a half, were never to be the same again.

Government Neutrality

The third commitment, to government neutrality, was a direct result of this nationalization process. For the Supreme Court was now forced to say precisely what church-state separation meant in any given situation, and they found this task to be far from easy. The reason is that those who wrote the First Amendment never spelled out precisely how the promotion of religious freedom (mandated by the free-exercise clause) was to be distinguished from the promotion of religious belief (forbidden by the establishment clause). Some say the framers were deliberately ambiguous, either because they themselves could not agree or because they saw a positive advantage in leaving the question open for future generations. In any case, many began to believe during the 1940s and 1950s that the best way to guarantee religious freedom was to make the distinction between religion and government as absolute and complete as humanly possible and to understand the establishment clause as "building up a wall of separation" between the two, a metaphor used almost casually by Jefferson in an 1802 letter to the Baptist Association of Danbury, Connecticut.

Many others, however, were attracted to a very different metaphor coined in 1832 by James Madison, who spoke about "the line of separation between the rights of religion and civil authority." The image of a line had the advantage of being much more flexible than that of a wall, its elements constantly changing so as to make it difficult, as Madison noted, to trace with such distinctness as to avoid collisions and doubts. The line image does not conjure up a confrontation between two antagonistic institutions, separated for all time by an impregnable barrier that must be defended by one and attacked by the other. Madison's metaphor makes it much easier to see that what is really the case is that citizens, who in fact may belong as individuals to both institutions, are engaged in a common quest to determine where the line is to be drawn at any particular point in the nation's history. Supreme Court decisions also assume a different image when looked at through Madison's eyes: they are not like large stones mortared into a solid wall but like points where the line appears to the majority of justices to be fixed at any given time.

Over the last forty years, the justices of the Supreme Court have in general been much more attracted to Madison's benign metaphor of a movable line of separation rather than to Jefferson's impregnable wall metaphor (though both appear in their decisions), very likely because they wanted to avoid charges of hostility or indifference to religion. As a result there has gradually developed over the years a concept of benevolent neutrality, allowing a zone of permissible accommodation and legislative discretion—a kind of "play in the joints" between the two clauses, to use former Chief Justice Burger's apt phrase. The Court has thus continued to support paid chaplains for legislatures and the armed services, exemption of religious property and income from taxation, and the legal observance of religious holidays; and it has approved such practices as making available school facilities for meetings of student religious clubs, supplying secular textbooks for children in parochial schools, busing children to these schools, and giving tax allowances for fees paid to either public or parochial schools.

In practice, therefore, separation (or neutrality) means today a prohibition against sponsorship and interference, but it also means the avoidance of government entanglement through pragmatic maneuvering between the permissible accommodation of religious freedom and the impermissible promotion of religious belief. In other words, the degree of government participation in the sanctioning and support of religious practices must be balanced with the corresponding impact of these practices upon freedom of belief and conscience. Guided by these principles, the Court has judged certain accommodating practices to be forbidden under the First Amendment. For public schools these include reading the Bible, reciting officially prescribed prayers, mandating a moment of silence for prayer, and posting the Ten Commandments; for religious schools these forbidden practices include government financing of secular courses, "released time" for religious instruction in public facilities, and supplying secular textbooks and equipment directly to the schools.

There is one large anomaly in the Court's search for the best way to be neutral toward religion, namely the difference it has found between charitable and educational institutions with respect to the constitutionality of financial assistance. Federal, state, and local governments routinely fund church-related hospitals, orphanages, and old-age and nursing homes, but the funding of secular education in church-related elementary and secondary schools has always been regarded by the Supreme Court as forbidden accommodation. Indeed, these schools have become the single greatest symbol of church and state in the United States, one that pervasively affects the whole fabric of society.

The reason for this is obviously not the concept of separation itself, since other nations that have separated religion and government find no difficulty at all in providing nondiscriminatory aid to all church-related schools. Many American jurists have argued, moreover, that such public funding would be a means of promoting not religion but religious freedom, that is to say, the freedom of religious choice. For the burden of sharing the enormous cost of public education, properly assessed upon all taxpayers, greatly reduces the practical freedom to choose a school not supported by public funds. Not to lift this restraint, so the argument goes, is to discriminate against religious schools precisely because they are religious, thereby greatly weakening the force of the free-exercise clause.

The root reason thus lies elsewhere. This consistent refusal to allow public funding of secular education in parochial schools seems to be based on the conviction that in practice it really would be impossible to distinguish in any principled way the promotion of religious freedom on these elementary and secondary levels from the promotion of religious belief. The Court, in other words, has been concerned here not with actualities but with potentialities: the possibility that religion *could* be fostered in classrooms supported by state funds and the likelihood that any effort to see to it that religion was *not* fostered would lead to too much state entanglement with the religious institutions.

This explains why the Court, when deciding cases in this area, usually speaks of the divisive political potential of funding parochial schools and emphasizes the dangers of political division along religious lines. These dangers are not constitutional, however, but political. Nondiscriminatory aid to these schools could indeed be justified by the First Amendment if this amendment were taken out of the political context. Within this context, however, there is simply too much opposition in the nation to any overlap of church and state in this particular educational area. Elementary and secondary schools have become *the* symbol of the American ideal of church-state separation. It is almost as if there were some tacit agreement by a very large segment of society that if an absolutely strict separation should be maintained here, an impregnable wall built wide and high, then the ideal itself will be secure, and movable lines, overlap, and accommodation may be more easily tolerated elsewhere in order that the *other* American ideal of benevolence toward religion might also be secure.

Summary

There is general agreement that the public care of religion is limited to care for freedom of conscience and religious association as well as to care for the internal autonomy of the churches. When will these limits be transgressed in one or other direction? When will permissible become forbidden accommodation? The Court's cases, Justice William Brennan once said, show "how elusive is the line which enforces the Amendment's injunction of strict neutrality, while maintaining no hostility toward religion. . . . Inevitably, insistence upon neutrality . . . may appear to border upon religious hostility."

The legal principle of neutrality, in other words, is not self-elucidating. The meaning of the concept (and commitment to it as a nation) has to be drawn from Supreme Court decisions rather than the meaning of the decisions from the concept. Unless citizens have a Court decision in regard to a specific government action, therefore, there is simply no way to know a priori whether that action is in fact neutral toward religion and thus constitutes neither sponsorship nor interference. On the one hand, linkages of any sort between religion and government must be looked upon with suspicion; on the other hand, because it is a cultural reality of great importance to the nation, religion must to some extent be regarded with benevolence and therefore legally accommodated.

A state or local government may decide to locate the line of separation between these two institutions at one or other point for purposes of a particular piece of legislation, but only those who are members of the Court at the time are empowered to judge whether or not this line has been properly placed.

See also CIVIL LAW, FUNCTION OF; DUE PROCESS; MURRAY, JOHN COURTNEY; PLURALISM; POLITICAL PHILOSOPHY; PUBLIC AND PRIVATE, RELATIONSHIP OF; RELIGIOUS FREEDOM; SACRED AND SECULAR, RELATIONSHIP OF.

Bibliography: S. Mead, *The Lively Experiment: The Shaping of Christianity in America* (New York: Harper & Row, 1963). R. McBrien, *Caesar's Coin* (New York: Macmillan, 1987). W. Miller, *The First Liberty* (New York: Knopf, 1986). C. Mooney, *Boundaries Dimly Perceived: Law, Religion, Education, and the Common Good* (Notre Dame: Univ. of Notre Dame Press, 1990). J. Murray, *We Hold These Truths* (New York: Sheed & Ward, 1960). A. Reichley, *Religion in American Public Life* (Washington: Brookings Institution, 1985).

CHRISTOPHER F. MOONEY, S.J.

CIVIL LAW, FUNCTION OF

This entry seeks to identify the function and goals of civil law as a human enterprise and a complex social activity reflecting human purposiveness. What do persons concerned with the meaning of human law believe they intend to accomplish within their society by their socially oriented activity called "law"? As theology, this inquiry takes up one aspect of a search to understand the complex relationship of church to "world."

The quest entails explicit attention to the evolution of theological thinking (development of doctrine) about law within human historical practice and the history of ideas. In the history of Christian theology and philosophy and eventually in the secularized social sciences, especially political science and legal philosophy (separated from but still not unrelated to theology and philosophy), what are the implicit and explicit conceptions of the goals and function of law? This history has occurred primarily in the West (embracing Europe and the Middle East and eventually the Americas). Now, in the present era of a truly worldwide church, the influences of cultures other than European will affect these conceptions more and more.

Modern and postmodern theology have come to focus ever more explicitly on social ethics. The moral manuals of the late Renaissance and early modern eras dealt with law insofar as obligations and ideals of the individual conscience of rulers as lawmakers or enforcers would raise questions about it in the practice of individual confession. Now, however, Christian ethics or moral theology gives extended thematic treatment to the societally shared obligations and ideals inherent in the systemic moral character of the political economy. So theological reflection on justice and law leads to official church response in magisterial teaching about the corporate obligations of democratic societies. For example, Pope John XXIII galvanized an effort toward cooperation for world peace by his 1963 encyclical *Pacem in terris.* So, too, by confronting "sinful social structures" and structural injustice in legal systems, contemporary liberation theology has evoked both criticism and new concern from Roman church authorities.

In spite of the long and complex process of historical development in theological understandings of civil law and its function, we do not find in the writings of any particular past historical era ready-made and explicit answers to our own modern and postmodern historically particular quest to understand the "function of civil law." One must interpret what is more-or-less implicit and nonthematic in the reflections of earlier eras to obtain an answer to one's modern and postmodern questioning.

Scriptural and Theological Reflection

In the Early Church

We do not find a fully thematic treatment of civil law and its function as distinct from religious law in the OT, and only the barest seed of such treatment in the NT. The sacred and the secular are seen as two aspects of one unified social reality.

Romans 13:1-7 provides a moral admonition (*paranesis*) concerning the Christian's duty of obedience to "governing authorities" (almost certainly assumed by the Pauline author to include persons who are *not* Christian believers, though these are not yet assumed to be bent on persecution of Christians). The ground given is that these imperial officials have "no authority except from God and those authorities that exist have been instituted by God."

This theme of divine origin of the authority of law and its affirmative claim on Christian conscience will recur in later Christian thought on law. The Pauline author adds that such rulers "are not a terror to good conduct but to bad." The civil authority is said not to "bear the sword in vain" relative to those who do evil. This function of civil law to command conscientious submission of Christian believers assumes the well-known Pauline reservations about the function of law in general (along with Mosaic Law) relative to faith—so dramatically embodied in Rom 5-7 and Galatians. But here a morally legitimate function of a government that is outside the Christian community is expressed in the assertion that those who "do what is good" need "have no fear of the authority." The Pauline author also implies a limit on the moral power of these authorities commanding through law: their aim must be to engender good conduct of subjects. This kind of limitation on the moral function of law to oblige recurs in later Christian theology: if the lawgivers command what is unjust and evil, their claims to divine authority are not clear.

Johannine Revelations, later than Romans, presents a deeper suspicion within the early church of the legitimacy and benevolence of Roman authorities and their law. Christian experience of early Roman persecution seems to be expressed. A hostile civil law's claim on conscience is limited because of unjust impact.

Later "spiritual" (rather than literal) interpretations of the saying of Jesus in Mt 22:15-22 ("Render to Caesar . . .") and of the "two swords" in Lk 22:38 provide medieval and some subsequent commentators on Scripture with a hook on which to hang their efforts to develop a political philosophy.

In the Patristic Era

The contradiction between the function of the civil law of the Roman Empire and church life was a dominant theme in the patristic era. Both church discipline and theological reflection were deeply concerned with the problems arising within the believing community (e.g., sin of apostasy) from failures to conscientiously resist the violent, legally enforced persecutions by imperial authorities. Thus prior to the Constantinian establishment and in the tradition of Revelations, civil law was seen to function as a hostile religious dimension of the larger society within which Christians struggled as a marginal and suspect foreign sect. Passive resistance to imperial law is a characteristic response for Christians (e.g., regarding the law of military service with its demand for a religious oath to the divine emperor, also with respect to any Christian participation in imposing the death penalty for crime, so obviously abused in persecution of Christian believers).

The Constantinian establishment of Christianity as the (de facto) religion of the empire radically changed the outlook of Christians on civil law and its function in relation to their religious community-life; the affirmative respect seen in Rom 13 was renewed. Now Christians participated more and more fully in enacting and enforcing the law of the empire and assumed this responsibility to be morally justified. As the church came to dominate the religious life of imperial society and simultaneously to organize itself in parallel through a more formal kind of canon law patterned on imperial Roman law, both church practice and reflection accepted as basically legitimate the moral authority and function of rulers and their Roman law.

Christians experienced a religiously unified society that had both religious and temporal dimensions. The civil and canon laws functioned symbiotically within it. Roman civil law functioned to control political and economic affairs, especially in the form of the *jus gentium,* which tolerated yet also unified and ordered diverse tribal legal traditions. Imperial law thus supported the missionary aims of the religious community as well as established ecclesial communities. A distinction between the two laws, civil and canonical, and their functions could thus be taken for granted, yet not as creating wholly separate realms opposed one to the other (the modern view).

Even in the beginning of this acceptance of a symbiosis between civil and religious legal organization, however, Pauline reservations about the moral meaning of law, including civil law, persisted. St. Augustine's two cities imply this. A Pauline suspicion of law appears as a warning against excessive regulation of Christian life and as a reaction to the impotence of imperial law in the face of barbarian invasions. Among some Christians, flight "from the world" into the deserts of Egypt symbolized an esoteric spiritual tendency to reject the world and its struggles, including the developing function of law.

In the Medieval Era

In legal practice. In the centuries of chaos after the fall of the old empire and before the dawn of the medieval period, an awareness of the functions of the developing canon law of the councils and the papacy as distinct from the function of civil law of the declining empire and other secular polities that replaced it was present but submerged. Only later in the high medieval period did clear separation of clerical from lay leadership and authority produce increasingly explicit theological and jurisprudential recognition, which the medieval authors discuss under the rubric of the "two swords."

The period between the fall of the old empire in the 5th century and the new reordering of communal life in the 11th through the 13th centuries had involved in many places the imposition of church authority by bishops (including the pope, on the Papal States) to fill a disastrous vacuum in lay authority. Church authority and lay governmental authority had frequently become merged in one person, for example, an abbot or a prince-bishop. In this situation, temporal-ecclesial authority and law sought to master the disastrous political, economic, and social chaos that ravaged European life in all its aspects after the fall of the old empire.

As feudalism developed in the medieval renaissance, however, the function of lay authority and the expression of this in civil law grew. But this growth continued to be inextricably mixed with the development of canonical regulation of church life. Thus, right up to the postmedieval Renaissance and Reformation there continued to be an operative, implicit cultural assumption among both rulers and thinkers that the two realms of law, the civil and the canonical, function as dimensions ingredient in the one civil-sacral social order. The new Roman Empire was called "Holy."

A fully thematic "separation" of "church" from "state" (which had forced itself on the consciousness of the early church under Roman persecution and which modern constitutional practice would come to take for granted after the laicization and secularization of the social and political orders of society following the Reformation) only begins to be hinted at in the medieval investiture controversies. In these struggles the church leadership, especially focused in the pope and the growing Roman Curia (Gregory the Great, Innocent III), demanded freedom from lay authorities to control church office and life even where the bishop was also a vassal of the king or emperor. An open conflict thus developed between the growing legal organizations of the "spiritual" and the "temporal" dimensions of feudal society. At a later point, the investiture controversies about jurisdiction even took on the form of claims of superiority of church authority over lay rulers and their law (e.g., Boniface VIII)—claims to integrist control of the spiritual over the temporal. Thus what began as a demand for freedom of church authority from temporal dominance evolved into an attempted assertion of spiritual dominance over temporal.

Yet a general thrust to achieve order out of civil and economic chaos was being realized in both clerical and temporal affairs. Clerical administration of canon law modeled on Roman law and, in the royal courts, a combination of Roman and traditional (tribal) law functioned to restore a vision of the common good of the one unified social order, a striving to achieve economic sufficiency and civil peace through justice. The functions of both canon and civil law in the 13th century became increasingly differentiated. Feudal law allowed the growth of towns and of a class engaged in commerce and production while preserving political control in the noble classes. Within the clerical leadership of the church there developed (with the rise of the new universities from the cathedral schools) a new differentiation between bishops and theologians; and within the schools there developed a differentiation in function and professional outlook (sometimes hostile) between the canonists and the theologians. A clearer differentiation between canonists and secular legists followed as well, especially in the late medieval and early Renaissance periods with the decline of classical feudalism and the early development of the centrally controlled national states—though the ideal of expertise in both canon and civil law persists even to modern times.

In the field of civil law, the influence of Roman law interacting with traditional (tribal) legal custom led to growing awareness of the need to balance two distinguishable functions of civil law. On the one hand, legal customs preserve and transmit the particular treasured social and political culture of a distinct ethnic group. On the other hand, rational predictability and uniformity in growing legal practice within developing national states demand a process of theoretical reasoning. On the continent of Europe this complex development took a decidedly legislative turn (codes), culminating in the early modern era in the Napoleonic codes. There the university faculties of law studying Roman law had a dominant theoretical influence on conceptions of law and its function both in civil and canonical legal evolution. But in England the evolution of a strong royal law distinct from the canon law of the church took the form of elaborate development of case law based on precedent in royal courts with lay judges: the common law (Bracton).

Judges drawn from the ranks of lawyers trained in the Inns of Court in London made practical legal decisions in disputes about feudal property interests and the contractual interests of commerce as well as about accusations of crime. This process received its theoretical rationalization in the judicial opinions of appellate judges, who gave reasons for upholding or reversing decisions at trial, rather than from university faculties. The common law functioned as an adversary system, drawing more explicitly from traditional customary law than from Roman law in resolving matters at issue between parties in the lawsuit.

Within this common law a variety of specialized functional areas of law became differentiated: law courts decided cases separately from courts of equity, and two distinct bodies of precedent were developed. An unwritten, case-by-case constitutional law (organic law controlling what counts as law versus what is "unconstitutional" and null as law) took shape, starting from such documents as the *Magna Charta.* The common law as a whole—constitutional law, common law, and equity—functioned to give a more predictable order to the more and more complex political and economic life of the kingdom, while matters such as marriage and the administration of trusts and estates after death seen to involve explicitly religious conscience remained in the courts of the church (under varying degrees of lay influence).

Medieval legal theory. In the 13th century the importance of the ideal of law as a source of renewal of society and of stability and freedom of the church appears dramatically in theology. St. Thomas Aquinas elaborated the most systematic theoretical (both theological and philosophical) account of the nature and function of civil law in the Treatise on Law (ST IaIIae, qq. 90–97) and the Treatise on Justice (ST IIaIIae, qq. 57–79). This theory of law and its function is relatively abstract, in contrast with the work of legists and judges in the service of kings and also with that of canonists in the service of the pope and bishops. Nonetheless it articulates certain important themes about the function of civil law that have been evolving throughout the history of Christian Europe and affecting the practice both of Roman legists and of civil- and common-law judges. In Aquinas' theology these themes constitute nothing less than a kind of basic theoretical constitutionalism.

Drawing on the Scriptures and the theology of the patristic thinkers, on the philosophy of Aristotle and the theories of the Stoics through Cicero, and on the works of the Roman legists and the canon lawyers, Aquinas provided a succinct point of departure for summarizing these themes:

> This is the definition of law by its four essential parts: an ordinance of reason for the sake of the common good commanded by the authority who has charge of the community, and promulgated (ST IaIIae, q. 90, a. 4).

The legitimacy of authority is a first condition of existence and function of valid law. The legitimacy of authority implies action by the whole people (thus the customary element in law) or by a person or persons legitimately acting on their behalf (thus later, the executive, legislative, and judicial elements in law).

Second, to be valid the law produced by this authority must function to produce the common good. Thus law must be aimed at producing justice through the ordered goodness of the activity of the members of the community who act together under the law. This means that edicts employing governmental force for selfish purposes of ruling classes are not law at all but only "a species of violence."

Third, valid law must be the product of prudent practical reason, and so law should appeal to the reason of those subject to it. But human law secondarily exists as a result of will, the command of the authority executing the dictates of practical reason, and so it implies the possible use of force to compel compliance in those who unreasonably resist. Human law precisely as a work of practical reason is rooted in the natural law, and so ultimately in divine law, God's own wisdom. But law and morality are not simply the same. Restraint on the valid content of human law extends to its function in the real world of imperfect, sinful human beings; not all acts of vice are to be forbidden by human law, nor are all acts of virtue to be enjoined by it, but only what, given the moral development and customs of a particular society, is reasonably possible in order to promote the common good.

Finally, promulgation of law to the members of the community making it adequately known is required for it to function through reason. In this theoretical constitutionalism of Aquinas, a crucial moral function of valid human law (its claim on the individual conscience of the community member to contribute to the common good by willing conformity to valid law) is achieved first of all through informed reason.

In the Treatise on the New Law and Grace (ST IaIIae, qq. 106-14) Aquinas incorporates a warning of Augustine about the potential burdensomeness of too much law (ST IaIIae, q. 107, a. 4, quoting St. Augustine, *Epist.* lv, 19; PL 33, p. 221). The moral primacy of individual conscience formed in good faith even if erroneous (ST IaIIae, q. 19) qualifies the power of valid law to command. Resistance to unjust rulers and their law can be morally justified (ST IIaIIae, q. 42, ad 3m).

In Reformation and Counter-Reformation Controversy

A new element appears in the theology of the Reformers, especially due to Martin Luther's understanding of two negatively oriented "uses of the law" (convicting the sinner and coercing the wrongdoer) in contrast with the justifying function of faith and grace. Luther's determined rejection of "works of the law" in religious life can seem to challenge the authority of all law, though Luther was intransigent in demanding submission to unjust rulers as worthy punishment of the subjects' sinfulness. Here, nonetheless, appears a basis for secularization of civil law and its function—though this will not take place until later in the Enlightenment.

Counter-Reformation Catholic theology, in response, takes up and develops the medieval theory of Aquinas on law and its relationship to virtue, reasserting the positive goal of law as the "common good" and also the importance of the virtues of "legal justice" and "distributive justice" for constituting the temporal common good. The unambiguous assertion of a "third use of the law" (to direct people toward righteousness) in John Calvin leaves the Reformed tradition stemming from Calvin more open than the Lutheran tradition to explicit consideration of law as a positive dimension of social life too. Both Catholic and Calvinist traditions assert, as well, the legitimacy of resistance to tyrannical government as a corrective of unjust law.

Among both Catholics and Calvinists there begins to be an explicit development from the Roman law conception of the *jus gentium* of a "law of nations" (or international law), and this includes affirmance of the constraints of the "law of war" and, eventually, challenge to war's terrible product, slavery. Law is to function to establish justice and its fruit, peace, among the newly emerged and mutually competing nation-states and with respect to their imperial conquest of non-European peoples. This development has somewhat different theoretical overtones, more explicitly theological in such thinkers as the Catholic Suarez and Vitoria, more philosophical in the Calvinist Grotius. But the conception of a just and peaceful common good of a world community under law to which all participants are to contribute begins its thematic development. And with it there is further elaboration of the grounds for lawful resistance to tyranny within nations.

In the Early and Later Modern Period

In the period of the Enlightenment the themes noted to this point take new forms, as a now thoroughly secularized civil law develops ever-greater complexity to serve the needs of a fast-developing economic and political culture. Regulation of human activity expands not only as an expression of civil authority but also in organizing the division of labor demanded by industrial and commercial development (private bureaucracy). The ideal of reform of law to achieve a common good more effectively finds varied expression in such philosophers as Locke, Hume, Bentham, and Mill and in legal philosophers such as Austin. An individualist conception of the person, however, begins to develop, and law is conceived as based more on contractual consent, whether real or postulated, than upon human solidarity.

Constitutionalism constraining law from injustice takes written expression in the United States, especially in the Bill of Rights. Latent social injustice supported by law is challenged radically and dramatically by Marx. Law increasingly pervades public and private life, and the practice-oriented specialized study of distinct areas of law and its function flourishes.

A search for equality and the participation of all persons in shaping and receiving the benefits of law through democratic forms comes to the fore as an explicit ideal of legal theory and practice. At the same time, this ideal is challenged by various forms of political absolutism that emphasize law as the source of order through totalitarian empowerment of rulers. The social encyclicals of Leo XIII (*Rerum novarum*) and Pius XI (*Quadragesimo anno*) begin a notable theologically based challenge to the continuing social injustice from both the Left and the Right but are limited in their influence on legal development, even among Catholics.

Some Contemporary Concerns and Questions

The function of law in contemporary First World societies constantly increases in complexity, and the study of these complexities becomes always more subspecialized. In the United States the realms of ordinary law study and practice thus become continually more distanced from such well-crafted challenges to achieve a just common good through law as are posed by the U.S. Catholic bishops in *The Challenge of Peace* and *Economic Justice for All.* Even more distant are the powerful Pastoral Constitution on the Church in the Modern World of Vatican Council II and subsequent papal encyclicals of Paul VI and John Paul II. The impact of John XXIII's *Pacem in terris* on the world scene in 1963 was a notable exception to this.

At the international level the ideal of world law fostering an international common good is only partially realized in the United Nations and the International Court of Justice at The Hague. The older law of treaties and war among national states staggers along, while a narrow nationalism that alienates states one from another still impairs the progress of a world law effectively establishing a common good for all peoples.

In the area of U.S. constitutional law, a search to find expression of the ideal of human rights and social justice implied in historically formulated provisions confronts a fundamentalist positivism in interpretation by conservative justices that seeks to maintain older privileged social, political, and economic forms of life. For example, judicial efforts of some (Brennan, Marshall) to establish priority of rights of persons is confronted by persistent efforts to assert protection of property rights that enshrine economic, social, and political privilege.

The ideal of law as promoting a common good increasingly participated in by all members of society and implicit in the Bill of Rights and the Fourteenth Amendment is both urged and challenged. Political efforts to criminalize abortion are often paired with advocacy of the barbaric death penalty and aggressive support of totalitarian regimes friendly to the United States.

The struggle to constrain violence, racism, sexism, and other impairments of personal dignity through law advances against subtle opposition.

In the vast area of ordinary common law deriving from previously decided cases that function as precedent, the need to deal with always-new economic problems and social crises within a morally pluralistic society has meant enormous proliferation of statute law. The effective claim of this mass of positive legislation on the conscience and moral (including religious) conviction of citizens is greatly diminished by contrast with the claim of law and its function in prior, less-complex cultures. And the intent of legislators to achieve an administratively convenient solution of apparently merely technical problems often simply ignores the lack of such law's appeal to reason and conscience of citizens. At the same time, the appeal of law to mere unthinking obedience has largely been dissipated. The essential role of lawyers in the adversary system by which law is developed through decision of disputes is often caricatured.

The rapid development of an affluent consumer society in the First World has produced a huge gap between those who are well off and those who are poor, both within the United States and in the expanding populations of the Third World (developing nations primarily in the Southern Hemisphere). The function of law to achieve distributive and social justice, that is, an ever-more-fair sharing among all people of goods necessary for human survival and thus for a minimal humane common good, seems more rather than less impaired as the economic development of the First World accelerates. Thus the ideal function of law to ensure justly ordered peace within a nation and among the rest of the world's materially deprived presents an ever-greater challenge to those who shape the law.

Within particular special legal disciplines such as criminal law, realization has grown that law functions to achieve a complex of competing and even sometimes mutually contradictory goals. This can demand trade-offs and constant experiment at the cost of stability of law. For instance, the goals of containment and punishment of convicts and deterrence of potential criminals compete in practice with an ideal of rehabilitation. On the one hand, measures to forestall predicted criminal behavior impair the ideal of justice, which forbids constraining or punishing any but those already fairly convicted of actual crime. On the other hand, especially in the area of commercial law, efforts are underway to replace adversarial resolution of disputes by trial before the courts with sophisticated dispute-resolution procedures aiming to make both parties win, thus strengthening ongoing relationships.

In every area of law the complex, mutually conditioning relationship of any one legal measure to all the rest and of one area of law to all others means that the search for justice and a fairly shared common good through law always demands a constantly renewed exercise of imaginative intelligence and prudent practical reason.

See also CANON LAW, FUNCTION OF; COMMON GOOD; CONSCIENTIOUS OBJECTION; HUMAN RIGHTS; JUSTICE IN THE WORLD; NATURAL LAW; POLITICAL PHILOSOPHY; SACRED AND SECULAR, RELATIONSHIP OF.

Bibliography: F. Murphy, *Politics and the Early Christian* (New York: Desclee, 1967). B. Tierney, *The Crisis of Church and State, 1050–1360, with Selected Documents* (Englewood Cliffs, N.J.: Prentice-Hall, 1964). T. Gilby, *The Political Thought of Thomas Aquinas* (Chicago: Univ. of Chicago Press, 1958). H. Berman, *Law and Revolution: The Formation of the Western Legal Tradition* (Cambridge: Harvard Univ. Press, 1983). W. McLoughlin and R. Bellah, eds., *Religion In America* (Boston: Beacon, 1968). J. Murray, *We Hold These Truths: Catholic Reflections on the American Proposition* (New York: Sheed & Ward, 1964). L. Fuller, *Anatomy of the Law* (New York: Praeger, 1968). M. Perry, *The Constitution, the Courts, and Human Rights* (New Haven: Yale Univ. Press, 1982). R. Unger, *The Critical Legal Studies Movement* (Cambridge: Harvard Univ. Press, 1983). "Church and World," "Justice," "Law," "Law and Gospel," "Natural Law," "Theology," in K. Rahner et al., eds., *Sacramentum Mundi: An Encyclopedia of Theology,* 6 vols. (New York: Herder & Herder, 1968–70).

JAMES F. BRESNAHAN, S.J.

CLASS

A class is an aggregate of persons within society whose members share common economic, social, and cultural characteristics. Classes comprise different strata of society, usually reflecting levels of inequality with respect to income, wealth, power, and prestige. Feudal societies of the Middle Ages showed extreme levels of inequality, with rights and privileges codified by law.

The writings of Karl Marx and Frederick Engels brought special attention to class distinctions in society. They viewed classes and class conflict as the key elements and driving force of history. Though Marx never wrote any systematic study on classes, he used two main criteria for defining classes. Classes, for Marx, were above all determined by their position or role in production. Groups that owned and controlled the means of production came to be the dominant classes, in conflict with those excluded from ownership and control. But Marx also believed that "class consciousness" was essential for the formation of a true class "in and for itself."

Most of Marx's writings, focusing on the changes brought about by the Industrial Revolution, stressed the bourgeoisie (capitalists) and the proletariat (working class) as the two most important classes of modern times. The triumph of the bourgeoisie established capitalist society. The overthrow of capitalism and introduction of socialism would not only bring the workers to power but would lead eventually to a classless society.

Marx recognized other classes in society but consistently stressed the capitalist-proletariat struggle. In *Das Kapital* he spoke of three major classes, the capitalists, the proletariat, and the landlords. Other writings included discussions of the petite bourgeoisie (small shop-owners, professionals, intellectuals, and others of the middle class), the peasants, and the *lumpenproletariat* (the marginalized of society who played no real role in the productive process). Though in Marx's time the peasant class still constituted the largest class in most countries, Marx believed that peasants lacked the class consciousness needed to play any major role in bringing about social change and that control of the economic base of society generally led to corresponding control of state power and ruling ideas. Erik Olin Wright and others have used Marx's method to analyze contemporary class structures and conflicts.

Max Weber challenged Marx's emphasis on economic factors, arguing for three distinct sources of power and status in society. He recognized the economic sphere as important. Even in this sphere, however, Weber believed that Marx's class distinctions oversimplified the great range of strata within classes, for example, the significant difference between a dishwasher and a skilled mechanic in the working class. In addition to the economic, Weber claimed that the social and political realms play equally important roles in determining social strata. The social realm he related to prestige, honor, and lifestyle. The political, where political parties and government bureaucracies have become increasingly significant, often determines power relations in society.

Though class distinctions often remain prominent in traditional and developing societies, most non-Marxist sociologists do not treat class distinctions and class conflicts as crucial in analyzing contemporary industrialized societies. Most North American discussions of class differences fall under the heading of "social stratification." Three distinct though interrelated approaches are used to determine classes or social level: subjective (what class or level people perceive themselves as belonging to); reputational (the class that observers assign to groups); and objective (income, wealth, occupational prestige, etc.). On the subjective side, polls taken in the United States at different times since

World War II suggest that most U.S. Americans view themselves as middle class, or at least less than 10 percent see themselves as belonging to the upper class or the poor. A study by Gilbert and Rahl based chiefly on economic norms recognizes a more objective distinction of classes in the United States: capitalist class, 1 percent; upper middle class, 14 percent; middle class, 30 percent; working class, 30 percent; the working poor and underclass, 25 percent.

Catholic church teachings until the late 19th century tended to view hierarchical class divisions as "natural." *Rerum novarum* (1891) recognized the disturbing presence of class conflicts brought on by the Industrial Revolution, as did *Quadragesimo anno* (1931) and later social encyclicals, including Pope John Paul II's *Laborem exercens* (1981). Stressing moral responsibilities on both sides, church teachings aimed at diminishing these conflicts. In the 1980s John Paul II and Vatican officials criticized Latin American liberation theologians for using a conflict model of social analysis and especially for references to "class struggle."

See also CAPITALISM; CLASS STRUGGLE; MARXISM; RERUM NOVARUM.

Bibliography: J. Landis, *Sociology,* 7th ed., chap. 5. (Belmont, Calif., 1989). See also other contemporary sociology textbooks, usually under the heading of "social stratification." D. Gilbert and J. Kahl, *The American Class Structure: A New Synthesis,* 3rd ed., esp. pp. 327–37 (Chicago: Dorsey, 1987). E. Wright et al., "The American Class Structure," *American Sociological Review* 47 (December 1982).

ARTHUR F. McGOVERN, S.J.

CLASS STRUGGLE

"Class struggle" generally refers to the hostility generated between dominant, oppressive classes in society and lower, oppressed classes. Class struggle is a notion most associated with Marxist social analysis. Karl Marx and Frederick Engels believed that class struggle operated as the driving force in history. Their *Manifesto of the Communist Party* (1848) asserted this forcefully: "The history of all hitherto existing society is the history of class struggles. Freeman and slave, patrician and plebian, lord and serf, guildmaster and journeyman, in a word, oppressor and oppressed, stood in constant opposition to one another, carried on an uninterrupted, now hidden, now open fight, a fight that each time ended, either in a revolutionary re-constitution of society at large, or in the common ruin of the contending classes" (Tucker, ed., pp. 473–74).

The idea of class struggle did not originate with Marx. Lorenz von Stein and other social critics had described the class struggles fomented by the Industrial Revolution. Marx, however, made it the cornerstone of his social analysis. He argued that how people produce, which forms the economic basis of society, shapes the whole life of society. This economic base or structure includes productive forces (natural resources, tools, and human labor), but classes are determined more directly by "relations of production," by the way in which systems of production are organized. Ownership and control over the means of production give rise to the dominant class or classes in society. Those excluded from ownership and control become the most oppressed or dominated classes. The dominant class gains not only economic control but political and ideological rule as well. "The executive of the modern State," Marx claimed in the *Manifesto,* "is but a committee for managing the common affairs of the whole bourgeoisie" (Tucker, ed., p. 425).

Marx believed that the Industrial Revolution had created two major antagonists: the bourgeoisie or capitalist class and the proletariat or working class. He credited the capitalist class with having created the most productive and efficient system thus far in history. He believed, however, that it would unwittingly bring about its own destruction through its own creation, the proletarian working class. These two opposed classes struggled against each other because their interests clashed. The capitalists sought to keep wages at the lowest possible level; the proletariat fought for higher wages and shorter work days. Even when workers' wages rose the struggle continued because the gap between owners' profits and workers' pay created resentment. Marx claimed that profits originated from exploitation of "surplus value" created by labor. Workers' wages were not determined by their contribution to production, by the time they gave to their work, but by the amount owners believed would be sufficient to keep them and their families in subsistence.

The exclusion of workers from ownership and control of the means of production constituted the objective basis for their situation as a class. Marx argued, however, that "class consciousness" was needed for workers to become a true class "in and for itself." The very struggles of the workers in defense of their interests helped them to develop this consciousness and to recognize their need for solidarity as a class. The bourgeoisie enlisted them in its own struggles against the monarchy and older forms of feudal rule, but in doing so it strengthened workers' class consciousness. Struggles to form unions and to obtain better wages and working conditions sharpened their class consciousness even more.

Marx recognized the presence of other classes in modern society: the petite bourgeoisie (small-business owners, professionals), peasants, and the marginalized of society (the *lumpenproletariat*). The conflict between capitalists and workers, however, would determine the future of industrial society. Though peasants still constituted the largest class in Marx's time, agriculture no longer served as the source of greatest wealth, and the peasants themselves remained too isolated and unorganized socially and politically to effect significant social change.

Challenges and Modifications of Marx's Ideas

In the late 19th century Marx's predictions about the impending collapse of capitalism, the decline of the middle class, and the increasing misery of the working class appeared misguided. Capitalism continued to flourish, the middle class grew larger and stronger, and workers turned their efforts to immediate gains of higher wages and better working conditions through their organization of unions. Eduard Bernstein at the turn of the century argued that Marxism should abandon its rhetoric of revolution and should work instead for a gradual evolution toward socialism through use of democratic political methods.

Lenin, however, challenged this gradualism. Class struggle was essential to Marxism, so also was a commitment to revolutionary change. Lenin recognized the tendency of workers to accept increments of change, but he castigated it as an ineffectual "trade-union consciousness." Workers should not be left alone in their struggles. Revolutionary theory must come "from without," from intellectuals, as the contributions of Marx and Engels demonstrated. Professional revolutionaries must lead the way and form a "vanguard party" to lead workers toward revolutionary change. These points, developed by Lenin in *What Is to Be Done?* (1902), became the dominant interpretation of Marxism once the Bolsheviks took power in 1917. Lenin reinforced the leading role of the vanguard party by insisting also, in *State and Revolution* (1917), on a "dictatorship of the proletariat" led by the Communist party.

Critics have raised serious objections to Marxist-Leninist views of class struggle. Max Weber challenged what he viewed as Marx's reduction of power struggles to economic factors. He viewed political power, especially the power of bureaucratic control within government, and social prestige as competing factors. In the days prior to the Russian revolution many Marxists challenged Lenin's attempts to rely on a vanguard party rather than on workers themselves as leading the struggle toward socialism. "Dictatorship of the proletariat," they argued, would become a "dictatorship *over* the proletariat."

The domination of the Communist party in the USSR and throughout Eastern Europe led other critics to argue that new forms of class struggle had emerged in those countries. Officially, the Communist parties claimed that continuing conflicts took the form of nonantagonistic struggles. But others viewed ruling party leaders and top government officials as constituting a new class of oppressors. The formation of a workers' Solidarity movement in Poland followed by the dramatic protests against Communist rule throughout much of Eastern Europe in 1989 and 90 indicated massive resentment of Communist-party rule.

In the United States, except among Marxist intellectuals, the idea of class struggle has never won a significant following, though most textbooks in sociology do distinguish between conflictual and functional theories of analysis. Conflict theory borrows from Marx a conviction that competition and conflict are markedly present in society (though manifest in racism and sexism as well as in worker-owner conflicts) and should serve as the focus of sociological analysis. Functional analysis, however, developed by Talcott Parsons, Robert K. Merton, and others, prevails as a more dominant form of analysis. Functional analysis sees society as an organic body with various occupations and groupings serving to enable society to function. Different reward systems are needed, according to this theory, to motivate persons to take up the work needed to form a well-functioning society. If physicians and corporate executives make more money and are held in greater esteem than factory workers, the difference reflects what society considers more important.

Church Social Teachings on Class Conflict

The first major social encyclicals focused upon the conflicts brought about by the Industrial Revolution. Leo XIII's *Rerum novarum* (1891) noted that "the enormous fortunes of individuals and the poverty of the masses" had created harsh conflicts within society (RN 1). Leo condemned the "callousness of employers," "the greed of unrestrained competition," and the dealings of "avaricious and grasping men" as causes of injustice and class hostilities. He sought to resolve the conflicts and injustices by offering several guidelines. He called upon owners to pay just wages and to guide their actions by Christian moral principles. He argued that the state should intervene to protect workers' rights. He acknowledged the right of workers to form unions but called upon them to accept their responsibilities and to avoid hostile conflicts. At the same time, he condemned socialist solutions that would do away with private property, and he rejected the socialist (Marxist) assumption that hostilities between classes are natural and inevitable (15). Cooperation and mutual responsibility, not class struggle, should characterize owner-worker relations.

Pius XI in *Quadragesimo anno* (1931) reaffirmed these principles. He acknowledged and called for the abolition of conflict between classes. Labor, he insisted, cannot be bought and sold like some piece of merchandise. "None the less the demand and supply of labor divides men on the labor market into two classes, as into two camps, and the bargaining between these parties transforms this labor market into an arena where the two armies are engaged in combat" (QA 83). He chastised capitalism, in which "immense power and despotic economic domination is concentrated in the hands of the few" (105). Like Leo XIII, however, Pius XI looked for solutions that would create harmony and not rely on class struggle to bring greater justice. He proposed an economic system based on "corporations" that would give workers a share in ownership and a voice in management (64–65, 81–97).

In more recent times John Paul II's *Laborem exercens* (1981) addressed the issue of class conflicts most directly. He recognized human work as essential to human development and established "the priority of labor over capital" as the central principle of his encyclical. In terms quite similar to Marx, the pope said that "labor" stands for those who work without being the owners of the means of production, and that "capital" refers to those who act as entrepreneurs and who either own the means of production or represent the owners (LE 14). The encyclical places the blame for class conflict historically on capitalists who exploited workers by keeping wages at the lowest possible minimum so as to maximize their own profits (11). John Paul II also accepts and even commends the "struggle" of workers to obtain their rights and just needs. Struggle "for" justice, however, differs sharply from struggle "against others." The pope affirms struggle in behalf of justice for all as praiseworthy. However, with the Marxist notion of class struggle clearly in mind, he judges struggle to bring one party into power as wrong (20).

Liberation Theology in Latin America

In the 1970s and 1980s, Latin America's liberation theology gained prominence and stirred controversy because of its stress on political involvement and its use of Marxist analysis. Though references to class struggle occurred in various writings of liberation theology, critics focused particularly on Gustavo Gutiérrez's *Theology of Liberation* (1973). Most of Gutiérrez's comments on class struggle simply stress that class conflict constitutes a fact of reality in Latin America. But Gutiérrez does say that neutrality is impossible, since to deny the existence of social divisions would mean accepting the prevailing system. "To accept class struggle," he says, "means to decide for some people and against others," and he calls upon the church to opt for the oppressed.

Some critics interpret Gutiérrez's comments as an endorsement of Marxist views on class struggle. The Marxist conception of class struggle includes (1) seeking victory by one class over another, (2) promoting resentment and hatred in place of love, (3) an implied encouraging of violent means, and (4) viewing class struggle as the driving force of history. Defenders of Gutiérrez would argue that none of these elements appears in Gutiérrez's discussion of class struggle. He calls for opting with the poor against oppressing classes but seeks a restoration of true unity in society, not the victory of one class over another. Far from advocating class hatred, he discusses explicitly how to preserve universal Christian love in the midst of class conflict. He does not endorse violence, and he does not say or imply that class struggle is the driving force of history.

Some critics, however, believe that the expression "class struggle" has become so identified with Marxism that any use of the phrase implies or at least risks implying an acceptance of Marxist ideology and the whole Marxist program of revolutionary tactics. In 1984 the Congregation for the Defense of the Faith, headed by Joseph Cardinal Ratzinger, issued *An Instruction on Certain Aspects of the Theology of Liberation.* The instruction criticized these certain aspects on several scores. It rejected, as misguided, efforts to separate Marxist analysis from the rest of Marxism and made several comments related specifically to class struggle. The acceptance of class struggle, the instruction asserts, leads to hatred and violence (*1984 Instruction,* sec. 8, nos. 7–9). Some liberation theologians, moreover, accept class struggle as "the fundamental law of history" (sec. 9, nos. 2–3). Liberation theologians make Marxist analysis the guiding force of "praxis" (political activity), which then becomes the sole criterion of truth. "Theological criteria for truth are thus relativized and subordinated to the imperatives of the class struggle" (sec. 8, nos. 1–4; sec. 10, no. 3).

John Paul II acknowledged liberation as a legitimate and important Christian theme, and in 1986 he wrote to the bishops of Brazil that the theology of liberation was "not only opportune, but useful and necessary." But in many talks, both prior to and since the letter, he warned against the introduction of "false ideologies" into liberation theology, especially ideologies such as Marxism that speak about class struggle. In several addresses given during a May 1990 visit to Mexico, John Paul II warned frequently against "conflictive notions of liberation." The church's option for the poor, he said, is not an ideological option, "nor is it a matter of being trapped in the false theory of class struggle as the moving force of change in history. Love for the poor is something arising out of the Gospel itself and must not be formulated or presented in conflictual terms" (John Paul II, *Origins,* May 24, 1990, vol. 20, no. 2, p. 31). The Vatican opposition to use of class struggle appears quite clear. John Paul II's more general opposition to "conflictual notions of liberation" would seem to require, however, some balancing with his statements in *Laborem exercens* about the legitimacy of "struggle for" workers' rights and just needs.

In a new introduction to a 15th-anniversary edition of *A Theology of Liberation,* Gutiérrez acknowledged the misunderstandings generated by his use of class struggle in the first edition. To clear up these misunderstandings, he rewrote and gave a new title, "Faith and Social Conflict," to the section of his book originally entitled "Christian Fellowship and Class Struggle." Probably with a view to justifying his earlier version, Gutiérrez cites several passages from church teachings that refer explicitly to the "fact" of class struggle (QA 82–83; LE 11, 14; and a 1968 statement by the French episcopal commission that "class struggle is a fact that no one can deny"). In the new edition Gutiérrez avoids expressions such as "combating the oppressing class" and "to participate in class struggle." He speaks rather of "opposing certain groups of people" who violate human rights and of "solidarity with" or a "preferential option for" the poor. Perhaps the controversy might have been avoided or at least diminished had he enunciated some ethical norms at the outset indicating morally acceptable and unacceptable means of struggle from a Christian perspective.

The dramatic breakdown of Communist party rule throughout Eastern Europe will most likely diminish the appeal of Marxist analysis and its references to class struggle. The reality of social conflict, however, will continue, and in Latin America conflicts have most often revolved around a class-related issue of land ownership and use. In many countries of Latin America the top 1 or 2 percent of landowners control 40 to 80 percent of all arable land, with 60 to 85 percent of rural households remaining landless or nearly landless (Riding). In Central America violent conflicts, arising often over the issue of land reform, claimed over 100,000 lives in the 1980s alone. Social conflict remains strong in countries like Brazil and Peru, which rank among the worst in the world in disparity of wealth between the rich and the poor. Marxism too often oversimplifies analysis with its focus on class struggle, but the necessity of addressing the causes of social conflict remains important.

See also CAPITALISM; CLASS; EXPLOITATION; INDUSTRIALIZATION; LABOR AND CAPITAL IN CATHOLIC SOCIAL THOUGHT; LIBERATION THEOLOGY; MARXISM; POLITICAL THEOLOGY.

Bibliography: R. Tucker, ed., *The Marx-Engels Reader,* 2nd ed. (New York: Norton, 1978). *Five Great Encyclicals,* including *Rerum novarum* and *Quadragesimo anno* (New York: Paulist, 1939). Congregation for the Defense of the Faith, *Instruction on Certain Aspects of*

Liberation Theology (Vatican City: Libreria Editrice Vaticana, 1984), also published in the *National Catholic Reporter* (September 21, 1984). John Paul II, *Laborem exercens,* in G. Baum, *The Priority of Labor* (New York: Paulist, 1982), and John Paul II's addresses in Mexico, *Origins,* vol. 20, no. 2 (May 24, 1990). G. Gutiérrez, *A Theology of Liberation* (Maryknoll, N.Y.: Orbis, 1973), original English edition and in 1988 a new 15th anniversary edition. A. Riding, "The Struggle for Land Reform in Latin America," *The New York Times* (Sunday, March 26, 1989), sec. 4.

ARTHUR F. McGOVERN, S.J.

COLLECTIVISM

Collectivism is both a view of the social group, most significantly, the state, and those practices that derive from this belief. These practices have found their most forceful and terrifying forms in this century. In this view of the state or social group neither the individual person nor any other group that he/she forms or joins has legitimacy apart from the collective. The collective may assume different forms: party, nation, race, or the people have been frequent candidates. Since the collective is the sole source of meaning and value, it arrogates to itself power in order to control the state with its subordinate groups. Since nothing in the entire society or within the secondary groups matters except insofar as it contributes to the collective or carries out its programs, collectivism is a menace to the individual. In the interaction between the person and the collective, the only secure relation is that he/she must fulfill an array of duties. With or without state power, the collective can subject persons to domination or, further, to totalitarian control. Rights are only those granted by the collective, so they offer no defense of the individual with respect to it, especially since the code of law and procedures of adjudication that would secure rights are created by the collective on its own behalf.

Collectivism also threatens the intermediate bodies of society and thus the vitality of the economic and other social processes that they sustain. The life of any group is only a subordinate goal. Within these groups, rather than self-determined participation, activity degenerates to response at the behest of often anonymous others. Rather than personal initiative, passive acceptance. Clearly the members' activity in collectivism stands at a remove from participation in a system of collegial, collaborative, or cooperative enterprises. The latter thrive through the particularity and initiative of their members; a collective renders its "members," or better said, its "elements," if not similar and passive, then anonymous and compliant.

The form of obedience found in a collective offends human dignity because (1) the person who is bidden to carry out a requirement has no effective alternative or no alternative group to which he/she may withdraw; (2) for an act of noncompliance, the system punishes the person in several ways, all of which point to that person's ceasing to matter from the constrained viewpoint of the collective. No heed is paid to the privilege of conscience. Since the collective assumes suprapersonal qualities, it tries to reduce those of its members. Its assertion of the form of its will requires that it attempt to eliminate the complexity introduced by the free wills of individual persons.

While totalitarianism concerns the range of state control over the societal, familial, and personal spheres and incorporates a collection of intrusive methods that is utilized across this range, and while authoritarianism is a style and pattern of unilateral administrative control, collectivism concerns the purpose, goal, and central agent of state or social control. As a result of its far-reaching and unique claim to legitimacy, collectivism tends toward totalitarianism and authoritarianism. These latter do not require collectivist ideology or organization.

Under a collectivist culture, emblems and stories do not emerge and continue as living traditions in broad strata of society; rather, the controlling elements of the collective either create or seize them for its purposes. The collective organism claims for itself a further, extensive power: it alone determines time. The usual measure of this time is the collective's progress or the development of the group that is the center of the group's ideology and control. This progress is also read back into the years prior to the collective's coming into control. Further, this control suppresses or alters the other strands of history. The collective's use of time reduces the lives of persons to the report of their function, and it erases alternate histories of neutral groups or of independent local communities. Belief in divine timelessness or in God as the Lord of history are tenets of faith that shelter those who suffer from this domination of time; indeed these truths stimulate hope and thus enable resistance.

The acquiescence to and acceptance of collectivism draws nourishment from several roots: the fear of the other; the lack of a lively allegiance as this is evidenced in a respect for cultural markers (e.g., the laws) that express restraining values which are the social controls on all common action; the breakdown or lack of preparation for discourse in a multicultural society; and the effective atheism that sees not the Lord but a large, vital, and mysterious group as the source and end of significance or salvation.

Surprisingly, several dangers accompany the collapse of major collective organizations earlier in this century and in recent years: believers and other citizens may fail to recognize the actual and defensive worth of those achievements that have been seized, maintained, and refined in the face of collectivist threats. Others may fail to be aware of the emergence of collectivist tendencies in areas of the world that have until now not been prominently involved in U.S. foreign policy. Or collectivist patterns may appear on the domestic scene. As the pretense of suprapersonal collectives has become manifest, anonymous norms have assumed a value for the sake of which persons must alter their lives. In this light, market indices and the pursuit of profit deserve further examination.

One tool that shows great force in assessing the inroads of collectivism is a sustained attention to the vitality of the body of the normal citizenry. Such attention sets in revealing light those times when the citizenry must routinely pay the price for the sake of the metaphorical body of the collective. The tragic loss of careers, lives, and entire groups for the sake of the collective has drawn ready recognition. New is the realization that extensive environmental danger, which slowly assails the health of the citizens, can be an indication of collectivist, organic ideology, whose "body" is, of course, immune to such damage. Traditional and recent Roman Catholic teaching supports this sustained attention to the vitality of the body as a critical social index.

Collectivism has arisen in particular in this century at that moment when persons, in their perennial search for a power beyond yet related to themselves and for a significance that spans their physical and lived worlds, have come to recognize the limits in the promise of Enlightenment rationalism, industrial production, international merchandising, and nationalist striving. These four historical developments both contributed to the breakup of secure and close agricultural communities and had the merit of offering a sometime response to a few of the needs of persons in this social transformation. How faith and the church counter collectivism is not simply a question of condemnation. The church, together with nonbelievers, faces a current challenge in collectivism, which raises the question how free persons work together in groups and through structures. Particularly in the past, practices such as the devotion paid to guild saints and pilgrimages to regional shrines have been some of the ways the church acknowledged the human significance of localities and subordinate social groups. The church must once again develop practices that, vivified by word and sacrament, convey this significance today. In its approach to collectivism, the church makes a considerable contribution precisely on levels where efforts may appear insignificant. To teach persons how to read the symptoms of collectivism is one way. Another is to teach them how the practices of their own lives (as these take place in their school organizations, work groups, and recreation groups) both stimulate their own freedom and prepare them in this way to stand firm against the mesmerizing advances of collectivism.

Because power, which results from the interaction of persons, must be eliminated on behalf of the collective's coercive force, a curious and deadly inversion takes place. The most personal values count least—thinking toward truth, considered free choice, tender love, humor—while exactly those traits that are accidental and external matter most, thus the importance of doctrinaire adherence and of uniforms. The more the collective can succeed in extinguishing the personal in individuals, the greater its temporary chance to survive as a quasi person.

Human rights, the basis for the welfare of persons in a community (*Redemptor hominis* 17.3), protect them from collectivism. Yet these rights are more than a static possession; they require a dynamic interaction. They flourish through the exercise of freedom along with others. Thus the teaching on rights coheres with the principle of subsidiarity (*Quadragesimo anno*). The church and other social structures must assist persons to attain the fulfillment of their capacities and the protection of their rights; the society and a fortiori subordinate groups in society exist only on the basis of their members and, most importantly, only for their good.

See also ECOLOGY; FASCISM; FREEDOM; HUMAN RIGHTS; REDEMPTOR HOMINIS; SUBSIDIARITY, PRINCIPLE OF; TOTALITARIANISM.

Bibliography: H. Arendt, *The Human Condition* (Chicago: Univ. of Chicago Press, 1958). A. Michnik, *Letters from Prison* (San Francisco: Univ. of California Press, 1985).

PHILIP J. CHMIELEWSKI, S.J.

COLONIALISM

For most of recorded history larger or more powerful nations have been assiduous in the creation of colonies, composed either of their own citizens or, more commonly, of other peoples subjugated by force. Since this panorama is so vast, "colonialism" (sometimes referred to as imperialism) in this article will be restricted to its classical version: beginning with the great sea voyages of the late 15th and 16th centuries, the creation of colonies by Europe and the United States in the Americas, Asia, and Africa, usually resulting in the domination of the subject peoples militarily, politically, and culturally. The 500th anniversary of this colonization was celebrated in 1992, although the number of colonies has declined precipitously since the end of World War II in a process that has come to be known as "decolonization."

In recent years, however, Catholic social thought has underscored new forms of colonialism, which usually replace military/political hegemony with a broad spectrum of subtle or overt economic or cultural structures of domination, a process that is called "neocolonialism." Special emphasis has been devoted to analyzing and attempting to overcome the strategy of using foreign aid as a means of impinging on the sovereignty rather than considering the welfare of the developing nations.

For example, in *Mater et magistra* (1961), Pope John XXIII concludes a discussion of justice between nations of different economic development with an urgent appeal to respect individual characteristics and rights of these nations (MM 169–70); if this is not achieved, he continues, it "clearly would be but another form of colonialism, which, although disguised in name, merely reflects their earlier but outdated dominion" (172). In *Pacem in terris* (1963) he devotes a section to the evolution of underdeveloped countries and reiterates strongly that it is vitally important that the rich nations in providing aid "should respect the moral heritage and ethnic characteristics peculiar to each, and also that they should avoid any intention of political domination" (PT 125).

More recently, the Second Vatican Council (1962–65) in *Gaudium et spes* pointed out the grim fact that many Christians in the wealthy nations enjoy great abundance while millions are tormented by hunger and disease; the bishops then stated emphatically that "this situation must not be allowed to continue, to the scandal of humanity" (GS 88). Soon after the council, in 1967, Pope Paul VI took up this scandal and devoted an entire encyclical to analyzing and suggesting pastoral praxis to eliminate such suffering (*Populorum progressio*).

On the 20th anniversary of *Populorum progressio,* Pope John Paul II availed himself of the opportunity to reiterate Paul's message and also to publish his own most comprehensive and substantive document thus far on geopolitics, while lamenting "the persistence of and often the widening of the gap between the areas of the so-called developed North and the developing South" (*Sollicitudo rei socialis* 14). Since there has been some displeasure in Rome regarding "social sin" as opposed to personal sin, it is an important advance that he identifies the "true nature of the evil that faces us with regard to the development of peoples" as the "structures of sin" (SRS 37; see also note 65, on the dialectic between personal and social sins). He also refers to these structures as "different forms of imperialism" (36) and forms of "modern imperialism" (37); this use of "imperialism" as a synonym for "colonialism" shows clearly that the pope did not hesitate to use terms with Marxist connotations. In the sentence that created the greatest furor in the United States, he describes the two superpowers thus: "Each of the two blocs harbors in its own way a tendency toward imperialism, as it is usually called, or toward forms of neocolonialisms: an easy temptation to which they frequently succumb, as history, including recent history, teaches" (22).

Another extremely important contribution to the overcoming of colonialism occurred with the Latin American bishops' conferences at Medellín, Colombia (1968), and Puebla, Mexico (1979), which have had a great impact on the universal church, especially regarding the option for the poor. These magisterial documents, along with the amazingly rapid spread of the theology of liberation to the entire Third World, have been the most important developments in the renewing and galvanizing of Catholic social thought and praxis and thus in contributing to the eradication of the terrible legacy and the blatant scandal of neocolonialism.

See also DEVELOPMENT; MARXISM; MEDELLÍN; LIBERATION THEOLOGY; PACEM IN TERRIS; POOR, PREFERENTIAL OPTION FOR; POPULORUM PROGRESSIO; POVERTY; SOLLICITUDO REI SOCIALIS.

ALFRED T. HENNELLY, S.J.

COMMON GOOD

Recent official Catholic teaching has presented two complementary interpretations of the meaning of the classical concept of the common good. First, *Gaudium et spes* stated that humans were created by God not for life in isolation but for the formation of social unity (GS 32). The communitarian character of human existence means that the good of each person is bound up with the good of the community. Thus the obligations of justice and love will only be fulfilled when each person contributes to the common good in accord with his or her abilities and in light of the needs of others (30). The common good is a social reality in which all persons should share through their participation in it. It is not simply the arithmetic aggregate of individual goods suggested by the utilitarian formula "the greatest good for the greatest number." In a utilitarian understanding, increased aggregate social good (e.g., gross national product) is compatible with the exclusion of some persons from participation in it. Emphasis on the participation of all in the common good is particularly important in a time characterized by "a daily more complex interdependence of citizens" (*Mater et magistra* 59). Unless directed by a moral concern that all persons share mutually in the benefits that come from social advance, this increased interdependence can become a negative force of domination and exploitation (*Sollicitudo rei socialis* 38).

This theme of participation of all persons in the benefits of the common good leads to the second main emphasis in recent magisterial discussion of the subject. Indeed, the common good is defined as "the sum total of conditions of social living, whereby persons are enabled more fully and readily to achieve their own perfection" (MM 65; see GS 26). Further, *Pacem in terris* stated that "it is agreed that in our time the common good is chiefly guaranteed when personal rights and duties are maintained" (PT 60). Emphasis here is on the way individual persons benefit from the enhancement of the common good. The distinctively modern notion of rights is invoked to specify the most fundamental demands of the common good. These rights specify the minimum standards for any society that is "well-ordered and productive" and in which the dignity of each person is realized (9). The duty to promote the common good, therefore, entails the duty to protect the human rights of all.

These two emphases reveal a complex relation between the developing Catholic social-ethical tradition and the theory and practice of modern liberal democracy. Commitment to the common good rejects the individualistic presuppositions of that form of liberal thought rooted in the Enlightenment notion of human autonomy. Solidarity (commitment to community) is directly opposed to some classical liberal understandings of freedom as absence of the constraints entailed by communal responsibility. John Paul II restated the traditional Catholic commitment to the value of community by saying that "solidarity is undoubtedly a Christian virtue. . . . [Solidarity is] a firm and persevering determination to commit oneself to the common good." At the same time, a positive estimate of the values of liberal democratic freedoms is evident in how John Paul II describes the common good: "the good of all and of each individual" (SRS 38–39). This echoes John XXIII's insistence that respect for human rights is a prerequisite for the achievement of the true common good. Community and solidarity are to be highly valued, but so are freedom and the dignity of each person. Therefore recent Catholic discussions of the common good stand opposed to the extremes of both individualism and collectivism.

The historical antecedents to this discussion help clarify the issues. Classical Greece viewed the *polis* and "the common" as the sphere of human flourishing. The private domain was a zone of deprivation and incomplete humanity. Aristotle saw the human person as "by nature a social and political being" (*Nicomachean Ethics* 1097b, l. 10), whose happiness is achieved in the exercise of the public virtues of citizenship. These virtues go beyond the minimal cooperation needed to keep society functioning materially to a richer form of fellowship where the higher goods of self-government, wisdom, and contemplation of the truth can be achieved: "A state exists for the sake of a good life, and not for life only. . . . Political society exists for the sake of noble actions, and not of mere companionship" (*Politics* 1280b, ll. 6–7; 1281a, ll. 3–4).

In Rome, Cicero said a commonwealth (*res publica*) was "not any collection of human beings brought together in any sort of way but an assemblage of people in large numbers associated in agreement with respect to justice and a partnership for the common good" (*De re publica* I, xxv, 1). He lamented the fact that the heroic virtue of the Roman republic had ended before his birth, and that once-great Rome was no longer such: "It is through our own faults, not by any accident, that we retain only the form of the commonwealth, but have long since lost its substance" (ibid., V, i, 2).

The biblical tradition adds a distinctive emphasis to these classical ideas. Augustine challenged the supremacy of the *polis* as the domain of final human fulfillment. Another domain—the city of God, the heavenly Jerusalem—is the ultimate good of every person. As Thomas Aquinas later put it, "God's own goodness . . . is the good of the whole universe" (ST I, II, q. 19, art. 10, 1). This theocentric definition of the human good had a radical effect: it desacralized what the classical sources made holy: the *polis.* In doing so it must oppose any ruler who claims divine prerogative. The commandment to love one's neighbor as oneself demands commitment to the common good. But this commandment does not make the neighbor—individually or collectively—a surrogate for God. The final good of every person transcends any good that can be achieved politically, economically, or culturally.

Thus the tension between John XXIII's two ways of describing the common good has theological roots. Love of neighbor, the "people of God," the "body of Christ," and the social nature of the human person are biblical and philosophical images that highlight the fact that individual persons only attain their destiny together in community. At the same time, persons have a destiny that transcends what they can achieve politically. The common good of the "earthly city" is of central concern to all who seek to love their neighbor. But this "terrestrial common good" is not of absolute value; only God has that status. Therefore respect for the transcendent dignity of the person is a precondition for the attainment of that earthly and political good that recognizes its own limitations.

The complementarity of the common good with the idea of human rights was explored from a Thomistic perspective by Jacques Maritain in the 1940s. Maritain's position can be called "personalist communitarianism," for it affirms that "personality tends by nature to communion" (p. 47). Positively, the fulfillment of personality is achieved only through knowledge and love of other persons. Subpersonal beings cannot form communities but only physical collectivities. For this reason genuine community can exist only where the dignity of persons is secured. Personhood and the good of community are mutually implicating realities. Negatively, as finite and limited persons, human beings need other persons and the larger society in order to thrive or even exist at all. These needs are for material goods such as food and shelter, for higher goods such as moral and intellectual education, and for God as the sustainer of their very existence and as the fulfillment of their capacity for relationship.

This understanding of human sociality was the basis of Maritain's understanding of the analogical nature of the common good. The central theological root of Maritain's discussion of the relation between the person and the common good is that the idea of the person is an analogical idea that is realized fully and absolutely only in its supreme analogue, God. The fact that persons are essentially relational beings has its supreme exemplification in the fact that God is not a monad but a Trinitarian communion of "subsistent relations." To the extent that a being is personal, it will be a being-in-relation-to-other-persons. In Martin Buber's language, the good of persons exists "between" persons in the relations that make them who they are. Thus to understand human society properly we must see it as located on an analogical scale between the perfect communion of persons that is the Trinity and the spatial juxtaposition of nonpersonal creatures that do not form societies in the proper sense at all. The historical existence of human beings stands in an intermediate position between these two analogues.

This analogical framework opens up a number of useful perspectives on the ethical and political meaning of the common good. Like Augustine's analysis, it implies that the full common good exists only in the communion of all persons with God and with each other in God. This demands the rejection of any theory that makes the good of the *polis* the highest good or that grants absolute sovereignty to the state. It is thoroughly antitotalitarian. Human beings are destined to a good that is beyond both civil society and the state. Both civil society and the state have an obligation to respect this transcendence of the human person by respecting human rights. Maritain's "personalist" interpretation of these rights, however, must be carefully distinguished from individualism. The freedom and dignity of persons are achieved in communal relationship with other persons, not in isolation. Thus respect for freedom and dignity demands support for the many forms of relationship in which personhood is realized: friendships, families, voluntary associations, civil society, politics, and relationship with God as well. Each of these relationships realizes a part of the terrestrial common good. Each is analogous to the ultimate common good: the union of human beings with God and with each other in God.

This can be called a pluralistic-analogical understanding of the meaning of the common good. It is pluralistic because pursuing it demands full respect for the many different forms of interpersonal and social relationships in which human beings achieve their good in history. The temporal common good is therefore a rich ensemble of goods. Each of them has a place within the framework of social existence, but none may be absolutized or allowed to dominate all the others. It is analogical because the good achieved in the communal relationships of family, friendship, civil society, or politics is a genuine but partial reflection of the full common good achieved in the communion of the kingdom of God.

Catholic social teaching expresses the relationship among the partial goods attained in diverse kinds of historical community in the principles of solidarity and subsidiarity. As formulated by John Paul II, solidarity is both a moral and a theological virtue. Morally, solidarity is a habitual disposition of mind and heart by which the interdependence of human beings is recognized not only as an empirical fact but as a moral demand to build up the bonds of genuine mutual relationship. Theologically, "there are many forms of contact between solidarity and charity, which is the distinguishing mark of Christ's disciples" (SRS 38–39). Because of the pluralistic nature of the common good, however, this commitment to the good of all persons is not to be realized in a single, undifferentiated community of the whole human race. Such a community would submerge the person in what Pius XII called "mass society" and would likely have totalitarian political implications. Rather, the good of persons is attained when they are able to participate in a rich diversity of communal relationships, ranging from those as small as the family to those as large as the national and global societies.

The principle of subsidiarity states that the larger forms of community such as political society should not replace or absorb those that are smaller but rather should provide help (*subsidium*) to them when they are either unable or unwilling to make their proper contribution to the good of the community. The government provides such help by directing, restraining, and regulating the activities of these other communities "as occasion requires and necessity demands" (*Quadragesimo anno* 80), to ensure that they in fact contribute to the common good rather than undermine it. Thus government has a limited but nonetheless indispensable role in the pursuit of the common good. Subsidiarity does not mean that a government that governs least governs best. It calls for as much government intervention as necessary to enable the other parts of civil society to contribute to the common good.

The Declaration on Religious Liberty (*Dignitatis humanae*) contains the clearest discussion of the contribution of government to the common good in recent official teaching. It follows John Courtney Murray by maintaining that the whole of civil society in its communal plurality is responsible for building up the common good, while the state is charged with the protection of "public order." Public order is itself a moral concept: it is that basic degree of social union that is necessary for a genuinely civil society to exist at all. There are three prerequisites for such union: justice (which secures for people what is due them, namely their human rights); public peace (which will only be genuine peace when it is founded on justice); and public morality (the standards of public behavior on which consensus exists in society (DH 7). Government, therefore, does not have the responsibility for promoting the full common good of the people, for doing so would lead to massive intervention in spheres such as family life, the arts, education, and religion. Each of these sectors of civil society has its own proper contribution to make to the common good, and government must respect and encourage these contributions. But government is responsible for the achievement of that part of the common good that enables society to function as a community of fellow citizens. Human rights as defined by the U.S. bishops—"the minimum conditions for life in community" (*Economic Justice for All* 79ff.)—specify what these preconditions for a community of citizens are. They include both the civil-political and social-economic-cultural rights enumerated both in the United Nations' Universal Declaration of Human Rights and in *Pacem in terris.* Pursuit of the common good and protection of human rights are complementary practical objectives when rights are understood this way.

Recent discussions, however, have also stressed the inadequacy of an understanding of the common good that is limited by the boundaries of the nation-state. The common good is increasingly a transnational reality. John XXIII observed that "at this historical moment the present [international] system of organization and the way its principle of authority operates on a world basis no longer correspond to the objective requirements of the universal common good" (PT 134–35). Paul VI called for a much greater commitment by developed countries to the alleviation of the plight of poor nations through a reorientation of trade, aid, and investment policies (*Populorum progressio* 43ff.). John Paul II argued that the rivalry between the Eastern and Western blocs that dominated world politics through the cold war period was the principal impediment to the achievement of the international common good and greater global solidarity. He characterized this rivalry as a "structure of sin" because of its negative impact on the economic prospects of developing countries (SRS 36). Attainment of the universal common good, therefore, calls for reconfiguration of these structures based on a preferential concern for the poor and on a healing of the East-West political and military rivalry.

John Paul II has also introduced a concern for the protection of the environment into his discussions of the common good (SRS 34). Technology is assessed positively, but it will have harmful effects on the biosphere and ultimately on human beings unless it is at the service of moral values. John Paul II's call to include the good of the biosphere in the understanding of the common good is a genuinely new emphasis in church teaching that is likely to see further development in the future.

See also COLLECTIVISM; COMMUNITY; ECOLOGY; HUMAN RIGHTS; PERSON, DIGNITY OF; POOR, PREFERENTIAL OPTION FOR; RIGHTS AND DUTIES; SOLIDARITY; SUBSIDIARITY, PRINCIPLE OF.

Bibliography: D. Christiansen, "The Common Good and the Politics of Self-Interest: A Catholic Contribution to the Practice of Citizenship," in D. Gelpi, ed., *Beyond Individualism: Toward a Retrieval of Moral Discourse in America* (1989). C. Curran, "The Common Good and Official Catholic Social Teaching," in O. Williams and J. Houck, eds., *The Common Good and U.S. Capitalism* (1987). H. Daly and J. Cobb, *For the Common Good: Redirecting the Economy toward Community, the Environment, and a Sustainable Future* (1989). D. Hollenbach, "The Common Good Revisited," TS 50 (1989). C. de Koninck, *De la primauté du bien commun contre les personnalistes* (1943). J. Maritain, *The Person and the Common Good,* trans. J. Fitzgerald (1947). J. Murray, *The Problem of Religious Freedom* (1965). M. Novak, *Free Persons and the Common Good* (1989).

DAVID HOLLENBACH, S.J.

COMMUNISM

The idea of communism is very old, dating back to ancient times. The semimythical Lycurgus, appalled by the gap between the few rich and the many poor, sought a more equitable distribution of land and a simpler mode of life for his Greek city, but Sparta corrupted his ideal of common sharing of meals, property, education, and military training by subordinating all individuals to the harsh requirements of a despotic, collectivized garrison state.

Plato is most famous for his advocacy of communism in *The Republic.* Insisting that governing, like the practice of medicine or navigation, is for experts, he prescribed communism of wives and property, not for all but only for the dedicated guardian class. Plato was not interested in social justice or the attenuation of class conflict. His sole purpose was to preserve the philosopher-rulers and their military auxiliaries from having their vision of the good contaminated by owning gold and worrying about family affairs. Plato's communism was limited to consumer rather than producer goods; unlike Marx's, it was decidedly elitist and antidemocratic. Far from presupposing an equitable distribution of material goods in a future society of hedonistic prosperity, Plato's purpose was ascetical and thus was more akin sociologically to the rules of Christian medieval monastic orders than to the policies of modern communism. The fact that Aristotle criticized Plato for making his philosopher-rulers (both male and female) miserable shows that the communism of *The Republic* bears not the remotest similarity to the practice of communist societies in the 20th century, in which old exploiting regimes were replaced by a "new class" invested with special socioeconomic privileges denied to the masses of the people.

Some have discerned the seeds of socialist thought in the OT—in the Mosaic Law and the writings of the Jewish prophets. Moses, Isaiah, Amos, Tobit, Hosea, and others made it clear in countless passages that God's commandment required the chosen people to have compassion for the poor and the needy, the weak and the fatherless, and that the rich who ignored the pleas of the oppressed and the hungry would be punished. Despite their scathing denunciations, however, the scriptural authors did not propose common ownership of property but preached respect for the possessions of those blessed with material goods. One small Jewish sect, the ascetical Essenes, did practice common ownership. It is suggested that their communist egalitarianism may have influenced John the Baptist and some early Christian communities in which possessions were voluntarily shared.

The inhabitants of Thomas More's *Utopia* were Christians who favored a community of property because they thought that was the life-pattern of Christ and his followers. In the NT Jesus reiterated the Mosaic Law, which had emphasized charitable almsgiving and the avoidance of covetousness. Although the Gospels reflect a powerful and loving concern for the poverty-stricken, Jesus did not condemn private ownership for the sake of social justice. To the rich young man who asked what he must do to inherit eternal life, he answered, "If you would be perfect, go sell your possessions and give to the poor." He then went on to tell his disciples how difficult it is for those who trust in riches to enter the kingdom of God (Mt 19:16-27; Mk 10:17-27; Lk 18:18-27). Throughout Christian history these passages have been interpreted to mean that wealth is not intrinsically evil (unless accumulated by evil methods, including exploitation of the helpless) but that inordinate attachment to material riches can bar the way to salvation. Jesus foretold how at the final judgment the blessed will be separated from the damned on the basis of one criterion: who did and who did not feed the hungry, clothe the naked, and shelter the shelterless (Mt 25:31-46). One cannot, however, derive specific Catholic political or economic doctrines from passages that pertain to the inner spiritual disposition of persons and not to the organization of society.

Such fathers of the church as Sts. Basil, John Chrysostom, Ambrose, Clement of Alexandria, and Gregory the Great denounced the rich who callously hoard a superfluity of goods while ignoring the cries of the needy. It was widespread patristic teaching that God had originally given the earth as a common right for all; that property, like slavery, war, and coercive government, is a human institution introduced as a result of sin; and that avarice had created deep, unjust disparities between rich and poor.

In the Middle Ages St. Thomas Aquinas synthesized Christian doctrine on the moral obligations of property with Aristotle's classic defense of private ownership as a practical exigency of human nature (since what is commonly owned is usually neglected), but with the proviso that it be used liberally for the benefit of others. To Aquinas only almsgiving could morally justify the customary institution of private property. In medieval society there had not yet developed the political-administrative structures that would emerge later and that would be able, in a more democratic age, to employ taxation as an equalizing instrument to reduce if not eliminate unjust disparities. It is also worth noting that in feudal Christian Europe the charging of interest was, as Aristotle had noted, unnatural; it was considered exploitative of human needs and therefore sinful. That stigma was lifted with the rise of bourgeois capitalism when levying a fee for borrowed money came to be looked upon not necessarily as vile usury but as a potentially socially useful facilitator of productive risk taking in the economic order. The change of view was reasonable, but it did not prevent the continued gouging of the disadvantaged by unscrupulous moneylenders. Moreover, it cannot be denied that the development of modern capitalist industrialism would lead to new forms of exploitation of the many laborers who had to earn their bread by the sweat of their brow by the few wealthy who did not.

Modern socialist and communist thought undoubtedly have some roots in Jewish and Christian beliefs, in Thomas More's satire on 16th-century mores, and in the writings of other Enlightenment philosophers, radical idealists, and utopian socialists—Rousseau, Condorcet, Mably, Babeuf, Saint-Simon, and others—who saw property as the source of all inequality, injustice, and social evil. The brand of communism that assumed a ruthless totalitarian form in the 20th century is traceable to a spirit of egalitarianism and a contempt for traditional institutions that were characteristic of the French Revolution, as well as to a demand for justice on behalf of the working proletariat and a hatred not only of the intolerable conditions of early European industrialism but also of the bourgeois capitalist system that produced them. (For a description of dialectical materialism, economic determinism, the critique of capitalism, the laws of scientific socialism, and the prediction of the final revolutionary conflict "to put the worker in his place" and usher in the classless communist society, see MARXISM.) Karl Marx was not bent on violent methods and in his younger days may have hoped that his utopian goals could be attained through a "peaceful" dialectic of subverting the bourgeois capitalists, but he certainly did not abhor violence if it should be required to ensure the success of the revolution. By no means was Marx a pacifist.

It was Lenin, coming out of a tradition of Russian revolutionary conspiratorial activity that had mirror-imaged tsarist secret police methods, who invested 20th-century communism with its twisted predilection for violence and terror. Lenin was a Marxist to the core, but he expanded the theory, updating it for the age of imperialism, the highest, final stage of monopoly-finance capitalism, which had divided the non-Western colonial territories for the purpose of plundering their resources, thereby instigating wars among the capitalist states. Lenin despised such Marxist revisionists as Eduard Bernstein and Karl Kautsky, who highlighted the errors in Marx's predictions and advocated an evolutionary path to socialism via the democratic ballot box. Lenin called that "adding a kopeck to the ruble." The elitist Lenin believed that Marx's proletariat, somnolent and stupid, grateful for the crumbs they could win from the capitalists' tables, would never never rise up to overthrow the regime oppressing them. He would create a revolutionary party, the "vanguard of the proletariat"—professionally trained conspirators with a discipline of steel and a passionate readiness to resort to every device of propaganda, agitation, espionage, subversion, deception, sabotage, betrayal, terror, assassination, and force—totally uninhibited by any bourgeois prattle about ethics, honesty, and fair dealing. Lenin outdid Machiavelli by describing his antihumanist strategy in a 1905 pamphlet, *What Is to Be Done?* It is now widely regarded as a tragedy that his deranged blueprint and policies found a home in Russia in 1917.

According to orthodox Marxist theory, the revolution should occur first in the industrially most advanced countries such as Britain, the United States, and Germany. George Plekhanov, a leading Russian socialist, insisted that Russia must undergo a liberal bourgeois revolution before making the transition to socialism. Marx had offhandedly suggested in an obscure footnote that there might be a peasant revolution in a backward agricultural nation like Russia. The Great War, which began in 1914, brought disaster to a corrupt tsarist regime, which abdicated to Alexander Kerensky's constitutional government in March 1917. Lenin, a keen opportunist and brilliant strategist, took full advantage of domestic instability and disillusion with the war; his manipulative skills, daring, and propaganda slogan, "bread, land, and peace," brought the Bolsheviks to power in November 1917. Once in command Lenin emphasized the first term in Marx's "dictatorship of the proletariat" and created a more ruthlessly efficient police state than the tsars had ever known. His experiment in "war communism" from 1917 to 1921 brought peace with Germany at a heavy price in Russian population and territory, but it also produced total economic and social chaos, such that Lenin was compelled in the New Economic Policy to bring back the expropriated landowners and capitalist managers to salvage the situation.

Meanwhile the socialist parties in the Socialist International split between those who had supported the national defense efforts in the war and who favored a nonviolent democratic approach and those who believed that international class solidarity took priority over national sentiment and who therefore decided to transfer their basic political loyalty to Moscow, where the revolution had triumphed. The former retained the name "socialists"; the latter became known as "communists."

After Lenin's death in 1924 the Communist party divided for a time between two of his associates—Leon Trotsky, a radical theoretician of permanent world revolution, and Joseph Stalin, who prescribed a more cautious nationalist doctrine of building socialism in one country. The communist ("Sparticist") revolution in Germany, led by Karl Liebknecht and Rosa Luxembourg, was crushed in Berlin in January 1919 when the German Social Democrats allied themselves with the military to defeat Bolshevism. Postwar confusion brought communists to power in Hungary under Lenin-trained Bela Kun in March 1919, but Kun instituted a red terror that so alienated peasants and workers that his regime was overthrown five months later. Communist failures in Central Europe did not augur well for the future of Trotsky. Lenin had warned the party against Stalin, but the latter gained controlling power through his role as secretary, which enabled him to appoint his loyal (or fearful) supporters to key posts at all levels. Trotsky was expelled from the party in 1927 and exiled abroad in 1929, to be vilified as Soviet Enemy No. 1 and hounded by Stalin's agents until he was finally murdered in Mexico in 1940.

Stalin elaborated Lenin's concept of the conspiratorial party as the sole custodian of the "dictatorship of the proletariat." The state, far from "withering away" as Marx had predicted, was now to be strengthened as a bastion of socialism against "capitalist encirclement." Between 1928 and the Nazi invasion of 1941, Stalin, in a series of "five-year plans" and with some help from Western capitalists, carried out a "forced socialist march" to accelerate industrialization by centralizing control of the economy, nationalizing plants, and fixing unrealistically high production quotas. These policies made for gross inefficiency, a prodigious waste of resources, and widespread worker resentment because capital investment priority went to heavy industry (steel, machine tools, and other areas important for military power and future capital formation), while consumer goods got very little attention. During that same period agriculture was collectivized at a tremendous human cost. Millions of wealthier landowners (*kulaks*) and peasants were murdered, starved from famine, or put into forced labor camps (*gulags*). Eventually, it was necessary to give the peasants on the collectivized farms (*kolkhozes*) private plots and a few animals. As Aristotle might have predicted, these private holdings were worked much more intensively than "the common" and produced a substantial portion of all dairy products and vegetables needed to supplement the grain harvests from the collectives and state farms (*sovkhozes*).

Stalin established a totalitarian system in which secret police groups descended from Lenin's *Cheka* (the NKVD and OGPU, forerunners of the later Committee for State Security or KGB) terrorized the population while the party exercised a monopoly of power in all sectors of society. Party organization paralleled that of the state at all levels—a "government behind the government," a master puppeteer pulling the strings of governing officials. Stalin, the central decision maker in a vast empire, nurtured for his own glory a cult of personality that replaced the history of the tsars in children's schoolbooks. He himself, though a Georgian, pushed a program of "Russification" for all ethnic groups and took over much of tsarist culture, except that as a militant atheist he drove the Orthodox church and its patriarch underground until he needed to revive the old Russian nationalist spirit in World War II. To consolidate his power he ordered the Great Purge of 1935–36, in which millions were arrested and hundreds of thousands executed, with the highest percentage of victims in the topmost echelons of the party and the armed forces.

When war seemed imminent in 1939, Stalin bought time by entering a pact with Hitler that paved the way for Germany's attack on Poland and the forcible incorporation of eastern Poland and the Baltic states (Estonia, Latvia, and Lithuania) into the USSR. During the Second World War Churchill, Roosevelt, and Stalin formed an uneasy alliance between communism and democracy to defeat nazism. Although the Soviet Union suffered heavy losses, the war's close brought Red Army and thus communist control of East Germany, Poland, Hungary, Romania, and Bulgaria in 1945. "Socialism in one country" gave way to an extended Russian-dominated empire—the "communist bloc," into which Czechoslovakia was incorporated in 1948.

The political, economic, and military vacuum in Europe resulting from the war, combined with profound ideological, political, and strategic differences between East and West, led to the formation of hostile alliances (North Atlantic Treaty Organization, or NATO, and the Warsaw Pact) and a long period of acrimonious rivalry and arms competition known as the "cold war." In China, Mao Zhedong's Communist party completed its protracted peasant revolution ("the Yenan Way") and came to power in 1949 after Chiang Kai-shek's Kuomintang (National) forces retreated to Formosa (Taiwan). For a decade after the 1950 outbreak of the Korean War, the West faced what appeared to be a formidable and unbreakable Sino-Soviet communist alliance bent on extending influence into the erstwhile colonial territories by supporting guerrilla insurgents fighting for national liberation from the West. The conflict became particularly acute in Southeast Asia (against France and Britain) and North Africa (against France).

Up to his death in 1953, Stalin justified his "iron curtain" and his megalomaniac police-state methods by citing the threat of capitalist encirclement. Literature, drama, art, music, and the teaching of history were kept under strict ideological control and compelled to pay homage to Stalin as "supreme leader." No less than before the war, his central planners (Gosplan) emphasized the development of heavy industry for military power purposes while meeting only the minimal needs of consumers—housing, food, clothing, and other basic necessities. Soviet military forces subjugated the peoples' democracies of Central Eastern Europe. Indigenous communists trained in Moscow exploited those economies to Soviet advantage, distorted national cultures to conform to Stalinist orthodoxy, and persecuted religion, infiltrating the clergy and severely curtailing the activities of "the Church of Silence."

Totalitarian control was fully preserved during the Khrushchev years (1955–64) but with reduced reliance on terror and somewhat greater emphasis on the production of consumer goods, combined with efforts to persuade the people that communism represented the wave of the future and would eventually encircle and overcome capitalist economies. Khrushchev condemned the cult of personality and the brutality that had marked Stalin's dictatorship. This policy of "lifting the lid" on terroristic suppression inspired talk of "liberalization" and "national roads to socialism" after the pattern of Tito's Yugoslavia (which had broken away from the Soviet bloc from 1948 onward).

Nevertheless the Hungarian freedom uprising of late 1956 was quickly crushed by Soviet tanks with tens of thousands of casualties, a tragic episode that prompted Pope Pius XII to reiterate rather pointedly the traditional Catholic doctrine of the "just war." In the early 1960s Fidel Castro turned Cuba into a communist state in the Soviet orbit. To obtain a U.S. protective guarantee for Castro against invasion, Khrushchev reversed his adventurous gamble of placing missiles in Cuba that threatened the United States. In contrast to Stalin, who had contended that modern war would destroy capitalism and ensure the triumph of socialism, Khrushchev apparently was convinced that nuclear war would mean mutual suicide.

Khrushchev mounted a vigorous propaganda campaign for general and complete disarmament, an unrealistic and nonnegotiable goal within the anarchic international system. He called for "peaceful co-existence" between the communist and capitalist states and after years of acrimonious debate agreed to a limited nuclear test ban treaty. This not only reduced the fear and danger of radioactive fallout but also ushered in an intensive, protracted period of East-West arms control negotiations, which at times curbed and at other times accelerated the arms race between the superpowers. Both the United States and the Soviet Union justified building their nuclear arsenals, as Pope John XXIII noted in *Pacem in terris,* "not for aggression they affirm—and there is no reason for not believing them—but to dissuade others from aggression." At the same time, Khrushchev vowed that the Soviet Union would support "just wars of national liberation" (that is, revolutionary guerrilla insurgencies) in Asia, Africa, and Latin America.

The early 1960s witnessed a growing rift between the two leading communist powers over the Soviet policy of withdrawing aid from China while extending aid to Third World "bourgeois nationalists" as well as a dispute about Marxist orthodoxy and leadership of the world revolution. Mao Zhedong accused Khrushchev, in a typical dialectical contradiction, of timidly seeking détente with the West and of engaging in "risky adventurism" by placing nuclear missiles in Cuba. In Western Europe highly organized and well-financed communist parties were unable to win a place in governing cabinets despite consistently popular strength at the polls—close to a quarter of the electorate in France and at times nearly a third in Italy.

While advocating peaceful co-existence Khrushchev carried on an unrelenting ideological attack on capitalist imperialism for granting only the appearance of political independence to the erstwhile colonial territories while actually keeping them in economic bondage. He criticized the European Economic Community as an instrument of neocolonial exploitation of the less developed countries within the oppressive international framework of military alliances and bases organized by the United States. (Marxist and other global theorists of "world capitalism" and *dependencia* would soon draw the dichotomy between the industrialized "core" of wealthy states and the poor, dependent countries of the "periphery." They accused the working class in the industrialized world of abandoning "international proletariat solidarity" and linking up with the bourgeoisie to enhance their standard of living by exploiting the workers of the Third World.) To compensate for another failed communist prediction—namely, that since Western prosperity depended on plundering the colonies, decolonization would cause depression—communist apologists attributed continued Western economic growth to the artificial stimulus of the "arms race."

The Soviet Union, under Leonid Brezhnev from the late 1960s to the early 1980s and during the brief tenures of Andropov and Chernenko, was more determined than ever to achieve at least military parity with, if not superiority over, its external adversaries (which now apparently included China and an economically powerful Japan). During the latter part of that period there was considerable concern in the West that the military balance (or "world correlation of forces," as the Soviet leadership put it) was tilting toward the East. As the American polity became more isolationist in the wake of a disastrous, nation-rending Vietnam War, Soviet influence increased in the Horn of Africa, southern Africa, Southeast Asia, and the

Central America-Caribbean region. As subsequent developments would show, Moscow's emphasis on the expansion of military capabilities (which drew a response in kind from the United States and its NATO allies) proved fatal to the Soviet economy. During the latter part of the Brezhnev era Western fears of Soviet military capabilities and expansionist tendencies reached a climax following the Soviet invasion of Afghanistan. Uncertainty was compounded by the rise of Islamic fundamentalism, an increase in international terrorist activity (assassinations, bombings, aircraft hijackings, and the seizure of hostages), and perceived threats to Middle East oil supplies on which the industrialized world depended. In Western Europe millions protested new missile deployments, while scientists and strategic analysts throughout the world argued about the feasibility of weapons based on "new principle physics" that might provide defense against missiles in space. The Soviet-Western debate reached new heights of invective rhetoric, and even the communist leadership in Beijing warned the West of Soviet designs. The less developed countries, which in the Cold War had constituted a leftist-leaning "neutralist bloc" in the United Nations, began to divide between oil-exporting and oil-importing states, between pro-Soviet and pro-Chinese governments, and between the least advantaged or poorest and the newly industrializing countries that were being drawn to the Western trading orbit. Communist parties in Western Europe were embracing a "Eurocommunism," which involved a tilt toward nationalism and democratic socialism as well as a declaration of greater independence from the USSR and criticism of its policies.

World tensions and fears of nuclear war confronted an anguished Catholic church with a profound dilemma. For nearly a century, the popes had expounded a social philosophy that acknowledged the good and condemned the evil to be found in all political and economic systems. In the best Thomist tradition, the papal teachings reflected a quest for a middle way between the antihuman excesses of capitalism and of socialism, of the unbridled individualism in liberal democracy, and of the suppression of individual freedoms in totalitarian states. The church abhors materialist philosophies and attitudes in all systems as well as agnostic or atheistic hostility to religion, whether militantly promulgated or insidiously insinuated. (See "The Social Encyclicals" and "Liberation Theology Controversies" under MARXISM; see also TOTALITARIANISM.) Nuclear-age popes have continued to recognize significant differences not only between Christian teaching and Marxism but also between Western democracy and Soviet communism. Pope John XXIII conceded that actual socioeconomic movements may contain some elements deserving of approval and thus prove better in performance than the false philosophies from which they derive and which they still formally profess, and he also described some two dozen human rights and freedoms on which the record of the Western democracies was clearly superior to that of communist societies (PT 9–27, 159).

Pope Paul VI, dealing with the problems of the developing nations, seemed somewhat more critical of liberal capitalism with its emphasis on profit, competition, and property as an unlimited right than he was of Marxist socialism (*Progressio populorum* 26, 57, 58). Pope John Paul II warned sternly against a social system that uses "the tactical and deliberate lie, which misuses language, which has recourse to the most sophisticated techniques of propaganda, which deceives and distorts dialogue and incites to aggression" (World Day of Peace Message, 1983). In response to communist charges that Third World poverty was due to rapacious capitalism, he said: "You will not allow yourselves to be intimidated . . . by oversimplified explanations which are more ideological than scientific," but then admonished the West to effect structural reforms to help the world's poor ("Homily at Yankee Stadium" 4, *Origins* 9, 1979, p. 311). The popes always tried to refrain from exacerbating the conflict between the systems for the sake of peace in an interdependent world.

Despite the growth of its military power, the Brezhnev era was characterized as one of "stagnation" by Mikhail Gorbachev, who came to power in 1985. He quickly decided that drastic changes had to be made if the Soviet communist system was to survive into the 21st century as a viable world power. The defense industry was the only productive sector in the economy. The Communist party *apparatchiki* and other members of the fortunate *nomenklatura* (government, military and police officials, factory and farm managers, scientists, engineers, and leading figures in literature, the performing arts, and sports) enjoyed special privileges—better housing, clothes, medical care, vacations, access to well-stocked commissary stores—while satisfying the basic consumer needs of the general population remained a lower priority. Centralized planning, with all decisions regarding investment, production quotas, labor and material allocations, prices and wages set at the top of the bureaucracy, was increasingly inefficient. Managers, anxious to please the planners more than the customers, emphasized quantity over quality and falsified their books. Gorbachev scathingly condemned the lack of initiative, incompetence, absenteeism, alcoholism, and corruption that had become marks of the system. He promulgated radical new policies of *glasnost* (openness and publicity in place of rigidly controlled news, *Izvestia,* and party-line truth, *Pravda*) and *perestroika* (which implied significant political-administrative restructuring and economic reform).

Gorbachev wanted to preserve the Marxist socialist way by modernizing Soviet communism so that it would be more attractive politically in a democratic age and better able technologically to compete with the United States, Japan, and an integrating European Community. By no means was he interested in converting the Soviet Union into a Western-style liberal democratic state. To achieve his goals he had to end the costly East-West arms competition, particularly in strategic defense employing exotic new technologies as well as intermediate-range nuclear missiles in Europe, which could pose a threat to Soviet territory. Gorbachev wished to attract outside aid to prevent the eventual collapse of the Soviet Union as a military white elephant invested with unusable power and lagging behind in innovative productive and service capabilities being developed in the United States, Japan, and the European Community.

Gorbachev was thus willing to negotiate arms agreements which, unlike earlier SALT treaties that had set ceilings on arms but led to hardly any reductions, would actually destroy substantial quantities of weapons and provide for unprecedented safeguards in the form of on-site inspections. He withdrew Soviet troops from an enervating war of attrition in Afghanistan and announced unilateral cuts in numbers of troops and tanks stationed in Europe. At home he introduced a degree of multicandidate (although still one-party) elections for a new popularly elected assembly and later tolerated the emergence of an opposition party. He broke the monopoly control of the Communist party and gradually transferred power from the party to the government, thereby weakening the party and strengthening the legal institutions of the state at the level of the union and the republics.

Gorbachev's diplomacy fundamentally transformed the international situation. He repudiated the imperialism of his predecessors in Central and Eastern Europe. The Communist party collapsed in Poland and Hungary. The Berlin Wall was leveled, and soon thereafter communist governments were ousted in Czechoslovakia, Romania, and Bulgaria. The Soviet leader hastened the liquidation of the German Democratic Republic and acquiesced in the unification of Germany within the framework of the Atlantic alliance while the communist Warsaw Pact was dissolved. Although Gorbachev played a historic role in the dramatic changes, his policies were only one of several evolutionary forces and were often in response or reaction to the new political, social, economic, and religious currents stirring the world. These included the desire for democratic freedoms and human rights, growing skepticism about the morality and utility of military power, mounting demands for improved living conditions, increasing concern for the human environment, and a spreading conviction that central economic planning on the communist model had utterly failed. The long-silent churches of Central and Eastern Europe—Catholics in Poland, Czechoslovakia, and Hungary along with Lutherans, Calvinists, Orthodox, and Jews in East Germany, Romania, Bulgaria, and even the Soviet Union—had in recent years become more assertive on behalf of religious and political freedom. Their strength declining, communist parties in Western Europe hastened to repudiate and repent their past, change their names and symbols, and vow their attachment to democratic methods. After the fall of the Marxist-Leninist regime in Ethiopia, communist governments survived only in China, Vietnam, North Korea, and Cuba.

Gorbachev's policies generated opposition on the Right from party ideologues, conservative bureaucrats, and military leaders who accused him of deviating from Marxist orthodoxy, threatening their careers, fomenting political turmoil, ruining the economy, jeopardizing state security, and presiding over the disintegration of the once-mighty Soviet empire. From the Left he was blamed for the economic chaos because he failed to move toward a market economy with sufficient speed. Gorbachev's problems were seriously compounded by a resurgence of ethnic nationalism and separatism despite the boasts reiterated by every leader since Lenin that the Soviet Union had resolved the nationality question. The military-rightist coup of August 1991 was aborted, after which the central government under Gorbachev gradually lost power and authority to a new "commonwealth" of independent but interdependent republics. (The complete independence of the Baltic republics—Estonia, Latvia, and Lithuania—had already been recognized just as the Communist party of the Soviet Union was being legally dismantled by a Gorbachev who had continued to defend its ideals.) In December 1991 the USSR ceased to exist as a subject of international law. The emerging "Commonwealth of Independent States," led by the Russian Republic under President Boris Yeltsin, faced daunting problems—nationalist rivalry from Ukraine and other republics, the prospect of economic disaster, and profound disagreements over finance, trade, foreign diplomatic representation, ethnic minorities, human rights, and the control of military, especially nuclear, forces.

Although the "collapse of communism" had become a universal cliché, nevertheless the social question and the problem of the poor to which Marxist-Leninist communism had, as a false prophet, professed to be the solution, remained. In December 1987 Pope John Paul II had noted the "persistent and often widening gap" between the wealthy and the poor, not only between the industrialized North and the developing South but within all countries, since all are marked by glaring inequalities in food, nutrition, hygiene, health, housing, water, literacy, education, economic opportunity, working conditions, and life expectancy. He deplored the fact that both liberal capitalist and communist collectivist systems have in different ways reduced individuals and nations to abject dependence and deprived them of legitimate human rights and freedoms. The pope insisted that both systemic concepts of the development of individuals and peoples were in need of radical correction (*Sollicitudo rei socialis* 12–22).

Writing in 1991, Pope John Paul II traced the fall of oppressive communist regimes to the peaceful protests of workers and others whose human rights had been violated. Without relying on force, using only the weapons of truth and justice, they rebelled against the inefficiency and dehumanizing results of a system that had corrupted the moral and cultural life of nations by trying to impose upon them the spiritual void of atheism, a "secular religion" whose illusory goal was to create a paradise on earth (*Centesimus annus* 23, 24). Situations of injustice still prevail, he noted. Should the countries that abandoned communism and other developing countries now adopt a "victorious capitalism" as their model, he asked. Only if that means a positive, responsible market system that allows free human creativity juridically limited by the requirements of genuine service within a framework of social justice that recognizes the spiritual, religious, and ethical dimensions of life. "The Marxist solution has failed, but the realities of marginalization and exploitation remain in the world, especially the Third World, as does the reality of human alienation, especially in the more advanced countries. Against these phenomena the Church strongly raises her voice" (CA 42).

See also ALIENATION; CAPITALISM; CENTESIMUS ANNUS; CLASS STRUGGLE; DEMOCRACY; MARXISM; SOLLICITUDO REI SOCIALIS; TOTALITARIANISM.

Bibliography: R. DeGeorge, *Patterns of Soviet Thought: The Origins and Development of Dialectical and Historical Materialism* (Ann Arbor: Univ. of Michigan Press, 1970). R. Conquest, *The Great Terror: Stalin's Purges of the Thirties,* rev. ed. (New York: Macmillan, 1973). R. Conquest, *The Harvest of Sorrow: Soviet Collectivization and the Terror Famine* (New York: Oxford Univ. Press, 1986). J. Cort, *Christian Socialism: An Informal History* (Maryknoll, N.Y.: Orbis, 1988). A. Dallin and G. Breslauer, *Political Terror in Communist Systems* (Stanford, Calif.: Stanford Univ. Press, 1972). M. Fainsod, *How Russia Is Ruled,* rev. ed. (Cambridge: Harvard Univ. Press, 1963). M. Goldman, *USSR in Crisis: The Failure of an Economic System* (New York: Norton, 1983). M. Gorbachev, *Perestroika* (New York: Harper Collins, 1988). A. Gray, *The Socialist Tradition: Moses to Lenin* (New York: Longmans, Green, 1947). A. Meyer, *Leninism* (Cambridge: Harvard Univ. Press, 1957, rpt. Westview Press, 1986). A. Nove, *The Soviet Economic System,* 3rd ed. (Winchester, Mass.: Allen & Unwin, 1986). A. Ulam, *The Bolsheviks: The Intellectual and Political History of the Triumph of Communism in Russia* (New York: Macmillan, 1965). A. Ulam, *Stalin: The Man and His Era* (New York: Viking, 1973).

JAMES E. DOUGHERTY

COMMUNITY

Human persons find themselves placed in a variety of relationships and associations with one another. These relationships and associations constitute community to the extent that they enable those who are so related to share common interests, intentions, purposes, sentiments, or understanding, and/or to participate in common activities. Although "community" can be treated in certain contexts as synonymous with "society," it is frequently taken to encompass bonds of affective and personal commitment among its members that enable their interactions and relationships to be conceived in terms that are less formally and institutionally structured than those generally connoted by the term "society." In this use, "community" still includes reference to the range of human associations and relationships for which society is considered to provide a more formal institutional structure.

When "community" is understood in this most generic sense, a person can be a participant in more than one community; these various communities can be differentiated from one another with respect to what they enable their participants to share. One can thus belong, at the same time, to the cultural community of one's ethnic and linguistic heritage, to the civic community of this town or nation, to the intimate community of one's family and friends, to the worshiping community of this congregation or parish, to the working community of one's particular occupation, trade, or profession, as well as to any number of communities delimited by their participants' shared interests and activities in art, music, sports, and the like. In this context of multiple participation, the particular communities of which one is a member may each carry different weight with reference to the fundamental moral significance and function of community. "Community" can be defined, in this sense, as that set of relationships that provides the primary locus for the formation of a person's identity as a moral agent in relation to all others; this formation encompasses the development of those modes of understanding, intention, affection, and action that enable one to participate in the activities that sustain the relationships that provide the bases for the community's existence, identity, and attainment of its end(s).

In its presentation and explication of the moral significance and function of community, Catholic social thought has developed particular emphases upon themes that show how community stands in direct and intrinsic relationship to a proper and adequate understanding of the human person. The philosophical exposition of these themes, generally set within a conceptual framework of natural law, has most often given primary focus to concepts, considerations, and arguments that (1) explicate and ground the claim that human persons are intrinsically social and (2) elaborate the implications this claim has for the ordering of human social activity. These implications have been framed principally in terms of the constitution and function of social institutions and the delimitation of the ways that members of a community appropriately participate in the workings of such institutions. Among these institutions the family takes primacy as "a kind of school of deeper humanity" and "the foundation of society" (*Gaudium et spes* 52). The theological exposition of these themes has principally clustered around a varied but interrelated set of concepts, images, and symbols—for example, creation, covenant, *koinonia,* kingdom of God—that also affirm an intrinsically social character to human existence but that also explicitly root this human exigency toward community in the graciousness of God's salvific activity. In consequence, the church receives special consideration within this theological exposition, since it is understood as the community that preeminently owes its existence to God's salvific initiatives (*Lumen gentium* 2).

Within both philosophical and theological expositions of the moral significance and function of community, the concept of the dignity of the human person has played an especially prominent role. The Genesis account (1:26–27) of the creation of the human person in God's image (*imago Dei*) stands as the starting point for theological treatment of the concept of human dignity (GS 12; *Economic Justice for All* 32). Three aspects of this treatment are of particular importance in the elaboration of the intrinsically social character of human existence and its rootedness in God's salvific activity: (1) an insistence that the full acknowledgment and achievement of this dignity for individuals is possible only within the context of each one's membership and participation in the life of a community (GS 24–27); (2) the correlation of the source of human dignity in God's gracious act of creation with the final destiny—sharing in God's own life—to which humanity is called and which requires the active cooperation of human persons (GS 34; *Populorum pro-*

gressio 15–17); (3) the identification of the conditions for the acknowledgment and attainment of this dignity with the protection of the full range—political, economic, and social—of human rights and with the exercise of the corresponding responsibilities to others that these rights entail (*Pacem in terris* 35).

To the extent that Catholic social thought has cast its philosophical discussion of the intrinsically social character of the human person in terms of Aristotelian and Thomistic categories, it has viewed the concept of human dignity and its bearing upon the moral significance and function of community in terms of a finality that is inherent to human persons. This finality has its ultimate focus upon the attainment of a personal communion with God that enables and perfects our communion with one another as well as with the whole order of creation; it also encompasses a range of specific and limited goods that play an essential role in the constitution of the authentic human good possible for us to attain within the finite conditions of human existence (GS 39). This finality also assigns to the common good a special ordering function in the attainment of the authentic human good, particularly with respect to the concrete workings of human social, political, and economic institutions. As an ordering principle, the common good is neither the mere sum total of the goods sought by individuals nor is it the good of the whole—be it a particular community or the entire human species—for which individual parts may be sacrificed. "It is the good *human* life of the multitude, of a multitude of persons; it is their communion in good living. It is therefore common to *both the whole and the parts* into which it flows back and which, in turn, must benefit from it" (Maritain, p. 41).

This placement of the meaning and attainment of human dignity within an account of human good, which aspires to comprehend its plurality through the ordering principle of the common good, stands in contrast with an understanding of the dignity of the person that takes the freedom of individuals to make their own choices to be its central, if not sole, constitutive feature. This latter understanding of human dignity has played an important role in the establishment and operation of the institutions of Western liberal democracy: autonomy, that is, the freedom of individual self-determination, functions as a central conceptual underpinning for the social-contract views that have generally been taken, in popular as well as academic argument, as both the morally appropriate and practically persuasive justification for these institutions and for the individual's participation in them. One consequence of such social-contract views has been to place the exercise of an individual's freedom of self-determination in strong tension, if not inevitable conflict, with the responsibilities that membership in a community and participation in its institutions entail for the individual. In particular, to the extent that contractarian views make the moral significance and function of social relationships turn upon questions of whether and to what extent the origin of such relationships lies in the free self-determination of individuals, these views also place at the moral periphery one's membership and participation in communities whose bonds of relationship are matters that are not readily and simply subject to free self-determination, for example, ties of family, language, ethnicity, and culture.

The mutual and intrinsic relationship of community to the value and dignity of the person, which is central in the development of Catholic social thought, has provided a basis for both the implicit and explicit criticisms that church pronouncements have made of both the contractarian understanding of the social relationships that undergird human community and the atomistic individualism it serves to encourage (e.g., PT 78; GS 74;

Octogesima adveniens 26, 35). These criticisms are set within a framework that acknowledges the value of freely undertaken human associations and the centrality of consent for the moral legitimacy of political authority within any particular human community (GS 75; OA 45–46). Presupposed is an understanding of the dynamics of human freedom in which the value of the exercise of human freedom is measured not merely by its satisfaction of the principle of individual autonomy but also by its congruence with an intrinsic ordering of human persons to participation in common good.

The understanding of the dynamics of human freedom that is presupposed in Catholic social thought on community has been paralleled in important ways by a set of challenges that a number of thinkers, both secular and religious, have recently posed to the cultural and academic dominance of a contractarian understanding of the moral character of social relationships. These challenges have frequently been taken to function as a "communitarian" critique of contractarian views. Consonant with an affirmation of an intrinsic mutual relationship between the persons and community, these authors have encouraged a retrieval of the idea of common good: the "public argument" (Murray, p. 8) that constitutes the civic and civil moral conversation at the heart of the reflective life of a community must have the common good as its focus, particularly as that argument bears upon decisions and actions that affect the life and well being of each and all the members of the community.

In addition to encouraging this retrieval of the common good, certain versions of the communitarian critique have also proposed a narrative mode of understanding as the most appropriate way to comprehend the structure of the intrinsic mutual relationship between persons and community. Within this mode of understanding, learning the narratives that exhibit the finalities embedded in the constitutive practices of the community and acquiring the skills requisite for participation in those practices are the primary activities that shape a person's identity—most crucially, one's identity as a moral agent. The moral identity of persons is thus primarily located by reference to the practices, including those of reflective inquiry, in which one participates as a member of a particular community and which constitute that community's moral tradition.

The narrative approach to understanding community as the matrix for the formation of the moral identity of its members frequently places great stress upon the historical particularity of the moral tradition that the practices of any community embody; in consequence, its account of community stands vulnerable to charges that it does not offer an adequate basis upon which universal moral claims that bind all persons can be pressed. This criticism, on the philosophical side, sees in the narrative approach no more than yet another formulation of moral relativism; on the theological side, it sees the narrative approach limiting the applicability of crucial Christian moral claims to those who are within the ambit of sectarian community.

However, this narrative approach also offers possibilities for enriching a number of the concepts and themes involved in the continuing development of Catholic thought on community. For instance, this approach helps to underscore the importance that the church, precisely as a worshiping community, plays in the formation of moral identity. The enacted events, images, and stories that constitute the worship of the Christian community mediate to its participants the salvific activity of God and have power to shape the moral agency of those who worship so that their dispositions, actions, and affections may more and more be drawn into accord with the responsive pattern of agency that is most fully exhibited in Jesus Christ. A second possibility for enrichment lies in the accounts of the dynamics of tradition that the narrative approach has been required to develop in response to criticism that the historical particularity of the moral practice and the reflective moral inquiry of any community does not offer an adequate basis on which to press universal moral claims. Of particular interest are those accounts (e.g., Alasdair MacIntyre's *Whose Justice? Which Rationality?*) in which maintaining and developing a viable moral tradition requires commitment, on the part of those who represent the traditions of their particular communities, to sustain and take part in a continuing public conversation with one another about our common human good, that is, a commitment to engage in what John Courtney Murray characterizes as "public argument."

There are a number of other current philosophical and theological discussions that also offer potential resources for the enrichment of Catholic thought on community. Three that deserve particular attention can be briefly noted here. First, theological proposals to interpret the relations among the persons of the Trinity on the model of community suggest that the fundamentally social character of the human person created in the image of God has its roots not just in God's act of creation but also in the Trinitarian life of God. Second, both feminist and liberation thinkers have explored the positive and the negative dimensions of the ways in which the social location of individuals, the ideological commitments embedded in a particular culture, and the structure of relationships of power within a society all function in the formation of the identity of persons. Although they join their voices to the sharp criticism that Catholic social thought has leveled at contractarian understandings of social relationships having atomistic individualism at their base, feminist and liberation thinkers also fault Catholic thought for containing understandings of community that presuppose hierarchical models for the structuring of social institutions and relationships. These models are seen as inevitably functioning to exclude those at the margins of community from participation in the determination of their own destinies. An important basis for such criticism has been a model of human connectedness in which solidarity with those who are powerless and outcast forms a touchstone with which to test the moral adequacy of a community's institutions and practices. Third, ecological and environmental concerns have suggested significant ways in which our thinking about community may need to include not only our relationships to one another as persons but also our relationships to all animate life and its environing world.

See also BASE COMMUNITIES; COMMON GOOD; FAMILY; PERSON, DIGNITY OF; RIGHTS AND DUTIES; SOCIETY; SOLIDARITY.

Bibliography: L. Boff, *Trinity and Society,* trans. P. Burns (Maryknoll, N.Y.: Orbis, 1988). D. Hollenbach, "The Common Good Revisited," TS 50 (1989) 70–94. F. Kirkpatrick, *Community: A Trinity of Models* (Washington: Georgetown Univ. Press, 1986). A. MacIntyre, *Whose Justice? Which Rationality?* (Notre Dame, Ind.: Univ. of Notre Dame Press, 1988). J. Maritain, *The Person and the Common Good* (New York: Scribner's, 1947). J. Murray, *We Hold These Truths: Catholic Reflections on the American Proposition,* rpt. with an introduction by W. Burghardt (Kansas City, Mo.: Sheed & Ward, 1988).

PHILIP J. ROSSI, S.J.

COMMUNITY ORGANIZATION

Community organization is a strategy that encompasses the improvement of social circumstances, the intensification of political processes, and the development of persons as cooperators. Community organization has proved itself a highly effective means for achieving that element of the principle of solidarity that involves personal and group responsibility for the common good; its immediate activity most frequently pursues relatively narrow concerns that contribute to the constitution of the common good in a particular community. The process is social; that is, it is an ordered and targeted dynamism that takes place in those segments of the life of persons that span the range between the family and the constituted, official, civic life. The process includes a set of tactics and categories of analysis that an "organizer" often assists the community in learning and utilizing and, more important, an organic (i.e., proceeding from the free development of a particular group of persons) interaction of the members of the community who commit themselves to the organization (here understood as a structure).

Community organizations are commonly imagined as connected with a particular locality, for example, a neighborhood or housing complex. However, they may be specified by place, work, or need. Examples of work specification are a union local and a nonunionized workplace; the welfare rights organization provides an instance of a group determined through social needs where the members have no common residence, do not share an employment, yet have a broad range of common requirements.

Labor organizing, urban political organizing in the 19th and early 20th centuries, and rural community organizing are the origins of current community organizing. At the local level community organizing found its origins with the settlement house workers and the agricultural extension agents. These varieties of the organizing of community span a range that includes (1) development in a specific locality, (2) planning to achieve certain social tasks, and (3) radical social action on the part of those who have been victims or disadvantaged. Much community organizing, as the term is usually used, refers to a combination of the first and third characteristics.

A recent development has attempted to establish a group of interested persons in, and teach them about, a particular area by focusing on long study and visible commitment to a local parish and its structures, hence the name of the development: church-based community organizing. Some elements of this advance have been stimulated by those movements in Latin American pastoral practice and theology that revive the people in their faith by means of a grounding in Scripture, especially as it focuses on a people who attain freedom through the Lord's intervention, and that animate the members of a given community to seize responsibility for their world on the Samaritan model (see-judge-act), which Joseph Cardijn made familiar and effective in urban and industrial settings.

Another key development has been the stimulus given to the process and structures of planned organizing through the Campaign for Human Development (CHD). In fact, community organization is one possible means for achieving what the U.S. Catholic bishops have urged (e.g., in *Economic Justice for All*) as an astute, contemporary North American articulation of an element of subsidiarity, namely, participation.

In terms of the ethics of community, the organizing process helps both the participants in the community and those who attempt to build a pastoral theology on the basis of the varied processes (1) to understand how a member belongs to a community, namely, how he/she becomes involved in processes that reveal common needs, goals, and paths of change; (2) to grasp how members view their own personal and collective potentials; and (3) to comprehend how mutual recognition and public attestation (liturgy) of these processes stimulate and confirm the growth to responsibility.

A particular religious (and ethical) contribution that may add to the effectiveness of community organizing efforts is to understand the broad requirements for social or civic change. Certainly members of the community must pursue the readjustment of power and resources and the recontouring of the accompanying organizational policies. This is, however, insufficient for perduring change; the members of the community must reestablish the basis of decision making. Beyond the new policies and power arrangements a different set of values must govern, one shared by many of the parties.

A community organization must address the full humanity of each of its members; this requires that persons learn to use means to reach particular, often material, social ends. This is a necessary learning, one not to be assumed. In addition, the desire and ability of persons to interpret particular emblems and manifestations in this world, indeed, to endow aspects of their achieved world with particular significance, must be a central area for the work of the organizers. Most importantly, they must learn what it means to free themselves, to take the initiative, to act in freedom, to act responsibly, to cooperate. Further, that community organizing is a phenomenon that is a response to alienation in a democratic society hints at the further Christian significance of community organization: reconciliation. Community organization can be an engine for social change in reconciling not simply opponents, though that is to be hoped for, but in drawing together again the previously anonymous and mutually opaque fragments within and outside the community.

Further advances in theological reflection on community organization must appropriate what black Christians have achieved through the organizing of their communities, even in those periods before the highly visible 20th-century phases of the pursuit of civil rights.

Many of the efforts of community organizations have targeted an official for the sake of some social good or, in the case of workers' organizations, some company official on the way to some economic good. The advantages of such a strategy are clear: the focus of the community's efforts is sharply delineated and thus highly visible. Given this, the community can marshal its limited resources effectively. Even successes, however, are dangerous. The organized members must not forget that they can seek both political and, in the case of labor organizations, managerial restructuring, which secures their voice. Cultural advantages can also be sought. The greater difficulty in securing some goods does not make them less important. Furthermore, the targets of the organized community may be within the society or culture itself. Local movements against the drug subculture constitute an example. Here, however, there arise those dangers that accompany any situation in which a group directs its force against particular individuals.

The role of the organizer is a complex one. He/she is frequently an outsider who arrives in a given community in order to help it organize itself. His/her organizational skills—including at least knowledge on an array of tactics, commitment, education—and charism place him/her in the dangerous position of taking the initiative from the people in matters of strategy and policy. Such a pattern would mean that despite particular successes the organization would fail, since the skills of the people themselves would not attain their own independent charge. The priority given to experiential learning on the part of many organizers provides one barrier against the organizer's control of strategies and policies, for attention to and learning from the members of the community are the very force that drives the instruments of organizing. Faith can maintain and foster a nonmanipulative commitment to a group of people. Many organizers in the United States operate out of a faith that proceeds into a messy, complex world by way of justice for the love of a specific community as it moves through a particular time and place.

A further ethical question arises in terms of the theology of power. If (according to H. Arendt) power grows precisely when people face and speak to one another and if community organizing targets particular persons to be the enemy, then does the proper use of power for the common good become dependent upon an illegitimate force or even upon violence? From another vantage one may ask whether the understanding, often found in talk about community organizing, that focuses on pressure and counterpressure hinges on a physicalist model that reduces both opponents and community members to tools; this would contradict the goal of community organizing: to develop active citizens. The organizers must proceed carefully so that the organizations they serve do not adopt the tactical traits of the opponents. One can recognize the importance of marshaling external forces through events and alliances while affirming that power is not simply external but lies within the members of the organization and emerges from them.

Often enough the group must accomplish something visible in order to stimulate the organization's self-awareness, to foster the community's self-reflection, and to change the actual pattern of living. Minority members on a school board make a difference, so does a playground, so do accident prevention programs. Yet less- and hardly-visible changes must also be goals, at least as complements to the manifest ones: the regular practice of hope and faith in the common effort and in the course of civil dialogue makes a significant difference. Concerning goals such as these, the members of the community and the organization must come to a reflexive awareness.

Mobilizing popular opinion so that it favors the particular position taken by the members of the community organization is dangerous if it remains only a tactic. The mechanism suggests a more important connection in the life of the pluralist society: because they remain citizens and share a common lot and responsibility with the other members of a particular city or region, the members of the organization should *educate* these others about the situation. The U.S. Catholic bishops adverted to this in 1970 when they described the role of the Campaign for Human Development. The CHD provides seed money for self-help through community organizations; according to the bishops these organizations attain another important goal when they contribute to the education of the nonpoor population: insofar as a community organization *communicates* with the majority of society, it contributes to the common good.

Leaders and other members must distinguish causes from tactical targets. City bosses, narrow-visioned managers, and stubborn union officials still wield power, but they are not always the most weighty causes or even causes at all of specific local troubles. The more long range the causes and the more complex their bearing on the lives of the community's members, the more the community organization should engage in activities that form a wider network with other community organizations as well as with other associations, for example, those connected with a delimited range of issues independent of specific communities.

An extension of this appraisal indicates that a danger for community organizing is believing that the specific features of the urban crisis are the results simply of the decline of community. The city is that place where citizens pursue their common good on the basis of informed argument, within several histories, and directed by their hopes. Not just the neighborhood, not just the economic sector, but the city matters to the daily life of its inhabitants. Organizers and members must ask how the subsystem that is the basis for their collective action fits into the sociocultures that find their articulation and order in the city. If the members do not raise these questions and do not attempt to answer them, then their very successes will blind them to the larger processes that will fashion their lives even more extensively. Along these lines that point toward greater complexity, organizers and members of the organization must ask what is the significance of the city in the Christian tradition.

A further question: a democratic culture often sets a premium on carrying out populist aspirations, yet the goals, programs, and decisions of the populist movement or grass-roots organization are still a matter for ethical evaluation. The hope is that persons of faith will challenge and enliven community organization through the imperatives derived from gospel and tradition.

To build community and to develop leadership are the goals that pastoral-sacramental theology and community organizing have in common. To the parish or chaplaincy apostolate, community organizing offers a range of skills and patterns in reaching out to those who may be distant from faith and church life and who share a world with believers. Conversely, the common and extensive practice of pastoral-sacramental ministry can vivify community organizing and the people of the community by offering both Word and sacrament as they emerge from and take root in the day-to-day lives of the members of the community. Liberation theologians have indicated some of the paths between the lived world of the people and the life of Word and sacrament. Community organization provides a tradition within which North Americans can make still other discoveries for the life of the Christian community in a pluralist society in terms of inculturating the gospel and the life of the church.

Community organizing is not only pursuing social politics but is also engaging in the quest for radical social reform. Neither the visibility of some tactics nor the use of some forms of conflict indicate the radical character of this reform. Rather, community organizing's radicalism lies in the profound commitment of its participants to persons and their needs. This requires arduous trust and fidelity, attentive care and service, and lasting hope.

See also ALIENATION; BLACK THEOLOGY; CAMPAIGN FOR HUMAN DEVELOPMENT; CULTURE; FORCE; HOPE; LAITY, ROLE OF; SCRIPTURE, USE OF IN CATHOLIC SOCIAL ETHICS.

Bibliography: H. Arkes, *The Philosopher in the City: The Moral Dimensions of Urban Politics* (Princeton: Princeton Univ. Press, 1981). N. Betten and M. Austin et al., (*The Roots of Community Organizing: 1917–1939* (Philadelphia: Temple Univ. Press, 1990). C. Curran, "Saul D. Alinsky, Catholic Social Practice, and Catholic Theory," in *Directions in Catholic Social Ethics* (Notre Dame: Univ. of Notre Dame Press, 1985).

PHILIP J. CHMIELEWSKI, S.J.

COMPETITION

Competition is a rivalry between individuals or groups or nations; it arises whenever two or more parties strive for something that all cannot obtain. Thus economists see it as inherent in the human condition given the reality (since Adam and Eve) of unlimited wants and limited resources to satisfy those wants.

In free-market economic systems this natural competition has a specific function: it regulates prices and quality. However certain conditions must exist for competition to perform this task: (1) there are many buyers and sellers; (2) they have known alternatives; (3) they have equal bargaining power; (4) new buyers and sellers can freely enter the market. When these conditions exist competition will keep the price near the level of the costs of production and will keep quality at a level close to the state of the art. Competition is the regulating mechanism in the marketplace; it keeps one person's or group's greed from exploiting others.

However, as the history of free-market capitalism has demonstrated, the tendency of business is to avoid the pressure and instability of competition by reducing the number of competitors in the market through mergers, by advertising to convince consumers that there are really no alternatives to their product, and by increasing their market power through growth, which makes bargaining power unequal and makes entry into the market for newcomers difficult if not impossible. This makes the situation not one of free-market competition but of monopolistic or oligopolistic competition, or in economic jargon, "imperfect competition." From the perspective of the economic system the effect is that the regulating mechanism has been turned off, opening the way for the excesses of economic power such as the exploitation of workers and of poor nations condemned in Catholic social teaching.

Over time Western free-market capitalist democracies have responded with varying degrees of government regulation to protect the public interest. Catholic social teaching over the past hundred years reflects the realities of competition at various times. Competition itself is not rejected, only its excesses. The focus is on the effects of competition (or the lack thereof) in the workplace, within national economies, and in international trade. Catholic social teaching presents a vision of an alternative society based on cooperation and solidarity as the truly human social order.

Excesses

In 1891 Leo XIII saw the social order as one in which workers "have been given over, isolated and defenseless to the callousness of employers and the greed of unrestrained competition" (*Rerum novarum* 2; see *Mater et magistra* 11–12).

John XXIII in 1961 called unregulated competition (as well as class struggle) "utterly opposed to Christian teaching and also to the very nature of man" (MM 23). In *Pacem in terris* (1963) he called economic competition among nations a threat to the universal common good (PT 130ff.).

In 1967 Paul VI observed the effects of international competition on poor nations and condemned the abuses of the system, which considers "competition as the supreme law of economics" (*Populorum progressio* 26). In 1971 he deplored as a feature of unlimited competition the wasteful creation through advertising of "superfluous needs" while many are still unable to satisfy basic needs (*Octogesima adveniens* 9). He characterized societies as "hardened by competition" against the needs of the poor (OA 15), and he cited competition among nations for economic, technological, and military power as an obstacle to justice and peace in the world (45).

In 1983 the Canadian bishops deplored the human costs of competition: "Under these conditions of excessive competition, only the 'strong' are able to survive while the 'weak' are eliminated from the market and participation in society" (ECPC 2). The U.S. bishops in 1986 cited increased competition in world markets as a factor in U.S. unemployment (*Economic Justice For All* 146).

Concentration of Power

Pius XI wrote in 1931 of "immense power and despotic economic dictatorship . . . consolidated in the hands of a few" (*Quadragesimo anno* 105). "Free competition has destroyed itself; economic dictatorship has supplanted the free market," he observed (QA 107–9; see also MM 35–36). Easy gains in "a market unregulated by law" give scope for caprice and greed that "nullify the wisest forecasts of producers" (QA 132). He also pointed to the threats to political freedom and international peace inherent in concentrations of economic power (107).

Paul VI returned to the same theme in 1967, observing that competition in international trade cannot produce just results when the parties are too unequal. "An economy of exchange can no longer be based solely on the law of free competition, a law which, in its turn too often creates an economic dictatorship. Freedom of trade is fair only if it is subject to the demands of economic justice" (PP 58–59).

The Canadian bishops noted the same phenomenon in the structural crisis of the 1980s as they observed the intensified concentration of economic power in the hands of a few transnational enterprises, enabling them to exercise monopoly power (ECPC 2).

Usefulness

Pius XI did not condemn competition per se, however, calling it "justified and certainly useful provided it is kept within certain limits" but rejecting it as the directing principle for economic life (QA 88; see also MM 35–36).

Pius XII, addressing the Italian Federation of Commerce in February 1956 echoed this conditional approval of free competition: "Freedom of economic activity cannot be justified and maintained except on condition that it serves a higher freedom, and has the ability, when need arises, to renounce a part of itself, in order not to fall short of the moral imperative." Otherwise, he concluded, all economic and political freedoms are likely to be lost.

In 1967 Paul VI applied the same conditional approval to competition in international trade: "Without abolishing the competitive market, it should be kept within the limits which make it just and moral, and therefore human." He proposed international agreements to provide more equality among trade partners (PP 61).

John Paul II in *Redemptor hominis* (1979) deplored the inability of current systems to deal with the widening gap between rich and poor, calling for transformation of structures based on the principle of solidarity. He listed as an example the sector of trade "where the laws of healthy competition must be allowed to lead the way" (RH 16). This would require conversion of mind, will, and heart and "resolute commitment by individuals and peoples that are free and linked in solidarity."

The U.S. bishops in 1986 specified that the needs of efficiency and competition in the workplace must be moderated by consideration of the effects of work schedules and compensation on family bonds (EJA 93). In the same letter the bishops noted that "competition alone will not do the job. It has too many negative consequences: for family life, the economically vulnerable, and the environment" (296). They called for a renewed commitment by all to partnership for the common good.

An Alternative Vision

Catholic social teaching's fundamental assumptions about human nature and the human family are at the root of the ambiguity about models of society based on competition. Though the value of freedom inherent in free-market capitalism accords with Catholic social teaching's emphasis on the primacy of the individual, the individualism that pits people and groups against one another is contrary to the sense of community, organic unity, and solidarity that infuses the Catholic tradition.

Thus in the social teachings discussions of competition are accompanied by descriptions of a different type of society, even though competition is recognized as necessary in the world as it is. As the sense of global interdependence grew in recent decades, the papal and episcopal writers stressed this alternative vision more strongly.

Pius XI in *Quadragesimo anno* (1931) proposed an organic, corporatist model of society based on the principle of subsidiarity as a way to reconstruct the social order (QA 88–98). John XXIII in *Pacem in terris* (1963) presented a vision of society governed by harmonious, orderly relations between persons and nations rooted in truth, justice, charity, and freedom (PT 80, 98, 163–66; see *Gaudium et spes* 26). The same vision imbued the writings of Paul VI, who called for world authority to establish a world order of justice (PP 76–80) and challenged Christians in every walk of life to transform the social structures in the spirit of justice and peace (OA 48). John Paul II's encyclical *Sollicitudo rei socialis* (1987) called for overcoming the "structures of sin," which shape modern societies, by "the exercise of human and Christian solidarity" (SRS 40). Finally, in their pastoral letter the U.S. bishops called for a new American experiment, the creation of a society based on a new sense of partnership on all levels (EJA 295–325).

See individual popes and encyclicals. *Also see* ADVERTISING; BUSINESS ETHICS; CAPITALISM; CONGLOMERATES; CORPORATIONS; INDUSTRY; EXPLOITATION.

Bibliography: G. Stigler, "Competition," in J. Eatwell et al., eds., *The New Palgrave: A Dictionary of Economics,* 4 vols. (London: Macmillan, 1987), vol. 1.

AMATA MILLER, I.H.M.

COMPUTERIZATION

A computer is best understood, perhaps, as a system with three major components: hardware (the physical equipment required for operation, which typically includes processor, memory, screen, printer, and in some cases a link to a larger network of computers, e.g., a modem); software (a set of rules that governs information processing); and data (the information that the user "inputs" so that it can be processed by the software).

Historical Background

Computers are tools, and as their early history suggests, they are best suited for tasks that require very many computations, any single one of which is relatively simple, within a very short time period. Before the development of the electronic (digital) computer during World War II, researchers at the Massachusetts Institute of Technology (MIT) designed an electromechanical (analogue) computer to solve the equations by which electrical utilities balanced user demand with generator output on a second-by-second basis. During the 1920s utilities began to find that human operators could not solve the equations quickly enough to handle the growing complexity of consumer use-patterns.

The first digital computer (ENIAC) was designed at the University of Pennsylvania during World War II to solve another problem related to speed. The university's engineering school had hired about one hundred women to calculate the complex ballistics tables that predicted trajectories for specific artillery shells. However, the press of the war and its flood of new weapons created a continuous backlog, which ENIAC was intended to handle. The Penn design was in turn adapted by a team of MIT researchers for a computer with a much more challenging mission: to imitate, by a large number of very rapid calculations, the complexities of air turbulence in real flight in order to train pilots in a cockpit simulator.

In the intervening four decades computer software has been designed for a vast assortment of tasks. It remains true, however, that programs designed to perform arrays of relatively simple computations maximize computer strengths and minimize computer limitations. Computers have proven effective for managing many routine forms of information for businesses, governmental departments, and similar organizations, while applications for individual use in areas such as word processing and financial management have made personal computers popular.

Ethical Issues

Increasing experience with computerization, however, has begun to attract attention to a number of significant problem areas. The ethical dimensions of these issues have received surprisingly little attention from ethicians and moral theologians. In fact, the disparity between the extensive scholarship devoted to biomedical ethics and the minuscule attention given to computerization represents a major blind spot in contemporary Christian social thinking. The problem areas stemming from computerization can be grouped under five headings: police-state violation of privacy, workplace relations, information overload, black-box rigidity, and the more extreme claims being made for "artificial intelligence."

Police-state violation of privacy. Organizations such as Computer Professionals for Social Responsibility have begun to articulate the societal and ethical challenges posed by government-operated data banks. Should the FBI, for example, be permitted to maintain a comprehensive data bank that includes the arrest and conviction records of U.S. citizens, with open access for local law-enforcement agencies? Should such a data bank be permitted to be integrated with other information about citizens (credit records, etc.) so that "fishing expeditions" aimed at creating lists of potential suspects (according to some predesigned profile of data characteristics) could be conducted by the FBI or other user agencies? Who would have access to such data? Who would be given authority to add to or delete from such files? What would prevent false information from being inserted (accidentally or maliciously) in someone's file? What happens to the constitutional rights of citizens whose profile would land them on a suspect list? Such questions render the ethical dimensions of data-bank usage nearly self-evident, particularly for citizens of a democracy.

Workplace relations. It has been repeatedly observed over the past decade and more that computerization revolutionizes the workplace. Its positive contributions (e.g., permitting second-by-second control of processes, organizing information) explain some of its popularity. Computers can also be used, however, to scrutinize employees in such fine-grain detail that some offices and factories begin to resemble little police states. Scrutiny systems become ethically questionable when they are used to sweat workers by forcing them to a demeaning or debilitating pace—as when secretaries are monitored to see that they maintain a given level of keystrokes per hour and the level is set excessively high—or when the detailed level of scrutiny approaches an invasion of legitimate privacy. The ethical issues found here are not new; workplace justice has proven a thorny question since the onset of industrial capitalism. Computers, however, so enhance the scrutinizing power of management that they bring the ethical questions to a heightened level of intensity. Finally, increasing evidence of worker disabilities (e.g., carpal tunnel syndrome) arising from computer use poses a problem that should not be underestimated or overlooked.

Information overload. On the surface the problem of information overload appears functional rather than ethical. Both individuals and businesses have found that they can ask computers to provide too much detail in analyzing data, so that instead of being assisted decision makers are overwhelmed by a flood of undigestible output. The ethical problem arises when automated programs are designed to cope with overload by replacing human decision making. Such programs sometimes enhance efficiency, but they can also open those who rely on them to the serious ethical issues attendant on black-box rigidity.

Black-box rigidity. Very large programs have begun to be designed for situations in which a large number of interactive variables must be taken into account. Some govern physical processes such as the machine tool-cutting of metal parts for engines; others (expert systems) govern decision-making processes such as piloting an airliner or a bank officer deciding whether and at what rate of interest a customer might receive a loan. Such programs are extremely complex and, once designed and installed, tend to take on the character of a "black box" (i.e., a technology one uses without understanding how it works). This can cause functional problems when the original designers leave the scene and current users grow ignorant of the specific assumptions programmed into the algorithm. As circumstances change such assumptions often become obsolete. Then, when the computer gives "the answer" to a problem in the changed environment, there may be no one present who understands how the faulty elements within the black-box algorithm have distorted calculations.

The problem takes on an ethical dimension when we note that assumptions embedded within algorithms necessarily embody the bias of those who designed them. It is quite possible, for example, that an algorithm programmed to decide who can and cannot get government housing loans would contain racist assumptions or that a program designed to allocate specific repair requests to various members of a firm's repair team would reflect some designer's assumption that repairmen are inherently lazy. Because the algorithms are so complex and so expensive to reopen once they are installed, the operation of biases within them and their inherent tendency to remain rigidly in place raises the question of who should have a chance to debate computerized assumptions and how often decision-governing algorithms should be reopened and renegotiated. Given the cost of such procedures and the tendency of those who benefit from existing assumptions to enforce the status quo, this appears to be one of the more difficult ethical dilemmas stemming from computerization.

"Artificial intelligence." A centuries-old mechanistic dream—the longing to reduce animal and human complexity to the level of artificial constructs—has been revitalized by some thirty years of research and development aimed at designing artificial-intelligence (AI) programs that imitate some aspect of human consciousness (e.g., on a very simple level, programs that "play" chess). Funding levels for research have been substantial and have fostered a group of scholars who have invested themselves and their careers in the search for programmed models of consciousness.

Claims that given enough memory capacity and processing speed, algorithms could replicate *every* aspect of human consciousness represent an extreme but vigorous position within the AI community: the desire to reduce all nonrational modes of experience (e.g., sensuality, mysticism, intimacy) to intentionally programmed and univocally defined codes. From this perspective, AI extremists embody an ancient desire to overcome human unpredictability and ambiguity—the tug and pull of human passions, debates, and inner longings. This hankering to reduce all human experience to rational codes may prove a more significant ethical problem than the more obvious uses of data banks for police-state surveillance. Ultimately, however, both spring from the same source: a hatred of pluralism and ambiguity and the need to control reality according to whichever plan the designer espouses.

Conclusion

The ethical issues raised by computerization appear, then, to be new forms for old dilemmas. Given their remarkable capacity to organize information and procedures quickly, computers can lure those in power to avoid the truculent processes by which people with diverse values, dreams, beliefs, and goals debate one another about rules that will govern some version of a common good. Debate with people whom those in power find offensive or inferior has been resisted for millennia. Computer abuses represent only an enhanced capacity for such despotism.

It should be noted, however, that recent research suggests that the capacity of computers for precision programming may well be too effective, rendering top-down power moves so intolerable that social groups will be forced to find ways to conduct the very debates just mentioned in order to avoid social anarchy. Should these findings prove accurate, it may well be that the ethical problems generated by computers will help foster a new maturity in societal moral thinking.

See also AUTHORITY, POLITICAL; BUSINESS ETHICS; CORPORATIONS; EXPLOITATION; PLURALISM; PRIVACY, RIGHT TO; TECHNOLOGY; TOTALITARIANISM.

Bibliography: S. Zuboff, *In the Age of the Smart Machine: The Future of Work and Power* (New York: Basic Books, 1988).

JOHN M. STAUDENMAIER, S.J.

CONFÉDÉRATION DES TRAVAILLEURS CATHOLIQUES DU CANADA (1921–1960)

The Confédération des Travailleurs Catholiques du Canada (CTCC) was the French Canadian and Catholic trade-union federation that has had a profound impact on Quebec's working-class life and culture for almost seventy years. Though its existence spanned slightly less than four decades, its successor bodies, the Confédération des Syndicats Nationaux (CSN) and the smaller Centrale des syndicats démocratiques (CSD), represent a continuing influence of the original parent federation. Although these latter bodies are secular by definition, the confessional heritage is part of the sacred memory of this sector of Quebec's union movement.

Much historiography on the CTCC is inclined to judge the movement harshly. It is called clerical, socially paternalistic, negatively antisocialist, and divisive of the province's work force. Although there is much truth in this assessment, some of Quebec's important labor historians are calling such a view into question. According to Jacques Rouillard, the CTCC constituted from its beginning a genuinely French Canadian working-class alternative to the American-based English-speaking unions of the American Federation of Labor (called the Trades and Labour Congress in Canada). There is truth here as well. The CTCC was a child of both Quebec nationalism and Catholicism. However, both of these ingredients, so dear to its more conservative founders, were shaped and transformed by the increasingly proletarian character of the movement. Working-class reality would reshape both nationalism and Catholicism to the point where the CTCC would become the most militant and radical voice of laboring Quebec.

Catholic and national unions had existed in the province since the beginning of the century as alternatives to English-speaking and secular imports, but it was not until they amalgamated their forces at the Hull Congress of 1921 that the CTCC was born. The clerical presence dominated, and the goal of the new federation was defined constitutionally "to promote and safeguard the general interests of Catholic unionism in Canada" (*Programme-Souvenir,* 1922, p. 65). The movement would be guided by episcopally appointed chaplains, and the bishop had the right of veto over all congress resolutions. Non-Catholics could belong but could not hold offices in the new body. Doctrinally the union upheld the prevailing social Catholic views of class inequality, social paternalism, the harmony of labor and capital, and a negative attitude toward strike action. The CTCC upheld the open shop and saw as a duty the resisting of international unionism with its secular and seemingly socialistic values. All in all, the new union was constructed to be a defensive arm for the church's perception of an ideal society.

Nonetheless, the reality of proletarian life intervened, and the institutional church's conservatism and control fell before a gradually increasing militancy from lay leadership and the union's rank and file. Chaplain infighting disillusioned many in the union, and worker struggles of the interwar period pushed the CTCC toward a more fighting spirit. A broad program of legislative reform was demanded, and the traditional social Catholic leader of the CTCC, Alfred Charpentier, led the campaign for a factory union-shop policy. Strikes at the Eddy plant at Hull (1924), the four-month work stoppage in the shoe factories (1926), and the grim Dominion Textile strike (1937) were stark testimony to a union rank-and-file challenging of the institutional church's more conservative notions of social doctrine. In these major confrontations divisions within the church were manifest, with many of the union-local chaplains standing in solidarity with their striking comrades.

However, it was in the postwar decades that the CTCC reached its rank-and-file maturity. Membership blossomed until almost one in three of Quebec's unionized work force belonged. Many of these new members were in the expanding metallurgical trades. Further, a new leadership was emerging that would challenge old perceptions and ecclesiastical control. The long process of deconfessionalization had begun in earnest. Discrimination against non-Catholics was eliminated, and serious negotiations with the industrial-based CIO (Congrès du Travail du Canada, or CTC) for unification purposes replaced the old prewar hostilities of the rival unions.

Easily the major political reason for radical changes within the CTCC was the long-term premiership of Maurice Duplessis and his antiunion program. Matters came to a head in the renowned asbestos strike of 1949. Led by Jean Marchand and Gérard Picard, the CTCC's new militant leaders, the asbestos miners in the eastern counties fought the bosses, police, and government. All the unions and sectors of the church rallied to the cause, as did Quebec's anti-Duplessis intellectuals. However, it was the union that led the conflict and the church that dragged its feet. Sparked by its gradual and painfully earned gains, the CTCC decided to act on its own. Slowly it pulled away from the church at the same time that Quebec itself was becoming increasingly secularized. Old-style corporatism was dropped from the union's program, and worker participation in management was advocated in its stead. By 1960 the union voted for full secularization. The name Catholic was dropped, and the new federation was called the Confédération des Syndicats Nationaux. The social doctrine of the church was replaced by a more general commitment to Christian principles, and the chaplains were gradually phased out. These changes were not hostile, and the church accepted them reluctantly but gracefully.

Since 1960 the CSN has grown more openly nationalistic in support of its French Canadian heritage, and it has adopted a democratic socialist stance. It still eschews strictly partisan politics but has played the central role in the famous common front and general strike strategies of the 1970s. Though no longer expressly Catholic, its history has ensured that a subliminal Catholic spirit of justice and liberation remains alive and well within the CSN federation.

See also CHURCH, SOCIAL MISSION OF; CLASS STRUGGLE; CORPORATISM; LABOR AND CAPITAL IN CATHOLIC SOCIAL THOUGHT; PATERNALISM; STRIKE, RIGHT TO.

Bibliography: J. Rouillard, *Histoire de la C.S.N.* (Montreal: Boréal, 1981). J. Rouillard, *Histoire du Syndicalisme Québécois* (Montreal: Boréal, 1989). *Histoire du mouvement ouvrier au Québec* (Montreal: CEQ, 1979). P. Trudeau, ed., *La Grève de l'Amiante* (Montreal: Éditions du Jour, 1970 [1956]).

OSCAR COLE ARNAL

CONGLOMERATES

A conglomerate is a large-scale corporation created and constituted by the merger and acquisition of smaller companies with diverse products and markets for the purpose of extending and diversifying markets. A particularly modern (postwar) economic phenomenon, it was only in the 1980s that their emergence raised significant ethical and social concerns. The encyclical tradition has not addressed conglomerates specifically, but the moral issues raised by their existence are related to many dominant themes that are treated in modern Catholic social thought: economic justice for all, the concentration of economic power, subsidiarity and centralized organization, workers' rights to participation, and concerns of human dignity.

The predominant moral theme raised by conglomerates is the issue of justice. Justice, defined as securing and protecting human rights and dignity for the well-being of the common good, is the standard by which any economic structure is to be judged. This is given the strongest statement in the U.S. bishop's letter on the economy (1986): "Basic justice demands the establishment of minimum levels of participation in the life of the human community for all persons" *Economic Justice for All* 77). The test of the moral adequacy of conglomerates as a form of economic organization is their ability to meet the basic standards of justice. The Catholic social tradition raises doubts and cautions about whether conglomerates are able to meet these criteria.

Conglomerates are distinguished by the way they centralize and concentrate economic power and decision making. While the motivations for forming conglomerates are usually economic efficiency, greater potential for using capital effectively, and protection against market declines, conglomerates run the danger of decreasing competition through the exercise of market powers, excluding a broad base of participation in decision making, and of creating greater distance between management and workers. These conditions serve to generate considerable economic as well as moral conflict.

In *Quadragesimo anno* (1931) Pius XI warns that when wealth is concentrated in the hands of a few, and these few are not owners of capital but act as trustees and managing directors of invested funds, these directors are able to "administer according to their own arbitrary will and pleasure" (QA 105). Furthermore, Pius asserts that the excessive competition that has given rise to conglomerates has created a situation in which only the strongest can survive economically. This is contrary to the biblical imperative that the dignity and value of all individuals, most especially the poor, need to be protected by economic organizations. In the encyclical tradition economic competition is affirmed only in that it allows for the participation of and ensures the protection of all the actors in the economic arena. Conglomerates run the risk of obscuring some of the rights of the full range of participants in economic society.

Both *Populorum progressio* (1967) and *Octogesima adveniens* (1971) develop an extensive understanding of economic institutions. Paul VI shows an alarm for the harmful effects of multinational corporations' growing control of capital resources and the increasing concentration of wealth. He calls for breaking down the concentration of wealth in the international arena and asserts the need to find new forms of economic organization that reflect a greater concern for human dignity and economic rights. The cornerstone of the pontiff's thought is that each person is an intrinsically valued member of society and therefore belongs to the entire community of persons. Each individual without exception is called to promote the full development of the whole human society. Both of these encyclicals are pessimistic about the ability of the free economic market alone to bring about these changes. In *Octogesimo adveniens,* Paul indicates that some type of political control and intervention in the market will be necessary to effect the necessary changes that will secure these goals.

The implications of Paul's ideas for conglomerates are significant. They suggest that market extension through diversification ought to be aimed at providing greater choices and better products to larger numbers of persons. The data on whether conglomerates actually achieve this is inconclusive, although there are indicators that suggest some limitations exists on consumer choices because of conglomerates. At least the danger of this possibility exists.

The idea of subsidiarity and participation are other moral norms of the Catholic social tradition that relate to the existence of conglomerates. As economic organization and power become centralized the danger of distancing decisions from the realities of the people they affect becomes more possible. Subsidiarity, the principle that activities and decisions ought not be assigned to a larger and higher society when they can be performed successfully by smaller and lower communities, is more difficult to achieve as power and decision making become heavily centralized. Participation is also threatened by conglomerates in that the range of input into economic decisions can become diminished the more heavily power and decisions are controlled by a small number of individuals and groups.

See also COMMON GOOD; COMPETITION; CORPORATIONS; PERSON, DIGNITY OF; POPOLORUM PROGRESSIO; PROFIT; QUADRAGESIMO ANNO; SUBSIDIARITY, PRINCIPLE OF.

JAMES A. DONAHUE

CONSCIENCE

Conscience is part of everyone's daily life and is often taken for granted. Discussions about conscience, however, easily become complex. This is due to the nature of the subject matter and reflects the widely varying perspectives and presuppositions of the discussion's participants. For these reasons the long and interesting history of reflection on conscience has left many open questions and resulted in general agreement on only some of the major aspects of personal conscience.

Conscience refers to certain basic interior experiences and activities inherent in the mature human person. One of these is the inner self-accusation that follows a wrongful deed or omission by the person. This aspect of conscience has been termed "consequent" or "judicial," since it reflects upon and judges personal decisions that have already been made. Here conscience registers guilt for decisions that were both erroneous and responsible and innocence for those that were right or at least legitimately excusable. Conscience also considers decisions that need to be made and judges whether a possible course of action would serve the good that ought to be done. In this case conscience is termed "antecedent" or "legislative." Assuming it is made in good faith, this antecedent judgment of conscience is binding upon the person. This principle has deeply influenced contemporary assessments of religious and ethical pluralism (*Dignitatis humanae* 3; *Human Life in Our Day* 147).

It is axiomatic that conscience must make pending decisions in light of moral certitude that the action being contemplated is morally right. Deciding in the absence of such certitude involves a willingness at least to leave good and evil to chance; this is inconsistent with a conscientious commitment to the good. From this basic point is derived the principle that conscience must be rightly informed about decisions it makes (*Gaudium et spes* 16; R. Hofmann, "Conscience," in *Sacramentum Mundi* 1:411–14).

At the same time, freedom is inherent in conscience. Only in freedom can a person be committed to doing and promoting the good and avoiding evil. Only in light of freedom can judgments be attributed to the person as such and take on properly moral value. It is freedom that gives rise to the responsibility proper to conscience. Without freedom one cannot speak of conscience or moral responsibility (GS 17; DH 3).

Although there is wide agreement on these basic points, there is considerable contemporary controversy about conscience. This is evident in the size and contentious quality of some of the literature on this subject and such associated topics as the relationship between moral norms and personal freedom or between ecclesiastical authority and freedom of conscience. In part these discussions are evidence that the unfinished debates of the past are continuing today. They certainly reflect the fact that conscience, always at the heart of personal and ecclesial life, remains an immediate and perennial concern for clergy and laity alike. But the vigor and unresolved quality of these debates and the anxiety sometimes associated with them can also be likened to a series of tremors emanating from the tectonic plates beneath these discussions. The grinding of opposing philosophical and theological positions has riven a once harmonious discussion, released a great deal of energy for good and for ill, and rearranged the terrain on which the edifice of conscience must be constructed, understood, and maintained. This has implications for all areas in which conscience is decisive: personal, pastoral, ecclesial, and theological.

This article will attempt to illuminate this situation through a review of its principal causes, components, and implications. In this connection four elements would seem particularly important: (1) the inherited approach to conscience, specifically, that of the classical or manual writers; (2) the impact of personal and pastoral experience, especially concerning marital sexual problems; (3) the appearance of significant disagreement on fundamental philosophical and theological issues underlying an understanding of conscience; and (4) the emergence of competing approaches to conscience. It is hoped that an exploration of these issues will clarify the theological discussion and contribute to the responsible exercise of conscience that is essential to ecclesial and personal life.

The Inherited Approach

The inherited approach to conscience can be understood by how it specified the obligation proper to conscience. Right formation of conscience was normally to be obtained from the natural moral law. In principle, any person in possession of rational capacities was held able to consider the social and personal nature of the human being and arrive at a correct understanding of the good to be done and the evil to be avoided in the course of daily life. In practice, however, it was thought unlikely that people would actually succeed in doing this. For that reason, in order that the truth needed for correct moral judgments should be known easily and with certitude by all, it was considered necessary that people be informed or taught by qualified authorities, either the "approved authors" of respected theological works or those holding official positions of authority in the church. These authorities would conduct the required studies into the natural moral law, and sometimes the Sacred Scriptures and tradition as well, and formulate the principles that were to regulate moral living. In the case of ecclesiastical authorities, the assistance of the Holy Spirit was seen to help guarantee the correctness of what they officially taught (J. Fuchs, *Natural Law: A Theological Investigation,* New York: Sheed & Ward, 1965, pp. 144–62; Paul VI, *Humanae vitae* 4, 5, 28).

Personal conscience was then called upon to receive the teaching presented by the authorities and to rely upon it in the course of moral decision making. It was for conscience to determine which teaching or principle was applicable to a pending decision and to apply it correctly so as to act rightly then and there. Hence conscience was often referred to as the "subjective and proximate norm" of morality. In practical terms this view limited conscience to a reception and application of teachings prepared and proposed by the authorities. Prudence would aid the person in the task of application.

None of this was seen to violate freedom of conscience, which all agreed was required if moral obligation was to exist at all. Moral obligation, however, was specified by the moral principles and teachings proposed by the authorities. Thus it was quite consistent that these authors expected conscience to accept and apply the taught norms as an expression of an authentic personal freedom. In this way conscience manifested its commitment to the good and true and was simultaneously assured of being rightly informed.

Given this relationship between obligation and freedom of conscience, the scope for legitimate diversity in the concrete judgments of conscience depends upon the specificity or generality of the teaching at issue. Where the moral teaching is framed in very specific and even universal terms, there is little or no room for acceptable variation in these judgments; in such cases a nonconforming judgment presumably reflects an erroneous conscience. This is certainly exemplified in the area of sexual morality; direct abortion is another case in which there is little or no room for divergence.

The entire area of social morality, however, constitutes an opposite situation. Moral teaching on these questions never descends to particulars with the notes of certitude and universality. On the contrary, it is commonplace for official teaching to be expressed in terms that are general or at least specific in a tentative way. It often calls upon people to take upon themselves the responsibility of determining what is actually to be done (*Lumen gentium* 43; *Populorum progressio* 32, 81). This injunction requires not only a grasp of general teaching but a technical competence appropriate to the matter at hand. Official teaching on social questions typically acknowledges the legitimacy of divergent views even in the case of more specific applications (*The Challenge of Peace,* Summary) and has in fact tolerated vigorous debate on them. For these reasons, even sharp conflicts in this important area usually do not spill over into more fundamental domains in which moral obligation and the authority of the church themselves would become the issues.

This reference to the broader spectrum of Catholic teaching shows that the critical variable is neither conscience's freedom nor its responsibility to be rightly informed. No responsible author of any school of thought disputes these points. Rather the crux is how moral obligation is determined and related to conscience. Practically, the issues are the degree of specificity of the teaching presented to conscience as its norm of rightness, whether the norm can legitimately be modified or adapted to the circumstances of the moral agent, and who determines what is right and by what criteria. Stresses and conflicts appear much more readily and with greater force where teachings are proposed specifically, as open to no exceptions and based on largely abstract premises that leave little to the judgment of the agent. In practice this means that social teachings usually do not occasion serious tensions. They do surround marital and sexual teachings as well as those bioethical questions involving reproduction and direct killing. Attention must therefore be paid to the presuppositions and method employed in formulating these teachings. For our purposes the discussion can be limited to the area of sexual morality.

The inherited and also official teachings require marital sexual behavior in all cases to adhere to an essentially procreative and interpersonal "nature of the act" and condemn as intrinsically immoral all direct behavior that does not. This approach rests upon the assumption that such an abstract norm is a safe and sure guide to morally right judgments in all circumstances. At the same time, this system presumes that the moral life is lived primarily in the realm of actions and the judgments that lead to them. What matters is that people do the right things and avoid acts judged immoral. Finally, it assumes that the task of determining what is right and wrong is best transferred from the moral agent to others. Ordinary people are seen as lacking the necessary intellectual capacities and are also viewed as being vulnerable to the push of sexual feelings and the pull of arbitrary whims. This helps explain the tendency to offer the taught norm as a protection against the chaotic or arbitrary in human life. The authorities are regarded as having scientific, spiritual, or juridical qualifications that enable them to arrive at the knowledge of right and wrong in human life. Accordingly, the experts' theological qualifications, the assistance of the Holy Spirit, and the authority attached to official positions in the church are often invoked when people are urged to receive and apply what is being taught to them. When the latter two considerations are strongly asserted, the merits of a teaching tend to be correspondingly diminished as a factor to be weighed (HV 4, 11, 12, 14, 17, 28; *The Church in Our Day,* 222–41; *Human Life in Our Day,* 37–45).

The Impact of Experience

Against the background of this inherited and once prevailing approach to morality and conscience, it is no wonder that the issue of contraception proved so troubling and indeed acted as a catalyst of important changes in many related areas of Catholic life. Contraception involves activities and motives that collide with a contrary teaching formulated in specific terms that allowed no exceptions whatsoever. Pope Paul VI authoritatively reiterated the classic teaching on this issue in his 1968 encyclical, *Humanae vitae,* and in the process explicitly renewed the identification of the Catholic ecclesiastical magisterium with that teaching. Catholic couples nevertheless continued to confront problems that could be addressed only through a reliable means of precluding conception. This situation involved enormous stress between the prevailing official doctrine and what seemed to many to be the urgent requirements of health, family, or marriage. Yet married people had to resolve the issue in some fashion and act accordingly. It is a matter of fact that many Catholics decided to proceed in a manner out of step with the officially taught norm that condemns each and every directly contraceptive act as immoral. What is more, many made these decisions as matters of conscience, believing sincerely that no better choice was concretely available to them.

This situation was significant pastorally and theologically. First, it constituted an ongoing experience of resolving a moral dilemma in conflict with official church teachings. People instead considered the concrete circumstances confronting them and tended to listen to advisors who took those circumstances as well as their good faith into account when advising them. Of course this involved a very different approach to the determination of right and wrong needed in conscientious decision making. Deciding in favor of contraception also accustomed people to resolving the dissonance felt when they decided and acted inconsistently with officially taught moral norms. Given the continuance of contraceptive activities in many marriages, such experiences accumulated significant formative power in many people's moral and ecclesial lives.

Married people were not the only ones affected; in the course of pastoral care the clergy were also forced to confront and resolve similar stresses. It is safe to say that this had a transforming effect on many of them as well. Finally, Catholic theologians could hardly remain aloof from what was happening. Many applied themselves to the task of understanding these events, explaining them in theological terms, and suggesting ways to resolve this crisis of moral teaching and practice. Moral theology was particularly influenced by the encounter with contraception-related problems (J. Mahoney, *The Making of Moral Theology: A Study of the Roman Catholic Tradition,* Oxford: Clarendon, 1987, pp. 259–301).

The Appearance of Disagreement

The process of responding to this crisis was conditioned by at least five important factors. The first was the earlier work of many scholars in such areas as the Sacred Scriptures, liturgy, history, textual interpretation, and philosophy. This work supplied many of the scholarly tools and foundational insights that would enable a later generation of theologians to propose new ways of understanding and resolving contemporary problems in Catholic life. The second factor was the rejection of the inherited approach of the manuals, which many considered unable either to give an adequate, convincing account of Catholic faith and moral life or to help the church respond to contemporary challenges. The third was the Second Vatican Council, which was for many theologians a vindication of the seminal work done by their oft-maligned predecessors earlier in this century and a mandate for more confident if also more humble attempts to engage the church positively and constructively with the world, its problems, and possibilities. The fourth was the increasing recognition that the circumstances faced by many people objectively limit what can reasonably be expected of them at least for the time being. Finally, there have been vigorous attempts to correct nonconforming activity among married people and their clergy and oppose revisionist thinking among Catholic theologians.

The interplay among these five factors has produced at least three general positions, each with its own proposal for resolving the crisis. The first is mainly concerned with defending the inherited doctrine. This is often done on largely traditional grounds: the moral imperative of the natural law to preserve the nature of the marital act from any manipulation or intrusion and the ecclesial imperative to accept and conform to authoritative church teaching in this area. A related approach introduces a distinction between doctrine, defended as clear, fixed, and universally binding, and the pastoral or pedagogical arena, in which the limits of the human condition can be recognized and addressed. Pastorally one may sometimes find a "conflict of duty" and consequently allow behaviors ruled out by moral doctrine; similarly, one might also reinterpret the specific obligation imposed by moral doctrine in light of the "law of gradualness" (see "The French Bishops on 'Humanae vitae,'" *Catholic Mind* 68 [January 1969] pp. 47–54; John Paul II, *Familiaris consortio* 34). The second position belongs to those contemporary theologians who argue that the inherited approach must be replaced with one that is less abstract and is open to consideration of intention and circumstances in the formulation of moral norms (B. Hoose, *Proportionalism: The American Debate and Its European Roots,* Washington: Georgetown Univ. Press, 1987, pp. 1–40; J. Gallagher, *Time Past, Time Future: An Historical Study of Catholic Moral Theology,* New York: Paulist, 1990, pp. 245–68).

Finally, a number of Catholic scholars, many of them philosophers, have fashioned what might be called a countercontemporary position. They hold that official Catholic teachings on marital sexuality are correct but reject the reasoning usually associated with them. They have constructed an entirely new system of moral decision making and have used it to defend the official teaching on contraception. This same system is the theoretical basis for their attacks against contemporary theologians' efforts to revise sexual ethics and to justify that revision on the basis of a more inductive approach to the determination of morally right behavior (Germain Grisez, *The Way of the Lord Jesus,* vol. 1: *Christian Moral Principles,* Chicago: Franciscan Herald, 1983).

In a parallel development, some have been urging that the cardinal virtue of prudence is the foundation and source of all moral judgment. Even though this view predates the contraception crisis and is not directly involved in the above disputes, it is immediately pertinent. In affirming that one's basic moral imperative is always to know the real and realize the good, proponents of this view assert that morality depends on personal character and virtue; in a Christian context this suggests that conversion is also essential. This means that morality is inherently rooted in the person and implies that no set of specific behavioral teachings can ever be accepted as constituting completely adequate criteria to govern the formation of conscience. At best, such written or expressed norms only seek to systematize or put into words what prudent people would do when acting prudently; they also have pedagogical use in assisting people to grow in prudence. The proposal to recognize morality as ultimately being a matter of personal virtue certainly raises further questions. It also stands in sharp contrast to all approaches that understand morality to be properly dependent upon written or verbally formulated behavioral moral norms (R. McInerny, "Absolutes, Relatives, and Inlaws," *Theology Digest* 28 [1980] 321–31; J. Pieper, *The Four Cardinal Virtues,* Notre Dame, Ind.: Univ. of Notre Dame Press, 1966, pp. 1–40).

The Emergence of Competing Approaches

It is apparent that despite the broad consensus about the need of conscience to be free and to be rightly informed, very sharp differences have emerged about how and on what terms a right conscience is to be achieved. These differences reflect disagreements on at least three overlapping fundamental points. First, to what extent should moral norms reflect the contingent and historical aspects of reality? Or should they instead be kept secure from the flux of history and the insecurities of judgment in changing circumstances? Second, who should have the task of deciding what behavior is morally right? Some wish to reserve this to the experts or authorities who can claim important advantages in making this judgment. The opposite view acknowledges the necessity of learning from others but nevertheless insists that, in the final analysis, judgment belongs to the moral agent, since only the agent can know and weigh the intentions and circumstances that are properly involved in the right determination of all concrete moral decisions. Third, is morality inherently a matter of personal character and virtue, especially charity and prudence? This would make an inner norm decisive. Or must the moral agent adhere to an externally formulated norm of behavior if rightness is to be achieved?

When one considers the range of views about conscience in the contemporary Catholic community, one finds an underlying diversity of assumptions and convictions about foundational matters: the nature of the real; how and with what certitude the real becomes known to human beings; the nature of the good in morality; the criteria by which one should determine what behavior is morally right; who is to be trusted with this judgment; and the function and authority of official church teachings about morality. Each position entails a characteristic approach to the moral enterprise and therefore to the delineation of moral obligation presupposed in the formation of conscience.

See also BIRTH CONTROL; FREEDOM; GRACE; MAGISTERIUM; METHODOLOGY, MORAL; MORAL LIFE, CHRISTIAN; NATURAL LAW; PASTORAL CARE.

Bibliography: B. Butler, "Authority and the Christian Conscience," *American Benedictine Review* 25 (1974) 411–26. *Clergy Review* 60 (1975) 3–17. C. Curran and R. McCormick, eds., *Readings in Moral Theology No. 3: The Magisterium and Morality,* pp. 171–87 (New York: Paulist, 1982). E. D'Arcy, *Conscience and Its Right to Freedom* (New York: Sheed & Ward, 1961). P. Delhaye, *The Christian Conscience* (New York: Desclée, 1968). J. Dolan, "Conscience in the Catholic Theological Tradition," in W. Bier, ed., *Conscience: Its Freedom and Limitations* (New York: Fordham Univ. Press, 1971). L. Janssens, *Freedom of Conscience and Religious Freedom* (New York: Alba, 1965). C. Pierce, *Conscience in the New Testament* (London: SCM, 1955).

WALTER J. WOODS

CONSCIENTIOUS OBJECTION

Conscientious objection generally refers to the refusal to bear arms for conscience's sake or to engage in any cooperation with military training and service. While today the term is extended to wider applications such as conscientious objection to capital punishment, to the killing of animals, to abortion, to abuses of the environment, and to capital gains, we will confine ourselves to the military context, where the term has assumed its common meaning. We will especially touch upon the place that conscientious objection has taken in Catholic social teaching.

Conscientious objection to military service dates to the early Christian era (although in the modern era it stands at times without explicit connection to Christian motivation). The early Roman writer Celsus complained in A.D. 173 about Christians who refused military service: "If everyone were to do as you, there would be nothing to prevent the emperor from being left in utter solitude, and with the desertion of his forces, the empire would fall into the hands of the most lawless barbarians." One could name many witnesses to this early conscientious resistance. For example, Maximilian Martyr was beheaded in 295 for his opposition to military service.

Theologians ascribe various motives to this early Christian witness, seeing it partially as a reaction to idolatrous practices in the Roman army; nevertheless, in many cases it was the killing itself that constituted a frequent and clear basis for the objection. Martin of Tours gave his famous reply: "Hitherto I have served you as a soldier. Allow me now to become a soldier of God. . . . I am a soldier of Christ. It is not lawful for me to fight" (Sulpicius Severus, *The Life of Martin* 4.3).

After the Early Chistian Era

After the early Christian era, as the just-war teaching entered the Christian Church conscientious objection was less universal but not totally absent. The Franciscan movement of the 13th and 14th centuries and some Anabaptist sects of the 17th and 18th centuries encouraged resistance to all shedding of blood. In our own time the Quakers, Mennonites, and the Church of the Brethren, often designated as "peace churches" because of their universal proscription against participation in war, have given rise to a significant tradition of conscientious objection. Also in the 20th century, the nonviolent movement of Gandhi has influenced religious-based movements of conscientious objection as well as secular movements.

Within Catholicism even before the Second Vatican Council there have been outstanding witnesses to conscientious objection. Franz Jagerstatter, the Austrian peasant who refused to join what he knew was an unjust war; Thomas Merton, the young writer whose becoming a Catholic was immortalized in his famous book *The Seven Storey Mountain*; Gordon Zahn, the early pacifist who became an outstanding influence on the Catholic peace movement—all of these represent the countless anonymous Christians who throughout our century have felt constrained by faith and conscience to resist military conscription.

The Teaching of the Second Vatican Council

After Vatican II the Roman Catholic church (as well as many of the Reformation churches), while not abandoning just-war teaching and while not embracing a totally pacifist posture, have nevertheless evolved clear teachings recognizing the rights of conscience and the limitations of the state in its prosecution of war.

Vatican Council II, in its Pastoral Constitution on the Church in the Modern World, explicitly recognized the ethical validity of conscientious objectors: "We cannot fail to praise those who renounce the use of violence in the vindication of their rights and who resort to methods of defense which are otherwise available to weaker parties too, provided that this can be done without injury to the rights and duties of others or of the community itself (*Gaudium et spes* 78). Addressing itself to the state, the council added: "It seems right that laws make humane provisions for those who for reasons of conscience refuse to bear arms, provided however, that they accept some other form of service to the human community" (GS 79).

These statements both illustrated and helped to bring about a seemingly genuine development of doctrine. For example, the U.S. Catholic bishops toward the end of the Vietnam conflict, basing themselves on these statements, asked that provision be made for "*selective* conscientious objectors." By this term they meant those who object in conscience not to all war but to a particular war that they believe does not fulfill the criteria of the just-war teaching. Specifically the bishops asked that government grant "a modification of the Selective Service Act making it possible for selective conscientious objectors to refuse to serve in wars they consider unjust, without fear of imprisonment" (*Human Life in Our Day*). They reiterated this teaching in *The Challenge of Peace,* saying that selective conscientious objection is "a moral conclusion which can be validly derived from the classical teaching of just-war principles" (CP 233).

An Evolution of Teaching

That all of this constituted an evolution of Catholic thought can be seen by comparing these exhortations to the earlier and far less tolerant position of Pope Pius XII, who in a 1956 Christmas message affirmed that if the decision for war is reached by freely elected leaders of government, "a Catholic citizen may not appeal to his conscience as grounds for refusing to serve and to fulfill duties fixed by law." This view granted a presumption of rightness to the state that may have been more common in that historical moment. By the time of Vatican II, however, such a presumption was seen as unbefitting the democratic state, in which the responsibility of citizens was clearly extended to the scrutinizing of public policies. The council gave very clear emphasis to a primacy of the individual conscience vis-à-vis the modern state, declaring that "conscience is the most secret core and sanctuary of the human person" and that "in the depths of their conscience human beings detect a law which they do not impose upon themselves, but which holds them to obedience" (GS 16).

In the past, conscientious objectors have often suffered from being forced to bear the burden of proof as regards their sincerity. Today the pastoral situation has shifted. For today it should be more clearly recognized that even the just-war teaching gives a prima facie obligation not to kill. The U.S. Catholic bishops rightly situated the just-war teaching within the context of a moral "presumption against war" (CP 22–25). Such a renewed understanding clearly places the burden of proof, at least in the case of Christians coming before their own pastoral counselors, less on those who in conscience cannot kill and more on those who would conscientiously decide to participate in war.

This evolution of Catholic thought from Pius XII to Vatican II occurred amid a growing awareness of the horror of modern weaponry. It was only after outlining the destructive capability of modern weaponry that Vatican II called for "a completely fresh reappraisal of war" (GS 80). This reappraisal focused, in its beginning phases at least, on the essentially indiscriminate nature of modern weaponry.

Conscientious Objection and Modern Weaponry

It is this indiscriminate character of warmaking and its obvious violation of just-war teaching that has given new importance to the whole issue of selective conscientious objection. The reasoning for this is very coherent: one of the council's strongest condemnations was against indiscriminate warfare, and its formulation has already become classic: "Every act of war directed to the indiscriminate destruction of whole cities or vast areas with their inhabitants is a crime against God and human beings, which merits firm and unequivocal condemnation" (GS 80). For all practical purposes this condemnation placed the church clearly against nuclear war. Catholics faithful to this central teaching would necessarily find themselves in a new class of selective conscientious objectors, that of nuclear pacifists. However, it should be clear that "nuclear pacifist" is somewhat of a misnomer, since such a posture is really derived from the just-war teaching's insistence on keeping intact the protection of civilians from all direct acts of war.

This category of selective conscientious objection has application beyond nuclear weaponry, extending itself to *any* indiscriminate acts. Thus the U.S. Catholic bishops recognized what a well-known analyst of Catholic peace teaching, Gordon Zahn, has termed "situational conscientious objection": "No Christian," the bishops declare, "can rightfully carry out orders or policies deliberately aimed at killing non-combatants." This obviously refers not only to nuclear bombings but even to localized actions of war that would be indiscriminate either in intent or in direct effect. The explicitation of such teachings in our time may be given fresh emphasis as a result of situations such as the My Lai atrocity of the Vietnam War. But the teaching itself is surely not new, encoded as it is for many years now in international law, Geneva conventions, and even in the manuals of military behavior of nations throughout the world.

Other Forms of Conscientious Objection to Warmaking

This moral aversion to indiscriminate warfare and to the modern weaponry that leads to it has spawned new forms of citizen conscientious objection such as tax resistance and opposition to working in defense industries or in other areas of the military-industrial complex. The U.S. Catholic bishops in their pastoral letter on peace gave this latter form of conscientious objection a moral legitimation: "All Catholics . . . can and should use the moral principles of this letter to form their consciences. . . . Those who in conscience decide that they should no longer be associated with defense activities should find support in the Catholic community" (CP 318).

Since legally very few states make humane provision for selective conscientious objection, it not infrequently happens that the objector, if he or she is to follow conscience, must engage in civil disobedience. Thus conscientious objection and civil disobedience in the present legal context frequently coincide. The social and ethical basis for this civil disobedience can be found in Christian tradition. John XXIII in his encyclical *Pacem in terris* summarized that tradition: "Since the right to command is required by the moral order and has its source in God, it follows that, if civil authorities legislate for or allow anything that is contrary to the will of God, neither the law made nor the authorization granted can be binding on the conscience of the citizens since God has more right to be obeyed than human beings" (PT 51).

The basis for civil disobedience as a form of conscientious objection can be found as early as Thomas Aquinas, who gave his analysis of what constituted an unjust law: "Laws may be unjust in two ways: first, by being contrary to human good. . . . The like are acts of violence rather than laws; because, as Augustine says (*De Lib.* art. i.5), a law that is not just seems to be no law at all. Wherefore such laws do not bind in conscience, except perhaps in order to avoid scandal or disturbance. . . . Secondly, laws may be unjust through being opposed to the Divine good: such are the laws of tyrants inducing to idolatry, or to anything else contrary to the Divine law: and laws of this kind must nowise be observed, because, as stated in Acts 5:29, we ought to obey God rather than humans" (ST Ia, IIae, 96, 4). It is, in fact, this saying of the apostles quoted by Aquinas that can be said to be the foundation for all Christian acts of conscientious objection.

Legal Status

We have focused on Catholic sources in this treatment of conscientious objection. It should be clear, however, that the Roman Catholic church's teaching on conscientious objection is shared by other denominations, many of whom have formulated teachings on the validity of conscientious objection through national and international governing bodies. In the United States alone, by the mid-1980s over forty-seven religious denominations had joined the National Interreligious Service Board for Conscientious Objectors (NISBCO), which came into being in 1940 as a response to military conscription.

The legal status of conscientious objection is complex and diversified in the various nations. While some provision for pacifists was found in a few countries' legal codes in the 19th century, it is only in recent times that legal protection has become common, especially in the West. (The United Nations' Commission on Human Rights voted in favor of the right of conscientious objection at its meeting in March 1987 and again in March 1989.) The United States has had conscript laws as far back as the Civil War. Some would attribute this early and relatively liberal policy to the powerful Quaker influence in the formation of the colonies. While in our time protection for the conscientious objector has been extended in many nations to include the nonreligious objector, the same protection has not been extended to the selective objector who applies the just-war teaching to particular wars or to individual situations. This remains a task to be achieved.

See also ARMS RACE; CHURCH-STATE RELATIONS IN THE UNITED STATES; CIVIL LAW, FUNCTION OF; CONSCIENCE; COOPERATION, PRINCIPLE OF; DISARMAMENT; PACIFISM; PEACE.

Bibliography: NCCB, *The Challenge of Peace: God's Promise and Our Response* (Washington: USCC, 1983). USCC, *Declaration on Conscientious Objection and Selective Conscientious Objection* (Washington: USCC, 1971). G. Zahn, *Another Part of the War: The Camp Simon Story* (Amherst: Univ. of Massachusetts Press, 1979). E. Egan, *The Catholic Conscientious Objector: The Right to Refuse to Kill* (Erie, Pa.: Pax Christi, 1981). J. Forest, *Catholics and Conscientious Objection* (New York: Catholic Peace Fellowship Pamphlet, 1981). F. Meehan, "The Catholic Conscience Faces the Military Draft," *The Catholic Mind*, vol. 78, no. 1345 (September 1980) 10–14. G. Zahn, *The Life and Death of Franz Jaegerstetter* (Springfield: Templegate, 1986). A. Muste, *Of Holy Disobedience* (Wallingford, Pa.: Pendle Hill Pamphlet, 1952).

FRANCIS X. MEEHAN

COOPERATION, PRINCIPLE OF

While the concept of cooperation is found often in an exhortative sense in the Vatican II documents concerning ecumenical relations (*Unitatis redintegratio* 12; *Spiritus Domini* 80–94; *Apostolicam actuositatem* 27) and missionary work (*Ad gentes* 35–41), it more often appears traditionally in the principle of cooperation with evil. The principle offers several distinctions that together determine whether someone's assistance in another's wrongdoing is licit or not.

Cooperation depends upon determining the exact object of the cooperator's activity and being able to distinguish that from the object of the wrongdoing. As can be seen in the principle of double effect, the object, the most fundamental concept in traditional Scholastic moral theory, describes the exact activity under investigation.

Kelly demonstrates the specific determination of an object in the case of a nurse assisting in an illicit operation: "In itself, the work done by the nurses is not morally wrong. It is exactly the same work that they would do at a perfectly moral operation; hence, it would come under the classification of indifferent or morally good actions. To render this kind of assistance to one who is performing or about to perform an evil action and evil purpose, is called material cooperation" (pp. 332–33).

For centuries the manualists carefully examined the object of moral activity. Thus in the case of the servant who transported letters between his master and his lover, the object of the servant's action is transporting letters, which is morally indifferent and not like the object of his master's illicit intentions. Similarly, Catholics who made Masonic emblems are free of moral blame, precisely on the grounds that the emblems are, in themselves, indifferent. Likewise, priests could administer Communion to sinners because the object itself, administering Communion, is indifferent. In a similar vein, the Holy Office judged on the question of cremation (DS, no. 3278).

In the tradition, moralists specified exactly the object that the cooperator performs to assist in wrongdoing. The actions of a nurse assisting in an illicit operation, of a priest distributing Communion to a sinner, of an artisan making a Masonic emblem, or of a servant bearing amorous letters from a master to his mistress are not the same as the actions of a doctor performing a direct abortion, of a sinner receiving Communion, of a Mason identifying himself with an insignia, or of a master communicating with his mistress.

After identifying the cooperator's object, several considerations are examined to determine the liceity of the cooperator's activity. The first distinguishes between formal and material cooperation, which concerns whether the cooperator intends the object of the wrongdoer's activity. If the cooperator does, then the cooperation is formal and therefore illicit. The distinction argues that the nurse's, the priest's, the servant's, and the artisan's activity remain licit as long as they do not intend the illicit objects being performed by the wrongdoers. If cooperation is not formal, it is simply material and permitted.

Recently some authors have claimed that formal cooperation can be ascribed even when the cooperator does not approve of the wrongdoing. The distinction comes from those manualists (Noldin and Gury) who argue that there are two types of formal cooperation, explicit and implicit. Explicit involves an act of the will. Implicit does not. Implicit comes from the fact that no explanation can distinguish the cooperator's object from the wrongdoer's object. Davis gives "deliberate adultery" as a case of formal, implicit cooperation when someone commits an act of adultery knowingly and argues against having intended it as such.

Implicit formal cooperation means that the deed done can admit of no other explanation than what the activity itself expresses. The object of the act itself can have no more immediate intention. Thus were I to stab repeatedly an innocent person, I could not claim that I did not intend to kill the person. The object of the activity itself does not admit another explanation. Similarly, someone who injects a patient with a lethal drug cannot claim that the patient's death was not intended. However, by administering a painkiller that could endanger a patient's life, one could claim intent to alleviate the patient's pain but not to cause the patient's death.

Implicit formal cooperation is argued only in those few cases where the object of the cooperator's action cannot exclude a particular meaning. Therefore, the manualists did not attribute implicit formal cooperation to the nurse who hands a doctor an instrument in an illicit operation. Nor did they impute it to the priest distributing Communion to a sinner. Nor did they designate this as the activity of artisans who made Masonic emblems, of judges who rendered verdicts in divorce cases, or of people who wished to be cremated. The assertion that a particular act of cooperation is implicitly formal requires an object like the actual removal and destruction of a fetus, cremation in a sacrilegious ritual, or the actual reverence of a Masonic emblem. These cases clearly involve the cooperator's intention and admit no other justifiable explanation without accusing the agent of hypocrisy.

The second consideration concerns the distinction between immediate and mediate cooperation. Cooperation is immediate when the object of the cooperator is the same as the object of the wrongdoing. Thus were the servant actually to engage in illicit sexual acts for his superior or the nurse actually to abort a fetus, the object of each activity would be illicit. Generally speaking immediate cooperation is always wrong, though the manualists see, even here, exceptions. These exceptions concern constraint, wherein the cooperator's object is the same as the wrongdoing despite the cooperator's unwillingness. Being unwilling, the cooperator has not intended the object of wrongdoing. Conversely, when cooperation is mediate the cooperator's object remains distinguishable from the wrongdoing and is therefore licit.

When a cooperator's object of activity has been both material and mediate, then three other considerations together help determine the question of liceity. Thus the third consideration distinguishes between proximate and remote cooperation. This distinction recognizes the prudence in maintaining distance in cooperation. It asks just how mediate the cooperation is. Here the tradition demonstrates more how proximate the cooperation may be as opposed to how remote it must be: a servant can pass letters, an anesthesiologist can administer gas, a priest can give Communion, and so on.

The fourth consideration concerns the degree of necessity involved in the cooperation. To the extent a wrongdoer cannot accomplish the activity without assistance, to that degree the fifth consideration, grave reason, must proportionately be stronger. In some instances a grave reason is simply to maintain employment. But other reasons concern more generally the diminishment of evil that could occur through cooperation (DS, nos. 3190–93; Davis, pp. 343, 349–52; Kelly, pp. 332–35). Here a considerable weighing of values occurs, determining the degrees of proximity and need against a justifying grave reason.

In its history the principle is prompted by three fundamental concerns. First, there are subordinates, for example, the servant or artisan, whose livelihood is dependent on the varying degrees of legitimate cooperation. Second, there are emergencies in which greater harm would result without cooperation, for example, the priest distributing Communion and the decision to cremate. Third, there are those whose presence, though apparently compromised, nonetheless prevent institutions from further corruption. These cases, for example, the judge who presides over divorce cases and the nurses and anesthesiologists who assist in illicit operations, are considered licit not solely or even because of the financial needs of the cooperators but rather because of the hope that their presence in the institution will lead to less wrongdoing in the future.

The principle offers a thorough calculus for moral decision making. Against other principles, this one engages many more areas of ordinary life than the principle of double effect, is much more sophisticated than the principle of the lesser evil, and certainly is more dynamic than the principle of toleration. Nonetheless, many avoid it because, as Davis said of determining the liceity in objects of material cooperation, there is "no more difficult question than this in the whole range of Moral Theology" (p. 342).

See also ABORTION, SOCIAL IMPLICATIONS OF; CHURCH-STATE RELATIONS IN THE UNITED STATES; DOUBLE EFFECT, PRINCIPLE OF; PARTNERSHIP; PLURALISM; TOLERATION, PRINCIPLE OF.

Bibliography: H. Davis, *Moral and Pastoral Theology* (London: Sheed & Ward, 1958). G. Kelly, *Medico-Moral Problems* (St. Louis: Catholic Hospital Association, 1958). J. Keenan, "Prophylactics, Toleration, and Cooperation: Contemporary Problems and Traditional Principles," *International Philosophical Quarterly* 29 (1989) 205–20.

JAMES F. KEENAN, S.J.

COOPERATIVE ASSOCIATIONS

A cooperative is a nonprofit economic organization whose goal is to provide some particular benefit to its members: the reduction of costs or the securing of a certain income. The basis for membership is a capital contribution to which the member retains ownership. A further, implicit contribution of the members in consumer cooperatives is that they will purchase from the cooperative. In addition, the members' contribution to the cooperative often includes some direct service in operations. In a producer cooperative, however, the organization handles the sales of the goods extracted or manufactured. Typically, the wholesale purchases of a cooperative make it possible to reduce the costs of consumption goods to the members or of goods needed for further (e.g., agricultural) production. Cooperatives attract people of moderate means because these persons desire benefits attainable on the basis of the small capital outlay they can muster. In general, the returns on the cooperative's capital are distributed to the members. This distribution is frequently not on the basis of the number of shares held (in any case, the number of shares per person is usually very small) but rather on the basis simply of membership or in proportion to the amount of purchases. The one-person-one-vote principle establishes the overall control of the organization.

The Rochdale Pioneers in Great Britain initiated in 1844 the modern cooperative movement. The significance of the Rochdale group lies in (1) their early and successful combining and application of proven cooperative practices, (2) the continuation and extension of their system, and (3) their impact on Jose-Maria Arizmendi of the Basque region in the north of Spain, who, along with his collaborators, developed an extremely successful system of both consumer and producer cooperatives that is adapted to industries grounded in highly developed technologies, includes service companies, and stimulates research capacities. In many ways, for example in federating producer and consumer cooperatives, these Mondragon cooperatives differ decidedly from previous models.

The cooperative system is hardly foreign to the U.S. situation. In the 19th century the Knights of Labor attempted to make use of this organizational form as an avenue to social reform. Further, the U.S. system of agricultural cooperatives and their federations is a pronounced instance of the possible range for a cooperative system.

The failure of the Knights and the success of agricultural cooperatives indicate the requirements for the successful development of this economic form: the elementary organization for cooperative consumption or production requires adjunct financial, educational (e.g., managerial), and technical support. The Mondragon system meets these requirements by providing services itself through units of a cooperative federation.

The benefits of the cooperatives go beyond cost reduction or secured additional income. The idealistic forebears of the Rochdale movement bequeathed one legacy that the Pioneers maintained: cooperatives can be a tool for strengthening ties or for venturing to bring about social reform. At the furthest reach of cooperative models, Mondragon indicates the contemporary effectiveness and range of such social benefits. The Mondragon federation of cooperatives is a complex and novel system that has moved into copartnership and has established a regular, participatory management. It has explicitly structured, ongoing democratic processes lacking in other producer or consumer cooperatives. It has been one organization that has strengthened local ties and propelled the region out of a period of economic crisis.

Church social teaching, primarily in *Rerum novarum* and *Quadragesimo anno,* was one of the fonts from which the designers of the Mondragon system drew their inspiration. The Antigonish movement is another development whose origin lies in church teaching and mission. The movement contributes to social and communal betterment (here in an area subject to the disadvantages of economic change) by means of adult education toward concerted action that often takes the form of cooperatives.

At the turn of the century ethicist and canonist Arthur Vermeersch in his *Manuel Social* highly recommended cooperatives as one means by which weak persons could attain a mutual benefit amidst the complex and dangerous forces of industrial society.

The well-known Bishops' Program of Social Reconstruction of 1919, issued under the guidance of Msgr. John A. Ryan, urged the establishment of further cooperatives because they assisted the workers, certainly in reducing prices and also in giving them training in business methods and a capacity for cooperative action.

Mater et magistra urges cooperatives in the farming and all other productive sectors as a means for mutual aid (MM 146). In this tradition the U.S. Catholic bishops in *Food Policy in a Hungry World* urge the support of cooperatives and make explicit reference to these twin benefits: distributing economic power more widely and extending participation. The document regards both of these as paths by which those who lack power can enter into participating in the systems of society.

Cooperative programs achieve both solidarity and subsidiarity insofar as they make possible, through self-help and self-education, concerted action for mutual benefit.

Another application of the cooperative model is the credit union. In this structure the members obtain a reduction in the cost of loans. The fact that credit unions are often connected with a particular place of employment draws attention to the social bond that exists among the members of the cooperative. This social bond was a key element in the cooperative credit associations developed by Friedrich Wilhelm Raiffeisen, which became the mode adopted in the United States. Such a bond provides some parameters or a general set of tastes that clearly shape policies or, at least, create enough space for the tolerance required in the deliberation by the members. It also increases the ease of locating and keeping members. The social bond may be a problematic element today given the increasing variety of the ethnic makeup in the United States, the disappearance of many workers' organizations, and the fragmentation of social intercourse.

Some considerations also arise concerning member contributions: if the member must contribute in terms of work time, this may be an unrealistic expectation given the increased job and family commitments of many in the United States today. If members have the option of buying out his or her work requirement, this may introduce invidious distinctions or otherwise erode the spirit that makes possible the noneconomic benefits of the organization. Given the extension and overlapping of markets for inputs, goods, and services, the cost reduction or return on membership share may be too small to keep present members or attract new ones. The mechanism of the cooperative may then require collaboration with similar organizations beyond the locality or region in order to take advantage of new information, sources, and markets. Particularly with regard to producer cooperatives or worker cooperatives along the lines of Mondragon where the workers' share is considerable, since the income and secured portion of wealth meets the members' and their families' present and future needs, the organization must strive to develop safety mechanisms to protect these livelihoods from grave loss.

See also BISHOPS' PROGRAM OF SOCIAL RECONSTRUCTION OF 1919; COPARTNERSHIP; CREDIT UNION; DEMOCRACY; LABOR AND CAPITAL IN CATHOLIC SOCIAL THOUGHT; QUADRAGESIMO ANNO.

D. Ellerman, *Worker Ownership: Economic Democracy or Worker Capitalism?* (Somerville, Mass.: Industrial Cooperative Association, 1985). R. Mason, *Participatory and Workplace Democracy: A Theoretical Development in Critique of Liberalism* (Carbondale and Edwardsville: Southern Illinois Univ. Press, 1982). M. Schirber, "Cooperatives," *New Catholic Encyclopedia* 4:298–302. NCCB, "Food Policy in a Hungry World," *Origins* 19 (November 23, 1989) 414–20.

PHILIP J. CHMIELEWSKI, S.J.

COPARTNERSHIP

Copartnership takes the form of a number of structured processes whereby those who work toward a common object assume on the basis of their work activity an increased competence and responsibility in the policies and operation of the office, plant, or firm for the sake of a mutual benefit. Copartnership requires at least the setting up of structures whereby owners and managers can be held accountable for decisions and policies.

Laborem exercens speaks of the participation by workers in an economic enterprise in terms of three patterns of copartnership: (1) joint ownership of the means of work, (2) sharing in management, and (3) sharing in the profits of business (LE 14).

Insofar as copartnership extends into the system of ownership, this advances toward one element that undergirds the common good, namely, coparticipation in property, which helps avoid the concentration of economic and thus political power (*Economic Justice for All* 114).

Comanagement as consultation with workers can remain at the level of the solicitation and gathering of information, suggestions, and viewpoints; this would stop short of an actual share in decision and control by workers. A move beyond this comanagement to a further development of copartnership requires greater attention to the quality of democratic process in the participatory activity. Two questions are of immediate importance: (1) in the plant is there at least an equal voice secured for workers, and (2) can the workers place items on the agenda?

Responsible comanagement in the firm requires effective voice at several levels: in the actual work position, in the management of a particular plant or office, and in the management of the firm, that is, in the decisions of central management and significant owners.

Copartnership in the workplace requires a right to and actual participation in decisions concerning the practical matters involved in the time, space, and techniques of the arrangement of the workplace and its processes. Having a voice in these decisions implies both that persons are engaged in very particular institutions and that they develop themselves, especially that they develop their ethical dispositions and habits of activity.

Profit-sharing programs are a restricted form of copartnership. Although the participants in these programs receive additional income or even some wealth by way of getting a share of the profits, and although these may lead to an increased commitment to the office's or plant's operations on the part of the employees, regular channels for the experience of initiative, decision making, and accountability are not integral to profit-sharing structures.

An objection to profit sharing is that practically it involves doubling the chances of loss for the worker: to the perennial danger of job loss there is now added the danger of sharing losses. This is a threat not just to the income but to the limited wealth of the workers. Yet at the same time, a greater range of options and choice has been introduced; there may be new dangers, but active and responsible persons now have structures through which they can address such threat. Decision about losses and how to allocate them now become part of the workers' mature evaluation and planning: work sharing, pay changes, distribution of dividends, and plant closings. Properly supervised loss-insurance plans and internal corporate programs provide a practical and effective response to this crisis.

There are critical differences between stockholding and profit-sharing schemes in copartnership programs and those in cooperatives. Although some social bond frequently links the members of a cooperative (e.g., those living in a certain area), this is not necessarily the case; membership ensues upon purchase of a share or the secured contribution to production. In contrast, membership in any of the various copartnership programs derives from one's work activity in a particular company or facility; there is an intrinsic link between person and structure. Although cooperatives may provide an alternate income, it is often minimal; they strive primarily to reduce some range of costs. In contrast, through participation in a profit-sharing plan the workers intend to provide themselves a further source of income. Cooperatives are managed according to policies approved by an assembly or by representatives of the membership. Comanagement schemes (although assemblies and representatives may figure into the constitution of the organization) require a near-continuous interaction, ideally at several levels in the plant and firm. Cooperatives are owned broadly on the basis of purchase. Comanagement schemes strive for ownership. In the most interesting version, found at Mondragon, the characteristics of property have changed. Only workers in the firm purchase the shares; yet a facility in entrance and exit remains. The share itself has come to be a repository of decision and committed responsibility that depends on the worker's activity.

Securing the voice of the person in the course of the work process means that the system of control, production, and service does not elide the personal capacity for decision. The chance to partake in wealth through shared ownership means that the person and his/her dependents have another source of income and a more established security; that is, this element of copartnership guards the requisite of all persons for a security in which to develop a life that contributes to the common good. Such security requires (given the vagaries of history) the variety of defenses (here, multiple sources of income) and the capacity to project a future, the lasting basis for which a share in the corporation provides.

Because persons learn collaboration and responsibility most readily in their immediate surroundings in the firm, that is, at the actual place of work, the attempts to institute regular cooperation between managers and other workers must come within the effective purview of the workers themselves. From a broader vantage, the simple purpose for economic participation, that each person may realize that he/she works for him/herself, will lead to reforms in enterprises and the reshaping of the economy (LE 14–15).

Earlier arguments (e.g., of Msgr. John A. Ryan) for copartnership were cast in terms of distributive justice. Other arguments point to the contribution on the part of workers to the maintenance and increase of productive property. Still others seek to assure a voice for each person in any action toward which he/she makes a contribution. Here the reasoning, by moving to a more central point, avoids the highly charged dispute concerning the determinant of property ownership. Recommendations that urge comanagement flow, in part, from such a position. Moving to a position still more central to the person is the argument that in any process where the person invests his/her activity, there he/she engages his/her personhood; at that point, he/she will not be treated as an object; he/she must be able to act as a subject. Thus comanagement allows not only a fair, equal voice to the worker but also, for example, the ability to initiate matters on the basis of each person's capacity for discovery.

Profit-sharing programs, shared ownership, and, most importantly, coparticipation then constitute the structures for securing the full range of personal activity.

Another, more social argument for coparticipation says that all those who both share the common lot in a society and collaborate in attaining the common good and who, at the same time, are affected by the operations of a particular company should be able to participate in decisions about that company. This would reduce the threat of their being rendered objects vis-à-vis the firm's processes and decisions. The U.S. Catholic bishops move toward supporting such copartnership when they urge further regional and national collaboration (EJA 307–11, 318).

The idea of copartnership, whether in Nell-Breuning's understanding of codetermination or that found in *Economic Justice for All,* repeatedly indicates the importance of structures extending beyond the particular plant and firm into the locality and region so that the economic functions of that plant or firm may serve not only all who work there but the others whose lives it affects. Some unions have maintained a concern for regulating standards of craft and workmanship, the benefits of which accrue beyond the contracting parties to the purchasers and other recipients of the firms' goods and services. Further, unions through training programs and broader education have had an impact on persons and public that have exceeded the effort and remuneration specified in the contract. Copartnership more extensively structures these transcontractual advantages as regular concerns for the common good and for social impact.

The North American Catholic support for copartnership antedates the first Roman statement in *Quadragesimo anno* (1931); in 1919 under the influence of Msgr. John A. Ryan, the Administrative Committee of the National Catholic Welfare Conference and later, the bishops' board, approved the well-known Bishops' Program of Social Reconstruction. The document urged participation by workers in management and wider distribution of ownership. *Quadragesimo anno* was the first global call that workers were to share in ownership, management, and profits.

After the Second World War, Jose-Maria Arizmendi developed a system of small-sized industrial and service "cooperatives" in an underdeveloped area in the north of Spain. Oswald von Nell-Breuning was instrumental in the effort to establish workers' participation (*Mitbestimmung,* or codetermination) at multiple levels of the factory and firm in the heavily industrialized, highly unionized, and strongly centralized West German economy.

John XXIII returns to the teaching of Pius XI in advocating that workers share in ownership and management. In *Mater et magistra* the pontiff makes reference, in addition, to Pius XII's broadcast on September 1, 1944, which favored partnership in larger firms (MM 84). According to *Mater et magistra* workers should gradually acquire a share in their enterprises (77). In this way they assume responsibility and perfect themselves, that is, attain the full exercise of their human capacities (82). Section 91 goes on to specify partnership in terms of shared management.

Gaudium et spes continues the teaching of both Pius XI and John XXIII. In this document the council emphasizes the personal and social development for which human work is the critical fulcrum; it urges "the active participation" by workers "in the running of an enterprise" (GS 68). John Paul II in *Laborem exercens* stands firmly in this line; he urges joint ownership, partaking in management, and sharing in profits by workers.

The U.S. Catholic bishops have more recently urged forms of copartnership, establishing its basis in the threefold moral significance of work (EJA 97) and referring to *Laborem exercens.* The first element of this significance, "the distinctive human capacity for self-expression and self-realization," develops through copartnership so that it more extensively contributes to the common good.

The varied programs of copartnership are closer to the North American experience than many contemporary observers recognize. Cooperatives have prepared the way; employee stock ownership programs are a moderate, transitional version. More directly, when John Paul II affirms that the person, independent of the type of work he/she undertakes, is the subject (LE 7), the democratic character of this channel of Roman Catholic social teaching is very close to the egalitarianism latent or expressed in many U.S. social and political patterns.

The bishops make clear the connection between their extended treatment of partnership and the recommendation for structures of participation (EJA 296). They explicitly sketch their idea of worker-management partnership (300). Their recommendation moves beyond the collaborative determination of work conditions, profit sharing, and stockholding when they indicate that whether employed or not, more people in the country should become shareholders. This means of economic participation is one design for achieving the twofold goal: (1) responsible collaboration (2) as effort toward the common good in all sectors of society.

Any program of copartnership must proceed on the basis of helping people learn their own abilities to partake in such processes. Such education is critical. Otherwise even well-designed structures will collapse and the workers will grow disenchanted.

Particularly insofar as worker participation in a given plant or firm is successful, a critical juncture is reached: either the organization can attend to the necessities of others within the (immediate) range of the plant's or firm's activity, or it will become caught in its own concerns. A rivalry with members of other firms or rival industries may ensue. Since workers' participation constructs systems around those who are employed, the danger exists that a particular system may fail to consider certain elements of the common goal, for example, care for those who are infirm, children, and elderly persons. Not all those whom the firm's or the plant's decisions affect may work there; thus it is more difficult for these to partake in decision making. Unfair procedures raise the likelihood of unjust results.

Codetermination designs the structure of collaborative decision and activity so that two sides participate: management and workers. A difficulty with this system is that participation in ownership (the third pole of the firm), especially in those contemporary replacements for strict ownership that set strategy and policy for the corporation, has not yet been adequately designed.

For decades Catholic social teaching has supported unions; more recent developments in this position and the reflection on it have begun to urge forms of copartnership. The two systems are mutually sustaining. Forty years of codetermination in the strong union setting of West Germany provides some evidence of this. The system of worker participation by way of the union, the local, collective bargaining, and contract provides a legally regulated minimum by which the worker has a say and holds authorities responsible for wage, terms of work, workplace conditions, and other decisions. Beyond and alongside the union model, copartnership can offer means for broad regular consultation and responsibility that supplements merely periodic or office-led activity and adds active, positive collaboration to reactive, problem, or grievance-linked procedures. Nevertheless, there remains a double danger: just as the bishops denounce efforts to prevent the continuation of existing union locals or the formation of new ones, so too all developments in copartnership that are used to subvert union effectiveness must be condemned.

Another development that would further strengthen effective cooperation would be to ensure the workers an appropriate participation in the knowledge concerning technical processes. The lack of knowledge leads to the absence of responsibility; the lack of a common knowledge about the processes to which all contribute results in the undermining of copartnership.

To assist working persons in grasping the analogy between the still-remaining or newly emergent civic concerns on the one hand, where participation has been traditionally and widely accepted, and the concerns in the world of work on the other, is one means to encourage the learning of the skills of participation.

See also COOPERATIVE ASSOCIATIONS; DEMOCRACY; GOODS, ACCESS TO; LABOREM EXERCENS; MATER ET MAGISTRA; NELL-BREUNING, OSWALD VON; OWNERSHIP; RYAN, JOHN AUGUSTINE.

Bibliography: N. Betten, *Catholic Activism and the Industrial Worker* (Gainesville: Univ. Presses of Florida, 1976). R. Dahl, *A Preface to Economic Democracy* (Berkeley: Univ. of California Press, 1985). D. Ellerman, *The Democratic Worker-Owned Firm: A New Model for East and West* (London: Unwin Hyman, 1990). J. Vanek, *Self-Management: Economic Liberation of Man* (Harmondsworth: Penguin, 1975).

PHILIP J. CHMIELEWSKI, S.J.

COR UNUM

The pontifical council for Christian and human development, Cor Unum, was established by Pope Paul VI on July 15, 1971, in a letter written to then Secretary of State Jean Cardinal Villot, who was also appointed its first president. Cor Unum is a permanent office or dicastery of the Holy See, functioning under a president assisted by a vice president. The council consists of approximately forty members—bishops, priests, religious, and laypersons—from the various regions of the world. Some members represent various agencies within the church in the sociocharitable and development fields, while others are members in their own name because of personal expertise in the same areas. The council is assisted by a group of consultors chosen because of personal competence and experience in related areas. The executive arm of the council is its secretariat, located within the state of Vatican City.

The purpose of Cor Unum is to assist the pope in his response to the duty of charity, to promote the formation of God's people in the true meaning of charity, to set the true progress and advancement of peoples in the context of evangelization. In the fulfillment of its mandate Cor Unum is responsible for the harmonization of the energies and initiatives of all the Catholic aid organizations at the international level. Thus it relates closely with the major confederations such as Caritas Internationalis, Coopération Internationale pour le Développement et la Solidarité (CIDSE), the Society of St. Vincent de Paul, the International Association of the Ladies of Charity, and the International Catholic Migration Commission as well as with many other national-level aid and development agencies of the church operating internationally.

Cor Unum is at the disposition of the bishops' conferences and of individual bishops in their relations with Catholic aid organizations. It relates with other Christian churches and ecclesial bodies where possible so that people may benefit from mutual charitable initiatives, and thus it has regular contacts with the competent commission of the World Council of Churches. Through its relation with the various components of the system of the United Nations organization working in the area of aid and development, Cor Unum seeks to facilitate their relations with Catholic aid organizations. Cor Unum, as well as Catholic aid organizations, seeks always a united, effective, and prompt response to disasters. Whenever the pope wishes to undertake special activities or initiatives in the charitable sphere, it is Cor Unum's responsibility, at his request, to serve as his instrument to put such activities or initiatives into effect speedily. In this manner in the light of the current needs of humanity does the bishop of Rome seek to maintain the Catholic church, the community of baptized believers, in that ideal of one heart (Latin, *cor unum*) and one soul, of which St. Luke wrote in the Acts of the Apostles (4:32).

See also AID; ALMSGIVING; CHARITY; MAGISTERIUM.

JOHN S. KNIGHT

CORPORATIONS

A modern corporation is a legal and contractual mechanism for doing business using capital from investors that will be managed on their behalf by directors and officers. Created either for a limited period or in perpetuity by the state that grants its charter, it is treated in many respects as a natural person before the law. Thus it can buy and sell, own property, incur debts, and sue and be sued. According to their specific purposes and the laws of the chartering state there are many types and classes of corporations, for example, for-profit, not-for-profit, commercial, educational, and religious corporations.

Advantages of the corporate form are (1) capacity to bring together capital from many investors; (2) limited liability (only what owners have invested is at risk); (3) durability (its life outlasts the founders); (4) capacity for growth, making it possible to realize cost savings from large-scale production.

The type of corporation mentioned in Catholic social teaching is the for-profit business corporation, which dominates the business sector of most industrial economies today and which has become global in its scope. This kind of corporation is legally owned by its shareholders, who retain some ultimate rights. However, the real power is vested in the board of directors, who governs the corporation and chooses the management, which is accountable to it.

Certain concerns about corporations have been raised in Catholic social teaching as well as by economists and other social scientists: the separation of ownership and control, the lack of social accountability, the dangers of bigness itself, the depersonalization of the workplace in large industrial corporations, the role of multinational corporations in poor nations, the role of corporate stockholders.

In the tradition of Catholic social teaching ownership carries with it responsibility (*Populorum progressio* 23), and Pius XI saw the corporate form as giving "occasion to the most sordid license" because of the "reduced obligation of accountability" inherent in this legal form. Because of the opportunity to hide behind the shelter of a joint name, he said, "the worst of injustices and frauds are perpetrated . . . and directors of business companies, forgetful of their trust, betray the rights of those whose savings they have undertaken to administer" (*Quadragesimo anno* 132).

The U.S. bishops in 1933 acknowledged that "the big corporation has its place" given the demands of modern technology. However, they stated that "their intolerable abuses, especially their clandestine manipulation of trust funds and earned surplus, must cease if we are to restore the social and economic order." They called on Catholic scholars to "put forth concrete plans that will insist on the rigorous application of moral principles to big corporations," placing limitations on them so as to protect smaller entities from absorption by the larger and providing a "graded hierarchical order between various subsidiary organizations" ("Present Crisis" 72, in Byers, ed., pp. 414–15).

This preference for smaller economic entities persists in Catholic social teaching, rooted as it is in the principle of subsidiarity (QA 79; *Mater et magistra* 53; *Economic Justice for All* 99). It appears again in the concerns of the U.S. bishops over the increasing presence of nonfarm corporations that drive out smaller farmers and that lack a sense of responsibility for the good of the community or the food system as a whole (EJA 225, 234).

Pius XII judged the impersonal unity of the modern industrial corporate form as alien to the personal-centered order intended by God and thus as a threat to the whole social order (Pius XII, "Christmas Messages," in Byers, ed., pp. 99–109).

In their 1986 pastoral the U.S. bishops called on "giant corporations" to govern their activities according to the moral principles specifying the human significance of work: work as the principal way people exercise the human capacity for self-expression and self-realization, work as the ordinary way for human beings to fulfill their human needs, work as a way in which people contribute to the well-being of the larger community (EJA 97).

During the 1960s the activities of modern multinational corporations in poor nations attracted attention. Paul VI in 1967 questioned the "industrialists, merchants, leaders or representatives of larger enterprises," who "are not lacking in social sensitivity in their own country," about why they "return to the unhuman principles of individualism when they operate in less-developed countries." He called on them to be "initiators of social progress and human advancement" by training indigenous workers, bringing them into management positions, and establishing just employer-employee relations (PP 70).

In 1971 Paul VI addressed the emergence of multinational enterprises as "new economic powers" largely independent of the national political powers "and therefore not subject to control from the point of view of the common good." He saw them exercising "a new and abusive form of economic domination on the social, cultural and even political level," a new form of the "excessive concentration of means and powers" condemned by Pius XI in *Quadragesimo anno* (*Octogesima adveniens* 44).

John Paul II, writing a decade later, pointed to the actions of multinational/transnational enterprises as one of the causes of the ever-widening gap between the incomes of rich and poor nations. In his treatment of the growing interdependence of world economies and its impact on workers, he described how multinationals "fix the highest possible prices for their products, while trying at the same time to fix the lowest possible prices for raw materials or semimanufactured goods." This sets the context in which local employers may have to determine wages and working conditions for their own workers "below the objective requirements of the workers" (*Laborem exercens* 17). He included the multinational corporations as one of the components of the "indirect employer" responsible for the whole orientation of labor policy (LE 18) and thus the object of the whole challenge of the Catholic social teaching on justice in the workplace.

In their 1986 pastoral the U.S. bishops recognized the power of U.S. transnational corporations and financial institutions to help determine the justice or injustice of the world economy. The bishops pointed out that these corporations can make a positive contribution to development in poor nations (EJA 280) and to global solidarity even though profit maximization "has often tempted" them to behavior that increases inequality and instability (116) and creates or perpetuates dependency or maintains repressive regimes in power (279).

The bishops indicated how a constructive role can be played: "By collaborating with those national governments that serve their citizens justly and with intergovernmental agencies, these corporations can contribute to overcoming the desperate plight of many persons throughout the world" (116). They urged U.S. and international support for efforts to develop a code of conduct for multinational corporations "that recognizes their quasi-public character and encourages both development and the equitable distribution of their benefits." Transnational corporations should be required to abide by these codes (280). The bishops also laid out a vision of partnership in the U.S. economy based on the tradition of Catholic social teaching, and they outlined the proper role of managers and shareholders in corporations (305–6).

The bishops deplored the effect of corporate decisions to relocate production abroad at the expense of U.S. jobs and communities (146). They recognized that the primary legal responsibility of managers in U.S. corporations is to exercise prudence in the interest of a profitable return to investors. Then they added, "But morally this legal responsibility may be exercised only within the bounds of justice to employees, customers, suppliers and the local community" (305). With size goes power and social responsibility (111). Corporations were also called upon as one of the institutions in a national strategy to encourage self-help among poor people through provision of seed money, training and technical assistance, and organizational support for projects such as low-income housing, credit unions, worker cooperatives, and neighborhood and community organizations (200).

Commenting on the role of shareholders, the bishops urged serious, long-term research and experimentation to find more effective ways of dealing with the "complex and insufficiently understood" question of how to relate the rights and responsibilities of shareholders to those of other people and communities affected by corporate decisions (306).

Turning to the obligations of the church, its institutions, and its members as shareholders in corporations, the bishops exhorted them to be both morally and financially responsible stewards. "As part owners they must cooperate in shaping the policies of those companies" through dialogue with management, voting at corporate meetings, introducing shareholder resolutions, and participating in investment decisions. They praised the efforts of dioceses and "other religious and ecumenical bodies" that work together toward corporate responsibility goals (354).

See individual popes and encyclicals. *Also see* BUSINESS ETHICS; CAPITALISM; COMMON GOOD; COMPETITION; INDUSTRY; PERSON, DIGNITY OF; PROFIT; SUBSIDIARITY, PRINCIPLE OF.

Bibliography: D. Byers, ed., *Justice in the Marketplace: Collected Statements of the Vatican and the United States Catholic Bishops on Economic Policy, 1891–1984* (Washington: USCC, 1985). P. Drucker, *The Concept of the Corporation* (New York: New American Library, 1964). R. Hessen, "Corporations" in Eatwell et al., eds., *The New Palgrave: A Dictionary of Economics,* vol. 1. M. Velasquez, "Ethics, Religion, and the Modern Business Corporation," in T. Gannon, *The Catholic Challenge to the American Economy* (New York: Macmillan, 1987).

AMATA MILLER, I.H.M.

CORPORATISM

"Corporatism" refers to a type of social organization that establishes "vocational" or "occupational" groups of trades or professions that include both workers and employers. This type of organization was recommended by Pius XI's encyclical *Quadragesimo anno* in 1931. Such groups were intended to revive the guilds of the European Middle Ages, which had gone into decline and at the time of the French Revolution were suppressed. A revival of this form of social organization was seen by Pius as a way of joining working people and their employers/company owners and thus overcoming the division of people into the two camps of workers and employers. In the view of the pope, this division of the labor market resembled two armies in combat and was leading society to ruin. The aim was to unite the two groups rather than have them set over against each other. It was thought that just as proximity unites people into municipalities, so those who practice the same trade or profession ought naturally to unite in vocational groups.

Through the development of these groups, common interests would predominate and harmony prevail. The corporations were to be the middle way between an individualistic and exploitative capitalism and a threatening atheistic socialism.

Like all documents of the social teachings of the church, *Quadragesimo anno* has to be looked at in its context, which is primarily that of Italy and Europe at the time of the Great Depression. It is important to note the urgency of the economic situation of the time in which the pope wrote. Italy was already suffering the consequences of fascism's economic policies. Then all economies were devastated by the stock market crash of 1929, which brought on the Great Depression. It was a time of factory closures, rising unemployment, and growing social unrest.

In the encyclical, articles 81–87 spell out the idea of these occupational groupings. People were to be free to choose the forms the groupings would take, provided justice and the common good were taken into account. In cases of conflict between employers and employees, separate deliberations and separate votes would be held. According to Oswald von Nell-Breuning, S.J., the drafter of the encyclical who wrote a commentary on it in 1932 (English translation 1936), the pope conceived the vocational groups as public legal corporations, of which, by law, everyone practicing a profession or trade would be a member. The encyclical does not actually say this. It does say that the groups should be autonomous, and it claims the same liberty in establishing forms of organization and rules as the free associations (unions) fostered by Leo XIII in *Rerum novarum.* In a 1971 commentary on the drafting, Nell-Breuning said that he thought this section (QA 81–87) on vocational groupings was "progressive, liberal, definitely democratic, against individualism and against statism; in short, correct."

The entire idea of corporatism, however, was complicated by the fact that a type of corporative organization was being introduced in Italy by the Fascist government at the time of the writing of *Quadragesimo anno.* Articles 91–96 of that encyclical were, according to Nell-Breuning, written by Pius XI himself and make reference to the corporative structure being fostered by the Italian Fascists. Pius describes them as follows: "The corporations were granted legal recognition by the state and became the organs that concluded labor contracts and agreements. The state's recognition granted them a kind of monopoly status. Joining the organization was optional but payment of its taxes and acceptance of its labor contracts were not. The corporations were made up of representatives of the unions of workers and employers. They were organs of the state, and had the power to direct and co-ordinate the activities of the unions. Strikes and lockouts were forbidden under this arrangement. Public authority would intervene in the absence of agreement between the workers and employers/owners."

The pope noted certain advantages to these arrangements: collaboration of classes, repression of socialist efforts and organizations, and the moderating influence of a special ministry in the government. Pius then went on to point to some of the fears fascist corporatism raised: the state substituting itself for private initiative, the excessively bureaucratic and political character of this type of corporatism, and the risk of serving particular political aims rather than moving toward a better social order.

Pope Pius XI later complained about Mussolini's negative reaction to what Pius called his "benevolent nod" in *Quadragesimo anno.* Pius must, then, have understood his own remarks in articles 91–96 as being positive or at least generous. Much later, Nell-Breuning said that he became convinced that Pius XI did not understand fascism. It appears true that elements of fascism had some appeal for a pope looking for a third way between socialism and capitalism. Yet the totalitarianism and violence of Italian fascism made him critical.

It is unfortunate that authoritarian regimes such as those of Salazar in Portugal, Dollfuss in Austria, Petain in France, Franco in Spain, and Vargas in Brazil claimed to be embodiments of the social order recommended in *Quadragesimo anno.* These governments promoted corporations as organs of state control with political roles. They were in practice not autonomous and violated the principle of subsidiarity that Pius XI included in *Quadragesimo anno* (79ff.). This principle claims that it is wrong for more centralized bodies to take over what can be efficiently done by smaller bodies at a lower level. The papacy never disavowed the claims of these regimes as distortions of the encyclical. It is not surprising, then, that the idea of corporatism became confused with these distortions, and after the defeat of the fascist powers it was no longer possible to use the term constructively. Pius XII still occasionally endorsed the idea but did not elaborate or develop it. John XXIII reiterated the principle of subsidiarity and complemented it by the notion of "socialization," which referred to the multiplication of social relations in modern life and the need for their coordination. Pope John opened the door for more creativity in dealing with the tension between necessary state intervention and more decentralized initiative.

In the United States the name used was not "corporations" or "vocational groupings," but "industry councils." It was thought that this was a better translation in the context of an industrial society. The pope's plan for social reorganization came to be known as the "industry council plan." In the American church there was debate over what forms the councils should take. Some thought the plan called for very strong social controls such as price-fixing. Others thought this would be economically unwise. The European Catholic social thinkers criticized the Americans for interpreting the encyclical too literally and urged them to carry out their own social analysis so as to inform Rome of American realities. Discussion of the recommendations of *Quadragesimo anno* continued in the United States into the 1950s.

See also FASCISM; LABOR AND CAPITAL IN CATHOLIC SOCIAL THOUGHT; MODERN CATHOLIC SOCIAL THOUGHT; NELL-BREUNING, OSWALD VON; PIUS XI; QUADRAGESIMO ANNO; SUBSIDIARITY, PRINCIPLE OF.

Bibliography: J. Coleman, "Development of Catholic Social Teaching," in C. Curran and R. McCormick, eds., *Readings in Moral Theology No. 5: Official Catholic Social Teaching* (New York: Paulist, 1986). J. Cronin, "Forty Years Later: Reflections and Reminiscences," in *Readings in Moral Theology No. 5.* O. von Nell-Breuning, "The Drafting of *Quadragesimo Anno,*" in *Readings in Moral Theology No. 5.* O. von Nell-Breuning, *Reorganization of Social Economy* (New York: Bruce, 1936). J. Pollard, *The Vatican and Italian Fascism, 1929–32* (New York: Cambridge Univ. Press, 1985).

MARIE J. GIBLIN

COVENANT

Covenant knits together the entire Bible and is intrinsic to biblical community and its social patterns. Covenant is nothing other than an agreement or treaty, sometimes with conditions attached to it, seeking loyal cooperation between parties in response to a dispute or crisis. Covenant is one of many theological themes with nontheological origins, the result of acculturation. In the Bible covenants sealed an agreement between individuals important enough to represent extended families (Gen 21:22–32, Abraham and Abimelech), between tribes or nations (Josh 9, Israel and the Gibeonites), between God and Israel (at Mount Sinai, Exod 24).

Two important covenant themes thread through the Bible: one unconditional and more universal (with Noah, Abraham, and David), the other conditional and restricted (with Israel at Sinai). God promised Noah a stable universe for the entire human race under the symbol of the rainbow (Gen 9:9–17); God promised Abraham land and abundant offspring who would be a blessing for "a host of nations" with the one condition of circumcision (Gen 12:2-3; 15; 17); with David God made an unconditional, everlasting covenant, promising a kingdom wide-reaching in its domain (2 Sam 7; Ps 132; Isa 55:3-5). The Mosaic or Sinaitic covenant had legal conditions (Exod 20–23) and was restricted to Israel, "my special possession, dearer to me than all other people" (Exod 19:5-6).

The Davidic and particularly the Sinaitic covenants take center stage in the Bible, to be reinterpreted ever more symbolically and interiorly. This refinement followed Israel's intuition of Yahweh as ruler, shepherd, parent, and spouse.

The model of the suzerainty treaty of the Hittite people (14th–13th centuries B.C.) and the Assyrians (7th–6th centuries B.C.) enabled Israel to view the Mosaic or Sinaitic covenant within God's great acts of salvation. Within Exodus, Deuteronomy, and Josh 24 we can detect these elements from the suzerainty treaty form: identity of the great king (Exod 20:2; Deut 5:6; Josh 24:2b); beneficent deeds of the suzerain or Yahweh (Exod 19:4-6; Deut 1:6–4:49; Josh 24:2-13, 17-18); requirements or laws (Exod 20:3–23:13; Deut 5–26; Josh 24:14-20, 23-24); witnesses (Deut 4:26; 30:19; Josh 24:22, 27); blessings and curses for (dis)obedience (Deut 27–28; Josh 24:19-20); ratification and renewal at sanctuary (Exod 24; Deut 30–31; Josh 24:25-28). Covenant thus rested upon Yahweh's gracious, redeeming actions for Israel, ritually renewed at major festivals (Lev 23; Deut 13); laws provided Israel with the opportunity of a grateful response. Deuteronomy began to stress the interior sealing of the covenant with circumcision of the heart (Deut 10:16; 30:6), asking Israel to "love the LORD, your God, with all your heart, and with all your soul, and with all your strength" (Deut 6:5; 30:11-14).

When the covenant had degenerated into legalism (Jer 7; 26) the classical prophets sought to revive the ancient spirit, calling again for circumcision of the heart (Jer 4:4), explicitly naming the reform a "new" covenant (Jer 31:31-34). Jeremiah preserves the larger context of a new exodus from bondage (Jer 31:2-14) amid Yahweh's new wonders for Israel (Jer 31:22b). Ezekiel uses more ritual language in calling for "a new heart. . . and a new spirit" (Ezek 36:26-38).

Somewhat contemporary with Ezekiel but much closer in spirit to Deuteronomy, Hosea, and Jeremiah is the other prophet of the Babylonian Exile, Second or Deutero-Isaiah (Isa 40–55). This prophet expressed the bonding between God and Israel as parent-child (Isa 43:1-7) and husband-wife (Isa 54:1-8); God is the kinsperson (in Hebrew, *go'el,* now translated "redeemer"), related by blood and therefore obliged to intervene and save. In this context family or marital intimacy comes side by side with universal outreach, especially when the word "covenant" appears. With a world vision Isa 54:9-10 refers to the covenant with Noah; God swears "never again [to] deluge the earth [nor] to be angry with you." "My covenant of peace [shall not] be broken, says the LORD, who has mercy on you." The exiles are to "look to Abraham, your father, and to Sarah, who gave you birth" (Isa 51:2). God renews with all Israel "the everlasting covenant, the benefits assured to David" (Isa 55:3). The prophet identifies completely with the suffering people scattered among the foreigners, and through the prophet Israel becomes "a covenant of the people, a light for the nations" (Isa 42:6; 49:6). In the fourth Song of the Suffering Servant the foreign nations comtemplate the silent, persecuted servant: "pierced for our offenses, crushed for our sins; upon him was the chastisement that makes us whole" (Isa 53:5). The Hebrew word meaning "to make whole" is from the root of *shalom,* as in "the covenant of *peace*" with Noah (Isa 54:10). This servant "gives his life as an offering for sin" (Isa 53:10). Second Isaiah merges the major covenant traditions, so that the restrictions of the Sinaitic covenant are removed and its blessings reach the world.

The prophetic influence of Jer 31:31-34 shows up prominently in the Dead Sea Scrolls. The Israelites who produced them are sometimes called "covenanters"; they considered themselves living in "the days to come" of Jer 31:31, with the covenant inscribed upon their hearts, as they write in their "Manual of Discipline" (1QS 5:1–6:2). They were in training for the final day of the Lord, the war between light and darkness, by perfectly fulfilling the Law of Moses and reciting it day and night (see Josh 1:1-11).

Jesus, too, moves in the direction of Deuteronomy, but also (and here quite differently from Qumran) identifies himself with the Suffering Servant of Isaiah. Like the servant of Isaiah Jesus declares that he comes "to serve and to give his life as a ransom for many" (Mk 10:45). In curing the sick Jesus reached across legal boundaries to touch them and be identified with them. Thus Jesus "fulfill[ed] what had been said by Isaiah the prophet: 'He took away our infirmities and bore our diseases'" (Mt 8:17). At the Last Supper, according to Luke and Paul, Jesus combined the new covenant of Jeremiah with the Suffering Servant theme of Isaiah: ". . . my body, which will be given for you . . . the new covenant in my blood, which will be shed for you" (Lk 22:19-20; see 1 Cor 11:24-25).

Paul develops the "new" covenant of Deuteronomy, Isaiah, and Jeremiah. Again, as with the OT prophets, neither Jesus nor Paul thought of "new" as a completely new creation, breaking with the "old" (see Mt 5:17-20). To Israelites still belong "the adoption, the glory, the covenants, the giving of the law, the worship, and the promises" (Rom 9:4). Yet the "new" is far superior (2 Cor 3). By reaching back to Abraham Paul sees salvation exclusively through faith in Jesus (Rom 4), and through the blood of Jesus Jews and Gentiles are reconciled with God (Eph 2:11-22). Yet the break between Judaism and Christianity did become final by the time of the Epistle to the Hebrews (ca. A.D. 100). Jesus is explicitly called a "mediator of a better covenant" (Heb 8:6), and after quoting Jeremiah's words about the new covenant (the longest OT quotation in the NT), Hebrews adds: the "'new' covenant [makes] the first one obsolete" (Heb 8:13). Jesus, by his blood, is the high priest of the new covenant (see Heb 4:14-16; 9; 10).

Covenant, therefore, not only drew from social and political conditions of many ages but also had a history and sustained the direction of biblical theology. It worked its way between the tension of a personal God, parent and spouse for the chosen people Israel (Mosaic covenant), and a universal God, creator and savior of the world (covenants with Noah, Abraham, and David). Covenant expressed itself ritually in Temple worship and in the Eucharist; prophets, including Jesus, enabled the covenant to be ever "new" in the heart of society. NT theologians eventually separated the new covenant from the old, yet leaving the latter a "mystery" waiting for the triumph of God's mercy in the lives of all people (Rom 11:25, 30-32).

See also BEATITUDES; COMMUNITY; CREATION; DECALOGUE; GRACE; REVELATION; SCRIPTURE, USE OF IN CATHOLIC SOCIAL ETHICS; SOLIDARITY.

Bibliography: K. Baltzer, *The Covenant Formulary in Old Testament, Jewish, and Early Christian Writings* (Philadelphia: Fortress, 1971). P. Hanson, *The People Called: The Growth of Community in the Bible* (San Francisco: Harper & Row, 1986). D. Hillers, *Covenant: The History of a Biblical Idea* (Baltimore: Johns Hopkins, 1969). D. McCarthy, *Treaty and Covenant*, 2nd ed. (Rome: Biblical Institute Press, 1978). J. McKenzie, "Aspects of Old Testament Thought: Israel—God's Covenanted People," in *New Jerome Biblical Commentary* (Englewood Cliffs, N.J.: Prentice-Hall, 1990). J. Swetnam, "Why Was Jeremiah's New Covenant New?" *Vetus Testamentum Supplement* 26 (Leiden: Brill, 1974).

CARROLL STUHLMUELLER, C.P.

CREATION

To ask what bearing creation has or ought to have on ethics is to ask a large, basic, and urgent question that has generated much discussion and little consensus. Given the unsettled state of theological ethics both within and beyond Roman Catholic circles, even the presumption on which the question rests—that creation does somehow bear on ethics—cannot be taken for granted. For it depends in part on the closely related methodological question, also a focus of debate, about the specifically Christian character of Christian morality.

Those who would argue for Christian specificity have located it in some particular source, usually a canon within the canon of the NT, or in a particular motivation, most often identified with agape, or in a particular content, the new commandment of love perhaps, or in a particular context within which Christian morality is practiced, such as the mystical body or the kingdom of God. What is noteworthy about these recent approaches is that none of them draws in any but a very indirect way on creation as such. They all focus from different angles on the *new* creation in Christ, on grace and redemption, rather than on nature as created. In this they differ, often deliberately, from the older natural-law ethics, which, unsatisfactory though it was in many respects, did make creation an intrinsic component in its account of the human good.

Meanwhile, even if it cannot be presumed that the created universe should inform specifically Christian ethical thought, there can scarcely be any question but that Christian ethicists are called upon to say something about the created universe. Ecological and environmental issues, together with those arising from developments in genetic engineering and other forms of biotechnology, are as practically urgent as they are theoretically complicated. Insofar as solutions depend on a reorientation of attitudes, feelings, and spirituality, there is a real need for rediscovering imaginative, symbolic expressions capable of displacing the basically utilitarian outlooks on the nonhuman world that were promulgated by the makers of early modernity. The narrative image of enlightened people possessing and mastering nature by means of morally neutral science is a myth that has entered deeply into Western patterns of thought and feeling. Yet however well intentioned, current attempts to introduce one or another pre-modern or non-Western myth that would resacralize nature are at bottom foreign to biblical religion and at odds with the Christian doctrine of creation. More promising and appropriate is Maximus the Confessor's image of a cosmic liturgy through which human beings offer the earth, and themselves with it, in thanksgiving to God. But although such a doxological vision can serve to inspire reverence and channel action, as the works of Teilhard de Chardin have done, sustained and serious theological thinking is needed if ethics is to have anything plausible to say.

The theological context within which questions about creation can be raised as ethical questions is defined by the relation of the supernatural to the natural—yet another controversial topic. Against what was no doubt a mistaken tendency to divide reality into two adjacent but mutually exclusive layers, recent theology has rebelled by stressing the truth that grace is a reality within the universe that actually exists. As with any reaction, however, there is danger of exaggeration in the opposite direction: to the extent that avoiding separation erases distinction, either the natural will tend to be thought of as by its nature graced or else, what comes to the same thing, the supernatural will be conceived as a natural endowment. But this equally mistaken departure from the classic Catholic position cannot, in the long run, support either a theology or a spirituality of creation that honors what is natural because it *is* natural. In fact, the much criticized (because much misunderstood) distinction between nature and the supernatural, between the order of creation and the order of grace, made a systematic entry into Western theology for just that reason—because it was necessary, in order to affirm and understand in all seriousness the sheer gratuity of divine love, to affirm and understand *in its own terms* the naturalness of the created world. It is true that the implications of what came to be known as the theorem of the supernatural were worked out with the help of Aristotle's philosophy, which has now been all but completely discarded in favor of either a biblical mode of thought and speech or, at most, a philosophy framed in personalist rather than in ontological terms. In itself, however, the distinction between natural and supernatural is not one that Aristotle could have drawn. Its foundations are laid in Scripture, and an equivalent distinction has in fact been drawn by those 20th-century theologians who uphold the integrity of the natural as such on the biblical ground that in proclaiming Christ's resurrection the apostolic Church proclaimed as well a resurrection, God's vindication and reaffirmation, of creation itself.

At its best, then, the tradition of distinguishing between natural and supernatural orders coincides with Scripture in affirming that the created order is significant in its own right not despite but because of the fact that God is gracious and in Christ makes all things new. Not even sin can uncreate what the Creator has found very good. To affirm and understand the naturalness of the natural is thus to affirm and understand the primary, albeit not the final and definitive, expression of the infinitely understanding love that is God. Two misconceptions need to be avoided on this score. (1) Since love implies a beloved as well as a lover, it might seem that God *needed* to create in order to have something to know and love, in other words, that the world is necessary for God to be God. Christianity teaches otherwise. Whether this or any other world exists or not, reciprocal relations of understanding love already exist. They exist eternally *in* God and they *are* God, the three divine persons of the Trinity. (2) A different though related idea, also derived from philosophical speculation rather than from Scripture, is that since love is good, and good is essentially self-diffusive, the created world is an extension or outpouring or fulfillment of God's being. Again Christianity teaches otherwise. It is true that creation, like grace, is purely a gift. But what is given in grace is God's own self, whereas in creation what is given is precisely not God but finite existence. That the world is created, then, means that its very being is not necessary but contingent and dependent: its nonexistence is possible, it does not have to be, and it would not be at all except for God's free act of deciding it shall be, that is, of deciding to create. Furthermore, the world does not have to exist *as* it does; the way it exists is likewise contingent, dependent on the free decision of its Creator. Both these affirmations are included in the traditional doctrine that God creates neither out of God nor out of anything else but *ex nihilo,* out of nothing at all.

That God creates freely, however, rather than from need or necessity, does not mean that the divine decision to create is a capricious or arbitrary fiat. God is infinitely *understanding* Love. Far from deciding on whim, the God who acts in creating acts wisely, because the decision to create is in accord with divine intelligence. It follows that the universe, which exists solely because of unbounded Love, thereby manifests by existing intelligibly the unbounded Intelligence, who causes it to be in an intelligible order. What God creates is not an aggregate of isolated objects but a cosmos, a universe of beings. Each of them is finite, contingent, nonnecessary; each is related intelligibly to others; and each is *what* it is in virtue of those relations, which in their totality constitute a world order. That is the link between creation and ethics—the notion of the world as an ordered whole.

Because this order, the whole dynamic constellation of the actually existing universe, is the object of God's creative love, it is a greater good than the good of any particular being ordered within it. Even so, it has no capacity of its own to survive. The more evident it becomes that responsibility for the survival of one stretch of this ordered whole, the earth, rests with that being which is created "in the image of God" its Creator, the greater need there is for spelling out in concrete terms what it means for humans to have not only a proper place within an ordered world but also an active role in ordering it for better or worse. But if created order is to be respected, preserved, and promoted, *how* it is ordered must first and above all be understood. Ethics therefore cannot responsibly ignore the natural sciences, which are natural not only in that they endeavor to understand "nature" in the loose sense of the nonhuman world, but also in that each of them has as its aim an understanding of the nature of one zone of order within the world—physical, chemical, zoological order, and so on, as the case may be. This is not to say that there is a direct route from scientific to ethical discourse. There is not, the principal reason being that what it is to understand scientifically, and what reality it is that scientists understand, are not themselves scientific questions, nor yet ethical ones. They are philosophical. Explicit, technical philosophy has been deprecated in recent times by some theologians and ethicists, but without its support the very notion of the created universe as an ordered whole can be little more than rhetoric.

Regarded philosophically, an order is an intelligible set of the relations of things one to another. In the universe that actually exists there are two general types of natural order that are of concern to ethics. (1) One type of order has its ground in the fact that finite beings exist in different ways. What it is to be a dog is not the same as what it is to be a daisy. Moreover, each kind of created beings has its own acts or operations. Dogs bark and bite, daisies grow and bloom. And the activity of any finite being is a function of its nature, the kind of being it is. One way, therefore, in which each kind of being takes part intelligibly in the order of the universe is its "flourishing," its being ordered toward an end proper to itself. This is not a matter of extrinsic final causality in what is commonly thought to be the Aristotelian sense but of the intrinsic organization of complex unities. Such, for example, are the orderly processes that lead from oak to acorn to oak. As an aspect of each being's having one nature or essence rather than another, this sort of orderly directedness or finality may be termed "horizontal." (2) But universal order includes another sort of finality, which does not result from the nature of any individual being as such but from concrete plurality, from the fact that there exist many beings of any given kind. The orderedness of certain kinds of molecules is sometimes subsumed within the orderly processes that make oaks and acorns what they are; acorns, in turn, sometimes enter into the biological processes that constitute the flourishing of squirrels. The molecules go on with their properly chemical activities, each according to its kind, but they do so within a new, more complex, and higher pattern. The discontinuities and dependences by which one level of ordered activity is related to another lead to the notion of a "vertical" ordering, a graded series of beings and their horizontal finalities. Viewed dynamically, in evolutionary terms, the order of the world is such that subatomic particles enter into and participate in the being and functioning of chemical elements; elements enter into compounds, compounds into cells, and cells into the astonishing variety of plant and animal life. Horizontally, then, oxygen is ordered to its proper being and functioning at the chemical level; vertically, however, it is ordered to respiration.

Among the beings that participate in the order of creation are men and women, and among the activities proper to human beings are not only recurring chemical reactions and unconscious biological processes but also the conscious operations of mind and heart: thinking, understanding, deciding, choosing, loving. These are not merely physiological events, which they subsume and to which they are not reducible. Such operations occur spontaneously; their occurrence is what makes the difference between human and animal being; and each has its horizontal finality: intelligent thinking heads for what is intelligible, deliberating for what is worthwhile, and so on. But their occurring also has an internal, vertical finality of its own. Attention and observation are ordered to and subsumed by acts of understanding; judging that a situation has been correctly understood is ordered to and subsumed by deliberating on what is to be done about it. Because of these vertically further levels of activity, there are two components in concrete human reality, a constant and a variable. One is human nature, which like other natures can be understood in its horizontal finalities by studying any individual. The other, variable component is human history, humankind's making of humankind. It varies because the natural capacities with which human beings have been gifted can be actualized in different ways, and one of these capacities is that of determining freely, though within a limited range, the course that the actualization of the others will take. Each of us is the author of his or her own life-story. Corporately, moreover, we are responsible for the unfolding stories of our families, communities, civilizations, and cultures. That nobody is an island is not poetry only but ascertainable fact. Any person's self-actualizing and self-surpassing, the exercise of his or her natural freedom, is conditioned not only by past decisions and the habitual "second nature" that results from them but also by the language, tradition, and education through which meaning and value are shared. In short, human self-making is a cooperative project.

Where ethics is concerned, it is of the greatest importance to maintain both that the constant and the variable, nature and history alike, are equally real and equally intrinsic to human being, and also that they are distinct, because from the relations between them many of the most fundamental issues of ethics arise.

On the one hand it has been claimed, in various ways and with various degrees of sophistication, that ours is the species whose nature is to have no nature. The existence into which each of us is thrown is meaningless chaos; there is no intelligent basis on which to choose; deciding, insofar as it is genuinely human, is neither good nor evil, neither reasonable and intelligent nor the opposite, but simply free. Such a claim means in effect that each individual is what Christianity holds God alone to be: a creator *ex nihilo.* Against this absolutization of the vertical dimension in human self-surpassing, an ethics that takes the doctrine of creation seriously must insist that the horizontal patterns of human development—physiological, psychological, cognitive, and moral—have their own essential fulfillment and flourishing, that they condition the exercise of natural human liberty, and that to violate them is not self-constitution but self-destruction.

On the other hand, to distinguish between human nature and human history is to hold that beyond life, construed as the horizontal flourishing of recurrent biological operations, there is the good life, the life of excellent cognitive and moral self-making. Human persons live humanly, not by bread alone but by and for what they come to know is real and what they judge is valuable. They live, that is, not only in a habitat but also in a world that owes its character to their own specifically human activity: to insights, plans, assessments, evaluations, decisions, and commitments—and to the failure of these in stupidity, irrationality, and sin. To this world of meaning and value belong, for example, marriage and the family, as contrasted with mating and the herd; so likewise do all the other institutions and traditions that make societies and civilizations what they are. Each of these products of cooperation in living excellently has a historical unfolding that may flourish or decay. Each, in its progress or decline, differs radically from the repetitiveness of beehives and anthills, which properly speaking have no history.

Now the human good, as a historically developing reality distinct from the spontaneities of biological life, belongs to the order of the universe as created. Christianity would add that the universe has been disordered and is being redeemed, that there also exists within it an order of grace, and that beyond even the good life there is the beatitude of sharing God's own life. Nevertheless, in the same way that grace, as the traditional phrase runs, perfects nature without deleting it, so too grace heals and enhances human self-making in history without violating the natural source of history in human freedom and intelligence. For this reason any Christian ethics that would endeavor to direct and redirect human history through rational persuasion will have to take account of the natural order, human and nonhuman, in all its overwhelming complexity. Schematic though it is, the foregoing sketch suggests that at least four broad categories need to be made use of: (A) the various levels of horizontal finality in the nonhuman world; (B) the vertical ordering of nonhuman being and activity to human life; (C) human life in its natural, spontaneous, horizontal finalities; and (D) the vertical self-surpassing that individually and socially constitutes the good life of intelligence, reasonableness, and responsibility in its historical progress or decline. It also suggests that many of the most debated issues in ethics are specifications of the general question whether horizontal finalities, (A) and (C), can rightly be altered or truncated on the ground that to do so promotes a higher level of being and activity, in particular the historical self-constitution of human persons (D).

For the most part the ethical dimension of environmental or ecological problems has to do with interference in the nonhuman order of creation (A). Further distinctions plainly need to be drawn, however, and on where to draw them there is little agreement. To cure a viral disease may be to thwart the flourishing of an organism that, by exercising its proper nature, makes the human organism ill; likewise, testing the vaccine that thwarts the virus may affect the flourishing of some species of mammals. The claim that animals have rights and viruses have not rests on an analogy with human politics that is open to serious doubt. Equally dubious is the instrumental analogy on which the nonhuman creation is conceived as a vast congeries of tools separate from, over against, and valuable only in relation to the human uses to which they can be put. Closer to the Christian understanding of creation than either of these mutually opposed views is the analogy proposed by some environmentalists: the earth as a single, organically interdependent ecological system, within which even the self-directed course of human civilization (D) is only one element. It would follow that decisions to alter the cycles and patterns and ongoing processes that are actually occurring at a given time will be right or wrong depending on how they affect not the human race in isolation, much less any particular group or individual, but the being and functioning of the whole. Such an argument is entirely consonant with the theological affirmation mentioned earlier that what God creates, sets in order, approves, and loves is in the first instance not any particular being or kind of being but the dynamically interrelated entirety of finite being. Accordingly, to set the common good, not simply of human society but of the earth, ahead of any particular good is to take responsibility for co-creating what God creates. But such a responsibility demands intelligence. Adequately to understand the actual circumstances and probable consequences of any human act or practice that alters what is called the balance of nature—which is to say, any act or practice whatever—is clearly an enormous task. Just as clearly, however, it has to be undertaken if human decisions are to be informed by something other than sentiment.

The task at hand is all the more daunting by reason of the fact that the earth as an ecological unit includes more than the horizontal flourishing of species. It includes as well the complex vertical process that moves from the capacities of nature—"natural resources," that is, but also the human capacities for invention, planning, decision, devotion, and sacrifice—to the recurring and developing actualization of a global standard of living. In a word, *economics* is a component of the ecological whole to which human beings belong. Understanding how an economy develops belongs as much to understanding the order of creation as does understanding how a virus develops; both are processes that combine unvarying regularities with statistically intelligible variations, and the probability that either of them will flourish can be raised or lowered by decisions that depend on how well its flourishing is understood. Insofar as an economy results from genuine human self-surpassing, from intelligent, reasonable, and responsible decision, that economy will be a harmonious continuation and enhancement at the social and historical level (D) of the vertical finality of physical, chemical, and biological nature (B) toward the good life.

To do more than hint at the content and implications of conceiving the world as an ordered whole has not been possible within the scope of the present entry. It will, however, have done its work insofar as it shows that creation, so conceived, bears on ethics to the same extent as does intelligent grasp of how the actual world is actually ordered. For only on correct understanding can responsible decision rest, and it is by deciding responsibly that men and women make themselves worshipers in the great liturgy through which the created world's unfolding good glorifies the God who creates.

See also AGRICULTURE; BANKS AND BANKING; CULTURE; ECOLOGY; ECONOMIC ORDER; GRACE; NATURAL LAW; REPRODUCTIVE TECHNOLOGIES, SOCIAL ASPECTS OF.

Bibliography: O. O'Donovan, *Resurrection and Moral Order* (Grand Rapids: Eerdmans, 1986). K. Melchin, *History, Ethics, and Emergent Probability* (Lanham, Md.: Univ. Press of America, 1987). B. Lonergan, *Method in Theology,* chap. 2 (New York: Herder, 1972). *A Third Collection,* chap. 3 (New York: Paulist, 1985). *Collection,* Collected Works, vol. 4, chaps. 2, 3, and 7 (Toronto: Univ. of Toronto, 1988).

CHARLES C. HEFLING, JR.

CREDIT

Modern industrial economies rely on credit to finance both business investment and the purchase of durable consumer goods such as houses, automobiles, and household appliances. Catholic social thought has expressed concern with the danger of monopoly control of credit. In warning of the increasing concentration of private property, Pope Pius XI wrote: "This dictatorship is being most forcibly exercised by those who, since they hold the money and completely control it, control credit also and rule the lending of money. Hence they regulate the flow, so to speak, of the lifeblood whereby the entire economic system lives, and have so firmly in their grasp the soul, as it were, of economic life that no one can breathe against their will" (*Quadragesimo anno* 106).

See also BANKS AND BANKING; COMMON GOOD; COMPETITION; CREDIT UNION; INFLATION.

CHARLES K. WILBER

CREDIT UNION

In U.S. law a credit union is a lending institution chartered to make credit more available to people of small means. To obtain a federal charter and tax-exempt status, membership in a credit union must be limited to groups having a common bond and capable of sustaining a modest savings and loan activity, primarily for consumer loans. The common-bond provision means that a preexisting group (employees of the same firm, members of the same association, residents of the same place) must be identified as the "field of membership" of a credit union, membership being limited to members of that group. The first credit unions in the United States were founded in New Hampshire and Massachusetts in 1908 and 1910 respectively. Both were in Franco-American parishes, after a model initiated in Quebec by Alphonse Desjardins in 1900 (see A. Desjardins, *The Co-operative People's Bank, La Caisse Populaire,* New York: Russell Sage Foundation, 1914).

The Canadian institution drew in turn on precedents in Europe such as the Raiffeisenkassen in Germany. Unlike the Rochdale cooperative experiment in England, which ultimately was subverted, the Raiffeisen model and its variations took root and spread. They were a prominent feature of social Catholic pastoral action, especially in rural areas. They responded to the need for credit among segments of the population at high risk from loan sharks and ineligible for conventional loans. They first appeared as an adaptation of features of the cooperative movement, the mutual-aid societies ("friendly societies" of workers), and the capitalist banking system. Borrowing ideas from Herrmann Schulze-Delitzsch, a social Protestant named Friedrich Wilhelm Raiffeisen (1818–88) created this new type of intermediary between lenders and borrowers for the relief of hard-pressed German farmers.

The Raiffeisen model was characterized by limited territory (parish or township), no capital, no dividends, volunteer administration, and unlike the Canadian and U.S. adaptations, unlimited liability. This meant that all the members were equally responsible for the debts of the association. The key to its effectiveness, apart from the integrity and zeal of its organizers, was this liability in solidarity that the members assumed. By pledging their own most valuable collateral (land, buildings, tools, farm animals), they were able to attract loans from banks or other primary lenders at favorable rates. In turn, when they sat on committees approving the loan applications of their neighbors, they had every interest in seeing to it that the credit was invested wisely and productively. (The orientation to consumer credit was not characteristic of the rural credit-union movement in social Catholicism.) This spurred developments such as learning and disseminating new techniques that broke the hard cake of rural custom in progressive ways.

Pastorally, of course, credit unions associated with the parish deflected the efforts of anticlerical liberals and socialists to win the farm population for their programs. As was the case with Pope John XXIII's peasant father, when one could buy the land one farmed with a loan from the parish credit union while cultivating a cash crop (silkworms in his case) at its suggestion, one had little reason to listen to anticlericals who preached the demise of religion as the precondition of any progress. Such pastoral effectiveness usually presupposed, on the one hand, a farm crisis or a socialist threat, and on the other, the formation of a regional or national association of peasants, or of an agricultural or industrial labor organization, which could mobilize resources (managerial and educational, sometimes political clout as well) and make them available to the local association and its credit union. Here again Germany provided a model in its Christian but nonconfessional peasant associations (from the 1870s on). In France a pioneer was Louis Milcent (1846–1918), secretary of the Oeuvres des cercles catholiques d'ouvriers. After 1879 when he left Paris for the Jura, he was active in the theoretical labors of the Fribourg Union (q.v.) and developed a practical concern for the peasants in his region, setting up an organization for them in the market town of Poligny. By 1885 he had founded the first rural credit unions in France.

In Italy the credit-union movement was started by a Jew, Leone Wollemberg. Along with another Italian Jew, Luigi Luzzatti, he inspired a zealous Capuchin in France, Ludovic de Besse (1831–1910), during de Besse's visit to Italy in 1888 with the idea of "people's credit." Only later did the French Capuchin learn of the German origins and success of the movement. He propagandized ceaselessly for setting up credit unions; but Louis Durand (1859–1916), the lawyer from Lyons who actually shaped the Catholic credit-union federation in France from 1893 on, parted ways with de Besse, who was willing to work within a broader and not strictly Catholic movement. Durand was an anti-Semitic, anti-Masonic, anti-liberal monarchist. While rejecting Leo XIII's *ralliement* he accepted his social teaching, especially the need to combat usury (*Rerum novarum* 5). During Pius X's pontificate, he was a stalwart of social-Catholic integrism and confessionalism. By way of the French Catholic example the Raiffeisen model was adopted in Spain and found its way back into northern Italy. At this point the credit-union movement took root there in Catholic parishes and grew exponentially.

After World War I the movement continued to develop. One of its most remarkable adaptations occurred in the Basque country after the Second World War within the innovative industrial cooperative movement named after its place of origin, Mondragon. It was the brainchild of José María Arizmendiarrieta (or Arizmendi, 1915–77), a local priest who had already founded a vocational school and helped launch a cooperative manufacturing enterprise. Discovering a provision in the banking laws that allowed a premium of 0.5 percent to be paid on workers' savings, he set up the Caja laboral popular in 1959 as the bank for workers' cooperatives. The savings are pooled to provide funds for investments in new and existing cooperatives of production; the other main thrust of this new departure in credit institutions concerned the health and retirement needs of the cooperatives' members until this function was spun off in a separate cooperative. The pension plan is supported by payroll deductions just like the government social-security plan from which cooperatives were excluded by law. The entrepreneurial division of the Caja laboral popular has pioneered in creating a system of "social entrepreneurship."

See also AGRICULTURE; ANTI-SEMITISM; CREDIT; ENTERPRISE; OPERA DEI CONGRESSI; SOLIDARITY.

Bibliography: C. Moody and G. Fite, *The Credit Union Movement: Origins and Development, 1850–1970* (Lincoln: Univ. of Nebraska Press, 1971). H. Rollet, *Action sociale des catholiques en France (1871–1914)*, 2 vols. (Bruges: Desclée, 1947–58). W. Whyte and K. Whyte, *Making Mondragón: The Growth and Dynamics of the Worker Cooperative Complex* (Ithaca, N.Y.: ILR, 1988).

PAUL MISNER

CULTURE

This article organizes the discussion of culture under five headings. The first and longest section contextualizes the topic within contemporary church history and world events. The second section stresses the heart of the matter: the gradual emergence of the anthropological concept of culture since the second half of the 19th century and the growing acceptance of this concept as an operational, architectonic principle in Catholic thought. The third section sketches culture's assimilation into

Catholic social teaching, especially the papal magisterium. The fourth section underscores the contribution of Third World, especially Latin American, Catholicism, to the linking of culture with transformative or liberative action. The fifth section suggests some possibilities for the concept of culture as its discoveries and implications affect almost every understanding, theoretical or practical, of the Christian presence in the world.

Contextualizing the Term in Catholic Discourse

In the years following the Second Vatican Council the term "culture" emerged as a vastly influential concept in dialogue with virtually every area of contemporary thought. Modern communications, mass media, and worldwide migrations created a "global village" in which the discrete cultures, peoples, and religions of the world interacted as never before. Since the second half of the 19th century cultural anthropology has provided rich data regarding the customs, rites, religions, and values of the human race. Initially ethnographers set their gaze on primitive cultures, but more recently on modern ones. These intercultural relations and new knowledge inevitably entered into dialogue with Christian life and practice as well as with theology and social thought.

In its search for terms for dialogue with the modern world, the Second Vatican Council stressed the concept of culture as uniquely suitable for bridging a Catholic understanding of faith and tradition rooted in Christian humanism with the changing circumstances of time and the explosion of knowledge. The notable importance given to culture in the documents of the Second Vatican Council, especially sections 53 to 62 of the Pastoral Constitution on the Church in the Modern World (*Gaudium et spes*), is a benchmark in the understanding of the increasingly influential role of the concept of culture in subsequent church teaching, theology, and social thought.

The wider church and Catholic thinkers have taken this development seriously. Consequently there are few areas of theology and pastoral praxis unaffected. Judging from the increasing literature on the subsidiary term "inculturation," it appears that the trend has only just begun. The use of the term "inculturation" (the confrontation of the gospel message with cultures and their interpenetration) has experienced a meteoric rise in the consciousness of Catholic researchers, writers, and teachers. The opening words of the Pastoral Constitution on the Church in the Modern World, perhaps the most quoted words of the Second Vatican Council, augured the increasingly influential role of the concept of culture in Catholic social thought: "The joy and hope, the grief and anguish of the men of our time, especially of those who are poor or afflicted in any way, are the joy and hope, the grief and anguish of the followers of Christ as well" (GS 1).

Many Catholic leaders, writers, and teachers have taken up the challenge of the Second Vatican Council in regard to the anthropological concept of culture, making it an—if not the—integrating or architectonic principle for understanding the church's mission and social teaching today. None has done this with greater energy and forcefulness than Pope John Paul II (Gremillion, pp. 187–213). He expressed this conviction in his very first encyclical, and the social teachings developed in his pontificate have been variations on this one theme: "For the church all ways lead to man" (*Redemptor hominis* 14).

The demise of colonialism and the rise of worldwide liberation movements highlight the relativity and limitations of Western culture and strip it of some of its hegemony. This occurs *within* Western cultures themselves, for example, as immigrants, women, and other marginated groups struggle for justice, denouncing oppressive patterns and structures (e.g., patriarchy), and also *between* Western and non-Western cultures as the latter strive to overcome the effects of socioeconomic, political, and cultural oppression (e.g., neocolonialism, dependency). At the same time, however, the pervasive power of the culture of modernity—a kind of "super culture" linked with First World technology, science, and economics—has forced Third World cultures to defend themselves by stressing their distinctiveness and developing various forms of cultural resistance, for example, cultural nationalism and religious fundamentalism. The result of these trends is a heightened awareness of culture—of the vast array of feelings, values, and approaches to life shared by human beings (Azevedo, pp. 53–55).

The fluidity of change in the contemporary world is also manifested in various postmodern trends exposed by social science, especially cultural analysis. Broadly speaking this refers to a dissatisfaction with the modern world's debt to the rationality of the Enlightenment, to science and technology, to the notion of progress, and to capitalist (liberal) as well as Marxist ideologies. Disvalues and dehumanizing trends such as totalitarianism, consumerism, materialism, ecological disasters, individualism, and cultural narcissism are explained in part by these pervasive expressions of modernity.

A countervaling cultural movement now unfolds, and over against these negative trends spiritual values, human dignity, and solidarity are juxtaposed. It shows itself in many forms, for example, the ecological movement and experiments in radical lifestyles such as that of the Catholic Worker movement or Mother Teresa's Brothers and Sisters of Charity. In Latin America and elsewhere the basic ecclesial communities offer a new vision of church that takes cultural and social analysis quite seriously. Fascination with Eastern religions, the occult, parapsychology, and new religious movements manifest the dissatisfaction with mainline Christianity, whose attitudes and interests reflect too narrowly their Western roots and the pervasive influences of modernity.

World events have also contributed to a deeper awareness of cultures in general and especially of the culture of modernity. The decline of socialism in Eastern Europe, the cautious opening of China to the West, the energy of Islam as a world religion, the complex Middle Eastern situation, the dramatic sociopolitical changes in Latin America, and more importantly, the search for a new world order as superpower relations are transformed raise a number of issues regarding culture on the one hand and emergent sociopolitical and economic structures, democratization and modernization, on the other. Catholic social thought increasingly views these realities through the lens provided by social science, especially cultural anthropology.

The Anthropological Concept

A. L. Kroeber and Clyde Kluckhohn have traced the history of the term "culture" in Western thought in *Culture: A Critical Review of Concepts and Definitions.* For centuries the term referred principally to "high" culture, that is, to the fine arts, humanism, intellectual enlightenment, and classical education. This use of the word has not been entirely supplanted, but beginning in the 19th century ethnologists began an exhaustive analysis of so-called primitive cultures. Their concept of culture was eventually applied to Western societies, leading to the supplanting of the word "civilization" by "culture" in 20th-century analyses of important changes taking place in the modern world. Culture became an operational concept and heuristic tool yielding insights into a whole range of contexts such as industrialization, urbanization, and political movements. Kroeber and Kluckhohn's standard definition of 1952 is still representative of the myriad definitions of culture in use today: "Culture consists of patterns, explicit and implicit, of and for behavior acquired and transmitted by symbols, constituting the distinctive achievement of human groups . . . ; the essential core of culture consists of traditional (i.e., historically derived and selected) ideas and especially their attached values; cultural systems may, on the one hand, be considered as products of action, on the other as conditioning elements of further action" (p. 66).

In recent years anthropologist Clifford Geertz's definition of religion has specified the nature of the interaction of religion and culture. It has brought the issue of culture into the heart of religious and theological studies: "Religion is a system of symbols which act to establish powerful, pervasive moods and motivation in men by formulating conceptions of a general order of existence and clothing these conceptions with such an aura of factuality that the moods and motivations seem uniquely realistic" (Geertz, chap. 4).

Geertz's approach to religion as a powerful distillation of culture and his interest in moods, motivations, and the "aura of factuality" have repercussions on morality, especially social morality. Catholic social thought had traditionally resisted viewing morality as a product of culture. Pius XII, for instance, insisted that "principles of Christian life and morality transcend cultural limitations" (*Evangelii praecones* 60). Such a view must today be qualified in many ways in light of the contemporary understanding of culture's role in religious and moral development.

The Evolution of the Concept in the Magisterium

It can be said that the remote antecedents for the emergence of culture as an increasingly influential concept in Catholic social thought is the church's and, before that, ancient Israel's long history of encounters with cultural diversity. The church's survival in history has a great deal to do with attitudes toward values, feelings, and ideas perceived as somehow alien or extraneous to the prevailing, received ones and with how tensions arising from cultural clashes are eventually resolved. Certainly the conflict between the Apostle Paul and the Judaizers as narrated in Acts of the Apostles is a classic example. Church history as well as the history of theology is replete with instances of what A. Shorter calls "interculturation," or the interpenetration of cultures in Christian theory and praxis (p. 13). The church's millennial encounter with cultures has endowed it with a vast reservoir of experiences.

Historical sources reveal abundant instances of the church's cultural sensitivity in centuries past. For example, this statement of the Fourth Lateran Council of 1215 manifests the urgency and clarity with which a key and often thorny cultural issue, that of language for ministry and worship, was addressed in medieval times: "Since in many places within the same city or diocese people of various languages are mingled, possessing under one faith a variety of rites and customs, we firmly order that bishops of such cities and dioceses provide suitable men who according to the diversities of rituals and languages will perform for them the divine ministries and celebrate the sacraments, instructing them both by word and example" (cited by Pius XII in the apostolic constitution *Exsul familia* 653).

Another brilliant example of the gradual development of cultural sensitivity in the church is that of the Spanish and Portuguese evangelizers of the Americas who, despite the many dehumanizing features of the *conquista,* struggled to graft Iberian Catholicism onto the pre-Columbian cultures. Theirs was a relatively successful venture that today accounts for well over a third of all the world's Roman Catholics.

In the 19th century the insistence of the popes beginning with Leo XIII that *indigenous* clergy be trained and ordained for mission territories eventually (almost one hundred years later) led to the existence of what Karl Rahner has called a "global church," reflected in the fact that for the first time in history the majority of the world's bishops are from the Third World. The Second Vatican Council foreshadowed this trend, which will be dramatically confirmed in the next ecumenical council. This simple fact has enormous implications. One of them is that North Atlantic and European epistemologies, perspectives, and worldviews rooted in Western civilization will continue to exist in tension with a variety of alternative ones.

As early as 1622 the Congregation for the Propagation of the Faith declared: "Do not regard it as your task and do not bring any pressure to bear upon the people to change their manners, customs and uses unless they are evidently contrary to religion and sound morals. . . . People love and treasure . . . their own country and what belongs to it. . . . Consequently there is no stronger cause for alienation and hate than an attack on local customs" (quoted in Surlis, p. 12).

The immediate context for the emergence of culture in Catholic social thought, however, is found in papal teaching from Leo XIII onward, especially in Leo XIII's *Inscrutabili* (1878), Benedict XV's *Maximum illud* (1919), and Pius XII's *Evangelii praecones* (1951). In 1936 Pius XI was quoted as having said in conversation: "It is necessary never to lose sight of the fact that the objective of the Church is to evangelize, not civilize. If it civilizes it is for the sake of evangelization" (Surlis, p. 14). This statement reflects the distinction gradually being made between the Christian civilization of the West and evangelization. The implications of this distinction became clearer after the Second Vatican Council in the Decree on the Church's Missionary Activity (*Ad gentes*), in Paul VI's *Evangelii nuntiandi* (1975), and John Paul II's *Redemptoris missio* (1991).

The distinction between "civilizing" (or Romanizing or Americanizing) and evangelizing has many consequences. Perhaps the more notable are in the area of liturgy, where liturgists like Anscar J. Chupungco have striven to develop principles for the proper adaptation of the liturgy based upon respect for cultures. Important initiatives have been taken by the Roman Congregation for Divine Worship leading to new rites such as the Zairean Rite of the Mass. But there is a great deal of dissatisfaction with the adaptations made to date, indicating that the consequences of taking culture seriously in liturgical renewal will be many more.

Catholic social teaching has also given increasing importance to the concept of culture and the distinctions and sensitivities that come with it. The phrase "Christian civilization" and the word "Christendom" have all but disappeared in Catholic social discourse, tainted as they are with European imperialism and colonialism. Taking its cue from the Second Vatican Council, Catholic social thought from Pope John XXIII onward has insisted that true and full humanity is achieved only through culture. Integrally related to the concept of culture, therefore, are two fundamental categories of Catholic social thought: (1) human dignity and (2) the social purpose of private property. Pope John Paul II has repeated the phrase of Pope Paul VI over and over again: "What we hold important is man, each man, and each group of men, and we even include the whole of humanity." These two categories explain the insistence on human rights, the structural socioeconomic and political analyses, and the concept of social sin in John Paul II's most accomplished and original statements on social questions: *On Human Work* (*Laborem exercens*) in 1981 and *On Social Concern* (*Sollicitudo rei socialis*) in 1987, and *Centesimus annus* in 1991.

In the thought of John Paul II the concept of culture serves to link two interrelated aspects of the church's mission. In 1982 he founded the Pontifical Council for Culture, and in an address to that council one year later he expressed the role of culture in the linkage between evangelization and social justice: "There are two principal and complementary aspects which correspond to the two levels on which the Church carries out its activity: that of the *evangelization of cultures* and that of the *defense of man and his cultural development.* Both tasks demand that new means for dialogue between the Church and the cultures of our time be developed" (Carrier, p. 28).

The Latin American Contribution

Both the missiological and social aspects of the concept of culture have been taken up by the world church especially in the Third World. The role of culture in the thought of the second (Medellín, 1968), third (Puebla, 1979), and fourth (Santo Domingo, 1992) general conferences of Latin American bishops provides an excellent example. The three conferences conceived of dialogue with culture as primordially dialogue with the poor, since the poor are the vast majority of Latin Americans. Concern for the defense of humanity, especially human dignity, also means to "opt for the poor," for the poor are quintessentially human. It is from their perspective that one most fittingly grasps the socioeconomic, political, and cultural realities of Latin America (Carrier, p. 71). The option for the poor, rooted in a new sensitivity to culture, becomes a powerful epistemological tool.

Properly understood, respect for culture does not and should not distract from action on behalf of justice or socioeconomic and political liberation. Rather the two in the thought of Puebla and Medellín are integral to each other, exigencies of an authentic option for the poor. Concretely this dual commitment—to culture and to social action—is seen in (1) the growing respect given various forms of popular religiosity among the Latin American peoples and (2) the rise of basic ecclesial communities focused on liberative or transformative action.

Culture as Catalyst in Catholic Thought

The contributions of the concept of culture to Catholic thought has not been limited to social thought. As we have seen, it arose first in the context of mission and was eventually assimilated into social teaching. Now the concept is working its way through theology, thus penetrating the Christian community's very self-understanding. Important concepts in the field of the sociology of knowledge and hermeneutics combine with the anthropological concept of culture to create a host of challenges in every area of theology. The far-ranging consequences of this intellectual sea change can only dimly be surmised as humanity and the church enter a new millennium. The role of culture may be likened, perhaps, to that of history in 19th-century critical studies. As historical consciousness worked its way through almost every area of knowledge including theology, nothing remained quite the same in its wake.

See also EVANGELII NUNTIANDI; EVANGELIZATION; HUMANISM; INCULTURATION; LIBERATION THEOLOGY; MEDELLÍN; POOR, PREFERENTIAL OPTION FOR; PUEBLA.

Bibliography: M. Azevedo, *Inculturation and the Challenges of Modernity* (Rome: Gregorian Univ. Press, 1982). H. Carrier, "Understanding Culture: The Ultimate Challenge of the World-Church," in J. Gremillion, *The Church and Culture Since Vatican II* (Notre Dame: Univ. of Notre Dame Press, 1985). H. Carrier, "The Contribution of the Council to Culture," in R. Latourelle, *Vatican II, Assessment and Perspectives* (New York: Paulist, 1989). A. Kroeber and C. Kluckhohn, *Culture: A Critical Review of Concepts and Definitions* (New York: Vintage, 1952). C. Geertz, "Religion as a Cultural System," in *The Interpretation of Cultures* (New York: Basic Books, 1973). A. Shorter, *Toward a Theology of Inculturation* (Maryknoll, N.Y.: Orbis, 1988). P. Surlis, "The Relation Between Social Justice and Inculturation in the Papal Magisterium," in A. Roest Crollius, ed., *Creative Inculturation and the Unity of Faith* (Rome: Gregorian Univ. Press, 1986).

ALLAN FIGUEROA DECK, S.J.

D

DEBT

Personal Debt

The emergence of Catholic social teaching in the 19th century converges with a manual-based moral theology that drew heavily on the language of law and rightly ordered acts. It will be some time before this teaching links economic matters to the common good (Pius XI, *Quadragesimo anno,* 1931). Leo XIII's *Rerum novarum* (1891) finds its normative criterion for the evaluation of economic life in the concept of equity (RN 51). Equity derives from justice rather than from the notion of the common good. Thus moral reflection on debt focuses on debt as a contractual matter. It deduces its principles from contract law and from a concept of society based on natural law. Justice is defined as *suum cuique tradere*—to render to each, each one's due. Following Aristotle, Thomas Aquinas had indicated three forms of justice: legal, commutative, and distributive. Commutative justice regulates the rightful relations between individuals and between individuals in relation to the community. The moral analysis of debt, rooted in reflections on ownership and property, draws on the implications of commutative justice. The debtor assumes certain obligations with regard to the property of another. These obligations can arise from a variety of sources—from a loan, purchase, theft, and so forth. Ordinarily, debt concerns that which is due to another as a right of justice arising from the fact that one (1) actually possesses something that belongs to another or (2) has unjustly caused damage to another.

Commutative justice requires that when the property of another is held as a loan, it must be returned to its owner in its entirety. Whoever refuses to pay back or to compensate or does so only partially or with wrongful delay acts unjustly. The gravity of the injustice committed depends on the value of the property involved and also on the material circumstances of the creditor. The obligation to pay ceases when the debtor has no assets from which to make payment. A bankrupt is excused from paying the debts in full as long as the insolvency continues. Should the bankrupt later become affluent, the obligation to pay still binds in conscience. The obligation to pay ceases when it is morally impossible for the debtor to do so; for example, if payment of the debt would cause great harm to the debtor or to someone else, or if payment would cost the debtor or the debtor's family their good name. The debt ceases permanently if freely remitted by the creditor. The barring of a debt by civil authority by statute of limitations does not constitute a remission of the debt; the debtor is still under a moral obligation to pay, while the civil authority declares that it will not help the creditor to recover what is due.

The development in social teaching of the concept of common good and the principle of subsidiarity modifies the contractual language of the moral tradition and increasingly emphasizes the dignity of the person (both debtor and creditor) and their partnership in the social order. Pius XI stresses the social nature of private property and teaches that private ownership should be in harmony with the needs of the common good (QA 49). His chief concern is the proper role of the state in the just distribution of property and wealth. Yet by emphasizing the normative character of the common good he makes it clear that economics depends upon moral science. The U.S. bishops in 1986 make the same point: "The economy is not a machine that operates according to its own inexorable laws, and persons are not mere objects tossed about by economic forces" (*Economic Justice for All* 96). The emphasis on common good challenges an individualistic ethics and an economic ethics that claims its own laws.

Pius XI introduces the classic formulation of the principle of subsidiarity (QA 79–80; see also John XXIII, *Mater et magistra* 54). It is a violation of justice if larger political entities absorb the functions that smaller groups can ably carry out. This principle underlines the natural dignity of all the social actors. John XXIII presents the provision of credit and reasonable interest rates for farmers as an example of state-enabling that derives from this principle (MM 134). The social and personal implications of credit and interest are here indicated. Creditor and debtor are social partners.

International Debt

The social partnership of the pre–Vatican II era becomes an international partnership in the perspective of the Second Vatican Council (*Gaudium et spes* 69). However, international partnership already finds mention in the pre–Vatican II teaching. Pius XII during World War II considers the reconstruction of the worldwide economic order. This world order would "respect the rights of those smaller states to political freedom, to economic development . . ." (CM 1941). John XXIII urges cooperation between wealthy and poorer countries (MM 170; *Pacem in terris* 121, 125). He also allows for greater economic pluralism than his predecessors and asks that whatever the economic system, "it allow and facilitate for every individual the opportunity to engage in productive activity" (MM 55).

Paul VI develops the implications of international partnership in regard to debt in *Populorum progressio* (1967). Dialogue between creditor and debtor nations is necessary in order to avoid domination of one by the other or the denial of dignity or freedom (PP 54). This emphasis on the process of the agreement (through respectful dialogue) as distinct from the content of the agreement (loan and terms) is a central aspect of submissions on the international debt question ever since (EJA 258). Paul VI urges that dialogue focus on the real needs of the debtor and on the debtor's ability to use and service the loan (PP 54). The debtor should not be overwhelmed by debt repayment. The conditions of repayment should be "satisfying to both sides, namely, by balancing free gifts, interest-free or low-interest loans, and the years for gradually repaying the loan" (PP 54).

The Medellín Document on Peace (1968) critiques the lack of cooperation and dialogue in the progressive debt situation of Latin America. Eleven years later, the inhumanity of the prevailing economic system is challenged by the bishops gathered at Puebla: "We see the continuing operation of economic systems that do not regard the human being as the center of society, and that they are not carrying out the profound changes needed to move towards a just society" (Puebla, Final Document 64).

In the face of overwhelming repayments and meager resources, the question of nonpayment arises. Paul VI confronts this question by recalling Leo XIII's teaching

(RN 63) that if the positions of the contracting partners are too unequal, the consent of the parties does not suffice to guarantee the justice of the contract. Paul VI claims that what is true of the just wage for the individual is also true of international contracts, "for commercial transactions can no longer depend solely on the law of free competition since it all too frequently creates economic dictatorship" (PP 59). The Administrative Board of the United States Catholic Conference expresses caution in the application of Paul VI's teaching (USCC Administrative Board, "Statement on Relieving Third World Debt," *Origins* 19 [1989] 305–14; henceforth RTWD). The board maintains that "a moral presumption exists in personal and social relations that debts should be paid" (RTWD 39). However, the dubious legitimacy of some debtor governments, the failure of some governments to represent the real interests of their populations, the record of what has already been paid due to high interest rates, and the social cost imposed on the poor all combine to suggest that "in many instances the presumptive obligation to repay should be overridden or modified" (RTWD 41).

This statement and others refer to the moral perspective of the Scriptures with particular reference to the institution of Jubilee Year (Lev 25:8-17), in which debts were to be forgiven and lands restored (RTWD 35; see also EJA 36). The debtor was not to be kept in a condition of permanent debt and thereby in a condition of permanent dependence (D. Hollenbach, "Liberating Jesus for Social Involvement," *Biblical Theology Bulletin* 15 [1985] 151–57). While biblical institutions and images do not provide clear solutions to complex debt situations, "the biblical imagery does provide a starting point, a way to understand creditor-debtor relations, which a purely empirical assessment of the debt problem will never offer" (RTWD 36).

The pontificate of John Paul II has developed and clarified the concepts of Catholic social teaching that undergird the ethical perspective on the debt question. The pontifical commission Iustitia et Pax provides a synthesis of these concepts in *At the Service of the Human Community: An Ethical Approach to the International Debt Question,* section 1 (Vatican City: Polyglot Press, 1986; henceforward ASHC). The commission outlines six ethical principles:

1. *Create new forms of solidarity.* This principle acknowledges the increased interdependence of countries. Interdependence requires "expressions of solidarity, which respect the equal dignity of all peoples rather than lead to domination by the strongest, to national egoism, to inequalities and injustices." This global interdependence had been alluded to by Paul VI (PP 3) and by the 1971 synod of bishops (*Justitia in mundo* 7). In the teaching of John Paul II the appeal for solidarity holds a dominant place (*Redemptor hominis* 16; *Sollicitudo rei socialis* 26, 33, 40). Solidarity is characterized by respect and action, which combine to build up a human community marked by equity and justice (John Paul II, "Peace Is a Value with No Frontiers," *Osservatore Romano* 30, December 1985).

2. *Accept co-responsibility.* All of the economic actors share responsibility for causing (and resolving) the international debt problem. The principal of subsidiarity is applied here in the global context. Causes can be internal to the countries involved: abuses of investments must be admitted; exclusive concern for profit must be acknowledged. Causes can be systemic: "from evolutions in the international environment." Critique of capitalism and collectivism have been a regular if not constant feature of Catholic social teaching. Accepting responsibility involves the admission of human limit and unfreedom. Personal sin asserts itself in sinful structures (Congregation for the Doctrine of Faith, *Instruction on Christian Freedom and Liberation* 42).

3. *Establish relations of trust.* Mutual trust is indispensable to an ethical approach to the debt question: "It nourishes belief in another person's good faith, even when difficulties prevent the person from respecting his commitments, and makes it possible to continue treating him as a partner." Failure to trust objectifies the other. Where there is lack of trust, the creative subjectivity of the other person is destroyed (John Paul II, SRS 15; *Laborem exercens* 5). Situations of domination and subjugation follow from this.

4. *Know how to share efforts and sacrifices.* An equitable sharing of adjustment efforts and sacrifices is required of all partners. The scandal of the suffering of millions of disadvantaged must be acknowledged. Meeting their needs must be of primary importance (EJA 274).

5. *Foster the participation of all.* Because the resolution of the debt question is not exclusively a financial matter, political and economic leaders must work alongside the financial and monetary officials. Subsidiarity and participation require that all members of society be heard and be involved in the process. Solidarity is all-inclusive. Debt resolution is therefore a political question.

6. *Identify emergency and long-term measures.* Two undertakings are required: emergency measures to rehabilitate debtor countries; long-term measures such as the reform of the financial and monetary institutions in order to avoid a repetition of the crisis. The emergency situation exists because in many countries the national debt and the interest and principal payments are so high in proportion to available resources that repayment obligations damage the national economy and cause severe hardship, especially for the poor. This situation is worsened when protectionist policies, high interest rates, and low prices of raw materials make the debt all the more difficult to service. The struggle to repay creditors has some countries on the brink of bankruptcy (ASHC, sec. 2).

The U.S. bishops summarize in a helpful way the recent history of the debt crisis: "*Historically,* the three major economic actors share the responsibility for the present difficulty because of decisions made and actions taken during the 1970s and 1980s. In 1972 the Soviet Union purchased the entire U.S. grain surplus, and grain prices trebled. Between 1973 and 1979, the Organization of Petroleum Exporting Countries raised the price of oil eightfold and thereafter deposited most of the profits in commercial banks in the North. In order to profit from the interest-rate spread on these deposits, the banks pushed larger and larger loans on eager Third World borrowers needing funds to purchase more and more expensive oil. A second doubling of oil prices in 1979 forced many of these countries to refinance their loans and borrow more money at escalating interest rates. A global recession beginning in 1979 caused the prices of Third World export commodities to fall and thus reduced the ability to meet the increasingly burdensome debt payments out of export earnings" (EJA 272). The bishops go further and say that the global financial system contributed to this crisis: "the global *system* of finance, development, and trade established by the Bretton Woods Conference in 1944—the World Bank, the International Monetary Fund (IMF), and the GATT [General Agreement on Tariffs and Trade]—was created by the North to prevent a recurrence of the economic problems that were perceived to have led to World War II. Forty years later that system seems incapable, without basic changes, of helping the debtor countries—which had no part in its creation—manage their increasingly untenable debt situation effectively and equitably" (EJA 273).

The ethical approach to international debt gives rise to various proposals. Emergency proposals involve four areas: development assistance, trade, finance, and investment. *(a)* Development assistance: Industrialized countries should improve their financial and technical assistance of development in the Third and Fourth Worlds. This aid should not be for military expenditure. *(b)* Trade: Industrialized countries should remove protectionist barriers that hinder exports from developing countries. International trade conditions and fluctuating prices of raw materials should be analyzed in order to remove dominance and exploitation. *(c)* Finance: Interest rates should be brought down to facilitate reimbursement by debtor countries. Reimbursement conditions should be compatible with the debtor's ability to meet basic needs. Debt remission should not undermine the financial, economic, and political credibility of the "less advanced" countries or put a stop to new flows of capital from banks. *(d)* Investment: The multilateral financial organizations—IMF, the World Bank, regional banks—should increase the representation and participation of developing countries in the economic decisions that affect them. The IMF should modify its adjustment requirements by integrating a "human factor"; the austerity measures it sometimes requires for its "seal of approval" establishing creditworthiness often exacerbate the already difficult circumstances of the poor. Debtor countries should apply internal equity considerations in order that their own poor are not penalized (ASHC, sec. 3).

One long-term proposal concerns the formation of a political authority "with the responsibility and power to promote the global common good" (EJA 261). This proposal echoes Paul VI's appeal for a "World Fund" and for worldwide collaboration among nations (PP 51). M. Cardinal Roy, in 1970, proposed the institutionalization of aid-flows between nations and suggested that world aid should be a matter of distributive justice, a system of taxation in the coming planetary society (M. Cardinal Roy, "Message on the Occasion of the Launching of the Second Development Decade," November 1970). Dissatisfaction with the Bretton Woods institutions (EJA 277) and the appeals for global solidarity add a dimension of urgency to this proposal.

See also BANKS AND BANKING; COMMON GOOD; ECONOMIC ORDER; ECONOMIC PLANNING, SOCIAL IMPORTANCE OF; JUST WAGE; PRIVATE PROPERTY; SOLIDARITY; SUBSIDIARITY, PRINCIPLE OF.

Bibliography: *External "Dolares" Eternal "Dolores": Christian Reflections on the Debt Crisis,* Pro Mundi Vita Studies 1 (January 1988). O. Williams and J. Houck, eds., *The Common Good and U.S. Capitalism* (Lanham, N.Y./London: Univ. Press of America, 1987).

PATRICK CARROLL, O.S.M.

DECALOGUE

It is important to read the Decalogue as the Bible presents it. In Exod 20:1-17 the Ten Commandments are words that God speaks to Israel at the base of Mount Sinai. In Deut 5:6-21 they are the words of Moses, who reminds Israel of what God had revealed to him at Mount Horeb (Sinai). In both cases the Decalogue is embedded in the story of Israel's experience of God following its liberation from slavery in Egypt by God's power. To detach the Ten Commandments from the narrative framework in which the Bible places them distorts the story of Israel's escape from Egyptian bondage and risks misunderstanding of the commandments themselves. Liturgists, moralists, and catechists have taken the Decalogue out of its setting for a variety of reasons, with the effect of misconstruing the value of the Ten Commandments.

In the biblical tradition the Decalogue is the basis upon which Israel's continuing relationship with God becomes possible. God's deliverance of Israel from slavery in Egypt established that relationship. The Ten Commandments were to set the pattern for Israel's life so that it could maintain that relationship. The metaphor that ancient Israel chose to express the relationship was the covenant. While this metaphor comes from the legal sphere, it is wrong to understand the Decalogue merely as a summary of Israel's legal obligations toward God. The Ten Commandments were not restrictions that limited Israel's freedom; rather, they were to lead Israel to the fullness of life in the land that God gave them. Also, obedience to the Ten Commandments was not so much submission to the divine will as a response of love. God's goodness and love, experienced by Israel in the liberation from Egypt and the gift of the land, elicited a response of love from a grateful Israel. The commandments, then, are not arbitrary stipulations but a central component of God's self-revelation at Sinai.

The Bible does not suggest how the commandments were to be divided or enumerated. The references to the "ten words" do not appear either in Exod 20 or in Deut 5 but rather in Exod 34:28, Deut 4:13, and Deut 10:34. While Exod 34:1, 4, 29 and Deut 5:22 mention the two tablets, there is no hint about which commandments belong to which tablet. The Roman Catholic and Lutheran churches follow Origen, Clement of Alexandria, and Augustine, who considered the prohibition of worshiping other gods and the making of images as one commandment while separating the prohibition of coveting the wife and possessions of one's neighbor into two commandments. The Jewish and Reformed traditions join the commandments prohibiting covetousness into one and separate the prohibitions of false worship and the making of images into two.

There is no strictly logical order to the commandments, though at the beginning of the series they group around Israel's obligations toward God, and the commands that follow deal with obligations the Israelites have toward each other. None of the commandments is unique in Israelite tradition. What is unique is their association in this series of ten. The simplicity of the commandments is striking; their straightforward thrust avoids the need for expert legal interpretation. Finally, the Bible recognizes the comprehensiveness of the Decalogue. At the conclusion of its version of the Ten Commandments, Deuteronomy notes that God "added no more" (5:22).

The cultural setting of the first millennium B.C. set the parameters of the commandments dealing with God. The first three prohibit any type of action that implies human control over the divine. Ancient peoples set up images in their sanctuaries to assure the divine presence in them, but no image could compel the divine presence in Israel. The mythological worldview in the ancient Near East envisioned many gods. In contrast, the commandments insist that Israel serve its God alone. The God of Israel is no guarantor of oaths. The Israelites were to avoid taking unnecessary oaths in the name of their God. The prohibition of working on the Sabbath shows that the God of Israel determines the pattern of Israel's life.

The commandments that deal with the Israelites' obligations toward each other have parallels in the law codes of other ancient Near Eastern peoples. These commandments suggest themselves when people begin to live together in groups. To maintain group solidarity the members of that group need to trust one another and to respect one another's property, for what society could endure for very long if the people in that society lied to one another, stole from one another, did not respect marital bonds, and condoned murder? What made ancient Israel's approach to these common obligations unique was its assertion that people's relationship with God was dependent upon the fulfillment of these obligations. A person's relationship with God was a by-product of just intersocietal relationships. Any breech in human relationships within Israel compromised the people's relationship with God. The Ten Commandments have no penalties attached to them because the ultimate penalty for stealing, lying, murder, or adultery is not a penalty the community can impose but a penalty God can impose.

The first commandment (Exod 20:2-6; Deut 5:7-10) requires absolute loyalty from Israel. When the Israelites entered the land promised to their ancestors and adopted a settled agricultural life, some chose to serve the gods of the indigenous Canaanite population. They believed that these gods controlled the fertility of the soil. They had to learn that their God controlled every sphere of life, and they had to submit to this control. The prohibition of images that was part of this commandment underscores the uniqueness of Israel's God, who could not be portrayed in any form. Nothing created can represent the God of Israel.

The second commandment (Exod 20:7; Deut 5:11) sought to prevent people from attempting to manipulate God. The peoples of the ancient Near East believed that the name of a god contained certain implicit power (see Num 22–24). The commandment forbids the Israelites from using the power of God's name for any worthless purpose. God's sovereignty was incompatible with any attempt at control by human beings. This commandment does not attempt to protect God but Israel. It forbids the pointless and false use of the divine name, which reflects a lack of seriousness toward God. By the NT period it had become the custom to avoid pronouncing the divine name in any circumstance.

The third commandment (Exod 20:8-11; Deut 5:12-15) is set in a positive form. It contains two obligations: that of making the Sabbath holy and of working for six days only. (The word "sabbath" derives from the Hebrew word for rest.) The Israelites are to make the Sabbath holy (set apart) by ceasing all work on that day. The tradition gives a reason for the observance of this commandment. The Book of Exodus sees limitation of the Creator, who rested on the seventh day, as motivation for the observance of the Sabbath rest. Deuteronomy reminds the Israelites that they were once slaves in Egypt with no rest from their servitude. The Sabbath was a reminder of their former bondage and the freedom that God granted them.

The fourth commandment (Exod 20:12; Deut 5:16) reflects the values of a traditional society that honored and respected its elders. The equal status of the mother is significant and is exceptional in the cultural context in which this commandment emerged. The promise appended to the commandment is unique in the Decalogue. It carries with it an implied threat that a lack of respect for one's parents may lead to an abrupt end to one's days in the land that God promised to Israel.

The fifth commandment (Exod 20:13; Deut 5:17) forbids the act of murder for personal and illegitimate reasons. The commandment forbids the type of killing that is incompatible with those who are in a covenantal relationship with the God of Israel. It does not forbid capital punishment, which was part of the ancient Israelite criminal law (Deut 17:2-7; 19:12), nor does it prohibit war (see Deut 20–21). Other legislation (Deut 19:1-13) deals with manslaughter (accidental killing).

The sixth commandment (Exod 20:14; Deut 5:18) deals specifically with adultery and not with other forms of illicit sexual activity. Other laws deal with these (see Deut 22–25). This commandment prohibits sexual relationships between two persons, one or both of whom are married to another party. The Bible considers adultery a serious breech of the loyalty that Israel owes to God (Jer 5:7; Hos 4:2; Job 24:13-17). It views the violation of marital fidelity as threat to the integrity of Israel's relationship with God.

The seventh commandment (Exod 20:15; Deut 5:19) is a prohibition of theft. There is some debate whether the command forbids simple theft or focuses on the taking of a person by force and the sale of that person for profit. Both types of crime undermine social relationships. Simple theft is forbidden elsewhere in Israelite law (see Exod 22:1-13).

The eighth commandment (Exod 20:16; Deut 5:20) forbids giving false statements in legal cases. Since testimony given against one's neighbors in a legal proceeding determines their future, it is critical that all evidence be factual. The biblical tradition takes the integrity of the legal system seriously. This commandment shows that truthfulness in legal testimony is not just necessary for a functioning judicial system; it is a requirement from God.

The ninth and tenth commandments (Exod 20:17; Deut 5:21) are unlike the others, since they deal with motivation rather than overt acts. Thus they form a fitting conclusion to the Decalogue, since they prohibit fostering the kind of desire that leads to overt acts against the other commandments. These two commandments are a type of summary of the others. Violating either is the first step that leads to the violation of any of the others.

The Decalogue reflects the insight that the God of Israel is a God who governs all spheres of life. This God requires obedience. It is important to see the Decalogue in its covenantal context. The obedience that God requires of Israel flows from God's saving and liberating acts on Israel's behalf. These acts established a relationship between God and Israel. The Decalogue became the means by which Israel was to maintain that relationship. Finally, the Decalogue's stipulations show that the status of Israel's relationship with God was a product of harmony within its human community.

See also CAPITAL PUNISHMENT; COVENANT; MORAL LIFE, CHRISTIAN; SCRIPTURE, USE OF IN CATHOLIC SOCIAL ETHICS.

Bibliography: W. Harrelson, *The Ten Commandments and Human Rights* (Philadelphia: Fortress, 1980). E. Nielsen, *The Ten Commandments in New Perspective,* Studies in Biblical Theology, 2nd series, 7 (London: SCM, 1968). J. Stamm and M. Andrew, *The Ten Commandments in Recent Research,* Studies in Biblical Theology, 2nd series, 2 (London: SCM, 1967).

LESLIE J. HOPPE, O.F.M.

DEMOCRACY

The historical record on the relation of Catholicism and democracy is mixed. Recent developments, however, have aligned Catholic social thought explicitly—and it seems permanently—with the position that democracy is the political form most in keeping with the Christian message.

When we examine the structure of the early church, it appears to be neither a democracy nor a centralized hierarchical structure but something in between. Peter and his successors were understood to have received a special commission from Christ ("Thou art Peter and upon this rock I will build my church," Mt 16:18), but the apostles and their successors, the bishops, were also given a universal mission by Christ ("Going therefore teach ye all nations," Mt 28:19), and the early Christian communities were described as direct recipients of divine grace and inspiration ("Where two or three are gathered in my name, there am I in midst of them," (Mt 18:20). The Christian communities often acted as quasi-independent self-governing entities to make decisions, especially in times of persecution. The apostles elected a replacement for Judas, and in the Council of Jerusalem, which was to decide on whether circumcision was required for Gentiles, decisions were made by consensus (Acts 15). The early church partook of elements of all three of the classic forms, monarchy, aristocracy, and democracy, and when later Christians looked back to it as a model they could find evidence of all three forms of government.

Also relevant to later ideas of limited government that were important in the development of liberal democracy was the dualism, both of loyalties and of institutional structure, that was implied by Christian belief in an independent source of legitimation of government that both gave a special religious character to political authority and limited its area of authority ("There is no power but of God. The powers that be are ordained of God," Rom 13:1-2; "We must obey God rather than men," Acts 5:29).

When the church emerged from the catacombs in the 4th century and first was tolerated and then formally established as the religion of the Roman Empire, there was a danger that it would be swallowed up in the imperial bureaucracy, and indeed something close to that process took place in the Eastern church. Yet even in the East collegial decision-making structures existed, notably the ecumenical councils, seen principally as assemblies of bishops and patriarchs, although usually called by the emperor and with a special place for the representative of the pope. In Western Europe and North Africa, councils of bishops enacted legislation with or without participation of temporal authorities, and Rome demanded—but did not always receive—a special role in resolving disputes. Bishops were selected in various ways, most commonly by a vote or consensus of the diocese, and although the episcopal dioceses were in communion with Rome the pope was not seen as exerting a strong governing role in the diocese. Often the strongest influence was the local ruler, but in theory, as argued explicitly by Pope Gelasius at the end of the 5th century, there were two structures of rule, a dualism of spiritual and temporal authority.

The centralization that is associated with the modern Roman Catholic church dates from the 12th century. A revitalized papacy developed a system of law, courts, records, and bureaucracy that made Rome increasingly important in the government of the church, and in such documents as *Unam sanctam* of Pope Boniface VIII (1302) all power was seen as concentrated in the papacy.

Yet there were also more democratic elements in the practice and the theory of medieval Catholicism. Gratian's *Decretum,* the basic text used by all canon lawyers, insisted that "bishops are to be elected by the clergy and requested by the people" (D 62, can. 1) and that "no bishop should be assigned to the people against their will" (D 62, can. 1) and cited as a condition for the validity of a law that it must be "approved by the practice of those under them" (D 4, can. 2). A Roman law provision that originally applied to water rights, "what touches all, should be approved by all," was incorporated in the official canon law collection, the *Liber Sextus,* in 1298, and new religious orders such as the Dominicans developed elaborate systems of election and representation for their internal governance. In the church-state conflicts between the spiritual and temporal powers each side appealed to the legitimizing role of the consent of the people to weaken the claims of the other side, and in the 14th and 15th centuries writers of the conciliar movement such as Nicholas of Cusa drew on the democratic elements in the church tradition—elections, consent to law, and original equality in natural law—to argue that the council as the representative of all the members of the church was superior to the pope.

St. Thomas Aquinas (1225–74) combined both hierarchical and democratic elements. On the one hand, law is made by "the whole community or the person who represents it" (ST I–II, q. 90, art. 3), and the best form of government is one in which "all participate in the selection (*electio*) of those who rule" (ST I–II, q. 105). On the other hand, government by a monarch is best because it promotes unity and follows the patterns of God's monarchical government of the universe (*De regimine principum,* chap. 3). The pope leads the church to a higher spiritual goal of humanity, but (at least in one interpretation—there are conflicting texts) he can only intervene in temporal affairs "with respect to those things in which the temporal power is subject to him" (ST II–II, q. 60, art. 6). Law is morally obligatory and reflects the divine purposes in the world, but an unjust law that violates natural or divine law is no law at all but an act of violence (ST I–II, q. 96, art. 2). All men are equal in sight of God and even slaves have rights, but "there is an order to be found among men" according to which even before the Fall the more intelligent were to lead the less intelligent (*Summa contra Gentiles* 4.81; ST I, q. 92, arts. 3–4). Authoritarian, constitutionalist (Aquinas as "the first Whig"), and democratic conclusions can be drawn from Aquinas' writings and from the tradition of medieval Catholicism.

The process of papal centralization was carried much further in the period of the Counter-Reformation with the imposition of a common liturgy (the Roman Rite), discipline, and control over appointments of bishops (in the Middle Ages exerted principally through the requirement of papal confirmation of episcopal elections). That control was shared with Catholic monarchs through the *jus patronatus,* the right to name candidates for episcopal sees to the Vatican, and through concordats, or treaties, that guaranteed the rights of the church, especially state support for Catholicism and enforcement of religious uniformity, as well as special rights in the areas of education and marriage. Yet this apparent endorsement of absolute monarchy was qualified by the Jesuit and Dominican opponents of the theory of the divine right of kings, including Robert Bellarmine and Francisco Suarez, who argued that royal authority came from God through the people. Some of their arguments for a conditional transfer of authority contributed to the constitutional tradition that led ultimately to Locke's *Second Treatise of Civil Government,* but none of the Catholic writers argued, as Locke did, for religious toleration. The Catholic writers still endorsed the rule of the monarch but argued for moral and constitutional limits on his exercise of rule.

In the 18th century the anticlericalism of the French Revolution produced a deep suspicion of democracy on the part of the Vatican. The French revolutionaries opposed the privileges of the church and attempted to force the clergy to accept the Revolution in the *Civil Constitution of the Clergy,* which in the name of the people subordinated the priests to civil authority.

In the 19th century the Italian republican nationalists were denounced by the Vatican because their goal of Italian unification required the forcible takeover of Rome and the Papal States. When Rome was seized by the nationalists in 1871, Pope Pius IX imposed a ban on Catholic participation in Italian politics. His successor, Pope Leo XIII, did not lift that ban but encouraged French Catholics who had opposed the Third Republic because of its anticlericalism to involve themselves in French political life through the so-called *ralliement* policy. And in Bismarckian, Germany, Catholics organized the Catholic Center party in resistance to the Iron Chancellor's anti-Catholic *Kulturkampf.* In 1885 the Vatican's opposition to liberal republicanism was modified somewhat with the publication of Leo's encyclical *Immortale Dei* (*On the Christian Constitution of States*). Leo wrote that "no one of several forms of government is to be condemned. . . . Neither is it blameworthy in itself in any manner, for the people to have a share, greater or less, in the government; for at certain times and under certain laws, such participation may not only be of benefit to the citizens, but may even be of obligation" (36). Yet this does not mean that Leo had suddenly become a democrat. In both this encyclical and in *Libertas (On the Nature of Human Liberty),* issued in 1888, he reaffirmed his predecessors' denunciations of freedom of worship, of expression, and of teaching, accusing the liberals of making "the state absolute and omnipotent" and of proclaiming that "man should live altogether independently of God." Indeed, the pope denounced liberalism as "the sullied product of a revolutionary age of man's unbounded urge for innovation." Yet having opposed religious freedom in principle, he added that the church "does not forbid public authority to tolerate what is at variance with truth and justice, for the sake of avoiding some greater evil or preserving some greater good." (This is the passage that gave rise to the distinction later made by Catholic theologians between the "thesis" or ideal situation of Catholicism as the established true religion, and the "hypothesis" or pragmatic compromise of religious toleration in a situation of religious pluralism.) For the 19th-century papacy, continental liberal democracy was opposed because it advocated separation of church and state and removal of public support for Catholicism, secularization of education and marriage, and efforts to replace the Catholic religion with an all-encompassing rationalism and anticlericalism.

In other European countries with parliamentary governments—Belgium, Holland, Germany, Austria—Catholic parties participated in political life, and in the German case the Center party became one of the bulwarks of parliamentary government, while in France and Italy parties of Catholic inspiration were not active because of Vatican opposition. After the *non expedit* ban on Catholic participation in Italian politics was lifted in 1919 a socially oriented priest, Don Luigi Sturzo, organized the Popular party, which had spectacular success but was dissolved in 1924 by the Vatican after Mussolini came to power, and Sturzo went into exile. In France many Catholics (including the young army officer Charles de Gaulle) were monarchists and opposed to the parliamentarism of the Third Republic, but a small party of Christian Democratic inspiration, the Popular Democratic party, was organized in the 1930s and involved young leaders who were later to be active in the resistance to nazism and in the creation of a Christian Democratic party, le Mouvement Républicain Populaire (MRP) after World War II.

The single person who did most to relate democracy and human rights to the Catholic tradition and to argue against a link between Catholicism and authoritarianism was French philosopher Jacques Maritain. Converted to Catholicism in 1906 and to Thomism in 1912, Maritain only began to write about politics in the late 1920s following the condemnation by Pius XI of Action Française, a right-wing movement with which Maritain had been sympathetic. The best known of his books applying Thomist principles to democracy are *Integral Humanism* (French ed., Paris: Aubier, 1936), *Scholasticism and Politics* (New York: Macmillan, 1940), *The Rights of Man and the Natural Law* (New York: Scribner's, 1943), and *Man and the State* (lectures delivered at the University of Chicago in 1949 and published by the University of Chicago Press in 1951). There Maritain argues that integral or personalist and communitarian democracy is the best application of Christian and Thomist political principles, and that the modern democratic state is the result of the "leavening influence of the Gospel principles in human history."

Maritain distinguished his religiously based personalism from what he considered to be the egoistic individualism of "bourgeois liberalism" and the collectivism of Marxism—thus maintaining a continuity with earlier papal writings that had criticized both philosophies. However, he drew from the Thomist tradition to argue for a religiously pluralistic and socially concerned democratic state that was almost indistinguishable from the contemporary democratic welfare states of Europe. Along with other Catholic political thinkers of European background such as Yves Simon (*The Philosophy of Democratic Government,* Chicago: Univ. of Chicago Press, 1951) and Heinrich Rommen (*The State in Catholic Thought,* St. Louis:

Herder, 1945), he was responsible for a new development in Catholic thought that became part of the ideological foundations of the Christian Democratic parties of Europe and Latin America—the argument that democracy was not simply one of several forms of government, all of which were acceptable to the degree that they promoted "the common good," but that it was the one political structure that was most in keeping with the nature of humankind and with Christian values.

During World War II the Vatican began to take a more positive attitude toward democracy. Pope Pius XII in his 1944 Christmas message drew direct links between political freedom, democracy, and the Christian tradition. However, the real breakthrough in papal thought on liberal democracy took place with the publication of John XXIII's encyclical *Pacem in terris.* After what appears to be a classically conservative beginning, a discussion of "order between men," the pope states that every human being is a "person" by virtue of which "he has rights and duties of his own, flowing directly and simultaneously from his very nature." Among those rights is "the right to worship God according to one's conscience," which the pope describes as "the right to honor God according to the dictates of an upright conscience, and therefore to worship God privately and publicly."

The encyclical makes a similar argument on democracy, stating that "the dignity of the human person involves the right to take an active part in public affairs and to contribute one's part to the common good of the citizens" and that "the human person is entitled to the juridical protection of his rights." In the next section the pope says that "it is impossible to determine, once and for all, the most suitable form of government," but he refers again to the advantages of participation and of ministers holding office only for a limited time, in effect arguing for periodic elections.

A more explicit endorsement of democracy took place at the Second Vatican Council in 1965. The Pastoral Constitution on the Church in the Modern World *(Gaudium et spes)* included a formal commitment of Catholicism to democracy: "It is in full accord with human nature that juridical-political structures should, with ever better success and without discrimination, afford all their citizens the chance to participate freely and actively in establishing the constitutional bases of a political community, governing the state, determining the scope and purpose of various institutions, and choosing leaders" (GS 75).

The council also adopted the Declaration on Religious Liberty *(Dignitatis humanae),* which restated in more forceful terms what Pope John XXIII had said in *Pacem in terris.* Arguing that "the human person has a right to religious freedom," the council declared that "the right to religious freedom has its foundation in the very dignity of the human person" and defined that right as freedom "from coercion on the part of individuals or of social groups and of any human power in such wise that in matters religious no one is to be forced to act in a manner contrary to his own beliefs. Nor is anyone to be restrained from acting in accordance with his beliefs, whether publicly or privately, whether alone or in association with others, within due limits" (DH 2).

Religious freedoms were not the only liberties endorsed by the council. Again drawing its arguments from the development of "a keener awareness of human dignity" and repeating what had been argued in *Pacem in terris, Gaudium et spes* endorsed the contemporary aspirations for "a political-juridical order in which personal rights can gain better protection. These include rights of free assembly, of common action, or expressing personal opinions, and of professing a religion privately and publicly. For the protection of personal rights is a necessary condition for the active participation of citizens, whether as individuals or collectively, in the life and government of the state" (GS 73).

The formal commitment of the Catholic church to democracy and human rights as well as to religious freedom meant the abandonment of a long-standing tension between the Vatican and liberal democracy. The council's 1965 statement on democracy contained footnotes to Pius XII's wartime Christmas messages, but it marked a much clearer and unambiguous commitment to democracy and political participation than ever before. The Vatican's opposition to liberal democracy—much of it fueled by now-obsolete struggles over education and financial support—had disappeared. While in many ways this was simply a recognition of ideological and political changes that had taken place at the grass roots and in the national communities in Europe and Latin America, that it was now formally endorsed at the highest level had an important impact on the conduct of church leaders and the clergy in subsequent decades. The bishops themselves had received a kind of political and moral education as a result of their attendance at the council from September until December for four years, and, especially in Latin America, it affected their attitudes toward their own moral role as defenders of democracy and human rights. Catholic seminaries and educational institutions used the council's decrees as an educational reference point, and traditionalist conservatives and integralists could no longer cite Vatican declarations to legitimate their views.

The endorsement of liberal democracy by the institutional church was not a wholly uncritical one, and there has been an attempt to maintain some continuity with earlier statements. This is particularly true in the case of economic liberalism or free-market capitalism. In 1967, for example, Pope Paul VI wrote an influential encyclical, *Populorum progressio (On the Development of Peoples),* which attacked capitalism as a system that "considers profit as the key motive for economic progress, competition as the supreme law of economics, and private ownership of the means of production as an absolute right that has no limits and carries no corresponding obligation." The pope quoted Pius XI on "the international imperialism of money" and argued that "unchecked liberalism" is itself a form of dictatorship (PP 26).

Pope John Paul II is often described as a conservative in theology and ecclesiology, but he criticized liberal individualism and free-enterprise economics in his encyclical *Laborem exercens,* written in 1981 on the 50th anniversary of Pius XI's *Quadragesimo anno,* which endorsed the priority of labor in economics. *Libertas conscientiae,* the Congregation for the Doctrine of the Faith's *Instruction on Christian Freedom and Liberation* (1986), sums up the state of contemporary Catholic social thought in its commitment to solidarity (the human obligation to contribute to the common good) and to subsidiarity (the promotion of the initiative of individuals and intermediate communities) (LC 73). The instruction reiterates the Church's commitment to democracy, arguing that there can only be "authentic development in a social and political system which respects freedoms and fosters them through the participation of everyone" while guaranteeing a "proper pluralism in institutions and social initiatives" (LC 95).

What do these statements and the developments since Vatican II tell us about the contemporary relation of liberal democracy and Catholicism? In a sense there is now a philosophical identity of the basis from which both liberalism and Catholicism draw their justification of democracy—the dignity of the human person. Liberalism allows for a variety of philosophical and religious outlooks as grounds for that dignity—whether it is the free individual in "the state of nature which has a law of nature to govern it" of Locke's *Second Treatise* (par. 6), the self-legislating free moral person of Kant, the freely choosing, self-developing, and increasingly socially conscious individual of Mill, the product of the thought experiment of John Rawls, who becomes more and more aware of the duty to others, or the Christian endowed with an immortal soul and a special right and duty to make moral and political choices for which God will hold that person responsible.

Yet there are also differences. Social responsibility and social development seem to come later in most liberal theories, products of a rather desiccated process of moral universalization. The belief in humankind's common creation by God and in an objective common good lend Catholic political thought a more pronouncedly social orientation, so that Christian democracy, for example, has never had the problems with the modern welfare state experienced by liberalism because of its more individualistic beginnings.

There is also a continuing tension between Catholicism and liberal democracy because of the structure of authority and decision making in the church itself. It is true that Vatican II's Dogmatic Constitution on the Church *(Lumen gentium)* defined the church as "the people of God" and stated that "the order of the bishops is successor to the college of the apostles in teaching authority . . . together with its head, the Roman pontiff, and never without this head" (LG, chaps. 2, 3), and since Vatican II there has been a partial decentralization of the internal structure of the church. National councils and international synods of bishops have taken a more active role, and the laity has been more deeply involved in decision making. However, the church has not become a democracy, and those like Leonardo Boff who have argued for an increase in internal democratization have had difficulties with the Vatican. There is still a tension and probably there always will be between a hierarchical church that sees itself as a guardian and interpreter of divine revelation and a sociopolitical structure that decides public questions on the basis of free discussion, majority rule, and individual rights. Yet while there are limits to the acceptance of democracy in the internal governance of the church, in the political sphere it is now clear that Catholic social thought endorses democracy as the form of government required by the nature of humankind as free moral beings endowed by their Creator with the capacity and duty to govern themselves.

See also CHRISTIAN DEMOCRACY; DIGNITATIS HUMANAE; GAUDIUM ET SPES; JOHN XXIII; MARITAIN, JACQUES; PACEM IN TERRIS; POLITICAL PHILOSOPHY; VATICAN COUNCIL II.

Bibliography: W. Abbott, ed., *Documents of the Second Vatican Council* (New York: Herder & Herder, 1966). M. Fogarty, *Christian Democracy in Europe, 1820–1953* (London: Routledge, 1947). E. Hanson, *The Catholic Church in World Politics* (Princeton, N.J.: Princeton Univ. Press, 1987). J. Maritain, *The Rights of Man and the Natural Law* (New York: Scribner's, 1943). J. Maritain, *Man and the State* (Chicago: Univ. of Chicago Press, 1951). H. Rommen, *The State in Catholic Thought* (St. Louis: Herder, 1956). P. Sigmund, *Nicholas of Cusa and Medieval Political Thought* (Cambridge, Mass.: Harvard Univ. Press, 1963). P. Sigmund, ed. and trans., *St. Thomas Aquinas on Politics and Ethics* (New York: Norton, 1988).

PAUL E. SIGMUND

DEMOGRAPHICS

As a modern field of study demographics employs statistical measurements and mathematical methods to examine both the structure of human populations, for example, their distribution by age, sex, and marital status, and their dynamic aspects, for example, births, deaths, and migratory movements. Demographic studies rely heavily on census data, registration of vital statistics, and sophisticated polling techniques. The concern of such studies is not simply with the number and distribution of people in the population in terms of age, sex, wealth, educational level, and so forth but also with the relationship of particular populations to the material resources and cultural goods available to them.

Demographic studies have been of special interest to those responsible for identifying markets for salable goods as well as to insurance agencies. The increased knowledge about and importance of population problems have made such studies crucial to governments and private agencies concerned about the protection of the environment and the use and distribution of natural resources. The Second Vatican Council in *Gaudium et spes* (87), Pope John XXIII in *Mater et magistra* (186–92), and Pope Paul VI in *Populorum progressio* (37) and *Humanae vitae* (2) showed awareness of demographic studies, John with more skepticism than Paul. In assessing demographic studies it is important to note that they do not predict the future, nor do they prescribe moral courses of action. They are attempts to show what the social consequences of human behaviors will be if present trends continue.

See also DEVELOPMENT; ECOLOGY; ENERGY; GOODS, DISTRIBUTION OF; NATURAL RESOURCES; POPULATION; POPULORUM PROGRESSIO; STEWARDSHIP.

JAMES P. HANIGAN

DETERRENCE

Deterrence denotes the attempt to reduce another's incentives to act in undesirable ways by threatening to carry out harmful, sometimes punitive responses to such actions. By aiming to inhibit another's activity those who deter attempt to modify another's behavior, seeking to secure some measure of cooperation by raising the costs of undesirable actions. Deterrence thus takes the form of a conditional or hypothetical threat: if specified conditions are violated, if cooperation cannot be sustained, then threats will be carried out. Ideally the goal is to create a situation in which deterrent threats will not have to be exercised. In theory, those who are threatened cooperate because alternatives to cooperation include harmful consequences. In this way those who deter resort to coercive measures with untrustworthy individuals or groups to secure a desired state of affairs or to prevent an undesirable state of affairs.

Judgments about the morality of deterrence have focused on deterrent threats in the criminal justice system, conventional war, and nuclear war. This entry will focus on ethical responses to nuclear deterrence.

Nuclear deterrence is a means of preventing the outbreak of nuclear war, and some conventional wars, by threatening to use nuclear weapons in response to aggressive military actions. Nations make threats of nuclear reprisal or attack, the outcome of which a potential aggressor would consider a disproportionate price to pay for political or military objectives. In a general sense nuclear deterrence is paradoxical: nations threaten to wage war in order to prevent war from being waged.

Threats of nuclear attack are premised on two main uses of nuclear weapons: counterpopulation and counterforce attacks. The former refers to the use of nuclear weapons against civilian targets, that is, cities. The latter refers to the use of nuclear weapons against military targets, related industries, and communication facilities. United States policy has been a mixture of counterforce and counterpopulation targeting since the 1950s.

Moral evaluations of nuclear deterrence raise the basic question, can we do evil that good may come? Answers to this question vary, depending on the relation between consequences and principles in one's moral theory. Variations also hinge on the application of just-war tenets to the dangers posed by nuclear-deterrent threats interpreted in light of the rule of double effect. Moral assessments of deterrence can be clustered into four groups.

1. The first group would focus on the morality of intention implied by deterrent threats. Axiomatic in this approach is the

principle of moral equivalence between action and intention: whatever is wrong to do is wrong to intend, regardless of the consequences that follow from such intentions. Acts of war proscribed by just-war tenets are wrong to intend for deterrent purposes. Evidences about intentions are best found, according to this view, in the targeting policies of military planning.

It follows that deterrent policies premised on counterpopulation targeting are immoral because they include the intention to kill civilians, contrary to the protections provided by the *jus in bello* criterion of discrimination. Judgments vary about whether counterforce nuclear war can be confined to just-war restraints; those who believe that such war is conceivable usually conclude that nuclear deterrence is acceptable only on the condition that it conform to plans for a just and limited use of nuclear force. Further, such plans seem credible, since they are part of a realistic application of military force against aggression. Those who condemn all possible uses of nuclear weapons are bound by the principle of moral equivalence to condemn the intention to use them as well.

One variation of this approach holds that nuclear-counterforce war ought to conform to just-war restraints but that such war may escalate to disproportionate levels for unintended reasons. This prospect has salutary effects, the argument continues, proportionate to the overall goal of preventing the outbreak of war. Thus the menace of nuclear war can be credibly deterred without having to intend to use nuclear weapons in an indiscriminate fashion.

As developed by Paul Ramsey, this approach distinguishes the end of fighting a war from the end of deterring a war. Within war itself, parties must behave according to just-war criteria, which only permit counterforce nuclear warfare. But it is realistic, Ramsey held, to think that counterforce nuclear war will unintentionally escalate to disproportionate levels, inadvertently raising the costs of war. This prospect, seen in advance by both adversaries, is entirely proportionate to the preventive aims toward which deterrence is ordered—or so Ramsey argued.

2. A second general approach evaluates nuclear deterrence by ranking consequences over principled intentions. Usually representatives of this camp hold that the beneficial consequence of nuclear deterrence—the prevention of nuclear war— outweighs considerations surrounding intention and moral purity. A more radical version of this approach would hold that in international relations appeals to morality are bankrupt, since moral canons are not widely shared. Even in this instance, however, judgments rest on maximizing benefits over burdens to justify the utility of deterrent policies. In either case appeals to consequences tend to express fewer reservations about the morality of counterpopulation targeting so long as it can be shown that such targeting is the most effective way of reducing the risk of nuclear war.

Generally this second approach buttresses its claims by arguing that counterpopulation targeting is a safe policy, since neither side gains an advantage by striking the other's cities first. When neither side has incentives to use nuclear force first, relations are stabilized and the risk of war is considerably reduced. This view is thus critical of those who espouse counterforce policies, arguing that such policies are premised on the advantages wrought from a first-strike attack. (With only counterforce weapons, each side has incentives to go first, lest the adversary's first strike neutralize the other side's counterforce arsenal.) When each side has incentives to strike first in a crisis, political relations are destabilized, contrary to deterrent designs.

3. A third general approach begins by assessing the morality of deterrent intentions but insists that we must separate intentions to use nuclear weapons from the intention to possess them for deterrent

purposes. This means that we must separate evaluations of use from those of deterrence. It also means that we might condemn the use of nuclear weapons while retaining them for the purpose of deterrence.

This position is premised on one of two claims. Some hold that the threat to use is not equivalent to the intention to use and that we err by conflating threats with intentions. Others hold that deterrent intentions are not equivalent to the intention to use because deterrent intentions are paradoxically structured; they are structured so as to *prevent* use. By either account, a judgment about the use of nuclear weapons ought not affect the moral question of their possession for deterrent purposes.

The goal of separating the question of use from that of deterrent intentions is to ensure that any condemnation of use does not automatically yield a condemnation of possession of nuclear weapons for deterrence. Accordingly, those who embrace nuclear pacifism are not bound to reject nuclear deterrence outright. This allows them to eschew the tendency of some nuclear pacifists and other strict pacifists to argue for unilaterally dismantling the nuclear arsenal. Rather, those who embrace this third view seek to join two strong moral claims, both of which are shaped by just-war criteria: first, the use of nuclear weapons is immoral given the restrictions imposed by the *jus in bello*; second, unilateral disarmament may render a nation vulnerable to intimidating threats, perhaps tyranny, contrary to the right to self-defense inherent in the *jus ad bellum*. Often assailed as a policy of "bluffing," this view holds that possession without the intention to use is the best path between these two moral verdicts.

4. A final approach holds that just-war restraints may proscribe the use of nuclear weapons in the normal course of war but may be overridden by appeals to consequences when the only alternative is defeat at the hands of a tyrannical foe. In this case, appeals are made to consequences only under specified conditions, not generally speaking. Such an approach might be premised on the alleged superiority of Western polities over their enemies, allowing measures of defense that would be condemned if the other side used them instead. Or it can be premised on the belief that no defense against nuclear attack is possible outside of a nuclear response. Deterrent threats of nuclear attack may include immoral intentions, but such judgments may be suspended if the alternative is victory or intimidation by a diabolical enemy.

See also ARMS RACE; DISARMAMENT; DOUBLE EFFECT, PRINCIPLE OF; PEACE; WAR.

Bibliography: T. Schelling, *Arms and Influence* (New Haven: Yale Univ. Press, 1966). P. Ramsey, *The Just War: Force and Political Responsibility* (New York: Scribner's, 1968). P. Morgan, *Deterrence: A Conceptual Analysis* (Beverly Hills, Calif.: Sage, 1977). M. Walzer, *Just and Unjust Wars: A Moral Argument with Historical Illustrations* (New York: Basic Books, 1977). L. Freedman, *The Evolution of Nuclear Strategy* (New York: St. Martin's Press, 1981). W. O'Brien, *The Conduct of Just and Limited War* (New York: Praeger, 1981). NCCB, *The Challenge of Peace: God's Promise and Our Response* (Washington: USCC, 1983). D. Hollenbach, *Nuclear Ethics: A Christian Moral Argument* (New York: Paulist, 1983). J. Finnis et al., *Nuclear Deterrence, Morality, and Realism* (Oxford: Clarendon, 1987). R. Hardin et al., eds., *Nuclear Deterrence: Ethics and Strategy* (Chicago: Univ. of Chicago Press, 1985). R. Miller, *Interpretations of Conflict: Ethics, Pacifism, and the Just-War Tradition* (Chicago: Univ. of Chicago Press, 1991).

RICHARD B. MILLER

DEVELOPMENT

The whole question of development is a complex issue: who decides what development means and for whom? The answers vary and are ultimately subjective. Nonetheless, in the last several decades a particular view has predominated. This perspective took shape in the immediate post–World War II period. Known as "the developmentalist perspective" or "the modernization paradigm," it reigned with little criticism until the 1960s. Decidedly Western and linear, it assumed that development and economic growth were synonymous. According to the theorists who supported this view, underdevelopment was caused by a lack of capital. The solution, therefore, was to promote economic growth by an infusion of capital, which would lead to industrialization and eventual prosperity. Underdeveloped nations would enter into a process of social and economic transformation whereby they would gradually achieve economic maturity through technological advancement (Rostow). Conversion to more modern values socially, politically, and culturally was seen as integral to such a transformation. The mood conveyed by this perspective was one of optimism and hope.

The optimism spawned by the modernization paradigm was barely visible by the mid-1960s. Economic stagnation coupled with political and social unrest afflicted most Third World countries that had adopted this model of development. As a result, a pointed critique of developmentalist policies and practices emerged from social scientists in Latin America. Their critique is referred to as the "dependency school" perspective. According to dependency-school theorists, the uneven development that occurred in the Third World as a result of the modernization paradigm was an inevitable result of fundamentally unjust relations between core nations (Western Europe, the United States, Japan) and nations found on the periphery of the world economy (most nations in Latin America, Asia, Africa). They described these relations as neocolonialist. Clearly, core nations dominated the economies of developing countries through investments, trade, subsidies, and military aid. Simultaneously, they forged internal political alliances with ruling elites, who attempted to ensure a stable social climate for their interests, often through repressive measures. Such economic and social relationships actually negated the possibility of genuine development. The dependency approach to underdevelopment continues to provide an alternative to the growth-oriented model still preferred by most Western nations and Third World elites.

Currently a highly discussed approach to the development theory, related to the dependency school, is the world-system approach. Attributed primarily to Immanuel Wallerstein, this perspective proposes that there is one world economy—a capitalist economy. This world system, which initially emerged in the 16th century, is composed of core states or center nations, semiperipheral and peripheral nations, and a few areas of the world as yet untouched by capitalism. While this perspective sees the hegemonic power of some of the core states to be in decline, it also sees the peripheral nations' position in the system deteriorating to such an extent that revolutionary transformation of the world capitalist system into a socialist world system is their only hope (Blomström and Hettne, p. 191).

Modern development theory has often neglected the primary role women play in the development process. DAWN, a global network of professional researchers, policymakers, and activists, has raised serious questions about the impact of development on the poor of the world, especially women. It points out that women constitute the majority of the poor in the world and suffer from additional burdens imposed by gender-based hierarchies and subordination. They urgently recommend that women's voices be heard in the process of defining development as well as in the process of designing policies, plans, and strategies for implementation required in a "people-centered" approach to development (Sen and Grown).

Catholic social teaching has clearly been influenced by modern development theory. At times it has reflected the optimism of the developmentalist perspective; at other times it has expressed the more critical vision characteristic of the dependency-school and world-system perspectives. Too often it has failed to acknowledge the pivotal role women play in the development process. Nevertheless, since Pope John XXIII Catholic social teaching has underscored the fundamental need to build a more just global economic system and has been critical of development policies and procedures that hurt the poor.

For example, in *Mater et magistra* (1961) Pope John XXIII insists that development transcends purely economic growth and must include "a corresponding social development" so that every member of the human community can develop as fully as possible (MM 73–74). Optimistic about the possibilities for cooperation and harmony among nations, John XXIII urges the more developed nations of the world to assume greater responsibility for those nations suffering from poverty, hunger, and a lack of basic human rights. He sees aid as one way for more advanced nations to reach out in compassion to their less developed brothers and sisters (157–60). Likewise, he cautions that aid be given without strings attached, thereby condemning neocolonialist strategies of domination (170, 172).

In *Pacem in terris* John XXIII reiterates his plea to economically developed nations to come to the aid of less developed countries (PT 121). Writing in 1963 during the early years of the United Nations' First Development Decade, he is hopeful aid will eventually enable poor countries to arrive at a level of development commensurate with their dignity as human persons (121–22). He condemns political and cultural domination as a motive for lending aid (125). Ultimately John XXIII's position is predicated on the assumption that economic relations can be improved only if the wealthier nations share the fruits of the international capitalist system more equitably.

Gaudium et spes, one of the most important documents of the Second Vatican Council, also reflects John's optimism about economic development. It urges that such development be "guided and coordinated in a reasonable and human way" (GS 63). It acknowledges, however, the growing gap between rich and poor nations, and it points to the need for numerous socioeconomic reforms and articulates certain principles of justice that its authors considered applicable to the question of development. Those principles include the recognition that the ultimate purpose of economic activity is not profit or domination but the service of people (64), the importance of democratic participation in economic decision making nationally and internationally (165), and the need for Christians to act justly and charitably when it comes to their involvement in modern socioeconomic development (72).

Following the lead of Pope John XXIII and the Second Vatican Council, Pope Paul VI's *Populorum progressio* is Catholic social teaching's *Magna Charta* on development. Paul VI was so concerned about this issue that he created the Pontifical Commission on Justice and Peace to further just social development. Like John XXIII, he sees authentic development as more than mere economic growth. For Paul VI it must include political, social, and cultural development. Further, it should promote the good of all persons (PP 6, 14, 40, 42).

Less optimistic than his predecessor about the future of global economic development, Paul VI insists that "development demands bold transformations, innovations that go deep" (32). He criticizes the economic fragility caused by one-crop economies in the Third World (7), excessive land ownership that hurts the common good (24), and a capitalist economic system that deifies profit, competition, and private ownership of the means of production (26). He urges rich nations to place their superfluous wealth at the service of poor nations (40) and calls for a "World Fund" to aid the most destitute by utilizing part of the money spent on arms (51). He demands that the debt repayments of developing countries be ameliorated (54) while denouncing unjust trade relations between rich and poor nations (56–61). Finally, he chastises multinational corporations for their lack of social sensitivity in less developed countries (70).

Like the theorists associated with the dependency school, Paul VI presents a comprehensive denunciation of the unjust relations that exist between core and peripheral nations. In truly prophetic fashion, however, he does not merely denounce injustice. He offers an alternative vision. This vision is rooted in his belief that "development is the new name for peace" and that the key to such peace is solidarity and a new humanism that will integrate the fruits of technological advancement with "the higher values of love and friendship, of prayer and contemplation" (17–20). The result of these "humanistic relations" will be a profound global solidarity built on the understanding that genuine peace is impossible without authentic development, that is, without an economy put at the service of human beings (83–86).

Reiterating Paul VI's vision that "development is the new name for peace," the Latin American bishops met at Medellín, Colombia, in 1968. They affirm with him the importance of global solidarity (*Justice* 3). They seek a *new* continent predicated on the development of a *new* people, who in freedom and with responsibility create new and reformed structures in light of the gospel (3). The construction of this new society will demand democratic participation in decision making, especially among the lower classes (7). It must also transcend the limitations of liberal capitalism and the Marxist system, both of which the bishops condemn. They call for a radical transformation of the way business is carried out in Latin American countries and plead for just economic and social change on a national and international level (11). Then and only then will development policies and procedures give witness to solidarity and the option for the poor (*Poverty* 10). Such a posture suggests they have been influenced to some degree by social scientists who represent the dependency-school perspective.

Perhaps the most poignant remark Paul VI makes regarding development in *Octogesima adveniens* (1971) is his criticism of "bureaucratic socialism, technocratic capitalism, and authoritarian democracy" as incapable of addressing global injustice and inequity. His hope lies in the "rebirth of utopias," that is, a new vision of future human relations founded on the transformative possibilities of the present (OA 37). He also repeats his plea for revised international relations between developed and developing countries and boldly questions the adequacy of Western models of growth (43).

Justitia in mundo, the document that resulted from the synod of bishops' Second General Assembly in 1971, remains faithful to the church's vision of integral development. It denounces the industrial and technological world order, which favors concentration of wealth, power, and decision making in the hands of a few (JM 9). Pointing to international systems of domination, the synod supports the will for and right to development among both developing and socialist nations (13–18). In addition, the synod affirms the aims of the Second Development Decade and urges that national autonomy be respected and mutual cooperation be fostered in order to achieve real and just development (71).

Meeting in Puebla, Mexico, in 1979, the Latin American bishops continue the condemnations of both liberal capitalism and Marxist collectivism they made at Medellín eleven years earlier, this time by classifying both as forms of idolatry and institutionalized injustice (Final Document, "Evangelization, Liberation, and Human Promotion," 4.4, 5.5). For development to be truly liberating, the bishops insist it must "transform human beings into active subjects" (4.3). Essential to this transformation is conversion to a preferential option for the poor on the part of the whole church. In calling for such conversion the bishops commit themselves to a process of development that is inherently just and mutual (Final Document, "A Preferential Option for the Poor," 1.1, 1.3).

John Paul II's lengthy discussion of the concept of development appears in *Sollicitudo rei socialis,* published in 1987. Written to commemorate the 20th anniversary of *Populorum progressio,* John Paul II seeks, like his predecessors, to present a view of authentic development as something more than economic self-sufficiency; it must also include cultural, political, and human development as well (SRS 9, 15).

Citing the fact that the global economy has become more unjust in the last two decades, John Paul denounces the economic, financial, and social mechanisms that accentuate underdevelopment (16). The housing crisis, unemployment, underemployment, and the international debt crisis are singled out as blatant examples of this underdevelopment (17–19). According to John Paul II, the reasons these roadblocks to development persist are political: the ideological opposition between East and West—between Marxist collectivism and liberal capitalism (20–23).

The authentic development that John Paul II envisages transcends the deficiencies of underdevelopment and the excesses of superdevelopment. Describing development as both an individual and a social duty, John Paul sees it encompassing respect for cultural diversity, openness to the transcendent, and respect for human rights (27–32). Most importantly, authentic development is inherently moral in character. As he views the issue, truly moral individuals must act to see to it that genuine development is realized (33–35). This will require individuals to recognize those "structures of sin," which "rooted in personal sin" give rise to immoral institutions (36). Individuals and nations exacerbate the life of these structures by pursuing excessive power and profit (37). Conversion to solidarity, that is, a deep and tenacious commitment to the common good by each person within every society, will conquer the many obstacles to full development (38–39). This solidarity is aligned with the virtue of charity and, as a specifically Christian virtue, promotes gratuity, reconciliation, and forgiveness, thereby overcoming those "evil mechanisms" and "structures of sin" responsible for underdevelopment (40).

According to this encyclical, reforms in international relations are needed, but they must be predicated on "the option or love of preference for the poor" (42). This love can lead both individuals and nations to the cooperation solidarity demands. Only in this way can authentic development be secured in the coming decades.

The concept of development in Catholic social teaching moves across a continuum of modern development theory. Except for the utopic vision ushered in by Paul VI and supported by the Latin American bishops' statements at Medellín and Puebla, it hovers between the optimism of John XXIII and the cautious spiritualizing of John Paul II, both of which fundamentally support a developmentalist perspective. One thing is certain at this juncture in history: the church must continue to read "the signs of the times" in its ongoing efforts to promote a truly integral and liberating development for all nations.

See also AID; BANKS AND BANKING; CAPITALISM; DEBT; ECONOMIC ORDER; INDUSTRIALIZATION; LIBERATION THEOLOGY; POPULORUM PROGRESSIO; TRANSNATIONAL CORPORATIONS.

Bibliography: W. Rostow, *The Stages of Economic Growth: A Non-Communist Manifesto* (Cambridge: Cambridge Univ. Press, 1960; 2nd ed., 1971). M. Blomström and B. Hettne, *Development Theory in Transition: The Dependency Debate and Beyond: Third World Responses* (London: Zed, 1984). G. Sen and C. Grown, *Development Crises and Alternative Visions: Third World Women's Perspectives* (New York: Monthly Review Press, 1987).

MARY HEMBROW SNYDER

DIETZ, PETER E.

Peter E. Dietz (1878–1947), known as the "labor priest," dedicated his priestly ministry to bringing Roman Catholic social teaching, principally *Rerum novarum,* to the United States labor movement. Born on July 10, 1878, on Manhattan's Lower East Side, Dietz as a boy went with his German immigrant father to the meetings of the nascent union movement and there experienced firsthand the laborers' need to organize. At sixteen, Peter discerned his vocation to the priesthood. Ten years later, in 1904, he was ordained by James Cardinal Gibbons for the Cleveland diocese.

Dietz had many personal trials during that ten-year period, including struggles with debilitating depression and difficulty determining the proper expression for his vocation. During his two years of study (1900–1902) at the Society of the Divine Word's seminary in Moedling, Germany, he became convinced that his own country's democratic traditions made America the place where Catholic-inspired economic reform could succeed. He left Germany animated by a vision of a specific priestly mission: using Catholic social teachings to shape economic reform in an American democratic society. After a year's study at Catholic University, he was accepted by the Cleveland diocese and ordained in 1904.

The newly ordained Dietz became active in the Ohio Central Verein and soon thereafter in its national organization. He was the first editor of the English section of the *Central Blatt and Social Justice,* in which he outlined an action plan for social reform. He held the position only from 1909 to 1910, when he left because of a disagreement over strategies for reform with Frederick Kenkel, social education director of the Verein's central bureau. Unlike Kenkel, Dietz insisted upon developing a program of specific actions to accompany study.

Dietz shifted his energy to founding the Militia of Christ for Social Service, an organization for Catholic members of the American Federation of Labor (AFL) and other trade unions. The Militia's principal objective was to establish the Roman Catholic church's support of economic and social reform on the laborer's behalf and to counter Protestant and, even more importantly, socialist influence on the trade unionist. Dietz's long-range goal was to coordinate efforts between the Militia and the AFL through a formal alliance, but labor leaders rejected the plan. Even without the AFL's organizational support, Dietz sought to establish a broad-based movement that would transform the American social order into a Christian one. The Militia did, at its strongest, enlist several hundred labor leaders but never fulfilled Dietz's aspirations for a nationwide network. Active branches existed for several years, primarily in midwestern cities like Milwaukee, Chicago, and St. Louis.

Dietz had at the time of the Militia's founding also involved himself in the American Federation of Catholic Societies (AFCS). He had, in fact, represented the AFCS at the 1910 AFL convention, where he and labor leaders formed the Militia. In 1912 Dietz became executive secretary of its newly founded Social Service Commission. The Militia's magazine, *Social Service,* which Dietz edited, became part of the AFCS *Bulletin* under the title "Newsletter."

Dietz had initially hoped to incorporate the Militia into the commission and thereby provide it with a national forum and badly needed financial backing. That hope never materialized. He also wanted the commission to implement a comprehensive plan of action on behalf of labor reform, but broad episcopal support was lacking. He did remain the *Newsletter* editor until 1918, when the AFCS withdrew support for the Social Service Commission. The National Catholic War Council (NCWC), founded in 1917, eventually subsumed the AFCS and, in 1919, became the National Catholic Welfare Conference. Msgr. John A. Ryan, Dietz's longtime friend, headed its Social Action Department, and Dietz remained only an observer.

Dietz had also committed his energy from 1915 until 1922 to founding a school dedicated to educating laymen and laywomen about Catholic as well as social and political principles for U.S. economic reform. From 1915 to 1917 the American Academy of Christian Democracy, located in Hot Springs, North Carolina, sought to educate its women students in Catholic social thought and the American political system. Dietz's fervent hope was that the graduates would transform their knowledge into action.

The school moved in 1917 to a Cincinnati hospital in hopes of attracting more students. Later that year, it moved to Ault Park, Ohio, to gain access to more faculty. Though the academy graduated some fifty women who took the name "White Cross Nurses," it constantly struggled to retain faculty and locate financial backing. In 1922 Dietz received enough AFL support to convert the academy into the American School of Labor, whose primary mission was to educate Catholics about Leo XIII's teachings about trade unionism. In that same year, however, an irreconcilable conflict arose with Cincinnati's Archbishop Henry Moeller, who ordered Dietz to leave his diocese. Evidence suggests that powerful Cincinnati businessmen convinced the archbishop of the labor priest's destabilizing influence.

Dietz returned to Milwaukee in 1922 and a quieter parish life. Here he founded St. Monica's parish in Whitefish Bay, Wisconsin, and he served that community until his death in 1947. At St. Monica's he organized the state's first parish credit union in 1928. Other parishes used his procedure in establishing their own credit unions.

Peter Dietz's story bears a certain poignancy. His influence consistently appears, as the ideas that he originated are realized by others much later. The Association of Catholic Trade Unionists traces its objectives back to Dietz's Militia for Christ. His attempt to coordinate Catholic social reform came to a fuller realization in the NCWC's Social Action Department under John Ryan. The official Catholic statement on economic reform that Dietz sought came in the Bishops' Program of Social Reconstruction of 1919 and much later in the U.S. Catholic bishops' pastoral letter *Economic Justice for All* (1986). His Academy of Christian Democracy and National Labor College anticipate the American Catholic labor institutes by twenty years. His tireless efforts as editor serve as an important witness to the need for a strong Catholic press to help shape Catholics' commitment to social reform. As Aaron Abell pointed out, "Just as John A. Ryan was the academician, so Peter E. Dietz was the organizer, of the American Catholic social movement." Though his aspirations always outstripped his resources, he clearly laid the groundwork for those who enlisted the church in the work of economic and social reform. The inscription on Dietz's gravestone, "Champion of Labor—Founder St. Monica's congregation," captures precisely his life's work.

See also ASSOCIATION OF CATHOLIC TRADE UNIONISTS; BISHOPS' PROGRAM OF SOCIAL RECONSTRUCTION OF 1919; CREDIT UNION; RYAN, JOHN AUGUSTINE.

Bibliography: M. Fox, *Peter E. Dietz, Labor Priest* (Notre Dame, Ind.: Univ. of Notre Dame Press, 1953). J. Mitchell, *Critical Voices in American Economic Thought* (New York: Paulist, 1989). A. Abell, "The Reception of Leo XIII's Labor Encyclical in America, 1891–1919," *The Review of Politics* 7 (October, 1945) 464–95.

SANDRA YOCUM MIZE

DIGNITATIS HUMANAE

From their beginnings Christians have differed over the freedom that religious belief confers and the freedom that ought to be granted to religious belief. This article will consider the freedom that ought to be granted to religious belief, as the Catholic church has debated the issue over the last century. It will first contrast Pius IX's and the Second Vatican Council's magisterial judgments on what is called civil religious freedom, then trace prudential and philosophical arguments that led from one to the other and close with a theological argument that is still in development.

Two Contrasting Positions

In his 1864 *Syllabus of Errors* Pope Pius IX condemned any suggestion that "the teaching of the Catholic Church is opposed to the well-being of society" (Syl 40.6). More particularly he condemned several secular propositions that tried to improve on earlier church teaching. He anathematized suggestions that "the Church ought to be separated from the State and the State from the Church" (55), that "it is no longer expedient that the Catholic Religion shall be held as the only religion of the State, to the exclusion of all other modes of Worship" (73), that non-Catholics in Catholic countries "shall enjoy the public exercise of their worship" (79), that "the Church has not the power of availing herself of force, or any direct or indirect temporal power" (24), that "every man is free to embrace and profess the religion he shall believe true, guided by the light of reason" (15), and that any of the above claims, if accepted and implemented, would benefit either the church or the state (76). Pius closed by discouraging any suggestion that "the Roman Pontiff can, and ought, to reconcile himself to, and agree with, progress, liberalism, and civilization as lately introduced" (80). This pithy rejection of modernity, including discussion within the church, merely echoed in method and substance earlier papal condemnations of freedoms of speech, press, assembly, and worship. The *Syllabus* condemned both prudential interpretations of the modern world (73, 76) and principled theories (40, 55, 79, 15, 24, 80) as contrary to Catholic teaching.

In 1965 the Second Vatican Council, in its Declaration on Religious Liberty, declared that "the human person has a right to religious freedom. This freedom means that all men are to be immune from coercion on the part of individuals or of social groups and of any human power, in such wise that in matters religious no one is to be forced to act in a manner contrary to his own beliefs. Nor is anyone to be restrained from acting in accordance with his own beliefs, whether privately or publicly, whether alone or in association with others, within due limits" (DH 2). The decree itself advanced two arguments in support of religious freedom. The first is a philosophical argument addressed to all peoples. The second is a theologically based argument directed to the believer.

The philosophical argument rests on an affirmation that is frankly admitted to have arisen first in the secular order, outside the church (1). It is an insight into the personal and political implications of human dignity. First, all people are under a God-given obligation to search after the truth and to embrace that truth once found. "Truth, however, is to be sought after in a manner proper to the dignity of the human person and his social nature" (3). This means that truth is to be sought publicly in conversation with others. A necessary condition for the exercise of this obligation is freedom from external coercion. Religious bodies have a right to internal discipline and external witness. However, "in spreading religious faith and in introducing religious practice, everyone ought at all times refrain from any manner of action which might seem to carry a hint of coercion" (4). The text further claims that religious freedom advances the secular good by developing the citizen's sense of social responsibility (6). Although the church also argues for its own religious freedom based on its privileged position as the true church of Christ, even on that basis it claims in the public forum only the same freedom that other religions rightly demand, that is, the unencumbered freedom to preach and witness (13).

Second, modern notions of human dignity include an understanding of the state as limited. The role of government is restricted to protection of rights, "promotion of general conditions favorable to the fostering of religious life," and protection of the equality of citizens before the law, never allowing a violation of that equality for religious reasons (6). Any limitations on religious expression are to be based on the narrow norm of public order: peace, the violation of rights, and public morality (7). That is, religious witness in word and act is to be limited only by the same norms that apply to all moral acts. Religious life is accorded as much freedom as possible and restrained as little as possible, and then only to avoid major disruptions of the civil order.

Dignitatis' theological argument begins with the admission that modern notions of religious freedom are not to be found in Scripture. What Scripture does offer is a deep grounding for human dignity compatible with, and supportive of, civil religious freedom (9). And this support is mutual. "Religious freedom makes no small contribution to the creation of an environment in which men can without hindrance be invited to Christian faith, and embrace it of their own free will, and profess it effectively in their whole life" (10). Further, *Dignitatis* confers on modern religious pluralism a type of theological permanence by appeal to Mt 13:30, 40-42, the parable of the wheat and the tares that will only be separated at the end-time. It then endorses the example of Jesus' and the early church's noncoercive advancement of the gospel, although it admits that "in the life of the People of God as it has made its pilgrim way through the vicissitudes of human history, there have at times appeared ways of acting which were less in accord with the spirit of the gospel and even opposed to it." "Nevertheless," *Dignitatis* concludes, "the doctrine of the Church that no one is to be coerced into faith has always stood firm" (12).

Notwithstanding this last doctrinal claim, debate has continued since *Dignitatis* on exactly what has changed in Catholic magisterial teaching. The following discussion traces three levels of development in the church's debate of religious freedom. The first concerns changing magisterial evaluations of modern public policies, such as establishment and disestablishment, and evaluations of the moral health of modern societies. The second level involves philosophical theories advanced in support of religious freedom. The third involves theological theories supporting religious freedom. On all three levels we find three distinct evaluative attitudes. One is the attitude of intolerance, a judgment that a given policy, society, or theory is evil, joined to a commitment to its suppression or defeat. The second attitude is tolerance, based again on an evaluation that the item is evil but without a commitment to its suppression. The last is the affirmation of the goodness of the policy, society, or theory joined with a commitment to its advancement. The *Syllabus* recommended political intolerance (a policy) and dogmatic intolerance (concerning theory). *Dignitatis* rejected both political intolerance and political tolerance, while it mitigated Pius IX's intolerance toward dogmas or theories.

Prudential Arguments

In 1865 the bishop of Orléans, Félix Dupanloup, dampened the *Syllabus'* reverberations by introducing a distinction between the "thesis" and the "hypothesis" of papal teaching. Papal teachings generally proclaim the ideal, the permanent, the thesis. Still, the ideal must be measured against the actual social situation to which the teachings are applied. Prudential examination of societies can allow Catholics to embrace policies that are less than ideal, the hypothesis—here the separation of church and state and general grants of religious freedom.

Leo XIII reiterated Pius' condemnations of religious and social freedom generally and, by systematizing them, in fact strengthened them (*Libertas*). Still, Leo's papacy was somewhat less embattled, signaled in part by his early encouragement of Thomistic studies. From Dupanloup's suggestion and in an atmosphere of renewed philosophical studies, three distinct types of prudential or context-sensitive arguments emerged.

The first turned on the fact that most modern societies are religiously pluralistic. Given that pluralism, the attempt to impose civil penalties on even small minority religious groups would most likely lead to civil war. For the sake of public peace as a natural good, it was argued, the higher-order good of the full implementation of Catholic doctrine, including curtailment of heretical expression, must be suspended. This argument was then expanded after the Second World War in the recognition that international reconstruction would require the full participation of all people of good will, including non-Christians. A just, albeit partial, reconstruction would only be possible if Catholics chose not to impose establishment and intolerance. These national and international peace arguments attempted to shunt the possibility of political intolerance into an apparently inconceivable future, tempering non-Catholic concerns over Catholic political intentions.

A second prudential argument appealed to the gradual but actual evolution of the state and of human society. While the church might rightly have taken over the state's coercive arm in periods of political anarchy, the maturation of political power after the Renaissance now requires that the church return control of direct coercion to the states. Similarly, although Catholic peoples in the midst of the Industrial Revolution were ignorant, impotent masses in need of paternal protection, modern education and the increasing ethical responsibilities of all persons demands an end to coerced protection.

Finally, a third context-sensitive argument relied on differing readings of the political threats posed by the last and the present centuries. Granted that at one point anti-Catholics conspired to suppress the church and rip its members from its protection, 20th-century forms of state totalitarianism have threatened to suppress not only the church but the entire Western affirmation of human dignity and the very notion of God. The post-Reformation compromise that allowed the prince to decide the faith of his subjects is no longer even minimally viable.

Common to these arguments were prudential, historically sensitive judgments on civil society that disallowed the imposition of the Catholic "ideal" for the foreseeable future. Catholics could remain dogmatically intolerant while being politically tolerant. That is, they could accept civil religious freedom as the lesser of two evils, the greater evil being political chaos or domination by totalitarian atheists.

Philosophical Arguments

Prudential arguments could justify Catholics who chose not to press the coercive option, including popes in the Papal States. Yet Catholics in pluralistic societies required more. The continuing religiously sanctioned suppression of non-Catholics in Spain, Portugal, and elsewhere left other Roman Catholics vulnerable to challenges from groups such as the American Nativists. From the other side, the Vatican responded to nonestablished Catholic pleas for a softening of Catholic theory with the claim that the prejudice they faced in their adherence to Catholic teaching was simply an aspect of living under the cross of Christ.

The social and pastoral inadequacy of this response led to the realization that

Catholic theory itself must provide a ground for embracing civil freedom as a positive good, not simply as the lesser of two evils. But how to change dogma or theory while still affirming the truth of the ordinary Catholic magisterium? Thomistic studies, with its recognition of distinct human realms—one based in nature and the other in the supernatural—and its added claim that the supernatural does not contradict or reverse the natural, offered a needed rational scalpel. This led to three distinct philosophical arguments and eventually became the heart of *Dignitatis.*

First, a reclaimed Thomistic understanding of civil law (the juridical order) allowed movement beyond Thomas' own recommendation that law be used against the willful heretic. Civil law properly governs only external acts. It is ineffective, inappropriate, and even dangerous when applied to the internal realm of belief. Also, civil law is an instrument of the temporal, not the supernatural, order. As an instrument of the passing order, no specific institutionalization of church-state relations can ever claim to be ideal, noncontingent, or thesis. Similarly, as an instrument of the temporal order, the use of civil law cannot be considered a permanent right of the church.

Second, philosophical definitions of the state were judged to have legitimately changed. As temporal realities, the state and philosophies of the state could change without challenging the permanence of Catholic theological principles. The 19th-century papal arguments against religious freedom were unavoidably interwoven with philosophical theories of the state that are now clearly archaic. Those theories that positioned the state simply as an extension of the church may have been prudentially adequate responses to politically anarchic worlds. However, they now clearly violate a deeper Catholic understanding of autonomy proper to the natural and supernatural orders. Again, theories of the state as the paternalistic preserve of elites are now incompatible with modern notions of human dignity. Modern theories of the limited competence of the state in moral matters and of its complete lack of competence in religious matters (DH 3), it was argued, could be accepted as insights legitimately developed in the secular order, even if at times in conflict with the church.

Finally, again in the temporal order, a complex notion of human dignity has replaced evaluations of the masses as ignorant and passive. This new evaluation has exposed a deeper implication of a Thomistic theory, namely, that the moral authority that grounds the state rests ultimately with the people, not with civil or religious elites. Society, as distinct from the state, now is affirmed as the center of moral deliberation and determination. This argument of the rightful emergence of the people as society's moral center linked the notions of the limited state and the general human obligation to seek the truth. It became the heart of *Dignitatis'* philosophical justification of civil religious freedom.

Dignitatis left those who claim that both papal policies and theories are not open to reversal, such as Archbishop Levfebre, little choice but to reject the council as heretical. Similarly, postconciliar attempts to reconcile the philosophical claims of the *Syllabus* and *Dignitatis* have generally eviscerated *Dignitatis'* strong affirmation of civil religious freedom. Catholic evaluations of specific institutions and its theories of both civil law and political institutions did indeed shift. The council moved beyond philosophical intolerance, even beyond philosophical tolerance, to an affirmation that better philosophical insight first developed beyond its borders. But what of theological dogmatic intolerance, the claim that 19th-century pontiffs temporally and substantively held the theological high ground against all challengers?

The Lingering Theological Argument

As mentioned above, *Dignitatis* simply claimed that the church's theological notion of human dignity is compatible with secular civil freedom and asserted by scriptural appeal the permanence of pluralism and the inappropriate religious use of coercion. It left untouched the claim that valid, salvific theological (and not just moral) insight might arise beyond the church's clearly identified magisterial authority. During and after the council some supporters of religious freedom called for a more thorough grounding of *Dignitatis'* affirmation in theological terms, both to give it a stronger and more permanent support and for the implications that civil freedom might have for the internal life of the church. Confusion over the claim for dogmatic theological intolerance, however, blocked and continues to block the development of those arguments.

The difficulty revolves around the truth status of magisterial theological claims considered over time, parallel to *Dignitatis'* recognition of the temporal lag between morally correct anthropological and political philosophies and the church's acceptance of them. Can correct theological insight first arise outside the Roman church, even in temporary opposition to the church? An affirmative answer appears to jeopardize three related theological claims: first, that belief in Jesus Christ is necessary for salvation; second, that Christ is present to his people in and through the church; and, third, that the Lord's promise to be with his people is actualized in the infallible teaching of the church. While some rejections of political and dogmatic tolerance, much less freedom, might express Catholic jingoism or bias, a more pressing concern is the religious confession of God's ongoing presence within contemporary society. The council did affirm not only that the salvation of non-Catholics was possible, but even that non-Catholic churches aid in salvation. Does that entail simply a dogmatic tolerance at each moment of Catholic history—a recognition that non-Catholics possess salvific truth as only incomplete reflections of what the Roman church already possesses? Or does it also mandate a theological equivalent of *Dignitatis'* philosophical argument, in this case that theological insight can and does arise outside magisterial boundaries and that the magisterium must be attentive to those developments?

Since the council the magisterium has deepened its commitment to religious freedom as an immunity. As Achille Mestre has argued, Vatican participation in the formation and implementation of the Helsinki accords and its encouragement of the removal of civil penalties for religious belief in countries such as Spain has institutionally bound the church to the fate of civil religious freedom. Further, the papacy and large sectors of the church have settled into the conviction that theology is not only to motivate social transformation but even is to supply in varying degrees the shape that political and cultural transformations are to assume. Likewise much of *Dignitatis'* theory of the state has taken a familiar position within Catholic teaching (although the church's appropriation of *Dignitatis'* notion of civil law is still spotty).

What, however, of theological insight and empowering will, arising outside the magisterium, as an agent in time of magisterial development? Both the theories of dogmatic theological intolerance and of a cosmos-wide enabling theological freedom can preserve the affirmation that Christ continues with and directs God's people. Both can preserve, if viewed over time, the claim of infallibility. Each, however, suggests a distinct manner for resolving disagreement and conflict. *Dignitatis* has left us an affirmation of a civil institution, but even more, with a problem of the church's ongoing affirmation of God's presence.

See also FREEDOM; MAGISTERIUM; MURRAY, JOHN COURTNEY; PERSON, DIGNITY OF; PLURALISM; RELIGIOUS FREEDOM.

Bibliography: J. Murray, *Religious Liberty: Catholic Struggles with Pluralism,* ed. J. L. Hooper (Louisville, Ky.: Westminster/John Knox, 1993). J. Dionne, "The Religious Liberty Issue," in *The Papacy and the Church: A Study of Praxis and Reception in Ecumenical Perspective* (New York: Philosophical Library, 1987). P. Huizing, "Religious Freedom: A Bibliographical Survey," trans. T. Westow, *Religious Freedom: Canon Law* Concilium 18 (New York: Paulist, 1966). A. Mestre, "L'Eglise catholique et la liberté relieuse depuis 1975," *Recherches de Science Religieuse* 78 (Janvier-Mars, 1990) 73–96. R. Regan, *Conflict and Consensus: Religious Freedom and the Second Vatican Council* (New York: Macmillan, 1967). D. Wolf, *Toward Consensus: Catholic and Protestant Interpretations of Church and State* (New York: Doubleday, 1968).

J. LEON HOOPER, S.J.

DISABILITIES, PERSONS WITH

The Scriptures of both Judaism and Christianity are marked by a salient concern for persons with disabilities. Job presents "justice" as the foundational ideal of Hebrew spirituality. The first mandate of this virtue is to be "eyes to the blind and feet to the lame" (Job 29:15). The Torah shows specific concern for those with disabilities (Lev 19:14; Deut 27:18). Jeremiah lists "the blind and lame" first among those of the remnant of Israel that will be saved (Jer 31:8).

Prominent in the Jesus movement were "the lame, blind, dumb, and crippled, and many other sufferers" (Mt 15:30). Acts notes the presence of "many paralyzed and crippled folk" (Acts 8:7). The delegates of John the Baptist were told of Jesus' care for the "blind," the "lame," the "lepers," and the "deaf" as a mark of the authenticity of his mission (Mt 11:5). There was also nothing stinting about the biblical concern for disabled persons. When you were having a party, you should invite them "and so find happiness" (Lk 14:13).

Ideals are always roughly born and subject to contrary headwinds. Negative myths regarding persons with impairments are present in both Jewish and Christian biblical sources. Persons with disabilities are forbidden to make the offerings in the temple (Lev 21:18), and even handicapped animals are, symbolically, unsuitable for offerings to the Lord (Deut 15:21). Jesus was confronted with the idea that inherited disabilities were due to the sins of parents, an idea that he rejected (Jn 9:1–3). For this reason, the message was insistently pressed that those who are naturally and economically deprived enjoy a position of privileged affection with God and with all who love justice.

This accent on disabled people flowed directly from the basic theological anthropology of Judaism and Christianity. All persons (and not just kings) were born in "the image of God" (Gen 1:26), and therefore, all persons are created equal, a revolutionary idea that, as Elain Pagels says, "Aristotle, among others, would have considered . . . absurd" (*Adam, Eve, and the Serpent,* p. xx, Random House, 1988). An immediate application of this was made to those with disabilities; they too were sacraments of encounter with the mystery of God. They too shared in and reflected God's infinite lovability. All of evolution had relied on the need to identify with the powerful in order to survive. Judaism and Christianity pioneered a cultural revolution, saying that it is only by identifying with the weak, the poor, and the disabled that we can survive. Justice entails precisely this fundamental option for the dispossessed, whatever the reason for their plight. In varying ways, what this leitmotif of biblical theology offered was in Thomas Ogletree's words "an altogether different basis for securing human life, dignity, worth, and wholeness" (*Hospitality to the Stranger,* p. 148, n. 13, Fortress, 1985). Persons are valued not for transient qualities of health or prestige but as images of infinite Goodness. The option for the disabled is thus not an extraneous piety in Judaism and Christianity but an essential corollary of the moral core of these religions.

Who Are Those with Disabilities?

In terms of modern ethics "disability" refers to those who suffer a physical or mental impairment that is not easily corrigible. Visual and hearing problems that are remediable do not constitute a disability in the strict sense. Disabling problems associated with aging, however, are included in the concept of disability. Thus the category is a large one, increasing in size with extensions of longevity in the technologically developed world and with physical and mental impairments due to nutritional deprivation in poverty zones in the First and Second Worlds as well as in the Third World. Given the widespread polluting of the planet and its atmosphere, discussion of the rights of persons with disabilities extends into the future in a way that it could not do in the past. We must now think of the rights of those who, because of our malfeasance, will be born into a poisonous and disabling world. Discussion of the rights of persons with disabilities involves not only individual (or commutative) justice but primarily social and distributive justice.

What Are Rights?

The term "right" denotes a moral claim that we can make on others. There are two sources of rights, (1) earned entitlements and contracts and (2) essential needs. The first source is stressed in cultures infected with possessive individualism; the second is stressed in the biblical tradition (see G. Theissen, *Biblical Faith: An Evolutionary Approach,* Fortress, 1985). Both of these sources are intermediary and not ultimate. The ultimate source of rights is the worth of the individual person. We honor contracts with people and we respect their earned entitlements and essential needs because they are worth such fidelity. Their worth grounds this right. (On rights see Daniel C. Maguire, *A Case for Affirmative Action*, Dubuque, Shepherd Inc., 1992.)

The worth of persons, then, means that they deserve in strictest justice and not out of optional charity what they essentially need. Humanity is a shared glory, and we deny others their share if we deny them what they essentially need; however, no one has a justice claim to have frivolous needs met. If we deny persons their essential needs, those things they need to survive and thrive as persons, we implicitly deny their humanity. If persons are seen as not worth what they essentially need, they would be without rights. The logical implications of such a denial are murderous.

Rights are either *economic* or *political.* Economic rights respond to essential needs such as food, housing, medical care, and the opportunity to work. Political rights involve such activities as voting, social organization, and freedom of expression. Neither economic nor political rights are limited to the hale and well. Obviously, persons with mental disabilities will have limited opportunity to exercise political rights, but social and distributive justice require that political and economic arrangements favor disabled persons, especially those who are politically disenfranchised by their disability.

The history of morals indicates that we are slow to acknowledge rights generated by essential needs. Regarding those with disabilities, we have only recently begun to meet their basic need to have access to public facilities, work opportunities, and special educational assistance. Technology requires perfectionism and intolerance of defect. This impatience easily transfers to persons with disabilities and reinforces exclusionary practices. Such practices are not only unjust to those persons but also attack the common good by ostracizing talented people who often have compensatorily enhanced abilities in certain areas precisely because of their handicaps.

Clearly, the persons with mental disabilities are the most exquisite challenge to justice. First, we must beware of classifying as "retarded" those who are merely socially and educationally deprived. Second, those who do have genuine mental impairment have full human rights to a joyful and peaceful existence. Crypto-utilitarian arguments for helping them so that their care will be more cost effective for society are fallacious and destined to fail. Those who cannot be helped to live semi-independent and cost-effective lives still have full human rights and dignity. Cost-reduction benefits to society are not the grounding of those rights. Our unique preciousness as persons is not related to our efficiency or economic productivity.

Third, mentally disabled persons may be capable of marriage and in some cases of having children; however, the supreme art of respectful dissuasion may be needed to discourage reproduction when parenting is not practicable, even with the social support and ongoing counseling that these persons deserve in strict justice.

Public policy should give special attention and benefits to the families with members who have a disability. These families are meeting unique economic and emotional challenges and a just polity would make tax allowances and special services available to them.

See also AGED, CARE OF; BEATITUDES; HEALTH CARE; HUMAN RIGHTS; MENTAL HEALTH, ETHICAL ISSUES IN; PERSON, DIGNITY OF; POOR, PREFERENTIAL OPTION FOR.

Bibliography: M. Maguire, "Parenting and Tragedy," *New Catholic World* 99, no. 4 (February, 1982) pp. 109–111. D. Maguire, *The Moral Core of Judaism and Christianity: Reclaiming the Revolution* (Minneapolis: Fortress, 1993).

DANIEL C. MAGUIRE

DISARMAMENT

1. In Catholic social ethics disarmament represents both a global objective in international politics and an important instrument of security policy. The global objective is—as in many international political declarations—general and complete disarmament. In practice, however (aside from voluntary unilateral measures or those taken in accordance with peace treaties), disarmament means that two or more states strive for legally regulated partial reductions of armaments. During the last few years of waning East-West tensions, disarmament efforts have proceeded at an unexpectedly rapid pace.

Disarmament is closely related to arms control, the goal of which is the international regulation of modernization in military power. However, arms control has a wide range of means at its disposal in addition to arms reduction. Both arms control and disarmament seek not to reduce the defensive posture of states but to enhance peace, security, and stability. Disarmament seeks to establish maximal security at the lowest possible level of armament. Stability is the criterion for the overall shape of military power (strategic stability as a goal for disarmament) as well as for its composition by specific weapon systems. For example, weapons that require quick military decisions in political crises should be deployed as little as possible, for they may intensify the crisis (crisis stability).

In a climate of mistrust and political animosity, disarmament requires enforcement. All contracting parties must feel certain that the agreement will be kept. For this reason verification becomes crucial to disarmament policies. However, reaching agreements on specific verification procedures (particularly on-site inspections) is problematic, as it requires granting states access to each other's military installations.

2. For the most part, arms-control proposals have been introduced at a multilateral level. Treaties concerning the peaceful use of certain geographical regions (e.g., Antarctic continent in 1959; outer space in 1967) or the prohibition of the emplacement of nuclear weapons and other weapons of mass destruction on the seabed (Seabed Treaty, 1971) fall into this category. Certain nuclear testing procedures have been prohibited by the Limited Test

Ban Treaty (1963). Proliferation of nuclear weapons runs counter to the 1968 Non-Proliferation Treaty.

Furthermore, the United States and the Soviet Union and now the Russian Federation and other successor states of the Soviet Union have entered into several bilateral agreements on arms control: SALT, the ABM Treaty, and START I and II (1991–93). These treaties limit and reduce strategic weapons and antiballistic missile systems. The INF Treaty of December 1987 represents a breakthrough in that it became the first genuine disarmament agreement. The United States and the Soviet Union agreed to dismantle all intermediate-range missiles. START now envisages the drastic reduction of strategic nuclear potential. Another success is the Treaty on Conventional Forces in Europe (CFE, 1990–92). This treaty drastically reduces the number of tanks, armored vehicles, artillery systems, combat aircraft, and combat helicopters deployed between the Atlantic Ocean and the Ural Mountains. The agreement aims to eliminate the potential for surprise attacks and large-scale offenses through arms reduction and transparency measures.

In addition, it also envisages limiting conventional forces personnel levels in Europe. The "Convention on the prohibition of the development, production, stockpiling, and use of chemical weapons and on their destruction" (1992) eliminates an entire category of weapons of mass destruction. Disarmament policy currently faces the following challenges: (1) The START treaties must be ratified and implemented. Following the break-up of the Soviet Union, the USA now has four treaty partners: Russia, Belarus, Kazakhstan, and the Ukraine. (2) The Convention on chemical weapons must come into effect and be implemented. (3) The CFE treaty has come into force and must now be implemented. (4) Preventing the spread of weapons of mass destruction has become the most important issue. Many states are demanding that the NPT be extended for an unlimited period of time at the next review conference (1995). (5) States unable to fulfill their disarmament obligations require disarmament assistance. This has become an important area of disarmament policy.

3. Catholic social thought takes a twofold approach to disarmament. First, it views disarmament as a means of war prevention. In this case, it is assumed that an uncontrolled arms race—especially in weapons of mass destruction—has a destabilizing effect and that "the resulting so-called equilibrium is in fact no reliable and genuine peace" (*Gaudium et spes* 81). Disarmament is the instrument for reversing the arms race, which could otherwise lead to war. The arms race currently takes place under conditions of (nuclear) deterrence, the implications of which (e.g., competing theories of deterrence and nuclear targeting) draw increasing attention from Catholic social ethics. Disarmament is regarded to be a way to reduce the threat of war inherent in deterrence policy and even a way out of deterrence itself.

In addition, Catholic social ethics advocates disarmament as a demand of justice. The arms race is an unacceptable waste of resources. "The arms race is one of the most horrible wounds on mankind; it heaps unbearable suffering upon the poor (GS 81). For this reason Vatican II, the popes, and the bishops repeatedly have insisted that "disarmament should begin, not with unilateral efforts but based on mutual, contractually measured steps with veritable and effective guarantees" (82). They explicitly agreed to the form of a treaty and to agreed measures of verification.

The church freely acknowledges that disarmament inevitably encounters substantial obstacles in a climate of mistrust. After all, military armament is the expression of fundamental antagonism. In fact, the development of arms control and disarmament shows that breakthroughs could only be achieved where common interests supersede this antagonism. Catholic ethics has repeatedly emphasized the importance of confidence-building measures that in turn require efficient institutions for international cooperation and, indeed, an entirely new way of thinking about peace.

4. Pope Pius XII had already thought it necessary "to limit—under efficient control—armaments" (1957 Christmas address). Pope John XXIII wrote in his encyclical *Pacem in terris* that "justice, good sense, and respect for the dignity of mankind beg for an end to the arms race; for simultaneous arms reduction of both sides" (PT 112). Pope Paul VI referred repeatedly to disarmament issues. In his address to the United Nations first special session on disarmament (1978), he said that "it would be a tragic illusion to believe that the arms race might continue indefinitely without causing a catastrophe." Pope John Paul II underlined before the United Nations second disarmament session (1982) that deterrence could only be acceptable ethically if it were a step on the way toward a progressive disarmament.

In the early 1980s the Catholic bishops of the United States received worldwide attention for their pastoral letter *The Challenge of Peace.* The letter attempted to concretely respond to the peace teaching of the church and especially of Vatican II. Writing in an environment of the new search for military strength, which they regarded as an impetus for the arms race, the American bishops addressed the questions of nuclear deterrence and modern warfare. They pleaded for numerous concrete steps toward arms control and disarmament: for example, "support for negotiated bilateral deep cuts in the arsenals of both superpowers" and "negotiations for a comprehensive test ban treaty." According to the bishops, the Non-Proliferation Treaty of 1968 needs more effective implementation. They even call for "a willingness for each side to take some first steps" to make disarmament possible. *The Challenge of Peace* has both advanced and made more specific Catholic postwar peace ethics. The call for disarmament is a significant part of it.

In sum, church teaching considers disarmament one of the key political instruments for achieving stability of peace and preventing war. The positive effects would be even more significant if disarmament could allow redistribution of resources—from national defense to the development of poor countries.

The Challenge of Peace as well as various peace addresses of other episcopal conferences—in particular, "Out of Justice, Peace," delivered by the German bishops in 1983—prove that disarmament ultimately has a theological dimension: Christians believe in God, who through Jesus Christ promised peace to the entire creation. By their actions, Christians want to prove their belief in a peaceful future. It is for this reason that they take all possible steps to justice as well as to overcome the threat and use of violence between individuals and among peoples. Thus disarmament is a challenge growing out of Christian faith.

See also ARMS RACE; DETERRENCE; JOHN XXIII; PACEM IN TERRIS; PAUL VI; PEACE; PIUS XII; WAR.

HANS LANGENDÖRFER, S.J.

DISCIPLESHIP

Possibly no other theme in the Christian tradition is more prominent than that of discipleship. Though the term is certainly current in the ancient world, Jesus clearly gives it a new meaning. In one way, it is possible to summarize the substance of Christian life as nothing else than the effort to make discipleship one's whole way of life.

The Biblical Background

Disciple (*talmîd*) is nearly absent from the OT, and the established LXX tradition does not use the Greek equivalent (*mathētēs*) at all. The reason the term is lacking in these texts is that the ideal was not to attach oneself to a human master but to be a disciple only of God. After the return from exile, however, those who were responsible for the teaching of the Law were considered to be masters, and their personal authority was recognized by their followers. Unlike the classical Greek world and Hellenism, this relation between master and pupil was essentially formal.

In the NT the term for disciple (*mathētēs*) is common in both the Gospels and Acts. Other than a few references to the disciples of Moses (Jn 9:28), of John the Baptist (e.g., Mk 22:16), and of the Pharisees (e.g., Mt 22:16), all references to discipleship are limited to those who have accepted Jesus as their master. Unlike the students of the rabbis who searched for a master and then had to prove their qualifications for study before being accepted by the teacher, the disciples of Jesus are sought out and called by Jesus himself. "Come, follow me!" is Jesus' cry, and "they immediately abandoned their nets and followed him" (Mk 1:17-18). Jesus calls his "students" together without any regard for their educational background or qualifications. Not only does he call Levi the tax collector to be a disciple, but Jesus also calls women who served him and who later remained with him until the end. Unlike the rabbis who welcomed their students so long as they were ready to accept what the rabbis had to say, Jesus welcomes his disciples on the basis of their faith in who he is. Thus faith is the central factor in the relation between Jesus and his disciples, not the knowledge and authority of the teacher. For his disciples, then, Jesus is the Lord and not just a teacher.

To be a disciple of Jesus is always characterized in the NT as a witness and an attachment to the person of Jesus. To follow him is to cut all ties with the past (Lk 5:11), to give up one's family (Lk 14:26), and to take up the cross and share in the very destiny of the master (Mk 8:34). They are to associate with the poor, the sick, the outcast, and the disabled (Lk 4:18-19), and they are to love even their enemies (Lk 6:27-28). By following Jesus and by conforming their lives to his teachings, the disciples already begin to participate in the coming new age that must be lived out under the conditions of the old. Finally, the call to become disciples does not imply that those who follow are to remain at the side of Jesus; rather, they are sent out to preach the good news of the coming reign of God to all people.

Papal, Conciliar, and U.S. Episcopal Documents

Only a few specific references to the theme of discipleship occur in these documents prior to Vatican II. There are probably two reasons why such a paucity of passages exists. First, after the Council of Trent in the 16th century the manuals of doctrinal and moral theology became the standard texts in Catholic theology. The theologians who wrote and revised these manuals until the advent of Vatican II divided up the Christian life in their discussions, and many of the important themes pertaining to the moral life were relegated to either doctrinal or spiritual theology. Whenever discipleship was treated in these books, however, the emphasis was placed on obedience to Christ and to his vicars on earth. Second, in the century before Vatican II the social teaching of the church used two principal images to express the nature of the Christian life: the image of the shepherd and the passive flock and the image of an ordered cosmos, which so predominated in St. Thomas Aquinas' theology in the 13th century. Consequently, the descriptions of discipleship that characterized the NT biblical tradition are greatly lacking in these documents.

In the documents of Vatican II and in the subsequent social documents written by both the popes and the U.S. episcopal conference, one again finds frequent references to discipleship. No doubt the council's insistence on the reintegration of doctrinal, moral, and spiritual theology and its demand that theology be nourished by Scripture certainly contributed to a new emphasis on the following of Jesus (*Optatam totius* 16).

The primary image for understanding the Christian life and the church at Vatican II was that of a journey or pilgrimage (*Lumen gentium* 8). This image fits well with many of the NT themes used to describe discipleship to Jesus. The emphases on holiness (LG 10, 42), being sent to preach the good news (17), being called by God (40), and witnessing to the person of Jesus through acts of charity and humility (42) once again become important qualities of discipleship. Three other themes are also frequently used in conjunction with discipleship in these documents. First, because the Christian life is construed as a journey, discipleship is repeatedly described in terms of conversion—a lifelong attempt to withdraw from sin and to commit oneself to Jesus (e.g., the NCCB documents *To Live in Christ Jesus* and *The Challenge of Peace* 47–54). Second, a distinguishing mark of discipleship is seen as commitment to solidarity with the poor (*Sollicitudo rei socialis* 40). Finally, the NT motif of discipleship as a community of believers seeking to commit themselves to the following of Jesus in society is a dominant subject in several of these documents (e.g., *Redemptor hominis* 86–87; CP 52–54).

Recent Catholic Theology

Since Vatican II several theologians have attempted to make discipleship a central theme for integrating all of theology. They have argued that responding to the call of Jesus is the first meaningful and faithful act of the Christian life. Consequently they take the disciple of Jesus in the community of disciples as the starting point, subject, and goal of all theological reflection. In this way, discipleship has become one crucial way to develop a dialogue between faith and culture, including politics and economics.

Several feminist theologians have recently recovered the biblical roots of discipleship in their attempts to argue for a discipleship of equals in society and in the church. They rely heavily on the text in Gal 3:28 where Paul claims that there is no distinction between race, class, and gender in the community of disciples. In addition, they rely on the Synoptic tradition, in which discipleship to Jesus replaces old family ties and traditional family structures and creates a new community or family of equals (Mk 3:31-35).

See also COMMUNITY; FEMINISM AND CATHOLIC SOCIAL THOUGHT; METHODOLOGY, MORAL; MORAL LIFE, CHRISTIAN; POOR, PREFERENTIAL OPTION FOR; SIN; SOLIDARITY; THOMAS AQUINAS, CONTRIBUTION OF.

Bibliography: E. Fiorenza, "The Biblical Roots for the Discipleship of Equals," *Journal of Pastoral Counseling* 14 (1979) 7–15. E. McDonagh, *The Making of Disciples: Tasks of Moral Theology* (Wilmington, Del.: Glazier, 1982). "Mathētēs," in *Theological Dictionary of the New Testament,* vol. 4, G. Kittel, ed. (Grand Rapids: Eerdmans, 1967).

JAMES J. WALTER

DIVORCE

The Judeo-Christian Tradition

Divorce was and is permitted in the Jewish tradition, but stable marriage is aspired to and favored. "I hate divorce, says Yahweh, God of Israel" (Mal 2:16). In Jesus' time there were two contesting schools of thought. The school of Shammah held a strict view in which a man could not divorce his wife unless she had done something really infamous. The school of Hillel took the view that any slight misdemeanor on the part of the wife, such as not cooking the food properly, gave the husband an excuse for divorce.

It was against this background that Jesus was questioned by the Pharisees. His answer was definite and appealed to the nature of marriage as it was in the beginning.

"Some Pharisees approached him and asked 'Is it lawful for man to divorce his wife?' They were putting him to the test. He answered them, 'What did Moses command you?' They replied, 'Moses allowed us to draw up a writ of dismissal in cases of divorce.' Then Jesus said to them, 'It was because you were so hard hearted that he wrote this commandment for you. But from the beginning of creation he made them male and female. This is why a man leaves his father and mother, and the two become one flesh. They are no longer two, therefore, but one flesh. So then, what God has united, human beings must not divide'" (Mk 10:2-9). This firm and unequivocal reply set an ideal for Christianity that has been preserved ever since. Both in the Second Vatican Council and John Paul II's apostolic exhortation *Familiaris consortio* there are warnings against divorce.

Recent History of Divorce

This clear antidivorce position of Christianity has come under strain in the last thirty years. Right up to the 19th century matrimonial matters remained in the hands of the church, but thereafter the civil courts began to grant divorce. Initially the numbers were small. They increased after the two world wars but then settled down.

There was, however, a uniform rise in Western societies after 1960, and in the last thirty years there have been unprecedented increases in divorce. I shall quote figures for the United States and Britain, two of the three leaders in the divorce tables.

TABLE I
Divorce Rate per 1,000 married women by age
United States between 1960 and 1984

Age	1960	1965	1970	1975	1980	1984
Total	9	11	15	21	22	21
Under 20	34	30	28	41	46	53
20–24	23	26	35	44	52	51
25–29	14	18	27	40	43	40
30–34	11	13	20	29	34	32
35–44	9	10	14	20	23	22
45–54	5	6	8	10	10	11
55–64	2	3	3	4	4	4
65 and over	1	1	1	2	2	2

In this table the massive increase in the twenty-five years from 1960 is shown particularly for marriages under age 20, which we shall see are particularly vulnerable (Glick and Lin, p. 737). More specifically, a study in 1987 (Norton and Moorman, p. 3) indicates that women who were married between the ages of 25 and 29 had an ultimate likelihood of divorce of 53.6%; age 35–39, 55.5%; and age 45–49, 36.4%. Thus an approximate figure for divorce in the United States is one in every two marriages.

In table II divorce in the European Community is shown for the years 1981 and 1986 (Social Trends, 1989, Central Statistical Office, HMSO).

TABLE II
Divorce per 1,000 existing marriages

	1981	1986
United Kingdom	11.9	12.9
Belgium	6.1	7.3
Denmark	12.1	12.8
France	6.8	8.5
Germany (Fed. Rep.)	7.2	8.3
Greece	2.5	3.0
Irish Republic	0	0
Italy	0.9	1.1
Luxembourg	5.9	7.5
Netherlands	8.3	8.7
Portugal	2.8	
Spain	1.1	

It will be seen that all countries show a rise from 1981 to 1986. In fact, the leading three countries for divorce in the world were the United States, the USSR, and the United Kingdom. In the United Kingdom the percentage of marriages that were expected to be dissolved was 37%.

Reasons for Divorce

Such high divorce rates are a cause of great concern, and there is much speculation regarding the reasons. The easiest explanation is to consider the 1960s a period of acute sexual permissiveness, which destabilized family life. Here the cause is given as moral instability, but while the flight from religion undoubtedly plays a role in divorce, the cause for such a steep rise is much more complicated. Social scientists have been arguing the reasons and have put forward three propositions, namely, general, specific, and practical considerations.

General reasons. Students of marriage are agreed that the nature of marriage is changing drastically. A generation or two ago the instrumental theory of marriage was being offered (Parsons and Bales). Under this theory the husband was the head of the family, the breadwinner, the person who dealt with the outside world on behalf of the family, while the woman was the childbearer, child-rearer, housekeeper, and catalyst of affection. Provided the couple observed these social obligations and avoided adultery, then the marriage was considered to be sound.

In the last thirty years this picture of marriage has been rapidly disappearing. Women's emancipation has assumed major proportions, and the hierarchical structure of the husband-wife relationship has changed into an egalitarian one. Women are now working in large numbers and have gained economic independence. Even more important, the emphasis within marriage has shifted from fulfillment of roles to emotional and sexual satisfaction. Thus in a space of a quarter century there are historic changes affecting marriage and the family that have yet to be understood, absorbed, and interpreted. Above all, the education and support for marriage along these new lines has yet to be achieved, and the gap between change and education for change has been filled by divorce. Another feature of women's emancipation is that wives are no longer prepared to put up with behavior by their husbands that would have been acceptable two or three generations ago. Thus the degree of aggression, violence, and alcoholism that is tolerated has been reduced.

Specific reasons. Within the context of these major general changes, social scientists have shown that divorce is specifically associated with youthful marriages under the age of twenty, premarital pregnancy, limited education, and mixed marriages by religion, race, social class, and economic and educational background. The lower the socioeconomic position the higher the divorce rate.

Practical considerations. The need for couples to separate from their parents emotionally so as to avoid interference is vital. Furthermore, they have to negotiate successfully the task of running the home, managing money, and developing leisure and work patterns, particularly when both spouses are working.

Emotionally they have to cope with expressing feelings, showing affection, negotiating conflict, and fulfilling each other sexually. Expressing feelings has become a major component of contemporary marriage. Wives have generally been better at affectivity than husbands, and this may present a conflict. Sexuality has assumed a much greater importance than as a biological force for procreation. Sexual fulfillment is vital for a satisfactory marriage. Neither the expression of affection nor sexual satisfaction can be ignored.

All these issues are important in the early years of marriage, but with the passage of time couples may change socially, emotionally, and sexually and begin to become alienated. Over time this alienation may bring the marriage to an end, as the couple share little in common with the passing of years. In the past this did not matter so long as they adhered to their social roles. Now it is the quality of the relationship that matters, and such an estrangement may bring the marriage to an end. The reasons for marital breakdown are now vast, and couples have to work very hard to preserve the quality of their relationship in changing circumstances.

Consequences of Divorce

In the 1960s, when divorce really began to escalate, the main thrust of public opinion was the urgent need for couples not to be locked in unsatisfactory marriages. Great importance was attached to the need for spouses to be freed from the shackles of a marriage that did not work, and so the laws were changed to make divorce easy. Little thought was given to the consequences of divorce.

Thirty years later we have come to see that the consequences are severe and a high price has to be paid. The conflict of divorce is stressful and has adverse physical and emotional reactions. Doctors and pastors often see the depressions, suicidal attempts, even suicides, that are associated with divorce. There is a private agony, particularly when one spouse is still in love with the partner and cannot accept his or her departure. There is economic deterioration as single parents, usually women, cope with their new situation.

Above all, there are adverse consequences for the children. Longitudinal studies in the United States and Britain have shown that children from divorced families have a higher incidence of poor performance at school, antisocial behavior, and emotional disturbance at home and school. Children of divorce who have been followed up in adult life show they are academically and economically disadvantaged, their health suffers, their social performance is poor, and when they marry they have a higher rate of divorce themselves, thus continuing in a vicious cycle. Perhaps of all the moral issues that Christianity faces, divorce stands out as the most carefully studied, showing that the religious insights of its damage are supported by the social and psychological studies.

Then there are the consequences of second marriages. The majority of divorcees remarry, but the evidence is that second marriages are even more prone to breakdown than first ones. There is also evidence that coping with stepchildren in the new family is particularly difficult.

Prevention

Marriage and the family are not only the units that form society, whose stability is of the utmost importance, but they are also the nurture ground of love, which is central to Christian faith. Divorce presents a particular challenge to the Christian community, and we need to answer it effectively.

In order to do so it is important to remember that Christian marriage is first and foremost a secular reality that becomes a divine mystery. The divine mystery depends on understanding and appreciating accurately the secular reality. It is no good longing for the return to a past when the divorce rate was much lower. We have to appreciate that marriage is changing, and it is this changed reality that has to become the object of the articulation of Christian virtues.

Since the Second Vatican Council, marriage is seen as a "community of love," and this change from a legal to an affective approach coincides with the secular reality, which is moving toward marriage as a loving reality that is lived in the egalitarian relationship between the spouses, the support that husbands must give to the realization of the potential of their wives, and the emphasis that couples are putting on affectionate and sexual fulfillment. A whole new world is emerging in which the gospel values of commitment, faithfulness, forgiveness, and love have to be realized. Christian meaning has to be built on the current secular reality of marriage. Of course, marriage between Christians is a sacrament imbued with grace, but this grace has to work on the human values pursued by the couple.

So what can Christianity offer to the rest of the world? First, it is necessary for the church to affirm and reaffirm the importance of marriage and family life. Second, it has to ensure that children are prepared for personal relationships of love, which would include courses of preparation for marriage. Above all, the wedding must not be seen as the conclusion but the beginning of the church's involvement with the married. After the wedding couples need to be supported, particularly in the early years of marriage, which are so vital to the stability of marriage. This support needs to take a variety of forms, from discussion groups through preparation for baptism, First Communion, and confirmation, with the background awareness for the couples of the relationship between their growth in marriage and their growing responsibility toward their children. Finally, we need a liturgy for marriage in which couples are reminded at regular intervals of the link between their marriage as a secular reality and a divine mystery.

But all this work on prevention must be accompanied by a theology of marriage in which couples are helped to see that their minute-to-minute relationship with each other socially, emotionally, and sexually is their living expression of love, which is the moment-to-moment encounter with God. They are truly a "domestic church," in which their relationship with each other is the infrastructure of their relationship with God.

Care of the Divorced

The number of the divorced runs into millions. The Roman Catholic community is not spared the ravages of divorce, and there are millions of Catholics all over the world who are divorced and who remarry. Some will be fortunate enough to have their marriages annulled and so are allowed to enter a second marriage with the blessing of the church.

Others will not be so fortunate. The church is faced with the dilemma of protecting the sanctity of marriage on the one hand and being compassionate to divorced persons on the other. At present those who remarry without their first marriage having been annulled and who do not live as brother and sister cannot receive Holy Communion. This is a harsh discipline that alienates many Catholics not only from Holy Communion but from the life of the church itself. The subject has been discussed extensively, and Häring in his recent book *No Way Out?* using the principle of *oikonomia,* advocates admission to Holy Communion. Clearly the church is faced with a major problem here, and there is need for the utmost care and compassion for those who are divorced and remarried. Each pastor has to work within the framework of his conscience. But the divorced are a large group of men and women who need to be integrated into the life of the church and their experience used as part of the battle so that contemporary marriage may be achieved without so much divorce.

See also EVIL, SOCIAL; FAMILY; LOVE; MARRIAGE; MORAL LIFE, CHRISTIAN; SEXISM; SPIRITUALITY; VATICAN COUNCIL II; WOMEN.

Bibliography: P. Glick and S. Lin, "Recent Changes in Divorce and Remarriage," *Journal of Marriage and the Family* 48 (1986). A. Norton and J. Moorman, "Current Trends in Marriage and Divorce Among American Women," *Journal of Marriage and the Family* 49 (1987). T. Parsons and R. Bales, *Socialisation and Interaction Process* (London: Routledge, 1956). B. Häring, *No Way Out? Pastoral Care of the Divorced and Remarried* (St. Paul Publications, 1990).

JACK DOMINIAN

DOUBLE EFFECT, PRINCIPLE OF

The principle of double effect is an instrument that distinguishes permitted from wrong "objects" of activity. It concerns only those objects with two effects, and it presupposes that some "objects" are always wrong. According to some periods of the tradition, there are objects of activity that are prohibited without exception, called "intrinsically wrong." Schueller gives two general categories for these: either they frustrate "a natural (God-given) faculty," or they are performed without the "required authorization" (*ex defectu iuris in agente*). The former include lying and some forms of contraception; the latter include divorce and direct killing of the innocent. These intrinsically wrong objects cannot be intended.

The object, a Scholastic concept, concerns the moral matter under investigation and is different from its intended effects. Aquinas, for example, distinguishes between the object of lying, which is intrinsically wrong, and the effects of various species of lies. The object of lying is saying something other than what one has in mind. The effect intended, however, depends upon the species: a jocose lie intends humor, an officious lie intends protection, a mischievous lie intends harm. The sin of lying is not in the effect intended, but rather in the object intended. The sin is intending to say something other than what one has in one's mind (ST 2–2, 110, 1–3).

Distinguishing the object from the effects is pivotal for understanding the principle, since the principle serves one object with two effects. Two particular examples demonstrate well the function of the principle. The first is the case of the dying patient in intractable pain, with no hope of recovery. An intrinsically wrong object of activity is direct killing of the innocent, and therefore to give the patient an injection of a lethal drug is always prohibited. But can one give the patient a painkiller, even if the patient could suffer heart failure as a result? The principle permits this because the object, administering a pain reliever, is distinct from one of its effects, possible death; the administration of such drugs is ordinarily for pain relief and not for killing. Conversely, the object of injecting a lethal drug can not be distinguished from its effect: the very meaning of the object is to kill.

The second case concerns destruction in a just war. An intrinsically wrong object of activity is the direct bombing of civilian populations, which would be considered the direct killing of innocents. But is the direct bombing of munitions factories or other military targets within civilian populations the same object as the direct bombing of civilian populations? The principle argues that they are distinctive.

These two cases involve one object that within a specific context has two effects. In the first case the object, administering morphine, has two effects, alleviating pain and possibly killing an innocent. In the second, the object, bombing a munitions factory, has the effects of destroying an enemy source of war and killing innocent employees.

Maintaining the liceity of one's conduct in activity that borders on the morally wrong is the function of the four conditions of the principle. For this reason the first condition argues that the object cannot be intrinsically wrong. In the first case, injecting a poison into a person is intrinsically wrong and cannot be permitted. But, injecting painkillers is, in itself, permitted. Similarly, the bombing of a civilian area is intrinsically wrong and cannot be permitted. But the bombing of munitions factories in a civilian area is, in just war, permitted because the object is the bombing of the factories, not the civilian area. The latter is, the traditionalists argue, circumstantial.

The second condition argues that though the evil effect is foreseen, it cannot be intended. Thus one could not administer the painkillers if the activity is nothing more than an excuse to kill the patient. If, however, the amount of painkillers is dangerous but necessary to alleviate the pain, then their administration is permissible even if death is probable though not intended. Similarly, the bombing of munitions factories in a civilian area is not permitted if one launches the attack as an excuse to kill the civilians as well as destroy the factories. If, however, the attack is launched and the civilian deaths are not intended though a number of deaths are anticipated, the attack is still permitted.

The third condition contends that the good effect cannot follow the bad effect. This prevents a prohibited object from being employed as a means. The good effect in the first case is the alleviation of pain. Thus, though by injecting a poison one could bring about a good effect such as alleviating pain, one cannot because the evil effect, killing the patient, is the means to the good effect, the alleviation of pain. Likewise, the good effect in a just war is defeating the enemy. Thus though one could defeat the enemy by destroying its civilian population, the principle prohibits the use of intrinsically wrong means.

The final condition requires proportionate reason for this nearly morally wrong activity: to the degree that one risks someone's death in order to alleviate their pain, to that degree the patient's condition and pain ought to be grave. To the extent that there is likelihood of innocent deaths, to that extent the munitions factory ought to be a necessary target for winning the just war.

In recent years there have been several attempts to argue that the principle of double effect is reducible. Knauer, for instance, writes that the principle determines the moral rightness or wrongness of any action, but he makes the argument on the grounds that only the fourth condition, proportionate (he calls it "commensurate") reason, defines the rightness or wrongness of an action. For him there are no intrinsically wrong acts, as traditionally understood. Schueller and Ugorji disagree. The principle is only used in those cases that approximate intrinsically wrong activity. The tradition stands against Knauer. Medina (1528–80), Lessius (1554–1623), Laymann (1575–1635), and Molina (1536–1600) all argue that a bad "object" makes superfluous all discussion about the permissibility of harmful effects. The Salmanticenses in the *Cursus theologicus* (1647) held the same first condition. In fact, the standard manuals, whether by Gury (1874), Noldin (1922), Davis (1934), or Kelly (1958) hold the same condition: the object cannot be one that is already prohibited.

A curious contemporary phenomenon is the frequent appeal to the principle. But the principle only makes sense when an object is proximate to an intrinsically wrong object and when one of the two effects could be considered an intrinsically wrong object were it intended. By invoking the principle unnecessarily, they place four conditions on their activity that are not required in ordinary moral decision making.

The principle applies only when the object under discussion bears a considerable degree of moral questionableness. During World War II, the principle needed to be invoked for the bombing of Cologne. There the bombing of the train station would at once have solely two clear and major effects: the destabilization of the shipment of arms and heavy loss of innocent civilian life. Two clear effects, each with considerable weight, one a value, the other a disvalue. But the principle of double effect was not needed for the invasions of Normandy or Anzio. There many civilians would be killed, but this was not like the moral questionableness of targeting a military strategy in a civilian area. Thus, in the whole subject of war, the principle is rarely invoked outside of the instance presented.

Similarly, the principle is invoked in hospital care and the administration of morphine. There clearly the administration of perhaps deadly doses of morphine requires us to invoke the principle because it has at once solely two clear and major effects: the easing of pain and the possible death of a patient. But the principle is not needed were one to perform dangerous, near-life-threatening surgery. Even though death could occur one does not invoke the principle of double effect because it is not needed.

In the two cases cited the principle is invoked because the object is very close to performing wrong activity directly. But we need to do this rarely, for rarely is our proximity to directly performing wrong activity necessary. For this reason moral theologians argue that the tradition has in the past and ought to in the future invoke the principle rarely.

See also COOPERATION, PRINCIPLE OF; KILLING; NATURAL LAW; TOLERATION, PRINCIPLE OF; WAR.

Bibliography: P. Knauer, "The Hermeneutic Function of the Principle of Double-Effect," *Natural Law Forum* 12 (1967) 132–62. B. Schueller, "The Double Effect in Catholic Thought: A Reevaluation," *Doing Evil to Achieve Good* (Chicago: Loyola Univ. Press, 1978). L. Ugorji, *The Principle of Double Effect* (Frankfurt am Main: Peter Lang, 1985). J. Keenan, "The Function of the Principle of Double Effect," *Theological Studies* 54 (1993) 294–315.

JAMES F. KEENAN, S.J.

DUE PROCESS

The expression "due process" is short for "due process of law," used in the United States Constitution for the restraints upon the actions of government to keep them within the limits of fundamental fairness. No person shall "be deprived of life, liberty, or property, without the due process of law" (Fifth Amendment; also the Fourteenth in reference to the states). The origins of due process lie deep within the Anglo-American common-law tradition.

"Due process" has a range of meanings from quite general to very particular. Most generally it signifies the procedures that are appropriate or suitable to ensure justice and fairness in the situation or conflict at hand. More technically, in judicial proceedings "due process" refers to the rules and principles established within a system of jurisprudence to enforce and protect the rights of persons. For example, it means that the tribunal must be competent to pass on the subject matter of the suit, that the defendant be within the jurisdiction of the court, that the judge be impartial, and that a person at jeopardy have the right to counsel, the right to be present at the proceedings, the right to be heard and to contest every material fact that bears on the matter involved.

Due process is said to be both substantive and procedural. Substantive due process means that no fundamental right or freedom shall be denied without adequate justification. Procedural due process implies that every individual will be accorded specific protections in administrative and judicial proceedings. For example, it includes the right to be informed of actions that might prejudice one's rights, to be heard in one's own defense in penal matters, to confront one's accusers, and not to be judged by those accusers.

Due process, therefore, is a broad and analogous concept in the realm of justice and fairness; its concrete specification depends on the context and content of the particular claim or dispute.

Due Process in the Church

Due process, known by slightly different names, has long roots in the Christian tradition. Matthew's Gospel records a very early procedure for the resolution of conflicts within the community: "If your brother (or sister) sins against you, go and tell him his fault between you and him alone. If he listens to you, you have won over your brother. If he does not listen, take one or two others along with you, so that, every fact may be established on the testimony of two or three witnesses.' If he refuses to listen to them, tell the church" (Mt 18:15-17).

Throughout its history the church's canon law has demonstrated concern for the proper jurisdiction and fair operation of its courts. Canon law is replete with procedures, rules of evidence, and protections for defendants. Two major collections, which are in substantial continuity despite the seven and a half centuries that separated them, bear witness to this canonical concern for due process: Book 2, "Judgment," *Decretals of Pope Gregory IX* (1234) and Book 7, "Processes," *Code of Canon Law* (1983).

Actual practices within the church have not always been in complete conformity with the canonical tradition. In evidence of that, the commission for the revision of the Code, when beginning its work after the Second Vatican Council, recognized the need for better protection of rights in the church. The commission elaborated a set of principles to guide the revision, which were approved by the episcopal synod of 1967. Three of those ten principles explicitly called for the protection of the rights of persons in the church (principles 1, 6, 7).

Canon 221 of the 1983 Code is the primary statement of the due-process rights of church members: "1. The Christian faithful can legitimately vindicate and defend the rights which they enjoy in the Church before a competent ecclesiastical court in accord with the norm of law. 2. The Christian faithful also have the right, if they are summoned to judgment by competent authority, that they be judged in accord with the norm of law. 3. The Christian faithful have the right not to be punished with canonical penalties except in accord with the norm of law."

Many specific procedural protections are contained in Book 7 of the *Code of Canon Law* (cann. 1400–1752). However, most administrative actions, that is, actions taken by bishops or other church officials within the scope of their executive authority, are not subject to judicial review (can. 1400.2). In practice, the only recourse for those aggrieved by such actions is administrative appeal, that is, recourse to the superior of the one who took the offensive action (cann. 1732–39).

In addition to administrative recourse, the Code repeatedly recommends alternative procedures to resolve disputes and settle grievances in the church. It calls for equitable solutions to be arrived at through negotiation, mediation, or arbitration (cann. 1446, 1713–16, 1733). Permanent offices or councils can be established in each diocese to provide these services (can. 1733.2).

Three good examples of contemporary due process have emerged from the National Conference of Catholic Bishops in the United States. In 1969 the NCCB adopted and recommended a document entitled *On Due Process,* which contained detailed procedures for conciliation and arbitration. Such procedures were subsequently established in many dioceses, but in very few are they readily available to the people and actually effective. In 1979 the NCCB approved a set of procedures for use by its own Committee on Conciliation and Arbitration. And in 1989 the NCCB approved guidelines to forestall or resolve the differences between bishops and theologians.

Modern Catholic social teaching speaks strongly of human rights and their just juridical protection (*Pacem in terris* 27, 75–79; *Gaudium et spes* 29). It implicitly endorses the concept of due process and, at least once, refers to it explicitly (*Justitia in mundo* 24). This teaching challenges the church to make due process a reality in its own inner life.

See also CANON LAW, FUNCTION OF; CIVIL LAW, FUNCTION OF.

Bibliography: *On Due Process* (Washington: USCC, 1972). *Committee on Conciliation and Arbitration Procedures* (Washington: USCC, 1979). "Doctrinal Responsibilities: Approaches to Promoting Cooperation and Resolving Misunderstandings Between Bishops and Theologians," *Origins* 19:7 (1989) 97–110. *Due Process in the Dioceses in the United States, 1970–1985* (Washington: Canon Law Society of America, 1987).

JAMES A. CORIDEN

E

ECOLOGY

Ecology is a branch of biological science that studies organisms' relations to one another and to their surroundings. The planet Earth is a type of community of life characterized by interdependence and delicate balance. A deeper understanding of this has been accelerated by environmental deterioration. This has been accompanied by the accusation that Christianity has been the significant influence in shaping exploitative attitudes toward nature. Factors such as these have forced a reappraisal of creation, humanity, and God in ecology theology and ecological ethics.

Ecological Awareness

At the level of theological reflection and church statements there is much to justify the comment made in 1986 that "the Catholic Church's voice on the ecological crisis has been muted" (McDonagh, p. 108). The bulk of creative writing in the field has come from within the Protestant tradition, for example, Moltmann and Gustafson. Nevertheless, "muted" neither means silent nor blind. Over the past two decades injustice toward the environment has been an issue for liberation theologians as it has been for Bernard Häring, Thomas Berry, and particularly for feminist writers such as Rosemary Radford Ruether.

It could also be argued that for Catholics, concern for the natural environment has tended to surface in the form of creation spirituality. This may indicate a growing need to interpret and express religious experience with a greater flexibility than is perceived to exist in theological disciplines. It may also be part of a gradual shift of moral sensibility and imagination currently occurring in Western culture.

In official documents we can detect a gradual emergence of ecological awareness since Vatican II in *Octogesima adveniens* 21 (1971), *Justitia in mundo* 11 (1971), and *Redemptor hominis* 15 (1979). John Paul II treats the issue more extensively in 1987 when treating of international interdependence. Ecological concern is shown in "positive signs"—awareness of limited resources and respect for the integrity and cycle of nature (*Sollicitudo rei socialis* 26). We have the same sentiments from the U.S. bishops in *Economic Justice for All* (1986) and a full pastoral on the environment from the bishops of the Philippines (1988). Finally, in 1990 we had the first papal document devoted exclusively to environmental concerns in the message for the World Day of Peace, *Peace with God the Creator, Peace with All of Creation* (WDP).

Ecology and Theology

Recent scholarship has clarified understanding of the two strands that make up the biblical account of creation. On the one hand there is the call for man and woman to be an image of God, to "be fruitful, multiply, fill the earth and conquer it" (Gen 1:28). Linked to the disharmony between nature and humans resulting from sin, this mandate has been interpreted as one of mastery and exploitative domination of nature by humankind. Dualist and Gnostic influences, Enlightenment philosophy, the myth of progress, and modern industry and technology have reinforced this anthropocentric view of nature. The material world—tainted, without value, even debased—exists mainly if not solely for human purposes.

On the other hand, a more adequate and integrated perspective sees God calling humankind to "cultivate and take care" of a creation that is good (Gen 2:15). Stewardship entails bringing "into play those abilities and gifts which distinguish the human being from other creatures" (WDP 3). It involves the caring and responsible management of the resources of the earth—authentic dominion. As tenants rather than owners, we humans have a responsibility from and accountability to God—a theocentric framework. Ours is a gift that if used wisely will ensure that the earth is not only abundant and beautiful but, more importantly, will give glory to God.

Human stewardship revolves around harmony with creation as the condition of peace. This is because the divine call established a fixed relationship between humans and the rest of creation. The deliberate choice to go against the Creator's plan by sin destroyed the existing harmony and led to various forms of alienation, especially in earth's rebellion against humans. "When man turns his back on the Creator's plan, he provokes a disorder which has inevitable repercussions on the rest of the created order. If man is not at peace with God, then the earth itself cannot be at peace" (WDP 5).

This biblical vision entails a renewed appropriation of the inherent goodness of all creation. It rejects any view of the material world as evil together with any associated attempt to justify exploitation and destruction. Evil, moreover, stems neither from the original creation nor from God. The source of wickedness, suffering, and death is grounded in a historical reality—the irresponsible, destructive use of human freedom (Gen 3). Similarly, it must be admitted that, historically, Christianity may have helped give a relative value to nature and that other political, philosophical, and economic factors aggravated such a process. Ultimately, once again it is human choices that have led to the ecological crisis.

We are more aware that the intrinsic goodness together with the aesthetic goodness of creation go beyond its instrumental (utility) worth. Our relationship of care is not solely one of looking after nature so that it looks after us. We are also meant to cultivate and preserve nature as something beautiful and worthwhile in itself that both reveals and glorifies God. It involves contemplating the earth with wonder so that we may hear the still, small voice of God. Aesthetic and spiritual nourishment come as much from the sacrament of God's creation as from human culture.

This renewed Christian ecological vision seems to shift the focus from the relationship between creation and humanity to that between the whole of the created universe and God. It also highlights interdependence within creation. We humans are unique in that we participate in and depend on the created order. Yet we are also agents meant to cooperate with and to harness nature's capacities for mutual benefit. As co-creators we have the task of developing the potential both of nature's resources and of our human gifts. What is better appreciated is the interconnected quality of creation that indicates a God-given order. There are boundaries to human activity essential to preserve the balance and harmony needed for the survival of the planet, its resources, and its inhabitants present and future.

Creation, too, is seen as fallen with humans through their choices against God's design and as looking toward redemption. Perhaps the Pauline vision of creation subject to futility yet yearning for completion finds its contemporary expression in the degraded earth crying out in pain. "The profound sense that the earth is 'suffering' is also shared by those who do not profess our faith in God" (WDP 5).

The new harmony, then, is found in Christ's reconciliation of all creation to the Father and his handing over the kingdom to the Father "so that God may be all in all" (1 Cor 15:28). Redemption of the person and of the universe are inextricably linked. Humans are now co-redeemers. It is the human person who is the medium of Christ's redemption as the *imago Christi,* especially through the community of believers. Humans alone can receive and give love, transcend themselves by knowledge, freedom, and the gift of the self. As God's stewards we heal, bring to fruition, and transform the good but flawed world of creation by respecting the divine plan.

Ecology and Ethics

A coherent and adequate theology of the environment must address the question of values, attitudes, and action. Within Catholic social teaching there are resources that can assist in shaping a Christian ecological ethic.

The first of these is *private property.* Its foundation is that the goods of the earth belong to all. Earlier Thomistic tradition held that the rights of private ownership were subordinated to and derived from the social needs of the community or the common good. Leo XIII, partly influenced by a fear of socialism and partly by Lockean theory, saw private property as an individual's natural and inherent right to use for private aims. From Pius IX until John XXIII and *Gaudium et spes* there is a reassertion of the social context, of boundaries on the ownership and use of private property, and of renewed stress on the universal purpose of creation's goods. Over the past twenty years there has been an increasing concern in church documents for the equitable distribution of nature's resources at the level of basic needs—central in ecological awareness.

Solidarity is another significant concept that has been developed in the recent writings of John Paul II.

In *Laborem exercens* (1981) we see the various levels of solidarity between persons in the setting of a just society.

In *Sollicitudo rei socialis* (1987) the parameters of solidarity are broadened. De facto there is an increasing interdependence in the world—physical, economic, political, social, and environmental. This calls for a renewed and deepening awareness of moral interdependence. Solidarity is now a virtue of a "*firm and persevering determination* to commit oneself to the *common good*; that is to say to the good of all and of each individual, because we are all really responsible for all" (SRS 38). Responsibility to the environment is part of the ethical framework for true development. It bears fruit in peace and is achievable only through true conversion and God's grace. We have here, then, the first church document at this level that approaches ecological issues in the setting of just and sustainable development.

The papal message for the World Day of Peace (1990) sees environmental degradation not just as a matter of better management or use of resources but ultimately as a moral and religious question. It is about meaning and values. A morally coherent worldview must have interdependence as its foundation. This demands the need to "keep alive a sense of 'fraternity' with all those good and beautiful things which Almighty God has created" (WDP 16). No peaceful society can afford to neglect as a moral guide the order of creation "with its own integrity, its own internal, dynamic balance, which should be used while safeguarding its integrity" (WDP 8).

The dignity of the *human person* and the value of life are also central in Catholic social and moral thought. In the ecology discussion "respect for life, and above all for the dignity of the human person is the ultimate guiding norm for any sound economic, industrial or scientific progress" (WDP 7).

Overall, church teaching and most theological writing tend to distance themselves from the position of some radical environmentalists and ecotheologians. In rejecting "anthropocentrism" (hierarchy and superiority of humans over nature) authors such as Berry see human "solidarity" with nature as entailing equality and mutuality. Human dignity, then, appears to be devalued. Nevertheless, one must account for the fact that on the earth humans alone are spiritual subjects—capable of reflective knowledge, of appreciating goodness as value, of ordering the various types of good, of moral activity that entails seeking the good, and of self-determination through freedom of choice. If the earth's future is closely associated with enlightened and conscious human decisions, then human beings have a special if not unique role in that process.

The wider arena of Catholic moral theology contributes other significant considerations in environmental responsibility. The sheer magnitude of the ecological problem means that moral theology and personal response must go beyond acts or omissions to "the attitudes and/or ideologies that might help to explain the deeper causes of the symptoms" (Häring, p. 173). It must involve inner renewal or *conversion.*

Conversion must go beyond a more internationally coordinated approach to the distribution and management of the earth's goods, essential though that may be. It must be more than the need to influence and shape more enlightened and responsible environmental policies at the local, national, and international levels of public and social life. Conversion involves an attack on greed and selfishness, whether individual or collective, that underlies ecological breakdown and structural forms of poverty. It entails a radical shift in outlook and how we each order our values. It means that "simplicity, moderation and discipline, as well as a spirit of sacrifice, must become part of everyday life" (WDP 13). It is, at heart, a spiritual challenge, a sign of God's spirit at work in the world.

Conversion is only possible under the grace and power of God. It demands that humans acknowledge personal responsibility and guilt for the state of the degraded and abused environment. To stand repentant and needing forgiveness before God, each other, and creation is the essential condition for a new start. Only in this way can we rediscover the true biblical vision of *shalom*—the peace, wholeness, totality, and harmony of all creation restored and healed in Jesus Christ.

A responsible use of the environment highlights the place of *character* and *virtue* in the moral life. Character gives our lives moral orientation by directing us to certain kinds of activities. Our basic commitments, dispositions, value responses, ways of seeing the world, and social relations shape and help define who we are and our actions. We are formed by our choices, growing in virtue by repeated patterns of actions that become habitual, even effortless. We are also molded by our Christian community and by the key images and metaphors that capture and convey its life, particularly through prayer and our relationship with Jesus. The contemporary shift in moral sensibility also influences the sort of people we are. Some see it as a renewal of the feminine part of consciousness, where there is emphasis on the nurturing, intuitive, and reconciling aspects of human life over the aggressive, logical, and controlling dimension.

Christian discipleship, then, is not primarily a matter of individualistic moral perfection. It has a communitarian, relational context, reflecting and sharing in the life of the triune God. It aims at the integration of freedom and mutuality on the understanding that our personal moral choices are inescapably social, sometimes public, even cosmic in their effects. Discipleship is principally a response to God in Jesus, especially as embodied in the person in need and by using the gifts of the Father as occasions for grateful stewardship.

The language of *rights* is used by some as a reaction to "anthropocentrism" and to ensure that the natural world is a factor in moral consideration. Animals (e.g., species) and nature (e.g., trees, wilderness) are seen to possess rights to protect them from human ravishment. While understanding the metaphorical usage, the literal attribution of rights to animals and inanimate nature has some serious difficulties. A right as a moral power to do, omit, own, or demand something of value requires the capacity for free choice, the ability to acknowledge the rights of others, to recognize correlative duties within a mutual relationship, and to bear moral and legal responsibility. For all that, cruelty to animals and the abuse of God's creation is a perversion of the caring relation between humans and nature, an offense against God, since it contravenes the reasonable and good use of God's gifts according to the divine plan.

Conclusion

The appreciation of the inherent goodness of nature and the perception of harmonies and values within nature as indicators of human behavior capture something of a pre-Cartesian, Stoic view of the world. We can discern in empirical experience and nature's processes evidence of God's purposes and of how we should relate to other created things and to God. This may seem to dislodge the distinction between "fact" (grounded in scientific truth as objective) and "value" (moral/aesthetic truth as subjective).

Nevertheless, we must beware of any form of determinism. How can we know that we have accurately recognized God's purposes and the true relations within the created order? What place does human intelligence have in using, correcting, supplanting, enhancing, even transcending, nature? This also involves the use of other ethical sources, Scripture, tradition, philosophy, and so forth, and how one weighs these in moral evaluation.

We must also be careful of romanticizing nature. It can be both gracious and cruel, arousing wonder by its beauty as much as by its destructive power. Moral standards can be derived from a creation that is intrinsically good and manifests the immanent God. But we must also account for and overcome the existence of moral evil—a historical reality. Giving too much weight to respect for nature can dilute human responsibility. Humankind has sinned against the environment, but it has also sinned against itself and against God.

Creation-centered theology and environmental respect alone, then, cannot answer the need for repentance, healing, and redemption from evil within ourselves and in our choices. Respect for and joy in creation cannot accomplish earth's healing on their own. We need redemption from beyond us, from the transcendent God who purifies and empowers us to purify the earth and bring it to wholeness. The risen Lord restores, heals, and forgives actual historical choices and their effects, enabling us to be truly converted. Only in this way are we enabled to shape the future by decisions that truly reflect our call to image God and to share in the task of reconciling all things in Christ.

See also ANIMALS, RIGHTS OF; CREATION; DEVELOPMENT; LAND; NATURAL RESOURCES; PRIVATE PROPERTY; SPIRITUALITY; STEWARDSHIP.

Bibliography: J. Carmody, *Ecology and Religion: Toward a New Christian Theology of Nature* (New Jersey: Paulist, 1983). J. Gustafson, *Ethics from a Theocentric Perspective* (Chicago: Univ. of Chicago Press, vol. 1, 1981, vol. 2, 1984). D. Hall, *Imaging God: Dominion as Stewardship* (Grand Rapids, Eerdmans, 1986). B. Häring, *Free and Faithful in Christ,* vol. 3 (New York: Crossroad, 1981). S. McDonagh, *To Care for the Earth* (Santa Fe: Bear & Co., 1986). J. Moltmann, *God in Creation* (New York: Harper & Row, 1987).

THOMAS RYAN, S.M.

ECONOMIC ORDER

The economic order has always presented Christians with a challenge. The economic dimensions of human life are as ordinary and necessary as any others, yet either too little economic success or too much often endangers more important goals in life. The questions of economic life for Christians touch both personal and institutional relationships, and the answers of the tradition at different times in its history exhibit a basic continuity and yet show differences related to the status of the religious community within the wider society. Thus the responses made within a religious state, whether in ancient Israel or medieval Christendom, differ from those given within a secular state. And even within the latter situation we find responses when Christians are a persecuted minority, as in the first centuries of the church, that differ from those made today when Christians live within a modern democracy. As a result, the task of analyzing a Christian view of economic order is a complex one. It requires careful attention not only to the content but to the context of earlier answers to the questions involved.

The Hebrew Scriptures

The most basic fact of life in the Hebrew Scriptures was the relation of Israel to Yahweh in the covenant. Thus, like other dimensions of life, the economic order of Israel was to be structured in fidelity to the demands of the people's fundamental relationship with God. Throughout most of the literary traditions in the Hebrew Scriptures, it is presumed that if Israel remains faithful to the demands of the covenant it will prosper economically. If it breaks the covenant economic failure along with social and political breakdown is the result.

The dominant and most pervasive view of the economic order in the Hebrew Scriptures is that incorporated in the Torah, the Law. Here, fidelity to Israel's relationship with Yahweh is spelled out in some detail not only for the nation's worship, dietary laws, and familial relations but also for the economic life of the people. The rationale for this was clear: when the Israelites lived as aliens and slaves under the pharaoh, it was the Lord who saved them and brought them through the desert to a land of their own. Thus whatever prosperity individuals experience, they are to remember that it is from Yahweh that this economic success comes. Additionally, Yahweh's particular concern for the most marginalized leads to a number of economic restrictions on the prosperous.

All of the literary strands of Israel's traditions indicate a particular concern for the widow, the orphan, and the stranger in the land (Exod 22:21-22). The God who tells Moses "I have seen the miserable state of my people in Egypt" (Exod 3:7-8) is the same Lord who "sees justice done for the orphan and the widow, who loves the stranger, giving him food and clothing" (Deut 10:18). The Deuteronomic code specifies several concrete economic restrictions. When harvesting, any sheaves overlooked in the field are to be left for the widow, the orphan, and the stranger. In harvesting grapes in the vineyard, the Law requires that the harvesters not go through the vineyard a second time to harvest what they may have left at first but that they leave it there for these needy ones in the nation (Deut 24:19-21).

Some scholars (e.g., N. Gottwald, *Tribes of Yahweh,* Maryknoll, N.Y.: Orbis, 1979) conclude that the religion of Yahwism arose as a peasant-based reaction within Canaan and that this sociological starting point helps explain the strong egalitarian emphasis in the Hebrew tradition. In any case, the basic conviction that all things belong to the Lord led to laws concerning the Sabbath Year (Exod 23:11; Lev 25:1-7), the seventh year in which fields were left fallow with only the poor eating from them, and in which all debts were to be forgiven (Deut 15:1-11). The Jubilee Year, the most radical of the economic laws, required that all property be restored to its original owners every fiftieth year (Lev 25:8-17). There is no evidence that the Jubilee Year was ever actually implemented, but it represents a radical limitation on the meaning of economic ownership and a fundamental denial of the possibility of self-sufficiency, economic or otherwise, in this primarily agrarian society.

The emphasis of the Hebrew prophets in economic life raises the level of concern about economic dimensions of the Law and demands a strong and effective economic ethic. Isaiah gives an indictment against those who "refuse justice to the unfortunate and cheat the poor among my people of their rights" (Isa 10:2). Amos excoriates the wealthy of his day for their lavish personal expenditures and their abuse of the poor (Amos 2:6-7; 5:11). Cultic fasts and other religious observances are meaningless without a firm commitment to the economic well-being of the poor (Isa 58:6-7).

Alongside the restrictions on economic life in the interest of justice are elements in the Law that conduce to economic growth. Economic historians have long noted the importance of the use of money for exchange rather than barter as a key factor in economic development in the ancient world. The monetization that occurred in Israel as a part of the centralization of worship had, then, positive economic effects (Gordon, p. 18). Similarly, when compared with other Near Eastern societies and even the earlier history of Israel, the enhanced though still minimal social status of resident aliens and women allowed for a broader-based social and economic mobility. The Law also secured the legal status and predictability of claims on personal property for both owners and debtors (Deut 24:10-13), a basic prerequisite for economic development. Similarly, differences in economic restrictions on the sale of houses in a walled town and in rural areas indicates that at least a degree of economic mobility occurred in the towns in ways not allowed in the countryside due to the view of land in the covenant.

Of course, fidelity to the covenant is not the only concern for the economic life of Israel, and two other, related issues need to be kept in mind. The first is that the Hebrew Scriptures indicate or imply that the business acumen of an individual will be conducive to prosperity. Jacob not only cleverly wins the inheritance from his brother, Esau, but while in voluntary exile he becomes wealthy due to his business skills as a breeder and herdsman (Gen 30:32-43). Similarly, the tradition looks favorably on Joseph's rise from slavery into broad political and economic power under the Egyptian pharaoh due to Joseph's own talents and cleverness (Gen 47:13-26). Joseph is clearly dependent upon Yahweh in the interpretation of the pharaoh's dream, but the text also gives Joseph much credit for his own administrative abilities and their positive effect amidst economic scarcity. Thus, although the upright person is to live in accord with the covenant, the Scriptures praise the economic acumen of those who are both faithful and successful.

A second critical view of economic life, one that brings into question the relation of covenantal fidelity to economic success, is presented in the Book of Job. Job is a thoroughly faithful Israelite who in the face of great suffering and deprivation is tempted to curse his God. Job can answer the questions of his doubting friends by pointing to his virtuous record, but he cannot then make sense of the calamities that have befallen him. The dramatic power of the story arises from the extent of the general presumption throughout Israelite history, and indeed throughout the Near East in that period, that virtue and economic success will go hand in hand. It is Job's unbending fidelity to Yahweh in the face of the greatest of sufferings that speaks the strongest message of the story. No human success—economic, familial, social, or otherwise—is to stand in the way of the fundamental fidelity of every Israelite to

Yahweh. Thus while the relation of economic prosperity and religious faith may be more complex than that anticipated by the Deuteronomic view of the world, the primacy of faith remains the basic message.

In summary, we can say that unlike some other world religions Judaism has never held that an escape from the economic realities of life is the ideal for a religious person. Rather the religious relationship with Yahweh comes in the midst of the living of daily life, and economic dimensions of that life are as religiously significant as any other.

The Christian Scriptures

Jesus' life and the lives of the NT writers occurred under Roman control of both political and economic institutions. As a result, many of the practical concerns for the structuring of an economy in accord with the will of Yahweh seemed of little relevance. Because there was simply no realistic hope for influencing economic structures in society, what we can learn about structuring an economic order from the NT must often be discerned from texts that had another purpose in mind.

Scripture scholars remind us that it is extremely difficult to distinguish what Jesus "really taught" from the later theologizing of NT writers. Still, it is widely agreed that Jesus extended a call to discipleship, which necessarily involves a denial of self, service to others, and a fellowship not only with one's social peers but also with social outcasts and sinners (Donahue, in Haughey, p. 88). Thus this call of Jesus to discipleship entails a commitment to the other, particularly the other who is most in need socially and economically. While this basic commitment does not define any economic institutions, it stands in judgment of every economic system.

Equally fundamental to Jesus' mission was the proclamation of the kingdom of God. While the reign of God undoubtedly calls for the disciple to recognize a personal dependence on God, contemporary scholars caution against an overly spiritualized interpretation. "Kingdom" is a political metaphor, and the motif of an actual place where the reign of God finds a home is never completely absent. It was not until later centuries when Christians had access to political power that the political implications of the reign of God became more carefully articulated, as had occurred in ancient Israel during those periods when it enjoyed self-rule.

The Synoptic Gospels include a wealth of materials relevant to the economic life of the disciple, but it is Luke who exhibits the strongest interest in questions of what we would today call "economic justice." While the danger of accumulated possessions is clear throughout the Synoptics, Luke is most insistent on this position. The rich man who built bigger and bigger barns is called a fool by God for laying up such treasures on earth (Lk 12:15-21). The Sermon on the Mount in Matthew counsels disciples to live simply, but Luke's version of the sermon goes further. It is not "the poor in spirit" (Mt 5:3) who are blessed but "the poor" (Lk 6:20). The disciples are to lend, even to their enemies, without expectation of return (Lk 6:35). In the parable of the rich young man, Jesus answers the inquiry by telling the young man to sell all that he has and distribute it to the poor (Lk 18:18-23). Jesus does not present this radical challenge to all disciples—Zacchaeus found approval upon his willingness to give away half that he owned (Lk 19:1-10)—but Luke represents the economically more radical strand of the Christian tradition, one that is highly suspicious of wealth in any form and holds up a stronger economic ethic as a higher ideal. However, in none of the Synoptics does Jesus require all disciples to sell all they own, although he does insist that they live simply and offer assistance to the poor and outcasts.

Throughout any consideration of what the Gospels have to say about the economic order, we must remember that the

Palestine of Jesus' day was a generally poor, agricultural society. While dates, olives, and dried fish were exported to other parts of the Roman Empire, the vast majority of the population lived very simply, as was typical in most ancient agricultural societies. Thus the presence of abject poverty for widows, orphans, resident aliens, and others who suffered from the structured injustices and random misfortunes of life was an ever-present reality and not something that needed attention only now and then.

Of the various patterns of economic life actually implemented in Christian communities, the most radical challenge to the prevailing economic system reported in the Christian Scriptures is that of the Jerusalem community, which for some time held all goods in common (Acts: 4:32-35; 2:44-45). Two distinguishable elements are cited in the text. The first is that "everything they owned was held in common." The second is that "all those who owned land or houses would sell them, bring the money from them, and present it to the apostles." The first condition is consistent with a variety of productive economic arrangements. The second represents a more radical call to sell off capital assets (productive land, and houses that could be lived in or rented) and implies, though it does not explicitly state, that eventually the only source of income for the group would be the work of its members and charitable contributions. Even a dependence on employment is not certain, as the text goes on to say that "they went as a body to the temple every day" (Acts 2:46). Some commentators (see Gordon, p. 78) interpret this to mean that members of the Jerusalem community gave up their normal employments. The outcome reported in Acts is that none of the members was ever in want. Still, it is also clear from the text that when Paul sought the endorsement of leaders in Jerusalem for his missionary effort, the one condition they placed upon him was that he raise funds to help sustain the community at Jerusalem in concrete economic terms. Differences in interpretations of the experience of the early Jerusalem community are key elements in differences in later centuries among Christians advocating alternative approaches to the economic order.

While Paul gladly took up his pledge to assist the needy in Jerusalem (Gal 2:9-10), his own teaching on economic matters was quite different from that embodied in the Jerusalem community. He does not propose the pooling of possessions in the other Christian churches, and he himself attempts to remain economically independent so as not to burden the communities he visits and serves. When Paul receives economic assistance for his work, it often comes from wealthy individuals, some of them still apparently active entrepreneurs (Acts 16:14; 17:4, 12). Paul's own teaching on economic issues makes it clear that justification in Christ will not turn the Christian away from day-to-day economic concerns, although it will lead the community to bear one another's burdens, particularly those of the weakest members.

The Early Church

As the early church grew, made converts, and established communities throughout the Mediterranean world, Christians found it necessary to reflect on the meaning of their belief for all dimensions of their life within the Roman Empire, including economic life.

There were diversities of outlook on economic life among early church leaders and theologians, yet there were many basic themes common to all of the fathers of the church. Most fundamentally, all understood that the material world was created by God and that by God's intention it should be common to all. As Ambrose of Milan puts it, "God has ordered all things to be produced so that there should be food in common for all, and that the earth should be the common possession of all" (*De officiis ministrorum* 1.28, PL 16:62).

Springing from this basic doctrine of creation is the conviction that all persons, rich and poor, are equal in ways more fundamental than their economic inequalities. The Fathers point to the fact that both the poor and the rich are born naked and neither can take any material goods with them when they die (Ambrose, *De Nabuthe* 1, PL 14:731; Augustine, *Sermon 75* 5.6, PL 38:523). Similarly, because God created the world and gave it as a common possession, individuals who own property are best understood as stewards of what they possess and not absolute owners. While the Fathers did not advocate physical poverty as an end in itself, they frequently preached simplicity in the use of economic goods. As Clement of Alexandria asked, "Tell me, does a table knife refuse to cut if it is not studded with silver or have a handle of ivory? . . . What difference does it make if the wash basin be only of clay? Will it not hold water anyway to wash the hands?" (*Paidagogos* 2.3, PG 8:436).

We can see in this and similar themes in the Fathers the influence of Greek and Roman philosophical traditions, where the basic values of the gospel are joined with more detailed arguments for their reasonableness. Thus, the Stoic notion of self-sufficiency is related to Jesus' call for simplicity in the Sermon on the Mount. As Clement put it, "Those concerned for their salvation should take this as their first principle, that, although the whole of creation is ours to use, the universe is made for the sake of self-sufficiency, which anyone can acquire by a few things" (*Paidagogos* 2.3, PG 8:437). As Augustine taught, "We possess many superfluous things, unless we keep only what is necessary. For if we seek useless things, nothing suffices" (*Enarratio in Psalmum 147* 12, PL 37:1922). Similarly dependent on Stoic notions of nature and morality is Ambrose's argument for the basic equality of rich and poor because both are born naked. Natural facts are understood as data for moral interpretation: "Just as the foot is the measure for the sandal, so the physical needs of each person are the measure for what one should possess" (Clement of Alexandria, *Paidagogos* 3.7, PG 8:609). Employing natural facts (such as physical needs and equality at birth) as fundamental sources for Christian ethics anticipates a fully elaborated natural-law morality in the medieval Scholastics.

The most fundamental fear of the early church concerning economic goods was that they lead so easily to a hardness of heart. Several of the Fathers observed that the owner of property who continually covets more is the servant of wealth and not its master. Once possessed by one's possessions, the individual can no longer remain faithful to God. Such discussions make it clear that the church fathers were wrestling in the name of the Christian community with questions of the legal and moral meaning of private property in an era when many were both wealthy and Christian. Ambrose taught that the distribution of property rights arose from human arrangements and not from the natural order of things, where all things were held in common (*De officiis ministrorum* 1.28, PL 16:61–62). In this, he anticipated the codification of this position by Thomas Aquinas. And whatever else ownership of property means, it had to mean that the owner was still responsible for the common use of that property to meet the needs of others as well as one's own. As Augustine put it, "The superfluous things of the wealthy are the necessities of the poor. When superfluous things are possessed, the property of others is possessed" (*Psalmum 147* 12, PL 37:1922). "Those who give something to the poor should not think that they are doing so from what is their own" (*Sermon 50* 1.2, PL 38:326). Gregory of Nyssa went as far as to say that the wealthy should share "a third or a fifth" of their possessions with the poor (*De pauperibus,* PG 46:466).

There were reasons other than simple obligation for the wealthy to share with the poor. Christ identified himself with the poor, and the Pauline image of the body of Christ ensures that assistance given to the poor is given to Christ himself. Ambrose argued that sharing one's wealth with the poor actually places God in debt to the wealthy and that the surest way to relieve the fear of theft of one's wealth is to "store it in the hearts of the poor" (*De Nabuthe* 7, PL 14:741). Similarly, Chrysostom taught that the poor who are helped by the rich today will intercede for the rich on the day of judgment.

While most patristic teaching on economic life takes the form of moral appeals to individual Christians, there is also evidence of organized, institutional responses for relief of the poor. Tertullian expected each community to maintain a kind of "community chest" from voluntary donations, which would be part of the community's effort to meet the needs of the poor (*Apologeticus* 39.1.5–7, PL 1:468–70). Ambrose, who was Roman prefect in northern Italy before being called to be bishop, employed similar institutional instincts and established similar efforts within the Christian community in Milan.

While the holding of property in common was not understood as a requirement for all Christians, it was Chrysostom who boldly proposed this as a general way of life. Citing the example of the early Jerusalem community, he preached to the Christians of Constantinople that the best way to fulfill the obligations of property was to hold all goods in common. He argued that it would be much less expensive to meet the needs of everyone at a few common tables than it would be in individual tables in houses throughout the city, an efficiency modern economists call "economies of scale." Chrysostom asserted that pooling wealth in Constantinople would bring more than a million pounds of gold and this would be more than enough to care for everyone. In addition, it would convince pagans of the wisdom of the Christian faith (*In Acta Apostolorum* 11.3, PG 60:98). However, while all the fathers of the church showed varying degrees of suspicion of commerce and market transactions, none of the others went as far as Chrysostom in proposing the holding of property in common as a general solution.

The Fathers were unaware that the issues of economic productivity are relevant to the welfare of the poor. Of course, they are not unique here, as this is a modern notion and one only rarely adverted to in ancient or classical literature of any sort. Economic historians note that the increasing wealth of the early Roman Empire came largely due to increased specialization made possible by the broader-based markets that the empire brought about. Still, there seems to have been little change in the actual techniques of production (in agriculture, the trades, etc.). The system of absentee ownership of large agricultural tracts grew throughout the first four centuries of the early church, and it is not surprising that the Fathers would be very critical of wealthy landowners who expended little of their own effort in the production process. Thus while modern economists lament the patristic presumption that the wealthy simply "found" their wealth here (e.g., Augustine, *Sermon 124* 5.5, PL 38:686), this was far more true in the agricultural situation of the early church than in the production of goods and services in the modern world.

In sum, although the Fathers imposed both strict limits on the meaning of ownership and strict obligations to assist the poor, Clement of Alexandria expressed a widely held patristic presumption when he taught that "it is not impossible to conduct the affairs of the world in a fitting way in keeping with the laws of God" (*Paidagogos* 3.11, PG 8:656–57).

One of the most important institutional developments in the patristic era was the rise of Christian monastic communities. Without doubt, the founders of such communities wanted primarily to create a setting for the renunciation of all possessions, both external and internal, a place where community members could seek God with a singleness of purpose not possible amid the complications of daily life in the Roman Empire. For many this undoubtedly included the judgment that, particularly after Constantine's conversion rendered church membership socially advantageous, Christian communities in the cities were assimilating too much of the Roman worldview and had lost much of the religious clarity of the primitive Christian communities of the NT era. Additionally there are numerous reports of individuals entering monastic life in the 4th and 5th centuries partly in response to economic difficulties caused in large part by the concentration of land ownership and the consequent impoverishment of subsistence farm economies.

From an economic point of view the monastic communities of the early centuries represented an opportunity for community members to organize their economic life together in ways not otherwise possible within the broader economic structure of the empire. It was of course impossible to ignore the economic and class distinctions of the empire altogether. Augustine's *Rule* is not untypical in making concessions to monks who had formerly been members of the wealthy class, but the rule always described such concessions as due to the fragility of these monks (*Regula* 4–5, PL 32:1379). Other monks who do not receive the same in food, clothing, or blankets are described as more robust individuals and more fortunate because of this. It was part of the genius of early monastic rules to make limited concessions to human fragility and yet to structure life to strengthen community habits known to be more conducive to the search for God.

Within the discipline of the monastic community, physical work had a high place, due not only to necessity but to its spiritual value as well. At a time when the agricultural economy of the empire stagnated, the monasteries were often recognized as highly productive agricultural undertakings. The lives of the Egyptian Desert Fathers (ca. 395) include a number of stories about the agricultural productivity of monastic communities and their consequent ability to help the poor of the region. Thus, for example, a text from the late 4th century reports that "from the labors of the brethren they dispatch whole shiploads of wheat and clothing to Alexandria for the poor, because it is rare for anyone in need to be found living near the monasteries" (*The Lives of the Desert Fathers,* B. Ward, ed., trans., N. Russell [London: Mowbray, 1980] 18, "On Sarapion"). While the stories about the productivity of monastic agriculture are always related to faith in God as the underlying reason, there is little doubt that many monastic agricultural efforts were more productive than most others in their region and time. With the prevalence of the *Rule of Benedict* from the Carolingian period onward, Benedictine monasteries (including later Cistercian communities) became responsible for sizable economic enterprises, primarily based in agriculture. Here too, the religious importance of common labor linked monastic observance with economic productivity for centuries to come.

The Middle Ages

In spite of the diversity of perspectives encompassed in the Middle Ages, constraints of space require a focus on the views of Thomas Aquinas. His views on economic order are typical for the era, and his subsequent influence in economic and other moral matters has been undeniably immense.

Aquinas' moral analysis is founded on his conception of the natural law, a view that combined Aristotle's notion of the *telos* (goal or end) of a human life with the Stoic notion of structure in the universe. For Thomas, the eternal plan of God resulted in creation of humans and all other creatures, with each having a nature based on God's intention for it. As rational creatures, human persons can come to understand their nature and can know what fulfills themselves. Thus these moral standards have the character of a law, the natural law (ST I-II, q. 91, a. 2). Moral life requires that reason discipline the passions, something as necessary in economic interaction as in other aspects of human life.

Thus in considering the economic ownership of property, Aquinas argues that private ownership is not required by the natural law but is also not contrary to it. Such ownership represents a helpful addition to natural law (ST II-II, q. 66, a. 2). In endorsing private property, Aquinas distinguishes two aspects of the relationship between persons and property. The first is the power to procure and dispense (i.e., make decisions about) material goods, and the second is the actual use of what is possessed. Aquinas gives what we today would call "efficiency" reasons to support his claim that property is appropriately private with regard to the first aspect. First, each person is more willing to exert an effort to obtain private property than to procure commonly held property. Second, there is more order in society when it is clear who has responsibility for physical possessions. Third, each person can live in a more peaceful state of mind when control over physical goods is uncontested. A similar defense of private property based on its practical advantages was later made by John Duns Scotus, Bernard of Siena, and most medieval Christian scholars.

In regard to the second aspect, the use of goods, Aquinas follows the patristic tradition in arguing that the use of all goods is to be common, due to God's intention in creating them: that they meet the needs of humanity.

This distinction between the power to obtain and make decisions about goods and the actual use of the goods is problematic for modern minds because the individual's freedom in making decisions about goods is severely limited by the common use to which goods must be put if we are to remain in accord with the natural law. It is, however, quite consistent for Aquinas to argue (ST II-II, q. 66, a. 7) that if a poor person is in dire need and can find no way to meet those needs except by taking the goods that the rich person holds in excess of needs, it is morally legitimate for the poor person to take those goods from the wealthy one. Thomas quotes Ambrose to the rich man ("It is the hungry man's bread that you withhold"), but the argument is not a modern appeal to the rights of the poor. Rather, Thomas argues that because it is the nature of material goods to meet human needs, a man who owns more goods than he needs violates the nature of those very goods if he refuses to allow them to meet the needs of the poor. In effect he forfeits his ownership of those goods. The poor man's taking of property in this situation is, as Thomas puts it, neither theft nor robbery. This teaching on the common use of goods represents the single greatest clash between the classical Christian economic ethic and the prevailing view of economic life in the modern world.

Aquinas' view of exchange, following Aristotle, requires that all contracts "observe equality of thing and thing" (ST II-II, q. 77, a. 1). That is, the payment for a good should be equal to the worth of the good. The general notion is that the seller may not take advantage of extreme needs of buyers by charging prices higher than normal—unless the need for the good by the seller has also increased and the higher price would simply be equal to the now higher "worth of the good." This undercuts any simple reliance on the market to set prices. Still, at other points Thomas seems willing to allow for market conditions to raise the price (ST II-II, q. 77, a. 4), and this seeming contradiction in Thomas has left commentators uncertain of how to apply the rule of just price in practical situations.

Aquinas' view on usury largely follows that of the patristic era and of Aristotle himself. Thus Aquinas follows the distinction between goods that are consumed in their use (e.g., food and drink) and goods that are not (e.g., the use of a house for a year). Aquinas includes money in the first category of goods because its principal use is for exchange, where it is consumed (or alienated) in the process of giving it to the other as goods are received in exchange. As a result, Aquinas argues that as it would be immoral to sell wine separately from the use of the wine (in effect, charging the other for the right to hold the wine for a time and then return it unconsumed), so it is immoral to charge for the right to hold money for a time prior to its return.

It is instructive to note that modern Catholic moral theology has had little difficulty in setting aside this traditional teaching on usury but is left with a significant difficulty in developing the meaning of the common use of property in a modern economic system. The difference, of course, is that a relatively minor shift was necessary to recognize that money represents control over real resources and that, like the rented house, real resources still exist after they have been used for any period of time. The teaching on private property could only be set aside at the price of a far larger shift in the underlying notion of natural law.

The Transition to Modern Economic Life

The cultural changes that have taken place in the modern world have been immense. They have presented to Christianity as great a challenge as the prevailing culture of the Roman Empire presented to the small Christian communities of the earliest days of the church. In the transition from medieval Christendom to the modern world, Christians have had to rethink some basic presumptions in every area of human life: the character of the human person, science, technology, politics, social organizations, economic life, and even Christianity's understanding of its own history. In some of these areas an accommodation has been made to modern insights while leaving the fundamentals of Christian belief intact. Thus, for example, while the challenge posed by the science of Galileo and Copernicus seemed at the time to threaten Christian belief, later developments in biblical scholarship and in the theological understanding of science have led to an intellectual calm in this area for mainline Christian churches during the late 20th century. Similarly, after centuries of identifying itself with the monarchies of Europe and resisting modern democratic challenges that were often identified with atheism, the Roman Catholic church has endorsed the self-determination of peoples and political democracy in the 20th century. However, contemporary debates about Christianity and economic order indicate clearly that no such resolution has yet occurred in this dimension of modern life for Christians.

With the rise of merchant trade and of substantial cities at the end of the feudal era, economic life took on a new dynamism. As slow as these changes appear to the 20th-century eye, they were the beginnings of a challenge to a static interpretation of economic life within Christianity. The leaders of the Protestant Reformation were among the first Christians to embody a significantly new approach. While Martin Luther's notion of the calling of the Christian urged all to daily work (and repressed monasticism and mendicancy), its relation to the existing political and economic order was not revolutionary. John Calvin, however, expressed an appreciation of commercial activity from the perspective of Christian theology. While he approved of neither greed or individualism, Calvin shifted ground on the traditional condemnation of usury, allowing for "productive credit." His ideal of the church as a "holy community" led him to initiatives in establishing textile manufacturing in Geneva as a source of employment for those without jobs (Troeltsch, p. 641ff.). Still, both Protestant and Catholic perspectives condemned the greed that seemed typical of successful economic actors, and they consistently condemned the individualism that so often characterized the most dynamic sectors of economic life.

With the further spread of merchant capitalism in 16th and 17th centuries and the Industrial Revolution in the 18th and 19th centuries, the pace of economic change accelerated, and subsequent shifts in cultural patterns created dramatic challenges for traditional communities. This first became apparent in the nations that industrialized early, but by the end of the 19th century these economic forces transformed nearly all European societies. With the rapid developments of manufacturing productivity, large numbers of agricultural laborers moved to industrial jobs in the cities in the face of loss of employment in rural areas and with the hope of better opportunities in urban factories. The disruptions were immense, with many leaving their traditional homes, values, and religious settings and finding themselves in dependent economic relationships, competing for harsh, low-wage jobs in the cities. In the face of widespread dislocation and misery in urban settings, socialist reformers, usually atheists, offered an attractive alternative to workers. The upheavals in Europe from the French Revolution through the end of the 19th century included a cacophony of voices addressing both political and economic organization.

Christians responded in a variety of ways. The rise of the liturgical movement under Prosper Guéranger and the revival of monasticism in Europe were directly related to the crying needs of an industrialized culture (R. W. Franklin, *Nineteenth-Century Churches: The History of a New Catholicism in Württemberg, England, and France,* New York: Garland, 1987). Intellectuals within Catholicism formed a number of formal study groups of leading social thinkers such as the Geneva Alliance (1870) and the Fribourg Union (1884). Bishop Wilhelm von Ketteler, Bishop Mermillod, René de la Tour-du-Pin, Albert de Mun, Charles Périn, and others provided leadership in Roman Catholic circles organized to address the economic problems of the day. While all of these men were reformers, some were clearly monarchist in their orientation, and all were deeply concerned by the threats to Catholic community represented by both prevailing industrial capitalism and the effectiveness of the socialist left wing in Europe. Particularly among German Catholics, the proposed long-term solution was that of "corporatism," a socioeconomic order based on vocational groups that were to include owners, managers, and workers in the same organization. However, the immediacy of the problems and the resistance of the modern world to such corporatist solutions led many leading Catholics such as von Ketteler to a different proposal: to press social Catholicism toward a focus on improved government social policy (Mueller, p. 88). The debates and differences were intense. It was in response to this situation that Leo XIII published his best-known encyclical, *Rerum novarum* (1891), in an attempt to pose a Roman Catholic answer to "the social question."

Leo clearly condemns the excesses of the free market and rejects both capitalism and socialism. He laments the demise of the older workmen's guilds and attacks the rise of individualism, which leaves the worker "isolated and defenseless, to the callousness of employers and the greed of unrestrained competition" (RN 2). In response, Leo advocates Catholic "workmen's associations" to press for better working conditions and wages. Leo argues for the traditional "just wage" and rejects the free-market argument that a voluntary acceptance of a job legitimates the wage rate regardless of how low it is. Rather, Leo argues that it is "a dictate of nature more imperious and more ancient than any bargain between man and man" that the wage must be enough to support the worker in "reasonable and frugal comfort" (34). He recommends strong government action when the voluntary interactions of workers and owners do not result in appropriate economic solutions. In this he reiterates the traditional Catholic conviction that the state, when properly constituted, plays an important role in supporting social and economic structures discerned through a religious perspective.

At the same time, Leo warns against socialism. He repeats the traditional endorsement of private property, and in his enthusiasm for contradicting what he (erroneously) understands to be the socialist condemnation of all private property, he makes a stronger case in its favor than the tradition had previously done: Leo describes private ownership as "sacred and inviolable" (35), and he claims that humans have "by nature" the right to private property. The earlier tradition, of course, interpreted the dispensation of goods in nature to be common and saw private property as a (justifiable) addition to the natural law.

In *Quadragesimo anno* (1931) Pope Pius XI set out to reiterate and clarify the teaching of Leo XIII. Pius distinguishes the "right of property" from its use and states that there are duties attached to property ownership (although he does not specify them). Rather, in defending private ownership he argues that the misuse of property does not destroy or forfeit the right of property itself, and he defends the practice of transmission of property in inheritance as one that "cannot be taken away by the state" (QA 49).

Pius XI sets out to propose a reconstruction of the social order and in doing so "it is principally the State we have in mind" (78). Pius does not expect all solutions from state intervention but finds the state the only vehicle able to overcome the evils of individualism in modern social economic life. It is in addressing the reliance on governmental organization at various levels that Pius introduces his now well-known "principle of subsidiarity" as a mechanism for deciding what level of governmental or organizational action is appropriate to a particular problem. The principle states that "it is an injustice, a grave evil and disturbance of great order for a larger and higher organization to arrogate to itself functions which can be performed efficiently by smaller and lower bodies" (79). It is a typically Catholic principle in that it exhibits a willingness to rely on governmental structures for a solution and at the same time cautions against turning too quickly to solutions imposed politically from above.

Pius XI's solutions are close to those proposed by the Jesuit economist Heinrich Pesch, the architect of "solidarism." Pesch depended on the Thomistic and Aristotelian notion of virtue as a proper mean and argued that only industrial councils ("vocational groups") could strike a mean between capitalist individualism and socialist collectivism. This search for a "third way" was fairly typical of European Catholics addressing the social problem before Vatican II, when a different attitude toward the modern world took hold within Roman Catholic circles.

Vatican II and Beyond

In his encyclical *Mater et magistra* (1961), Pope John XXIII explicitly reiterates the basic teachings of Leo and Pius XI and goes on to propose principles for a 20th-century Catholic economic ethic. Like his predecessors, he bases this ethic on the dignity of all human persons as children of God and attempts to work out a position aligned with neither free-market capitalism nor totalitarian socialism. In doing so, he responds more carefully to the nuances of public arguments outside the church than did his predecessors. Thus he distances Catholic social teaching from totalitarian communism in defending "the right of private property, including that pertaining to goods devoted to productive enterprises."

He also extends the teaching on private property by quoting favorably in the encyclical a portion of a speech in which Pius XII taught that private property is "required by the plan of divine wisdom and the law of nature" (MM 109, 111). This is an even stronger statement than Leo's claim and far exceeds that made by Thomas Aquinas. In Thomas's categories, this asserts that private property is required not only by natural law but explicitly by eternal law as well. Whether excessive or not, it illustrates how the context of Catholic ethics (in this case the struggle between communism and capitalism) influences moral teaching.

In addition, where Aquinas had balanced the right of privately owning goods with their common use, in *Mater et magistra* Pope John strikes the balance between the right of privately possessing goods and "a continuing effort . . . to spread the use of this right through all the rank of the citizenry" (113). Although he in no way contradicts the traditional teaching on common use that "in the right of private property there is rooted a social responsibility" (119), he argues here for the widespread ownership of goods. The intention seems to be that if *all* persons possessed sufficient goods then the requirements of common use imposed on property held by the wealthy would not have to come into play.

However, while Pope John advocates increasing economic productivity, he rejects a rising level of production as an adequate standard of welfare. He argues that the distribution of goods remains crucial for justice (83), and he makes the traditional argument that the economic order must be structured to the common good.

A more significant development is Pope John's teaching on "economic rights." The use of the language of "rights" or "natural rights" is widespread in the modern world. Catholic social teaching since Leo XIII has slowly come to endorse this language as a contemporary expression of traditional teaching about natural law, with natural rights now being understood as the legitimate claims of individuals based on the natural law. Thus it is not surprising that church documents now express much of Catholic social teaching about the economic order in terms of "economic rights." The list of rights in *Pacem in terris* (1963) includes the right to "free initiative in the economic field," the right to work, the right to safe working conditions, the right to a wage determined in accord with justice, and the right to own private property (PT 18–21). This list was expanded with the publication two and a half years later of the Pastoral Constitution on the Church in the Modern World (*Gaudium et spes*) at the close of the Second Vatican Council. There the council fathers argued for a broader list of economic rights to guarantee "everything necessary for leading a life truly human": the right to food, clothing, and shelter, the right to choose a state of life freely, the right to education, to employment, to safe working conditions, and to labor unions (GS 26, 65, 68).

Pope Paul VI continues the development of Catholic social thought on economic life in his encyclical *Populorum progressio* (1967). He follows the lead of Pope John in beginning with "the signs of the times," identifying increasing poverty, inequality, unrest, and cultural damage in the developing nations as problems that the church needs to address. He quotes *Gaudium et spes* on the doctrine of "common use" of all goods and goes on to declare that "all other rights whatsoever, including those of property and of free commerce, are to be subordinated to this principle" (PP 22). It is a "grave and urgent social duty" to redirect all these other rights in the modern world "to their primary finality." In doing so, Pope Paul brings explicitly to the heart of modern Catholic social teaching the doctrine of common use, which had played so central a part in the teaching of the patristic and medieval periods.

Pope Paul criticizes the "unchecked liberalism" implicit in extreme views on the profit motive, competition, and property rights (26) and at the same time warns developing nations against the temptation of an economic prosperity that endangers religious faith (41). He also extends the teaching of Leo XIII on the relation of freedom and justice. Leo warned that a worker's voluntary acceptance of a low-wage job did not justify the wage, and Paul VI extends this insight into the problem of inequalities in power between nations in international trade to argue that "what was true of the just wage for the individual is also true of international contracts. . . . Freedom of trade is fair only if it is subject to the demands of social justice" (59).

In *Octogesima adveniens* (1971), Paul VI provides two further important developments. The first is a more nuanced treatment of the human sciences in which he urges Christians to play an active part in their development and to become more cautious about their methodological restrictions and ideological presuppositions (OA 38–40). Second, he provides a far more careful treatment of the debates between Marxism and "liberal ideology" than any other pontiff to date. Within socialism he distinguishes "various levels of expression," from a generous aspiration for justice, to historical movements, to a full-blown secular ideology that Christians cannot endorse. He rejects the Marxist notion of class struggle but recognizes a more attractive dimension of Marxist scientific activity and rigorous analysis, while still noting a tendency toward "totalitarian and violent society" (31–34). Similarly, he recognizes the importance of personal initiative, efficiency, and defense of the individual that occur within the liberal ideology but rejects the "erroneous affirmation of the autonomy of the individual," which lies at the very root of philosophical liberalism (35).

Pope John Paul II published his treatment on human work, *Laborem exercens* (1981), on the 90th anniversary of *Rerum novarum.* In it, he stresses the subjective meaning of work for human activity. He calls for "the priority of labor over capital," so human workers would never be treated like "capital," the tools and materials needed for production (LE 12). John Paul criticizes the economies of both East and West for the treatment of workers (a theme he develops far more extensively in *Sollicitudo rei socialis* (1987) and repeats Paul VI's reaffirmation of the centrality of common use in the understanding of property (LE 14). In doing so he provides a modern interpretation of common use within market economics. Wages are the means by which the vast majority of people have access to "those goods which are intended for common use" (19). The unemployed who cannot find work are to have access to these goods through unemployment benefits, a crucial obligation for society (18).

Pope John Paul II calls for a larger view when he describes all of the capital in an economy as "a great workbench at which the present generation of workers is working day after day" (14). He also goes on to develop the conception of the "indirect employer" of workers, which includes the state as well as the "persons and institutions of various kinds" who have any influence on the working conditions (17). This notion of indirect employer may prove to be among the most fruitful of those employed by Pope John Paul II in that it forges a moral link between individual employers and the array of structures (from labor negotiations, to state health and safety requirements, to national laws and international declarations) that influence the character of any employment situation.

The Situation in the United States

The relation of the Roman Catholic church to economic life in the United

States has been significantly different from that in Europe for a number of reasons. In the United States the church has not been identified with monarchy, and the relation between state and church has never been seriously conflictual. American Catholics began as minority immigrants and only slowly were assimilated into the American mainstream. As a result, the Catholic church quite naturally became associated with the cause of the working classes. In addition, the industrial struggles between workers and management in the United States, while severe and bloody at times, were more quickly resolved in favor of a non-Marxist labor movement than was the case in Europe. For all of these reasons, the American Catholic church has traditionally shown a greater openness to identifying with the economic struggles of its members. For similar reason, the economic success of American Catholics and others, particularly in the 20th century, has led church leaders to a strong appreciation of the benefits available within a regulated market system.

The development of official teaching of the U.S. Roman Catholic bishops on economic life has undergone a multitude of influences. The publication of Leo XIII's *Rerum novarum* was significant but caused no great shifts in the American Catholic church, although it did press some bishops to end their earlier opposition to the formation of labor unions (Mueller, p. 93). The Protestant social gospel movement (see W. Rauschenbusch, *A Theology Social Gospel (1917),* Nashville: Abingdon, 1945) of the 19th and early 20th century made a theological argument for economic reform, though by no means through the traditional Roman Catholic natural-law tradition.

Still, the U.S. Catholic bishops did not publish any substantial opinions on the economic order until the end of World War I (1919), when the leadership of the National Catholic Welfare Conference (predecessor to today's National Conference of Catholic Bishops) called for a program of social reconstruction (*Our Bishops Speak,* Milwaukee: Bruce, 1952, pp. 243–60). In it the bishops called for the legal guarantee of the right of workers to organize, a living wage, an eight-hour day, the establishment of cooperative stores, and "equal pay for equal work by the two sexes." They identify the three main defects of the U.S. economy: inefficiency and waste in production and distribution, insufficient income for the great majority, and unnecessarily large incomes for a small minority. Under the pressures of the Great Depression, the administrative committees of the National Catholic Welfare Conference took even stronger positions in 1933 in condemning the excesses of the market system, which had brought so many Americans to unemployment and poverty. The bishops attack "callous and autocratic possessors of wealth and power who use their position and the riches to oppress their fellows" (*Our Bishops Speak,* p. 298).

American Catholic intellectuals were themselves greatly interested in the resolution of the social question within the American context. The Central Verein was an influential German Catholic organization whose general proposal for a solution followed the lines of corporatism and solidarist solutions in Europe, but their impracticality within the United States presented the main problem. An alternative approach, the one that ultimately won out, was that represented by John A. Ryan, a priest and professor at The Catholic University of America. Ryan's approach was to call for a number of democratically imposed economic reforms, many of which are now taken for granted in the United States as basic to any humane economy. Beginning with the Catholic natural-law tradition and its emphasis on order and harmony, he argued for labor unions, a minimum wage, health insurance, social security, health and safety laws, and a host of other elements. His loyalty to Rome led him to accept the occupational council system proposed in *Quadragesimo anno,* but his own energy was directed toward greater government intervention to prevent abuses in the economy, an emphasis that the Catholic bishops of the nation came to share. Both the "solidarist" and "meliorist" approaches to the social question were represented within the Catholic Economic Association (later, the Association for Social Economics) and its journal, *Review of Social Economy.*

In the period since the Second Vatican Council, the mainstream of Catholic social thought and economic life has been influenced by a spectrum of opinion from the conservative voices on the Right within the United States to the more radical thought of liberation theologians speaking from Latin America.

The best-known neoconservative Catholic voice on economic matters in the United States is Michael Novak. In *The Spirit of Democratic Capitalism,* he charges that the Roman Catholic tradition has been too critical of the cultural resources of the modern world. He argues that the Catholic church in the United States has much to teach the rest of the church universal because of its success in wedding a strong sense of the individual with traditional community values. Novak asserts that three distinguishable systems make up the modern nation: the economic, political, and moral/cultural systems. Each needs to have its own relative autonomy from and influence over the others, with none of the three dominating. Thus he criticizes church leaders and other intellectuals who wish to impose too many standards from the moral/cultural system onto the economic and political systems (Novak, pp. 182–86).

Central to Novak's argument is the claim that entrepreneurs and business leaders are not the evil, profit-maximizing, greedy people their critics make them out to be. Novak argues that Americans are, in fact, a communitarian and generous people, and points to a number of empirical observations like those of Alexis de Tocqueville in the 19th century to illustrate his point. The implication, then, is that a communitarian people such as this will be able to assimilate without danger the individualizing effects of a free-market economy as long as the moral and cultural institutions of the society remain vibrant and maintain that communal sense. The only alternative he sees is for the churches to try to reestablish the homogeneity that Christianity sustained in the Middle Ages, something to which Novak attributes the ongoing poverty of Latin America (Novak, pp. 272–82).

A radically different interpretation of the poverty in the Third World is provided by liberation theologians. Predominately a Catholic development, liberation theology grew up in Latin America following Vatican II. This perspective begins with two fundamental facts about Christian life and beliefs. The first is that Christians, like Jesus himself, must be identified with the poor and oppressed. The second is that good Christian theology must be a reflection upon Christian life and not an abstract construction prior to it. The result is that Christian theology is authentic only if it is a reflection on the ongoing struggles for liberation of the poor and oppressed of the world. Theology, then, is critical reflection on liberating praxis (Gutiérrez, pp. 13–15). It is in this way that liberation theology makes a "preferential option for the poor," requiring an identification with the poor and their struggles in order to understand adequately the world around us. Critics of liberation theology have accused it of putting too much stress on economic liberation to the neglect of the Christian's relation with God, but liberation theologians such as Gutiérrez have insisted from the beginning of this theological movement that there are three "levels of meaning" implicit in the term. Liberation entails (1) economic and political liberation from the oppression of existing structures, (2) the liberation of humanity as a historic task throughout the ages, and (3) the liberation of humans from sin and into communion with God (Gutiérrez, p. 176).

While liberation theologians do not endorse Marxist beliefs universally, most do depend heavily on Marxian social science, in particular the dependency theory of underdevelopment. According to this understanding, the nations of the Third World are underdeveloped not because they simply have yet to catch up with the developed nations of the world but because they are and will remain in a subordinate relationship to those developed nations. Thus only with a radical change—only with democratic socialism and a break in the current hegemony of First World economies throughout the Third World—can those latter nations find a path for their own economic flourishing.

When the U.S. Catholic bishops set out to write a pastoral letter on economic life in the early 1980s they were fully aware that the spectrum of judgment within the U.S. Catholic community ranged from neoconservative to liberationist. They had before them the statements not only of individual liberation theologians but of the Latin American bishops conference at Medellín (1968) and Puebla (1979). They were also aware of the difficulties caused for the World Council of Churches when many Protestants objected to the radical economic and political stands taken by that body in the 1960s and 1970s (Paul Abracht, "From Oxford to Vancouver," *The Ecumenical Review* 40, no. 2, April, 1988, pp. 147–68). As a result, the bishops opted to refrain from the ideological debates about capitalism and socialism and instead sought a narrower focus, one indicated by the ultimate title for the work: *Economic Justice for All: Catholic Social Teaching and the U.S. Economy* (1986). In it the bishops appeal to biblical themes—creation in God's image, the covenant, the reign of God, discipleship, poverty—as well as to ethical resources available from the traditional Catholic commitment to the natural law—the dignity of the human person, human rights, love and solidarity, participation, and commutative, distributive, and social justice. As a result, the bishops conclude that a just economic order must encourage the participation of all persons and must guarantee a number of economic rights, including at least minimal levels of food, clothing, shelter, medical care, and basic education (EJA 80). When an economic system is working well, nearly all adults assure themselves of these basics through gainful employment, and for that reason the bishops call for a strong economy and insist on "the right to earn a living" and the related rights to healthful and safe working conditions, wages sufficient to human dignity, and the possibility of property ownership. When, however, the individual is either unable to work or unable to find work, then society has a duty to provide for basic needs in the economic sphere just as it has a duty to guarantee the fundamental freedoms in the political sphere (80).

The bishops endorse the notion of an "option for the poor," but this is in important respects different from that espoused in liberation theology. For liberation theologians it plays the role of an *epistemological* principle, asserting that only from the perspective of the poor can the Christian truly understand the contradictions of the economic order. For the U.S. bishops the option for the poor is principally an *ethical* principle, one based on human dignity. "The obligation to provide justice for all means that the poor have the single most urgent economic claim on the conscience of the nation" (86). The bishops do not call for equality of income or wealth (74) but do call for an end to the marginalization and powerlessness of the poor in American society. They call for a new cultural consensus that would invigorate a project similar to the experiment with political rights at the nation's founding: "a similar experiment in securing economic rights: the creation of an order that guarantees the minimum condition of human dignity in the economic sphere for every person" (95). While the federal government has an important role to play in that process, the bishops are careful to articulate the roles of working people, labor unions, owners, managers, and citizens more generally in this process.

The bishops address four concrete policy problems—employment, poverty, food and agriculture, and the relation to developing nations—but in doing so they make it clear that they speak with a different authority than when they address general principles. "Our judgments and recommendations on specific economic issues, therefore, do not carry the same moral authority as our statement of universal moral principles and formal church teaching" (135). The bishops urge that the nation make employment its highest priority. This would mean not only achieving a strong economy at the level of macroeconomics but also establishing targeted employment programs through cooperation of business, labor, and government to assist the unemployed, particularly the long-term unemployed. The bishops describe the changing characteristics of poverty in the United States, with higher proportions of women and children than in the past, and call for a social solidarity that will assist the poor without creating a dependency imposed by paternalistic programs. The bishops defend the existence of economic inequality on the basis of incentives, risk, and other factors but judge that the level of inequality in the United States is morally unacceptable (185). They call for better national policy to encourage conservation and to diminish the negative economic effects on moderate-sized family farms caused by current government policy. The bishops call for a morally responsible role for the United States in international economic relationships, both nation-to-nation and within international organizations.

The close of the bishops' pastoral letter on economics captures quite well the current state of Catholic social thought on economic life. The bishops remind their readers of the importance of a commitment to a kingdom of love and justice and the centrality of personal conversion in a morally responsible economic life. At the same time, they presume that the economic system will be characterized by the activity of free persons within markets that are circumscribed by laws designed to prevent the worst abuses to which an otherwise completely free market would lead. As a result, critics on the Left are dissatisfied because the bishops do not condemn capitalism, while critics on the Right are irritated because the bishops call for a more robust communal structuring of economic life than capitalism by itself provides. The bishops, however, press ahead in proposing a new and more adequate vision for what economic and political life together might be. They do not call for a return to an earlier era when economic relationships seemed less problematic, nor do they advocate a sectarian withdrawal from the mainstream of American public life today. Rather, they challenge their readers both within and outside the church to begin "a new American experiment: a partnership for the public good" (295). This would include greater cooperation within firms and industries, between the mediating structures of voluntary associations at local and regional levels, and a national partnership in the development of policies conducive to the establishment of justice and the attainment of common good in our public life.

Many challenges and questions remain, at both a theatrical and practical level, for the understanding of the economic order for Catholic social thought and for Christian social thought more generally. The single most encouraging dimension of the situation in the late 20th century is that there is now more attention directed to the problems of economic life and their relationship to Christian faith than ever before in history.

See also CAPITALISM; GOODS, ACCESS TO /DISTRIBUTION OF; JUST WAGE; LABOR AND CAPITAL IN CATHOLIC SOCIAL THOUGHT; LIBERATION THEOLOGY; MODERN CATHOLIC SOCIAL THOUGHT; OWNERSHIP; POOR, PREFERENTIAL OPTION FOR; PRIVATE PROPERTY; RIGHTS AND DUTIES.

Bibliography: NCCB, *Economic Justice for All Catholic Social Teaching and the U.S. Economy* (Washington: USCC, 1986). J. Haughey, ed., *The Faith That Does Justice* (New York: Paulist, 1977). B. Gordon, *The Economic Problem in Biblical and Patristic Thought* (Leiden: E. J. Brill, 1989). C. Avila, *Ownership: Early Christian Teaching* (Maryknoll, N.Y.: Orbis, 1983). E. Troeltsch, *The Social Teaching of the Christian Churches* (1911), 2 vol. (Chicago: Univ. of Chicago Press, 1976). F. Mueller, *The Church and the Social Question* (1963) (Washington: American Enterprise Institute, 1984). C. Curran, *American Catholic Social Ethics* (Notre Dame: Univ. of Notre Dame Press, 1982). G. Gutiérrez, *A Theology of Liberation* (1971), (Maryknoll, N.Y.: Orbis, 1973). I. Garcia, *Justice in Latin American Theology of Liberation* (Atlanta: John Knox, 1987). M. Novak, *The Spirit of Democratic Capitalism* (New York: American Enterprise Institute/Simon & Schuster, 1982).

DANIEL RUSH FINN

ECONOMIC PLANNING, SOCIAL IMPORTANCE OF

Catholic social teaching on economic planning concerns roles and relationships of agents on various levels from local to international. These agents include in widely varying degrees governments and other public agencies; financial institutions; corporations and businesses; workers, especially as represented by labor unions; and various movements and agencies working for social change.

From the time of Leo XIII Catholic social thought has criticized both liberal capitalism and Marxist collectivism as practiced by dominant powers, asserting that neither free markets alone nor state-controlled central planning is the best way to organize the economy. Major references to economic planning in Catholic social thought include *Gaudium et spes* 70; *Populorum progressio* 33–42, 50–55; *Laborem exercens* 17–18; *Sollicitudo rei socialis* 36; *Economic Justice for All* 115, 280, 315–17; ECPC 3. These references reflect attempts to modify assumptions of both systems.

Catholic social teaching on the dignity and social nature of the human person and on the nature of society and the state provides the basis for much of its critique. According to this tradition human dignity is realized in community, in each person's vocation to participate as a co-creator with God in a divine plan for bringing about a community of justice and peace, and the state plays a positive though limited role in promoting the common good. The principle of subsidiarity has meant both that higher bodies such as the state should refrain from acting where smaller bodies are sufficient and that public authorities should intervene where smaller bodies are unwilling or unable to ensure economic justice for all.

While affirming a place for private property and the free market, Catholic social teaching has also emphasized social responsibilities attached to ownership. Since Pius XI it has recognized the possible necessity in some situations for socialization or nationalization of some sectors of the economy—whenever private ownership puts so much power into the hands of a few that governments can no longer protect and foster the common good—with the proviso that measures be taken to ensure broad participation in decisions and ownership.

Since Vatican II the requirements of serving the common good in the context of a globally interdependent economy have come to the fore; among other measures the establishment of an effective international authority has been advocated. Economic as well as political democracy has been defined positively in terms of a human right to participation rather than solely as a right to freedom from state intervention. In recent years Catholic social teaching has struggled with the implications of an option for the poor, which evaluates economic plans on the basis of their effect on poor people and places priority on maximizing their opportunities for participation in economic life, including decision making.

As presented in Catholic social thought, the issue is not whether economies should be planned but rather who participates in planning, in what ways, and for what ends. In practice, economic planning already takes place at many levels, from families to corporations to governmental agencies (EJA 317). The role of government in planning, according to Catholic social thought, is to coordinate planning for the common good, with as many people as possible participating through a variety of organizations. As Gregory Baum observes in a commentary on documents issued by the Canadian Catholic bishops, "The necessary centralizing trend, the growing need for responsible and democratically controlled economic planning, must be counter-balanced by a decentralizing trend, the cutting down to size of the giant transnational corporations" and the fostering of "various forms of community ownership and workers' ownership of the industries" (Baum, "Canadian Catholic Social Theory," p. 256). This tension is central in Catholic social thought on economic planning as a just and rational coordination of economic activity with the widest possible participation in planning as in all other facets of socioeconomic life.

See also CAPITALISM; COLLECTIVISM; COMMON GOOD; POOR, PREFERENTIAL OPTION FOR; PRIVATE PROPERTY; PUBLIC AND PRIVATE, RELATIONSHIP OF; SOCIALIZATION; SUBSIDIARITY, PRINCIPLE OF.

Bibliography: G. Baum, *The Priority of Labor: A Commentary on "Laborem Exercens," Encyclical Letter of Pope John Paul II* (New York: Paulist, 1982). G. Baum, "Toward a Canadian Catholic Social Theory," *Cross Currents* 35:2–3 (Summer/Fall, 1985) 242–56. M. Carnoy and D. Shearer, *Economic Democracy* (Armonk, N.Y.: Sharpe, 1980).

BARBARA HOGAN

EDUCATION, ROLE OF

The church has always been concerned with education, since among its other essential functions the church is a teaching body. The University of Paris was founded and chartered by the church in 1205, and that of Bologna almost simultaneously, thus beginning the long history of university education in the West. (The Muslims had earlier academies, mainly religious, in the Middle East.) The center and core of these early Catholic universities—Oxford and Cambridge, Salamanca, Coimbra, Louvain, Vienna, Munich, Cologne, Pavia, and many others—was initially the professional theology and philosophy faculties, followed quickly by faculties in civil and canon law and medicine. The trivium and quadrivium were propaedeutic studies for all of these.

After the Reformation and the Enlightenment the Catholic universities were secularized and became state universities. They remained, however, the primary centers of higher education and many kinds of professional preparation. Science and, later, engineering assumed an ever more important role with the advent of scientific and industrial revolutions.

In the last century Louvain regained its Catholic charter, and several Catholic institutes were founded in France at Paris, Lille, Tour, Lyon, and Toulouse. New Catholic universities were founded in Holland (Nijmegen) and Italy (Sacro Cuore in Milan), with state-supported Catholic and Protestant theological faculties at German and other state universities.

Finally, in North and South America and, sparingly, in the Far East (Korea, Japan, Taiwan, the Philippines) new Catholic universities and colleges were established over the past two centuries. The United States claims almost half of these—they are funded privately, chartered by the states, and generally under lay control. There are currently about 250 such institutions in the United States and about 500,000 students in mainly coeducational settings. The two best Canadian Catholic universities, Laval (in Quebec) and Montreal, recently repeated history by becoming state universities with Catholic theological faculties.

From the very beginning of universities, one of their most significant roles has been the preparation and credentialing of professionals: clergymen and clergywomen, lawyers, medical doctors, scientists, politicians, business leaders, teachers, and many kinds of paraprofessionals. There is generally a twelve-year educational cycle that precedes this professional education. Most nations provide six-to-eight-year elementary and four-to-six-year secondary schooling as preparation for their best students, who apply for higher or professional learning in the universities.

Obviously, this elementary and secondary education is quite different in scope and excellence depending on the economic and social levels of the given country. There is also a wide disparity of educational quality within countries. And in spite of worldwide educational efforts (except in the least-developed countries) there remain more than a billion illiterate people—mainly poor—with an even larger number who are functionally illiterate.

It would be difficult to project a promising and humanly fulfilling career of lifetime work today without some education beyond high school. Particularly in the most demanding high-technology climate in the world's history, the qualifications required of all who work—professionals, nonprofessionals, semiprofessionals—are higher than ever before. Therefore quality education on all levels becomes a necessity for any person or nation that does not want to live on the fringes of social and economic progress.

The astounding postwar economic success of such Asian countries as Japan, Taiwan, Korea, and Hong Kong is explained by an excellent educational system through all levels that produces a population of almost universally literate and capable citizens. In contrast, in the most affluent and advanced country on earth, the United States, too many black and Hispanic minorities, through educational deprivation in ghetto schools and the high rate of dropping out of school, are becoming an underclass with fading hopes for the future. Education makes all the difference.

In modern times, there has been a growing tension between humanistic and technological or vocational education. The latter is focused on how to do something; the former on how to be someone. One could say that both are necessary. On the one hand, it is important, through humanistic education in literature, art, history, mathematics, and science, to understand the full dimensions of being human and humane. On the other hand, a human needs to make a living, which implies vocational education as well. It should be possible to achieve both these goals through humanistic and vocational education. To educate exclusively for one or the other would be to undereducate for life in modern society.

Another perennial controversy is whether education can or should teach values. This seems to be a fruitless dichotomy; education is by its very nature a great values for humans, cherished throughout human history. Moreover, learning without values could be a dangerous asset for humans. Trained intelligence, which can be a human benefit, can be a threat if badly used. An intelligent thief or brigand is a worse threat than a stupid one.

Most educators would see the advantage of stressing values in all levels of education. Obviously, honesty is to be preferred to dishonesty. Patriotism is better than perfidy. Justice is better than injustice, caring better than uncaring, knowledge better than ignorance. These basic values are at the heart of human progress and prosperity. How can one visualize education without them?

Such values may more easily be inculcated in religious schools, but it would seem an important part of all education to teach these values in all schools. It should be noted that these values are better exemplified in the lives of teachers than by the words they utter. As St. Augustine said, "Our words speak, but our example cries out."

Education on all levels seeks to draw out the potential good in all of us, to replace error with truth, to move from ignorance and incompetence to knowledge and competence. Beyond knowledge, education should lead to wisdom, which is the foundation of all human good and happiness.

See also BUSINESS ETHICS; CHURCH, SOCIAL MISSION OF; CULTURE; HUMANISM; INCULTURATION; MORAL LIFE, CHRISTIAN; REASON, ROLE OF.

THEODORE M. HESBURGH, C.S.C.

EMPLOYMENT AND UNEMPLOYMENT

Employment is the main source of income for most people in modern industrial economies. The income earned from employment is their primary means of obtaining the food, clothing, shelter, education, and other goods and services necessary to lead a life of human dignity. Also, employment is an important way that people participate in the workings of their societies. Unemployment takes away people's ability to provide for their needs and excludes them from participation in the economy.

Thus it is understandable that employment and unemployment have been central concerns of Catholic social thought. *Rerum novarum, Quadragesimo anno,* and most of the statements of the U.S. Catholic bishops, including *Economic Justice for All,* give major emphasis to the importance of employment and the tragedy of unemployment. As the U.S. bishops said in *Economic Justice for All*: "Full employment is the foundation of a just economy. The most urgent priority for domestic economic policy is the creation of new jobs with adequate pay and decent working conditions. We must make it possible as a nation for every one who is seeking a job to find employment within a reasonable amount of time. Our emphasis on this goal is based on the conviction that human work has a special dignity and is a key to achieving justice in society. Employment is a basic right, a right which protects the freedom of all to participate in the economic life of society. It is a right which flows from the principles of justice. . . . Corresponding to this right is the duty on the part of society to ensure that the right is protected. The importance of this right is evident in the fact that for most people employment is crucial to self-realization and essential to the fulfillment of material needs" (EJA 136–37).

The encyclicals, pastoral letters, and council documents that make up Catholic social thought are fundamentally moral documents. They are not treatises on economics. Concern for the effects of the economy on the lives of millions of human beings led to their issuance. They argue that concern for human dignity in social solidarity is at the core of Christian faith (*Mater et magistra* 219–20; *Gaudium et spes* 63; EJA 28). Because economic institutions and policies have a major impact on human dignity they are not only technical but moral concerns as well. Therefore a Christian perspective on economic life must be shaped by three questions: What does the economy do for people? What does it do to people? And how does it permit people to participate? In addition, in pursuing the common good special concern must be given to the economy's impact on the poor and powerless because they are particularly vulnerable and needy.

The concept of the common good is rooted in a communitarian vision of society (Hollenbach). Because of this it emphasizes both the dignity of the human person and the essentially social nature of that dignity. Both civil and political liberties on the one hand and social and economic needs on the other are essential components of the common good.

Gaudium et spes defines the common good as "the sum of those conditions of social life which allow social groups and their individual members relatively thorough and ready access to their own fulfillment" (GS 26). The common good is not the aggregate of the welfare of all individuals. Rather it is a set of social conditions necessary for the realization of human dignity that transcend the arena of private exchange and contract. For example, "such goods as political self-determination, participation in the economic productivity of an industrialized society, and enjoyment of one's cultural heritage can be obtained by an individual only through participation in the public life of society" (Hollenbach, p. 147). Such conditions or goods are essentially relational. To exist they must exist as shared. Claims on these goods are social rights such as freedom of assembly, work, and adequate health care.

In short, individual persons have rights to those things necessary to realize their dignity as human beings who are made in the image and likeness of God. These rights are derived from the person's membership in a community, not from his or her nature as an isolated individual. God made the earth and everything in it for the use of all, not for some individuals to benefit greatly while others are excluded. One of the most important rights that every person shares and the one that concerns us here is the right to employment.

Economists on Employment

In contrast, free-market economic theory is rooted in an individualist conception of society. Society is seen as a collection of individuals who have chosen to associate because it is mutually beneficial. The common good is simply the aggregate of the welfare of each individual. Individual liberty is the highest good, and if individuals are left free to pursue their self-interest, the result will be the maximum material welfare.

The core of economic analysis is the model of competitive-market capitalism. In this view an uncoerced person can be depended upon to act rationally to maximize his or her individual self-interest; more importantly, an automatic, self-regulating mechanism to manage economic affairs is possible if it is built on that self-interested human nature. Free individual choices are expected to overcome scarcity and result in the common good through the automatic adjustments of free exchange in markets. The forces of competition ensure that the economy produces those goods that people desire and that those goods are produced in the most efficient way.

The fact that all economies, including the most advanced industrial ones, are characterized by widespread poverty, unemployment, and low wages poses a problem to free-market economists. The claim that free competition ensures material welfare for all, including those at the bottom, seems to ring hollow. Free-market economists explain these problems in two ways. First, there are countries that restrict the free operation of markets. If these countries would remove the restrictions to the free play of self-interest, much of the poverty would be eliminated by the resulting economic growth. Second, in those countries with free-market systems, continuing poverty is explained as the result of the niggardliness of physical nature and the improvidence of human nature.

This was the dominant view of economics in both England and the United States until the 1930s, and during the 1980s it once again became the ruling economic belief in much of the world, including the rapidly disintegrating communist countries. This free-market view can be summarized under a few propositions held by these economists.

1. People are motivated primarily by self-interest, described best by Adam Smith as an "innate propensity to truck, barter, and exchange."

2. A free-market economy, through the forces of competition, converts that self-interested behavior into the common good by forcing profit-maximizing firms to produce what self-interested consumers demand and to do so in the most efficient way.

3. A free-market economy requires freedom of choice—of where to invest, of what job to take, of what product to purchase, and so on.

4. Problems in the economy, including poverty, either are due to government interference with the free market or are the result of physical and human nature. The scarcity in physical nature requires time to overcome. The perversity of human nature means some people will always fail and thus be poor; some people are lazy, immoral, or improvident.

5. Public authorities can and should do little besides enforce the rules of the game and provide those goods, for example, defense, that the private sector is unable to produce.

6. There is an inherent stability in the market economy, and equilibrium will generally be at a position of full employment. What may appear as destructive effects of market operation, the loss of jobs or industries, are transitory by-products of the market's creativity in constantly forcing increases in efficiency and productivity.

7. The propositions that hold for national economies hold in the international sphere as well. A regime of free trade through international markets with little government involvement will be most successful in improving world income.

However, this optimistic view of the free-market economy has been plagued by the periodic recurrence of large-scale unemployment. When the unemployment rate in the United States and Europe exceeded 25 percent in 1933, economists and policymakers were ripe for a new vision and a new social philosophy. The easy assumption about the individual's sole responsibility for poverty rang hollow as millions of hardworking persons suddenly found their basic material welfare severely threatened.

The period from 1930 to 1975 was marked with turmoil. These forty-five years of the mid-20th century saw the first days of a depression in the Western world that threatened the collapse of the entire free-market system. Glaring inequities of wealth and income became stark realities in the face of breadlines and widespread poverty. Meeting basic needs was only a dream for many. There was a rash of mortgage foreclosures that expelled countless small farmers from their land. All of this occurred in the midst of an absurd idleness of capital equipment, despite the obvious need for production.

Economists had believed that free-market economies were self-stabilizing, but the English economist John Maynard Keynes was now arguing that such free-market systems were inherently unstable. His argument, in essence, was rather simple. The economists before Keynes' time had assumed and had even abstractly "proven" that through the medium of markets, tens of thousands of economic participants would go about their daily economic activities in such a way as to achieve, unknowingly, a full-employment economy. But Keynes now argued that this theory was only a special case of a more general theory, and that equilibrium with unemployment was the general expectation.

One of the cornerstones of Keynes' theory was his treatment of investment. Classical and neoclassical economists believed that the level of investment was closely tied to the interest rate. If an economy started to fall into a recession, the interest rate would decline, causing investment to increase, thus preventing the recession. Keynes, however, argued forcefully that investment decisions were much more closely linked with what he called "animal spirits." The term suggested fragility and instability, even when it was in large measure narrowed to refer to profit expectations or business optimism. Keynes had ample evidence for his case in the depression of the 1930s, for even though investment was sorely needed and the interest rate had fallen below 1 percent, there was still minimal investment. No sane business would invest, regardless of the interest rate, if convinced that the project would incur losses.

In addition to his argument about the interest rate and investment, Keynes rejected the free-market economist's notion that wage reductions would lead to increases in employment. Instead he argued that wages are a part of aggregate demand in addition to being production costs. If wages fall, aggregate demand and sales will fall. If sales fall, profits will decline and firms will demand less labor. The depression experience of the 1930s in the industrial world made these points convincing to all who were not wedded to free-market economics.

Thus Keynes argued that decentralized decision making by millions of consumers and businesses would add up to full employment only by accident. There are no automatic mechanisms pushing the capitalist economy toward full employment. To Keynes it was not at all surprising, therefore, that the economy was mired in a state of high unemployment with no mechanism to lift itself out.

Keynes, however, did not leave the economy to flounder. He proposed that the necessary ingredient for stability was appropriate government fiscal and monetary intervention, consisting primarily of expenditure, taxation, and credit policies. He showed that the government could ease the recession-racked economy back toward a full-employment equilibrium by providing the initial stimulus to restore confidence and return some much-needed purchasing power to participants in the economy. As a result, any unemployment caused by deficient aggregate demand could be overcome by government action to increase aggregate demand.

Proof of the Keynesian demand-management propositions came with the monumental spending requirements of World War II. In short order the vacant factories were taken out of mothballs, dusted off, and retooled, and were soon producing the equipment needed for the U.S. war effort. Idle men and women were either handed a rifle to use or were put at the seat of a rifle-making machine. There was practically no unemployment. The war experience was thus the first piece of clear evidence that the government could have a major impact on aggregate demand and could offset the demand deficiency of the private sector.

The appearance of inflation as a major problem in the 1970s led to a repudiation of Keynesian macroeconomic policies and a renewal of free-market policies in the 1980s. In England and the United States, new governments embraced free-market views and focused on inflation as the major economic policy problem. As a result large recessions developed in both countries during the early 1980s, reaching unemployment levels higher than any time since the 1930s. Even with sustained economic recovery the decade of the 1980s had higher average unemployment rates than any decade since the 1930s.

Thus the prevailing policy priority in the United States and many other industrial countries is to accept higher unemployment rates in the attempt to achieve lower inflation rates. Certainly inflation is an important economic problem, but the use of a recession and unemployment as the solution results in even greater evils. It is here that Catholic social thought has something important to contribute to the debate.

Catholic Social Thought on Employment

The social teachings of the church, beginning with Pope Leo XIII, extending through Pope Pius XI, Pope Paul VI, and now Pope John Paul II, especially in *Laborem exercens,* assist us in finding the roots of the unemployment problem. They point out the flaws in the way we view the economy and therefore have structured it—atomistically, oriented to self-interest, measuring quality of life by material benefit and a commodity mentality.

In 1891 Pope Leo XIII wrote, "The present age handed over the workers, each alone and defenseless, to the inhumanity of employers and the unbridled greed of competitors" (RN 6). Forty years later, during the depression of the 1930s, Pope Pius XI said, "The ultimate consequences of the individualist spirit in economic life are . . . : Free competition has destroyed itself; economic dictatorship has supplanted the free market; unbridled ambition for power has likewise succeeded greed for gain; all economic life has become tragically hard, inexorable, and cruel" (QA 109). In 1961 Pope John XXIII proclaimed, "Work, inasmuch as it is an expression of the human person, can by no means be regarded as a mere commodity. . . . [It] is not to be thought of in terms of merchandise, but rather according to the laws of justice and equity" (MM 18).

In 1981 Pope John Paul II summed up the market vision of the economy as economism—the failure to remember the primacy of persons in community over things (LE 13). In our failure to remember the primacy of persons we have lost sight of the centrality of work—the obligation and the right of all persons throughout the world to work in order to satisfy their own needs and to work for the common good. *Laborem exercens* was written because despite the fact that "from the beginning of the industrial age, the Christian truth about work had to oppose the various trends of materialistic and economistic thought . . . the danger of treating work as a special kind of 'merchandise' or as an impersonal 'force' needed for production . . . always exists, especially when the whole way of looking at the question of economics is marked by the premises of materialistic economism" (7).

Labor is not merely a factor of production or a means to the end of increased production. The right and obligation to work is not to be determined by the vagaries of the market, whether that market is domestic or international. We are to understand the meaning of our existence and our dignity in terms of our work as co-creators, first of all for the common good—the human community—and also for ourselves. Therefore all people must have the opportunity to work, and all work should express human solidarity.

The communitarian nature of Catholic social thought repudiates the position that the level of unemployment should be left to the dictates of the market. Emphasis on the common good means that the community has an obligation to guarantee the right of employment to all persons. Thus the state, as an instrument of the community, has an important role to play in ensuring the effectiveness of that right.

Pope John XXIII summarized the basic teaching on the role of the state as given by Pope Leo XIII in 1891: "The state, whose purpose is the realization of the common good in the temporal order, can by no means disregard the economic activities of its citizens. Indeed, it should be present to promote in a suitable manner the production of a sufficient supply of material goods, . . . safeguard the rights of all citizens, but especially the weaker, such as workers, women and children, . . . contribute actively to the betterment of the living conditions of workers, . . . see to it that labor agreements are entered into according to the norms of justice and equity, and that in the environment of work the dignity of the human being is not violated either in body or spirit" (MM 20–21).

In *Laborem exercens* Pope John Paul II discusses the role of the indirect employer—all the agents at the national and international level that are responsible for economic policy. "The role of the agents included under the title of indirect employer is to act against unemployment, which in all cases is an evil and which, when it reaches a certain level, can become a social disaster" (18).

Drawing upon the principle of subsidiarity—where responsibility begins at the level of the individual and works upward through local groups to the national and international level as needed—Pope John Paul II elaborates the community's obligations to overcome unemployment: "In order to meet the danger of unemployment and to ensure employment for all, the agents defined here as *indirect employer* must make provision for overall planning with regard to the different kinds of work by which not only the economic life, but also the cultural life of a given society is shaped; they must also give attention to organizing that work in a correct and rational way. In the final analysis this overall concern weighs on the shoulders of the state, but it cannot mean one-sided centralization by the public authorities. Instead, what is in question is a just and rational coordination, within the framework of which the initiative of individuals, free groups, and local work centers and complexes must be safeguarded" (18).

Of necessity, when speaking to the whole world, papal encyclical letters remain relatively abstract and general. When addressing specific economic issues in a particular country, national conferences of bishops can be more concrete in their analyses and recommendations. The U.S. bishops have done so on a number of occasions—from the Bishops' Program of Social Reconstruction of 1919, through the *Statement on Unemployment* (1930) and *The Economy: Human Dimensions* (1975), to *Economic Justice for All: Pastoral Letter on Catholic Social Teaching and the U.S. Economy* (1986), to name the best known.

In *Economic Justice for All* the bishops summarize Catholic social thought and conclude that "employment is a basic right" (137). They then describe and analyze the specifics of the unemployment situation in the United States in the mid-1980s. Applying Catholic social thought to this concrete reality, they develop specific recommendations to realize the right of work for all. Recognizing that "the movement from principle to policy is complex and difficult and that although moral values are essential in determining public policies, they do not dictate specific solutions" (134), the bishops caution that their "judgments and recommendations do not carry the same moral authority as [their] statements of universal moral principles and formal church teaching" (135).

The bishops do not claim to provide the last word on the unemployment debate. Rather their goal is to give an example of why and how moral concerns are an important part of economic issues. In effect they are saying: Here is our attempt to apply moral values. If you are not satisfied, then try it yourself. Their recommendations are not economically naive. While free-market economists have decried them as "statist," most other economists—influenced by the work of Keynes—have received them as thoughtful and reasonable recommendations. It is worthwhile to list some of these recommendations:

1. "the fiscal and monetary policies of the nation—such as federal spending, tax, and interest rate policies—should be coordinated so as to achieve the goal of full employment" (156).

2. "expansion of job-training and apprenticeship programs in the private sector administered and supported jointly by business, labor unions, and government" (159).

3. "increased support for direct job creation programs targeted on the long-term unemployed and those with special needs" (162).

The validity of specific policies such as these is dependent on an accurate assessment of empirical reality and therefore is open for debate. However, underlying these proposals are the less contingent propositions that full employment should be a priority goal of economic policy, that government must play an important role in carrying out such policy, and that it is the duty of all citizens to support some such policies.

Conclusion

In Catholic social thought employment is the major way in which most people in industrial economies both earn a living and participate in their communities. Therefore, as members of a community people have a moral right to employment, and their communities have a moral obligation to construct economic institutions and policies so that this right can be exercised. Catholic social thought rejects the free-market argument that the level of employment should be determined entirely by the workings of the marketplace. It also rejects the use of recessions and unemployment as a means of fighting inflation. Labor is people, not simply a commodity to be bought and sold as the vagaries of the market dictates. Rather, markets and other economic institutions and policies should be shaped and regulated according to "whether it protects or undermines the dignity of the human person" (EJA 13).

See also CAPITALISM; COMMON GOOD; ECONOMIC PLANNING, SOCIAL IMPORTANCE OF; INFLATION; KEYNESIANISM; LABOR AND CAPITAL IN CATHOLIC SOCIAL THOUGHT; RECESSION; WORK, THEOLOGY OF.

Bibliography: D. Byers, ed., *Justice in the Market Place: Collected Statements of the Vatican and the United States Catholic Bishops on Economic Policy, 1891–1984* (USCC, 1985). NCCB, *Economic Justice for All: Pastoral Letter on Catholic Social Teaching and the U.S. Economy* (USCC, 1986). G. Baum, *The Priority of Labor: A Commentary on "Laborem Exercens"* (Paulist, 1982). J. Cronin, *Catholic Social Principles* (Bruce, 1950). D. Hollenbach, *Claims in Conflict: Retrieving and Renewing the Catholic Human Rights Tradition* (Paulist, 1979). C. Strain, ed., *Prophetic Visions and Economic Realities* (Eerdmans, 1989). C. Wilber and K. Jameson, *Beyond Reaganomics: A Further Inquiry into the Poverty of Economics* (Univ. of Notre Dame Press, 1990). O. Williams and J. Houck, eds., *The Common Good and U.S. Capitalism* (Univ. Press of America, 1987).

CHARLES K. WILBER

ENERGY

Energy resources play an essential part in the production of basic goods and in general economic expansion and thus in meeting basic human needs in the modern world. The availability of inexpensive energy sources such as coal, oil, and natural gas fueled the Industrial Revolution and the dramatic progress of Western society into the 20th century. At the same time widespread use of such fuels has led to serious pollution of air, water, and land through the emission of harmful chemicals into the air, "acid rain" which threatens animal and plant life, and the threat of global warming. Furthermore, supplies of fossil fuels, particularly oil, have been severely depleted internationally, resulting in higher prices that severely tax the resources of poor persons and nations and contributing to international tensions.

Conservation of scarce energy resources has been recommended along with the transition to renewable and ecologically safer energy sources. Several alternative sources have been proposed—nuclear, solar, water and wind generated, geothermal—although each alternative has its own dangers or expense. Controversy has in particular surrounded the development of nuclear energy. Proponents suggest that nuclear energy can be produced safely with minimal raw material and with less expense in the long term. Opponents of nuclear energy point to the dangers of radiation in mining, producing, and disposing of radioactive material as well as to the danger of accidents in nuclear power plants. Opponents note further that nuclear energy may aid in the proliferation of nuclear weapons, since such weapons may be produced from nuclear waste products without a great deal of advanced technology. As yet, however, none of the alternative energy sources has proved cost effective for widespread use. Their development would require increased governmental support.

In 1981 the U.S. Catholic bishops suggested six moral principles that should guide decision making in the production and use of energy: (1) Any use of energy resources must uphold the right to life—in regard both to the safety of those who produce energy and to the needs of those who use the energy. (2) Men and women must accept an appropriate share of responsibility for the welfare of creation as "responsible stewards," both for the present and for future generations. (3) People must accept limitation in a Christian spirit, including the acceptance of sacrifice for the sake of others and of the common good. (4) Humanity must strive for a more just society through practices and structures that ensure an equitable distribution of energy resources. (5) Special attention must be given to the needs of poor people and members of minority groups. (6) Wide participation must be ensured in the processes of making decisions about energy production and use.

See also ECOLOGY; NATURAL RESOURCES; STEWARDSHIP.

Bibliography: USCC, "Reflections on the Energy Crisis," *Origins* 10 (April 23, 1981) 705–19.

MARK O'KEEFE, O.S.B.

ENLIGHTENMENT, THE (INFLUENCE OF)

The name "The Enlightenment" is a widely used description of a period in European intellectual history in which a decisive break was made with the ancient and medieval past in favor of a new trust in human reason and science. Thus broadly understood, it has been enormously influential, and its influence is as inescapable as science itself or modernity. More narrowly the term is often limited to the period of roughly the 18th century and is associated with the emergence of a new reliance on instrumental reason as a result of the rise of science and with neoclassical models in art and literature. In addition to scientists, the dominant thinkers of the era were philosophers and political theorists. Early groundwork for modern liberal democratic states is among the most important historical contributions of these Enlightenment thinkers. In this narrow sense the Enlightenment ended with the French Revolution and Napoleon even though many of its themes persisted, intertwined with themes from the Romanticism that then emerged.

Catholic response to the Enlightenment went through a number of stages and continues to be controversial. In the 18th century some direct influence was felt in parts of Germany and northern Europe, but little in the south. The movement was often deplored in the 19th century, where the passing of the medieval world was often identified with denial of church authority and/or with atheism (*Syllabus of Errors*). Leo XIII emphasized the links between the Enlightenment and the French Revolution and the influence of "certain philosophers of the [18th] century, professors of a foolish wisdom, who set themselves to root up the foundations of Christian truth and started a system of philosophy calculated . . . to inflame . . . desires after unlimited license" (*Nobilissima Gallorum gens* 1). Traces of its influence were among the ideas identified as "modernism" and condemned early in the 20th century (*Pascendi*). Indirectly, however, Enlightenment ideas and suppositions subtly influenced Catholic teaching. There was a congruence between the Enlightenment's belief in the reliability of reason and its overall desire for certainty and some aspects of post-Reformation Catholicism. The manualist tradition's "probabilism" in moral theology and emphasis on certainty that characterized much neo-Scholasticism thus showed the unintentional influence of the Enlightenment in the hardening of its own characteristic intellectualism. For example, *Rerum novarum,* groundbreaking in so many ways, may have arrived at its unusual and no longer viable declaration that private property was ordained by natural law on the basis of a Lockean Enlightenment influence.

Gradually, however, positive elements of the Enlightenment were recognized. Democratic government, human rights, and reliance upon scientific evidence for claims made about the empirical world became more acceptable in church circles. At the same time, ideas such as denial of the supernatural, distrust of any authority or tradition, emphasis on individualistic autonomy, and belief in progress and in human perfectibility continued to cause tension. In recent years, however, all of these latter ideas—except the denial of the supernatural—have come under secular attack; though they remain common assumptions they are no longer taken for granted, even in secular philosophy.

By Vatican II, talk of the Enlightenment would have seemed anachronistic, but some of its ideas, previously scorned, were given belated approval. Practical social ideas were separated from the more problematic metaphysical ones and integrated into church life. The most important and most widely recognized of these was religious liberty; related ideas such as separation of church and state and ecumenism were also accepted and institutionalized. The movement toward a popularly understandable vernacular liturgy, toward some decentralization of authority, and away from grossly sentimental and even superstitious practices and customs can also be traced partly to Enlightenment influence. More broadly, the entire thrust of Vatican II was an opening of the windows that had been self-consciously closed against new ideas—those arising from the Enlightenment, the Reformation, and so forth, or sprung from those that had. Needless to say, the exact shape of *aggiornamento* continues to remain unclear.

See also ATHEISM; LEO XIII; NATURAL LAW; PRIVATE PROPERTY; REASON, ROLE OF; RELIGIOUS FREEDOM; RERUM NOVARUM.

Bibliography: M. Buckley, *At the Origins of Modern Atheism* (New Haven: Yale Univ. Press, 1987). H. Jedin and J. Dolan, eds., *The Church in the Age of Absolutism and Enlightenment* (London: Burns & Oates, 1981). H. Küng, *Does God Exist?* (New York: Doubleday, 1980).

ANTHONY BATTAGLIA

ENTERPRISE

The word "enterprise" appeared only recently in papal social thought and has not been listed in any earlier dictionary of Catholic theology, even though according to Friedrich von Hayek and Joseph Schumpeter it is the defining element in capitalism, the most successful (but flawed) economic system that the world has yet experienced. Oswald von Nell-Breuning, S.J., has written that out of respect for his father, a businessman, Pius XI laid the groundwork favorably in *Quadragesimo anno* by reference to the triad of *intellectus, res, opera*: "Man's productive effort cannot yield its fruits . . . unless mind, material things, and work combine and form as it were a single whole" (QA 69). This triadic allusion recognized that enterprise means the use of intelligence (*intellectus*) to combine various factors of material capital (*res*) and labor (*opera*). In Nell-Breuning's view the treatment of this subject at Vatican II in *Gaudium et spes,* because of lack of time, relapsed into a dualistic rather than a triadic mode, so that Vatican II took a step backward, remaining "tied to the traditional but inadequate dual model of property and labor," while omitting any mention of the entrepreneur. This omission aroused considerable dismay among European laypersons.

It also evoked a controversy inasmuch as the formulation of Vatican II mentioned only the following bearers of economic functions: "owners, employers, managers and workers." This list omits the entrepreneur; contrary to the usually strict council rule in this regard it mentions the representatives of capital prior to those of labor and fails to note that "employer" is redundant, since that function is normally exercised either by an owner or a manager.

The precise Latin phrase alluding to enterprise used in *Gaudium et spes* (68) is *participatione in inceptis. Inceptus* refers not at all to what in English we call the virtue of enterprise, or even to the entrepreneur, but rather to "the enterprise" as consisting in the first place of the human beings who work together in association and in the second place of the entire ensemble that makes up a business, from the persons who constitute it, through its capital and operating balance sheets, to its procedures and its products. In this conception of enterprise, the most important element is the association of persons who cooperate in production by making contributions of different kinds, especially by employing their person (labor) or property (capital), and whose various interests the return from this production is intended to serve. Thus, Vatican II wished to emphasize that the enterprise is not merely the sum total of physical assets or of funds shown in the balance sheet but rather the living association of persons working together for their common interest. As Nell-Breuning points out, however, the definition used at Vatican II pointed to the roles only of labor (the workers) and capital (the owners), and omitted the role of the person of enterprise.

But what, precisely, is meant by the term "enterprise," so often overlooked in Catholic social thought? What is distinctive of the entrepreneur or, better put, the person of enterprise? It is clear enough that enterprise, when attributed to a person, points to a virtue, a habitual disposition or skill. But what sort of virtue is it?

In *Sollicitudo rei socialis* Pope John Paul II made by far the clearest and most profound statement concerning the right to economic enterprise in the whole of papal social thought to that time. He rooted enterprise in the image of the Creator, which has been impressed upon the human person, and speaks of it as a right endowed by the Creator (co-equally with the right to religious liberty): "the right to personal economic initiative." He denies to the state any right to oppress this natural inclination, which in the economic order makes each human to be (in the appropriate sense) a creator. The pope points out that the right to economic initiative is important for the common good as well as for the individual. In the individual, its oppression "absolutely destroys the spirit of initiative." Against the common good, its oppression produces "passivity, dependence and submission to the bureaucratic apparatus," producing "frustration or desperation" and propelling "emigration," real or psychological (SRS 15). The pope uses "spirit of initiative" as an important specification of "the creative subjectivity of the citizen."

The new departure of *Sollicitudo* had been foreshadowed by the pope's early phenomenological inquiry, *The Acting Person,* which examined the human capacity to originate action as the clue to human identity. This theme would be elaborated more fully, and in an explicitly economic context, in paragraphs 31–32 of *Centesimus annus,* which highlight initiative and entrepreneurial ability as an "essential part" of work.

Now if humans are endowed with a spirit of initiative, what is the habit that disposes them to exercise this spirit? Clearly enterprise is an intellectual virtue. As Israel Kirzner has written, following Hayek, "discovery" or discerning or noticing are the primary modes of enterprise. As Nell-Breuning puts it, enterprise first of all consists in *intellectus,* the innovative insight by which the entrepreneur "combines the productive factors of labor and capital." The German publication *Ordo Socialis* in its pamphlet *The Entrepreneur* by Peter H. Werhahn offers Schumpeter's definition: The creative entrepreneur is one "who, by means of ever new combinations of the factors of production brings about innovation and makes economic growth possible." This definition brings to light the early meaning of enterprise as defined in the *Oxford English Dictionary,* closely derived from the Latin and the French for "take in hand": "A piece of work taken in hand, an undertaking; *chiefly* . . . a bold, arduous or momentous undertaking." Nowadays, however, with the recognition that enterprise is a universal endowment whose exercise in an age of growing populations and growing needs is a humble daily necessity, enterprise is not viewed as rare or momentous but as ordinary and common to all. In the transition from a feudal order (or socialism) to a democratic and capitalist order, the social structure itself calls for the exercise of intellectual initiative in politics, economics, and culture.

Yet enterprise is more than an intellectual virtue whose essence consists in discerning new possibilities, for an entrepreneur is judged not only by what he/she discovers but also by what he/she actually brings into being, realizes, or produces. In this respect, enterprise is also a moral virtue whose essence is to apply discovery to practice and to move from insight to effective action. Thus, enterprise is parallel to prudence in being both an intellectual and a moral virtue.

We may distinguish, then, four different senses of the noun "enterprise": (1) an undertaking or task; (2) a business firm (a voluntary association) established to undertake specific, concrete tasks over a period of time; (3) the personal virtue constituted by the readiness to discover and to realize new possibilities of economic activity; and (4) the fundamental human right to exercise this virtue. Until Pope John Paul II, the third and fourth of these meanings, personal virtue and fundamental human right, have been almost wholly neglected in Catholic social thought. Reflection on the social and cultural conditions required to nourish this virtue has barely yet been undertaken in theological circles.

Finally, it is necessary to lay bare some common errors: (1) It is a mistake to speak of entrepreneurs as "capitalists" as if they were owners of capital; they may well be users of the venture capital of others or managers of an entrepreneurial organization whose capital is owned by others. (2) The innovation exercised by entrepreneurs may consist less of developing new products than of anticipating and meeting new demands and new circumstances in everchanging markets. (3) The virtue of enterprise is practiced not only by those whose primary function in an organization is labeled "entrepreneur" but also by workers who are daily alert to using "the discovery process" in their work, or even by purchasers who must discover the best among the many choices available to them in the marketplace. (4) The defining characteristic of a capitalist economy is the development of social institutions and cultural supports for promoting the personal practice of enterprise. Such social and cultural institutions would include, for example, patent and copyright laws, the protection of trademarks, financial incentives for invention, easy access to the legal incorporation of new business, open entry into old markets and openness to the establishing of new markets, and an instruction in innovation and creativity throughout the educational system. The mere existence of markets, private property, and the profit motive is virtually universal. These things characterize traditional, precapitalist societies (even socialist societies) as well as capitalist societies. The specific difference that defines the capitalist society, then, is the widespread exercise of the virtue of enterprise over and above the mere existence of the market economy.

See also CENTESIMUS ANNUS; CORPORATIONS; CREDIT; ECONOMIC ORDER; INVESTMENT; PERSONALISM; PROFIT; WORK, THEOLOGY OF.

Bibliography: F. Hayek, "Economics and Knowledge," "The Use of Knowledge in Society," and "The Meaning of Competition," reprinted in *Individualism and the Economic Order* (Chicago: Henry Regnery, 1972). F. Hayek, "Competition as a Discovery Procedure," in Hayek, ed., *New Studies in Philosophy, Politics, Economics, and the History of Ideas* (Chicago: Univ. of Chicago Press, 1978). I. Kirzner, *Discovery and the Market Process* (Chicago: Univ. of Chicago Press, 1985). I. Kirzner, "Socio-Economic Life," commentary on *Gaudium et Spes,* chap. 3, in H. Vorgrimler, ed., *Commentary on the Documents of Vatican II,* vol. 5: *Pastoral Constitution on the Church in the Modern World* (New York: Herder & Herder, 1969) esp. pp. 299ff. O. von Nell-Breuning, *Reorganization of Social Economy: The Social Encyclical Developed and Explained* (New York: Bruce, 1939) esp. pp. 115f. M. Novak, "The Virtue of Enterprise," *Crisis,* vol. 7, no. 5 (May 1989) pp. 19–25. John Paul II, encyclical letter *Sollicitudo Rei Socialis* (Washington: USCC, 1987). Pius XI, encyclical letter *Quadragesimo Anno,* in *Seven Great Encyclicals* (Glen Rock, N.J., 1963). J. Schumpeter, *Capitalism, Socialism, and Democracy,* 3rd ed. (New York: Harper & Row, 1950) esp. pp. 131ff. P. Werhahn, *The Entrepreneur: His Economic Function and Social Responsibility* in *Ordo Socialis No. 4* (Köln, FRG: Association for the Advancement of Christian Sciences, 1990).

MICHAEL NOVAK

ENVIRONMENT

See CREATION; ECOLOGY; ENERGY; KINGDOM OF GOD; LAND; LAND RIGHTS; POPULATION.

EPISCOPAL CONFERENCES, CONCEPT OF

Ever since the earliest times in the history of the church, the bishops of a region have come together in formal meetings, called synods or councils, in order to proclaim and uphold Christian doctrine and to give practical orders and directions for the life of their communities. In the 19th century a new and less formal type of these associations of bishops began to emerge, and they became known as episcopal conferences: they were gatherings of the bishops of a certain region or nation, without any legal power but with some appropriate norms and rules for their operation.

Vatican Council II approved of them and encouraged their establishment: "This most sacred Synod [i.e., council] considers it supremely opportune everywhere that bishops belonging to the same nation or region form an association and meet together at fixed times. Thus, when the insights of prudence and experience have been shared and views exchanged, there will emerge a holy union of energies in the service of the common good of the churches" (*Christus Dominus* 37).

The new Code of Canon Law, promulgated in 1983, has given a constitutional form to the conferences: "The conference of bishops, a permanent institution, is a grouping of bishops of a given nation or territory, whereby, according to the norm of law, they jointly exercise certain pastoral functions on behalf of the Christian faithful of their territory in view of promoting that greater good which the Church offers to human persons, especially through forms and programs of the apostolate which are fittingly adapted to the circumstances of the time and place" (can. 447).

The theological foundation for the episcopal conferences is in the collegial nature of the episcopate. As no one can be a Christian alone, no one can be a bishop alone. To be a bishop means to be a member of the college of bishops, which is a *communion,* a social body. This college is not a voluntary union that a bishop may or may not join; it exists on the strength of the Spirit, who appoints and consecrates the overseer (the original meaning of the ancient Greek word, *episcopoi,* bishops) of the communities. The conferences are therefore nothing else than an external expression of this preexisting reality.

Every diocesan bishop occupies a neuralgic post in the universal church. He is the center of unity for his own people, and through him his people are united to all other churches. Clearly such relations cannot be merely theoretical; they cry for practical expressions. As no bishop could fulfill his task without conversing with his own people; no bishop can be a bond of unity with other churches without sustained and ongoing contact with other bishops.

Although the primary purpose of the episcopal conferences is to serve the welfare of the local churches within their territories, they can certainly be of invaluable help to the primacy. As Peter was helped by Paul's advice, so the successor of Peter can be helped in his solicitude for all the churches by the successors of the other apostles.

The conferences, useful as they are, suffer also from some limitations. The diocesan clergy, who are the *presbyterium* around the bishop in every diocese, have no constitutionally assured ways or means to bring their concerns before the conferences. Religious institutes, which may carry a significant share in the pastoral work of the dioceses (especially through their educational apostolate), have no guaranteed access to the conferences. Nor do laypersons, women or men. When the bishops of a conference deliberate and decide about the life of the church, they are not bound to hear any voice other than their own. The temptation to speak and act as if they were the church can be very real. Also, the people outside their assembly can perceive themselves as being called to a merely passive role in God's kingdom. This constitutional limitation, however, can be remedied by the conferences through a policy of consultation and openness.

See also EPISCOPAL LETTERS, FUNCTION OF; NATIONAL CONFERENCE OF CATHOLIC BISHOPS, UNITED STATES; SYNOD OF BISHOPS; VATICAN COUNCIL II.

Bibliography: H. Legrand et al., eds., *The Nature and Future of Episcopal Conferences* (Washington: Catholic Univ. Press, 1988). T. Reese, ed., *Episcopal Conferences: Historical, Canonical, and Theological Studies* (Washington: Georgetown Univ. Press, 1989). The list and addresses of all episcopal conferences can be found in *Annuario Pontificio,* Vatican City: Libreria Editrice Vaticana, published annually.

LADISLAS ÖRSY, S.J.

EPISCOPAL LETTERS, FUNCTION OF

Among episcopal letters issued by individual bishops or by groups of bishops the so-called pastoral letters have a particular significance. They are public documents addressed to the faithful; they are convenient instruments for the bishops to exercise their teaching office.

That the episcopal office includes the right and duty to teach has been the belief of the church from the earliest times and was confirmed again by Vatican Council II: "As successors of the apostles, bishops receive from him [Christ] the mission to teach all nations and to preach the gospel to every creature" (*Lumen gentium* 24).

Early examples of pastoral letters by an individual bishop are the ones written by St. Ignatius of Antioch (d. ca. 110) to various churches in the Middle East over which he may have had some supervisory authority. In modern times no better instances of the same can be found than the pastoral letters of Emmanuel Célestin Cardinal Suhard, archbishop of Paris (1940–49); they had a great impact on the shaping of the religious life in France after the Second World War.

The establishment of episcopal conferences all over the world after Vatican Council II led to widespread development of pastoral letters by groups of bishops. Two letters of the bishops of the United States, *The Challenge of Peace* (1983) and *Economic Justice for All* (1986), are prime examples of such communication.

To determine the authority of a given episcopal pastoral letter, its content ought to be examined. If it is a proclamation of Catholic beliefs as they have been "handed over" by the apostles, its authority is the same as that of revelation; hence the proper response to it can be an assent of faith. If it is a declaration of anything less than the apostolic tradition, its weight and authority ought to be assessed in the light of the common beliefs of the church and the teaching of the other bishops in communion with the See of Rome; hence the proper response is to receive it with religious loyalty, since the episcopate is not without the assistance of the Spirit, and then to evaluate it according to the ordinary theological criteria; that is, in the light of our tradition and the teaching of other bishops and the See of Rome, giving its proper scope also to the *sensus fidelium*: the supernatural instinct of the faithful.

The ultimate function of such letters is to proclaim the Christian doctrine, to help the faithful to follow an evangelical way of life, and to protect and uphold the dignity and rights of all human persons.

See also EPISCOPAL CONFERENCES, CONCEPT OF; MAGISTERIUM; PASTORAL CARE.

Bibliography: The full texts of the pastoral letters of the U.S. bishops with brief introductions can be found in H. Nolan, ed., *Pastoral Letters of the United States Catholic Bishops,* 1792–1988, in five volumes (to date), Washington: NCCB/USCC, 1984–89. Information about the pastoral letters of other hierarchies can be obtained from the secretariat of the respective conference.

LADISLAS ÖRSY, S.J.

ESCHATOLOGY

Derived from the Greek *eschatos* (furthest, last), the term "eschatology" is taken to refer to the religious vision of the ultimate destiny of humanity and of the world. Recent exegetical and theological studies have raised important questions about the doctrinal and ethical implications of the eschatological vision of the Scriptures.

Old Testament

Whether it is possible to speak of eschatology in the OT is largely a question of how one defines the term. Early in the 19th century, "eschatology" referred to the church's teaching about death, resurrection, judgment, the end of the world, heaven, and hell. This form of eschatology was dismissed by K. Barth as a "harmless little chapter at the end of dogmatic theology" (*Der Römerbrief,* Munich, 1922, p. 486). It is commonly understood among exegetes today that eschatology in this sense is not an issue in the OT. But if eschatology is understood to refer to the development of a future-consciousness throughout the centuries of biblical history, then eschatology is an issue that lies close to the very core of the revelatory process and is intrinsically related to the theology of covenant and promise. The covenanted people hopes for a future, salvific act of God that will bring about the decisive relation of the people with its God.

The unfolding of this future-consciousness in Israel was tied to the political history of the people, reflecting the ambiguities of that experience. Not only is there a positive hope, but there is a sense of a coming divine judgment as well (Amos 7:1-9; 8:1-4; 9:1-6). The latter became an important aspect of the prophetic tradition from the fall of the northern kingdom onward. The phrase "the day of Yahweh," which at first expressed the positive hope for the life-giving intervention of God, now indicates that the hope of the people will be fulfilled only in the wake of divine judgment.

Viewed in these terms, eschatology is a vision that sees Israel's present condition as unfinished and as open to completion through the full coming of God into Israel's life. But Israel's destiny is seen to be linked to that of the nations and that of the cosmos itself (Isa 2:2-4; 19:18-25; 56: 6ff.; 60; Zech 9:1-8). Thus in the later prophets the future dimension of biblical faith becomes truly universal and eschatological in scope. It envisions not only the destiny of Israel but the destiny of all humanity and the world (Isa 65:17). Eschatology, therefore, is intimately tied to a theology of history, for it reflects the sense that history is essentially open ended and incomplete until it finds its consummation in the aim God has set for it in the very act of creation.

While this fulfillment lies in the future, it is not clear what form it will take (some earthly political configuration or some sort of transcendent future) nor when it will be realized (in the near future or in the distant future). The future fulfillment, often expressed in terms of harmony, peace, reconciliation, and justice, remains the object of hope. As such, it is basically unknown and mysterious and becomes the object of many metaphorical projections throughout biblical history (new covenant, kingdom, life, peace, justice, banquet, marriage feast, etc.). In each instance, the conviction is that the resolution of history is rooted in God's life-giving action.

While the expectations of the prophetic tradition were concerned primarily with the destiny of the people as a whole, the influence of Greek thought during the Hellenistic period led to speculation on the destiny of the individual, at least in a limited degree, in the Wisdom literature (Wis 2:3; 3:1-4; 9:15). Greek anthropology with its concept of an immortal soul made it possible to think of some sort of survival after death for the individual person. Here are found the roots for the development of notions of individual judgment, retribution, resurrection, and the possibility of an afterlife that is something other than mere existence as a shade in Sheol.

In the apocalyptic reflections of the intertestamental period (from the beginning of the 2nd century B.C.E.) the hope of the prophetic tradition is developed in new directions. A crucial factor in understanding the apocalyptic literature is the sense of desperation and futility from which it emerges. If the experience of Israel points to the futility of human endeavor, then hope, if it is to live on, can only be hope in God. Thus, one of the qualities of the apocalyptic mentality is the radicalization of hope precisely as hope in God and in nothing else. Everything that is inimical to God will be subdued, and the rule of God will be definitively established. If the prophets, for the most part, looked to a future historical situation as the fulfillment of the promise, apocalyptic raised the question of a future that transcends the framework of any historical experience. In this stage of development, the vision of a truly universal and cosmic fulfillment emerges, and with it the possibility of a resurrection of the dead (Dan 12:2-3; 2 Macc).

In summary, the OT ends with no uniform vision. Its faith is radically open to the future, but the contours of the future remain unknown. The expectations of a God-given fullness of life in a world marked by peace, justice, and reconciliation that run through this history are drawn together in the symbol of a future rule or kingdom of God that crystallizes the prophetic-apocalyptic dream of the future.

New Testament

It can be said that Jesus took up the hopes of his people (his kingdom-preaching) and that he transformed these hopes in the light of his own experience of God (the *Abba* experience). The symbol of the kingdom in Jesus' usage becomes the preeminent symbol of a condition in which the power of God's indiscriminate love and forgiveness comes to rule in human life and human relations. What the Jewish tradition had hoped for as a future fulfillment in God's kingdom Jesus associated immediately with his person and ministry (Mt 11:5; Lk 10:23ff.; 4:21). Thus in its dialectical use of both present and future language, the Synoptic tradition suggests a provisional form of the kingdom in the work of Jesus' ministry, even though the definitive form of the kingdom remains to be realized in the future and is often associated with the appearance of the Son of Man on the clouds of heaven (Mt 26:64; Mk 14:62; Lk 22:69). If the meaning of Jesus' preaching is called into question by his execution, new light is shed on it from the perspective of the Easter experience of the disciples. A new dimension of eschatological consciousness emerges rooted in the earlier traditions but now taking a specifically Christian form in the light of the disciples' faith in Jesus as the risen Lord. The confession of Jesus as the Christ was formulated in the categories of OT hope even though these categories had to undergo significant transformation in the process.

The eschatology of the early Pauline tradition reflects the sense of an imminent end (1 Thess 5:2ff.) and describes the parousia in vivid, apocalyptic terms (1 Thess 4:16-18). The Pauline material offers helpful clues concerning the role of apocalyptic thought and the shifting emphasis placed on the present and future dimensions in early Christianity.

The Gospel of John reveals two eschatological patterns. The dominant pattern has been described as "vertical." Here, eschatological language relates not to a chronological future but to the deep significance of the present experience of faith and grace. Judgment and salvation are realized in our present relation to Jesus (Jn 3:18; 3:36; 5:24). The second pattern has been described as "horizontal" and is more in line with the theology of salvation history commonly associated with the Bible. This pattern situates the final experience of salvation on the "last day" (Jn 6:39–40).

Shaped in its entirety as a work of apocalyptic, the Book of Revelation opens the reader's vision to a "new heaven and a new earth" (Rev 20:11–21:5). Though the scenario is emphatically apocalyptic, the message is a powerful word of hope and consolation to a community that finds itself in dire circumstances. Despite all appearances to the contrary, the power of God's life-giving, creative love will be victorious over the powers of evil.

Appropriating the Insights

If one can speak of a "rediscovery of eschatology" in exegetical studies, at least in the sense just described, the appropriation of this discovery in Christian life and theology has been slow and uneven. Among exegetes and biblical theologians the process has moved in a number of directions, each suggesting a model, which would lead to diverse evaluations of the significance of the biblical data. The "consistent future" model of J. Weiss, A. Schweitzer, and M. Werner with its emphasis on the radical, eschatological nature of Jesus' preaching gave way to varieties of "realized" or "existential" eschatology in C. H. Dodd and R. Bultmann. While Bultmann's view removed eschatology from any relation to public history and made it exclusively an issue between the individual believer and God, O. Cullmann argued in favor of a "salvation history" model that attempted to incorporate both present and future, both existential time and chronological time, both personal and public history, into an overarching historical model that moved from creation to consummation.

The attempted Christian-Marxist dialogue of the 1960s led to significant developments among systematicians. In Protestant circles W. Pannenberg argued for a theological model that would give priority to the future and would reverse the common understanding of historical causality. It is the magnetic pull of the future that causes the present rather than the present that causes the future. Thus eschatology would lead to fundamental methodological changes in the whole of theology. In his *Theology of Hope* J. Moltmann saw the eschatological promise of God as the revelation of a future that contradicts every historical present. Hope is not merely a changed consciousness but an active movement to change reality under the pressure of the future. C. Braaten, inspired by both Pannenberg and Moltmann, has argued for a radical rethinking of doctrine and ethics from the perspective of an eschatological vision of reality.

Relatively independent of exegetical studies, Roman Catholics such as J. Pieper (*Über die Hoffnung,* 1935), G. Marcel (*Homo viator,* 1944), and C. Bernard (*Théologie de l'espérance selon Saint Thomas d'Aquin,* 1961) had developed the theological understanding of hope largely from the resources of Scholastic theology. With a more direct reference to the modern exegetical situation, in the late 1950s Roman Catholic systematician H. von Balthasar described eschatology as the "storm center" of theology, arguing in favor of a consistently Christological reconstruction of eschatology in a highly personalist style. K. Rahner argued in favor of a similar reworking of eschatology with the Christ-mystery as the unifying principle. In the context of the Christian-Marxist discussions, Rahner described Christianity as the "religion of the Absolute Future." The Christian vision of a transcendent future should generate inner-historical "utopias" among Christians, moving them to change the world for the better. The eschatological future is the self-transcendence of history into the mystery of God, in whom alone history finds its consummation. J. Metz, in reaction to the allegedly excessive individualism of Christian existentialists such as Bultmann and Rahner, developed a theology of the world and a political theology. Here, in a way reminiscent of Moltmann and Braaten, the vision of God's future generates criticism of the present condition of society and leads to a search for forms of human existence more appropriate to the life of eschatological faith.

From a totally different perspective and independently of the biblical renewal, evolutionary and cosmological concerns are reflected in the attempt of Teilhard de Chardin to bring the vision of faith into closer relation with the concerns of contemporary science. His work inspired attempts to relate the sense of cosmic history with the biblical sense of an open-ended future in a cosmic process that finds its ultimate fruit in the mystery of Christ. This called forth attempts to redefine the relation of matter to spirit, of anthropology to Christology, and of natural evolution to christification (the transforming union of the world with God through love). The challenge was picked up by Rahner and others in the 1960s, and more recently by R. Pendergast and T. Berry. Here the total context of cosmic reality becomes the primary matrix for defining the problems and outlooks for human and cosmic history.

At the level of magisterial teaching, Vatican II used the *eschaton* as a crucial ecclesiological category, seeing the church as the historical instrument of the kingdom, which lies in the future (*Lumen gentium* 8, 44, 48–51). While maintaining a vision of a transcendental future as proper to Christianity, the council attempted to draw from that vision the motivation for Christian engagement in building the world (e.g., *Gaudium et spes* 39).

In the aftermath of Vatican II eschatology has inspired a variety of movements: theology of the world, theology of liberation, and theology of revolution. While none of these attempts can claim adequacy, eschatological reflection has brought significant enrichment to many areas of Christian theology.

Eschatology and Ethics

Inspired by Pannenberg, Lutheran systematician C. Braaten calls for a fundamental restructuring of ethics that sees the kingdom of God as the normative starting point and sees the concrete content of that kingdom to consist in love. "The contents of ethics are principles of action calculated to embody as concretely and approximately as possible the realities of the future kingdom in the provisional and transitory contexts of the present" (*Christ and Counter-Christ*, Philadelphia, 1972, p. 131). The eschatological vision provides the sense of an ideal in the light of which all present orders are brought to judgment. With a similar emphasis on the love-command, P. Ramsey makes a limited use of apocalyptic themes in raising a critique of human "hubris" and naive progressivism in contemporary society. Placing primary emphasis on the experience of peace in the Christian community, S.

Hauerwas attempts to draw out the ethical implications of eschatology in his vision of a "peaceable kingdom" (*The Peaceable Kingdom,* Notre Dame, 1983).

For mainline Roman Catholic ethicians (J. Fuchs, C. Curran, R. McCormick), eschatology is not a structural element in ethics but principally a source of motivation for ethical activity whose material content may be known independently of Scripture. Eschatology can provide strong motivation for world building and can move even to heroic action, but it provides no specific ethical materials. V. Genovesi argues for a more sustained attempt to develop ethics out of the dialectical structure of historicity as reflected in the relation between memory of the past and imagination of the future. His would be an ethics in which hope would function as the "driving force" of Christian ethics. But in general, the sweeping reformulation suggested by Braaten and Genovesi is little reflected in the work of ethicians.

Liberation theology (G. Gutiérrez) can be seen as a sustained attempt to draw ethical insights from eschatological metaphors. By reading the texts of Exodus and the prophetic tradition in specific sociopolitical situations, liberation theology draws a much closer relation between religion and political reality than is commonly done. The struggle for justice is not identical with but closely allied with God's grace, which frees us from sin. The vision of a better future conferred by God is presented as the source for strong motivation to engage in the transformation of the world of present sociopolitical reality.

One cannot speak of a uniform appropriation of the eschatological vision in exegesis, systematics, or ethics today. Areas that seem most in need of basic reformulation are:

1. *Anthropology.* Eschatology is seen as language about ultimate human fulfillment in relation with God. This suggests the need for a deeper sense of the nature of human reality and its ultimate potential and the need to explore the relations between common human hopes and the vision of hope developed through the biblical revelation. The Christ-mystery provides a particular way of understanding the meaning of the human that may not coincide with the vision of particular humanistic philosophies. One may wish to speak of "Christian humanism," but it may still be necessary to look to Christ to discover the authentic human self-understanding.

2. *Social reality.* The anthropological vision of the biblical tradition is highly relational. The salvation categories of the Bible are first of all communal and only later individual. This implies that a purely individualistic formulation of salvation and eschatology is inadequate to the concerns of the tradition. We are confronted not with an either/or choice but with a dialectical relation between the individual and the social. Issues of individual destiny must be reformulated in the context of the collective.

3. *Cosmic context.* The relational anthropology of the biblical tradition suggests further that human fulfillment cannot be dealt with independently of the cosmic context, which provides the biological base and context for human life and development. What is the relation between the theological categories of creation and eschatology? And what is the relation, if any, between these and scientific cosmologies? Issues of human destiny need to be reformulated in their total cosmic context.

4. *Nature and grace.* Baroque and neo-Thomist interpretations of the relation between nature and grace are in need of fundamental rethinking. While grace is the actualization of human potential, independently of grace the meaning of the *humanum* remains ambiguous. How will the relation between these appear in the light of the needed redefinitions of matter and spirit, for example, especially in the light of new understandings of the relation between creation and eschatology?

5. *Human works.* Does anything "remain" of our historical activity? Do we exist simply in a time of moral testing, leaving all our creations behind with death? Does the intrinsic fruit of our historical activity, regardless of how deeply transformed, enter into the reality of the kingdom? How do our efforts to change the world relate to the divine change for which we hope?

See also ANTHROPOLOGY; COVENANT; CREATION; ECOLOGY; KINGDOM OF GOD.

Bibliography: C. Braaten, *Eschatology and Ethics* (Minneapolis: Augsburg, 1974). V. Genovesi, *Expectant Creativity: The Action of Hope in Christian Ethics* (Washington: Univ. Press of America, 1982). Z. Hayes, *Visions of a Future: A Study of Christian Eschatology* (Wilmington, Del.: Glazier, 1989). A. Lonergan, ed., *T. Berry and the New Cosmology* (Mystic, Conn.: Twenty-Third Publications, 1987).

ZACHARY HAYES, O.F.M.

EUTHANASIA, SOCIAL IMPLICATIONS OF

The English word "euthanasia" is derived from the Greek for "good death" and connotes the process of providing for a good or merciful death. The Catholic tradition has generally distinguished active, direct, or positive euthanasia, which is the killing of a dying patient, from passive, indirect, or negative euthanasia, which is the withholding or withdrawing of life-sustaining medical treatment, thus allowing a person to die of disease or trauma. Today the word is most often used only to mean the killing of a dying person (active or direct euthanasia), and it is better to avoid confusion by limiting the term to actual killing. Medical ethics also distinguishes voluntary from involuntary euthanasia, according to whether or not the person killed individually chooses this means of death.

This essay will treat four aspects of the problem: (1) theological foundations, (2) the received tradition, (3) critical questions, and (4) the social dimension.

Theological Foundations

Two theological principles have traditionally been applied to questions of care for the dying: first, God's sovereignty over human life; second, the redemptive value of human suffering. In textbooks of Catholic medical ethics of the past, these principles were often used as a sort of proof text for the ethical judgments the authors made even though those judgments were made on other than theological bases (Kelly, 1979, pp. 232–35, 274–77).

Recently Catholic scholars have criticized this way of making moral judgments. They have hesitated in claiming to know exactly what it means to say that God is sovereign of human life. Surely it does not mean that God wants us to do nothing at all to relieve human suffering. The example of Jesus requires the opposite conclusion. Theological principles like these cannot by themselves solve our ethical questions.

Yet theological principles remain important. They tell us how we are related to God as Creator. They are hermeneutic themes (Kelly, 1979, 436–48) or maieutic hints (J. Fuchs, "Christian Faith and the Disposing of Human Life," TS 46 [1985] 683). When we use them this way we see that our faith tradition is clearly ambivalent, or bivalent. It pulls us both ways. We are both creatures and co-agents with God. We are called both to find meaning in human suffering and to alleviate it when it is right to do so. Theological principles like these help us to understand the meaning of human life.

This is important in the context of care for the dying. We are required to accept some treatment but not all treatment. God gives us some authority but not total authority. We are to find meaning in suffering but not to worship it and seek it. Theology thus provides a base for understanding who we are, even when theological principles like these cannot give clear answers to our dilemmas.

The Received Tradition

The Catholic tradition has developed its approach to euthanasia over many centuries. This tradition rests on two bases: first, on a recognition that not all medical treatments that prolong biological life are truly beneficial to the patient (the distinction between ordinary and extraordinary means of preserving life), and second, on the judgment that there is a clear and compelling moral difference between killing and allowing to die, so that while allowing to die is often morally right, the direct killing of an innocent person, as in (active) euthanasia, is always morally wrong. The official position of the hierarchical magisterium continues to be based on these two sets of concepts (Sacred Congregation for the Doctrine of the Faith, *Declaration on Euthanasia,* 1980; USCC, *Ethical and Religious Directives,* 1971).

The ethical distinction between mandatory and optional treatment or between ordinary and extraordinary means of preserving life goes back several centuries and is most often associated with Pope Pius XII, who repeatedly stressed it during his pontificate (C. Speicher, "As We Have Said," Ph.D. diss., Duquesne Univ., 1991, pp. 86–122). The distinction proposes a reasonable middle ground between an extreme sanctity-of-life position that permits no cessation of efforts to prolong life, insisting that life itself is the greatest possible value to be sustained at all costs, and a totally lax quality-of-life position that permits cessation of treatment and even active killing for trivial and hedonistic reasons.

The Catholic tradition has recognized *both* the sanctity of life—life is indeed sacred—*and* the ethical import of the quality of life—life need not be prolonged under all circumstances; that is, at some point a lack of the ability to carry out humanly meaningful purposes, which some would term a lack of quality of life, means that life can be let go.

While we are obliged to take "ordinary" care to preserve our lives, we are not obliged to use medical measures that are morally "extraordinary." It is essential to understand that this is a moral and not a medical distinction; there are no simple technical or statistical criteria for determining the difference. Means that are usually thought of as medically ordinary may be morally extraordinary. Thus what would be an ordinary or mandatory means when used in caring for a person whose chance of renewed health is great (e.g., an antibiotic for pneumonia) would become extraordinary in the care of a patient who has little or no chance of recovery (the same antibiotic for a person dying of terminal cancer). There is no moral obligation to preserve life at all costs.

The tradition includes many factors that may be considered when making this decision: the chance of success, the degree of pain and the patient's fear, the financial cost, the social cost, the needs of others, and the patient's readiness for death. The distinction between ordinary and extraordinary means as developed and applied within the Catholic tradition is very wide and very flexible. People do not have a moral obligation to preserve their lives if the means needed to do so offer little benefit or impose significant burden.

The second distinction on which the received tradition is based is that of killing and allowing to die, a distinction provided through the principle of double effect as that principle was developed by moralists up to the middle of this century. According to this distinction the direct killing of an innocent person is never morally right, but allowing-to-die is sometimes morally right.

There are five different kinds of actions to be considered. First, one may decide to withhold certain medical means that would prolong life. If the means in question is indeed "morally extraordinary," the act (the decision not to use it) is generally accepted as morally right. Second, one may decide to withdraw a life-sustaining treatment that has already been started. The Catholic tradition has seen this second kind of action to be the equivalent of the first. Morally it is the nonuse of medical treatment, and if the treatment is morally extraordinary (optional) it may be withdrawn. Both the first and the second action have often been referred to as negative, passive, or indirect euthanasia, though as suggested above, it is less confusing to avoid this terminology. The forgoing (withholding or withdrawing) of morally extraordinary medical treatment does not kill the patient; rather it allows the patient to die of the underlying disease.

Third, one may take positive means aimed at relieving the patient's suffering but not directly intended to cause death. The distinction is sometimes difficult to make, of course, as increasing doses of a sedative may shorten life. But it is certainly a moral act to relieve pain, and this sort of medication is not morally wrong as long as consideration is given to the patient's wishes, desire for consciousness, and readiness for death. The Catholic received tradition, according to analysis through the principle of double effect, considers the act itself not to be an act of killing but rather to be a giving of medication that relieves pain. This use of medication has sometimes been called "double-effect euthanasia" (Thomasma and Graber). The intention is not to relieve pain by bringing death, by killing, but rather to relieve pain even though death may "indirectly" result. This is morally right.

Fourth, one may act in conjunction with the patient by assisting the patient to commit euthanasia. The patient wishes to kill himself or herself and makes this known to another, asking that person to provide the necessary means. The patient actually consumes the drug or utilizes the method provided. This is assisted suicide or assisted euthanasia in the strict sense. One person helps another commit suicide. The received Catholic tradition judges this killing of an innocent person to be always morally wrong.

Fifth, the health-care practitioner or some other person may take an action that directly brings about the death of a patient. This, like the fourth action, is a "direct" killing according to the principle of double effect and is judged to be always morally wrong.

Critical Questions

The received Catholic tradition has considered the distinction between killing and allowing to die to be definitive and has argued consistently against (active) euthanasia. The act itself, which is a direct killing of an innocent person, is unexceptionably wrong. No set of circumstances or consequences can make it right. Whereas the principle of double effect permits the rightness of some instances of allowing to die ("indirect killing"), that same principle never permits active euthanasia, which is wrong in itself. The criteria used to determine the difference here are largely physical or biological and involve an analysis of the action itself that is done.

But a number of ethicists, including some Catholic moral theologians, have questioned this; they argue that direct killing (active euthanasia or assisted suicide) may be morally right in some cases (Maguire; C. Curran, *Politics, Medicine, and Christian Ethics,* Philadelphia, Fortress, 1983, pp. 161–62). Many of those who argue for this change in the received tradition agree that there is an important difference between killing and allowing to die. But they insist that the distinction is not sufficient by itself to make all acts of euthanasia morally wrong. This revisionist position is basically consistent with the normative method known as proportionalism, which rejects the notion that actions in and of themselves can be judged immoral (intrinsically immoral acts). Thus some Catholic moral theologians now argue that once the dying process is irreversibly begun the proscription of killing loses some of its moral weight. It may be more loving, and thus more consistent with the Christian moral demand, to actively and mercifully abet the process of dying than to permit continued pain and suffering.

The Social Dimension

Both the received tradition, which concludes to the absolute wrongness of (active) euthanasia, and the proportionalist revision, which may conclude to its rightness in some cases, have tended to ignore or at least to underemphasize some aspects of the social dimension of this important question. The received tradition has made its judgments mainly by looking at the act-in-itself. Though it has often pointed out social harms that might result from euthanasia, comparison with other of its bioethical judgments—contraception, for example—makes it clear that these social harms are of no real importance in the actual moral analysis. They are added on; euthanasia would be forbidden even if it could be shown the practice would serve the common good. The proportionalist revision, while theoretically open to including social implications in its operative method and often better than the received tradition at pointing them out in its arguments, has sometimes overstated the positive social effects of a practice of euthanasia and ignored or understated its potential social harms. And arguments in favor of euthanasia, especially in the secular U.S. arena, consistently emphasize primarily the individual's right of individual choice; this emphasis, so very widespread in the United States, supports the neglect of the social context.

Two aspects of the problem call for social ethical analysis. One is the legalization of euthanasia. The other is the rightness or wrongness of individual acts of euthanasia. Neither question can be answered in isolation from society. The moral problem of euthanasia is but one example of why health-care ethics ought not be categorized as a branch of "personal" as opposed to "social" ethics.

The rejection of the absoluteness of the distinction between killing and allowing to die need not lead to the conclusion that the legalization of euthanasia is socially desirable and therefore right. There are valid reasons for insisting that no changes in the law be made in this regard. Any increase in the number of exceptions to the general principle against killing makes other exceptions easier. Human life is of intrinsic and incalculable value. It is a sacred gift of God. When a society decides that certain kinds of killing are moral, there is an ever-increased chance that the society will extend such permission even further. Our nation has decided that killing is legally permitted in properly declared wars, in court-ordered capital punishment, in abortion, in self-defense, and in some circumstances in defense of private property attacked criminally. Active euthanasia is not the same kind of killing as these others, but to permit it legally would add one further allowable exception to the law forbidding killing.

In addition, it must be emphasized that the distinction between killing and allowing to die has been one of the pillars on which the present U.S. consensus that legally permits the forgoing of certain treatments is based. The absolute legal prohibition of active euthanasia thus serves as a protective barrier against going too far and serves as a valid argument against those who think that forgoing treatment is itself euthanasia. If we remove that barrier, there may be fear on the part of some that we have gone too far already. There may thus be a backlash against the present consensus that forgoing treatment is in many cases legally and morally right. The legalization of active euthanasia may actually lead politically to a restriction of the present consensus and thus to an increase in the sufferings of dying patients.

Another reason against the legalization of active euthanasia concerns the integrity of the medical profession. Doctors are not now allowed to kill their patients. Permission to do this might lead to mistrust of physicians.

Finally, there is the ever-present danger, especially in a time of necessary resource allocation, that active euthanasia would serve as a socially acceptable form of cost containment. Though laws would at first limit the practice to voluntary euthanasia, it would be hard to draw the line there, since one might logically insist that those incapable of choosing should also have the right to be freed of the dying process, which conscious persons might legally escape. The temptation to eliminate poverty cheaply by eliminating the poor might be hard to resist.

There are, of course, arguments on the other side. One of these concerns the muddle courts get into when trying persons accused of euthanasia, which is legally first-degree murder. We often hear of court cases where juries find family members innocent of killing their suffering relatives even though they admit having done so. And some are jailed for actions that seem to most of us to be those of a distraught and loving relative and possibly even acts of moral courage. But the fact that the law is not able to deal adequately with certain exceptional cases does not of itself warrant the claim that euthanasia should be legalized. Sensitive juries and sensitive district attorneys would seem to be better ways of dealing with exceptions.

A second argument in favor of the legalization of euthanasia is that if euthanasia is morally right in some cases, it ought to be legal as well. The individual should have the legal right to choose how to die. But if we include social factors in the moral analysis of the act of euthanasia, it is not at all clear that euthanasia is morally right for individuals living in societies like the United States. Dying is not merely an individual event; the way people die and the structures that surround dying have important social ramifications. Dying persons are members of society, and just as society has responsibilities to them, they have responsibilities to it. While allowing for the possibility of rare exceptions, it would seem that persons dying within an advanced medical-care system need not and ought not have recourse to euthanasia.

This conclusion presumes agreement with the arguments already made against the legalization of euthanasia. If it is true that this would be contrary to the common good in the United States and similar nations, then dying persons ought to avoid lending support to euthanasia legalization by asking for active aid in dying unless their own personal need for such help can be shown to prevail. This approach to the issue is in keeping with a proportionalist method. The remaining question is whether or not the need of dying patients is such that the avoidance of continued pain and suffering should compel us to legalize the practice of euthanasia despite its undoubted social dangers. If it is, then legalization is morally warranted, but it ought to limit the practice to those cases where the patient has entered the dying process in the immediate sense and has personally requested euthanasia.

But is the need of dying persons such that it compels us to agree to a social practice of euthanasia? Proponents of legalized euthanasia point out the undoubted horrors of persons uselessly invaded for months or years by medical treatment and of persons dying in great pain from lengthy illness. But nothing in either the Catholic received tradition or U.S. law requires this. Such medical treatment is morally extraordinary and may be withheld or withdrawn. It is important in this context to point out that this includes medical nutrition and hydration when this serves only to keep an unconscious patient biologically alive or is used to "force feed" a dying patient who has stopped eating (Shannon and Walter).

Such persons need not be killed; they may be allowed to die of the underlying disease. Nor is physical pain necessary. Nothing forbids the use of medication to the point of unconsciousness if this is necessary to eliminate pain, even if, as has already been noted, the medication indirectly hastens the moment of death. In the absence of medical nutrition, which may rightly be forgone in many cases, the dying process is not artificially prolonged.

Thus the received tradition and the proportionalist revision need not differ widely in their approach to euthanasia. Some contemporary moral theologians will doubtless want to argue that there are exceptions. If the absolute proscription of the act-in-itself of active euthanasia is rejected, as seems warranted, then in cases where modern medical care is not available euthanasia may well be morally right. But these cases are not likely to be present in the U.S. social context and in other similar societies, provided the morally proper forgoing of extraordinary treatments and the use of sedation are provided. In this context, euthanasia is unnecessary. Loving care can be given to the dying while pain is relieved. Moral responsibility to individual patients does not demand the socially hurtful practice of euthanasia.

See also AGED, CARE OF; DOUBLE EFFECT, PRINCIPLE OF; HEALTH CARE; KILLING; METHODOLOGY, MORAL; PIUS XII; RIGHTS AND DUTIES; TECHNOLOGY.

Bibliography: R. Gula, *What Are They Saying About Euthanasia?* (Mahwah, N.J.: Paulist, 1985). D. Kelly, *Critical Care Ethics: Treatment Decisions in American Hospitals* (Kansas City, Mo.: Sheed & Ward, 1991). D. Kelly, *The Emergence of Roman Catholic Medical Ethics in North America: An Historical, Methodological, Bibliographical Study* (New York: Mellen, 1979). D. Maguire, *Death By Choice* (Garden City, N.Y.: Doubleday, 1973). T. Shannon and J. Walter, "The PVS Patient and the Forgoing/Withdrawing of Medical Nutrition and Hydration," TS 49 (1988) 623–47. R. Sparks, *To Treat or Not to Treat: Bioethics and the Handicapped Newborn* (Mahwah, N.J.: Paulist, 1988). D. Thomasma and G. Graber, *Euthanasia: Toward an Ethical Social Policy* (New York: Continuum, 1990).

DAVID F. KELLY

EVANGELII NUNTIANDI

The apostolic exhortation issued by Pope Paul VI on December 8, 1975, *Evangelii nuntiandi (On Evangelization in the Modern World),* was intended to draw together the results of the fourth synod of bishops, which had been devoted to the theme of evangelization. It also marked the close of the 1975 Holy Year, in which evangelization had been a special theme, and commemorated the tenth anniversary of the close of the Second Vatican Council. It is generally considered to be the single most important papal document on mission in modern times.

Background

The Decree on the Church's Missionary Activity (*Ad gentes*), promulgated by the Second Vatican Council, was a landmark in the church's thinking about mission. It moved the understanding of mission from the periphery or frontier of the church's life to its center, proclaiming the church itself as "essentially missionary" (AG 1, 2). It rooted the church's mission in the trinitarian life of God and saw the sending of the Son as the paradigm that gave the church both its identity and its task.

Despite its laudable theological elements, however, *Ad gentes* did not address the many problems that missionary activity was beginning to face. The widespread move toward independence among many colonialized nations led the peoples of those countries to question both the motives and the methods of the church's mission. Despite a growing indigenization of hierarchies in those countries, the churches tended to remain dependent on the churches of North America and Europe for personnel and financial support. This large-scale dependency was stunting the growth of the churches in those areas, since with personnel and money went the power of decision making. The theology of the particular or local church that had been proposed by Vatican II only highlighted this issue. Many compared the style of the church's mission to that of the colonialism exercised in the economic and political sphere. A discussion ensued in missiological circles about whether missionaries should be sent out at all. Indeed, a major conference of mission-sending religious institutes in 1969 questioned the very motives for mission in light of this colonial history.

Second, the widespread perception in Latin America that the efforts at development by North Atlantic countries largely contributed to a continuing dependence moved missionaries and theologians in the Latin American countries away from a theology of development to what became known as a theology of liberation. This was already apparent at the Second General Conference of Latin American bishops at Medellín in 1968, and was crystallized in 1971 by the appearance of Gustavo Gutiérrez's *Teologia de la liberacion* (English title, *A Theology of Liberation,* 1973). Theology of liberation called for a more integral understanding of salvation, embracing not only the spiritual and individual realms but the political and collective as well. It represented a major new direction in theology with clear consequences for the church's role in society. To some this new direction seemed to be an ideologizing of the gospel as a form of left-wing, even Marxist, politics. For others it represented a postcolonial response to injustices in society and offered a way of living out the church's call to mission. Liberation theology represented, then, the new face of the church's mission.

A third development at this time that needed reflection and response was what would come to be known as "inculturation." Although the word would not be used until the 1978 synod of bishops, the effects of trying to incarnate the gospel more fully in cultures were already being felt. *Gaudium et spes* had already put forward a positive evaluation of culture in the Second Vatican Council (GS 58) and both this document and *Ad gentes* had encouraged adaptations in different cultures. A major development, especially in Latin America and Africa, had been the emergence of the small ecclesial communities (variously styled basic Christian communities, base ecclesial communities, small Christian communities) as the fundamental ecclesiastical unit for many people. Concern was expressed in some circles that these communities were setting themselves up in opposition to parochial and diocesan structures of the church. Others, however, saw them as a revitalization and deepening of Christian commitment. Another major concern on the part of bishops was the freedom to make adaptations. There was a feeling that Rome was, on the practical level, ambivalent at best toward permitting departures from uniformity in liturgical and other matters.

A final factor was the growing awareness of how much of the Catholic church was to be found outside North America and Europe. The growth of what missiologist Walbert Bühlmann had called "the Third Church" or what Karl Rahner was to call in 1979 "the world church" meant that there was an agenda to be addressed that to this point had been subordinated to that of the older churches in North America and Europe. Many bishops coming from Asia, Africa, and Latin America hoped that the 1974 synod, devoted to the theme of evangelization, would be the forum for allowing this agenda to come to the forefront.

The 1974 synod, then, opened with an array of expectations on the part of participants that could not reasonably be addressed within the span of a single month. The conduct of the synod itself, with strict control on the part of Vatican authorities, only served to heighten the level of frustration on the part of the bishops. No consensus could be reached on important matters, and so the results of the deliberations were handed over to the pope in unfinished form with the hope that he would cast them into a meaningful and useful document. Paul VI's closing address to the assembled body, however, did not seem encouraging. He sharply reasserted the primacy of the pope over the bishops and had largely negative remarks to make about liberation theology.

The apostolic exhortation that was issued a year later came as a pleasant surprise. Far more irenic in tone, it represented a distillation of the best of what had been presented on the issue of evangelization and offered cautious but positive encouragement to cultural adaptation and liberation theology.

Content

Evangelii nuntiandi is divided into seven chapters dealing with different aspects of the evangelization process. An introduction (1–5) gives the background and purpose of the document. The pope notes that it is being issued on the occasion of three events. The first is the conclusion of the 1975 Holy Year, when emphasis was placed on the church fulfilling its mission to be a messenger of the good news of Jesus Christ. The second is to mark the tenth anniversary of the conclusion of the Second Vatican Council, whose purpose was "to make the Church of the twentieth century ever better fitted for proclaiming the Gospel to the people of the twentieth century" (2). The third is to give a fresh impulse to evangelization as a result of the reflections of the 1974 synod. Those reflections were directed by three questions: "In our day, what has happened to that hidden energy of the Good News, which is able to have a powerful effect on man's conscience? To what extent and in what way is that evangelical force capable of really transforming the people of this century? What methods should be followed in order that the power of the Gospel may have its effect?" (4). Paul VI then expresses these concerns even more pointedly: "Does the Church or does she not find herself better equipped to proclaim the Gospel and to put it into people's hearts with conviction, freedom of spirit and effectiveness?" (4).

The first chapter (6–13) links the evangelizing activity of Jesus to that of the church. It attempts to synthesize, first of all, Jesus' own evangelizing activity. Characteristics of this activity are the proclamation of the kingdom of God; a proclamation of salvation "which is liberation from everything that oppresses man but which is above all liberation from sin and the Evil One" (9); a call to a profound conversion of mind and heart via the road of suffering and abnegation; a tireless preaching of the good news; a manifestation of the kingdom of God in signs and wonders; the emergence of a community around Jesus that in turn goes out to evangelize. It is in this last characteristic of Jesus' activity that the discussion turns to the church, for whom "the task of evangelizing all people constitutes the essential mission, . . . her deepest identity. . . . She exists in order to evangelize" (14). The reciprocal links between Christ and the church in the evangelization process are then explored. The church is born out of Jesus' own evangelizing activity and is in turn sent by him to evangelize. The church does this first by witnessing in its own life to Jesus' message: being attentive to the Word, living in charity, breaking bread together. But the church also continues to need to be evangelized: "She needs to listen unceasingly to what she must believe, to her reasons for hoping, to the new commandment of love." She needs to be "evangelized by constant conversion and renewal, in order to evangelize the world with credibility" (15). Having continued to be evangelized, the church sends out its own evangelizers. Evangelization is a task that belongs to the whole church. The chapter closes with a reflection on the profound link between Christ and the church, on how one cannot claim to love Christ without at the same time committing oneself to and loving the church.

With the origins of evangelization thus set out, the second chapter presents a definition of evangelization (17–24). It begins by noting the complexity of the evangelization process, remarking that in times past evangelization has even been identified with one or other part of the evangelization process. This remark reflects the debates earlier in the century about whether evangelization should be seen primarily as a conversion of souls or as establishing the local church. *Ad gentes* made a point of rising above that debate by saying that evangelization embraced both of these activities and grounded the entire process in the saving activity of Christ working through his church.

The discussion of evangelization here builds on *Ad gentes* and discussions of the church in *Lumen gentium* and *Gaudium et spes* but clearly also addresses concerns that either arose or were sharpened in the years immediately after Vatican II. It begins by noting that the preaching of the good news is aimed at the renewal of humanity in all its dimensions. This remark reflects the concern for a holistic sense of salvation, promoted both in theologies of development or human promotion and theologies of liberation. At the same time the pope reminds his readers that this renewal comes first and foremost through baptism and lives lived according to the gospel. He sums up how evangelization brings about this renewal by saying that "the Church evangelizes when she seeks to convert, solely through the divine power of the Message she proclaims, both the personal and collective consciences of people, the activities in which they engage, and the lives and concrete milieux which is theirs" (18). Thus the pope reemphasizes the primacy of the spiritual task of the church's evangelizing efforts but notes at the same time its social consequences. Indeed, a true preaching of the gospel has to affect and sometimes even upset "criteria of judgment, determining values, points of interest, lines of thought, sources of inspiration and models of life" (19).

Evangelization, then, is directed not only at individuals but at the collective patterns of life in which human communities live—in a word, at cultures. "Culture" here is understood in the modern, social-scientific sense of the totality of a way of life and not in the restricted sense of the high culture of art, music, and literature. The pope articulates succinctly the relationship between gospel and culture, reiterating *Gaudium et spes* on this matter: the gospel is independent of any culture, but it is heard and lived out by persons always connected to a culture, and cultural elements are an inevitable part of their building up of the kingdom. While the gospel is independent of any culture, it is not incompatible with any of them (20). He goes on to note that there is a dramatic split between the gospel and culture in our times, thereby reflecting the concerns voiced by many bishops at the 1974 synod from both the First World and the Third World about the gap of relevance experienced by many people today, either because of secularization or because of the alien cultural forms in which the gospel is presented to them.

The defining of evangelization then turns to another crucial point, namely, the role of witness of life in proclamation. Living in a manner consistent with what is preached has always been a concern in evangelization, but another point is also touched upon here. This has to do with situations where direct proclamation is not possible or is even forbidden by law (as is the case in some Buddhist and Muslim theocracies and in some avowedly atheist states). Pope Paul affirms the witness of life as a form of evangelization: "Such a witness is already a silent proclamation of the Good News and a very powerful and effective one. Here we have an initial act of evangelization" (21). In the next paragraph he reaffirms that explicit proclamation is still necessary, since witness in itself is necessarily incomplete; witness of life without explanation of the motives for such living gives only part of the message. But he closes with a caution. Proclamation has often been made synonymous with evangelization, when in fact "it is only one aspect" of it (21). Thus the pope sets forth an important relationship between modes of communicating the gospel, a relationship often debated by missiologists.

But there is more to the evangelization process. It involves not only witness and proclamation but requires conversion and is completed by the listener entering into the ecclesial community, accepting its sacraments, and in turn accepting the call to apostolic initiative. The chapter closes reemphasizing the holistic character of the evangelization process, recalling that all of the elements discussed—renewal of humanity, witness, proclamation, conversion, entrance into the community, and apostolic initiative—are necessary for the evangelization process to be complete.

The third chapter (25–39) deals with the content of evangelization. The pope begins by distinguishing between the essential content of evangelization—content that cannot be modified—and secondary elements that may change with the circumstances or contexts of evangelization. He concentrates here on the essential content. To evangelize means, in the first instance, "to bear witness, in a simple and direct way, to God revealed by Jesus Christ, in the Holy Spirit: to bear witness that in his Son God has loved the world—that in his Incarnate Word he has given being to all things and has called men to eternal life" (26). But evangelization bears "as the foundation, center and at the same time summit of its dynamism—a clear proclamation that, in Jesus Christ, the Son of God made man, who died and rose from the dead, salvation is offered to all men, as a gift of God's grace and mercy" (27). He goes on to insist that this is not an immanent salvation addressed only to the here and now, but one that reaches its fulfillment in communion with the divine Absolute, "a transcendent and eschatological salvation, which indeed has its beginning in this life but which is fulfilled in eternity" (27). Expanding on this, he emphasizes that the message of the gospel is a message of hope in the promises given by God in the new covenant. This expectation is concretized in the church and its sacraments. Here he gives a brief nod to the importance of the "planting of the church," a major item of discussion in the missiology of the 1930s and 1940s. While emphasizing the transcendence of salvation, Pope Paul also takes the opportunity to reaffirm that salvation must nonetheless touch the whole of life. "This is why evangelization involves an explicit message, adapted to the different situations constantly being realized, about the rights and duties of every human being, about family life without which personal growth and human development is hardly possible, about life in society, about international life, peace, justice and development—a message especially energetic today about liberation" (29).

With that final word there follow several paragraphs (30–38) devoted to the question of liberation as a form of salvation. The pope begins by acknowledging the injustices that plague human life and recalls the discussions of the 1974 synod: "The Church, as the Bishops repeated, has the duty to proclaim the liberation of millions of human beings, many of whom are her own children—the duty of assisting the birth of this liberation, of giving witness to it, of ensuring that it is complete. This is not foreign to evangelization" (30). The rest of the discussion is thereby framed in this positive assessment of liberation.

The pope then moves to discuss a number of the questions that liberation theologies raise. He notes first of all that there are profound links between evangelization and human advancement via development and liberation, both in the human or anthropological order and in the theological order. Human beings are not abstractions but live in concrete social and economic circumstances. And creation cannot be separated from redemption. Redemption must touch the totality of human life, for justice lies at the heart of our love for neighbor. But that should not devolve into reducing the church's mission to the temporal project of liberation from unjust structures and from oppression. To do so would rob the church of the fullness of its message and reduce it to an ideological system. Here again Paul VI takes the opportunity to reaffirm the religious finality of the Christian message. He then sums up the approach liberation should take: "It cannot be contained in the simple and restricted dimension of economics, politics, social or culture life; it must envisage the whole man, in all his aspects, right up to and including his openness to the absolute, even the divine Absolute; it is therefore attached to a certain concept of man, to a view of man which it can never sacrifice to the needs of any strategy, practice or short-term efficiency" (33). This latter comment seems addressed to those who would accept a Marxist anthropology in articulating a theology of liberation.

Having given these caveats, he hastens to add that "the Church is certainly not willing to restrict her mission only to the religious field and dissociate herself from man's temporal problems" (34). But one must realize that while the church links salvation and liberation they can never be identified, since not every notion of liberation is compatible with the "evangelical vision of man" (35), as outlined in paragraph 33. Indeed, liberation will fail "whenever its profound motives are not those of justice in charity, whenever its zeal lacks a truly spiritual dimension and whenever its final goal is not salvation and happiness in God" (35).

He then briefly touches on the question of oppressive and unjust structures and their relation to personal conversion. While it is important to work to change those structures, the most perfect structures will still fail if the human heart is not converted as well (36).

In regard to the means used to achieve liberation, the pope rules out flatly the use of violence, especially the force of arms (37). He then concludes this discussion of liberation by recalling the church's role and resources for collaborating in the work of liberation. The church equips those who work for liberation "with the inspiration of faith, the motivation of fraternal love, a social teaching which the true Christian cannot ignore" (38). He closes the chapter with a brief affirmation of and plea for religious liberty as a fundamental human right.

Chapter four takes up the methods of evangelization (40–48). Paul begins with two already discussed: witness of life, and preaching or explicit proclamation. After reaffirming what had been said about these in chapter two, he recommends use of modern media, especially visual media, to help communicate the message (42). He then speaks of the use of the Liturgy of the Word as an appropriate forum for evangelization, both within the context of the celebration of the Eucharist and in non-Eucharistic settings (43). This is followed by a discussion of renewed catechetics, especially as directed at children and young people (44). He then returns to the use of mass media and recommends their use, mainly on the basis of their effectiveness at reaching large numbers of people (45). This is balanced by a reminder of the importance of one-to-one contact in evangelization (46). Then comes a section on the importance of the sacraments in the evangelization process as a means of supernatural grace (47).

The chapter closes with an important reflection on popular religiosity as a means of evangelization. The pope prefers the term "popular piety" to popular religiosity, since this form of religion engenders a whole series of attitudes—"patience, the sense of the Cross in daily life, detachment, openness to others, devotion" (48) —in the believer. While noting that popular piety does have its limitations and can sometimes degenerate into superstition, he is generally positive about it as a means for greater evangelization; indeed, it can be "a true encounter with God in Jesus Christ" (48).

Chapter five lists what are called the beneficiaries of evangelization, that is, those to whom evangelization is addressed (49–58). The pope begins by reminding his readers that the message of the gospel is intended for everyone. In preaching the gospel difficulties are often encountered, sometimes of such a nature that there may be a wrongheaded tendency to narrow the scope of evangelization (this seems to be addressed to those calling for a moratorium on sending out missionaries), or the restriction of missionary activity by governmental powers.

The rest of the chapter is devoted to what he calls "examples" of the types of people to whom evangelization is addressed. These include those who have not heard of Christ and his gospel (51) as well as those who have been baptized but do not practice their faith (52). The pope then turns his attention to evangelizing those in other religions. He begins by reiterating the respect and esteem that should be accorded those who follow other religious ways (he seems to be thinking here principally of the great literate religious traditions). While praising their achievements he reaffirms the missionary responsibility of the church to proclaim the message of Christ and chides those who say that "the time of the missions is now past" (53). He then notes how important it is to continue to evangelize and nourish those who already believe, with a few words also to Christians not in full communion with the Roman Catholic church. To the latter the church gives witness to "the fullness of revelation whose deposit she guards" (54).

Attention is then turned to nonbelievers, as the pope explores the phenomenon of modern atheism. He notes the complexity of contemporary atheism both in its origins and in its manifestations. At the same time he notes a hunger for the gospel growing out of the emptiness of secularism and consumerism. Some of the attitudes engendered by a secularist society affect the baptized as well, leading to an indifference toward faith and religious practice. The pope pledges special efforts toward evangelizing both of these groups.

In what might seem to be an unusual positioning, the pope uses the end of this chapter to address the question of the small Christian communities (58). He notes their variety and their presence throughout the church. He notes further that some of them live in harmony and communion with the pastors and structures of the local church and have come together for differing reasons: to escape anonymity in mass society, to create more homogeneous units, to respond to a shortage of priests. Other communities, however, see themselves as distinct from the church and engage in criticism of the church, especially its hierarchy. These communities "are radically opposed to the church" (58). He notes that these latter communities do not deserve the name "ecclesial." The former group, however, can be a hope for the universal church if they seek nourishment in the Word of God, avoid hypercritical attitudes, and remain in communion with the local church and its hierarchy.

Chapter six takes up the question of who are the agents of evangelization (59–73). Paul VI begins by reiterating the teaching of the Second Vatican Council: evangelization is the task of the entire church and not just a specialized few within the church. It is also a fundamentally ecclesial act, not the work of the isolated individual. He uses this opportunity to reaffirm both the universality of the church and the integrity of the individual or local churches, taking care at the same time not to reduce the universal church to the sum of its parts (62).

He then returns to the question of evangelization and culture and speaks of "transposing" the gospel message into a new culture. This transposition needs to occur "in the field of liturgical expression, and in the areas of catechesis, theological formulation, secondary ecclesial structures, and ministries" (63). How this transposition is to be achieved is a delicate matter. "Evangelization loses much of its force and effectiveness if it does not take into consideration the actual people to whom it is addressed, if it does not use their language, their signs and symbols, if it does not answer the questions they ask, and if it does not have an impact on their concrete life" (63). But essential content must not be lost on the pretext of translating it.

This digression on the question of inculturation is followed by a return to the discussion of the relation of the local or individual churches to the universal church, where the importance of communion with the See of Peter and the magisterium is reaffirmed (64–65).

Attention is then turned to the concrete agents of evangelization. They are each treated in turn: the pope (67), the bishops and priests (68), religious (69), laity (70), the family (71), and young people (72). A final section is devoted to the diversified ministries of the laity, reaffirming their place in the church (73).

Chapter seven deals with the interior attitudes that should characterize the agents of evangelization (74–80). These include an awareness of and submission to the Holy Spirit (75), an authentic witness of life (76), a quest for unity within the church and among Christians (77), a reverence for truth (78), a motivation of love (79), and zeal (80). The apostolic exhortation closes with entrusting the church's evangelization effort to Mary, the Star of evangelization (82).

Significance

Evangelii nuntiandi has established itself as the most important document on the church's mission and evangelizing activity of the modern era, surpassing even *Ad gentes* in this regard. It continues to be cited widely and has inspired a number of documents from episcopal conferences on evangelization, among them one from the U.S. bishops on mission in 1986. It is the most quoted papal document in the Final Document of the Puebla meeting of the Third General Conference of Latin American bishops.

Evangelii nuntiandi contributed significantly to a shift in the discussion of the necessity of missionary activity, ending the calls for a moratorium on sending missionaries and giving a clearer motivation for undertaking mission. Its effect is evident in the 1981 meeting of mission-sending institutes, a successor to the 1969 meeting mentioned above. In that 1981 meeting the tenor of the discussion had clearly shifted from the "why" of mission to the "how" of mission.

But perhaps more important than this institutional effect, the document contributed to the definition of a number of aspects of Catholic social teaching. Seven of these deserve mention.

1. *A holistic sense of evangelization. Evangelii nuntiandi* consolidates what was implicit in *Ad gentes* regarding what constitutes evangelization. *Ad gentes* devoted a chapter to the theological foundations of missionary activity and a chapter to the three stages of missionary activity (Christian witness, preaching the gospel and assembling the community, and forming the community of God) but did not go into the detail that is found in *Evangelii nuntiandi.*

The exhortation defines evangelization as a process that involves many moments—from witness and preevangelization, through explicit proclamation, conversion, entry into and growth within the Christian community, to responding to the call to become an agent of evangelization oneself. By focusing on the complexity of the process, *Evangelii nuntiandi* is able both to embrace the wide range of definitions given to evangelization and to provide a schematic view of their interaction. By so doing, it presents a holistic sense of evangelization in at least three senses.

First, it is holistic in locating evangelization at the heart of the church's identity and activity. This continues a process already begun in the documents of Vatican II but here given greater definition and clarity. By returning again and again to ecclesiological concerns such as the role of the sacraments and the relation of the particular churches to the universal church, and by giving examples of what an evangelical vitality looks like in concrete communities, Paul VI makes of evangelization not just something that creates the Christian community but also something that sustains it and is a hallmark of its fidelity to the gospel. By emphasizing evangelization as the principal activity of the church, he gives ecclesiology itself a certain cast—as outward looking, self-critical, concerned with the totality of creation.

Second, it is holistic in that it broadens the concept of evangelization beyond the idea of the first acceptance of the gospel. Evangelization comes to embrace the entirety of Christian life as the gospel message calls the believer to an ever-deeper commitment to discipleship. Thus evangelization is a need that the Christian never entirely outgrows. It becomes a way of both examining and living the Christian life.

Third, it is holistic in its repeated insistence on redeeming the totality of human existence—personal and collective, spiritual and social, immanent and transcendent. While it is careful to give clear precedence to the spiritual and the supernatural, it makes abundantly clear that this cannot be achieved without redeeming the social and the natural. As it is succinctly put, the order of redemption cannot ignore the order of creation.

The holism marking this document's approach to evangelization has helped, therefore, to clarify the meaning of the concept and the tasks to which it calls the believing community. By situating it in the heart of the church's identity and activity, *Evangelii nuntiandi* has helped bring an end to missiological debates about the purpose of evangelization (e.g., the conversion of souls versus the planting of the church).

2. *The continuing necessity of evangelization.* By both broadening and clarifying the meaning of evangelization, *Evangelii nuntiandi* helped end the discussion in Roman Catholic circles about the need to continue missionary activity. It achieved this principally by reexamining the process of evangelization and thereby shifting attention away from a too narrowly conceived understanding of evangelization. Some might maintain that this broadening diluted the energies to go out to peoples who have never heard the gospel as opposed to reaching out to those in dechristianized societies. But that would seem to be a reversion to a restricted view of evangelization. By reminding Christians of the continuing need to be evangelized themselves, Paul VI recalls that no one is master of the evangelization process or of the gospel itself—not even the church. All are subject to the gospel and to Christ. By thinking of evangelization in this fashion, the temptation to see it as territorial conquest is diminished significantly.

This document does not break new ground on the matter of encounter with other religious traditions. It reaffirms the church's duty to share the good news with all but does not discuss how the evangelizer is to interact with the "seeds of the Word" found in those traditions. This remains one of the most perplexing and enigmatic areas in church teaching.

3. *Witness of life. Evangelii nuntiandi* represents an advance over the teaching of the council on the matter of witness of life

(AG 11–12). The council concentrated mainly on the ways the witness of life is achieved but cast the whole phenomenon as part of the preevangelization moment. Paul VI here places the witness of life within the ambit of evangelization itself as the first (albeit incomplete) step in the process. This subtle shift is significant because it legitimates witness of life as a missionary activity in its own right. This has become important in situations in which direct proclamation simply is not possible. It has also opened new ways of approaching those in the other great literate religious traditions on the basis of dialogue. The witness of life not only gives a greater authenticity to Christian presence in largely non-Christian environments, it also allows dialogue to move to another level, which could be blocked by considering witness of life as only a preliminary stage to proclamation. This attitude toward the witness of life, called "dialogue of life" in many places, has opened new possibilities of evangelization not so easily recognized before.

To be sure, *Evangelii nuntiandi* continues to assert the importance of explicit proclamation. But by making witness of life part of rather than preliminary to the evangelization process, it gives an important legitimacy to witness that has helped unfold its potential. While this form of witness has come under attack from time to time, its value in situations of dialogue has been incalculable.

4. *Liberation. Evangelii nuntiandi* was the first papal document to address theologies of liberation in detail. In many ways the questions it posed and the responses it gave continue to shape the Vatican attitude toward liberation, as evidenced, for example, in the two instructions on liberation theology issued by the Congregation for the Doctrine of the Faith in 1985 and 1986.

Evangelii nuntiandi shows a hesitation, even an ambivalence, toward the concept of liberation. On the one hand, it affirms the intentions of those who seek to bring about liberation from oppression and injustice and sees those concerns as consonant with the gospel. On the other hand, it is clearly uncomfortable with inserting the concept into traditional Christian vocabulary about salvation. Part of the discomfort comes from the many different ways in which the term is used; part comes, too, from the unidentified anthropology that informs some liberation theologies—namely, Marxism. There is a concern that concentration on social injustice may diminish concern for individual sin and the need for conversion and that focus on thiswordly needs for liberation may obscure more fundamental notions of spiritual salvation. And finally, there is a concern about the means that may be employed to achieve liberation and the arguments adduced to support them. This centers primarily on the use of armed force against oppression and the condoning of intentional violence. *Evangelii nuntiandi* tries to thread its way through these concerns, addressing each along the way. It ends its discussion of liberation on an uneasy note, one that has sounded through Vatican disquisitions on the topic ever since. However, if one employs the criteria that this document proposes—being in solidarity with those who are oppressed, working for integral liberation, never forgetting the primacy of the spiritual, not becoming naively optimistic about how reformed structures will end oppression, and eschewing violence—then there clearly is room in Catholic social teaching for a positive evaluation of liberation theology. Liberation can form part of a legitimate approach to evangelization.

5. *Basic ecclesial communities. Evangelii nuntiandi* was also the first papal document to address the basic ecclesial communities. It duly noted the variety of types and the variety of motivations for forming them. It devotes its attention to one issue of this phenomenon, namely, their relation to the sanctioned structures of the church.

Communities that distance themselves from the hierarchy and from parochial and diocesan structures cannot call themselves ecclesial; they are to be considered only as sociological units. The document does have positive things to say about those communities that do adhere to church structures, but most of its attention is directed to ways that these communities might deviate from the church rather than contribute to its upbuilding. What emerges is not so much clear teaching on what the communities are and can be as what they are not. In a way, the discussion is somewhat amorphous, perhaps because this discussion is at best peripheral to a treatment of evangelization and probably only appears because it was discussed during the 1974 synod.

6. *Cultural adaptation.* Cultural adaptation was a frequent theme in the allocutions and writings of Paul VI and it appears again here. It echoes the stance of *Gaudium et spes* regarding the relation of gospel and culture: while the gospel is compatible with every culture, it is beholden to none of them and indeed transcends all cultures, although it is only manifested to us through them. *Evangelii nuntiandi* presses beyond the desirability of translating the gospel into terms intelligible to each culture to the utter necessity of doing so. It establishes culture in the modern, social-scientific sense in its descriptive rather than its normative understanding. At the same time, it makes clear that bringing the gospel into a culture does not leave the culture unchanged if true evangelization has taken place; the very marrow of the culture is transformed. Likewise it insists that the essential message of the gospel cannot in any way be altered or diluted in what it calls the transposition process.

Culture and the process of inculturation have continued to be a favorite papal theme. To some extent there has been some movement away from the notion of culture found in *Evangelii nuntiandi* back to the older, more normative understanding of culture. Such can be found, for example, in the 1989 document of the International Theological Commission on Faith and Inculturation, which retreats somewhat both on the issue of culture and on popular piety.

7. *Popular piety.* Popular piety is here treated for the first time in a papal document of this level. The evaluation is largely positive. Popular piety is often derided as an incomplete or deviant form of faith; *Evangelii nuntiandi* makes the point that popular piety is itself a vehicle for evangelization more than a phenomenon to be evangelized. It shows considerable sophistication in understanding the phenomenon and thereby contributed significantly to shaping the CELAM discussion at Puebla in 1979, resulting in a more balanced approach. *Evangelii nuntiandi* probes beneath the practices to get at the attitudes informing popular piety and so is able to discern its value and its potential.

See also BASE COMMUNITIES; DEVELOPMENT; INCULTURATION; LIBERATION THEOLOGY; PAUL VI.

Bibliography: W. Bühlmann, *The Coming of the Third Church* (Maryknoll, N.Y.: Orbis, 1976). Congregation for the Doctrine of the Faith, "Instruction on Certain Aspects of the 'Theology of Liberation,'" *Origins* 14 (September 13, 1985) 193–204. Idem, "Instruction on Christian Freedom and Liberation," *Origins* 15 (April 17, 1986) 713–28. G. Gutiérrez, *A Theology of Liberation* (Maryknoll, N.Y.: Orbis, 1973). International Theological Commission, "Faith and Inculturation," *Irish Theological Quarterly* 55 (1989) 142–61. J. Lang and M. Motte, eds., *Mission in Dialogue* (Maryknoll, N.Y., 1982). NCCB, *To the Ends of the Earth* (Washington: USCC, 1986). Paul VI, *On Evangelization in the Modern World* (Washington: USCC, 1976). SEDOS, ed., *Foundations of Mission Theology* (Maryknoll, N.Y.: Orbis, 1972). USCC, ed., *Synod of Bishops, 1974* (Washington: USCC, 1975).

ROBERT SCHREITER, C.PP.S.

EVANGELIZATION

"Evangelization" is a term referring to the comprehensive process in which the gospel is announced, the message is accepted, and the recipient becomes a member of the believing community. The use of the term is of relatively recent origin and reflects important developments in the church's understanding of its mission to "go out and make disciples of all nations" (Mt 28:19).

The process to which evangelization refers is rooted, of course, in the NT. It is to be understood as a continuation of Jesus' own message and ministry, summarized in Mk 1:15 as "the kingdom of God has come near; repent, and believe in the Good News." The "Good News" (Greek, *euangelion*) is that God is drawing near and is offering a liberating salvation to all who would turn away from sin and alienation and come to the living God. One accepts this salvation by accepting Jesus and by following after him in discipleship, living and acting as he did. The accounts of the appearances of Jesus after the resurrection include in them a commission to continue Jesus' ministry. Indeed, this is the principal task of the church: to continue the announcement of the good news (hence, to evangelize) until Jesus comes again.

To a great extent the task of evangelizing was seen as preaching the good news to those who had not heard it, especially those in faraway places and distant lands. Secondarily, such preaching was directed to those who had heard the good news but no longer followed after Jesus in discipleship. Emphasis was placed on three moments in the process: the explicit proclamation of the good news, the repentance or conversion of the listener, and the development of a local church through baptism and the other sacraments. A term more commonly used than "evangelization" throughout much of Christian history was the "spreading of" or "propagation of" the faith. Thus when Pope Gregory XV in 1622 founded a vehicle for coordinating the church's mission activity, it would be called the Sacred Congregation for the Propagation of the Faith. The newer understanding is reflected in the renaming of that congregation by Paul VI in 1967 as the Sacred Congregation for the Evangelization of Peoples.

A series of papal encyclicals, beginning with *Maximum illud* in 1919, prepared the way for the teaching of the Second Vatican Council, where the term evangelization begins to be used. It appears in *Lumen gentium* 17 at the end of the chapter entitled "The People of God," where it is used to speak of those who have not yet become part of the church. The meaning of evangelization, however, is developed most completely in *Ad gentes,* the Decree on the Church's Missionary Activity.

Ad gentes is a watershed in the development of the teaching of the church on evangelization. It presses the responsibility of evangelization beyond the church's response to Christ's commission to preach, locating it first of all within the Trinity itself, in the sending out of the Son and the Holy Spirit to reveal the divine mystery. Such a view has two important implications. First, in evangelizing, the church is not only living in obedience to its Lord's command, it is participating in the very life of the Trinity. It partakes in a deep and intense way in God's own life and activity. Second, such participation reveals the true identity of the church: it is intended by its very nature to be missionary (AG 1, 2). These insights give a very different contour to the church's self-understanding. Its evangelizing activity is not merely intended to extend its boundaries; it is intended rather to be the most complete form of the church's self-expression.

Ad gentes goes on to describe the evangelization process, summing it up under three headings: Christian witness, preaching the gospel and assembling the people of God, and forming the Christian community—a more-or-less traditional understanding of the evangelization process but one formed clearly within the ecclesiology of *Lumen gentium.* Its principal contribution to the development of church teaching, however, lies in the doctrinal foundations it sets down for evangelization, namely, its Trinitarian origins with the implications flowing from this for the church's understanding of itself.

The most complete development of the church's understanding of evangelization is to be found in Pope Paul VI's 1975 apostolic exhortation *Evangelii nuntiandi.* This was issued as the result of the pope's reflections on the discussions held during the 1974 synod of bishops and was devoted to the theme of evangelization in the modern world. *Evangelii nuntiandi* builds upon the work of the Second Vatican Council but extends it in significant ways. It remains the church's charter document for evangelization.

Evangelii nuntiandi relies on the doctrinal principles set out in *Ad gentes* and does not devote a great deal of space to repeating them. Its value lies in its attention to the complexity of the evangelization process and some of the implications it draws from that. In *Evangelii nuntiandi* 18, Paul VI summarizes his understanding of evangelization: "The Church evangelizes when she seeks to convert, solely through the divine power of the Message she proclaims, both the personal and collective consciences of people, the activities in which they engage, and the lives and milieux which are theirs."

Evangelii nuntiandi provides two principal insights into the evangelization process itself. First, the witness to the Christian message offered by the life of the evangelizer is more than a mere preparation for the gospel; it is part of the evangelization process itself. This insight has helped confirm the experience of those who would evangelize in situations where direct proclamation is not feasible or even desirable. It legitimates their activity and at the same time reveals the intricate ways in which the good news comes to be heard. Second, *Evangelii nuntiandi* emphasizes that the evangelizing process does not end with the establishment of the church but with the sending out of a new generation of apostles. Thus the fruit of evangelization is not the church but rather a continuation of the evangelizing activity. This insight was implicit in *Ad gentes'* understanding of the church as essentially missionary, but it was left to *Evangelii nuntiandi* to express it more clearly and forcefully.

Understanding the process of evangelization is not the only contribution of *Evangelii nuntiandi.* It also offers important insight into the question of to whom evangelization is directed. It was noted above that traditionally evangelization was aimed at the unbeliever and those who had lapsed from belief. This document extends evangelization to include those who already believe but need a never-ending deepening of their faith. Put simply, the church itself is in need of constant and continuing evangelization in order to be true to its Lord, Jesus Christ. By making this point, Pope Paul VI shifts the gestalt of evangelization from just being the outreach of the Christian community to an understanding of the ongoing process of growth in discipleship. In so doing, evangelization does not lose its cutting edge but rather is allowed to be seen as the radical process it is. All are in need of constant and continuing evangelization. Such an approach gives the church itself a special meaning: it is not to be seen as an end in itself but rather as a pilgrim on the path toward ever-greater entry into the divine mystery. The church, then, must be self-critical, ever reforming, and open to a continuing and deeper conversion into Christ.

Given this understanding of evangelization, it becomes clear that evangelization is not the task solely of the hierarchy or specialized agents like missionaries. Evangelization is a task incumbent upon every member of the church, for evangelization defines best what it means to be a member of the church.

Evangelii nuntiandi's final contribution to understanding evangelization is its holistic approach. Evangelization is, to be sure, directed toward converting the individual away from sin to a life of God. But Pope Paul VI goes to great pains to emphasize that conversion is intended also for the collective of humanity. It is directed to the cultures in which people live with all their attendant socioeconomic and political structures. Indeed, it aims to convert human "criteria of judgment, determining values, points of interest, lines of thought, sources of inspiration and models of life" (EN 19). Thus the struggle for liberation that has become part of the local church's agenda in so many places can be seen as a form of evangelization.

"Evangelization" has come to be seen, then, as a comprehensive term for the church's outward movement in carrying out the mission of Jesus Christ. It involves all in the church, not just a specialized few. It carries forth the message of an offer of salvation by God in Jesus Christ, a salvation that touches not only individual human hearts but whole societies and cultures. It is a never-ending process of conversion—for those hearing the message for the first time, for those who have forgotten or rejected it, for those who try to grow into greater fidelity to it. For the church not to evangelize is to lose its very identity and purpose for being.

See also EVANGELII NUNTIANDI.

Bibliography: Vatican Council II, Decree on the Church's Missionary Activity (*Ad Gentes*). Paul VI, *On Evangelization in the Modern World (Evangelii Nuntiandi).*

ROBERT SCHREITER, C.Pp.S.

EVIL, SOCIAL

The tradition of identifying and condemning social evil has been a long one in the Catholic church. We see it in the medieval theologians of Salamanca, de Vitoria and Soto, who attacked the American slave trade and its links to unemployment in Spain. It is manifest in the struggle of Henry Cardinal Manning in England in the 1880s fighting for the industrial poor, especially the dockers. Leo XIII's encyclical *Rerum novarum* (1891) marked the entry of the magisterium into this arena. In it we find a pattern common to much of the social teaching of this century. Church leaders note conditions of work, health, and housing that undermine the dignity of men and women made in Christ's image (RN 2). They make some effort to explain the genesis of such evil and to find possible remedies for it (RN 32–34). Leo's intervention was received as an ignorant affront to the prevailing economic theories, thus setting a pattern frequently repeated since then.

This call to stand in Christ's name with the poor and the powerless against evils that oppress them has become stronger and clearer since *Rerum novarum.* One of the few condemnations uttered by Vatican II was aimed at forces that cheapen and destroy human life: genocide, abortion, torture, and the like (*Gaudium et spes* 27.3). In their synodal document of 1971 the world's bishops spoke up for the most powerless: migrants, ethnic minorities, and the abandoned (*Justitia in mundo* 21–26). Pope John Paul II carried this insight even further when he spoke of the Christian's duty to the poor. "This is an option, or a special form of primacy in the exercise of Christian charity, to which the whole tradition in the Church bears witness" (*Sollicitudo rei socialis* 42). This growing sense of identification with the lot of the poor has also led the church in many nations from being seen as part of the establishment to being in the position of a critic of the regime, even a subversive element in the eyes of some ruling powers (JM 24).

Because much of this magisterial teaching has been made as a response to concrete situations of injustice, there has been little extended theological reflection on the nature and origins of evil as a social phenomenon. Though the distinction between physical and moral evil is made, moral evil (normally used interchangeably with "sin") as a human, religious characteristic acts as the focus of the church's magisterial writings in the area of justice. This article will follow the same approach.

The ultimate roots of conflict in a shattered world are located unambiguously in the internal wound of sin, according to *Reconciliatio et paenitentia* (RP 2). Misuse of freedom (GS 13) and conflicting desires in the human heart (GS 10) lead men and women to try to build existences independent of God but which leave them alone, dishonored, and exploited (RP 5). Sundered from what alone can bring them fulfillment, they inevitably find themselves abusing and destroying the bonds that tie them to the created world and other people (GS 13).

Though the Thomistic view of evil as a lack of a due good underlies modern magisterial documents, we find a significant change in emphasis from the time of John XXIII. Evil and its effects are presented in progressively more personalistic terms. In 1891 Leo XIII was loath to encourage worker activism (RN 16) because he still viewed society in terms of God-given hierarchical authority. Ninety years later John Paul II defended the Christian value of work in terms of its aptness to promote key human values such as personal dignity and its creative contribution to the coming of God's kingdom through the integral development of society economically, politically, culturally, and religiously (*Laborem exercens* 4–8). Sin is what distorts or destroys such integral development. Social evil is repeatedly depicted in such personalistic terms in *Gaudium et spes* and in the writings of Paul VI, for example, in his address on war to the United Nations in 1965. "You cannot love with weapons in your hands. Long before they mete out death and destruction, those terrible arms . . . cause nightmares, distrust and dark designs. . . . They lead astray the mentality of peoples."

Another thread that has grown particularly strong since John XXIII is the drawing of the antithesis between world solidarity shattered by the effects of sin and Jesus' reforging of solidarity by his free taking on of human suffering and the effects of sin.

It was John XXIII who first emphasized the concept of socialization, namely, an increased interdependence among all the nations of the world. Pointing to unequal distribution of land and resources, he stated that efforts to eliminate such disparities were essential for any hope of lasting world peace (*Mater et magistra* 155, 157). John Paul II insisted that church social doctrine is critical of both liberal capitalism and Marxist collectivism (SRS 21; *Octogesima adveniens* 26) because each has failed to provide genuine dignity for people by destroying these inequalities. Instead, their exaggerated concern for security has hindered world cooperation (SRS 22), building up tensions that reveal themselves in "war by proxy" all over the globe (SRS 20). Instead of providing global leadership and solidarity in overcoming these evils, the West has abandoned itself to a growing and selfish isolationism, while the East has ignored its duty to alleviate human misery (SRS 23).

In *Laborem exercens* John Paul II provided his own critique of the classical Marxist theory of class struggle as the inevitable historical vehicle for the birth of a classless society. Though agreeing with Marx upon the central role of human labor in the productive process, he proposed a far wider concept of work that included manual work, organization, and domestic labor. In this wider view, class warfare is an anachronism, the real struggle being one for solidarity, a struggle to establish common rights. He insisted that history moves forward not by rigid rules but through free human choice. The world we live in, broken up into power blocs and dominated by imperialism, is not a world shaped by inevitable evolutionary forces but rather one "subject to the structures of sin" (SRS 36).

The strategy of Christ is clearly contrary to such divisiveness. As a man Jesus experienced the basic human condition, rejection and loneliness. Yet he went much further, freely embracing the mystery of apparent rejection and separation from God on the cross (RP 7). That passage of suffering on behalf of all humanity was at the same time his entrance into glory and resurrection. God's plan to call all people into lives as children of God is now forever linked to the cross (*Dives in misericordia* 7). Suffering for the Christian can therefore be creative, even joyful, for its meaninglessness is now transformed into something salvific for our brothers and sisters.

It is against this background of human sinfulness that the magisterium has attempted to tackle the difficult question of tolerance of a lesser evil, for example, war, to protect a greater good, say the freedom of a nation. The possibility of using force to overthrow an unjust regime occurred first in Pius XI's *Firmissimum* (1938). Paul VI warned that the impulse to overthrow unpopular tyrannies could in fact usher in even worse evils, though he did reluctantly admit of such a possibility when it is the only way to overturn a long-standing tyranny that is causing great personal and communal damage (*Populorum progressio* 31).

In striving to determine what true economic good is, magisterial teaching centers itself on the maxim that the human person is "the source, the center and the purpose of all economic and social life" (GS 63). This norm must not be construed in terms of a liberal individualism. Global interdependence means that the fate of each human being resonates for good or ill to the fate of all others. So individual good or happiness is always balanced against the rights and needs of the entire human community. This approach characterizes the discussion of nuclear warfare (*The Challenge of Peace* 3, 103; GS 80), deterrence theory (GS 81.1; *Pacem in terris* 111), pollution and conservation (JM 11; OA 21; SRS 34), scientific and economic development (GS 57.4; 63.2), and the responsibility of the media (OA 20).

Human dominion over the world is not unlimited. The concept of development has become so narrowly linked to growth in material goods that there is a real danger in not seeing that this kind of growth is not being accompanied by a corresponding development of moral awareness. People are not becoming more responsible and generous (OA 41; *Redemptor hominis* 15.3). True dominion over the world must resemble that of Christ, that is, it "consists in the priority of ethics over technology, in the primacy of the person over things, and in the superiority of spirit over matter" (RH 16). This is so central a truth that even a system that produced great wealth and distributed it fairly would still be evil if it took away human dignity by removing all responsibility and personal initiative (MM 83).

Reflection on these teachings has led to a richer appreciation of the meaning of sin. Whereas Leo XIII portrayed sin as disobedience to God's will and the law of the church, modern magisterial teaching has adopted a far more integralist view of sin. Since sin destroys personal equilibrium, it is a suicidal and self-destructive act whose effects will radiate out to poison all human relationships. In this sense every sin is both personal and social (RP 15). Sins that have pervaded the life of a community, for example, bribery in the police force, are the result of the accumulation and concentration of many personal sins (RP 16). This is the way in which individual sins enter into the structures of the world, touching all by their contagion, interfering with the development of peoples and nations (SRS 36). In our time two such structures of sin that create immense damage are an all-consuming desire for profit and a thirst for power (SRS 37). The only way to fight such evil is to work for conversion to a sense of interdependency, solidarity, and commitment to the common good (SRS 38).

Though Vatican II was rather uncritical in its espousal of the Western model of development, it did move the church toward giving up its privileged position and benefits in some societies. The bishops of the 1971 general synod moved even further, saying that since working for justice was a constitutive part of the preaching of the gospel, then the church must begin by acting justly in its own life and structures and toward its own members (JM 40). Even to speak with credibility to the poor and oppressed, its members must be sparing in their lifestyles (JM 47). In a similar vein John Paul II recalled the observation of Paul VI that for the church to evangelize it must be evangelized in itself (*Evangelii nuntiandi* 13), steeped in the spirit of reconciliation among its own members and toward other Christian churches (RP 9). To achieve this the church must work hard to educate Christians about the demands of justice. There is no more effective vehicle for this than the liturgy, for here the power and word of the Lord can expose and conquer evil, helping to form consciences anew. Similarly, a renewed understanding and use of the sacrament of penance will help to keep the social dimensions and power of evil before the minds of those who strive to be followers of Christ (JM 58).

See also ECOLOGY; JUSTICE IN THE WORLD; LABOR AND CAPITAL IN CATHOLIC SOCIAL THOUGHT; MARXISM; POOR, PREFERENTIAL OPTION FOR; RERUM NOVARUM; SOLLICITUDO REI SOCIALIS.

NEIL VANEY, S.M.

EXISTENTIALISM

A name given to a broad spectrum of philosophical positions, the word "existentialism" is sometimes used rather loosely and probably should be taken as a vague word for a tendency rather than for a clearly identifiable school of thought. Nevertheless, the position can be fairly characterized as having two poles. Existentialists have in common, negatively, a rejection of traditional Western philosophy's emphasis on the reasonableness of the world and the power of the mind to know it. This is the metaphysical or epistemological pole of the movement. The other is ethical or psychological. Existentialists emphasize the importance of the individual's real-life choices and especially the necessity of taking responsibility here and now for the project of finding or giving meaning to one's life. The resulting emphasis upon the individual's specific, life-changing decisions often dramatizes the frustration of the intellect and the anxiety involved in accepting the real human condition. It is contrasted with the "essentialist" idea, often only implicit, that life is primarily made worthwhile by having the right thoughts or believing the right doctrines—or even that such thoughts and beliefs are valuable, important, or useful.

The philosophical discussion of matters such as these can be quite abstract, but the issue has always had a practical side. Although examples of this tendency can be found throughout the history of Western philosophy and theology—for example, emphasis upon faith rather than belief in St. Paul—existentialism as an overt philosophical movement is a rather recent emphasis. Although Blaise Pascal is often named as a forerunner, its modern emergence is usually traced to mid-19th-century Lutheran philosopher/theologian Søren Kierkegaard; it became popular in Europe in the period after World War I. The word itself was popularized by Martin Heidegger and became associated theologically with the hermeneutics of Rudolph Bultmann. Bultmann taught that the message of the gospel was not to be identified with information about Jesus but was rather the call to live a certain kind of life, the apostolic church's understanding of the kind of life to which Jesus had called his disciples.

The term entered popular speech in the United States in the decades after World War II, largely through the version associated with French philosopher Jean-Paul Sartre. This version was atheistic and antinomian; it was attacked in *Humani generis* as "a new and erroneous philosophy which . . . concerns itself only with existence of individual things and neglects all consideration of their immutable essences." In the United States the moral position called "situation ethics" was sometimes identified as existential in this negative sense.

More recently the term has taken on a positive meaning in theology as it has become associated with Karl Rahner, a one-time student of Heidegger's, and with moral theologians such as Bernard Häring. Rahner was treated as suspect by ecclesiastical authorities in the 1950s, but his reputation was rehabilitated at Vatican II. He uses the term "supernatural existential" in the context of the traditional question of the relation of nature and grace. He means by this an openness to the supernatural, which is a capacity of human beings. By calling it an "existential" he emphasizes that it is not a "thing" or a part of human nature. Rather the term indicates a meeting of nature and grace within the real, existing human being. Rahner has also popularized references to existentialist ethics, emphasizing the element of experiential decision making.

Bernard Häring and others used categories from philosophical existentialism to emphasize themes such as freedom of conscience and the primacy of love in moral theology. The term "personalism" was coined to apply to similar positions. In spite of the stature of figures such as Rahner and Häring, or perhaps because of it, the term "existentialism" has become more and more a dated term for a past movement in philosophy. In the United States (and in English in general) it has always had a somewhat foreign sound; some of the same points have been made by more native movements like pragmatism. Terms related to existentialism like "phenomenology" and "personalism" continue to have wider use.

See also ATHEISM; GRACE; PERSONALISM; REASON, ROLE OF.

Bibliography: K. Rahner, "Concerning the Relationship of Nature and Grace," *Theological Investigations,* vol. 1 (London: Darton Longman & Todd, 1961). B. Häring, *The Christian Existentialist* (New York: New York Univ. Press, 1968).

ANTHONY BATTAGLIA

EXPLOITATION

Exploitation is the refusal or failure to respect the subject-character of a person or persons in the satisfaction of the dominant will of another. Exploitation occurs when persons are prevented through the willfulness of others or through social structures from being the rightful subjects of their own history. Exploitation is possible in all fora of human intercourse, for example, in the place of work, between the sexes, and between nations.

"Exploitation" may also be employed to describe (in moral discourse) the use of natural resources, animals, and so forth. Here, exploitation refers to a manner of using that is adjudged as abusive or without proportionate reason in the satisfaction of the agent's will and without concern for the common good.

See also ANIMALS, RIGHTS OF; CLASS STRUGGLE; COMMON GOOD; FORCE; GREED; HUMAN RIGHTS; LIBERATION THEOLOGY; PERSON, DIGNITY OF.

PATRICK CARROLL, O.S.M.

F

FAMILY

There are many things that Christians, like the rest of humankind, have not been able to understand fully. The various arrangements called "family" are among these partially understood matters of human living. Like many other religious traditions, Christianity has wanted the family to be a stable institution, providing for the economic, educational, interpersonal, and psychological needs of people. Most of the time, however, Christian leaders have taken the existence of the family for granted, challenging its form only when it appears to deviate from a monogamous model and assuming its basic internal justice. Though the family has generally been considered to be a major social institution, Christian theology has not addressed it with anything like the amount of attention given to the state or to the church itself. Indeed, the family is barely visible in Christian theology and ethics, and insofar as there is a Christian understanding of the family, it has not developed very much over the centuries. Hence, to consider the family in the context of the past one hundred years of Roman Catholic social teaching requires some reflection on what is missing in the tradition as well as what is present.

Theological Beginnings

Modern Catholic social teaching in the form of official church documents began in response to specific historical situations. These situations were identified primarily in economic and political terms, and though families were importantly affected by these situations, the analysis used in the documents ordinarily did not bear on the structure of the family itself. The reason for this may well be the same reason that has kept contemporary philosophical theories of justice from including the family—a reason that Susan Moller Okin identifies as the failure to take gender seriously in most considerations of justice (*Justice, Gender, and the Family*). It is certainly the case that a hundred years ago as well as now many of the key problems of labor, management, market, and politics have been problems for women as well as for men, and problems intricately connected with gendered patterns of life in the family as well as the wider society.

But the absence of much concern for the family in Catholic social teaching may go further back than one hundred years. We may understand it better in the light of a much longer tradition of Christian teaching (and lack of teaching) about the family. While within the limits of this essay it is not possible to trace the whole tradition, some perspective on it can be gained by attending at least briefly to its historical beginnings. Rowan Greer's important study of the relationship between theology and life in the early church provides an interesting picture in this regard (Greer, esp. chap. 4). As Greer shows, the church in late antiquity manifested at least three attitudes toward marriage and family, the combination of which yielded a deep ambivalence. First, there was seeming rejection of family ties, sometimes even open hostility (pp. 77–78). The Christian message was a "sword" of "division," setting family members against one another (Mt 10:34-39; Lk 12:51-53). Christians had loyalties beyond the family. They were to call no one "father" on earth (Mt 23:9), and they might even risk being handed over to persecution by offended members of their families. They were asked in some sense to "hate" father, mother, spouse, children, to "forget" wives or husbands, to leave all things in pursuit of something greater, more important, than ordinary family life. They lived in anticipation of a new age, which would exclude marrying and giving in marriage (Mt 12:25; 22:30; Lk 20:35). All family bonds and responsibilities were relativized in favor of an imminent realm of God in which unity with God and all persons would transcend the special human relations that were in place before its coming.

Second but closely related to this first attitude, the early Christians saw the church itself as their family (Greer, pp. 97–99, 104–5). For those who were previously without a family (e.g., widows and orphans), now there was the protection of the church (Acts 6:1; 1 Tm 5:3ff.; Jas 1:27). For those who had to leave their former families, the church itself was their new home (Mk 10:29-30). The Christian community offered a kind of membership, of belonging, that abolished all barriers of nation and gender and economic status. Here there "is neither Jew nor Greek, there is neither slave nor free, there is neither male nor female; for you are all one in Christ Jesus" (Gal 3:28). While this was a promise for the future, it also could be experienced in the present.

Finally, in tension with the first and second attitudes, Christians also believed that marriage and family in the ordinary sense could be affirmed, not abolished, in their new life of faith (Greer, pp. 99–100, 105). While some might be called to "leave all things," yet for others, existing family units, households, might be affirmed (Acts 10:2; 11:14; 16:15). Thus rules were given for households, rules in the form of the Hellenistic Jewish *Haustafeln* (Eph 5:21ff.; Col 3:18ff.; 1 Pet 2:18ff.). Following such rules, Christians could counter the charges of their enemies that they were domestic troublemakers. The socially disruptive antifamily trends in the Christian community were thus moderated. In the affirmation and confirmation of existing family ties, moreover, family relations might in some respects be transformed. Greer, for example, thinks 1 Cor 7:4 was aimed at overturning societal conventions of inequality in marriage, for Paul indicated that "the husband rules over his wife's body *and* that the wife rules over her husband's body" (Greer, p. 100).

But the message remained ambiguous, with the attitudes of rejection, substitution, and affirmation continually in tension. In the 3rd century all three attitudes contributed to a Christian stance that was in opposition both to the extreme antimarriage, antisex asceticism of some Gnostics and to the apparently libertine practices of others. Marriage was affirmed as good by the Christian church, as part of creation, though celibacy was considered better. Marriage was, of course, the choice of the majority of Christians, and the church taught a discipline for it—the discipline of exclusivity and permanence.

From the 4th century on the negative attitude of Christianity toward the family was expressed most clearly in the monastic movement. Monasticism took the place of martyrdom as the ultimate form of Christian self-sacrifice in relation to the things of the world. It developed as a protest against the domestication of Christianity as a way of life, and it sought to sustain the tension of waiting for, and leaning toward, a future that is promised, participated in, but not yet realized. Monasteries became surrogate families, offering a life more closely approximating (it was thought) the realm of God to come. At the same time, the church recognized pastoral requirements to strike a balance in Christian evaluations of marriage and family. For example, bishops and abbots began to discourage anyone from entering a monastery without a spouse's consent. Periodically, church councils recalled Christians to the respect due to marriage and to familial bonds and duties.

Nonetheless, the themes of asceticism, of desire for the vision of God through contemplation, and of the church itself as a substitute family converged to hold in place through centuries a view of marriage and family as subordinate to other forms of Christian living and other spheres of Christian works. When the church affirmed the family's importance, it invariably did so in terms of the functional roles of the family in socializing children or in keeping order in society. The family could prepare persons for more important things in life—for roles in society or in the church, for lives of prayer or good works. Especially for men, the family was something to move beyond.

Greer argues that despite the seeming contradictions, there is theological coherence in the varied attitudes of the early church toward marriage and family (pp. 111–16). That is, the religious and spiritual ideal and ultimate goal of the Christian life included utter and perfect union with God, universal unity among human persons, and a unity of body and soul that would finally constitute incorruptibility. Celibacy stood as a kind of metaphor for this ideal, and as such it served to relativize every limited framework for human relationships (including marriage and family). But depending on whether one took a theological stance favoring opposition to society or transformation of society (both of which could be consistent with the Christian ideal), a Christian assessment of family life could be either negative or positive.

It is difficult to see how even positive attitudes proved seriously transformative, however. The results of Christian teaching left the general standards and structure of the Roman Empire regarding marriage and family little changed. Whatever the potential for new mutuality in marriage, whatever the beginning dissolution of barriers within and among families, the *paterfamilias* by and large still reigned, and the household remained ordered as the culture required. The Christian view of the family was essentially a static view, whether this was because affirming the family was aimed at social respectability or because the church remained relatively uninterested in the family.

It was not until the 14th century that a significant shift came that allowed a major new positive evaluation of marriage and family life (Yost, pp. 169–80). Humanists in the Renaissance proposed a profound change in focus from otherworldliness to social responsibility, from renunciation and withdrawal to self-discipline and achievement in a world where family and productive labor were combined. The Protestant Reformation in some ways completed this movement and articulated a new understanding of the place of the family in Christian life. Now the work of Christians as Christians was not primarily in the cloister or the sanctuary but "in the market place, behind the plow, and in front of the stove" (Lazareth, p. 133). Still, Christian assumptions about the structure of the family changed very little.

In the Roman Catholic tradition, moreover, much of the pattern of evaluation established in the early church and reinforced in the centuries that followed remained in place. Though marriage was given the dignity of a sacrament in the 12th century, it remained a lesser calling in the Christian community, still subordinate to celibacy and still primarily instrumental in relation to church and society. Key developments in the theology of marriage and family tended not to alter the basic assessment of their place in Christian life but to reconsider very particular issues such as the nature of the marital bond and the purpose of sexual activity. By the time the modern tradition of Catholic social teaching began at the end of the 19th century, little had been done to reevaluate the basic possibilities of marriage and family.

The 20th century has in some sense brought a quantum leap in the church's positive affirmation of the family. Again and again in papal encyclicals, statements of episcopal synods, the documents of Vatican II, and so forth, the family has been hailed as the foundation of society and even "the first cell of the church," the "domestic sanctuary" of the Christian community (see, e.g., *Apostolicam actuositatem* 11; *Gaudium et spes* 52; synod of bishops' "A Message to Christian Families in the Modern World," *New York Times* [October 26, 1980] 18). Yet these high assessments are moderated by cautions about excessive self-love, the worship of pleasure, and illicit practices against human generation (*Gaudium et spes* 47). John Paul II, following the 1980 international synod of bishops on the family, praised the family as an authentic way of Christian living, but in comparing marriage with celibacy he reaffirmed the church's defense "throughout her history" of the "superiority of this charism [celibacy] to that of marriage, by reason of the wholly singular link which it has with the kingdom of God" (*Familiaris consortio* 16). The Roman Catholic tradition of official teaching remains at least ambivalent about the family.

Yet there are theological resources in the Catholic tradition that can challenge the traditional attitudes of Christian leaders toward marriage and the family. The very concerns that led Christians of the past to relegate the family to secondary importance in the Christian life can now be revisited in the light of both contemporary understandings of the family and modern theological developments in Christian self-understanding. For example, undergirding traditional preferences for celibacy over marriage were a number of assumptions that many Christians would today reject. These assumptions included: Marriage and family are "things of this world" that must be transcended for the sake of the kingdom of God; they are less conducive (than a celibate lifestyle) to growth in a whole and absolute love for God and to a universal love of all humankind; marriage is ordinarily related to sex, and human sexuality is in some way dangerous and suspect; the sphere of the family is primarily women's place and therefore subordinate in principle to men's spheres, to the public worlds of church and society (see Margaret A. Farley, "The Church and the Family: An Ethical Task," *Horizons* [Spring 1983]).

Today Christian theology is less likely to think of a "divided heart" in terms of human love versus love of God and less likely to conceptualize marriage as only an "indirect" way to union with God. Catholic theology in particular is more likely to see special relations as participations in and helps to Christian *agape,* not hindrances in the mode of an either/or. And while the last word is not in (nor will it probably ever be) regarding the meaning of human sexuality, theological perspectives on sexual desire and activity and relations are both less pessimistic and less idealistic-romantic than they were in the church of the past. As for the place of women and the dichotomy between public worlds and private, these are questions that Christian theology has only begun to address; these are questions that more appropriately take us into the last hundred years of Catholic social teaching.

A revised theological interpretation of marriage and family is, however, still largely in the making. Whose voices are to speak in this regard is no doubt part of the question for the church and its families.

But the "barely visible" place of the family in Christian theology is itself not irrelevant to the similar near-invisibility of the family in Christian ethics. (Of course, there is a great deal in Christian moral theology and ethics about certain questions that have relevance for marriage, but these are questions of sexual ethics such as contraception, divorce and remarriage, and not questions regarding the overall place of the family in the Christian life or the justice of the family itself.) Against this background, then, we can turn to the modern tradition of official Catholic social teaching—to the teaching on the family insofar as it appears in church documents since *Rerum novarum*.

Social Ethics and the Family

The family is important to Leo XIII and his successors. It never holds center stage in an overall social analysis of historical situations, but it also never drops away from the horizon of concerns that prompted the major social encyclicals. It might be argued that the church's solicitude for the family in this social-ethical tradition has been, however, largely part of a defensive religious agenda, one that is little conducive to rethinking the nature and form of the family. Perceived threats to the family are threats from outside the family itself—from theories and movements that proclaim the end of the family as a social institution, from political forces that want to infringe on the role of parents as educators of their children, from economic trends that leave families impoverished, from state intervention in family decisions about sexual morality, and so on. Against such threats the church has articulated a fundamental human right to marry and to found a family, to procreate and to rear children. As David Hollenbach's study of the family in modern church social teaching suggests, these rights have been upheld in a complex history of church opposition to certain forms of socialism and to state coercion of the family regarding procreation (Hollenbach, esp. chap. 4). It is difficult not to observe, however, that the church's efforts to protect the family from state intervention almost always include a concern to protect the church's own role in relation to the family, a role of regulator as well as advocate. In spite of this or because of it, the concern of the church for the family in modern civilization is still one in which the family is only marginally visible and in which the internal structure of the family is uncritically assumed.

The clearest elements in the official church's family theory of the last hundred years include (1) the meaning of the family for individuals, (2) the family's relationship to society, and (3) the proper roles of persons within the family. These elements interact with one another in the sense that what is proposed for one is often systematically dependent on the other for its warrants. For example, arguments for family rights over against the state are grounded in the essential importance of familial relations for the human dignity and flourishing of the individual. Similarly, the division of spheres of life into private and public worlds leads to and also depends on a gender differentiation of roles.

First, then, the documents in this tradition present marriage, family life, and parenthood as forms of human activity and relationship that are intimate to the identity of individual persons. (I am heavily dependent here upon the overview and analysis of these materials in Hollenbach, ibid.) While not everyone is called to marry or to have children, for those who are, marriage and procreation are essential dimensions of the concrete realization of their transcendent worth as individuals. The family is a natural institution, anterior to any other human society, a privileged form of human community with bonds that are qualitatively different from other forms of association. (These assertions are common to the whole tradition, but see, for example, RN 12; GS 52; U.S. bishops' pastoral letter, "Economic Justice for All: Catholic

Social Teaching and the U.S. Economy," *Origins* 16 [November 27, 1986] no. 93.) Marriage and family are rooted in the core of human personhood, having their foundation in the biological, interpersonal, and social dimensions of the person. Because of this fundamental human meaning for marriage and family, individuals have a right to marry and to found a family, rights that must not be infringed on by the actions and policies of the state.

Leo XIII argued that "no human law can abolish the natural and original right of marriage" (RN 12). This claim was repeated again and again through the documents of the tradition. Pius XII, John XXIII, and Paul VI, for example, all insisted on the fundamental and inalienable right to marry and to procreate. "When the most inalienable right of matrimony and procreation is taken away human dignity is destroyed" (*Populorum progressio* 37; see also, for example, John XXIII, *Pacem in terris* 15; GS 52, 87).

But the only relation of the family to the wider society is not its negative rights to be let alone. In fact, so important to this tradition is the second element of its family theory—that is, the complex relationships of the family to the state—that the other two elements (the meaning of the family for individuals and its internal role assignments) tend theoretically to serve this one. (I have arbitrarily identified these elements as 1, 2, and 3, only for the sake of addressing them here.) The relationship of family and state is significantly reciprocal. On the one hand church leaders have argued that the family is necessary to society. It is the basic "cell of society," the foundation of social order. Through marriage and family the members of society are propagated, and it is in the context of the family that children are to be reared, educated, and fashioned into good citizens. Leo XIII even argued that children learn obedience to the state by learning obedience to their fathers (*Arcanum* 26). But, as John Paul II insisted, "the social role of the family certainly cannot stop short at procreation and education" (FC 44). Families should devote themselves to "manifold social service activities," especially in favor of the poor, and their responsibilities extend even to "political intervention" on behalf of the "rights and duties of the family," "transforming society" in whatever way they can (ibid.).

On the other hand, because the family is an "imperfect" society, unable to provide for all of its own needs, it is in turn dependent upon the state. Growing attention has been given in the tradition to the responsibilities of society to support its families, primarily in their economic needs. At the very heart of the church's modern social teaching is the recognition of economic rights, which ground the claim of all persons for minimum levels of well-being. From the early calls for a "family wage" by Leo XIII and Pius XI, to the expanded concern of Pius XII for the postwar impact on families of unemployment, homelessness, inflation, and sickness, to the recommendations by John Paul II for "other social measures" such as grants to mothers, to the careful insistence by the U.S. bishops in *Economic Justice for All* that economic policies must strengthen and stabilize family life—the tradition has not wavered from a commitment to the basic economic welfare of families insofar as this was understood (see, for example, Pius XI, *Quadragesimo anno* 71 and *Casti connubii* 117–18; Pius XII, *Christmas Address,* 1952; John XXIII, *Mater et magistra* 33 and *Pacem in terris* 16).

But another aspect of the relationship between family and society is more problematic for many family members today. For all of the reciprocity of needs and duties, rights and responsibilities between the family and society, the theoretical relationship between them (as articulated in this tradition of social teaching) is finally extrinsic. The two social arrangements remain autonomous in significant ways—some of which are aimed to prevent the absorption of the family by the state, some of which sustain a dichotomy between a "public" world and one that is "private." It is the latter, of course, that is troubling today. As Hollenbach has noted, it has prevented the tradition from translating its insights (for example, regarding the basic conditions for the realization of human dignity) from one sphere to another—in particular, from society to the family (Hollenbach, p. 319ff.). As other theorists have noted, the gender assignment of roles in these two spheres has undergirded invalid and harmful interpretations of women's and men's realities. The theory of gendered, separate spheres has yielded a practice of gendered injustice.

This brings us, then, to the third element in the church's modern family theory—its understanding of the internal structure of the family. Despite some acknowledgments of cultural diversity in marriage and family profiles, the tradition has been consistent in maintaining that the structure of marriage and even of the family is basically God-given, discernible as an immutable part of nature, knowable by Christians through reason and revelation. Both Leo XIII and Pius XI began their considerations of marriage with the presupposition that "not by man were the laws made to strengthen and confirm and elevate it [matrimony] but by God, the Author of nature, and by Christ our Lord, by whom nature was redeemed. Hence these laws cannot be subject to any human decrees" (*Casti connubii* 5). More than two-thirds of a century later Vatican II found it necessary to speak of "distinguishing eternal realities from their changing expressions" (GS 52; see also GS 48), but there was still clarity about the "eternal realities" of marriage and family. In 1981 the synod of bishops indicated that it had "learned much about the many and varied cultural conditions in which Christian families live" but concluded that "the Church must accept and foster this rich diversity, while at the same time encouraging Christian families to give effective witness to God's plan within their own cultures," evaluating all cultural elements to "insure that they are consistent with the divine plan for marriage and the family" (*A Message to Christian Families in the Modern World*).

The immutable structures of marriage and family have been thought to embrace not only the free consent of partners, sexual exclusivity, openness to procreation, and indissolubility; they have also included a hierarchical relationship and differentiation of roles for husbands and wives. It is only these latter structural aspects that will be considered briefly here. At first in this tradition it was assumed that the order of the family "includes both the primacy of the husband with regard to the wife and her children, and the ready subjection of the wife and her willing obedience" (CC 26). This was based on what was thought to be their different "natures" and on the need for unity in the family (which in turn would foster unity in society). Though women and men are equal under God, they are not equal before one another. They differ, thought Leo and Pius, in that "the husband represents Christ, and . . . the wife represents the Church, [therefore] let there always be, both in him who commands and in her who obeys, a heavenly love guiding both in their respective duties" (*Arcanum* 11; *Quod apostolici muneris* 8; CC 26–27). Moreover, women "are not suited for certain occupations; a woman is by nature fitted for home-work" (RN 42). Women are physically weaker than men, and less rational. Hence women do better with children, constituting the "heart" of the family while men are the "head." "As he occupies the chief place in ruling, so she may and ought to claim for herself the chief place in love" (CC 27). Both could not rule together because unity was thought (in any social organization) to depend on the clear authority of one. If one alone is to carry authority, it ought to be the one whose nature is suited to ruling, the one who could best represent the fatherhood of God and the leadership of Christ.

The tradition in its beginnings, then, provided a theory of family structure that at the same time held a theory of separate spheres—the private and the public. Even though the husband was the *paterfamilias,* in whose care and under whose authority the family lived, still, the home belonged ironically to women and children. Or at least it was generally inappropriate for women to work, let alone have authority, outside the home. And the tradition spoke very little about the appropriate actual work expected of men within the home.

Clearly some of this theory changed in the course of a century. Gradually the tradition modulated and then dropped explicit arguments for essential inequality of nature between women and men. Gradually, too, the line of demarcation between the public and the private blurred. Yet the modern tradition of Catholic social teaching has not yet fundamentally transformed its view of the roles of women and men or of the structure of the family. Pius XII saw better than his predecessors the internal relations, mutual influences, between the family and society. He acknowledged that women had a role to fill not only in the home but in the world of politics and business. Still, he thought that the equal dignity of women and men required respect for their different "characteristic qualities which nature has given each of them" (address of October 21, 1945). Women were characterized by a "native bent to motherhood" and "delicate sensitiveness," so that finally "a woman who is a real woman can see all the problems of human life only in the perspective of the family" (address of October 26, 1941).

John XXIII acknowledged the appropriateness of women's participation in the public sphere and wrote approvingly of women's demand for "rights befitting a human person both in domestic and in public life" (PT 15). Yet his encyclicals did little with the questions of the family, and little movement appeared in the development of family theory. Vatican II struggled to represent new understandings of the equality between women and men. *Gaudium et spes* observed that the "active presence of the father is highly beneficial to their [the children's] formation," but added with seeming ambivalence, "the children, especially the younger among them, need the care of their mother at home. This domestic role of hers must be safely preserved, though the legitimate social progress of women should not be underrated on that account (52). Paul VI wrote in favor of political solutions that would "put an end to an actual discrimination [against women] and would establish relationships of equality in rights and of respect for their dignity," but quickly qualified this by saying, "We do not have in mind that false equality which would deny the distinctions laid down by the Creator himself and which would be in contradiction with women's proper role, which is of capital importance, at the heart of the family as well as within society" (*Call to Action* 13).

John Paul II has continued and even escalated the aspects of the tradition that see gendered roles as essential to human life in society and the family. In many different ways and on countless occasions he has asserted that while on the one hand "there is no doubt that the equal dignity and responsibility of men and women fully justifies women's access to public functions, on the other hand the true advancement of women requires that clear recognition be given to the value of their maternal and family role, by comparison with all other public roles and all other professions" (FC 23). And again, "With due respect to the *different vocations of men and women,* the Church must in her own life promote as far as possible their equality of rights and dignity: and this for the good of all, the family, the Church and society" (ibid., emphasis added). The watchword is now not inequality but complementarity, and as a result the gendered hierarchy of roles and separation of spheres remains entrenched in the tradition.

Whose Perspective? Whose Justice?

There are many strengths in the modern tradition of Catholic social teaching. Some of them can be brought to bear on issues of the family—but not unless the chasm between the family and other spheres of life is bridged, not unless the insights into justice that have developed in relation to society can be translated in relation to the family. Such a project is impossible as long as the basic presuppositions about the family and about the nature of women and women's work remain unchanged. These presuppositions have been challenged from many quarters, and here it is not possible to rehearse those challenges or to try to show the transformative possibilities of a more adequate theological and sociological theory. Nonetheless, this consideration of the modern tradition of Catholic social teaching about the family must not end without at least juxtaposing it with alternative views. Only thus can we see possible new stages in the life of the tradition.

Interesting analyses and arguments have recently been proposed by two secular theorists, positions that might engage the tradition of Catholic social teaching with fruitful results. We can simply note these positions, leaving a more detailed treatment of them and an adjudication of their claims against opposing traditions for another context. The first of these theorists has already been cited, Susan Moller Okin, and the second is the French revisionist Marxist Christine Delphy.

In her recent study, *Justice, Gender, and the Family,* Okin's dialogue partners as well as adversaries are not bishops and popes but contemporary philosophers of justice. Her starting point is the contention that contemporary philosophy almost invariably simply assumes the family as a social institution and assumes that it is just. On the contrary, she argues, the family is not a just society, and its injustice has negative effects on every other society as well as on the individuals who belong to the family. Hence it behooves those who are interested in theories of justice to pay attention to the needs of the family.

The central injustice in the structure of the family, according to Okin's analysis, is the division of labor between the sexes. Far from being a God-given natural way of relating between men and women, husbands and wives, the gendered division of labor constitutes a pervasive social problem. It inflicts increasingly serious damage on children and destroys the potential of the family to be the crucial first school in which children develop a sense of justice. Instead, children learn from the beginning to model their behavior according to roles whose assignments to people are inherently unfair.

There is nothing, Okin argues, in the nature of work that makes it impossible to adjust it to the fact that people are parents as well as workers (Okin, p. 5). There is also nothing in the nature of women or men that dictates that men should not be equal participants in the rearing of their children. Rather, the heavy weight of tradition works powerfully to reinforce sex roles that are commonly assessed as of unequal dignity and worth. To call these roles complementary is not to make them equal.

Moreover, it is a mistake to assume that "family" is itself a natural "given," anterior to society and with an internal meaning that needs no critiquing for its justice or injustice. This is a mythical account of the family, and it serves to sustain the dichotomy between the public and private spheres. Actually, however, the family is in an important sense made what it is by decisions of those in power in the wider society and in other social institutions (the church and the state "make" the family be what it is in a given time and place).

One of Okin's suggestions for assessing the justice or injustice of a sexual division of labor is to employ the philosopher John

Rawls's "veil of ignorance" and "original position" as a heuristic device (*A Theory of Justice,* Cambridge: The Belknap Press of Harvard Univ. Press, 1972). She also thinks Michael Walzer's "separate spheres" theory can be helpful precisely in seeing the impact of family injustice on other spheres of life (*Spheres of Justice,* New York: Basic Books, 1983). The nuances and refinements of Okin's analyses and proposals escape this brief description, but her challenge to philosophers and to church leaders is a serious one, one that can press further the complex questions to which no one should yet claim all of the answers.

Christine Delphy does something quite different from Okin, though her concern in *Close to Home: A Materialist Analysis of Women's Oppression* centers also in the problem of the sexual division of labor (trans. and ed. by Diana Leonard, Amherst, Mass.: Univ. of Massachusetts Press, 1984). What Delphy offers is a radical Marxist feminist analysis of the roles of women and men within the structure of marriage and family. She argues that it is the relationship of roles that is the problem, not first the content of the roles. The relationship of men's and women's roles is hierarchical in the division of labor and then of sex. Marriage, in Delphy's view, essentially includes a labor contract. A wife is engaged to do unpaid work for others—unpaid in the sense that it is not remunerated by either wage or any general form of exchange. The "return" that the wife receives is her maintenance. The service she renders is not a fixed service (since it can vary at the will of her husband), and the return for it is not correlated with the amount of her work (but, rather, with the class of her husband—for those of a preeminent class work less than those of a lower class, though the return they receive is greater).

A woman's class is, Delphy insists, uniquely determined—not on the basis of her occupation but her husband's occupation (or her father's, insofar as her background prior to marriage makes a difference). If a woman is unmarried, her class is influenced by her marital status, since the system pays women less than men even if they work for wages (a factor that accounts for the pressures on women to marry).

Patriarchy, therefore, is a system of social relations wherein women are subordinated to and exploited by men. It is not based on women's biology or their talents, but on an economic set of arrangements primarily. Hence, in Delphy's analysis, the structure of marriage and family is no less "made" than in Okin's. It is perhaps just as invisible without careful examination, and it can be overlooked in many of the ways Okin deplores. The more closely family structures are probed, the clearer become the questions of cultural diversity as well as the questions of possible commonality in human experiences of life in a family.

Delphy is not the first theorist to use Marxist tools to unveil an ideology of gendered relations. Her analysis is offensive to many women and men. Yet what she does is important precisely because it focuses on marriage and family in a way that disallows trite assumptions, that challenges too idealistic or romantic a theory, that raises the possibility of different eyes for seeing what traditions have long taken for granted. Her proposals, like Okin's, shatter the set rules of discourse and move directly to questions of justice.

The goals of Okin and Delphy are not really different from the professed goals of those who carry forward the tradition of Catholic social teaching. A barely visible yet crucial human association like the family needs all the eyes and the voices, all the unlikely partners in observation and commitment, that can be found. Of course every analysis, every interpretation, every prescription, must be tested against the concrete experience of family relationships and family life and against the central beliefs of the traditions whose faith has proved healing over time.

The Catholic tradition of social teaching regarding the family needs honest critique and genuine development. It brings to human and Christian discernment an approach that at its best is committed to inductive exploration of concrete situations and a covenanted loyalty to religiously grounded values. It has never turned completely away from families in their various experiences of sorrow and joy, isolation and comfort, violence and harmony. Now more than ever it is concerned with not only the survival but the good function of families and the individuals within them. Whether from a modest natural-law perspective or a graced insight into the new ordering of creation promised by Jesus Christ, the church has clues for a culture and its families. This should not be surprising in a tradition that professes to offer community to all—at a deep level of shared being, at a practical level of service and political advocacy, and in all the ways discernible for realizing a call to a just and universal communion.

See also CHILDREN, RIGHTS OF; CHRISTIAN FAMILY MOVEMENT; HOMOSEXUALITY, SOCIAL IMPLICATIONS OF; MARRIAGE; PUBLIC AND PRIVATE, RELATIONSHIP OF; SEXISM; WOMEN.

Bibliography: S. Okin, *Justice, Gender, and the Family* (New York: Basic Books, 1989). R. Greer, *Broken Lights and Mended Lives: Theology and Common Life in the Early Church* (University Park, Penn.: Pennsylvania State Univ. Press, 1986). J. Yost, "The Traditional Western Concept of Marriage and the Family: Rediscovering Its Renaissance-Reformation Roots," *Andover Newton Quarterly* 20 (March 1980). W. Lazareth, *Luther on the Christian Home* (Philadelphia: Muhlenberg, 1960). D. Hollenbach, *The Right to Procreate and Its Social Limitations: A Systematic Study of Value Conflict in Roman Catholic Ethics* (Ph.D. diss., Yale Univ., 1975).

MARGARET A. FARLEY

FASCISM

Defining fascism, whether in terms of ideology, the social bases of its mass support, or the characteristic policies of fascist regimes, is very difficult. Indeed, the development of studies of European fascisms to date has been accompanied by a long, ongoing debate about the essential nature of fascism, with some scholars like the Canadian Allardyce arguing that the European fascist movements do not possess sufficient common characteristics to arrive at a definition that will encompass them all.

Nevertheless, it is more generally accepted by historians that European fascisms, especially both the major regimes—fascist Italy and Nazi Germany—and minor movements in other parts of Europe including Scandinavia, France, and Britain did possess common characteristics that add up to a loose definition of fascism as a radical right-wing political ideology, movement, and in some countries, regime. The conservative, authoritarian regimes of Salaazar in Portugal and Franco in Spain are generally not regarded as being fascist in the strict sense, and the precise nature of "Austrofascism" under Dollfuss remains a matter of debate.

The outstanding characteristic of all these movements was an emphasis on the central importance of nationalism and the nation-state. From this flow logically most of the other common denominators of European fascisms, including a pronounced militaristic rhetoric and paramilitary organizational style, due also to the fact that many of the early adherents of fascist movements were veterans of the First World War. The territorial settlement at the end of the war created a sense of frustrated nationalism that was successfully exploited by emerging fascist movements in central European states, which thus advocated an aggressive and expansionistic foreign policy. Most European fascisms were strongly racialist, whether on the basis of pseudoscientific theories, as in the case of German nazism or simply militant anti-Semitism, which was the case for most of the rest. The major exception was Italian fascism, whose notions of race were essentially cultural and which did not adopt racial anti-Semitism as public policy until the end of the 1930s.

The supreme need for the "rebirth" or "regeneration" of the race/nation required both a new ruling elite and a charismatic leader, the *duce* in Fascist Italy and the *Führer* in Nazi Germany, and a form of political organization that exalted the claims of the state over those of its citizens, hence the emergence of authoritarian or totalitarian dictatorships. The overriding claims of the nation also usually dictated the necessity of some type of corporatist economic structure, the disciplining and harmonization of the conflicting interests of capital and labor in an institutionalized straitjacket.

With these common characteristics, European fascism was naturally the antithesis of other ideological systems—liberalism, democracy, and socialism. The anti-Bolshevik "crusade" was an essential ideological ingredient of alliances between fascist regimes in the 1930s.

Finally, fascism may be located within a distinct time period, 1919 to 1945, though it should be understood that the ideological roots of fascism go further back in time, and that fascist-type movements have continued to exist on the margins of political life in a number of post-1945 European states.

Italian Fascism

The first fascist movement to come to power and establish a regime was Mussolini's *fasci di combattimento* in Italy. Indeed, it is precisely from the word *fascio,* meaning "group" or "bundle," that the generic terms for the phenomenon, fascist (*fascista*) and fascism (*fascismo*), are derived. The experience of the Italian *fasci* exemplifies that fascism was a European phenomenon, born out of the disturbed economic, social, and political conditions of post–First World War Europe. Mussolini, like the majority of the others who founded the first *fascio* in Milan (March 13, 1919), was a veteran of the war and a rabid nationalist. Initially the Italian fascists were also strongly anticlerical, antisocialist, and antimonarchist and from the first used violence against their political enemies.

Like embryonic fascist movements elsewhere in Europe in the immediate postwar years, the *fasci* remained a small minority isolated within a very restricted geographical area—the cities of northern Italy. The breakthrough for the *fasci* came in the countryside and towns of northern and central Italy in the latter half of 1920, 1921, and 1922. Here the fascists were able to insert themselves into the violent, bitter conflicts between the local landowning classes and the Catholic and socialist peasant leagues. Taking the part of the local landowners and the rural establishment generally, the fascist squads managed to conquer large areas, thanks to a combination of brutal violence and the collusion of local police and the judicial and military authorities.

Mussolini's subsequent seizure of power during the so-called march on Rome in October 1922 was the result of a skillfully engineered exploitation of the paralysis of the Italian parliamentary system coupled with increasingly credible threats to use force. As was the case with other fascist movements, Italian fascism came to power legally and with the connivance of the establishment—the king, the church, the more senior liberal politicians, and the armed forces. These were to constitute the basis of the "consensus" on which the regime was maintained in the 1930s and early 1940s.

The transition from the old, liberal parliamentary regime to a one-party, totalitarian dictatorship was long and drawn out, partly because Mussolini had no blueprint for the future when he became prime minister and partly because of the resistance of the democratic antifascist opposition. But by 1929 most of the institutions of the new fascist regime—secret police, Special Tribunal, Grand Council of Fascism, laws criminalizing antifascism—were in place. But it was only in the 1930s that Italian fascism completed the development of its most characteristic economic and social institutions—the "corporate state." And it was also in the 1930s that fascist foreign policy reached its aggressive, assertive, and ambitious stage. The conquest of Ethiopia in 1936 gave Mussolini the confidence to intervene in the Spanish civil war, to proclaim that "the Mediterranean is an Italian lake" with all the implications that contained in terms of further conquests, to enter the Rome-Berlin Axis in 1936, to sign the Pact of Steel in 1939, and in June 1940 to enter the war on the side of Germany. A succession of disastrous military defeats eventually led to the collapse of the regime in July 1943.

The restored fascist regime set up under Mussolini two months later, the Fascist Social Republic, was, as its name suggests, largely a republican reedition of the first fascist dictatorship but with some rather opportunistic leanings to the left, and a reinvigorated commitment to anti-Semitism. In the final analysis, the Social Republic was a puppet state, totally dependent on the German occupying forces, and when those surrendered in April 1945 the republic perished and with it Mussolini.

National Socialism and Other Fascist Movements and Regimes

This fairly detailed examination of Italian fascism is justified by the fact that most (though by no means all) of the other fascist movements in Europe in the 1920s and early 1930s were strongly influenced by this first fascist movement to successfully transform itself into a regime. Other fascisms modeled their organization, image, propaganda, and policies on Italian fascism: Moseley's Blackshirts in Britain, Pavelic's Croatian Ustasha, Gombos's fascist group in Hungary (to some extent), and Jose Primo De Rivera's Falangists in Spain. And though not truly "fascist" dictatorships, the Catholic, conservative authoritarian states created by Dollfuss in pre-Anschluss Austria, Salazaar in Portugal, and Franco in Spain borrowed heavily from Italian fascist institutions and policies. Even Adolf Hitler was an admirer of the *duce,* and there are some discernible influences of Italian fascism to be detected in the development of the German nazi movement in the 1920s. But German nazism, it must be emphasized, was a very special, *sui generis* brand of fascism that, in its turn, was to strongly influence the development of fascist movements in Holland, Belgium, and Scandinavia.

One of the primary differences between German national socialism and Italian fascism was the former's adherence to a virulent racialism and anti-Semitism that provided it with a constant and powerfully coherent ideological core lacking in Mussolini's movement. There were other important differences—Hitler was a more self-confident leader than Mussolini and had a longer time in which to develop the structures and policies of his movement before coming to power.

National socialism's evolution corresponds almost exactly to the three phases of the Weimar republic's politicoeconomic history. During the republic's first four years of dislocation and disruption it was a regionally based *putschist* movement; during the relative stability of the mid-to-late 1920s it became an unsuccessful minor antisystem party attempting to reconstruct itself organizationally and tactically after the abortive coup in Munich of 1923; during the crisis-ridden depression years of the early 1930s it became an ultimately triumphant mass movement, its political and electoral achievements based on charismatic leadership, an impressive party organization developed during the dog years of the later 1920s, and the politicization and radicalization of the German middle classes that provided it with it most important source of mass support. But national socialism found a breakthrough to power on a purely electoral basis elusive, and like Mussolini before him, Hitler only came to power as chancellor through the machinations of the nation's conservative elites, who sought in the political crisis of the 1930s and through the "borrowing" of Hitler's movement a means to regain the power they had been deprived of during the 1918 revolution.

But also like Mussolini though with greater speed and control, Hitler dispensed with his coalition partners, and he established a one-party dictatorship within six months of having taken office in what was formally a democratic republic. This "legal revolution," as it has been defined by Karl Dietrich Bracher, was based on the institutional power that Hitler's appointment as chancellor had given him combined with the use of violence and terror exercised by his paramilitary forces, now given free rein by the legal protection Hitler could afford them. The "stick" elements of the dictatorship were integrated with the "carrot" of economic recovery and a series of highly popular diplomatic and military moves that removed the shackles of the universally hated Treaty of Versailles and other elements of the postwar peace settlement. Domestic and foreign policy were conjoined within the context of ideology: the steadily intensifying persecution of the Jews in Germany, the militarization of both society and the economy, the creation of a "Greater Germany" and the beginnings of empire, first by diplomacy, then in 1939, by war—all these corresponded to the central tenets of national socialist racialism and imperialism.

The Second World War itself represented to Hitler far more than it did to Mussolini the culmination of aims and policy developed from the early 1920s onward. Above all, the invasion of the Soviet Union and occupation policies in the east, including the "final solution," saw the unrestrained application of the most uncompromising aspects of Hitler's thought. However, the Soviet Union's failure to collapse as expected and its ultimate military recovery, the overextension of German military power, and the entry of the United States into the war doomed the ultimate national socialist project. The bankruptcy of the movement, both crystallized in and symbolized by Hitler's suicide in the Berlin bunker in 1945, following as it did the death of Mussolini, removed from power in Europe that mass fascism that had exercised so much influence, fear, and fascination for nearly a quarter of a century.

Catholics, the Church, and Fascism

Fascism in its varying local forms exerted a powerful attraction for Catholic clergy and laity alike. Its appeal for the restoration of "order" and "hierarchy" in society, coming as it did during the economic, social, and political chaos of the immediate postwar years and the traumatic shock of the introduction of democratic institutions, struck a deep chord. Similarly, its militant and usually violent anticommunism was a welcome development in the early 1920s, when the Bolshevik threat had assumed the form of Soviet-style regimes and an accompanying "red terror" (albeit, short lived) in various parts of eastern and central Europe; in Italy the threat, in the form of two years of working-class militancy, had less substance but was felt just as palpably.

Another very important factor in the response of Catholics in eastern and central Europe was fascist anti-Semitism: it cannot be denied that anti-Semitism was widely prevalent among the clergy and laity of most eastern and central European states and in France as well. "Theological" anti-Semitism was reinforced by both the economic role of Jews in peasant communities and their apparently strong influence in Masonic and socialist movements. Another not-inconsiderable attraction for Catholics was the patriotic/nationalist stance of the fascists. In Slovakia and Croatia in particular the church was closely identified with frustrated national aspiration, hence the fact that the Croatian episcopate and clergy welcomed the establishment of an autonomous Croatian state under the leadership of Pavelic and the fascist Ustasa in 1941.

Economic considerations were also important, though the Italian case was perhaps unique. Here the crude defense of economic and class interests by the fascists appealed to the clericofascists, a group of conservative politicians inside the Catholic Partito Popolare who abandoned the party and helped to sustain fascism during its consolidation of power in the mid-to-late 1920s. Elsewhere such considerations were also important but usually took the form of Catholic support for corporatist ideas and institutions. Mussolini's Corporate State in Italy, which was almost unreservedly endorsed by Catholic Action and the Catholic University of Milan, was emulated in the Standestaat of Chancellor Dollfuss in Austria. Furthermore, Catholics were persuaded to support the corporatist-type institutions of Salazaar's Estado Nuovo and Franco's post–civil war Spanish regime.

Catholic support for fascism measured in terms of party membership and votes is difficult to calculate and in any case varied enormously from place to place. Though, for example, there was strong Catholic electoral support for Italian fascism and German nazism, both the Partito Popolare and the Catholic parties in Germany/Bavaria proved most resistant of all the non-fascist parties to the electoral inroads of fascism and nazism. And in the Second Spanish Republic, conservative Catholic opinion gave little visible support to the Falange of Jose Primo De Rivera, being satisfied with the traditionalism and conservatism of CEDA, the official Catholic party. In Slovakia in the late 1930s and early 1940s the clergy-dominated HSL's increasingly adopted fascist forms and policies not out of conviction but under pressure from Nazi Germany, which exercised a protectorate over the country.

The response of Catholics to fascism was, of course, strongly influenced by the attitude of the papacy. This meant for most of the period Pius XI, whose election in February 1922 was followed by a softening in the criticisms of Italian fascism by *L'Osservatore Romano,* the official Vatican daily newspaper. Pius XI's innate conservatism, his experience of bolshevism as nuncio to Poland between 1918 and 1921, and his intolerance of Catholic lay political independence made him critical of the Partito Popolare and inclined him to view the anticommunist stand of fascism during Italy's "Red Two Years" with considerable sympathy.

Mussolini skillfully exploited the change of leadership in the Vatican by publicly renouncing fascist anticlericalism and introducing a package of measures beneficial to the church shortly after his appointment as prime minister. By the autumn of 1926 his efforts had borne fruit in the form of the opening of negotiations between Italy and the Vatican to resolve the sixty-year-old "Roman question." The resulting Lateran Pacts of 1929 ensured the incorporation of Catholic support into the consensus on which the regime was based in the 1930s and brought great international prestige for Mussolini and Italian fascism. The pope's willingness to treat with Mussolini was motivated by a burning desire to bring about a "Christian restoration of Italian society in a Catholic direction" (his own words), an aim shared by the hierarchies of other countries in Europe. An inherent antipathy towards liberalism and the parliamentary institutions it had created, a feeling shared by many Catholic clergy and laity as a result of the church-state conflicts that had erupted wherever the liberals gained political power, made it easy to negotiate with fascism. And the authoritarian state, which fascism promised, seemed to offer a return to the safe, ordered Christian society that had disappeared in so many European countries after the French Revolution.

Fascism, at least Italian fascism in the early 1920s, appeared to be an essentially conservative, restorative force despite its adolescent excesses. Fascism's willingness and capacity to "deliver the goods" in the form of the restoration of ecclesiastical influence, privileges, and property seemed to confirm this (and this phenomenon was not restricted to Italy). But the relationship that developed between the Vatican and Italian fascism was at best a marriage of convenience. Though there was considerable support from the church and Catholic intellectuals for such policies as "ruralization," public morality campaigns, and corporatism, there were tensions and these broke out into serious crises from 1929 onward. In 1929 Pius XI implicitly criticized Mussolini's attempts to monopolize the education of youth in his encyclical *Rappresentanti in terra*; in 1931 as a result of more serious conflicts over the role of Catholic Action, the only nonfascist mass organization permitted to exist in Mussolini's totalitarian state, the pope published an encyclical, *Non abbiamo bisogno,* which was explicitly directed against Italian fascism and which criticized the nationalistic and militaristic elements of fascist ideology.

In that same year *Quadragesimo anno,* though addressed to the whole world, also implicitly attacked Italian fascist corporatism as being inconsistent with Catholic social teaching and in particular with *Rerum novarum* on the grounds that it was excessively political and statist in content. Finally, in 1938, Mussolini's introduction of the racial laws precipitated another confrontation, which was only brought to an end by the pope's death in February of the following year.

If Pius XI's relationship with fascist Italy was an uneasy marriage of convenience, that with Nazi Germany was bitter and troubled. It began well; the Vatican, using the Lateran Pacts as a model, negotiated a deal with Hitler's new government whereby the long-sought-after *Reichskonkordat* was signed in return for the support of the Catholic Zentrum party for the Enabling Act, which ultimately provided the legal basis for the Nazi dictatorship. In addition, the Zentrum agreed to dissolve itself. But the *Reichskonkordat* proved less effective in defending the rights of the Catholic church in Germany than the Lateran Pacts did in Italy. The ink was barely dry on the agreement when Hitler turned the processes of the *Gleichschaltung* against the German Catholic press, trade unions, and youth organizations. The neopagan elements of national socialism, which had prompted the ban by many German bishops on Catholic membership in the party at the beginning of the 1930s, now came more openly into evidence, and in 1937 the pope condemned the persecution of the German church in his encyclical *Mit brennender Sorge.*

The Vatican's unhappy experience with Nazi Germany strongly colored its attitude toward the international tensions that surfaced in Europe in the mid-to-late 1930s. While not budging from his condemnation of atheistic communism, Pius XI showed increasing hostility to Hitler's regime and its foreign policy. Thus when civil war broke out in Spain, where the Vatican might have been expected to wholeheartedly endorse Hitler's efforts to support Franco in his battle against the "godless republic," its policy was tempered by its fear of the spread of national socialist influences into the Iberian peninsula. Similarly, the Vatican's ambivalent stance during the Italian invasion of Ethiopia can in part be explained by the anxiety that the international crisis that the war created would lead to a rupture in Franco-Italian relations and drive Mussolini into the arms of Hitler, which is precisely what did happen.

Despite this setback the Vatican did not abandon its attempts to minimize German influences on the fascist regime in Italy, nor did it cease to encourage the emergence of fascist Italy as the leader of a "third force" in Europe between German neopaganism and Russian atheistic communism. Mussolini's introduction of racial anti-Semitism in 1938, which Pius XI angrily and publicly condemned, and the signing of the Pact of Steel in 1939 signaled the failure of these efforts.

Pius XI's successor, Eugenio Pacelli, has often been accused of being more "soft" on both German national socialism and Italian fascism. Even worse, he has been castigated, not entirely without reason, for failing to take a strong enough stand against the German extermination of the Jews, against collaboration with that policy by regimes like Petain's Vichy government in France, and against the atrocities committed by the Ustasha against the Serbian minority in Croatia. However inadequate his efforts were to prevent these evils, it cannot be doubted that he condemned them and the racialist doctrines from which they sprang.

Conclusion

The Catholic response to fascism, as we have seen, is largely explicable in terms of a traditional antipathy toward liberalism, democracy, and socialism and also in terms of the church's general unhappiness with the advance of urban industrial society. It also makes sense in the context of the disturbed economic, social, and political conditions that prevailed in Europe in the interwar period. In these circumstances, fascist movements with their youthful, vigorous, and idealistic stance had a strong appeal for Catholics. It needs to be reiterated, however, that many Catholics, both clergy and laity, consistently condemned and actively opposed fascism, paying with their lives for this in some cases.

The fact that not a single founder or major leader of fascism was a convinced, practicing Catholic should have provided clear evidence of the fundamentally unchristian character of this new political movement. But various fascist movements and regimes seemed to hold and practice beliefs very dear to Catholic hearts. There was, for example, a considerable degree of convergence between Catholic and fascist ideas on the role of women, the family, contraception, abortion, and the importance of rural society and values, even if the underlying motives were often very different; however, the church condemned the Nazi experiments in eugenics, *lebensborn,* and euthanasia.

Anti-Semitism was another point of convergence between fascist and Catholics in many countries, though the church usually but not always expressed its reservations when such a sentiment went beyond mere discriminatory legislation and became vicious and violent. Very often it was too late, and in Germany and Poland the Catholic response to the Holocaust was, at best, one of passivity and indifference. In Hungary and Italy, however, most Catholics behaved in an honorable and humanitarian fashion. Having made agreements with what appeared to be essentially anticommunist, conservative, and patriotic movements, church leaders and individual Catholics woke up to find that they were riding a tiger of extreme racialism, an experience that was shared by other conservative groups.

The Catholic flirtation with fascism in the 1920s and 1930s proved to be an unhappy and painful experience. Yet on the whole it did not have long-term, damaging effects. In Italy, Germany, and France the church survived with its prestige and moral authority largely intact. In Hungary and Yugoslavia, however, the flirtation with fascism was to have tragic consequences, providing the postwar communist regimes with an excuse to systematically persecute the church and imprison its bishops and clergy.

The church also seems to have learned the lessons of its relationship with fascism: though it continued to support authoritarian regimes in Portugal and Spain in the post–Second World War period and would have preferred such a system in Italy, elsewhere it finally embraced liberal democracy. Moreover, enthusiasm for corporatist experiments was abandoned and the postwar popes have limited themselves to a discreet critique of the capitalist system in their statements on economic and social questions.

See also ANTI-SEMITISM; CORPORATISM; ECONOMIC ORDER; HOLOCAUST, THE; PIUS XI; PIUS XII; QUADRAGESIMO ANNO; TOTALITARIANISM.

Bibliography: K. Bracher, *The German Dictatorship* (Harmondsworth, 1973). M. Blinkhorn, ed., *Fascists and Conservatives* (London, 1990). A. De Grand, *Italian Fascism* (Lincoln/London, 1982). F. Friedlander, *Pius XII and the Third Reich* (London, 1966). E. Helmreich, *The German Churches and Hitler* (Detroit, 1979). W. Laqueur, ed., *Fascism: A Reader's Guide* (New York, 1976). D. Muelberger, ed., *The Social Basis of European Fascist Movements* (London/New York, 1987). J. Pollard, *The Vatican and Italian Fascism, 1929–32* (Cambridge/London, 1985). P. Sugar, ed., *Native Fascisms in the Successor States* (Santa Barbara, 1971). R. Wolff and J. Hoensch, eds., *Catholics, the State, and the European Radical Right, 1919–1945* (New York, 1987). R. Griffin, *The Nature of Fascism*, 2nd ed. (London, 1993).

JOHN F. POLLARD*

*The author is grateful to his colleague Dr. Don Watts for his help with the section on German National Socialism.

FATHERS OF THE CHURCH, INFLUENCE OF

Assessing the influence of patristic social thought in a short space would seem an impossible task. The number of the Fathers, both Greek and Latin, whose social teaching has to be taken into account is large. Clement of Alexandria, Basil the Great, Gregory of Nazianzus, Gregory of Nyssa, John Chrysostom, Ambrose of Milan, Augustine of Hippo, Leo the Great, and Gregory the Great would figure prominently in the list. Further, the issues in which their thought exercised its impact are numerous; they include the origin, nature, and foundation of power; the object, nature, and kinds of laws; the source, tasks, and purpose of justice; the nature and duties of the state; the civil obligations of Christians; the relationship between church and state; slavery; labor; property and wealth; interest and usury; almsgiving; war and peace. Moreover, since most of the Fathers' sociopolitical writings are homilies and commentaries on the Bible, it is difficult to ascertain accurately whether a particular author's use of their ideas is an indication of his or her indebtedness to the Fathers or to the biblical heritage they transmit, unless of course he or she justifies a certain position by an explicit appeal to the authority and reasoning of an individual Father. Finally, while the expression "patristic social teaching" may suggest that there exists a uniform body of teachings on social matters among the Fathers, the fact of the matter is that there is a diversity of opinions among them, even in important issues (e.g., civil obligations of Christians, the relationship between church and state), and such a diversity exacerbates the difficulty in assessing the influence of patristic social thought.

Bearing these difficulties in mind, this article seeks to show how postpatristic theology receives the social teachings of those who are called "fathers of the church" on account of their orthodoxy of doctrine, holiness of life, and ecclesiastical approbation. Our discussion will include both Greek and Latin Fathers, with the exclusion of Augustine, whose influence is treated under a separate entry elsewhere.

The Economic Order

Under this heading we will consider the influence of patristic teachings on wealth, the right of ownership, almsgiving, usury, and slavery.

Wealth, Private Ownership, and Almsgiving

Roman law regards private ownership (*ius utendi et abutendi quantum iuris ratio patitur*) as a human right and defends the prerogatives of the owner without insisting on his or her social obligations. It is in this area that the Fathers made their most lasting and challenging contributions. Not only did they enjoin detachment from riches but also sharing them with the needy, and such sharing is seen not simply as a matter of generosity and charity but as a duty of justice. From the perspective of the impoverished one might speak of the just entitlement of the poor.

In general, the Fathers regard the right of ownership as a consequence of sin; they speak of a primitive state prior to the Fall in which private ownership is not known (see, e.g., Ambrose, *De officiis* 1.28.132; *De Nabuthe* 1.2; *Expos. evang. sec. Luc.* 7.124, 247). Even after the Fall ownership is more apparent than real. No one possesses anything as one's own; everything has been created by God for the whole humankind and belongs to God. If God allows anything to be owned, God can take it back (John Chrysostom, *In Ep. 1 ad Corinth. Hom. 10.2*). Therefore, rather than ownership one must speak of stewardship or use or power of disposition, which carry heavy obligations. Only if wealth is used for the benefit of all is private ownership legitimate. It requires a sense of justice and solidarity, a willingness to redress social inequities, a generous sharing of one's possessions. To give to the poor is nothing but restoring to them what is their due (Ambrose, *De Nabuthe* 12.53). Not to give alms is to steal (Basil, *Homily 6,* PG 21:272–77).

The Fathers do not recommend total poverty or total equality in an integral communism, nor do they condemn private ownership as such. What they attempt to do is reconcile the evangelical counsel of total renunciation with the practices of a society founded on private property by reminding their contemporaries of the universal destiny of wealth and the duty of almsgiving as an obligation of justice. Thus, for the Fathers, the fundamental and primary truth is not that private ownership is an exigency of natural or divine law but that all the goods of the earth are common to all humankind. Such universal destiny of wealth does not invalidate private possession but carries with it serious social obligations.

In strict adherence to the Fathers, Thomas Aquinas unequivocally affirms with a quotation from Ambrose that "whatever certain people have in superabundance is due, by natural law, to the purpose of helping the poor" and that "each one is entrusted with the stewardship of his own things, so that out of them he may come to the aid of those who are in need" (ST II[a] II[ae], q. 66, a. 7). Thomas acknowledges the advantages of private ownership, that is, the power to procure and dispense wealth in preserving and fostering efficiency, order, and peace; nevertheless, as far as the use of wealth is concerned, he affirms that "a person ought to possess external things, not as one's own, but as common, so that, to wit, one is ready to communicate them to others in their need" (ibid., q. 6, a. 2). Private ownership, though not contrary to natural law, is "an addition thereto devised by human reason"; it is a derivative law, subordinated to natural and eternal law. That is why, Thomas argues, it is lawful for a needy person, by reason of *evidens et urgens necessitas,* to succor his or her own need by means of another's property taken either openly or secretly. Such an act is not theft "because that which he takes for the support of his life becomes his own property by reason of that need" (ibid., q. 66, a. 7, ad 2).

Unfortunately, the patristic doctrine on property transmitted by Aquinas suffered an eclipse in the first half of the 19th century when theologians were excessively willing to accept capitalism's individualistic and exclusivistic concept of private ownership without spelling out its limits and its social obligations. It is Leo XIII who, though condemning the socialist attempt to do away with private possession of goods and affirming the right of private ownership "to be best adapted to human nature and to peaceful and tranquil living together" (*Rerum novarum* 17), recalls with approval a statement of Gregory the Great (*Hom. 9 in Evangel.* 7) that "whoever has received from the divine bounty a large share of blessings . . . has received them for the purpose of using them for perfecting his own nature, and, at the same time, that he may employ them, as the minister of God's providence, for the benefit of others" (RN 36).

Pius XI appeals to the authority of Scripture and the Fathers in enjoining the sharing of superfluous income: "The grave obligations of charity, beneficence and liberality which rest upon the wealthy are constantly insisted upon in telling words by Holy Scripture and the Fathers of the Church" (*Quadragesimo anno* 50). Pius XII, in his radio message for Pentecost, June 1, 1941, reiterates that it is the will of God that the right to own property, though from the natural law itself, should in no way obstruct the flow of "material goods created by God to meet the needs of all to all equitably, as justice and charity require" (AAS 33 [1941], p. 199). John XXIII repeats *Rerum novarum*'s appeal to the authority of Gregory the Great to underscore the social function of property (*Mater et magistra* 119).

Vatican II invokes the authority of Basil (*Hom. in illud Lucae "Destruam horrea mea"* 2, PG 6:656B); Lactantius (*Divinarum institutionum,* book 5, on justice, PL 6:565B); Augustine (*In Ioann. Ev.* 50.6, PL 35:1760; *Enarratio in Ps. 147* 12, PL 37:1922); and Gregory the Great (*Homiliae in Ev.* 20, PL 76:1165; *Regulae pastoralis liber* 3.21, PL 77:87) to affirm the universal destination of earthly goods: "In the use of things one should regard the external goods one legitimately owns not merely as exclusive to oneself but also as common property, in the sense that they can benefit others as well as oneself. For the rest, the right to have a share of earthly goods sufficient for oneself and one's family belongs to everyone. The Fathers and Doctors of the Church held this view, teaching that all are obliged to come to the relief of the poor and to do so not merely out of their superfluous goods" (*Gaudium et spes* 69).

Paul VI quotes Ambrose to make the point that private property does not constitute for anyone an absolute and unconditioned right: "You are not making gift of your possessions to the poor person. You are handing over to him what is his. For what has been given in common for the use of all, you have arrogated to yourself. The world is given to all, and not only to the rich" (Ambrose, *De Nabuthe,* c. 12, n. 53, PL 14:747 in *Populorum progressio* 23). Paul VI could have cited Ambrose's other equally controversial statement: "Natura ius commune generavit, usurpatio ius fecit privatum" (*De officiis* 1.132). The pope will extend this obligation of sharing among individuals to nations: "The superfluous wealth of rich countries should be placed at the service of poor nations" (PP 49).

The influence of patristic teaching is no less powerful on John Paul II's integral humanism and his teaching on the "option for the poor," "solidarity," and human rights. Regarding the right of private ownership, the pope echoes the teaching of the Fathers: "Christian tradition has never upheld this right as absolute and untouchable. On the contrary, it has understood this right within the broader context of the right common to all to use the goods of the whole creation: The right to private property is subordinated to the right to common use, to the fact that goods are meant for everyone" (*Laborem exercens* 14). The U.S. Catholic bishops' pastoral letter *Economic Justice for All* quotes Cyprian (*On Works and Almsgiving* 25) to affirm that "whatever belongs to God belongs to all" and that "from the patristic period to the present, the church has affirmed that misuse of the world's resources or appropriation of them by a minority of the world's population betrays the gift of creation" (EJA 34).

This contemporary extension of assistance to the poor on the individual level to the transformation of unjust societal structures should not be thought of as a distortion of patristic teaching on almsgiving. On the contrary, the insistence on solidarity with the poor and transformation of structures is a logical development of such a teaching. Of course, the Fathers were unable to raise the question of reforming social structures; facing economic injustices they spoke and could only speak of alms. Nevertheless, it is important to remember that for the Fathers, almsgiving is a duty of justice, a form of restitution to the poor of what is owed them, a way of reestablishing a social balance that has been disturbed by private ownership. Unfortunately, later theologians to a certain extent forgot this conception of the Fathers and tended to look upon almsgiving merely as a work of mercy. Today, however, in order to be faithful to the basic insights of the Fathers, one has to say that "almsgiving" requires creating sources of employment, redistributing the national income, organizing business in a truly human manner, and spreading the ownership of property in an equitable way.

Usury and Slavery

The Fathers' condemnation of lending with interest (usury) is unanimous, a very significant position indeed in view of the fact that both Roman law and the OT (at least the lending of money to foreigners; see Deut 23:20-21) permitted such a practice. Both Greek and Latin Fathers—in particular the Cappadocians, John Chrysostom, Ambrose, Jerome, and Augustine—severely proscribe lending of money (Jerome includes also articles of food) with interest.

Such patristic severity is reflected in the condemnation of usury by councils such as Lateran II (1139), Lateran III (1179), and Vienne (1314). Thomas Aquinas, following Aristotle's notion that money is simply a means of exchange, argues that taking interest for money lent is unjust because it is a selling of what does not exist, and that a person is bound to restore the money taken as interest (ST II^{a} II^{ae}, q. 78, a. 1; *De malo* 13.4). As late as 1745 Benedict XIV in condemning Scipione Maffei's book *Dell'impiego del Denaro* (1744), which defends the legitimacy of usury, reaffirmed the traditional teaching of the Fathers.

Of course today, since money is regarded as a productive means, lending with interest has become an acceptable practice. Interestingly, there has been a shift in linguistic usage: the old term "usury" no longer means lending with interest but with excessive interest. Nevertheless, the reasons for which the Fathers condemn usury are still valid: it is an injustice against the poor. In the words of Basil, "Indeed, it is extremely inhuman that one has to beg for the most basic necessities to support one's life while another is not satisfied with the capital he has, but excogitates ways of increasing his opulence at the expense of the poor in distress" (*Homily 2 on Psalm 15,* 1).

Slavery was a widespread practice in the Greco-Roman world. Despite their strong affirmation of the fundamental equality and freedom of all human persons, the Fathers (e.g., Gregory of Nazianzus, Augustine) regarded slavery as an economic necessity, a product of war, and a consequence of the Fall. Slavery was a form of private property, a social institution that the Fathers did not seek to overthrow. Rather, they sought to mitigate its cruelty and to encourage enfranchisement. In the question of slavery, one can only wish that the Fathers' teaching on the fundamental equality and freedom of all human beings had exercised a greater influence toward the abolition of this inhuman institution.

The Political Order

Under this heading we will examine the influence of patristic teaching on the relationship of church and state and on war and peace. In these two issues, however, the towering figure, at least in Latin Christianity, is Augustine, whose influence has been discussed in a separate entry.

Church and State

The Fathers elaborated their teaching on the relations between church and state to deal with the conflicts between the two institutions. Under the Arian emperor Constantius (337–61), who inordinately meddled with the affairs of the church, the doctrine of nonintervention was taught by Hosius of Cordova, Lucifer of Cagliari, Hilary of Poitiers, and above all Ambrose. Hosius in his famous letter (see Athanasius, *Hist. Arian.* 44, PG 25:744–48) affirms that the emperor insofar as he is a Christian must be submitted to the church and that there must be a separation between the functions of the church and the state. For Ambrose, there is a distinction between the *res publica* (the province of the emperor) and *religio* (the church), upon which the emperor has no authority and to which he must be submitted as a Christian. This is already the beginning of the doctrine of the submission of the prince of the church *ratione peccati,* a doctrine taught by the Greek Fathers Gregory of Nazianzus (*Orat.* 17.8, PG 35:976) and John Chrysostom (*In Ep. 2 ad Corinth. Homil.* 15, c. 4–5, PG 61:509). Furthermore, Ambrose insists that the emperor must serve the church, for example, by invoking councils, facilitating the attendance of bishops at them, ratifying their decisions, and watching over their implementations. The influence of Ambrose's teaching will be considerable in the West as it contributed to the resistance of the Latin church against the intrusions of the emperor. Augustine himself was inspired by Ambrose in his teaching on the autonomy and primacy of the church over the state. The Middle Ages will insist on the *ministerium regale* of the emperor to the church.

From the death of Theodosius (395) to the accession of Zeno (474), the relations between the church hierarchy and secular authorities were, at least in the West, more friendly and provided a favorable context for developing the doctrine of collaboration between church and state. No longer was there the need for insisting on the separation of the two powers, nor was the superiority of the church contested. Rather, the relationship between church and state was seen as that of mutual cooperation. This doctrine was espoused particularly by Augustine, who though still affirming the distinction and autonomy of the two spheres, insists that church and state exist for the sake of human persons and their eternal welfare and therefore must collaborate with each other to achieve their distinctive goals. On the one hand, the church aids the state with its prayers, its moral teachings, its ensuring that Christians perform their civic duties. On the other hand, the state secures peace for the church, endows it with material resources and privileges, and, if necessary, protects the church against its enemies by means of coercive power.

This view of the relation between church and state was adopted by Pope Leo the Great, who in his letter to Emperor Leo writes, "Royal power has been granted to you not only for the government of the world but principally for the protection of the Church" (*Letter* 156.3, PL 54:1130). This doctrine of close collaboration, which reserves to church authority the power to determine issues of faith and discipline, could be practicable only if the emperors were devoted to the church and respected its rights.

In the West Augustine's doctrine of the distinction, autonomy, and collaboration between church and state and of the legal primacy of church over state has had, as is well known, an enormous influence on medieval popes and theologians, even though "political Augustinism," that is, the tendency to absorb secular power into spiritual power, represents a distortion of Augustine's thought. Pope Gelasius (493–96) was still faithful to Augustine when he affirmed that there are two powers that govern the world, the *auctoritas sacrata pontificum* and the *regalis potestas.* Each in its own domain enjoys supreme authority (*principaliter*); each ought not to interfere in the affairs of the other. This reciprocal independence should not lead to isolation but to exchange of services. But the preeminence of spiritual matters implies the superiority of the church over the state. The prince must be submitted to the church as a Christian, but only in religious matters. Gelasius did not claim to have a *potestas directa in temporalibus.*

It must be recognized that in the American tradition of the "separation of church and state," which prohibits the establishment of religion and the hindrance of the free exercise thereof, the patristic teaching on the relation between church and state no longer applies. Nevertheless, the Fathers' insistence on the collaboration between the two organizations for the integral welfare, both material and spiritual, of their members still retains its validity and relevance.

War and Peace

Again in this issue, the influence of Augustine on later theologians, especially Thomas Aquinas, Francisco de Vitoria, and Francisco de Suarez, is enormous. The 1983 letter of the U.S. Catholic bishops, *The Challenge of Peace,* evinces the longlasting influence of Augustine's just-war doctrine (80–110). Of course Augustine was not the only Father to defend the legitimacy of military service and to determine the conditions for a just war. Ambrose had already distinguished between just and unjust war, the former being intended to repel an unjust attack or to repair the damage to the honor of the country (*De officiis* 1.27.129, PL 16:61). Furthermore, in the conduct of war, combatants must observe good faith and justice (ibid. 1.29.139, PL 16:63). Victory does not allow pillage.

Besides this just-war tradition, there is among the Fathers the nonviolence tradition as well. *The Challenge of Peace* recognizes and praises it. The letter quotes Justin and Cyprian of Carthage and cites the example of Martin of Tours in support of the pacifist option, but one can also appeal to the authority of other Fathers such as Ignatius of Antioch, Tatian, Tertullian, Lactantius, and Clement and Origen of Alexandria, and invoke the example of martyrs. It is important to call to mind the influence of this pacifist tradition of the Fathers on the later church, from Francis of Assisi to Vatican II, whose *Gaudium et spes* called upon governments to enact laws protecting the rights of those who adopt the position of conscientious objection to all war (GS 79). As *The Challenge of Peace* affirms: "While the just-war teaching has clearly been in possession for the past 1,500 years of Catholic thought, the 'new moment' in which we find ourselves sees the just-war teaching and non-violence as distinct but interdependent methods of evaluating warfare. They diverge on some specific conclusions, but they share a common presumption against the use of force as a means of settling disputes" (120).

Conclusion

What legacy in social teaching do the Fathers leave us? At the heart of patristic social message lies the predilection for the poor. For the Fathers faith cannot be separated from the practice of justice and charity to the poor. All earthly goods are for the use of all human beings; we are not owners but stewards of material goods; private property, when not shared with the needy, is unjustified; the sharing of goods is required by justice; the human person is by nature a social being called to live in community; the total fulfillment of the human person cannot be achieved unless both church and state collaborate together to promote justice and peace. These basic affirmations of the Fathers have become the perennial social teaching of the church.

See also ALMSGIVING; AUGUSTINE, INFLUENCE OF; COMMON GOOD; GOODS, ACCESS TO; GOODS, DISTRIBUTION OF; RERUM NOVARUM; STEWARDSHIP; WAR.

Bibliography: R. Musto, *The Catholic Peace Tradition* (Maryknoll, N.Y.: Orbis, 1986). R. Antoncich, *Christians in the Face of Injustice: A Latin American Reading of Catholic Social Teaching,* trans. M. O'Connell (Maryknoll, N.Y.: Orbis, 1987). P. Bigo, *La doctrine sociale de l'Eglise* (Paris: Presses Universitaires de France, 1965). A. Carlyle, *The Influence of Christianity upon the Political Ideas* (London, 1912). R. Charles, *The Social Teaching of Vatican II: Its Origin and Development* (San Francisco: Ignatius, 1982). I. Giordani, *The Social Message of the Early Church Fathers* (Paterson, N.J.: St. Anthony Guild, 1944). G. Hamman, ed., *Riches et Pauvres dans l'Eglise ancienne* (Paris: Bernard Grasset Editeur, 1962). P. Phan, *Social Thought,* Message of the Fathers of the Church 20 (Wilmington, Del.: Glazier, 1984).

PETER PHAN

FEMINISM AND CATHOLIC SOCIAL THOUGHT

Both feminism and Catholic social teaching are wide-ranging and constantly developing bodies of thought that seek, from different perspectives, to effect change in dominant economic, political, and cultural systems. Several ways in which these two bodies of thought diverge and converge will be explored here, beginning with a consideration of what is meant by "feminism."

"Feminism" has served as a name for the growing body of theory and social practice based on experiences in the women's movement worldwide, a phenomenon that can be interpreted broadly to include all that women have done to survive and to resist oppression throughout the centuries. Feminism does not refer to the feminine as a special category of women's issues; it is rather a systematic challenge to patriarchal or sexist economic, political, and cultural structures, that is, to systems in which women are subordinated and excluded from full participation in the life of the society. Beginning with women's experiences, feminism seeks greater well-being, mutuality in relationship, equality, and participation for women, raising questions about structures for organizing all of life. Feminists include men as well as women who are committed to these goals.

Within feminism there is much diversity. Although boundaries are fluid and most feminists draw on a wide range of influences in their thought, several major configurations of feminism can be discerned (Ruether, pp. 214–34, 99–115; Riley, pp. 43–73; Brubaker, pp. 290–331), all of which have much to contribute to Catholic social thought. Liberal, Marxist/socialist, and romantic philosophical traditions provide the basis for three often-delineated types of feminism; romantic feminism encompasses a diverse yet related group of radical or separatist and other cultural feminists who see differences between males and females as representative of masculine and feminine natures that are complementary opposites. Factors of socioeconomic class, race, ethnicity, and religion further contribute to the diversity within feminism that will be considered here.

Liberal feminism, rooted in the Enlightenment liberal tradition that forms the basis for capitalism and democracy as it is practiced in the West, emphasizes the equality and common human nature of all persons and seeks to extend to women as individuals political and legal rights within current systems. Marxist and socialist forms of feminism, drawing on the theories of Karl Marx but also on various strands of feminism in different ways, stress the need for transformation of economic structures in order to effect positive change for women of all classes. The type of feminism frequently termed "radical" considers gender discrimination the root cause of all forms of oppression; sees women's control of their own persons, especially their bodies, as the core issue; and advocates separating from patriarchal institutions in favor of cultivating a women's culture through women-centered alternatives. Some radical feminists suggest the natural (especially moral) superiority of women, paradoxically an assumption shared with both nonseparatist cultural feminists and conservative nonfeminists who emphasize a role of moral reform for women within current structures.

Class, race, ethnicity, and religion also bring diversity to feminism. Women of color and of many cultures and social classes worldwide have challenged white, middle-class North American feminists to broaden and deepen their analysis in light of the situations of all women, especially the poorest. While some feminists, with many others in the modern world, are distanced from religious worldviews, others work to transform mainstream traditions or to develop women-centered alternatives. Some feminists identify their work as feminist liberation theology, indicating their affinities as well as their differences with Third World and African American theologies of liberation written from male perspectives. African American women have used the term "womanist" to distinguish their views from both white feminist and black male perspectives. Many feminists in the global women's movement emphasize structural connections among sexism, racism, classism, heterosexism, abuse of the environment, and all other forms of oppression. In this view, patriarchy (literally, "rule of the fathers") is a system controlled not by all men equally but particularly by an elite group of ruling-class white males.

Official modern Catholic social teaching consists primarily of major statements by popes and by international gatherings of bishops; it is sometimes considered to include at lower levels of authority statements by national or regional conferences of bishops. Scholars have contributed as experts in the formulation of documents and as interpreters of the entire body of teaching, which is meant as a response to economic, political, and social concerns expressed by ordinary people in many ways. In general, the patriarchal organization of the church and of modern scholarship shapes the process by which official Catholic social teaching has been formulated; that it is finally written from a dominant male perspective is one of its most significant limitations from a feminist perspective.

Despite its limitations, Catholic social thought has formulated some valuable principles regarding conditions for realizing human dignity and some trenchant criticisms of existing social systems. Feminists and others, however, have pointed out that the church does not apply even its own criteria to itself; it does not provide a model of the participation in decision making that it advocates for society, thus raising the issue of the credibility of Catholic social teaching. For instance, in the view of the Vatican, the church is exempt from admitting women to orders and thus to full participation in its own leadership. Those to whom Catholic social thought is addressed can more easily dismiss its content, since the church does not practice what it preaches in its own social organization.

These limitations are part of a central methodological issue concerning the praxis (ongoing process of practice and reflection) out of which Catholic social thought is written. Feminist, Latin American, and other liberation theologies are exploring what it means for the church today to make an option for the poor in the face of massive inequalities of wealth and power worldwide. Liberation theologies raise issues such as the need for structural change in dominant economic, political, cultural, and religious institutions; the importance of initiatives taken by those on the margins of society in their own behalf; and the context of prior institutional violence in which revolutionary conflict takes place. Liberation theologies challenge the idea that action is an application of timeless theological principles, emphasizing instead the primacy of an ongoing praxis (in which critical reflection is one step) of commitment in particular struggles for liberation. They highlight the location of all theologies in particular contexts and social positions by which they are deeply conditioned, calling into question claims to universality that in fact make one perspective absolute while distorting or ignoring others, such as those of Third World peoples or of women.

While there has been some movement in Catholic social thought toward a liberation perspective, especially since the Second Vatican Council and by some regional groups of bishops, especially in Latin America and in Canada, an ongoing struggle of conflicting social theories can be discerned. From the time of Leo XIII Catholic social thought has criticized both "liberal capitalism" and "Marxist collectivism" as they have been practiced by dominant powers. At the same time, a pattern of including some elements of a liberation (radical, socialist) perspective in analyses of problems such as poverty but of finally proposing liberal or reformist strategies less challenging to structures of international capitalism can be traced. In addition, an earlier organicist worldview, which views society as an interdependent organism sustained by natural hierarchies and inequalities, continues to inform Catholic social thought with conflicting effects. It provides, for example, both a basis for criticism of liberal denials of social interdependence and a predisposition to support a stratified society, including a division of labor based on gender and race as well as class (Hobgood).

This pattern of conflicting paradigms, especially where women are concerned, is evident in the relation of Catholic "social" and "sexual" teaching. While recent social teaching has shown some movement toward a more inductive approach in which general principles leave room for differences in practical judgment (*Octogesima adveniens* 4, 49–50), teaching about sexuality and reproduction has continued to reflect an exclusively deductive approach in which principles are considered absolute and specific at the level of acts permitted or forbidden (Gudorf, "Seamless Garment"; C. Curran, "Catholic Social and Sexual Teaching," TT 44:4 [1988] 425–40). From a feminist perspective, that there is less room for moral agency in areas in which women might be decision makers points to sexist assumptions. A major contribution of feminism, epitomized in the feminist axiom that the personal is political, has been to uncover dichotomies such as those underlying conflicting approaches to sexual and social issues.

Feminists have begun to reinterpret all the theological categories that have informed Catholic social thought, particularly its theological anthropology or understanding of human persons, male and female. Church documents have affirmed that men and women share the same human nature, indicating a single-nature anthropology, but discussions of roles and characteristics thought to be proper to women suggest an organicist, dual-nature anthropology. They have defined femininity in terms that can reinforce patterns of female passivity and male activity, thus undermining women's moral agency (Brubaker, pp. 142–48). Motherhood, physical or spiritual, is said to be the proper and primary role of women, with the effect of making nurturing tasks and unpaid labor in the domestic sphere almost exclusively the responsibility of women. While some positive language concerning the equality of women, the participation of women in public life, and the women's movement as a "sign of the times" has appeared since the time of Vatican II (e.g., *Pacem in terris* 19), an insistence on different roles considered proper to the "nature" of women and primary for their salvation (PT 41; OA 13; *Laborem exercens* 19; *Economic Justice for All* 207) continues effectively to limit the possibility of women's participation outside the domestic sphere and to keep economic, political, social, and ecclesial power in the hands of men.

Thus, despite some changes at the level of language about women, a belief that men and women are essentially different and destined for different roles in society and in the church serves to legitimate the subordination of women in churches and in the larger society, functioning in a way analogous to "separate but equal" racial policies, which have historically resulted in structured inequality. The traditional organicist theological anthropology underlying Catholic social teaching helps to legitimate a gender system that provides cultural support for oppressive economic and political systems (Brubaker, pp. 23–24, 75–142; Gudorf, *Liberation Themes,* pp. 249–327; Riley, pp. 78–87).

Depending on who interprets the characteristics of normative humanity and the significance of differences, whether considered natural or cultural, both single-nature and dual-nature anthropologies can be used to deny women what they need to claim their places as full persons in every sphere of life. Paradoxically, radical feminists are among those who espouse a dual-nature anthropology, with the difference that they would reverse current power arrangements, since the characteristics considered unique to women are valued as more life giving than those ascribed to men. Affirming the essential sameness between men and women can provide a different but equally effective basis for the subordination of women, if concepts of normative humanity are based on male experience. While feminists differ in their evaluations of the significance of differences between women and men, they converge in their goal of challenging dominant concepts of normative humanity, male and female, and the ways that they have been used to keep women and other groups subordinate.

In regard to specific issues addressed in Catholic social thought, feminists can find common ground as well as major differences. Modern Catholic social teaching has criticized dominant economic and political systems, making connections that many feminists consider vital, for instance, between justice and peace or among economic, political, cultural, religious, and personal dimensions of issues such as "development" or liberation in the Third World (*Sollicitudo rei socialis, Populorum progressio*). Feminist challenges to Catholic social teaching, especially highlighting questions of theological anthropology, may be illustrated through a consideration of the issues of peace and economic justice.

Issues of war and peace reveal dilemmas rooted in assumptions about women's nature both for Catholic social thought and for some radical and cultural feminists who have suggested a role for women as natural peacemakers. Other feminist analysis uncovers complexity and ambiguity regarding women in relation to war and stresses that women's contributions to peacemaking must come from actual experiences of women, not from any idealized concept of women's true nature. Feminists have also drawn attention to the cultural roots of war in patriarchy, showing connections to domestic and other forms of violence in a society based on relations of domination and subordination (Riley, pp. 96–97; M. Condren, "To Bear Children for the Fatherland: Mothers and Militarism," in *Motherhood: Experience, Institution, Theology,* ed. Anne Carr and Elisabeth Schüssler Fiorenza, Edinburgh: T. & T. Clark, 1989, pp. 82–90). With other liberation theologians, feminists have explored the relevance of just-war criteria for violence in revolutionary situations (K. Lebacqz, *Justice in an Unjust World,* Minneapolis: Augsburg, 1987, pp. 93–99), raising challenges to the continuing influence in official Catholic social teaching of the traditional priority given to the preservation of order and to social change from the top down, through the personal conversion of individuals (Hobgood, pp. 322–24; Brubaker, pp. 121–22).

Assumptions about women's "nature" as well as definitions of work based on male experiences also undermine the adequacy of Catholic social teaching about issues of economic justice. These assumptions make women's work invisible, to the detriment both of women and of the completeness of the analysis offered of issues such as labor and Third World development. They obscure the relation of production and reproduction practices, the contributions made by women's labor in all its forms, and the conditions under which women labor, and they serve to legitimate a double work day of unpaid domestic and underpaid wage labor for women in all parts of the world, most of whom work in various settings out of economic necessity. Principles such as solidarity and the right of all people to participation in economic as well as political decision making are vitiated for women through qualifications based on such assumptions. Although development has been a major theme in the encyclicals of Paul VI (PP) and John Paul II (SRS), the vital roles of women in the economies of Third World nations and feminist critiques of dominant development theories have been overlooked. Since women and their dependent children are the poorest of the poor worldwide, an effective option for the poor requires a central place for women and women's perspectives in any analysis of the structures that create poverty in the modern world (Brubaker, pp. 75–148; Riley, pp. 91–98).

While feminism and Catholic social thought diverge on many points, converging movements may be seen perhaps most vividly in challenges that both face. Both women and religion occupy ambivalent positions in the modern world. Both are relegated by many to the less important "private" realm; at the same time, the Catholic church is still a powerful institution, and some women share in the privileged status of their class or race. Thus, both feminism and Catholicism are challenged by internal contradictions and connections yet to be made with the majority of the world's people, especially the women who are the poorest of the poor. In one sense, both are in the throes of discovering what it means to be a global or truly catholic movement with structures in which the human dignity of all persons can be fully respected and poor people participate as equals in shaping authoritative practice and theory. The global women's movement and groups concerned both with Catholic social thought and with feminism such as NETWORK and the Center of Concern (Washington, D.C.) have much to contribute to the development and liberation of both Catholic social thought and feminism, perhaps especially as they support forums where women of color and of the poor make their contributions. There will be no truly catholic (in the sense of universal) social thought until those at the margins of societies and churches are truly partners in decision making and in theological reflection on the urgent social questions that both feminism and Catholic social thought have sought, in different ways, to address.

See also SEXISM; WOMEN; POOR, PREFERENTIAL OPTION FOR; MARGINAL PERSONS; REPRODUCTIVE TECHNOLOGIES, SOCIAL ASPECTS OF; ABORTION, SOCIAL IMPLICATIONS OF.

Bibliography: P. Brubaker, *Rendering the Invisible Visible: Methodological Constraints on Economic Ethics in Relation to Women's Impoverishment* (Ph.D. diss., Union Theological Seminary, New York, 1989). C. Gudorf, *Catholic Social Teaching on Liberation Themes* (Washington: Univ. Press of America, 1981). C. Gudorf, "To Make a Seamless Garment, Use a Single Piece of Cloth," *Cross Currents* 34:4 (Winter 1984–85) 473–91. M. Hobgood, *Catholic Social Teaching and Economic Theory: Paradigms in Conflict* (Philadelphia: Temple Univ. Press, 1991). M. Riley, *Transforming Feminism* (Kansas City, Mo.: Sheed & Ward, 1989). R. Ruether, *Sexism and God-Talk: Toward a Feminist Theology* (Boston: Beacon, 1983).

BARBARA HOGAN

FORCE

The term "force," when used in descriptions of human interactions in the social world (or in an analysis of relations in ethics and politics), is in the class of terms that includes "power," "coercion," and "manipulation." Force may indicate application of physical pressure (as in brute force, violence) but need not be limited to such measures, that is, nonviolence may be force. Nonetheless, the term suggests that one influences the conduct of another even against that subject's will (Max Weber). When employed in the social sciences (and in a theological context) the term generally focuses on those means that disregard human freedom and integrity; it connotes the treatment of a subject as an object.

Karl Rahner's approach to force (brute force) is one congruent with the Catholic theological tradition. Force ought not exist, as it stems from concupiscence. In keeping with the tradition, Rahner expects that force (like concupiscence) will never be eliminated, but avoiding a Manichaean pessimism, he looks for a gradual overcoming of force. As it stems from sin, force remains problematic, a dangerous and ambiguous element of the social world. One must react against it while recognizing that physical force is a reality of God's creation. Force may be the condition of freedom, as we exist in a social space occupied by many subjects. Force reflects the self-assertion and resistance proper to a being; all beings, simply because they exist, have some power. Power and freedom, Rahner suggests, are mutually and dialectically interdependent. Freedom is clearly the higher value, but Rahner denies that we can, as Christians, absolutely renounce force. To do so would be to renounce the exercise of human freedom in the material realm; this would lead to the destruction of the subject. However, we can neither simply legitimate brute force nor can we easily eliminate nonviolent force.

A moral analysis of force recognizes that the exercise of force is a process of either salvation or perdition (Rahner). This analysis proceeds from one of two perspectives. It can proceed from the perspective of those who traditionally exercise force, that is, those in positions of authority. It is commonplace in the Catholic tradition to offer guidance to them. Recently, however, Catholic theological reflection has begun from the perspective of the powerless.

Those using force must recognize the persons at its mercy, reduce or eliminate force's results on them, and attempt to replace it with knowledge, love, or rationality. Force can, at best, be accepted as provisional; acceptance of force must be conditional. De facto possession of force does not legitimate it. Clearly force is exercised not "*because* I have but *although* I have it" (Rahner). Its consequences always remain unforeseen; one cannot justify it solely by one's original intent.

In several ways the analysis of war in the documents of the Second Vatican Council is an appropriate analogue for an analysis of force (see *Gaudium et spes,* chap. 5). The council advises critical caution in accepting the decisions of authority in wars. Other aspects of the council's approach are equally significant. It accents creation of social contexts and structures that make less necessary the use of war or, analogously, brute force. The council recognizes the necessity of making provision for those who conscientiously dissent from armed force. Finally, the council recognizes the necessity of legitimate defense for a society in the absence of a transnational power sufficient to protect the welfare of its people; analogously one can argue to the use of force in certain cases of injustice.

Recent Catholic responses to structural injustice, especially the injustice of poverty, have confronted the reality of force in international affairs and domestic social settings. Insofar as force is operative in the economic development of Latin America or in the feminization of poverty in the United States, it is problematic; Catholics ought to condemn such oppression. Insofar as force will be an integral part of alleviating oppression, it must be seen as an expression of human freedom in the material realm. The use of force cannot be reserved only to those in traditional positions of authority. By the same token, force used by the oppressed will remain dangerous and ambiguous; it is, nonetheless, a self-assertion proper to all human beings.

See also CONSCIENTIOUS OBJECTION; DEVELOPMENT; FREEDOM; GAUDIUM ET SPES; PACIFISM; POOR, PREFERENTIAL OPTION FOR.

Bibliography: K. Rahner, "The Theology of Power," *Theological Investigations* (Baltimore: Helicon, 1966) 4:391–409. D. Dorr, *Option for the Poor: A Hundred Years of Vatican Social Teaching* (Maryknoll, N.Y.: Orbis, rev. ed., 1992). D. O'Brien and T. Shannon, eds., "Medellín Conference Documents," *Renew the Earth: Catholic Documents on Peace, Justice, and Liberation* (Garden City, N.Y.: Doubleday, 1977) 547–79. D. Wrong, *Power: Its Forms, Bases, and Uses* (New York: Harper & Row, 1979).

STEPHEN J. CASEY

FREEDOM

Freedom is commonly understood as the unrestrained and uncompelled capacity of persons, individually or collectively, to act or refrain from acting, or to act in one way rather than another. Implicit in this understanding is belief in a fundamental initiative, or power to originate action and direct it intelligently. The term "freedom" may be applied to this power in itself, to the absence of circumstances impeding or preventing its exercise, or to the presence of conditions enabling or facilitating its exercise. Questions concerning the existence and nature of such power belong to metaphysical and theological inquiry concerning the compatibility of free will or free choice with natural or divine determinism. Questions concerning conditions affecting its exercise are major components of moral, social, and political philosophy. Throughout history these two kinds of questions about freedom, although usually distinguishable, have often been closely interrelated.

Early discussions of freedom are clearly rooted in the common experience of a social order comprising free persons and slaves. Broadly speaking, the former did as they chose while the latter did as they were told, although it was recognized that the behavior of slaves was not and could not be totally constrained or that of free persons totally unconstrained. Nevertheless, in classical thought freedom came to be associated with a particular kind of social character whose outstanding traits are the opposite of servile. Basic among these was a disposition to form opinions and choices independently and to express them candidly while expecting others, equally free, to do likewise. The maintenance of social stability and coordination among persons claiming both freedom and equality necessitated a high quality of collective deliberation aimed at the adoption of social policies and practices based not on submission to sheer authority or mere force but on mutual agreements including reasonable compromises. In all of this we perceive the traditional elements of democracy and its dependence on what are called in modern states "freedom of speech" and "freedom of assembly."

The irony of such liberal and egalitarian views and procedures flourishing in communities materially sustained by the labor of slaves did not go entirely unnoticed. One attempt to relieve it was based on the assumption articulated by Aristotle to the effect that slavery is the natural social state of persons lacking sufficient rationality to choose wisely and deliberate usefully. In one form or another that opinion has served for two and a half millennia as an effective rationalization for reconciling social consciences with political and economic oppression. It embodies the important truth that a tolerable society predicated upon the freedom of its members does depend on the general achievement of a certain level of intellectual culture. Hence the importance for such a society of what came to be known as "liberal education," that is, the education appropriate for free persons in a free society. Hence too, the eagerness of oppressors to make such education unavailable to those whom they hope to oppress.

Deeper reflections on the ethics of freedom in the classical period were stimulated by Sophist teachings that seemed to imply that social and moral restraints on the exercise of freedom are simply conventions that clever people can be trained to manipulate through public discourse so as to expand the scope of their own power and bring less clever people under its control. Plato challenged the underlying idea that it is a perfection of freedom simply to satisfy one's own desires by overcoming the opposing claims of others. He did so by transposing the question of freedom from the external social to the internal psychological domain, noting what has since become a commonplace, that one can be enslaved not only by other persons, but by one's own unruly passions of aggression and acquisitiveness. Such a concept of interior enslavement implies a hierarchy in the psychological order, wherein reason rules and when necessary overrules the passions. In a famous and controversial analogy Plato argued that social order requires the same hierarchy, a rule of reason over aggressive and acquisitive drives. The validity of this argument is not contingent on the arguable way Plato himself developed it, envisaging the ideal republic as an intellectual aristocracy or the absolute monarchy of a philosopher king. It is nevertheless true that Plato's thought has lent itself to legitimate uses by proponents of both democratic and oligarchic schemes of government.

With the decline of the Greek city-state as an achievable ideal and the rise of successive imperial regimes embracing vast multitudes and various cultures, one finds the political sphere increasingly regarded as offering more threats than opportunities to freedom. Freedom came to be widely regarded as a cherished individual resource of defense against the vicissitudes of social circumstance. The Stoics in particular responded by developing Plato's conception of interior freedom in a distinctively thoroughgoing way. If circumstances threaten to frustrate human desires and one is unable to change the circumstances, one is nevertheless free to change the desires. Freedom is thus valued as the power of voluntary adjustment to limited possibilities, acquiescing in the inevitable while desiring only the attainable. To make such a theory work demands unrelenting emphasis on the discipline of feelings by reason and fosters that habitual distrust of feelings that finds expression in the Stoic ideal of dispassion. Such an attitude is well suited to life in a world over which one has little sense of control and in which the most advantageous exercise of freedom takes the form of modest adjustment and patient resignation. Freedom thus conceived is, as the Stoics insisted, not excluded even by imprisonment or enslavement; among them it took on a religious value as submission to the Divine Reason ordering the cosmos. Both the social circumstances and the religious outlook of early Christians made them highly receptive to Stoic ideas concerning the right use of freedom. Such ideas, along with their Platonic antecedents, have been strong and lasting influences on Christian conceptions of personal and social morality.

Another major influence on Christianity was Neoplatonism, which interpreted the human condition as resulting from the soul's descent from a supreme spiritual principle into the confines of matter and saw freedom's highest expression as a love aspiring to the spiritual heights from which it had declined, a concept whose influence on Christian mysticism can hardly be overestimated. Among those most responsive to that influence was St. Augustine, whose conception of Christian freedom nevertheless took a different direction, dictated by his understanding of the Bible. Since the biblical God was one who imposed moral laws and judged human beings by their obedience to them, that same God must have endowed them with freedom of choice. And since the Christian gospel offered redemption to a humanity deemed universally sinful, humanity's free access to God must have been forfeited by disobedience. Hence restoration to God was not within freedom's grasp but depended entirely on God's unmerited favor. Salvation was bestowed gratuitously on whomever God predestined for it; for others there could be only the damnation earned by sin. Such a theology deprived human freedom of the dignity it enjoyed in classical thought. At the same time, Augustine's emphasis on universal human sinfulness did not foster optimism about social cooperation. Communities were assumed to be motivated, like gangs of thieves, by the crude self-interest of their members, whose potential mutual destructiveness it was the main task of government to restrain. Augustinian thought engendered a worldview in which the implications of human freedom were more ominous than inspiring and human social arrangements were esteemed more for the restrictions they imposed on abuses of freedom than for any opportunities they might offer to exercise it constructively. Authoritarianism in the church was further encouraged by the conviction that without orthodox belief and observances, guaranteed by ecclesiastical authority, there could be no salvation. Given such a conviction, toleration of religious differences could scarcely be acknowledged as a benign policy.

Augustine's domination of Western theology was reflected in Christian diffidence about human freedom. In the Middle Ages, however, renewed study of classical authors, and especially the discovery of Aristotle, stimulated a more positive attitude toward freedom both as the fundamental condition of all morality and as a social value to be protected and enhanced by government. Certain political thinkers, most notably Marsilius of Padua, interpreted the authority of law as a creation of the people rather than a direct bestowal of God and accordingly emphasized the importance of representativeness in government. In the case of church government, this emphasis took the form of conciliarism, a movement that was ultimately defeated by advocates of papal supremacy. The concept of a political life in which citizens properly exercised their freedom by participating in their own government and, if necessary, by resisting autocratic pretensions was destined to thrive, but not, for a long time, within Roman Catholicism.

In the post-Reformation era, while a strong emphasis on private judgment, personal conscience, and egalitarian community became characteristic of a number of Protestant groups, Catholicism relied increasingly on intensified discipline, centralized Roman authority, and the protection of Catholic monarchs to avert a further disintegration of Christendom. It was partly as a result of this development that Catholicism typically found itself on the opposing and ultimately losing side of the great revolutionary movements that ushered in the modern age of democracies. The bitter hostility to Catholicism that was a major component of the French Revolution's secular and anticlerical heritage provoked an intensely reactionary response. Even John Locke's famous doctrine of religious toleration, which profoundly influenced the founders of American democracy, made an ironic exception of Catholicism as inherently inimical to religious freedom. Nineteenth-century liberalism incurred virtually indiscriminate condemnation by the most reactionary of all modern papacies, introducing an era of extreme doctrinal and disciplinary rigidity and insitutional detachment from the main movements of social reform in the modern world.

Nevertheless, progressive Catholic social thinkers became increasingly sensitive to the economic enslavement and political powerlessness of indigent and laboring masses in modern industrial societies. These social perceptions, sharpened by awareness of their revolutionary implications, found official Catholic expression in a series of social encyclicals, increasingly liberal in their premises, that have appeared from Leo XIII to John Paul II. These documents have shown a growing awareness that human freedom depends on a certain provision of economic security and a deepening conviction that government's duty to serve the common good requires effective measures to guarantee such economic security for all citizens. It has also been increasingly acknowledged that government is most likely to discharge this duty when it is most representative of and answerable to its citizens of all classes and conditions. In this way, republican and democratic policies have increasingly commended themselves to modern Catholic social consciences, while the thriving condition of Catholicism in modern democracies has soothed antiliberal anxieties.

Catholicism's last great obstacle to integration in democratic societies was overcome by the Second Vatican Council, which extolled the sovereignty of personal conscience, denounced despotic and totalitarian political structures, and most momentously, embraced the ideals not only of toleration but even of positive ecumenism in its Declaration on Religious Liberty.

In the years following the council Catholicism has emerged most impressively as a religious force actively seeking and preaching freedom for the economically and politically oppressed, both within nations and among nations. Long recognized as an ally of colonialism, and close collaborator with postcolonial aristocracies, the Catholic church has vigorously affirmed the responsibility of affluent nations not only to refrain from exploiting their poor neighbors but to contribute actively to the relief of oppressive conditions in developing nations. Although never one of the strongest religious opponents of slavery, Catholicism became much more active in combating slavery's aftermath of racial discrimination during the present century. One of the most eloquent signs of a new Catholic sensitivity to the moral primacy of conscience has been the church's relinquishment of its previous tendency uncritically to endorse the military ambitions of civil rulers, and its new insistence on individual responsibility to subject warfare to moral criticism and refuse participation in wars believed to be unjust.

The extent to which Catholicism has responded in recent decades to the value of human freedom within this world, especially in the circumstances of political and economic life, is attested by the popularity and proliferation of an intellectual development almost without precedent in the church's history, typified by the movement known as liberation theology. Stimulated by moral outrage at systematic exploitation of the masses in developing nations, especially in Latin America, this movement has effectively translated for a new generation the biblical theme of salvation from terms mainly of otherworldly eschatology into concepts of political and economic reform aimed at replacing oppressive regimes with social structures designed to extend freedom. It is not easy to think of any major theological development in the church's history that has expressed and occasioned so thoroughgoing a reinterpretation of the practical implications of the gospel.

Heightened Catholic respect for human freedom has generally been accompanied by a realistic awareness that unrestrained economic liberty in modern industrial societies leads almost inevitably, owing to differences of opportunity, to ever-greater inequality in the distribution of goods, and thus ultimately to virtual enslavement of the poor. That recognition has served as a caution against absolutizing the freedom to acquire and amass private property and by the same token as a stimulus to cultivate socialist—including Marxist—analyses of unjust economic arrangements. This trend remains a highly controversial one among Catholics, especially in the United States, and the recent sharp decline of esteem for Marxism throughout much of the world is bound to affect that controversy. Nevertheless, official church teachings have candidly recognized that economic liberalism in its extreme form of laissez-faire capitalism tends to be highly destructive of liberty for most members of most societies. In this context especially, the practical inseparability of the social values of freedom and equality and the difficulty of achieving a fair balance between them become unmistakable.

Although Catholicism's greatly intensified interest both theoretical and practical in human freedom is partly a reflection of similar tendencies in modern secular thought, Catholic thought even at its most radical has steadfastly resisted that unqualified glorification of individual human freedom that has attracted many modern adherents and found expression in influential philosophical movements, especially among existentialists. Catholic praise and pursuit of freedom have adhered to religious tradition in insisting that human freedom is a means to rather than the end of human life and a means whose concrete value always depends on the service it renders to values that transcend it.

Modern Catholicism's rapid emergence as a powerful champion and eloquent advocate of human freedom has seemed to some observers to be accompanied by an embarrassing paradox. For at the very time when the church has appeared as an outspoken critic of authoritarian and despotic structures in secular regimes, it has maintained as its own structure of government the most absolute of monarchies, embracing a social order in which class privilege is conspicuous, especially in the subordination of laity to clergy and, in general, of women to men. In recent years criticism of these seeming moral inconsistencies has intensified, only to encounter intensified resistance and censoriousness from the church's central authorities. It is difficult to suppose this mounting tension between outwardly directed respect for freedom and inwardly directed distrust of it can long persist without significant adjustments one way or the other.

See also AUTHORITY, POLITICAL; CONSCIENCE; DEMOCRACY; HUMAN RIGHTS; POLITICAL PHILOSOPHY; POLITICAL THEOLOGY; RELIGIOUS FREEDOM; TOLERATION, PRINCIPLE OF.

JAMES GAFFNEY

FRIBOURG UNION

On October 18, 1884, Prince Karl von Lowenstein and Count Franz Kuefstein of Austria, along with the Marquis Rene de la Tour du Pin and Louis Milcent of France, gathered in the residence of Bishop Mermillod of Fribourg, Switzerland, to found an international organization of Catholic social thinkers to be known as "L'Union catholique d'études sociales et économiques." Faced with increasing turmoil in Europe, they astutely observed the need for a coherent social theory distinct from that of capitalism or socialism in order to restore justice to the social realm.

In yearly meetings held in Fribourg from 1885 to 1891, Social Catholics from Austria, Belgium, France, Germany, Italy, and Switzerland drew upon the thought of Thomas Aquinas to forge this new vision to which they gave the name "régime corporatif" (corporative system). Leadership of the group devolved on Bishop Mermillod, Counts Blome and Kuefstein, and La Tour du Pin, while to the three theologians, Georges de Pascal, Augustin Lehmkuhl, S.J., and Albert Maria Weiss, O.P., fell the task of articulating the theoretical foundations of this corporative system.

The twenty to thirty-two members who met yearly worked in a spirit of intense loyalty to the Church and to Leo XIII, who was briefed regularly on the results of their meetings. Not content with mere theory, they also sought practical solutions to the social ills surrounding them. Working in secrecy so as not to acerbate the conflict with Catholic liberals such as Charles Perin of Louvain, they produced documents on just wages for workers, insurance reform, labor unions, agricultural cooperatives, and private property as well as on the role of the state and of international legislation in the preservation of social justice. Many of their insights were incorporated into Leo XIII's *Rerum novarum* and remain at the heart of contemporary Catholic social thought.

Their description of the corporative system, accompanied by savage attacks on the free-market economy, was misconstrued by many of their opponents as a romantic desire to resurrect the medieval social order. Drawing on the Thomistic notion of society as bound together in a "unity of order," they sought to incarnate in modern structures the spirit underlying the whole medieval enterprise. The corporative system is constituted by the natural grouping of persons according to their professional duties, rights, interests, and social functions. Only when all of these natural groupings are represented in the political arena can justice prevail in a truly "organized" corporative system.

Faithful to their Thomistic roots, the Fribourg Union writers never hypostatized the political community in their attempts to counter the atomizing effects of modern liberalism. Even while consciously comparing society to an "organism," they rejected totalitarian schemes of state socialism in which the individual is entirely subjugated to the state. The solidarity they prized was that of individuals pursuing together the common good while retaining their dignity and autonomy as persons.

In such a society, the state will necessarily play an eminently positive role. Using insights from Thomas' *De regimine,* the Fribourg Union repudiated liberalism's minimalistic and negative concepts of the state's role and called upon the public power to intervene positively whenever needed to safeguard the demands of justice and of the common good. At the same time, care must be exercised to respect the initiative of individuals and of intermediary bodies in a corporatively organized society. This principle soon became known as the "principle of subsidiarity." The ultimate concern of the state is with justice, and it is the Fribourg Union's deliberations on Thomas' "general justice" that provides the theological framework for future discussions of the newly emerging term, "social justice."

The legacy of the Fribourg Union remains a mixed one. Its concrete proposals proved inadequate in the face of the vast changes taking place in industrial society. Fascism's use of the organic metaphor to defend totalitarianism further discredited the Social Catholics' efforts to erect a "corporative system." At times elements of modern liberalism clouded their understanding of Thomas' political theory. In spite of this, they successfully preserved vital elements of the traditional Christian vision of a good society: the social purpose of property, the positive but limited role of the state, the centrality of justice, the primacy of duties over rights, the principle of subsidiarity, and most importantly, the crucial role of the common good as the unifying force of the political community.

See also COMMON GOOD; COOPERATIVE ASSOCIATIONS; CORPORATISM; ECONOMIC ORDER; LEO XIII; MODERN CATHOLIC SOCIAL THOUGHT; RERUM NOVARUM; THOMAS AQUINAS, CONTRIBUTION OF.

Bibliography: C. Massard, *L'Oeuvre sociale du Cardinal Mermillod: l'Union de Fribourg* (Louvain: Edit. Univ., 1914). N. Paulhus, *The Theological and Political Ideals of the Fribourg Union* (Ann Arbor: Univ. Microfilms, 1983). R. Talmy, *Aux Sources du Catholicisme Social: l'École de La Tour du Pin* (Tournai: Desclée & Cie., 1963).

NORMAND PAULHUS

G

GAUDIUM ET SPES

"The joys and the hopes, the griefs and the anxieties of the men and women of this age" (*Gaudium et spes* 1) are primary concerns of the church according to Vatican II's best-known and most controversial document, the Pastoral Constitution on the Church in the Modern World, or *Gaudium et spes.* The document that the council never intended to write became a symbol for major changes in Catholic social thought. *Gaudium et spes* called the church into dialogue with the modern world, which included addressing pressing social problems. It provided a new vision for the relation between church and world, claiming that church and world learn from each other in reciprocity (GS 4, 11). As *Gaudium et spes* attempted to examine social, political, and cultural realities in light of the gospel, human experience, and history (46), was it indeed a breakthrough containing elements of radical discontinuity with earlier Catholic thinking? Or, as others suggest, did this optimistic document remain hopelessly wedded to reformist, Western, middle-class thought, incapable of truly illuminating the joys, hopes, griefs, and anxieties of the non-Western and less-developed parts of the world?

This essay situates *Gaudium et spes* within Vatican II and the context of Catholic social teaching prior to the council, explores changes in methodology signaled by the document, summarizes major themes within the document with an eye to both continuity and discontinuity with earlier Catholic social teaching, discusses the impact of the document on postconciliar Catholic social thought, and finally reviews criticisms of the document in light of later historical developments.

Context

Gaudium et spes is indicative to many of a profound change in the church before and after Vatican II. Yet the document draws on strengths of prior years of Catholic social thought. The document develops teaching found in Leo XIII, Pius XI, Pius XII, and John XXIII. The indebtedness to Pius XII, for example, is evidenced in numerous footnotes within the document. The document also repeats important themes from John XXIII's *Mater et magistra* and *Pacem in terris. Gaudium et spes* reflects the development of a more open style of Catholicism evidenced by social encyclicals, the theological insights of pioneers such as M.-D. Chenu, Yves Congar, and Karl Rahner (who was instrumental in shaping an early, rejected draft for the council), and the use of biblical sources and historical/critical scholarship by Catholic scholars.

Although *Gaudium et spes* continues a tradition of Catholic social thought, many claim it also significantly modifies the church's traditional stance to modern society. It presents, for example, a more positive concept of the world than that found in 19th-century writings. More than the writings of any previous council, *Gaudium et spes* demonstrates an awareness of change in the world and the impact of the secularizing process on moral problems. The sections devoted to culture signaled to many a sharp turn for an institution associated with the rejection of modern culture. In spite of the document's clear indebtedness to previous Catholic social thought, most see a change between the opening of the council by John XXIII in October 1962 and its conclusion by Paul VI in December 1965. *Gaudium et spes* became a primary symbol of that change.

This transition is reflected in the internal workings of the council itself as it shaped *Gaudium et spes,* the only major document of Vatican II that had its origins in a suggestion from the council floor. No preparatory commissions had been ordered to consider the topic of the "church in the world." At the opening of the first conciliar session, the relation between church and world was still not included in the list of conciliar subjects, although a speech by John XXIII on September 11, 1962, may have set the stage for its inclusion. In describing the upcoming council, John XXIII discussed the internal nature of the church as well as pressing social problems such as inequalities among nations, marriage, social justice, peace, and underdevelopment.

A shift within the council occurred at the end of the first session. Joseph Cardinal Suenens of Belgium asked the council to consider issues more "external" to the church. The following day Cardinal Montini spoke supporting Suenens' suggestion. The presence of bishops from underdeveloped countries and the influence of cardinals such as Montini, Suenens, Lercaro, and Konig and the bishops Wojtyla and Garrone further heightened awareness among council members of the need to address problems of hunger, poverty, war, and the like. When Paul VI opened the second session he explicitly charged the council to consider the church's relation to the world as one of its objectives. From these initiatives came the formulation of Schema XVIII, later designated Schema XIII, which eventually emerged as *Gaudium et spes.*

The internal changes within the council as it developed *Gaudium et spes* mirrored the changes in the church after the council. From a somewhat rigid traditionalism witnessed in the topics of the preparatory commission, to the inclusion of the relation between the church and the world, and finally to the development of the forward-looking document *Gaudium et spes* is significant movement in three years of deliberation.

Changes in Methodology

Gaudium et spes proposed as its methodology an examination of social, cultural, and political realities "in the light of the gospel and of human experience" (46). The church, according to the council, has "the duty of scrutinizing the signs of the times" (4). In order to adequately read the "signs of the times," bishops and priests are asked to use modern tools of science to aid the faithful (62). The phrase "signs of the times" was used frequently by John XXIII. As employed by the council it signaled the context for theological reflection and pastoral action. The introductory statement, for example, provides a moving cultural analysis of the contemporary world (4–10). The phrase also hints at the methodological changes that will be found later in the document.

That the council begins *Gaudium et spes* by analyzing the signs of the times rather than by exploring abstract ideas of church and the common good suggests a methodological change from classicism to a historically conscious approach. The world, as viewed by council members, has passed from "a rather static concept of reality to a more dynamic evolutionary one" (GS 5), and they seem to approve. History in the document is a place of ongoing revelation and not, in the classical manner of previous documents, a mere locus for applying universal principles. The spirit of God is present in history.

The increased historical sensitivity of the document yields a decreased reliance on natural law. Earlier social documents tended to frame concepts using natural-law methodology. The teachings of Leo XIII, Pius XI, Pius XII, and John XXIII were all based in natural law. Within Catholic tradition human reason, natural law, and creation were the primary sources of moral wisdom. *Gaudium et spes,* however, seems to move away from a notion of the existing natural order in which moral wisdom is discerned from human nature or from creation alone. Significantly the phrase "natural law" appears at only three points in the document (74, 79, 89).

If a methodological shift away from natural law occurs in the document, to what methodologies does it turn? Increased historical consciousness means, in part, reliance on the tools of the human sciences. Historical sensitivity to the framers of the document also means understanding the human in terms of the history of salvation. Part 1 of the document explores the human and human community on the basis of creation, sin, incarnation, and redemption. The teachings in the pastoral constitution then, will attempt to be based on biblical revelation. The council will try to employ a methodology that relates the biblical message and faith more directly to secular life and its problems (43).

The increased reliance on biblical revelation as a grounding for the church's social mission is reinforced by the Christological emphasis of the document. The council's strategy is to understand humanity in terms of Jesus Christ. Each chapter in part 1 ends with a Christological summary of themes (22, 32, 39, 45). Jesus is viewed as the perfect man, the new human being.

The pastoral constitution wishes to conduct its examination not only on the basis of the gospel but also "in the light of . . . human experience" (46). As social teaching moved in the document away from the deductive and a natural-law ethic to the inductive and the historical, the human person became primary. The influence of personalism may be noted throughout the document. In the constitution's section on politics the person is viewed as the link between church and world (76). The document's treatment of marriage is highly dependent on personalist thought. In its discussion of conjugal love and transmission of life, for example, the document teaches that the moral character of procedures are determined by objective criteria "based on the nature of the human person and his acts" (51). The official commentary states that acts are to be judged not by "merely biological aspects, but insofar as they refer to the human person integrally and adequately considered."

A shift to the human person and the subjective is also seen in the pastoral constitution's treatment of conscience. Whereas earlier documents insisted on moral laws, commandments, or norms as objective sources of morality, the constitution looks at conscience as an important reference point for personal morality. Crucial to human dignity is the right to act "in accord with the upright norm of one's own conscience" (26). In making a distinction between the substance or meaning of a moral truth and its formulation, the council again suggests implicitly that the believer turn to his or her conscience for guidance (62). Some might suggest that the council also opens the door to dissent as an appropriate act of conscience in opposing the formulation rather than the substance of morality.

The shifts in methodology cited above also suggest a new role for the layperson. The pastoral constitution urges laypeople to become well versed in the "sacred sciences" (62). It also is modest about the church's own competence, suggesting that pastors are not always "such experts, that to every problem which arises . . . they can readily give . . . a concrete solution" (43). An implication of the methodological shifts to increased historical consciousness and personalist thought is a more active role for laity in defining their own history in the world.

Structure

Gaudium et spes provides an example of the engagement with the world to which it calls its reader. The structure of the pastoral constitution models the methodology it recommends to others as well as underscores important themes in the document. Using a pastoral tone and nontechnical language, the introductory statements (1–10) model its assertion that we are obligated to know the "signs of the times," as the constitution first describes the state of the world before setting forth its more explicitly Christian message.

The constitution is divided in two main parts, "The Church and Man's Calling" (11–45) and "Some Problems of Special Urgency" (46–90). The theological anthropology and Christian ideals of part 1 are the basis for the discussion of special problems in part 2, grounding its treatment of human dignity, human community, and human activity in the gospel and the person of Jesus Christ, all of which provide the basis for the church's social mission. The first two chapters, "The Dignity of the Human Person" and "The Community of Mankind," integrate the personal quality of the human with the social, although personalism remains dominant. As mentioned earlier, the return to Christology at the end of each chapter in part 1 underscores the strategy of viewing humanity in light of Jesus Christ. Part 1 clearly views the social mission of the church from a biblical, Christological, theological, and personalist understanding.

Part 2 addresses "Some Problems of Special Urgency." The five chapters of the second section each begin with an attempt to read the signs of the times. Significantly, the pastoral constitution itself, as well as the crucial chapters of part 2, begins with a historical approach to reality rather than an abstract account. The problems addressed by the council are marriage and the family, the development of culture, socioeconomic life, political life, and peace and international cooperation.

Major Themes

The issues explored in *Gaudium et spes* are numerous. It is beyond the scope of this essay to deal with the constitution's themes in depth; such treatments are included throughout this volume. In attempting to ascertain whether the pastoral constitution represents continuity or discontinuity with traditional Catholic social thought, a brief summarizing of a sample of issues will be explored.

Part 1 begins with a treatment of human dignity, providing a theological anthropology that grounds the rest of the document. The human person is defined in a dynamic manner that stresses authentic freedom and marks a move to the subject. The constitution notes that we are created in God's image yet also caught in sin. Human freedom, intelligence, and moral sensitivity are made more acute in "the face of death" (18). A communitarian theme emerges as the council fathers claim that "by their innermost nature persons are social beings and unless they relate themselves to others, they can neither live nor develop their potential" (12). Human dignity and our nature as social beings also suggest a fundamental equality and "every type of discrimination, whether social or cultural, whether based on sex, race, color, social condition, language, or religion, is to be overcome and eradicated as contrary to God's interest" (29). Central to the role of the church as defined by the pastoral constitution is the safeguarding of human dignity.

Closely tied to the notion of human dignity and authentic freedom is the document's treatment of conscience. Part of human self-development as one grows in "truth and goodness" is to tend to conscience, "the most secret core and sanctuary of a man" (16). Conscience is viewed as the voice of God (16), and the council claims that the gospel respects "the dignity of conscience and its freedom of choice" (41). Other sections of the document will refer to the need for the conscience to be properly formed (31, 43, 87).

The treatment of conscience within a broader theological anthropology shifts the emphasis away from the focus on moral laws found in most earlier documents. Now the conscience becomes the subjective norm for moral action. Clearly the pastoral constitution rejects the treatment of conscience in the moral theology of the earlier manual tradition. The rationalistic and legalistic tone of earlier moral theology is replaced with a more personalist and subjective understanding of conscience and the human person.

Human dignity also grounds the document's discussion of human rights. Although human rights are discussed frequently in the document, a systematic treatment is never presented. We do learn, however, that the human has inviolable rights and duties (26) and that the church is to defend human rights (76). The treatment of human rights found in the constitution corresponds to that found in both of John XXIII's encyclicals, *Mater et magistra* and *Pacem in terris.* The two encyclicals and the pastoral constitution all recognize political, economic, personal, and religious rights as encompassing the basic human rights to which persons must have access.

Having "set forth the dignity of the human person," the council turns its attention in part 2 to "particularly urgent needs characterizing the present age" (GS 46). The first issue, marriage and family, generated some of the more heated debates of the council proceedings. The council's move to a more personalist methodology is clearly reflected in its treatment of marriage and family. Marriage is described as a "community of love," an "intimate partnership of married life and love," which is "rooted in the conjugal covenant of irrevocable personal consent" (47, 48).

The treatment of marriage offered by the pastoral constitution holds traditional formulations as well as major conceptual shifts. Doctrine related to marital fidelity, respect for life, and reproduction remains rather traditional. The brief treatment of birth control, which states that "sons of the Church may not undertake methods of birth control which are found blameworthy by the teaching authority of the church in its unfolding of the divine law" (51), offers nothing new. Marriage is also treated within the context of family as in previous documents. Marriage, according to the constitution, is by its nature "ordained toward the begetting and educating of children" (50).

However, the language used to define marriage also signals major shifts in the church's understanding of the marital relationship. Especially significant is the replacement of the notion of marriage as a contract with language of intimate partnership and covenant. Whereas the Code of Canon Law of 1917 defined marriage as a contract defined by its object, the constitution places conjugal love and covenantal relationship at the heart of its formulation, using personalist language to move marriage beyond the earlier legalistic framework.

Surprising to many is the refusal to use the customary ordering of the ends of marriage in its treatment on marriage and family. Earlier magisterial pronouncements frequently spoke of primary and secondary ends of marriage. In this formulation love of spouse is subordinated to reproductive functioning and the consequent rearing of children. The pastoral constitution views children as the fulfillment of spousal love rather than its purpose.

Sexual intercourse is also framed more positively than the treatment given in earlier documents. The constitution recognizes joy in marital intercourse as a positive value for "these actions signify and promote that mutual self-giving by which spouses enrich each other with a joyful and a thankful will" (49).

What impact did these shifts effect following the council? The notion of marriage as covenant, some suggest, might allow for consideration of the possible death of some marriages, since the document seemed to open the door to consideration of psychological, moral, and emotional health as pertinent in granting annulments, for example. However, Paul VI, shortly after the council, claimed that marriages exist as "juridical reality even if subjective elements die" (Farley, 225). The 1983 Code of Canon Law did, however, adopt some of the covenant language of *Gaudium et spes* while keeping a basically juridical view of marriage. Many express regret that the council chose to avoid difficult issues such as celibacy, divorce, mixed marriages, and a fuller treatment of birth control.

The council next directs its attention to a less controversial issue, the development of culture. The tone of the section is positive, with the council fathers expressing optimism that the development of culture will "make the conditions of life more favorable for all" (58). Culture is defined in broad terms as human "effort to bring the world itself under his control by his knowledge and his labor" (53). Culture is what humans create and culture in turn creates humans. Culture and the church exist in reciprocal relationship, mutually requiring the other. Given the importance of culture it is crucial that all possible should participate in public affairs, education, and other activities of culture.

The section on culture further marks the methodological shift to an increased historical consciousness. Cultural pluralism and the historical-social boundedness of culture and the church's role within culture is affirmed (53). In order to understand God's activity in the world, the church must understand its own "specific historical environment" (53). The council fathers urge development of expertise in the human sciences as part of Christian obligation (57). A historical-critical approach to religious self-understanding is implied as well as an opening for the later development of theologies of inculturation.

The chapter on socioeconomic life clearly continues lines of thinking developed in Catholic social thought in the preceding seventy-five years and introduces themes that would be further developed in the decades following Vatican II. The pastoral constitution owes much to the economic thinking of John XXIII and introduces themes that have been further developed by Paul VI, John Paul II, the synod of bishops, and various bishops' conferences. The chapter's confident tone affirms industrial development, global expansion and growth, and technological advances.

The pastoral treatment begins its discussion of economic life with the notion of human dignity explored in the earlier theoretical section. From respect for human dignity flows "the welfare of society as a whole" (63). The pastoral constitution contrasts the plight of the poor with the wealthy (63), decries the injustice in international trade and the unequal powers of trading partners (83, 85), and establishes as a key principle "the common purpose of created things" (69).

Continuity with earlier economic teachings is evident. Property as an "expression of personality" (71) restates existing teaching. However, the right of private property is relativized and applicable after basic human needs are met (69). The document is open regarding "forms of ownership," claiming ownership patterns should be "adapted to the legitimate institutions of people according to diverse and changeable circumstances" (69). The teaching on ownership and private property continues the shift in Catholic social thought away from the more conservative treatments of Leo XIII and Pius XI, and it sets the stage for the more radical structural analyses proffered, for example, by the documents of the General Conference of bishops of Latin America in Medellín in 1968 and in Puebla in 1979.

Appealing to the notion of human dignity for its grounding of economic principles is also in keeping with earlier treatments. However, the pastoral constitution further develops Catholic social thought in this respect by linking the notion of human dignity with human labor. Human labor is "superior to the other elements of economic life. For the latter will have only the nature of tools" (67). The notion that a person becomes a partner in creation through work (67) and the priority of human labor will be further expanded by John Paul II in *Laborem exercens.*

The short section devoted to political life seeks to promote the value of participating "freely and actively in establishing the political bases of a political community" (75). The section uses the notion of the common good to encourage protection of human rights, participation in political life, respect for the rights of minorities, and the right to choose one's own form of government. Political pluralism is also noted and affirmed.

A call for an "evaluation of war with an entirely new attitude" (80) is made in the fifth chapter. Overshadowed somewhat by John XXIII's *Pacem in terris,* the council fathers reiterate John's plea for outlawing war by international cooperation, and they condemn total war, as had both Pius XII and John XXIII. John XXIII's denunciation of the arms race is reaffirmed by the document, claiming that it especially "injures the poor" (81). The constitution also introduces themes that will be pursued in greater depth by the U.S. bishops in their pastoral letter *The Challenge of Peace.*

Implicit use of the just-war tradition is made throughout the document. National self-defense is allowable as a last resort after other means of settlement have been attempted (GS 79). The just-war principle of discrimination is applied in its strong condemnation of acts aimed at "the destruction of entire cities or of extensive areas along with their population" (80).

A noteworthy development in the section on peace is the posing of conscientious objection as an alternative to the just-war tradition. The document acknowledges the rights of those "who for reasons of conscience refuse to bear arms" (79). *Gaudium et spes* was significant for the debate during the Vietnam War regarding conscientious objection and for the growing Catholic pacifist community of the 1970s.

Disappointing to some was the document's treatment of deterrence, which does not provide an outright condemnation (81), and its caution in not considering unilateral disarmament as a viable option (82). Missing also from the document are treatments of wars of liberation and civil wars.

Impact

For those who claim that *Gaudium et spes* was a bold breakthrough in the church's teaching, to what developments do they point in contemporary thinking and action? The personalist emphasis of the document has continued to dominate postconciliar moral theology. Questions of conscience and church authority are central to the writings and discussions of moral theologians since the writing of the pastoral constitution. The personalist view of marriage with its emphasis on conjugal love has become the dominant view in moral theology since Vatican II. The constitution's view of individual conscience has influenced the teaching on conscientious objection, and since 1965 the church has taught that the Christian may follow either the just-war or pacifist traditions.

Some writers claim that the pastoral constitution was responsible, in part, for the growth of Catholic feminist theology.

Anne Patrick contends that central theological affirmations such as the equality of all persons and the more dynamic historical consciousness found in the document implied an affirmation of the full personhood of women. This emphasis is now being increasingly articulated by Catholic women, many of whom have become theologians themselves (Patrick, p. 58).

For many the impact of *Gaudium et spes* is especially evident in the socioeconomic realm, and the claim is made that ideas found in the document have become major new themes during the years following Vatican II. Although the pastoral constitution focuses primarily on the individual, it begins to recognize social structures. The document opens with a significant statement affirming the church's option for the poor. Official church documents since Vatican II have been especially concerned with the church's mission in socioeconomic realms. The synod of bishops' 1971 document, *Justitia in mundo,* emphasizes reform of social structures. In *Evangelii nuntiandi* (1975) Paul VI explicitly links evangelization with the church's social and political mission. John Paul II in the 1981 encyclical, *Laborem exercens,* locates oppression as stemming from the conflict between labor and capital. Using principles found in *Gaudium et spes* such as the superiority of labor (GS 67) and the necessity for worker participation (68), John Paul II further develops an analysis of labor's priority over capital and of structuralist themes found in the pastoral constitution. Some will claim that the constitution also paved the way for liberationist documents such as those from the General Conference of bishops of Latin America in Medellín in 1968 and in Puebla in 1979.

Criticisms

Critics claim that *Gaudium et spes* was at best a reformist document and did not signal radical changes in the church. Theological movements in Latin America, Asia, and Africa as well as feminist theologies and theologies of the environment reveal both the limitations of the document and the inconsistencies in church practice following the writing of the constitution.

Some have criticized the church for failing to implement its concerns regarding empowerment of the laity, claiming that slow progress has been made. The constitution encouraged the laity "to receive an appropriate formation in the sacred sciences" (62), and training centers were encouraged for laity but have yet to be implemented. The decentralizing emphases of the document are far from institutional reality. As one observer writes, "Statements about collegiality and lay responsibility ring hollow when not structurally assembled" (Fagin, p. 23).

The impact of the constitution on later teaching and practice concerning marriage and the family also receives mixed reviews. As noted earlier celibacy, divorce, and mixed marriages are left out and the issue of family planning is treated in a very cursory manner (50). Although the 1983 Code of Canon Law adopted some of the constitution's covenant and partnership language the treatment remains essentially juridical. The most damaging criticism however, comes from a Third World perspective. The teachings concerning marriage and family seem relevant to those who can afford to meet the basic needs of family members. As Moser and Leers write, "The ideal it puts forward in family terms presupposes adequate income, a house with several rooms, good health, emotional stability and a lot of free time" (Moser and Leers, pp. 47–48).

Little attention is given in the document to environmental pollution, the depletion of nonrenewable resources, and general environmental exploitation. The council fathers' language concerning nature and the relation of humankind to nature is rather disturbing. Humanity should "consolidate its control over creation" (9), "subject to himself the earth and all that it contains" (34), "subdue the earth" (57), and hold "increasing domination over nature" (63). In Lynn White Jr.'s 1974 article, "The Historical Roots of Our Ecologic Crisis," the language of dominating, subduing, and controlling nature is blamed for current environmental crises. The council fathers seem oblivious both to the environmental problems already evident in the world and the impact of framing the human/nature relationship in terms of domination. Later theologies of the environment will significantly reframe the human/nature dynamic.

The document contains serious problems from a feminist perspective. Explicit concern for women rarely appears in the constitution. The document acknowledges discord resulting from "new social relationships between men and women" (8), claims that discrimination based on sex is "to be overcome" (29), and recognizes that women are employed outside the home and should participate in cultural life (60). This limited analysis provides little insight into the concrete situations of women, demonstrating a blindness to rape, domestic violence, poverty, excessive workload, and so forth. It also does not offer an internal criticism of the church's own structures and ways in which the institutional church might not affirm the full personhood of women.

Women "should be able to assume their full proper role in accordance with their own nature" (60), according to the framers of the constitution. Recent feminists have articulated the tension in this and later social teaching between an "affirmation of women as human persons entitled to full social rights and a view that women are uniquely essential to raising of children" (Andolsen, p. 12). John Paul II will continue to claim in *Laborem exercens* that women's nature differs from that of men.

Feminist theologians will also criticize the use of generic masculine nouns throughout the document. In addition, God is referred to as "father" most consistently, defining divine reality in masculine terms. Thus although norms concerning equality are found in the document, the application of the norms to women is inadequate and not substantially developed in later teachings.

Donal Dorr claims that *Gaudium et spes* is missing a coherent Third World theology and "body of experts to articulate such a theology" (Dorr, p. 120). The constitution is written from a First World perspective even when Third World problems are addressed. The agenda for the council was determined largely by debates within European theology during the late 1950s and early 1960s. Although Third World bishops were present, they did not have the same impact as the progressive bishops and theologians from successful European countries such as Holland, Belgium, France, Germany, and Switzerland, who were supported by the bishops of the United States and Canada. Missing from the document is adequate attention to problems of pollution, mass unemployment, urbanization, struggles of oppressed racial groups, Third World indebtedness, and inflation. Wars of liberation, revolutionary movements, peace movements such as the movement led by Gandhi in India, the revolution in Vietnam, the successful revolutions of Cuba and China, are not mentioned. In short, the document views the world through the eyes of reform-oriented Christians of Western, developed, capitalist countries.

The constitution is optimistic. The council fathers believed that modern, industrialized, technological, development-oriented society could bring worldwide betterment: "For the first time in human history, all people are convinced that the benefits of culture ought to be extended and actually can be extended to every one" (9). Industrial development, technological advances, and the growth orientation of modern society are all affirmed. The essentially optimistic view seems to assume that the development of the Third World can happen by generalizing the development strategy of the West without involving major changes in the world economy. Reform of economic structures is preferred, although the document is reticent to spell out what those reforms might be.

It is unfair to claim that the bishops were completely uncritical of social structures. They recognize that people are often "spurred toward evil by the social circumstances in which they live" (25), thus acknowledging the existence of social or structural sin. They decry inequality (29, 66) and call for social change (26, 42, 66, 85, 86). However, the persistent emphasis on the person throughout the document yields a weak analysis of structural realities and of social sin.

Critics further claim that the treatment of political participation presupposes the political conditions of the West and that human rights are mentioned but not given a systematic treatment. Although poverty is addressed, liberationists could rightly claim that it is an outsiders' perspective and that a theology or spirituality of poverty is not developed. And Tissa Balasuriya will claim that no true dialogue with other religions or cultures is found that might offer real alternatives to the "white, Western, capitalist, male mind-set that still dominated Catholicism" (Balasuriya, p. 148).

Although the document clearly contained seeds for later developments in liberation theology, many Third World critics claim it endorsed liberal values and the liberalism of the progressive West. As Gregory Baum writes, "This liberal notion of the self-development of persons corresponded to the aspirations of the Western middle classes, but did not shed light on the emancipatory struggles of people, including the working class, who were structurally oppressed" (Baum, p. 14).

One may believe that *Gaudium et spes* ushered in a new day for the church by highlighting the social mission of the church, by further orienting the church to the concerns of the poor, by affirming the centrality of the person, by empowering the laity, and by further opening the church to the world around it. Or one may claim that *Gaudium et spes,* though well intended, remained a document reflecting liberalism, a naive optimism concerning Western-style development and expansion, and an inadequate response to the problems of the Third World, women, and the environment. Whichever is the case, *Gaudium et spes* remains one of the most significant and challenging documents in the history of Catholic social thought.

See also CHURCH, SOCIAL MISSION OF; CONSCIENCE; CULTURE; JUSTICE IN THE WORLD; METHODOLOGY, MORAL; MODERN CATHOLIC SOCIAL THOUGHT; PERSON, DIGNITY OF.

Bibliography: B. Andolsen, "A Woman's Work Is Never Done: Unpaid Household Labor as a Social Justice Issue," in B. Andolsen et al., eds., *Women's Consciousness, Women's Conscience* (San Francisco: Harper & Row, 1985). T. Balasuriya, *Planetary Theology* (Maryknoll, N.Y.: Orbis, 1984). G. Baum, *Theology and Society* (New York: Paulist, 1987). J. Coleman, ed., *One Hundred Years of Catholic Social Thought: Celebration and Challenge* (Maryknoll, N.Y.: Orbis, 1991). C. Curran and R. McCormick, eds., *Readings in Moral Theology No. 5: Official Catholic Social Teaching* (New York: Paulist, 1986). D. Dorr, *Option for the Poor: A Hundred Years of Vatican Social Teaching* (Maryknoll, N.Y.: Orbis, 1983). G. Fagin, ed., *Vatican II: Open Questions and New Horizons* (Wilmington, Del.: Glazier, 1984). M. Farley, "Divorce, Remarriage, and Pastoral Practice," in C. Curran, ed., *Moral Theology: Challenges for the Future* (Mahwah, N.J.: Paulist, 1990) 213–39. P. Huizing, "Canonical Implications of the Conception of Marriage in the Conciliar Constitution *Gaudium et spes,*" in W. Roberts, ed., *Commitment to Partnership: Explorations of the Theology of Marriage* (New York: Paulist, 1987). R. Latourelle, ed., *Vatican II: Assessment and Perspectives, Twenty-Five Years After,* vol. 2 (New York: Paulist, 1989). R. Lucien et al., eds., *Vatican II: The Unfinished Agenda: A Look to the Future* (Mahwah, N.J.: Paulist, 1987. A. Moser and B. Leers, *Moral Theology: Dead Ends and Alternatives* (Maryknoll, N.Y.: Orbis, 1990). T. O'Connell, *Vatican II and Its Documents: An American Reappraisal* (Wilmington, Del.: Glazier, 1986). A. Patrick, "Toward Renewing the 'Life and Culture of Fallen Man': *Gaudium et Spes* as Catalyst for Catholic Feminist Theology," in J. Dwyer, ed., *"Questions of Special Urgency": The Church in the Modern World Two Decades After Vatican II* (Washington: Georgetown Univ. Press, 1986). G. Schner, ed., *The Church Renewed: The Documents of Vatican II Reconsidered* (Lanham, Md.: Univ. Press of America, 1986). L. White, Jr., "The Historical Roots of our Ecologic Crisis," in D. Spring and

E. Spring, eds., *Ecology and Religion in History* (San Francisco: Harper & Row, 1974).

LOIS ANN LORENTZEN

GENOCIDE

"Genocide" is a term used with increasing frequency in the vocabulary of ethicians and social scientists, yet it remains a term in search of precision. The Convention on Genocide approved by the General Assembly of the United Nations on December 9, 1948, makes an effort to set forth its parameters. As viewed by this United Nations document, genocide definitely involves activities whose goal is to liquidate in whole or at least in large measure members of a distinguishable national, ethnic, racial, or religious group. Activities envisioned in the convention as having a potential for becoming genocide include direct killing, serious bodily or mental harm, imposition of living conditions that in due time will result in death, forcible prevention of births, and transferring children of the persecuted group to another community.

In the period preceding the United Nations declaration, the right of humanitarian intervention on behalf of populations subjected to conditions deemed life threatening by the international community had been considered part of the law of nations. The Nuremberg trials following World War II, whose shock waves directly stimulated the process of framing a United Nation declaration, contain frequent reference to instances of previous international intervention on behalf of groups threatened with extinction. Examples include efforts to end the atrocities in the Greco-Turkish war in 1827, a U.S. intervention to counteract anti-Semitism in Syria and Rhodes in 1840, a French push to check religious hostilities in Lebanon in 1861, and protests directed to the Turkish government at the turn of the century for its treatment of Armenians and other Christian minorities.

Surveying these varied efforts by governments to protect selected groups coming under sustained attack for whatever reason, scholars have attempted to develop theories of genocide. There has been some success but also considerable controversy. Eric Wolf, for example, developed the notion of "pariah people" to describe groups of indigenous people who frequently stood in the way of colonizers and hence were prime candidates for genocidal attack. Other scholars have replaced this term with "stranger peoples," feeling that Wolf's use of the term "pariah" reduced the victims to subhuman status. But even "stranger peoples" is not without difficulty, according to Leo Kuper. It still places the burden of the definition on the victims and derives meaning from the standpoint of the host society. Kuper prefers "hostage peoples." This focuses the analysis of genocide far more on the perpetrators of the injustice and also better highlights the arbitrary nature of the fate generally endured by the victims.

Other analyses that have shaped contemporary thinking about genocide include the following: Jean Paul Sartre, out of his involvement with the French struggle in North Africa, has strongly emphasized the intimate links between colonialism and genocide. In contrast, political philosopher Hannah Arendt attributes the growth of genocide to the rise of an ethos of secularization, of disenchantment with the world, and of rationalization having its origins in Western religion. Thus, for her, far from being a regression to barbaric paganism, bureaucratic dehumanization and mass murder are clearly within the mainstream of Western culture. A number of scholars propose what is called the "elite" theory of genocide, which argues that genocide is most frequently the work of totalitarian regimes. It results from the elevation of political survival by these elites to the highest value in society. The Catholic bishops of Burundi used a form of this analysis in explaining the origins of the massacre of the Hutu people in their country in a pastoral letter issued in January 1973. Finally, there are sociological approaches to genocide, which see it essentially as a response to social dysfunction for the dominant group, and psychological theories advanced by Konrad Lorenz and others that present it as a manifestation of inherent human destructiveness.

Much research remains to be done in clarifying the notion of genocide. Especially important is understanding its relationship to the Nazi Holocaust, which most scholars, especially Jewish scholars, tend to place in a separate category.

See also ANTI-SEMITISM; ARMS RACE; BLACK THEOLOGY; FASCISM; HOLOCAUST, THE; MARXISM; TORTURE.

Bibliography: L. Kuper, *Genocide* (New Haven/London: Yale Univ. Press, 1981). I. Charney in collaboration with C. Rapaport, *How Can We Commit the Unthinkable? Genocide: The Human Cancer* (Boulder, Colo.: Westview, 1982). I. Horowitz, *Genocide: State Power and Mass Murder* (New Brunswick, N.J.: Transaction Books, 1976).

JOHN T. PAWLIKOWSKI, O.S.M.

GOD, IMAGES OF

Recent Catholic social thought, both in official church teaching and in theological research, is characterized by a return to the Scriptures in order to "attend to the Bible's deeper vision of God, of the purpose of creation and of the dignity of human life in society" (*Economic Justice for All* 29). Far from being a revival of a precritical use of scriptural proof texts or a retrenchment into the ghetto-like mentality of fundamentalism, this development, together with an increased readiness to engage in more critical, sophisticated social analysis, has given greater force to the philosophical ("natural law") argumentation, which has always been a hallmark of Catholic moral theology and ethics. It has also helped to provide a genuinely theological and spiritual foundation for the church's understanding of its social mission in the modern world. The Scriptures and the images of God they present us with are able to appeal to, touch, and activate the imagination of faith on a level different from and often more powerful than that of simple argumentation. First, some important pertinent themes and perspectives of church teaching will be explored, and then a brief indication of relevant developments in liberation and feminist theology will be given.

Official Church Teaching

Modern Catholic social teaching had its real beginning in 1891 with the publication of *Rerum novarum,* in which Leo XIII addressed the widespread poverty and exploitation of workers in industrialized countries. The issues of economic justice, the human dignity of the individual, and the common good, especially the rights and the care of the poor, have remained central ever since, even as other issues such as world peace and ecological responsibility have gained importance. Since Vatican II a variety of papal encyclicals, synodal declarations, and pastoral letters have reflected upon these issues with the help of biblical theology. New images of God have gained significance; traditional images and concepts are seen from new perspectives. Among them, several are worth noting: (1) the kingdom of God, (2) the transcendence of God, (3) the universal fatherhood of God, and (4) the God of creation.

1. No theme is as central as that of *God's kingdom* as proclaimed and established by Jesus Christ. The reign of God is the key biblical image that establishes the essential relationship between faith and the promotion of justice. To speak of God's kingdom or reign is to image God as a personal agent active in human history and bringing about the divine will, which is the saving transformation of the entire creation. The preaching and personal destiny of Jesus Christ are understood to be the revelation of God's original purpose in creating the

world and the fulfillment of God's covenantal promise to redeem it from the powers of death, which threaten to destroy it because of human sin. God's coming reign is vividly described by Jesus with many images and metaphors, especially in the Sermon on the Mount and in the parables, which figure prominently in recent documents (e.g., the U.S. Catholic bishops' *Challenge of Peace* and John Paul II's reflections in *Dives in misericordia* on God as the "Father of mercies," based on the story of the Prodigal Son and developing the essential connection between mercy and justice). God is not merely the transcendent source of being or the ultimate foundation of moral principles. God is the one who comes to us here and now in our history to establish the kingdom: the "God of the kingdom." Like *Gaudium et spes,* many official documents continue to distinguish in a traditional way between "earthly progress" and the "growth of God's kingdom," but they emphasize clearly that our hope for the final fullness of God's kingdom in the "new earth must not weaken but rather stimulate our concern for cultivating this one," where the "kingdom is already present in mystery" (GS 39). The kingdom is this world as it embraces and is transformed by God's rule (justice).

The God of justice is not seen primarily in the rather individualistic, juridical terms of a former piety concerned with "saving one's soul" but as one who executes justice for the needy and demands it of the whole people (EJA 38). The "sovereignty of God" means the reign of such justice as an eschatological, prophetic challenge to all other notions of justice and liberation in opposition to all forms of oppression. God's justice becomes personally visible in the face and actions of Jesus as unexpected, unearned mercy, gracious love of the poor, and solidarity with the outcast. Its demands are concrete and immediate, especially emphasized by the Lord's identification with the least of one's brothers and sisters.

Largely inspired by liberation theology (which it has viewed with some suspicion), official church teaching has taken up the central OT images of the Exodus and of God as "liberator of the oppressed and the defender of the poor" (*Justitia in mundo* 30), emphasizing that God's justice and the salvation it brings necessarily incarnate themselves in the concrete political, social, and economic liberation of those who suffer oppression. Thus the church is called to serve the kingdom and to be a means of its establishment on earth (*Populorum progressio* 13). In order to proclaim the gospel authentically it must proclaim the liberation of the whole person, of all men and women, and has the "duty of assisting the birth of this liberation, of giving witness to it, of ensuring that it is complete" (*Evangelii nuntiandi* 30).

The good news of God's kingdom, God's liberating reign, is directed to all, but in a special way toward the poor. Thus God is seen as one who identifies with those who are powerless. God hears the cry of the poor. In the community God's covenant justice is to be manifest above all in the way the poor and unprotected are treated. Mindful of the way that God had freed them, the people of the covenant are to care for the poor, the oppressed, and the stranger (EJA 36). In Jesus, God "takes the side of those most in need" and disciples are therefore called upon to make a similar "option for the poor" (EJA, introduction, no. 16). Pope John Paul II likewise speaks of the "option or love of preference for the poor" which faith demands (*Sollicitudo rei socialis* 42).

God's reign will bring about universal peace. The U.S. bishops noted that after the experience of the Exile, Israel's "God was no longer identified with military victory and might" (CP 31). Increasingly, "images of peace and the demands upon the people for covenantal fidelity to true peace grow more urgent" (CP 32). In the prophetic literature of the OT God is pictured as peacemaker, the one whose rule would usher in a final age of universal peace, the true fulfillment of the covenant promise and messianic hope. The NT bears witness to the fulfillment of God's promise in the person and ministry of Jesus and also to the mission of the believing community to carry out Christ's mission of peace in history (CP 56–68).

2. The *transcendence of God* is seen above all in relationship to the inviolable dignity, freedom, and equality of all human persons, precisely because they are created in God's image. At the "center of all Catholic social teaching are the transcendence of God and the dignity of the human person" (CP 15). In every human being "authentic freedom is an exceptional sign of the divine image" (GS 17). Thus the transcendence of God does not imply the denigration of the human creature. On the contrary, it is the foundation and final fulfillment of human freedom and dignity (GS 21; EJA 32). God's transcendence is not merely an abstract characteristic of the divine reality. It is humanity's own calling and destiny, for in grace all are "called to one and the same goal, namely, God" (GS 24). God's transcendence and the transcendent nature of the human person mean that all persons are fundamentally equal and enjoy certain basic rights. Every form of discrimination and social or political exploitation is contrary to God's intent (GS 29). The transcendence of God and the human orientation to it prompt the church to emphasize that no particular political structure or social program can claim to constitute humanity's true and final fulfillment nor understand humanity's true dignity and freedom as radically as Christian faith (GS 41). Thus the transcendence of God functions as a critique of ideology in the service of humanity's true liberation (*Octogesima adveniens* 26–37; SRS 41–45; Puebla 535–61).

3. The image of God as *father,* which has certainly become problematic, is often used to express the unity of the human race as a single family. Despite its patriarchal and authoritarian overtones, it is a central NT term referring to the one God and, more specifically, to God's personal and loving care for all men and women. The important theological insight here is the linking of the oneness of God with the unity of the human race (GS 24; OA 17). Christians may not call upon God as father without recognizing that all men and women are brothers and sisters in Christ, made alive and drawn together in community by the Spirit. In this vein, the solidarity of the human race has become a central theme in recent church documents (SRS 40; EJA 61–95, 363–65; Congregation for the Doctrine of the Faith, *Instruction on Christian Freedom and Liberation* [1986] 71–96). Rejecting both the unbridled individualism of modern liberalism and the collectivism of those political systems and structures that ignore the dignity and freedom of the individual, church teaching stresses the interpersonal, communitarian nature of human life (GS 32; *Instruction on Christian Freedom and Liberation* 73; EJA 63; SRS 21, 26, 32–33). Such communion implies mission on behalf of communion: human community in God's image is called upon to be universally inclusive (*Christifideles laici* 32, 41–43).

The mystery of the Trinity is seen as the ultimate ground of such solidarity in loving communion. Communion is a "new model of the unity of the human race, which must ultimately inspire our solidarity," a "reflection of the intimate life of God, one God in three Persons" (SRS 40; see also GS 24, EJA 64).

The vision of a universal brotherhood and sisterhood of humanity as children of the one God and the Trinitarian model of communion, which emphasizes equality and mutuality, provides the theological foundation for the theme of the common good. This concept, long important in catholic social thought, has undergone much development recently and plays a crucial and critical role in virtually all official church social teaching since Vatican II.

4. The image of God as *creator* figures prominently in the growing awareness of our responsibility for the earth, its resources, and authentic development. The creation stories of Genesis are often used in recent church teaching to stress human stewardship (EJA 32). By creating human beings in God's own image, God shares the divine power of dominion, entrusting the creation to their watchful care (SRS 29). Authentic, morally responsible development of peoples is an obligation (PP 15–16; SRS 31–32) that includes respect for all God's creatures (SRS 33). The dominion spoken of in the Scriptures is not a warrant for exploitation (EJA 34; *Christifideles laici* 43). Human work is seen as an unfolding of the Creator's work (GS 34; EJA 32) and as an essential aspect of authentic human self-actualization and development (*Laborem exercens* 4–6). Human beings are called to cooperate with God in "completing the work of creation" and for this reason, every "worker is, to some extent, a creator" (PP 27). Human labor is "a participation in God's activity" (LE 25), a "share in the creative activity of God" (EJA 32), who gives human beings the power to "transform and perfect the world in solidarity" (Medellín, "Justice" 3). The cultivation and development of the earth through the arts, sciences, and technology is an "essential dimension" of the human vocation (SRS 30). True development has as its goal a universal "civilization of love" (SRS 33).

Important New Theological Approaches

While one can detect shifts of perspective and new emphases with respect to the Christian concept of God in all areas of recent scholarship, it must here suffice to draw attention to two contemporary theological approaches that have produced fruitful new ways of imaging God and that continue to have a significant influence on the development of Catholic social thought: liberation theology and feminist theology.

Liberation theology. Theologians like G. Gutiérrez, J. L. Segundo, C. and L. Boff, and J. Sobrino insist that we can only speak of God adequately when we speak of the kingdom, which belongs in a privileged way to the suffering poor, and through them, to all. The God of Jesus Christ is the God of the kingdom, the God who comes to liberate the oppressed and to establish justice. The image of God as liberator and vindicator is central. God's very being and presence (signified in the divine name YHWH) means solidarity with and liberating action on behalf of the people. In his words and deeds Jesus identifies himself especially with the poor and outcast. The incomprehensible mystery of God is revealed precisely in God's hidden, suffering solidarity with the oppressed. In the cross and resurrection of Jesus, God's identification with those who suffer from sin and oppression reaches its fulfillment and manifests its saving power. The theologians mentioned above all stress that while the liberation of Christ cannot be identified with (reduced to) political, social, and economic liberation, it is and must be historically identified in such concrete forms of human liberation.

God chooses the poor to reveal Godself. Thus for Gutiérrez the Beatitudes—"Blessed are the poor"—are not so much a statement about the poor as a revelation of God. The God of Jesus Christ is the God of the poor, the God who takes sides with the poor against oppression. Today, in the irruption of the poor in the life and consciousness of the church, God reveals a new way for Christianity. The widespread suffering of the poor ruptures comfortable theologies and ecclesial structures and demands a new locus and mode for speaking about God. The poor and oppressed are the most concrete image of God. Only in solidarity with the poor can we find and image God correctly. Christ's identification with the poor makes the same demand on the church. It calls for a preferential option for the poor. At the same time it is concretely through the poor that God reveals the universality of the divine love. This love is determined to embrace oppressors and liberate them from the situation of oppression by exposing the alienation and inhumanity of their deeds and calling them to turn away from their sin. The church as sacrament of God's love, at once universal and "preferential," must become the church of and for the poor.

Feminist theology. The feminist critique of language about God makes the important connection between the predominantly male imagery in Scripture, traditional theology, and liturgical piety and the social-political reality of patriarchy. Theologians such as R. Reuther, E. Johnson, E. Fiorenza, and A. Carr argue that male language about God in Scripture and tradition has often been used to legitimate the oppression of women. They point out the need to develop female images or symbols of God that are truly reflective of and adequate to Christian experience. "Forgotten" biblical images, God as mother and the female personification of God as Wisdom, have been retrieved. Even more important than particular images, none of which can adequately represent God, are the issues of inclusivity, mutuality, equality, and freedom, which must be the center of any truly Christian image of God. It is here on a more basic level that many feminist theologians urge us to turn to the experience of women and how it reveals God. Their voices, in turn, can stimulate the faith imagination of the whole community as it attempts to discern and to speak about God.

Carr has pointed out several themes, born of the experience of women, that have become prominent in recent feminist reflection on God and underlie such images of God as mother, sister, friend, partner, and lover. (1) *The liberating God,* who comes to reconcile and establish true human community in which all persons can take their rightful place as free and responsible agents. (2) *The incarnational, embodied God,* who in the flesh of Christ reveals that there is no ultimate dualism in the world (matter/spirit, body/mind, male/female) or between God and the world (transcendence/immanence, divine freedom/human freedom). (3) *The relational God,* whose liberating power is present and manifest not so much in discrete interventions as in and through human (cooperative) action. (4) *The suffering God,* who is really touched in some way by the plight of the oppressed and marginalized, who is one with them and whose solidarity offers hope and courage. (5) *The God who is future,* whose active presence in human history promises a future for women and all others who have been excluded in their struggle for dignity and freedom. (6) *The God who is Trinitarian mystery,* whose very being reveals that "mutuality, reciprocity, cooperation, unity and peace in genuine diversity" is the foundation and goal of all reality (Carr 148ff., here 157).

See also COMMON GOOD; COVENANT; CREATION; FEMINISM AND CATHOLIC SOCIAL THOUGHT; KINGDOM OF GOD; PERSON, DIGNITY OF; POLITICAL THEOLOGY; STEWARDSHIP.

Bibliography: J. Haughey, ed., *The Faith That Does Justice: Examining the Christian Sources for Social Change* (New York: Paulist, 1977). D. Hollenbach, *Claims in Conflict: Retrieving and Renewing the Catholic Human Rights Tradition* (New York: Paulist, 1979). D. Hollenbach, *Justice, Peace, and Human Rights: American Catholic Social Ethics in a Pluralistic Context* (New York: Crossroad, 1988). V. Araya, *God of the Poor: The Mystery of God in Latin American Liberation Theology,* including bibliography (Maryknoll, N.Y.: Orbis, 1983). R. Chopp, *The Praxis of Suffering: An Interpretation of Liberation and Political Theologies* (Maryknoll, N.Y.: Orbis, 1986). R. Haight, *An Alternative Vision: An Interpretation of Liberation Theology* (New York: Paulist, 1985). A. Carr, *Transforming Grace: Christian Tradition and Women's Experience,* including bibliography (San Francisco: Harper & Row, 1988). K. Tanner, *The Politics of God: Christian Theologies and Social Justice* (Minneapolis: Fortress, 1992).

JOHN R. SACHS, S.J.

GOODS, ACCESS TO

Access to goods and services by individuals, corporations, nations, and other economic units is achieved through a number of direct and indirect routes. In traditional economies the personal acquisition of consumption goods typically results directly from personal labor, for example, in traditional subsistence agriculture and handicrafts. In a market economy access to consumer goods can be realized directly through exchange, for example, of one good for another or of labor for consumer goods, and is therefore dependent upon access to markets for employment and for the purchase and sale of goods. Exchange is normally accomplished through the medium of money, and in modern economies access to goods and services depends upon the monetary value of wealth and incomes. In addition, access to money, for example, through credit, indirectly influences access to goods and services as do changes in the value of money itself. Access to goods and services is also made possible by financial transfers such as government subsidies, access to government expenditure programs, and private philanthropy.

Access to goods and services in the international economy depends not only on wealth and incomes but also on access to foreign currency, which is earned by the sale of export goods and services in international markets or obtained through foreign borrowing, direct foreign investment, and public and private foreign aid. Export earnings in turn depend upon access to foreign markets, prices in those markets relative to domestic costs, and the value of local currency relative to that of foreign currencies.

Wealth, income, access to credit, to markets, to financial transfers, and the value of money are in turn dependent upon a number of personal, historical, economic, social, political, and cultural determinants that influence ownership and control of property, especially of productive assets, as well as employment and investment opportunities, social status, political influence, and social policies and programs. All have been the subject of greater or lesser degrees of Catholic social teaching, and all are also determinants of poverty, understood as the lack of adequate access to goods and services.

Access to goods and services and the determinants of that access have been a concern of Western social thought dating to biblical tradition and Greek philosophy. Aristotle contrasted the legitimate exchange of goods and services based on their usefulness in meeting a hierarchy of personal needs against the unnatural and unconstrained market activity of the professional trader in pursuit of monetary surpluses that exceeded the limits of natural usefulness. Lycurgus, the legendary Spartan lawgiver, is said to have redressed economic inequalities in ancient Sparta by redistributing productive land and by substituting internationally worthless iron money for gold and silver in order to deprive the rich of the opportunity to import foreign luxuries. The Book of Leviticus describes measures to remove obstacles to the accessibility to goods by the poor—measures taken in a sabbatical year when all debts were to be forgiven and in a jubilee year when productive land was to be redistributed from the rich to the poor and indentured servants and slaves were to be freed. Modern Catholic social thought follows in the Western tradition of identifying and evaluating the structural and personal determinants of access (or the lack thereof) to goods and services and of furthering policies to redress obstacles to access in different economic systems.

It is difficult if not impossible to calculate useful absolute measurements of poverty, and Catholic social teaching has generally not tried to do so. A poverty level of income is dependent upon cultural, social, and regional differences as well as upon health, education, native talents, and other personal characteristics subsumed in the concept of human capital, along with household characteristics such as the number of wage earners and dependents. The incidence of poverty also varies by gender, race, and age as well as by occupational status. Although disparities in incomes and wealth in the most developed market-based economies have generally not reached levels sufficient to destabilize their economic systems, poverty continues to persist and to affect specific regions and social groups disproportionately. For developing areas of the world, the World Bank estimates that about one-third of the population, mostly in rural areas, live below poverty lines calculated for individual countries, and that the numbers of poor will remain stable in the developed countries while continuing to increase in Sub-Saharan Africa and to decrease significantly in Asia and slightly in Latin America.

In medieval Scholastic thought access to goods and services by all social groups was not something that had to be negotiated, bargained, or fought for. Economic activity for human sustenance in a traditional society could be considered an organic component of a well-organized society in which all members responsibly carried out their respective duties and in return were institutionally assured of access to sufficient goods and services for a dignified existence. By the time of the first papal social encyclical, *Rerum novarum,* the market economy and industrial capitalism had long since overwhelmed the possibilities of an economy functionally organized according to the criteria of medieval Scholasticism.

Catholic social teaching respects the principle of exchange of goods and services, including labor, and rejects socialist models of systemic nonmarket distribution as well as claims for absolute equality of access to goods and services. However, it has never accepted the marketplace as a sufficient determinant of just access to goods and services in a modern economy. Wages and prices set in the market, even when freely negotiated, are not automatically judged to be just wages and prices, since markets are neutral with respect to the motivations and basic human needs of their participants as well as to the sources and levels of profits, earned and unearned. In Catholic social thought individual self-interests are always subordinate to a common good. Moreover, capitalism as an ideology has been consistently criticized in papal documents when it treats labor as a commodity offered in exchange for access to goods and services through an income that is fixed by the market's evaluation of that labor. In Catholic social teaching access to the goods and services necessary for the sustenance of human dignity is a natural right that takes precedence over the terms of contracts determined by market forces. Wages and prices that determine access to goods and services in the marketplace are themselves subject to a higher law grounded in the dignity of the human person. In the earlier social encyclicals, for example, *Rerum novarum* of Leo XIII and *Quadragesimo anno* of Pius XI, that dignity was derived principally from natural-law reasoning about the intrinsic value of the human person, while the encyclicals of John Paul II, for example, *Laborem exercens,* utilize an interpretation of the Book of Genesis to further ground that dignity in the Christian doctrine of co-creation. Although the principle of co-creation adds a functional dimension of work to justify economic rights, the value of that work as a claim on goods and services derives from the value of the worker as subject, not from the value of the worker's labor as an object of market exchange.

Although Catholic social teaching, like its Scholastic antecedents, acknowledges a social responsibility to work and recommends social limits on consumption to express a spirit of poverty, it does not accept involuntary dehumanizing levels of poverty as a naturally defensible outcome of market-based economies. Instead it looks beyond market outcomes to the determinants of access to the goods and services traded in markets and supports public intervention in economic life to overcome structural deficiencies and normative limitations of market behavior in meeting human needs at both domestic and international levels.

At the level of national or domestic economies Catholic social teaching has stressed the economic rights of workers to employment and to a just or "living" wage and has supported the rights of workers to organize in order to press their claims on employers and policymakers. Catholic social teaching has supported social programs that increase the access of the poor to essential goods and services, especially those in the areas of nutrition, health care, and education, that increase human productivity and the possibilities for gainful participation in economic activity. At both national and international levels Catholic social teaching has urged a "preferential option for the poor" on the part of public and private sectors to redress existing imbalances in access to goods and services. At the level of the international economy Catholic social teaching, both in papal documents like *Populorum progressio* and *Sollicitudo rei socialis* and in regional documents like those issued by the synods at Medellín and Puebla and the U.S. Catholic bishops' pastoral letter, *Economic Justice for All,* has urged increased access to the markets of the more developed countries for the products of the less developed, especially products that are labor intensive, at prices that will allow the less developed countries to realize a substantial share of the gains from trade and improve their capacity to import while increasing employment and incomes.

While acknowledging potential contributions of foreign investment to employment and incomes of developing countries, Catholic social teaching has also been critical both of the destabilizing effects of mobile foreign capital on local markets for labor and final products and also of the diversion of local resources from production to meet basic local human needs. More recently the church has joined others in urging creditor banks, international institutions, and governments of more developed countries to renegotiate the terms of international debts of less developed countries in order to alleviate the disproportionate burden on the purchasing power of the poorest debtors and the poorest citizens of the debtor countries.

However, the social encyclicals have also consistently defended the right to private property, including ownership of productive capital. As a major source of personal security as well as of productive capital and of access to credit and social mobility, private property is a major determinant of access to goods and services in market-based economies. Market-based economies that have relatively wide dispersion of property ownership tend to have less disparity in incomes between the richest and the poorest. So it is not surprising that the right to private property has never been understood as absolute or unqualified in Catholic social teaching but has instead always been circumscribed by its subordination to the common good, which takes moral precedence over unconstrained individual self-interest.

Tension in the relationship between individual self-interest and the common good is reflected in shifts of emphasis from one to the other in Catholic social teaching about private property over the years. In *Rerum novarum,* for example, Leo XIII emphasizes the personal importance of private ownership of productive capital in response to the socialist challenge of the late 19th century, while in *Populorum progressio* Paul VI acknowledges the legitimacy of agrarian reform and nationalization of productive assets in the face of the extreme concentration of private domestic and foreign ownership of productive capital in many developing countries in the second half of the 20th century.

In short, Catholic social thought as expressed in official documents has sought criteria for access to the products of economic activity in a Christian understanding of the human person rather than in ideological or analytical economic models and systems. In so doing it has been critical of the workings of existing systems in meeting human needs and has directed attention to fundamental human objectives of economic life that are too easily overlooked in conventional analysis and ideological debate.

See also CREDIT; GOODS, DISTRIBUTION OF; GREED; INCOME; LABOR AND CAPITAL IN CATHOLIC SOCIAL THOUGHT; POOR, PREFERENTIAL OPTION FOR; POVERTY; WELFARE/WELFARE STATE.

Bibliography: J. Calvez and J. Perrin, *The Church and Social Justice* (Chicago: Henry Regnery, 1961). "Religion and the Economy: Theory, Practice, Vision," *Religion and Intellectual Life,* vol. 4, no. 1 (fall 1986).

ERNEST BARTELL, C.S.C.

GOODS, DISTRIBUTION OF

Because of its concern with distributive and social justice, Catholic social teaching on economic activity has concerned itself more with normative issues of distribution than with issues of production, growth, and efficiency. The historical, philosophical, and biblical sources of Catholic teaching on justice in economic activity have themselves focused on human rights and responsibilities in the use of goods and services, not on the technicalities of production. Economic distribution as a topic of analysis can include the apportionment of almost any human good including utility, pleasure, power, status, and freedom of choice. However, it most commonly refers to the distribution of income and wealth, and there are many intersections between the analysis of economic distribution in social science and the ethical criteria in Catholic social thought about the concentration of ownership of wealth and income, about economic equality, and about poverty.

Economists distinguish between the functional distribution of income and the size distribution of income. The functional distribution of income refers to the shares of income generated in an economy that accrue to those factors of production that are the source of the income-generating output. These are traditionally classified to include wages and salaries of employed labor, the dividends, interest, and rent that accrue to financial and real capital, and profits that reward entrepreneurship. The size distribution of income refers to the shares of total income accruing to economic units (e.g., individuals, families, and households) from all productive sources including wages, dividends, and interest on savings. It is this notion of distribution that is implicit in most Catholic social teaching on the subject. Although in traditional agrarian societies and in contemporary low-income economies most economic units depend on only one functional source of income, the relationship between the functional distribution of income and the size distribution of income in more developed modern economies is complicated by the fact that the same individuals or households are increasingly reliant on more than one source of income. The same household may receive income from wages and salaries, interest on savings, dividends on stock, payments from pension funds, mutual funds that invest in corporate securities and government bonds, rent from real property (including the imputed rent from owner-occupied dwellings), and transfer payments from government entities such as subsidized health care, education, housing, and food.

Moreover, as economic life becomes more complex traditional functional categories of the sources of income (e.g., employment and property) become less homogeneous and meaningful as distributional indicators of economic well-being. On the one hand, income from employment includes the hourly wages paid to casual labor as well as the seven-figure salaries paid to top management of major corporations. On the other hand, property income as conventionally defined and measured fails to include that portion of the income of the self-employed that is a return on personal capital, nor does property income include that portion of personal income that is really a return on investment in human capital, for example, through education and training that are increasingly required for various occupations.

As conventionally defined, the functional distribution of income in the major developed economies has been marked through this century by an increase in the share of income from employment with most of the increase attributed to salary rather than wage earnings, while the distribution of income by economic units, (i.e., individuals and households) remained relatively stable in most major developed countries, including the United States and Canada, from World War II until the 1970s, despite wide swings in government policies concerning taxes, transfer payments, regulation of financial markets, and social policies during that period. Between 1969 and 1985, however, the income share of the bottom 40 percent of families in the United States, according to one estimate, fell from 18 percent to 15.5 percent, its lowest level since the 1940s.

One's position in the relative distribution of income does not necessarily make one rich or poor, so there is a need for fixed measures that can serve as benchmarks of poverty. It should be noted, however, that it is difficult if not impossible to calculate useful absolute measurements of income or wealth that have univocal normative or ethical value. A poverty level of income, for example, is dependent upon cultural, social, and regional differences and standards as well as upon health, education, native talents, and other personal characteristics subsumed in the concept of human capital, along with household characteristics such as the number of dependents and wage earners. The size distribution of income among individuals and households also varies by gender, race, and age as well as by occupational status.

Nevertheless, different measures of "absolute poverty" (e.g., the U.S. Department of Labor's regional household estimates) have been used for different policy purposes. In the United States after allowance is made for social transfer payments, the poverty rate among households headed by men dropped from about one-third to about 7 percent between 1949 and 1979. The drop would have been even greater if it were not for the worsening inequality in the relative distribution of income during the last decade of the period. There is, however, at lower levels of income in the United States a disproportionate share of women, elderly, children, blacks, Hispanics, and single-parent households headed by women and the chronically unemployed. These categories also overlap, so that there is, for example, a relatively greater representation of elderly minority women among those living at poverty levels of income.

Internationally, during the first two decades after World War II growth rates in a number of developing countries, especially in Latin America and parts of Asia, were higher than in many of the most developed nations. However, since the 1970s the distribution of income by country has become more concentrated in favor of the richest nations of North America, Western Europe, and East Asia, while sub-Saharan Africa continues to lag further behind. Today, the richest fifth of the world's population has an average per capita income that is roughly fifty times higher than that of the poorest fifth of the world's inhabitants. It should also be noted that within many of the less developed countries, especially in Latin America, the distribution of both income and wealth is more concentrated than in the richest nations. The World Bank estimated in 1990 that roughly one-third of the population of the developing countries of the world, over one billion people, were living below the poverty lines it calculated for each of the developing countries based on national costs for nutrition and other basic and customary needs. However, it also estimates that only 3 percent of the total consumption of these countries would have to be transferred to the poor to lift them above the poverty line.

There are many competing theories in social science that attempt to explain the distribution of income that results from the production process in a given economy. None of them is satisfactory by itself, but together they do identify a wide range of determinants that influence both the functional and the size distribution of income.

In neoclassical economics there is still a tendency to emphasize the functional distribution of income and to impute a positive normative value to the shares of factor income that result from competitive market prices, for example, from wage rates for labor and interest rates on capital set in competitive markets. Within the strict assumptions of the neoclassical model of competitive free markets, each of the factors of production will be paid the value of its marginal product as determined in those markets. This means that increases in wage rates for a given labor force will result from increases in the productivity of labor and in the demand for labor. The same will be true for the price of capital. Moreover, equal pay for equal effort and skills will prevail at all levels of output, and the prices paid for goods and services will be no higher than the costs of production including competitively determined profits for the risk taking and services provided by entrepreneurs. Under these conditions it can be shown that productive resources in the economy will be fully and efficiently employed, economic growth will be maximized, and all the income generated in the economy will be distributed to the factors of production through the market price-mechanism, without need for direct intervention in the marketplace.

Catholic social thought has consistently rejected as the ultimate arbiter of a just income distribution this invisible hand of the market, which is indifferent to the motives, needs, and human characteristics of those who use it, depend on it, and influence its allocation of resources and distribution of income. There is economic analysis to support that rejection. Once it is acknowledged, for example, that wage rates and the prices of other factors of production vary, not only with effort and productivity but also with the simple fact of varying degrees of scarcity of the factor in the marketplace, the link between human endeavor and the ethical content of market-determined income distribution is weakened. Taxi drivers in New York earn more than taxi drivers in Calcutta, not because they are necessarily harder workers or better drivers but because labor is less abundant relative to opportunities for employment in New York than in Calcutta. The link between morality and market-determined functional shares of income is further weakened by the fact that the assumptions required for the efficiency of the neoclassical model are not realized in the real world of uncertainty, unemployment, unequal access to market information, speculative profits, unearned rents, monopoly practices, union negotiations, geographic and institutional barriers to factor mobility, and other market imperfections.

The macroeconomic concepts of aggregate investment, consumption, and savings in Keynesian and post-Keynesian analyses that are used to explain the persistence of unemployment also call attention to the importance of factor shares of income distribution to economic growth and to the composition of economic output. With a given level of savings in an economy, according to a representative macroeconomic argument, an increase in investment spending on capital goods by entrepreneurs will bid resources away from production of consumer goods by raising prices, thereby lowering the purchasing power of wages and salaries. However, the reduced effective demand by consumers resulting from the inflationary bite from workers' incomes will subsequently have a depressing effect on the economy through lower spending on consumption goods, unless prices of final products and wages adjust to productivity gains from the new investment in such a way as to restore effective demand through increased consumer buying power among workers. In other words, when macroeconomic considerations are introduced, income distribution is no longer simply the passive result of production in a particular economic system but instead emerges as an important determinant of the level of production itself.

Moreover, income distribution influences the composition of output and hence of employment opportunities. The experience of developing countries has demonstrated that countries with relatively equal shares of income among economic units will tend to devote a larger share of their resources to the production of goods to meet basic needs, while countries with a highly skewed distribution of income will tend to allocate a relatively larger share of resources to the production and import of luxury goods. In light of interrelationships like these it has been argued that capital as a factor of production cannot be meaningfully measured apart from market prices that are the result of the distribution of income, so that it becomes circular to claim that the functional distribution of income by factor shares (e.g., of capital and labor) is determined passively by market forces.

The analysis of income distribution can be expanded still further by the introduction of institutional, political, and social practices and customs of a given society that affect the concentration of ownership and control of productive resources, influence the legislation and administration of tax and expenditure policies, and determine access to information, contracts, jobs, and credit. Under these circumstances, income distribution can be analyzed as the result of investment and other spending decisions that are themselves products of much more than competitive market forces. Moreover, these decisions determine the quantity and composition of goods produced and therefore help determine the prices of those goods, which often include noncompetitive markups that further distance the distribution of income from the neoclassical model.

Classical Marxist analysis emphasizes the conflict between social classes, namely, between workers and capitalists, as a primary determinant of income distribution. However, in the more developed countries of the world workers increasingly benefit from property income, for example, through pension-fund investments, and from social programs like social security and health insurance funded by tax revenues, while massive amounts of corporate capital are increasingly controlled by salaried corporate executives rather than by stockholders. A link between social class and income distribution may, however, still be significant in developing countries marked by traditional patterns of ownership of land and other productive resources, including access to financial capital.

Dependency theories of development have attempted to explain the persistent and growing income inequalities among nations through analysis of structural characteristics of the international markets as well as through class analysis. There is, for example, some statistical evidence to suggest that the prices received by many developing countries for their traditional exports (e.g., agricultural products and minerals) to developed countries are not only unstable but also fail to keep pace with the prices of imports of manufactured goods from the developed countries. This may be due to the fact that primary products (with the notorious exceptions of oil and diamonds) are typically sold in competitive markets, while manufactured products are sold at administered prices in imperfectly competitive markets. Under such circumstances improvements in the productivity of labor in poor countries that export mostly primary products will be passed on to buyers in the form of lower product prices, while productivity gains in the manufacture of industrial goods that are administratively priced can be retained in the form of higher wages and profits. As a result, developing countries fail to capture their potential share of the gains from international trade.

It is also argued that dependency is reinforced by global profit-maximizing behavior of transnational corporations upon whom less developed nations depend for investment capital, access to foreign markets, modern technology, and employment opportunities as well as expertise and training in management and marketing. Mobile international capital, however, is apt to move with some volatility throughout the international market economy without offering significant local access to modern technology, seeking countries with the cheapest labor, the lowest taxes, and the best opportunities for quick repatriation of locally generated profits. The international mobility of capital presumably also makes it easier for transnational corporations to demand costly concessions from host countries, which are often enhanced through bribery and collusion with local business elites. Foreign capital seeks political stability and high rates of return to compensate for perceived political risks. It is thus vulnerable to the support of authoritarian regimes prone to violations of human rights and repression of economic and political participation by the poor.

The success of the newly industrialized nations of southeast Asia through export production by foreign firms plus the international debt crisis of the 1980s, which has brought direct foreign investment to a near halt in most debtor countries, have challenged if not overwhelmed traditional dependency analysis of international income distribution. As annual debt-service payments of Latin American debtor countries has made that region a net exporter of capital, the structural dependency that was the subject of criticism in the social encyclicals of Paul VI, in the documents of Medellín and Puebla, and in the writings of liberation theologians has been eclipsed by the financial dependency of the debtor nations in the 1980s and 1990s.

The complex interrelationships among the determinants of both functional and size distribution of income, both domestically and internationally, create space for the application of a variety of normative criteria by which to judge and alter the distribution of income and wealth. Some of the criteria refer to the functional implications of relative measures of income distribution, for example, the tension between income and growth, while others are grounded in religious and philosophic premises, for example, criteria in Catholic social teaching for a living wage and for the "preferential option for the poor" grounded in biblical interpretations and natural-law reasoning about the human person.

A relatively unequal size distribution of income is justified functionally by the incentives that the prospect of higher incomes create for human effort and risk-taking entrepreneurship. However, it is not clear how much income is needed to elicit effort and entrepreneurship. Salaries of top executives in Japan, for example, are not nearly as high a multiple of average wage rates as they are in the United States. Moreover, economic incentives are not the only ones that elicit effort, and it may be argued that a dominant reliance upon economic incentives is as much a reflection of materialistic cultural values as of natural human characteristics.

Inequality in the distribution of income is further justified as a prerequisite for high rates of economic growth by arguing, much as classical economists did, that it is the rich who will generate the high rates of saving and investment that are necessary for high rates of economic growth. It is further argued that the benefits of high growth will trickle down to the poor through the markets in the form of higher wages and employment and will reduce poverty in a much less conflictive way than redistribution through taxes and transfers, land reform, and other forms of government intervention in the economy that are perceived to be deterrents to growth and elements of a zero-sum game of winners and losers.

Critics point out that the incomes of the rich, especially in developing countries, are often squandered on luxury consumer imports, financial and land speculation, and capital flight, none of which generate productive domestic investment, growth, and trickle-down effects. On the contrary, it will be argued that poverty simply breeds poverty through poor nutrition, health care, and education. A direct infusion of investment in human capital through social expenditures on health, nutrition, and education as well as investment in productive physical infrastructure—along with increased access to ownership and control of productive assets through employee stock-ownership programs, land reform, credit programs for small and informal sector businesses, and other policies favoring broader participation—will stimulate growth and higher incomes for the poor through increases in labor productivity and will strengthen the political and social stability that are prerequisites for private investment.

The methods used to finance infrastructure, social programs, and other redistributive policies can themselves influence the resulting redistribution. Deficit financing of public expenditures, for example, is likely to be inflationary as more money chases the same goods, and the resulting inflation can erode the purchasing power of the money incomes of the very people the social expenditures are designed to help. Public borrowing to finance social expenditures may redistribute the burden of those expenditures through the accumulation of domestic and foreign debt to a future generation of taxpayers, although if the social expenditures reduce future expenses to society or increase future productivity of labor and other resources, the future redistributive tax burden may in principle be offset.

At the international level policies favoring free trade will tend to reward the most efficient producers and the consumers of their products but may impose harsh costs of adjustment on those displaced by enlarged competition. Thus highly paid workers with ethically desirable working conditions in previously protected markets of developed countries may suffer the cost of redistribution to less developed regions with low wages, poor working conditions, and high unemployment, making difficult the ethical evaluation of an ongoing and frequently unstable process. Since many of the policy alternatives affecting distribution at both domestic and international levels need not be mutually exclusive, public policies for distribution face the challenge of incorporating the appropriate mix of tax, transfer, and spending programs, in order, for example, to balance social programs financed by taxation of incomes and wealth with the stimulation of market incentives for savings, productive investment, and entrepreneurship within the political, economic, social, and cultural framework of a given society.

In addition to functional criteria, other normative premises have been introduced into the analysis of equity or justice in income distribution. Rationalist criteria have been used either to justify in terms of individual self-interest the maximization of the income of the worst-off member of society or to justify an option for equality in the distribution of income under certain specific assumptions about ignorance, uncertainty, and the diminishing marginal utility of income. Catholic social teaching in papal and episcopal documents has concerned itself both with the relative inequality of incomes and wealth within and among nations and with absolute shares of goods and services available to specific groups in society, especially workers, heads of households, and the very poor among individuals, households, and nations. In so doing the church has also rejected both the primacy of self-interest and absolute equality in distribution as norms and has not generally prescribed specific measures for acceptable absolute or relative shares of income. Nor has it relied upon either functional arguments for growth and efficiency or rational arguments of self-interest to define the criteria for an ethically acceptable, that is, just, distribution of income.

In earlier papal documents such as *Rerum novarum* of Leo XIII and *Quadragesimo anno* of Pius XI, the claims of distributive justice on behalf of specific groups arise principally from a shared humanity in the tradition of Scholastic natural law. More recent papal social encyclicals, especially those of John Paul II, rely more heavily on biblical arguments. *Laborem exercens,* for example, utilizes an interpretation of the Book of Genesis to justify the distributive rights of workers, not on the objective value of their services in the market, but on their subjective roles as co-creators of the material universe. In addition, more recent papal documents, for example, *Populorum progressio* of Paul VI, as well as episcopal documents like *Economic Justice for All* of the U.S. bishops and the documents issued by the Latin American bishops at Medellín and Puebla, draw upon the social sciences to illustrate and explain distributional injustices in both domestic and international economies.

Whether the argumentation is philosophic, scriptural, or empirical, the criteria for justice in distribution within Catholic social teaching consistently include a communal or collective dimension that transcends the individual and serves as both limit and incentive for individual behavior. Expressed in Catholic social teaching on the common good and on solidarity, it is this transcendent, shared reality that especially distinguishes the criteria for distributional justice in Catholic social thought from those in rational analyses of economic justice based on individual self-interest, as maximized in the marketplace or realized through some other individualistic calculus. Consequently, it is not surprising that Catholic social thought has consistently defended a role for governments in the implementation of criteria for justice in economic distribution. The extent of that role in the social documents of the church has varied with changes in methodological approaches, historical situations, and regional differences throughout the history of Catholic social teaching.

Nevertheless, despite the heavy emphasis on the social dimension of justice in distribution, papal documents have consistently rejected socialist systems of intervention in economic life as models for the development and application of criteria for economic distribution. In the earlier papal documents the rejection was based heavily on the atheistic roots of Marxism. In the writings of John Paul II the rejection is also grounded heavily on the repression of human freedom as well as the bureaucratic inefficiencies and corruption that have accompanied the implementation of socialist models in practice. Structural analysis of international dependency in the documents of Medellín and Puebla and class analysis of domestic imbalances in the ownership and control of land and other productive resources in the writings of some Latin American liberation theologians have pointed toward socialist solutions among others. The social documents of the church, however, have been consistent in rejecting violent class struggle as a solution to distributional inequities and careful to avoid endorsement of state-dominated systemic socialist solutions. At the same time, there has never been a clear evolution of a "third way" to distributional justice between classical capitalism and classical socialism in Catholic social teaching. The recent documents mentioned above have tended to support reformist policies rather than systemic solutions to redress distributional injustices, and in that sense they have anticipated the delinking of specific policies from ideological systems that has accompanied recent transitions to democracy from authoritarian regimes of both the Right and the Left in Latin America and Eastern Europe.

See also CAPITALISM; COMMON GOOD; COMPETITION; GOODS, ACCESS TO; GREED; JUST WAGE; LABOR AND CAPITAL IN CATHOLIC SOCIAL THOUGHT; POVERTY.

Bibliography: Y. Brenner et al., eds., *The Theory of Income and Wealth Distribution* (New York: St. Martin's Press, 1988). D. Byers, ed., *Justice in the Marketplace* (Washington: USCC, 1985). P. Davidson and J. Kregel, eds., *Macroeconomic Problems and Policies of Income Distribution: Functional, Personal, International* (Brookfield, Vt.: Gower, 1989). G. Gutiérrez, *A Theology of Liberation: History, Politics, and Salvation*, trans. and ed. by C. Inda and J. Eagleson (Maryknoll, N.Y.: Orbis, 1988). J. Rawls, *A Theory of Justice* (Cambridge: Belknap, 1971). The World Bank, *World Development Report, 1990: Poverty* (New York: Oxford Univ. Press, 1990). O. Williams, and J. Houck, eds., *The Common Good and U.S. Capitalism* (Lanham, Md.: Univ. Press of America, 1987).

ERNEST BARTELL, C.S.C.

GRACE

The Western Christian doctrine of grace, both Roman Catholic and Protestant, has been molded in the fires of controversy. The polemics of the 5th and 16th centuries favored Paul over the Synoptics and John and tragically obscured at times the rich understandings of grace in the OT. Thanks to the ecumenical openness of Vatican II, Catholic theologians of the West have come to appreciate the riches of the Eastern churches' more Johannine sense of divinizing grace, just as liberationist concerns have led to a new exploitation of Synoptic themes of grace as they bear on emancipation from oppressive situations and the furthering of God's reign. In this article particular attention is given to the social dimensions of God's grace.

Scripture

In the OT the fidelity (*'emet*), loving kindness (*hesed*), and gracious favor (the verb *hanan*) of God as the initiating covenant partner with Israel provide, together with the divine righteousness (*sedakah*), the most reliable basis for that people's personal and social existence. If only Israel will trust God's commitment to the people and, when failing to trust it, return repentantly to the God who singled out this people for very special favor, then God's people will flourish in the land and become a "light for the nations" (Isa 42:6). God's grace as sovereign, freely bestowed blessing, presence, and protection is extended to individuals (e.g., David), groups of people (e.g., orphans and widows, the remnant), and to all of Israel. Often enough the favor extended to individuals is favor that will redound to the well-being of the people (e.g., kings and prophets). "Grace" as a noun is not the focus of attention, however, but rather the creator-God's full involvement in the history of Israel, expressed by a range of attributes. But the call to Israel to bless its God, which runs through the OT, especially in the Psalms, amounts to a call to recount thankfully the story of God's saving dealings with God's people, signalized by the Exodus drama and the gifts of Law and Prophets. Israel's commonweal is epitomized in its freely thanking God for those things God has freely done for Israel. Here grace meets grace.

In the Synoptic Gospels the primary image of God's favor and freely loving commitment to the people is the kingdom or reign of God. By proclamation of that reign, evocative portrayal of its gracious world in parables, and healing deeds of power, Jesus expresses the already-present character of that reign, while his fateful conflict with antagonists and the persistent web of human poverty and oppression signal that God's reign in its full, public actualization is still to come. On his own initiative Jesus gathers disciples about him (e.g., Lk 5:10), the beginning of a new, eschatological people, and sends them forth to share in his ministry. This and all his initiatives of grace appear to be overwhelmed by the forces of evil on the cross. But God uses apparent defeat to fashion a new presence of Jesus as grace in human history, one that evil can never expunge.

John's Gospel emphasizes the gift of God in Jesus as eternal life (Jn 5:24), as truth that sets free (Jn 8:32), as love like Jesus' (Jn 15:20), and, finally, as "glorification," that is, the paradoxical revelation of God's saving power in the lifting up of Jesus on the victorious cross (Jn 17:1-5). As the drama of sign and glory unfolds, people's reception or rejection of God's life and truth and love fatefully divides them into those who belong to Jesus by faith ("my disciples") and those who reject him ("the world").

The primary focus for Paul is the saving act of God in Jesus' crucifixion and resurrection. This act breaks down the division between Jew and Gentile: in Christ, the last Adam, divine favor exists for both groups in equal abundance and with equal access. God's act in Christ means that the Spirit has been poured forth into the hearts of those who have been justified (Rom 5:5) and are being sanctified and are on their way to definitive salvation when Christ returns (Rom 6:22). Those who believe and are baptized belong to the household of faith (Gal 6:10) as adopted children (Gal 4:5) and belong as well to the sphere of Christ and the Spirit (1 Cor 2:12), while those who remain in their sin belong to the sphere of the "flesh," the old aeon (Gal 1:4). In his arguments with Judaizers in Galatia (those who insist that Gentiles must become Christians by first becoming Jews) Paul stresses the already-now character of God's grace in Christ. When correcting the charismatic enthusiasts of Corinth he accentuates the not-yet-definitive nature of their justification and sanctification. But underlying all these particular tactical moves, Paul, in deep continuity with the ministry of Jesus, proclaims the complete abundance of grace for all who open themselves to it (Rom 6:20), the sovereign freedom of the God who shares this grace in the bestowal of the promised Spirit (Rom 6:23), and the thoroughly inclusive nature of this grace (Gal 3:27-28). The only "outsiders" are those who close themselves to the gift. All are called to be "insiders." In Paul's view (consonant with the rest of Scripture) God's grace is both personal and social, internal and public.

History of Theology

The tension between personal grace and social grace was exhibited in Augustine, probably the single most influential figure in the development of the Western understanding of grace. While the author of the *Confessions* highlights the personal journey of conversion undergone by an individual, the Augustine of *The City of God* dwells on the intimate dependence of God's city on true worship for its common good. Yet even Augustine's explorations of personal grace accentuate its strengthening of the inner core of a person in a world that is in imminent danger of collapse, and this social-historical concern is as important as the dispute with Pelagius for understanding Augustine's theological concerns. It has been argued that Augustine's preoccupation with original sin and the need for internal, justifying grace in his dispute with Pelagius meant that he failed to do justice to an insight dear to Pelagius that grace is structural and external (as well as personal and internal). However, Augustine's rich sensitivity to the sacramental nature of Christian life needs to be kept in mind in this regard.

Thomas Aquinas contributed to the developing doctrine by reflecting even more than did Augustine on the intrinsic reality of "nature," or creaturely reality, as it is transformed by grace. He recognized that God's involvement with creatures as source of grace consists not only of the communication of the divine Gift, the Holy Spirit, but also of the transformation of the inner structure of nature. According to Thomas, human nature naturally desires that communication and transformation, even though they strictly transcend the powers of the creature (a paradoxical conception that later neo-Scholastic thought will not be able to sustain). With the help of Aristotle but with immeasurably deeper debt to the NT and Augustine, he organized his treatise on the *one* grace of God in Christ by distinguishing (but not separating) the indwelling of the Holy Spirit and created grace; the elevating (divinizing) and healing functions of grace; its operative, cooperative, and "free" (charismatic) dimensions; grace as habit and act; grace as prevenient and subsequent; and, finally, the phases of grace: justification, sanctification, and beatification. Thomas' most social consideration of grace appears in his treatment of the grace of headship, which is proper to Jesus Christ as source of life of his body, the church. Here personal grace and "capital," or social grace (grace shared with others), are not distinct (ST III, q. 8, a. 5). A second major resource for a social theology is Thomas' elaboration of the notion of habit, since a social structure consists of the pattern of human interactions fashioned by the interlocking of habitual assumptions, attitudes, and behaviors (ST Ia-IIae, qq. 49–54; 110–11). Roles in groups and institutions are a primary example of such habituated behavior and perception. Thomas' analysis of habitual grace (and vice) offers perspectives for an exploration of the ultimate horizon and pervasive deep-structure of any institution or group: the habit of grace or of sin that constitutes the moral quality of any "social construction."

Because of the disintegration of social structures in the 16th century, the Reformers lost from view the communal and relational horizon that tacitly framed Aquinas' explorations of grace and favored a more individual understanding of grace: the church is the community of the saved, not the community that communicates justifying grace through one's entrance into it. Furthermore, in a widespread dualistic interpretation of Luther's doctrine of the two kingdoms, civil society is viewed as the place of law and works and not the place of faith and grace.

Official Catholic Social Teaching

The explicit notion of grace does not loom large in the hundred-year-old tradition of the official church's social teaching, even less the notion of social or structural grace. Because of the primary focus on this-worldly human relationships and the desire to appeal to all people of good will in papal encyclicals, the Catholic understanding of the created order, its origin, progress, and destination hold pride of place. The dignity of the human person created in the image of God; the intrinsic value of the creative labor of human beings; the primacy of the common good, which in turn fosters the only authentic personal good; attention to the "signs of the times"; the stewardship relationship of humankind to all created goods; the essential contribution authentic human achievements make to the fashioning of the "new heaven and new earth" despite the transitory character within history of even the best of those achievements; the eternal goal of human life as ultimate horizon that illuminates and orders all human activity—all these constantly recurring themes and more led the authors of official Catholic social teaching from *Rerum novarum* (*On the Condition of Workers,* 1891) to *Sollicitudo rei socialis* (*On Social Concern,* 1987) to stress the so-called acquired virtues of prudence, justice, fortitude, and temperance while not denying the yet-more-fundamental infused virtues of faith, love, and hope. These latter supernatural or "theologal" (i.e., God-oriented) virtues are seen as enfleshed in day-to-day life in acts of restraint, of courage, of the righting of crooked relationships, and of wise deployment of means (industry and technology) in the light of human-friendly ends (values).

Insofar as the social teaching is aimed at identifying and urging the correction of grave and widespread social injustice, the kind of grace that is implicitly appealed to is healing and cooperative grace, for what the world desperately needs is the grace and labor of reconciliation. That reconciliation can take the form of a new and more just distribution of the earth's goods and the fruits of human industry, fresh risks for peace to offset the daily risks of war so cavalierly engaged in, and at the root of these moves the conversion of hearts that their owners might hunger for this new order and risk themselves for this new peace. The more regional yet internationally significant teachings of the Latin American bishops at Medellín (1968) and Puebla (1979) and the U.S. bishops writing on war and peace (1983) and economic justice (1986) offer eloquent testimony that grace consists essentially in righteousness or justice, in the sense of right, life-giving relationship, and that a primary way of knowing God, the Ultimate Grace, consists in doing justice and thus fostering grace in our world.

The most explicit appeal to the structural dimensions of grace and sin are to be found in Pope John Paul II's encyclical *On Social Concern* in which he writes about a world divided into two blocs as "subject to structures of sin" (SRS 36); he contrasts this with a world of healthy interdependence and solidarity (ibid.). He points out that these structures are rooted in, and consolidated by, the personal sins of individual people. On an earlier occasion John Paul II had spoken of sinful situations and social sin while admitting that structures and situations are not the subjects of moral acts, and therefore cannot be formally good or bad (apostolic exhortation *Reconciliation and Penance,* 1984). The two primary evils signalized in *On Social Concern* are the all-consuming desire for profits and the thirst for power with the intention of imposing one's will on another. In each case a destructive absolutizing of relative goods (profits, power) comes into play. The positive call involves patient and courageous steps in favor of the common good, or as it is phrased in Pope Paul VI's 1967 encyclical *Populorum progressio* (*On the Development of Peoples*), the integral development of the whole individual and of all people (PP 42). John Paul II sees the opposite of structural sin residing in interdependence as a moral category and solidarity as a moral virtue and a moral attitude. Presupposing the help of divine grace, people can overcome structural sin only by diametrically opposed attitudes and behavior: for example, the poor becoming united, learning to support each other, and publicly demonstrating in nonviolent ways for their rights (SRS 39). Many points of contact exist between solidarity as a Christian virtue and charity, especially when in the light of faith solidarity seeks to go beyond itself in total gratuity, forgiveness, and reconciliation. Solidarity has its most profound source in the communion of the Trinity, which comes to expression in the communion that is the soul of the church's vocation to be a sacrament (40). While not using the expression "social grace," the present pontiff comes closest to it of all papal social teachers in the way he speaks of solidarity as a virtue rooted in the recognition of the interdependence of individuals and nations. Among the practical guidelines are the church's traditional doctrine of the preferential option for the poor (42), and the reform of the major international social structures such as the international trade system and the world monetary and financial system (43).

Contemporary Catholic Theology

Grace formally refers to the utterly free self-bestowal of the transcendent God on humankind and to that gift's transformation of the freedom of individuals and groups of individuals. Thus structures and situations cannot be called grace in the formal and primary sense. Persons are the formally graced ones in human history, just as only persons formally sin. However, situations and structures are grace insofar as they express in spatiotemporal terms the presence of grace or to the extent that they help maintain, protect, and foster the free cooperation of people with God's gracious action in history. The primary situation or structure of grace (social grace) in history is the church as the creation of the Holy Spirit and the indefectible sign of the victorious death and resurrection of Jesus Christ. The preaching of the Word and the communal worship events called "sacraments" are particular social graces par excellence. Families of faith and love are social grace for those who belong to them. Those who struggle in faith, love, and hope for social justice, who combat in nondestructive ways the racism, sexism, classism, and imperialism of our world are in their witness social grace for others, putting them in a place of decision by challenging them to social conversion.

Liberationist theologies of the Third World have urged an integral liberation of humankind involving (1) sufficient economic well-being to support human dignity, (2) the transformation of consciousness (conscientization) that allows oppressed people painfully but effectively to become agents of their own history and oppressors to be converted to a solidarity with the oppressed, and (3) the forgiveness of sin and participation in divine life (G. Gutiérrez). While distinguishable, these dimensions of human liberation are as interrelated as are body, psyche, and spirit in human beings. The experience of divine grace as elevating provides the assurance that it is *ultimately* safe to change longstanding structures of human interconnection when they are oppressive and to suffer the persecution of the defenders of those structures. Nothing we can do, nothing that happens to us, will cause our God to desert us, for the divine life is our home and infinite protective "boundary"; the grace of forgiveness we have received empowers us to seek, in the struggle for social justice, not triumph but reconciliation. When supported and nourished by hopeful love, our prudence (strategic savvy), justice (disposition to *do* the right thing), fortitude (inner strength for the struggle), and temperance (feel for how "small can be good") are genuinely social virtues (ST Ia-IIae, q. 61, a. 5) and expressions of social grace. In contemporary terms, *communicades de base,* twelve-step programs, and groups of women helping one another name their experience and relate to oppressive structures in their lives are significant instances of local social grace, grace in the form of "group life."

Indeed, one promising area for continuing theological reflection on social grace concerns the roles it can play in institutional and group dynamics. Some of the paradoxes inherent in group life (e.g., the fact that members must risk trusting one another in order to find out whether the group is trustworthy) and the profound ambivalence at work, consciously or unconsciously, in social situations (namely, the desire to belong to a reality larger than self and the fear of annihilation on the one hand, and the desire to be autonomous and the terror of possible abandonment on the other) connect with the two fundamental dimensions of grace as divinizing and forgiving. For the gift of the Holy Spirit ("one Person in many persons": Heribert Mühlen) provides both infinite home for and blessing on our restored uniqueness while simultaneously opening us in self-transcendent love to our neighbors in need.

See also AUGUSTINE, INFLUENCE OF; COVENANT; CREATION; EVIL, SOCIAL; HOPE; LOVE; SIN; THOMAS AQUINAS, CONTRIBUTION OF.

Bibliography: L. Boff, *Liberating Grace,* trans. J. Drury (Maryknoll, N.Y.: Orbis, 1979). T. Clarke, ed., *Above Every Name: The Lordship of Christ and Social Systems* (Ramsey, N.J.: Paulist, 1980). R. Haight, *The Experience and Language of Grace* (New York/Ramsey/Toronto: Paulist, 1979). J.-M. Laporte, *Patience and Power: Grace for the First World* (New York/Mahwah: Paulist, 1988). E. Schillebeeckx, *Christ: The Experience of Jesus as Lord,* trans. J. Bowden (New York: Seabury, 1980). K. Smith and D. Berg, *Paradoxes of Group Life: Understanding Conflict, Paralysis, and Movement in Group Dynamics* (San Francisco/London: Jossey-Bass, 1987).

BRIAN O. McDERMOTT, S.J.

GREED

Greed in the sense of an intense selfish desire for money and material goods is virtually synonymous with the classical capital sin of avarice and as such is consistently condemned in Catholic social thought as a motivating force for economic behavior. Greed is sometimes identified with the pursuit of self-interest in general and of economic profits in particular that drive the free-market model of economic activity. It is true that neoclassical models of economic efficiency and growth are built on the assumption that individual economic actors have material desires that exceed their resources to satisfy them and that rational behavior in these circumstances will strive to maximize returns from those resources.

Self-interest need not be either unreasonable or unlimited and can be constrained voluntarily by a hierarchy of personal values and socially by structures and institutions that place greater priority on social values than on unrestrained personal interests. Catholic social thought respects individual human freedom and the legitimacy of free-market behavior, but it has never accepted the marketplace as a sufficient determinant of social justice, since markets are indifferent to the motivations and values of their participants as well as to the sources and levels of profits, earned and unearned. Consequently, in Catholic social thought the common good has always taken precedence over unreasonable individual self-interest.

See also COMMON GOOD; GOODS, ACCESS TO; GOODS, DISTRIBUTION OF; PROFIT; SIN.

ERNEST BARTELL, C.S.C.

H

HEALTH CARE

Catholic social teaching has traditionally understood health care as a fundamental human good. Such goods are so fundamentally related to human dignity, that is, so essential to the flourishing of the human person and the community, that their presence or absence enhances or diminishes a host of other goods important for individual and community. Therefore, Catholic teaching claims that persons have a basic right to health care. "Every person has a basic right to adequate health care which flows from the sanctity of life and the dignity of human persons" ("The Right to Health Care"). This right to health care is classed among the social and economic rights of persons: "the rights to life, food, clothing, shelter, rest, medical care, and basic education" (*Economic Justice for All* 80), distinguished from civil and political rights such as freedom of speech, worship, assembly.

This traditional approach establishes some essential insights into the nature and importance of health care. For example, it rejects as unjust a system—such as that of the United States—where substantial numbers of residents are denied access to basic health care. But this traditional approach needs to be amplified to further delineate the contours of a just health-care system. The virtual explosion of health care's evolution since the turn of the century demands a fuller development of other principles present in Catholic teaching to assist modern societies in fashioning and maintaining a health-care system that serves human dignity in its individual and in its community dimensions.

Individual/Common Good

Solidarism is equally opposed to individualism and collectivism. In principle, individualism subordinates the community to individual good, and collectivism absorbs the individual into the good of society. Solidarism insists that there is a mutuality and ongoing tension in the relationship between individual and society. Neither individual nor society is primary and superordinate to the other in all respects. The dignity of the individual demands that the common good of society flow back upon it and even transcend the social whole in many respects. But in other respects the person as individual, or part, remains inferior and subordinated to the whole and must serve the common good.

In defining health care no single perspective—neither the communal nor the individual—can be decisive on all issues. For example, we cannot subordinate the individual's right to refuse participation in experimental procedures to society's interest in medical progress. But in devising public policy for a nation's health care the perspective of the common good must be the determining factor, and this will inevitably demand the sacrifice of some individual needs (Callahan, pp. 103–34). Only appropriate examination of specific issues can determine which perspective deserves priority. In cultures such as the United States, where the individual perspective tends to dominate all analyses, special care is needed to give the perspective of the common good its due weight.

Beneficence: Love Within Limits

Powerful forces drive modern health care to an ever-increasing consumption of resources. This thrust to consumption represents a synergy of factors, for example, health care's growing identification with technology and the technological imperative; the emphasis on freedom of choice by providers and consumers with its aversion to control; the escalating expectations concerning quality and quantity of care; the presence of extensive market and profit opportunities; the growing population of elderly and their extensive need for care.

To this powerful dynamic for increasing consumption Catholic teaching brings the message of restraint and limits. "We experience ourselves as creatures subject in many ways to limits. . . . We must repeatedly and unavoidably make choices from the many possibilities that call to us—choosing this option and foregoing those other options" (*Gaudium et spes* 10). Because health care is so inequitably distributed within many nations and around the globe, the effort to expand access to basic health care can become the dominant and exclusive theme of health-care reform. The expansion of universal access to basic care warrants priority. But Catholic teaching insists that this effort to expand health care by realizing equitable access go hand in hand with effective restraint on health care's expansive dynamic. The urgent imperative to correct injustices in allocation should not become an ally of the expansionist tendency of modern health care.

The commandment of beneficence stands at the heart of Christian morality. Beneficence is always the realization of love in a world of limits. As finite beings we can only grasp limited possibilities to serve our neighbor's good. We cannot effectively serve all the interests of an unlimited number of persons (Schüller, p. 70). Given the tendency of health care to resist the reality and consciousness of limits, it is especially important to recognize an underlying characteristic of beneficence: making hard choices in a world of limits.

Due Proportion

Two levels of proportion are important in fashioning public policy concerning health care: the level of macroallocation and the level of microallocation.

The *macroallocation process* strives to determine what proportion of community resources should be reasonably expended on health care relative to other basic elements of the common good, for example, housing, employment, transportation, environment, international relations, infrastructure, art and culture, and national defense. Each of these basic needs sets necessary limits to the others. Health care's share of resources and the rate at which it may justly escalate are rightly constrained by the limits of overall resources available for the common good and the demands of other basic needs such as education, housing, and defense. At this level of allocation it is important to recognize that many societal goods not immediately associated with health care (standard of living, education, employment, housing) ultimately contribute more to the community's health than do direct health-care services.

The *microallocation process* strives to take the resources determined by the macroallocation process and achieve their reasonable and balanced distribution across the quasi-infinite health needs of the community. The needs that must be balanced on this micro level of allocation can be thought of in a number of ways, for example, in terms of populations: age, gender, socioeconomic groups, and ethnic groups; as well as in terms of modalities of treatment: promotion, prevention, education, acute, emergency, long term, home, institutional, mental, medical, and social.

The goal of this two-layered process is (1) on the macro level a *well-rounded society* where health care takes its proportionate place among the other services required by the common good and (2) on the micro level a *well-rounded health-care system* where various publics and services receive their proportionate amount of resources. Applying this principle of due proportion will always leave needs unmet—at the macro and the micro level—because of our situation as limited creatures. A consistent challenge will be to distinguish the unmet needs calling for reform—those arising from factors such as injustice or inefficiency—from the unmet needs calling for acceptance—those arising from the human condition of limits. The determination of reasonable proportion on both the macro and the micro levels will remain a never-ending responsibility for a society and a challenge that demands more specific principles and extensive social and political systems and processes.

Advocacy for Societal Change

Health-care professionals and institutions tend to focus their awareness and resources on direct service to individual need. Such direct service with its demands for excellence, compassion, and response to the full range of human need beyond the merely physical will remain central to the health-care mission. But Catholic teaching calls health-care professionals and institutions to a vision and program of action beyond this horizon of aid to individuals; it demands a service to deficiencies in the systems and structures of society's health-care practice. In large and complex societies it is the systems themselves more than the behavior of individuals that account for widespread, patterned justice or injustice. Health-care professionals and organizations are called to public policy advocacy concerning the issues of macro and micro allocation elaborated above. "Our service efforts cannot substitute for just and compassionate public policies. . . . The pursuit of economic justice takes believers into the public arena. . . . We are called to . . . conversion and common action, to new forms of stewardship, service, and citizenship" (EJA 26–27).

Subsidiarity, Integration, and Unity

There is extensive potential for fragmentation and disintegration in a reality as complex as health care. The more health care bases its practice on the needs of individuals and the more it emphasizes freedom for patients and practitioners as a central concern, the greater the potential for fragmentation and the more resistance there will be to the discipline of an integrated system.

Catholic tradition—locating the central issues of health-care public policy in the arena of the common good—identifies a lack of integration here as a grave and fundamental flaw and calls for systemic, fully social response that is proportionate to the size, complexity, and density of the issue. A classic expression of this is the "principle of subsidiarity" (EJA 99). This can be stated in two modes: negatively it implies that society should limit individual initiative only to an extent that is absolutely unavoidable; positively, that society should take in hand everything that can be done only, or can be done better, by society than by the individual or group (Nell-Breuning, pp. 114–15).

Applied to health care, this principle demands that as much uniformity, centralization, and regulation be institutionalized as required to provide for the common good—that much and no more, no less. Fire protection, national defense, and education all demand different degrees of control, centralization, and uniformity to be effective and just as a part of national life. Because health care deals with such a fundamental good for individual and society;

because of its dynamic to consume without restraint; because of extreme complexity, density, and breadth; because of its potential for abuse and injustice—health care demands a high degree of integration, control, and coordination (Callahan, pp. 98–99).

Preferential Option for the Marginalized

Even in well-ordered human systems the tendency persists for resources to flow toward wealth and power. The more complex the issue and the more it involves expensive realities, the greater the danger that some groups—the economically poor, women, children, minorities, the elderly—will be disadvantaged. Concerning health care, the situation of the marginalized is doubly grave: while their health needs are notably greater than the general public's, their access to needed care is substantially less.

Catholic social teaching recognizes this dynamic to marginalize the poor and the powerless and calls for a persistent counterdynamic—a preference for the poor. "As followers of Christ, we are challenged to make a fundamental 'option for the poor'. . . . We are called to respond to the needs of all our brothers and sisters, but those with the greatest needs require the greatest response" (EJA 16). The persistence and power of this tendency to neglect the health-care poor can only be resisted by a formalized and consistent approach to this problem.

Workplace

Health-care institutions are often the community's largest employers. They represent a major work-culture in the community. The importance and meaning of work has been a consistent and central concern of Catholic social teaching. Work has vital importance for the individual, for the family, and for society and has been identified as "a key, probably the essential key, to the whole social question" (*Laborem exercens* 3).

A key distinction is made between work as objective and work as subjective (LE 5, 6). Work as objective focuses on the product of labor, whereas work from the subjective viewpoint considers the human person's experience of work. The subjective meaning of work deserves priority in the fashioning of the health-care workplace. The central issue here is that work and service give persons the opportunity to experience themselves as active agents in the creation of their world, as "subjects who decide about themselves." Such experience requires a workplace characterized by worker empowerment through systems of communication, participation, and co-responsibility (LE 6, 7; EJA 299–301).

Health care has some major barriers in its self-understanding and institutional setting that make it difficult to fashion a workplace that gives priority to "work as subjective." First, health-care institutions tend to be powerfully shaped by systems of professional hierarchy that honor the subjective meaning of work for the few but ignore it for the majority. Second, the traditional patient-centered rhetoric and self-understanding of health care tend to mute the importance of a worker-oriented culture. Finally, the market dynamics and financial pressures of modern health care tend to keep a focus on the product, not the agent, of labor.

In addition, health-care institutions tend to strongly mirror the patterns of discrimination present in the larger society of which they are a part. Patterns of preference and privilege—especially those involving gender, race, and ethnicity—tend to be reflected at all levels of the organization: trustees, management, professional staff, and employees. Catholic teaching calls for explicit and programmatic efforts to reverse these patterns of bias (EJA 73, 167, 199).

Global Health Solidarity

Nowhere is it truer than in health care that misery and opulence live side by side.

Currently the world's wealthy nations spend four hundred times more per capita on health than the globe's poorest nations can afford. To such colossal imbalance of global resources Catholic social teaching urges: "If our country is to guide its international economic relationships by policies that serve human dignity and justice, we must expand our understanding of the moral responsibility of citizens to serve the common good of the entire planet. . . . Locked together in a world of limited material resources and a growing array of common problems . . . all the economic agents in our society, therefore, must consciously and deliberately attend to the good of the whole human family" (EJA 65). Our social teaching challenges developed nations to move beyond narrow pursuit of ever-loftier national health status while millions perish globally for lack of the most primitive care. While serving locally we must work for greater global health equity.

See also COMMON GOOD; COMMUNITY; HUMAN RIGHTS; MENTAL HEALTH, ETHICAL ISSUES IN; METHODOLOGY, MORAL; POOR, PREFERENTIAL OPTION FOR; RIGHTS AND DUTIES; SOLIDARISM.

Bibliography: D. Callahan, *What Kind of Life* (New York: Simon & Schuster, 1990). Catholic Health Association, *No Room in the Market Place* (St. Louis, Mo.: CHA, 1986). L. Churchill, *Rationing Health Care in America* (Notre Dame, Ind.: Univ. of Notre Dame Press, 1987). C. Curran, "The Right to Health Care and Distributive Justice," in *Transition and Tradition in Moral Theology* (Notre Dame, Ind.: Univ. of Notre Dame Press, 1979). M. Kelly, ed., *Justice and Health Care* (St. Louis, Mo.: CHA, 1984). John Paul II, *Laborem exercens.* B. Schüller, *Begründung Sittlicher Urteile* (Düsseldorf: Patmos, 1980). O. von Nell-Breuning, "Social Movements," *Sacramentum Mundi,* vol. 6 (New York: Herder & Herder, 1970). NCCB, "Pastoral Letter on Health and Health Care," *Origins* 11, no. 25 (December 3, 1981) 396–402. USCC, "The Right to Health Care," *Origins* 15, no. 12, p. 86ff. NCCB, *Economic Justice for All* (Washington: USCC, 1986).

JOHN W. GLASER

HOLOCAUST, THE

Church historian Franklin Littell has argued that the Holocaust is as much a central event in Christian history as in Jewish history because so many baptized members of the church took part in its implementation and it took place in countries assumed to be part of Christian civilization. The same issue was raised in simpler terms, yet more graphically in a way, to Alexandre Donat, author of *The Holocaust Kingdom,* by a fellow inmate in a concentration camp: "How can Christianity survive the discovery that after a thousand years of its being Europe's official religion, Europe remains pagan at heart?" It is becoming increasingly evident that the Holocaust poses a central ethical challenge for Christianity as well as Judaism.

The Holocaust, now called the *Shoah* (the "annihilation") by many Jewish writers, involved the mass extermination of human life in a guiltless fashion. Such widespread human destruction not only became thinkable under the Nazis but technologically feasible for the very first time. The possibility now existed for dispassionate torture and the murder of millions, not merely as the act of a crazed despot, not merely as an irrational outbreak of xenophobic fear or a desire for national security, but as a calculated effort to reshape history supported by intellectual argumentation from the best and the brightest minds in a society. It represented an attempt, according to Jewish philosopher Emil Fackenheim, to wipe out the "divine image" in human history. The death camp was not an accidental by-product of the Nazi effort. It was its very essence.

The fundamental challenge of the Holocaust lies in its continuing challenge for a reevaluation of the basic understanding of God's relationship to humankind and the implications of this reevaluation for the basis of moral behavior. Clearly the Nazis aimed at creating a "superperson" who would be freed once and for all from all traditional moral restraints, especially those imposed by religious beliefs such as sin, redemption, and revelation. All reality was reduced to anthropology and politics. God was dead for the Nazis as an effective moral force in the universe. Ultimately what theologian Michael Ryan terms the Hitlerian "salvation history" confined itself absolutely to the limits of time. It resigned itself to the conditions of finitude while claiming total power within that context. The Nazis now felt they and they alone could decide who was fit for the new humanity about to be born. Those who were deemed unfit, the Jews first and foremost but also Poles, Gypsies, homosexuals, the mentally and physically impaired, could be eliminated however and whenever the Nazis willed.

Some scholars believe that the pseudoreligious, pseudomessianic movement that was Nazism had direct roots in earlier intellectual currents in Europe. They cite in particular deists, Voltaire and the French encyclopedists, the Young Hegelians, the romanticists, and the new scientists who through their escalating discoveries left the impression to many that a triumphant material civilization was dawning. This new era was to be marked by liberation from the "shackles" of previous notions of God and divine authority over human conduct.

The Nazis were intent on achieving a total transformation of human values by appealing to the new sense of human freedom that was dawning in many parts of the Western world and to what they saw as the long-suppressed vitalistic side of humanity. The latter they sought to energize through their well-known mass public rallies, which became naturalistic liturgies of a sort and focused in a special way on the cultivation of power as a basic virtue. The "new person" to be created by the Nazi program was to be in touch once more with the basic life forces of the universe as the Nazis understood them, power being among the primal drives of the human spirit.

Nazi ideology poses basic challenges to traditional Western morality, which is closely tied to the traditions of Judaism and Christianity. The first and foremost challenge has to do with continued belief in the covenantal God of the biblical tradition. Many Jewish scholars (e.g., Emil Fackenheim, Elie Wiesel, Irving Greenberg, Richard Rubenstein) have focused on the God question. They have been joined in this effort by a few Christian scholars such as David Tracy, Johannes Baptist Metz, and Rebecca Chopp. Is it possible to maintain any sense of a God who continues to command humanity, to demand from it adherence to certain prescribed moral norms of conduct? Most Holocaust commentators agree that traditional interpretations of the "commanding" power of the divine need reformulation, perhaps radical reformulation, in light of the Holocaust. Some now speak of only "fragmentary experiences" of God or of replacing the notion of a "commanding God" with that of a "compelling God." The process of reformulation is far from complete. The discussion continues in earnest.

One consequence of the rethinking of God's "commanding presence" in the world after the Holocaust is the emergence of a general view among many within the discussion that human responsibility has definitely been enhanced in terms of creation's future well-being. But this leads to several other questions. How, first of all, do we best respond to this new burden of human responsibility? One prominent ethicist Stanley Hauerwas has placed great emphasis on a renewed cultivation of the traditional virtue of humility that acknowledges the fundamental giftedness of all human powers over creation. Others, while agreeing with the need to maintain a sense of giftedness in terms of human capacity, nonetheless feel that more is necessary. Humanity today finds itself in a significantly new situation in terms of its role as guardian over creation. The Holocaust has clearly shown that God does not, perhaps cannot in light of the creative course that has been chosen, stop human activities that threaten basic survival. That now clearly depends on humankind. Thus an affirmation of human *co-creatorship,* rather than humility, is the requisite moral response to the Holocaust.

Emphasis on human co-creatorship, however, raises a further problem. On the one hand, Elie Wiesel has stressed that it is not only God who comes out of the Holocaust in tarnished fashion but belief in the basic goodness of the human person as well. The Holocaust thus demands serious reflection on the anthropological basis of morality. Simplistic assertions about prevailing human goodness will not do. On the other hand, as the Austrian Catholic philosopher Frederich Heer has underscored, we must be doubly careful after the Holocaust of falling back into conventional Augustinian notions that tend to view humanity and the world primarily in terms of sinfulness. This "fatalistic tendency," so commonplace in Christianity, played a part in creating indifference if not outright collaboration with Nazi destruction and could pave the way for even further destruction in the future if not curbed. After the Holocaust, we need to strike a careful anthropological balance between human goodness/human creativity and the inherent potential for human destructiveness. We also need to recognize that any effective morality must address both the rational and the vitalistic aspects of human beings. Liberal thought with its high idealism was unable to withstand the power generated by the Nazi mass rallies because its moral emphasis was primarily rational. Liturgy hence will need to play an important role in post-Holocaust morality, including sustaining human commitment at times when God appears absent and injustice seems destined to remain in place.

Other areas of morality for which the Holocaust carries significant implications include (1) the use of power; (2) the role of religious tradition in public culture, especially in pluralistic societies; (3) the increasing use of depersonalized public language, which easily can remove victims of injustice from the universe of moral obligation; and (4) how societies develop "early warning signals" to detect the seeds of anti-Semitism and fascism. Overall, the Holocaust must be seen as posing a continuing challenge to Christian morality unlike any other single event of the 20th century.

See also ANTI-SEMITISM; EUTHANASIA, SOCIAL IMPLICATIONS OF; EVIL, SOCIAL; FASCISM; GOD, IMAGES OF, PIUS XII; TOTALITARIANISM; WAR.

Bibliography: H. Friedlander and S. Milton, eds., *The Holocaust: Ideology, Bureaucracy, and Genocide* (Millwood, N.Y.: Kraus, 1980). J. Pawlikowski, *The Challenge of the Holocaust for Christian Theology,* rev. ed. (New York: Anti-Defamation League, 1982). P. Haas, *Morality After Auschwitz: The Radical Challenge of the Nazi Ethic* (Minneapolis: Augsburg/Fortress, 1988).

JOHN T. PAWLIKOWSKI, O.S.M.

HOMELESSNESS

The phenomenon of homelessness is by no means new. Isaiah (58:7) speaks of "the homeless poor," and the blind and the lame who cried out to Jesus from the roadside would have been part of this group. Across the ages homelessness has continued as a concomitant of extreme poverty. In India and other Third World countries the sight of men, women, and children sleeping on city sidewalks is commonplace. Nor are such sights unknown in the First World.

But the phenomenon is more shocking to the conscience in industrialized nations because of their greater resources, resources through which—in the United States at least—poverty could be eradicated altogether if only the commitment were made. Because of the dramatic rise in the number of people without shelter in this country, the very word "homeless" became a household word during the 1980s. Previously the more usual terms were pejorative, like "vagrants" and "bums," and they are still used by those who stereotypically regard the homeless as men and women too lazy to work rather than as human beings caught in a complex web of social and economic factors over which they have little control.

By the beginning of the 1990s estimates of the numbers of homeless ranged from half a million to three million. It is a population that began to become increasingly diverse in the third quarter of the 20th century. For the first half of the century it was composed in large part of alcoholic middle-age men. With the development of psychotropic drugs in the 1950s, however, many mentally impaired adults were discharged from psychiatric institutions. In theory community health networks were to provide needed support and residential care, but because of budgetary constraints this theory never became a reality in most communities. Without guidance as to continuing the medications that had once stabilized their behavior they often turned to alcohol or drugs in an attempt to self-medicate, which only aggravated their illness. Because of aberrant behavior that sometimes involved breaking the law, a number found themselves in local jails where they were (and still are) subject to abuse by other prisoners.

More recently homeless families composed primarily of single mothers and their children have expanded the ranks of the homeless. By the end of the 1980s it was estimated that this group constituted one-third of the total homeless population. A major reason for their plight is the shortage of affordable housing. Federal spending for subsidized housing dropped dramatically during the Reagan administration, and the shortage has continued into the 1990s. Some cities have waiting lists of several years for public housing units and for section-eight vouchers that pay part of the rent for privately owned properties. A 1989 survey of twenty-six cities by the National Coalition for the Homeless found the lack of affordable housing cited again and again by service providers as the main cause of homelessness in their areas, areas representative of all parts of the country.

While the cost of nonsubsidized housing has steadily climbed, the shelter allowance of those on public assistance has not. Welfare mothers in private housing have little choice but to use the food and clothing portion of their grants for rent. Nor does the high cost of housing affect only those on public assistance. A 1990 study by the Economic Policy Institute concluded that as many as one-third of all Americans are shelter poor; that is, obliged to spend so much on housing that they are unable to pay for other necessities. Connected with the state of being shelter poor is the emergence of the working homeless. Caught between low wages and high rents, some are evicted and find themselves and their possessions on the street, with the added cruelty that their possessions are often stolen by passersby. Others double up in the already crowded households of relatives or friends, creating a category that advocates refer to as the hidden homeless.

The severe lack of affordable housing is not just the result of diminished spending at the local, state, and federal levels. At one time there were numerous inexpensive residential hotels in cities around the country. Called SROs (Single Room Occupancy), they allowed single men and women of small means to live with a sense of dignity and independence.

In the 1970s, however, as formerly low-income neighborhoods began to become gentrified, developers converted SROs into high-priced condominiums. New York City alone lost over 100,000 residential hotel rooms: two-thirds of its total. San Francisco's was halved between 1975 and 1988. Displaced residents living on Social Security or other entitlement benefits lacked the means to afford comparable accommodations elsewhere.

In regard to younger homeless people, substance abuse of drugs like crack cocaine greatly compounded their difficulties by creating a distinct disability, which for homeless pregnant women involves the risk of bearing infants who are themselves drug addicted. Adding still further to the complexity of the situation is the scarcity of free drug-rehabilitation facilities for addicts who seek help. Those that exist have long waiting lists. Private facilities are prohibitively expensive for people who lack medical insurance, and Medicaid, the medical insurance of the poor, does not pay for residential treatment.

An especially painful aspect of the increased diversity of the homeless population has been the growing number of people with AIDS (acquired immunodeficiency syndrome). Many had previously been self-supporting. Losing jobs and then homes as their illness progresses, they frequently find themselves with nowhere to go except to public shelters. There, neglect, hostility, and health hazards (other infectious diseases, poor nutrition, inadequate sleep) may well await them.

As the homeless began to make greater use of outdoor public spaces, municipal authorities responded with a variety of strict countermeasures. In the spring of 1990, for instance, city and state workers in Portland, Oregon, ejected homeless people encamped under bridges and highway viaducts. Some municipalities have enacted ordinances against sleeping in public. Similarly, transit authorities go to great lengths to deter the homeless from seeking shelter in train, bus, and subway stations. In Washington, D.C., metal grates were placed over subway entrances after homeless people began to sleep there during the winter months.

Litigation on their behalf has helped to secure some degree of protection for the homeless. The first significant step in this direction was a suit brought in 1979 by a young New York lawyer, Robert Hayes. The suit claimed that homeless men were being forced to live in crowded and unsafe conditions in the few existing city shelters. The New York State Supreme Court subsequently ruled that the city would have to provide safe, clean shelter to all homeless persons who requested it. The court's decision led to the creation of a vast complex of congregate shelters utilizing armories, gymnasiums, and other city-owned properties.

Congregate shelters housing hundreds of human beings have proven, though, to be plagued with drawbacks. Originally created as temporary emergency facilities, in numerous instances they have become an end in themselves; lacking other options, many people live in them for years. On the other hand, because of violence the more vulnerable shun them entirely. Understaffed by caseworkers, moreover, large shelters provide only a minimal level of social and medical services. Finally, because municipal shelters in some cities are open only at night, the health of the sick homeless deteriorates still further as they wander the streets during the day.

Private organizations have helped to fill the gap with respect to what is not provided by local governments. Responding in the manner of Mt. 25 ("When I was a stranger you welcomed me") churches have opened their doors to provide meals and sleeping space, as have synagogues. A number of dioceses have established shelters of their own, including shelters for high-risk groups such as pregnant women and people with AIDS.

A broad coalition of churches and synagogues in New York known as the Partnership for the Homeless introduced the concept of coordinating the efforts of religious groups in order to maximize their ability to provide assistance to as wide a range of homeless people as possible. The model has spread to other cities like Los Angeles, San Diego, and Boston. Shelters operated by private and religious groups tend to be superior to city-run shelters because of their small size and the greater degree of personal attention that can be offered. Religious and private organizations have also been able to create limited amounts of transitional and permanent housing.

But advocates agree that without substantial outlays for housing from government sources aimed at long-term rather than stopgap solutions, the numbers of homeless will not decrease. One step in the direction of greater federal support was the passage by the United States Congress of the Stewart B. McKinney Homeless Assistance Act of 1987, which authorized funds for twenty program areas. Although the act is viewed as an important beginning, the actual amounts allocated year by year have been relatively small and aimed at emergency services rather than at permanent housing. The act does provide for some transitional housing, but the value of the latter is lessened if there is no permanent housing from which the transition can be made.

Although homelessness is most visible in large cities and their suburbs, it exists in small communities too. According to the National Coalition for the Homeless' 1990 survey, in Wenatchee, Washington, which has a population of approximately fifty thousand, there were over one thousand homeless people. Shelter requests rose 25 percent between 1989 and 1990. Providers estimated that a third of their clients were mentally disabled and that three-quarters were substance abusers.

Rural regions in Appalachia and the South also have homeless people, with homelessness sometimes taking the form of housing so substandard that it lacks running water, heat, and electricity. Healthcare workers in southern Kentucky, for example, have spoken of people living in chicken coops and abandoned school buses. The homeless and near-homeless in rural areas of the United States face an added disadvantage in that most programs for the poor are concentrated in urban areas; without transportation, these people remain isolated in their poverty.

If homelessness is primarily a concomitant of poverty, its solution may lie in a more equitable distribution of the country's wealth that would ensure adequate health care, housing, and education to all. Such an approach has long been part of the thinking of the Scandinavian countries. In the United States, however, the momentum has been in the opposite direction: the gap between rich and poor has been widening. And as congregate shelters take on more and more an appearance of permanence, there is the danger that homelessness is becoming institutionalized. If it is true that a nation is to be judged by its treatment of its most vulnerable citizens, the United States would have much to answer for.

See also ALIENATION; ALMSGIVING; CHARITY; DIGNITATIS HUMANAE; HEALTH CARE; MENTAL HEALTH, ETHICAL ISSUES IN; POOR, PREFERENTIAL OPTION FOR; PRISON.

Bibliography: *American Nightmare: A Decade of Homelessness in the United States* (New York: National Coalition for the Homeless, 1989). P. Rossi, *Down and Out in America: The Origins of Homelessness* (Chicago: Univ. of Chicago Press, 1989). R. Landers, "Why Homeless Need More Than Shelter," *Editorial Research Reports,* vol. 1, no. 12 (March 30, 1990). E. Quigley, "The Homeless: How Can the Problems of the Homeless Be Overcome?" *Congressional Quarterly Researcher* (formerly *Editorial Research Reports*) vol. 2, no. 29 (August 7, 1992). N. Boxhill, *Homeless Children* (New York: Haworth, 1990). M. Burt, *Over the Edge: The Growth of Homelessness in the 1980s* (Washington: Urban Institute, 1990). C. Caton, *Homeless in America* (New York: Oxford Univ. Press, 1990).

GEORGE M. ANDERSON, S.J.

HOMOSEXUALITY, SOCIAL IMPLICATIONS OF

Framing the Issues

It is not the purpose of this article to discuss the morality of homogenital behavior. The strengths and weaknesses of the scriptural, natural-law, and psychological arguments usually proposed against such activity have been well analyzed elsewhere, just as the wide spectrum of current theological opinion on this issue has been well documented (see this article's bibliography). It may be said in passing, however, that despite the substantial progress that has been made in defining more precisely the numerous points needing consideration in any attempt to render a fair and informed moral assessment of homogenital acts, much remains to be settled. Moreover, even as the psychological, theological, and ethical data on this specific matter of genital sexuality continue to accumulate, attention is being drawn to related moral questions of a pressing and broader public nature: the social implications of being a homosexual man or woman and the need to safeguard the rights of gays and lesbians in societies where they are often the objects of fear, ridicule, and intolerance.

While many Roman Catholic moralists (e.g., Lisa Cahill, Charles Curran, Philip Keane, Richard McCormick) suggest that homogenital acts may be evaluated as *premoral* wrongs, not objective *moral* evils, when they express the faithful love shared by a truly or irreversibly homosexually oriented couple who are striving for permanency in their relationship, these same theologians nonetheless strongly maintain the normative nature of heterosexual expressions of marital love with its procreative potentiality. From the viewpoint of these so-called revisionist theologians, the problem for Christians does not lie in supporting heterogenital expressions of committed love as normative; rather, as has been stated by Ralph Weltge, the real question has to do with "how the norm is used in church and society, what is done by design or default to those who violate it. The homosexual bears pressures, indignities and injustices which demand relief. The question is how to take up his [or her] cause without either sacrificing the norm or sanctioning its use as a cover for persecution" (Weltge, p. 60).

Magisterial Call for Respect and Tolerance

The problem of persecution and discriminatory practices against gays and lesbians is by no means illusory. Within the last fifteen years documents from both individual U.S. bishops and the National Conference of Catholic Bishops, as well as from the Sacred Congregation for the Doctrine of the Faith, have repeatedly urged not only compassion and pastoral concern for homosexually oriented people but also recognition and protection of their human rights. One notes, for example, the position taken in the U.S. bishops' statement of 1976, *To Live in Christ Jesus:* "Homosexuals, like everyone else, should not suffer from prejudice against their basic human rights. They have a right to respect, friendship and justice. They should have an active role in the Christian community" (quoted in *Homosexuality and the Magisterium* 9). In 1978, Archbishop John R. Roach pressed this point even more urgently: "It is a matter of injustice when, due to prejudice, they [gays and lesbians] must suffer violation of their basic human rights. Like all persons, they have a right to human respect, stable friendships, economic security, and social equality. . . . Consequently, both religious and civic leaders must seek ways to assure homosexuals every human and civil right which is their due as persons, without, however, neglecting the rights of the larger community" (quoted in *Homosexuality and the Magisterium* 11).

Protestation against the persecution of gays and lesbians appears, as well, in the highly controversial *Letter to the World's Bishops on the Pastoral Care of Homosexual Persons,* which was prepared by the Congregation for the Doctrine of the Faith in 1986: "It is deplorable that homosexual persons have been and are the object of violent malice in speech or in action. Such treatment deserves condemnation from the Church's pastors wherever it occurs. It reveals a kind of disregard for others which endangers the fundamental principles of a healthy society. The intrinsic dignity of each person must always be respected in word, in action and in law" (10).

The congregation seems, however, not to heed its own admonition. In several places the letter's insensitive or at least incautious assertions help to explain the sound criticism it has received. To begin with, there is no justification for the letter's apparent assumption that all or most homosexuals are engaged in or advocate promiscuity. This seems, however, to be the clear implication of a statement like the following: "Even when the practice of homosexuality may seriously threaten the lives and well-being of a large number of people, its advocates remain undeterred and refuse to consider the magnitude of the risks involved" (9). Regrettable, too, is the fact that gays and lesbians are advised that through a process of self-denial and conformity to the sacrificial love of Christ, they will achieve "a source of self-giving which will save them from a life which constantly threatens to destroy them" (12). We must wonder what is being implied about the lives of homosexuals, as opposed to heterosexuals, that places them in such a precarious position.

Decriminalizing Private Sex Acts

Concern about the human and civil rights of homosexuals necessarily raises the question of public policy in at least two areas: the decriminalization of sex acts, and the passage of legislation prohibiting discrimination against gays and lesbians simply because of their sexual orientation. Regarding the first issue, in countries or states where homogenital acts are prohibited by law, a strong case may be made for the decriminalization of such acts, at least when they are performed in private by consenting adults. Apart, then, from statutes needed to protect minors from exploitation, to maintain public decency, and to regulate prostitution, laws forbidding voluntary and private acts of oral/anal sex by members of the same (as well as opposite) sex should be repealed because they do more harm than good in the public order. In general, such laws are ineffective, haphazardly invoked, and capriciously implemented with widely varying penalties; in addition, the enforcement of such laws usually involves recourse by police to illegal tactics like entrapment; finally, these laws perpetuate a situation quite conducive to the further harassment of homosexuals by blackmail or extortion (Malloy, pp. 145–62).

Gay- and Lesbian-Rights Legislation

In turning to the broad question of civil laws designed to protect the rights of lesbians and gays, it seems that the church's magisterial warnings against the persecution of homosexuals have generally not produced ecclesial support for civil legislation prohibiting discrimination on the basis of sexual orientation. In fact, it is a matter of public record that most often the local and regional hierarchy actively work to have such legislation defeated. The repeated claim of these opponents is that passage of the legislation would indeed be tantamount to asserting that homogenital acts are socially acceptable and morally permissible. Hence the legislation must be resisted or rejected lest the impression be given that the church is in any way sympathetic to "the homosexual lifestyle" as a legitimate social or moral option. The Congregation for the Doctrine of the Faith seems particularly strong in opposing this kind of civil-rights legislation. Not only does it reject the view that "homosexual activity is equivalent to or as acceptable as the sexual expression of conjugal love," but, in addition, the congregation asserts that such a view "has a direct impact on society's understanding of the nature and rights of the family and puts them in jeopardy" (9). Further, after characterizing the legislation in question as an attempt "to protect behavior to which no one has any conceivable right," the congregation sounds an ominous note in observing that when such legislation is introduced, "neither the Church nor society at large should be surprised when other distorted notions and practices gain ground, and irrational and violent reactions increase" (10).

In 1992, the congregation sparked further controversy by its document entitled "Some Considerations Concerning the Catholic Response to Legislative Proposals on the Non-Discrimination of Homosexual Persons." The document was sent originally to the American bishops and then, in a slightly revised form, was made available for wider publication. In a statement accompanying the revised version of the document, Joaquin Navarro-Valls, a Vatican spokesman, said that it was "not intended to be an official and public instruction . . . but a background resource offering discreet assistance to those who may be confronted with the task of evaluating draft legislation regarding non-discrimination on the basis of sexual orientation."

The Foreword of the document expresses the concern that legislative initiatives "which would make discimination on the basis of sexual orientation illegal . . . may in fact have a negative impact on the family and society." After advising bishops to "keep as their uppermost concern the responsibility to defend and promote family life" (9), the document states that "there are areas in which it is not unjust discrimination to take sexual orientation into account, for example, in the placement of children for adoption or foster care, in employment of teachers or athletic coaches, or in military recruitment" (11; also see 15). (An obvious question to be asked here: what assumptions lie behind this assertion?)

Next, the document states that while "all persons have the right to work, to housing, etc.," nonetheless, "these rights are not absolute. They can legitimately limited for objectively disordered external conduct." In fact, this limitation of rights is sometimes "not only licit but obligatory," whether we are dealing with "culpable behavior" or with the actions "of the physically or mentally ill. Thus it is accepted that the state may restrict the exercise of rights, for example, in the case of contagious or mentally ill persons, in order to protect the common good" (12). One can only wonder about the infelicitous comparisons proposed in this section of the document.

Finally, the document expresses the fear that making it illegal to discriminate against homosexual persons "can easily lead, if not automatically, to the legislative protection and promotion of homosexuality." In this scenario, homosexual persons would expect or insist upon special consideration by trying to use their homosexuality "as a positive source of human rights, for example, in respect to so-called affirmative action or preferential treatment in hiring practices" (13). It seems fair to say that the document presents a number of concerns and fears, but offers no proof that extending legislative protection to the civil rights of homosexually oriented individuals or couples necessarily threatens the rights currently enjoyed and protected by others. Attention, therefore, must be given to these questions: what rights are in fact threatened and how is this threat manifested, and in what ways would the common good suffer?

On the other side of the issue, argumentation in favor of antidiscrimination legislation on the basis of sexual orientation takes a different tack; it regards such legislation not as approbation of any specific genital activity but simply as protection for homosexual persons and their civil rights. In itself, then, support for the legislation does not imply or necessitate agreement with any intentions, motivations, or value judgments that might or do lead to genital actions that have traditionally been regarded as morally wrong. This is not to suggest, however, that all civil-rights legislation centering on the issue of sexual orientation automatically warrants approval and support. Obviously, a bill's precise formulation is a matter of legitimate concern, and the fact that a broad spectrum of complex issues may fall within the purview of the proposed legislation means that every law deserves careful consideration even as it demands prudent analysis.

Some bills have focused on protecting gays and lesbians from discrimination in access to housing, employment, and public accommodations. Even around these basic concerns, there is continuing controversy in certain quarters. Regarding employment, for example, the Department of Defense for fifty years mantained a policy against admitting homosexuals into the armed forces, and these men and women were subject to disciplinary action and dismissal from the military if their sexual orientation was discovered. In 1993, a new policy, popularly referred to as "don't ask, don't tell," was introduced, whereby recruits and military personnel will no longer be asked about their sexual orientation, and so long as homosexuals do not announce their orientation and refrain from homosexual conduct (e.g. handholding, kissing, engaging in the sex act, attempting to marry a person of the same sex), they will not be subject to investigation or separation from the military. It remains unclear how this new policy will be received and implemented. Particularly strong sentiments surface, as well, in discussions about the teaching profession. It is commonly urged that proclaimed or declared homosexuals should be prohibited from teaching and counseling positions, at least on the primary and secondary levels of education, but it is never made clear exactly what is meant by the terms "proclaimed" or "declared." Has the proclamation/declaration been made to society at large, to one's family and friends, to one's employer, or to one's students? Significantly, the reason offered to justify not having "known" homosexuals working within these levels of education is not a concern over the possible seduction or solicitation of students, since, in fact, pedophilia and child abuse occur more often among heterosexuals. Rather, there is a fear that gay and lesbian teachers might prove too attractive and influential as role models with the result that they may confuse and hence mislead impressionable youths (Malloy, p. 159; Harvey, pp. 110, 114).

Perhaps the gay-rights questions that are the main focus of public debate and attention today are those that center most closely around the traditional understanding of marriage and family life. In a move to give some legal status to the personal union existing between two members of the same sex, several cities have already passed while others are considering legislation recognizing not marriages as such but what are called "domestic partnerships." In general, the policies regarding domestic partners require that gay and lesbian couples file a declaration of their relationship and somehow indicate that they are responsible for each other's welfare. Under these conditions, the same-sex couples enjoy a variety of prerogatives: they may, for example, file joint income-tax returns, share property rights, receive health coverage and medical benefits from a partner's policy, claim inheritance, and possibly even seek a form of alimony should the relationship be dissolved.

While there continues to be generally strong societal and religious opposition to recognizing homosexual marriages as such, Philip Keane urges that both society and the Catholic church "should be open to finding other ways of supporting stable homosexual unions" (p. 89). At the same time, however, Keane shares the common view that homosexual couples should not be allowed to adopt children. Presumably, in the judgment of many, such couples should also be denied foster care of children. The rationale for such prohibitions needs further investigation, especially since single-parent adoptions are possible, even, it would seem, by homosexually oriented individuals. Perhaps it is feared that children raised by two members of the same sex will be confused and embarrassed by this arrangement when it is contrasted with the family constellation common to most other households. Or perhaps it is assumed that a same-sex couple would provide role modeling that will entice a child into a homosexual lifestyle. How well founded such fears and assumptions are is unclear; but if they are going to be allowed to dictate public policy, they certainly demand greater scrutiny.

Decisions about homosexuals and the adoption, foster care, or custody of children are best made just as they are when dealing with heterosexuals—on a case-by-case basis. In and of itself, one's sexual orientation says nothing about one's ability to be a fine parent or guardian. Furthermore, greater clarity and more justice in this matter may result if decisions are made that reflect greater emphasis on the needs of children for loving parents than on the need of adults to have children. No one has a right to a child, but children have a right to the nurturing of love.

Conclusion

Determining the proper responses to the issues and questions presented here is no simple task. The following observations may help, however, to focus future discussions and to initiate appropriate courses of action:

1. We need to remember that few rights, like few values, are absolute. This means that the great majority of rights that humans enjoy are relative and hence must be carefully weighed, balanced, and arranged into some kind of hierarchy of importance. Realistically, conflict among competing rights and values is sometimes unavoidable.

2. In the interest of the truth and justice that liberate, religious leaders should either support or oppose lesbian- and gay-rights legislation solely on the basis of a bill's intrinsic merits; this means that just as a church can ill-afford to capitulate to attempted manipulation by any pressure groups, so also is it ill-advised to recoil from the demands of its mission simply out of fear of misguiding or scandalizing its members. The faithful are best served, and scandal and confusion are best combated, by efforts at sound education.

3. It seems problematic to claim on the one hand that the lack of long-term stability in a large majority of same-sex relationships is evidence, in itself, of an inherent weakness or flaw in the nature of homosexual love (Malloy, pp. 234, 339), and then to oppose on the other hand any attempt to establish some kind of institutional support-system for these relationships that might prove helpful to their stability and permanence.

4. There is neither merit nor justice in the mentality that claims to tolerate gays and lesbians so long as they know their place and keep to it; for too long a similar mentality made victims of other minorities, racial and ethnic.

5. There is something invidious about the claim that there is really no need for any gay-rights legislation, since all that is necessary is that homosexuals keep their sexual orientation to themselves and a few trusted others. If they do this, they will have no difficulty exercising their civil rights. Indeed, John Harvey is of the opinion that "for the undeclared homosexual there is no discrimination, and a gay-rights bill would induce no changes" (p. 115). A similar observation appears in the 1992 document of the Congregation for the Doctrine of the Faith: "As a rule, the majority of homosexually oriented persons who seek to lead chaste lives do not publicize their sexual orientation. Hence the problem of discrimination in terms of employment, housing, and the like does not usually arise" (14). This suggestion that the way for homosexuals to avoid discrimination is to remain undeclared, invisible, and "closeted" or hidden, is not beyond questioning. Are homosexuals truly safe, or even free, in their secretiveness when they must always live with the fear of being discovered? And even if this were a safe way to live, we must ask if it is a healthy way to live humanly, psychologically, and spiritually. And is it not itself a form of oppres-

sion to require as the price to be paid for the exercise of their civil rights that gays and lesbians live in silent deceit, pretending to be other than who they truly are? Having to live in such a way would seem to be demeaning and debilitating to homosexuals themselves, and it certainly does nothing to challenge others in society to greater moral sensitivity and maturity. In fact, advising homosexuals to remain invisible only reinforces the vicious circle in which society is trapped: when homosexuals surrender to society's general intolerance by remaining invisible, they effectively allow the stereotypical images by which they are portrayed to go unchallenged; in turn, these images feed the very homophobia that results in the intolerance and discrimination that already make so many homosexuals' invisibility necessary or expedient.

6. Finally, just as no homosexual should feel forced to remain invisible, so also should none be forced into visibility. There is, then, something reprehensible in the recent phenomenon known as "outing," whereby some of the most radical homosexual groups have undertaken to reveal the homosexuality of politicians and celebrities in various fields, either to "claim" them openly as role models or to punish them as hypocrites when they not only hide their homosexuality but are also publicly critical of the cause of homosexuals.

See also AFFIRMATIVE ACTION; CHILDREN, RIGHTS OF; CIVIL LAW, FUNCTION OF; FAMILY; HUMAN RIGHTS; MARRIAGE; PASTORAL CARE; TOLERATION, PRINCIPLE OF.

Bibliography: J. Gallagher, ed., *Homosexuality and the Magisterium: Documents from the Vatican and the U.S. Bishops, 1975–1985* (Mt. Rainier, Md.: New Ways Ministry, 1986). V. Genovesi, *In Pursuit of Love: Catholic Morality and Human Sexuality* (Wilmington, Del.: Glazier, 1987). J. Harvey, *The Homosexual Person: New Thinking in Pastoral Care* (San Francisco: St. Ignatius Press, 1987). P. Keane, *Sexual Morality: A Catholic Perspective* (New York: Paulist, 1977). E. Malloy, *Homosexuality and the Christian Way of Life* (Lanham, Md.: Univ. Press of America, 1981). R. McCormick, *The Critical Calling: Reflections on Moral Dilemmas Since Vatican II* (Washington: Georgetown Univ. Press, 1989). R. Nugent, ed., *A Challenge to Love: Gay and Lesbian Catholics in the Church* (New York: Crossroad, 1983). R. Weltge, ed., *The Same Sex* (Philadelphia: Pilgrim, 1969).

VINCENT J. GENOVESI, S.J.

HOPE

Since early in their history Christians have been advised always to have their answer ready for people who ask them the reason for the hope that they enjoy and embody (1 Pet 3:15). While it may be said that Christians traditionally have not sufficiently heeded such advice, the situation appears recently to have changed. As Christians have come to appreciate more fully their existence as "the pilgrim people of God," so, also, have they come to realize their need for what may be termed a "pilgrim ethic."

In their effort to construct such an ethic, Christians have turned to the virtue of hope, for hope, as suggested by Bernard Häring, is really "faith and love on pilgrimage," the "internal dynamism" that keeps Christian faith and love alive and active (Häring, p. 48). To explore this idea, we note first that the ultimate unity of the twofold commandment of love succeeded in revealing the necessary relationship between faith (our personal response of love for God) and the service of our neighbor out of love. Thus it is that the only faith that embodies the spirit of true Christianity is the "living faith" of Jas 2 or the faith that does the work of love (Gal 5:6). But up to this point the integrity of Christian living is not yet complete. Still missing is the vitality of hope, which is experienced as "the glow of faith and the fire of love," an energy "which allows, liberates and encourages faith to be active in love, even when reason can see no reason except to despair, to be cynical, and to hate" (Genovesi, p. 138).

The interplay that hope has with faith and love may be further articulated. Thus for the actions that characterize the lives of

Christians, faith is the authority, love is the reason and motive, and hope is the dynamism. As Christ calls Christians to faith, so faith calls them to hope, and hope calls them to love in a way that is meant to transform the earth (Genovesi, p. 135).

To focus on Christian hope is to highlight the fundamental eschatological nature of Christian living, which means simply that while Christians are to make their way through this world and at the same time make the most of it for everyone, they understand, nonetheless, that finally they are not of this world; their lives, rather, are properly shaped by the *eschaton* or end-time when the reign of God will be fully realized. Mention of God's reign suggests, of course, a question regarding the responsibility Christians have for, and the contribution they make to, the final and full appearance of that reign.

Historically, Christians have differed in their understanding and explanation of the roles played by God and human beings in the establishment of God's reign. At least this much may be suggested, however. To facilely ascribe all responsibility for this enterprise either to God or to human beings would seem both to discredit respectively human beings or God and to assault the true nature of Christian hope. Thus, were human activity to be totally without effect upon the establishment of God's reign, Christians might reasonably conclude that their labors lack lasting significance in the eyes of God. "And if divine significance is not attached to the accomplishments of human beings, we must seriously question whether human achievements have any lasting significance for individuals themselves" (Genovesi, p. 112). If they do not, then really there is little to motivate us, little to be responsible for, and little to hope for.

At the same time, however, were Christians to imagine that the reign of God is solely and completely theirs for the making and the taking, they would have forgotten that, like faith and love, hope, too, is a relational reality. This means at the very least that as people of hope we Christians live with "an interior sense that there is help on the outside of us" (Lynch, p. 31). Given this realization, we are freed not only to work for, but also to receive, what God has promised us.

It appears, then, that we must affirm in a more nuanced way the co-responsibility that God and human beings share for our world and God's reign. Such an affirmation, however, recognizes and invokes the need for ongoing prayerfulness in an attempt to discern the changing parameters that define the limits both of our power and of our obligation to resist and overcome present evils and to creatively lay the foundations for the ultimate fulfillment of God's reign. We bravely and boldly take up the challenge to make history, but we do so gracefully and gratefully, always aware of the paradox that in moving forward "we tread in the footsteps of the God who is to come to us from the future" (Schillebeeckx, p. 190).

See also ESCHATOLOGY; IMAGINATION, ROLE OF; KINGDOM OF GOD.

Bibliography: V. Genovesi, *Expectant Creativity: The Action of Hope in Christian Ethics* (Lanham, Md.: Univ. Press of America, 1982). B. Häring, *Hope Is the Remedy* (New York: Doubleday, 1972). W. Lynch, *Images of Hope: Imagination as Healer of the Hopeless* (New York: Mentor-Omega Books, 1966). E. Schillebeeckx, *God the Future of Man,* trans. N. Smith (New York: Sheed & Ward, 1968). K. Ward, "Reinhold Niebuhr and the Christian Hope," in *Reinhold Niebuhr and the Issues of our Time,* ed. R. Harries (Grand Rapids: Eerdmans, 1986).

VINCENT J. GENOVESI, S.J.

HUMAN RIGHTS

To the modern "ethos of freedom and equality" (C. F. von Weizsaecker), the appeal to human rights almost appears as a fundamental category of political and ethical thought. Yet although we have grown accustomed to formulating elementary demands for political freedom, national and international social justice, and participation in the formation of public opinion and in the process of political decision making in the language of human rights, we must not overlook the fact that today this ethos, while it may be gaining in recognition, is by no means yet a universally accepted code of norms. It is true at present that thanks to the most recent developments in the field of supranational law and the growth of public sensibility toward human-rights violations, these rights are subject to more effective international protection than ever before. Nevertheless reports on the situation in various countries continually presented by human-rights groups and organizations provide all too often proof that elementary human rights, not only of individual persons but also of ethnic or religious minority groups, are under serious threat today in many countries in the world.

This article aims to outline the most important aspects of the development of human-rights thinking in both the secular and the ecclesiastical areas (I) as well as the consequences of such thinking for legal codification (II); furthermore it also discusses the basic ethical and systematic structure of a theory of human rights (III) and then the extent to which this can serve as the basis for a future international ethos that transcends the cultural and religious diversities between people of different geographical places of origin and smooths the path for a form of human-rights protection that is globally effective and legally enforceable (IV).

I The Development of Human-Rights Thinking

The origins of ethical thought in universalistic categories going beyond the bond of the both obligatory and protection character of ethical norms for particular groups of people, may be found both in the Judeo-Christian religion and in Greco-Roman philosophy.

The theological anthropology of the Old Testament is marked by the idea of man created in the image of God (Gen 1:26f.). This endows man with the specific dignity that distinguishes him from the rest of both animate and inanimate creation. The OT theme of the conclusion of a covenant between God and humankind firmly establishes this dignity in an additional fashion by God's unique devotion to those God created, who are therefore fundamentally and definitively withdrawn from the arbitrariness of others. This applies not only for those belonging to the people of Israel but also to the neighboring heathen peoples. Human dignity is in this sense, then, inviolable and inalienable. It cannot be taken from anyone endowed with it, nor can the person renounce it. This fundamental thought, found as early as in the OT and theologically justified there too, that is, that human dignity may, under certain circumstances, be gravely violated by one's own actions or by action on the part of others but can never be disposed of completely, remains the point of departure for the secular theory of human rights too, developed in the modern era and based on natural law. It is the "Archimedian point" on which this whole theory has its foundation and which creates conditions in which human rights can be valued and respected irrespective of any legal positivist decision.

Some consequences of the realization of the dignity of each individual person can be seen in the OT, for example, in the special protection accorded not only to widows, orphans, and the weak but also to strangers (Exod 23:9, Lev 19:34) from potential despotism on the part of the powerful.

The moral message of the NT confirms and reaffirms the theological anthropology of the OT. The loving devotion of God for God's creatures, which culminates in the redemptive death of Jesus Christ, gives human beings a particular facility for passing on the love they have received as a gift: "I give you a new commandment: love one another; you must love one another just as

I have loved you" (Jn 13:34). The Christian command to love given in the NT therefore also springs from the same roots as the Jewish form of the command encountered in the OT (Lev 19:18): it is founded in the dignity of the human person with which the Creator distinguishes God's creatures from all other created things. Since belief in the good news is able in a special way to motivate Christians morally and give them strength, it is this belief that liberates them from attachment to self, something that all too often hinders them from actually performing that which is recognized as morally the right thing to do. Respect for certain human rights then can be understood in this perspective as a particular form of basic attitude that relates to greater justice and indeed greater well-being for one's fellow human beings. Thus the NT ethos displays in principle the same openness for human-rights thinking as is seen in the Jewish understanding of the Torah, which takes as its point of departure the realization of the worth of the whole of (human) creation—even though the term "human dignity" is itself not biblical and although systematic legal and political consequences were only derived from this openness in modern times.

In the philosophical sector, starting points for human-rights argumentation are first found in Stoicism (Zenon, Epictet, Seneca, Cicero). Stoicism considers all human persons as equal and views each individual's own rationality and free will as the very base of such equality. The respect due to every rational being (Cicero: "homo res sacra hominis") forms the cornerstone of criticism of a practice of political power that sets itself objectives other than the major one of ensuring the public good of the community. Particularly in Stoicism, the idea of a natural law is developed, a law that can be recognized by humans by virtue of their rationality and that is morally binding on them over and above and independent of any positive legal order. (The very first approaches to thinking based on natural law are of course much older and can be found as early as in the Sophists.) This model of a "suprapositive" legal foundation—natural law as rational law—influences to a great extent philosophical concepts in early Christianity and also later plays a decisive role in the theoretical discourses of European humanists of the modern era on the foundation of human rights. The Stoics themselves do not go so far as to give such rights an established character; rather they see slavery, for example, as compatible in principle with the theory of the equality of every person.

Up until the early modern era, Christian philosophers and theologians draw on only selective points of the approaches that characterized the ancient Christian and Hellenic world to reach ethical conclusions orientated toward human rights. While as early as during the time of the Greek patristic teachers Gregory of Nyssa speaks of the "regal dignity" of human beings, the thought, for example, that religious freedom is a fundamental right allowing each individual to live according to his or her own religious convictions is one that is rejected by Augustine in the post-Constantine era, even though before the Edict of Milan in 313 Christians in practice claimed such a right in relation to the Roman emperor, as long as they were in a situation where they were trying to liberate their religious community from persecution. In the 11th century, John of Salisbury demanded the separation of spiritual and secular power, thereby developing theses which in their basic elements anticipate the call heard in the modern era for a division of powers in order to achieve a rational limitation of power, and which give theoretical support to the medieval model of treaties limiting the power of authority (see II)—in a similar way as in the 14th century treatise *Defensor pacis* of Marsilius of Padua.

In his tract *De regimine principum,* Thomas Aquinas views the freedom of the individual, the right to life, and the right to property as the basis of any just power. Bartolus of Saxoferrato in the 14th century also includes freedom of thought and freedom of association here. According to William of Ockham, liberty and property (understood to mean a claim to those vital material things necessary for a minimum social standard of living) are rights endowed upon the human person by God, intrinsically bound to human dignity and therefore inalienable. Nicolas of Cues too recognizes natural rights common to all people and to which all state power must be subject. Cusanus, like Ockham, demonstrates ideas that in essence are a preparation for the later teaching regarding the sovereignty of the people.

In 1486, during the era of the Renaissance and of humanism, G. Pico della Mirandola's tract *De dignitate hominis* appears. Among the Reformers, it is particularly the work of Calvin that offers food for reflection on human rights. Friedrich Spee von Langenfeld in his work *Cautio Criminalis* makes a contribution of particular historical importance to overcoming the persecution of witches and to the abolition of torture as a legal means of interrogation.

In the situation of radical political and social change that characterized the early period of the modern era, political philosophy devotes itself in particular to the theoretical derivation of certain rights and freedoms of the individual. The medieval religious and political unit had grown increasingly fictitious, and with the Reformation, it was obvious to all that it was crushed completely; the feudal-corporate order, which had guaranteed certain rights and privileges to individual sections of society via a form of corporative representation of interests, was being dissolved by the dawn of absolutism. The monarchial sovereign is placed in direct opposition to the legally by far weaker underlings who found the scope for action they had enjoyed up until then—and which was in any case already severely limited—increasingly under threat.

The argumentation propounded by the late Spanish Scholastics (Francisco de Vitoria, the Salamanca school), which is very much characterized by the idea of a natural law, works on both the concept of a natural unity of humankind—reverting back to the Stoic-Christian teaching on the equality of all human beings—and on that of the legitimacy of political power being derived from the will of the people. This argumentation is thus already influenced by the contractual theoretical foundation model for political power. Amalgamations into one state are according to this theory, therefore, founded on an original contractual agreement among free subjects to guarantee their elementary basis for life; the mandate accorded to the person bearing political power is based on that person's guaranteeing the rights of the citizens, rights that emanate from the social contract concluded—in particular the right to the protection of their lives and their physical integrity but also the right to marriage, to family, to legal protection, to property, and to freedom of association.

The literature of the 16th and 17th centuries, geared against absolutism and in the main stemming from the pens of Calvinistic and secular theorists of the natural law (F. Vasquez, Grotius, Althusius, Wolff, Pufendorf, Thomasius, Milton, Blackstone, especially Locke, and in France Voltaire and Montesquieu), is also part of this mode of thought. Now, however, it goes further than that and, on the basis of human dignity, proclaims explicitly natural, individual human rights and basic freedoms, which predate and supersede the state. Thus corresponding legal claims to life, freedom, and a minimum social standard of living no longer appear as they did during the medieval legal system based on contractual limiting of authority (see II), that is, as having been granted as privileges; rather they become endowed with a character that makes their claim to validity independent of historical and political conventions. Not even the social contract is the real source of the constitution of individual rights but rather serves to transform naturally evident rights into civic rights.

Under the influence of the Reformation, mainly that of Calvinist groups, it is initially freedom of religion and freedom of conscience that in particular begin to take center stage in human-rights argumentation. The first phase in the development of the theory of human rights, however, is in general mainly characterized by strong accent being placed on individual rights to freedom understood as protection and defense from possible state intervention, but also already including the demand for participation in the process of political decision making, with Christian and theological argumentation increasingly fading into the background. The historically effective breakthrough of human-rights thinking is given in the 17th and 18th centuries by the revolutions in England, America, and France (where this became particularly manifest in the 1789 Declaration of the Rights of Man and the Citizen), although at this time the fact that they are basically popular movements means they still greatly concentrate on forming an internal legal basis and are lacking in the main in supranational perspectives. The Jacobin constitution drafted in 1793 during the French Revolution—which indeed never came into force—recognizes not only rights of freedom and participation but also certain claims to economic and social rights.

In German-speaking Europe, the philosophy of idealism, in particular that of I. Kant, also works, in parallel with these philosophical and political developments in America and Western Europe, toward establishing the basis of the picture of the human person according to the Enlightenment and toward giving consideration to the idea of the autonomy of each moral subject. In the light of this philosophy, human rights appear as a condition for the possibility that human beings can fulfill that for which they were morally determined; thus it is from this aspect that J. G. Fichte also defines the claim to social rights, for example, the right to work, to be educated, and to have at least a minimum standard of living. Gradually, however, this philosophy takes its leave of the reasoning that these fundamental rights are enshrined in the natural law, favoring instead, particularly in Hegel, a form of argumentation based to a large extent on legal positivism. The understanding then of basic rights is transformed from one that stresses the fact that these rights are of a character that predates and supersedes the state, to one that works on the opinion that these rights are granted by the constitution and thus may, in principle, be reversed by the constitutional authority. Outside of Germany, too, it will be at least the second half of the 19th century when legal-philosophical positivism becomes dominant, and only after the Second World War following the excesses of violence and inhumanity encountered in the totalitarian systems of national socialism and Stalinism that it is restrained—once again in favor of a revitalization of the concept of natural law.

The position of the Catholic church with regard to human rights—conceived mainly as liberal protective and defensive rights against state influence and against the limitation of personal freedoms—is seen in the wake of the French Revolution and then throughout the 19th century as in the main negative (see, for example, Pius IX's *Syllabus of Errors,* 1864). The theory of human rights developed during the Enlightenment is reproached for wanting to give free scope for action in which the individual is no longer subject to any moral obligation whatsoever. In addition, the church's rejection in this area is strengthened by a stressed areligious or antichurch form of attack used in the argumentation of several contemporary advocates of human rights thinking.

As a consequence of the industrialization of the 18th and 19th centuries, the understanding of human rights propagated during the Enlightenment meets with further criticism: in its liberal-individualistic accent it is said to overlook the fact that in order to make use of individual free scope for action, corresponding legal guarantees of freedom are not enough; required in addition are certain social and material prerequisites without which this room for maneuver cannot possibly be used. Social justice therefore also includes protective rights for the economically weaker members of society that must guarantee these positive claims will be met to a certain minimal level of performance by the state. Economic and social rights too are at this time said to have human-rights character. The socialist movement—of F. Lassalle and in particular of K. Marx and F. Engels—accuses those defending the classical idea of human rights of supporting particular rights that are not of use to all but rather only to the economically stronger bourgeoisie (human rights as class rights); Marx rejects in particular the institution of private ownership, since this enables the individual to pursue private interests removed from and possibly in opposition to the interests of the community at large. In contrast to social democracy, the Marxist approach can in the final analysis, however, not accept an understanding of human rights extended to the social dimension, since it rejects the thinking that the proletarian movement represents the general or unpartisan interests of all but favors instead the theory of the class struggle.

Catholic social teaching in the 19th century (particularly after *Rerum novarum* in 1891) distances itself from Marxism but shares the concerns expressed by socialist critics, particularly Lassalle and social democracy, and the so-called "Catheder socialists" (including G. v. Schmoller), in those areas where this criticism speaks out for elementary social needs of the individual in the face of the social consequences of an individualistically orientated market liberalism that is not cushioned by state social legislation. In the ensuing period the social dimension of the basic rights, together with traditional liberal protective and defensive rights, becomes part of both the legislature and the constitution of a growing number of countries throughout the world.

The 20th century is characterized by what might be termed a "universalization" of human rights, to the extent that these rights transcend the particular legal order of individual states and develop into an integral layer of a basic normative consensus in the field of supranational law. This was true only to a limited degree at the time of the League of Nations—here the accent is, in view of the conflicts that played a major role in the outbreak of the First World War, on the desire to give effective protection to ethnic and religious minorities, with the proclamation of the right to self-determination formulated in W. Wilson's 1918 Fourteen Point Plan to fall back on. Even during the Second World War (the 1941 Atlantic Charter), but in particular after it (the Charter of the United Nations of 1945 and the 1948 U.N. Universal Declaration of Human Rights, considerably influenced by J. Maritain), a form of argumentation, closely connected with the resurrection of frameworks of legal philosophies based on the natural law, begins to have a commanding influence on political decision making, giving consideration to the multidimensionality of human rights, stressing their claim to validity as predating and superseding the state, and striving for their comprehensive implementation worldwide. The renaissance of natural-law thinking, however, cannot conceal the fact that despite verbal consensus, the understanding of human rights still remains disputed at this time between the developing antagonistic systems in East and West. This is quickly seen in the ensuing period wherever the principles of the Universal Declaration of Human Rights are to be translated into practical policies and a real legal system. Even while this declaration is being formulated there is basic dissent on the question of whether freedom rights or social rights are to be given priority.

The position of the Catholic church with regard to human rights is subject to radical change with the encyclical *Pacem in terris* (1963), following important modifications in the traditional stance taken during the pontificate of Pius XII. While the 19th-century popes look on human rights with skepticism and rejection, John XXIII makes them the fundamental point of departure for his social and ethical argument, based on both the philosophy of the natural law and biblical theology. The pope defines the scale of human rights in the most extensive way possible, gearing himself very markedly toward the individual human-rights demands formulated in the United Nations' Declaration of Human Rights (in the development of which he himself played a part) and interpreting these rights on the whole as having been entrusted also to Christianity to be implemented on an ever wider basis. This implementation of human rights in both their liberal and social dimensions therefore becomes the decisive criterion for the ethical evaluation of the social order. The following passage makes clear that the encyclical is very closely linked with the natural-law interpretation of human rights: "Any society, if it is to be well-ordered and productive, must lay down as a foundation this principle, namely, that every human being is a person, that is, his nature is endowed with intelligence and free will. By virtue of this, he has rights and duties, flowing directly and simultaneously from his very nature. These rights are therefore universal, inviolable and inalienable" (PT 9).

Among the individual human-rights demands, John XXIII stresses the right to life and to freedom from bodily harm as well as the right to those commodities necessary for an appropriate standard of living (food, clothing, a home, education, health care, unemployment aid, and help in old age). He further stresses the right to freedom of opinion and information, freedom of religion and conscience, freedom to choose one's profession, freedom of migration, and the right to impartial legal protection for these rights. Among the rights to political participation, John stresses freedom of assembly and freedom of association. The pope also views the right to private property as one derived from the nature of humankind, while pointing out that consideration has to be given to the social obligation of holding any property. In general, in view of the social nature of humans, the pope views the individual rights and claims in correlation to corresponding social obligations on the part of the individual and in line with the aims of the social order, which serves the common good. This allows in theory for the application of certain claims to human rights, in cases of conflict, to be limited in the interests of the common good.

The Second Vatican Council, with its declaration in favor of freedom of religion (in *Dignitatis humanae*) and to human rights as a whole (in the pastoral constitution *Gaudium et spes*), means the correction of the Catholic stance initiated in *Pacem in terris* now has consensus within the church as a whole. In the council documents, too, a connection is noted between individual rights on the one hand and the "just requirements of public order" (DH 2) on the other; here however the question remains open concerning what priorities would be set in case of conflict and to what extent it might be possible to limit the at least prima facie endowed rights of the individual.

The postconciliar development of the church's teaching gives increasing importance to the area of human rights in its social message. At the same time it increasingly disregards reference to natural-law categories in the foundation of human rights and stresses the possibility of a specifically theological approach. The encyclical *Populorum progressio* deals with the ethical tasks of development aid already thematized in the pastoral constitution and presents an argument that makes possible both the proclamation of the "right to development" contained in the document of the 1971 Roman bishops' synod, *Justice in the World* (*De iustitia in mundo*), and later is the *topos* of the church's "preferential option for the poor." The 1975 document, *The Church and Human Rights,* of the papal Justice and Peace Commission attempts not only to give an overview of the philosophical and theological approaches to human rights in the ecclesiastical sphere, but also goes further to the level of pastoral orientation and practical initiatives. In John Paul II's 1979 encyclical, *Redemptor hominis,* Christology is the point of departure for the development of teaching on human rights derived from the dignity endowed on human beings by God.

II Human Rights as an Element of the Legal Order

In the medieval feudal order, where the idea of legally defensible individual human and basic rights was unknown, it is the instrument of a power-limiting contract that appears as an important principle in political and legal formation, with the help of which the central power of royalty is limited in favor of corporate rights (initially, in particular those of princely feudal lords). A significant example of legal development in Britain was the *Magna Charta* signed in 1215, although similar legal structures are found throughout Europe until the late Middle Ages. Everywhere the aim is to secure the free scope for action that has been passed down against absolutist tendencies on the part of the supreme ruler and also to establish a right to resistance against any potential misuse of power.

In the end, with the creation of the modern state in the early period of the modern era, it is absolutist interests that finally triumph over the corporate state order. The corporate right to speak on legal internal matters of state is repressed, with the result that those who had exercised this right are deprived of political power. The elaboration of theses explicitly mentioning human rights in political-practical philosophy (see I) reacts to this development and allows basically new social and ethical arguments to be worked out rather than merely harking back after the restoration of a social order that no longer exists. In revolutionary England in the 17th century it is already human rights that are being used to justify the demand for equality of voting rights for all citizens and the demand for (limited) freedom of religion. The Habeas Corpus Act of 1679 creates an effective protection of the citizen against arbitrary arrest and ensures the right to a proper trial; the Bill of Rights of 1689 lays down important privileges, previously contractually secured but now seen as individual civic rights against royal power.

The nation-building process in the United States is linked to the development in England. In the United States after the Declaration of Independence, various individual states use the Bill of Rights (the most famous being the Virginia Bill of Rights of 1776) to do important preparatory work for the establishment of a free, democratic constitutional order based on the principle of division of powers. (In spite of the comprehensive catalogue of basic freedoms contained in this constitution, it will be the second half of the 19th century before the institution of slavery is abolished everywhere in the United States.) The declarations of human rights made during the French Revolution—particularly the first, made in 1789—act, after 1800, as an exemplary model for national constitutions throughout Europe (or draft constitutions, as in Germany in 1848-49).

After 1945, the founding of the United Nations showed that human rights are now recognized as fundamental rights and that it is one of the most important tasks of this new organization to ensure their implementation (United Nations Charter, art. 1, par. 3). The two 1966 international covenants on civil and political rights as well as economic, social, and cultural rights are an attempt to make up for the shortcoming inherent in the principles of the 1948 Universal Declaration of Human Rights, namely that because of the political and moral character of this document, its principles have no direct legal effect. East and West also remain (see I) disagreed on the question of an appropriate interpretation of the importance of the statutory rights—and this in spite of the fact that the preambles to both covenants make reference to the principles of the U.N. Charter. Moreover, the extensive right to self-determination for all peoples laid down in the first section of the covenants maintains generous room for maneuver, within which the social and political development in the signatory states is to be examined in relation to their conformity with the treaties.

The covenant on economic, social, and cultural rights contains claims to rights of the individual, in particular to work and humane working conditions, to social security, the protection of the family, an adequate standard of living, the enjoyment of physical and mental health, as well as to training and education and to participation in cultural life. The treaty on civil and political rights bans torture and slavery, reaffirms the principles of the Habeas Corpus Act, the principles of freedom of movement both at home and abroad, freedom of thought, conscience, religion, and opinion, freedom of association and society, the principles of protection of marriage and the family, the right to take part in the process of public political formation of opinion, and the protection of ethnic, religious, or linguistic minorities. Both the civil-rights pact (art. 4, par. 1) and the social pact (art. 4), however, contain a general clause according to which the limitation of certain statutory rights of the individual for the common good or for reasons of public order may be compatible with the principles of this agreement (*ordre* public reservation). The social pact furthermore recognizes (art. 2, par. 1) that the complete realization of the rights claimed in it can only be possible "progressively" depending on the conditions in the country concerned, particularly from an economic point of view. To verify whether those obligations contained in the covenants are adhered to, a system of reports is provided for, as well as, in the case of the civil-rights pact, an institutionalized form of complaints against certain countries, according to which one party to the covenant may lodge a complaint against another party-state for actual or suspected violations. The optional protocol to the civic-rights pact moreover recognizes individual complaints from citizens against measures taken by the government of their own country that they hold to be in conflict with the provisions laid down in the pact. This is a clear attempt at guaranteeing human rights in one country independently of official government protests on the part of another state and at ensuring that the individual whose rights may have been violated is granted a status coming close to that of a subject in international law.

Apart from the 1966 covenants, which became internationally binding for the signatory states after ratification by a minimum number of states in 1976, further international agreements on specific problem areas in the protection of human rights have been concluded at the U.N. level (refugee and antitorture convention, convention on the prevention and punishment of the crime of genocide, against slavery, racial discrimination, and discrimination of women, among others). To secure human rights at supranational law, other regional human-rights protection systems have been developed below the U.N. level, for example, the European Convention on Human Rights and the European Social

Charter, the American Convention on Human Rights, and for Africa the Banjul Charter of Human Rights and the Rights of Peoples.

In Europe, in the light of the most recent political developments, the importance of the CSCE process (Conference on Security and Cooperation in Europe) has grown further, a process in which not only the countries of Eastern and Western Europe take part but also the United States and Canada. The "Basket III" of the 1975 Helsinki Final Act contains only declarations of intent with regard to implementing and respecting human rights, and these do not have binding international effect; they may thus be viewed on the same level as similar political and moral obligations such as the U.N. Declaration of Human Rights. During the CSCE follow-up meetings, however, on the human dimension it became clear that in spite of the lack of possible sanctions in international law, the CSCE process was endowed with the potential for bringing about considerable political change in the situation in the countries of Eastern Europe. At the moment political analyses are, in view of the concept of a European peace order and of overcoming the division into two military blocks, concentrated on the question of the extent to which the CSCE framework can serve as the political and institutional core of such an order and how far the spectrum of tasks to be dealt with there should be extended.

III The Theory of Human-Rights Argumentation

It is not only in the official teaching of the Second Vatican Council and the postconciliar popes that a more biblically based approach takes precedence over access to human rights seen in terms of a natural law conceived as rational law, which has always been a characteristic element in Catholic argumentation in the field of moral theology. In the ecumenical dialogue going on between the Christian churches too, as well as in the philosophical and political disputes between representatives of the countries of the North and the South and East, the idea of human-rights claims and demands being based on the natural law is a controversial one (see IV). In the field of philosophy, the possibilities and the extent of an ethical approach based on (human) rights that are to be postulated as at least morally valid are under debate. This has, in part, direct consequences for the question of how human-rights demands are viewed in relation to one another, whether they have a hierarchical order, and how one should proceed in cases of dispute involving individual demands, either among one another or in reference to the interests of the community at large (the common good), that is, whether, for what reason, and to what extent individual rights can be limited. In dispute is whether all or at least certain human-rights demands can be given the status of absolute rights or whether they have a prima facie structure where a system of priority rules would be needed to decide which right was to be given such priority in case of conflict; whether a system of human-rights principles develops from a single moral principle (e.g., love in the sense of *agape, dilectio*) or is based on a range of particular principles equal in rank but independent of one another (justice, fairness, goodwill, faithfulness, justness, thankfulness, truthfulness, mercifulness, and others). Contributions to this discussion are also made by representatives of deontological and teleological approaches to moral theology when they deal with the question of the normative ethical consequences of a call to human dignity.

In the light of a teleological approach to the question of human rights based on the natural law—an approach that in principle is not limited to Christians alone but ought to be acceptable to all rational beings—particular moral principles can be understood in the final analysis as special expressions of one single moral principle (love as *agape*) with different interrelations in different actions. The reason behind the obligation to love is seen in the dignity of the human person to which this love must be referred. This dignity is founded on the idea of the human person as a subject and on the person's ability to determine his or her own way of living and to choose actions from among various options. At the same time the fact that a human person is a subject is a condition for the person's being able to receive any moral demands at all. Individual human rights here, too, receive their character as moral obligations, and thus are at their core independent of legal positivization. They are in fact particular expressions of that to which every individual being can make claim in the name of his or her dignity as a human person—and thus they are also valid reciprocally according to the so-called Golden Rule (relationship between rights and obligations). Action that helps the individual to be ensured that human-rights standards are, in one's own person, respected is of central importance for one's well-being. Commitment to human rights is therefore one of the most important expressions of moral integrity in actions designed to promote the good of one's neighbor. Human-rights guarantees give individuals the possibility of maintaining their status as moral subjects in elementary legal matters and social affairs of life; the extent to which human rights are realized therefore directly affects the opportunities available to human persons to become morally mature.

Among human rights, exceptional importance is attached to the right to freedom of conscience, the right not to be forced to act against the moral judgments of one's own conscience. While most human rights have a more-or-less direct connection with the various dimensions of a person's external freedom, an attack on freedom of conscience affects the internal freedom and therefore the moral integrity of the subject. The attempt to force someone to act against conscience is equal to direct encouragement to sin. Such an attempt is, even from the point of view of teleological argumentation, always and under all circumstances morally reprehensible; thus the moral ban on torture is always valid. Even when torture does not represent an attack on the morality of the person being tortured, but rather is an attempt to prevent terrible evil being inflicted on a great number by a malicious act on the part of the wrongdoer (e.g., in the case of a nuclear terrorist who is aware of the morally reprehensible nature of the action), a practically general ban on torture can be maintained in the sense of a *lex lata ad praecavendum periculum generale,* since the misuse of even so limited permission to use torture in certain very hypothetical cases may be considered much more probable than proper recourse to such permission. The general validity of the ban on torture can therefore be accounted for not only from a deontological viewpoint but also using consistently teleological argumentation.

Many individual human-rights demands may be designated as "intermediate principles" (*mittlere Prinzipien,* O. Hoeffe), which are not on the same level as their historically concrete implementation in specific political, social, and legal conditions against a contingent background, but rather show the importance of ethical assessment criteria in relation to these. The observation that such concrete conditions appear incompatible with certain human-rights standards therefore demands these conditions be examined and if need be, changed or abolished. Should certain actions or living conditions conflict with these standards, proof would have to be given that they are nonetheless legitimate and not vice versa, that is, that the human-rights claim that criticizes such actions or conditions is for its part justly being made. This "burden of proof" regulation shows its importance particularly in cases where attempts are being made to dismiss human-rights claims of individuals in the name of the interests of society at large (see below).

All individual human-rights demands as are met today in context of philosophy, theology, and politics can be divided up and categorized according to different criteria. The differentiation most often made is among (*a*) rights to freedom seen as rights of defense against state intervention in certain areas of private life (*status negativus*), (*b*) claims to social rights to a minimum provision of commodities that permit participation in the life of society (*status positivus*), and (*c*) rights to take part in the process of the formation of political opinion and option (*status activus*). Rights to freedom and partly to participation are also termed "human rights of the first generation" and social and economic rights those of the "second generation," as opposed to what is termed today the "third generation of human rights"; under discussion, for example, are the right to peace, to cultural and economic development, to the integrity of environment. From the point of view of the legal system, a problem arises in that new category—that these rights are conceived as collective as opposed to individual rights and refer to political and moral aims that are to a high degree of a general character, so that in contrast to human rights of the first and second generations, the question of who is in possession of these rights and what exactly they entail has not been answered satisfactorily.

In determining the internal relationship of these categories of rights, decisive importance is attached to the question of whether and to what extent one particular right can be seen as a prerequisite for the possibility of enjoying another particular right. Thus the opportunities a person has for making use of political rights to freedom and participation depend considerably on the person's having a secure minimum social standard. For one whose daily activity consists of trying to secure the basic minimum for one's family for the next day, freedom of the press and of opinion very quickly become merely formal rights that have no effect on the practical reality of one's life; thus the guarantee of elementary social rights must be seen as condition for any individual possibly being able to develop freely. Social and ethical responsibility would be cut in half if it were only to be considered as a legal and institutional obligation to respect the freedom of others without trying to promote the well-being of our fellow men and women who are not as fortunate. The fact that the question of how social claims to certain rights can be adequately met is, particularly because of the influence of many outside conditions in the economic capability of a country, much more complex than simply guaranteeing rights to freedom and by no means detracts from the human-rights character of such claims; it rather demonstrates that the demand to change those economic conditions, if need be, toward more just division of wealth and of the competition conditions on the world market, does indeed have a human-rights dimension and thus makes the urgency of it even more pressing. In the same way, the demand for a democratic constitutional order with basic rights, guaranteed independent of party political interests, can be derived from the right of the individual (as a rational being) to be heard in matters that affect him or her and thus from the right to participate in the political decision-making process; only constitutional orders of this kind offer adequate insurance that political participation cannot be linked in an underhand way to attachment to predefined party political positions.

Given the growing interconnection today of all human relations in the environment around the human person and in view of the fact that humanity today is despoiling this environment in various ways to the endangerment of future generations, it is necessary to extend the classical understanding of human rights to guarantee the right of our children's generation today and of those yet to be born to live under conditions worthy of a human person. Human-rights argumentation moreover must not become so narrow in meaning that the individual value of nonhuman creation, in particular of animals, and the necessity of protecting them from arbitrary cruel treatment is lost from view. Human persons are also morally responsible for the way they treat the nonhuman world around them. Unjust structures or the despoiling of the natural environment must not become legitimized in the forefront of human-rights argumentation, for example, by calling on the right to freedom in the economic sense. The character of human rights as rights that apply to all creatures endowed with human dignity tends indeed, rather, to prohibit a few from enjoying unhindered advantages that detrimentally affect the possibility of guaranteeing human-rights standards for many other persons.

Thus the difficult question must be asked as to what are the internal limits of validity of individual human-rights demands when in conflict with comparable other individual demands (thus for example there is often a strained relationship between demands for freedom and demands for equality), with the interests of the common good, or in cases where a conflict occurs because of the same claim being made by two different parties. A decisionistic choice between different rights, which are conceived as in their own way absolutely obligating, seems inconsistent from an ethical point of view and unacceptable from a political point of view, since there would be a danger arbitrary decisions might be taken. It is the duty of political justice to develop solutions that, even though they may put limits on particular rights, preserve their core intact. From this principle, however, the problem becomes more difficult of how to act in situations where limits on certain human rights are only sensible if the rights are suspended completely rather than merely partially (e.g., in the case of quarantine in which the freedom of movement of individuals is, in certain circumstances, removed for long periods).

One solution is offered by the above-mentioned "burden of proof" regulation as well as by the systematic questioning whether there exists a situation in which the satisfaction of one individual human-rights demand (e.g., social security at least at a minimum level) would be the precondition for the implementation of another (e.g., political participation). Limitations placed on basic rights may be justified rationally as soon as it can be demonstrated that a certain temporary limitation of freedoms is urgently necessary to secure the political stability of a state structure, or to bring the social level of a society up to the standard required for these basic rights to be exercised as a general commodity available to all and not only reserved to a small number of the privileged. This same principle may be valid today for the relationship between economic freedoms and ecological demands; it is also applicable to states of emergency. Thus the argument can also be contradicted whereby the task of the state to "satisfy according to its possibilities" is said to apply only to social-demand rights. The concrete formulation of a catalogue of basic *freedoms* also points out that the conditions that make claiming these rights possible must also be fulfilled.

Nevertheless one can see from this that in serious situations the legal guarantees of freedom may often depend to a large degree on the political judgment of the representatives of the legislative and the executive on the general state of society and thus on the empirical nonlegal conditions, against which the bearers of political responsibility may err in a fatal fashion. The explosive nature of this is intensified by the fact that because it is possible to limit basic rights, the danger is always present that use will be made of this possibility to justify authoritarian and totalitarian practices. Within the context of constitutional orders the question is therefore posed of what individuals or institutions are competent, if need be, to decide on the need and the legitimate extent of either the limitation or indeed the complete suspension of basic rights. How can one separate the area where majority decisions as well as considerations in line with a general assessment of the advantages and disadvantages of limiting a basic right suffice from the area of the inalienable core of a basic right? To what extent is, in case of deeply rooted conflicts between different convictions, the legitimation of political decisions on their conformity with procedural regulations sufficient? (Here in discussions on political ethics the question of "civil disobedience" is introduced.)

From a social-philosophical viewpoint, O. Hoeffe suggests as a solution to conflicts of this kind the criterion of distributive advantage as a principle of political justice. Political structures (including giving human rights the positive character of basic rights by laying them down in constitutions) should be considered just when in spite of disadvantages each individual living under such a structure enjoys comparatively more advantages. Hoeffe's proposal comes close here to a social and ethical approach based on the rights of the individual, since the well-known accusation made against utilitarianism—that it is prepared to sacrifice the well-being of the individual for the sake of collective advantage—cannot be made against the argument of distributive advantage. One would therefore expect that everyone would be able to agree with such a system of justice. On the other hand, the criterion of distributive advantage is based to a high degree on the concept of society at large; it too therefore admits no conclusion gauged via direct analysis, but rather via empirical analysis, of the extent to which a given legal and social order may be considered to comply with human rights. The same is true for the formal principles of justice proposed by J. Rawls: "First principle: Each person is to have an equal right to the most extensive total system of equal basic liberties compatible with a similar system of liberty for all. Second principle: Social and economic inequalities are to be arranged so that they are both: (*a*) to the greatest benefit of the least advantaged, . . . and (*b*) attached to offices and positions open to all under conditions of fair equality of opportunity" (J. Rawls, *A Theory of Justice,* Cambridge, Mass. 1971, p. 302).

IV Human Rights as the Foundation of an International Ethos

Since 1945 considerable improvements have taken place in the protection of human rights. At the level of formation of the legal order, human rights have been and are being positivized, on the one hand, in national constitutions and, on the other hand, within supranational legal systems (regional systems for the protection of human rights, the United Nations covenants on human rights; see II). Within the set legal framework, national and international jurisdiction is entrusted with ensuring that human rights are guaranteed, yet the dominant role still exercised by reservations stemming from national sovereignty makes more difficult the task of achieving the global and adequately effective implementation of human rights by an international or a supranational authority—difficult to an extent that is intolerable. Such an authority would have to be with consensus of the international community and thus be based on a minimum of commonly shared ethical principles that could build the basis of an international ethos, irrespective of the differing civilizations in the various cultural, political, and religious areas of the world. The question must be asked as to what obstacles exist to any attempt at making human dignity and human rights the normative basis of such an ethos acceptable. It cannot be denied that there are in the world today fundamental normative differences in position.

In view of this it is necessary, on the one hand, to create the conditions for a possible global human-rights-based legal and social order and, on the other, to ensure that the individual cultural development in different areas of the world does not fall victim to the attempt to lay down such a universal ethos in politics and law, which thus could be seen as a violation or engenders the suspicion of cultural imperialism.

The way the West justifies human rights does not meet with automatic agreement, either in the non-Christian religions of the world or in certain culturally different worldviews stemming from other sources or secular ideologies. This is partly because of the great importance they attach to rational structures of arguments: for this reason they are the main target of every kind of fundamentalism. Furthermore they are also accused, particularly by the countries of the South of having a one-sided and individualistic orientation, among other things, that does not take due account of the fact that the individual is bound by many different family and other social ties.

In the social and religious conception of the social order represented by Islam, in which the modern model of a separation between religion, or church, and state (as is generally the case in Europe) is rejected, the principle of religious tolerance is accepted to the extent that Islam allows non-Muslims too to practice their religion individually within Islamic society, on condition that they are "keepers of the word," that is, Jews and Christians or members of another religion with a written revelation. Non-Muslims, however, are certainly not considered equal to Muslims as far as their civic rights go. They have a lower status, which can be seen in particular in the field of marriage and family law as well as in the fact that they are barred from holding public office. Quite controversial, also, appears the question of the extent to which the concept of "holy war" (*jihad*) against non-Muslims who do not belong to a revelatory religion is limited to defense against attacks on Islam or can also be understood as a way of unleashing an offensive war with the aim of carrying out missionary activity for Islam. In any case, long-term coexistence not only with Christianity but also in particular with polytheistic religions is unimaginable; the relationship between the religions is characterized, rather, by competition and even confrontation. The social position of women in Islam must also be seen as unequal and discriminatory. Muslim scholars today discuss the necessity and the possibility of reinterpreting Islamic tradition in a way that is opposed to the renaissance of fundamentalism in the Islamic world and that is geared toward consciously welcoming the development of human-rights standards in the Western world.

To apply the paradigm of human rights to the Far Eastern conceptions of the world represented by Hinduism and Buddhism is even more problematic than is the case with Islam. This is true in part because of the fact that Buddhism is marked by many different schools—from a kind of state ideology to a philosophy stressing perspectives critical of the state—and also because it is not distinguishable enough from the opinions represented by Confucianism and Shintoism. Nevertheless, basic social and ethical aims such as peace and social justice are acceptable also to a Buddhist or a Hindu and can be classed as guiding factors in the ethical behavior of the individual in his social and political environment; these religions may not thus be said to be identified by a belief in, in principle, withdrawing from the world and renouncing the tasks it might entrust them with. What is missing is an explicit approval of the human-rights *topos* as the cornerstone of an agreed social order.

In spite of these theoretical difficulties, however, one can see practical agreements in the world today on the human-rights character of basic goods—in national constitutions, in international proclamations, and in conventions binding in international law—on the trio of claims to liberal, social, and participatory rights. This existing consensus may justify hopes that it may indeed lead to better, justice-based international protection for human rights—even if it means an extensive renunciation of sovereign claims. To the extent that human-rights standards are in conflict with religiously motivated claims to authority, the question must also be asked here of how the probable or actual social consequences of the underlying religious conceptual model can be made compatible with a future and where possible a global ethos of human rights. Wherever the practice of religion has inhuman consequences, for example, in violent missionary methods or in the political or social persecution of those who think differently, one at least must be allowed to pose the question of whether fanaticism is not threatening to take the place of genuine religious conviction.

International law as it stands at the moment contains an explicit ban on intervention (art. 2, par. 7 of the United Nations Charter) and thus does not have this method at its disposal as a legitimate instrument of pushing through human rights in other countries. This certainly does not only mean a ban on the use of military force but also means that nonmilitary foreign policy or economic strategies may not be used if they represent an intervention into the internal affairs of another country. It is no rare occurrence that countries in which human rights are often brutally suppressed attempt to defend themselves against international political efforts to ensure these rights are protected by pointing to the intervention ban. The international ban on intervention, and the interests of a fully effective protection of human rights in the absence of an international authority capable of getting its judicial decisions carried out, are thus caught in sometimes tragic conflict with each other. This does not alter the fact that in earlier decades of this century and in particular during the last century, at least a moral right was claimed to "humanitarian intervention," but sometimes in places it was merely used in an attempt to hide power seeking and domination. The misuse of a legitimate right to intervention is therefore excluded by the intervention ban in the U.N. Charter, but equally excluded is the possibility of justly putting across one's arguments—for example in the case of serious, long-term human-rights violations in another country. Thus it is difficult to decide whether the present comprehensive ban on intervention or a more narrowly expressed ban that would admit certain exceptions would be of more benefit to the international community as it is today.

In the present world it is often possible to observe a connection between situations of social injustice, human-rights violations, the poverty of refugees, and—at least in the short term—danger to international peace. Any policy of the economically developed countries of the North aimed at really protecting and promoting the rights of the individual and of peoples in the disadvantaged world, irrespective of superficial national interests, would have to be understood as development aid in the sense of "help toward self-help." The proper understanding of "development" here should not be limited to the financial dimension but should be undertaken as an overall policy, tackling, for example, all forms of discrimination of minorities and any regression into nationalistic or racial arrogant ideologies. In view of the growing interdependence of the international community, this would also be a wise long-term strategy to break down potential conflicts that otherwise might endanger the political peace and economic prosperity of the North. It nevertheless remains a fundamental moral demand from which one should not pull back even if one's own advantage is considered less-directly affected. If human-rights policy desires to remain credible and fit for consensus in the long term, it must have not a pragmatic base but, rather, solely one that gives adequate consideration to ethical categories.

See also DIGNITATIS HUMANAE; ENLIGHTENMENT, THE (INFLUENCE OF); NATURAL LAW; PERSON, DIGNITY OF; RELIGIOUS FREEDOM; RIGHTS AND DUTIES; TOLERATION, PRINCIPLE OF; TORTURE.

Bibliography: Commission Theologique Internationale/Commission Pontificale "Iustitia et Pax," *Les chrétiens d'aujourd'hui devant la dignité et les droits de la personne humaine* (Cité du Vatican, 1985). M. Crahan, ed., *Human Rights and Basic Needs in the Americas* (Washington, 1982). A. Hennelly and J. Langan, eds., *Human Rights in the Americas: The Struggle for Consensus* (Washington, 1982). D. Hollenbach, *Claims in Conflict: Retrieving and Renewing the Catholic Human Rights Tradition* (New York, 1979). J. Waldron, ed., *Theories of Rights* (Oxford, 1985). I. Brownlie, ed., *Basic Documents on Human Rights,* 2nd ed. (Oxford, 1981). T. Buergenthal, ed., *Human Rights, International Law, and the Helsinki Accord* (Montclair, N.J., 1977). P. Sieghart, *The International Law of Human Rights* (Oxford, 1983). T. Meron, ed., *Human Rights in International Law: Legal and Policy Issues* (Oxford, 1984). V. Nanda, ed., *Global Human Rights: Public Policies, Comparative Measures, and NGO Strategies* (Boulder, Colo., 1981).

THOMAS HOPPE

HUMANISM

In its widest sense "humanism" refers to the appreciation and enhancement of the quality of being human. For Western culture the foundations of this awareness are to be found in the achievements of Greek and Roman civilizations, attaining its clearest articulation in the classical period of Greek philosophy. Plato saw the true homeland of human reason not in the world of material things and sense perception but rather in the invisible world of the Ideal Forms. This separation is both the strength and the weakness of his interpretation. By setting one realm over against the other, Plato disclosed the potential of human reason as a power available to reach to the ultimate conditions of its own existence. The weakness is Plato's location of everything humanly worthwhile in a world apart from the material world of the senses. Aristotle's philosophy marks a further major step in this developing awareness of the scope and nature of human reality. By perceiving the Forms no longer as an independent sphere but as the source itself of the intelligibility of *this* world, Aristotle drew attention to the intrinsic blueprint that governs the operation of each being as it strives to fulfill its own potential. A significant part of this early achievement in art, literature, law, and philosophy was lost to the West for the next 1,500 years. The predominant influence remained Plato's philosophy, especially as given a mystical expression by Plotinus and a Christian interpretation by Augustine. Together with Stoic moral philosophy, this formed the cultural atmosphere breathed by Christianity in the patristic era and, following the destruction of the Roman Empire in the West, provided the framework for the synthesis of church and culture in the form of medieval Christendom.

Humanism, in its stricter historical sense, must be seen against this background. From the 11th century, civil life began to emancipate itself from the direct tutelage of the church. Interest was initially directed toward pre-Christian political and legal sources as alternatives to canon law, in order to discover a foundation for the newly emerging secular governments. This was especially a lay enterprise centered on the recently founded universities and the courts of European princes. Faith also sought to explore its own resources through the systematic use of human reason. The rediscovery of Aristotle enabled Aquinas to give new precision to the relationship of grace and nature. From this time on, the ancient classics were increasingly sought as the best source of models and information for better understanding *humanitas* before the introduction of *Christianitas.* The result was an emerging appreciation of "nature" as the field of the diverse, the changeable, and the individual.

In the early 14th century there was a heightened interest in the literary, cultural, educational, and aesthetic classical works.

This early Renaissance humanism turned more explicitly to the *studia humanitatis.* Plato and Aristotle remained the rival philosophers. The Platonic strand developed a more artistic and imaginative form of humanism, linked in many cases to religious views that turned to Augustine and other patristic sources, both Greek and Latin, for their inspiration. It defended the dignity of the individual over against the more impersonal and naturalistic Aristotelian philosophy of the Latin Averroists. Pico della Mirandola (1463–94) in his *Oration on the Dignity of Man* founded human dignity on the "freedom of choice" that enables persons to be "maker and molder" of themselves (3). The opposing view, influenced also by Stoic determinism, regarded the human being as a natural being in an ordered world, with faith exiled to its own separate realm. This position gradually gave way to a defense of individual dignity, based, as Petro Pomponazzi (1462–1525) argues in *On the Immortality of the Soul,* not on a substantial distinctiveness through the possession of an immortal soul but on the ability of the human intellect to "think discursively, and comprehend universals, which organic and extended powers cannot do at all" (chap. 9). These divergent and unreconciled views were to set the stage for the continuing debate about the scope and nature of human reality to the present day.

In the 16th century Renaissance humanism became more intensely a cultural and educational program. The classical experience of the ancients could be recaptured, they reasoned, if the texts were approached with the appropriate literary methods and skills. In the light of this general principle, Erasmus (ca. 1466–1536) argued for a return to the original texts of Scripture and the patristic era as a means of recapturing the purity of the experience of the early church without the stultifying accretions of the medieval period. This was also the century of the Reformation. The Swiss Reform movement was initially heavily influenced by Erasmus and the humanists in their efforts for the moral reform of the church. Luther, however, followed quickly by Zwingli and the other Reformers, while continuing to employ and promote the educational techniques of Renaissance humanism, sharply distinguished their theological concern with "justification by faith alone" from the humanists' optimistic reliance on free will.

Rene Descartes (1596–1650) gave to the broad understanding of humanism its distinctive modern shape by distinguishing two distinct substances: *res extensa,* the quantifiable material world of space and time, the field of science; and *res cogitans,* the subjective realm of feeling, perception, mind, and choice. The hierarchically perceived order of God, nature, and humanity of the previous era was now shattered. For Descartes, faith and reason were separate but not contradictory, although with reason in the ascendancy. Faith itself was understood as essentially a matter of the "will," or of the "heart" according to Blaise Pascal (1623–62), to be defended by rigorous analysis and the deductive powers of reason. As the influence of science increased, especially after Isaac Newton (1642–1727), "reason" became more and more identified with the empirical induction and verification processes of the physical sciences. The Enlightenment in the 18th century, inspired by a growing confidence in scientific inquiry, subjected the then-current religious teaching of the churches to ever sharper criticism. Epitomized in Voltaire (1694–1778) and the *Encyclopédie* (1751–65), this attack saw Christian faith as the enemy of rational autonomy and the emancipation of society from the traditional regime of church and state. The English-speaking tradition of humanism, associated with such figures as David Hume (1711–76), John Stuart Mill (1806–73), Thomas Huxley (1825–95), William Morris (1834–96), John Dewey (1859–1952), and Bertrand Russell (1872–1970), became increasingly committed to a secular form of society within which the rights of individuals would be protected against all encroachment and infringement. This liberal humanism seeks to give full weight to life in the world and to develop responsibility for its progress. In more modern times this has been coupled with the express purpose of eliminating from the understanding of the "human" everything that does not meet the scientific criteria of empirical verification.

On the Continent also, humanism in many instances adopted a militantly anti-Christian or atheistic stance, moving from the deism of the Enlightenment with its pleas for tolerance, to its political culmination in the French Revolution with the enthronement of Reason in Notre Dame Cathedral in 1793 for the cause of "liberty, equality, and fraternity." One very influential strand developed the materialistic pole of Descartes' dualism of mind and matter to reduce everything, including mind, to mechanistic terms. Ludwig Feuerbach (1804–72) focused attention on this world and its needs. The concept of God, he argued, is a projection of the "infinity" of human consciousness. Theology therefore must be dissolved into anthropology. Karl Marx (1818–83) radicalized this "alienation" by uncovering the exploitation of labor from which it arises. Religion he considered to be an opiate to relieve the misery of the poor by turning their thoughts to a nonexistent better world to come. Friedrich Nietzsche (1844–1900) carried the consequences of the "death of God" to their logical conclusion by demanding an end to the inimical-to-life morality of Christianity and the revaluation of all values in favor of a Dionysian affirmation of the inexhaustibility of life.

In a broader framework, leaving aside the antagonism of scientific reason and emerging political freedom to traditional Christianity, recent centuries have witnessed a clearer understanding of the complexity of human reality. Immanuel Kant (1724–1804) pointed to the preconditions of human knowledge and moral conscience. Georg Wilhelm Hegel (1770–1831) made explicit the historical nature of all human thought. Progressively, the details of this new appraisal have been outlined: such features as its economic and political infrastructures, the place of feeling and imagination, the influence of the unconscious and other hidden factors, the all-embracing context of language and culture, the priority of praxis, the material and ecological basis of human life, and the scope of human technological and scientific powers. The life-world has thus become increasingly differentiated so that more and more of what it means to be human has been brought into explicit awareness, and the power to assume control over the material conditions of life has, for better or worse, been harnessed.

The Christian churches have slowly begun to take note of these changes. Pope Leo XIII in *Rerum novarum* (1891) addressed the historical issue of the social conditions of work in the modern industrialized world and initiated by his proposed solution a move away from abstract, predetermined theories of human nature toward a renewed sensitivity to the developing consciousness of what it means to be human. This thinking attained its fullest official expression in *Gaudium et spes,* seen especially in its attempt to overcome the otherworldly accent of the past and to emphasize the Christian commitment to the construction of the "earthly city" (GS 20–21, 40–45); its strong defense of human freedom (14–17) and solidarity (24–32); its attention to new historical conditions (4–10); and its statement on the bond between human values and the kingdom of God (33–39). Paul VI in *Populorum progressio* called for a humanism embracing each person and "open to the values of the spirit and to God" (PP 42, see also 20–21). His principal source for this appeal was Jacques Maritain (1882–1973), who advocated an integral humanism created by a refraction of the values of the gospel within society in order to realize the concrete possibilities that history makes available in any given era. Pope John Paul II has continued this approach. In *Sollicitudo rei socialis* he presents integral development as an "essential dimension" of the human vocation, which is only ensured when the goods of the world are subordinated to the "transcendent reality" of the person (SRS 28–30). This formulation retains a dichotomy of spirit and matter, even though in a less pronounced form than the earlier dualism of body and soul, natural and supernatural. Faith is still seen as inhabiting its own transcendent, self-sustaining sphere from which superior vantage point it is then able to influence and direct secular events. Human freedom, initiative, and responsibility continue to be undervalued. In social ethics the challenge to this style of thinking has come from political and liberation theology. A new Christian humanism must acknowledge the operation of the material and cultural conditions that underpin all realization of human potential. Faith itself is immersed in this historical process as it attempts to express and live the salvation offered in the gospel. It is not only a hierarchy of values that is important to this task, but also their progressive integration into the creative enterprise of the human assumption of responsibility for the future of the world. The spiritual is a quality of the material world that must be enhanced by the proper exercise of human freedom in union with the spirit of Christ, if creation is to attain its fulfillment. Revelation entails a liberating challenge to the injustice and sinfulness of all established human structures and systems. Science is not an alternative worldview but a means, together with all other forms of human knowledge and skill, to enhancing this quality of human life. Such a humanism is never a task once and for all completed, but is an ongoing incentive to renew practice and articulate faith in the light of an ever more authentic grasp of the gospel message.

See also ANTHROPOLOGY; AUGUSTINE, INFLUENCE OF; ENLIGHTENMENT, THE (INFLUENCE OF); GAUDIUM ET SPES; MARITAIN, JACQUES; PERSON, DIGNITY OF; SOLLICITUDO REI SOCIALIS; THOMAS AQUINAS, CONTRIBUTION OF.

Bibliography: H. Blackham, *Humanism* (Penguin, 1976). K. Robbins, *Religion and Humanism* (Oxford: Basil Blackwell, 1981). W. Ullmann, *Medieval Foundations of Renaissance Humanism* (London: Paul Elek, 1977).

NEIL BROWN

HUNGER

In the simplest and most direct conception, hunger is not a difficult idea to define: hunger is the condition caused by lack of food. But as with so many apparently simple concepts, the idea of hunger becomes infinitely more complicated when applied to the real world, the world of malnutrition and poverty, of suffering and deprivation, and, at the most graphic level, the world of distended bellies and starving babies. While the present essay will attempt to address the issue of hunger in a reasoned and dispassionate way, it is important to keep in mind that hunger is very much a problem of politics and policy—very much a practical and living ethical issue calling for a response from every informed global citizen.

Definition and Dimensions

No one can say for sure how many hungry people there are in the world. One reason for this is that there is no universally accepted definition of hunger. Recent scholarship has offered the concepts of food shortage, food poverty, and food deprivation to organize the disparate data on hunger and its prevention and to bridge the differing perceptions of hunger's cause held by those who emphasize the distribution of food and hunger and those who focus on the symptoms of undernutrition.

Food shortage. The clearest picture of hunger is found in food-short countries: here we encounter absolute shortage where there is simply not enough food to sustain the population within a given region. Most often, natural disaster, war, or societal disruption lies at the heart of food shortage. Recent data prepared by the United Nations shows that in 1986, 1,570 million people, or 31 percent of the world's population, lived in forty-nine countries where the total dietary supply was less than that required for health, growth, and productive work. Of these forty-nine countries, thirty-one were located in sub-Saharan Africa, six in South Asia, and six in the Western Hemisphere.

Such measurements adequately reflect the devastating prevalence of hunger in today's world but do not show the depth of nutritional deprivation. For the most poignant faces of hunger we must consider the faces of famine. These are the widespread, persistent, and often near-complete food shortages that attract the attention of the media and that for many in the Western world are synonymous with world hunger. In 1988 at least five countries with a combined population of 204 million people—4 percent of the world's population—suffered famine within their national territory. In many cases the victims of war are inseparable from the victims of famine, as the famines most resistant to relief are those created or aggravated by violent conflict. Indeed, combatants in many contemporary wars have intentionally disrupted the flow of food, using food as a weapon in acts of almost inconceivable cruelty. In 1987 wars were fought in twenty-three countries, seventeen of which experienced significant disruption of the food supply. And in 1988 and 1989 the continuing armed conflict in the southern Sudan took the lives of an estimated 260,000 people by starvation while relief agencies were forced by military menace to suspend operations.

It is important to note, however, that although famine provides the most familiar image of hunger, famine accounts for only 10 percent of hunger-related deaths. Other forms of chronic persistent hunger, less graphic and sadly less compelling, are as yet neither recognized nor adequately addressed—but they are just as deadly.

Food poverty. An equally important element in the overall hunger equation is the concept of food poverty: the food-poor hungry live in households that are unable to pay for food or that lack access to the resources needed to feed themselves even when food is generally available within their region. Their poverty can issue from a wide variety of factors: insufficient land, low wages, unemployment or low prices for produce or manufacture, and a score of others. Amartya Sen, the foremost contemporary philosopher and economist working on hunger issues, identifies these factors as failures of entitlement: whether through direct cultivation, participation in an exchange economy, or protection by social insurance, individuals of all societies possess some means of access, or entitlement, to food. In many societies, however, this entitlement is insecure and is liable to failure in periods of economic or social turbulence. The result is food poverty. It is this condition that allows the unconscionable spectacle of occasional or even widespread hunger in areas enjoying general food availability.

The best available research indicates that in 1988 just over 1 billion people in developing countries lived in households too poor to obtain caloric intake necessary for work, and 455 million lived in households too poor to obtain the caloric intake necessary for minimal activity among adults and for the healthy growth of children.

Food Deprivation. All hungry people are food deprived. This category includes, of course, the individuals who live in regions of scarcity or reside in food-poor households. But more difficult to identify are individuals deprived of nutrition available within the households. This deprivation may result from ignorance, abuse, or neglect and often falls most brutally on the most vulnerable.

Above all, deprivation indicators show humanity's failure to provide for its children. 21 million infants—16 percent of the world total—are born underweight, while 168 million children, or 29 percent of the world total, are underweight for age. Women, characteristically disempowered within the family unit, are often the last to be fed even though they are major contributors to family food supply; they too suffer disproportionately from food deprivation.

Taken together, these three perspectives on food scarcity provide a coherent profile of global hunger. Though the numbers are different according to each definition and measurement, the overarching message is the same: more than one billion people are hungry today.

Who Are the Hungry? Where are these one billion people living in conditions of chronic hunger? And what is their livelihood, however meager? These one billion people live in nearly two million villages or urban agglomerations in more than one hundred countries. Seventy-five percent of the hungry live in rural areas; the remaining quarter live mostly in sprawling urban slums and shantytowns. The poorest of the poor are landless farmers—families with no land who survive as tenants and laborers.

Food Supply and Population

Hunger, of course, is not a static and quantifiable commodity but is rather a relationship of people to food. The grim litany of statistics presented above suggests an obvious question: Is there enough food to feed the world's population?

For the great bulk of history the answer to this question would have been an unequivocal no. Population grows geometrically while food supply, for centuries, could grow only arithmetically. These elementary facts gave rise to the apocalyptic theories of Malthus, who reasoned in his famous treatise *Essay on Population* (1798) that only through periodic calamities such as famine and war, which abruptly reduced population, could food supply and population remain in equilibrium.

In a superb historical irony, however, Malthus published his theories just as they were becoming obsolete. Since the late 18th century humanity has developed techniques to draw more food from the land and to distribute it more efficiently, allowing for a hitherto unimaginable increase in food supply *and* population. In the roughly two centuries since Malthus, the population of the world has increased from about one billion to about five billion; by 2000, the global population is expected to reach six billion. But the production of food in that same period, and especially in the most recent generations, has accelerated even more dramatically.

Indeed, the planet's food supply—often called earth's "carrying capacity"—appears now to be sufficient to feed every living man, woman, and child. Recent research suggests that the world's current food output could sustain six billion people—or 120 percent of world population—on a basic predominantly vegetarian diet. However, if we improve the diet slightly to include more animal products, we exceed our carrying capacity, for at that standard there is only food enough to feed about four billion people, or 80 percent of world population. And if we suppose a richer diet incorporating a wider variety of foods, there is only sufficient food to feed about two and a half billion people, or 50 percent, of the world's population. Remember, though, that if more people had the ability to buy food, it is almost certain that more food would be produced for sale. That is, although current food supplies are adequate to feed the entire global population, more and richer food could be produced if social, ethical, or economic imperatives so demanded.

Hunger and Poverty

Hunger, then, is not a function of overall global food shortage and, as shown above, is often not even related to local food scarcity. Instead, recent research indicates that hunger is a function of poverty and disempowerment. The hungry lack entitlement to food—arable land, cash income, social insurance, or the like—and are in some cases unable to command food due to prejudices within the family structure. The development of food surpluses has been accompanied by increasingly complex and stratified societies with correspondingly greater opportunities for entitlement failure. More than ever, it is the daily inadequacy of food entitlement—and not the failure of nature—that lies at the root of deprivation and hunger. Thus we are returned to the epigram with which this essay opened: hunger is a human-made problem, not a condition of nature. Hunger is a problem of policy and politics. Hunger is poverty.

One needs only review the habits and condition of the world's poorest to confirm this assertion. According to the most recent World Bank statistics, the poor spend at least half of their annual income on food; this figure is often as high as 70 to 80 percent. And of this disproportionate food budget, more than half again goes to the local food staple (rice, corn, and the like), indicating the inadequacy of the diet of the poor. Poverty is usually the fundamental cause of malnutrition. And the greatest toll is often borne by women and children as the distribution of consumption within poor households tends to favor males and income-earning adults. The poor suffer from a broad range of debilitating disadvantages—they have less access to publicly provided goods and government relief; they tend to receive less and poorer education; they are often set apart by cultural and/or racial barriers. As characteristics of poverty, these unfortunate realities are somewhat beyond the scope of the present essay. But as contributors to the chronic, perpetual poverty that prevents billions of people access to food, the effects and causes of poverty are close relatives to the effects and causes of hunger.

Hunger in the United States

The discussion thus far has centered on the problem of hunger in the Third World. Although most of the world's hungry reside there, and nearly all starvation takes place there, it is important to remember that hunger can be found all over the world, even in the United States, the world's leading food producer.

Hunger in the United States goes mostly unnoticed. There is little outright starvation here to capture headlines and sympathies. But the rise of homelessness and pervasive hunger in the past decade cries out for attention and effective response. The best recent reports indicate that twenty million people—one in twelve Americans—suffer from hunger at some point in each month. Hunger is a frequent attendant of poverty in the United States. Throughout the late 1980s, over thirty million Americans lived below the poverty line. Unlike their counterparts in the Third World, the poor of the United States must divert substantial sums of their income to non-food commodities: rent, for example, absorbs as much as 78 percent of the poor family's income in some U.S. areas. Even in families where both adults work full time, income may not be sufficient for a nutritionally adequate diet. Hunger in the United States leads to babies being born with low birth weight, stunted growth in children, poor education records and even illiteracy—and thus the cycle of poverty and hunger is replicated. The hungry include a broad range of the population: they are children, elderly people, and the working poor.

Better than any other example, the case of the United States shows that hunger is not a function of scarcity but of poverty or entitlement. The United States produces and retains large surpluses of the highest quality grain in the world, and remains by far the largest exporter of food in the world—yet its poor go hungry, not from lack of food but from lack of food entitlement.

Some Ethical and Theological Perspectives

Catholic social doctrine takes us one step beyond the natural social doctrine in that it considers the eternal destiny of the human being. Christ himself affirmed that he had come neither to destroy the law nor to change it, but to perfect it. The church, like its founder, proclaims that humans do not live by bread alone, and so, like Christ, the church has the deepest and most loving compassion for those who hunger. In the words of Mother Teresa, "Jesus Christ is clothed in the distressing disguise of the poor."

In Mt 25 the question is raised, "Lord, when did I see you hungry?" and the answer is given, "Whatever you did to these the least of my brethren, you did to me." Thus, it is the teaching of the church that we stand face to face with Christ when we deal with those who hunger. At the same time, the church warmly recommends to her members the practice of the spiritual and corporal works of mercy, and among the latter, the one that comes first in the list clearly and precisely states: "feed the hungry."

This responsibility to those who hunger rises not only from our Christian faith but resides as well in the fundamental principle that each individual is a person and as such has rights and duties that are the consequences of his or her nature. These rights and duties are universal and inviolable. One of these rights is the right to life, which itself is dependent upon access to food. To deny such access is to deny the right to life. Hence to speak of the right to life and the dignity of the individual is to say nothing if there is not effective protection of this right.

It is from the two lines of argument outlined above that a moral imperative is constituted. Morally, the developed world has an obligation not only to feed the hungry but to share with society's most vulnerable the benefits of its economic, scientific, and social development so that one day self-determination and self-sufficiency are achieved. "Am I my brother's keeper?" Simply stated the answer is yes.

Prospects for the Future

In the coming decade 850 million people will be born in the Third World. The chance that one of these people will be born poor and grow up in hunger will depend on a variety of factors, above all where he or she is born. But this does not mean that policy choices and individual actions are unimportant—far from it. As we have seen, the choices of individuals and governments all over the world can make a critical difference for the world's poor; indeed, they can make the difference between hunger and subsistence, between life and death. Now more than ever before, it is possible to contemplate and work toward a world of decreasing hunger, and even a world without hunger.

As research from the Brown University Feinstein Hunger Program makes clear, there are several reasons for optimism. In the current generation, humanity has altered its relationship with the food supply in fundamental ways, making the end of hunger an attainable proposition. For example, humanity passed the first threshold of theoretical food sufficiency in the 1960s and is now approaching a second threshold of improved diet sufficiency. Our population is within our carrying capacity; we can feed ourselves. Moreover, the end of hunger may be reachable because for perhaps the first time in history it is possible to contemplate the end of food scarcity, famine, and mass starvation. With the exception of the intentional creation of famine as a weapon of war, a combination of effective early warning systems, global emergency food reserves, and improved experience with distribution has brought the end of famine well within sight.

But just because hunger can be eradicated does not mean that it will be. Even as the proportion of hungry people in the world decreases, the number of people hungry continues to rise. Progress has been slow—unacceptably slow. It has been persuasively argued that the slow pace of change can be explained by the great number of people and institutions that have a stake in perpetuating hunger. The so-called "hunger industry" is a diverse collection: people who use hunger as a weapon; employers in both rich and poor countries for whom cheap labor is a comparative advantage; farmers and agribusiness people who market grains to the hungry; and even international relief and development organizations.

And within the community of those concerned are enormous divergences in explanatory analyses and policy recommendations: in broad terms, one sector addresses the problem incrementally, one specific case at a time; while the other sector addresses the greater context, calling for fundamental social change as a prerequisite for problem solution. The debate between reformist and radical analysis in issues of hunger and development is lively and important to real understanding of causes and solutions.

The present essay passes no judgment on this debate and makes no specific recommendations for ending hunger. Many examples of the various analyses and solutions are included in the attached bibliography. For the present, it is enough to emphasize that the problem *can* be solved, that the solution is within our grasp, and that humanity has a moral obligation to end hunger.

See also DEVELOPMENT; DISARMAMENT; GOODS, ACCESS TO; LAND RIGHTS; PACEM IN TERRIS; POPULORUM PROGRESSIO; POVERTY; RIGHTS AND DUTIES.

Bibliography: A. Berg, *Malnutrition: What Can Be Done?* (Baltimore: Johns Hopkins Univ. Press, 1987). W. Byron, ed., *The Causes of World Hunger* (New York: Paulist, 1982). Gourevitch and Savitt, *Education for Development: The Hunger Report, 1989–90* (New York: Interfaith Hunger Appeal, 1989). D. Grigg, *The World Food Problem, 1950–1980* (Oxford: Oxford Univ. Press, 1985). Kates et al., *The Hunger Report: 1988* (Providence, R.I.: Feinstein World Hunger Program of Brown Univ., 1988). Kates et al., *The Hunger Report: Update 1989*. F. Lappe and J. Collins, *World Hunger: Ten Myths* (San Francisco: Institute for Food and Development Policy, 1979). M. Lipton, *Why Poor People Stay Poor* (Cambridge: Harvard Univ. Press, 1977). W. Murdoch, *The Poverty of Nations: The Political Economy of Hunger and Population* (Baltimore: Johns Hopkins Univ. Press, 1980). *Paths to Peace: A Contribution. Documents of the Holy See to the International Community* (Brookfield, Wis.: The Liturgical Press, 1987). A. Sen, *Poverty and Famines: An Essay on Entitlement and Deprivation* (Oxford: Clarendon, 1981). R. Sivard, *World Military and Social Expenditures, 1987–88,* 12th ed. (Washington: World Priorities, 1987). World Bank, *Poverty and Hunger: Issues and Options for Food Security in Developing Countries* (Washington: The World Bank, 1986). World Bank, *Poverty: The World Development Report 1990* (New York: Oxford Univ. Press, 1990).

ROBERT J. COLL

I

IMAGINATION, ROLE OF

It is commonplace to hear about principles of Catholic morality or principles of Catholic social teaching. But where do the principles come from? How are they applied in concrete life? Such questions point to the role of moral imagination in Catholic thought. Classical Catholic moral theology with its high emphasis on casuistry clearly knew that it had to creatively and imaginatively apply its principles.

Historically, the Catholic theology of moral imagination can be said to be grounded in the Aristotelian-Thomist dictum that all knowledge begins with sense knowledge. On the basis of this dictum, all human moral judgment becomes, at least in part, a creative understanding of concrete reality. Aquinas' much misunderstood insistence that human intelligence is active (*intellectus agens*) as well as receptive thus becomes the starting point for a Catholic moral theology of imagination. John Henry Newman's theory of the illative sense as a key in the human assent process also illustrates the importance of moral imagination.

Among contemporary theologians, Karl Rahner's work on imagination is perhaps most notable. Rahner calls his brilliant retrieval of Aquinas' theory of knowing "a metaphysics of imagination," and he makes it clear (Rahner, p. 254) that a central element in the vocation of the moral theologian is to be an artist. Rahner insists that the focus on art and imagination cannot be construed as meaning that moral theology can abandon clear moral principles. His point is that principles are never enough, especially when we deal with social issues. From the viewpoint of Catholic metaphysics, our concrete moral judgments are always more than a simple deduction from moral principles.

The hermeneutic philosophy of Paul Ricoeur has also contributed much to the contemporary moral theology of imagination. Of particular importance is Ricoeur's notion that in human learning there must be a playful phase, a moment of second naiveté or suspended judgment (*epoché*), before we can move to true judgment. Ricoeur's works stress metaphor as the key to learning, but at the level of Ricoeur's metaphysics, metaphoric learning is the exercise of imagination.

Daniel Maguire has aptly made the case for the role of imagination in all of moral theology. It is clear, however, that imagination takes on a very special importance in the field of social thinking. The nature of social issues is such that people often have to struggle to really see why the social issues are morally important. The nature of many social issues (racism, sexism, economic injustice) is also such that meaningful social change is very often the result of a new vision based on playful association of previously unconsidered possibilities. In the introduction to their 1983 pastoral letter, *The Challenge of Peace,* the U.S.

bishops made it clear that Catholic social principles do not provide definitive answers to many aspects of the nuclear-weapons issue. This meant that the bishops had to rely, at least implicitly, on the exercise of moral imagination as the basis for their teaching on nuclear arms. So does most other Catholic social thinking.

See also CONSCIENCE; EDUCATION, ROLE OF; HOPE; METHODOLOGY, MORAL; REASON, ROLE OF; SPIRITUALITY; THOMAS AQUINAS, CONTRIBUTION OF; VALUES.

Bibliography: K. Rahner, *Theological Investigations* 2 (Baltimore: Helicon, 1964). P. Ricoeur, *The Philosophy of Paul Ricoeur: An Anthology of His Work* (Boston: Beacon, 1978). P. Keane, *Christian Ethics and Imagination* (New York: Paulist, 1984).

PHILIP S. KEANE, S.S.

INCOME

The *Encyclopedia of Economics* says: "Income is most familiar to people as the amount of money received from participating in the labor market, that is, earnings from paid employment. Most would recognize that items such as interest payments on savings accounts or dividends from stocks also represents income. And it would be generally agreed that earnings from self-employment, for example, the receipts of doctors and lawyers less their expenses of doing business, represent income" (J. Meigs, "Income," in *Encyclopedia of Economics,* ed. D. Greenwald, McGraw-Hill, 1982, p. 481). *The American Heritage Dictionary* simplifies this definition thus: "The amount of money or its equivalent received during a period of time in exchange for labor or services, from the sale of goods or property, or as profit from financial investments." Catholic social doctrine divides "income" thus defined into two distinct considerations.

As first considered, "income" means "wage," which is the "remuneration for work done" (John Paul II, *Laborem exercens* [1981] 19). "Wages" would not include income from financial investments and some cases of money or its equivalent earned from the sale of goods or property. The work done, of course, may consist in producing goods and/or selling them, or in selling property (e.g., real estate); but more often the remuneration comes "in exchange for labor or services." "Whether the work is done in a system of private ownership of the means of production or in a system where ownership has undergone a certain 'socialization,' the relationship between the employer (first and foremost the direct employer) and the worker is resolved on the basis of the wage, that is, through just remuneration for work done" (LE 19). Catholic social doctrine proclaims "the principle of the common use of goods" (LE 19; cf. Pius XII, *The Fiftieth Anniversary of "Rerum Novarum"* [1941]; Second Vatican Council, *Gaudium et spes* [1965] 69; Paul VI *Populorum progressio* [1967] 22; Congregation for the Doctrine of the Faith, *Libertatis conscientia* [1986] 90. See also the reference to Thomas Aquinas below). For the majority the *just* wage is the way in which they gain their rightful "access to those goods which are intended for common use" (LE 19).

Determining if wages are just is easy in those cases when manifestly they are not, and highly complex and difficult when the basic requirements of justice have been met at least minimally and the issue that remains is simply how large a share one may have in "the common use of goods." Nevertheless, "in every case, a just wage is the concrete means of verifying the justice of the whole socioeconomic system and, in any case, of checking that it is functioning justly. It is not the only means of checking, but it is a particularly important one and, in a sense, the key means" (LE 19).

Income must provide for the needs of the family if the socioeconomic system may be judged as functioning properly. Therefore, "just remuneration for the work of an adult who is responsible for a family means remuneration which will suffice for establishing and properly maintaining a family and for providing security for its future. Such remuneration can be given either through what is called a family wage—that is, a single salary given to the head of the family for his work, sufficient for the needs of the family without the other spouse having to take up gainful employment outside the home—or through other social measures such as family allowances or grants to mothers devoting themselves exclusively to their families. These grants should correspond to the actual needs, that is, to the number of dependents for as long as they are not in a position to assume proper responsibility for their own lives" (LE 19; cf. GS 67).

Both direct and indirect employers bear responsibility for guaranteeing just wages. Practically speaking, the direct employer (the person, business, corporation, or the like that hires the worker) may not be able to guarantee a just wage or find doing so unduly difficult. In that case, primary responsibility would devolve upon the "indirect employer," which shares responsibility in any case. The indirect employer consists in "all the agents at the national and international level that are responsible for the whole orientation of labor policy" (LE 18). Catholic social doctrine prescribes that together direct and indirect employers guarantee just wages.

Income from financial investments and the like, as distinct from wages, is just when the private ownership of the means of production, natural resources, and other goods intended for common use promotes the common good: "The right to private property is subordinated to the right to common use, to the fact that goods are meant for everyone" (LE 14). Catholic social doctrine further proclaims that the ownership of capital (financial investments) may never rightly bring about the opposition of capital to labor because the ownership of capital is justified only when that ownership promotes work, that is, creates the opportunities to work in more human and efficient ways resulting in greater wealth justly distributed. Therefore, capital justly owned and managed serves labor or work rather than opposing labor. When capital so functions, owners justly receive income from their investments. In determining the justice of systems of private ownership and in maintaining the limited right to private property, the church still appeals to the principles that St. Thomas Aquinas set out, for example, in *Summa theologiae* IIa-IIae, q. 66, aa. 2, 6; q. 134, a. 1, ad 3; *De regimine principum,* bk. 1, chaps. 15, 17.

See also COMMON GOOD; FAMILY; GAUDIUM ET SPES; LABOR AND CAPITAL IN CATHOLIC SOCIAL THOUGHT; LABOREM EXERCENS; POPULORUM PROGRESSIO; PRIVATE PROPERTY; SOCIALIZATION; THOMAS AQUINAS, CONTRIBUTION OF.

RICHARD R. ROACH, S.J.

INCULTURATION

"Inculturation" is a new word in the church's theological vocabulary. The reality has been operative in the church from the very beginning. The term reflects other terms such as "accommodation" and "indigenization," which simply connote that the church, like its founder Jesus Christ, must embody itself in the world. As was said at Vatican II, "In order to be able to offer to all men the mystery of salvation and the life brought by God, the Church must become part of all these groups for the same motive which led Christ to bind Himself, in virtue of His Incarnation, to the definite social and cultural conditions of those human beings among whom He dwelt" (*Ad gentes* 10).

The basic analogy used at Vatican II for the church's insertion in the world is that of the Incarnation. The analogy is found in the pastoral constitution, *Gaudium et spes,* and in the decree on the missionary activity of the church, *Ad gentes.* "In his self-revelation to his people culminating in the fullness of manifestation in his incarnate Son, God spoke according to the culture proper to each age. Similarly the Church has existed through the centuries in varying circumstances and has utilized the resources of different cultures in its preaching to spread and explain the message of Christ, to examine and understand it more deeply, and to express it more perfectly in the liturgy and in various aspects of the life of the faithful" (GS 58; cf. AG 1).

The word "inculturation" is first used to mean the church's mission as that of incarnation. The use of the word is the consequence of two basic characteristics of the Vatican Council: Its emphasis on the church's mission to the world and on the role and importance of culture. This concern with culture led to a more specific understanding of the church's mission. For the first time, it seems, the church has been led to envisage social and cultural life as a whole, as the central meeting point of all its problems—economic, political, domestic, philosophical, religious. The church claims for itself a culturally redemptive presence in the world. "The good news of Christ continually renews the life and culture of fallen man" (GS 58).

This emphasis of Vatican II on the church's mission to the world and the important role of culture in human affairs led Paul VI in his apostolic exhortation *Evangelii nuntiandi* to affirm that culture must be the chief concern of the church's missionary activity, for "what matters is to evangelize man/woman's culture and cultures" (EN 20). In his visit to Africa, while emphasizing that the Christian faith is one, Paul VI affirmed that "the expression, that is, the language and mode of manifesting this one faith, may be manifold; hence, it may be original, suited to the tongue, the style, the character, the genius, and the culture, of the one who professes this one faith. From this point of view, a certain pluralism is not only legitimate, but desirable. An adaptation of the Christian life in the fields of pastoral, ritual, didactic and spiritual activities is not only possible, it is even favored by the church. The liturgical renewal is a living example of this. And in this sense you may, and you must, have an African Christianity" (address at the closing of the all-African Bishops' Symposium).

With all this concern for culture it is not surprising that the word "inculturation" would be introduced into the church's vocabulary. It seems that the word was first introduced by Cardinal Sin of Manila at the synod on catechesis in Rome in 1977 and was first used in an official papal document by John Paul II in his apostolic exhortation on catechesis in October of 1979. Since then the pope has used this term many times in various addresses. In 1980 in Nairobi, Kenya, he affirmed that "inculturation, which you rightly promote, will truly be a reflection of the incarnation of the word, when a culture, transformed and regenerated by the gospel, brings forth from its own living tradition original expressions of Christian life, celebration, and thought" (The African Bishops' Challenge 6). In 1982 the pope established a Pontifical Council for Culture, and on that occasion he wrote, "There is an organic and constitutive link existing between Christianity and culture." Such a link implies that faith itself is deeply affected by culture. "A faith which does not become culture is a faith which has not been fully received, not thoroughly thought through, not fully lived out" (letter to Agostino Cardinal Casaroli, secretary of state, May 20, 1982, quoted from the English-language weekly edition of *L'Osservatore Romano*).

When used to describe the church's mission, the word "inculturation" has meant basically the continuation of the mystery of the Incarnation. Seen from the perspective of the social sciences, "inculturation" has received a more varied meaning: the term is tied to the concept of culture.

Culture as such is practically impossible to define, for it touches every dimension of human existence. With no fixed or agreed-upon definition, it may be described as "a set of symbols, stories (myths) and norms for conduct that orient a society or group cognitively, affectively, and behaviorally to the world in which it lives" (D. Browning, *The Moral Context of Pastoral Care,* Philadelphia: Westminster, 1983, p. 73). For Clifford Geertz, culture "denotes an historically transmitted pattern of meanings embodied in symbols, a system of inherited conceptions, expressed in symbolic forms by means of which men communicate, perpetuate, and develop their knowledge about and attitudes toward life" (*The Interpretation of Cultures,* London, 1975, p. 89).

Culture is the result of man and woman's ability to communicate and construe reality; it also pertains to the development of man and woman perceived as social beings. Etymologically the word comes from the Latin *colere,* which means "to till the fields," and analogically and by extension man and woman's mind and mental faculties.

Individuals and societies are deeply affected by culture. The social and anthropological sciences have coined a variety of words to describe the interaction of individuals and societies with culture. In cultural anthropology the word "enculturation" describes the process through which one is integrated and achieves competence in one's own culture. Here the emphasis is on adaptation, nurturing, and growth.

The process whereby an individual is integrated into a particular society and achieves competence in its culture can also be called "socialization." Socialization provides for the internalization of the meanings of a culture and the process of self-interpretation. Socialization involves the process of being inserted into a social-cultural environment, which in fact produces one's self-identity. That process of insertion demands the internalization of a culture's self-understanding, self-image, and valuing. The word "acculturation" is used to describe the process wherein two cultures come into contact and the necessary changes and transformation that ensue.

The word "inculturation" can mean both socialization and acculturation. It connotes the process of integration and of encounter, of being transformed and of transforming. When used in church documents the term combines the meanings of "enculturation" and "acculturation." It implies that the church as an embodied reality must, in its mission of evangelization, insert itself in various cultures. In that process the church will transform a culture but it will also be transformed (cf. AG 22).

A true process of inculturation demands an ongoing and living exchange between the church, which is also a specific culture, and other cultures. Authentic inculturation demands on the part of the church a willingness to dialogue with all cultures. Dialogue means concern, respect, and hospitality toward the other; acceptance of the other's identity, modes of expression, and values. True dialogue does not invade; it does not manipulate, for there can be no such thing as dialogical manipulation. Dialogue achieves a communion of horizons, which leads to self-disclosure and self-understanding. The task of the church in the coming decades is to be faithful to its mission of preaching the Christ-event in such a way as to transform and penetrate the various existing cultures but to do so in such a manner as to be open itself to transformation.

See also ANTHROPOLOGY; EVANGELII NUNTIANDI; EVANGELIZATION; GOD, IMAGES OF; PATERNALISM; PLURALISM; PRAXIS; SOCIALIZATION.

Bibliography: J. Gremillion, ed., *The Church and Culture Since Vatican II: The Experience of North and Latin America* (Notre Dame, Ind.: Univ. of Notre Dame Press, 1985). M. Azevedo, *Inculturation and the Challenges of Modernity* (Rome, 1982). A. Chupungco, *Cultural Adaptation of the Liturgy* (New York, 1982). A. Crollius, *Inculturation: Its Meaning and Urgency* (Africa: St. Paul Publications, 1986). P. Schineller, *A Handbook on Inculturation* (New York: Paulist, 1990).

LUCIEN RICHARD, O.M.I.

INDIVIDUALISM

See CAPITALISM; MONOPOLY; PRIVATE PROPERTY; PUBLIC AND PRIVATE, RELATIONSHIP OF; QUADRAGESIMO ANNO.

INDUSTRIALIZATION

"Industrialization is the system of production that has arisen from the steady development, study, and use of scientific knowledge. It is based on the division of labor and on specialization and uses mechanical, chemical, and power-driven, as well as organizational and intellectual aids in production. The primary objective of this method of organizing economic life, which had its genesis in the mid-eighteenth century, has been to reduce the real cost per unit, of producing goods and services" (J. Hughes, "Industrialization: I. Economic Aspects," in *International Encyclopedia of the Social Sciences* 7, D. Sills, ed., Macmillan, 1968, p. 252). We must not read this definition as limiting "the concept solely to manufacturing, as agriculture is also subject to mechanization (as well as other modes of technical rationalization), and so are services such as transportation and communication" (W. Moore, "Industrialization: II. Social Aspects," op. cit., p. 263).

Industrialization on a large scale began during what is popularly called the Industrial Revolution. Although details are disputed, Great Britain is considered the site of the beginning of this revolution during the period from 1750 to 1825. The revolution spread throughout Europe and to all nations of European origin. Japan was the first non-European nation to industrialize (1859–1910). At present all major nations are trying to industrialize according to their needs and resources.

The Industrial Revolution imposed horrendous suffering on the workers engaged in the industrial process, but industrialization as such was not responsible. Industrialization primarily designates technology employed in manufacture and other human work. As such it is morally neutral. Greed and the injustice of the system caused the workers' suffering. The church condemned these evils, not technology as such, through its teaching, which came to be called its social doctrine. The church recorded the suffering of the workers, along with the accurate diagnosis of the problem, in the encyclical *Rerum novarum,* of Pope Leo XIII (1891):

"In any case we clearly see, and on this there is general agreement, that some opportune remedy must be found quickly for the misery and wretchedness pressing so unjustly on the majority of the working class: for the ancient working-men's guilds were abolished in the last century, and no other protective organization took their place. Public institutions and the laws set aside the ancient religion. Hence, by degrees it has come to pass that working men have been surrendered, isolated and helpless, to the hard-heartedness of employers and the greed of unchecked competition. The mischief has been increased by rapacious usury, which although more than once condemned by the Church, is nevertheless, under a different guise, but with like injustice, still practiced by covetous and grasping men. To this must be added that the hiring of labor and the conduct of trade are concentrated in the hands of comparatively few; so that a small number of very rich men have been able to lay upon the teeming masses of the laboring poor a yoke little better than that of slavery itself" (RN 3).

The Church still responds to the challenge of industrialization by insisting that we use all technology, of which industrialization is a part, justly and humanely. In the words of the Second Vatican Council:

"Human activity proceeds from man: it is also ordered to him. When he works, not only does he transform matter and society, but he fulfills himself. He learns, he develops his faculties, and he emerges from and transcends himself. Rightly understood, this kind of growth is more precious than any kind of wealth that can be amassed. It is what a man is, rather than what he has, that counts. Technical progress is of less value than advances towards greater justice, wider brotherhood, and a more humane social environment. Technical progress may supply the material for human advance but it is powerless to actualize it.

"Here then is the norm for human activity—to harmonize with the authentic interests of the human race, in accordance with God's will and design, and to enable men as individuals and as members of society to pursue and fulfill their total vocation" (*Gaudium et spes* 35).

See also ECONOMIC PLANNING, SOCIAL IMPORTANCE OF; EXPLOITATION; GAUDIUM ET SPES; INDUSTRY; LABOREM EXERCENS; OCTOGESIMA ADVENIENS; QUADRAGESIMO ANNO; RERUM NOVARUM; SOLLICITUDO REI SOCIALIS.

RICHARD R. ROACH, S.J.

INDUSTRY

Pope John Paul II defines "industry" by contrasting industry with agriculture. Both activities constitute work in the objective sense whereby human beings carry out the task of subduing the earth (Gen 1:28). "Thus agriculture constitutes through human work a primary field of economic activity and an indispensable factor of production. Industry in its turn will always consist in linking the earth's riches—whether nature's living resources, or products of agriculture, or the mineral or chemical resources—with man's work, whether physical or intellectual" (*Laborem exercens* [1981] 5). By linking the world's riches with human work, industry becomes "the firms that supply goods and services to a particular market" (R. Thomas, with W. Weber, *Microeconomics: Principles and Applications,* Dryden, 1990, p. G3).

"Industry" also means diligence, assiduity, and the like. For this second, quite distinct meaning, Pope John Paul II uses the term "industriousness":

"Work is a good thing for man—a good thing for humanity—because through work man not only transforms nature, adapting it to his own needs, but he also achieves fulfillment as a human being and indeed, in a sense, becomes 'more a human being.' Without this consideration it is impossible to understand the meaning of the virtue of industriousness, and more particularly it is impossible to understand why industriousness should be a virtue: for virtue, as a moral habit, is something whereby man becomes good as a man." In this second sense, industry overcomes that aspect of the capital sin of sloth that issues in laziness, particularly with respect to performing good works.

See also INDUSTRIALIZATION; LABOREM EXERCENS.

RICHARD R. ROACH, S.J.

INFLATION

Economists define inflation as a situation of continuously rising prices or, equivalently, of a continuously falling value of money (in terms of its purchasing power). In the past, periods of inflation were followed by periods of falling prices, but since the 1930s prices have tended to rise every year in the industrialized countries—sometimes slowly and sometimes rapidly (as in the 1970s). Hyperinflation (prices rising 50 percent per month or more) occurred in Germany in the 1920s and in Latin America in the 1980s.

Households experience inflation as erosion of the purchasing power of income (unless their income rises at the same rate as prices). For investors it heightens uncertainty about future returns. For lenders it shrinks the value of loans repaid, while for debtors it reduces the real sacrifice required to repay what they have borrowed. This cursory review of the effects of inflation suggests why it has social significance and why it becomes an inflammatory political issue.

In modern economies there is a trade-off between unemployment and inflation. To control inflation (which begins with a situation of demand for more goods and services than the economy is currently able to supply), the economy must be "slowed down," that is, demand must be reduced. That means production cuts, layoffs, and reduced income for some (usually the least skilled). Price controls can be instituted temporarily, but the underlying imbalance between demand and supply must be addressed, and it takes time to increase supply (especially in poor countries). Thus, implementation of anti-inflation policies as well as inflation itself bears most heavily on the poorest groups.

Thus inflation has been a concern of Catholic social teaching. Responding to the World War I inflation, the U.S. bishops in 1919 called for laws to abolish "monopolistic extortion," and for the establishment of cooperative stores to abolish "unnecessary middlemen" as means to restrain price rises after wartime price controls were removed (*Social Reconstruction,* 21–22).

Pius XI, during the Great Depression, called for full employment and for maintaining "a right proportion among wages and salaries" and "in the prices at which the goods are sold that are produced by the various occupations." Only thus will the "social economy be rightly established and attain its purposes" (*Quadragesimo anno* 74–75).

In 1940 the U.S. bishops observed the harmful effects of rapid or frequent fluctuations in prices and wages, which "disturb the harmonious proportions between income and prices not only for owners and employers but also for the workingmen themselves" (*Church and Social Order* 45).

Pius XII, in the 1950s, a period when Western economies were experiencing both the benefits and the problems of growth, called for attaining the highest possible level of employment, but also for preventing the risk of inflation (Christmas message, 1952; to the International Association of Economists, September 9, 1956).

John XXIII, reaffirming the traditional teaching on the living wage in 1961, recognized that "maintenance of equilibrium between wages and prices" and "the need to make goods and services accessible to the greatest number" must be considered in determining a just wage (*Mater et magistra* 71, 79).

During the inflation of the 1970s the U.S. bishops wrote in a brief and strongly worded pastoral titled *The Economy: Human Dimensions* (1975) that "there are those who insist that we must tolerate high levels of unemployment for some, in order to avoid ruinous inflation for all. Although we are deeply concerned about inflation, we reject such a policy as not grounded in justice" (EHD 14). They went on to recognize the serious effects of inflation: a weakening of economic stability, an erosion of economic security, with most serious effects on the poor and those living on fixed incomes (15). Finally, they called for anti-inflation policies modeled on those of other industrialized nations, which managed incomes and prices through public policy and thus prevented high rates of joblessness (16).

In their 1986 pastoral the bishops reiterated the same call for effective policies to control inflationary pressures while expansionary policies needed to generate full employment are being pursued. (*Economic Justice for All* 156–58).

John Paul II, writing in 1979 when inflation was causing serious problems in both rich and poor nations, called "the fever of inflation and the plague of unemployment . . . symptoms of the moral disorder . . . in the world situation" (*Redemptor hominis* 16).

The themes are consistent over the years. Inflation is a serious problem, especially for the poor. Policies should be developed to control inflation while pursuing the goal of full employment, since "the major protection against inflation is a decent job at decent wages" (EHD 16).

See also COOPERATIVE ASSOCIATIONS; ECONOMIC PLANNING, SOCIAL IMPORTANCE OF; EMPLOYMENT AND UNEMPLOYMENT; INDUSTRIALIZATION; JUST WAGE; MATER ET MAGISTRA; MONOPOLY; QUADRAGESIMO ANNO.

Bibliography: M. Parkin, "Inflation" in J. Eatwell et al., eds., *The New Palgrave: A Dictionary of Economics,* 4 vols. (London: Macmillan, 1987) vol. 2, pp. 868–70. C. Lynde, "The Zero-Inflation Ploy: Gambling with Our Jobs," *Dollars & Sense* 159 (September 1990) 6–9.

AMATA MILLER, I.H.M.

INSURANCE

Insurance is a system of protection against risk. In private insurance individuals pay premiums in return for a guarantee of compensation in event of a specified occurrence. Social insurance is usually provided by government and designed for the protection of wage earners and lower-income persons. Unemployment compensation, workers' compensation, publicly funded medical insurance, and old-age pensions are examples.

In Catholic social teaching the right to security in cases of unemployment, ill-health, and old age is a basic human right derived from the right to life (*Pacem in terris* 11; also *Laborem exercens* 19; *Economic Justice for All* 80, 103).

In 1919 the U.S. hierarchy called for enactment of a "legal minimum wage" which would be gradually increased to meet future needs as well (*Social Reconstruction* 24). Until this level of wages was reached there should be comprehensive state insurance against illness, disability, unemployment, and old age funded by a tax on industry. However, this insurance was to be regarded as "merely the lesser evil, and should be so organized and administered as to hasten the coming of the normal condition" (SR 25). They also urged continuance of the life insurance offered to military personnel during World War I (26).

In their 1933 statement, *Present Crisis,* the U.S. hierarchy called again for insurance against unemployment and old age—to be provided by the employer, the employee, and the government (47–48).

In 1937, Pius XI, in *Divini Redemptoris* (*On Atheistic Communism*), advocated wages high enough so workers could "make suitable provision through public or private insurance for old age, for periods of illness and unemployment" (DR 52).

In 1940 the U.S. bishops again called for security for working people against unemployment, sickness, accident, old age, and death. The "first line of defense against these hazards" should be the possession of sufficient property to provide reasonable security. Industry should provide "not merely a living wage . . . but also a saving wage." By this time social insurance was recognized as a "necessary part of the program," "a social responsibility of industry jointly with society," since individual industries alone could not achieve this (*Church and Social Order* 32, 36).

The Australian hierarchy in their 1954 letter, *Standard of Living,* called for a "standard wage," which would enable a person to "begin to make suitable provision through public and private insurance, for old age, for periods of illness and unemployment." Once married the worker would receive an increase to provide for additional dependents.

Pius XII supported provision of insurance, but he cautioned that "the anxious desire for security should not prevail over the businessman's readiness to risk his resources to such an extent as to dry up every creative impulse" (to the Italian Federation of Commerce, February 17, 1956).

John XXIII in *Mater et magistra* (1961) applauded social insurance as a positive sign of social transformation (MM 48). He saw it as a means of redistribution, of reducing economic inequality (136), and of providing a security which had been rooted in property ownership in the past (105). He called for two forms of insurance for farmers: one for their produce and the other for farm families (135; see also EJA 247). Special insurance programs should also be provided for "family groups of artisans and farmers" and for cooperatives (MM 88).

John Paul II in *Laborem exercens* (1981) named provision of unemployment benefits as a fundamental duty of the group of agents he calls the "indirect employer"—all those responsible at the national and international levels for labor policy (17–18).

In 1986 the U.S. bishops cited lack of health insurance as an aspect of poverty, especially for older women in the United States (EJA 177, 180). They recommended examination of health insurance policies and income security programs in light of their effects on family stability (206).

The synod of bishops in 1971 stated that those who work for the church should "enjoy that social security which is customary in their region" (*Justitia in mundo,* chap. 3). In 1986 the U.S. bishops committed themselves "to the principle that those who serve the Church—laity, clergy and religious—should receive a sufficient livelihood and the social benefits provided by responsible employers in our nation" (EJA 351).

Thus the provision of means of security against loss of income is clearly a right supported in Catholic social teaching. The employer is the preferred provider, but government has a responsibility to share in the provision of insurance, especially for low income persons and specific groups such as farmers.

See also HEALTH CARE; HUMAN RIGHTS; LABOREM EXERCENS; MATER ET MAGISTRA; PACEM IN TERRIS; PUBLIC AND PRIVATE, RELATIONSHIP OF; SOCIAL SECURITY; WELFARE/WELFARE STATE.

Bibliography: S. Levitan, *Programs in Aid of the Poor,* 5th ed. (Baltimore: Johns Hopkins Univ. Press, 1985).

AMATA MILLER, I.H.M.

INVESTMENT

In popular terms an investment is the purchase of an income-earning asset such as stocks, bonds, or rental property. It is also used to refer to the purchase of assets such as stocks or real property that are bought in hopes that they will appreciate in value and can be sold later for a profit. In economics the term has a narrower meaning—the construction of capital goods such as delivery trucks, automatic lathes, or factory buildings that are used to produce other goods that are then sold.

In a free-market economy investments are directed by the profit expectations of the investor. Catholic social teaching has urged property owners to also consider the social impact of their investments. In addition, government has been called upon to engage in policies that will direct investment into uses such as education, low-cost housing, and job creation that will enhance the common good. During the Second Vatican Council the assembled bishops proclaimed: "Investments . . . must be directed toward providing employment and sufficient income for the people both now and in the future. Whoever makes decisions concerning these investments and the planning of the economy —whether they be individuals or groups or public authorities—are bound to keep these objectives in mind" (*Gaudium et spes* 70).

In detailing what they consider the moral priorities of the economy, the U.S. bishops emphasize that "the investment of wealth, talent, and human energy should be specially directed to benefit those who are poor or economically insecure" (*Economic Justice for All* 92). They go on to point out that investments have crucial moral dimensions. They can create jobs and they can eliminate jobs. They can be used to produce luxury goods for the rich and excessive military technology or they can be used to produce needed goods and jobs for the poor and to improve education, health, and the basic infrastructure of the economy.

The basic point made by Catholic social teaching is that investment should not be directed solely by private profit. Private investors need to balance individual profit with a concern for the common good. Also, government as the representative of the community should intervene to help direct investments into avenues that enhance the common good.

See also ECONOMIC PLANNING, SOCIAL IMPORTANCE OF; INDUSTRY; OWNERSHIP.

CHARLES K. WILBER

J

JOHN XXIII

Angelo Roncalli (1881–1963), as John XXIII (1958–63), is the pope of the Second Vatican Council (1962–65). This is not simply a fact of history: rather, the call for an ecumenical council represents the consequence of the theological and pastoral objectives of his pontificate. In his widely noted opening address (*Gaudet mater ecclesia*) of October 11, 1962, Pope John elucidates his primary intentions and objectives for this council: the renewal of the doctrines of the church in consistence with the present world (*aggiornamento*). *Aggiornamento* does not mean adapting the doctrines of the church to superficial terms of plausibility in the modern thinking but rather the effort to give a new form, through an exchange with today's culture, to the power of the gospel and the church's tradition. In this process, new elements can indeed gain shape that were only implicitly apparent in the body of tradition. This revival requires a genuine dialogue with the modern world. In this dialogue the church does not just take a normative or even didactically disapproving role; instead, its role is essentially a receptive one in recognizing and promoting the modern world's positive value and interpretation structures as its own in the perspective of the gospel. Freedom of religion and thought, the relationship with the development of democracy in modern history, and the definition of human rights are among the items on the agenda of the council in which the church proves the ability to engage in such a dialogue.

To Pope John, the idea of *aggiornamento* indispensably implies the timely public, political, and social engagement of Christians as well as the need for Catholic social teaching. Although it is separate from the teaching of faith, the church's social teaching cannot be separated from the latter. It is a necessary component of Christian teaching as a whole, unless the creative power of the Christian message for society is to be given up (*Gaudet mater ecclesia* 11). In the tradition of the popes since Leo XIII, John XXIII comments in two encyclicals on social and political questions and develops the social teachings of the church in accordance with the changing dimension of problems. The encyclical *Mater et magistra* (1961) in its first two parts recapitulates the development of Catholic social teaching since *Rerum novarum.* The third part deals with new aspects of the social question; in particular, the situation of agricultural workers (*campesinos*) and questions of development policy are discussed. The fourth section presents thoughts on a new way of life in truth, justice, and love. This section demonstrates that John XXIII considered the education toward social responsibility and the training in social practice as essential ingredients of Catholic doctrine and teaching.

The positive reactions to this social encyclical show that in spite of all loyalty to the tradition of the church's social teaching, a new era of Catholic social teaching begins (O. von Nell-Breuning). New emphases and aspects become noticeable; the scope of social problems is now seen on a worldwide scale. Consequently new questions arise for Catholic social teaching, for example in the field of development policy. The social philosophy based on natural rights loses its character as a dominating source for understanding the principles of the social order. Instead, the church's social teaching is developed as an integral component of Christian anthropology (MM 222). Due to this increasingly theological argumentation, the confrontation with socialism and liberalism loses its determinant character for the way Catholic social teaching manifests itself. With stronger impartiality than his predecessors, Pope John can express the weight of empirical and sociological arguments and analyses. The social-ethical argumentation tends to proceed in an inductive manner based on concrete social analysis, and not deductively by deriving moral demands from principles.

In the encyclical *Pacem in terris* (1963), Pope John turns to specific questions concerning the advancement and preservation of peace. The public interest in this encyclical results not least from John XXIII's revision of the church's traditional doctrine of just war. In view of the state of development of modern weapons technology, that is, the destructive potential of nuclear weapons, war no longer appears to be sensibly possible and justifiable as a means for restoring violated rights (PT 127). This statement certainly needs further explanation. The council did not adopt it in the pastoral constitution *Gaudium et spes.* The critical approach to the traditional doctrine of just war, however, is not the central theme of the papal letter. Extensively and for reasons of principle, the encyclical concentrates on the close connection between peace and justice. The realization of human rights through creating a political world order oriented toward the basic idea of the "common good" is stressed as a constituent element of a peace process.

This argumentation is an expression of the encyclical's attempt to mediate between the principle of common good that is normative for Catholic social teaching and the modern human-rights program. However, the encyclical regarding peace reaches beyond these considerations of principle by developing concrete ideas for advancing a peace process in the world: to Pope John, necessary requirements of a meaningful peace process include an end of the arms race, international agreements for effective disarmament, and a general ban on nuclear weapons. The orientation of this peace message toward practical action is reflected (as in *Mater et magistra*) in the fact that it is not addressed to politicians, moral philosophers, and other experts but to all human beings of good will.

For church and theology, the legacy of John XXIII represents a permanent task. They are placed in the process of an open-ended search: continually pointing out the current relevance of Christian teaching in a dialogue with the cultures of the emerging world society; and demonstrating the power of the Christian message for shaping society in a rational discourse among those who share the interest in a practical approach in view of the problems of social reality ("human beings of good will").

See also HUMAN RIGHTS; JUSTICE IN THE WORLD; MATER ET MAGISTRA; NATURAL LAW; PACEM IN TERRIS; RELIGIOUS FREEDOM; "SIGNS OF THE TIMES"; VATICAN COUNCIL II.

HANS LANGENDÖRFER, S.J.

JUST WAGE

A just wage is remuneration for work that allows workers to support themselves and their families in human dignity. Synonyms for the term "just wage" are "living wage," "family wage," "just compensation," "just remuneration," and "equitable sustenance." A just wage is a compensation package that includes monetary payments, benefits, vacation and personal days, health insurance, and so forth.

History

The roots of the teaching on a just wage are found in the medieval teaching on the just price. The amount farmers or merchants received for a product had to cover the cost of their labor and materials, as well as provide for their living expenses and that of their families. In his treatment of justice in buying and selling, Thomas Aquinas followed the principle that justice demands that equality should reign in contracts of exchange. Thomas pointed out that justice was determined not only in the value of a thing or service exchanged but also in its estimated worth within a community. Subsequent Scholastic moralists analyzed the equality of a just price in light of the three Thomistic divisions of justice—commutative, distributive, and legal, or social. They stressed that all individual contracts were set within a social context, with employers and employees bound to serve the common good. However, most moralists prior to *Rerum novarum* (1891) linked the payment of a just price with personal stability in a social class and the upholding of the status quo. The just price became uncritically identified with local practice, without regard to the practical impact on the support of workers and their families.

The teaching on the just wage shifted into a new gear with Pope Leo XIII. He built upon the work of his precursor in addressing the social question, Bishop Wilhelm von Ketteler, by supporting the dignity of labor and the moral necessity for a just wage. In *Rerum novarum* Leo said that human dignity demands that workers be treated justly and that they receive in return for their exertion what is needed to support and preserve life. He rejected the so-called Iron Law of Wages, which said that wages, like prices, are determined in a free market by the random interaction of buyer and seller, and the availability of goods. Strict contractual justice may be satisfied by the contract, but not the fuller justice that flows from human dignity. Sufficient remuneration for labor supported the workers and their families in a reasonable and frugal manner. Basic needs included food, housing, clothing, physical well-being, provision for children and their rearing and education, opportunity to own property, and guarantees for the future. These are not luxuries but what human beings need in the practical order to express the innate dignity which is theirs.

Pius XI supported the right to a just wage for workers and their families in his 1930 encyclical on marriage, *Casti connubii* (117). *Quadragesimo anno* (1931) reiterated Leo's teaching as an expression of the fundamental dignity of each human being, who is always a member of society (QA 71). The fiscal situation of businesses must be considered; workers cannot demand excessive wages (QA 72). The common good is the context in which a just wage is set, while unemployment is an evil that is contrary to social justice. The principle of subsidiarity demands that each level of society contribute to the common good (QA 74–79). Pius XI distinguished between what was due in justice and what was given in charity. "The wage-earner is not to receive as alms what is his due in justice" (*Divini Redemptoris* 46; QA 137).

While Pius XII repeated the right to a just wage (Christmas address, 1942) as a basic principle of the internal order of nations, John XXIII advanced the development of the just wage by respecting historical and international socioeconomic factors (*Mater et magistra* 55, 68, 71). In *Pacem in terris* John gave the most comprehensive list of rights in Catholic social teaching (PT 11–27). One of the specific economic rights is to a just wage (20). Each right has duties. Just wages are set by mutual collaboration and with the protection of government (MM 21; PT 31, 64). Throughout John's treatment of human rights there is the insistent understanding of the interdependence of all persons, communities, and nations (PT 42, 121). Vatican II affirmed past papal teaching on the just wage as an expression of the inviolable dignity of the human person (*Gaudium et spes* 67; *Dignitatis humanae* 2).

Paul VI added to the understanding of equitable sustenance (*Octogesima adveniens* 14; *Populorum progressio* 6, 27) by stressing the integral development of persons. Material needs alone are not enough (PP 20). He acknowledged the aspirations to equality and participation, by workers and others in society. A just wage is set within a politically and economically interdependent world.

In *Laborem exercens* (1981) John Paul II stresses the opportunities for "co-creation" with God through human work. Labor has priority over capital because capital is the result of human work. Therefore the just wage is central to social ethics (LE 19), since it secures a fair relationship between worker and employer. And since human labor is a necessary condition for the founding of a family, just remuneration for work must support the worker's family and provide for each member's future (10). A just wage has social consequences and becomes a tool in evaluating the justice of entire socioeconomic systems (10). In his commemoration of the 100th anniversary of *Rerum novarum,* John Paul affirms the centrality of the dignity of human work and of workers in socioeconomic systems (*Centesimus annus* 6). He sees the right to a just wage as one of several essential human rights (CA 4, 8, 15, 34, 43, 47).

Theology

The right to a just wage is grounded in the basic themes of Catholic social doctrine. A fundamental presupposition is the dignity of the human person. Each person's dignity is both transcendental and concrete; each person's dignity is lived out and upheld within a social context. The equality and dignity of all persons therefore demand that more humane and just conditions be brought about in society. The concrete expression of human dignity is best found in the human rights tradition, that is, each person, because of his or her dignity, has certain rights (and duties) that are universal, inviolable, and inalienable. They form a constellation of the conditions for the realization of human worth in action, in an ordered arrangement. This order is characterized by dynamic interconnectedness and integral development. No one right can be singled out without acknowledging its relationship—personal, social, instrumental—to other human rights. The order of human rights is directed toward the full and integral development of persons, as individuals and within human communities.

Within the order of rights, the just wage as a right is a social mediation of the individual's right to work. When workers receive fair remuneration they are empowered to carry out the other rights, for example, to bodily integrity, to the support of their families, to the building up of the common good.

The right to a just wage is not without its own duties. Each worker has responsibilities to provide a full and honest day's labor, to respect property and lawful authority, and to bring meaning and worth to toil through industriousness. Employers have the responsibility to give workers just remuneration, to respect the human limitations of their employees, to allow workers' associations, and to use all available technology prudently while making and keeping their company competitive and profitable.

It must be stressed that the just wage is repeatedly linked to support for workers *and their families.* The variety of families in each culture must be taken into consideration. All heads of households, whether female or male, whether married or not, deserve a wage that enables them to provide sufficiently for themselves and their dependents.

The threefold division of the principles of justice assist in balancing the tension of individual wage agreements (commutative justice) and the common good (GS 26). The just wage is rooted in the communitarian vision of society. The principles of distributive and social justice give order to the structures and institutions of civil government, and society as a whole, so that the right to a just wage for an individual worker can be enacted.

In the history of the just wage there is no one dogmatic application of the just wage (OA 4, 23; *Sollicitudo rei socialis* 41). Christians have the duty of enfleshing moral principles. Concrete love has to take into consideration the historical situation of needy and hurting people, a critical analysis of the economic and political systems, the inescapable reality of individual and social sin, and a sense of the mutual interdependence of all peoples. The just wage is an "in-principled" expression of love and solidarity (GS, explanatory note; *The Challenge of Peace* 8–12; *Economic Justice for All* 126–27).

Several conclusions, or axioms, can be drawn for the practical application of a just wage. (1) There is no single just wage. It must be regularly and concretely judged in every country, even in various areas of a country. (2) A just wage is a minimum, or better, *at least* a minimum. It is to allow what is needed for the full and integral development of workers. (3) A just wage is always a family wage. (4) It is necessary to have a public system of employee administration, which embraces worker participation and consultation, wage scales, job evaluation, opportunities for promotion and further education, signed agreements, grievance procedures, and annual review of the whole system. (5) A just wage includes the understanding of equal pay for equal work. There can be no discrimination based on race, sex, national origin, age, or marital status. However, benefits may be tailored to support dependent family members. (6) A just wage is conditioned by the employer's ability to pay, market forces, and the common good. Efforts to promote fair wages and full employment cannot be limited to individual companies but must include in any dialogue "indirect employers" (LE 17), for example, governments, central banks, trade unions, and international trade agreements.

In the Church

In theory and experience, a question seldom asked is: Should the church pay a just wage to its employees? The first affirmative expression of just compensation for church workers in an official ecclesial document is in the 1917 Code of Canon Law. Canon 1524 applied the teaching of *Rerum novarum* on just wages, instructing all administrators of church goods to give fair wages and decent working conditions to employees. Few commentators, and fewer pastors and administrators, took note of this canon. The Second Vatican Council did affirm a just wage for those employed by church agencies (*Ad gentes* 17; *Apostolicam actuositatem* 22). The passage in the *Decree on the Apostolate of Lay People* (AA) is marked by a generous and joyful spirit of appreciation for lay workers. It encourages pastors to give workers financial and pastoral support, spiritual formation, and incentive for advancement, *quam maxime.* The most explicit declaration of the church's responsibility to practice what it preaches is found in the 1971 document of the synod of bishops, *De iustitia in mundo.* "While the Church is bound to give witness to justice, she recognizes that anyone who ventures to speak to people about justice must first be just in their eyes" (JM 40). All who serve the church by their labor—laity, religious, and priests—are to receive just remuneration (JM 41). A living wage for priests is also affirmed by the second document issued by the 1971 synod, *De sacerdotio ministeriali.* The 1983 Code of Canon Law carries out the papal and conciliar teaching on the just wage in canons 231 and 1286. Finally, the U.S. bishops' 1986 pastoral letter, *Economic Justice for All,* stands in the American episcopal tradition of supporting workers and their rights. The bishops state that at all times the church, in its various parishes, dioceses, structures, and institutions, must apply its own principles that govern the just operation of any economic structure to its own workings (339, 349, 351–58). "Indeed the Church should be exemplary" (347). Only if the church does the works of justice "in-house" will the call for justice in the world be authentic and credible (CA 57).

See also BUSINESS ETHICS; FAMILY; LABOR AND CAPITAL IN CATHOLIC SOCIAL THOUGHT; MANUAL LABOR; RIGHTS AND DUTIES; WORK, THEOLOGY OF.

Bibliography: F. Almade, "Criteria for a Just Wage for Church Employees" (Ph.D. diss., Duquesne Univ., 1990). J. Cronin, *Social Principles and Economic Life* (Milwaukee: Bruce, 1959). M. Fogarty, *The Just Wage* (London: Herder & Herder, 1961). J. Healy, *The Just Wage 1750–1890: A Study of Moralists from St. Alphonsus to Leo XIII* (The Hague: Martinus Nijhoff, 1966). *Just Treatment for Those Who Work for the Church* (Cincinnati: National Association of Church Personnel Administrators, 1986). J. Ryan, *The Living Wage* (New York: Macmillan, 1906).

FRANK D. ALMADE

JUSTICE IN THE WORLD

Justice in the World (*Justitia in mundo*) is the first social document to come from a world synod of bishops. It was prompted by a request from Pope Paul VI to the 1971 synod for guidance in better articulating and promoting the church's engagement in the cause of global justice. Published on November 30, 1971, with the pope's approval, the document was both a response to his request and a personal appeal of the world's bishops to the people of God to become actively involved in the work of justice. It is very much a "call to action" rather than a doctrinal statement.

Coming as it does in the wake of five major contributions to Catholic social teaching during the first decade of the *aggiornamento* (*Mater et magistra,* 1961; *Pacem in terris,* 1963; *Gaudium et spes,* 1965; *Populorum progressio,* 1967; and *Octogesima adveniens,* 1971) and considering its brevity, the significance of *Justice in the World* might have been dwarfed in comparison. This was not to be the case, however. The circumstances of its origin, its methodology, and the positions it so boldly proposes have earned it a prominent place within the church's social teaching.

The synodal origin of the document accounts in part for its importance. Even more significant than its being the first synodal social document is the fact that it reflects the consensus of over 170 bishops representing the diverse social, cultural, economic, and political contexts and concerns of Africa, Asia, Eastern and Western Europe, Latin America, and North America. The majority of these bishops were elected by their own episcopal conferences as their spokesmen to the synod. Despite this divergence in background and experience, each of the document's five sections, voted separately, received over 80 percent approval. The negative vote was always less than 7 percent. Furthermore, this is not a First World document. The influence of the African, Asian, and Latin American churches, and particularly of the Medellín bishops present, is unmistakable, especially in the analysis of global injustice and in some of the dominant themes (e.g., liberation through development, structural injustice, the work of justice as constitutive of the gospel, and the church's mission).

The methodology employed in the preparation of the document is also of some importance, reflecting as it does the more consultative, dialogical, inductive, culturally sensitive approach of the postconciliar church. Prior to the synod, local episcopal conferences met to discuss a set of guideline questions ("Elements for a Reflection on Justice in the World") prepared by the council of the synod. What resulted from these discussions were sixty reports, which reflected a surprising convergence of views. There was strong agreement, for example, on the appropriateness of denouncing global injustice and addressing justice within the church itself, on the theology that should ground the church's involvement in social justice, and on the need for new approaches to education for justice.

In part, this remarkable convergence can be attributed to the influence of the social teaching of the previous decade (noted above) as well as the documents from the Second General Conference of Latin American bishops held at Medellín, Columbia, in 1968. In addition, the Pontifical Commission Justice and Peace had provided all episcopal conferences with major statements on social justice from the national and regional episcopal conferences of Asia, Africa, and Latin America, along with a number of papers dealing with social justice and development. All of this input served to prepare for the dialogue that was to take place at the synod both in the twelve work-groups and in the speeches delivered in the general sessions.

Justice in the World (JM) opens with an introduction that is followed by four additional sections: (1) Justice and World Society; (2) The Gospel Message and the Mission of the Church; (3) The Practice of Justice; and (4) A Word of Hope.

The introduction is in itself forceful and to the point. It begins by identifying the central issue that the synod bishops sought to address and clarify, namely, the mission of the people of God in furthering world justice (JM 1). Scrutinizing the "signs of the times," they come to this question aware of numerous and grave global injustices but also of a new consciousness arising among many of the oppressed propelling them beyond a fatalistic resignation to "liberate themselves and to be responsible for their own destiny" (4). In the face of unjust and intolerable social, economic, and political structures the bishops share the basic conviction, echoing *Gaudium et spes* and Medellín, that the "Church's vocation [is] to be present in the heart of the world by proclaiming the Good News to the poor, freedom to the oppressed, and joy to the afflicted" (5). Examining sacred history and the progressive realization of God's plan of liberation and salvation revealed therein, they come to the oft-cited conclusion that "action on behalf of justice and participation in the transformation of the world fully appear to us as a constitutive dimension of the preaching of the Gospel, or, in other words, of the Church's mission for the redemption of the human race and its liberation from every oppressive situation" (6). Herein lies the heart of the synod's message: the church *must* be engaged in this world to bring about justice for all.

The force and significance of this statement, which brings the introduction to a close, is not to be overlooked. By using the term "constitutive," the synod underscores the centrality and indispensability of the work of justice in the preaching and living out of the gospel and in the church's mission. Without it, the church would not be true to itself or to its vocation. Engagement in the cause of justice is neither peripheral to what the church is about nor is it optional. Furthermore, by saying that the work of justice is "constitutive" of the church's mission, the bishops of the synod claimed that the evangelizing work of the church is more than spiritual in nature. It is inextricably tied to realizing the kingdom even now amidst the economic, political, and social realities of human existence. This theological and ecclesiological stance, which culminates tendencies present in Catholic social thought since *Mater et magistra,* is not without controversy in the church community. There are those who see the church's mission as primarily spiritual in nature and are therefore resistant to its involvement in the political arena or who fear that the gospel will be emptied of its transcendent meaning and reduced to a religious justification for social change. If there were any doubts about papal endorsement of the synod's statement, they should have been dispelled by Paul VI's *Evangelii nuntiandi* (1976).

Theological justification for this controversial stance is taken up in a schematic way in the document's second section, "The Gospel Message and the Mission of the Church." Though one of the briefest sections, it may well be the most important, expressing as it does an incarnational theology. The church's mission on behalf of justice is ultimately grounded in the nature of God as disclosed in the Hebrew Scriptures and in the actions and teaching of Jesus as recounted in the Christian Scriptures.

The God of the Old Testament reveals God's self not only as liberator of the people of Israel but also as "liberator of the oppressed and defender of the poor" within Israel. God's nature and activity require both a response of faith and justice toward the neighbor. Precisely in the work of justice is God recognized as liberator of the oppressed.

Similarly, Jesus united in an indivisible way, through his life, preaching, and actions, love of God and neighbor. His total self-giving to God was manifested in and through his actions aimed at the salvation and liberation of human beings. Always he identified himself with the "least brethren" and proclaimed the intervention of God's justice on behalf of the needy and the oppressed. Pauline theology carries on the theme. Christian existence, for Paul, is summed up by faith in Christ effecting itself in love of neighbor. "According to the Christian message, therefore, man's relationship to his neighbor is bound up with his relationship to God; his response to the love of God, saving us through Christ, is shown to be effective in his love and service of men. Christian love of neighbor and justice cannot be separated. For love implies an absolute demand for justice, namely a recognition of the dignity and rights of one's neighbor. Justice attains its inner fullness only in love" (34).

This is the very essence of the Christian message, and it demands, according to the synod bishops, a dedication to the liberation of all people in their present existence. It is precisely because of Christ's mandate to preach this gospel, which demands justice, that the church "has the right, indeed the duty, to proclaim justice on the social, national and international level, and to denounce instances of injustice, when the fundamental rights of man and his very salvation demand it" (35). Echoing *Mater et magistra,* the synod unmistakably affirms that worldly existence is also part of the church's concern. As a religious and hierarchical institution, however, the proper role of the church is to defend and promote the dignity and fundamental rights of the human person (37), not to offer concrete solutions to situations of injustice. It is encumbent upon members of the church, as members of society, not only to fulfill their civic responsibilities but also to work concretely on behalf of justice.

What is the global situation, as the bishops perceive it, to which the church must respond? The first section of *Justice in the World,* "Justice and World Society," provides an analysis of the situation and in so doing raises several very important themes, namely structural injustice and the right to development and participation. The section begins with the observation that the world in which the church lives and acts is marked by a profound paradox. There are significant forces, grounded in the awareness of the basic equality and human dignity of all, working toward a unified world society. Contributing to this are new technological developments, global and instantaneous communication, an interdependent world economy, and the growing realization of the fragility and finiteness of the biosphere, which is a patrimony of all of humankind.

However, co-existent with this move toward unity there are also forces of division and hostility that seem to be increasing in strength. There are the long-standing antagonisms between and among nations, races, and classes, made more acute by new weapons of destruction, especially nuclear arms. There is also the "new industrial and technological order that favors the concentration of wealth, power and decision-making in the hands of a small public or private controlling group" (9). The result is economic injustice and lack of participation in those social, economic, and political structures vital to human well-being and development. Both prevent people from attaining their human and civil rights.

In this context the bishops offer a blunt critique of the notion of development that prevailed primarily but not exclusively in the First World during the previous quarter century. The assumption was that increased economic growth in the developed countries would ultimately benefit the disadvantaged in developing countries. This approach not only failed due to a variety of causes but also gave rise to "great numbers of 'marginal' persons, ill-fed, inhumanly housed, illiterate and deprived of political power as well as of the suitable means of acquiring responsibility and moral dignity" (10). Furthermore, the synod contends, development was a questionable goal to begin with. If the standard of living achieved by the richer nations, and the rates of consumption and pollution associated with it, were extended to the whole of humankind, irreparable damage would be done to the earth and its resources. This situation calls for new modes of understanding what it is that promotes human dignity.

What the synod fathers propose as a way of combating international systems of domination, and this is a major theme of the document, is a "determined will for development." Development here, however, is not to be understood solely in economic terms. Rather, it reflects Paul VI's usage in *Populorum progressio* when he speaks of the "right to development," or every person's right to growth toward maturity as a person. Development promotes the good of the whole person; it is an integral development (PP 14–21). The synod bishops explain that "the right to development must be seen as a dynamic interpenetration of all those fundamental human rights upon which the aspirations of individuals and nations are based" (JM 15). This appears quite similar to Paul VI's concept of the integral development of the whole person and of the whole of humankind. The right to development is seen as the means of liberation for developing nations.

By implication, the right to development means the right to those conditions that foster the realization of human rights and human dignity, individually and socially. Hence the specific content of the right to development will vary with different social, economic, and political contexts. Its requirements will need to be discovered in varying circumstances through an analysis of the prevailing institutionalized modes of human interaction. In any situation, however, as the bishops note, development requires the elimination of unjust social structures. Conversion of hearts and charity are not sufficient (16). Structural injustice and social sin are central themes of this document. While the concepts previously appeared in *Populorum progressio* (21) and *Octogesima adveniens* (45–46), and were very prominent in the Medellín documents, their usage here draws attention to them in an unprecedented way for the entire church.

Throughout this document, the world's bishops are quite clear that overcoming injustice is very much the responsibility of the developing nations themselves, though certainly not theirs alone. "In the face of international systems of domination, the bringing about of justice depends more and more on the determined will for development" (JM 13), and "in the developing nations . . . that determined will asserts itself especially in a struggle for forms of claiming one's rights and self-expression" (14). Taking their future into their own hands is itself a manifestation of their own personalization even though they might not fully achieve their goal (17). What is at issue here is another important theme of the document—developing people's right to participation in shaping the social, economic, and political structures that provide the context for their development. Participation in the process of social change is essential to realizing human potential and to promoting human dignity. To assist with participation in the international order marked as it is with unequal relationships, the synod endorsed a "responsible nationalism" in order to assist developing nations in acquiring their own identity. "From this basic self-determination can come attempts at putting together new political groupings allowing full development to these peoples" (17).

The synod concludes this section with a brief and fairly ambiguous paragraph calling for a "mediatory role" and the creation of an "ongoing atmosphere of dialogue" to overcome opposition and obstacles in the pursuit of justice (27–28). While there seems to be an implicit option for nonviolence here, it is unclear what the bishops mean by mediation and whether they intend it to be the primary mode of social change. Nor do they explore or suggest other avenues if mediation and dialogue should fail.

In the fourth section of *Justice in the World* the synod turns to the "practice of justice" in three principal spheres—the church itself, education, and the international order. With regard to the church's witness, the bishops make two major points. The first, in a somewhat ambiguous and underdeveloped paragraph, is that Christians, whatever the form of their involvement in social change, should witness to the gospel by emphasizing nonviolence, the priority of love and right (39). The second is that the church, if it is to be credible in its promotion of justice in the world, must itself be just. This requires a careful examination of respect for rights within the church, of how possessions and power are employed, and of the lifestyle of all members of the church (40–48). This section owes much to emphases in the Latin American church and is a significant development in Catholic social teaching.

"Education for justice" (which is reminiscent of "conscientization" in the Latin American church) has several components: a renewal of heart based on the recognition of individual and social expressions of sin; the inculcation of a truly human way of life; the awakening of the capacity to critique society and its values and to renounce those that violate justice; in developing countries, a heightening of awareness of concrete situations of injustice and the call to transform them; an enabling of the less-developed countries to take their destinies into their own hands and to form truly human communities. In addition, education for justice should be ongoing and experiential in process, and focused on respect for the person and on human dignity in content (51–55). "By these means the transformation of the world has already begun" (51). For the Christian this education takes place not only in the family and in other educational settings but also in the Liturgy of the Word, in catechesis, in the Eucharist, and in the other sacraments (54, 58).

Finally, the practice of justice calls for international action. The synod is quite specific here, delineating eight propositions for consideration: (1) recognition of an international order based on inalienable rights and the dignity of the person, and the adoption of and adherence to by all of the U.N. Declaration of Human Rights; (2) support of the United Nations and other international organizations as the first step in addressing the multiple aspects of international conflict; (3) fostering the aims of the Second Development Decade, especially rich nations' sharing a percentage of their wealth with the developing nations, fairer prices for raw materials, opening the markets of the richer nations with some preferential treatment for manufactured goods from developing nations; (4) creation of new institutional arrangements to allow developing nations equal participation in decision making regarding development; (5) support for the specialized agencies of the United Nations that address specific areas relating to poverty and marginalization; (6) encouragement to governments to direct more of their aid to "multilateral channels"; (7) reduction of the level of material consumption among the rich nations and the threat it poses to the earth's resources; (8) in order for the right to development to be fulfilled, respect for cultural diversity in the pursuit of development, self-determination in structuring economic and social development, full and equal participation for all in attaining the common good (64–71). Interestingly, most of these recommendations cast the developed nations as the primary agents of change.

The synod concludes this section by asserting that the preceding reflection on the church's involvement in action for justice will remain ineffective if it is not embodied in the life of local churches. In addition, it asks episcopal conferences to further pursue the lines of thought articulated by the synod and to put its recommendations into practice. Finally, it recommends to the Pontifical Commission Justice and Peace, to the council of the secretariat of the synod, and to competent authorities yet deeper study and bringing to a successful conclusion what the synod had begun.

Justice in the World ends on a hopeful note. In the fifth and final section, the synod bishops affirm the power of the Spirit working in the world and the belief that human efforts at bringing about justice will ultimately be perfected in the coming of the kingdom of justice and love. In the meantime, hope in the coming kingdom is already beginning to take root in the human heart. And while it proclaims the gospel, the church calls upon all, especially those who are poor and oppressed, to cooperate with God in bringing about liberation from sin and the transformation of the world (74–77). The synod ends where it began—by underscoring the absolute necessity of human efforts on behalf of justice as intrinsic to the preaching and living of the gospel.

There are critical questions left unanswered by *Justice in the World.* What, for example, is the relation between liberation and salvation? Who are the primary agents of change, and what are acceptable methods for bringing it about? What is the relationship between developed and developing nations in the work of justice? How are the poor and the marginalized to take their destinies into their own hands? Is there a role for confrontation when mediation and dialogue fail? Is the use of violent force and revolution ever justified? It remains for future social teaching to take up these issues. *Justice in the World* is a call to action and not a treatise on social justice or social change. And while it may be remembered for its understanding of development, its underscoring of participation, structural injustice, and social sin, and its call for justice within the church, it will probably be the synod's affirmation of action on behalf of justice as lying at the heart of the gospel and the church's mission that will be its lasting contribution to Catholic social teaching.

See also CHURCH, SOCIAL MISSION OF; DEVELOPMENT; EVANGELII NUNTIANDI; EVIL, SOCIAL; GAUDIUM ET SPES; MATER ET MAGISTRA; MEDELLÍN; MODERN CATHOLIC SOCIAL THOUGHT; POPULORUM PROGRESSIO.

Bibliography: J. Alfaro, *Theology of Justice in the World* (Vatican City: Pontifical Commission Justice and Peace, 1973). D. Dorr, *Option for the Poor* (Maryknoll, N.Y.: Orbis, 1983) pp. 177–89. J. Gremillion, *The Gospel of Peace and Justice* (Maryknoll, N.Y.: Orbis, 1976). D. Hollenbach, *Claims in Conflict* (New York: Paulist, 1979) pp. 85–89. P. Land, *Justice in the World: An Overview* (Vatican City: Pontifical Commission Justice and Peace, 1972). D. O'Brien and T. Shannon, eds., *Renewing the Earth* (Garden City: Doubleday, 1977) pp. 384–89.

RONALD HAMEL

K

KERBY, WILLIAM JOSEPH

Priest, sociologist, editor, Kerby is generally considered the founder of "scientific charity" for American Catholics. Born February 20, 1870, in Lawler, Iowa, Kerby attended St. Joseph's (now Loras) College in Dubuque. He studied for the priesthood at St. Francis Seminary in Milwaukee and was ordained in Dubuque on December 21, 1892. He was sent to pursue graduate studies at The Catholic University of America (CUA) in Washington, D.C., where he studied with Fr. Thomas Bouquillon, who insisted that moral theology was not simply a matter of abstract reasoning. Moral theology had to be grounded in social reality as discovered through the social sciences.

When CUA decided to begin a department of sociology, Kerby was chosen to head the department. He was sent to study in Europe in 1895, studying at the universities of Bonn and Berlin before receiving his doctorate from the University of Louvain in social and political science in 1897. He returned to head CUA's department of sociology for the next four decades, and he also taught at neighboring Trinity College. Kerby was one of the pioneers of academic sociology in America and was *the* pioneer of academic American Catholic sociology. In this early era sociology and social work remained closely connected.

Kerby became a strong advocate of social reform as a means of discouraging the development of socialism. He believed that given the economic situation of America in 1900, socialism would naturally triumph unless the church developed a positive program of social reform. Denunciation of socialism was no longer enough.

Kerby became involved in a number of local charitable groups but became distraught by what he perceived as the provincialism, defensiveness, and isolation of Catholic charitable groups. In 1910 he was among the founders of the National Conference of Catholic Charities (NCCC) and served as secretary from 1910 until 1920. His intent was to create a national consciousness and sense of solidarity among Catholic charitable workers, who were spread out across the country. Every two years he organized a NCCC conference that allowed for an exchange of ideas and experiences. In the 1920s he assisted in founding the National Catholic School of Social Service, for which he served as assistant director from 1924–29.

Besides organizing Catholic charities, Kerby also believed Catholics should unite with non-Catholic groups who were working for similar objectives. Kerby sat on the board of charities for the District of Columbia from 1920 until 1926.

Kerby also believed in the power of Catholic journals to educate the faithful. He was editor of the *St. Vincent de Paul Quarterly* from 1911 to 1917. He founded but did not edit the *Catholic Charities Review* in 1917, and he edited the *American Ecclesiastical Review* from 1927 until his death in 1936.

Kerby was the primary advocate of scientific Catholic charity in America, sending out numerous disciples from CUA. He most clearly articulated this notion of scientific charity in his *Social Mission of Charity* (1921), in which he defined charity as "science ending in love" (Kerby, p. 2). Kerby argued that while service to the poor was integral to the mission of the Church, such service could no longer be limited to simple and direct relief of the poor. In the modern age the causes of poverty had to be discovered and addressed rationally. Three things were required to make charity more efficient—study, organization, and training. Social workers, priests, and all those who worked with the poor needed to be trained in the social sciences. "Charity must be scientific" (p. 7). The social worker had to be able to identify the causes of poverty and seek to correct them. Second, "relief work is done most effectively through organization" (p. 119). By organizing workers and agencies, resources could be pooled, knowledge shared, and mutual support provided. In addition, organized charities could serve as better advocates of the poor in the social arena. Finally, Kerby called for trained social workers and the creation of schools in which to train them. In sum, Catholic charity had to be organized on a scientific basis if it was to be effective and efficient in 20th-century America. Through the efforts of Kerby, American Catholic charities were better organized and its personnel better trained, though there were frequent reactions against Kerby's clinical approach to charity.

Kerby was made a monsignor in 1934. He died in Washington, D.C., on July 27, 1936.

See also CATHOLIC CHARITIES USA; CHARITY; CHURCH, SOCIAL MISSION OF.

Bibliography: W. Kerby, *The Social Mission of Charity* (Washington: The Catholic Univ. of America Press, 1921, rpt. 1944). D. Gavin, *The National Conference of Catholic Charities, 1910–1960* (Milwaukee: Bruce, 1962).

JEFFREY M. BURNS

KETTELER, WILHELM EMMANUEL VON

The fourth child of landowning parents of the lesser nobility in Westphalia, Ketteler was born in 1811. He was educated by Jesuits in Switzerland, and he acquired a degree in law, did a year's military service, and entered the Prussian civil service in 1835. The decisive turn in his life came when the Prussian state arrested the archbishop of Cologne, Clemens August Droste zu Vischering, in 1837. He opposed the policy of the government in matters of mixed marriages as they were being applied in the western (Catholic) provinces. Ketteler resigned his position but could not resolve to follow an ecclesiastical vocation until 1841 (ordained 1844 in Münster). He was elected a delegate to the National Assembly in Frankfurt in 1848. Becoming in short order pastor of the main Catholic church in Berlin and then bishop of Mainz in 1850, Ketteler emerged as the leading spokesperson for German Catholicism. He participated in the Vatican Council of 1870, where he opposed the definition of papal infallibility, and he died at the height of the Kulturkampf in Germany in 1877. He was an opponent of absolutism wherever it raised its head.

Ketteler was the forerunner and inspirer of the powerful German Catholic social movement. Pope Leo XIII, apropos of *Rerum novarum,* called him "our great predecessor." He was certainly the most conspicuous example of forward-looking Catholic social thought in his time and stands at the head of the list of 19th-century bishops who took up the cause of the working class. His reputation in this respect rests principally on a series of publications. Singly they did not amount to more than episodes in his life as a diocesan bishop, but together they added up to a persistent campaign to awaken church and society to the real character of the social question of the 19th century. The first publication contained his six Advent sermons of 1848, entitled *The Great Social Questions of the Present.* His basic work, *The Labor Question and Christianity* (1864), was fully and sympathetically aware of Ferdinand Lassalle (1825–64), an early socialist political figure, and his analysis of the plight of the working class. Until 1869 Ketteler proposed only church and private activity in aid of a solution. Then he published two related writings: a historic address to about ten thousand workers held in the open during one of his diocesan visitations, "The Labor Movement and Its Goals in Relation to Religion and Morality"; and a report to the Bishops' conference at Fulda, "Pastoral Care of Factory Workers." He now endorsed central aims of the contemporary labor movement including government intervention through labor legislation. Thereafter, the First Vatican Council, the Franco-Prussian War, the foundation of the new German Reich, and the ensuing Kulturkampf urgently required his attention. Proof that, even so, he had not forgotten the labor movement came in his Lenten pastoral letter of 1877, the year of his death, and in an uncompleted draft later published entitled "Can a Catholic Worker Be a Member of the Socialist Workers Party?" Ketteler's answer was no, not as the latter was constituted by the 1875 congress at Gotha with its antagonism for "religion and morality."

In Ketteler's time, the labor question was still new, except perhaps in Britain where the longer-term effects were not exactly encouraging. No one knew how society was to cope with it or indeed whether there would be any workable solutions. As is customary with such emerging challenges, most people whatever their position declined to accept responsibility for the problem or its solution. Ketteler, too, had to feel his way, first raising the public awareness of the problem in church and society, and then sorting out various proposals for interpreting and dealing with the specter of the degradation of the working class. For the astute Ketteler, of course, it was clear that this would most likely mean further inproportionate damage to the Catholic part of the German population.

Ketteler naturally, and not inaccurately, saw the basic adversary to be modern Continental liberalism. Opposing the influence of traditional Christianity at every turn, 19th-century liberals also cast off the obligations in solidarity that the church had inculcated over the centuries, which had brought the Western world to the level of civilization (*Kultur*) that it had reached. When the scientist and National Liberal member of the Prussian diet, Rudolf Virchow, interpreted Bismarck's campaign to bring Catholics into line with the new Prussian-dominated Reich as an epochal cultural struggle (Kulturkampf), Ketteler could only agree, while wondering why this struggle was thought to be necessary. In its *intellectual* aspect, liberalism celebrated a freedom of thought that censored nothing but traditional religious thinking; *political* liberalism exalted the freedom of the individual and the power of the state against the church; what workers were suffering from, on their part, was a *social* liberalism, or individualism, that dissolved human ties and imposed a poor substitute, the ties of money. Liberals spoke much about rights, but the only right they regularly called "sacred" was that of private property.

Like other traditional Catholic opponents of liberalism (Juan Donoso Cortés, Edmund Jörg), Ketteler regarded socialism as an offspring of liberalism, equally materialistic and equally misguided because alienated from religion. Private property, though hardly "sacred" in the sense of its bourgeois defenders, had its uses. Utopian schemes that would necessitate the overturning of the whole prevailing system of production and, moreover, could only be established through violent revolutionary uprisings, were as inhumane as the conditions visited upon workers by economic liberalism. The socialist remedies would be as bad as the individualistic liberal maladies. (Ketteler did not have time to acquaint himself with Karl Marx's critique of capitalism in particular.)

One may nevertheless note that, by degrees, Ketteler acknowledged the common root of his Christian social outlook and that of some liberals, namely the value of human freedom in opposition to any kind of absolutism. Human freedom, however (and this was his quarrel with doctrinaire economic liberals), did not require absolute freedom of trade (goods, money, property) nor an absolute abstention on the part of the state from any regulation of the labor market. Some societal interventions into economic affairs were helpful and required to reestablish the primacy of human beings over markets and competition. In their characteristically opposed ways, both liberalism and socialism endangered this. The capitalistic mode of production as such, even though its prime beneficiaries and apologists tended to see it as in alliance with doctrinaire liberalism, was not necessarily tied to dog-eat-dog principles; it could prove to be a benefit to humankind under proper guidance.

Ketteler's influence was practically dominant in the world of German-speaking social Catholicism; and German-speaking social Catholicism was ahead of social Catholicism elsewhere, in keeping with Germany's industrial development in the latter part of the 19th century. Karl von Vogelsang (1818–90), convert and publicist in Vienna, appealed especially to Ketteler's earlier blanket opposition to liberalism and developed a corporatist vision that was scarcely less revolutionary and opposed to capitalism than was Marxist socialism, while the German Volksverein (q.v.), and the Christian labor movement it promoted around the turn of the century, made creative use of another approach that Ketteler had adopted in his 1869 address to workers. Here Ketteler had introduced two new elements into his previous social thinking. One was limited state regulation or intervention; the other was the trade-union movement along the lines of the British experience. This he saw as potentially an effective way to implement the principle of association on a voluntary basis within the structures of a modern, liberal society; one aimed for a gradual reform rather than a total replacement of capitalist industrial and commercial methods. At the same time, the labor movement in Britain drew on Christian religious inspiration, though it was not an organ of the church. Such a stance, as Ketteler thought, would be an indispensable condition for the success of a labor movement on the Continent as well. At least in the Catholic parts of Germany, an antireligious labor movement would gravely hamper its own prospects for success.

To the bishops later that year he recommended that a number of priests be trained in economics and familiarize themselves with the factory system. The church could not organize trade unions—they were not primarily religious organizations—but should stand ready to help Catholic lay leaders. If any of his episcopal colleagues were worried that they might be straying into economic rather than religious teaching, Ketteler maintained that the labor question "touched upon the deposit of faith." There was a materialistic, entirely self-centered principle at work in modern economics that "stands in flagrant opposition to basic humanity, let alone Christian dignity, just as it stands opposed to the purpose of material goods, as intended by God, to serve the needs of all humankind" (Ederer, p. 475).

After a season, this pioneer's inspiration bore fruit. It was too late to save the labor movement on the Continent from internecine strife, but it at least prepared the way for a vigorous (if separate and minoritarian) Christian trade unionism in Catholic Europe by the time of World War I.

See also CAPITALISM; CHURCH, SOCIAL MISSION OF; CIVIL LAW, FUNCTION OF; LABOR AND CAPITAL IN CATHOLIC SOCIAL THOUGHT; MODERN CATHOLIC SOCIAL THOUGHT; PERSON, DIGNITY OF; PRIVATE PROPERTY; SOLIDARITY.

Bibliography: W. von Ketteler, *Sämtliche Werke und Briefe,* ed. E. Iserloh (Mainz: von Hase und Koehler, 1977–). *The Social Teachings of Wilhelm Emmanuel von Ketteler,* ed. and trans. by R. Ederer (Lanham, Md.: Univ. Press of America, 1981). A. Birke in *Staatslexikon,* 7th ed. (1987) 3:394–96. E. Bock, *Wilhelm von Ketteler, Bishop of Mainz: His Life, Times, and Ideas* (Lanham, Md.: Univ. Press of America, 1977). E. Iserloh in *TRE: Theologische Realenzyklopädie* 18:109–13. P. Misner, *Social Catholicism in Europe* (New York: Crossroad, 1991). A. Rauscher, "Katholische Sozialphilosophie im 19. Jahrhundert," in *Christliche Philosophie* 1:752–67 (Graz: Styria, 1987). L. Roos, in *Zeitgeschichte in Lebensbildern* 4:22–36 (Mainz: Grünewald, 1980).

PAUL MISNER

KEYNESIANISM

Keynesianism, named after the depression-era British economist, Alfred Keynes, is a mid-century response to extreme economic individualism. Most economic historians credit this development of government-business collaboration with the stabilization and later growth of the industrial West (with the resulting rejection of both Marxism and 19th-century economic liberalism and social Darwinism).

The political economy of managed capitalism closely resembles modern Catholic social thought as it applies to macroeconomics. While acknowledging the distinction between European Christian Social Democracy and the European Social Democrats (Democratic socialists) the general sociopolitical thrust of both of these mid-20th-century reform movements in industrialized countries points in the direction of economic justice. Since the history of modern Catholic social thought represented in the papal encyclicals and various bishops letters virtually requires a mix or managed economy, it is fair to say that Keynesianism (managed economics) better represents the church's intention to advance the social good than does unregulated economic individualism.

Current debate ranges from continuing attacks from the Catholic Right (see Michael Novak, William Simon, and William Buckley) on the liberal center (bishops letter on the economy), to the positions of the Christian socialists and liberation theology. Papal pronouncements seem at various times to support any (or all) of the above positions, depending on what interpretation is given to the heart of Christian values.

See also BUSINESS ETHICS; CAPITALISM; COMMON GOOD; ECONOMIC ORDER; ECONOMIC PLANNING, SOCIAL IMPORTANCE OF; LABOR AND CAPITAL IN CATHOLIC SOCIAL THOUGHT; MODERN CATHOLIC SOCIAL THOUGHT; POLITICAL PHILOSOPHY.

MICHAEL D. WHITTY

KILLING

An ethical assessment of the taking of human life, or killing, requires attention to a number of concerns. On the one hand, the activity of killing must be distinguished from purely accidental, nonhuman agents as the cause of death. On the other hand, the moral responsibility of a human agent in the activity of killing must be carefully circumscribed. For the purposes of this entry, the activity of killing will be understood to refer to the taking of human life by a human agent. The ethical question that will be addressed will focus on whether and under what circumstances such an activity may or may not be justified.

Biblical materials on the subject of killing clearly condemn the taking of human life. The prescriptions in the Decalogue (Exod 20:15; Deut 5:17) condemn the activity of murder and view the protection of life from the framework of the intimate covenant established between God and humanity at Sinai. The inviolability of human life stems from the conviction that human beings are created in the "image and likeness of God" (Gen 1), a conviction that proscribes the "shedding of blood" (Gen 9:6). The tacit approval of some forms of killing, for example, of entire populations through the activity of the *herem,* or "holy war" (e.g., Joshua ordering the slaughter of the citizens of Jericho, Josh 6:21ff.), is perhaps best understood as a religious gesture acknowledging the supreme dominion of God over the vanquished, whose changed status forbade a return to ordinary life. The report of these episodes is generally not understood as constituting an approved practice but rather as a "moment" within the development of a larger, organic trajectory that normatively forbids all such killing.

New Testament materials continue to develop the theme of love of neighbor beyond the confines of tribal loyalties and extend love to the enemy (Mt 5:44; Lk 6:27). Not only the external action of killing is forbidden but also the interior disposition of hatred, which generates the external act: "Out of the heart come evil thoughts, murder, adultery" (Mt 15:19). Paul and John accentuate these proscriptions, and the following references are particularly pertinent: Rom 13:1-10; 1 Jn 3:11-12, 15.

From the theological perspective of the new covenant fashioned with humanity through Christ, and the doctrine of the Incarnation, the formal unity of the obligations to love God and to love one's neighbor (Mt 25) emerges as a clear implication of the task of covenant fidelity. Such a perspective further specifies an obligation to exercise stewardship over the gift of life, since the Christian community on its pilgrimage to the kingdom of God does not determine the moment of the Bridegroom's return, and hence it is unjust to deprive others of the gift of life. But, does the NT forbid all actions of violence, even those undertaken in self-defense or the defense of others?

According to Mt 5:38-41, Jesus forbids recourse to violence and admonishes recourse to "turning the other cheek." Seeking justice through the avenue of peace has a long and honored tradition. However, it is important to observe that the NT does not present an unambiguously clear rejection of recourse to the use of force under all circumstances. For example, in Lk 3:14, John the Baptist admonishes the soldiers to "rob no one with violence." Jesus praises the faith of the centurion without requiring renunciation of his profession. Similarly, the NT recognizes the authority of the sovereign not "to bear the sword in vain" (Rom 13:4). The justification of force is a perennial question in Christian theology, but its use is always an exercise in Christian regret. The contemporary understanding of the criteria for a just war recognizes the priority of peace and seeks to minimize violence as far as possible.

A related issue is the justification of the state to take life in order to protect the common good. The theological tradition has recognized that the state uses its authority in the form of law, and even the ultimate sanction of capital punishment, in order to deter further violence and to protect the common good of the society. Whether or not such actions are appropriate or necessary is the subject of much contemporary debate. As with the just-war theory, serious challenges to the applicability and relevance of capital punishment stem from a deepening appreciation of the intrinsic value of all human life and the pursuit of alternative means of resolving conflicts as well as alternative forms of punishment.

The theological tradition draws two important distinctions in order to clarify permissible and impermissible acts of killing. Any action intended to kill an innocent individual directly is forbidden and morally impermissible. Actions taken for the purpose of self-defense or the defense of another may require force sufficient to deter or to repel the attack. The use of such force proportionate to the nature of the attack may result in the death of the offender. Under these circumstances the killing of the unjust aggressor is morally permissible.

Because God exercises sovereignty over the gift of life, even the taking of one's own life is forbidden. Human beings are to be stewards of the gift of life, and no person can take measures to terminate one's own life. Objectively, such killing is morally forbidden and is to be positively discouraged. Judgments of an individual's subjective culpability and blame, however, must submit to an awareness that the suicidal person is often severely distressed and that the suicidal act is a desperate, tragic cry for help. Attention to these mitigating factors can help survivors cope with the loss that is incurred.

Moralists also draw an important distinction between killing and allowing to die. In the exercise of medical care, for example, it is sometimes necessary to forgo aggressive treatment modalities, when these are no longer medically beneficial to the patient, in favor of supportive or comfort measures. Allowing the patient to die is not an act of killing but rather a recognition of the inevitability of death and the intrinsic limits of human interventions to forestall death. Direct killing of the innocent, whether in the form of euthanasia to alleviate suffering or in the form of ending life deemed as unwanted or lacking in quality (e.g., direct abortion), is unjust and is proscribed.

Unjust taking of life can occur not only through direct measures but also through omission and neglect. For example, the failure to avail oneself of appropriate measures to sustain life or to accept appropriate, reasonable medical treatment can constitute an unjust taking of life. Thus the Vatican *Declaration on Euthanasia* defines euthanasia as "any action or omission" that has as its express purpose the direct ending or termination of life. Therefore, any action or failure to act that intentionally seeks to hasten the death of an individual is tantamount to direct killing, or murder, and is morally prohibited.

The provision of a treatment, however, to alleviate suffering that also may cause the shortening of life (e.g., the palliative use of morphine) is justified because such treatment is intended for the comfort of the patient, is balanced or proportionate to the patient's need, and the use of morphine is not the source of the patient's demise. The patient's death is an indirect, unintended effect of the medication whose primary purpose is to ease the suffering of the patient.

In summary, direct, unjust assaults on human life are viewed as morally impermissible. Indirect killing with careful attention to critical and reasoned justification can be morally permissible.

See also ABORTION, SOCIAL IMPLICATIONS OF; ANIMALS, RIGHTS OF; CAPITAL PUNISHMENT; DOUBLE EFFECT, PRINCIPLE OF; EUTHANASIA, SOCIAL IMPLICATIONS OF; HEALTH CARE; PACIFISM; WAR.

Bibliography: T. Aquinas, *Summa theologiae,* II-II, q. 64, articles 1–8. J. Blenkinsopp, "Commentary on Deuteronomy" in *The Jerome Biblical Commentary,* ed. R. Brown, J. Fitzmeyer, and R. Murphy (New Jersey: Prentice Hall, 1968). *The Code of Canon Law,* cann. 1397–98 (Michigan: Eerdmans, 1983). B. Häring, *The Law of Christ* 3:187–267 (Westminster: Newman, 1966). J. Huesman, "Commentary on Exodus," in *The Jerome Biblical Commentary* (as cited above). N. Lohfink, *The Christian Meaning of the Old Testament* (Milwaukee: Bruce, 1968). J. McKenzie, *Dictionary of the Bible* (Milwaukee: Bruce, 1965). A. Regan, *Thou Shalt Not Kill* (Butler, Wisconsin: Clergy Book Service, 1977). T. Tilley, "The Principle of Innocents' Immunity," *Horizons* 15/1 (1988) 43–68. J. Yoder, "Exodus 20:13—Thou Shalt Not Kill," *Interpretation* 34 (October 1980) 394–400.

JEREMIAH J. McCARTHY

KINGDOM OF GOD

"Kingdom of God" is a biblical term used to describe God's kingly rule. In Matthew's Gospel "kingdom of heaven" is the more usual expression, with "heaven" serving as a substitution for "God" in keeping with Jewish sensitivity about using the divine name too freely. The

Hebrew-Aramaic word for "kingdom" is *malkut,* and the corresponding Greek term is *basileia.* These words are sometimes translated as "reign" to express the dynamic character of God's kingship and to avoid the local and static connotations of "kingdom." But "kingdom of God" remains the common English rendering.

The "kingdom of God" refers to God's future display of power and judgment, and to the final establishment of God's rule over all creation. Then all people and indeed all creation will recognize and acknowledge the God of Israel as the only God and Lord. In early Judaism and the NT the kingdom is future and eschatological (pertaining to the end-time) in its fullness, though the NT writers recognize present dimensions to God's kingdom. When the Day of the Lord comes and God's kingdom is fully established, God's will shall be done on earth as it is in heaven (Mt 6:10).

Hebrew Bible and Early Judaism

The Christian (and Jewish) doctrine of God's kingdom has roots in the biblical statements about God's eternal kingship and in the understanding of monarchy in ancient Israel. The kingship psalms of the Hebrew Bible so frequently and insistently celebrate God's kingship ("the Lord reigns," Pss 93:1; 97:1; 99:1) that some scholars assume the existence of a special New Year festival in honor of Yahweh as king. The kingship psalms praise God as king over creation: "The Lord sits enthroned as king forever" (Ps 29:10); see also Psalms 96 and 97. God's kingly rule has been manifest especially in Israel's exodus from Egypt (Ps 114; Exod 15:1-18). That rule is also associated with judgment: "He will judge the peoples with equity" (Ps 96:10). In the debate over anointing Saul as king the chief hesitation concerns the relation of the earthly king to God's kingship: "they have rejected me [God] from being king over them" (1 Sam 8:7).

In early Judaism and early Christianity the kingship of God is assumed. But interest shifts to that time when God's kingship will be so manifest that all peoples and all creation must acknowledge it. Given the condition of political subjugation imposed on Israel from outside (Persians, Ptolemies, Seleucids, Romans), there was need to explain how God's lofty promises to Israel (see, e.g., 2 Sam 7) could be fulfilled. One explanation was that in the "last days" of human history God's kingship would be made evident in a spectacular way and Israel vindicated and granted what had been promised to it. In talking about this future manifestation of God's reign the Jewish writers used words and motifs from the biblical tradition (Day of the Lord, divine warrior, God as king, the anointed one, cosmic signs, etc.) in a new eschatological (or apocalyptic) context.

The essence of early Jewish and of early Christian ideas about God's kingdom can be summarized as follows: When the course of Israel's history has been accomplished (and that should be soon), God will vindicate Israel (or the faithful in it) by destroying evil and evildoers and by bringing about a new heaven and a new earth where goodness and justice will prevail. It is God's task to fulfill then the promises to Israel and to establish the kingdom for all to see and acknowledge.

There is no uniform scenario of events leading to the fullness of God's kingdom. According to Dan 12:1-3 God brings in the kingdom when the time is right (at the death of Antiochus IV); there will be a cosmic battle featuring Michael, a great tribulation, and the vindication of the righteous dead through resurrection to eternal life. In the Apocalypse of Weeks (*1 Enoch* 91:12-17), the final three (of ten) ages from Adam feature the establishment of righteousness in Israel, the judgment upon the whole world, and the new heaven and new earth where "sin shall no more be mentioned forever." *Assumption* (or *Testament*) *of Moses* 10 envisions that when

God's kingdom appears throughout all creation, Satan will be no more and Michael the archangel will avenge Israel's enemies; the kingdom's coming will be accompanied by cosmic portents, and the result will be punishment for the Gentiles and exaltation for Israel. The Qumran *Manual of Disciple* (cols. 3–4) portrays the present as the struggle between two spirits until the time of God's visitation. The children of light follow the angel of light and do the deeds of light, whereas the children of darkness follow the prince of darkness and do the deeds of darkness.

New Testament

That Jesus shared the hopes of his Jewish contemporaries for God's coming kingdom is indicated by the so-called Lord's Prayer: "Thy kingdom come, thy will be done on earth as it is in heaven" (Mt 6:10). His entire message is summarized in Mk 1:15: "The time is fulfilled, and the kingdom of God is at hand; repent, and believe in the gospel." His parables that explicitly speak of God's kingdom (see Mt 13) look forward to something amazingly large (mustard tree, huge amounts of bread, great harvests) and valuable (treasure in the field, pearl), thus suggesting that there will be a clearer and more obvious manifestation of God's kingly rule than there is at present. That manifestation will involve a judgment in which good and evil will be separated (dragnet).

These same parables indicate that the kingdom is present now even if in a small way (seeds, leaven) and demands total commitment on the part of those who perceive it (treasure, pearl). The present dimension of God's kingdom is emphasized in Lk 11:20 (Mt 12:28): "But if it is by the finger of God that I cast out demons, then the kingdom of God has come upon you." Jesus' exorcisms and healings are present aspects of the kingdom and represent victory over demonic forces. Whatever interpretation be given to Mt 11:12 ("From the days of John the Baptist until now, the kingdom of heaven has suffered violence, and men of violence take it by force"), the kingdom is enough of a present reality that it can be opposed. No saying is more important to our topic than Lk 17:21: "the kingdom of God is in the midst of you." Here Jesus asserts that the kingdom is already present ("among you"). The Greek preposition *entos* (among, in the midst of) has often been taken to mean "within," and the kingdom taken as a mystical or spiritual reality dwelling within the soul or the individual person—an interpretation that is not consistent with the teachings of Jesus or early Judaism. These "present" sayings imply that the kingdom is present or at least inaugurated in the person and ministry of Jesus. They need to be read alongside other Gospel sayings that look to the fullness of God's kingdom in the near future (Mk 9:1; 13:30; Mt 10:23). These "future" sayings have been taken as mistakes on Jesus' part, as adaptations to the conventions of the time, or as spiritual judgments urging people to make use of God's final grace-period.

The most dramatic sign of the inauguration or presence of God's kingdom was the resurrection of Jesus. Resurrection was part of the end-time scenario and applied to all the just (and wicked). The Christian claim is that a single person (Jesus) has been granted eternal life in its fullness (resurrection) before the other end-time events have taken place. Paul correctly interpreted Jesus' resurrection as the "first installment" or "down payment" toward the general resurrection (2 Cor 1:22; 5:5) and the "first fruits of the Spirit" (Rom 8:23). The basic insight of Paul's theology is that the judgment expected at the end of human history has been anticipated through Jesus' death and resurrection and that therefore the righteous "through faith" (Rom 3:25) can now stand in right relationship with God (justification). To some extent God's kingdom has already come through Jesus' resurrection.

Though all the NT writers kept alive hope for the future coming of God's kingdom in its fullness ("Thy kingdom come"), some laid even greater emphasis on its present aspects. Many sayings speak of "entering" or "being in" the kingdom of God (e.g., Mt 18:1-4), thus implying a link between the community of Jesus' disciples and the kingdom. Some Deuteropauline texts speak of the resurrection of believers as having already been accomplished (Col 2:12; Eph 2:6). John's Gospel represents the most "realized" eschatology: "Whoever hears my word and believes him who sent me has eternal life; he does not come into judgment, but has passed from death to life" (5:24). The future judgment takes place in the encounter with the revealing word of Jesus; there one must choose between God's world (light, truth, life) and "this world" (darkness, falsehood, death).

Throughout the NT the future and present dimensions of God's kingdom stand in tension. The fundamental hope for God's future kingdom in fullness is maintained ("Thy kingdom come"). But there is growing appreciation that in Jesus' ministry and especially in his resurrection from the dead the kingdom is also a present reality. Christians live in the tension between the "already" and the "not yet."

History of Interpretation

Four basic interpretations of the kingdom of God can be distinguished in the patristic writings: the eschatological expectation of a coming kingdom as in early Judaism and the NT (Apostolic Fathers), the spiritualizing view based on Lk 17:21 understood to mean that God's kingdom is "within us" (Origen), the political identification of God's kingdom with Constantine's Roman Empire (Eusebius), and the ecclesiastical approach that finds God's kingdom present in the church militant and triumphant (Augustine). In the Middle Ages the eschatological approach was revived in a new form by Joachim of Fiore and his followers, who looked forward to a new age under the Holy Spirit. In his commentary on Mt 3:2 Thomas Aquinas distinguished four senses in "kingdom of heaven": Christ dwelling in us through grace, Scripture, the present church militant, and the heavenly court. Albert the Great understood the kingdom to be God reigning in human hearts and over the saints in heaven.

The Protestant Reformers carried on the four patristic interpretations in various combinations, with Luther distinguishing the heavenly kingdom from the earthly kingdom, and the Anabaptists adopting the apocalyptic and political dimensions. In the Enlightenment Immanuel Kant envisioned an earthly kingdom in which virtue would reign and that could be produced by human efforts. The Social Gospel movement of the 19th century (Walter Rauschenbush) saw the building of a just society on religious principles as the manifestation of God's reign.

In the late 19th and early 20th centuries Johannes Weiss and Albert Schweitzer rediscovered the apocalyptic context of the kingdom of God in early Judaism and interpreted Jesus' teaching and activity in that light. Thus they restored the future coming of God's kingdom as the central theme of Jesus' preaching ("Thy kingdom come"). The subsequent debate concerned the extent to which God's kingdom is already present: realized (C. H. Dodd), in the process of realization (Joachim Jeremias), or inaugurated (Werner Georg Kümmel). Recent debate has focused on what precisely Jesus meant by the "kingdom of God": the climax of a series of future events, a way of talking about God's presence in strength (Bruce D. Chilton), or a symbol evoking the myth of God's kingship (Norman Perrin in his later publications).

Implications for Social Ethics

The kingdom of God has been a major topic in biblical research during the 20th century. The recognition of the kingdom as the central theme in the Synoptic Gospels and in Jesus' own teaching generated detailed studies of the biblical evidence. The discovery of the Dead Sea Scrolls and renewed attention to the writings of early Judaism (especially the apocalypses) provided the historical setting for understanding Jesus' preaching of God's kingdom. This research has important implications for Christian social ethics.

God's kingdom according to the NT is first and foremost eschatological; that is, it pertains to the last day when God breaks into human history and brings about a new heaven and a new earth. But it is also essential to Christian faith that in Jesus Christ—in his teaching and healing ministry, and especially in his resurrection—the kingdom has been made present. The terms "inauguration" and "anticipation" seem more appropriate than "realization" for talking about the present dimensions of the kingdom. Whether the end-time events unfold according to the scenarios in the Synoptic apocalypses (Mk 13; Mt 24–25; Lk 17, 21) or these images are simply metaphors bound to the imagination of Jesus' day can be determined only when God's kingdom arrives in its fullness. Nevertheless, some elements appear essential: resurrection of the dead, final judgment, rewards and punishments, and life in God's kingdom.

What Christians do in the present can best be seen by looking critically at the traditional identifications of God's kingdom. One strand going through Christian history is the spiritualizing, individualistic reading of Lk 17:21: "The kingdom of God is within you." This translation is rejected by modern exegetes because it is contrary to Jesus' other teachings and early Judaism. The renderings "among you" and "in your midst" are preferred because they reflect the social nature of God's kingdom even in the present. The future kingdom of God provides the horizon and goal for Christian action in the present. But it remains God's prerogative to bring it in its fullness. We do not bring it or build it up. The furthest that the NT goes is 2 Pet 3:12 (and even here there is a translation problem): "waiting for and hastening (or, earnestly desiring) the coming of the day of the Lord." Like John the Baptist, Christians can look toward, prepare for, suffer for (see Mt 11:12; Col 1:24; Mk 13:20), and remove obstacles from the coming kingdom. In the present the teachings of Jesus and the biblical writers provide the values and actions that are appropriate responses to Jesus' death and resurrection as well as fitting preparations for God's kingdom in its fullness.

Identifying God's kingdom with any earthly empire or kingdom was far from the minds of Jesus or the biblical writers. Jesus was executed as a political rebel ("King of the Jews") at the hands of the Roman governor Pontius Pilate and the Jewish leaders. While Paul (Rom 13:1-7) and other writers (1 Pet 2:13-17; 1 Tim 2:2) counseled cooperation with the imperial officials, the Revelation of John bitterly criticized the Roman Empire for overstepping the boundaries of Christian religious principles. The early Christians everywhere were a religious and political minority and had no expectation of constructing a political order on Christian principles alone. Nevertheless, they kept alive the early Jewish hope for a "new earth" where justice and peace would reign. Although the NT does not offer a "social teaching" in the full sense of the term, it does conceive Christian life in a social context and does lay down teachings with social consequences (e.g., concern for the poor, loving enemies, forgiveness, criticism of excessive wealth). Without providing the blueprint for the just society, it does contain the principles that serious Christians take as guides in contributing to the sociopolitical entities in which they participate.

The kingdom of God is not the same as the church. Yet the two are not unrelated. The kingdom of God presupposes a community of faith in which those who already recognize and act upon God's sovereignty dwell. The church is made up of those who aspire to the fullness of God's kingdom; they have been gathered in Jesus' name and are led by God's Spirit. Thus the church is a sign of the definitive reign of God. It bears witness to the kingdom and heralds its coming. It is proper to speak of building up the body of Christ (the church), provided the church is not equated with the fullness of God's kingdom. In describing what Christians and/or the church do with respect to God's kingdom, some modern theologians speak of "serving the kingdom" or "cooperating with the kingdom" or "spreading the kingdom." These are acceptable provided the biblical insistence on God's role is preserved and the temptation to Pelagianism is resisted.

Modern biblical research has restored the kingdom of God as the horizon and goal of Christian social ethics. It has highlighted Jesus' resurrection as the most dramatic anticipation of God's future kingdom. It has introduced caution regarding language about God's kingdom and with respect to the traditional identifications (soul, state, church). It has emphasized the role of hope ("Thy kingdom come") and taught us to look for the anticipations of God's kingdom in the present. It has reminded us that God's kingdom is essentially social both in the present and the future ("thy will be done on earth as it is in heaven"), and that Christian social ethics is formulated and practiced in the tension between the "already" and the "not yet" of God's kingdom.

These biblical-theological perspectives on God's kingdom were incorporated in the American Catholic bishops' pastoral letters *The Challenge of Peace* (1983) and *Economic Justice for All* (1986). Both letters not only attend to the biblical data pertaining to the topics but also treat the topics within the framework of biblical theology, with particular concern to preserve the tension between the "already" and the "not yet" of God's kingdom.

The letter on war and peace expresses the biblical teachings as follows: "The fullness of eschatological peace remains before us in hope, and yet the gift of peace is already ours in the reconciliation effected in Jesus Christ. . . . Because we have been gifted with God's peace in the risen Christ, we are called to our own peace and to the making of peace in our world" (CP 55). A similar balance between future hope and present responsibility is expressed in the letter on the economy: "Although the ultimate realization of God's plan lies in the future, Christians in union with all people of good will are summoned to shape history in the image of God's creative design and in response to the reign of God proclaimed and embodied by Jesus" (EJA 53).

See also BEATITUDES; COVENANT; DISCIPLESHIP; SCRIPTURE, USE OF IN CATHOLIC SOCIAL ETHICS.

Bibliography: B. Chilton, ed., *The Kingdom of God in the Teaching of Jesus* (Philadelphia: Fortress; London: S.P.C.K., 1984). R. Schnackenburg, *God's Rule and Kingdom* (New York: Herder & Herder, 1963). B. Viviano, *The Kingdom of God in History* (Wilmington: Glazier, 1988). W. Willis, ed., *The Kingdom of God in 20th-Century Interpretation* (Peabody, Mass.: Hendrickson, 1987).

DANIEL HARRINGTON

KNIGHTS OF LABOR

The Knights of Labor were founded in 1869 by Uriah Stephens in Philadelphia and were officially called the Noble and Holy Order of the Knights of Labor. They were one of the first national labor unions and became the foremost labor organization in the United States during the period from 1876 to 1886. In 1879 Terence V. Powderly became Grand Master Workman and ushered the Knights into their period of greatest prosperity. Unlike the later American Federation of Labor (AFL), who organized only skilled craftsmen, the Knights attempted to form "one big union" with membership open to all productive workers, skilled and unskilled, male and female, black and white. Only nonproducers such as bankers and stockbrokers were to be excluded. Unlike the AFL, which focused on short-term bread-and-butter issues, the Knights sought to reform the entire industrial order by ushering in a cooperative society in which the evil of "wage slavery" would be abolished. A society of small producers organized cooperatively would resolve most of the problems brought on by the Industrial Revolution.

The main tool the Knights intended to employ in the creation of the new cooperative order was education. Prior to real change the workers and other members of society had to be instructed in sound economic principles. The Knights sponsored lectures and study clubs to promote this end. The Knights initially opposed the use of strikes as counterproductive; while strikes might be momentarily successful, they hindered the long-range goal of a cooperative society. To obtain short-range goals such as the eight-hour day and improved working conditions the Knights advocated the use of primary and secondary boycotts. In 1885 alone, the Knights supported 196 boycotts, of which 59 were concluded successfully and another 114 pending. The Knights came to support strikes quite reluctantly. In 1885 the Knights won a major strike against railroad magnate Jay Gould, and membership in the Knights blossomed to its peak of over 700,000. In 1886 the loss of a second strike against Gould, the Haymarket Tragedy, and the creation of the AFL signaled the decline of the Knights. Though the Knights were not officially disbanded until 1917, their period of greatest prosperity and influence was over.

As the United States Catholic church was primarily a working-class people in the 19th century, a large number of Catholics had joined the Knights. The Knights' leader, Terence Powderly, was also Catholic. This presented the church with a problem, since the church's obsessive fear of socialism made it hesitant to endorse the workers' right to organize or to strike. Compounding this problem was the Knights' oath of secrecy. Early labor unions invoked secrecy to protect their members from antiunion employers. The church had been preoccupied with secret societies for more than a century following the condemnation of the Freemasons in 1734. Invoking the ban against secret societies, in 1884 Archbishop Eleazar Taschereau of Quebec had the Knights condemned in Canada. Bishop James Healy of neighboring Portland, Maine, published the ban and forbade any Knight from receiving the sacraments in his diocese.

The liberal wing of the United States church, led by Archbishop James Gibbons of Baltimore, sought to prevent the condemnation of the Knights in the United States. Powderly assured Gibbons that he would make any necessary changes in the Knights' constitution to prevent papal condemnation of the Knights. As several United States archbishops agreed with the condemnation of the Knights, the matter was referred to Rome for a final decision. In February, 1887, Gibbons delivered his famous "memorial" in defense of the Knights to Rome. In the memorial Gibbons acknowledged the reality of the grievances of American workers, who were oppressed by the "greed" and "avarice" of unprincipled monopolies and grasping owners. At the heart of Gibbons' argument was the claim that if the Knights were condemned, the American working class would abandon the church. Rome grudgingly allowed the Knights to be "tolerated." Gibbons emerged triumphant, placing the church squarely on the side of the worker.

The controversy surrounding the Knights of Labor, in conjunction with several other events, led to the promulgation of Pope Leo XIII's major social encyclical, *Rerum novarum,* in which the rights of workers were clearly and positively stated. The Knights and Powderly were not as fortunate. After 1887 the Knights declined, and in 1901 Powderly, his faith shaken by the controversy, openly abandoned the Catholic church by joining the Masons.

See also AMERICANISM; INDUSTRIALIZATION; LABOR AND CAPITAL IN CATHOLIC SOCIAL THOUGHT; RERUM NOVARUM; STRIKE, RIGHT TO.

Bibliography: H. Browne, *The Catholic Church and the Knights of Labor* (Washington: The Catholic Univ. of America Press, 1949).

JEFFREY M. BURNS

L

LABOR AND CAPITAL IN CATHOLIC SOCIAL THOUGHT

A customary use of the word "capital" generally describes an asset owned by an individual as wealth. This usage may be extended to an asset that is only potentially a source of income, such as a house, or to a person's specialized training for employment ("human capital"). Thus "capital is an asset that can generate an income stream for its owner." This description is contested by Marxist thought if it is taken to mean that "inanimate objects are productive in the sense of generating an income stream"; on the contrary, for this school capital is not a "thing" but a definite sort of social relation between those who control the means of production and those who do not (Bottomore, p. 60). Defenders of capitalism also challenge the common usage if it should imply that capital and wealth are equivalent. Capital here is just that portion of wealth "which is reinvested in productive activities." Not all wealth is useful in this way. So whereas for the Marxist the income stream, or profit, works to reproduce social relations of control that are masked as a thing, for the defender of capitalism profit is the socially beneficial "margin of new wealth created by the prudent investment of old" (Novak, p. 11). Alternatively, labor, or human productive activity, is conceived in the light of relations of control or as a constitutive dimension of a productive process that rewards creativity and risk taking for the common good.

The relation between labor and capital in Catholic social thought is often interpreted to be a feature of a "third way," institutionally to embody political and economic justice beyond Marxist and capitalist positions (see, e.g., Dorr, p. 235). Whether or not this is the case (and we will have occasion to address this question below), the definitional tussles sketched above suggest that it is important to place Catholic reflection in the context of debates over the normative primacy of (democratic) capitalist and (democratic) socialist institutional arrangements. Following an account of these debates in contemporary American Christian ethics, this essay will proceed to consider the relation between labor and capital in a number of crucial Catholic sources. A brief assessment of the success of Catholic social thought in maintaining its critical independence concludes the piece.

Capitalism Versus Socialism in Christian Ethics

The party of capitalism and the party of socialism part company only after both affirm that democracy is their dream and aspiration. Both insist that the direction of the ship of state is to be established by the citizenry through peaceful deliberation and participation. Democracy, on one side, diffuses power and preserves a wide range of freedom. On the other side, democracy affirms equality of membership in the political community and the equal stake citizens have in the fortunes of that community.

Robert Benne defines "capitalism" as "an economic system that relies on a workably competitive market as the dominant mode of making economic decisions; on private ownership of the means of production; on economic freedom to enter the market as producer and consumer, investor or laborer; and on a legal order that protects voluntary and peaceful exchange and that attempts to maintain the competitive nature of the system. Further, it relies on a rational and systematic pursuit of profit as a primary spring of social action. . . . Private ownership merely affirms that ownership is non-governmental. It leaves the door open for many kinds of ownership and management, including that by employees" (Benne, p. 68). This system is preferred because it (1) optimally promotes economic growth while (2) inhibiting concentrations of power and (3) supporting liberty, equality of opportunity, and the fair value of each.

Economic growth, supported by the efficient employment of economic resources, is a feature of good stewardship in the biblical sense. The goods of the earth, entrusted to human beings as their custodians, must be used in a way that eases or removes the pressures of grave physical necessity. On this score, Michael Novak notes that economic activity directed toward efficiency and growth can and does make use of "capacities for self-reflection, invention, and innovation [that] constitute in [humanity] the *imago Dei:* the image of God the Creator" (Novak, p. 161). A third claim is empirical: capitalist arrangements, founded on competitive market systems, have been enormously successful in producing expanding economies that benefit all members of capitalist society.

Capitalist institutions also allow a distinction between political and economic power and afford decentralization of power in society. While the economic system may need to be limited (as well as supported) by the democratic political system and the moral cultural system of a society, the fact that the economic system retains a real independence from the political sphere especially curbs concentrations of state power.

Capitalism, finally, supports justice. Economic liberty encouraged by the market is partly constitutive of freedom itself. Persons are free to enter or leave markets, subject only to constraints of ability, initiative, and market demands. There is wide latitude to pursue chosen vocations. We can spend our money as we choose. These freedoms are important in expanding those unobstructed spaces within which we may pursue our life projects. Economic opportunities are also distributed widely in free-market economies. "This opportunity to better oneself," Benne insists, "is *the* most important element that a society—or an economy—can offer. In the eyes of average people it far outweighs strategies of income redistribution." A system of economic reward for economic contribution both correctly recognizes relative excellence in meeting market demands and provides incentives for creativity in service of the needs and wants of others. To the extent that the system of rewards fails to secure the fair value of liberty and opportunity, and insofar as inequalities necessary for incentives fail to advance the prospects of the least advantaged members of society, the polity must pursue strategies of justice. These may include redistributive taxation so that the basic needs of citizens are met (Benne, pp. 74–77).

The democratic socialist may argue both that growth and efficiency are important and that market arrangements that support them are compatible with socialism. Cornel West is typical: "There . . . should be little doubt—given the glaring economic failures and political despotisms in the command economies of marketless communist regimes—that market activities of some sort, with price mechanisms that balance supply and demand and reflect cost and use-value, are the only modern alternative to large, powerful, unaccountable bureaucratic hierarchies of full-fledged control planning" (West, "A Christian Perspective," p. 85). Genuinely free markets in themselves are not the problem. What is?

The primary problem is the way in which the power of corporate business disproportionately engages or influences public and governmental processes. In assuming public functions (e.g., determining a society's technology, work patterns, market structures, resource allocation, and compensation) without making itself accountable to the public, that power, especially in its corporate aspect, is excessively concentrated and privileged. Presumably a bulwark against excessive political control, it eludes democratic containment in many of its practices of investment and production.

Now Christians, let us say, hold that all human creatures are made in God's image, and therefore bear an inherent and "alien" dignity independent of temporal criteria of human worth. They also recognize that human sinfulness needs to be checked by institutions that curb excessive forms of power. What follows from this for a Christian socialist like West is that human persons ought to be accorded the respect that supports their development with others of their God-given capacities within democratic arrangements that highlight "not simply participation within a given set of structures *but also empowerment to change the structures themselves.*" Given the antidemocratic character of corporate capitalism, this canon of respect can be realized only through some form of democratic socialism that combines markets, constitutional democracy, public ownership of major economic enterprises, and workers' control.

Just as the democratic-capitalist argument for decentralization masks the realities of the abundance of private economic power, so the argument concerning justice covers up the realities of severe injustice endemic to the capitalist system. Beyond the problem of disempowerment discussed above, socialists note how the protection of economic liberty overwhelms regard for the basic needs of human persons; how the particular stress on opportunities "to better oneself" deflects attention away from the deep structural inequality evident in the range of positions for which persons are to compete; and how the elevation of reward for contribution inevitably generates a criterion of human worth that is narrowly and inhumanly bound to degrees of human productiveness. Efforts on the part of the state to secure justice are limited by the political privilege the corporate sector enjoys. Its inordinate influence on political processes includes the power to shape citizen opinion and the political agenda; hence any pursuit of justice is likely to be bound to what the success of private enterprise can permit. Pleas for economic growth for the improvement of the prospects of all citizens, for example, may well be compatible with significant levels of inequality, poverty, and unemployment so long as such "growth" is pursued.

The social theory of Karl Marx, of course, informs the democratic socialism many Christians endorse. West sketches the rudiments of the Marxian legacy. "The Marxist theory of capitalist society claims: Capitalism is a historically transient system of production which requires human beings to produce commodities for the purpose of maximizing surplus value (profits). This production presupposes a fundamental social relationship between the purchasers and the sellers of a particular commodity, namely, the labor power (time, skill and expertise) of producers. The crucial commodity is bought by capitalists who own the land, instruments and capital necessary for production; it is sold by producers, whose labor power is needed for production. The aim of the former is to maximize profits; that of the latter, to ensure their own survival" (West, *Deliverance,* p. 108).

The "fundamental social relationship" in effect alienates workers from their work in that they do not participate in decisions about its style and substance; thus they cannot find themselves in what they are doing. They are alienated from what they produce in that their product, treated as a commodity to be bought and sold, is utilized in ways over which they, again, have no control. Since profits are taken from the buying and selling that support the wage-capital relationship, the worker finds that he or she is really just fashioning a world against himself or herself. Interest in one's work remains constricted to maintaining physical life; without links to other persons through common control over their work or a positive orientation to the end of their product, one is reduced to life in hostility and competition with one's fellows in the struggle for survival. Such Marxian insights would serve a theological analysis displaying how capitalist arrangements contradict a proper stance of reverence for individuals who, beloved of God, are fulfilled in communities of mutual support.

There is a marked contrast in the way the disputants normatively describe human work. This issue can be refined somewhat by considering Marx's vision of "free human production." He takes the relationship of exchange in a private-property system to be inherently self-interested and self-isolating. One produces only in order to own something one needs or wants. "I have produced for myself and not for you, just as you have produced for yourself and not for me. . . . Our mutual production means nothing for us as human beings. Our exchange, therefore, cannot be the mediating movement in which it would be acknowledged that my product means anything for you because it is an *objectification* of your being, your need. *Human nature* is not the bond of our production for each other. Exchange can only set in *motion* and confirm the *relationship* which each of us has to his own product and to the production of the other person. Each of us sees in his product only his *own* objectified self-interest and in the product of the other person, *another* self-interest which is independent, alien, and objectified" (Marx, p. 278).

Even the language of human need becomes dehumanized, since it is only what I want, your object, that gives your need for my object any value or dignity. My product is indeed the power I have over you, and vice-versa. A *human* language of need in relation to our human work would be spoken in this context of power "as a plea, as begging, and as *humiliation* and hence uttered with shame and supplication." Only an independent power over the other can bear our dignity. At the same time, this power over another is based upon our mutual bondage to the *objects* we produce, since they are but "the sensuous shell and concealed form" of what we need and desire, and since we become merely the "means and instrument" of what we produce to get what we may need or want. "Our *mutual* value is the *value* of our mutual objects for us. Man himself, therefore, is mutually *valueless* for us."

In contrast, suppose we had produced things as human beings. My production would express myself in my individuality and uniqueness. It would be part of my life, and I could see myself in the work I had poured myself into. In your use of what I produce, I have the direct satisfaction that I have satisfied a human need through my work. You would be able to affirm me, in and with my self-expression, as being a part of your life. As an individual I would have realized my true social nature, and "our productions would be so many mirrors reflecting our nature." My work within a system of private property is "an externalization of life because I *work in order to live* and provide for myself the *means* of living. Working is *not* living" (Marx, p. 281). That system makes it impossible to attain the condition in which full individual self-expression is realized in human service and fellowship.

Democratic capitalists would defend private ownership precisely because it respects the free creativity of human persons. The free-market system is praised because it requires attention to the needs and wants of others, rather than merely oneself, for the purposes of serving them. Productive activity in this context encourages cooperation, communication, and teamwork because economic liberty and free association are guaranteed. Appealing to what Tocqueville called "the principle of self-interest rightly understood," democratic capitalists can suggest that human selfishness is rightly checked by market arrangements. "To produce goods and services that make life better for others serves not only self-interest but the common good" (Lay Commission, p. 18). These claims challenge Marx's rhapsodic vision of the possibilities of human nature and call into question collective ownership; for the condition of human sociality is nothing other than liberty. Human work within capitalist institutions, supporting and supported by the values of other communities like the family, can achieve a form of fellowship in which inventiveness, initiative, and the "virtues of enterprise" are advanced. A system of communal control and ownership cannot match up.

Labor and Capital Since Rerum Novarum

How are the terms, arguments, and conclusions of these controversies related to the contributions of Catholic social thought regarding labor and capital? An answer to this question depends on an interpretation of these contributions. My approach will be rather conventional, plotting a line of development in papal and council teachings from *Rerum novarum* through the writings of John Paul II. I claim no special privilege for this approach; it remains, however, one significant way to expose relevant material.

Rerum novarum. "It is the soul which is made after the image and likeness of God; it is in the soul that sovereignty resides, in virtue of which man is commanded to rule the creatures below him, and to use all the earth and ocean for his profit and advantage. . . . In this respect all men are equal; there is no difference between rich and poor, master and servant, ruler and ruled. . . . No man may outrage with impunity that human dignity which God Himself treats with reverence, nor stand in the way of that higher life which is the preparation for the eternal life of Heaven" (RN 32). While this text directly supports Leo XIII's case for the right of workers to rest from their labor, it claims much in addition and in its own right. It establishes a fundamental claim to human dignity based on humanity's theocentric origin and destiny; moreover it asserts that that dignity is equally shared among all human beings, whatever their station or economic position. Finally, the text intimates both the transcendence of the human person over the temporal and material world as well as the person's immanent, productive involvement with it.

This sort of perspective governs Leo's critique of certain socialist and capitalist arrangements. The former is rejected because it denies a natural right to private property ("the results of labor should belong to him who has labored"), and because it commends the absorption of natural associations like the family into the state. Yet, following Aquinas, possession is distinguished from the human use of property, which must respond to the needs of others in charity or ("in extreme cases") justice. At the same time, a laissez faire capitalist endorsement of the unrestricted sanctity of the labor contract is criticized as well in the name of a "just wage"; "there is a dictate of nature more imperious and more ancient than any bargain between man and man, that the remuneration must be enough to support the wage-earner in reasonable and frugal comfort" (RN 34). Note also the attack on the "greed of unrestrained competition" (2). These points do not cut to the heart of the current controversies, however; democratic socialists may accept the institution of genuinely private property (as well as markets), and democratic capitalists allow for intentional strategies of justice.

A pair of tensions in *Rerum novarum* establish greater relevance and anticipate subsequent developments in papal social teachings. On the one hand Leo holds (and this also in opposition to the socialism he decries) that capital and labor, typically identified as "rich and poor," are organically related to each other. "Each requires the other; capital cannot do without labor, nor labor without capital" (15). Normatively a harmonious mutuality of responsibility ought to obtain, and the *state* should stand "above the interests of all classes and . . . keep a balance between them" (Dorr, p. 17). On the other hand, Leo concedes that in fact the wealthy do hold inordinate political power in virtue of their economic situation, and that the state must intervene both actively to assist the needy worker and to encourage a wide distribution of property ownership. The two proposals explicitly follow from labor's claim to equal concern and respect and seem to presuppose that political intervention is not so much neutral and harmony promoting as it is explicitly protective of the weak in a situation constituted by conflict.

A related tension between harmonious ideal and conflictual reality is present in *Rerum novarum.* Leo celebrates the equal access of all human creatures to virtue, which serves above all to unite capital and labor "in the bonds of friendship." Such virtue, in line with the example of Christ, "cannot fail to keep down the pride of those who are well off, and to cheer the spirit of the afflicted; to incline the former to generosity, and the latter to tranquil resignation" (20–21). But the pope also acknowledges the need for worker organizations that, apparently, presume and operate within a state of affairs where vigilance and just complaint, not tranquil resignation, respond to injustice and the absence of generosity.

At stake in these two cases is the fit between, if you will, ideal and nonideal theories of justice, and the ways in which ideal theory can function to curb a social analysis of injustice grounded in something like the dominance of economic power over the spheres of political power and human need (Walzer). The ideal account of political neutrality, organic harmony, and hierarchically defined virtue seems, perhaps, to cut against Leo's severe challenges to the status quo of 19th-century industrial capitalism.

Quadragesimo anno. It can appear that Pius XI complicates the story by (1) repeating the tensions noted above, and by (2) simply intensifying the critique of capitalism and socialism commenced by his predecessor. There is reason to go with this reading, but a closer look indicates development in relation to *Rerum novarum.* The state's neutrality now appears to be aimed more at establishing a politically wrought "common good" among persons and groups and less at preserving some preestablished organic harmony. Virtue and structural change in the direction of economic equality are commended but not integrated; however, commentators have pointed out that such an integration may be potentially present (Dorr, pp. 58–59). Free enterprise and private property are strongly affirmed. Socialism, even of the "moderate" sort, is roundly condemned. Still, Pius XI goes beyond Leo in attacking the corruption of free enterprise by "individualistic free competition," whereby the accumulation of economic power proceeds unrestrained. This leads to a struggle to dominate not only economic markets and labor but also the state. "Free competition has committed suicide; economic dictatorship has replaced a free market. . . . The

State which should be the supreme arbiter, ruling in queenly fashion far above all party contention, has become instead a slave, bound over to the service of human passion and greed" (QA 109).

Whatever the critique of socialism, then, and whatever concessions are made to the fact that the classes of labor and capital can, do, and may properly exist in a just society, the case can be made that *Quadragesimo anno* forcefully names what democratic socialists see to be the worm at the heart of capitalist institutional arrangements: the tyranny of private economic power over political matters bearing on a public good, as well as over the sphere of human need for the material conditions of a life lived with dignity. Yet Pius XI does not call for democratic socialist arrangements; rather, the public authority of the state is counted on properly to intervene on behalf of the common good and in accord with the principle of subsidiarity (79). The conditions of dignified life are sought in wage earners receiving their fair share of the fruits of production and increasing their possessions by thrift and prudent management (61). We find no explicit recommendation of public ownership, although perhaps we do have a cousin to workers' control in the plea for workers' sharing somewhat in the ownership or management of enterprise (65). Correcting the harsh excesses of "free competition" and establishing an order of relatively autonomous "functional groups" according to vocation are the means to overcome the injustices and conflicts that contingently characterize the relation between capital and labor (81–87). But the relation itself is not subjected to any direct and internal challenge in terms of democratic principles.

Mater et magistra and Pacem in terris. Doctrinal continuity with a twist characterizes John XXIII's 1961 document *Mater et magistra.* A right to private property is reaffirmed and tempered by appeal to what Pius XI referred to as the social character of ownership. A just wage and just distribution generally of material resources for the common good are called for along with worker participation in the operation of economic enterprises. *Quadragesimo anno's* definition of the principle of subsidiarity is quoted approvingly in full (MM 53). And all of this with a more international focus on injustice, and with something of a meliorist vision of how the prevailing economic order of the day was moving (115, 163; Dorr, 89–97).

Three features of the document indicate a shift in the practical force of Catholic social thought regarding the relation of labor and capital. First, a normative anthropology of the thoroughly social character of human life and flourishing is stressed in connection with John's description of "the multiplication of social relationships, that is, a daily more complex interdependence of citizens, introducing into their lives and activities many and varied forms of association" (59; see also 60–62). The former qualifies John's assessment of this complexity in social life; while acknowledging its dangers, he fundamentally sees it as an indication of "that human and natural inclination, scarcely resistible, whereby men are impelled voluntarily to enter into association in order to attain objectives which each one desires, but which exceed the capacity of single individuals" (60). In the logic of the document, these objectives are "the sum total of those conditions of social living, whereby men are enabled more fully and more readily to achieve their own perfection," that is, the common good (65).

Second, a tendency in *Rerum novarum* to describe human labor as for the purposes of the coordinate goods of making a living and personal self-expression is modified by weighting the second good more heavily. John notes that many workers prefer the development of professional skill over the possession of goods and that "this accords with the inherent characteristics of labor, inasmuch as this proceeds directly from the human person, and hence is to be thought more of than wealth in external goods. These latter, by their very nature, must be regarded as instruments. This trend indicates an advance in civilization" (106–7).

Third, John XXIII is bolder than his predecessors in envisioning the rightful ownership of means of production "by States and other public agencies" when the common good requires it. The three themes operate to show (1) how capital may be seen as a predicate of labor rather than as an independent reality standing over against it, and (2) how the social character of human life, as constitutive of human dignity, may properly ground the public ownership of enterprise in some cases.

Hollenbach has persuasively argued that *Pacem in terris* systematizes the preceding encyclical's account of the moral implications of the social meaning of human dignity. "It reemphasizes *Mater et Magistra's* stress on the fact that human dignity is internally conditioned by human interdependence, an interdependence which exists both within national borders and across them. The rights which protect human dignity, therefore, are the rights of persons *in* community. . . . Human dignity is not an abstract or ethereal reality but is realized in concrete conditions of personal, social, economic, and political life" (Hollenbach, pp. 65, 68). The document's presentation of rights includes, then, both the civic and political freedoms cherished by liberal capitalists and the social and economic rights championed by socialists.

Gaudium et spes. The Pastoral Constitution on the Church in the Modern World (GS) establishes the deep theological warrants for much subsequent Catholic reflection on the relation of labor and capital. It does this while following and developing the teaching of the past, particularly in the line of John XXIII. The central move in the document is to integrate a thoroughgoing Christocentrism with a thoroughly open and undefensive posture toward the entire world. The opening words set the course: "The joys and hopes, the griefs and anxieties of the men of this age, especially those who are poor or in any way afflicted, these too are the joys and hopes, the griefs and anxieties of the followers of Christ."

Consider two examples of this integration that are pertinent to our topic. (1) The anthropology of sociality is developed with specific reference to the doctrines of the Trinity and Incarnation (GS 24, 32). Against this background, John XXIII's discussion of increasing social complexity is extended and enriched. "This social life is not something added on to man. Hence, through his dealings with others, through reciprocal duties, and through fraternal dialogue he develops all his gifts and is able to rise to his destiny" (25). (2) Human work is grounded in the image of God, the true meaning of "dominion" in God's light, and the expectation of a new earth and a new heaven in Christ; this expectation "must not weaken but rather stimulate our concern for cultivating" our world. "For here grows the body of a new human family, a body which even now is able to give some kind of foreshadowing of the new age" (39). Labor unfolds the Creator's work and contributes to the divine plan, so that the name of God will be wonderful in all the earth (34). As such, development of self and world in work "is of greater value than any external riches which can be garnered."

Economic life follows these insights when productivity is understood fundamentally to serve the whole person (64); when productive work is adapted to human need, including the need for free and communal self-development; when the labor of the human subject is deemed "superior to the other elements of economic life" (67); when active participation by all in enterprise is promoted (68); and when patterns of ownership honor the universal purpose of created goods to provide for the benefit of all (69). The importance and power of these norms and their warrants emerge fully in the writings of John Paul II.

Populorum progressio. If you take seriously the notion that the whole world is God's good work and are accordingly struck with the injustice rampant in it, you cannot but say with Paul VI that "the social question has become worldwide." Of course, this theme is explicit in the writings of John XXIII, but his successor replaces gradualist optimism with a note of great urgency. The pope appeals to those with abundance to assume more responsibility toward the goal of "integral development" of poor nations. Three duties are announced: that rich nations offer significant aid for developing countries ("solidarity"), that inequitable trade relations be rectified ("social justice"), and that "universal charity" be exercised between peoples so that some do not advance at the expense of others (PP 44). Paul VI denies that private property is an "absolute and unconditioned right" but does not recommend the abolition of the competitive market. Still, his indictment of "liberalism" as a form of "individualistic capitalism" is reminiscent of the strong words of *Quadragesimo anno:* "it is unfortunate that . . . a system has been constructed which considers profit as the key motive for economic progress, competition as the supreme law of economics, and private ownership of the means of production as an absolute right that has no limits and carries no corresponding social obligation" (PP 26).

This is a controversial document. Defenders of democratic capitalism such as Michael Novak have challenged *Populorum progressio* for passing over the critical terms quoted above without sufficient reflection. "Is not profit another name for economic progress? . . . Is not competition better than state monopoly? Did not John Locke, Adam Smith, and John Stuart Mill . . . justify private property through its service to the common good, and, therefore, as a *relative* right?" (Novak, p. 135). Critics from the left like Donal Dorr, in contrast, worry that Paul VI relies too much on a "consensus" model of conflict resolution. "The encyclical lays so much stress on the value of collaboration of rich and poor, and on the duty of those 'at the top' to initiate this, that it does not pay enough attention to what the poor can and should do," including the possibility of (even nonviolent) confrontation (Dorr, p. 156). But Novak tries too hard to catch Paul VI in some either/or (democratic capitalism/bureaucratic state socialism) that the latter would resist and transcend; Dorr himself realizes that by "pointing out the injustices of the world and the obligation of the rich and powerful to remedy them, Paul VI was necessarily making the poor more aware of their rights and in some sense encouraging them to seek these rights actively."

Octogesima adveniens. Paul VI's open letter to Quebec's Cardinal Roy continues the universal appeal for justice with special reference to problems of urbanization and industrialization. An apparent advance from prior teachings is the focus on the political character of economic activity. At least we find it suggested that the activity of mobilizing and exercising political power for justice is a reality-creating event not restricted to states. "To take politics seriously at its different levels—local, regional, national and worldwide—is to affirm the duty of man, of every man, to recognize the concrete reality and the value of the freedom of choice that is offered to him to seek to bring about both the good of the city and of the nation and of mankind" (OA 46). Indeed, Paul announces that with regard to the economic realm, in order "to counterbalance increasing technocracy, modern forms of democracy must be devised, not only making it possible for each man to become informed and to express himself, but also by involving him in a shared responsibility" (47).

That Paul would be writing of a more decentralized, culturally specific, and dynamic conception of political activity can find some confirmation in his attack on "ideology." The former may be "the projection of a plan of society" that unites criticism of existing societies with "the forward-looking imagination both to perceive in the present the disregarded possibility hidden within it, and to direct itself towards a fresh future" (25, 37). The latter is an imprisoning intellectual system that totalizes and deforms the perception of social realities. Paul rounds up the usual subjects here: both Marxist and "liberal" ideologies are rejected outright, though features of the former (scientific social analysis and critique, historically tested praxis) come in for conjectural and hypothetical approbation, only to be exposed in the end as bound to suffocating systems of materialism and class struggle after all (33–34).

The problem with these hints and evidences is that they exist alongside themes that appear to pull in another direction. These include a traditional account of "the political society" as having a universal character, coordinating and completing more particular groupings in terms of the common good. This sort of move typically goes hand in hand with making the focus of politics the activity of the state in its promotion of greater justice through collaboration and dialogue among competing parties. In addition, in his discussion of labor unions, Paul VI regards as a "temptation" the employment of force through strikes to obtain "demands of a directly political nature" (14). How this claim comports with the yoking of economic to political considerations remains unclear.

Laborem exercens and *Sollicitudo rei socialis.* John Paul II states that he intends to be in "organic connection" with the tradition of Catholic social thought while seeking to discover new meanings to human labor. Regarding the first aim, the idea is to bridge the approaches of Leo XIII and Pius XI to the labor question within nations with the more international concerns about justice of their successors. As for the second purpose, the pope explores to a larger extent than his predecessors the significance of work in light of the biblical witness.

Genesis provides the source for the fundamental importance of work in human life. There we find narrated the story of humanity's creation in God's image as male and female; that image is partly constituted by the call to have dominion over the earth. "In carrying out this mandate, man, every human being, reflects the very action of the Creator of the universe" (LE 4). Thus the subjective side of work is decisive. The worker is a person, capable of acting rationally and according to a plan and able to decide toward a goal of self-realization in community with others. All work, then, ought to manifest and confirm the person who works, as such, and as one who holds dominion.

It follows that work cannot be seen as a form of merchandise to be sold to an employer, nor as an impersonal force needed for production. The degradation of the subject of work in Leo XIII's time was based on "grounds that human work is solely an instrument of production, and that capital is the basis, efficient factor and purpose of production" (LE 8). This error, or "economism," (considering labor solely according to economic purpose) is based on the prior mistake of subordinating personal and spiritual realities to material ones. This takes place, however, not only when profit and wealth become the end of economic activity and persons the means. "Dialectical materialism" also denies subjectivity in that the worker is taken to be a mere resultant of economic and productive relations governing a particular historical period (14).

So labor is prior to capital. Capital is not separate from and over against labor, precisely because in the process of production "labor is always a primarily efficient cause, while capital, the whole collection of means of production, remains a mere instrument or instrumental cause." Capital, an instrument, serves work and is the result of work. Prominence must always be given to the person over things (12–13).

The traditional account of private ownership is recast in terms of the preceding. Property is acquired through work in order that it serve work and human workers; therefore, a right to private property is subordinated to a right common to all to use the goods of creation for the fulfillment of persons. Hence one cannot exclude in principle the socialization of certain means of production under suitable conditions. Policies of joint ownership, profit and management sharing, and worker shareholding are also viable. At the same time, private ownership cannot be eliminated, and state monopoly or bureaucratic centralization is not in any proper sense "socialization." Here again, the priority of personal work is the linchpin. The laborer wants the fruit of his or her work to be used by oneself and others. He or she wants to be able to participate, as a responsible and creative being, in the work process as a whole. And he or she wants to be able to know that in one's work, one is working for oneself (14–15).

Laborem exercens has its problems. The biblical and theological account of the character of work as toil and a curse, while discussed, does not seem to be integrated dialectically with the general account of work as imaging dominion. That account itself is too liable to corruption in terms of the arrogance of human lordship over the natural and human environment. Some corrective in terms of, if you will, the manner of divine lordship as service, which persons are to image, is necessary but effectively absent in the document. Finally and most important, for all the talk about persons and subjectivity, the activity of women seems to be normatively restricted in the text to the requirements of their "nature" to be childbearers and mothers (19).

Still, it must also be said that John Paul II does a remarkable job of coherently and fairly reinterpreting past tradition. Themes such as human dignity, critical independence from capitalism and socialism, the relative right of private ownership, and moral concern for the poor are reaffirmed in a way that also addresses past difficulties and picks up undeveloped insights. Leo XIII's problem of the "fit" between ideal theory and the analysis of injustice is handled by replacing a vision of organic harmony and complementarity with one of personalism—and this is done by following faithfully Leo's own celebration of the fundamental dignity of humanity. John Paul II commends movements of worker solidarity to oppose the degradation of work and to pursue justice (8), and the theory of the priority of labor explains why this may be so; what is more, he can make way for proper political confrontation between labor and capital by insisting that, in principle, union struggles are and ought to be *for justice.* They are not just a reflection of class, nor are they meant to eliminate opponents. He worries that worker movements for justice may be subordinated to the decisions of political parties (20), but he does not thereby deny, as Paul VI may, the rightful political character of these movements. While he does not explicitly commend democratic economic arrangements, a theme lacking in Pius XI and hinted at by Paul VI, his thinking about labor's active self-responsibility moves palpably in this direction (whatever the relation of this consideration to patterns of justifiable markets and private ownership). Indeed, the U.S. bishops have powerfully pursued this tendency, as it reflects on the entirety of Catholic social teaching, in their 1986 pastoral letter *Economic Justice for All.* John Paul II also systematically develops the view, discovered in *Mater et magistra* and *Gaudium et spes,* that capital is a predicate of labor. His discussion of the "indirect employer" and the structural dimensions of wage and employment patterns makes good use of John XXIII's analysis of the increasing complexity of human interdependence (LE 17).

In *Sollicitudo rei socialis,* John Paul honors *Populorum progressio* through an analysis of international injustice that is greatly indebted to *Laborem exercens.* The division of the world into two systems or blocs, represented by liberal capitalism and Marxist collectivism, is cited as a decisive source of the world's misery. The fundamental materialism of each enables a competitive pursuit of wealth and power that subordinates the good of persons and peoples. Conceptions of the right to common use of the goods of creation and human solidarity on behalf of the poor are also employed in the pope's analysis and appeal.

Conclusion

The parties of capitalism and socialism continue to contend for the heart of Catholic social teaching, but that teaching has sought to maintain an independence that enhances rather than diminishes its relevance to social ethics. Perhaps the best way to understand this is to question the idea that the tradition since *Rerum novarum* provides or recommends, at least implicitly, some third institutional approach to the "social question." If there were such an approach emerging from the tradition, there would also be resources from within the tradition to challenge it. We find in Catholic social thought not so much a "third way" as a *tertium quid* that establishes a point of view from which the strengths, weaknesses, and above all half-truths of the competing systems may be clearly discerned and related to one another. For example, if capitalist work is as Marx says it is, it should to that extent be condemned; but if creativity and responsibility are available to laborers under democratic capitalism, that should be celebrated. Materialism must be rejected, wherever it is found. All systems bear a burden of proof in light of the notion that they, like the Sabbath and work, are for the human person and not the other way around. The person, a social being, a sacredness created by and destined for fellowship with God, is prior. It is this vision of human dignity in solidarity that trumps our lovely theories (including the church's in any particular time and place), that resists easy answers, and that elicits, as must be the case, the exercise of the virtue of political prudence in discerning possibilities for justice in the realities of our lives in the world.

See also ALIENATION; CAPITALISM; CLASS STRUGGLE; COMMON GOOD; PERSON, DIGNITY OF; SOLIDARITY; SUBSIDIARITY, PRINCIPLE OF; WORK, THEOLOGY OF.

Bibliography: R. Benne, "Capitalism with Fewer Tears," in B. Grelle and D. Krueger, eds., *Christianity and Capitalism* (Center for the Scientific Study of Religion, 1986). T. Bottomore, ed., *A Dictionary of Marxist Thought* (Harvard Univ. Press, 1983). D. Dorr, *Option for the Poor* (Orbis, 1983). D. Hollenbach, *Claims in Conflict* (Paulist, 1979). Lay Commission on Catholic Social Teaching and the U.S. Economy, *Toward the Future: Catholicism in Crisis* 2 (November 1984). K. Marx, *Writings of the Young Marx on Philosophy and Society,* L. Easton and K. Guddat, eds. (Doubleday, 1967). M. Novak, *Freedom with Justice* (Harper & Row, 1984). M. Walzer, *Spheres of Justice* (Basic Books, 1983). C. West, "Neo-Aristotelianism, Liberalism, and Socialism: A Christian Perspective," in B. Grelle and D. Krueger, eds., *Christianity and Capitalism* (Center for the Scientific Study of Religion, 1986). C. West, *Prophesy Deliverance* (Westminster, 1982).

WILLIAM WERPEHOWSKI

LABOREM EXERCENS

This encyclical on labor, commemorating the 90th anniversary of Leo XIII's *Rerum novarum,* was published on September 14, 1981, at a time when it appeared that the union movement *Solidarnosc* was the effective agent transforming Polish society. *Laborem exercens* contains several radical ideas: it offers a pejorative definition of capitalism, it suggests that the error of capitalism has been repeated in communism, it announces the priority of labor over capital, it argues that the title to the ownership of the means of production is always conditional, and it recommends that industries be owned by the people who work in them. Since these ideas are at odds with the liberal tradition of America, the encyclical created a certain puzzlement among American Catholics. Some Catholics expressed their reserve while others offered less offensive interpretations of the text (Houck and Williams). Even the U.S. bishops did not integrate all of these ideas into their 1986 pastoral, *Economic Justice for All.* The Canadian bishops, by contrast, followed the lead of *Laborem exercens* in their statements on economic justice.

Because of its controversial nature, I shall present a substantial resumé of the encyclical in which I concentrate on the new ideas and offer the precise quotations of the controversial points. In the resumé I shall follow the subtitles given in the official English version. At the end of the article I shall discuss a number of unresolved questions.

Resumé of Encyclical

Part 1. The introduction (LE 1–3) interprets the evolution of papal social teaching on economic justice from the "class" concern of Leo XIII and Pius XI, dealing with the maldistribution of wealth and power in Western countries, to the "world" concern of John XXIII, *Gaudium et spes,* and Paul VI dealing with the same maldistribution on the global level. What has remained constant in this shifting concern is the focus on human labor—the division of labor and the conditions of labor—which is "a key, probably the essential key"(LE 3), to the entire question of justice in society.

Part 2. The section on the role of work in human life (4–10) provides a theoretical basis for critical reflection on economics. Basing himself on Genesis and on philosophical reflections, the origin of which is not specified, John Paul II argues that according to God's design humans are destined to create their social world by labor, and by this labor to enter into their own self-realization. This process shapes every single person and moves forward the whole of human history. The laboring process "embraces all human beings, every generation, every phase of economic and cultural development, and at the same time it is a process that takes place within each human being, in each conscious human subject. Each and every individual is at the same time embraced by it. Each and every individual, to the proper extent and in an incalculable number of ways, takes part in the giant process whereby man 'subdues the earth' through work" (4).

Human labor has an objective and a subjective meaning. The objective meaning refers to the objects produced by labor, from agricultural products and manufactured goods to the tools of labor, or technology, and from there to the entire social world inhabited by men and women. And the subjective meaning of work refers to the self-realization of men and women through their labor. The human being works as a person, that is, as a subject "capable of acting in a planned and rational way"; and this laboring activity, "independently of its objective content . . . must serve to realize his humanity, to fulfill the calling to be a person that is his by reason of his very humanity" (6).

The role of labor in the self-realization of men and women also reveals the vulnerability of human life. "Man's life is built up every day from work, from work it derives its specific dignity, but at the same time work contains the unceasing measure of human toil and suffering and also of the harm and injustice which penetrate deeply into social life within individual nations and on the international level" (1). "It is possible to use work in various ways against man, . . . to make work into a means for oppressing man, and to exploit human labor, that is to say to exploit the workers" (9). Injustices in the division and organization of labor not only cause social inequalities, they also damage the lives of the workers and rob them of the dignity due to them.

To distinguish this theory of labor from Marxism, the encyclical insists on the "preeminence of the subjective meaning of work over the objective one" (6). However important the production of goods and the industries, *Laborem exercens* argues, the ethical criterion for evaluating an economic system is the impact it has on the subjects of labor, that is, on the workers, and this not only in terms of the material benefits they receive but also and especially in terms of the self-realization they experience as human beings. This ethical criterion is ultimately spiritual.

Applying this ethical criterion, the encyclical denounces the threat to the right order of values in capitalism and communism. In both economic systems workers are treated as objects and commodities. "Man is treated as an instrument of production, whereas he . . . ought to be treated as the effective subject of work and its true maker and creator" (7). Here the preeminence of the subjective has been undermined. Reflecting on the reversal of values, *Laborem exercens* offers its controversial definition of capitalism: "This reversal of order, whatever the program or name under which it occurs, should rightly be called 'capitalism.' . . . The error of early capitalism can be repeated whenever man is in a way treated on the same level as the whole complex of the material means of production, as an instrument and not . . . as a subject" (7). The error of early capitalism occurred and continues to occur, even in systems that call themselves socialist, whenever "labor is separated from capital and set in opposition to it, and capital is set in opposition to labor, as though they were two impersonal forces, two production factors juxtaposed in the same 'economistic' perspective" (13).

Since workers were the principal victims in the early phase of industrialization, they struggled to create a labor movement that would defend the cause of justice. The ethical response to the conditions of exploitation produced "the impetuous emergence of a great burst of solidarity among workers" (8). This movement, supported by *Rerum novarum* and subsequent papal teaching, had a great impact on modern society and led to the creation of various forms of neocapitalism and communism. A certain welfare capitalism in Western societies actually improved the lot of working people. Yet in recent years—the reader adds, since the turn to neoconservatism—exploitation and oppression have again multiplied in Western societies and the rest of the globe. Since the tools of science enable us to arrive at a complete picture of the damage done to people globally, of their marginalization, misery, and hunger, we realize that the multiple forms of injustice is today "much more extensive than those which in the last century stimulated unity among workers for particular solidarity in the working world" (8). What we need today is a new outburst of solidarity among the victims and with the victims.

The labor movement continues to be the dynamic element of capitalist and communist society. We are told that labor unions are an indispensable element of industrial society. They are not—as Marxists believe—the agents of the class struggle that inevitably governs social life: instead they are "the mouthpiece for the struggle for social justice" (20). Conscious of the ethical vocation that history has assigned them, labor unions must move beyond the struggle for improving their own circumstances and extend their solidarity to all victims of society. The struggle of the labor movement is not against the owning classes but for social justice; it is against the established order only to the extent that those responsible for it resist the demands of justice.

"In order to achieve social justice in the various parts of the world . . . there is a need for ever new movements of solidarity of the workers and with the workers. This solidarity must be present whenever it is called for by the social degrading of the subject of work, by exploitation of the workers and by the growing areas of poverty and even hunger" (8). This movement of solidarity among workers and with workers is fully supported by the church, because the church considers the solidarity with the victims or the poor as "its mission, its service, a proof of its fidelity to Christ, so that it can truly be the 'church of the poor'" (8).

The divinely given human vocation to work sheds light on the entire life of society, including the family and the nation. In a few remarkable paragraphs (10), work is presented as the foundation of the family and the nation. Work creates the material condition for family life, and work shapes the process of education in the family. In the family the members are meant to discover themselves as subjects, as responsible agents, and hence to cultivate an ethic of social justice. Similarly, the nation, "the great society to which man belongs on the basis of particular cultural and historical links," is made possible by work and in turn educates its members to work. The nation is "a great historical incarnation of the work of all generations" (10). What is implied in these paragraphs is that if the division and organization of labor become unjust, that is to say if they violate the subject character of the workers, then the family becomes damaged and destabilized and the nation suffers inequality and exploitation.

Since material support and human dignity depend on work, social justice demands full employment. *Laborem exercens* does not equate work with employment. Work refers to all society-building activities, including the care extended in one's own home. In this context, the encyclical makes one of its few references to women. "Work is familiar to women, who sometimes without proper recognition on the part of society and even of their own families bear the daily burden and responsibilities for their homes and the upbringing of the children" (9). Work is much more than a job. At the same time, *Laborem exercens* does not wish to separate work from employment. For work is the normal way through which people participate in the wealth of society and create the material conditions for their own and their families' existence. Chronic unemployment on a massive scale is therefore totally unacceptable, an unmitigated disaster. Even if the unemployed should receive support from the state, without employment they are deprived of what is due to them. If the unemployed, I wish to add, are inspired by the perspective of *Laborem exercens,* then they will use their time to offer service to others and contribute, possibly in imaginative ways, to culture and society.

Part 3. The section on the present conflict between labor and capital (11–15) analyzes the ambiguous origin and the distorting impact of this conflict and then offers ethical guidelines for how to overcome it. As mentioned above, the error of industrial capitalism was to set up capital over against and in opposition to labor. What emerged was the conflict "between the small but highly influential group of entrepreneurs, owners or holders of the means of production, and the broader multitude of people who lacked these means and who shared in the process of production solely by their labor. . . . The workers [were obliged] to put their powers at the disposal of the entrepreneurs, and these, following the principle of maximum profit, tried to establish the lowest possible wages for the work done by the employees" (11). To free themselves from this exploitation, the workers organized their movement of opposition.

According to *Laborem exercens,* Marxists have interpreted this conflict as the manifestation of a universal principle operative in history, the so-called class struggle, which was defined in purely economic terms and hence was capable of being expressed in scientific terms. In each local conflict the workers wrestling for the improvement of their conditions were looked upon as representatives of the entire working class, engaged in the class struggle that would overcome the class injustices in society and eventually eliminate the classes altogether. Marxism presented itself both as a scientific interpretation of history and a revolutionary political practice aimed at acquiring the power to transfer the means of production from private owners to the collectivity. "The real conflict between labor and capital was transformed into a systematic class struggle conducted not only by ideological means, but also and chiefly by political means" (11). Yet the Marxist science of history is an ideology based on an economistic understanding of human life and hence is essentially misguided; and Marxist political practice leads to collectivist societies that deprive the people of their freedoms.

By contrast, *Laborem exercens* interprets the conflict between labor and capital in ethical terms. As mentioned above, "the break" that took place when capitalism entered the industrial age was the inversion of the right order of values. What is wrong with liberal capitalism is a moral matter. The exploitation and marginalization of the proletariat must be overcome by a solidarity movement of workers, organized in the name of justice, that struggles for the introduction of economic institutions that respect the right order of values. This right order is called "the priority of labor over capital" (12).

The subjects of production are human beings. It is their labor that is the efficient cause of production, while capital, the whole collection of means of production, is merely an instrumental cause. It is clear that capital is meant to serve labor. The ethical principle of the priority of labor over capital assures that in the process of production and the division of labor the workers remain the subjects of production.

Laborem exercens develops in a new way a theme traditional in Catholic social teaching, namely that there is no intrinsic opposition between labor and capital. In fact, labor and the tools of labor are in need of each other. They actually belong together. More than that, as capital refers to the machinery of production, capital is the result of labor, it is accumulated labor, "it bears the sign of labor" (12). Laboring at their workbench, be it simple or ultramodern, "workers enter into two inheritances: the inheritance of what is given to the whole of humanity in the resources of nature and the inheritance of what others have already developed on the basis of these resources, primarily by developing technology. . . . By working, man 'enters into the labor of others' (Jn 4:38)" (13). Since in their labor workers depend on others who have worked before them and who now work with them, labor generates a sense of solidarity.

When *Laborem exercens* speaks of workers it refers first to industrial workers, that is, the working class, and then, in an extended sense, to all men and women working in the industries, be they office workers, secretaries, accountants, engineers, or managers. The wage-earning industrial workers become the prototype of all men and women engaged in the building of society. That is why the encyclical encourages even professionals to unionize in defense of the justice due to them.

There is nothing in the process of production as such that prompts the opposition between labor and capital. The separation and conflict between the two has been caused by the early industrial capitalists. Liberal capitalism is an industrial policy that turns workers into instruments or objects, and at the same time an ideology that understands the human being, the worker, in purely economic terms. In its own way, this ideology is as economistic and materialistic as Marxism.

The priority of labor over capital is a principle that affects the understanding of ownership. While the church has always defended the right to private property, it has done so in the broader context of the right, shared by all, to use the goods of the whole of creation. The Christian tradition has never upheld the right to private property as absolute or untouchable. According to *Laborem exercens,* the right to the ownership, whether it be private or collective, is conditional: the title to the ownership of the means of production is legitimate only on the condition that they serve labor.

"Property is acquired first of all through work in order that it may serve labor. This concerns especially the ownership of the means of production. Isolating these means as a separate property in order to set it up in the form of 'capital' in opposition to 'labor' . . . is contrary to the very nature of these means and their possession. They cannot be possessed against labor, they cannot even be possessed for possession's sake, because the only legitimate title to their possession—whether in the form of private or collective ownership—is that they should serve labor" (14).

Ownership of productive goods is ethical only if it serves labor. The priority of labor over capital demands therefore that "the right to private ownership undergo a constructive revision both in theory and in practice" (14). But what does the expression "serving labor" mean? Capital is in the service of labor when the process of production respects the subject character of the workers. Such is the dignity of the workers that they are entitled to participate in the decisions that affect the organization of labor and determine the use made of the goods produced. Yet "serving labor" means even more. Since the industries and social institutions such as schools or systems of communication are intertwined and interdependent in modern society, since—in other words—the whole of contemporary society is involved in the process of production, industrial capital must serve not only the industrial workers but the whole of society. The priority of labor thus makes possible "the achievement of the first principle of the economic order, namely the universal destination of goods, and the right to common use of them" (14).

To replace private ownership by state ownership is no guarantee that the priority of labor will be observed. As a Pole, John Paul II is well aware that a government may exploit the workers and manage the industries to enhance its own power and serve its political purposes. The greatest chance that the priority of labor be observed is in an economic system where the workers themselves share in the decisions regarding the organization of labor and the use of the goods produced, in other words, in an economic system that recognizes the subject character of workers. Ultimately workers are meant to be co-owners of the giant workbench at which they labor.

This argument for co-ownership is reinforced by "the personalist argument" (15), which demands that in his or her work in cooperation with others, the worker is fully aware of also working for himself or herself. "We can speak of socializing [the means of production] only when the subject character of society is ensured, that is to say, when on the basis of his work each person is fully entitled to consider himself a part owner of the great workbench at which he is working with everyone else" (14).

The encyclical, it is to be noted, is a reformist, not a revolutionary, document. John Paul II hoped that through the impact of the labor movement both Western capitalism and Eastern European socialism could be reformed. Thus *Laborem exercens* recommends that on the way to the socialization of the industries, societies should experiment with various ways of associating workers with the ownership of capital or allowing workers to participate in industrial decision making. These recommendations remain vague. Some sentences even suggest that John Paul II still envisages as a possibility the corporatism that was favored by some political thinkers, secular and Catholic, prior to World

War II and that received the stamp of approval by Pius XI (*Quadragesimo anno* 83).

Of course, even the co-ownership and co-responsibility of labor, that is, the democratization of the industries, is no guarantee that the priority of labor be fully recognized. A worker-owned industry pursuing its own progress and profit might remain indifferent to the well-being of society as a whole and thus cease to serve the common good. There is no form of ownership that by itself assures economic justice. Ownership remains forever conditional. What is called for is constant watchfulness.

The papal proposal, it is to be noted, does not demand that the worker-owned or worker-run industries be accountable to the government and thus remain open to democratic control by society. This omission, it would seem, is the difference between the papal proposal and the social project known as "self-managing socialism."

Part 4. This section deals with the rights of workers (16–23). In its treatment of unemployment, "which in all cases is an evil and which, when it reaches a certain level, can become a real social disaster" (18), the encyclical introduces the distinction between the direct and the indirect employer. The "direct employer" refers to the person or institution with whom the worker enters directly into a work contract, and the "indirect employer" refers to other factors that influence employment and the conditions of employment, such as labor legislation, industrial development, training schools, housing for the workers, and transportation systems. Against communist society, the pope insists on the role of the direct employer: workers have the right to enter into a work contract with a direct employer, to look for the kind of work most suited to their talents, and to change jobs if they so wish. Against capitalist society, the pope insists on the role of the indirect employer, that is to say, on the need to create a labor code, promote industrial development, provide schools for training or retraining, build housing developments, make transportation available, and so forth. Society is just when it recognizes the role of the direct employer and the worker's freedom of choice and at the same time acknowledges itself as ultimately responsible for overcoming the plague of unemployment. This proposal, radical in the North American context, has an affinity with social democratic theory.

Dealing with wages and other social benefits, *Laborem exercens* argues that "in the context of the present there is no more important way for securing a just relationship between the worker and the employer than that constituted by the remuneration of work" (19). At present, workers with the help of their unions have to struggle for adequate wages. Some commentators have suggested that with this emphasis on wages the encyclical joins liberal social theory, which sees the wage contract as essentially just and nonexploitative and rejects the Marxist theory (never applied in the communist countries), which regards wage labor itself as a cause of alienation. However, when *Laborem exercens* stresses the importance of wages, it does so "in the context of the present," that is to say, in historical conditions where the co-ownership and co-responsibility of workers have not yet been established. According to *Laborem exercens,* an industrial system that refuses to recognize the subject character of workers, that is, refuses to allow workers to participate in industrial decision making, cannot claim to be just, even if it provides high wages for the workers. It is, therefore, in the context of the present that *Laborem exercens* joins traditional Catholic social teaching in its demand for a just wage.

In the same section, the encyclical defends the indispensable role played by labor unions in modern society, a topic already referred to above. It also highlights the dignity of agricultural work and the special care needed on the part of society so that persons with disabilities and immigrants in a foreign culture are able to find employment.

Part 5. This section offers elements of a spirituality of work (24–27). Human work creates a special relationship to God the Creator, to the man Jesus Christ who toiled on this earth, and to his death and resurrection, which gives meaning to the hardships and struggles associated with labor. What is surprising about this section is that the recommended spirituality applies only to the work done by Christians and makes no reference to the struggle of labor for economic justice and the calling of labor to become the agent of social change, themes proposed in the encyclical. This section does not offer a spirituality for "the solidarity movement of and with labor."

Some Unresolved Questions

1. Because *Laborem exercens* deals with work from the perspective of the workers, it offers a positive appreciation of technology. "Technology is undoubtedly man's ally: it facilitates his work, perfects, accelerates and augments it" (5). At the same time technology can also become the enemy of man: this happens "when mechanization supplants him, taking away personal satisfaction and the incentive to responsibility and creativity . . . or when, through exalting the machine, it reduces man to the status of its slave" (5). The encyclical defines the limits of technology by the impact it has on workers. There is here as yet no acknowledgment that technological development is also limited by its impact on nature. *Laborem exercens* still uses the confident language that "the entire world of machinery . . . is the fruit of the work of the human intellect and an historical confirmation of man's dominion over nature" (5). The ecological crisis and the limits of nature became an important issue for John Paul II in his 1987 encyclical, *Sollicitudo rei socialis* (see SRS 34). Yet even in *Laborem exercens* "nature" is never simply an assembly of resources to be used in industrial production; "nature" is first of all "a gift of the Creator" (12), and hence worthy of admiration and a cause for thanksgiving.

2. The emphasis on the human being as worker and the universality of the process of work embracing all people, individually and collectively, has suggested to some readers that John Paul II, possibly addressing the Polish people wrestling to free themselves from the communist system, is recommending the so-called Protestant ethic to the Catholic community. It is true that *Laborem exercens* offers no extended reflection on leisure. Is leisure only a period of rest, play, and prayer intended to restore people's strength and allow them to return to work with new vigor? Or is leisure a period of time worthy in itself, when people open themselves to reflection, contemplation, and creativity? The latter seems more in line with the Catholic spiritual tradition.

3. The encyclical with its emphasis on industrialization is addressed in the first place to the societies of Europe and North America. It is there that "the solidarity movement of and with labor" is to be the historical agent of social reconstruction. Does *Laborem exercens* offer here a universal message? Should simpler cultures or communities that depend on subsistence economies abandon their ways and imitate the industrial civilization of the West?

4. Hannah Arendt has criticized Marxist theory for making work the universal category and not distinguishing between work and action. A similar ambiguity is found in *Laborem exercens.* Is the organization of "the solidarity movement of and with labor" part of work, or is it action, an activity of a different kind? The object of work, we recall, are the things people produce, from simple tents to the complex structures of modern society. By contrast, the object of action is the reordering of human relations. Work has to do with making, action with doing. But if there is a difference between work and action, then how can *Laborem exercens* declare that "by

work man occupies his existence on earth" (LE, Foreword)? Is human history the product of work, or is it produced by both work and action? This ambiguity remains unresolved.

Every ecclesiastical document leaves unresolved questions. *Laborem exercens* acknowledges that the papal social teaching is a developing intellectual tradition that "brings out from the heritage of the Gospel 'what is new and what is old'" (Mt 13:52), where the new remains "in organic connection with the whole tradition" (2). Unresolved questions stimulate new reflection, and depending on changing historical circumstances, new answers may eventually be integrated into the church's social teaching. One must suppose that eventually the Catholic church will come to recognize the massive injustice done to women.

See also ALIENATION; CLASS STRUGGLE; EMPLOYMENT AND UNEMPLOYMENT; LABOR AND CAPITAL IN CATHOLIC SOCIAL THOUGHT; MARXISM; MODERN CATHOLIC SOCIAL THOUGHT; SOLIDARISM; WORK, THEOLOGY OF.

Bibliography: G. Baum, *The Priority of Labor: A Commentary on Laborem exercens* (New York: Paulist, 1982). D. Dorr, *Option for the Poor* (Maryknoll, N.Y.: Orbis, 1983) pp. 233–51. R. Duncan, "On Reading 'Laborem exercens,'" *Homiletic & Pastoral Review* 86 (July 1986) 11–19. M. Hobgood, *Catholic Social Teaching and Economic Theory* (Philadelphia: Temple Univ. Press, 1991) pp. 171–86. J. Houck and O. Williams, eds., *Co-creation and Capitalism: John Paul II's Laborem exercens* (Washington: Univ. Press of America, 1983). H. Ginsburg, "The Teaching of John Paul II on Work and the Right of Workers," *Social Thought* 13 (Spring/Summer 1987) 46–59. C. Marzani, "The Vatican as a Left Ally?" *Monthly Review* 34 (July/August 1982) 1–41. D. Miet, *Solidarity and the Right to Work,* Concilium 160 (1982) 58–65. J. Schotte, "The Social Teaching of the Church: Laborem exercens, a New Challenge," *Review of Social Economy* 40 (December 1982) 340–57.

GREGORY BAUM

LAFARGE, JOHN

John LaFarge's life changed decisively in 1911. At thirty-one, a priest and a Jesuit for six years, LaFarge's health failed him, and the prospect of several years of advanced theological study at Woodstock College gave way to fifteen years of pastoral ministry in southern Maryland. His interests in rural life and racial issues date from these years. Moreover, LaFarge's providential detour from speculative theology into pastoral ministry set him squarely in the public arena, a place for which his upbringing had prepared him well and to which his talents as a publicist and popularizer were especially well suited.

John LaFarge was born February 13, 1880, in Newport, Rhode Island, the tenth child and third son of the noted American artist John LaFarge and his wife, Margaret Mason Perry LaFarge. His family life was intellectually stimulating, to say the least; his father knew William and Henry James and Henry Adams, while Teddy Roosevelt was a good friend of his older brother, Grant. Combined with his mother's distinguished lineage (she was the granddaughter of Oliver Hazard Perry and the great-great-granddaughter of Benjamin Franklin), this atmosphere seems to have impressed upon young John a sense of noblesse oblige. By the age of twelve, he had decided to be a priest.

After graduating Phi Beta Kappa from Harvard University in 1901, LaFarge began theological studies as a lay student at the Jesuit-sponsored Canisianum in Innsbruck, Austria. Ordained a priest there in 1905, he returned to the United States and entered the Society of Jesus later that same year. The next several years of Jesuit formation found him at a variety of tasks. LaFarge taught at Canisius College in Buffalo and Loyola College in Baltimore, studied Scholastic philosophy at Woodstock College in Maryland, and served as a prison and hospital chaplain in New York City. But the years he spent in rural southern Maryland after 1911 exposed him to pressing social problems, forced him to think them through with the tools of Roman Catholic philosophy and theology, and so provided him with the opportunity to develop his own social thought.

All of LaFarge's social thought rests upon two fundamental presuppositions. First, the human person, redeemed by Jesus Christ, is an essentially social reality, and consequently the doctrine of the mystical body has social implications; and so the church, while primarily a spiritual institution, has a temporal mission integral to it. Christian action is thus an implication of faith and a duty of charity. Second, Roman Catholic doctrine, action, and liturgy are linked together in a seamless web. Beliefs engender action and lead to worship; worship implants beliefs more deeply within the human heart and thus fructify action; action embodies beliefs within the world and flow both out of worship and back into it again.

Because of LaFarge's strong interest in liturgy—he was the chaplain to the Liturgical Arts Society from 1933 until his death in 1963—and because of his own conviction that liturgy and social action were intimately related, a brief survey of his liturgical theology is appropriate. For LaFarge, worship is not an escapist world set apart; rather, it is the link between Christian life and Christian action in the world Christ redeemed. Hence, LaFarge considered liturgy a safeguard against the pervasive threats of individualism and secularism. Indeed, LaFarge once referred to liturgy as "the indispensable 'starting point' and inspiration for any just social order, in large or in small." Liturgy engenders Christian action because of its capacity to implant Christian truths within the heart. Hence its primary power is affective, and LaFarge's particular interests within the liturgical renewal focused on strengthening the emotional impact of liturgy. He supported efforts to enhance the esthetic elements of liturgy because these elements incarnate human desires and spiritual truths in material forms and so make them available to the Christian assembly. Likewise, LaFarge urged adaptations designed to increase the participation of the faithful in the liturgy; active participation in praise and worship, he wrote, led naturally to active participation in social action. LaFarge linked the health of the liturgical movement to the health of the sodality, catechetical, and family life movements as well as to the health of movements with which he was most particularly concerned, namely the rural life and interracial movements.

In southern Maryland LaFarge found illustrated the profound problems affecting modern rural life that had been described already by Leo XII in *Rerum novarum* and that would be even more pointedly addressed by Pius XI in *Quadragesimo anno* and by Pius XII in his radio address of Pentecost Sunday, 1941. LaFarge's own writings on the problems of rural society, most of which appeared after *Quadragesimo anno,* reflect his own dependence upon the social teachings of the church both for his analysis of rural problems and for his proposed solutions to them. His debt to papal social teaching can be glimpsed in three areas.

Most generally, LaFarge subscribed to the Catholic view of society elaborated in these encyclicals and elsewhere as an organic and hierarchically ordered entity whereby the individual parts are integrally related to one another and to the whole and where private property has a distinctly social function. Indeed, LaFarge often remarked that the Roman Catholic view of society was essential to the solution of rural problems because only the church correctly understood that human society is constructed, as it were, from the bottom up: from the person to the family to the community to the nation. Second, LaFarge sought to steer a middle course between liberal capitalist and totalitarian communist errors. Always a vigorous anticommunist, LaFarge roundly condemned contemporary Soviet experiments in agricultural collectivization with their inevitable corollaries of violence and dehumanization. Likewise, however, LaFarge criticized the commercialization of American agriculture, a trend the Great Depression only exacerbated. Large-scale farms ate up acreage, drove down agricultural wages, increased the level of rural social problems, degraded the status of the rural family, forced farmers off the land, and, finally, generated urban social problems as displaced agricultural workers sought scarce jobs in the city. LaFarge's emphasis on the family is the third major point of intersection between the papal encyclicals and his own work on rural life. Because the family is the fundamental unit of society, LaFarge repeatedly wrote, farming is a livelihood, a means of living for a family and not a purely commercial activity; hence the family's needs should determine the proper "size of the agricultural economic unit."

LaFarge's proposed solutions to the problems of rural life were likewise congruent with established papal social teaching. Two themes run through his various proposals: land ownership and public-private cooperation based upon the principle of subsidiarity. Calling land a gift of God given for spiritual purposes first and economic ones second, LaFarge advocated the wide diffusion of land ownership, the ownership of farm land by those who worked it, and the maintenance of farm land in plots of sufficient size so as to support a farm family adequately. Land ownership guaranteed the integrity of the rural family and guarded against the transformation of farmers into rural proletarians. LaFarge likewise recommended a range of public-private cooperative ventures. Cooperatives among farmers would be established, for example, as parish-based rural credit unions, producer organizations, and agencies of cultural improvement and religious education and expression. Cooperatives between farmers and consumers would establish marketing mechanisms and challenge the idea that the needs of the market are ethically neutral. Cooperatives between rural constituencies and state and local governments would encourage legislation to stop the disappearance of the family farm into large-scale combines and to overhaul tax structures that would penalize absentee landlords of commercial farms rather than small family farmers.

As southern Maryland introduced LaFarge to the problems of rural life, so it acquainted him with the many problems facing African Americans. Working as sharecroppers, tenant farmers, and unskilled laborers, and trapped in cycles of debt and dependency, blacks in southern Maryland occupied the lowest levels of society. Their situation deeply touched LaFarge, and he sought solutions in Roman Catholic social teaching. Unlike the problems of rural societies, however, papal social teaching had not directly confronted the situation of America's racial minorities, and so LaFarge creatively extended papal teaching to this particular area of his concern. Extracting from the several social encyclicals their emphasis on the dignity and sanctity of the human person, their placement of the human person within the organic structure of human society, and their insistence on protecting family life, and combining these with his own absolute conviction that "all other activities, all other problems," could be solved by adequate education "sooner or later," LaFarge constructed a coherent approach to the "interracial question" that guided his thinking and action for the rest of his life.

For LaFarge, racial prejudice was a willful moral refusal to recognize a member of a group as an individual and a concomitant ascription of group stereotypes to individuals. Further, racial prejudices shaped social institutions, and these institutions in turn confirmed and extended prejudice. Finally, racial prejudice had the sociological function of unifying social groups that might otherwise fragment. While granting that such racial prejudices are grounded in emotional experiences, LaFarge more often stressed the origins of prejudice in simple misinformation; while this conclusion may seem naive with the hindsight history affords us, it nonetheless enabled LaFarge to emphasize the importance of education in eradicating racism.

The role of the Catholic church in combating racial prejudice was consequently clear. If racial prejudice was a moral evil, it had to be denounced as a sin. If racial prejudice became crystallized in institutions, another institution, the church, was required as a corrective counterweight. And if racial prejudice acted as a perverse mechanism of social unity, only the church could supply the vision upon which authentic social unity could be built. But combating racial prejudice, LaFarge repeatedly emphasized, was likewise important to the church itself. Any hope of evangelizing African Americans would stand or fall with the church's commitment to improving their social conditions. Concerted Catholic action on behalf of racial justice was thus not just a litmus test of the church's commitment to justice generally, it signaled to American blacks that they were welcome within the church, and it made clear the church's conviction that spiritual welfare could not be divorced from material well-being.

While LaFarge discussed the critical elements of land ownership and black family life, education was far and away his most important prescription for elevating the condition of the American black. LaFarge hoped to develop native black leaders, firmly schooled in Catholic social principles, who would lead their brothers and sisters to equality. Accordingly, he founded the Cardinal Gibbons Institute in southern Maryland in 1922. Conceived as a Catholic version of such southern black schools as the Tuskegee Institute, Cardinal Gibbons offered a vocational-technical education combined with a solid course of general studies. Plagued by mismanagement and by financial difficulties as well, even before the onset of the Depression, the Institute closed in 1933. It was reopened as a parish secondary school in 1936 by one of LaFarge's pastoral associates in southern Maryland, Horace B. McKenna, S.J.

LaFarge also believed that educating whites was crucial to eliminating racial prejudice. By "clearing up" what he called "certain misconceptions" whites commonly held about the living and working conditions of African Americans, LaFarge not only hoped to spotlight the institutionalized racism to which whites seemed at best indifferent (such as discrimination in labor unions and banking practices, to say nothing of the more obvious violence of lynching), he sought as well to inform the consciences of those most able to reshape tainted social institutions. This educational effort would advance on two fronts: presenting the authentic Catholic teaching regarding the human person, and describing the actual effects of racial bias. Taking his own advice, LaFarge plunged into a study of history, sociology, psychology, and church teaching and became an extraordinarily able educator of the white (and black) public through such books as *Interracial Justice* (1937), *The Race Question and the Negro* (1944), and *The Catholic Viewpoint on Race Relations* (1954). In addition, his educational apostolate extended through literally dozens of articles and speeches in such periodicals as *America, The Interracial Review,* and *The Catholic Mind.*

While educating whites and blacks constituted LaFarge's chief answer to the interracial question, he also acknowledged the importance of public-private cooperation. He advocated such government assistance as funding vocational education for black youth. However, before the engagement of government, LaFarge wrote, a whole range of private cooperative ventures needed to be developed, such as scholarship programs in Catholic schools that would enlist the financial backing of white Catholics. Undoubtedly, however, the most important such private cooperative efforts were the Catholic Interracial Councils. Established in New York on Pentecost Sunday, 1934, the Catholic Interracial Council was an outgrowth of the Catholic Laymen's Union, an organization of black professionals LaFarge founded in 1927. A kind of Catholic Action program locally chartered to cooperate with other local groups in combating racial discrimination, the councils sought to implement the educational mission LaFarge described and to eliminate racially prejudiced practices from any institution, organization, or society of the Catholic church. By 1958, approximately forty such councils had been established in the United States. LaFarge served as national chaplain to the group until 1962.

This brief survey of the social thought of John LaFarge omits much. In addition to the professional associations given above, LaFarge was likewise a member of the National Academy of Arts and Sciences (Boston), the American Catholic Historical Society (second vice-president in 1934), the Catholic Association for International Peace, the St. Ansgar's Society, and the Catholic Laymen's Union. He also published widely in such areas as Catholic education, communism, world peace, and labor issues. While he contributed to numerous national and international journals of opinion, much of his published work appeared in *America* magazine, for which he was an associate editor from 1926 until his death, except from 1942 to 1944 (when he was executive editor) and from 1944 to 1948 (when he was editor-in-chief).

John LaFarge died on November 24, 1963, in New York City.

See also AGRICULTURE; COOPERATIVE ASSOCIATIONS; LAND; QUADRAGESIMO ANNO; RERUM NOVARUM.

Bibliography: John LaFarge, *The Jesuits in Modern Times* (1928); *Interracial Justice* (1937); *The Race Question and the Negro* (1944); *The Manner Is Ordinary* (1954); *The Catholic Viewpoint on Race Relations* (1956); *An American Amen* (1958); *Reflections on Growing Old* (1963).

MICHAEL GRAHAM, S.J.

LAITY, ROLE OF

Prior to Vatican II ordinary parishioners could be forgiven for assuming that the role of the laity was to "pay, pray, and obey." Though the history of the Church is rich in examples of lay initiative, this was the popular perception characteristic of the "devotional Catholicism" that reached its zenith in the first half of the 20th century. Even the burgeoning social movements sponsored by the National Catholic Welfare Conference were characterized by clerical leadership, well remembered through the cherished legacies of John A. Ryan, Raymond McGowan, Edwin O'Hara, John Cronin, Francis Haas, John LaFarge, and George Higgins. There were notable exceptions, of course, like Dorothy Day and Peter Maurin, whose Catholic Worker movement helped create a model for the lay apostolate, uncompromising in both its political radicalism and its evangelical authenticity. Nevertheless, prior to Vatican II the role of the laity, even in Catholic social action, seemed but an extension of that of the clergy.

Viewed within the history of Christianity as a whole, this diminished role of the laity must be regarded as a temporary aberration, an anomalous episode to be explained by prevailing social conditions and not as a normative element in Catholic tradition. Medieval Christendom systematically distinguished the secular from the sacred, the temporal from the spiritual order, but organized both orders according to the principle of hierarchy. Prior to the democratic revolutions that ushered in the era of modernity, relationships between the spiritual hierarchy and the laity were mediated through the temporal hierarchy; hence there was no need for focused theological reflection on the role of the laity as such, as opposed to the role of secular princes and magistrates. The passing of the ancien régime, however, emancipated peasants and workers from their secular bondage to the hereditary lay aristocracy.

In the short term it also left a vacuum that clerical leadership was poised to fill, once the Napoleonic adventure had succeeded in discrediting democracy in Europe. But in the long term these upheavals also rendered problematic the status of ordinary Catholic citizens as laity within the church. Were they anything more than the mass of nonclerical Christians, passively dependent upon the clergy for both access to the means of grace and guidance with reference to their temporal duties?

In the English-speaking world the emergence of the laity follows a somewhat different trajectory from that of Continental Europe. Being a persecuted minority without civil status in Great Britain, ordinary Catholics learned to survive without benefit of established clerical leadership. In British North America, particularly in the colonies that declared their independence in 1776, Catholicism tended to develop, as in Maryland, under lay sponsorship. In the immediate aftermath of the American Revolution, which the Catholic communities supported without hesitation, the church in the United States operated as a loose confederacy of self-governing communities, whose de facto structures of accountability had more in common with New England Congregationalism than with the ultramontanism beginning to sweep Europe. Nevertheless, the kind of lay leadership modeled particularly by prominent converts like Elizabeth Bayley Seton and Orestes A. Brownson arguably was far more consistent with the weight of Catholic tradition than the current expectations of the church that they had embraced.

As historian Jay P. Dolan has pointed out, theological arguments for justifying the lay activism characteristic of the early period of American Catholicism were not to be received by the whole church until Vatican II. What Dolan has aptly described as a "republican blueprint" for an American Catholicism was increasingly overtaken by the rise of the immigrant church in the United States, beginning in the 1840s. The displaced European masses now struggling to make a new start in "the land of opportunity" had more pressing concerns than trying to defend the prerogatives of lay leadership within the church. Thrown into the sheer chaos of rapid industrialization and tempted by the seductions of urban anomie, they looked to the clergy for moral support and patronage. The pastor was soon rightly regarded by the faithful not only as the most educated person in the parish but also as the one most likely to assist them whenever they got into trouble with the authorities. It made sense for immigrant Catholics to "pay, pray, and obey," for the disciplined, family-oriented lifestyle that resulted from adhering to the prudent counsels of their pastors turned out to be the surest if not the quickest path to upward social mobility.

When Vatican II broke upon the scene in the early 1960s, certainly the college-educated elite were not unaware of the lay Catholic movements of Europe and their impact on culture and politics just before and for a long time after World War II. But the condemnation of the so-called Americanist heresy by Pope Leo XIII in 1899 had cast a pall over the work of visionaries like Isaac Hecker, the founder of the Paulist Fathers, who hoped to unleash a flood of conversions based on what he took to be the unique affinities linking lay Catholic spirituality with sturdy Yankee virtue. As a result, when the documents of Vatican II, particularly the Dogmatic Constitution on the Church *(Lumen gentium)* and the Decree on the Apostolate of the Lay People (*Apostolicam actuositatem*), were read in America, few were the lay activists capable of appropriating the histories of their own local communities, Yankee or otherwise, as resources for Christian renewal. The documents were piously accepted as theological abstractions, all too often lacking contextual resonance in the laity's own experience.

What the documents have to say about the role of the laity, of course, is terribly important, if not decisive, for the future of Catholic social thought. Reread in light of the struggles of the post–Vatican II church, particularly the controversies surrounding Latin American liberation theology and the recent pastoral letters of the National Council of Catholic Bishops, the documents are striking for their refusal to see the role of the laity simply in terms of a conventional division of labor. The unity of the Christian vocation is boldly affirmed by pointedly defining the laity as "sharers in the priestly, prophetic and kingly functions of Christ" (LG 31, 34–36). The lay apostolate thus consists of "penetrating and perfecting the temporal sphere of things through the spirit of the Gospel" (AA 2), in support of which the ordained clergy exercise their own responsibilities consistent with the principle of subsidiarity. The assistance given by the clergy, of course, includes the ecclesiastical hierarchy's duty to preserve order, that is, to promote, coordinate, and hold accountable various forms of the lay apostolate in keeping with the common good of the church (AA 24). But initiative rests with the laity themselves, who by virtue of their share in the church's collective vocation as the people of God, must accept primary responsibility for acting within their own distinctive spheres of competence.

Many of the controversies that have occurred in the aftermath of Vatican II can be understood as attempts to clarify, in one way or the other, the ambiguities of the council's abstract directives regarding the role of the laity. When, for example, Gustavo Gutiérrez criticized Jacques Maritain's interpretation of Catholic action, he was attempting to remove an artificial barrier restricting the clergy's involvement in social movements with secular political implications. Similarly, when Archbishop Rembert Weakland resisted the efforts of neoconservative Catholics to confine the NCCB's role to enunciating the general principles of Catholic social teaching, he was rejecting the idea that the laity should be left with exclusive responsibility for drawing specific policy applications from these principles. Affirming with Vatican II the laity's distinctive competencies in various secular arenas thus cannot be allowed to undermine, either in social action or in critical reflection upon it, the unity of the church's vocation in the world. In this case, the studied ambiguity of Vatican II's statements seems designed to preserve the possibility of shared responsibility or mutual accountability for the church's mission and ministry as a whole.

The role of the laity, like that of the clergy, thus is best understood in terms of certain open-ended metaphors hallowed by tradition and given new life in the documents of Vatican II. "People of God" is one such metaphor; "leaven" and "salt of the earth" are others; and finally there is the tantalizing vagueness of "participation." No theological *tour de force* has yet been able to reduce these to a rigorous system of roles and responsibilities, rights and duties. Nevertheless, the empowering spirit that they were meant to convey does still come through, precisely because of their open-endedness: "Upon all the laity, therefore, rests the noble duty of working to extend the divine plan of salvation ever increasingly to all men of each epoch and in every land. Consequently, let every opportunity be given them so that, according to their abilities and the needs of the times, they may zealously participate in the saving work of the Church" (LG 33). Some quarter of a century after the closing of the council, the possibilities latent in this vision of the church have hardly been exhausted.

See also AMERICANISM; BASE COMMUNITIES; CATHOLIC WORKER, THE; LIBERATION THEOLOGY; MARITAIN, JACQUES; "SIGNS OF THE TIMES"; SUBSIDIARITY, PRINCIPLE OF; VATICAN COUNCIL II.

Bibliography: W. Abbott, ed., *The Documents of Vatican II,* trans. ed., J. Gallagher (London: Geoffrey Chapman, 1967). Y. Congar, *Lay People in the Church: A Study for a Theology of the Laity,* rev. ed. (Westminster, Md.: Newman, 1965). J. Dolan, *The American Catholic Experience: A History from Colonial Times to the Present* (Garden City, N.Y.: Doubleday, 1985). G. Gutiérrez, *A Theology of Liberation: 15th Anniversary Edition* (Maryknoll, N.Y.: Orbis, 1988). J. Hennesey, *American Catholics: A History of the Roman Catholic Community in the United States* (New York: Oxford Univ. Press, 1981). J. Maritain, *Integral Humanism: Temporal and Spiritual Problems of a New Christendom* (Notre Dame, Ind.: Univ. of Notre Dame Press, 1973). D. O'Brien, *Public Catholicism,* The Bicentennial History of the Catholic Church in America Authorized by the National Conference of Catholic Bishops (New York: Macmillan, 1989).

DENNIS P. McCANN

LAND

Land is one of the most important natural resources of God's creation, providing food, water, wood, natural beauty, and other benefits to meet the needs of and to enhance human life. The early chapters of Genesis portray a human life in close harmony with the earth and its fruits; the alienation of humanity from the land and the transformation of human dominion and stewardship into domination and subjugation arose only as a result of sin.

It is clear from the OT that the land was a central reality for the people of Israel, who had wandered as a landless people and for whom later exile from the land raised fundamental questions of meaning. For Israel the land was God's land, which God had given to the people in sacred trust to be passed on as a precious inheritance: "The land shall not be sold in perpetuity, for the land is mine; for you are strangers and sojourners with me" (Lev 25:23). In the story of Naboth's vineyard (1 Kgs 21) Naboth represents the traditional view of land as a sacred inheritance, while Ahab and Jezebel have a "foreign" view of land as a tradable commodity.

The ideal of the Sabbath Day and the Sabbath Year (Exod 23:10-12; Lev 25:4-5) represented not only rest for the people but also rest for the land. The land was understood to be a good in itself and not just property or a commodity. The Jubilee Year, every fifty years, mandated the return of the land to its original owners lest the people be permanently alienated from their inheritance (Lev 25:28). The prophets railed against those who coveted the land and who ruthlessly built up estates from the land acquired from the desperation of the poor (Mic 2:1-5; Isa 5:8-10).

Despite the vital importance of the land to human life and the biblical demands for a responsible stewardship, several threats to the land and signs of human alienation from the land have arisen in contemporary times. These include the concentration of landholdings in the hands of large agribusinesses and nonresident owners, transfer of prime farmland to nonagricultural uses, erosion, and pollution caused by the overuse of chemical fertilizers and insecticides (*Economic Justice for All* 217). In this context two central questions arise: Who should own the land? How should the land be used?

Land ownership. The question of land ownership occurs as a result of increased concentration of land in the hands of fewer people (EJA 225, 234). In the United States this has been manifest in the decline of the family farm and the rise of large agribusinesses, which are often able to control costs and prices for smaller farmers by diversifying into seed and fertilizer sales on one end of the food-production chain and food processing on the other end. The result of the growth of these agribusinesses has not improved productivity and, in fact, has resulted in less crop variety, which depletes the richness of the soil. Such businesses are often less concerned about the conservation of prime farmland and the long-term effects of chemical fertilizers and insecticides. Similar concerns regarding land ownership arise in other countries in the concentration of land into the estates of the wealthy. The problem of land ownership has resulted in the call for land reform and, in some instances, for land redistribution through expropriation. While respecting the right to private property, the social encyclicals have also consistently upheld the social character of property and the right of the state to expropriate land to meet the needs of the poor (*Populorum progressio* 24; *Gaudium et spes* 71).

Land use. The question of land use and conservation arises within the context of a responsible stewardship of and respect for the land. The concern is for an ecologically sound use of the land that will produce food adequate to meet the needs of all while conserving the land itself for future generations to use and enjoy. A number of particular concerns arise, including the loss of prime farmland to unplanned urban sprawl and highway systems and the ecological damage caused by careless deforestation of timberland and strip mining. Of primary concern is the depletion of soil through erosion and the pollution of land and water by the overuse of chemical fertilizers and insecticides. These problems are not unique to large agribusinesses but may also arise as a result of the desperation of smaller farmers who, in order to survive in the face of low prices, must try to maximize crop productivity in the short run without adequate concern for the long-term effects on land and water of the use of chemicals and the failure to rotate crops adequately (EJA 227).

In response to the problems presented by land ownership and use, seventy-two Catholic bishops of the midwestern United States in 1980 recommended ten principles of land stewardship: (1) The land is God's. (2) People are God's stewards on the land, "co-creators with God in guiding the land's productive power and in conserving the land's natural gifts" ("Strangers and Guests," no. 55). (3) The land's benefits are for everyone—both for present and future generations. (4) The land should be distributed equitably. (5) The land should be conserved and restored. (6) Land-use planning must consider social and environmental impacts. (7) Land use should be appropriate to land quality; for example, prime farmland should not be used unnecessarily for urban expansion or highways. (8) The land should provide a moderate livelihood. (9) The land's workers should be able to become the land's owners. (10) The land's mineral wealth should be shared.

See also AGRICULTURE; ECOLOGY; LAND RIGHTS; NATURAL RESOURCES; OWNERSHIP; STEWARDSHIP.

Bibliography: W. Brueggemann, *The Land* (Philadelphia: Fortress, 1977). J. Hart, *The Spirit of the Earth: A Theology of the Land* (New York: Paulist, 1984). Catholic Bishops of Midwestern U.S., "Toward Community in the Heartland: Strangers and Guests," *Origins* 10 (June 26, 1980) 81–96.

MARK O'KEEFE, O.S.B.

LAND RIGHTS

In 1492, Europeans and the American Indians discovered each other. To each, there opened a New World. For centuries Christopher Columbus has been described as the discoverer and the Indians as the discovered. Throughout the world, indigenous peoples were dispossessed of their lands without consent and without adequate compensation. Their societies were destroyed and slavery was common. In 1537 Paul III in the bull *Sublimis Deus* condemned those who held that "the inhabitants of the West Indies and the southern continents should be treated like irrational animals and used exclusively for our profit and service." He declared that the "Indians as well as any other peoples which Christianity will come to know in the future, must not be deprived of their freedom and their possessions even if they are not Christians and that, on the contrary, they must be left to enjoy their freedom and possessions."

In colonial times the European powers carved the globe into spheres of influence. Having asserted sovereignty by act of state, the colonizer would assert control over the local population and resources.

Native systems of land title would continue but only until they were extinguished by will of the sovereign. Especially where the native population lived a communal lifestyle, hunting and gathering, without a political system operating beyond the territory occupied by the local language group, the colonizers would take over the land as if it were *terra nullius.* The assertion of sovereignty often resulted in the expropriation of native lands without consent or fair compensation.

After the Second World War the United Nations committed itself to a decolonization process. Native peoples with an identifiable population and land base were entitled to self-determination. Local populations could make a free choice whether or not to be integrated into the adjacent society administered by the colonizing power. When separated by blue water or by identifiable boundaries, such populations could decide to separate and seek their own development.

In this postcolonial era, indigenous people have become more political in their struggle. Their rights are an international issue. Their claims to land rights, sovereignty, and self-determination are being heard but are restricted by prevalent notions of private property, national sovereignty, and assimilation. In many countries a just and proper settlement is still to be reached. Land rights is an issue in countries where an indigenous population is in the minority and the law of the new settlers has in the past paid insufficient regard for the traditional owners' right to land. It is also an issue where indigenous people are the majority but where communal notions of native land title are giving way to individual notions that are more compatible with the demands of foreign investors.

In international law self-determination has applied chiefly to people emerging from the colonization process being guaranteed a choice of future. It is not allowed to just any group. There must be an inquiry whether there is enough homogeneity or unity or common desire to hold the state together, whether it has economic resources and political capacity. Though there is still no definition of "peoples" in international law, the right of self-determination, carrying with it the entitlement to partition of territory, is exercisable only by a territorial community the members of which are conscious of themselves as members of such a community.

The international community of nations will not agree to interference in the domestic affairs of a territorial community to the extent that outside agencies would be able to adjudicate the claim of indigenous peoples to separate themselves from the nation-state, especially when the nation has long been recognized as a member of the world community of nations with boundaries intact. It would be even less likely if the indigenous population is scattered throughout the land and is made up of diverse groups without a long-established nationwide political structure, having intermarried with descendants of the settlers over centuries. Land rights for these groups can provide the economic and spiritual base for them to make a realistic choice between their traditional lifestyle and that of other nationals.

In his world travels, Pope John Paul II has spoken often about indigenous land rights and the need to negotiate agreements with indigenous people. To Australian aborigines he said: "Let it not be said that the fair and equitable recognition of Aboriginal rights to land is discrimination. To call for the acknowledgment of the land rights of people who have never surrendered those rights is not discrimination. Certainly, what has been done cannot be undone. But what can now be done to remedy the deeds of yesterday must not be put off till tomorrow. The establishment of a new society for Aboriginal people cannot go forward without just and mutually recognized agreements with regard to these human problems, even though their causes lie in the past."

In its recent document *The Church and Racism* the Pontifical Commission for Justice and Peace has spoken of aboriginal peoples as being "marginalized with respect to the country's development" (Pontifical Commission, p. 19). A dual right of first occupants is to be guaranteed: to land and to a social and political organization that allows them to preserve their cultural identity while remaining open to others. One risk to be avoided is their "being forced to assimilate without any concern for their right to maintain their own identity." The rate of their integration into the surrounding society must be their decision.

In seeking an appropriate social and political organization for indigenous people, we have to move beyond the primitive notion that assimilation is a precondition for justice for all. Equality does not equal uniformity. Equality of treatment requires recognition of differences that indigenous minorities themselves want to maintain in order to develop according to their own specific characteristics while still having regard for others and for the common good of society and the world community. An assured land base is essential. Any decision to be integrated into the surrounding culture must result from a guaranteed free choice based on the right of minority group members to live together according to their specific cultural and religious characteristics. This requires the provision of realistic alternatives backed by the equitable provision of government services to indigenous people, whichever choice they make.

Indigenous people are not simply self-identifying groups in the community who are in need of welfare assistance. As descendants of the first occupants and as the primary custodians of indigenous culture and heritage, they have a right to continue the management of their community affairs on their lands as autonomously as possible provided they do not act contrary to the common good or interfere with the rights of others, and provided all community members are afforded a realistic choice between their community life and the lifestyle available to other nationals. Though the provision of such choice may require extra resources from government, the cost is justified and necessary given the history of dispossession of land and kin that was the precondition of the birth of the modern nation-states that include indigenous peoples within their borders. The evils of assimilation and discrimination will be overcome only by indigenous people determining their future, even if it be inevitably as a part of a nation-state in which they are numerically a minority.

Recognizing indigenous land rights, a postcolonial legal system is able to reverse some of the wrongs from previous generations and to wrap a protective husk around the relationship of the indigenous people with their land (often spiritual as well as economic), affording them the protections and opportunity needed to determine their own future and to manage their own affairs, no longer foreigners nor second-class citizens in their own land. Land-rights laws usually preclude tribal elders alienating the land or relinquishing control. The land is to be maintained for future generations. The land is held in trust for the benefit of all tribe members. Special provisions govern access to the land by miners and other developers because such commercial activity can disrupt the spiritual life and traditional lifestyle of the people. The risk of such disruption should be permitted only with the consent of the people.

See also AFFIRMATIVE ACTION; ABORIGINES, AUSTRALIAN; COMMON GOOD; CULTURE; HUMAN RIGHTS; LAND; MINORITIES; RIGHTS AND DUTIES.

Bibliography: John Paul II, discourses to indigenous people: to the Indians of Ecuador, in Latacunga, January 31, 1985, in OR, English ed., no. 9, 4.3 (1985) 5–10; to the Indians of Peru, in Curzco, February 3, 1985, in OR, English ed., no. 12, 25.3 (1985) 3–4; to the Aborigines of Australia, in Alice Springs, November 29, 1986, in OR, English ed., no. 49, 9.12 (1986) 16–18; to the North American Indians, in Phoenix, September 14, 1987, in OR, English ed., no. 38, 21.9 (1987) 21–22; to the Indians of Canada, in Fort Simpson, September 20, 1987, in OR, English ed., no. 40, 5.10 (1987) 11–12. John Paul II, 1989 World Day of

Peace Message, "To Build Peace, Respect Minorities." Pontifical Commission, "Iustitia et Pax," *The Church and Racism: Towards a More Fraternal Society* (Vatican City, 1988). F. Brennan et al., *Finding Common Ground,* 2nd ed. (Melbourne: Collins Dove, 1986).

FRANK BRENNAN, S.J.

LEO XIII

Gioacchino Vincenzo Pecci was born on March 2, 1810, in Carpineto, south of Rome. After studies at the Roman College (later the Gregorian University) and the College of Ecclesiastical Nobles, he joined the papal service. He served ably as governor of Benevento and then Perugia in the Papal States and was appointed nuncio to Belgium in 1843. With short visits to London, Cologne, and Paris, he first came into contact with industrialized Europe and constitutional government. He was appointed bishop of Perugia in 1846 and was named a cardinal in 1853 but was kept from any curial posts because he was suspect to Cardinal Antonelli, Pius IX's secretary of state.

Elected pope on February 20, 1878, he was confronted with the problem of upholding the rights of the church against the increasing hostility of the liberal European states. From Pius IX he inherited the Roman Question, the situation of the Holy See from 1870 when the city of Rome fell to the forces of the kingdom of Italy to 1929 when the Lateran Treaty was signed. Like Pius, Leo continued to see the dangers to the church of socialism, communism, and Freemasonry, which underlay the problems for the church especially in France and Italy. Nevertheless, he sought to open dialogue with the modern world in a series of encyclicals. Reflecting the program he had already adapted for his seminary in Perugia, he called for the Thomistic revival in *Aeterni Patris* (1879) to provide the church with a consistent theological approach to modern problems. In *Humanun genus* (1884) he saw Masonry as the "sect" at war with the church and seeking secretly to gain control of governments; it was at the base for the laicism seeking to destroy the church in Europe and eventually led to socialism. In *Immortale Dei* (1885) he carefully distinguished between the spiritual and temporal spheres but was hesitant in his support of democracy in *Diuturnum* (1881).

On the diplomatic front, in 1887 Leo XIII negotiated the end of the Kulturkampf, the effort that Bismarck had begun in 1872 to subjugate all church affairs, including education, to the German state. In 1892 he urged French Catholics to rally to the Third Republic in *Au milieu des sollicitudes,* part of the policy of his secretary of state, Mariano Cardinal Rampolla, to gain French support against the Triple Alliance of Italy, the Austro-Hungarian Empire, and the German Empire and ultimately to end the Roman Question. Later in 1892, he sent Archbishop Francesco Satolli to the United States, where he remained as the first permanent apostolic delegate to hierarchy, then divided on a series of issues including the social question.

Leo XIII's contribution to the social teaching of the church flowed from his orientations in theology and church-state matters. In 1886, he had named as cardinal Archbishop James Gibbons of Baltimore. The United States was then experiencing the same Industrial Revolution as Western Europe, but with a difference—the working class remained loyal to the church. In Rome Gibbons successfully defended the Knights of Labor, an early American labor union, and sought to prevent the condemnation of the works of Henry George, who urged a single tax on the unearned increment of the value of property as a solution to the nation's social ills. Instead of a condemnation, Gibbons later urged that the pope issue an encyclical addressing the respective rights and obligations of both capital and labor. The result was *Rerum novarum* in 1891.

The practical success of the U.S. church in retaining the working class was the major influence on Leo's decision to issue an encyclical. But the theoretical approach came from another source. In 1885 Gaspard Mermillod, bishop of Lausanne (who was named a cardinal in 1890), formed the Fribourg Union to study the social question within the context of Thomistic thought and to draw up concrete proposals for legislation on the problem. This provided the framework for the first papal social encyclical.

In *Rerum novarum* Leo XIII steered a middle course between socialism's denial of private property and capitalism's denial of the rights of labor. He couched his thought in decidedly Thomistic language and, against state absolutism, asserted the principal of subsidiarity, that between the state and the individual or family there were other associations, including the church and "private societies" organized for special purposes (RN 52, 72). A century later his assertion might appear paternalistic that "certain occupations . . . are less fitted for women, who are intended by nature for the work of the home—work indeed which especially protects modesty in women and accords by nature with the education of children and the well-being of the family" (60). Yet, in the historical context of capitalistic exploitation of women in the work force, he stood as their defender.

The encyclical went through three drafts, the final one of which was the work of Camillo Cardinal Mazzella, former dean of Woodstock College in Maryland. Mazzella inserted passages more strongly emphasizing the right to private property than earlier versions, probably at the bidding of Archbishop Michael A. Corrigan of New York, who wanted his own position strengthened against the suspected socialism of one of his priests, Edward McGlynn, who had been excommunicated in 1887, in part for his support of Henry George and who, incidentally, was reconciled to the church by Satolli on the basis of *Rerum novarum.*

Leo repudiated socialism for seeking to take all private property away from individuals and give it to the community. Instead, he affirmed the right of all to private property. "The end to which workers immediately look," he wrote, "is to procure property for themselves and to retain it by individual right as theirs and as their very own." Workers should, therefore, receive a wage sufficient to support themselves and their families, and to save enough to purchase property (9, 65). The state, furthermore, was obliged to safeguard private property "through the bulwark of its laws" (55).

Both labor and capital had mutual rights and obligations. Workers were "to perform entirely and conscientiously whatever work has been voluntarily and equitably agreed upon" and to shun violence and association with "vicious men" who falsely held out vain hopes and promises (30). Employers were to treat workers not as slaves but with "the dignity of human personality . . . ennobled through what we call the Christian character," and were to provide time for workers to attend to their religious obligations, ensure a workplace free from "enticements of sin" and temptations against thrift, and not to impose "more work . . . than strength can endure, nor that kind of work which is unsuited to a worker's age or sex." Concretely, employers should "give every worker what is justly due him" (31–32).

Leo XIII shaped the role he attributed to the state in terms of his principle of subsidiarity. The state had the obligation to safeguard the rights of individuals and groups as parts related to the whole; it should "protect equitably each and every class of citizens, maintaining inviolate that justice especially which is called *distributive*" (49). It should intervene whenever "any injury has been done to or threatens either the common good or the interests of individual groups, which injury cannot in any other way be repaired or prevented" (52). Although the pope thought that the strike, a standard instrument for workers to assert their rights, was an "evil," he argued that "the authority of the law" should "anticipate and completely prevent the evil from breaking out by removing early the causes from which it would seem that conflict between employers and workers is bound to arise" (56). Leo was, therefore, acknowledging that strikes frequently grew from injustice.

Against the absolute state's repression of associations, Leo defended as a "natural right" the existence of confraternities, societies, and religious orders (73). Among other associations subsidiary to the state that had rights were workers' organizations. But here he showed a decided preference for the European model of Catholic unions under the auspices of the clergy and bishops (74–78).

The limited role that Leo XIII attributed to the state in the social question must be seen in the context that the governments he knew firsthand were denying the rights of the church and other organizations. He had little knowledge of constitutional democracy such as existed in the United States. In 1895 he warned the United States in *Longinqua* that the American separation of church and state was not to be seen as an ideal. Four years later, he issued *Testem benevolentiae* against Americanism (q.v.), a movement he suspected of denying external authority. Likewise, he forbade Catholic membership in various fraternal organizations because he not only thought them Masonic but also feared for Catholics to engage in prayer or quasi-religious rituals with non-Catholics.

See also AMERICANISM; JUST WAGE; KNIGHTS OF LABOR; RERUM NOVARUM.

Bibliography: Leo XIII, *Rerum Novarum* (Washington: NCWC Publications Office, 1942). J. Murray, "Leo XIII on Church and State: The General Structure of the Controversy," *Theological Studies* 14 (1953) 1–30. J. Kelly, *Oxford Dictionary of the Popes* (Oxford: Oxford Univ. Press, 1986).

GERALD P. FOGARTY, S.J.

LIBERALISM

See FREEDOM; KETTELER, WILHELM EMMANUEL VON; PIUS XI; POLITICAL PHILOSOPHY; PUBLIC AND PRIVATE, RELATIONSHIP OF; QUADRAGESIMO ANNO; RIGHTS AND DUTIES; SOLIDARITY.

LIBERATION THEOLOGY

Latin American liberation theology first appeared around 1960, facing vigorous pastoral opposition. (At almost the same time, black theology of liberation appeared in the United States, followed by similar yet different theological perspectives from different parts of oppressed and marginalized humanity.) Liberation theology in Latin America arose from the poverty of the great majority of the Latin American population and the understanding that the reality of the misery was due to a profound social injustice, together with the understanding that this was contrary to the preaching of the life-kingdom, central to Jesus' gospel, and of the need to live with joy and hope the grace of God's love.

From the beginning this effort to understand our faith had three important questions: What does it mean to do theology? What is the meaning of poverty in biblical revelation? How can we witness resurrection in a context of poverty and death? Those questions are still present. They will be our guide in this brief work.

Talking About God

Every theology is talk about God; in the final analysis, God is its only subject matter. On the other hand, the God of Jesus Christ is presented to us as a mystery. A sound theology is therefore conscious of attempting something difficult, not to say impossible, when it seeks to think this mystery and speak about it. This fact accounts for the well-known statement of Thomas Aquinas: "We cannot know what God is, but only what God is not." At the same time, however, God is a mystery that must be communicated and may not be left hidden, because it means life for every human being. How, then, are we to find a way of speaking about God?

Adopting the viewpoint of the theology of liberation, I will say that we must begin by contemplating God and doing God's will and that only in a second step are we to think about God. By this I mean that worship of God and the doing of God's will are the necessary conditions for thinking about God. Only if we start in the realm of practice will we be able to develop a discourse about God that is authentic and respectful.

Contemplation and commitment within history are fundamental dimensions of Christian practice; thus there is no way of evading them. The mystery reveals itself through prayer and solidarity with the poor. I call Christian life itself the "first act"; only then can this life inspire a process of reflection, which is the "second act." Contemplation and commitment combine to form what may be called the phase of *silence* before God. Theological discourse, on the other hand, is a *speaking* about God. Theology is talk that is constantly enriched by silence.

The great hermeneutical principle of faith, and therefore of all theological discourse, is Jesus Christ. The incarnation of the Son of God is the basis of the hermeneutical circle: from human being to God and from God to human being, from history to faith and from faith to history, from human words to the word of the Lord and from the word of the Lord to human words, from love of our brothers and sisters to love of the Father and from love of the Father to love of our brothers and sisters, from human justice to the holiness of God and from the holiness of God to human justice.

Theology is a critical reflection, in the light of the Divine Word received in faith, on the presence of Christians in the world. As such, it must help us to see how we are to relate the life of faith to the demands made upon us in the building of a human and just society. It will make explicit the values of faith, hope, and charity contained in this commitment. In the final analysis, theology helps make service of the church's evangelizing mission more evangelical, more concrete, more effective. Theology is in the service of the church's work of evangelization and develops within it as an ecclesial function.

In the framework of theology of liberation the distinction of two phases (first act and second act) is a key element in theological method, that is, in the procedure that must be followed for reflecting in the light of faith. It is not a matter simply of theological methodology but rather implies a lifestyle, a way of being and of becoming a disciple of Jesus.

In the book that tells us of the acts of the first Christian community, the Christian manner of life is given a particular and original name: "the way." The word is used without any further qualification. To "follow the way" means to conduct oneself in a certain manner; the Greek word *hodos* can mean both conduct and way or path. Christians are distinguished by their behavior, their lifestyle.

Reflection on the mystery of God can be undertaken only by following in the footsteps of Jesus. It can therefore be said that our methodology is our spirituality, that is, our way of being Christians. Perhaps it is because of this connection between Christian life and theological method that the basic ecclesial communities of Latin America are playing an increasingly active role in this development of a theology. For these communities the commitment to the poor is a capital issue.

All theology starts with the act of faith. In this context, however, "faith" is understood not simply as an intellectual acceptance of the message but also as a vital reception of the gift of the Divine Word heard in the ecclesial community, as an encounter with the Lord, and as love for our brothers and sisters. Here we see the real meaning of St. Anselm's words.

The primacy of God and the grace of faith give the work its raison d'être. In that light we realize that if Christians seek to understand their faith, they do so, in the final analysis, in order to be able to "follow Christ"—that is, to feel, think, and act as he did. An authentic theology is always a spiritual theology as understood by the fathers of the church.

The fontal character of the *sequela Christi* is already a long-standing concern in Latin American theological thought. But the concern has become more urgent and richer in the rush of events in recent years (the persecution and assassination of many Christians for their commitment to the poor). In the context of the struggle for liberation, which seeks to establish love and justice among all, a new way is perhaps opening up for the following of Jesus in Latin America.

Ever since the Enlightenment a large sector of modern theology has taken as its point of departure the challenge launched by the modern (often unbelieving) mind. That mind confronts our world of religion and calls for a radical purification and renewal of it. Bonhoeffer took up the challenge and formulated in a penetrating way the question that is at the origin of a number of theological undertakings in our time: "How are we to proclaim God in a world come of age?"

But in Latin America the challenge does not come first and foremost from nonbelievers but from "nonpersons"—that is, those whom the prevailing social order does not acknowledge as persons: the poor, the exploited, those systematically and lawfully stripped of their human status, those who hardly know what a human being is. Nonpersons represent a challenge, not primarily to our religious world but to our economic, social, political, and cultural world. Their existence is a call to a revolutionary transformation of the very foundations of our dehumanizing society.

In this context, then, the question is not, How are we to talk of God in a world come of age? but, How are we to proclaim God as a Father (or Mother) in a nonhuman world? What is implied when we tell nonpersons that they are sons and daughters of God? These questions were the ones being asked in one fashion or another back in the 16th century by Bartolomé de Las Casas and many others once they had come into contact with the native Americans.

In other words, the question being raised today in Latin American is this: How are we to speak of God in face of the suffering of the innocent? This is more or less the theme of the Book of Job. We can in fact claim that a language for speaking about God is arising among us today out of the unjust sufferings but also the hopes of the poor of Latin America.

The World of the Poor

It can be said that in recent decades the church's life and thought in its Latin American setting have been marked by what we may call "the irruption of the poor." This phrase means that those who until now were "absent" from history are gradually becoming "present" in it. This new presence of the poor and oppressed is making itself felt in the popular struggles for liberation and in the historical consciousness arising from these struggles. It is also making itself felt on the social level in the rise of the basic ecclesial communities and in the theology of liberation.

The poor who are irrupting into our history are a people both oppressed and Christian. Latin America is in fact the only constituent part of the so-called Third World that has a majority of Christians. This makes the situation especially painful and constitutes a major challenge to the Christian faith and to the church. These two dimensions must be present in our theological reflection.

The Latin American situation is characterized by a poverty that the Latinoamerican bishops in Puebla call "the most devastating and humiliating kind of scourge" (Puebla, no. 29) and "anti-evangelical" (1159). In the well-known phrase of Medellín (1968 bishops' conference), the situation is one of "institutionalized violence" (Peace, no. 16). It therefore becomes necessary to analyze and denounce the structural causes of the injustice and oppression in which the poor of Latin America are living.

We are becoming increasingly aware today of what is at stake in this situation, namely, that poverty means death. It is of all this that we are speaking when we talk of poverty and the destruction of individuals and peoples, of cultures and traditions. We are speaking especially of the poverty of the most deprived: Indians, blacks, and women, these last being doubly marginalized and oppressed if they are also Indian or black. We are not, therefore, as has been claimed at times, confronting only the challenge of a "social situation," as if it were something—death—that has nothing to do with the fundamental demands of the gospel. No, we are confronted here with something opposed to the reign of life that the Lord proclaimed: with something, therefore, that a Christian must reject.

We are convinced that there is no Christian life without songs to God, without thanksgiving for God's love, without prayer. In the Latin American setting we may ask, How are we to thank God for the gift of life in a situation that bears the stamp of premature and unjust death? There are no easy answers to this question. It is certain, however, that, as the lives of the poor prove, such a situation does not do away with songs of thanksgiving. It does not silence the voice of the poor. It can even be said that Latin America is living in a time of judgment, a propitious moment, a *kairos*, a call to set out on new ways in fidelity to the Lord.

Theology always makes use of one or another kind of rationality, although it is not identified with it. The rationality corresponds at any given moment to the cultural universe in which believers are living. Every theology inquires into the meaning of God's word for us at the present historical moment.

Talk of present-day poverty in Latin America leads to an effort to know it both descriptively and by determination of its causes. This determination is effected through analyses and interpretations in the area of the social sciences (we connot identify social sciences and Marxist analysis). The episcopal documents at Medellín and Puebla, as well as other episcopal documents, have been engaged in precisely that kind of determination. The appeal to the social sciences in the theology of liberation has for its primary purpose to promote a better understanding of the social reality of the Latin American people, the reality in which, as a matter of historical fact, many are living out their faith and hope.

It is in the light of the life that we must assess the situation of premature and unjust death in which the great majority are living in Latin America. The assessment will make clear to us that the deeper meaning of what we call "total liberation" is, in the final analysis, the acceptance of the kingdom of life. In this context, "life" includes all dimensions of the human, in keeping with the all-embracing will of God. It is therefore contrary to the situation of unjust death in which the poor and oppressed are living.

For this reason, because the gift of life leads us to reject unjust death, the ultimate motive at work in what is called "the preferential option for the poor" is to be found in the God in whom we believe. There can be other worthwhile motives: the emergence of the poor in our time, the social analysis of their situation, human compassion, acknowledgment of the poor as agents of their own history. But, to tell the truth, for Christians the basis of this commitment is theocentric. Solidarity with the poor and the oppressed is based on our faith in God, the God of life who is revealed in Jesus Christ.

To Announce the Gospel

The "scandal of the cross" sheds light on the situation of unjust death in which so many in Latin America are living. The realization that the Lord loves us and the acceptance of the unmerited gift of the Lord's love are the deepest source of the joy of those who live by God's word. Evangelization is the communication or sharing of this joy. It is the sharing of the good news of God's love that has changed our lives. The point of departure for the work of evangelization is thus always an experience of the Lord—an experience of the Father's love that makes us his sons and daughters and transforms us by making us more fully the brothers and sisters of all human beings.

To proclaim the gospel is to call men and women into an *ecclesia*; it is to gather them into a community. Only in a community can faith be lived out in love; only there can it be celebrated and deepened; only there can it be experienced as simultaneously fidelity to the Lord and solidarity with all human beings. The God proclaimed by Jesus Christ is a God whose call is universal and addressed to every human being. At the same time, however, God has a preferential love for the poor and dispossessed. Universality is not only not opposed to this predilection but even requires it in order to make clear the meaning of the universality itself. The preference, in turn, has its proper setting in the call that God addresses to every human being.

Three dimensions or levels may be distinguished in the process of liberation: liberation of a social, political, cultural, and economic kind; specifically human liberation with its various aspects; and liberation from sin. In the final analysis the process is single but not monolithic; various dimensions, aspects, or levels must be distinguished and not confused with one another. Neither separation nor confusion, neither verticalism nor horizontalism.

Only in this way is it possible to preserve both the unity that the free and unmerited initiative of God has bestowed on every area of human history and the relative autonomies without which the coherence of human action and the gratuitousness of grace cannot be asserted with sufficient clarity. The end result is what liberation theology speaks of as a total liberation in Christ.

Liberation is at bottom a gift of the Lord. St. Paul tells us that "for freedom Christ has set us free" (Gal 5:1). This means liberation from sin, which is a self-centered turning in upon oneself. Sin is in effect a refusal to love others and, consequently, a refusal to love the Lord. According to the Bible, sin, or the breaking off of friendship with God and others, is the ultimate cause of the want, injustice, and oppression in which human beings live (see Medellín, Justice, no. 3).

The claim that sin is the ultimate cause is in no way a denial that these situations have structural causes and are objectively conditioned. But at the same time, it must also be kept in mind that no social transformation, however radical, automatically brings with it the suppression of all ills.

From this it follows that the coming of the kingdom cannot be identified with the historical embodiments of human liberation. The growth of the kingdom is indeed a process that takes place in history through liberation, to the extent that liberation means an important fulfillment of the human person and is a condition for a new and fraternal society. Without the liberating events of history, the kingdom does not grow; the process of liberation only destroys the roots of oppression and of the exploitation of one human being by another. This is not the same thing as the coming of the kingdom, which is first and foremost a gift.

From the viewpoint of theological reflection, the challenge we face in Latin

America is to find a language about God that grows out of the situation created by the unjust poverty in which the broad masses live (despised races, exploited social classes, marginalized cultures, discrimination against women). This language must at the same time be fed by the hope that heartens a people in search of its liberation. It is in this context of sufferings and joys, uncertainties and certainties, generous commitments and ambiguities, that our understanding of the faith must be continually renewed.

It can be said, I think, that a prophetic language and a mystical language are being born in this soil of exploitation and hope. The problem here, as in the Book of Job, is to speak of God in the context of the suffering of the innocent. The language of contemplation acknowledges that everything has its origin in the Father's unmerited love. The language of prophecy denounces the situation of injustice in which the peoples of Latin America are living, and denounces as well the structural causes of this situation. Without prophecy, the language of contemplation runs the risk of detachment from the history in which God is acting and in which we encounter God. Without the mystical dimension, the language of prophecy can narrow its vision and weaken its perception of that which makes all things new.

The aim of these two languages is to communicate the gift of God's reign as revealed in the life, death, and resurrection of Jesus. Being a witness to the resurrection means choosing life and indeed all expressions of life, because nothing is outside the comprehensive embrace of God's reign. This witness to life (life material and spiritual, individual and social, present and future) is particularly important in a continent marked by premature and unjust death. It is also particularly important in efforts to achieve liberation from oppression. Witnesses to the resurrection can therefore join Scripture in asking the ironic question: "Death, where is your victory?" That is the question suggested by a testimony like that of Archbishop Romero, to name but one among many.

We celebrate this life in the Eucharist, the action that is the primary work of the ecclesial community. When we share the bread we commemorate the love and fidelity that brought Jesus to his death, as well as the resurrection that put the seal of approval on his mission to the poor. The breaking of the bread is at once the point of departure and the point of arrival of the Christian community.

The aim of the theology of liberation is to be a language about God, and to be this in the communion of the church. It is an effort to make the Word of life present in a world of oppression, injustice, and death.

See also BASE COMMUNITIES; BLACK THEOLOGY; EVANGELIZATION; EVIL, SOCIAL; KINGDOM OF GOD; MEDELLÍN; POOR, PREFERENTIAL OPTION FOR; POVERTY; PRAXIS; PUEBLA; WOMEN.

GUSTAVO GUTIÉRREZ

LITURGICAL MOVEMENTS, SOCIAL INFLUENCE OF

While the liturgical movement can be viewed comprehensively, from its 19th-century origins in the work of Prosper Gueranger, who refounded the French abbey of Solesmes in 1833 and there began projects of liturgical research and liturgical restoration, through its spread across much of western Europe and North America, to its gradual endorsement by the papacy and its confirmation in the Vatican Council II constitution *Sacrosanctum concilium* (1963), this essay has a narrower focus. It will look at the points at which particular Catholic social movements and local liturgical movements intersected. It will also take account of the factors supporting and sustaining that interaction. While the names Lambert Beauduin (1873–1960) and Virgil Michel (1890–1930) are prominent from the viewpoint of liturgical history, the two monks—one Belgian, the other American—who are identified with promoting the social significance of the liturgical renewal were at center stage for only a short time in effort to establish liturgical foundations for Catholic social movements.

Beauduin, priest of the Belgian diocese of Liege, was a seminarian when Leo XIII's encyclical *Rerum novarum* was promulgated in 1891. The local ordinary, Bishop Victor Doutreloux, welcomed and promoted the teaching; under his sponsorship Liege had already sponsored three local congresses on social issues from 1887 to 1890. In 1894 he authorized the establishment of a fraternity of priests, the *Congrégation des Aumoniers du Travail,* to begin an apostolate of direct social interaction with dechristianized industrial workers. The leader of that project was Beauduin's seminary professor of moral theology, Canon Antoine Pottier. In 1899, two years after his ordination, Lambert Beauduin joined the labor chaplains, and he pursued a priestly ministry to laborers until 1906. The labor chaplains' project itself had begun to fall into disfavor and to manifest malaise after the death of Doutreloux (1901) brought Leo XIII's ironic selection of the antidemocratic Martin Rutten as bishop of Liege; Rutten's appointment came following government intervention with the Vatican to diffuse the labor movement.

In 1906 a spiritually disillusioned Beauduin entered the Abbey of Mont Cesar at Louvain. There, Beauduin's biographer notes, "his insight into the beauty of a liturgically-oriented spirituality hit him like a thunderbolt and eventually ignited the Belgian liturgical movement" (Quitslund, p. 10). In 1909, at the Malines National Congress of Catholic Works, Beauduin found opportunity in a church-sponsored convocation dealing with social, political, and economic concerns to promote Pius X's teaching that active participation in the liturgy is "the indispensable source of the Christian spirit." He was able to press that vision in congress resolutions and also to gain the support of his Benedictine superiors to commit Benedictine monasteries to the liturgical apostolate, publicly promoting liturgical spirituality among diocesan clergy and the laity.

Just three years after the Malines congress, the young Flemish priest Joseph Cardijn, who had studied for a time at Louvain, began his work as chaplain to a Girls' Club, slowly developing a method for lay spiritual formation for Catholic Action, which culminated in the Young Christian Student (YCS) and Young Christian Worker (YCW) movements. An English visitor to Belgium in 1938 heard articulated at Mont Cesar the judgment that "the task of the liturgical movement and of Catholic Action alike is just that of *remaking the community,* first the community of the parish, then the community beyond" (Larke). Within two decades, the two Belgian-based movements had claimed each other.

The YCS and YCW movements had spread to the United States by 1938. In 1942, at one of the early North American Liturgical Weeks, the mutuality of the liturgical and Catholic Action movements was explained. A promoter of Catholic Action drew attention to the direct role of the liturgy in the spiritual formation of Chicago "cells" for Catholic Action when he described the structure of the cell meetings. Liturgical reflection was seen as essential, since the Christian spirit by which to "observe, judge, and act" (the YCW-YCS strategy) comes "principally and indispensably from the liturgy" (Boyd).

To put the North American Liturgical Weeks themselves in context, Virgil Michel's earlier leadership in the U.S. liturgical movement must be cited. In 1924–25 Michel, a monk of St. John's Abbey in Collegeville, Minnesota, was sent for postdoctoral studies to Rome, where he met Lambert Beauduin, and to Louvain, where he became acquainted with the liturgical apostolate of Mont Cesar abbey. He was caught up in the spirit of the liturgical movement, returned to the United States, and convinced his abbot, Alcuin Deutsch, to give the movement its early North American base. The Liturgical Press was established in 1926, with a translation of Beauduin's *La Piété de l'Église* as its first publication and the monthly journal *Orate Fratres* (subsequently *Worship*) as its main vehicle for regular communication with the clergy.

According to Michel's analysis, the social problems of the United States in the 1930s were exacerbated by the Great Depression but had hardly been caused by it. He saw the root of social breakdown in the rampant individualism that was part of the national character. The true Christian spirit, by contrast, was communal, fed by its vision of the mystical body of Christ, a reality experienced and celebrated in the church's liturgy. In the spirit of Beauduin, Michel was convinced that every effort at the reconstruction of the social order would find its dynamism in a revitalized liturgical piety. His message quickly found a hearing.

The North American liturgical movement had a visible center at Collegeville, but at the end of the 1930s it had many local leaders among the clergy of both rural and urban dioceses. The National Catholic Education Association provided a broadened base for the dissemination of the message, partially through the direct influence of Virgil Michel himself, who had collaborated extensively with religious educators to promote a Catholic liturgical piety. The notion of the centrality of the liturgy for true Christian formation was also being promoted by lay and clerical leaders of many Catholic Action endeavors. By 1939 an initial national liturgical gathering was held under the sponsorship of U.S. Benedictine abbots. In 1940 the first of a three-decade series of North American Liturgical Weeks was held in Chicago under the sponsorship of the newly constituted North American Liturgical Conference, whose membership and annual program reflected a broad coalition of interests.

The reciprocal influence of Catholic social movements and the liturgical movement in North America is well documented in the pages of both *Orate Fratres* and the *Proceedings* of the Liturgical Weeks from the 1930s through the 1960s, although no definitive study of this relationship has been done. A partial listing of Catholic social movements self-identified with the liturgical movement would include the German Central Verein, the National Catholic Rural Life Conference, the Antigonish Cooperative Movement, the Catholic labor movement, the Catholic Worker movement, Friendship House, the Grail movement, the National Catholic Conference for Interracial Justice, and the Christian Family Movement, as well as the Young Christian Student and Young Christian Worker movements. Leaders of these movements—among them Msgr. Luigi Liguitti, George Higgins, John LaFarge, Edward Marciniak, Catherine De Hueck Doherty, Reynold Hillenbrand, and Martin Hellriegel—were prominent voices in the Liturgical Weeks. Virgil Michel, until his premature death in 1938, was a regular correspondent and conversation partner with these and other prophets for social change like Dorothy Day.

It is one of the ironies of contemporary church history that in the aftermath of the Second Vatican Council convened to revitalize the church, fifty years of existential mutuality between renewed liturgical piety and effective lay commitment to "social reconstruction" was virtually forgotten. The 1963 Constitution on the Sacred Liturgy, *Sacrosanctum concilium,* and the 1965 Constitution on the Church in the Modern World, *Gaudium et spes,* take scant account of the relationship between the "true Christian spirit" formed by the church's liturgy and the Christian people's vocation to be leaven in the mass of human society. The statement of the 1971 Synod *Justice in the World* says liturgy "can greatly serve education for justice," but it accords no primacy to liturgical spirituality.

The existential and theological reconstitution of the intimate connection between the church's liturgy and its mission has only begun twenty-five years after Vatican II. Issues of liturgical reform and liturgical inculturation have tended to overshadow the deeper meaning of authentic liturgical spirituality.

See also COMMUNITY; COOPERATIVE ASSOCIATIONS; GAUDIUM ET SPES; JUSTICE IN THE WORLD; LAITY, ROLE OF; MICHEL, VIRGIL; RERUM NOVARUM; VATICAN COUNCIL II.

Bibliography: *Proceedings of the North American Liturgical Weeks* (Washington: The Liturgical Conference, 1940–). *Orate Fratres* (Collegeville, MN, 1926–). W. Boyd, "Liturgy and Catholic Action," *Proceedings* (1942). M. Collins, "Contemplative Participation," in *Contemplative Participation: Sacrosanctum Concilium Twenty-Five Years Later* (Collegeville: The Liturgical Press, 1990) pp. 75–86. A. Haquin, *Dom Lambert Beauduin et Le Renouveau Liturgique* (Gembloux: Editions J. Duculot, 1970). H. Larke, "The Liturgical Movement and Catholic Action in Belgium," *Orate Fratres* 13 (1938–39) 59–65. P. Marx, *Virgil Michel and the Liturgical Movement* (Collegeville: The Liturgical Press, 1957). S. Quitslund, *Beauduin: A Prophet Vindicated* (New York: Newman, 1973). M. Searle, ed., *Liturgy and Social Justice* (Collegeville: The Liturgical Press, 1980). M. Zotti, "Cardijn: A Priest Who Believed in the Priesthood of the Laity," *The Living Light* (June 1987) 307–15.

MARY COLLINS, O.S.B.

LOVE

The two dominical commands to love God and to love our neighbor as ourselves are central to Christianity. It is then surprising how often love is not a central principle of systematic theology or even of Christian ethics. Social ethicists usually concentrate more on justice than on love. Faced with the daunting task of securing even minimum standards of justice for all people, some hold that love is superfluous or better relegated to interpersonal relations.

The word "love," in ordinary usage, has wide application: we love apples, our cat, our parents. We love ideal objects like justice and truth. We love specific activities such as playing, praying, even loving itself. We love institutions and groups such as the church, our nation, our alma mater. We also love metaphysical objects such as life and God. And so on. There is no known schema that adequately classifies all the objects we love or all the ways we love. We can speak of sensual, bodily, psychological, spiritual, and religious loves. We distinguish some loves by roles or agents, for example, parental, spousal, or divine loves. The tradition distinguishes between *agape, eros, epithemia, philia,* and charity.

Authors use a great variety of terms to describe love: intimacy, bonding, attachment, co-existence, interdependence, union, affirmation, active support, benevolence, promoting the good, concern, self-giving, self-transcendence, selflessness, self-forgetfulness, availability, acceptance, reverence, respect, presence, openness, desire, inclination, joy, and so forth. Each captures some aspect. There are no well-established definitions either for love in general or for its specific forms, and even individual authors are not always consistent.

In Scripture, the word "love" has roughly the same range of uses as in contemporary English. For example, it refers to raw sexual attraction, romantic love, familial affection, friendship. God's love is described as an effective, elective, redeeming love that includes judgment and forgiveness. God's love is directed to a special people, but it singles out some individuals and extends to all of creation. Israel's love for God presupposes and is commanded as part of the covenant; it is a fully engaging love given to no other god.

NT references to love are more frequent and complex than those of the OT. One should not say, as many do, that *agape* is God's love. *Agape* can be disordered, practiced by sinners, directed to the world or darkness, and motivated by gifts. Christ's death on the cross powerfully exhibits God's love for us. Jesus' own love for his friends is to be the source or measure of their love. This is possible because "the love of God has been poured out in our hearts through the Holy Spirit who has been given us" (Rom 5:5). For John and others, love means a mutual indwelling of God and human beings. It is almost a life-force that flows between love partners. On the one hand, *God's* love "is brought to perfection in us" (1 Jn 4:12); on the other, *our* love is perfected through confidence in God.

In the NT, love of God is linked with neighbor-love, though the latter alone is also said to be sufficient. John requires love mainly for the "brothers," while the Synoptics' Jesus recommends associating with sinners and not friends. Thus Christian love has selective aspects, but it is also universal. That is, preferential love for those whom God gives us is appropriate, but no one should be excluded. Love may be unilateral or mutual. Christian love goes "downward" with a preference for the religiously and socially least valued persons (the sinners and the lowly), "laterally" toward our sisters and brothers, and "upward" with a preference for the highest valued persons (God and Christ). Christian love patiently takes abuse, yet asserts itself against evil and for the good. It is willing to sacrifice itself, yet it can count on a reward.

Love is well described as an emotional participation in the beloved in its dynamism toward fulfillment. It is useful to set aside some common misunderstandings. Love is not simply doing good. Nor is it yearning for or striving after the beloved, since love has its moment of repose. Love is not identical with neediness; like God, we can love with full hearts. Love is not identical with any bodily states of feeling, though it will often be accompanied by such states. Love is not an intellectual value judgment of the worthiness of the beloved; rather love first leads us to feel the beloved's value. Love does not mean losing our identity in another. It is not equivalent to preference, because we can love persons whom we do not prefer. Love is not a bond of interests, since we can share the evil interests of others.

We should distinguish between deeds that are loving and the emotion that is love. The former might include anything that is right. Since we can do the right thing for many different reasons, not every loving deed is done from love. Love, rather, is a form of emotional participation. The value of the object "affects" or lays hold of us *and* we are inclined toward it. We consciously transcend ourselves to share in the being of the beloved, and we are moved by the beloved. In the poetic language of Dante: I both "in-you me" and I "in-me you." By contrast, "indifference" means that we are not affected by or inclined toward the beloved's value. Allowing the beloved to say its word of importance to us is a form of self-emptying conversion, since therein we are changed by the other. We then respond to the beloved, adding to it our affirmation of its goodness. We speak our yes to it, and we cooperate with it when we can.

Love is an activity through which the higher value of the beloved comes to appearance and, where possible, is realized. It may be directed to any "object"—personal or not—that bears values. Love unites with whatever is proper to the ideal essence of the beloved. It reveals the value that is already real, as well as the value that is yet to be realized. Love does not project onto the beloved something that does not (really or ideally) belong to the beloved. Far from being blind, love is essential to full objectivity. Loving devotion enables the lover to see value that others cannot see. Theology would be crippled without the access to God that love gives.

Love is grace. It is not conditional, demanding that the object first achieve some value. The affirmative nature of love explains love's power to change its object. Love is not merely a warm approval of what is already present. Its affirmation fosters the beloved's *own* tendency to perfection and resists any self-destructive tendencies. Love can, therefore, oppose particular qualities, deeds, and expressions that are not consonant with the beloved's ideal essence. Love is thus creative and redemptive. The union of the lover with the beloved enables the beloved to become in ways not possible without the offer of love.

One crucial distinction is "for whom" we ultimately are acting. *Agape, eros,* and *philia* can be distinguished by this criterion. *Agape* is directed to the beloved for the beloved's sake, *eros* for the sake of the lover, and *philia* for the sake of a "friendship" relation. Each is a genuine love of the beloved, moving to the enhancement of the beloved's value, but each has a different ultimate goal. Moreover, each can be a religious love, that is, a love that cooperates with God's own love.

Love among human beings is not limited to either self or others. Two common errors should be noted. The first is to reduce all love of others to a subtle form of self-love; for example, as a way to increase one's own happiness or self-esteem. Christians sometimes say they love others in order to achieve their own salvation—something quite different from loving others for their own sakes. The second error is to deny love for oneself. Christians frequently speak as if the only worthwhile love is a love for others. Though self-love is rarely recommended in the Scriptures and though the tradition often equates it with selfishness, self-love is crucial in every human being's life. It is the legitimate fostering of one's own fulfillment. Persons have a special responsibility for themselves, a responsibility that others cannot fulfill. As counselors readily attest, many people hate themselves. Social ethicists should be alert to conditions that promote self-hate.

To affirm self-love, however, is not to deny that the greatest fulfillment comes in devoting ourselves to God and to the good of others. When we consent to the need or value of the beloved, we consent to moving beyond ourselves, thereby overcoming our self-centeredness and thus becoming more free. Love expands the spirit by enabling it to participate ever more broadly and deeply in the world and in God.

In social ethics it is established that various groups have their own reality and dynamism. These groups can be both subjects and objects of love. For example, Christians can love their church; the church can love God; and God loves the church as well as its individual members. We can love individuals *as* members of a group, for example, our family; and both the group and members of the group can and should have a preferential love toward each other.

Though universal love of all human beings is essential, this is not enough for the fullness of Christian life. Jesus had friends to whom he revealed himself in a special way. While we should love those who are most valuable, for example, God, Jesus, the saints, we must also love those who are most distant from their own ideal value, for example, sinners, the despised, the helpless. Thus a preferential love for the poor or marginalized is requisite because of their need.

Given and responded to, love creates a moral solidarity of persons with one another. With every act of love offered and accepted a community grows, and those who are loved become more able to love in return. Thus the kingdom of God is fostered by love.

See also CHARITY; GRACE; IMAGINATION, ROLE OF; JUSTICE IN THE WORLD; MUTUALITY; SOLIDARITY, SPIRITUALITY; VALUES.

Bibliography: E. McDonagh, "Love," in *New Dictionary of Theology.* J. McKenzie, "Love," in *Dictionary of the Bible.* G. Outka, *Agape* (New Haven: Yale Univ. Press, 1972). E. Vacek, *Love* (Washington: Georgetown Univ. Press, 1994).

EDWARD COLLINS VACEK, S.J.

M

MAGISTERIUM

Lacking the more specialized meaning that it has acquired in recent centuries, the term "magisterium" was understood in the medieval period as referring in general to the authority of teachers. Accordingly, St. Thomas Aquinas distinguished within the church between the pastoral magisterium of bishops and pope (*magisterium cathedrae pastoralis*) and the scholarly magisterium of theologians (*magisterium cathedrae magistralis*). Although some theologians have suggested a return to this earlier theological usage, there is general acceptance of the current, narrower, and quasi-technical meaning of the term: the pastoral teaching office of bishops and pope, which according to Catholic doctrine is the teaching authority and mission that they have as successors of the apostles (*Lumen gentium* 24). In a more recent linguistic development, exemplified in the Second Vatican Council, the term refers also, derivatively, to bishops and pope themselves as pastoral teachers (*Dominum et vivicantem* 10).

The formal object of the pastoral teaching office is matters of faith and morals (*res fidei et morum*), and it is in terms of *doctrina de fide vel moribus* that the First Vatican Council defined the object of papal infallibility (DS, 3074). Nevertheless, although some theologians have maintained the opposite, the scope of magisterium and that of infallibility are not co-extensive; for the office of pastoral teaching and the gift of infallibility, which is given primarily to the entire church (LG 12, 25) and derivatively to their pastoral teachers, are neither identical nor identically related to divine revelation.

With regard to the word "*mores*" there is some unclarity, because before, during, and after the Council of Trent it was used both in the sense of morals and in that of religious practices, and this ambiguity was not absent even from Vatican I when it came to define papal infallibility. Some scholars therefore understand it to refer to what might be called today "Christian practice."

If magisterium and infallibility are neither identical nor co-extensive, they are also not completely separable in Catholic theology. Because of the charism of infallibility that accompanies it under certain conditions, magisterium can be operative in two ways. The office is exercised in a solemn or extraordinary way when a doctrine is defined by an ecumenical council or by a pope teaching *ex cathedra;* all other exercises of teaching authority by bishops or pope—whether individually, in ecumenical councils, or otherwise—are ordinary.

Nevertheless, the distinction between extraordinary and ordinary magisterium is not co-extensive with that between infallibly taught and noninfallibly taught doctrine. A doctrine can be taught infallibly not only through an exercise of extraordinary magisterium but also when bishops throughout the world, preserving "amongst themselves and with Peter's successor the bond of communion, in their authoritative teaching concerning matters of faith and morals . . . are in agreement that a particular teaching is to be held definitively and absolutely" (LG 25). Although with regard to the ordinary exercise of papal magisterium no pope has claimed infallibility, there has been at times a tendency in the church, notably during the pontificate of Pius XII, to attribute infallibility to such exercise of magisterium.

From the early ages of the church, in fulfilling their office bishops have joined together in regional synods and provincial councils; and acknowledging this traditional mode of exercising episcopal authority, Vatican II called for the institution of episcopal conferences to be spread throughout the world (*Christus Dominus* 37). Recently, however, there has arisen in certain quarters of the church a question of whether episcopal conferences have a mandate to teach; for it is maintained by some that only individual bishops in their respective dioceses, the college of bishops, the pope, and the Vatican departments that represent him have such a mandate. Implied in this view is that teachings of episcopal conferences cannot claim the authority of exercises of magisterium. Whatever the resolution of this presently controverted question, the term "mandate to teach in the church," even as applied to the pastoral teaching office, must certainly be understood analogously rather than univocally if the different agencies and levels of magisterial teaching are to be adequately accounted for.

Although there is no marked attempt among theologians to recover the medieval use of the term "magisterium," the current use seems to generate a view of the church in which *ecclesia docens* is seen as pope and bishops and *ecclesia discens* as the rest of the church. This conception is widely rejected by contemporary theologians, who without derogating from the role and the importance of the pastoral teaching office or from the diversity of gifts and callings in the church (1 Cor 12:4-30) see the entire church as *ecclesia discens et docens.* On the one hand, the development of doctrine in the pilgrim church and the proclamation of the gospel in accord with "the signs of the times" are possible only if those who exercise magisterium are learners as well. And on the other hand, having their own special calling from God, laypersons have by reason of their knowledge, competence, and preeminence a right and indeed an obligation to manifest their opinions on what pertains to the good of the church (LG 31, 37).

This principle about teaching in the church, although enunciated by Vatican II with regard to the laity, applies as well to all others who are not holders of the pastoral teaching office (deacons, priests, religious). In a special way it applies to theologians, as was eminently clear in Aquinas' twofold distinction of ecclesiastical magisterium.

It is noteworthy that the narrowing of the meaning of "magisterium" in modern times has been accompanied by a narrowing of the understanding of the theologian's office, to the point where in *Humani generis* (36), relying on Pius IX, Pius XII taught that the most noble office of theology is to show how a doctrine defined by the magisterium is contained in the sources of revelation in that sense in which it has been defined. To the controversy in the post–Vatican II church, then, between the Vatican and theologians over the latter's role in the church, the change in the meaning of "magisterium" may not be completely unrelated.

A common mode of exercising ordinary papal magisterium, beginning with Gregory XVI's *Mirari vos* of 1832, is the encyclical letter. In 1891 Leo XIII's *Rerum novarum* initiated what was to become the celebrated tradition of Catholic social teaching, embodied largely in papal encyclicals (a notable exception: Paul VI's 1971 apostolic letter *Octogesima adveniens*) and extending into the present papacy with John Paul II's *Laborem exercens* (1981), *Sollicitudo rei socialis* (1987), and *Centesimus annus* (1991). The social encyclical tradition developed, it is worth noting, when moral theology was a privatized science of personal morality and social morality was virtually overlooked by theologians. Especially in more recent times, episcopal conferences have also made important contributions to the advancement of Catholic social teaching, such as in the U.S. bishops' *Challenge of Peace* (1983) and *Economic Justice for All* (1986).

With regard to morals, it is common teaching among theologians that there are moral principles in divine revelation that could be solemnly defined or taught infallibly by the ordinary magisterium. Insofar as morality is divinely revealed (primary object) or insofar as a moral teaching pertains to the guarding or explaining of the deposit of faith (secondary object), morals are the object of infallibility. While some theologians have maintained that the entire natural moral law is virtually contained in revelation and can therefore be the object of infallibility, most, it seems, distinguish between basic moral principles and particular norms of behavior and maintain that the latter are not part of the proper object of infallibility.

Since the scope of infallibility and that of magisterium are not identical, that certain moral matters cannot be addressed infallibly does not mean that they cannot or should not be taught at all through the pastoral teaching office. On the contrary, it is generally held that pope and bishops should address in the light of the gospel the critical moral questions of every age, although to many of these neither divine revelation nor human reason can provide absolutely certain answers. For as in all human affairs, so in moral matters prudent and wise counsel is necessary even though it generally cannot be marked by absolute certainty.

See also EPISCOPAL CONFERENCES, CONCEPT OF; EPISCOPAL LETTERS, FUNCTION OF; LAITY, ROLE OF; REASON, ROLE OF; SYNOD OF BISHOPS.

Bibliography: C. Curran and R. McCormick, eds., *The Magisterium and Morality: Readings in Moral Theology No. 3* (New York: Paulist, 1982). J. Mahoney, *The Making of Moral Theology: A Study of the Roman Catholic Tradition* (Oxford: Clarendon, 1987). F. Sullivan, *Magisterium: Teaching Authority in the Catholic Church* (New York: Paulist, 1983).

NORBERT J. RIGALI, S.J.

MANUAL LABOR

"Human work which is exercised in the production and exchange of goods or in the provision of economic services, surpasses all other elements of economic life, for the latter are only means to an end" (*Gaudium et spes* 67). In this statement from the Second Vatican Council, the English word "work" renders the Latin "labor." Furthermore, the work designated, although not exclusively manual, at least in the principal instance is manual labor: "We believe by faith that through the homage of work offered to God man is associated with the redemptive work of Jesus Christ, whose labor with his hands at Nazareth greatly ennobled the dignity of work. This is the source of every man's duty to work loyally as well as his right to work; moreover, it is the duty of society to see to it that, according to the prevailing circumstances, all citizens have the opportunity of finding employment. Finally, remuneration for work should guarantee man the opportunity to provide a dignified livelihood for himself and his family on the material, social, cultural and spiritual level to correspond to the role and the productivity of each, the relevant economic factors in his employment, and the common good" (GS 67).

Commonly we distinguish manual labor from intellectual labor. The distinction is valid if not taken to imply a disjunction or separation. The engineer at a desk developing a complex program for a system of computers may be said to be engaged in intellectual labor, which differs from the manual labor of the service person who is engaged in repairing the engineer's car; but the difference in no way means that the service person is not thinking or that the engineer is not growing physically weary.

Catholic social doctrine, as noted above, proclaims that work (labor) is both a duty and a right. Work also ought to be a good whereby we become the persons God, who created us in his image, calls us to be (*Laborem exercens* 9). As a result of our ancestral sin (Gen 3:17-19) and the sins that have followed, work entails toil. Toil designates that dimension of work that is not in itself fulfilling; instead toil is the cross of labor. If we use this cross to unite ourselves with our Lord in his passion and death, it, too, serves our sanctification. But we must not be satisfied with passively carrying our daily cross. Instead we must seek to alleviate the burden, particularly in the lives of others (LE 27).

When dehumanized and degraded, manual labor becomes almost entirely toil. As recounted in the Book of Exodus when the Israelites were so reduced, their condition was referred to as "the whole cruel fate of slaves" (Exod 1:14). Manual labor should not be such a cruel fate, but as Pope John Paul II aptly observed, it was long thought such: "The ancient world introduced its own typical differentiation of people into classes according to the type of work done. Work which demanded from the worker the exercise of physical strength, the work of muscles and hands, was considered unworthy of free men, and was therefore given to slaves" (LE 6).

For the Christian anything like this attitude is wholly unacceptable: "By broadening certain aspects which already belonged to the Old Testament, Christianity brought about a fundamental change of ideas in this field, taking the whole content of the Gospel message as its point of departure, especially the fact that the one who, while being God, became like us in all things devoted most of the years of his life on earth to manual work at the carpenter's bench" (LE 6).

As labor whereby persons till their own land or are justly employed or become artisans or develop and exercise skills, work (albeit inseparable from toil) enhances and expresses human dignity. Advanced industrialization with attendant automation can reduce toil but may also reduce the truly human dimensions of manual labor, instead making the human person into an extension of the machine (LE 8). This very real problem lies not in the technology as such but in how we choose to use it. It is not right to make a human being into merely a cog in a machine.

Catholic social doctrine requires that we complement all labor with proper rest. Obviously this requirement is particularly urgent for those who work manually. Manual labor must not be such as to destroy the human body and must be so conducted that the human body can restore itself through proper rest (LE 25).

Finally, in the older moral manuals (textbooks primarily for seminarians) manual labor, practically speaking, was identified with servile work (*opera servilia*), which we are obliged not to engage in on the Lord's day. Since the Second Vatican Council the requirements for our observance of Sundays and holy days are commonly stated without this exclusive focus on manual labor: "Such days are to be kept holy also by avoiding needless labor and unnecessary commercial dealings, that is, activity of a kind that hinders the spirit of celebration and joy in the Lord that should mark such days" (*The Teaching of Christ: A Catholic Catechism for Adults,* 2nd ed.) Lawler et al., eds., Our Sunday Visitor, 1983, p. 297).

See also EMPLOYMENT AND UNEMPLOYMENT; GAUDIUM ET SPES; LABOR AND CAPITAL IN CATHOLIC SOCIAL THOUGHT; LABOREM EXERCENS; OCTOGESIMA ADVENIENS; QUADRAGESIMO ANNO; RERUM NOVARUM; SOLLICITUCO REI SOCIALIS.

RICHARD R. ROACH, S.J.

MARGINAL PERSONS

Marginal persons are so called because they have no role of participation in their political system. This lack of participation is rooted in the absence of social power. Marginality may derive from overt or covert processes of exclusion or noncommunication in a society. Marginal persons possess no role of responsibility in resolving either their own problems or the problems of society in general. Their marginality may reveal itself in a social passivity, as, for example, in low levels of productivity, education, or subsistence. Marginal persons do not form a cohesive group in society, nor do they establish ties of solidarity with others. Lack of internal integration and wider social solidarity perpetuate the sense and condition of powerlessness in the marginalized.

Marginal persons may live in circumstances of poverty and underdevelopment. Liberal democrats attribute this to laziness and free choice. Structural analysis, however, suggests that poverty and underdevelopment are *caused* by marginality. Therefore handout aid will never change this poverty. Marginal persons, themselves, must change. Conscientization seeks to help marginal persons discover the causes of their marginalization and organize themselves to overcome powerlessness and injustice. Marginal persons become agents of change. Integration, not incorporation, is the goal. Radical social change occurs when the creative subjectivity of marginal persons is empowered, acknowledged, and integrated into the dynamic social fabric.

See also ALIENATION; AUTHORITY, POLITICAL; CLASS; COMMUNITY; MINORITIES; PARTNERSHIP; POOR, PREFERENTIAL OPTION FOR.

PATRICK CARROLL, O.S.M.

MARITAIN, JACQUES

Jacques Maritain (1882–1973), French philosopher, convert to Roman Catholicism, was one of the major figures in the Thomistic revival that stemmed from Leo XIII's 1879 encyclical *Aeterni Patris*. Maritain's work from beginning to end was an effort to discuss philosophical issues under the inspiration of the work of St. Thomas Aquinas. His contributions to social thought must be seen in this light. But Maritain's thought also reflects the times in which he lived and the contemporary controversies in which he engaged.

Politically, he began far to the right, moved leftward until, at least on one interpretation, he moved rightward again with *The Peasant of the Garonne* (1968). The condemnation of *l'Action Française* forced him to consider the authority of the Catholic church to intervene in secular matters when the spiritual, too, is involved. He became a defender of the condemnation, but in the case of the civil war in Spain was a vocal foe of attempts to identify one or the other side with Catholicism. It is the seeming paradox of his work that, permeated as it is with his Catholic faith, he is a champion of the hope that believers and nonbelievers can arrive at practical agreements.

Natural law. Maritain accepted and developed the Thomistic view that there are truths about the social order that all human beings can recognize. Perhaps his most interesting discussion of the difficulties with this claim is to be found in *Man and the State* (1947). The Universal Declaration of Human Rights was approved by nations with radically different understandings of human nature and destiny. In what could such agreement on fundamental human rights consist? Was it simply a verbal agreement?

Maritain argued that such an agreement was due to natural law. Of course, he could not mean that all those who had signed the Universal Declaration would accept the account of natural law Maritain might give. He distinguished between an account or theory of natural law (gnoseological natural law) and the given community of human nature (ontological natural law), which was the ultimate basis for the otherwise surprising concurrence.

Machiavellianism. In an essay called "The End of Machiavellianism," which is found in *Religion and Culture,* Maritain firmly rejects an amoral approach to politics. He was encountering the view that since most people are bad the only effective social organization is one that accepts this somber fact. It is naive to expect human beings, citizens, to act on the basis of the moral good; consequently, self-interest must be recognized as the engine that drives human behavior. The fact that Machiavellianism does not work is a powerful argument against it. Furthermore, it cynically presupposes the morality it dismisses. It leads to the view that political and social action are techniques that can be deployed independently of the moral quality of the agent. This is the most fundamental delusion of all according to Maritain.

Person and common good. Maritain was a determined foe of the totalitarian regimes that led to World War II, and his essay on Machiavellianism was prompted by what he took to be the assumptions of totalitarianism. It is a paradox that a theory of social action that emphasizes self-interest should end by submerging the individual in the mass. Maritain's insistence on the common good and of the human agent regarded as person is at the heart of his view of social organization.

In *The Person and the Common Good* (1946), Maritain contrasted the human being considered as individual and the human being considered as person. His thinking on these matters cannot be divorced from the impact of the totalitarian regimes of the 1930s. Maritain insisted that, as person, the human agent has an end that transcends the political or social good. It is as individual that he is part of a whole. Considered as a person, the human agent is a whole and transcends the social order.

Democracy. It had long been Catholic teaching that there is a variety of forms of political life that are compatible with the faith. Monarchy, aristocracy, democracy—none has pride of place. With Maritain, we see the shift to the primacy of democracy. Democracy, he held, is the best political expression of Christianity. When he wrote *Integral Humanism* in 1934, he took a very dim view of capitalism and seemed to favor something like democratic socialism. Subsequently he visited the United States and was exiled here during World War II; all in all he spent twenty years in America. In *Reflections on America* (1958), a kind of love letter to the United States, he noticed how little the realities of American life fitted the stereotype of capitalism. But it was democracy that most engaged his attention, and he began to speak of democracy as a secular faith, of sins against it, of political heretics. Many were startled by the analogy between religion and politics when it was carried to such detail.

In *The Peasant of the Garonne,* Maritain wrote that he had known only three true radicals in his life, Saul Alinsky, Eduardo Frei, and himself. It is an enigmatic remark but suggests something of the way Maritain himself saw his work in social thought. Linking a president, a social agitator, and a professor might seem strange, but Maritain also played public roles, representing France at UNESCO when the Universal Declaration was drawn up and serving as French ambassador to the Vatican from 1945 to 1947.

After his death Maritain's reputation dropped a bit, but his work was never eclipsed. Indeed, a resurgence of interest in his thought is evident. There are two international Maritain associations, dozens of national groups, and the Jacques Maritain Center at Notre Dame has been in existence since 1947. Maritain's teaching on the human person influenced Paul VI, and the centrality of person in the social encyclicals of John Paul II can also be traced at least in part to Jacques Maritain.

See also AUTHORITY, POLITICAL; COMMON GOOD; DEMOCRACY; HUMAN RIGHTS; MODERN CATHOLIC SOCIAL THOUGHT; NATURAL LAW; PAUL VI; PERSON, DIGNITY OF.

RALPH McINERNY

MARRIAGE

Historically Christianity has understood marriage to be the only appropriate channel for human sexuality; it is a relationship of social and domestic partnership typically characterized by sexual intercourse and shared parenthood. Christian marriage has built on cultural institutions in which lineage and inheritance along male descent lines were the major structures of social organization. Marriage, Christian or not, has functioned both to provide a controlled mechanism of descent and to link distinct lineage-based kinship groups in a patriarchal system. In the 20th century companionship, friendship, and love have moved from their traditional subsidiary status in marriage to become central to the way its meaning is understood. In the Roman Catholic tradition, at least six factors have shaped the developing interpretation of marriage. These are (1) the sacralization of aspects of ordinary life, including marriage; (2) ascetic attitudes toward sexuality; (3) the use of nature as a norm for human acts and relationships; (4) the elaborate systemization of moral and ecclesiastical law; (5) a struggle to balance the physical and the spiritual or intersubjective aspects of personhood; and (5) a Western cultural origin.

Sacralization

Christianity has had a tendency to sacralize basic human experiences and institutions, as a way both of allowing discipleship to transform all spheres of life and of setting Christians apart from the culture. The text often cited in support of the sacramentality of marriage (Eph 5:25-32) is an analogy meant for the edification of particular Christians in particular marriages and does not in itself contain any "doctrine" of marriage as sacrament. Yet the association of marital love with Christ's love for the church does demonstrate how early Christians subsumed marriage into a religious worldview and linked it with religious symbols. More specifically, the NT and early Christianity held up a distinctive expectation that marriage would be permanent, in contrast to the dissoluble contract of ancient Hebrew, Greek, and Roman cultures (Mt 5:31-32; 19:3-9; Lk 16:18; Mk 10:2-12; 1 Cor 7:10-11). Christians also adopted a moderate asceticism and advocated celibacy as a higher vocation (1 Cor 7:1-2, 7, 36-40). In doing so, they rejected dualistic philosophies and religions that commanded celibacy while at the same time making the statement that sex, marriage, and kinship do not define the whole meaning of human life. By loosening the dominance of kinship and marriage in creating identity, Christianity opened the way for women into nontraditional roles. The NT also portrays men and women as more equal or reciprocal partners in marriage than did either ancient Judaism or the surrounding cultures (Mk 10:11-12; Lk 16:18).

The NT nonetheless includes some patriarchal instructions for the marriage relationship. The *haustafein* (household codes) enjoined the submissiveness of wives to husbands (as of slaves to masters and children to fathers) within the household as the basic unit of Roman society (1 Cor 11:2-34; Eph 5:24; Col 3:18; 1 Tm 8). These texts represent accommodation to the larger society by which second-generation Christianity sought acceptance and betray the egalitarian thrust of Jesus' own ministry and of Gal 3:28. Yet at another level they do reflect some attempt to transform secular marriage by Christian values, for example, by reciprocity within the household hierarchy (Eph 5:25; Col

3:19, 21; 4:1). Basic gospel themes of equality and solidarity—as well as extra-biblical, experiential critiques of women's oppression—instruct Christians today to find better, more culturally subversive ways in which to do that than the accommodationist NT patterns represent.

Historically the sacramentality of marriage was to become detached from its biblical base in the eschatological idealism of communal life and to become tied instead to canonical regulation. In the first three centuries of the church there was no specifically Christian marriage ceremony or institution of marriage. While certainly not seeing marriage as incompatible with Christianity, early authors devoted more attention to the praise of virginity than to the wedded state. In the 4th and 5th centuries pastoral concerns rooted in actual cases prompted the development of a legislative process to guide marriage relationships at the practical level. At the same time, marriage liturgies were created, and the ceremony was moved from the home to the church. Priests, whose presence at marriages was not originally required, became gradually more involved, taking over from the bride's father the blessing of the couple. The priest eventually became an indispensable part of the Christian celebration of marriage, although it remained (and still remains) the case that it is the bride and groom who actually confer matrimony on each other. By the 10th century there was in place the foundation of the judicial system governing marriage, requiring among other things that every marriage take place by means of a public liturgy.

Peter Lombard in the 12th century may have been the first to specifically designate seven sacraments, including marriage. In response to the Reformers' understanding of marriage as a good and divinely created but secular estate, the Council of Trent (1563) formally defined marriage as one of seven sacraments. Theological views of sacramentality and indissolubility have been heavily molded by juridical interests in defining clear criteria of the existence or nonexistence of the marriage bond, and in locating a particular moment at which it begins to exist irreversibly (see below, on canon law). Abstract predications about marriage must be replaced by a more experiential approach that recognizes both the provisional and the progressive nature of marriage as a human relationship, and the paradoxical bearing of gospel ideals on all human enterprises.

Ascetic Attitudes

In the developing tradition, ascetic strands (1 Cor 7:7-9, 29, 39) were exaggerated until they resulted in a fairly negative attitude toward sexuality in general as well as toward marriage as a lesser state than virginity or celibacy. For instance, Tertullian of Carthage in the 2nd century exhibited a rigorist stance toward sex, instructing his wife not to remarry after his death. In his later years, influenced by the Montanist heresy, he forbade second marriages completely. Although only Jerome among the church fathers would again approach such vehemence on that subject, they all strongly preferred virginity (e.g., Gregory Nazianzus, John Chrysostom, Augustine, John Damascene). Augustine was to defend marriage against its pagan detractors, the Manicheans, by speaking of its three goods: the procreation and education of offspring (*proles*); sexual faithfulness (*fides*); and the indissoluble bond, which in Christian marriage stands for the union of Christ and church (*sacramentum*). Augustine's contribution has formed the heart of Christian teaching about marriage. Yet Augustine exhibited some of the same repugnance for sex and marriage as that of the dualists against whom he argued. Even while defending marriage as good and as a legitimate sexual outlet, Augustine thought all sex was irremediably tainted morally by the unruliness of sexual desire.

Despite its possible adequacy to the realities of his time and that of several later generations, the Augustinian understanding of matrimony looks appallingly insufficient today, even harmful. Familiar critiques focus on Augustine's negativity toward sexual passion in general, his limited view of sex as good only when deliberately procreative, and his and his culture's suppression of the interpersonal value of sexual intimacy as well as their complacent assumption of gender inequality.

Nature as a Norm

Many Christian authors have followed the philosophers in seeking in nature some purpose of sex that could justify what they otherwise thought to be a suspicious activity. In the 2nd century Clement of Alexandria, like the Stoics, said that marriage is necessary for the procreation and raising of children and that sexual intercourse is good when it has conception as its aim.

The 12th-century theologian Thomas Aquinas is the foremost articulator for the Catholic tradition of the view that moral activity should follow the essentially good inclinations of human nature, and that sexual morality, too, is a morality of natural law. Marriage is for Aquinas a natural human reality raised to the level of a sacrament by Christian faith and doctrine. He appropriated Augustine's three goods from the *Sentences* of Peter Lombard, so perpetuating their influence. He also incorporated Aristotle's philosophy into Christian theology and ethics, which led him to define sexual morality partly in terms of "natural" and "unnatural" acts, differentiated according to whether the heterosexual and procreative structure of sexual intercourse is preserved. "Natural" sex acts are morally good only if they occur within marriage, because only married couples can provide a proper upbringing for children. Sexual passion is good as long as it is rightly ordered (to procreation). More innovatively, Aquinas saw marriage as a "friendship" of the most intense kind. Nonetheless, women were subordinate, and procreation, not love or sexual pleasure, remained the only legitimate reason for sexual relations, and the primary purpose of marriage until the 20th century.

Systemization of Moral and Ecclesiastical Law

Roman Catholicism is characterized by an interest in the regulation of sexual relationships, particularly marriage, and in giving moral guidance to the faithful in specific areas of sexual and marital conduct. The early medieval penitential books were resources for confessors that listed sins along with appropriate penances and encouraged a good deal of precision in the assessment of sexual behavior. The system of canon law asserted juridical control over marriage in the interest of protecting the institution, sometimes to the detriment of the needs of individuals.

Since the Middle Ages the church has assumed that marriage is created by consent to a contract; the contract constitutes both the substance of the marriage and the sacrament. At the same time, the church has attempted to maintain that marriage is an effective sign of Christ's presence to the church, a presence defined as saving love, not as a stipulation of rights and duties.

Historically, discussion about the nature and establishment of marriage reflected three different perspectives on what is most essential to the reality and experience of marriage: sexual intercourse; spiritual communion and living together (consistent with the marriage of Mary and Joseph); and a social institution for the raising of children. In medieval Scholasticism, the theologians tended to defend consent to a mutual personal and social relationship, while canonists sided with the more practical criterion of sexual intercourse. Already in the early Middle Ages when the church had complete jurisdiction over marriage, influential families had brought to it cases for adjudication. This made it necessary to determine precisely what constituted the bond, and indissolubility became linked to consummation.

Through the 9th century indissolubility was not understood in a way that absolutely precluded divorce. There was no one discipline on marriage shared by the universal church. But in some regions divorce and remarriage were permitted after adultery, abandonment, impotence, or the enslavement or capture (in war) of one spouse, as well as when one spouse converted to Christianity (the so-called Pauline privilege, see 1 Cor 7:12-15, which permits divorce only if both parties were unbaptized at the time of the ceremony). In the 12th century Gratian's decretals and Pope Alexander III established what continues to be Roman Catholic practice: marriage is valid and sacramental by virtue of the partners' consent and hence indissoluble. Yet a valid unconsummated marriage can be dissolved on the condition of a legal declaration within the church that it is "null and void." What is indissoluble in principle differs from what is indissoluble in fact. Perhaps this inconsistency is a juridical way to handle the insight that indissolubility is an eschatological ideal for married persons, but both indissolubility and sacramentality, because grounded in an actual human relationship, also must develop over time.

The Church's stipulation that any marriage of two baptized persons is by definition sacramental (and hence indissoluble) is a result historically of a struggle for jurisdictional control over marriage between the ecclesiastical and civil authorities in 18th- and 19th-century Europe. Since contracts fell under the jurisdiction of the state, the church insisted that for Christians the contract is the sacrament and that marriage thus comes within the concerns of canon law. A theological conundrum and practical problem that today results is the situation of so-called "baptized unbelievers," whom the church must regard either as administering to one another a sacrament they do not accept or as having no right at all to marriage, which is otherwise regarded as a natural human prerogative.

Interpersonal Aspects

Christian views of marriage have long struggled to harmonize its physical and intersubjective aspects. Early emphasis on procreation has given way to appreciation of the importance of the relationship of spouses. In the 20th century a major influence in Roman Catholicism has been "personalism," with its stress on love as the meaning of marriage. Personalist influences have been strong in recent magisterial teaching, but their ramifications for particular questions of ethics and of canon law have not yet been fully determined.

Stimulated, for instance, by the work of Herbert Doms and Dietrich von Hildebrand in the 1930s, personalist authors find the meaning of both sex and marriage in the love relationship of the couple. Although it at first reacted negatively to this threat to the primacy of procreation, the magisterium itself has become gradually influenced by the modern emphases on the dignity of the person and on the importance of interpersonal relationships to human society and welfare, and even by the emerging awareness of the dignity (if not full equality) of women. *Casti connubii* (1930) kept procreation in first place as the goal of sex and marriage and condemned birth control, but still spoke of marital love as in a sense the real purpose of matrimony. Since the 1960s the magisterium has treated love and procreation equally as ends of marriage. The pastoral constitution of Vatican Council II, *Gaudium et spes* (1965), describes marriage as a "community of love" and "covenant of conjugal love." *Humanae vitae* condemns contraception but elevates love to a level with procreation and furthers the "mutual self-gift" language, so pervasive in John Paul II's descriptions of marital love. But at the practical level, Catholicism's appreciation of the fundamental nature of reciprocal love in marriage must be characterized as ambivalent. Particularly since contraception is excluded even when needed to plan births for the welfare of the couple and the family, the norm of procreation continues to govern love's sexual expression. Moreover, women's procreative contribution and the necessity that they be ever ready to accept a new birth continues to define their primary role as maternal and domestic. The limitation of women and men to stereotypical gender roles undermines the equality that true mutuality presupposes.

John Paul II reinforces the tradition of *Humanae vitae. Familiaris consortio,* for example, idealizes marriage as primarily a "covenant of conjugal love" and an occasion of a mutual gift of self, not as ordered above all to procreation. Yet throughout his writings the pope is adamantly against artificial birth control. Although he recognizes the emergence of women as social actors outside the family, he reserves the true fulfillment of women to motherhood (*Familiaris consortio*).

The 1983 Code of Canon Law. The new code assimilates Vatican II personalist themes while leaving essentially intact the juridical mechanisms and criteria by which marriage is controlled. Marriage is defined as both a covenant and a contract. This language replaces the 1917 code's definition of marriage as a contract by which spouses consent to reciprocal rights to each other's bodies with regard to those acts naturally leading to procreation. Marriage is now the establishment by consent of "a partnership [*consortium*] of the whole of life," and is ordered both to the spouses' good and to the procreation and education of children. But the 1983 code retains the earlier criteria for the validity, sacramentality, and indissolubility of marriage.

Western Cultural Origin

The Catholic tradition on marriage has been largely a Western product. Its cultural origins can be seen in the stress on permanent monogamy and in the development of legal criteria for the existence of marriage that focus, for instance, on a distinct moment of consent. As Catholicism becomes increasingly a self-consciously universal and culturally pluralistic church, it will have to face challenges to customary definitions of marriage and of its purposes. One way to begin to meet such challenges is to attempt to discern the essential values of the historical tradition while still following the NT mandate to transform all relationships and to be critical of every human institution and tradition.

To return to Augustine's categories, marriage has functioned historically in Christianity as an appropriate sexual outlet, as a nurturant source of the next generation, as a secure institution that undergirds the interdependence of the sexes and of the generations, and as a symbol of humanity's equally secure dependence on divine salvation. The Catholic Christian tradition has, with its historical interest in practical guidance, progressively marked out ways to guide marriage concretely as a sexual, unitive, and parental relationship. Catholicism affirms and presents as normative for married couples the goodness of sexual desire and pleasure along with the need to look further in defining the human meaning of sex; shared parenthood; love as affective intimacy, companionship, and mutual cooperation and support; serious commitment to monogamous fidelity and permanency (represented as indissolubility); and confidence that God's forgiveness and reconciliation are available in marriage as an interpersonal partnership opening onto social roles (represented as marriage's sacramental quality). Although an initiating ritual of marriage is important as an effective sign of serious intent and social accountability, the marriage relationship is formed gradually by both consent and consummation (though not necessarily by specifically sexual consummation only). This tradition and its norms reflect the emergence in the modern period of an awareness of the interpersonal, affective dimensions of marriage; of the goodness of sexuality; and of women's more equal role in marriage.

While the "Christian view of marriage" will not be able to supply clear and culturally transcendent answers to all questions of sexual and marital ethics, it can lend a critical perspective on particular cultural realizations. Moreover, the embodiments of Christian marriage achieved by different Christian communities can prophetically enlarge one another. Discipleship requires that Christian marriage always embody gospel values: repentance for our sins, forgiveness and mercy in imitation of God, and equality and solidarity in our relationships with others. Christian marriage can be a sacrament, an avenue of God's graceful approach to humanity. It can convert sex, marriage, and family into relations through which the worth and dignity of each person is realized and in which a mutually supportive solidarity leavens cultural situations of marriage and kinship.

See also BIRTH CONTROL; CANON LAW, FUNCTION OF; DIVORCE; FAMILY; FEMINISM AND CATHOLIC SOCIAL THOUGHT; LOVE; PERSONALISM; WOMEN.

Bibliography: T. Mackin, *Divorce and Remarriage* (New York/Ramsey, N.J.: Paulist, 1984); *The Marital Sacrament* (New York/Mahwah, N.J.: Paulist, 1989); *What is Marriage?* (New York/Ramsey, N.J.: Paulist, 1982). L. Örsy, *Marriage in Canon Law: Texts and Comments, Reflections and Questions* (Wilmington, Del.: Glazier, 1986). W. Roberts, ed., *Commitment to Partnership: Explorations of the Theology of Marriage* (New York/Mahwah, N.J.: Paulist, 1987). E. Schillebeeckx, *Marriage: Human Reality and Saving Mystery* (New York: Sheed & Ward, 1965).

LISA SOWLE CAHILL

MARXISM

Marxism comprises the sociopolitical and economic ideas of Karl Marx, Friedrich Engels, and their followers. It connotes also the worldwide socialist movements that developed and sought to embody these ideas. Karl Marx (1818–83), the controversial social thinker who gave Marxism its name, was born in Trier, Germany. His father, a Jewish lawyer, converted to Protestantism to avoid anti-Semitic laws and had his son Karl baptized at age six. The young Marx studied law and philosophy at the University of Berlin and was attracted by the dialectic philosophy of G. W. F. Hegel. He joined a group of young Hegelians who challenged the more conservative views of Hegel, especially in respect to religion. After obtaining a doctorate in philosophy Marx turned to journalism and developed a critique of Hegel's political philosophy, a critique that led him to espouse social revolution. He joined forces with Friedrich Engels, and they collaborated on several works: *The Holy Family, The German Ideology,* and *A Manifesto of the Communist Party.* Much of Marx's life was spent in exile in London, where he wrote *Das Kapital.* Engels, who supervised his father's factories in England, wrote more popular versions of Marxist thought and supported Marx financially. Marx, the more original of the two, developed a social analysis based on a materialist view of history and a challenging critique of capitalism.

Marxist Analysis

Marx's materialist view of history: historical materialism. Marx believed that economic factors are most decisive in shaping society and creating change in history. Most studies in history assume that political leaders and political power act as the dominant forces in bringing about change. Marx thought otherwise. The key to understanding history, and the particular form a society takes at some point in history, can be found in the way humans produce—that is, their "modes of production." The modes of production depend on the natural resources, labor skills, and tools available at a given time. More importantly, however, they depend on how work is socially organized—that is, the "relations of production."

The relationships developed in organized work, with some owning and controlling the means of production while others work under them, create certain social classes. The state and its laws, and the cultural or religious ideas that prevail, reflect and serve the interests of the dominant class. "The mode of production of material life conditions the social, political, and intellectual life process in general" (Tucker, ed., p. 4). Thus in medieval society the principal mode of production involved agriculture with peasant serfs tilling the soil for wealthy landowners. The landowning lords were the dominant class, and the serfs the most oppressed class. The laws protected the owners. The prevailing political, cultural, and religious ideologies all served to justify the established order. The king ruled by divine right. God intended that some persons should be rulers and some ruled, some rich and some poor. Humans should accept their status in life, knowing that eternal salvation counts far more. These features of medieval society, as seen from a Marxist perspective, relate ultimately to how society is organized economically.

Changes occurred as new modes of production developed. Industrial production became more important and lucrative than farming. Manufacture of goods shifted from hand-made to factory-made. The owners of the factories and the bankers, the capitalist class, became dominant. The workers, the proletariat, became the new, most oppressed class. Class struggle ensued. The capitalists, or bourgeoisie, used the state to protect their property and the free-market system; they developed new ideologies to justify their system.

History thus moves, for Marx, through a dialectical process of change. The prevailing order of ideas and institutions is questioned and negated, giving rise to a new order. As new modes of production arise, they conflict with old ways of organizing society. "At a certain stage of their development, the material productive forces of society come into conflict with the existing relations of production" (Tucker, ed., p. 4). Class struggles intensify; the once-dominant class is overthrown; a new stage of history comes into being. Marx believed that capitalism would give way to socialism. The capitalists would be overthrown by the working class they had created. The capitalist mode of production produced wealth effectively, but the wealth benefited only a few. The workers, forced to subsist on minimum wages and often pushed into unemployment by capitalist crises, would revolt and usher in a new age of socialism and a classless society.

Marx's critique of capitalism. If Marx's materialist view of history gave an overview of change over time, his more-focused economic critique sought to uncover the secrets of capitalist production. Using a dialectical method—going from "appearances" to a deeper grasp of reality—Marx challenged the basic assumptions of the prevailing economic theory. He sought particularly to demonstrate "scientifically" that exploitation is *intrinsic* to capitalism, that profit can be explained only by the surplus value created by workers. Surplus value is the uncompensated labor the wage worker gives to the capitalist owner without receiving any value in exchange. What workers receive in wages is determined not by the value of their work or the time they put in (labor-time) but by the amount they need to sustain life (labor-power). The difference between the two, between the value created by work and the amount the worker needs in order to subsist, is surplus value. Marx stated his position quite graphically: "Suppose the working day consists of 6 hours of necessary labor and 6 hours of surplus labor. Then the free laborer gives the capitalist every week 6×6 or 36 hours of surplus labor. It is the same as if he worked 3 days in the week for himself, and 3 days in the week *gratis* for the capitalist" (Tucker, ed., p. 365).

Marx did not intend, however, simply to make a moral judgment on exploitation. He argued that the internal contradictions of capitalism create crises that will eventually lead to its collapse. Marx considered overproduction, combined with lack of buying power, as an ultimate cause of all economic crises. Capitalism is driven by a law of constant expansion. Its natural dynamism pushes it to seek ever-greater profits by producing more and by producing more cheaply (e.g., by intensifying labor and by replacing human labor with machines). Competition also drives capitalists to save on labor costs, reduce wages, and push smaller capitalists out of business. But this very expansion, Marx believed, contains the seeds of capitalism's destruction. Smaller wages to pay and fewer small capitalists to compete with also mean less buying power. Consequently, factories must be closed when goods lie unsold, and mass unemployment results. Crises wrack the whole system. Eventually the jobless masses will revolt, if only to survive.

Marx's views on the inevitable collapse of capitalism left him quite vulnerable to critics who respond that he has been refuted by history. Workers did not revolt, at least not in the highly developed capitalist countries where revolution was predicted. Workers' wages did not remain at a subsistence level. Union negotiations took the place of revolution; long-range corporate planning diminished problems of unforeseen overproduction. Neo-Marxists have offered various explanations for the continuance of capitalism: heavy investment in military weapons, the stimulation of false needs through massive advertising, the intrusion of the state to subsidize private business and placate the masses. However, a theory of capitalist "imperialism" developed by Lenin, Rosa Luxembourg, and others became the most frequently used explanation for capitalism's survival.

The development of an imperialist stage of capitalism, according to Marxist theorists, involved several factors. First, capitalists created monopolies that gave them more control over markets and prices, reducing the chaos that had led to recurring crises earlier. Second, banks merged to create greater control over investment. Third, foreign countries provided not only new markets for goods but a new locus for investing surplus capital. Fourth, international cartels formed and reached agreements on spheres of interest that permitted giant corporations to avoid price wars and loss of profits. Fifth, the most striking and obvious imperialism took the form of direct political conquest of colonies. Colonies gave assured control over raw materials, provided a guarantee of new markets, and permitted a new exploitation of cheap labor.

Developments in Marxism

Engels' materialist worldview. Marx's early writings condemned religion as an "opium of the people." Belief in God, he believed, made humans servile, worked to pacify the poor, and served to justify the status quo. Religion would disappear once socialism occurred; people would no longer need appeals to some higher being to overcome their feelings of alienation. It was Engels, however, who developed this atheism into a more complete worldview, a dialectical form of philosophical materialism.

Engels (1820–95) wanted to show that Marxism offered a truly "scientific" explanation of the world. Marx had demonstrated the "laws of motion" in human history, based on "material" economic factors. Engels sought to prove that philosophical materialism, viewed dynamically and dialectically, explained the laws of motion that govern all reality.

Theists had claimed for centuries that the universe could not exist without a God who brought it into being and into motion. Engels countered that "matter in motion" has existed eternally and that the inner tension and the dynamics of matter itself suffice to explain motion and change. Similarly, God is not needed to explain the origin of human life. It evolved out of lower forms of life.

Older materialist philosophies, however, failed to account for the dynamism within matter. Engels proposed three dialectical laws, borrowed from Hegel, as keys to understanding change. "The union and struggle of opposites" shows that within a given unity a tension of conflicting forces also is present, for example: attraction and repulsion on magnetic fields, positive and negative charges in the atom, oppressing and oppressed classes in a given society. "The transition from quantity to quality" shows that changes occur quantitatively up to a certain point, at which point a "leap" to a new quality takes place. For example: quantitative changes in the temperature of water lead to steam or ice, which represent qualitative changes; gradual changes in production lead to a revolutionary change in the whole structure of society, as in the change from feudalism to capitalism. "The negation of the negation" demonstrates a process of the dying of one form of life leading to a new form of life: a grain of barley buried in the ground brings forth new barley; in mathematics, minus *A* times minus *A* equals *A* squared; in history, a formerly oppressed class overthrows the ruling class.

Engels believed that this dialectical process in nature had been proved or confirmed by three great scientific discoveries of his day. The cell was discovered to be the basic structural unit of all living organisms and shown to develop dialectically through a process of multiplying itself. The law of conservation and transformation of energy showed that nature was a continuous process with one form of universal matter-in-motion changing into another. Darwin's theory of evolution proved not only the evolution of species but also their transformation through a series of dialectical leaps.

Lenin and the Russian revolution. The immediate followers of Marx, the German Social Democrats, moved away from revolutionary tactics and began using the electoral process to achieve gains. Though they made significant political gains and Social Democratic parties developed in other European countries, they failed to take power and achieve socialism. Lenin (1870–1923), confronted with a tsarist regime in Russia, believed that only revolutionary change would bring about socialism. With the Bolshevik revolution in November 1917 a Marxist socialist regime came into power, and Lenin became "the" authoritative interpreter of Marx.

Lenin drew upon ideas from Marx and Engels but stressed those he felt fitted the Russian situation. Key points in his doctrine would form the basis of Marxism-Leninism. Many Marxists argued that the Party should assist workers to achieve goals and strategies they set for themselves. Workers would become revolutionary once objective conditions created the right situation. Lenin opposed such a strategy. Revolutions do not just happen spontaneously. A revolutionary movement requires a clear, unified theory, and such a theory will not just develop automatically. Theory must come "from without," as shown by the contributions of Marx and Engels themselves. Successful revolution also requires professional revolutionaries: a small, disciplined, secret, and well-organized "vanguard party" with skills in agitation, propaganda, organizing, and theorizing. Professional revolutionaries are needed who can raise the consciousness of workers and enable them to see the necessity of revolution. These ideas, developed especially in Lenin's *What Is to Be Done?* (1902), became the basis for the leadership role of the Communist party in guiding revolutionary actions and in governing socialist governments once established.

Lenin also reaffirmed the atheistic worldview articulated by Engels. Marxism is materialism, Lenin asserted, and as such it is relentlessly hostile to religion. He insisted on the unity of every aspect of dialectical materialism, a philosophy cast from a single piece of steel such that not even one basic premise could be eliminated from it without departing from objective truth. He insisted also on atheism as essential to party membership.

In *State and Revolution* (1917) Lenin added other points as essential to true Marxism. He argued that socialism could only be attained through revolution followed by the establishment of a "dictatorship of the proletariat." Marx had at times used the expression "dictatorship of the proletariat" but intended it only as a transitional stage and as rule by workers. Lenin made the Communist party the controlling factor in socialist rule and claimed that a dictatorship of the proletariat was needed to suppress counterrevolutionaries and to guide the buildup of socialism.

All of these points stressed by Lenin focused on one central feature: power concentrated in the hands of the leadership of the Communist party. The Party brings in revolutionary theory, guides revolutionary strategies, safeguards philosophical materialism, and controls the government and all of society once in power. Lenin undoubtedly wanted workers themselves to one day truly run society, but critics believe that the means he used set the stage for Stalinism and for the massive dissent that finally erupted in Eastern Europe at the end of the 1980s.

New Forms of Marxism

If Leninist Communist-party Marxism became the most dominant form of Marxism and what most people associate with Marxism, other trends in Marxism also developed. Differences emerged even within the ranks of orthodox Marxist-Leninists. Followers of Leon Trotsky formed independent Marxist groups opposed to Stalin's views on socialist society. Mao Zedong formed a peasant-based guerilla movement in China and fused Marxist ideas with his own. In Yugoslavia Tito created a distinctive form of socialism that emphasized workers' self-management of industries and market competition. In the 1970s Communist parties in Italy, France, and Spain proposed a new form of "Eurocommunism" that discarded Lenin's "dictatorship of the proletariat" and called for adherence to democratic principles.

Critical Marxism. Many Marxist intellectuals developed new forms of "critical Marxism" that questioned not only Stalinist rule but Engels' philosophical materialism and other points considered essential in dominant Marxism. Hungarian philosopher George Lukacs (1885–1971) defended Lenin but questioned the reduction of Marxism to fixed, objective theses. Marxism is above all a method of analysis open to new data and new conclusions. Attempts to read Marxism as a form of economic determinism misses Marx's own emphasis on dialectics, which takes into consideration the causality of many interacting factors (the political, the ideological, the economic, etc.). The Italian Marxist Antonio Gramsci (1891–1937) was a contemporary of Lukacs, but his writings gained prominence only after World War II. Like Lukacs, Gramsci rejected treating Marxism as a set of objective laws and set theses. Especially in relation to strategies, politics must be viewed as an "art," not a science, and Marxism should not let itself be tied down to materialism. Gramsci also stressed the importance of "hegemony" in achieving socialism. The working class must win over society to socialist ideals and socialist institutions *before* revolution. Hegemony, or control, should come through consent, not force. Gramsci's idea of "organic intellectuals" working directly with the poor would find special resonance among Latin American liberation theologians.

The discovery and publication in the 1930s of manuscripts by the young Marx played a significant role in stimulating new studies and new interpretations of Marx. Marx's *Economic and Philosophic Manuscripts* (1844) pointed to a humanism that underlay his later economic writings. *The*

German Ideology (1845) showed how he initially formulated his materialist view of history. Western Marxists used new insights from Marx, combined with Freud and other thinkers, to analyze modern society. The "Frankfurt school" produced a number of neo-Marxist thinkers: Herbert Marcuse, Jurgen Habermas, Max Horkheimer, and others. German Marxist Ernst Bloch offered a new interpretation of Christianity that would greatly influence many European theologians. Bloch argued that Christianity, far from simply serving as an obstacle to change, opened up a messianic hope for the world. Utopian hopes and dreams inspire change and give motivation to Marxism as well as to Christianity.

In Eastern Europe many "dissenting" Marxists used the writings of the young Marx to criticize the bureaucratic statism they found in their own countries. In Czechoslovakia appeals to Marx's humanism influenced efforts there to create "socialism with a human face" prior to Russia's invasion in 1968. In Poland Leszek Kolakowski developed critiques of Marxism that eventually led him out of the country and ultimately to a rejection of Marxism itself. The "praxis" group in Yugoslavia challenged rigid and distorted Stalinist interpretations of Marxism, questioned Engels' materialism, and called for a return to the real Marx.

In 1989, the startling collapse of Communist regimes in Eastern Europe underscored a growing disaffection with Marxism in general. Different aspects of Marxist analysis, however, continued to exercise an influence, especially in reference to poverty and oppression in Third World countries.

Church Social Teachings and Marxism

Resistance to social change characterized the official stance of the Catholic church through most of the 19th century. Pope Pius IX's *Syllabus of Errors* (1864), with its condemnation not only of socialism but of "progress and modern civilization," manifested this resistance in its most intractable form. The French Revolution had left deep scars in the church psyche. Thousands of priests were deported or fled from France; abbeys were razed; statues and mementos were destroyed or defaced. The church looked to monarchies for protection, and the Vatican's own Papal States made the pope a civil monarch as well as sympathetic with monarchical rule. Some individual Christians and small Christian groups did attempt to awaken the official church to the plight of the working class but with little initial success. Bishop Wilhelm Emmanuel von Ketteler (1811–77) became the first prominent official church figure to speak out progressively on social issues. His work, the efforts of Catholic theorists in the Freibourg Union, and interventions by Cardinals James Gibbons of Baltimore and Henry Edward Manning of Westminster, drew the attention of Pope Leo XIII, who promulgated the church's first major social encyclical.

The social encyclicals. Pope Leo's *Rerum novarum* (1891) confronted two major problems created by the capitalist revolution—the plight of the working class and class conflicts. It acknowledged the problem that Marxists attacked: wealth concentrated in the hands of relatively few owners, the mass of workers impoverished, and the two classes in conflict. But Leo rejected the socialist solutions proposed by Marxists and others. Socialism, Leo argued, takes away humans' natural right to private property. Socialism proposes futile solutions, believing that all inequalities can be overcome, and it wrongly assumes that hostilities between classes are natural and inevitable. It also gives too much power to the state, risking a complete absorption of the individual and family by the state. As steps toward resolving the conflicts generated by the Industrial Revolution, *Rerum novarum* proposed several means. Since the encyclical argued that loss of religion and decline of morality were major factors in creating the problem, it called for a return to Christian morality and attention to church teachings. It called on owners and workers to accept mutual obligations and duties, noting especially that owners must pay a "just wage." Though wary of too much state control, the encyclical argued that the state does have an obligation to protect the interests of the working class. Perhaps most importantly, it acknowledged the right of workers to form labor unions.

Pope Pius XI's *Quadragesimo anno* (1931) reemphasized many of these same points. It sharply criticized the prevailing capitalist system in which "immense power and despotic economic domination is concentrated" (QA 105). Pope Pius again rejected socialism. "No one can be at the same time a sincere Catholic and a true Socialist" (QA 120). While this condemnation clearly applied to Marxist socialism, Pius also spoke of a "mitigated" form of socialism whose social reforms often paralleled those based on Christian principles (QA 114). The pope proposed, as a middle way between individualistic capitalism and collectivist socialism, a new form of corporation in which workers would share in ownership and decision making.

Pope Pius XI also promulgated the encyclical *Divini Redemptoris* (1937), directed explicitly against atheistic communism. Several ideological or philosophical principles of Bolshevik communism came under attack: (1) communism proposes a false messianic idea and deceptive promises about what a new society will be; (2) it holds that only matter exists, a view that rules out all belief in God, the soul, and hope in an afterlife; (3) class struggle and consequent violent hate and destruction become a crusade for progress; (4) there is no recognition of any individual rights in respect to the collectivity; (5) it rejects all hierarchy and divinely constituted authority including the authority of parents; (6) the natural right to property is abolished; (7) marriage and the family are completely undermined; (8) dominance of the collectivity makes production of goods its only goal and gives unlimited discretion over individuals; (9) morality is reduced to being simply a product of the economic order; (10) the state is given unlimited power though Communists claim that it will "wither away" (DR 8–14).

These charges, which summarize the major church criticisms of Marxism-Leninism, led to a condemnation that would characterize Catholic anticommunism for years to come. "Communism is intrinsically wrong, and no one who would save Christian civilization may collaborate with it in any undertaking whatsoever" (DR 58). Pope Pius XII would act on this condemnation. In July 1949, with a fear of communist power in Italy, the Holy Office forbade Catholics to join the Communist party or to encourage it in any way. Moreover it forbade the faithful to publish, distribute, or even read books and papers that upheld communist doctrines.

In the 1930s some Catholic thinkers, like Emmanuel Mounier in France, used Marxist analysis to critique capitalism while rejecting Marxist-Leninist solutions. Some Protestant theologians went even further. Paul Tillich espoused a religious socialism that accepted the basis of Marx's analysis of capitalist society and allied itself with the proletarian movement. Tillich criticized, however, the tendency of communism to absolutize its truths and authority; hence religious socialism must always stand in criticism of misdirected political socialism. Reinhold Niebuhr even spoke of himself for a time as a "Christian Marxist." He defended Marxist analysis and Marxism's claim to represent the attitudes of the working class. Like Tillich, however, Niebuhr criticized Marxism's absolutism and its deification of the proletariat. In later years, Niebuhr grew increasingly critical of Marxism and espoused a "political realism" that he thought could best be achieved through democratic politics, proximate solutions, and a pluralism of social strategies for change.

The 1960s and 1970s witnessed the emergence of new attitudes and ways of thinking in the church. The encyclicals of John XXIII reflected the pope's own positive and optimistic views. Vatican II recognized that efforts to transform the world were part of the church's mission. Some leading Catholic scholars in Europe undertook serious studies of Marxism, and several prominent Catholic theologians participated in Christian-Marxist dialogues. Pope Paul II's *Populorum progressio* (1967) sharply criticized affluent nations and their trade policies with poorer nations. *The Wall Street Journal* denigrated the encyclical as "warmed-over Marxism." In an "80th year letter" (*Octogesima adveniens*) marking the anniversary of *Rerum novarum,* Paul VI distinguished several aspects of socialism. He offered also, for the first time in the history of papal social teachings, several distinctions regarding Marxism. He noted that Marxism could be considered as (1) the active practice of class struggle, (2) exercise of political and economic power by one party, (3) a materialist ideology, or (4) a scientific method of examining social reality (OA 33). The pope went on to warn that these different aspects of Marxism have generally been linked together and that Marxist class struggle has led to violence and totalitarian societies. Some liberation theologians, however, would cite this letter in justification of their own appeals for use of Marxist analysis.

Liberation theology controversies. Through most of its history in Latin America the Catholic church played a predominantly conservative role, with bishops often aligned politically with the landowning class. Dramatic changes occurred in the 1960s. Many priests, religious women, and lay leaders began to live with and work with the poor. In the process they became more "conscienticized" about the massiveness of poverty in Latin America, and many became radicalized in their perceptions of the causes of this poverty. The Latin American bishops, meeting at Medellín, Colombia, in 1968, charged that the misery that beset large masses of their people was an "injustice which cries to the heavens." Some of their documents used a new language of "liberation" to address this issue. They spoke theologically of God sending Jesus "that he might come to liberate" all people from the slavery to which sin had subjected them, from hunger, misery, oppression, and ignorance. They pledged the church's support for the downtrodden of every social class. They attacked international imperialism and spoke of Latin America's "dependence" on foreign monopolistic powers.

Gustavo Gutiérrez, a Peruvian diocesan priest, developed the theme of liberation in his groundbreaking work *A Theology of Liberation* (1971, original; English trans., 1973). In his work Gutiérrez argued that dependency on capitalist countries of the North was a primary cause of Latin America's underdevelopment. On theological grounds, he argued that the Bible revealed a God who acted in history to defend and liberate the poor. The Exodus story showed Yahweh liberating the Israelites from oppression in Egypt; the prophets of the OT denounced injustice; Jesus identified with the poor (Mt 25: "I was hungry and you gave me to eat"; Lk 5: "Blessed are the poor for theirs is the kingdom of God"), challenged those who lay burdens on the marginalized, and was crucified as a threat to the prevailing order.

Liberation theology's call for political involvement by the church, but even more especially its appeals to the usefulness of Marxist analysis in addressing Latin America's problems, stirred immediate controversy within the church. The active involvement of many priests and religious in the Christians for Socialism movement—established in 1972 to promote the socialism introduced in Chile by a Marxist president, Salvador Allende—awakened still further controversy. Liberation theologians claimed that Marxist analysis could be separated from Marxist atheism and from advocacy of class hatred, but critics argued that any use of Marxism risked accepting its whole ideology.

Pope Paul VI appointed an international theological commission to study liberation theology and issued his own *Evangelii nuntiandi* (1975) to formulate what he viewed as sound and unsound uses of "liberation." John Paul II, however, brought far greater attention to the issues raised by liberation theology. When he addressed the Latin American bishops meeting in Puebla (Mexico) in 1979, he insisted that "Jesus was not a revolutionary" and that "the church's mission is not political."

John Paul II's encyclical *Laborem exercens* (1981) drew upon ideas from Marx: the primacy of work, work as self-realization, capitalist treatment of workers as mere tools of production, and capital (owners) as causing class conflict. The pope quite clearly, however, rejected Marxism itself: its atheistic, materialist philosophy, its efforts to bring *one* class into power, and most especially its placing of all control over society in the hands of a bureaucratic, one-party elite (LE 14).

In 1984, the Vatican's Congregation for the Defense of the Faith issued *An Instruction on Certain Aspects of the Theology of Liberation.* The instruction, written primarily by Joseph Cardinal Ratzinger but approved by the pope, criticized what it saw as a reduction of the faith to politics on the part of some liberation theologians. It focused sharply also on what it considered the Marxist imprint on liberation theology.

Certain forms of liberation theology, the instruction asserted, accept uncritically the "scientific" claims made in the name of Marxist analysis, failing to undertake any careful critique of the method (*An Instruction,* sec. 7). Liberation theologians are misguided in thinking that Marxist analysis can be separated from the rest of its ideology—from its atheism, materialism, and reliance on violence. "No separation of the parts of this epistemologically unique complex is possible. If one tries to take only one part, say, the analysis, one ends up having to accept the entire ideology" (7.6). Liberation theologians also make Marxist analysis the guiding force of "praxis," which then becomes the sole criterion of truth. "Theological criteria for truth are thus relativized and subordinated to the imperatives of the class struggle" (10.3). Finally, the main praxis called for by Marxism and accepted by liberation theology is one of class struggle, which leads to hatred and violence. Liberation theology accepts the theory of class struggle "as the fundamental law of history" (9.2–3), and the conception of class struggle "goes hand in hand with the affirmation of necessary violence" (8.7–9).

Supporters of liberation theology have questioned these interpretations, noting that the instruction challenges "uncritical" use of Marxism but effectively says that no use of Marxism is justifiable, since its parts are inseparable. Supporters argue that liberation theologians do use Marxist analysis critically, that many social scientists use elements of Marxist analysis without accepting its whole ideology, that praxis (active involvement) is judged "*in the light of* the Word of God," that liberation theology does not advocate violence and hatred and does not view class struggle as "the fundamental law of history." In an effort to offset misunderstanding related to the use of the phrase "class struggle," Gutiérrez rewrote his section dealing with this in the 15th anniversary edition of *A Theology of Liberation.*

In the 1980s writings by liberation theologians made fewer references to Marxist analysis, focused strongly on the "spirituality" of liberation, and stressed politically the new opportunities for mobilizing the poor democratically (with the demise of military rule in many countries). In 1986 John Paul II wrote to the bishops of Brazil that "the theology of liberation is not only opportune but useful and necessary." He also cautioned, however, that the points made in the Vatican instructions of 1984 and 1986 should be observed. In subsequent talks during trips to Latin America, the pope continued to warn about the dangers of introducing "a foreign ideology" (Marxism) into theology and of using conflict as a model for social change.

The future of Marxism itself appeared quite problematic at the outset of the 1990s given the seeming breakdown of Marxist-Leninist rule throughout most of Eastern Europe. What happens to Marxism will obviously greatly affect church responses to Marxism.

See also ATHEISM; CAPITALISM; CLASS STRUGGLE; COMMUNISM; LABOR AND CAPITAL IN CATHOLIC SOCIAL THOUGHT; LABOREM EXERCENS; LIBERATION THEOLOGY; POLITICAL THEOLOGY.

Bibliography: R. Tucker, ed., *The Marx-Engels Reader* 2nd ed. (New York: W. W. Norton, 1978). V. Lenin, *Selected Works, in Three Volumes* (New York: International Publishers, 1967). T. Bottomore et al., eds., *A Dictionary of Marxist Thought* (Cambridge: Harvard Univ. Press, 1983). D. McLellan, *Karl Marx, His Life and Thought* (London: Macmillan, 1973), and other works by this noted Marxian scholar. *Five Great Encyclicals,* including *Rerum novarum, Quadragesimo Anno,* and *Divini Redemptoris* (New York, Paulist, 1949). J. Gremillion, ed., *The Gospel of Peace and Justice,* church teachings from 1961–75 (Maryknoll: Orbis, 1976). Congregation for the Defense of the Faith, *An Instruction on Certain Aspects of the Theology of Liberation* (Vatican City: Libreria Editrice Vaticana, 1984, also published in the *National Catholic Reporter,* September 21, 1984). G. Gutiérrez, *A Theology of Liberation* (Maryknoll: Orbis, 1973; 15th anniversary ed., 1988). A. McGovern, *Marxism: An American Christian Perspective* (Maryknoll: Orbis, 1980). A. McGovern, *Liberation Theology and Its Critics* (Maryknoll: Orbis, 1989).

ARTHUR F. McGOVERN, S.J.

MATER ET MAGISTRA

Dated May 15, 1961, the 70th anniversary of *Rerum novarum, Mater et magistra* was not officially published until July 1961. In it Pope John XXIII offered a "reevaluation of the social question in the light of Christian teaching." Like *Pacem in terris,* the complementary encyclical of two years later, *Mater et magistra* is marked by the paternal, pastoral, and optimistic approach that characterized John's pontificate (see Thiéfry, pp. 898, 909; Campbell-Johnston, pp. 386–87, 410; Dorr, pp. 77–86).

The teaching of *Mater et magistra* has been described as "social humanism" (Thiéfry, p. 1009). John's appreciation of the tradition stemming from *Rerum novarum* began with the influence of Monsignor Radini-Tedeschi on the young Angelo Roncalli between 1905 and the outbreak of the First World War (Hales, p. 13). Heinrich Pesch is credited with developing a humanistic view of the ends of economic activity that found its way into *Quadragesimo anno* and *Mater et magistra* (Campbell-Johnston, p. 381). The extraordinary changes in the world since the Second World War provide the immediate social, economic, and political context of *Mater et magistra.* The local situation in Italian politics is also relevant (Hebblethwaite, p. 361). Important also were the *Semaines Sociales,* particularly that held at Grenoble in July 1960 on the theme "Human Person and Socialization" (Campbell-Johnston, pp. 381, 383; Thiéfry, pp. 906–7). Pietro Pavan is credited with a large share in the drafting of John's encyclicals (Hales, p. 92), but the pope himself pondered long and earnestly over *Mater et magistra* and *Pacem in terris.* Their style and approach is undoubtedly his own and the beliefs they expressed were also his.

This article on *Mater et magistra* follows the fourfold division of the text itself.

Part 1: Context in Papal Social Teaching (1–50)

Mater et magistra defends papal intervention on social, economic, and political questions. As mother (*mater*) as well as teacher (*magistra*), the church is concerned not only for the spiritual well-being of humankind but also for the material needs. Christianity, the "meeting-place of heaven and earth," has as its basic moral norm the twofold command to love God and neighbor. Like Christ, the disciples feel compassion for the people (Mk 8:2) and express it in practical acts of service. The church is concerned with physical hunger as well as with hunger for the "bread of life."

Mater et magistra situates itself within the history of church teaching on social and economic questions that begins with *Rerum novarum* in 1891 and continues through *Quadragesimo anno* in 1931 and the 1941 Pentecost message of Pius XII. Leo XIII's *Magna Charta* of social teaching is highly valued by John. The "dark background" helps to explain Leo's encyclical. The question of morality in economics was uppermost, since the might of the strongest and the laws of the market prevailed. Masses of people were living in ever-increasing hardship without what Leo judged to be the necessary conditions for dignity and serenity in family life. *Rerum novarum* offered "for the first time a complete synthesis of social principles" (15).

Leo's originality lay in extending the realm of human rights into the economic field (Hales, p. 42). For John, Leo proclaimed and defended the legitimate rights of the workers, outlined the basic economic and social principles for the reconstruction of human society, spoke of work as a specifically human activity to be regulated according to justice and equity, defended the natural right to private ownership of property while pointing out the obligation to society intrinsic to that right, and defended the duty of the state to involve itself in economic matters as part of its concern for the common good and to protect the rights of citizens, particularly its weaker members. In defending trade unions founded to safeguard the workers' legitimate professional interests, Leo made a lasting contribution to the development of the "law of labor" (21; Quinn, pp. 287–93).

For John the fundamental principles of *Rerum novarum* were those of human solidarity ("the nature of the human person" and "the needs of human nature") and Christian fraternity ("Christian teaching" and "the principles and spirit of the gospel"). On both of these grounds *Rerum novarum* is critical of unrestricted competition in the liberal sense as well as of the Marxist creed of class warfare.

The teaching of *Rerum novarum* was strengthened and developed by Pius XI. *Quadragesimo anno* reiterated the principles of Leo's encyclical, stressed directives that were still applicable and clarified points—regarding private property, the wage system, and the question of "moderate" socialism—that had caused confusion. The historical scene had altered considerably, which required Pius XI to reformulate Christian social thought in the light of changed conditions. *Quadragesimo anno* saw the remedies for "unbridled ambition for domination" and an economic regime that was "hard, cruel and relentless" in an orderly reconstruction of society. This "order" would include economic and vocational bodies independent of the state, public authority, and international cooperation. Pius XI balanced the principle of intervention by public authority with the principle of subsidiarity. In *Mater et magistra* John XXIII frequently refers to this and applies it, as Pius did, in the socioeconomic field. In *Pacem in terris* John will extend the use of the principle of subsidiarity to the political field, both national and international.

Pius XII issued a statement, *La solennità,* on Whitsunday, 1941, the 50th anniversary of *Rerum novarum.* He asserted the church's competence to decide whether the bases of a social system are in accord with "the unchangeable order which God our creator and redeemer has shown us through the natural law and revelation." In reaffirming the teaching of *Rerum novarum* Pius gave further directive moral principles on the use of material goods, on labor, and on the family (41–45).

John XXIII saw his task as one of maintaining fidelity to this tradition of Catholic social teaching while making further applications of its principles in the light of the changes that had taken place between the end of World War II and the beginning of the 1960s. The previous twenty years had seen more changes than the fifty years before that, changes that *Mater et magistra* summarizes as "a radical transformation in the internal structure of States and in their relations with one another" (46). There follows John's "social analysis" of the social, economic, and political world in which *Mater et magistra* appeared.

In *science, technology, and economics* new realities included nuclear energy, synthetic materials, automation, the modernization of agriculture, space travel, and extraordinary developments in communications and transport.

In the *social field* new realities included social insurance and social security, "more responsible trade unionists," improvements in education, a wider distribution of essential commodities, greater opportunities for advancement, a breaking down of class barriers, and a keener interest on the part of more individuals in world affairs. In noting outstanding discrepancies *Mater et magistra* announces the issues that dominate its own concern: a progressive lack of balance between agriculture on the one hand and industry and public services on the other; varying economic prosperity within the one political community; disparity in wealth possessed by different countries.

In the *political field* also the postwar years had seen radical changes. More citizens had become involved in politics, public authorities were involved more than ever in social and economic matters, colonialism was coming to an end in Asia and Africa, the nations of the world were more interdependent, and a network of international societies and organizations was well established.

All commentators sense a new tone in *Mater et magistra,* a feeling of optimism and a welcome for what is good. Many passages are engaging, encouraging, cordial, and affectionate (85ff., 156, 148ff., 160, 182, 184, 236f.). The encyclical does not emphasize what is wrong, although John expresses strong negative feelings and viewpoints also (68ff., 176, 253, 260). Dorr writes: "From the point of view of their formal teaching the social encyclicals of John XXIII show no very radical departure from the tradition of social teaching of his predecessors. But there are subtle differences in tone and emphasis which give these encyclicals a different effect when seen as interventions by the pope at this particular time" (p. 90). But for others there is more than a new mood or tone. John is not just commemorating, he is innovating (Hales, p. 45).

Part 2: Explaining and Developing (51–121)

In the tradition of Christian humanism, *Mater et magistra* is concerned for every aspect of the human person. John's intention in this encyclical has been described as "the humanization of social and economic institutions so that all may lead a fuller and more personal life as a help to a more moral and holier one" (Quinn, p. 272). This concern gives unity to the encyclical's teachings. It underpins John's preoccupations: freedom and initiative, eliminating inequalities between individuals and groups, and cooperation (on this last point see Dorr, p. 80).

Socialization (51–67)

There is nothing new in John's point that the primary place in the economic order be given to "the personal initiative of private citizens" either as individuals or in association. But *Mater et magistra* accepts the involvement of the civil power if social progress and the well-being of all citizens are to be achieved. Scientific and technological progress require the acceptance of increased public involvement in the economic sphere.

Although the Latin text of *Mater et magistra* does not use the word "socialization," official translations did. For many commentators the radical newness of *Mater et magistra* and its distinctive contribution to the development of Catholic social teaching lies in John's acceptance of what he calls the "increase in social relationships" (59), which is both sign and cause of the growing intervention of the state (Campbell-Johnston, pp. 382–87). It is natural for people to combine with their fellows. The conviction that the human being is a person and therefore "social," has been identified by Pietro Pavan as the basic principle of all papal social teaching (*New Catholic Encyclopedia* 13:360; see also Campbell-Johnston, pp. 395–400; *Gaudium et spes* 23–32; and the writings of Jacques Maritain).

There are many advantages in this process of socialization, says *Mater et magistra.* It facilitates the achievement of economic and social rights: work, health, education, housing, leisure. There are disadvantages, too, in that it can easily lead to a narrowing of the sphere of a person's freedom of action. For John "socialization" refers not just to the "welfare state" but to a broad social and cultural change that must balance the initiative and choices of free people with the "laws" of economic and social progress. The thing to do, he says, is to realize this progress toward the advantages it brings and away from the disadvantages. The full development of the human personality, true community, and right order all flow from governments balancing the free and active collaboration of individuals and groups with timely state intervention. In this way the individual person will be respected and society will achieve the "organic reconstruction" for which Pius XI called.

"Socialization in itself is neither good nor evil" (Campbell-Johnston, p. 384; Dorr, p. 93), but greater moral maturity is necessary for its proper progress. A healthy vision of the common good will be required in those with public authority. The negative things John mentions are not reasons for questioning modern development itself but arguments for control and balance (Dorr, p. 81).

The notion of "subsidiary function" spoken of by Pius XI remains a central principle. It is unjust, evil, and upsets right order when higher associations arrogate functions that can be performed efficiently by lower ones (53, citing QA 79). State involvement must not deprive individual citizens or intermediate associations of their freedom of action. Rather must it promote that freedom by protecting essential personal rights. If personal initiative is lacking, political tyranny and economic stagnation ensue. The human being is no longer truly respected as the "subject" of economic and social life. One might ask whether John has not been proved prophetic by the events that led to the collapse of East European style communism. If the good offices of the state are lacking, then "incurable disorder" ensues, namely the exploitation of the weak by the strong. This last is a major reason for the church's critique of Western liberal capitalism.

Pius XII warned against the Leviathan of "socialization" (*Sozialisierung*), and John XXIII acknowledges the point of this warning. He is anxious to stress the safeguards he sees against this eventuality and to distinguish his understanding of socialization from that condemned by his predecessors. In fact, the implied sociology of *Mater et magistra* is so "socialistic" that not only Leo but Pius XI or Pius XII would have been astonished by the claims that John was making (Hales, p. 43), "giving to the State functions which Pius (XI) would never have dreamed of giving it and recognizing personal claims of the individual upon the community which would not have occurred to him" (Hales, p. 45; Dorr, pp. 95–96).

The Just Wage (68–81)

John echoes the feelings of Leo XIII when he speaks of his overwhelming sadness at millions of workers living in subhuman conditions. In "violent and offensive contrast" is the wealth, luxury, and privilege enjoyed by a few. Justice and equity have been sacrificed to increased profit, "ill-conceived national prestige," and the arms race (69). Can it be right that less important services are better remunerated than harder work, out of proportion to the contribution such workers make to the good of the community, to profits, and to the national economy generally? Remuneration must not be left to the laws of the market to be arbitrarily fixed. Echoing his predecessors, John says that a wage that is in accordance with justice and equity is one that allows a worker to live a truly human life (Leo XIII) and to fulfill his family obligations in a worthy manner (Pius XI). Other relevant factors are the economic contribution of the worker (a new criterion), the state of the company and the requirements of the national good (two criteria introduced in QA), and the common good of the universal family of nations (another new criterion with MM). These are principles that must be observed always and everywhere, although their application is variable depending on the quality and quantity of available resources.

Justice and equity will be met, John believes, if economic progress is always accompanied by a proportionate social progress (73). For Pius XII, the true goal of a nation's economy is the personal development of the members of society. John shares this vision. Thus the expansion of a company should mean not only the return of profits into the business to make it even more profitable but also some participation of the workers in that economic success. What might seem quite a radical proposal—that workers gradually come to share in the ownership of their company—is to be found already in the writings of Pius XI: neither capital nor labor can claim all the profits that accrue to the exclusion of the other (Thiéfry, pp. 1017–21).

The Structure of Industry (82–103)

The question of work is not simply an economic one, a point already stressed in *Mater et magistra* (18, 71). Human persons have a natural need to express themselves in work and to perfect their own being. An economic system that removes human dignity, responsibility, and initiative is by that very fact unjust. Pius XII, keen to make positive suggestions about a just economic system, spoke of cooperatives of smaller businesses and partnerships in larger ones. *Mater et magistra* develops his suggestions at some length.

The work and lifestyle of the family farm, of artisans, and of cooperative enterprises must all be safeguarded and encouraged. The latter two must be ready to adapt their equipment and methods to meet new situations. Proper training and professional organization will help them to do this. Echoing the views of earlier social movements of artists and artisans and perhaps anticipating the "small is beautiful" movement of twenty years later, John reckons that the state, by protecting artisans and cooperative associations, is "upholding true human values and contributing to the advance of civilization" (89). This kind of occupation keeps alive a sense of responsibility, a spirit of cooperation, and a desire to continue the production of work that is new, original, and of outstanding merit. The human subject is not then swallowed up by an overreaching state machine. Active participation at the level of structures and institutions, another recurring theme in *Mater et magistra,* protects the freedom of the humblest persons in an increasingly complex society.

As regards larger enterprises, John says that the wish for "worker participation" in such businesses is justified. It is not possible to lay down hard-and-fast rules for every situation, but there is no doubt about the need to give workers a say in running the business for which they work. Both natural justice and modern conditions require it. A company should be "a true community of persons." Because of their greater responsibility the education of workers and of young people is vital. Through trade unions workers should exert their influence throughout the state and not just within their own spheres of employment. This is because any single enterprise is simply a part within a whole. There is mutual dependence within a nation's entire economic and social life, making cooperation between all individuals and groups more urgent than ever (Quinn, pp. 278–82). National and international authorities and institutions should represent workers also. On the structural evolution of national economies John preserves the teaching of Pius XI and Pius XII while remaining silent on the technicalities of such evolution, either for irenic reasons or to leave more freedom for the ways in which things might develop (Thiéfry, pp. 909–10; Quinn pp. 282, 287–93).

Mater et magistra expresses its admiration for guilds and unions, especially Christian ones, and (characteristic of John) encourages cooperation with non-Christian groups so long as they respect natural law and freedom of conscience. John adds another distinctive touch by explicitly expressing his admiration for the International Labor Organization.

Private Property (104–21)

John's arguments for private property are based on its benefits to the individual, the family, and society. "The right of private ownership of goods, including productive goods, has a permanent validity" (109). It belongs to the natural order that the individual is prior to society and society is ordered to the good of the individual; this is required for initiative. Other freedoms are suppressed where the freedom to own is suppressed; therefore, the "exercise of freedom finds its guarantee and incentive in the right of ownership" (109). We have noted already that freedom is a basic preoccupation of *Mater et magistra.*

For Pius XII the "essential freedom of the individual" depends on the right to private ownership of goods. John argues that social and political movements that previously had rejected this right were now coming to acknowledge its importance. Pius argued that human dignity requires the right to private ownership, which arises from "the moral dignity of work." *Mater et magistra* wants this right extended to all classes of citizens with a more widespread distribution of property, something that is, John says, not difficult to achieve (115). He is perhaps uncritical in his optimism about the inevitable benefits of pursuing a free-enterprise system (Dorr, pp. 83–86).

Public and state ownership is not unlawful and is even expected for some productive goods. The growth in public ownership is accepted by *Mater et magistra* as required by the exigencies of the common good, the principle of subsidiarity being sufficient to set due limits to state ownership.

Traditional too is the encyclical's insistence on the social function of private ownership, a function that John says is inherent in that right. The understanding of the human being as the steward of God's providence is to be found in *Rerum novarum.* It is a patristic and biblical teaching. State involvement does not replace this social function of private ownership; it *is* an inherent function. There is still room for charitable support (Mt 6:19-21; 25:40). Individuals and groups are more effective in promoting spiritual values than public authority. Although *Mater et magistra* breaks new ground in speaking of the *intrinsic* social function of private property, in developing the point John speaks of charity, whereas Pius XI offered a structural answer (QA 45–51; Thiéfry, pp. 906–7; Dorr, p. 78).

Part 3: New Questions of the Day (122–211)

Already Pope John has gone beyond his predecessors. What is revolutionary is (1) the welcoming of the much wider role played by the modern state and (2) an enormous enlargement of the traditional papal picture of the natural rights of the individual (Hales, p. 46). Part 3 concerns itself with "new aspects" of the social question.

Agriculture (123–49)

A matter dear to the heart of John XXIII is the fate of rural life in the modern world. Movement from the land is a "complex problem" not explained by economic expansion alone. Urban life offers comfort, novelty and adventure, easy money, greater freedom, and many amenities. By contrast farming has become "a depressed occupation."

In writing about rural life John raises practical issues and gives specific directives. Essential facilities must be developed in country areas, and a becoming standard of living must be made possible there. Agricultural production and business must be reformed. A sound agricultural policy will include a just method of taxation that acknowledges the peculiar difficulties of farmers, credit facilities, and insurance schemes, as well as social insurance and security to reduce discrepancies in the standard of living. Prices should be protected in view of the fact that price rewards labor and is not simply a return on invested capital—a point already noted in *Quadragesimo anno.* While all should be in a position to afford the agricultural products that serve primary human needs, this is no reason for keeping farmers in permanent inferiority. The industries ancillary to agriculture should be developed and other industries established in rural areas.

Although there is a variety of rural situations throughout the world, the ideal model is "a community of persons working together," above all, the family farm (142). Who can doubt the influence on John XXIII in these pages of Sotto il Monte and his personal experience of rural Italy? Still, John is not romantic about rural life. He envisages a progressive modernization of agriculture that will retain the values of working close to the earth. Farmers, too, should be organized into associations that express their solidarity and give them a say in questions that affect their lives. But farming remains a calling that is noble, conferring dignity on those who practice it and surrounding people with allusions to God the Creator and Provider. Patience, perseverance, and responsibility are required as well as a capacity for adaptation in view of scientific and technical progress. Farming is an answer to God's call to realize the providential, saving plan in history.

Associations of farmers must be guided by moral principles and respect for the common good. John expresses his satisfaction with all involved in cooperatives, professional groups, and worker movements that work on behalf of the agricultural community. "These pages of MM are unique in the whole corpus of papal social teaching. Never have the needs of a particular branch of the economy been so seriously the concern of a papal encyclical" (Hales, p. 51).

Inequality Within Political Communities (150–56)

Social and economic policies must be directed toward reducing and eliminating inequality among citizens of the same political community. The common good and the interests of the state as a whole require even and simultaneous development of the different sectors of the economy. This development must be gradual and harmonious. Besides the work of public authorities there is a role for individuals and for private enterprise. The principle of subsidiarity must, once again, be respected. In this way disproportions can be adjusted. The elimination of such discrepancies is demanded by human solidarity and by Christian fellowship. The international dimension of this question must be recognized, and the pope has a special word for the Food and Agriculture Organization.

Hales comments: "no pope, in the whole of papal history, has ever made so many specific and practical suggestions in the realm of social organization as Pope John made in MM and PT" (Hales, pp. xi–xii; Thiéfry, p. 903). In spite of this, *Mater et magistra* is largely silent on fundamental issues like agrarian reform, nationalization of industries, and public health care, although it accepts in a general way the process of socialization. There is no reference in *Mater et magistra* to women as a group suffering particular injustices. Two years later in *Pacem in terris* John does have something new to say on the position of women (PT 41). But *Mater et magistra* is the least polemical of documents, there being no formal condemnation of those "isms" that were the *bêtes noires* of earlier papacies. *Mater et magistra* expresses the church's concern to be involved without trying to do people's jobs for them or prevent free research on still unsolved problems.

Inequalities Between Nations (157–84)

Mater et magistra is the first encyclical to address itself to the issues of international relations and development. It therefore opens a new chapter in the church's social teaching, linking the issues of development and peace in a way that will be repeated in John's later encyclical *Pacem in terris.* This notion finds its first comprehensive treatment in *Populorum progressio.* John XXIII is concerned with the countries of "the Third World," whereas Pius XII was preoccupied in the second half of his papacy with the countries behind "the iron curtain." John was "more concerned to correct the errors of the West than to blame the errors of the East" (Hales, p. 131), his social teaching being "not so much an opening to the left as a decisive move away from the right" (Dorr, p. 103).

The relationship between political communities that are economically advanced and those in process of development is, says John, the most difficult problem today. Human solidarity makes it impossible to be indifferent to the lack of elementary human rights. Growing dependence of nations means that the preservation of peace will be impossible if glaring inequalities persist. John appeals to the humanity shared by all and to the specifically Christian notion of the mystical body of Christ, which is poor and unfortunate in those who are poor and unfortunate (1 Jn 3:16-17). There is an obligation on all who are well off to help those who are not, and it is "an outrage to justice and humanity to destroy or to squander goods" that others need (161). Emergency aid is essential, but a permanent remedy must also be sought (163). He fails to mention, however, that Western prosperity is itself dependent on cheap labor and the raw materials that serve to keep the Third World in its poorer condition (Dorr, p. 85).

Mater et magistra warns underdeveloped countries to consider the experience of wealthier nations. Productive efficiency is vital, but so too is fair distribution. Social progress must keep pace with economic progress. The individuality of nations must be respected and developed. There is a danger of ulterior motives in aid and of "a new form of colonialism" that would be a menace to world peace (171–72). Necessity and justice demand "political disinterestedness" in aid (173). The promotion of development in this spirit will be a precious contribution to the formation of a world community (174). Developed countries can be indifferent to what *Mater et magistra* calls the "hierarchy of values," with material well-being predominating in people's concerns, whereas economically less developed countries often preserve an awareness of more important human values.

What John does here is to apply the principle of subsidiarity to the new issue of development. The church's concern with development follows from its universality. It affirms the unity and difference among nations. It brings economic and social advantages, improved institutions and environment, and promotes human dignity, honesty, and virtue. Becoming the "lifeblood" of people, the church does not regard itself as a foreign body but as the source of rebirth, resurrection, and freedom in the very depth of human being, affirming and developing what is noblest and best in people. *Mater et magistra* is happy to see Catholics involved in development work and to see the developed nations providing education to African and Asian students as well as sending missionaries and development workers to those parts of the world.

Population Growth and Economic Development (185–99)

The continual rise in population seems to be "a world problem," with a feared shortage of the necessities of life. This is especially so in underdeveloped countries where the standard of living seems set to worsen unless the birth of humans be curbed in some way. John XXIII is reluctant to accept that the problem is as real as this stark diagnosis would have it. There is no "immediate or imminent world problem," he says (188). Resources are "well nigh inexhaustible," and human intelligence is gifted to exploit these resources. The real solution lies not in "expedients which offend against the divinely established moral order and which attack human life at its very source" but in renewed scientific and technical effort (189).

There is a real problem in the poorer nations, but this is due to more fundamental factors, namely, deficient economic and social organization and the lack of effective solidarity. No solution or statement of the problem is acceptable that "does violence to the human being's essential dignity" and is "based on an utterly materialistic conception of the human person and his/her life." A true solution will respect human dignity generally, the worth of each individual human life, and the need for worldwide cooperation. Education in cultural and religious values, a sense of responsibility, confidence in Divine Providence, and a determination to accept the sacrifices involved in rearing children—all of these make up the solution to this question (195). Genesis (1:28) includes two complementary commandments: "increase and multiply" and "fill the earth and subdue it." The latter does not legitimize the destruction of nature but its use for the service of human life. There is, says John, a contradiction in modern thinking, between the "fearful specter of want and misery" and the way in which scientific, technical, and economic resources "are being used to provide terrible instruments of ruin and death."

John thus links decisively the questions of population, economic development, and the arms race. A provident God has given the means for a dignified solution to the question of population growth. If the human being turns instead to means that are opposed to right reason, his social nature, and the intentions of Providence, then the problem will remain difficult and even insoluble. (See Hales, pp. 78–79 and Thiéfry, pp. 1028–29, both of whom feel that MM does not seriously tackle this issue as a real world problem.)

The International Order (200–211)

John is happy to add a level of "world authority" to Leo XIII's hierarchy of individual, family, association, and state. His enthusiasm for one world community is complemented and perhaps anticipated by the critique of nationalism in the writings of Pius XI and Pius XII, the latter considering "the denial of the unity and solidarity of the human race as one of the major heresies of modern times" (NCE 13:354; see PP II.2).

Nations are more than ever dependent on one another. Many are convinced that international understanding and cooperation are vitally necessary but unsure as to how it is to be achieved. Lack of mutual trust gives rise to "mortal fear" and has as a consequence the buildup of arms for defense and deterrence. This commits a vast expenditure of human energy and natural resources on projects disruptive of human society rather than beneficial to it. Ideological differences are the root cause of this mistrust, John argues (205). If the moral order is denied then there can be no one law of justice and no agreement between peoples. All will speak of justice but understand different things by it. Appeals to "justice" can serve sometimes to increase rather than to decrease tensions, making it seem that violence is the only way to achieve justice.

The moral order must be recognized and respected. The spirituality of the human person—his or her capacity for thought and freedom—demands a moral and religious order. There can be no "civilization" without God. Spiritual and moral values are vital if scientific and technical progress is to be used in the service of civilization rather than involving the whole race in irremediable disaster. There are signs of hope in people's dissatisfaction with worldly goods, in greater consciousness of human rights, in aspirations to more just and more human relations, in awareness of limitations, and in a striving for spiritual values.

Part 4: Toward a New Social Order (212–64)

A theory of society must take account of the whole person as well as of human weaknesses. A fundamental modern error is to dismiss religion as a feeling or a fantasy, as an anachronism and an obstacle to progress. But the sense of religion is deeply rooted, revealing the human person for what he or she is: created by God and tending toward God. Apart from God, the source of justice, truth, and love, the human being is a monster. *Mater et magistra* refers to the persecution of Christian believers and calls on all who see clearly to return to their senses. Human greatness is from God, and on God alone will the temporal order endure.

The church's social teaching has a permanent validity because its basic principle—that the individual human being is the foundation, cause, and end of every social institution—is raised to an order of reality that is above nature and that therefore enjoys a "sacred dignity." This social teaching is of universal application because there is a common human nature, and it must take account of varying conditions. Natural law places in the hands of the church the key to a truly human social order. Addressing himself beyond the church, John calls on people of goodwill everywhere to spread this doctrine and put it into effect.

The church's social teaching is an integral part of the Christian view of life. It should be studied in seminaries and parishes and especially in lay associations. In stressing the role of the laity, *Mater et magistra* develops a line of thought that originates in *Quadragesimo anno.* It is essential to show that the church's social teaching does provide solutions to present-day difficulties. Besides formal instruction there must be experimental knowledge and positive action. Learning by practice follows the Christian workers triad of *see, judge, act.* There may be differences of opinion about particular applications, but there can still be respect and esteem. What is important, says John, is to find the points of agreement and to do the good rather than arguing over the best.

While harnessing nature the human being is in danger of forgetting and of destroying himself says Pius XI in *Quadragesimo anno.* A giant of the physical world, the human being is a pygmy in the supernatural and eternal world, says Pius XII. Material progress and well-being are good things but are only instruments for the attainment of the human person's end. What does it profit to gain the world and lose one's soul (Mt 16:26)? The observance of Sunday as a day of rest safeguards the dignity of the human being as creature of God and image of God, answering a need that is religious, moral, and physical.

A life of activity in the world can be harmonized with spiritual perfection, and it would be a gross error to think otherwise. The challenge is to humanize and Christianize modern civilization, thereby serving humanity in union with God to God's greater glory (1 Cor 10:31; Col 3:17). To seek spiritual perfection and eternal salvation, far from being a distraction from involvement in the world, actually enhances the power of human affairs and of institutions to reach their immediate and more specific ends (Mt 6:33). The person of light will have a sure grasp of the fundamentals of justice in life's difficulties (Eph 5:8). Loving Christ, such a person will love all fellow human beings with a sureness of touch (1 Cor 13:4-7). In these paragraphs John XXIII anticipates the pastoral constitution *Gaudium et spes* on the twofold end of human life and activity: temporal and eternal (Campbell-Johnston, p. 380; Dorr, p. 79).

Christian people share in the divine life and their work has redemptive power, leavening this civilization with the ferment of the gospel. Our time, concludes *Mater et magistra,* one of deadly errors and deep disorders, is also one of immense possibilities and great hope. Cooperation in the tasks outlined by *Mater et magistra* will bring about a realization of Christ's kingdom in this world. As mother and teacher of all nations, the Church illumines, enkindles, and inflames, it warns and spreads its wisdom. John concludes with a prayer for prosperity, happiness, and peace.

Conclusion

There were many issues on which *Mater et magistra,* because of its pastoral character, did not speak (Thiéfry, pp. 907–8). John was careful about using terms that cover diverse and changing realities. Described as "post-Marxist" (Thiéfry, p. 911), the encyclical goes beyond polemics and is positive, constructive, and pastorally receptive in relation to new social phenomena. John XXIII was not blind to real and unresolved problems, but he preferred to highlight the advantages and benefits flowing from new social realities. Concentrating on the question of *what* needs to be done, he is not always specific about *how* it is to be done. His natural optimism assured him that it could and would be done. Later religious leaders, including John Paul II, have been far more cautious about the "inevitable" improvements that democratic capitalist society can bring (Dorr, pp. 81–86, 89). Nevertheless *Mater et magistra* is "a turning-point in Catholic social teaching," witnessing to development within that teaching and redefining the "natural allies" of the church on social and political issues (Dorr, pp. 103–4).

Pope John frequently referred to *Mater et magistra* in subsequent public statements. The preconciliar schemas for Vatican II as well as its first session ignored *Mater et magistra* (as well as RN and QA). John issued a stronger challenge in *Pacem in terris,* and both *Mater et magistra* and *Pacem in terris* were influential in important sections of the Pastoral Constitution on the Church in the Modern World (GS, pt. 1, chap. 2; pt. 2, chaps. 3–5). Paul VI recognized the contribution of *Mater et magistra* as diagnosing clearly for the first time the worldwide dimensions of the social question (PP 3). Subsequent papal documents echo this point, note *Mater et magistra*'s historical significance, and refer to other teachings found in it: *Populorum progressio* 28, 33, 46; *Octogesima adveniens* 5, 46, 47; *Sollicitudo rei socialis* 1, 9, 42.

See also AGRICULTURE; COLONIALISM; DEVELOPMENT; JOHN XXIII; JUST WAGE; PACEM IN TERRIS; SOCIALIZATION; SUBSIDIARITY, PRINCIPLE OF.

Bibliography: *Text:* AAS 53 (1961) 401–64.

English translations: London: CTS. (1963) J. Gremillion, ed., *The Gospel of Peace and Justice: Catholic So-*

cial Teaching Since Pope John (Maryknoll, N.Y.: Orbis, 1976) pp. 141–200.

Studies: R. Camp, *The Papal Ideology of Social Reform* (Leiden: Brill, 1969). M. Campbell-Johnston, "The Social Teaching of the Church," *Thought* (Autumn 1964) 380–410. D. Dorr, "Pope John XXIII—A New Direction?" in Curran and McCormick, *Readings in Moral Theology No 5: Official Catholic Social Teaching* (New York: Paulist, 1986) pp. 77–109. E. Hales, *Pope John and His Revolution* (London: Eyre and Spottiswoode, 1965). P. Hebblethwaite, *John XXIII: Pope of the Council* (London: Geoffrey Chapman, 1984). *New Catholic Encyclopedia* 9:441; 13:352–61. K. Quinn, "Trade Unions in 'Mater et Magistra,'" *Gregorianum* 43 (1962) 268–94. M. Thiéfry, "L'Encyclique 'Mater et Magistra': ses caractères, synthèse de ses enseignements,'" *Nouvelle Revue Theologique* 83 (1961) 897–913, 1009–33.

VIVIAN BOLAND, O.P.

MEDELLÍN

From August 26 until September 9 of 1968 the bishops of Latin America met in a conference held in Medellín, Colombia. In the course of their fifteen-day meeting they reflected on the situation of the church in their continent and wrote a series of texts, often called the Medellín Documents. For many people, however, the word Medellín implies more than a two-week meeting or a set of documents. It refers to a process of change that affected both the church and society in Latin America and ultimately the church as a whole. At Medellín the bishops of Latin America took a hard and critical look at the churches they represented and the societies in which they lived and decided that deep-seated change was necessary in both. A religious institution once characterized by theological conservatism and cultural traditionalism began to remake itself as an agent of evangelical justice and social change. This process of transformation is still going on. To really understand the revolutionary significance of Medellín, however, it is necessary to review briefly the history of the Catholic church in Latin America.

Catholicism came to Latin America in 1492 as an integral part of the Spanish and Portuguese conquest of the Western Hemisphere. The Catholicism the European invaders brought with them was marked by centuries of prior struggle with the Moors for control of the Iberian peninsula. When the Christians finally expelled the last bastion of Muslim influence from Spain under Ferdinand and Isabella, tellingly referred to in Spanish as *Los Reyes Católicos* (the Catholic monarchs), they were convinced that their triumph over Islam was a reward for their fervent faith. The Catholicism of the Spanish and Portuguese, then, was central to their self-understanding as a people as well as a proud symbol of victory.

It was this triumphal Catholicism that Columbus and the later *conquistadores* would import to Latin America. Largely untouched by the Reformation, Spanish and Portuguese missionaries set about evangelizing an entire hemisphere in the early 16th century. They worked in close conjunction with their respective monarchies. The result was a symbiotic relationship between the "cross and crown." The church expected the state to support its efforts at evangelization, while the state expected the church to legitimate its political agenda in the Americas. Consequently, the often ruthless exploitation of indigenous peoples in the Americas by the Spanish and Portuguese monarchies was only occasionally challenged by the institutional church, although a few noble exceptions stand out, especially that of the 16th-century Dominican theologian and bishop, Bartolomé de las Casas.

Both church and state in Latin America were extremely hierarchical and conservative. Until the Spanish colonies gained their independence in the early 19th century as autonomous republics, high colonial officials were always imported from Spain and Portugal. Likewise, bishops came from Europe, not the Americas. Both political and ecclesiastical leaders saw their primary task as defending the interests of the crown and the Catholic church. The institutional church consequently identified itself with the interests of wealthy European and Creole social elements. This later group was made up of the pure-blooded children of peninsular Spanish and Portuguese colonists born in the Americas. Although there were large numbers of indigenous peoples in many parts of Latin America as well as a growing black population because of the Spanish and Portuguese slave trade, the official church was far removed from the lives of these later peoples, most of whom were powerless and oppressed.

The position of the church as the dominant ideological and religious force in Latin America was only nominally affected by the emergence of independent republics in the early 19th century. Native-born oligarchs merely replaced Spanish and Portuguese colonials. This newly ascendent class of exporters and landowners recognized its need for the institutional church, whose symbols and rituals were a useful common currency in economically and racially divided societies. Catholicism was something both the wealthy and poor shared in common, although their respective understandings of Catholicism were distinct. Many of the new republics recognized Catholicism as the state religion. This concession allowed the state to influence ecclesiastical policy when necessary, especially in the appointment of bishops. Thus from the early part of the 19th century until the latter half of the 20th century, the Catholic church in Latin America acted as a conservative force that was identified in the minds of most people as a staunch defender of the established order.

The position of the church in Latin America began to shift in the 1950s as many countries underwent economic and social change. Encouraged by international banks and advisors from developed countries, members of national oligarchies attempted to move their countries beyond the exclusive export of natural resources and agricultural products, the two traditional sources of income for most Latin American countries. They wanted to create industrial economies that could supply both domestic needs and find a place on the world market. The export of raw material would continue, but this income would be augmented by manufacturing products for export as cheaply as possible. To do so required a large pool of laborers willing to work for minimal wages. Attracted by the possibility of a new life, large numbers of peasants migrated to cities like Lima, Santiago, and Sao Paolo, transforming quaint colonial towns into sprawling cities in a matter of a few years. Urban growth was prodigious, along with the proliferation of slums, increased economic disparity, and political tension. As economic plans faltered in the 1950s and 1960s, the stage was set for political conflict that manifested itself in calls for radical social change. For many of the poor it was obvious that the prevailing social order was unjust and exploitative. Those in power reacted to these challenges with repression as they desperately tried to hold on to their traditional privileges. The church thus found itself in the unenviable position of being the religious mainstay of a dysfunctional and unjust social system. It was obvious that the institutional church had to change its social orientation or risk becoming an oppressive anachronism. But charting a course of action was difficult given its traditional social role.

The church found a way out of its dilemma from an unexpected source—the Second Vatican Council. Documents like *Lumen gentium* and *Gaudium et spes* spoke of the Christian's obligation to create a more just and humane world. Although such an option had always been open to Catholics theoretically, the conservative political sensibilities of many members of the hierarchy made it difficult for Catholics in Latin America to associate with progressive social movements without evoking the ire of the institutional church. Vatican II changed this state of affairs by redefining secular history as a crucial forum in which human beings are called to collaborate in God's creative plan. For Catholics in Latin America who were anxious to address the acute ills around them, Vatican II came as a harbinger of good news. Progressive members of the episcopal hierarchy and ordinary laypeople were provided with the catalyst they needed to inject themselves into the social and political debates taking place in their nations.

When the bishops gathered in Medellín in 1968 their primary objective was to implement the insights of Vatican II in their continent. They differed in their respective interpretations of the council, but most of the bishops welcomed its message. It is not an accident that they entitled the Medellín Documents *The Church in the Present-Day Transformation of Latin America in the Light of the Council.* The conference was opened by Pope Paul VI, the first pope to visit Latin America. He urged the bishops to implement the Second Vatican Council in real and efficacious ways and to reassert the church's moral authority throughout the continent. Yet in many ways Medellín went far beyond Vatican II. Rather than producing somewhat abstract documents like those of the council, the Latin American bishops wrote highly analytical documents that focused not only on the church in Latin America but also on the overall socioeconomic situation of their continent.

What the bishops produced was a set of texts whose poignancy and passion surprised their very authors. Some of the assembled bishops began to advocate innovative theological and social ideas that marked a radical break with their traditional role as the religious guardians of the status quo. They recognized that the church had to say and do something about the growing poverty and oppression of the majority of Latin Americans. They were surrounded by a social and economic situation that, in their own words, "cries to heaven for justice."

The Medellín Documents are theological texts, not social scientific studies, but the theology of the bishops is written in the light of their actual context. They discuss the concrete challenges that confront Christians living in societies marred by oppression and violence. Following the insights of Vatican II, the bishops presume that theology flows from the Christian's immersion in the world, not from a concern with mere ideas. What the bishops at Medellín called for was a vigorous expression of faith made credible by Christian action on behalf of a new social order. They were aided in this task by a new generation of Latin American theologians such as Gustavo Gutiérrez and Juan Luis Segundo who, in their respective ways, had begun to shape an innovative theological agenda for the Latin American church. Their ideas captured the imagination of many bishops at Medellín, who incorporated them into the texts of the conference.

In the prologue of the Medellín Documents the bishops describe Latin America as a continent caught up in a process of profound social transformation. Rather than questioning the legitimacy of this state of affairs, they assert its necessity. They recognize that the aspirations of people for social change and real justice are manifestations of God's spirit acting in history. Furthermore, they call on Christians to take a prominent place in the remaking of their continent, along with other people of goodwill, even nonbelievers. This was a significant shift from past policy when the institutional church set up parallel social agencies and Catholic political parties in many Latin American countries. These specifically Catholic entities were generally conservative and wary of allying themselves with non-Christian social movements. In the Medellín Documents, however, the bishops ask Christians to put aside factionalism and unite with all people of goodwill in order to overcome the injustices around them. The bishops also make it clear that the church has no monopoly on solutions. They call for a pluralistic, open search for a qualitatively different social system.

Perhaps the most incisive discussion in the Medellín Documents is the section entitled "The Latin American Situation and Peace." The bishops unreservedly denounce "the extreme inequality among social classes" that divides Latin America into "haves" and "have-nots." At the same time, they speak of a continent afflicted with violent frustration as the "have-nots" constantly see their aspirations for economic justice and political recognition ignored by social elites. As the bishops point out, a small but powerful social class has consciously excluded the majority of people in Latin America from exercising real control over their lives. This has led, in the bishops' words, to "a lamentable insensitivity of the privileged sectors to the misery of the marginated sectors." As the bishops indicate, to advocate social change or economic justice in many Latin American countries is to run the risk of detention, torture, and death at the hands of repressive forces. Tragically, the violence of the rich leads some of the oppressed to a type of counterviolence. The result is a spiral of hostility that sometimes draws whole societies into a morass of conflict. Searching for a way out of such conflictual situations, the bishops propose the creation of societies in which every person's dignity and political rights are respected regardless of class, race, or gender. Quoting Pope Paul VI, they call for countries united by "the strong and peaceful energy of constructive works" rather than nations beset with factionalism and political strife.

In a section of the Medellín Documents entitled "Document on the Poverty of the Church: Latin America Scene" the bishops made one of the most important statements of the conference. They clearly indicate that the church must ally itself with the poor. It must opt to stand with them and act as their advocate. They understand that such a position is risky and unprecedented, but opting to be one with the poor is the only way that the church can function as a credible evangelical force in the midst of poverty and oppression. The bishops, therefore, speak of the need to reform church institutions and redirect the energy of the Christian community in ways that benefit the poor. They speak of the need to understand and challenge the existing sources of injustice while proposing intelligent, feasible action that can lead to a new social order. In their own words: "We ought to sharpen the awareness of our duty of solidarity with the poor, to which charity leads us. This solidarity means that we make ours their problems and their struggles, that we know how to speak with them. This has to be concretized in criticism of injustice and oppression, in the struggle against the intolerable situation that the poor person often has to tolerate, in the willingness to dialogue with the groups responsible for that situation in order to make them understand their obligations" ("Document on the Poverty of the Church" 10). Given the colonial history of the church in Latin America, such a statement indicates a profound change of attitude and policy.

The bishops who wrote the Medellín Documents effectively redefined the church in their continent and set in motion historical events that they could not totally foresee. In the immediate post-Medellín period a sense of euphoria and optimism prevailed in the Latin American church. Many Christians, both clergy and laity, became deeply involved in various efforts to reshape their societies. Such involvement, however, led to a reaction from more conservative sectors of society and the church. Some members of the upper classes, convinced that the church had been infiltrated by Marxists and furious at what they perceived to be the treason of an old ally, lashed out at progressive elements in the church. From the late 1960s to the present, Latin American Christians have experienced something unprecedented in their continent—persecution and martyrdom for their beliefs. During the 1970s and 1980s when many Latin American countries were controlled by right-wing military dictatorships, many Christians were singled out as dangerous subversives. Clergy, religious women, and thousands of laypersons have paid with their lives for their adherence to the gospel and the Medellín Documents.

At the same time, many bishops of a more conservative theological and social persuasion began to distance themselves from the perspective of the Medellín conference. This led to growing tension in the Latin American church between conservative and progressive elements that would be addressed in 1979 at the Puebla conference. Opposition to Medellín, however, did not stop its message from taking effect. In fact, opposition and persecution only strengthened the resolve of many Christians to follow through with their evangelical commitment. The persecution they experienced pointed to the structural injustice endemic in so many Latin American countries and the desperate need for new societies based on a Christian vision of society. What Medellín ultimately produced was a more committed Christian community that continues to make the gospel a real and transforming force in the lives of millions of men and women in Latin America.

See also BASE COMMUNITIES; CLASS STRUGGLE; DEVELOPMENT; EPISCOPAL CONFERENCES, CONCEPT OF; JUSTICE IN THE WORLD; LIBERATION THEOLOGY; MARXISM; POOR, PREFERENTIAL OPTION FOR; PUEBLA.

Bibliography: The entire text of the Medellín Documents can be found in *Second General Conference of Latin American Bishops, The Church in the Present-Day Transformation of Latin America in the Light of the Council: II Conclusions,* 2nd ed. (Washington: Division for Latin America, United States Catholic Conference, 1973).

CURT CADORETTE, M.M.

MENTAL HEALTH, ETHICAL ISSUES IN

The special circumstances of mental-health patients intensify ethical issues frequently found in health care. Decisions about therapy or treatment refusal are compounded by the fluctuating or uncertain competency of mental-health patients. Making matters worse, the very definition of mental health presents confusions for an exploration of the ethical issues in mental health. "Mental health" is a general term used to refer not only to the absence of mental disorders but also to the ability of an individual to negotiate the daily challenges and social interactions of life without experiencing cognitive, emotional, or behavioral dysfunction. The wide range of dysfunction contests more narrow definitions of health and its incumbent obligations. For example, shall mild personality traits such as passive-aggressive tendencies be considered a disease? Or, shall private or public resources be spent to overcome minor but undesirable personality characteristics?

The cause of mental illness is more difficult to establish than other illnesses. Mental health can be affected by numerous factors ranging from biologic and genetic vulnerabilities, to stress, to educational, political, and psychosocial conditions. The difficulty of determining what causes mental illness relegates it to low social priority, in part because Western medicine is dominated by a "medical model" of biologic causality. Western medicine is more willing to spend resources for technological cures where the cause of illness is easily and readily identifiable than to direct resources to ill-defined diseases. Consequently, mental health has experienced a budgetary famine. Despite the difficulty of establishing why people become mentally ill, the fact remains that they are suffering and require society's attention.

Autonomy

Adult competent persons possess legal and ethical rights to make health-care decisions, but mental illness often impedes competence. Beginning with the admission process and permeating any modalities of therapy, the extent to which the mentally ill person should participate in decision making is disputed. This often results in overriding the patient's wishes. The autonomous self-determination of adult patients, however, has long been the cornerstone of bioethics and is justified, among other reasons, by assumptions that the Golden Rule's dictate ("Do unto others") demands we respect others' choices and that the well-being of the patient is best known to the patient, not health-care professionals. Religious arguments foster autonomous choices because humans most image God in free choice. Autonomous decision making requires that the patient remain free from coercion and retain the capacity to make decisions. With persons who are mentally ill these qualities are often assumed not to be present, yet when we assume this we usurp their participation in their own health-care decisions.

Little debate exists about the legitimacy of overriding decision making for patients who obviously lack freedom or capacity: those who are overmedicated, psychotic, or suffering from dementia. More troubling, however, are patients with depression—a major risk factor for suicide—and with history of suicide attempts but who are nonetheless deemed competent by psychiatric evaluation. In these cases nonvoluntary admission or commitment for mental-health treatment has been regarded as unethical by some who maintain admissions should be voluntary except where the patient is a danger to self or others. Even when no danger exists, clinicians must balance a tension: promoting autonomous decision making of patients and acting paternalistically to seek the benefit and well-being of the patient.

Proxy consent. Quite aside from the content of what the patient wishes, the procedural question of establishing the appropriate decision maker is critical. Clinicians must investigate whether the patient has advance directives, such as having designated a proxy who holds a durable power of attorney. At a minimum, proxies have an obligation to determine the previous wishes of the patient, because the Golden Rule requires that the wishes of the competent be followed. Overriding a patient's wishes, if ever justified, must be done in the realization that the patient may be facing possible social stigmas and discrimination.

Confidentiality. Within the context of shared decision making among patient, family, and health-care professionals, questions arise over the extent to which confidentiality is imposed on the professional. Obligations of confidentiality are overridden when a proxy needs information about the patient to make an appropriate decision. Also, if a clinician is morally certain that a patient poses a harm to others and there is a clear way of averting the harm, then overriding the obligations of confidentiality is required.

Treatment Refusal

The right to refuse medical treatment even when the therapy, experimental or otherwise, is potentially beneficial is widely accepted. Our bodies may not be invaded without consent. Additionally, there is unanimous agreement that experimental treatments can be refused, not only because they are invasive but because it is not even clear whether the risks outweigh the benefits. While no one disputes that vulnerable populations must be excluded as research subjects when their use is simply because they are available, nonetheless some dispute remains about the use of vulnerable populations if they are the only group that stands to benefit by the experimental therapy. When research offers little risk to the subject and great benefit to others, a stronger obligation in fairness exists for any subject to participate.

Nonexperimental therapies also can be refused for a variety of reasons. Some treatments are simply futile, that is, they do not accomplish any therapeutic benefit or have fallen into discredit, such as the early psychiatric use of insulin to induce comas. Other treatments are used in nontherapeutic ways that are never acceptable, such as punishment, suppression of political dissent, or convenience of the staff. Yet even when therapies are beneficial they may be refused, for example, drug therapies that provide benefits such as (1) tranquilizing patients experiencing uncontrollable anxiety or manic states, (2) reducing mental confusion or disassociation, (3) lifting types of depression, and (4) restraining patients. It may be perfectly rational to refuse these drugs, as they all have burdensome side effects. When they are given, the least restrictive alternatives must be exhausted before more severe mind-altering pharmaceutical therapies are employed, as there is no one therapeutic approach that will heal the whole person. In any case, obligations always exist to foster optimal human functioning.

Perhaps the most disputed areas of psychiatric treatment border on those therapies that have the greatest impact on human functioning. Shock therapy, or electroconvulsive therapy (ECT), initially proved medically risky, often producing broken bones and severe memory loss. Now that the procedure is physiologically safer, questions persist as to whether this therapy is permissible insofar as it obliterates short-term memory.

Therapies that alter personal identity are most controversial. Early psychosurgery attempts (including prefrontal lobotomies, which destroyed or removed brain tissue for the express purpose of altering behavior) are now understood to be objectionable to the extent they destroy functioning most associated with human identity (i.e., free will). The principle of totality, which requires the removal of only clearly diseased matter, provides criteria restricting destruction of vital body parts when both the disease and the cure are uncertain. Recent uses of lasers to ablate seizure foci and techniques to remove emotional response to pain have been accepted because they are less likely to alter the patient's human functioning. Psychoanalytical therapies enabling clients to have insight into subconscious, hidden feelings and whose goal is to change the person's value system are more troubling when they promote values inconsistent with a Christian vocation.

Access and Rationing

Access to mental-health services and priorities within mental-health care present the newest dimensions of ethical controversy. Most Western nations have moved toward consensus regarding society's obligation to provide access to an adequate amount of health care. However, what constitutes adequate health care, or a package of basic comprehensive care, is still open to dispute.

A broad definition of mental illness that includes treatments of minor personality disorders is not the only issue that creates allocation problems. The magnitude of treatment plans required for the care of the mentally ill is staggering. Cure or reduced incidence for one category of mental illness alone, such as childhood mental-health disorders, entails expending monies for good prenatal and pediatric care, increased special-education programs, reduction of motor-vehicle crashes, educational and social support for children in high-risk groups, and reduction of alcohol and drug abuse among parents. These objectives mitigate mental illness by focusing on the aspects that can be changed by human behavior and better social arrangements. Straining any priority-setting solution is the fact that severe mental disorders have recently received relatively low priority, as evidenced by deinstitutionalization in the United States. The ethical priorities in mental health are not unrelated to the issue of who will provide the care. It is not altogether clear that psychiatrists who practice pure psychotherapy are those best able to provide care, and perhaps a more equitable distribution of medical care entails finding the appropriate level of provider to give the needed therapy.

Addressing the concerns of rationing care for the mentally ill must involve, among other things, the following concerns. First, any rationing policy must be cognizant of some meaningful indices of cure and rehabilitation, requiring evidence of appropriate utilization with no incentives to overtreatment. Second, such a policy must possess an "option for the poor" that insists that the least well off should not be the focus of the rationing program. The poor, already burdened, must not be further burdened, and inequity can be allowed to the extent that it favors this group. Third, the policy must incorporate a process that is open and that judges with nonbiased criteria.

See also FREEDOM; GOODS, ACCESS TO; HEALTH CARE; NATURAL LAW; PRIVACY, RIGHT TO; VALUES.

Bibliography: K. O'Rourke and P. Boyle, *Medical Ethics: Sources of Catholic Teachings* (St. Louis: Catholic Health Association, 1989).

PHILIP BOYLE

METHODOLOGY, MORAL

In moral matters, a methodology describes the processes by which a community of persons adopts, founds, validates, and communicates a moral way of life.

The processes must be such that they can be intelligently followed by persons who consider adopting the way of life. For this to be so, the processes must constitute a meaningful system in which starting points, sequences, and conclusions are clear and connected with one another. That is, they must constitute a coherent system. The coherence is required not simply for its own sake but because it lays down an ordered path that may lead persons into the way of life. The first function of an adequate methodology, therefore, is to provide for internal coherence within the system.

Internal coherence, however, has sometimes been pursued by making one factor dominant and suppressing the proper character and relative autonomy of other elements within the system. For example, the manualist method of Roman Catholic moral theology, which was standard prior to the Second Vatican Council, achieved a high degree of coherence. However, it tended to force the Scriptures into the structures of its deductive arguments, reducing them to a collection of proof texts. Any attempt to correct the methodology by giving a due place to the Scriptures must also respect the proper structures of moral reasoning. The coherence must be such as to respect the particular character of all the components. The methodology provides for the founding of the way of life by establishing this kind of appropriate coherence between the various elements that make up that life and the foundational principles that support them.

If the way of life is to be validated the methodology must provide structures for appropriate testing. Thus it must be possible to respond systematically to objections, either by refuting them or by incorporating corrections, in such a way that the system does not sacrifice its own internal coherence. In other words, the methodology must provide structures of self-correction. The system that the methodology presents will accordingly be an open system.

A morally good action is also a witness, or "example," to others. It manifests possibilities for fulfillment that a personal agent has discovered, confirmed by experience, and sought to achieve through that action. In this sense, every genuine moral action includes an element of communication. The possibilities for fulfillment must be communicated within the community and to others outside; thus, a further function of a methodology is to provide for structures of communication.

Hence, the basic criteria for the adequacy of a methodology are the indications that it has fulfilled its functions: the presence of appropriate coherence, openness and capacity for self-correction, and communicability.

Four Areas of Methodology

In contemporary Roman Catholic reflection on morality, there are several areas where important questions of methodology arise. It will be necessary to consider the following: moral theology, the social doctrine of the church as represented in the works of scholars and in official church teaching, liberation theology, and political theology.

The term "moral theology" as used here means the systematic exposition of how human life should be lived according to the requirements of the Christian faith. The meaning and status of the social doctrine of the church have been the subject of debate. There have been three major objections to the term "doctrine." In the first place, so it has been said, the expression gives a timeless, irrevocable status to what are, in fact, responses by church authorities to particular historical situations. Furthermore, the construction of a church doctrine seemed to be aimed at creating an ideology; a kind of third way between communism and liberal capitalism. Finally, it was feared that such doctrine would be a religious legitimation of a particular form of society, primarily the European. However, the term has been vindicated in recent statements of the magisterium. For example, the encyclical *On Social Concerns* (*Sollicitudo rei socialis*) of Pope John Paul II rejected the notions that the social doctrine of the church is a "third way" between capitalism and Marxism and that it is an ideology (SRS 41). There is an inevitable tension in social doctrine between universality and particularity. Some official documents have acknowledged clearly the difficulty of a universal message for a complex world (*Octogesima adveniens* 4). Other, more recent texts are more confident in proposing a unified teaching for all. It is, in any case, necessary to distinguish between permanent ethical principles, contingent historical judgments, and directives for action ("Guidelines" 3; SRS 3, 41). A particular issue in need of further study is how the contingent historical judgments are to be made, and who makes them. If earlier documents gave a primary if not exclusive role to the magisterium, more recent statements recognize clearly the role of the experience of the Christian community (*Centesimus annus* 3). It is difficult to distinguish clearly between "social doctrine" and "social teaching," which are used as practically equivalent in official documents. For the sake of convenience the term "social teaching" will henceforth be used for both doctrine and teaching.

Other important methodological questions are whether social teaching is a part of theology—specifically a part of the section of moral theology that deals with justice—or whether it is an autonomous part of theology in its own right, or not theology at all but natural ethics. As late as 1961 it was regarded officially as natural ethics. The current position of the magisterium, as reflected in statements of Pope John Paul II, is that it is essentially theological, the "application of the word of God to the life of men and society," and specifically moral theology (SRS 41). It has, however, within that discipline, a degree of autonomy ("Guidelines" 4). Granted that social teaching has a certain autonomy, does this mean it has its own specific methodology? Within its particular zones of interest—for example, the political order, the economy, ecology—social teaching must have a specialized methodology corresponding to the particular subject matter and form of inquiry. However, there are certain basic methodological questions common to both social teaching and moral theology in general, and these will be the subject of analysis here.

Liberation theology has provided what may well be a profoundly significant innovation in taking liberating practice as the fount and end of theological theory. This methodological option means that liberation theology has a powerful moral element in its very foundation. However, until recently there has been relatively little systematic study of the implications of this for moral theology. Sympathetic critics point to the need to recognize the relative autonomy of moral reasoning within the unity of theology as presented by liberation theologians (Vidal). More recently, some authors have made a significant beginning (Dussel, Moreno).

An important contribution of political theology has been its insistence that all theology has an inherently social and historical dimension (Metz). It has identified as major defects the isolation of theology in the private sphere and its separation from a totally distinct social doctrine. The social teaching of the church was developed against the background of a division between individual morality and social morality, a division that had not existed earlier in the tradition. The movements toward a more unified methodology represent a concern to recapture in a new way a unity that had been lost.

The Basic Structures

There are certain enduring structures within the Catholic moral tradition. They are like zones within which positions are taken, objections are posed, and transformations take place. Internal coherence is achieved when the various zones are appropriately integrated. Coherence is lost when the content of particular zones is distorted and/or when zones are not adequately related to one another. Some examples will make clear what is meant by this. The basic structures are the following:

1. *The interest.* This is the dominant concern that guides moral reflection in the bringing about, for persons, of a good life in the comprehensive sense. This includes both becoming good persons and carrying through right actions. Such a good life is sought as a constitutive element of salvation. Moral truth, as a truth about the genuinely good life, is a saving truth (Demmer).

2. *The vision.* This refers to a way of seeing personal life and human history as a meaningful whole. For the Catholic tradition, the vision arises fundamentally from faith, but faith stimulates reason. A key element is eschatology, the conception of ultimate fulfillment. The eschatological vision may be mediated by "utopias" (OA 37), which open imagination to possibilities in the present moment of human history that may be realized in the future. The vision leads to questions about the transcendent end or goal of life. The Christian tradition has seen ultimate personal fulfillment in a union of total love with God. There is an aspiration for the infinite given to the human person by God, which is freely fulfilled by the same God in the gift of divine love. The vision leads further to questions about the fundamental values or goods that guide human choices. For example, the values identified in contemporary social teaching are truth, freedom, justice, solidarity, peace, and charity, all of which are understood to be inherent in "the dignity of the human person" as constituting the basis of a true humanism ("Guidelines" 43; *Centesimus annus* 55).

Hence the vision raises questions about the kind of person one is called to become. This calls for a Christian anthropology, an understanding of the human person and of what the fulfilled human person is to be. In particular, there is required a conception of Christian liberty as a positive response to the modern history of liberty. The person as subject has increasingly become the focus of reflection in Catholic moral theology. Further, there arise questions about the virtues or empowerments that a life according to this vision would require. A vision of the person is incomplete without some vision of the cosmos or nature of which the person partakes. Recent documents emphasize "the need to respect the integrity and the cycles of nature" (SRS 26; *Centesimus annus* 37). A cosmic frame of reference has become part of the accepted methodology. Attention to the human person leads to reflection on the person of Christ as the full realization of humanity. Thus the vision includes Christology. Ultimately the character of the vision that guides moral theology must relate to the character of God. For example, is God naked will or totally undetermined freedom or rationally ordered will, a divine lawmaker or a God of love? The question of who God is, is the most basic question of moral theology.

Much of the criticism that has been directed against the methodologies of the recent past has pointed to a lack of cohesion between aspects of the vision and other structures. For example, the faith-vision was not well integrated with a moral theology and social teaching based principally on natural law. As a corrective to this arose the contemporary concern with a more thoroughly scriptural foundation (*Optatam totius* 16). A second example is the inadequate integration of the eschatological vision as symbolized in the "kingdom" and the goods and values that human activity seeks to realize in the world. The Second Vatican Council proposed a corrective, integrating the transcendent fulfillment and the social, moral life that is projected toward it. Earthly progress is not to be identified with the growth of the kingdom, but insofar as it promotes a better order in human society it is of vital importance to the kingdom of God. The values of dignity, brotherhood, and freedom will not be annihilated but found again in the fulfillment (*Gaudium et spes* 39; *Centesimus annus* 25). A third example of lack of cohesion in earlier theological models was the separation of the supernatural and natural ends of life. In this view the fulfillment of the supernatural end was extrinsic to the fulfillment of the natural. This two-level conception of life has now been set aside. The unity of life before God is founded on the openness to the infinite given to the person by God and fulfilled by the free gift of divine love. The unity of life is grasped in the unity of consciousness of the personal subject who lives it.

For liberation theology, an eschatological vision of the kingdom, or reign, of God as ultimate fulfillment for the poor, beginning now in community, is a basic, unifying point of the committed moral life (Dussel). For political theology the Resurrection is an eschatological symbol that stands in contradiction to the structures of the present. It is both a challenge and basis of hope in the possibility of transformation.

3. *Faith and reason.* The presystematic reflection by persons in the community on faith and its requirements is the starting point of moral theology. In this sense faith and reason give rise to moral theology. There is now a general agreement in Catholic theology that faith and reason are not opposed but complementary. In contemporary methodology, the relationship between faith and reason could be explained as follows. The moral theologian begins within the realm of faith, but faith leads to questions of reason about how life is to be lived. Answers to these questions call for direct, positive evidence. Thus the structures of these rational processes cannot be identified with faith and must be recognized as having a legitimate relative autonomy (Böckle).

There is also the question of autonomy of content. Does moral reasoning operating in the context of faith deliver material norms that are essentially the same as those of a genuine human ethic (Fuchs)? Or does Christian faith yield specifically Christian moral norms (Ratzinger)? The latter position would mean that there are some moral insights and norms that are available to believers but not to others. Many theologians in the Catholic tradition hold that there are no specifically Christian material norms but that there are specifically Christian intentionality and motivation. Others, however, insist that there is a "faith-ethic" in the sense that Christian faith provides identifiable norms that are not available to reason. Some pointers to a solution have emerged in contemporary discussion.

There is no such thing as "pure reason," so there can be no such thing as absolutely autonomous moral reasoning. Faith leads to and calls for thought. Reason contributes to answering the questions that faith stimulates. Faith can confirm, criticize, or subject to further inquiry the deliverances of reason. There is no reasonable person "as such" whose "genuinely human morality" we might consult. Morally reasonable persons live, think, and act within historical traditions. The starting point for a solution to these questions must therefore be in the living traditions of historical faith-communities as they respond to challenges from other traditions and seek to communicate with them.

For neo-Scholastic methodology the characteristic task of reason was deduction from principles. Contemporary moral methodology gives a much more important place to the inductive process. The same approach is acknowledged in official documents (*Mater et magistra;* GS; "Guidelines" 7; *Centesimus annus* 3).

The proper structure of moral reasoning has also been the subject of criticism and correction. In some older methodologies the deductive style of moral reasoning was modeled after legal or theoretical-metaphysical reason. The corrective has been to stress the particular character of practical reason. Where theoretical reason seeks to grasp reality as it is, practical reason directs toward what is to be. The emphasis on practical reason is necessary and welcome; it has, however, brought to light some difficult epistemological questions. For example: what is the nature and criterion of practical moral truth? The neo-Scholastic model presumed a correspondence theory of truth: what had to be shown was that the object of an act conformed to the appropriate norm that conformed to the objective moral order. An alternative concept or truth is evident in more personalist kinds of moral theology, according to which truth is found in the relation of the person to the Divine Persons. Others propose a transformational notion of truth, whereby truth is realized in a positive transformation of life (Tracy). For liberation theology, liberative practice provides the criterion of truth.

According to Karl Rahner the relation between theory and practice cannot be construed in terms of a sequence in which theoretical principles are followed necessarily by practical conclusions. A conception like this, according to Rahner, is the basis of theological integralism, which means a system in which theoretical considerations dominate completely and there is a failure to recognize the freedom and creativity characteristic of all truly human action. Integralism in this sense entails a failure to recognize that the practical intellect has a certain relative autonomy. Its act of apprehension takes place only within a free decision (Rahner, p. 322).

How is practical reason related to theory? Some have made a distinction between "moral theology" and "pastoral theology." Moral theology accordingly has the task of providing principles and norms (theory); pastoral theology deals with the person in his or her real situation (practice). Such distinctions seem to imply that in respect to theoretical knowledge a certain action might be wrong, but from the pastoral perspective, as a personal action of a particular subject it might at the same time be right. This appears to imply a two-truth theory, which would be unacceptable. Some pointers to a solution have emerged. In the first place, the notion of truth is analogous. Practical truth is not univocal with theoretical truth. Further, we must recognize that both forms of reason do not exist in themselves; that is, they must not be "reified" as if they existed apart in themselves. Rather, they interpenetrate in the unified consciousness of the subject. Again, it is not necessary that the sequences of practical reason be forced into syllogisms. A responsible moral agent may be able to follow a sequence that has other, less rigid and artificial structures (Demmer). Such sequences may capture more of the complex human reality and, at the same time, be intersubjectively communicable. In this context, the structures of narrative have been fruitfully employed. Some contemporary authors propose a greater role for imagination (Keane).

Although the tradition of natural law referred to reason and experience as sources of moral wisdom, the significance of experience and its acceptability as evidence have been disputed. Some representatives of the neo-Scholastic deductive model would seem to have allowed no place for experience at all. The necessary place of experience is recognized in contemporary theology and acknowledged in official documents. However, much work is still needed to clarify the meaning and significance of experience in this context. There are, for example, many different kinds of morally significant experiences: the intimations of the moral law in individual conscience (Newman); the experience of "ought" (Böckle); the joys, hopes, grief, and anguish especially of those who are poor and afflicted (GS 1); suffering, contrast experiences (Schillebeeckx); conversion (Lonergan; "Guidelines" 7). A method is needed to describe and interpret experiences. Many have found the phenomenological method particularly helpful in this respect. In particular, Karol Wojtyla employed this method to study the relationship between act as experience and the person.

Another important question concerns the method by which the data of experience may be processed so as to yield arguments that may lead to the transformation of a received position. That such transformations have occurred is not in doubt. The process by which this happens has not been sufficiently studied. Historical studies have shown that the system of "probabilism" (Medina, 1577) functioned in this way. A traditional position could be defended by apparently overwhelming evidence in the form of lengthy lists of citations from the Fathers. It seemed, therefore, that a new view could never muster sufficient evidence to prevail against the older, "more probable" position. Probabilism, however, would allow an opinion to be followed when it was supported by evidence that was genuine, even though of lesser weight than that supporting the older view. That is, an opinion could be followed even though it was "less probable" than the older position. In this way a new position could be accepted into the moral life of the community. Thus development of moral doctrine in the light of new experience was made possible (Klomps). The theory of probabilism has been invoked in some contemporary debates. For example, it has been urged that the theory of "proportionalism" could be accepted as a probable opinion on the grounds that it is supported by serious arguments and accepted by many competent moral theologians. To some theologians this argument is not convincing. The theory of probabilism itself needs to be further refined and developed if it is to meet contemporary requirements. At present, it would be fair to say that Catholic moral theology lacks an adequate theory of development.

4. *Culture.* Bernard Lonergan distinguished classical culture, where the controlling norm is thought of as "a universal fixed for all time," and a modern culture, which "thinks of the controls as themselves involved in an ongoing process" (*Method*

in Theology, p. 29). Some moral theologians invoke a similar distinction between a "classicist" and a "historically conscious" methodology (Curran, p. 101). For example, Catholic social doctrine in its earlier (pre-1960) form exemplified a classicist methodology. It proceeded by a form of argument where the major premise was a principle derived from the law of God, often in the form of an interpretation of the natural law by the magisterium. The minor premise was a contingent judgment on a set of facts about human society. The conclusion was an imperative, requiring or prohibiting some specific action. The same pattern can be found in some church documents of the period on, for example, sexuality and moral questions of medicine. The natural law itself was often interpreted as a metaphysical timeless order. Thus conclusions could be drawn that were valid for all time and independent of history.

In the second, historically conscious, method, history is the basic referent rather than timeless nature. Theology is concerned with discerning the plan of God in history, in particular by "scrutinizing the signs of the times" (GS 4). Permanent moral principles are not denied, but there is much greater awareness of contingent historical factors and the necessity of continuously updating moral teaching. It has been noted that the historically conscious model is much in evidence in recent documents on church social teaching but that in official documents on sexuality and biomedical ethics a classicist methodology is still evident.

5. *Community.* It is in the tradition of a community that a vision lives on; a moral life requires a moral community. For moral theology and social teaching the relevant community is the church. Thus an ecclesiology is an essential element of the methodology. Moral theology grows out of the experience and insight of the community, and its purpose is to develop that community insight. The consensus of the community, the *sensus fidelium,* thus sets limits for moral theology. It cannot claim to be a completely autonomous science, for this would mean rejecting its own source. Consequently, it also acknowledges those formal structures of authority that the faith of the community sustains and recognizes, specifically the magisterium. For the most part the moral tradition is taken for granted without question by the community. There are times, however, when the need to deal with new questions throws up conflicting proposals. In these circumstances it may happen that no agreement is forthcoming. It is in such situations that the magisterium may need to intervene so as to identify what truly belongs to the vision and practice of the Christian community and what does not. It is commonly held that the church has not taught infallibly in the areas of moral theology and social teaching. Pronouncements in these areas belong to the authentic (authoritative, noninfallible) teaching of the ordinary magisterium. Such teachings are in principle open to modification and change. There are some theologians, however, who argue that the ordinary magisterium has taught infallibly on some matters of morality (e.g., contraception). In the absence of a formal definition of doctrine by the magisterium, this position is as strong as the arguments advanced to support it. It should be remembered that many of the basic elements of the tradition (e.g., some of the contents of the vision) express definitive commitments of the church, even though they have never been the subject of formal definition. It is important to recall that the role of the magisterium is not limited to condemning errors; it has a positive, prophetic, teaching function in proclaiming the tradition.

Debates in this area are often narrowly focused on whether or not dissent is legitimate. It would be more appropriate to develop a methodology by which the common search for truth could be pursued, with due respect for authority and for those offering a new contribution (Örsy).

As John Henry Newman argued in his famous letter to the duke of Norfolk, the onus of proof lies with the conscience that questions the official position. What is needed is a more systematic account of what kind and weight of evidence could constitute a proof in such cases.

6. *Community mission.* The communities that share the Christian vision have all understood it to mean that they must commit themselves to a mission. All these communities have accepted the mission of preaching the message of the kingdom. Some, including the Roman Catholic church, have adopted as an essential element of their mission a responsibility for shaping the course of human history, that is, a commitment to the "authentic development of man and society" (SRS 1). Thus the Catholic church has sought to promote justice and peace, to transform culture, and to influence institutions, for example, in favor of the family and human rights. Liberation theology gives a distinctive orientation to the task, namely the liberation of the poor. The focus on liberation in its earthly and transcendent senses has been incorporated into official social teaching (*Evangelii nuntiandi* 31). The *Instruction on Christian Freedom and Liberation* (1986) has developed the theme at length, and papal teaching has affirmed the preference for the poor (SRS 42; *Centesimus annus* 11). Recent theology and official teaching have sought to integrate the two aspects of the project, evangelization and human promotion (*Centesimus annus* 5). The 1971 synod of bishops, for example, stated, "Action on behalf of justice and participation in the transformation of the world fully appear to us as a constitutive dimension of the preaching of the gospel."

It is within the community's historical mission that the individual person's moral life is stimulated and sustained. Hence, the structure and direction of the personal moral life are formed by the community. At the same time, Catholic moral theology has always been attentive to the inner life of the person. There have been significant methodological developments in this respect also. In keeping with the renewed emphasis on the Scriptures, the key elements of the personal moral life have been interpreted in terms of conversion and discipleship. To provide a systematic explanation of these biblical notions, some moral theologians have drawn on Bernard Lonergan's analysis of conversion. Others have provided an account of the moral life as a process of continuous conversion (Häring).

In terms of a theological understanding of the personal moral life, the standard methodologies of the manuals presented a particular problem. This was the lack of cohesion between the consideration of the transcendent goal, or ultimate end, and the moral life itself. The moral life consequently came to be conceived of as a series of separate acts with no enduring connection. Moral methodology hence focused on particular discrete acts and thus generated what is known as "act morality." A corrective to this has been developed in terms of the theory of the fundamental option and fundamental stance. The theory combined elements from personalist and transcendental Thomist philosophy with notions drawn from depth psychology to explain the basic orientation of life toward (or away from) God. The basic orientation is the enduring, continuous core of the moral life. It is expressed in particular acts but cannot be identified with those acts. A change of fundamental option and stance may be signaled by a particular act but generally only when that act is the final episode in an extended story of acts. The theory has been widely accepted. However, significant criticisms are that it fails to account sufficiently for the social dimension of the moral life, that it withdraws the moral subject from history, and that it tends to weaken a sense of responsibility for particular acts.

7. *Historical, material norms.* From the vision are derived basic requirements and prohibitions. The former express positive

possibilities of affirming the vision, realizing the values, and living the virtues. The latter exclude what denies the vision, negates the values, or corrupts the virtues. These requirements and prohibitions are expressed in what are called "formal norms." Examples are the commandments to love God and one's neighbor as oneself, to foster life, to live justly.

These requirements and prohibitions need to be expressed in more specific historical, material norms. They are historical in the sense that they include in their formulation ways of accounting for the complexity and contingency that surround concrete actions in time. They are material in that they include descriptions of actions.

In Catholic moral theology the content of norms has been frequently provided by appeal to the natural law. There have been significant changes in this area. In social teaching and specifically in papal encyclicals a move away from reliance on natural law is evident. In recent encyclicals, especially since *Peace on Earth* (*Pacem in terris*) in 1963, there has been a strong appeal to human rights. The fundamental point is the dignity and rights of the person rather than the natural law (SRS 26; *Centesimus annus* 55).

In other documents nature and natural law still appear but in a modified way. An interpretation that identified nature with physical and biological structures has been rejected. The change was reflected in an important text of Vatican II (GS 51), which stated that objective norms are to be "based on the nature of the human person and his acts." Later documents continued in like vein. The instruction on bioethics, *Respect for Human Life in Its Origin and on the Dignity of Procreation* (1987), says of the natural law, "Therefore this law cannot be thought of as simply a set of norms on the biological level; rather it must be defined as the rational order whereby man is called by the Creator" (Introduction, 3). According to this interpretation biological structures are morally relevant, not because they are natural but because they are of the person. In the same document, the norms relevant to human procreation are "laws inscribed in their persons and in their union" (Introduction, 5). The move from nature to person is now generally accepted in Catholic moral theology.

To formulate historical norms there is need for interpretative models, which can pick out from the turbulent reality of life those factors that are morally significant. For example, in the tradition we find models of "the human act," which identify such elements as interior act, exterior act, end, intention, circumstances, and consequences. Other models indicate why and how these elements are morally relevant. For example, in teleological models the human action is significant as a movement toward a fitting goal, or as productive of beneficial or harmful states of affairs. In deontological models it is significant as an act ruled by law, principle, or moral order. In the first case a morally wrong act is one that turns away from the goal or that produces a surplus of harmful over beneficial states. In the second, a morally wrong act is one that does not conform to the law, principle, or moral order.

In contemporary texts of Catholic moral theology, the terms "teleological" and "deontological" are used to construct a typology of current methodologies. Of the teleological type, the most notable is that known as "proportionalism." In the deontological type are included a range of methods, which are often revisions of a natural-law approach. The typology is not completely adequate. Proportionalism, for instance, is more precisely described as a mixed teleology, since it includes nonteleological considerations. Similarly, many if not all methods of the deontological type include teleological considerations. These are invoked in the construction and founding of historical norms, while deontological methods are used in applying the norms to concrete circumstances in the process of decision making.

A major point of debate is whether there are historical, material norms that are both universal and negative. On one side of the debate is the theory of proportionalism. This theory can best be understood in the context of the Catholic moral tradition. This tradition has worked out or has adopted from other philosophical and legal traditions a number of programs or axioms for processing complex situations. These have been constructed on the basis of experience and refined through application to cases. Some of these axioms are (*a*) law founded on the presumption of a common and universal danger; (*b*) the principle of proportionality as expressed in the principle of the double effect and the principle of totality; (*c*) the principle of choosing or counseling the lesser evil; (*d*) epikeia (equity); and (*e*) the "moral systems," by which one weighed conflicting opinions to determine the weight of evidence in their favor. It may be noted that the most recent work on methodology takes these traditional programs, including the study of cases, with a new seriousness (Demmer).

Proportionalism can be understood as a modern movement that draws on and modifies some of these traditional notions in order to justify and interpret moral norms (Knauer, Schüller, McCormick). Some exponents have developed extended arguments to show that the theory has a basis in the work of St. Thomas Aquinas (Janssens). A basic thesis of proportionalism is that an act cannot be declared morally wrong in itself, in the abstract. A judgment must consider all the circumstances of the act, including, especially but not only, the consequences. A morally wrong act is one that brings about a (premoral or ontic) harm without a proportionate reason, that is, without producing a proportionately greater beneficial effect. This method would uphold "virtually exceptionless" norms, that is, norms that prohibit harm-causing actions for which no proportionate, justifying reason can be conceived (Evans, McCormick).

Proportionalism has won acceptance by many moral theologians but has met vehement resistance from others. In the English-language literature on the subject the other side of the debate is represented in a particularly forceful way by what could be called the theory of "basic human goods" (Grisez). This, like proportionalism, is a correction of an early theory that proved to be inadequate in the face of new challenges. And like proportionalism, it seeks new ways to ground moral norms. It holds that the moral obligation (ought) cannot be derived from theoretical truth, for example, from a metaphysical interpretation of nature. Rather, one must reflect on rational judgments that actions ought to be done or not done. Such judgments are founded on one or more basic human goods. The basic human goods are aspects of the fulfillment of persons and correspond to potentialities inherent in human nature. The basic human goods are all equally primary and so are incommensurable with one another. Thus goods (and bads) cannot be measured against one another so as to determine the greater good and lesser evil. This is presented as a basic objection against proportionalism. In simplified terms, moral wrong consists in choosing against or excluding a basic human good. This method yields absolute prohibitions, for example, of abortion and nuclear deterrence.

The debate about proportionalism concerns the basis of moral norms. In the moral community norms are proposed to persons. Hence it is also essential to consider the strengths and limitations of persons as moral subjects.

8. *The person: conscience.* A person as a moral agent must seek to answer the questions, what kind of person am I called to become and what actions are the appropriate expression of such a person? The term "conscience" refers to that operation of moral consciousness that formulates this

personal call. The consciousness of a person asking those questions is borne by an inner dynamism toward the true and the good. In seeking to discern the nature and content of the call, conscience takes into account the whole range of structures of the community's moral tradition and draws upon the witnesses to genuine fulfillment offered by the moral community, expressed in its norms and confirmed by its appropriate structures of authority. Conscience thus engages in a process of learning, or "formation." According to the Second Vatican Council, conscience "discovers" a law that the person has not made and that he/she must obey (GS 16). The law is not externally imposed but arises from within and comes to light in the active process of discovery. Conscience does not autonomously create the moral law. But neither is conscience merely passively receptive. It expresses the orientation of the whole person to vision, value, and virtue. Hence the dignity of the person lies in following this law (GS 16). Conscience can often be mistaken, since the learning process may remain incomplete, with or without blame on the part of the person. When the person is without blame in this respect conscience may err, but it still retains its dignity (GS 16). That means that conscience, even when in error, must be respected both by the person and by others.

Conscience, as an element of the unified moral consciousness of the person, includes an awareness of positive capacities but also of the limitations of the person in moral and spiritual strength. These latter call for particular consideration. A classic statement on respect for personal capacities was made by Pius XII. The pope declared that a person is normally bound to use only ordinary means of treatment. He explained that a stricter obligation would be too burdensome for most and would make the attainment of the higher, more important good too difficult.

Some more-recent theories have probed more deeply into the limits on personal capacity. For example, Josef Fuchs has developed the notion of the "sin of the world." According to this author, limitations on human possibility may derive from the sin of the world; limitations that are due to human concupiscence, to the distortions that sin has brought to social structures, and to the weakness of persons (Hoose, p. 61). Theories of compromise have been developed to account for the possibility that the reality of a person's situation may be so constraining that he/she may be simply unable to follow the objective norm without making his/her situation even worse (Curran).

One theory of this type has been mentioned, albeit briefly, in an official church document (*Familiaris consortio* 34). This is known as gradualism, or "the law of gradualness." The basic idea might be explained as follows. The moral life should embody progress in the realization of genuine values. The values are not mere ideals. Persons are called to express them in their decisions insofar as they are able. However, conditions at a particular time may prevent their making a fully adequate response. In such circumstances, moral responsibility requires that one strive to create the conditions that would make a full response possible. This approach seems to offer possibilities for a responsible pastoral approach to situations of acute difficulty.

9. *Communication.* There can be no doubt within the Catholic tradition that the moral way of life that it has discovered ought to be communicated. This follows from the basic option for evangelization and from the church's assumption of responsibility for human history. Morality, in the Catholic tradition, can neither be purely private nor the particular morality of a sect. However, the methodology of communication presents questions that are not yet adequately answered. These questions concern first of all the addressees of the communication. Is the communication addressed to all persons of good

will or to all who share Christian beliefs or specifically to Catholics? The second area of concern is the social context in which the moral teaching is to be expressed. Attention must be given to the social and political institutions and the practices in which the moral teaching is to be embodied and that have influenced its formation. The process of communication between church and society is not merely one way. This is clearly recognized in contemporary moral theology in its willingness to learn from other disciplines. The third is the mode of communication. In some official documents of the church (e.g., *On Human Life, Peace on Earth*) the natural law is invoked as the basis for communicating with all persons of good will.

More recently, however, in official documents there has been a move toward a more explicitly religious, biblical foundation of the social teaching, integrated more or less well with natural law or other philosophical bases. Significant examples are the pastoral letters of the U.S. bishops *The Challenge of Peace* and *Economic Justice for All.* Inquirers legitimately seek to be informed of the complete process by which conclusions have been reached. The problem remains, however, of translating positions that have been formed within the specific Catholic tradition into terms that would be meaningful to others who share the same pluralistic society but do not share the same Catholic tradition. Further questions arise when the church, in seeking to carry on its historical mission in society, calls for the embodiment of certain moral norms, for example norms prohibiting abortion, in the law of the state. The criticism is frequently made that the church is seeking to impose its own values on society. The response is that such claims are based on a common human morality, not on specifically religious or Catholic principles.

10. *Structures of reconciliation.* The moral way of life of the Christian community is lived out by persons in history. Since, in the Catholic vision, human history is a salvation history through which humankind is saved from the power of sin by grace, the moral life must be seen as a way of salvation or reconciliation. Since all are involved in the reality of sin, all are called to participate in the process of reconciliation. Therefore an adequate methodology must recognize reconciliation as an essential and fundamental characteristic. Moral theology from the 16th to the present century was focused on reconciliation in the specific form of the hearing of confessions. This gave it a strong theoretical and practical cohesion. The recent widening of perspective, with its integration of the personal and social, requires a rethinking of how the process of reconciliation is to be carried out. Methodologically, moral discourse within this tradition functions so as to open up possibilities of transformation. In the language of individual sinfulness this is done by providing the person with structures by which the refinements of personal responsibility may be discerned. This is characteristic of the language of the confession of sins. It focuses attention on personal responsibility as the source of sin. At the same time it illuminates that responsibility as offering the possibility, in grace, of breaking with sin. In contrast, the language of social sin focuses attention on the embodiment of the effects of sin in social structures. It points out what must be transformed in those structures if they are to enhance rather than crush the possibilities of the human spirit (*Centesimus annus* 38).

See also CONSCIENCE; ESCHATOLOGY; GOD, IMAGES OF; MORAL LIFE, CHRISTIAN; NATURAL LAW; REASON, ROLE OF; SCRIPTURE, USE OF IN CATHOLIC SOCIAL ETHICS; VALUES.

Bibliography: F. Böckle, *Fundamental Moral Theology,* trans. N. Smith (Dublin: Gill & Macmillan, 1980). Congregation for Catholic Education, "Guidelines for the Study and Teaching of the Church's Social Doctrine in the Formation of Priests," *Origins* 19 (1989) 169–92. C. Curran, *Tensions in Moral Theology* (Notre Dame, Ind.: Univ. of Notre Dame Press, 1988). K. Demmer, *Moraltheologische Methodenlehre* (Freibourg, Switzerland: Universitätsverlag, 1989). E. Dussel, *Ethics and Community,* trans. R. Barr (Maryknoll, N.Y.: Orbis, 1988). G. Grisez, J. Boyle, and J. Finnis, "Practical Principles, Moral Truth, and Ultimate Ends," *The American Journal of Jurisprudence* 32 (1987) 99–151. R. Gula, *Reason Informed by Faith: Foundations of Catholic Morality* (New York: Paulist, 1989). B. Hoose, *Proportionalism: The American Debate and Its European Roots* (Washington: Georgetown Univ. Press, 1987). V. MacNamara, *Faith and Ethics: Recent Roman Catholicism* (Dublin: Gill & Macmillan, 1985). K. Rahner, "Theological Reflections on the Problem of Secularization," in *Theological Investigations,* trans. D. Bourke (New York: Herder & Herder, 1973) 10:322. K. Wojtyla, *The Acting Person* (Boston: D. Reidel, 1979).

BRIAN V. JOHNSTONE, C.SS.R.

MICHEL, VIRGIL

George Michel, born June 26, 1890, was the second child of Fred and Mary Griebler Michel of St. Paul, Minnesota. He entered the novitiate of St. John's Abbey in Collegeville, Minnesota, in July 1909, taking the religious name of Virgil, made solemn monastic profession in September 1913, and was ordained in June 1916. He died November 26, 1938. His contribution to Catholic social thought was distinctive because it was grounded in his conviction that social regeneration was intrinsically related to the liturgical life of the church.

The young Virgil Michel was sent to The Catholic University of America in Washington, D.C., for graduate studies (S.T.B., 1917; Ph.D. in English literature, "The Critical Principles of Orestes A. Brownson," 1918), to prepare for teaching at St. John's University. Concurrently he did summer studies in education at Columbia University in New York. Subsequently (1924–25) he did postdoctoral studies in medieval and modern philosophy at the Benedictine Institute of San Anselmo in Rome and at the Catholic University at Louvain in Belgium, where his interests focused in social philosophy and ethics. In these years he made contact with the European liturgical movement and began what would become his distinctive orientation of relating social theory and liturgical spirituality. At San Anselmo he met Dom Lambert Beauduin, O.S.B., the "founder" of the 20th-century European liturgical movement, who opened up for Michel a theological vision of the mystical body of Christ within the larger human community. In Belgium he came into more direct contact with the apostolate of liturgical promotion through the work of the monks at the Abbey of Mont Cesar.

Upon his return to the United States in the autumn, 1925, he took up the teaching of philosophy, the academic administration of St. John's University, the founding of The Liturgical Press, and the founding and editing of the liturgical journal *Orate Fratres,* later *Worship.* Social thought, Catholic education, and promotion of the liturgy were the three matters that engaged him intensely until his early death. For him they were intimately related. In 1935 he summarized his vision in an aphoristic syllogism: "Pius X tells us that the liturgy is the indispensable source of the true Christian spirit; Pius XI says that the true Christian spirit is indispensable for social regeneration. Hence the conclusion: The liturgy is the indispensable basis of Christian social regeneration." As an educator he was tireless in showing how this was the case.

In addition to promoting his vision through *Orate Fratres,* during the 1930s he collaborated with his confreres and the sisters of the order of St. Dominic at Grand Rapids, Michigan, in the development of religious-education textbook series for elementary and secondary schools and for colleges. He also wrote several books on social theory, and during the same decade he produced more than a dozen pamphlets on labor, capital, economics, ownership, and social reconstruction aimed at reaching adult Catholics. His social analysis focused on the distortions and dangers inherent in totalitarian states and capitalist individualism alike. By way of contrast, he saw revitalized liturgical life as eminently social and as capable of disclosing to people the mystery of a fully participative social order. To people who objected to his conjunction of liturgy and social reconstruction, Virgil Michel argued that no one has really entered into the heart of the liturgy who is not "seized with a veritable passion for the reestablishment of social justice in its wide ramifications."

Michel's goal was to engage adult Catholic laity and their pastors in a more profound understanding of lay Christian identity and mission in the world and to move the laity from a posture of dependency to "full stature in Christ." While he affirmed the current promotion of Pius XI's vision of Catholic Action as "the participation of the laity in the apostolate of the hierarchy," he was not comfortable with the restricted self-understanding implied in the papal call for officially organized and approved lay activity. He argued for a more comprehensive vision of the lay vocation as grounded in Christian baptism and lived out as leaven in the most ordinary domestic and social settings. Officially sponsored Catholic Action was only one possible manifestation of the comprehensive calling to be a member of the mystical body of Christ. The radical vocation of the adult Catholic was to remove or to ameliorate the social conditions that make profound human community impossible and to promote whatever would contribute to a redeemed social order. For Michel, that meant full and active lay participation in the sacrifice of Christ.

In addressing the social consequences of the individualism so characteristic of United States culture ("the amorphous mass-rabble aggregate that individualism has made of democracy"), Virgil Michel regularly used the central symbol of Christian sacrifice to talk about new possibility. The sacrifice of Christ was self-offering. The Mass was the real sacramental symbolic continuation of that self-offering by all those who were "in Christ." Christian life with its concern for the common good was the social manifestation of that hidden mystery of redemptive sacrifice celebrated at the altar. In an era in which sacramental theology focused on the priest's offering of the sacrifice, Dom Virgil consistently redirected attention to the sacramental and real sacrifice of the whole body of Christ for the life of the world.

It is generally agreed that Virgil Michel's legacy to Catholic social thought is his consistent articulation of the connection between liturgy and social justice that provides a theological foundation for the church's social ministry. Many have noted that it is precisely this original vision that distinguished the North American liturgical movement from its European counterpart in the 1940s and 1950s. Ironically, the Second Vatican Council (1962–65), which did so much to revitalize both the church's liturgical life and its understanding of its mission in the world, had the unfortunate effect of separating for Catholics in the United States what Virgil Michel and his collaborators had worked so hard to integrate in theory and in practice. *Sacrosanctum concilium* (The Constitution on the Sacred Liturgy, 1963) preceded by two years the conciliar consideration of *Gaudium et spes* (the Pastoral Constitution on the Church in the Modern World). Neither concern informed the other in any significant way in the development of the preparatory documents, during the conciliar debates, or in the finally approved constitutions. Subsequent implementation of the liturgical reform focused on lay participation in worship in isolation from social action. Catholic social activists in turn were wary of overinvolvement in liturgical reform, seeing it as a distraction from the call to "action on behalf of justice," which had been forcefully promoted through the statement of the 1971 synod, *Justitia in mundo* (Justice in the World). Twenty-five years after the council and fifty years after the death of Virgil Michel, a new generation of Catholics is rediscovering the need to reestablish the link between liturgical participation and social ministry and is finding in the works of this depression-era Benedictine monk a foundation on which to build.

See also COMMON GOOD; COMMUNITY; EVIL, SOCIAL; GAUDIUM ET SPES; JUSTICE IN THE WORLD; LAITY, ROLE OF; LITURGICAL MOVEMENTS, SOCIAL INFLUENCE OF; VATICAN COUNCIL II.

Bibliography: R. Franklin and R. Spaeth, *Virgil Michel: American Catholic,* with bibliographic essay (Collegeville, Minn.: The Liturgical Press, 1988). J. Hall, *The Full Stature of Christ* (Collegeville, Minn.: The Liturgical Press, 1976). K. Himes, "Eucharist and Justice: Assessing the Legacy of Virgil Michel" *Worship* 62:3 (May 1988) 201–24. P. Marx, *Virgil Michel and the Liturgical Movement,* appendices 1 and 2: "Virgil Michel's Bibliography" and "Bibliographic Essay" (Collegeville, Minn.: The Liturgical Press, 1957). *The Legacy of Virgil Michel* (Collegeville, Minn.: The Liturgical Press, 1991).

MARY COLLINS, O.S.B.

MINORITIES

The term "minorities" is disputed, mercurial, and freighted with hegemonic connotation. Historically its usage has been determined by the acquisition of social, cultural, racial, economic, and political power. In the United States during the late 19th and early 20th centuries, native-born white people applied the term "minorities" to linguistically and culturally distinct foreign-born immigrants who sought inclusion in the larger society. These native-born people not only defined the standards for social, cultural, economic, and political assimilation, they controlled the processes of measurement. Three groups deemed unassimilable were assigned a caste-like status: the first peoples of the North American continent or Indians, peoples of African descent, and Jews. Women were rendered invisible.

By the mid-20th century native-born or immigrant peoples of color in the United States—including African Americans, Africans, Asians, East Indians, Latin Americans, Mexicans, Pacific Islanders, Semitic peoples of the Middle East, and peoples from the Caribbean—were labeled "minorities." This usage continues to stigmatize "minorities" as less than and ontologically different from the dominating race and class. These people of color resist the label; Indians in particular reject it as they seek relations with the United States as sovereign peoples. The reduction of each of these cultural and linguistic groups to numerical minorities serves to maintain existing social, cultural, economic, and political arrangements. While women may constitute a numerical majority, they become most visible when paired with "minorities" (as in the expression "women and minorities") or when assigned "minority status" themselves. In the highly racialized contexts of the United States and South Africa, women of color are called "minority women" and viewed as separate and different from white women. The term "minority" carries political denotation: in South Africa the numerical minority is the political majority; in the United States gerrymandering protects the interests of a privileged majority. In Eastern Europe, the Middle East, India, Asia, and the Soviet Union, so-called ethnic, cultural, and religious "minorities" resist the label in their struggles for political independence.

See also ANTI-SEMITISM; BLACK THEOLOGY; FEMINISM AND CATHOLIC SOCIAL THOUGHT; HUMAN RIGHTS.

M. SHAWN COPELAND

MODERN CATHOLIC SOCIAL THOUGHT

Modern Catholic social thought is the moral reflection of Roman Catholics on human relations in society since the 18th century. While other entries in this volume focus on particular aspects of this thought, the following discussion provides a general outline of its meaning, history, concepts, and unity.

Meaning

Each term in the phrase "modern Catholic social thought" has several connotations. Unless these are pointed out, the overall meaning of this thought can be obscured.

"Modern"

Anticipated by developments in late medieval and Renaissance Europe, the so-called modern world of Western civilization emerged in the late 18th century. At that time revolutionary democracy, nascent industrialism, empirical science, and the cognate ideas of liberalism, capitalism, and rationalism profoundly altered the long-standing social practices and institutions of Europe's ancien régime. Though the precise character and pace of these alterations varied from nation to nation, a broad and irrevocable social transformation was underway.

Modern Catholic social thought began as a response to this transformation. As such, when the word "modern" is applied to this thought it signals a period of time; no endorsement of modern social ideas and practices is implied. In fact, debate over the meaning and moral propriety of modernity has been a key element of Catholic social thought since the 18th century.

"Catholic"

Over the past two hundred years, countless Roman Catholics have thought seriously about social change *as* Roman Catholics. That is, their thinking has been self-consciously informed by concepts, symbols, stories, and structures that mark the historical experience of the Roman Catholic community.

These thinkers have represented several groups within the church. These groups include professional authors and academics, members of the church hierarchy, and leaders of popular movements.

Professional authors and academics have played a central role in shaping modern Catholic social thought. As journalists, essayists, theologians, philosophers, jurists, and social scientists, Catholic professionals have influenced this thought in many ways: through research, writing, classroom teaching, public speaking, academic colloquia, and church consultations.

Members of the church hierarchy have contributed essential texts to the corpus of modern Catholic social thought. These texts encompass not only papal encyclicals, apostolic letters, and addresses but also documents from the Second Vatican Council, the Pontifical Commission on Justice and Peace, and the Vatican Congregations for the Doctrine of the Faith and Catholic Education. Roman Catholic bishops have likewise produced a large number of letters from within their regional group meetings, national episcopal conferences, and world synods.

From one perspective, the most important popular voice of Catholic social thought is the parent who organizes a household, nurtures children, and maintains family and neighborhood relationships with insights drawn from living the Catholic faith. In terms of direct influence on Catholic social thought, however, a more self-conscious popular-level contribution has come from movements led by the clergy and the laity.

Since the 18th century leaders of popular movements such as Frederic Ozanam and the Society of St. Vincent de Paul, Peter E. Dietz and the Militia of Christ for Social Service, Dorothy Day and the Catholic Worker movement, and Cesar Chavez and the National Farm Workers' Association have had a strong impact on Catholic social thought. Other movements less identified with a single leader—for example, Pax Christi and the Latin American base communities—have done the same, as have movements inspired by Catholicism's many religious institutes such as the Jesuit Action populaire, the Franciscan Third Order, Benedictine liturgical reform, and Mother Teresa's Sisters of Charity.

Thus modern Catholic social thought is the product of the whole church: professionals and nonprofessionals, hierarchs and nonhierarchs, clergy and laity.

"Social"

No absolute separation of personal and social morality is recognized in Catholic thought, yet an academic distinction between the two has existed in Catholic moral theology throughout the modern period. Catholic scholars interested in matters of personal morality have generally focused on so-called "fundamental" issues such as the nature of human acts, the determinants of moral action, the definition of moral norms, the exercise of practical moral judgment, the role of conscience, and human moral development. Those concerned with social morality have tended to concentrate on topics such as the nature of the social order, the origin of social power and authority, the definition of justice, human relations within social institutions, and current affairs.

Due to this academic division of labor, issues of Catholic personal morality have typically been discussed through the categories of "fundamental" moral theology, while issues of Catholic social morality have more often been explored with the aid of history, social philosophy, political and economic theory, sociology, and law. Consequently, while fundamental moral theology and modern Catholic social thought are not separate enterprises, the latter has been more interdisciplinary, exploratory, and wide ranging; it has never been simply a deduction from the former.

The wide-ranging character of modern Catholic social thought is largely unrecognized. The periodic and highly publicized appearance of papal encyclicals commemorating Leo XIII's *Rerum novarum* has created the impression that Catholic social thought is solely concerned with economic morality. Yet Leo XIII himself devoted more encyclical attention to political issues than economic (on his list of nine recommended encyclicals dealing with social morality, Leo XIII placed *Rerum novarum* eighth!).

Since the 18th century sincere and knowledgeable Catholics have reflected on many topics bearing on human relations in society. One way to organize these topics is to group them into five spheres of social interaction: religion, politics, family, economics, and culture.

Catholic thinkers have had a longstanding interest in social issues dealing with the order and operation of religious institutions. These matters include power and authority relations between hierarchy, clergy, and laity; the quality of episcopal leadership, clerical discipline, and lay participation in the church; the role and conduct of theologians; the nature of intercreedal relations; and the purpose and method of missionary work in non-Western cultures.

Political issues have also been a major concern. Topics often raised are the origin and purpose of the state authority; the limits of state power; the merits of diverse political systems; the moral requirements of citizenship; the definitions of law, justice, freedom, and rights; church-state relations; international politics; and war and peace.

Catholics have likewise thought seriously about family life in society. This list of issues includes the character and purpose of marriage; relations between husband and wife; marital sexuality; contraception, abortion, and sterilization; the care of children; and the social role of the family.

Catholic thought on economic life is voluminous. Among the topics discussed are the merits of various economic systems and theories, particularly capitalism, socialism, communism, and corporatism; the balance between the agricultural, industrial, and service sectors; the justification for property ownership; the meaning of work; relations between rich and poor, employer and employee, capitalist and laborer; the economic implications of charity, justice, and rights; the morality of wages, working conditions, benefits, unions, strikes, and co-partnership; international trade; the link between First World consumerism and Third World poverty; and the economic roles of the church and the state.

Cultural matters have also been a frequent Catholic concern. These encompass the character and limits of public expression; pornography, propaganda, and art; forms of recreation; the content and structure of private and public education; health care; and relations between racial groups, women and men, and Western and non-Western cultures.

Through its many concerns and interdisciplinary explorations, modern Catholic social thought has been a major source of creativity within the church. Indeed, this thought has been central to the history of Roman Catholicism since the 18th century.

"Thought"

When modern Catholic social thought is discussed, the words "teaching," "doctrine," and "ethics," are frequently interchanged with the word "thought." The confusion generated by these substitutions can be reduced by making three distinctions.

First, Catholic social thought can be distinguished from social teaching and doctrine. The status and role of bishops in official Roman Catholic ecclesiology suggest that the phrases "social teaching" and "social doctrine" be used in reference to letters produced by the church hierarchy. If so, modern Catholic social thought would include the teaching and doctrine of the hierarchy but would not be limited to it.

A further distinction can be made between social doctrine and social teaching. In their 1983 pastoral letter, *The Challenge of Peace,* the United States bishops distinguished between the letter's universal moral principles and its prudential policy choices: the former bind in conscience, and the latter, while requiring serious attention by Catholics, do not bind in conscience. This suggests that the phrase "social doctrine" could be limited to the universal moral principles articulated by the church hierarchy, while the phrase "social teaching" could indicate the combination of these universal moral principles with the hierarchy's prudential policy choices.

Finally, a distinction can be made between Catholic social thought and Catholic social ethics. If the word "ethics" refers to the academic study of morality, then Catholic social thought would encompass the ideas of the whole church while Catholic social ethics would refer to the work of professional Catholic ethicists.

Social doctrine, teaching, and ethics, then, can be considered parts of the larger whole called "Catholic social thought." Official ecclesiology may well insist that the parts stand in an order of priority; but each is still a part, not the whole.

Over time, these several parts have provided modern Catholic social thought with many sources and methods. Theology, philosophy, and Scripture have been the major wellsprings. Yet Catholic social thought has also drawn upon the lessons of history and the resources of the social sciences. Similarly, while this thought has often been associated with a deductive method, its growing attention to history and social science has increased the importance of inductive and dialectical methods.

Modern Catholic social thought is, then, a broad enterprise. Beginning in the 18th century, it has included the work of professional authors and academics, the church hierarchy, and popular leaders. It has addressed moral issues not only in economic life but also in religious, political, family, and cultural life. And it has pursued these issues with a variety of sources and methods.

History

Although the claim that modern Catholic social thought began with Leo XIII's 1891 encyclical *Rerum novarum* needs modification, it does suggest a way to organize the history of this thought. A characteristically Leonine approach toward social affairs did exist within the church from 1878 to 1958. Using this period as a marker, one can then speak of a pre-Leonine period of Catholic social thought from 1740 to 1877 and a post-Leonine period from 1959 to the present.

Pre-Leonine Period

Catholic social thinkers of the pre-Leonine period witnessed the cataclysmic changes in social ideas and practices symbolized by the French Revolution. A general sense of the religious, political, economic, and intellectual context of these changes is helpful before identifying the history of Catholic social thought at this time.

On the eve of the French Revolution the Roman Catholic church was recoiling from several setbacks. Among the most significant were the expulsion of the Jesuits from all the lands ruled by Bourbon monarchs and the tightened legislative control of the church in the lands of the Hapsburgs. During the Revolution itself numerous French clergy and laity were imprisoned, killed, or deported; papal communications were restricted or banned; and massive tracts of church property were expropriated. A respite occurred with the Restoration of 1814, at which time a new generation of English, German, French, and Italian theologians sparked a Roman Catholic intellectual revival.

Between 1740 and 1789 absolute monarchs (Maria Theresa and Joseph II in Austria, Frederick the Great in Prussia, Catherine the Great in Russia, Louis XV in France) governed lands still emerging from feudalism and populated by subjects only vaguely aware of their national identity. The revolution that toppled the French ancien régime sent shock waves across Europe. After 1814 social forces unleashed by the French Revolution continued to incite political upheaval against the restored governments of Prince von Metternich's Holy Alliance. Significant political changes took place as a result of the 1830 bourgeois revolution in France, the independence movements in Belgium, Poland, and Ireland, the socialist revolutions of 1848 and 1871, and the unifications of Germany and Italy.

Prior to the Revolution, the European economy was vitalized with precious metal imports from Mexico and Peru. For a time the commercial revolution reinforced mercantilism, the state-controlled halfway house between medieval economic traditionalism and the modern market system. But the English steam engine and factory system eventually unleashed the economic forces requisite for early industrial capitalism. Adam Smith surveyed this phenomenon in 1776 and launched his classical economic analysis. After the Revolution, new steel production, rail transportation, and agricultural machinery altered work and home life. An impoverished, volatile industrial proletariat arose. David Ricardo adjusted Smith's economic analysis, but Karl Marx's scientific socialism introduced a radical intellectual and practical revision.

During the pre-Leonine period, the philosophical Enlightenment begun by men such as Thomas Hobbes, René Descartes, and John Locke spread through the polemical tracts of the French *philosophes* and Italian *illuministi*. Jean-Jacques Rousseau and David Hume produced this movement's first self-critique. Later, Immanuel Kant challenged Continental philosophy, while English politicians and philosophers discussed Edmund Burke's conservative response to the French Revolution and Jeremy Bentham's radical utilitarianism. At the end of the period, philosophers debated Hegel and

Schelling's idealism, Auguste Comte's new positive science of society, John Stuart Mill's refined utilitarianism, and Charles Darwin's biological studies.

Modern Catholic social thought began in this volatile social and intellectual environment. Responding to these changes, Catholic authors and academics, members of the church hierarchy, and popular leaders began developing forms of social thought that would have a lasting impact on both Europe and the church.

One form of social thinking among Catholic authors during this period recommended a return to patterns of social life and thought characteristic of old Europe. People like Joseph de Maistre (1753–1821), Vicomte de Bonald (1754–1840), François René de Chateaubriand (1768–1848), and Juan Donoso Cortés (1809–53) called for rebuilding a hierarchically organized community of mutual aid where people with customarily acknowledged roles and powers would work together, deferentially, for the preservation of the whole. Some conservatives, like de Maistre and de Bonald, were reactionaries; they saw little or nothing of lasting value in the social changes of modernity. Others, like Chateaubriand, were more moderate; they acknowledged certain modern ideas but insisted that they be incorporated—slowly—into the dominant structure of traditional values and practices.

Many moderate conservatives had concrete proposals for social improvement. As a way of upgrading the conditions of workers, Franz von Baader (1765–1841) called for government restrictions on industry and trade (his 1834 *Ueber den Proletairs* memorandum to the Bavarian government was one of the first European documents to bring working-class problems to the attention of state authorities). Alban de Villeneuve-Bargemont (1784–1850) advocated public housing, savings banks, and agricultural cooperatives.

Another line of Catholic thought was represented by Félicité de Lamennais (1782–1854) in France and Emmanuel von Ketteler (1811–77) in Germany. An early critic of social problems created by industrial capitalism, Lamennais devoted much of his attention to the advantages of political democracy for the church. Von Ketteler, a powerful critic of both liberal capitalism and radical socialism, encouraged state legislation for fair wages and hours, safe working conditions, and worker associations. In related fashion, Charles de Coux (1787–1864) supported independent trade unionism, while Philippe Gerbet (1798–1864), Henry Dominique Lacordaire (1802–61), and the American Orestes Brownson (1803–76) criticized the social effects of early capitalism.

In a sense, these Catholic thinkers were "liberals." Unlike conservative Catholics, a number of them supported the separation of church and state. Others shared the moderate conservative concern for the condition of the workers but went a step further in supporting autonomous labor unions. Though scarcely liberal in the sense given the term by the European *philosophes,* these Catholic social thinkers were distinct from their conservative counterparts.

A "radical" line of Catholic social thought also existed during the pre-Leonine period. Catholic socialist Philippe Joseph Buchez (1796–1865) applied a class analysis to the economic problems of Europe and advocated social equality through a system of producer cooperatives. Influenced by utopian socialist Charles Fourier, Hippolyte de la Morvonnais (1802–53) encouraged an international network of local producer *phalanxes.* In Belgium François Huet (1814–69) constructed a broad model of economic distributivism.

In 1740 Benedict XIV (1740–58) initiated and encouraged the modern papal practice of writing encyclicals to "preserve the Catholic faith and either preserve or restore the discipline of morals." Following his lead, nine popes produced seventy-seven letters prior to the pontificate of Leo XIII. Despite the fact that these letters are largely forgotten today, their discussions of social issues pertaining to religious, political, family, economic, and cultural life are a vital part of the history of modern Catholic social thought.

Several pre-Leonine encyclicals dealt with social ideas and practices regarding religious life. In *Ubi primum,* Benedict XIV decried the breakdown of episcopal and clerical discipline in Europe. His *A quo primum* proscribed Christian-Jewish relations in Poland. Gregory XVI (1831–46) used *Mirari vos* and *Singulari nos* to condemn the notion of freedom of conscience in religion.

The political issue of relations between the church and the state was frequently raised in the pre-Leonine period encyclicals. Clement XIV's (1769–74) *Cum summi* and Pius IX's (1846–78) *Quanta cura* vigorously opposed church-state separation. In *Charitas,* Pius VI (1775–99) criticized the civil oath demanded of the French clergy.

Most papal discussions of family life during this period focused on the neglect of marriage regulations. Benedict XIV's *Nimiam licentiam,* for example, discussed the problems of mixed marriage and civil marriage. In *Traditi humiltati,* Pius VIII (1829–30) said marriage was a sacred and indissoluble union dedicated "not so much to generate offspring as to educate offspring for God."

Benedict XIV's treatment of avarice and usury in *Quanta cura* and *Vix pervenit* began the rich history of modern papal reflection on economic matters. In *A quo die,* Clement XIII (1758–69) argued that the poor deserve alms out of justice, not simply charity. Pius IX made the first papal response to socialism in *Qui pluribus* and *Nostis et nobiscum.*

Regarding cultural life, Clement XIII encouraged church and state censorship of books in *Christianae reipublicae.* Leo XII's (1823–29) *Charitate Christi* alerted its readers to the rise of drunkenness in modern Europe. Pius IX decried a similar increase in prostitution (*Nostis et nobiscum*). A wide-ranging critique of "liberal" culture was given in Pius IX's *Quanta cura* and its well-known appendix, the *Syllabus of Errors.*

It should be noted that the popes' omnibus condemnation of liberalism was, in part, a function of their personal experiences. Under the banner of liberalism, Napoleon's General Berthier captured Pius VI during the French occupation of Italy. The pope died a prisoner in 1799. Eight years later, Pius VII fell captive to Napoleon's General Radet. Though eventually released, the pope was imprisoned in Savonna for six years. The future Leo XII witnessed these events as a papal nuncio. As bishop of Montalto, Pius VIII was also imprisoned. Gregory XVI was driven out of the monastery of San Gregorio on the Caelian Hill while he was the abbot. During the revolutions of 1848, Pius IX was forced to flee Rome while the bishop of Parma was murdered in his residence.

Leaders of popular movements also influenced Catholic social thought during the pre-Leonine period. Various organizations for the assistance of European workers, such as Armand de Melun's patronage movement and Frederick Ozanam's Society of St. Vincent de Paul, were broad-based, influential organizations. In Germany, Adolf Kolping's (1813–65) Gesellenverein (associations organized and operated by workers themselves) attracted attention throughout Europe and had great impact on the development of Catholic social thought. This was true also of the German Center party. Created by Ketteler, this was the forerunner of the later Christian Democratic parties of Europe and South America.

Leonine Period

The accession of Leo XIII (1878–1903) to the papacy and his call for an institutional revival of Thomistic studies influenced Catholic social thought at all levels. It is useful to have a general sense of the social context wherein Leo XIII issued this call.

Responding to the First Vatican Council, his own seminary training, and the condition of European society at the end of the 19th century, Leo XIII mandated that Roman Catholic studies and instruction be built on the thought of the 13th-century theologian-philosopher Thomas Aquinas. Girded with the theological and philosophical principles of this neo-Thomism, Pius X (1903–14) criticized divergent theological systems under the epithet "modernism." At the same time, the church faced the German, Swiss, Belgian, Italian, and Hungarian Kulturkampf, the Austrian Los-von-Rom movement, and truculent church-state separations in France and Portugal. While the so-called Scholastic period of Thomistic studies and instruction continued from 1915 to 1958, its hegemony was increasingly challenged by the alternative *nouvelle theologie* created by such scholars as Teilhard de Chardin, Marie-Dominique Chenu, Yves Congar, and Henri de Lubac. This new line of thought developed just as the church began forging strong ties with democratic states in its fight against religious oppression in the Soviet Union and Eastern Europe.

The political context of the Leonine period was marked by major international turmoil. Prior to World War I the nation-states of Europe combined their antagonism toward the Roman Catholic church with aggressive African and Asian colonization policies. Conflict between "entente" and "central power" governments eventually triggered the First World War. When it was over, newly self-conscious ethnic groups clamored for self-rule, laboring classes were energized by the Russian Revolution, and the bourgeoisie sought reactionary means of political stabilization. Europe's parliamentary democracies successively collapsed under this collective turmoil, ushering in totalitarian regimes of right-wing fascist and left-wing communist ideologies. This political instability precipitated the Second World War. When it was over, Western Europe returned to the practice of parliamentary democracy, its international influence now eclipsed by the two superpowers.

The third stage of the Industrial Revolution, or "high capitalism," was underway at the beginning of the Leonine period. This stage was characterized by closely monitored assembly-line production, higher levels of foreign trade and investment, and a wave of inventions such as electrical power (1882), the gasoline engine (1884), the automobile (1885), the wireless telegraph (1897), and the airplane (1903). The field of political economy was replaced in 1890 by Alfred Marshall's mathematical economics. After a brief period of post–World War I economic growth, Europe and the Americas entered a deep depression. In 1936 John Maynard Keynes framed a theory of economic stimulation through government adjustment of interest rates, taxes, and deficit financing. This remained the most influential theoretical approach toward economics until well after the end of the Leonine period.

The intellectual context of the Leonine period also presented new challenges. At the outset of the period, Friedrich Nietzsche offered a penetrating critique of both Christianity and bourgeois culture, Ernst Haeckel and Herbert Spencer advanced materialist evolutionary theories, Sigmund Freud began his psychological studies, and William James introduced philosophical pragmatism. Other new philosophies emerged in the interwar years: Edmund Husserl's phenomenology, the Vienna Circle's logical positivism, Martin Heidegger's existentialism, and Henri Bergson's vitalism. After World War II, Sartre and Marcel expanded existentialism, while Merleau-Ponty continued phenomenology. The posthumous appearance of Ludwig Wittgenstein's writings enlivened analytic philosophy.

Throughout this period many Catholic social thinkers labored to reform society according to Thomistic principles. They considered this to be part of the larger project of rejuvenating the whole of Western civilization by means of the "perennial philosophy" from which it sprang. To others, the involvement of Roman Catholics in social affairs and their construction of schools, unions, and associations paralleling those of secular society seemed at once defensive and intrusive.

Many Catholic authors and academics contributed to this work. Some Catholic liberals like Heinrich Rommen (1897–1967) focused on matters of democratic political and legal theory. This area attracted much Catholic attention when Europe returned to parliamentary democracy after World War II. It was at this time that Jacques Maritain (1882–1973) and John Courtney Murray (1904–67) produced their important studies in Catholic political thought.

Other Catholic thinkers followed the earlier lead of von Ketteler, taking a liberal reformist approach toward economic problems. Franz Hitze (1851–1921) and John Ryan (1869–1945) were central figures here, as were the German solidarists Victor Cathrein (1845–1931) and Heinrich Pesch (1854–1926). Also important was Gaspar Mermillod's (1824–92) Fribourg Union, an annual meeting of French, German, Austrian, Italian, Belgian, and Swiss leaders and thinkers interested in ameliorating the social costs of the capitalist market economy through the organization of vocational groups.

Catholic conservatives also produced various lines of social thought during the Leonine period. Though the Fribourg Union acknowledged the value of vocational group organization, Austrian romantics like Karl von Vogelsang (1818–90) condemned capitalism entirely and sought its replacement with a compulsory state-controlled corporative system modeled on medieval guilds. In their visions and imperatives the Austrians were possibly more radical than conservative. Certainly they were far afield of the new liberal conservatives of the period who, like Charles Périn (1815–1905), supported the capitalist market system and rejected the idea of state intrusion in economic affairs.

Papal encyclicals took on a larger role in the overall articulation of Catholic social thought during the Leonine period. This was due, in part, to the diminished—and, in many cases, destroyed—power of local bishops in the new secular nation-states. Compared to their immediate predecessors, then, the Leonine period popes acquired a heightened programmatic self-consciousness, a broadened sense of pastoral responsibility for the whole of Western civilization, a greater preoccupation with specific moral issues, and a stronger claim to religious and moral authority. Encyclicals were a major instrument in this new papal orientation. Indeed, the sheer number of encyclicals written by the five popes of this period is staggering: 185 encyclicals in eighty years. Not all of these letters treated matters of religious, political, family, economic, and cultural life in society, but many more did than are typically noted in today's conventional list of so-called social encyclicals.

It was in his encyclical *Aeterni Patris* that Leo XIII called for the restoration of Thomistic studies in the Church. Theological and philosophical ideas deemed discordant with Thomistic principles were condemned in Pius X's *Pascendi dominici gregis* and Pius XII's (1939–58) *Humani generis.* At the same time, Pius X's *Il fermo proposito* and Pius XI's (1922–39) *Non abbiamo bisogno* encouraged the laity to improve society through what was called "Catholic Action."

Though primarily remembered today for his encyclical *Rerum novarum,* Leo XIII concentrated more of his attention on political theory, citizenship, church-state relations, and the concept of political liberty. The most important of these texts included *Diuturnum, Immortale Dei, Libertas, Sapientiae christianae,* and *Graves de communi re.* An abundance of arguments are put forth in these letters, from a Thomistic analysis of liberty and citizenship, through tentative support for political democracy, to a critique of church-state separation. The Leonine period popes also discussed the issues of nationalism (Pius XI's *Ubi arcano Dei consilio* and *Mit brennender Sorge*), war and peace (Benedict XV's [1914–22] *Ad beatissimi Apostolorum*), and citizen resistance to unjust authority (Pius XI's *Nos es moy conocida*).

Family life also concerned the Leonine period popes. Leo XIII addressed problems of family life in *Inscrutabili Dei consilio* and *Arcanum* (the latter being the first encyclical devoted exclusively to the meaning of Christian marriage). After identifying childbearing as the natural purpose of marriage, Pius XI proceeded in *Casti connubii* to condemn artificial birth control, abortion, and sterilization. In the same letter, Pius XI decried adultery and the negative impact of women's emancipation on family life.

The rights and duties of employers and employees, the moral status of property ownership, and the positive economic role of the state were treated at length in Leo XIII's *Rerum novarum.* The American bishops covered similar ground in their 1919 Program of Social Reconstruction. These issues surfaced again in slightly different form in Pius XI's *Quadragesimo anno.* Here, the pope emphasized the social dimension of property ownership, the merits of corporatism, and the concepts of social justice and subsidiarity. Socialism and communism were condemned in Leo XIII's *Quod Apostolici muneris* and Pius XI's *Quadragesimo anno* and *Divini Redemptoris.* In *Quadragesimo anno,* however, Pius XI noted that the programs of moderate non-Communist socialism "often strikingly approach the just demands of Christian social reformers."

In the cultural sphere of social life, the Leonine period popes analyzed the evils of slavery and racism (Leo XIII's *In plurimis* and Pius X's *Lacrimabili statu*), the perceived problems of co-education and sex education (Pius XI's *Rappresentanti in terra*), and the potentially dangerous social impact of modern art, movies, and television (Pius XI's *Vigilanti cura* and Pius XII's *Miranda prorsus*). Responding to moral challenges created by modern medical technology, Pius XII reasoned that if in the treatment of a terminally ill patient suffering great pain "the actual administration of drugs brings about two distinct effects, the one the relief of pain, the other the shortening of life, the action is lawful" (address to the ninth Congress of the Italian Anaesthesiological Society). Reminiscent of the pre-Leonine period style of social criticism, Pius XII's *Summi pontificatus* presented a wide-ranging moral analysis of secular culture.

Leaders of popular movements had a formidable impact on Catholic social thought during the Leonine period. As an expression of his Catholic faith, Léon Harmel (1829–1915) transformed his spinning factory at Val-des-Bois into a community of co-partnership. He advocated this scheme to Leo XIII through several Roman pilgrimages (his 1889 journey drew over ten thousand Catholic employers and employees). Support for worker association was maintained in the Leonine period through such movements as the Jesuit Action populaire. Across the Atlantic, Peter E. Dietz's (1878–1947) Militia of Christ for Social Service linked American Catholic workers with the secular labor movement.

Radical grass-roots movements also existed during the Leonine period. In Germany Heinrich Mertens (b. 1882) and Vitus Heller (b. 1906) organized associations of Catholic socialists. In the United States a unique form of nonviolent Catholic anarchism surfaced in Peter Maurin and Dorothy Day's Catholic Worker movement. At the same time, Virgil Michel linked liturgical reform and the cooperative movement in his journal, *Orate Fratres.*

Other Catholic leaders continued to work on drawing democratic political principles into the orbit of Catholic social thought. Though condemned by Pius X in 1920, Marc Sangnier's (1873–1950) French Sillon movement had great impact along these lines, as did Luigi Sturzo's (1871–1959) Italian Popolari party and the German Center party under the leadership of Othmar Spann.

Post-Leonine Period

The Second Vatican Council (1962–65) was the watershed between the Leonine and post-Leonine periods of modern Catholic social thought. Though the earlier period's emphasis on Thomas Aquinas was not explicitly rejected at Vatican II, Thomists were compelled to give ground to a greater variety of theological sources, methods, and conclusions. Renewed attention to Scripture and patristic studies, greater openness to modern philosophical movements, and serious interest in the social sciences inspired this new moment in Catholic social thought.

The post-Leonine period spans the pontificates of John XXIII (1958–63), Paul VI (1963–78), John Paul I (1978), and John Paul II (1978–). The period has witnessed not only the momentous changes of the Second Vatican Council but also the new challenges of liberation and feminist theologies. Before the collapse of the Soviet Union, tensions between it and the United States rose and fell, each time entangling newly independent Third and Fourth World nations in its movement. While Eastern-bloc nations vacillated between economic centralization and experiments in decentralization, Western nations of the Northern Hemisphere have experienced unprecedented economic growth. Simultaneously, nations of Central and South America, Africa, the Indian subcontinent, and East Asia have struggled through periods of severe poverty. The development of Western science and technology has mushroomed during this period, led by nuclear physics, laser technology, cybernetics, computers, and robotics. In the area of philosophy, the analytical school has continued its domination of Western thought, while significant alternatives have emerged in the work of Herbert Marcuse, Jürgen Habermas and Gyorgy Lukács of the Frankfort school, the hermeneutics of Hans-Georg Gadamer, and Jacques Derrida's deconstructionism.

New developments in Catholic social thought have accompanied these social and intellectual trends. Skirting the neo-Thomist approach toward this thought, scholars like Johannes B. Metz have developed a political theology informed not by natural law but the theological concept of the kingdom of God. In the United States, heirs to the liberal legacy of John Courtney Murray have continued exploring the positive meaning of democracy and human rights not only for Catholic political thought but also for the order and operation of the church. The work of Bryan Hehir, David Hollenbach, and John Coleman exemplifies this trend.

A major contribution to Catholic social thought during this period has been liberation and feminist theology. Through attention to human "praxis" and commitment to liberation of the oppressed, Latin American scholars such as Paulo Freire, Gustavo Gutiérrez, and Juan Luis Segundo have challenged the sources, methods, and conclusions of previous Catholic social thought. So too has feminist social ethics. Thinkers like Margaret A. Farley, Christine E. Gudorf, and Rosemary Radford Ruether have criticized the longstanding link in Catholic thought between human beings' reproductive biology and their social role.

Thinkers critical of these developments have created a sizable social literature of their own. Combining the "moderate" conservatism of a pre-Leonine-period figure like Alexis de Tocqueville with the "liberal" conservatism of a Leonine-period thinker like Charles Périn, Michael Novak has insisted on the merits of the capitalist market economy for Christian social life. Roger Charles has reasserted the value of Thomism for modern Catholic social thought, while James Shall has questioned the naive optimism of much contemporary Christian political thought by recovering an Augustinian sense of the human limits of social reform.

During this period the social writings of the church hierarchy have expanded beyond papal pronouncements to conciliar documents and social statements of bishops around the world. As in the past, these writings have covered a wide variety of social concerns.

In the religious sphere of social life, the conciliar document *Dignitatis humanae* presented a forthright endorsement of freedom of conscience in religion (thereby reversing earlier papal teaching). In their 1971 statement *Justitia in mundo* (*Justice in the World*), the general assembly of bishops declared "action on behalf of justice" a "constitutive dimension of the preaching of the Gospel." As such, Paul VI insisted the same year that "it is up to the Christian communities to analyze with objectivity the situation which is proper to their own country" (apostolic letter *Octogesima adveniens*). In the apostolic exhortation *Evangelii nuntiandi,* the same pope insisted that just as non-Western cultures can learn from Christian missionaries, so too must missionaries (and the church) learn from non-Western cultures.

The central political statement of the Church hierarchy in the post-Leonine period has been John XXIII's *Pacem in terris.* Here, the pope endorsed a wide range of political and economic rights within the context of promoting peace and condemning the arms race. On the last issue, the United States bishops' pastoral letter *The Challenge of Peace* noted the importance of both pacifism and just-war theory for resolving the problem of war in the nuclear age. American bishops from several states (Florida, Tennessee, Pennsylvania, Ohio, Missouri, and California) have written separate letters against capital punishment.

The most influential statement on family life during this period has been Paul VI's *Humanae vitae.* In this letter the pope sustained Pius XI's proscription of birth control but added new reflection on the affective dimension of marital love. Noteworthy too has been the Latin American bishops' concern over the condition of the family in oppressive social environments (Medellín and Puebla documents). In the Puebla Document, for example, the bishops called for special attention toward impoverished youth.

The popes have also sustained their predecessors' interest in the morality of economic life. John XXIII's *Mater et magistra* emphasized the global dimensions of economic ethics, focusing particularly on the crisis of world agriculture. Paul VI (*Populorum progressio*) and John Paul II (*Sollicitudo rei socialis*) have explored the structural links between Third World poverty and First World patterns of investment and consumption. In *Laborem exercens,* John Paul II focused on the meaning and experience of work in contemporary society, seeing here "a key, probably the essential key, to the whole social question." As a creative dimension of work, he has also supported a "right to freedom of economic initiative" (SRS). At the same time, both the Canadian bishops (*Ethical Reflection of the Economic Crisis*) and the United States bishops (*Economic Justice for All*) have come to quite distinct conclusions on the moral propriety of capitalist initiative.

A sweeping moral analysis of Western culture occurs in the conciliar document *Gaudium et spes.* Unlike earlier hierarchical writings, this text sought to understand "the joys and the hopes, the griefs and the anxieties" of modern people. In *Pacem in terris* John XXIII abandoned the earlier papal emphasis on censorship and recognized a person's moral right to freedom "in expressing and communicating his feelings." Though a person may think and speak incorrectly, the pope insisted that a distinction be made between "error and the person who errs." Thus, errors must be rejected, but people in error must be allowed to speak so that they might "break through" their mistakes and make available to everyone "occasions for the discovery of truth." For the popes, *acting* on an error is another matter. In the case of homosexuals, while a same-sex affective orientation may not be evil per se, the sex act between homosexuals is (Vatican Congregation for the Doctrine of Faith, *On the Pastoral Care of Homosexual Persons*). Because no single culture enjoys "a monopoly of valuable elements," Paul VI insisted in *Populorum progressio* that people be open to knowledge from other cultures. On this score the Wisconsin bishops criticized both church and society for past abuse of Native Americans (*Honoring Treaty Rights*).

The post-Leonine period has experienced many popular social movements inspired by Catholic leaders. In the United States people such as Thomas Merton, Gordon Zahn, James W. Douglass, and the Berrigan brothers crystallized a Catholic peace movement. Pax Christi has supported peace efforts worldwide. As older links between the church and organized labor began weakening in the United States, Cesar Chavez mobilized successful grape and lettuce boycotts in support for his United Farm Workers Union.

Inspired by the pedagogy of the Brazilian educator Paulo Freire, countless clergy and laity have created the Latin American base community movement. With over eighty thousand of these house-churches in Brazil alone, this movement has influenced Catholic thinking on the nature and social structure of the church.

On a less conspicuous but no less meaningful level, Canadian Jean Vanier organized the L'Arche movement for enhancing the lives of disabled and nondisabled people around the world. Though sometimes dismissed in academic discussions of Catholic social thought, the charitable work of Mother Teresa has also had a deep influence on social thinking at the popular level.

This history of modern Catholic social thought is only a sketch; many voices, issues, and nuances are missing. Yet even a sketch is sufficient to show how this thought has been a significant source of dynamism within the Roman Catholic church over the past 250 years.

Concepts

Since the 18th century Catholic social thought has been a combination of theological orientations and moral insights forged in lively engagement with ideas and practices of the modern world. For the sake of analysis the major theological and moral emphases of this thought can be distinguished.

Theological Orientations

Modern Catholic social thinkers have used several styles of theological reflection. Some have placed primary emphasis on a particular branch of Christian theology such as Christology, ecclesiology, soteriology, or eschatology. Others have focused on discrete passages from Scripture, the patristics, or writings of the church hierarchy. Still others have taken their major inspiration from the perspectives of classic figures like Augustine, Aquinas, or Bonaventure.

One way to draw these styles together so as to appreciate the overall role of theology in modern Catholic social thought is to note several of the theological metaphors they share. Metaphorical images of God, society, and the human person have had significant though often subtle impact on the moral insights of modern Catholic social thinkers. Though not exhaustive, the following analysis highlights four of these metaphors.

One metaphor frequently employed in Catholic social thought is a pastoral metaphor, that of a shepherd and his flock. Here, God is imaged through the model of Christ the Good Shepherd. This image emphasizes God's character as a caregiver willing to suffer and die for the flock (the church).

Correspondingly, society is depicted as the flock's spatial milieu. This milieu contains pastures of nourishment and security for the flock but also wilderness areas replete with wolves. Society, then, is ambiguous; it is simultaneously necessary and dangerous. As such, it must be approached very circumspectly.

The role of the person in the pastoral metaphor highlights the human qualities of memory, simplicity, obedience, and patience. In an ambiguous social milieu where survival depends on retaining the long-standing customs of Christian faith and morals, the power of memory is highly valued. So too are the rustic virtues of simplicity, obedience, and long suffering. These virtues reflect what is required of a person as a "lamb" in the flock and an imitator of Christ the Good Shepherd.

Many Catholic social thinkers have drawn on the pastoral metaphor. The papal encyclicals of the pre-Leonine period were largely shaped by this image. Catholic conservatives have sometimes used it as support for their positive vision of a lost bucolic past. Even a more radical voice like the Catholic Worker movement has sometimes framed its commitment to nonviolence, agrarian cooperatives, voluntary poverty, and social decentralization with this metaphor.

A different image occurs when Catholic social thought is influenced by the language and premises of Thomism. Here, the metaphor of cosmological design predominates. Now God is imaged less as the Good Shepherd and more as the intelligent designer of the universe. This reflects Thomas Aquinas' theological vision of God as the rational creator, sustainer, and fulfiller of all things.

The image of society also changes with this metaphor. Society is now envisioned as a necessary and good part of God's universal order. Confident that divine purposes are embedded in social relations and institutions, human beings can—and should—exercise their reason in the reform of society. The church should advise this reform because it (now imaged less as the flock and more as the mystical body of Christ) has Christ—the ultimate source of knowledge about God's order—at its head.

Human beings represent the apex of God's earthly order. By exercising their rational powers, human beings can participate in God's rational design. All people have this power, but the debility of sin makes the added tenets of Christian faith and morality necessary for eternal life. These supernatural tenets build on (but do not replace) the natural moral law. There is no necessary conflict between supernatural faith and natural reason, or eternal law and natural law, because they emanate from the same noncontradictory God.

The cosmological design metaphor has had great influence on modern Catholic social thought. Many liberal thinkers of the pre-Leonine period employed this metaphor. The papal encyclicals of the Leonine period used it abundantly, as did many Catholic academics and popular leaders of that time.

A third important image in modern Catholic social thought has been the metaphor of dialogical journey. Here, God is modeled more as a historical journeyer with humanity and less as a shepherd or rational designer. This metaphor also carries with it a greater emphasis on God's dialogue with humanity through the promptings of the Holy Spirit.

This approach also encourages a different perspective on society. Unlike an ominous pasture or a natural order, society is imaged as the necessary, historically changing context for God's conversational pilgrimage with humanity. Here, God's message to humanity is made known through the power of the Holy Spirit within the social history of the world. At the same time, the church is referred to less as a flock or mystical body of Christ and more as the people of God.

This metaphor encourages a view of the person that reflects this sensitivity to historical experience. From this perspective faith is construed more as a response of the whole being to the experience of God's self-revelation than as the maintenance of customary beliefs or rational assent to divine principles. Similarly, the basis of morality is located more in an affective experience of moral value than in an unquestioning obedience to authority or the rational comprehension of natural law.

Anticipated in some liberal voices of the pre-Leonine period, use of the dialogical journey metaphor becomes widespread among Catholic academics and popular leaders after the Second Vatican Council. The writings of the church hierarchy begin employing the dialogical journey metaphor at this time too, though with a sometimes disjointed admixture of the Leonine-period cosmological design metaphor.

The metaphor of conflictual liberation also figures prominently in modern Catholic social thought. Here the model of God as social liberator comes to the forefront. Whether highlighting God's liberating work in the Exodus or Jesus' anger in the Temple, this metaphor draws a direct connection between the character of God and the social condition of human beings.

From this perspective society is linked to the theological notion of the kingdom of God. On one hand, the political, economic, and cultural structures of society can empower human beings, thereby facilitating God's kingdom. On the other hand, these structures can oppress human beings, in which case they become sinful. Creating the former and eliminating the latter involves conflict; and in this conflict, God favors the oppressed. Indeed, the church is often referred to as the "church of the poor."

With the conflictual liberation metaphor, personhood is primarily approached by looking at how an individual acts. This action—or praxis—approach sees in a human being's social behavior the expression of that individual's actual faith and morality. Thus if a human being acts oppressively in society, that individual's de facto faith and morality are oppressive. Such an individual's identification with Christianity is superficial or deceiving. Without a firm commitment to the liberation of the oppressed—imitating God's own commitment—personhood is distorted.

Intimations of the conflictual liberation model are found in some Catholic socialist thinkers of the Leonine period. The main source for this metaphor has been the Latin American liberation theologians and leaders of the base-community movement that have emerged during the post-Leonine period. European political theologians, North American feminist theologians, and Latin American bishops have used this image as well, though frequently combining it with the language and premises of the dialogical journey metaphor. It has also been employed by post-Leonine popular leaders who have encouraged nonviolent tactics of conflictual liberation.

These four metaphors are not the only images that have influenced the theology of Catholic social thought, nor is the focus on metaphor the only way to approach this topic. This approach does, however, give a sense of both the importance and the variety of theological orientations for the development of modern Catholic social thought.

Moral Insights

Modern Catholic social thought has offered a variety of moral insights pertaining to human relations in society. While all of these cannot be covered here, several major insights pertaining to religious, political, family, economic, and cultural life are highlighted.

In the religious sphere of social relations, Catholic thinkers have tended to place high value on ecclesial unity. What unity specifically requires, however, alters, as metaphors for the church shift between the self-enclosed Roman Catholic "flock," the triumphal "mystical body of Christ," the broad-based "people of God," and the empowered "church of the poor." Though much debate has ensued over ecumenism, post-Leonine period thought has generally become less exclusive and more inclusive—not only of non–Roman Catholic Christians but also of non-Christians. As part of this development, Catholic social thinkers have increasingly emphasized the notion of inculturation for contemporary missiology; that is, as missionaries introduce Christianity they should neither harm non-Western cultures nor fail to learn from them.

Catholic social thinkers have also tended to link the issue of ecclesial unity with that of ecclesiastical order. Respect for the spiritual and moral authority of the Petrine office (and the hierarchy in general) has typically been recognized as a desideratum for ecclesial unity. But here too, a more precise understanding of the nature and range of this authority has shifted under the shepherding, monarchial, collegial, and co-liberator models of church leadership. Not surprisingly, the last two models have motivated calls for more substantive inclusion of theologians, women, and the laity into the ecclesiastical order of the church.

These models have, in turn, impacted Catholic thought on the social responsibility of the laity. While all Catholic social thinkers have recognized this responsibility, it has been understood in different ways. The cosmological design metaphor encouraged the Catholic Action approach, wherein the laity took their cues for social action from the church hierarchy. The dialogical journey and conflictual liberation metaphors, on the other hand, have encouraged laypeople to analyze the situation in their communities and respond in a manner consistent with the message of Christ.

In the realm of political life, Catholic social thinkers have generally agreed that state authority is ultimately grounded not in a secular social contract between people and rulers but in a correspondence between the behavior of the state and the will of God. However, the locus of God's will in this area has moved from the juridical authority of the church (where it was in most pre-Leonine and Leonine period thought) to the concept of the common good (where it has been in most post-Leonine period thought). Thus while Catholic social thinkers have come to accept the separation of church and state, they do not accept the separation of church and society, meaning the refusal to allow the church any input in the social debate concerning the common good.

Catholic social thinkers have in large part agreed that the state has a responsibility to the common good. This latter concept has typically been understood to mean a combination of social goods and political processes necessary for human flourishing. But the same thinkers have not been unanimous in specifically identifying these goods and processes or on the exact moment when a state so disregards the common good as to forfeit its moral legitimacy.

Though Catholic social thought has encouraged citizen participation in political life, many models of participation have been recommended. Leaders of the Catholic Worker movement, for example, have discouraged citizens from paying taxes for war, registering for conscription, and complying with legislation involving violence against life. Motivated in part by virtues inspired through the shepherd and flock metaphor, the Catholic Worker model of political participation has refused to submit to what is perceived as the technologically violent system of urban America. At the same time, liberal Catholic academics and grass-roots leaders have encouraged Christian cooperation with the system. Theologically bouyed by a combination of the cosmological design and dialogical journey metaphors, they have endorsed such things as the application of just-war theory to situations of international conflict and nuclear deterrence.

The concept of marriage as a sacred and indissoluble union between one man and one woman has been affirmed by all Catholic social thinkers since the 18th century. During the post-Leonine period, however, disagreement has occurred over the proper model of spousal relations. Though church hierarchical writings have paid more attention to the affective dimension of spousal relations since Vatican II, the model of functional complementarity has remained fundamental. Supported by the metaphor of cosmological design, this model depicts men as uniquely responsible for the exercise of family authority and provides women with specific responsibilities in regard to the nurturing of children. Influenced by the dialogical journey and conflictual liberation metaphors, Catholic feminist ethicists have insisted on a more egalitarian model of spousal relations involving a sharing of authority and nurturing responsibilities.

Catholic thought on family life has also put great emphasis on the procreation, protection, and education of children. Catholic thinkers have typically placed the discussion of abortion, sterilization, and artificial birth control in this context. Since Vatican II, distinct perspectives have emerged on these issues, in part due to the application of different theological metaphors. Those employing the cosmological design metaphor have addressed these issues from the standpoint of the rational comprehension of natural (here, biological) laws. Those employing the dialogical journey metaphor have addressed these issues from the standpoint of an affective experience of moral value. Neither approach has denied the value of children, yet both have nudged the moral evaluation of abortion, sterilization, and artificial birth control in different directions.

Catholic thinkers have also described the family as the essential cell of human society. This being the case, general agreement has existed that the state should assist families in situations where they cannot provide for their own health and survival. In keeping with the concept of subsidiarity, however, state assistance must respect the ultimate prerogative of the family over its own welfare.

In the economic sphere of social relations, Catholic social thinkers have for the most part accepted the market system of economic production and distribution—as long as it is morally and legally directed toward satisfying the common good. This does not mean, however, that Catholic social thinkers have uniformly endorsed capitalism. Many have not. Rather, capitalism has more often been looked upon as one among many economic philosophies (along with moderate socialism, corporatism, and cooperatism) that can shape a market system.

It has been common in Catholic social thought to see the problems of liberal capitalism as inversely reflected in Marxist socialism. Both understand the economy in largely materialistic terms: one encourages individual hedonism, the other, group hedonism. Both understand the economy as operating automatically: one as a function of an "invisible hand," the other as a function of dialectical materialism.

The morality of individual ownership of nonproductive property has long been acknowledged in Catholic social thought. Individual ownership of productive property, however, has been treated a number of ways ranging from outright rejection by Catholic radicals, qualified acceptance among liberals, and unqualified acceptance among certain conservatives. At the same time, each group has agreed with the principle that the basic goods of God's creation should be available to all humanity.

Since the 18th century Catholic social thinkers have shared a particular interest in the social conditions of working people. Work itself has been increasingly heralded as a human activity of not only economic importance but also profound psychological and religious significance. As a consequence, employers have been called upon to respect employees by abandoning work structures and schedules harmful to religious and family life, overseeing occupational safety, providing just wages, permitting some degree of employee participation in decisions affecting the firm, and respecting workers' associations. At the same time, employees have been encouraged to perform their work honestly and avoid any direct physical harm to the employer's person or property. Catholics influenced by the shepherd and flock metaphor have tended to approach these issues of employer-employee relations from the standpoint of moral duties; those using the dialogical journey metaphor have generally looked at these issues from the perspective of human rights.

Aside from Catholic anarchists, most Catholic thinkers have acknowledged the state's role in monitoring the economic system. This has included ensuring that individuals are treated fairly and that balanced support is given to the agricultural, industrial, and service sectors of the economy. On an international level, states have been increasingly called upon to provide direct aid to underdeveloped nations and recognize each nation's right to equal opportunity in international trade.

Catholic social thinkers have likewise insisted that the church maintain a special ministry to the poor, that it encourage a global perspective on economic issues, and that it divest itself of riches in cases of human need. The interpretation of such care, encouragement, and divestment has been a function of *which* metaphor is used in depicting the church.

Liberation theologians inspired by the conflictual liberation metaphor have insisted, for example, that the church and society make a "preferential option for the poor." While there have been different opinions among Catholic social thinkers over what such an option entails, it would seem to involve—from the Latin American perspective—the following five things in descending order of priority: a commitment to radical social change founded on an unqualified rejection of liberal capitalism and totalitarian Marxism, an anticipation of social conflict in view of this commitment, an adoption of lifestyles in solidarity with the poor, a commitment to living and working with the poor so as to help them act on their own behalf, and an experience of personal religious conversion through direct action with the poor.

The approach of modern Catholic social thinkers toward culture has also been influenced, in part, by theological metaphors. Those using either the shepherd and flock metaphor or the metaphor of cosmological design have tended to reject secular culture—the former taking a defensive posture, the latter taking an offensive posture. Catholics using the dialogical journey metaphor have sought to build bridges between the church and secular culture. Those taking strength from the conflictual liberation metaphor have for the most part rejected bourgeois culture and endorsed many (though not all) aspects of peasant culture. Catholic attitudes toward formal adolescent education have reflected this spectrum of options, with the merits and demerits of private and public systems debated at great length. All have agreed, however, that education should involve both beneficial secular knowledge and religious training.

These same tendencies can be traced across other cultural issues. On the topic of freedom of expression, Catholic thinkers have insisted that social communication be truthful. But during the pre-Leonine and Leonine periods many Catholics influenced by the pastoral and cosmological metaphors supported censorship on suspicion that social communication outside the church was false, while many post-Leonine period Catholics have encouraged open communication between the church and society. Consistent with the dialogical journey metaphor, this latter approach has contributed to the gradual opening of Catholic social thought—long articulated mainly by Western-educated white males—to the insights of non-Westerners, people of color, and women.

These distinct theological orientations have also influenced the development of Catholic thought on health care. This has been evident, for example, in the issue of withdrawing or withholding artificial means of feeding and hydration to terminally ill and dying patients. Catholics influenced by the cosmological design metaphor have tended to focus on the propriety of this act with an eye toward obedience to the natural moral law; Catholic thinkers shaped by the dialogical journey metaphor have generally addressed the morality or immorality of this situation with an eye toward the realization of moral value.

The relationship between theology and morality in modern Catholic social thought has been one of cross-fertilization in history. Theological orientations have shaped the morality of this thought and moral insights have fed back on its theology. One has never been the simple product of the other, nor have their interactions occurred outside of history.

Unity

Exposure to the numerous voices, issues, orientations, and insights of modern Roman Catholic social thought invites the question, What, if anything, unites it? Is there an identifiably "Catholic" way of thinking about human relations in society that draws all the parts together?

Behind this inquiry is the idea that when the phrase "social thought" has a modifier—whether "Catholic," "Christian," "Methodist," "Liberal," "Marxist"—the word signals some characteristic that gathers the parts into a whole. So one can rightly ask, Does modern Catholic social thought possess such a characteristic?

Some conclude that it does not. Due to the plurality of sources, methods, and conclusions in this thought, some people consider the claim for unity more an aspiration of the claimant than a characteristic of the literature. From this point of view, no substantive unity exists; the word "Catholic" is simply a label individuals apply—for any number of reasons—to their social thought.

The more common response has been to affirm the unity of modern Catholic social thought. But even here, people disagree over what the unifying element is. Several approaches can be identified.

One approach locates the unity of modern Catholic social thought in the social doctrine and teaching of the popes. Thus if the social ideas of a Roman Catholic reflect those of the pope, those ideas are "Catholic"; if they do not, they are not. If a distinction is recognized between doctrine and teaching, then a variant of this approach identifies the unity of modern Catholic social thought with both papal doctrine and teaching. The other variant finds the unity of this thought in papal social doctrine alone.

A different way of pinpointing the unity of Catholic social thought is to look not at ecclesiology, but method. Some people associate Catholic social thought with the moral theory of natural law. From this perspective, if the social ideas of a Roman Catholic are consistent with the natural law (the expression of God's eternal law available to humanity by the promptings of conscience and the teachings of the church), those ideas are "Catholic"; if not, they are not.

Yet another approach looks not at ecclesiology or method, but content. Many people consider the concept of human dignity the unifying factor in modern Catholic social thought. This concept flows from the Gen 1:26 identification of human beings as the image and likeness of God. From this source, human beings are thought to possess rights that bear directly on social relations.

Others locate the unity of this thought in the concept of the common good. The argument here is that all Catholic social thinkers postulate a society in which, in one form or another, the social goods and processes necessary for human flourishing are made available to as many people as possible.

Each of these affirmations of unity has weaknesses. By locating the unity of modern Catholic social thought in papal doctrine and teaching, one can miss the fact that the papal texts themselves have sometimes presented contradictory and inconsistent messages. Nor is natural-law theory a unifying factor. This theory is not utilized throughout modern Catholic social thought, even in hierarchical writings. The concept of human dignity, though ubiquitous in the post-Leonine period, scarcely appears in pre-Leonine and Leonine thought (at least up to the end of World War II). If modern Catholic social thought has a unity, the concept of the common good may come closest to describing it. Yet even here the typical understanding of the concept "common good" (strongly influenced by Thomistic categories) may be too narrow.

A more adequate way to describe the unity of modern Catholic social thought may be as an umbrella under which a variety of communitarian styles of social thought co-exist. This perspective would argue that Catholic conservative, liberal, and radical social thinkers have shared a communitarian impulse as noteworthy as their differences. This possibility can be reinforced by returning to the major theological orientations of this thought.

The several theological metaphors of modern Catholic social thought have shaped distinct ways of thinking about human relations in society. But on another level these metaphors have overlapped. The shepherd's ingathering, the creator's unified work, the journeyer's dialogic fellowship, the liberator's social commitment—all of these images of God have communicated a deep sense that the divinity has a will to gather, create, sustain, and transform human communities. This suggests that Catholic conservatives, liberals, and radicals—despite their obvious differences—have shared a profound theological commitment to nurturing community life. None of them has taken the community for granted.

Each theological model of society—ominous pasture, structure of divine purposes, historical context for dialogue, kingdom of God—has also shaped distinct forms of Catholic social thought. But at a deeper level these too may be related. In various ways each model has depicted society as a mutuality of service. Here again, while Catholic conservatives, liberals, and radicals have differed on how this mutuality of service is to be realized, none has understood society as simply a social contract.

In describing the person, it has made a difference whether one emphasized the human capacity to loyally retain traditions, intellectually grasp moral principles, affectively experience solidarity, or act in concert with the poor. But these capacities have also been linked. In their own ways each has accented the socially embedded character of human existence; each has insisted that humans are defined by the totality of their relations with other selves. Thus, Catholic conservatives, liberals, and radicals have again been joined; none of them has reduced the human person to an unencumbered chooser of autonomous ends.

If this communitarian impulse is correct, it explains why Catholic social thinkers as a whole have retained a distinct understanding of freedom, equality, rights, and justice in the modern world. In this understanding, freedom is not just the capacity to explore and satisfy one's wants but the power to achieve good in and for the community. Equality is not just the condition from which one can expect respect and opportunity but the power from which one can expect to participate in building these opportunities. Rights are not only a person's immunity from civil intrusion but also a person's entitlement to basic social goods and participation in social processes. Justice is not only fairness in contracts (commutative justice) but also fairness in social distribution (distributive justice) and the availability of opportunities to construct a good society (social justice). If one understands the concept "common good," or even the concept "human dignity," as encompassing this communitarian impulse, then their identification as the unifying factors of modern Catholic social thought is understandable.

Unfortunately, Roman Catholic individuals and institutions have not always respected these visions of freedom, equality, rights, and justice. There have been successes and failures; much has been achieved, much remains to be done. Nevertheless, these ideas have been an important part of modern Catholic social thought, part of what one might call the "communitarian" character of this thought.

The history of modern Catholic social thought is an unfinished drama over 250 years old. It is a story of Catholics who have at different times and places thought seriously about human relations in modern society. It is a story of disagreement and consensus, of multiple lines of argument held by people otherwise united in a commitment to bridge modern social experience with the conceptual, symbolic, narrative, and structural resources of the Roman Catholic community. And possibly, it is a story too of people united in an insistence that human beings are—by the grace of God—a community, and that social relations in the religious, political, family, economic, and cultural spheres of life must—with God's help—reflect that fact.

See also BISHOPS' PROGRAM OF SOCIAL RECONSTRUCTION OF 1919; CHURCH, SOCIAL MISSION OF; EPISCOPAL LETTERS, FUNCTION OF; FEMINISM AND CATHOLIC SOCIAL THOUGHT; LABOR AND CAPITAL IN CATHOLIC SOCIAL THOUGHT; MORAL LIFE, CHRISTIAN; SYNOD OF BISHOPS; VATICAN COUNCIL II.

Bibliography: A. Abell, ed., *American Catholic Thought on Social Questions* (Indianapolis: Bobbs-Merrill, 1968). J.-Y. Calvez and J. Perrin, *The Church and Social Justice: The Social Teaching of the Popes from Leo XIII to Pius XII (1878–1958),* trans. J. Kirwin (Chicago: Henry Regnery, 1961). R. Camp, *The Papal Ideology of Social Reform: A Study in Historical Development, 1878–1967* (Leiden: E. J. Brill, 1969). C. Carlen, ed., *The Papal Encyclicals,* 5 vols. (Wilmington, N.C.: McGrath, 1981). R. Charles, with D. Maclaren, *The Social Teaching of Vatican II: Its Origin and Development* (San Francisco: Ignatius, 1982). M.-D. Chenu, *La 'doctrine sociale' de l'eglise comme ideologie* (Paris: Les editions du Cerf, 1979). Congregation for Catholic Education, "Guidelines for the Study and Teaching of the Church's Social Doctrine in the Formation of Priests," *Origins* 19, no. 11, (1989). C. Curran, *American Catholic Social Ethics: Twentieth-Century Approaches* (Notre Dame: Univ. of Notre Dame Press, 1982). C. Curran and R. McCormick, eds., *Readings in Moral Theology No. 5: Official Catholic Social Teaching* (New York: Paulist, 1986). D. Dorr, *Option for the Poor: A Hundred Years of Vatican Social Teaching* (Maryknoll, N.Y.: Orbis, 1983). J. Eagleson and P. Scharper, eds., *Puebla and Beyond: Documentation and Commentary,* trans. J. Drury (Maryknoll, N.Y.: Orbis, 1979). J. Gremillion, *The Gospel of Peace and Justice: Catholic Social Teaching Since Pope John* (Maryknoll, N.Y.: Orbis, 1976). C. Gudorf, *Catholic Social Teaching on Liberation Themes* (Washington: Univ. Press of America, 1981). D. Hollenbach, *Claims in Conflict: Retrieving and Renewing the Catholic Human Rights Tradition* (New York: Paulist, 1979). B. Menczer, *Catholic Political Thought, 1789–1848* (Notre Dame: Univ. of Notre Dame Press, 1962). P. Misner, *Social Catholicism in Europe: From the Onset of Industrialization to the First World War* (New York: Crossroad, 1991). J. Mitchell, *Critical Voices in American Economic Thought* (New York: Paulist, 1989). J. Moody, ed., *Church and Society: Catholic Social and Political Thought and Movements, 1789–1950* (New York: Arts, Inc., 1953). M. Novak, *Freedom with Justice: Catholic Social Thought and Liberal Institutions*

(San Francisco: Harper & Row, 1984). M. Schuck, *That They Be One: The Social Teaching of the Papal Encyclicals, 1740–1989* (Washington: Georgetown Univ. Press, 1991). A. Vidler, *A Century of Social Catholicism, 1820–1920* (London: S.P.C.K., 1964).

MICHAEL J. SCHUCK

MODERNISM

"Coined in or around 1905, the term 'Modernism' was intended as a pejorative description of certain scholarly trends which had been developing . . . during the last decade of Leo XIII's pontificate. These trends arose out of the conviction that Catholicism was not incompatible with modernity," whereas "Catholicism under Pius IX had decided on a policy of retrenchment and hostility" (Gabriel Daly in *The New Dictionary of Theology*, p. 668). Contemporaneously there was a certain hue and cry about "social modernism." The main connection between the two "modernisms" was that the proponents of "integral Catholicism" harshly condemned both tendencies, scholarly and social, as unauthorized and ruinous departures from the status quo (identified uncritically with the tradition of the church). Hence the present treatment of modernism will have chiefly to do with the integrist outlook as related to certain developments in social Catholicism after *Rerum novarum.*

Christian democracy was the chief of these developments. In the 1890s this was a first stage of a Catholic labor movement, almost a reprise of the ideas that Félicité Lamennais had put out in 1830 about the union of pope and proletariat—of church and people—in emancipation from the dirigistic pretensions of the upper classes. In Italy *la democrazia cristiana* was first championed as an alternative to liberalism and socialism by Giuseppe Toniolo (1845–1918), an economist with deep interests in the Italian economy of the Middle Ages and Renaissance and a positive attitude toward the neo-Thomist anthropology and social teaching of the Jesuits of the *Civiltà Cattolica* (notably Matteo Liberatore, 1810–92). As the movement expanded, however, it ran athwart of the papal "*non expedit*" that forbade Catholic participation in national politics, whether as members of parliament or simply as electors. There was reason to think that this prohibition would soon have to be lifted. Romolo Murri (1870–1944), a priest from a diocese north of Rome, unfolded a prodigious activity in aid of organizing labor unions and in particular in propagandizing for the ideal of "Christian democracy." The lay Catholic establishment in the Opera dei Congressi did not see Catholic participation in national elections as immediately in the offing and did not appreciate the democratic propaganda emanating from Murri's publishing house. The hierarchy was similarly dubious about his great influence on the younger clergy and seminarians.

In this situation, Leo XIII issued the encyclical *Graves de communi re* (1901). He was not ready to permit normal political participation on the part of Catholics in Italy in view of the unresolved Roman Question (the temporal sovereignty of the pope vis-à-vis the kingdom of Italy and hence internationally). At the same time, he did not wish to disavow the turn to the people on the part of lay and clerical social Catholics, as evidenced in the embryonic labor organizations in town and country—something he had called for in *Rerum novarum* (48–61). So he endeavored to distinguish between the political aspects of Christian democracy and the socioeconomic ones, reserving his approval only for the latter. As far as the political aspect was concerned, he had long maintained that democracy could be a legitimate form of government but that no moral superiority in principle attached to it, no more than to monarchy or oligarchy. By contrast, that which he was pleased to call *Christian* democracy, that is, "beneficent Christian action in behalf of the people" (i.e., the lower classes; par. 7: "*actio benefica in popu-*

lum"), was indispensable in one form or another. A German Catholic politician of the Center party saw rightly when he declared, "In this sense, we (Catholics) are all democrats."

In Italy, then, there were those who, like Murri, declined to accept the papal tactic of definition as anything more than a stopgap disciplinary measure. They continued to believe that democracy was something more than an ethical adiaphoron and that it required the participation of members of all strata of society in the direction of government (something that a pope would not concede until the year of Murri's death, shortly after his reconciliation with the church). In Pius X's church (1903–14), however, claims of autonomy from hierarchical direction in the social sphere came to be regarded as "social modernism." Political democracy, with its doctrine of equal rights, was regarded in the same light. The confrontation with anticlerical *social* democrats made it easy for integralistic minds to tar any sign of unauthorized activity, whether in the world of scholarship or of economics or of politics, with the brush of modernism. A new generation of *Civiltà Cattolica* authors would publish articles condemning labor unionism in 1914.

What had happened was that the integrist reaction focused on those movements, like the Christian labor movement in Germany and Italy or the Sillon in France, where the claim to act autonomously in secular matters, independently of church authority, was accompanied by the claim to be acting on one's Christian religious responsibility and hence somehow in concert with Christianity. (By "integrism" or "integralism" is meant the conviction that all areas of both public and private life should be placed under the authority of the church, that is, the hierarchy. It was especially virulent during the period of intense church-state conflicts in the late 19th century: the annexation of the Papal States into Italy, completed in 1870, the Kulturkampf in German countries, the hostile separation of church and state in France in 1905.) The Center party in Germany was at least the indirect target of integrists in the German Catholic trade-union controversy (1900–14), which centered ostensibly on the interconfessional character of the unions (cf. the encyclical of 1912, *Singulari quadam*). For if Catholic and Protestant workers were involved in the same unions, the hierarchy could not expect to issue binding directives to correct false or dangerous ethical stances that the unions might adopt. In Italy Pius X kept up the pressure on the few but stubborn Murrian Christian Democrats, especially with the encyclical *Pieni l'animo* of 1906. Even moderates such as Toniolo and the publisher of Catholic newspapers, Giovanni Grosoli (1859–1937), whose services were highly appreciated by Leo XIII, were publicly reprimanded by Pius X.

In France the integrists were not content to encompass the condemnation of Marc Sangnier's Sillon. The principles enshrined in Pius X's letter to the French hierarchy, *Notre charge apostolique* (August 25, 1910, AAS 2:607–23) were to spell the end of any Catholic political or social movement not under the direct control of the hierarchy. Thus the Jesuits of the Action populaire (headed by Gustave Desbuquois, 1869–1946) came under suspicion and attack, as did the Semaines sociales. These integrist actions were coordinated by Raphael Cardinal Merry del Val (1865–1930), secretary of state to Pope Pius X (see Droulers, index). The operative principles were spelled out in *Notre charge apostolique.* The Sillon, it acknowledged, wished only to promote "the greatest possible participation of each person in the government of society" (AAS 2:615); this was seductive but unfortunately opposed to Catholic social teaching, which upheld the importance of obedience to external authority in a framework of relations of subordination. The ideal of social equality was "a chimera" (AAS 2:628) and a socialist one at that.

Workers must be taught to know their place. In France there were only fledgling Catholic labor groups and unions until after World War I, opposed tooth and nail by the relatively few Catholic industrialists (especially by the so-called Patrons du Nord). A model Catholic industrial patriarch, Léon Harmel (1829–1915), is the exception that confirms this state of the case. The massive paternalism of his peers suffered no breach when, in the wake of *Rerum novarum,* he defected openly from the expectations of his class and began to promote the Christian democratic movement. The Patrons entered into a working relationship with the ecclesiastical integrists so much in favor in Pius X's time. In 1909 and again in 1911, with the backing of Merry del Val, Julien Fontaine, S.J. (1839–1917), published accusations of a modernist conspiracy connecting the Semaines sociales professors with the would-be Christian labor organizers. Both stood accused of ignoring the natural law and hence of trying to destroy the social hierarchy, private property, and any social order. The integrists could not imagine a bishop leading factory workers into a strike against their employers; from this they concluded that the very notion of a union ready to strike even as a last resort was morally intolerable. Desbuquois of the Action populaire replied that Catholic bankers and industrialists were allowed to join trade associations that were active in the interests of their class without the need to receive any special guidance from their pastors; why could not Catholic workers do something similar, but on the side of justice? Thus he revealed the unquestioned paternalistic presuppositions that brought lay bourgeois and clerical integrists together.

The integrists lost their credit with the papacy when Pius X died. Finally in 1929 a public declaration of the Holy See was promulgated in defense of the right of workers to organize (in a letter to Bishop Liénart of Lille; see AAS 21:494–505 and Talmy 237–46). The sum of social modernism in the era of Pius X seems to have amounted to little more than efforts to promote the ideals of democracy and social justice among Catholics. Its most controversial issue, the legitimacy of labor unions, ended up with a papal vindication of the modernist side, confirmed in 1931 by *Quadragesimo anno.*

See also CHRISTIAN DEMOCRACY; LABOR AND CAPITAL IN CATHOLIC SOCIAL THOUGHT; OPERA DEI CONGRESSI; PATERNALISM; RERUM NOVARUM; SANGNIER, MARC (AND SILLON); STRIKE, RIGHT TO.

Bibliography: Articles by E. Hegel and N. Trippen in *Staatslexikon,* 7th ed. (1987) 3:109–11 and 1201–4; and by A. Zambarbieri and E. Poulat in DSMCI I/1:35–55 (1981). *Fonti e documenti* (annual, Urbino, 1972–, 1–). S. Agocs, "Christian Democracy and Social Modernism in Italy During the Papacy of Pius X," *Church History* 42 (1973) 73–88. R. Aubert in *History of the Church* 9:420–80, ed. H. Jedin (New York: Crossroad, 1981). P. Droulers, *Politique sociale et Christianisme: Le Père Desbuquois et l'Action Populaire* (Paris: Editions ouvrières, 1969). J.-M. Mayeur, *Catholicisme social et démocratie chrétienne* (Paris: Cerf, 1986). P. Misner, *Social Catholicism in Europe* (New York: Crossroad, 1991). E. Poulat, *Intégrisme et catholicisme intégral* (Tournai: Casterman, 1969). R. Talmy, *Le syndicalisme chrétien en France (1871–1931)* (Paris: Bloud & Gay, 1966).

PAUL MISNER

MONOPOLY

In Catholic social thought monopoly is seen as a natural outcome of unregulated markets. As early as 1891 Pope Leo XIII wrote that "the whole process of production as well as trade in every kind of goods has been brought almost entirely under the power of a few." Monopoly was seen as evil because it enabled "a very few rich and exceedingly rich men [to lay] a yoke almost of slavery on the unnumbered masses of nonowning workers" (*Rerum novarum* 6). Forty years later during the depression of the 1930s, Pope Pius XI said: "The ultimate consequences of the individualist spirit in economic life are . . . : Free competition has destroyed itself; economic dictatorship has supplanted the free market; unbridled ambition for power has likewise succeeded greed for gain; all economic life has become tragically hard, inexorable, and cruel" (*Quadragesimo anno* 109).

Monopoly is seen as a perversion of the right of private property. Christian tradition has never upheld the right to own private property as absolute and untouchable. As Pope John Paul II said in *Laborem exercens,* "The right to private property is subordinated to the right to common use, to the fact that goods are meant for everyone" (LE 14). Monopoly gives power to a few, enabling them to get rich at the expense of workers and poor consumers.

The state, as the representative of the community, is called upon to regulate markets so as to better achieve the common good. The existence of monopoly is evidence of the failure of markets to be self-regulating and of the state to perform its necessary functions. As early as 1919, in their Program for Social Reconstruction, the U.S. Catholic bishops argued for "prevention of monopolistic control of commodities, adequate government regulation of such public service monopolies as will remain under private operation, and heavy taxation of incomes, excess profits, and inheritances" (no. 38).

See also COMPETITION; CONGLOMERATES; CORPORATIONS; TRUSTS.

CHARLES K. WILBER

MORAL LIFE, CHRISTIAN

This article is intended as a general reflection on the place of morality within modern Catholic life and theology. In stating the matter in that way I am deliberately opting for a broad canvas. There has been much debate in Catholic theology in recent times about the Christian ethic. It has concentrated on specificity, that is, on whether Christianity proposes a different content to moral life from that proposed by human morality—in effect, by those who do not explicitly subscribe to Christianity. My concern here certainly includes that, but it is wider.

There is a general assumption among Christians that there is something that can be called a Christian ethic. A recent work begins with this assertion: "The foundations of Christian ethics must be evangelical foundations; or, to put it more simply, Christian ethics must arise from the gospel of Jesus Christ. Otherwise it could not be *Christian* ethics" (O'Donovan, p. 11). So convinced are many believers of this that they regard the promotion of its ethical vision as the chief point of Christianity, and they are bewildered if one even raises the question of specificity. It comes as a shock to them to find that some Catholic moralists regard efforts to insist on specificity as a mistake.

It helps to pause and look at the very conjunction of the words "Christian moral life," and "Christian ethics." Whether they be valid expressions or not, they ought not be taken for granted. If there be a Christian ethic it is one instance of a wider phenomenon—religious ethics. There are other religious ethical systems—Jewish, Muslim, Buddhist, animist, and so forth. Should we expect morality to occur with religion, and why?

Religion and morality are formally distinct. They have different concerns, different objects. They deal with different clusters of questions. There are many who acknowledge the ethical claim, who seek to listen to it and lead their lives in accordance with it, who develop ethical theories, but who firmly deny the religious dimension and refuse to have any truck with organized religious morality. They often claim that their morality is superior. In particular they claim that their moral motivation is purer, their state of moral development more advanced. An article in a relatively recent book on Christian ethics and contemporary philosophy begins with the remark that "the thesis of this paper is that religious morality is infantile" (Nowell-Smith, p. 75)—infantile above all in its general conception and as diminishing the responsibility and autonomy of the subject. Our approach to Christian moral life, then, might set it in the broader context of religious morality and puzzle over such questions as how do these two relatively independent areas, religion and morality, encounter each other; what happens to morality when it is incorporated into a religious system; what is the borrowing from one to the other?

Part 1: Context

The fact is that most religions have an ethical strand. But the ethical is only one part of the composite picture. Sociologists of religion list various elements that tend to recur—myth, cult, organization, ritual, behavioral rules of an ethical and nonethical kind. Religions incorporate the ethical in quite different ways. Their basic myth and their general cosmogony bear on it differently. Major themes that relate to morality—the creation of the world, of human beings and human institutions, of good and evil—are envisioned differently. In some religions evil is an aspect of God, in others there is a qualified semidualism, in others a full dualism in which there are two opposed cosmic systems. In some the deity is otiose or indifferent, in others it is generally benevolent and concerned; in some, creation is devoid of moral purpose, in others the deity is lord of history. Not all religions believe the soul to be immortal or dependent on the deity, and not all have notions of reward or punishment in an afterlife. So they enshrine different views of the origin of morality and of its possibility. They weigh it differently with respect to other elements of the system. They have different notions of salvation—perhaps the basic quest of religions—and in particular of the significance of moral life for that.

All this is the subject matter of the discipline of comparative religious ethics. We might ask how Christian ethics looks against this background. That sets our own concern in clearer focus. It sharpens our wits. It questions assumptions that may have lain unexamined in the expression "Christian ethics." It provokes us to pursue issues that affect the contours of our moral lives: why is Christianity an ethical religion; how, in what way, and to what extent; where does it get its morality from; how do we as Christians situate morality; how do we conceive of the relationship between God and morality; what is the significance of moral life for salvation—and what salvation; can we be moral and with what means; how does our Christian anthropology, in particular our view of good and evil in our human constitution, affect our view of the whole moral enterprise? It is because Christianity answers such questions in its own way that there is in the first instance something that can be called "Christian ethics." Not all these questions can be treated here, but I hope to advert to the major ones.

An Ethical Religion: A Religious Ethic

Not all religions are equally ethical: in some ethics plays a prominent role in the story—in the daily life, in the discipline, and in the way to salvation. It is a commonplace that biblical religion is ethical and biblical ethics religious. However Israel arrived at its Decalogue, that code is represented as standing at the very foundation of its history and as the direct and immediate communication of God. The context was the covenant. So, OT ethics is strongly historical: the sages may have had prudential reasons for some stipulations but they are subsumed under religious reasons; the law gives its orders in the name of the covenant God. God's demands for pity for the poor, the warnings against luxury and the abuse of wealth, are so insistent and overpowering that cult becomes worthless unless it goes hand in hand with ethical life. Behind those sayings lie God's authority and love for the people.

"What to me is the multitude of your
sacrifice?
says the Lord.
I have had enough of burnt offerings of
rams
and the fat of fed beasts; . . .
cease to do evil, learn to do good;
seek justice, correct oppression;
defend the fatherless, plead for the
widow" (Isa 1:11ff.).

"Shall I come before him with burnt
offerings
with calves a year old? . . .
What does the Lord require of you
but to do justice, and to love kindness,
and to walk humbly with your God?"
(Mic 6:6-8).

If your deity is capricious your religion might not give a high priority to morality, and ritual might well predominate. But the God of Israel was good, faithful, and merciful toward the poor. The covenant people were to be like God.

The religion-ethics dynamic is further accentuated in the NT. God is good, benevolent, has a care for the world, communicates with us, has a plan for a kingdom of justice and peace, wishes us to turn from selfishness and division and live with others in love. We are to show total and undivided obedience to God, but it is to a Father who has graciously approached us, who has first loved us in his saving action in Christ and called us to grace. The content of the ethics of Jesus may be found already in the OT or in extrabiblical sources, but it is the preaching of the kingdom that forms the fundamental presupposition and basis of it. The acceptance of the kingdom makes ethical demands on us. It is true that Jesus promises reward—not the reward of human favor (Mt 6) but of God's—and that just requital has its place in his preaching. But the overarching symbol is a merciful Father: God's mercy has been shown to us; we are called to show mercy in turn. By the Spirit who has been given to us we are enabled to live such a life: it is the fruit of God's Spirit. In the end this is what will matter—not bringing one's gift to the altar, not being able to call oneself a child of Abraham, not saying "Lord, Lord," but having fed the hungry, cared for the sick, visited those in prison (Mt 25).

There is no moral life in the Bible without reference to the faith that motivates one to respond to God. So it is today: the moral life of Christians is shot through with religion. Take some remarks that are the everyday currency of Catholic moral life: "I confess to Almighty God that I have sinned," "I absolve you from your sins in the name of the Father," "This murder is a crime against the sacred law of God," "I want to make my peace with God," "God can bring good out of evil," "We love others in God," "We see Christ in the neighbor," "What would Jesus have done in the circumstances," "Lord I am not worthy to receive you," "I have discerned this in the Spirit," "A Christian ought to . . ." In all there is an intriguing intermingling of religious and ethical considerations. Indeed it is not always possible to distinguish them: there are experiences and terms—sin, holiness, wholeness, sacrifice, worship, salvation—that are not clearly one or the other.

Such matters are not usually the focus when the issue of Christian moral life is discussed. The focus is rather the content of morality, the question of moral norms, and of whether Christianity does and must of its nature propose something different from other ethical systems. But it should be obvious that this more general context, the overall manner in which we conceptualize and situate morality, is of considerable importance. It is important both for morality and for faith: either or both can be distorted or diminished. Faith can be—and often is—reduced to morals or its understanding of the deity distorted. Morals can lose all autonomy. Rupert, in Iris Murdoch's novel *A Fairly Honourable Defeat*, "disapproved of belief in God which he felt to be a weakener of the moral sinews." But one can point to a whole battery of philosophers who felt that religion was antithetical to morality: Hume ("the steady attention alone to so important an interest as that of eternal salvation is apt to extinguish the benevolent affections and beget a narrow, contracted selfishness"), Kant (morality based on the will of God "would inevitably form the basis of a moral system which would be in direct opposition to morality"), Feuerbach ("whenever morality is based on theology . . . the most immoral, unjust, infamous things can be justified and established").

The task of religious ethics is not an easy one. It brings together two of the most profound, most significant, and to some extent most elusive human experiences; two great symbol systems; two languages, the language of ethics (right, wrong, duty, obligation) and the language of religious myth (salvation, grace, justification, sin). They are deep concerns of the human spirit, and it is hardly surprising that we find it difficult to hold them together in a manner that does justice to both: the deepest concerns do not easily yield themselves to neat definitions. How we hold the elements together has implications that go deep into our psyche. You see it in the notion of sin, for example, the shadow side of morality. It is a flash point because it brings together so many critical elements—God, moral law, failure, repentance, sanction, satisfaction, salvation, church discipline. The catechism definitions that we trade, the language and imagery we use, the prayers we teach our children, the role and significance we attach to the sacrament of reconciliation, affect not only our understanding of morality but of God. Which is why we constantly need a hermeneutic of our symbols and why also it is enlightening as well as humbling to do our morality—as our religion—in dialogue with other religious traditions.

So let me try to follow in a little more detail the general contours of Catholic morality. It might be helpful to stand back from it and ask such questions as what kind of deity emerges from the Catholic moral tradition—benevolent, accepting, understanding of human weakness, or the opposite? (What are one's memories of a Catholic childhood? Remember the famous sermon in James Joyce's *Portrait of the Artist as a Young Man.*) Does God first love us or do we have to merit God's love by moral righteousness? And if we do not, what then? One thinks of the remark of the bishop of Woolwich in his *Honest to God* that we cannot rethink our notion of God without rethinking our notion of morality, so much is one a function of the other. As an example take this paraphrase from the moral philosopher Cathrein, who greatly influenced the moral textbook and catechism of late 19th- and early 20th-century Catholicism. Law, he says, requires a sanction: if God wished the moral law to be kept the only way to do so would be to impose a reward and punishment for it; only the eternal punishment of hell or reward of heaven would be sufficient stimulus; to impose a lesser punishment would be contrary to the wisdom of God. It would be hard to overestimate the influence that kind of thinking has had—and it was the common coin of all the philosophers and theologians of the period—on our idea of God. It is at the root of our most basic fears. It *is* many people's concept of God.

Morality as Law of God

We are here on what has been called the theological frontier of ethics and are engaged in a particularly thorny piece of God-talk. The language that suggested itself most easily to the Christian tradition was that of law: morality is a law made by the ruler-God; sin is a crime, deserves punishment, and can only be discharged by pardon or penalty. Noldin gives a fair summary. "God constituted himself the human being's ultimate end; but by the very fact that he did so, he imposed on them an obligation of tending to the ultimate end. . . . The moral order instituted by God is the way by which one is to tend to the ultimate end and the means, by observance of which, one achieves it" (Noldin-Schmitt, pp. 38, 40). Neo-Scholastic moral theology went to some trouble to demonstrate that the eternal and natural laws exhibit the features of a *vera lex:* they are determined by someone in authority, they derive their binding force from the will of the legislator, they require a sanction, they can be dispensed from by the legislator. That particular metaphor has had grave consequences for Catholic moral life.

Such a religious morality is held together by a number of key concepts—morality as law of God, human righteousness as merit, beatitude as reward. The overall language model is a particular raid on the inaccessible mystery. Like all such, it is limited and bears the marks of its time and culture. It is an attempt to catch in symbolic form deep things of the spirit—belief in a transcendent, longing for salvation, recognition of the sacredness of the moral claim. The trouble is that we might read the symbol too sharply: to take it literally is to run the risk of distortion of our religious and moral sensibilities. One can only speculate what a different culture—Eastern for example—might have made of the biblical datum or how a female theological tradition—because the concepts and images have been severely male—might have shaped an understanding of the intermingling of the religious and the ethical. In the Roman Catholic tradition the language of "sacred law of God" remains the favored way of talking about morality.

Karl Rahner gave much thought to the Christian language of law-sin-guilt-punishment. He was unhappy about it because of the forensic model it espouses: it is predominantly and heavily the language of the law courts (Rahner, p. 214). How appropriate is that to catch God's relationship with us or to do justice to the notion of morality? A Christian, of course, needs to contextualize his/her moral life, like everything else, within his/her overall worldview, and the Catholic tradition sees God as origin, exemplar, final grounding, and ultimate end of all human choice. It needs somehow to say that. But we need to remember that one cannot without great logical caution transfer the everyday language of "law" or "will" to God and morality. We do not do justice either to God or to morality unless we somehow preclude the notion that God is a man with a "will" who issues commands like a monarch and arranges for punishment for those who do not obey. It is not surprising that it was along this particular fault line of the relationship of God-morality-salvation that the greatest upheaval in the history of Christianity occurred in the Reformation.

There are, of course, logical problems about morality as law. Already in Plato's *Euthyphro* they had been posed: "whether the pious or holy is beloved by the gods because it is holy, or holy because it is beloved by the gods." There are further objections that a divine-command theory of morality destroys responsibility and the very possibility of authentic response to the moral claim because it reduces morality to obedience to the will of a superior. There are varieties and nuances of divine-command theories, and much depends on what one's understanding is. But it has to be conceded that religious morality does open the way to crudities. One sees them in some of the more naive approaches to the "wiping away" of sin in confession. Moral fault cannot be wiped away or undone by God or by anyone else: what is done is done and one must take on the burden of one's failures. One can contextualize one's moral failures religiously, and the sacrament facilitates this. But to suggest that one can feel and behave as if one had not done wrong is to encourage the magical mentality and to do a disservice to morality and to the human spirit.

There were—and are—more nuanced understandings of law. For the great Scholastics it signified essentially guidance toward an end. "Law" is, after all, an analogical term, and we use it to describe the law of the seasons as well as the law of nature or physical laws. I can refer to morality as the law of my being, as a thrust in me, a tendency to move or grow in a particular direction—a thrust, for example, to act in a way that brings about human good or flourishing or development. And I can of course say that in this sense morality is the law or will of God my Creator. But there is all the difference in the world between thinking of human beings listening to a thrust in them to behave in a particular way and finding it appropriate to refer to this also as the will or law of God, and thinking of morality as the law of God because it is a set of ordinances issued by God. It is in the former sense that the great Scholastics could refer to morality as law, and in this attenuated sense as the law of God. We can still do so today provided we know what we are doing.

Morality as law, sin as crime, redemption as satisfaction to offended majesty, form a triad. It is one model. There are others. For example, there is in the tradition a kindlier view of our human and religious history that sees sin as sickness rather than as crime, as weakness rather than as willfulness, and that sees God as healer rather than as judge. Such a view does not regard us as born into guilt for something for which we were not responsible, as classic theology of an original Fall did. It does not regard us as answerable for the weakness and ambivalence with which we were born. It calmly accepts our evolution from prerational and unconscious animality with its indispensable drives, passions, and defense mechanisms. If this is the plan of our Creator it must be that God freely accepts the limitations, the imbalance, the lack of integration, to which we are all heir. It is the human condition. It can oppress ourselves and others. It can do harm. We need to be healed in order that the kingdom may come within us and around us. But there is a difference of perspective here that has far-reaching effects in human consciousness—in our sense of God, of ourselves, and of our relations to God.

It can be seen, then, how our particular creation and salvation-redemption myths—and even within the Christian tradition there are several of them—affect how we see the whole moral landscape. Salvation is a primary interest for religions: how it is envisioned and thought to be attained affects how moral life is situated. Not all religions place it in an afterlife, and not all relate it to morality. Traditional Catholicism did. For it, Christian life had one point, the heavenly salvation of the individual soul, and that was to be achieved by moral rectitude. So the moral theology manual began with the tract *De fine ultimo hominis,* which is the vision of God in heaven. What was the way thereto? Prümmer put that succinctly: "By virtue of his supreme authority God prescribed for us the way by which we can reach him and our own beatitude. That way is made known to us by the laws made by Him . . . whence it follows that we cannot reach our beatitude except by obeying just laws" (Prümmer, p. 98). Two issues especially arise here and suggest themselves for consideration—the stance of the Christian toward the world and the problem of merit and justification.

Salvation and the World

There are varieties of moral life. There are individual vocations and ideals. But let us speak generally. For most of its history Catholicism has regarded the world as a vale of tears, an exile after which "these poor banished children of Eve" would be shown the blessed fruit of the womb of the Virgin Mary—to quote a well-known and oft-used prayer. The world was a sad stage on which the drama of each one's individual salvation was played out. What happened to the world did not matter very much. What mattered was that each individual would strive to be preserved from its contagion and would ideally store up merit by the practice of virtue. The Christian was to ensure that nothing of his/her life in the world was lost to salvation by the practice of offering everything to God. If there was a thrust outward it was to save souls, to entice people away from moral depravity so that they too might reach salvation to the glory of God.

It is no longer so. There has been a shift in the community's perception and in theological reflection. One could interestingly trace the various theologies and the retrieval of biblical themes, particularly in relation to promise, salvation, history, and kingdom, that have brought about the shift. The net result has been that it has come to be seen that the church's concern is not just religious—the forms and structures of its own life—that it is not just an institution that offers salvation to the individual, not an ideology that legitimates the status quo, but that the church is for the kingdom and that the kingdom is for it a horizon and a judgment. It has to engage politically. Moral life has to become creative. In particular, justice can no longer be regarded as the preservation of the status quo. Hope cannot be for private salvation alone but for the cosmic peace. And because things will never reach the harmony that is God's dream for the human community but will always be under the eschatological proviso, Christians, far from trading opium, cannot settle for any human utopia but must be ever restless for the bringing about of the elusive kingdom.

Much of that received a blessing in Vatican II, notably in *Gaudium et spes* (39): "The expectation of a new earth must not weaken but rather stimulate our concern for cultivating this one." Even if in recent years there have been moments of hesitation—and interestingly, these at heart seem to focus on unease about the notion of salvation—post–Vatican II Roman statements have in the main retained this thrust. The emphasis on social analysis and on praxis as a hermeneutical key to the meaning of some of our central religious concepts—salvation, liberation, sin—has accentuated the new orientation. It has all modified our religious myth. It has given us a reshaped religious cosmogony. It tells a different story about the world, about body and soul, about human growth, about our environment, about the future. It offers us a different God. It gives a different orientation to Christian moral life.

Moral Life and Beatitude

The second issue that suggests itself for consideration concerns the model that the community has of the relationship between moral life and beatitude. It is an old problem. It will be remembered that it was a problem for Aristotle to link the perfection of moral life with the supreme perfection of contemplation: if perfect bliss is not simply a matter of moral flourishing, how are they related? For the Christian perfect bliss is union with God (*De fine ultimo hominis*). The Catholic tradition that saw morality as the law of the supreme legislator sat comfortably with the notion of bliss as reward for goodness and of loss of God as punishment for disobedience to the law—the "forensic metaphor." Part of his objection is that there is no intrinsic connection between moral life and beatitude: this is extrinsically granted by One who has power to legislate and reward. One has to win the favor of God: one could lose it. There is no need to labor the anxiety with which this has infected relations with God. However much a more benign pastoral practice has tried to soften the rigid logic of all this by appealing to more comforting areas of revelation, many Catholics down the ages have lived and died in fear of this God. Their hope was the confessional: the One whose authority gave binding force to the moral order could pardon, or wipe away, moral waywardness and had delegated this power to the church. That, too, crucially affected the perspective on Christian moral life.

Again, we are dealing with a model—but a dangerous model. At the theoretical level one finds something more satisfactory in Aquinas. He views moral life as a preparation for vision: only those who are morally good are in an apt condition to receive beatific vision. But vision is still a matter of reward. Rahner, Fuchs, and others take a different line suggesting—and here they are recovering an insight of Catholic philosophy—that those who respond morally to the individual (categorial) situations that life presents are in truth really, though unthematically, responding to the divine offer of God's own self. It is not, in Rahner's view, that one loves God and then—in accordance with the will of God—is disposed to do good to the neighbor. It is not that we have been commanded to love the neighbor and do so out of love of God. It is not that the love of God is the motive for love of neighbor. There is even a more radical unity between the two. The explicit love of neighbor *is* the primary act of the love of God: one can love God, whom one does not see, only by loving one's visible neighbor (Rahner, p. 247).

There is obviously much in the NT to support such a picture. It accords with and gives powerful philosophical sinew to the 25th chapter of Matthew: "Just as you did it to one of the least of these who are members of my family, you did it to me." It has the considerable virtue, too, of taking entirely seriously the spontaneous emergence of morality in interpersonal life rather than seeing it as issuing from divine edict. It gives that morality a profound metaphysical and religious interpretation, so much so that the whole incalculable mystery of our lives is seen to be contained within the drama of our love for one another.

I said that it was along this particular fault line that Christianity's greatest upheaval occurred. Luther had stood matters precisely on their head by his doctrine of grace and justification. For him moral life was more the result of justification than the means to it. The emphasis was on a God who first loved us and who reconciled us without any merit on our part: the Christian is at peace with God through graced faith in the redeeming Christ. Such forgiveness, however, is to beget forgiveness: the justified are to produce the works of justification in a eucharistic spirit. One thinks of the comment of Joachim Jeremias on the Sermon on the Mount as a splendid example. We do not appreciate the ethic of the Sermon, he says, because we have torn it out of its proper context. The context is the story of the kingdom, and that is one of forgiveness. Thus we are to preface every demand of the Sermon with the comforting assertion, "you have been forgiven," which is also a challenge to adopt the kingdom's way of forgiveness.

There seems to be a small revolution taking place in Catholic life on these matters. There is a more optimistic view of God's relationship to us. It does not please everyone. One hears complaints about the loss of a sense of sin or about the fact that people do not go to confession anymore or that whole congregations approach the Eucharist confidently without prior confession. Certainly one can record a shift in theological thinking. One finds theologians trying to introduce into this theology of deterrence by threat of eternal damnation some glimmer of hope, saying that faith does not imply a religious performance by which one attempts to please God but an abandonment of any performance on our part and an admission that we can do nothing ourselves (Böckle). Or that the purpose for which we must discern good and evil is not to secure God's welcome, which is assured us in any case (Burtchaell). One thinks also of Küng's reexamination of the Catholic position on justification and Rahner's large agreement with him. We have lived through interesting times—interesting in respect of our fundamental concern about the relationship of religious faith and moral experience.

Part 2: Content

I have raised some questions about the general context of Christian moral life. That seems to me to be as important as the question of content, which has dominated recent theological discussion. It deeply colors our sense of God and of our meaning, purpose, and possibilities. It runs far into our emotional life and evokes hope or fear, peace or anxiety. If crudely fashioned it can easily become a point of unbelief. It is especially useful for Catholics to stand back and view the contours of their lives, since in their tradition morality has occupied the high ground. Not only does one find a rigid position on the relation of works to salvation but also a very considerable emphasis on moral orthodoxy, on moral discipline, and on the competence of church authority in moral matters. The arena where these came starkly together was the confessional. It was there that the weight of church authority was felt. It was there that moral orthodoxy was checked and insisted upon and that discipline was imposed. To sin was to lose God's favor and to be exposed to damnation unless absolution was obtained. One who did not repent of mortal sin—as that was interpreted by church authorities and the manuals of moral theology—could not receive absolution. There was no other route to grace and normal church life; it was the second plank after shipwreck. It was a system that was terrifying in its simplicity and in its implications. The stakes could not have been higher.

The fear of the confessor himself was equally great. His training had been such that he was obliged to ensure that sins were confessed according to their number and lowest moral species, that is, in precise detail. His role, it was insisted, was not just declaratory—to be the visibility of the mercy of God. The confessional was a tribunal, the priest a judge. He was to judge the authenticity and adequacy of the confession, to impose a grave penance for a grave sin, to refuse absolution to those who were not disposed. So it was a large part of his professional competence to know what actions might jeopardize the salvation of his people. The teaching of the church and the moral theology manuals were his guide. If he found the system depressingly severe he raked through the textbooks to find authors of more kindly disposition whose "probable opinion" might afford him some latitude in dealing with the weaknesses of his penitents.

Neo-Scholasticism

It was this system that shaped the content of Christian moral life in the Catholic tradition in modern times, and it is reaction to it that is the starting point of contemporary reflection. The growth of the practice of private confession after Trent heightened the grace-sin drama, it highlighted the training of confessors, it exalted the role of the moralist. And the moralist concentrated on confessional dilemmas —on the fundamentals required for salvation. More disastrously, moral theology had over the centuries come adrift from its moorings in the great medieval syntheses. It had assumed a life of its own. It had become ever more assimilated to jurisprudence and had taken a positivistic turn.

So what was the Christian to do? What was to be the content of his/her moral life? The manuals set their sights low. They were concerned mainly to determine the boundary between mortal and venial sin. Their sources were church teaching, philosophical ethics (a version of natural law), and canon law. Canon law was prominent. The growing centralization of church power and authority in the late 19th and early 20th centuries had produced a detailed system of canon law that affected the daily life of the individual. Law bound under pain of sin, and it was the job of the moralist to weigh the significance of various laws. (One result was the recent bewilderment among Catholics about the abrogation of laws that they were once told bound gravely. To this day Catholics find it difficult to distinguish between morality and church law.) The concern was with what was necessary for salvation, and that generated a sharp distinction between law and counsel. Laws, Noldin says, are necessary to obtain eternal life, they bind all and bind by the will of God. Counsels only bind those who freely bind themselves and merely help one to reach eternal life more securely. It can be seen how sharply focused all morality was on personal salvation.

So the sources of the teaching were narrow. One would be hard put to find a reference to Christ in the general principles of morality. There was appeal to the Bible, not as an inspiring source of moral discernment but as providing authoritative corroborative texts for positions already assumed. That, however, was important. It meant that there was an ultimate source and grounding for morality in the will or law of God as found in revelation. That silenced argument and gave the system a confidence about its moral positions. The Catholic position then as now was one of qualified confidence in the power of reason. The main lines of morality, it says, can be discovered without recourse to an explicit revelation, but such a revelation is necessary in order that even the truths of natural law be discovered securely and with certainty. So there remains the need of a revelation. And since that has its obscurities, the faithful need the authentic interpretation of church authority. The effect is that the final appeal is not to the authority of human reason but to revelation—to the fact that God has made known authoritatively how we are to live. It also means that the reasons for a moral position proposed by the church may remain opaque, that in the end church teaching about morality does not have to defend itself at the bar of reason. It can adopt a superior attitude.

It has to be admitted that what the manuals presented was an arid and cheerless account of moral life. One could find in the Christian community more exalted teaching; it came under the rubric of spirituality and was treated in ascetical, mystical, and devotional works. But it was an optional extra, and it went with a cast of mind that suggested that the basic commandments were the rule of life for the faithful while the further reaches of Christian life were the preserve of priests and religious.

Renewal and Reaction

In the 1940s and 1950s there emerged a strong current of dissatisfaction with the morality of the manual and an urgent call for a renewal of moral theology (Thils, Tillmann, Mausbach, Gilleman, Häring, etc.). The central criticism was that what had been proposed as moral theology was merely a mixture of philosophy, psychology, and jurisprudence and failed to present the distinctive character of the Christian vocation. It was negative and minimalist, so the criticism went, concerned with what some called the science of sin rather than with the riches of Christianity. It lacked the dynamism and inspiration that one would expect from Christianity. Its basic error, it was said, was that it sought its inspiration and method in the wrong sources—in philosophy and natural-law ethics. The assumption was that religion should make a difference to morality, that it should give it a different content from philosophical ethics.

It was a primary tenet of the renewal movement that morality, if it was to be Christian, must be dependent on or derived from revelation. Above all, it was claimed that it must become biblical through and through. It must concentrate on the key themes of the Bible and not be satisfied with random quotations to bolster positions arrived at philosophically. It was a point of view that was canonized in the recommendations of Vatican II about the study of theology in general and of moral theology in particular: "Sacred theology rests on the written word of God, together with sacred tradition as its primary and perpetual foundation. . . . The study of the sacred page is, as it were, the soul of sacred theology" (*Dei verbum* 24). "Dogmatic theology should be so arranged that biblical themes are presented first. . . . Special attention needs to be given to the development of moral theology. Its scientific exposition should be more thoroughly nourished by scriptural teaching. It should show the nobility of the Christian vocation of the faithful and their obligation to bring forth fruit in charity for the life of the world" (*Optatam totius* 16).

Much of the discussion of the 1940s and 1950s was about the possibility of finding one basic Christian principle on which a whole structure of Christian morality could be built. Several candidates were advanced. Christian moral life, it was proposed, should be based on the new life of grace. This view depended on the accepted interpretation of grace as an entitative elevation of the soul and its faculties, which was seen as giving the human being a new *esse;* we should bring about in our lives the moral demands of the new being. Ethics and moral theology, it was said, differ in essence. Or, Christian morality should be primarily a morality of charity: the supernatural virtue of charity should be the root, form, and foundation of all moral life. Or, Christian life should be the following of Christ and moral theology the scientific presentation of that in individual and social life—Christ as the norm of morality. Or, Christian morality should be a morality of the mystical body or the elaboration of our sacramental vocation or, as Aquinas had said, an expression of the new internal law, which is primarily grace in us seeking to find its true realization. This renewal movement marks an important point of development in modern Catholic thinking about morality: the current debate centers on its wisdom and validity.

These approaches all insist that there is a specific content to Christian life that is different from and higher than the natural-law morality that had been favored by the manual—a position encouraged by the teaching of Vatican II that the fundamental vocation is that of baptism and that all Christians are called to the fullness of life in Christ. They all take the Bible as their starting point and are heavily dependent on reference to it. In spite of their claims, however, they did not adduce any significantly different content. They often confused content with motivation or with the general context and spirit of morality. Their use of the Bible was uncritical: it sometimes consisted merely in gathering together the scriptural texts and themes relevant to their subject, so that the bearing of Scripture on the moral argument was not clear.

There appeared in the late 1960s and early 1970s a reaction to this attempt to "Christianize" morality (Fuchs, Auer, Schüller). This was in part due to a dissatisfaction with what was seen as a lack of rigor in the writings of the previous two decades, especially in the use of the biblical material. The criticism noted that it is one thing to elaborate the moral teaching of OT and NT—that had been done successfully and inspiringly by several biblical scholars—but another to delineate what bearing this was to have on moral argument. On this methodological issue the renewal movement had been less than successful, so that the whole project of elaborating a morality "from the middle of the revelation" (Böckle) was put in doubt. An equally important factor in the reaction was the feeling that the attempt to "Christianize" morality gave the impression that Christians are a ghetto and Christian morality something esoteric. How could Christians then engage with all people of good will as Vatican II had proposed? There was also a desire to counter the biting criticism that Christian morality is a childish and unthinking acceptance of the Bible: revelation morality was stigmatized as a morality from beyond, naive biblicism, revelation positivism, theological positivism, obedience morality; this, it was alleged, was destructive of human autonomy and genuine moral response.

The concern was in part about the content of Christian moral life, in part about method, and in part about the Christian's understanding of the structure of moral experience. The immediate questions here push us back to deeper issues—to the stance of our religious story about God and human possibilities. Does our religion contain laws given and made binding by God? If not, if morality arises spontaneously in human nature, if human beings can distinguish right and wrong, does the binding force of such morality arise in human reason or does it arise from the binding will of God? Can we discern the content of such morality, or do we need a special revelation so that the Bible becomes an authoritative source of moral information? Is the content of moral life then what is available to human reason (in the present order of salvation), or is it different from or more than that—so that there is a morality that arises out of Christian faith and may in some manner be found in the Bible? Or does the nature of morality demand that the norms of Christian life be fundamentally intelligible without reference to such faith?

These authors take their stand on the autonomy of morality, albeit a relative autonomy. That position has two basic strands: (1) the norms of moral life are the same for Christian as for human morality and must therefore be accessible to reason; (2) morality makes its own demand and does not immediately require belief in God or appeal to the binding force of divine law. So morality arises out of the very human condition of being with others. And just as Christianity (as Vatican II also states) involves the recognition of earthly realities with their internal coherence and autonomy, so too it involves a recognition of the autonomy of morality. It is in essence the recognition that being with others makes a claim on us and that the acknowledgment of that is a primordial thrust of human reason and therefore a critical element in human wholeness.

(There were, as I have shown more fully elsewhere [MacNamara, chaps. 1, 2], historical reasons why theological thinking developed in this manner: the authors were not engaged in the luxury of speculating on the specificity of Christian morality but were responding to issues of the day. This is something entirely missed by Rigali in a recent article [Rigali, in Curran, ed., chap. 4]: he would rewrite history to suit his own purposes. Even a passing acquaintance with the literature reveals the two basic strands just mentioned: the frequent references to "revelation positivism" and the like show that heteronomy was a concern and why. The authors did not confuse it with the other issue of content, nor need we. It was and remains for religious ethics a crucial concern—as it was for Plato.)

The rejection of a Bible-based morality did not mean a return to the moral theory of the manualists. Theirs had been an impoverished form of natural-law morality. In particular, their dependence on the normativity of nature (physicalism) had come to be questioned. The emphasis now was on person; what is normative is what makes for the flourishing of the person in society. This easily expresses itself as a morality of agape: one of the insights of the renewal movement that perdured was Gilleman's suggestion (after Aquinas) that moral virtues are all a mediation of charity. To say that the person is the norm is, however, to leave many problems unresolved. There is a continuing debate between those who find the moral way in respect for individual human goods, none of which can be sacrificed or subordinated to another (Finnis, Grisez), and those who adopt a proportionalist calculus (Fuchs, Schüller). Both sides, however, reject the physicalist norm of the neo-Scholastics.

The autonomy position recognizes that Christians will situate morality—as everything else—metaphysically. Moral life is religious: the Christian must take "the natural ethical norms of life" into theological life (Schillebeeckx). It is in and through response to the other that one lives in love with God, the ground, ultimate justification, exemplar, and final intentionality of moral life. But morality has its own internal coherence. Christians are to contextualize it in a manner that does not impair or devalue that.

This position was viewed with alarm by other theologians (Ratzinger, von Balthasar, Stoeckle, Delhaye) who allege that it is a diminution of revelation, a denial of the church's teaching authority, and even an undermining of Christianity itself. Their stance stresses that the Bible is an indispensable moral authority for Christians, that there are in the Bible (as official church teaching declares) material moral norms that are universal and valid for all time—or at least Christian values and ideals and a Christian moral core. There is involved here, as well as the general issue of the bearing of the Bible on Christian discernment, the crucial issue of the source of church teaching, of its moral methodology. It is no coincidence that it was dissatisfaction with the methodology of *Humanae vitae* that occasioned some of the early articles of the autonomous position.

There is obviously much ethical material in the Bible. What is in question is how it is used or whether it can be regarded as authoritative. The autonomy position saw its significance as parenetic or as contextual. But the position of Ratzinger and the other critics reiterates the neo-Scholastic conviction that God is telling us through the Bible what to do, although different strands of it regard the biblical material as authoritative in different ways. To say the Bible gives us values, dispositions, or ideals is a weaker claim and gives more scope for a varied application to daily life than to say it gives universal rules (as does *Persona humana*). Values can be variously realized from one age to another; ideals do not bind with the same implacable rigor.

The difficulties of appeal to the Bible particularly for universal rules have been well documented. One faces problems about the dependence of the biblical writers on the philosophy of the time, about the cultural limitations of their horizons, about the distinction between normative and parenetic material, about exegetical and hermeneutical questions. In particular it is argued that in discriminating between still-valid percepts, for example, regarding adultery, and directives that the community has jettisoned, for example, regarding slaves or the position of women, one has to step outside the Bible and subject it to the criterion of common sense or of common moral experience.

Reflection

In reflecting on the current debate it is helpful to keep in mind three general overlapping questions: (1) How are Christians to understand morality? (2) What is the source of their moral code (is it "from above," decreed by God)? (3) How are they to go about moral discernment (by reference to the Bible or not)? The autonomy position insists on the recognition of morality as a human institution making its own claim. It seems to me to be important to drive that down as a deep pylon in Christian moral understanding. Christian faith enhances and transmutes that, but it is necessary to recognize that it can and does exist without faith. Faith situates it in an ultimate scheme of things. It tells stories—of the rationality, goodness, and fidelity of God, of hope in a final kingdom that will transform our earthly efforts, of a providence that can bring good out of evil, of ultimate forgiveness—which are kin to and which sustain and support the whole institution of morality. Faith offers powerful motivation: Christians are confronted in their holy books with the elemental stories of the patience and fidelity of God ("He makes his sun rise on the evil and on the good, and sends rain on the righteous and on the unrighteous," and "Since God has loved us so much, we too should love one another"); of the self-forgetfulness of Christ (who "emptied himself to assume the condition of a slave," who "laid down his life for us when we were still sinners"); of the presence of the Spirit in us ("keep away from fornication . . . your body, you know, is the temple of the Holy Spirit").

But all this material must be garnered and communicated to and by the community in a way that respects the internal coherence and autonomy of morality. The authority of morality is the authority of the truth. Its claim is the claim of the truth, and genuine moral response is some recognition of that claim. It is not simply obedience to the will of another, even to the will of God. Not all doing right is authentic moral response. To do the right, to avoid evil is something. But if we are concerned not only about what happens but about those who make it happen, then why people act, out of what kind of consideration, with what reason or motive, is important. There are levels of moral response as of moral development. There is a danger that in Christian ethics precisely moral considerations will be clouded. Reward, sanction, fear, can move and deter. They may be necessary to prevent evil. They may be the only thing that works in a situation. That is something, but it is not yet developed moral response. It is significant that both Christian and philosophical morality have recently shown a marked interest in the recovery of the category of virtue. Virtue concerns itself not only with what is done but with why and how.

What this means, therefore, is that for religious people there are different kinds of reasons for being moral. There are moral reasons. These are central to morality, all morality, including Christian morality. They are what morality is about. There are also religious reasons. One does good because it is the will of God or as an act of love of God or to imitate God or to bring about God's purposes or kingdom or to gain a heavenly reward. Both kinds of reason are good. But to be moral solely for (religious) reasons extrinsic to morality appears to lack true awareness of what morality means. Aquinas has the striking statement: "He therefore who avoids evil not because it is evil but because of the command of God is not free, but he who avoids evil because it is evil is free" (see 2 Cor 3).

The emphases of the autonomy position have set such matters in sharp relief. They have also rightly pointed up the problems of direct appeal to the Bible. But to admit to difficulty with the Bible as a source of authoritative moral rules is not to reject its authority in morals entirely but only to reject a certain kind of authority. It might be more profitable for Christian moral life to see the Bible primarily as nourishing faith rather than as imposing moral imperatives. We depend on the Bible for the great formative stories that tell us who God is, who we are, and what the world and the human community are about—for our cosmogony. They have a bearing on ethical judgment because they shape the self-understanding and the outlook on reality of the subject of moral discernment, of the "I" who judges. Judgments are not made in a vacuum. They are made by people who see the world in a particular kind of way: moral disagreement is due in part to the fact that we see the reality in question differently or weigh differently aspects of that reality. One's evaluative description of the field of action and the responsibility experienced in a situation depend on the sort of person one is. That in turn depends on the stories and symbols that shape one's consciousness and imagination. It is only if you can understand a people's story that you understand what they see as the logic of their choices.

Religious faith nourished by the Bible might be seen as forming or having the potential to form a particular kind of character and therefore to suggest values and to evoke certain kinds of awareness and sensibilities that affect moral judgment, so that the Christian subject's experience of life in Christ becomes the hermeneutical center of his/her ethics. One might see the Christian community, then, as having its own character shaped by stories of what God has done for it in Christ and therefore as having its own ideals and demands. And that is why there must be for us as there was for the Jews a close link between the liturgical recital of the good news of God's deeds and moral expectations.

So Christians are to discern as faith-people: they are to allow their faith to bear on their judgment. But we are not the first to seek the implications of faith for moral choice. We live in a tradition, and the Bible is the classic of that tradition. To make a sharp distinction between its religious and moral message is to do less than justice to the coherence and consistency of the life of the apostolic community. What we have in the Bible are impressions of that community's experience of the inbreak of the kingdom in Jesus, of its resultant self-understanding, and of its attempts to see that through into practice or behavior. So we need to notice how the faith-story issued in the ethical perspectives of the Bible. It has much to say, however elusively, about action; about living, loving, and dying; about world, flesh, and devil; about wholeness and flourishing; about welfare and happiness; about success and failure; about weakness and sin—concepts that are the common coin of the moralist.

Christian moral life calls, then, for dialogue between faith today and the complex faith of the apostolic community. It requires that we enter into the interplay of ethos and ethic that we find there to discover its dynamic of believing and doing. It is not only what the texts say to us that is important. It is why the writers say what they say. It is their understanding of themselves in the cosmos, their symbolic and social world, and the delicate way in which they see the implications of that for living. We need to allow the biblical text to open up for us the new and wider world of meaning that arises out of the experience of the divine irruption into history in Jesus Christ. We can only do so if we keep in mind that the ethical material of the Bible is rich, diverse, and chaotic. It comes at several levels. Its language is not that of a scientific treatise but of literature—imaginative, colorful. Its mode is indicative, imperative, parabolic, mystical. It is more story than history, more wisdom than law. It says what it has to say in a bewildering profusion of forms and genres. It has to be taken on its own terms.

One who enters the worldview of the Bible will receive not just encouragement and motivation for moral life but light on judgment. The faith of the apostolic community issued in sayings that remain instructive for us about the one thing necessary, about losing and finding one's life, taking up the cross, taking no thought for tomorrow, regarding others as better than oneself, seeking not one's own rights but those of others, laying down one's life, rejoicing in mourning and persecution. One who shares the story and does morality in fidelity to it finds a justification for choices about friendship with God, about prayer, poverty, detachment, celibacy, forgiveness, humility, as well as for a wider range of dispositions of joy, gratitude, hope, trust, patience.

There will be considerable areas of agreement between Christian and non-Christian, between all who have a concern for rights, justice, fairness, and benevolence. This will be especially so at the level of negative moral norms—"the minimum content of natural law" (Hart). But moral life cannot be adequately caught in negative norms. It is not only public but personal. It is not only about what one must do but what one can do, about individual potentialities and responsibilities. It is for several reasons more satisfactorily seen in terms of character—as a settled disposition of seeing and making judgments according to one's story, as an attention not only to what is done but to why, as an unrest until the perfect shape of moral wholeness is realized. The Christian tradition says that while the details of our lives will not coincide with Christ's, his fidelity to his story as expressed in the kingdom ethic of the Sermon on the Mount remains the only entirely valid norm of morality, against which all else is to be measured.

The Christian discerns the moral way within the community of faith. There is no need to apologize for that: all who do morality do it out of a particular worldview or stance that in some way affects judgment. Indeed, there is much talk nowadays in philosophical ethics that it is only within a community of shared vision that values and judgments can be satisfactorily vindicated. This is not to advocate some esoteric discernment. If there is, as Rahner says, a faith-instinct in moral matters it is the fruit of the stories and symbols that create the Christian imagination. The Christian "facts of life" are public facts. The logic of Christian judgment can be understood, even if not subscribed to, by those who do not share the vision. Nor is Christian morality a ghetto morality. The Christian seeks to affect society, to bring about the kingdom. That very mission calls for its own virtues: tolerance of others, a readiness to work with all people of good will, and patience when one's point of view is not accepted in the public forum. But with due respect for different perspectives, Christians have to do their morality in fidelity to their own religious myth. That enshrines their ultimate concern and provides their basic cosmogony. It would be strange if it did not have something to say about how life is to be lived.

See also GOD, IMAGES OF; KINGDOM OF GOD; MAGISTERIUM; METHODOLOGY, MORAL; NATURAL LAW; REASON, ROLE OF; REVELATION.

Bibliography: O. O'Donovan, *Resurrection and Moral Order.* P. Nowell-Smith, "Morality: Religious and Secular," in I. Ramsey, *Christian Ethics and Contemporary Philosophy.* Noldin-Schmitt, *Summa theologiae moralis,* vol. 1. K. Rahner, *Theological Investigations,* vol. 6, trans. Kruger. D. Prümmer, *Manuale theologiae moralis,* vol. 1. V. MacNamara, *Faith and Ethics.* N. Rigali, "The Uniqueness and the Distinctiveness of Christian Morality and Ethics," in C. Curran, ed., *Moral Theology: Challenges for the Future.*

VINCENT MacNAMARA

MURRAY, JOHN COURTNEY

Born in 1903, Murray emerged as perhaps America's leading Catholic social theologian in the 1950s and remained a watershed figure in Catholic social teaching until his death in 1967. He was a central architect of *Dignitatis humanae,* the Second Vatican Council's declaration on religious liberty, which proclaimed the immunity of the individual believer and religious communities from coercion by the state. He also formulated a wide-reaching Catholic public theology that made Catholic social teaching understandable within the social, political, and cultural context of the United States and simultaneously provided a critique of the American cultural and political ethos.

The central challenge that united all of Murray's social writings was the desire to heal the alienation that had grown up between the church and the modern world. Murray believed that temporal society was losing sight of its spiritual roots and that religion and religious values were being privatized within both Europe and the United States. He sought to reverse this privatization by delineating the legitimate autonomy that temporal society should have from dominance by spiritual authorities and by demonstrating that modern culture, society, and politics would founder unless they rested upon the transcendent dignity of the human person. The first step in Murray's social agenda lay in opening up a dialogue between the Catholic tradition and American society as a whole, and this could not be accomplished without facing the vexing issue that made non-Catholic Americans most suspicious of Catholic aims in the United States—the church's teaching that the state could not be neutral in matters of religion but instead had an obligation to promote the Catholic faith whenever it could productively do so.

The Church-State Question

Official Catholic teaching in the 1950s declared that the norm of church-state relations should be the "confessional state," in which government publicly recognized the unique status of Catholicism as the one true religion of Jesus Christ. This recognition would generally take three forms: the recognition of the full and unique freedom of the Catholic church, the recognition of government's obligation to repress false opinions in society that might lead men and women into error, and the duty of the state to publicly worship God through the rites of the Catholic church. Although the need to preserve order and the common good would necessitate that the government refrain from carrying out the latter two of these duties in religiously pluralistic societies such as the United States, this did not change the fact that governments should ideally promote the Catholic faith. The "confessional state" was the thesis in Catholic social theology; freedom of religion was merely an unavoidable accommodation necessary in certain countries.

Murray sought to challenge this reading of the Catholic tradition on church-state relations, and he did so by regarding the church-state question as an issue of doctrinal development. Looking back to the 4th-century writings of Pope Gelasius II and to Robert Bellarmine and John of Paris, Murray argued that the fundamental Catholic tradition on the relationship between church and state lay in the assertion that there are two distinct powers in society, the spiritual and the temporal. While the spiritual power has a priority in dignity, it has no direct claim to control the temporal power. Only through the conscience of the individual believer acting as citizen can the church legitimately touch the actions of government. This deeper Catholic tradition on the relationship between church and state had been lost sight of, Murray argued, in the church's reaction against 19th-century liberalism, which sought to erect a state that recognized no limits to its power and which grounded human rights not in the transcendent dignity of the human person but in the ability of the state to create rights. Murray proposed that the church should move beyond this period of reaction and recapture the ancient doctrine of the two powers, each autonomous in its own sphere. The only duty the state owed to the church was the recognition of the church's full freedom of action, not any obligation to publicly worship according to the Catholic rite or any obligation to repress heresy through the instruments of government.

The church's long tradition on the two powers provided one foundation for Murray's challenge to the doctrine of the "confessional state." But Murray found in the modern recognition of the dignity of the human conscience another reason for affirming that government's only rightful action toward religion is to promote religious freedom. Murray argued that freedom from coercion in religious matters is government's primary method of recognizing the dignity of the human conscience and the primary method of ensuring that the integrity of conscience is nurtured in society. For if freedom of conscience should operate in any sphere of human life, it should operate within the sphere of religious belief and action, where the human person must act on his/her own judgment and assume personal responsibility for the most fundamental of personal decisions. Government can help to provide this freedom for conscience by scrupulously refraining from interfering in any way with religious beliefs and actions except those that threaten the basic public peace and order of society.

Reforming American Society

Murray became embroiled in the doctrinal question of religious freedom as a result of his efforts to make Catholic social teaching understandable and effective within American society. And the bulk of his writings are devoted to his effort to create a public theology for the United States, a framework that critically evaluated American culture, politics, and society. Murray located in the Catholic tradition of natural law a language and set of concepts that could be used for dialogue among the religiously diverse people of the United States, and he believed that the Catholic tradition provided the basis for renewing the consensus that held the American nation together. He proposed that the United States could not properly exercise its enormous responsibilities in the world in the 20th century unless this consensus was refined, reformulated, and reinvigorated.

The first element of the American consensus that Murray sought to revivify lay in the order of culture—that set of common values that provided shared meaning and purpose to the heterogeneous population of the United States. He believed that three trends in the United States threatened to debase and destroy its culture: (1) technological secularism—the belief that the critical issues in American society can be solved by concepts of engineering and science without reference to a framework of shared values; (2) practical materialism—the belief that happiness springs from material accumulation and that the destiny of the United States lies primarily in dominating the material world and generating enormous prosperity; and (3) philosophical pluralism—the notion that all ideas have equal claim to acceptance within a pluralistic society and that it is wrong to entertain a notion of objective truth. In contrast to these trends in American culture, Murray proposed that a true public consensus had to be founded upon a notion of objective and enduring truth that located the rights of the human person in a transcendent framework. Such a framework would reject technological secularism because it provided no set of values within which to set the achievements of modern science. It would reject materialism as a distortion of the spiritual destiny and nature of the human person. And it would reject philosophical pluralism as a threat to the very capacity of the American people to come through dialogue to a meaningful consensus of shared values and goals.

The notion of an objective order of truth discoverable—at least in part—by human reason exercised in community also lay at the heart of Murray's effort to reform the political order in the United States. He argued that the American political tradition, rooted firmly in freedom and government by the people, had contributed greatly to human welfare throughout the world. And he believed that at the heart of the American political tradition lay the central political concepts of the natural law—the priority of society over the state; the limited role and powers of the state; the notion that human rights are rooted not in the power of the state to grant them but in the dignity of the human person created by God; and the assertion that the community is the source of all political power.

Murray further believed that in the First Amendment of the U.S. Constitution, the framers had farsightedly provided for the full freedom of religious belief and action that all governments should accord in matters of faith. But Murray had serious reservations about trends in the American political tradition in the 20th century, and he believed that the Catholic tradition of natural law provided a significant counter to these trends. He believed that the notion of democracy was becoming an idol in American life, with more and more people coming to assume that majority vote provided not only the best form of political organization but also the method for settling all questions of truth and justice. And he believed that a subtle secularism was creeping into the American political tradition, a secularism that held suspect any political stance by a citizen or public official that was rooted in religious beliefs and values. Murray argued that U.S. foreign policy discussions in the postwar world focused too much on the question, what are we against, rather than on the question, what are we for. And he concluded that U.S. policies on the use of military force were governed by an increasing oscillation between prolonged pacifism and fits of intense militarism rather than by the traditional principles of the just-war theory, which presented war as a last resort and always maintained strict limits in the prosecution of any war.

John Courtney Murray respected enormously the contributions that American society and politics had made to the world in the areas of constitutional order, the generation of wealth, and the maximization of legitimate freedom within society. But Murray was convinced that the United States could continue to flourish as a nation only if its culture, politics, and foreign relations reflected a consensus about fundamental values that was rooted in the transcendent dignity of the human person and was constantly being reformulated and reratified by the American people as a whole.

See also CHURCH-STATE RELATIONS IN THE UNITED STATES; NATURAL LAW; PLURALISM; RELIGIOUS FREEDOM; SECULARISM.

Bibliography: J. Murray, *We Hold These Truths: Reflections on the American Proposition* (New York: Sheed & Ward, 1960; reissued 1988). D. Pelotte, *John Courtney Murray: Theologian in Conflict* (New York: Paulist, 1976). R. McElroy, *The Search for an American Public Theology: The Contribution of John Courtney Murray* (New York: Paulist, 1989).

ROBERT W. McELROY

MUTUAL BENEFIT SOCIETIES

Mutual benefit societies originated in European villages as family-like support systems in which workers or artisans with common socioeconomic interests banded together to provide mutual assistance for such benefits as life insurance. Studies like *Constructing Brotherhood: Class, Gender, and Fraternalism* by Mary Ann Clawson (Princeton, N.J., Princeton Univ. Press, 1989) suggest that these European societies take on historical significance as egalitarian alliances among workers. Already organized, their purpose was often adapted by these workers to gain better working conditions.

European immigrants established similar organizations in the United States. Unlike their European prototypes, U.S. mutual benefit societies distinguished themselves through ethnicity and often enlisted members from all socioeconomic classes. Among the benefits provided, financial aid, funeral expenses, and life insurance were the most common. Although estimates suggest that only about 20 percent of an ethnic population joined these associations, mutual benefit societies in some cases did produce important organizational bases for labor-union movements, in others for the establishment of banks and credit unions that provided loans for immigrants, in still others for vital national churches or religious institutions such as schools and community social services, and in yet other cases for local political alliances.

U.S. mutual benefit societies sustained cultural identity while helping members integrate into American society by promoting self-help within the context of mutual assistance and ethnic pride for the individual and the community. Early in the 20th century societies serving a single ethnic group often formed a single national organization, while at the close of the 20th century some national organizations maintain their ethnic character and provide assistance to needy members.

See also ASSOCIATION OF CATHOLIC TRADE UNIONISTS; CREDIT UNION; INSURANCE.

SANDRA YOCUM MIZE

MUTUALITY

Mutuality, which refers to something shared by persons, is subject to great ambiguity in Catholic social teaching. As traditionally found in discussions of marriage, mutuality was understood formally, in terms of reciprocity. Each spouse had a set of obligations, functions, and roles paralleled by the obligations, functions, and roles of the other, which were different, and only equal proportionally. A prominent example is the obligation of wives to be submissive to their husbands and the reciprocal obligation of husbands to love their wives (Eph 5:22-25; *Partners in the Mystery of Redemption* 86). Mutuality here referred to the sharing of the joint project of marriage.

Under the influence of personalism a new understanding of marital mutuality has arisen. Mutuality has come to be understood by many as an interpersonal intimacy, rather than as formal reciprocity, and as therefore implying a certain degree of sameness and quality in spouses (*Gaudium et spes* 48; *Familiaris consortio* 18). Interpersonal intimacy is a sharing of self with the other, an openness and vulnerability to the other (FC 11, 15), which is difficult if not impossible when the sharers are understood either to be of essentially different natures or in dominant/subordinate positions to each other, as was the case in traditional marriage (*Casti connubii,* pp. 548–50). While social teaching now recognizes equal personal dignity as basic to marital intimacy, its understanding of sexual complementarity as entailing essentially different and hierarchically ordered traits and roles for men and women is in tension with lived equality between the spouses (FC 19; *Laborem exercens* 19).

Within Catholic social teaching on politicoeconomic life, acceptance of democratic theory has similarly led to a view of mutuality based on basic sameness and equality of power—between persons of different classes, races, and nations. Thus *Rerum novarum* and its anniversary encyclicals have insisted that mutuality, embodied as social justice, emerges from negotiation and cooperation among all: they therefore call for unions, other contemporary forms of worker solidarity, and types of profit, ownership, and management sharing that equalize power and encourage role sharing between employer and employees (RN, p. 131; *Quadragesimo anno* 93; *Mater et magistra* 82, 83, 93, 97–99, 146; LE 8). *Populorum progressio* insisted that the imbalance of power between rich and poor nations continued to impoverish the poor through imposition of unfair trade terms (PP 58–60). Similarly, Leo XIII's defense of social inequality (*Humanum genus,* p. 265) gave way to Pius XII's concern that inequality not prejudice justice and charity (1944 Christmas message, p. 14), which gave way to a general call for democracy—for the sharing of decision-making power among all—illustrating the need for all persons and groups to be represented in national and international decision making if justice is to be achieved (PP 65, 77; QA 24).

Thus social teaching no longer understands society in terms of a human body, in which the arms, legs, and various internal organs all fulfill their very different assigned functions and thereby share in the mutual life of the body under the assigned authority of the head (1 Cor 12:12-26; *Diuturnum,* p. 147; *Humanum genus,* p. 265). All citizens and nations must share in the same power and decisions, at least through their chosen representatives. But this recognition that members of society share a basic sameness of rights and require equality of power if just community is to exist is not reflected in social teaching on the family or on the structure and operation of the church.

There is, then, ambiguity in social teaching about the nature of both human intimacy and human community. If human intimacy at the center of marriage requires sharing not just of projects (such as raising children) but of selves, if it requires trust and vulnerability, then the church must renounce traditional hierarchically ordered gender roles and recognize the basic equality and sameness of men and women. Sex differences are not sufficient to ground differences in power and role. If the church truly understands itself as a human community, then like other human communities that desire justice, it must empower all its members to participate in decision making and renounce hierarchically assigned roles.

The church has traditionally seen the Yahweh/Israel covenant as the model of mutuality. In the covenant model Yahweh was the dominant partner, promising protection and care in return for the promised obedience and faithfulness of Israel. The covenant was mutual in the reciprocal sense, and this understanding of mutuality was extended to the relationship between Christ and the church, and between husbands and wives (FC 12).

An alternative model of mutuality is found in the Trinity, wherein the community in the Godhead is based on the full self-giving disclosure of three equal persons who share the same divine nature (Gallagher et al., chap. 1). If the kingdom Jesus announced was God's attempt to draw humanity into this same community so humanity could relate not only to Jesus but to God and the Spirit as Jesus himself did, then mutuality for humans is drastically different from the covenant model.

The church cannot continue to ignore the contradictions in its understanding of mutuality. Due to the breakdown of traditional communities and sources of intimacy in the developed world, there is an increasing hunger for intimacy and a growing awareness of the lack of interpersonal mutuality in society, which create escalating dissatisfaction with the formal mutuality of the covenant.

See also GAUDIUM ET SPES; LABOREM EXERCENS; MARRIAGE; MATER ET MAGISTRA; PARTNERSHIP; PERSONALISM; POPULORUM PROGRESSIO.

Bibliography: C. Gallagher et al., *Embodied in Love: Sacramental Spirituality and Sexual Intimacy* (New York: Crossroad, 1986). John XXIII, *Mater et magistra,* in *The Pope Speaks* 7:4. John Paul II, *Familiaris consortio,* in *Origins* 11:28, 29; *Laborem exercens,* in *Origins* 11:15. Leo XIII, *Diuturnum,* in *Actes de Leon XIII,* vol. 1 (Paris: Bonne, n.d.); *Humanun genus,* in *Actes de Leon XIII,* vol. 1 (Paris: Bonne, n.d.); *Rerum novarum,* in *Actes de Leon XIII* vol. 11 (Paris: Bonne, 1892). Paul VI, *Populorum progressio,* in *The Pope Speaks* 12:2. Pius XI, *Casti connubii,* in AAS 22 (1930). Pius XII, December 24, 1944, radio address, in AAS 37 (1945). USCC, *Partners in the Mystery of Redemption,* in *Origins* 17:45. Vatican Council II, *Gaudium et spes,* in *The Pope Speaks* 11:3.

CHRISTINE E. GUDORF

N

NATIONAL CONFERENCE OF CATHOLIC BISHOPS, AUSTRALIA

The Catholic bishops of Australia commemorated the 100th anniversary of Pope Leo's XIII's encyclical letter *Rerum novarum* by issuing a pastoral letter on the centenary date, May 15, 1991. Titled *A Century of Catholic Social Teaching*, the letter includes the following few paragraphs on ways in which this body of teaching has been received and applied in Australia:

"The publishing and dissemination of *Rerum Novarum* in 1891 coincided with a period of serious social, political and industrial upheaval in Australia. At the time, the Archbishop of Sydney, Cardinal Moran, was seen as one of our country's outstanding defenders of the rights of the workers, many of whom were suffering from the very kind of exploitation denounced by Pope Leo XIII. A number of the lay Catholics who contributed to the historic growth of those political and industrial organizations which were created to win a more just deal for working people in the following years and the early decades of the 20th Century, were influenced by *Rerum Novarum*.

"In a later period, after the appearance of Pius XI's encyclical *Quadragesimo Anno* in 1931, a number of movements of lay people, inspired by papal teachings as well as by the work of other socially conscious writers and activists, flourished. Their work helped to prepare both collaborators and a receptive readership for the series of annual social justice statements which the Bishops of Australia initiated in 1940.

"In 1987, the Bishops re-structured their justice, development and peace agencies, creating the Australian Catholic Social Justice Council and placing it and Australian Catholic Relief (formed in 1964) under the direction of a new Committee of the Australian Catholic Bishops' Conference—the Bishops' Committee for Justice, Development and Peace. One of the aims of the restructuring was to heighten the profile of Catholic Social Teaching in the Church in Australia and to widen the knowledge of that teaching in the Catholic community.

"In the past few years, both the Bishops' Committee and the Social Justice Council have published papers on general social teaching and particular issues. Australian Catholic Relief has also continued to be active in the social justice field, mainly through its development education programs. The major project of the Bishops' Committee itself, carried out on behalf of all the Bishops, has been a national consultation on the Distribution of Wealth in Australia. This resulted in the publishing early in 1991 of a draft statement titled *Common Wealth and Common Good.*

"Other committees and agencies of the Bishops' Conference also carry out work and produce publications with social justice implications. They include the Bishops' Committees for Missions, Aborigines, the Laity, Migrant Affairs, Health Care, Social Welfare and also the Australian Catholic Social Welfare Commission. Some of the activities and publications of the Pontifical Mission Aid Societies, which are immediately subject to the Sacred Congregation for the Evangelization of Peoples in Rome, also have a social justice content. Within the dioceses, individual Bishops and their social justice and peace committees and coordinators are also active in fostering interest in social questions and in making statements on issues of concern."

While this summary is far from all-inclusive, it does demonstrate that there has been a continuing and wide-ranging commitment by the Australian hierarchy to the church's social teaching during the century initiated by *Rerum novarum.* In the first half of that century this commitment did not often find expression in documents or statements issued by the bishops as a national group; but it was evident in the actions and words of a number of individual bishops, among whom the two most prominent figures were the Irish-born prelates Patrick Cardinal Moran, archbishop of Sydney (1884–1911), and Archbishop Daniel Mannix of Melbourne (1917–63). In the second half of the century, from 1940, many social-justice statements were made or authorized by the bishops as a group.

The historians Fr. James Murtagh and Patrick O'Farrell have described Cardinal Moran's role in the labor disputes of the final decade of the 19th century and in the simultaneous move to form a federation from the separate Australian colonies. "During the closing years of the century, which saw a vigorous growth of Australian nationalism and a great trial of strength between Capital and Labor, Australia's first Cardinal espoused the cause of the workers and played a leading role in the birth of Australian nationhood" (Murtagh, p. 63).

Speaking at a national forum celebrating one hundred years of Catholic social teaching (Adelaide, October 4, 1991), Australia's minister for justice, Senator Michael Tate, concluded that "there is a real link between practical improvement in 'the conditions of the working class' in Australia and the papal encyclical of 100 years ago."

Murtagh describes how Archbishop Mannix and the Australian hierarchy continued and developed the tradition established by Cardinal Moran "of vigorous social leadership on the part of the Catholic Church." This was done "especially through the forties and fifties in a series of annual statements, which examined current social questions in the light of Christian principles" (p. 133).

Under the influence of teachings and directives coming from the Holy See during the pontificate of Pope Piux XI, a number of lay-apostolate movements arose in Australia during the 1930s. These organizations took a strong interest in social justice principles and their application to Australia. The bishops decided in 1937 to establish a national secretariat for Catholic Action, with headquarters in Melbourne, staffed by two Catholic laymen, F. K. Maher and B. A. Santamaria. At the same time, an episcopal committee for Catholic Action in Australia was formed, with Archbishop Mannix as its president. In 1940 the Australian hierarchy directed that the Sunday within the octave of St. Joseph's Patronage should be known each year as Social Justice Sunday, when special attention would be given in churches throughout the country to the teaching of Catholic social principles. (Some years later it was decided to observe Social Justice Sunday later in the year, normally on the last Sunday in September.)

The bishops also issued what was described as an official statement of Catholic principles in 1940. Published under the title *Bishops' Statement on Social Justice* and drafted by Archbishop Justin Simonds of Hobart, the secretary of the episcopal committee, it was the first of the statements produced almost every year since that time by the Australian bishops or with their authority. Researchers and historians have lately shown special interest in these statements, which often attracted a great deal of public interest and at times gave rise to animated public debates. Commentators generally distinguish three periods and three distinct series of statements in the half-century since 1940.

Michael Hogan of the Department of Government and Public Administration, University of Sydney, sees the first period as running from 1940 to 1966 and has published, with commentaries, a collection of the annual statements issued in those years. The volume's title *Justice Now*! was in fact the title of the 1941 bishops' statement.

Professor Hogan later published a second volume, *Option for the Poor*, containing statements prepared for Social Justice Sundays between 1973 and 1987 (the second period) by a body established by the bishops and consisting mainly of laypeople. It was initially called the National Commission for Justice and Peace and subsequently the Catholic Commission for Justice and Peace (CCJP).

It would be logical to date a third period from 1987, when the Australian Catholic Bishops' Conference restructured its agencies in the justice, development, and peace areas, replacing the CCJP with the Australian Catholic Social Justice Council (ACSJC) and placing it and an already long-established overseas aid and development organization, Australian Catholic Relief (ACR), under the supervision of the newly formed Bishops' Committee for Justice, Development, and Peace (BCJDP). Publications issued after 1987 for Social Justice Sunday have been prepared by the bishops' committee itself or by the Social Justice Council, either alone or, as in 1988, in cooperation with other churches.

Looking back at the series of statements republished in Hogan's first volume, one could make a further subdistinction between the seventeen statements issued up to 1956, most of which were prepared in first-draft form by the National Secretariat of Catholic Action, and in particular (with the exception of the 1940, 1943, and 1949 statements) by Mr. Santamaria; and the seven statements published in the following decade, which were drafted either by one or more of the bishops or by other people to whom the task was delegated.

While some of the topics chosen from 1940 to 1956 are of little more than historical interest today, the series taken as a whole presents a panoramic view of Catholic social teaching as it had developed to that time and its application to Australia. Professor Hogan writes:

"Postwar reconstruction was firmly on the political agenda throughout the 1940's. Quite clearly the Catholic Bishops were claiming a role in the reshaping of Australian values and institutions which was to take place after the war. The Statements contain the outlines of a plan for the restructuring of Australia so as to provide a more just and equitable society. This plan took the form of an alternative ideology to that proposed by the major political parties and pressure groups of the time.

"It is relatively simple to catalogue the individual issues about which the Australian Bishops were concerned. They wanted to return rural life to its central position in Australian society. With this emphasis went a concern for the primary role of the family. There is a strong argument that Australia was under-populated, and that further immigration from Europe was necessary. The freedom of each individual is portrayed as one of the fundamental values; the totalitarianism of Hitler and Stalin is completely rejected. Yet this does not mean that liberalism is wholeheartedly embraced.

"There is a radical critique of the dynamics of modern capitalism, especially in the institutions of banking and credit. At the same time the polar alternatives to capitalism—socialism and communism—are rejected as completely unacceptable. The conduct of industrial relations in Australia by unions, employers, governments and industrial tribunals is criticized as confrontationist."

Hogan's description applies mainly to the statements published before the mid-1950s. Around that time, Catholic social activists in Australia and indeed the bishops themselves were divided over the way to fight communism in the trade unions and in the world of politics. The bishops did unite in issuing a pastoral letter on the menace of communism in April 1955. It was not one of the annual social justice statements, and the topics chosen for the annual statements from that time until the opening of the Second Vatican Council in 1962 reflect the hierarchy's wish to avoid any further divisions within the Catholic community. In the main they are on subjects about which there could be little dispute among Catholics.

As its title indicates, the 1962 statement, *What the Vatican Council Means to You*, went well beyond the area of social justice. In the three following years, when the council was in session and the bishops were fully occupied with its business, no social justice statements were issued. In the year following the close of the council, 1966, the bishops published a pastoral statement, *The Moral Code*, for Social Justice Sunday. This, the final statement in the first series of documents, was followed by a six-year period during which the practice of issuing annual statements was temporarily discontinued. It was a time in which the church in Australia, as elsewhere, was absorbing and attempting to come to terms with the substantial changes in church life ushered in by the council.

Following the formation in 1967 of the Pontifical Commission for Justice and Peace by Pope Paul VI, and the suggestion by the commission that national hierarchies set up their own commissions, the Australian bishops decided to entrust this work to the National Advisory Council of Australian Catholic Relief. In 1972 a separate National Commission for Justice and Peace was formed. As noted already, it later was called the Catholic Commission for Justice and Peace.

Between 1973 and 1987 the commission produced fifteen annual statements for Social Justice Sunday. Three of these (in 1983, 1984, and 1987) were prepared on an ecumenical basis. The commission's statements took account of the development of Catholic social teaching during and after the Second Vatican Council. Among the topics covered were population, morality in public life, the situation of Australian women, immigration, the Australian aboriginal people, unemployment, housing, the youth of Australia, and peacemaking in an armed world. They were issued with the endorsement of either the full conference of bishops or of the bishops' committee with specific responsibility for the commission.

As in the case of a number of the statements issued in the 1940s, several of the commission's statements gave rise to public controversy. Most of the documents included a brief note pointing out that the bishops recognized that not all people, even within the church, would necessarily agree with the positions taken by the commission on concrete social issues. The commission was also active in commenting on socioeconomic and human-rights issues as they arose and published a number of discussion papers on different aspects of social justice.

The Australian Catholic Social Justice Council has carried out a similar function to that of the CCJP since 1987. The first social justice statement published by the council, in the following year, was on the prison system. Prepared in cooperation with the Australian Council of Churches, the Anglican church, and the Uniting church, it made an important contribution to a major public debate on prison reform. Subsequently the council has produced three statements—on social justice in everyday life (1990), on immigration policy (1991), and on Australia's indigenous peoples (1993). In the meanwhile, the Bishops' Committee for Justice, Development, and Peace was conducting a nationwide consultation on wealth distribution in Australia. A short progress report on the consultation was issued for Social Justice Sunday in 1989, and the committee published the first draft of a statement on the subject, *Common Wealth and Common Good*, in January 1990. A final statement, *Common Wealth for the Common Good*, was published as the 1992 Social Justice Sunday statement from the Bishops' Conference.

While this survey has concentrated on statements prepared for the annual observance of Social Justice Sunday, it is worth noting that the bishops have made many other pronouncements on social justice issues over the years. A glance at the index of Nicholas Kerr's collection, *Australian Catholic Bishops' Statements Since Vatican II*, gives the lie to the myth propagated by some uninformed critics that the bishops have been silent on most matters apart from those involving abortion and sexual morality. Certainly the conference has spoken strongly on these matters and in defense of family life and will continue to do so; but many more statements have been made on other subjects such as Australian society, aborigines, racism, the media, the violation of human rights, poverty, refugees, unemployment, the recession, disarmament, and peace.

The Australian Catholic Bishops Conference takes very seriously its responsibility to propagate the church's social teaching and to convince the Catholic community, especially the laity, whose task it usually is to apply the principles to concrete situations, of the essential place that social justice occupies in the practice of the faith.

See also ABORIGINES, AUSTRALIAN; COLONIALISM; HUMAN RIGHTS; MARGINAL PERSONS; PERSON, DIGNITY OF; POOR, PREFERENTIAL OPTION FOR; POVERTY.

Bibliography: *A Century of Catholic Social Teaching* (Homebush, N.S.W.: St. Paul Publications, 1991). N. Kerr, comp., *Australian Catholic Bishops' Statements Since Vatican II* (Homebush, N.S.W.: St. Paul Publications, 1985). M. Hogan, ed., *Justice Now! Social Justice Statements of the Australian Catholic Bishops, 1940–1966* (Dept. of Government and Public Administration, Univ. of Sydney, 1990). M. Hogan, ed., *Option for the Poor: Annual Social Justice Statement of the Australian Catholic Commission for Justice and Peace 1973–1987.* (Dept. of Government and Public Administration, Univ. of Sydney, 1992). P. O'Farrell, *The Catholic Church and Community: An Australian History*, rev. ed. (Kensington, N.S.W.: N.S.W. Univ. Press, 1985). J. Murtagh, *Australia: The Catholic Chapter*, rev. ed. (Sydney: Angus & Robertson, 1959). B. Santamaria, *Against the Tide* (Melbourne: Oxford Univ. Press, 1981). P. Smyth, *Catholic Truth and Modernity—Social Justice Statements, 1940–1980* (Catholic Commission for Justice and Peace, Occasional Paper No. 2, 1984). G. Henderson, *Mr. Santamaria and the Bishops*, Studies in the Christian Movement (Sydney, 1982). M. Hogan, *Australian Catholics: The Social Justice Tradition* (Melbourne: Collins Dove, 1993).

EDWARD CARDINAL CLANCY

NATIONAL CONFERENCE OF CATHOLIC BISHOPS, CANADA

The Canadian Conference of Catholic Bishops/Conférence des évêques catholiques du Canada (CCCB/CECC), was established in 1943 as Canada's national conference of Roman Catholic bishops and was officially recognized by the Vatican in 1948. It is a service organization supporting individual bishops in carrying out their responsibilities to their dioceses and enabling bishops from across Canada to act collectively on matters of national or international concern. Currently (1990) the General Assembly of the CCCB/CECC has 121 members of whom 72 are active as heads of dioceses, 21 are auxiliaries, and 28 are retired. The bilingual and multicultural character of Canada's Catholic population is reflected in the conference membership with 70 Francophone members (50 active and 20 retired), 42 Anglophone members (34 active and 8 retired), and 9 active Oriental Rite members.

The various tasks of the CCCB/CECC are carried out through nine episcopal commissions. The largest of these is the

Episcopal Commission for Social Affairs, with eight member bishops representing the Anglophone and Francophone linguistic sectors and with a bilingual office under two lay co-directors. Since its founding in 1943 the CCCB/CECC has issued a considerable number of social documents and participated in numerous consultations on social topics ranging from native rights and land claims, the Canadian economy, peace and disarmament, unemployment, Third World aid and development, refugees, and responsible use of natural resources, to abortion, capital punishment, pornography, and divorce. To date, the most complete collection of social documents of the CCCB/CECC are the English-language volumes *Do Justice!* and *Love Kindness!* edited by E. F. Sheridan, S. J. Gregory Baum's essay "The Shift in Catholic Social Teaching" in *Ethics and Economics* presents a concise analysis of the history and development of the social thought of the Canadian bishops.

While the CCCB/CECC has been the principal forum for collaboration among Canadian bishops on issues of national social concern, the various regional bishops' conferences in Atlantic Canada, Quebec, Ontario, and the Canadian West have also influenced Catholic social thought and action within Canada's geographically, economically, and culturally diverse regions. Most notable has been the role of the Quebec bishops in helping Francophone Roman Catholics deal with the revolutionary transformations in Quebec society that came about during the "quiet revolution." Prior to World War II many bishops of French-speaking Quebec had actively or tacitly accepted a division of power in society that kept the control of the economic and industrial institutions of Quebec in the hands of an Anglophone minority. However, during the three decades following the Second World War this began to change. Citizens of Quebec progressively acquired the education, the skills, and the political means to take control over the full range of institutions that shaped their social living. A broad base of Quebec bishops supported and promoted these changes. During this period the bishops of Quebec issued a considerable number of documents, both in their own names and in the name of the Assemblée des Evêques du Québec (AEQ), to help Quebec Catholics deal with the social, political, and economic decisions that confronted them. The influence of the bishops of the AEQ has been felt not only in Quebec but also in the national conference as they exercised leadership in responding to the full range of social issues confronting Roman Catholics across Canada.

Roman Catholic involvement in social issues in Canada predates the founding of the CCCB/CECC. In the early decades of the 20th century Canadian clergy instituted programs of popular education such as the *Ecole sociale populaire* (founded in 1911) and the annual *Semaines Sociales du Canada* conferences (1920–62) in an effort to introduce the public to the norms and directives of papal social encyclicals. Programs of social and economic action such as the Antigonish cooperative movement at St. Francis Xavier University in Atlantic Canada and the Canadian Catholic Federation of Labor in Quebec sought to realize these principles in social, economic, and political life. One of the most heated social debates involving Catholic bishops in the 1930s and 1940s concerned the morality of Catholic participation in a Canadian socialist political party, the CCF (Cooperative Commonwealth Federation). The reaction of bishops to the CCF followed existing papal social teaching that placed great stress upon private property and that criticized communist and socialist movements in Europe. Bishops from across Canada criticized the CCF, implying that it was the type of socialism condemned by Pius XI in *Quadragesimo anno* (1931). The majority of Canadian Catholics interpreted these events as an official condemnation of the CCF. And while some Catholic support continued for the CCF through the 1940s and 1950s, the bishops' actions carried considerable weight among Roman Catholics in Canada. This critical stance toward socialism continued until the 1960s, when the CCF party was reconstituted as the New Democratic party and when the bishops themselves began to appeal to newer papal social encyclicals to promote concerns that typically had been identified with social democratic political movements.

With the formation of the CCCB/CECC in 1943 the Catholic bishops of Canada began a more regular program of initiating pastoral responses to social issues. The most significant series of social statements of the CCCB/CECC has been the annual Labor Day messages, which were initiated in 1956 and which would continue for two decades, through the years in which the social thought of the CCCB/CECC underwent its most dramatic transformations. Initially the Labor Day statements reflected Pius XI's critique of socialism. However, the bishops soon began to appeal to newer papal documents like *Mater et magistra* (1961) to focus their attention upon the concerns of workers, particularly those suffering under the injustices of industrial capitalism. And from 1961 to 1964 bishops of the CCCB/CECC made a concerted effort to reverse a tendency toward a wholesale condemnation of socialism and to place questions of domestic and international economic justice squarely at the center of Catholic moral responsibility.

In the years following the close of Vatican II the work of the CCCB/CECC began to show the influence of more revolutionary forms of social and political analysis. Conciliar and papal social documents were shifting away from an older natural-law approach that formulated "first principles" that would be applicable to all persons in all situations, toward a more inductive or empirical method that began from an analysis of concrete living conditions of people and that sought to promote human dignity within the context of these conditions. In large measure this shift was inspired by theologians from the Southern and Eastern Hemispheres who spoke of conditions of poverty, oppression, and human suffering that were being exacerbated by the application of older principles like the primacy of private property. As papal and synodal documents like *Populorum progressio* (1967), *Octogesima adveniens* (1971), *Justice in the World* (1971), and *Evangelii nuntiandi* (1975) came to be issued in subsequent years this change in method progressively gave rise to a new interpretation of the Christian gospel as a call for redressing structures that violated the dignity of the human person, who is fashioned in the image of God.

The principal source of this influence was Latin American liberation theology. During the early 1960s theologians in Latin America had begun to reflect upon the disastrous results of the United Nations Development Decades and to criticize developmentalist programs that sought to redress conditions of world poverty through measures that sustained or promoted North Atlantic economic institutions. Theologians like Gustavo Gutiérrez had begun to call for a "liberation" from "sinful social structures" of economic dependency and oppression that kept poorer countries in a state of systemic poverty, and they called for changes in the institutions governing international trade and monetary exchange.

In their statements issued between 1965 and 1975 the Canadian bishops sought to promote this awareness of "unjust social structures," internationally and within Canada. The annual Labor Day messages of this period reflect this preoccupation with systemic social injustice: *Solidarity in the Distribution of the World's Goods* (1965); *Poverty in Canada* (1966); *The Church's Solidarity with Workers and with Victims of Social Injustice* (1968); *New Power* (1969); *Liberation in a Christian Perspective* (1970); *A Christian Stance in the Face of Violence* (1971); and *Inequality Divides—Justice Reconciles* (1973). In addition, Catholic ecumenical involvement in this period brought Canadian bishops into contact with the social justice activities of the World Council of Churches. At the 1966 Geneva Conference and the 1968 Uppsala Assembly the WCC had experienced a transformation away from North Atlantic interchurch concerns toward "Two-thirds World" social justice concerns. Roman Catholic bishops worked with church leaders from the Canadian Council of Churches to produce a number of documents on international and domestic poverty (1969, 1970, 1973). And the 1970 document, *Brief to the Special Senate Committee on Poverty* signaled a new era in CCCB/CECC activities in which bishops worked to shape Canadian government policy more directly through consultations, briefs, and public representations to government hearings. In subsequent years the CCCB/CECC participated in a host of such ecumenical projects (e.g., Project North, GATT-Fly, the Task Force on Churches and Corporate Responsibility, the Interchurch Committee on Human Rights in Latin America, Ten Days for World Development, and the Interchurch Committee on Refugees).

The next phase of changes in the social thought of the CCCB/CECC arose as a result of the bishops' efforts to translate words into wide-scale action among Canadian Catholics. One of the major problems encountered in implementing action strategies was that sincere-minded Christians who lived in security and relative affluence often experienced great difficulty comprehending the systemic character of the conditions of injustice and oppression of the poor. Often middle-class Christians became impatient at the failure of the development programs of "experts" and blamed the victims, appealing to familiar Christian moral maxims on personal responsibility to condemn their laziness or their corruption. The bishops realized that only by getting close enough to the lived reality of systemic poverty could middle-class Catholics come to appreciate the structures of injustice under which the poor lived. And while the concern for the poor initially targeted the international scene, the bishops soon came to focus on the systemic poverty that existed within Canada itself.

A first sign of the bishops' recognition of this problem emerged in a document submitted on behalf of the CCCB/CECC to the International Synod of Bishops in Rome in 1971. The document, *Christian Formation for Justice,* put forth a "basic principle" that "only knowledge gained through participation is valid in this area of justice" (Sheridan, p. 219). In 1975 the Berger Commission review of the Mackenzie Valley pipeline proposals in the Canadian northland offered the occasion for the bishops to promote this principle. Energy development policies in the north were running roughshod over the land rights of native peoples and were proceeding with insufficient regard for the fragile ecology of the north. Canadian bishops called for Catholics to participate actively alongside native peoples and environmentalists toward the just settlement of land claims and the responsible management of the ecology and energy resources of the region. This praxis principle became the major thrust of the 1975 Labor Day message, *Northern Development: At What Cost?*

Through the late 1970s and early 1980s bishops of the CCCB/CECC sought to develop and apply a methodology for social ethical analysis that would be securely grounded in this praxis principle of Christian involvement in justice. In large measure this concerted effort arose out of the bishops' concern with the problems of systemic poverty within Canada and the debilitating impact upon the poor arising from the worsening economic recession. Canadian bishops feared that government officials drafted economic policies without gaining an adequate appreciation of their impact upon the poor. *From Words to Ac-*

tion (1976), *A Society to Be Transformed* (1977), and *Unemployment: The Human Costs* (1980) all sought to build upon this praxis principle. By the early 1980s the Social Affairs Commission of the CCCB/CECC had worked out a five-step pastoral methodology for analyzing social issues that would give priority to the concerns of the poor: (1) participate actively in solidarity with the victims of social injustice; (2) identify the social structures that sustain the conditions of human suffering; (3) evaluate the situation in terms of Christian moral norms and principles that focus on the dignity of the victims; (4) creatively explore new alternative visions and strategies; and (5) act along with others to implement the transformative strategies (Sheridan, pp. 412–13).

The fullest development and implementation of this methodology came with the December 31, 1983, release of the controversial statement, *Ethical Reflections on the Economic Crisis.* The document was issued to challenge and to stimulate public discussion and debate on existing government economic policies that targeted inflation rather than unemployment as the central economic problem of the recessionary period in Canada. *Ethical Reflections* succeeded in becoming the object of considerable public debate, attracting allies and critics alike from all sectors of Canadian society and commanding attention in Canadian media and in scholarly literature for years after its release. The document went further than any other CCCB/CECC initiative in making comprehensive and detailed recommendations for Canadian economic policy. Like the social documents of the American bishops that would follow in subsequent months and years, *Ethical Reflections* became the occasion for considerable debate on whether church leaders should appeal to religious authority to promote specific public policy strategies on technical issues in a pluralist society.

Since 1983 theologians and social ethicists have come to look upon the Canadian bishops' social documents as part of a wider transformation that has taken place in Roman Catholic theological and episcopal reflection on moral life. Canadian church leaders have joined their counterparts around the world in engaging in a form of prophetic advocacy to promote the human dignity of victims of bias and oppression. And they have done so at the risk of leaving behind an older heritage that sought to articulate universal moral principles that would apply equally to all people in all situations. Canadian bishops have come to realize that to speak responsibly to complex problems of social living requires understanding a tremendous amount of data on the particulars of specific historical and cultural contexts. They have come to acknowledge that moral norms that will be effective in realizing the dignity of human persons need to be tailored to the concrete problems in all their contextual specificity. Clearly many questions remain concerning the appropriate means for carrying this strategy forward in the context of contemporary ecclesial structures and pluralist social and political institutions. However, there appears to be little doubt that the Canadian bishops remain committed to the goal of promoting the human dignity of the powerless within the complexities of social living and to the praxis principle as the route toward the attainment of this goal.

See also CHURCH, SOCIAL MISSION OF; CONFÉDÉRATION DES TRAVAILLEURS CATHOLIQUES DU CANADA (1921–1960); EPISCOPAL CONFERENCES, CONCEPT OF; EPISCOPAL LETTERS, FUNCTION OF; MODERN CATHOLIC SOCIAL THOUGHT; NATIONAL CONFERENCE OF CATHOLIC BISHOPS, UNITED STATES.

Bibliography: G. Baum, *Catholics and Canadian Socialism* (Toronto: James Lorimer, 1980). G. Baum and D. Cameron, *Ethics and Economics* (Toronto: James Lorimer, 1984). G.-R. Pelletier and L. Racine, eds., *Les évêques et la crise économique* (Sherbrooke: Ed. de l'U. de Sherbrooke, 1984). G. Rochais, ed., *La Justice sociale comme Bonne Nouvelle* (Montreal: Bellarmin, 1984). E. Sheridan, ed., *Do Justice!* and *Love Kindness! The Social Teaching of the Canadian Catholic Bishops* (Sherbrooke/Toronto: Ed. Paulines & The Jesuit Centre, 1987, 1991).

KENNETH R. MELCHIN

NATIONAL CONFERENCE OF CATHOLIC BISHOPS, UNITED STATES

The National Conference of Catholic Bishops (NCCB) came into existence in 1966 to respond to the changes that the Second Vatican Council had precipitated. *Christus Dominus* (Decree on the Pastoral Office of Bishops in the Church), issued in 1965, recognizes the episcopal conference as a valid means for a region's or a nation's bishops to address collective pastoral concerns. The NCCB has canonical status and abides by guidelines set forth in *Ecclesiae sanctae* (1966). According to the NCCB's original statutes, approved December 19, 1970, by the Holy See, its purpose is "to foster the collegial concern of these bishops for the Church and society both in the United States and throughout the world." The U.S. bishops founded simultaneously with the NCCB the United States Catholic Conference (USCC), a civil corporation regulated by Washington, D.C., statutes concerning nonprofit organizations. The organization of two distinct but related institutions reflects the bishops' distinct but related obligations. The NCCB activities involve the bishops in their capacity as pastors concerned with intraecclesial issues, while the USCC unites the bishops with the remaining church membership as the "people of God," who have common responsibilities in service to society.

The two institutions replace the National Catholic Welfare Conference (NCWC) and its civil counterpart, the National Catholic Welfare Conference, Inc., both established in 1922. These organizations had replaced the National Catholic Welfare Council, founded in 1919. The NCCB/USCC maintains the Washington, D.C., location, which its antecedent had chosen to establish a Roman Catholic presence in the arena of national public policymaking. The two conferences continue to provide official Roman Catholic public discourse concerning contemporary U.S. social issues.

Organization

The United States hierarchy, specifically local ordinaries, their coadjutors, and auxiliaries, as well as other bishops serving the U.S. church in special capacities, constitute the NCCB/USCC membership. The bishops' dual membership and administrative power in both organizations blurs the theoretically distinct role assigned each conference. The NCCB and USCC have the same governing officers: a president, vice-president, secretary, and treasurer elected by the two institutions' joint membership. The two conferences' primary governing committees, the NCCB's Administrative Committee and the USCC's Administrative Board, consist of the same episcopal membership.

NCCB/USCC statements originate in standing or ad hoc committees. Only the NCCB issues statements pertaining to ecclesial matters, while both address social issues. NCCB committees consist solely of bishops, while USCC committees rely upon consultants outside the hierarchy and include members of the USCC permanent staff of laity, clergy, and religious, who implement and maintain national programs. As of 1989, that staff consisted of approximately four hundred people. A general secretary, who is a bishop or cleric nominated by the president and approved by the membership, oversees the NCCB/USCC staff.

Authority

The episcopal conferences provide the U.S. hierarchy with a forum to study and debate particular concerns of the local churches. The entire conference meets in plenary session, usually in the spring and fall. As clearly noted in its statutes, all episcopal conference decisions "are normally devoid of juridical binding force" (art. 13). Only those decisions passed by a two-thirds majority and existing in church law or common church teaching or authorized through special decree of the Holy See have binding juridical status (art. 14). In the spirit of "collegial co-responsibility," however, the members are expected to abide by decisions passed by two-thirds of the membership (art. 13). Statements issued, with rare exceptions, have reflected a consensus but depend upon the individual ordinary to implement on a diocesan level.

NCCB's Moral Vision

The collective United States episcopal voice heard through numerous conference statements has grown continually stronger in its defense of human dignity through a commitment to justice and peace from the "womb to the tomb." NCCB's more comprehensive pastoral letters connect the personal and social dimensions of Catholic moral life. The earliest, *Human Life in Our Day* (1968), affirms *Humanae vitae* in conjunction with other human-life issues. The document's first chapter affirms Paul VI's teaching on contraception and pledges commitment to strengthening family life. The second chapter, "Family of Nations," condemns modern warfare's destructiveness and questions U.S. involvement in Vietnam, even affirming for the first time selective conscientious objection.

To Live in Christ Jesus: A Pastoral Reflection on the Moral Life (1976) summarizes the hierarchy's "vision of the moral life and [their] perception of many of the critical issues of our day." Centered upon Jesus as definitive revelation of both God and humanity, the letter concerns individual Christian commitment and the faith's communal dimension within family, nation, and world. Social as well as personal sin are treated. The section on family reaffirms previous teachings on marriage, children, and the aged. Under the "Nation" heading, the bishops urge respect for the unborn, for women's dignity and rights, and for racial and ethnic groups; they also articulate a commitment to justice in employment, housing, and crime and punishment. Development, peace, and human rights focus the discussion of global concerns.

The Call to Action meeting (1976) resulted in the document *To Do the Work of Justice,* which provides another NCCB comprehensive statement. The areas targeted for concerted efforts are education for justice, support of family life as "vital agent" of community life in church and society, and the nurturing of parish life as experience of the church as community. Social responsibilities specified are pursuit of economic justice and human rights, including right to life; eradication of discrimination based on race, class, gender, or physical disabilities; and alleviation of world hunger.

Specific Issues

Abortion. Among specific goals in the bishops' social agenda, top priorities are stopping abortion and protecting the rights of the unborn. In 1966 and 1970 NCCB statements condemned the nation's move toward legal abortions. The year of the U.S. Supreme Court decision in *Roe* v. *Wade* (1973), NCCB issued three statements that initiated their drive for a constitutional amendment and sanctioned pro-life grass-roots organizations. The *Pastoral Plan for Pro-Life Activities* followed in 1975. The three-point plan includes education, church support for pregnant women and reconciliation for women seeking forgiveness for abortions, and continued commitment to alter public policy. The bishops reaffirmed the plan in 1985 and continue to maintain consistent efforts to halt abortion.

War and peace. The United States hierarchy's public stand on U.S. military policy has shifted notably, beginning in the Vietnam era. Using just-war criteria, the 1966 NCCB had declared U.S. involvement in Vietnam morally justifiable. In 1968 *Human Life in Our Day* raised serious questions about American involvement in Vietnam and suggested modification in U.S. criteria for conscientious objector status. The November 1971 *Resolution on Southeast Asia* reversed the 1966 position, stating that "whatever good we hope to achieve through the continued involvement in this war is outweighed by the destruction of human lives and of moral values which it inflicts." This statement, coupled with the USCC's October 1971 statement defending selective conscientious objection, launched the bishops' more critical stance on U.S. military policies.

The 1983 *Challenge of Peace: God's Promise and Our Response* presents the most comprehensive critical analysis of the moral dimensions of modern warfare to date. The bishops' ad hoc committee consulted laity, clergy, and religious, as well as technical experts, throughout the three-draft process. The final document adapts just-war criteria to judge the moral licitness of nuclear warfare. The pastoral letter unequivocally condemns targeting noncombatant population and rejects first strike as a moral option. While the statement never declares an absolute prohibition against the defensive use of nuclear weapons, it seriously questions a nation's ability to avoid rapid escalation once nuclear weapons enter a conflict. Deterrence is recognized as an acceptable policy only insofar as weapons are maintained only to deter attack. The threat posed by the nuclear arsenal must also become a motivating factor in bilateral disarmament. Five years later, in 1988, the NCCB published *Building Peace: A Pastoral Reflection on the Response to "The Challenge of Peace"* and an ad hoc committee's *Report on "The Challenge of Peace" and Policy Developments, 1983–1988.* The former calls the church to be a peacemaker, while the latter expresses dissatisfaction in governmental policy developments in deterrence. The report further clarifies the bishops' conditions for accepting deterrence.

Foreign affairs. The bishops have also involved themselves in peace and justice issues beyond their nation's borders. The 1967 Israeli-Arab Six Day War prompted a NCCB call to pray for peace. The 1973 resolution *Toward Peace in the Middle East* outlines a six-point solution including recognition of Israel's right to exist and of the Palestinians' right to a state and to compensation. The six-point plan was repeated in a 1978 USCC affirmation of the Camp David Agreements.

Challenges to the U.S. government's Latin American policy, though issued primarily through the USCC Administrative Board, further reflect the episcopacy's changing moral leadership in the global context of social justice. The 1974 *Statement on Solidarity on Human Rights in Chile and Brazil* demanded the halt of U.S. military aid until human rights violations ended. The statement is the first collective U.S. episcopal statement criticizing South American right-wing governments. A 1975 statement, *Panama–U.S. Relations,* and another in 1976 echo Panamanian Archbishop Marcos MacGrath, who places the canal question squarely in "the context of international social justice." The USCC's *Resolution on El Salvador* (March 1981) and NCCB/USCC president James Hickey's 1983 testimony as USCC spokesman before a House of Representatives subcommittee clearly reiterate the bishops' opposition to United States military aid in Latin America. The 1987 USCC *Statement on Central America* summarizes the episcopal position to date.

Minorities. NCCB statements on race relations within church and society in the United States have appeared periodically. One of the NCCB's first statements, *Pastoral Statement on Race Relations and Poverty* (1966), recognizes the direct relation between racism and poverty and expresses concern for the racial strife then erupting throughout the nation. In response to Martin Luther King, Jr.'s, assassination, in April 1968 the bishops issued the *Statement on National Race Crisis* directed toward Catholics and the wider society. The statement includes provisions for a USCC urban task force to coordinate Catholic efforts to create a "society, based on truth, justice, and love." The bishops also initiated the establishment of the National Office for Black Catholics, which opened in 1970.

The 1980s brought growing episcopal recognition of the nation's alienated Hispanic Catholics. The 1983 document, *The Hispanic Presence: Challenge and Commitment,* recognizes the community's invaluable contribution to the church, acknowledges intraecclesial concerns, and commits the church to the struggle for social justice. The NCCB also published a comprehensive pastoral plan in 1987 to meet particular Hispanic needs. The 1989 revision includes a response to the challenge that evangelical Christian sects present to the Hispanics' traditionally Catholic identity.

The bishops have consistently championed the rights of migrants and refugees. From the *Resolution on the Pastoral Concern of the Church for People on the Move* (NCCB, 1976) through its resolutions on Haitian refugees (NCCB, 1977), Southeast Asian small-boat refugees (NCCB, 1978), and Cuban and Haitian refugees (USCC, 1980), the United States episcopacy has placed itself on the refugees' side. In 1986 the NCCB reiterated its ecclesial obligation to serve the migrants and refugees in *Together, a New People: Pastoral Statement on Migrants and Refugees.*

An often overlooked minority, persons with disabilities, received affirmation in the *Pastoral Statement of the United States Bishops on Handicapped Peoples* (1978). The bishops called church members to fulfill their obligation of justice by welcoming disabled persons into society and the ecclesial community. The NCCB reaffirmed its commitment to their full participation in church and society on the 10th anniversary of their pastoral letter.

Economic justice. A variety of NCCB documents state the bishops' commitment to economic justice. Following the lead of its first year's *Pastoral Statement on Race Relations and Poverty,* the 1967 conference passed a resolution endorsing President Lyndon Johnson's War on Poverty. In 1969 the NCCB announced a Crusade Against Poverty and committed itself to direct action by raising self-help funds. The year 1970 marked the first Campaign for Human Development to gather seed money for projects to break "the hellish cycle of poverty." USCC statements on major welfare reform (1970), food policy (1985), tax relief for the poor (1986), federal budget cuts (1986), and homelessness (1988), among others, maintained the episcopacy's commitment to influencing public policy on behalf of the poor.

The bishops have also continued their traditional support of laborers, in this case, principally migrant workers. The 1968 NCCB statement on farm labor recognizes the economic difficulties encountered by both farmers and laborers and calls for cooperative efforts. In 1970 the USCC again provided the public application of the bishops' moral commitment in its call for a boycott of table grapes and of Farah products because of unjust labor practices. The 1985 NCCB membership sent a *Statement on Food and Agriculture* directly to President Ronald Reagan in support of farming families and laborers.

The bishops' definitive statement on the economy is the 1986 document *Economic Justice for All: Pastoral Letter on Catholic Social Teaching and the U.S. Economy.* Like the peace pastoral, the letter went through three drafts, and the participatory process engaged a wide spectrum of people from both church and the wider society. The pastoral begins with a biblically inspired Christian vision of human society based upon creation, covenant, and community. It then links that vision with Roman Catholic social teaching on justice shaped by natural-law ethic. The document then applies the ethical principles to four specific economic issues: employment, poverty, food and agriculture, and developing nations. Throughout the document a fundamental commitment to the most vulnerable in society, especially the poor, determines judgments of the economy. The bishops' commitment to build upon the pastoral's foundation is indicated by a 1988 *Report on the Ad Hoc Task Force on Food, Agriculture, and Rural Concerns.* This particular report reiterates concern for rural people's struggles, expresses alarm over the ecological consequences of current farming practices, and considers the global implications of honoring the basic human right to food.

Conclusion

The 1979 NCCB plenary session reviewed its own reason for existing. The ad hoc committee's report highlighted the conference's two basic functions: implementing the various conciliar decrees and interaction among the bishops in dealing with national challenges. The NCCB recognized that the implementation of Vatican Council decrees was basically complete; it therefore decided to direct more attention to particular national issues. The conference then produced two significant pastoral letters on key social issues, peace and economic justice, during the 1980s. Especially important was the collaborative process, which brought a wide spectrum of people into dialogue on these critical contemporary challenges. Although the precise role of the episcopal conference is under debate by local conferences and the Congregation for the Doctrine of the Faith, the NCCB is clearly committed to its public defense of human dignity from conception to death and to its quest for social justice.

See also ARMS RACE; CALL TO ACTION CONFERENCE; CAMPAIGN FOR HUMAN DEVELOPMENT; DETERRENCE; DISABILITIES, PERSONS WITH; DISARMAMENT; ECONOMIC ORDER; EPISCOPAL CONFERENCES, CONCEPT OF; EPISCOPAL LETTERS, FUNCTION OF; PERSON, DIGNITY OF.

Bibliography: H. Nolan, *Pastoral Letters of the United States Bishops,* vols. 1–5 (Washington: USCC, 1983–89). J. Benestad and F. Butler, eds., *Quest for Justice: A Compendium of Statements of the U.S. Bishops on the Political and Social Order* (Washington: USCC, 1981). "National Conference of Catholic Bishops: Statutes and Bylaws," *Jurist* 1 (1972) 109–17. *Collegiality and Service: NCCB and USCC* (Washington: USCC). T. Reese, ed., *Episcopal Conferences: Historical, Canonical, and Theological Studies* (Washington: Georgetown Univ. Press, 1989). E. McKeown, "The National Bishops' Conference: An Analysis of Its Origins," *Church History Review* (1980) 565–83.

SANDRA YOCUM MIZE

NATURAL LAW

"Natural law" (or "law of nature") is not a univocal concept. In the spheres of physics, of sociology, of psychology, and so forth, it is customary to speak of laws or regularities that are proper to each particular sphere; in what follows, however, we shall not speak of this but rather of the sphere of morality and law, where natural law denotes a binding obligation for the free human person. Binding obligation can have various origins: a divine or human institution but also, for example, a contract or custom. It can also have its origin in the essence of what it is to be human as such. It is in this sense that one speaks of nature and of natural law as "given by nature" in the legal or the ethical sphere.

Origins of the Christian Doctrine of Natural Law

Such an obligation is understood as somehow based in the reality of the human person. All attempts at natural-law thinking agree that from a legal and ethical perspective one does not experience the self as a being of total arbitrariness. The rejection of total arbitrariness implies the acceptance of suprapositive or prepositive elements in morality and law; it likewise implies that these elements of human experience and insight are accessible and that they are also fundamentally plausible, or capable of being justified. There exist, however, various opinions and theories about the mode of justification and the possibility of knowing the justification of concrete obligation; it is precisely here, both historically and systematically, that the problematic of natural law lies.

Besides this diversity, one must keep in mind that all attempts at natural-law thinking are never more than human attempts and thus are always exposed to the danger of mistaken understanding and/or ideological presuppositions. This danger is not excluded when one understands that in some way the divine is the true ultimate ground of natural law, whether in the teaching about the eternal ideas in Plato's *anamnesis* theory, or in the pantheistic understanding of the world in the *Stoa,* or in the Christian doctrine of the created participation of the human person in God's eternal wisdom.

The ideas of the pre-Christian understandings of the natural law (if one wishes to use this term already for this period) were taken up in the first Christian centuries. Beginnings already were made in the NT; in Paul, for example, we have the first two chapters of Romans (1:18-32; 2:14-16) in which he exhorts the Christians to behave correctly in this world in the sight of the non-Christians, who—although they do not know the Christian message—nevertheless (and thus "by nature") are capable of distinguishing between correct and incorrect behavior and thus of judging the ethical conduct of the Christians (cf. Rom 12:17; 1 Cor 10:32).

The great theologians of the first Christian centuries, above all Augustine and Ambrose, addressed themselves theoretically to the theme of the natural law. Their chief influence was not so much that coming from Greece, as found in the "eternal" ideas of Plato and Aristotle's observation that there exists in the city-state not only the law of statutes but also something that is right on the basis of nature (*physei dikaion*) and has the force of law (for Aristotle, *physis*-nature was the human person's gift of reason, which is capable of understanding and discovering what is right). Rather, these early Christian theologians were influenced by the Roman Stoics, whose pantheistic worldview tended to a certain identification of the human world (nature and reason) with the divine, and correspondingly, with an order of law and of morality that already existed in some manner and hence—in distinction to Aristotle—was universalist, that is, had the force of law for the whole of humanity and remained the same. The all-important point here is that one must recognize this order correctly and without ideological falsification. In a worldview structured in terms of creation and redemption, the Christians sought to transpose the Stoic understanding into a Christian understanding. Later, it was Thomas Aquinas who more than anyone else in the 13th century attempted to transpose and integrate the ideas of the Greek world (Aristotle), and especially of Roman philosophy and Roman law, into Christian philosophy and theology and into their understanding of morality and law.

The Roman understanding of natural law, however, was not uniform. Some considered that which is dinstictively human in human reality, namely, reason, to be the primal source of ethical and legal knowledge (Cicero, Gaius), while others understood physical nature, which is *the same in human and animal,* to be that which is most "natural" in human "nature" and to be the deepest guideline in human nature for correct behavior (Epictetus and above all Ulpian).

For Thomas Aquinas it was ultimately the creaturely participation in the wisdom of the creator God, that is, the divine reason, that was the origin of the natural law. In each case the task of practical reason is to co-ordinate the individual data with the concrete total reality of the human person and to make an ethical and legal evaluation and judgment in consideration of what it is to be a human being. But the theory of the jurist Ulpian, who held that the nature common to animal and human is "natural" in the deepest and fundamental sense, also found followers in the meantime. Thomas (unlike Albert the Great) could not refuse to accept to such an authority. In spite of his fundamental evaluation of reason as that which is distinctively human, he understood the natural tendency common to human and animal (above all self-preservation and propagation) as that which is fundamentally natural. Reason, therefore, must ask "nature" about the ethical and legal order that derives from *it* in order to discover what is correct in the total context of the human person. Thus, for example, in the sphere of sexuality reason alone must find in the construction of marriage (e.g., polygamy or monogamy) the correct way without questioning nature, since here the nature common to animal and human gives no (apparent) directive. This is the basis of Thomas' distinction between "in keeping with the reason" (*secundum rationem*) and "in keeping with nature" (*secundum naturam*). For example, when Thomas lets the nature alone determine ethical norms in the case of human sexuality without taking into account the total reality of the human person (*secundum naturam*), he has created a naturalistic fallacy that stands in opposition to his principle that for the human person it is fundamentally the *reason,* made in God's image, that determines the human correctness (*secundum rationem*) of ethical or legal norms in the total context of human reality. At this point, Thomas is inconsistent, because he pays heed to familiar authorities (Ulpian). This fact has put a burden on natural-law argumentation in Christian theology up to the present day.

For natural data cannot generate of themselves an ethical or legal obligation. They cannot be more than *relevant* for the rational discovery of the obligation. This is true even of the three "natural tendencies" of the human person to which Thomas draws attention: self-preservation, the maintenance of the species, and specifically human behavior (reason) (ST I-II 94, 2c); for the first two do not generate of themselves any concrete directive of conduct, since only reason can do this.

Thomas does not carry out consistently the distinction between the ethical *goodness* of the person and the ethical *correctness* of the person's conduct in the horizontal world. Both are called "good" by Thomas in general and without distinction—in keeping with the natural law. But natural law aims both to clearly distinguished them from each other and to relate them. This, however, was far removed from the world of ideas of Ulpian, for example, who was interested above all in an ethical and legal order deriving from an understanding of nature that was distinct from the practical reason.

When Thomas and his followers believed, on the basis of Ulpian's interpretation of nature, that they could read the ethical will of the creator God out of nature in (only) some spheres of life (e.g., with regard to the body and life, to sexuality, to the faculty of speech), they attributed to nature, understood as distinct from reason, an achievement of which it is not capable, namely, to indicate a legal or ethical order. This, however, is possible only as an order of the reason.

An Interpretation of the Christian Doctrine of Natural Law

To sum up: the natural law is not a law (formulated or capable of formulation) or a summary of such laws. It is not at all an external law, but, as Thomas says, an "internal" law (a *lex interna* or *indita*: cf. ST I-II 106, 1 ad 2, *Lex naturalis est lex indita homini*), namely, the possibility given to the human person's practical reason of undertaking the attempt of judging legal and ethical behavior. What we human persons try to judge and to formulate in such an attempt remains, however, always only a human attempt with which we have to live, for neither the God-given nature nor the divine gift of the practical reason can undertake in every case to guarantee the correctness of our ethical or legal project. The only infallible insight is the basic insight that humanity, and therefore human reason, demand that one do good and avoid evil in every sphere of human life. But no more than moral certainty attaches to the discovery, thanks to varied experience and the interpretation of what this means in an individual case in the concrete human reality.

In addition to this, the "nature" (human person) that is to be evaluated from an ethical and legal perspective is not a static entity. The human person known to us and his/her reality are something that develops out of the past and into the future. They are never, and were never, a definitive product of the creator God. The same is true of the human person's very capacity to interpret, evaluate, and orientate himself/herself. This changes to a certain extent. It follows that it would be an error to hold that a definitive codex of the legal and ethical norms of natural law could be drawn up with equal validity for all times.

It is therefore correct to say that natural law is historical and personal. We human persons have no other path to legal and ethical order than a historical and personal path. The word "personal," however, must not be understood in an individualistic sense, since human persons are essentially interpersonal and are related to one another in various ways. A splendid isolation does not exist, nor a Robinson Crusoe (for he would not be a person). The interpretation of the human person and of human society always takes place—hermeneutically—on the basis of a preceding interpretation and within an interpretation that is being carried out further in society, not indeed as the simple acceptance of such an interpretation but not independently of this.

It is therefore true only in a restricted sense to say that natural law is immutable. The formulation—"Do what is good and avoid what is evil" and its formally concretizing but tautological translation as "Be and behave in a manner worthy of the human person, humanely, rationally, in every sphere of life"—has a timeless validity that does not admit of any exception. But this is not true of its concrete translation into the varied historical, material reality of human life. Individual, interpersonal, social, and political situations of conflict do not find their solutions only through a supratemporal principle of the natural law. They demand the evaluation and the calculating consideration of all the elements that determine the situation of conflict. Only so is it possible to succeed in discovering a solution that corresponds to the situation, that is, a natural-law solution, one corresponding to the concrete human reality. Norms of natural law do indeed state something valid, but one must discover in concrete cases through a hermeneutical reading of these norms what this means in the ultimate concretization (and with a view to this concretization). This is the difference between a correct understanding of natural law and an explicit situation ethics.

It is true that natural law is not infrequently termed "divine" law and hence is called immutable. This can be justified, although not in the sense that formulated norms of natural law derive directly from God and are given to us in this form; rather, it can be justified only in the sense that the developing world of the human person and his/her variable ability to interpret this in the individual situations, and ultimately the capacity to make ethical and legal judgments, derive from the creator God and thus have their origin in God. The already existing reality of nature only indicates what God's will *in creation* is (that it should exist and that it should be *thus*). It is left to the created practical reason of the personal human being who is God's image in a *constitutive* manner (see ST I-II 94, 1; *In Eth. Nic.* I, lect. 1) what God's *ethical* will is, that is, what we human beings *ought* to do with the reality of "nature" that has been entrusted to us, as this unfolds and develops (B. Schüller). "Ought" is not a category of nature, but of the intellect that understands and judges.

Duns Scotus' interpretation of the natural law is different from that of Thomas, being more strongly voluntarist and personal. For Scotus natural law (like nature itself) is not *thus* in a precise and necessary manner but is contingent; nevertheless, it is just *thus*—although not in an arbitrary manner—that it is willed by God. The more personalistic ideas of a Duns Scotus find more understanding in today's personal concept of natural law than in the perspective of neo-Scholasticism. The voluntarism of W. Occam is even more accentuated than that of Duns Scotus. When one looks back over history, one sees a tendency to understand the natural law in a way that was more voluntaristic than Thomas understood it, especially in the 16th and 17th centuries, and above all in Francisco de Suarez (in his distinction from Gabriel Vázquez' Thomistic "rationalism") and, in dependence on Suárez, up to the most recent past.

Natural Law and the Church's Magisterium

The magisterium of the Roman Catholic Church, especially in the period between the mid-19th and mid-20th centuries, has largely accepted the Thomistic understanding. The ethical/legal distinction established by Thomas between a given natural order in keeping with creation and an order of reason has clearly been maintained. Ecclesiastical documents up to the present refer—above all in the sphere of life and death, of sexuality, and of the obligation to truth in speaking—largely to an ethical order given by created nature (hence by God) and therefore immutable (*secundum naturam*), while they refer in other questions—for example, those of the social and political order, in which it is not possible to indicate such an (apparent) ethical "order of nature"—to an ethical order of reason that must be discovered by the human person (*secundum rationem*). This twofold understanding of natural law is not satisfactory.

The traditional teaching on natural law is explicitly defended many times in the texts of the Second Vatican Council, as well as the twofold understanding of the natural law; yet it is possible to show that a tendency to change this teaching also exists. The council tends to refer human behavior less to set, formulated laws and norms than to the God-given task of more fully humanizing the human person and the world. This is a different perspective, one that issues quite different challenges. It displays a better and deeper understanding of the natural law. It can be shown to exist above all in *Gaudium et spes,* the Pastoral Constitution on the Church in the Modern World, but not in this text alone. This same perspective is dominant in the more recent social encyclicals. The concern here is to understand the contemporary (!) mode of reality of the world of the human person and to analyze and draw up projects with a view to the possibility of a fuller humanization of this world.

The council observes that faith helps Christians and their church in a particular way to be able to respond to this requirement. The Christian who analyzes the contemporary world of the human person and who draws up the project of a more human world does indeed act on the basis of his/her human reality, but does so "in the light of the gospel" (GS 48) and under the influence of grace. This does not mean that the Christian faith as such generates of itself the solution to the many problems of today's world. Faith does not take the place that belongs to the human person who understands herself/himself and draws up an ethical/legal project, nor does it solve her/his problems. Rather, it allows one to understand more deeply the relationship of God to the human person that began in Jesus, as well as what God expects of the human person and how Jesus understands the human person (the human person of the natural law!) in the reign of God, which has arrived with him. Accordingly, human existence and the human world are lived and realized before a horizon that the human person as such, still less as a sinner, cannot know and live. There is indeed a distinction between "being a human person" and "being in Christ," but they form one single reality and are not to be separated. Natural law is to be understood and to be lived as this kind of reality.

In this context, the magisterium of the church attributes to itself the right and the task of giving an authentic interpretation and exposition of the natural law in its concrete totality. This claim also was made at the Second Vatican Council. This is, however, problematic in view of the fact that the natural law as understood in this way is not revealed, nor does it belong in its material individual statements to the *Christian faith* in the stricter sense. For it is the proper task of the magisterium to watch over everything that belongs to the divine *deposit of faith* and also over everything without which this deposit cannot be defended. But it is certain that the detailed totality of the natural law does not belong to this.

This does not mean that those church authorities entrusted with leadership roles in the church ought not also watch over the compatibility of the ethical and legal behavior of Christians with their faith; nor does it mean that such authority ought not stretch out its guiding hand in such questions, to the extent that it has the material competence to do this. While the relevant ecclesiastical instructions are, at least in presumptive terms, to be looked on as true—to the extent that these are not revealed—they are, however, certainly not infallible and hence require from the Christian (only) a corresponding religious readiness to accept them (cf. LG 25). Such an activity of the church's magisterium, when carried out within its proper boundaries, can have an inestimable value for Christians.

Natural Law and Christian Faith

What has been said up to this point about natural law, the church, and revelation makes it perfectly clear that natural law, as far as this is known and formulated, is fundamentally a human cultural activity. Philosophy and theology must be aware of this. If one thinks in Christian terms about creation and hence about the origin of natural law in Christ, one sees in the natural law the beginning of God's self-revelation in Christ. This means that natural law is an analogous participation in the universal law of Christ that governs the world. The law of Christ presupposes *logically* the natural-law antecedent to itself. In the "new law of Christ," the primary element of which is the "grace of the Holy Spirit" (ST I-II 106–8), the new law of Christ signifies, as it were, the medium in which the grace of the Holy Spirit gives expression to itself in this world. This is how it is in itself (*quoad se*). *Quoad nos,* matters, that is, as seen from our perspective, stand reversed: for us human persons, there is no access to Christ and to the law of Christ other than via a certain knowledge of the natural law. This, however, is true only *logically,* for in terms of temporal sequence the acts of coming to know the natural law and the law of Christ can coincide in a mutual causality. Thus the contents of the natural law are the reality by means of which the law of Christ—the grace of the Holy Spirit—expresses itself in this world. In other words, one lives the faith in practice *through* the realization of the natural law—although this is consciously *before the horizon* of God's self-revelation in Christ.

Theologically, the expression "the redemption of the natural law" has been used, and this formulation makes good sense. It refers, however, not to the natural law as such, but properly to the concretely existent human person, for it is for the human person that natural law has validity. As sheer law (i.e., without grace), natural law would only bring about further sin for the unredeemed human person who is fallen ("under the power of sin," as Paul says). But in the human person who is under the power of the grace of the Holy Spirit, this grace is the path of genuine self-realization, for both grace and the "light of the gospel" bring about not only *knowledge* of the law, but also the free *performance* of the law in love.

As has been said, these reflections on the natural law refer to human nature as it is found de facto in the human person who exists today. But this human person stands a priori under the effective influence of the "sin of the world" (Jn 1:29; cf. Fuchs). As such, the human person is continuously borne by the creator God and entrusted to us to be realized—as far as possible—in the correct and good way.

Protestant theology generally tends to think differently on this point: namely, the human existence entrusted to us is the human person of origin (not of today's reality) as he/she comes forth from God's creative activity as an expression of God's will and of the commission God gives. This will and commission of God are held to be immutable, even today, although the human person now exists only "after the fall" and is therefore completely unable to achieve the realization of the human person of origin, that is, the human person becomes a sinner again and again. Unlike Catholic theology, this theology requires the theologoumenon that the constant nonfulfilment of the original will of God is personal *sin*. This theologoumenon is, however, blunted by the forgiveness that is always granted a priori to the sinner.

See also CONSCIENCE; ENLIGHTENMENT, THE (INFLUENCE OF); GAUDIUM ET SPES; PERSONALISM; THOMAS AQUINAS, CONTRIBUTION OF.

Bibliography: M. Crowe, *The Changing Profile of Natural Law* (The Hague: Nihoff, 1977). C. Curran, "Natural Law," in *Directions in Fundamental Moral Theology* (Notre Dame, Ind.: Notre Dame Univ. Press, 1985). I. Evans, ed., *Light on the Natural Law* (Baltimore: Helicon, 1965). J. Fuchs, "'The Sin of the World' and Normative Morality," in *Personal Responsibility and Christian Morality* (Washington: Georgetown Univ. Press). P. Keane, "The Objective Moral Order: Reflections on Recent Research," *Theological Studies* 43 (1982) 260–78. B. Lonergan, "A Transition from a Classicist Worldview to Historical Mindedness," in J. Biecher, ed., *Law for Liberty: The Role of Law in the Church Today* (Baltimore: Helicon, 1966). C. Curran and R. McCormick, *Readings in Moral Theology: The Distinctiveness of Christian Ethics* (New York/Ramsey: Paulist, 1980).

JOSEF FUCHS, S.J.

NATURAL RESOURCES

The natural resources of God's creation—land, water, air, animal and plant life, the beauties of nature—exist for the good of all of humanity and in themselves to give glory to God their creator. Human persons have been given a legitimate dominion over these resources to use them to meet human needs and enhance human dignity, but this dominion always exists within the context of a responsible stewardship. In their relationship with nature, human persons have both rights and duties. In their use of natural resources, human persons remain responsible to other persons in justice and in charity and ultimately to God. Socioeconomic relationships and systems must be so organized that nature remains sufficiently balanced, human needs are adequately satisfied, and poorer nations are able to gain a fair price for their natural resources as well as protect these resources from the overconsumption of wealthier nations (*Ethical Choices and Political Challenges,* I).

The abuse of natural resources through overconsumption, pollution, and consumerism fails to respect the limits of human dominion and the authentic place of humanity in harmony with the rest of the natural order. The refusal to recognize the rights of all people and of future generations to a share in the earth's natural resources manifests a failure to recognize the universal purpose of earthly goods and the social nature of the human person. Nature cannot be understood as a storehouse of commodities to satisfy every human desire; rather, human persons must understand themselves as part of the created and redeemed order that together groans until the day of salvation (Rom 8). In this context natural resources can be seen as sacraments of God's beauty and of God's solicitous care for the human family.

See also ECOLOGY; STEWARDSHIP.

MARK O'KEEFE, O.S.B.

NELL-BREUNING, OSWALD VON

Oswald von Nell-Breuning, S.J. (1890–1991), was a leading representative of structural social ethics in the tradition of Roman Catholic teaching and the emeritus professor of social and economic ethics at the Hochschule Sankt Georgen in Frankfurt am Main. In addition to publications in journals of economics, law, social policy, and opinion and also in trade-union periodicals, he has published articles in lexica as well as a range of books and compendia. The titles of his works number approximately eighteen hundred.

Developing some elements of the extensive accomplishment of Heinrich Pesch, S.J., in economics, he wrote a dissertation on stock-market morality under Joseph Mausbach (1928).

His early years of professional involvement were rooted in the political, educational, organizing, labor-union, and theological activities of the groups and movements constituting German Social Catholicism. In particular, he collaborated in the work of the People's Association for Catholic Germany. Upon the basis of the concrete programs of these groups there emerged his typically detailed and trenchant policy analysis.

Using the resources of the Königswinterer Kreis, an interdisciplinary seminar, Nell-Breuning developed a draft that resulted in the most significant sections of Pius XI's *Quadragesimo anno.* Subsequently he was a major translator and interpreter of official documents of Catholic social teaching for the German-speaking world. In addition, his attention to the span of this tradition has enabled him cogently to define and utilize its central principles, namely, solidarity and subsidiarity. Church social teaching he distinguished not by its content but rather by its authoritative origin. This authority requires responsible use within its sphere of competence and a willingness to learn from and cooperate with those who have mastered other areas.

The Western sections of Germany were prostrate after World War II. Amidst the threats of political, social, and economic chaos, Nell-Breuning strove steadily, both through his writing and in collaboration with representatives of varied sectors of society, to make a Catholic contribution to the establishment of an ethical order in society and state. He has sought to extend the political achievement for meeting common social needs (*Sozialpolitik*) and to advance beyond even these achievements to systemic changes. Both avenues proceed toward the establishment and maintenance of a state (*Sozialstaat*) upon which the citizens have a legal and ethical claim for assistance both in their needs and in attaining their personal self-development.

Markedly affected by the suffering of many Catholic workers in the union controversy at the beginning of the century, Nell-Breuning maintained regular contact with the German federation of unions while, over the decades, the unions and their members assumed a substantial and responsible role in the new society. As the unions developed, Nell-Breuning facilitated bilateral communication between the structure of the umbrella unions (*Einheitsgewerkschaften*) and the course of Church social teaching.

After decades of great tension between the two sides, he made significant contributions toward enabling workers and representatives of the Catholic church to address each other. His contribution (a draft for the document *Church and Workers*) to the 1975 German bishops' synod is the apex of this effort. An example of his impact on the unions occurred at the beginning of the 1960s. Nell-Breuning influenced the novel frame-contract for the construction industry, in which workers were secured, beyond wages, a regular increment of capital wealth.

Nell-Breuning's capacity to assist in shaping policy is not restricted to the world of unions. He worked as a scholarly advisor to the federal economics ministry for seventeen years and also was vice-chair for the federal advisory committee on housing.

Bold theoretical explorations led to his influence upon yet another formative force in West German social policy. In the face of great resistance, he read central texts of Marx in order to grasp how the insights there might deepen the Christian contribution toward common analysis, judgment, and action. History as the creation of actual persons and class analysis are two ranges of Marxian insights fruitful for Christian reflection. At the practical level such efforts facilitated his attention to and conversation with the Socialists in West Germany. Amidst great controversy, he stimulated and fostered cooperation with the Social Democratic party on policy issues.

One central area of Nell-Breuning's involvement in social and economic policy was his decades-long struggle for co-determination—multilevel participation by workers in the workplace, plant, and firm. He steadily argued for co-determination and helped achieve its several forms in federal law. He repeatedly advocated parity co-determination in order to guarantee that workers could act as free subjects.

Nell-Breuning continued to argue for even more extensive and intensive developments in co-determination: beyond the firm and through the setting-up of an enterprise constitution based upon the activity of work. Such a constitution would recognize and incorporate the three "poles" of an enterprise: those who provide (*a*) capital input, (*b*) enterprise skills, and (*c*) labor effort. The firm is an association of persons who provide these inputs. The constitution of the enterprise should be founded on this radical basis.

In his arguments for the continual adjustment of the market economy, he pointed to the need to maintain steady and even competition, to secure progressive social reform, to develop ecological responsibility, to maintain equity between the parties in the labor market, to assure just procedures within labor organizations, and to achieve a balance in the distribution both of income and of productive capital.

A hallmark of his procedure in these and other areas is a careful attention to the needs of persons in society over time. For example, since rapid changes constantly alter the disposable income of a person, this, not gross pay, should be the basis for assessing pension benefits and payment rates. Furthermore, Nell-Breuning urged the construction of a pension system based on the interaction of three generations. The system should assign a significant value to the contribution of those who provide children to society.

Amidst his advocacy of positions that would meet common needs or bring about structural change, Nell-Breuning focused on the person. Intimate to the person is his/her work activity. Repeatedly he probed the significance of work. He indicated how work is bound up with the very personhood of the individual, takes place in a social network, enables persons in society cooperatively to shape their limits, deploys free discovery in the creation of technology, and leads to service of one another. In addition, insofar as social and technological systems are profoundly altering the processes of work, he devoted increasing attention to the significance of leisure. This immediately concerned the shortening of the forty-hour week with its attendant possibilities and quandaries. He also examined the active time (*Sozialzeit*) between paid employment and recreation. Here lie increasing opportunities for participation as well as for personal devotion to others. In this way Nell-Breuning made possible a greater attention to unpaid work within the home, which benefits the whole of society.

Nell-Breuning aimed his chief efforts at the role of persons in the institutions and processes of society, not of the family or state. Here it is that he sought to bring his co-religionists, other Christians, other believers, and all other citizens out of ghetto certainties toward a shared responsibility for the culture across its entire range. The union or various co-determination structures are only two areas for such collaborative responsibility. Nell-Breuning underlined the relative independence of each social, cultural, and economic sphere; that is, each has its own operations and laws independent of any integrating authority.

He was instrumental in leading the members of the Christian community to assume their proper activity in these efforts—an activity that takes place in collaboration. This cooperation requires a sustained investment in the rigors of open discourse. In this he also emphasized the centrality of personal responsibility and broad participation. In ecclesiastical terms, this means a heightened respect for the role of the laity; in political terms, democratic systems; in social terms, free development of persons and subsidiary institutions.

Given the long decades of his intensive and varied work amid times marked by disasters and complex challenges, Nell-Breuning was a singular historical figure among those who, on the basis of gospel faith, collaborate in the construction of just social structures for the benefit of free persons.

See also CORPORATIONS; MARXISM; MODERN CATHOLIC SOCIAL THOUGHT; PESCH, HEINRICH; QUADRAGESIMO ANNO; SUBSIDIARITY, PRINCIPLE OF; VOLKSVEREIN; WORK, THEOLOGY OF.

Bibliography: F. Hengsbach, "Entschieden zur Sache: Werk, kirchliches Umfeld und politische Resonanz Oswald von Nell-Breunings, S.J.," *Theologie und Philosophie* 65 (1990) 321–48. F. Hengsbach, *Den Kapitalismus Umbiegen: Schriften zu Kirche, Wirtschaft und Gesellschaft—Ein Lesebuch* (Düsseldorf: Patmos Verlag, 1990). O. Nell-Breuning, *Gerechtigkeit und Freiheit: Grundzüge katholischer Soziallehre* (München: Olzog, 1985). O. Nell-Breuning, *Wirtschaft und Gesellschaft Heute,* 3 vols. (Freiburg: Herder, 1956–60).

PHILIP J. CHMIELEWSKI, S.J.

NEOCONSERVATIVES

In religious social thought, the roots of the so-called "neoconservative" movement in the United States go back to four key figures of the era 1930–65: Among Catholics, to Jacques Maritain (1882–1973) and John Courtney Murray, S.J. (1904–67); among Protestants, to Reinhold Niebuhr (1892–1971); and among Jews, to Will Herberg (1901–77). All four writers espoused a serious turn away from secular liberalism and toward the basic principles of Christianity and Judaism, with a corresponding turn toward political realism, or "practical wisdom."

All four had a profound sense of the transcendence of God, in whose light all worldly structures are relativized. Because of the primacy they gave to faith, these Protestants, Catholics, and Jews were called "neo-orthodox." Because of their sharp critique of secular and religious liberalism, they were called "new conservatives." There were differences and disputes among them, partly because of personality, partly because of differences in intellectual tradition and confessional style (there was not much communication across ecumenical lines in that era). But the four together represented an important movement in American intellectual life; Niebuhr and Murray were each singled out for a cover of *Time,* for instance, and the commentary on the works of all four is extensive.

All four were defenders of democracy, and while critical of many aspects of American life, they were also defenders of the originality of the American experiment in international social discourse. Classic works of theirs include Maritain's *Man and the State, Reflections on America,* and *Christianity and Democracy;* Murray's *We Hold These Truths* and his essays on religious liberty in the journal *Theological Studies;* Niebuhr's *Nature and Destiny of Man, Christianity and Power Politics, The Children of Light and the Children of Darkness, The Irony of American History, Christian Realism and Political Problems,* and others; and Will Herberg's *Protestant, Catholic, Jew* as well as his essays in the *National Review* and elsewhere, some of which have been collected by David G. Dalin in *From Marxism to Judaism.*

A short quotation from this last-named book may help to clarify one other bond between the "new conservatives" of the last generation and the "neoconservatives" of the present. Not only were both groups critical of the Left, some of them also underwent something like the conversion experience described by Will Herberg:

"My first encounter with the thought of Reinhold Niebuhr came in the later 1930s. I was then at a most crucial moment in my life. My Marxist faith had collapsed under the shattering blows of contemporary history—there is no need to tell a story now grown familiar. . . . At this point . . . I came upon Niebuhr's *Moral Man and Immoral Society.* . . . It came with the revelation of a new understanding of human existence in terms of a new understanding of human existence in terms of which I might reconstruct my life and thought. What impressed me most profoundly was the paradoxical combination of realism and radicalism that Niebuhr's 'prophetic' faith made possible. Here was a faith that transferred the center of its absolute commitment to what was really absolute—the transcendent God—and was therefore able to face the real facts of life unafraid, with open eyes. Here was a faith that called into question all human institutions and institutional vested interests, that permitted nothing of this world to parade as final or ultimate, and yet provided an intelligible ground for discriminate judgment. Here was a faith that warned against all premature securities, yet called to responsible action. Here, in short, was a 'social idealism' without illusions, in comparison with which even the most 'advanced' Marxism appeared confused, inconsistent, and hopelessly illusion-ridden" (Herberg, pp. 38–39).

In the wake of the Vietnam war, a new utopianism grew up on the American Left among radicals quick to elbow these four long-dominant "realists" aside as "essentially defensive or conservative" (Tom Driver). Although he himself had earlier been shoved aside by the new Left, the socialist Michael Harrington dubbed as "neoconservatives" those former socialists (or sympathizers) who had now become critical of the Left. His main targets were such significant Jewish thinkers as Irving Kristol, author of *Reflections of a Neo-Conservative* (1983) and (with Daniel Bell) editor of *The Public Interest;* Norman Podhoretz, author of *Breaking Ranks* (1980) and editor of *Commentary;* and others in the circles linked to those magazines. Thus the initial definition of neoconservativism singled out writers identified with the Left who had become critical of the Left; who were uneasy about the socialist project; who opposed radical utopianism (in the name of "realism"); and who rejected as a species of "bad faith" radical anti-Americanism. For these stands, neoconservatives were denounced as traitors to their former allies, backsliders, and reactionaries.

In the world of religious publishing, the term "neoconservatives" was quickly applied (by Peter Steinfels, e.g., in *The Neoconservatives*) to the Catholic writer Michael Novak and later to the Lutheran writer Richard John Neuhaus (Neuhaus has since converted to Roman Catholicism). Novak had for a time allied himself with the new Left, notably in *Toward a Theology for Radical Politics* (1969), as had Neuhaus in *Movement and Revolution* (with Peter L. Berger, 1969). Beginning to criticize the new Left in the *Rise of the Unmeltable Ethnics* (1972), Novak called for a new alignment of the Democratic party—"a politics of family and neighborhood" over against the academic and journalistic Left. In *To Empower People* (1977), Neuhaus again joined with Peter L. Berger to produce a theory of "mediating structures" that would serve partly to complement and partly to replace the hyperactive modern state. They defined mediating structures as "those institutions standing between the individual in his private life and the larger institutions of public life." These mediating institutions make up civic society and express the active social life of citizens outside the "megastructures" of the state and other bureaucratic institutions. The examples they focused on included "neighborhood, family, church, and voluntary association."

With his magisterial *Tranquillitas Ordinis: The Present Failure and Future Promise of American Catholic Thought on War and Peace* (1987), George Weigel was also added to the list of religious "neoconservatives." His commitment to the Murray Project—the continuation of the work on American democracy begun by John Courtney Murray, S.J.—confirmed his status as a critic of the Left and Right, most notably in *Catholicism and the Renewal of American Democracy.*

Although these three figures have evoked most of the critical comment, younger associates in the neoconservative circle (around *Crisis* and *First Things,* for example) include evangelicals like Dean Curry, Kent Hill, and Michael Cromartie; other Protestants like James Neuchterlein and Gilbert Meilander; and Catholics like Terry Hall and Robert Royal—and many others.

Neuhaus shared Weigel's commitment to the Murray Project, notably in his very influential books *The Naked Public Square* and *The Catholic Moment.* In addition, he has been editor (until its demise) of the triquarterly *This World* and its successor, the monthly *First Things.* While also writing extensively on democracy and human rights, Novak has become best known for his writings on capitalism and socialism: *The Spirit of Democratic Capitalism, Catholic Social Thought and Liberal Institutions, Will It Liberate? Questions about Liberation Theology, Free Persons and the Common Good,* and *The Catholic Ethic and the Spirit of Capitalism.* Novak was also a founder of *This World* and *Crisis,* two reviews widely described as "neoconservative."

For all their differences, the religious neoconservatives hold several beliefs in common: the primacy of religion over culture; the priority of culture over politics and economics; and the mutual interdependence of economic and political systems. They hold, empirically, that capitalism is a necessary but not sufficient condition for the success of democracy, and that democracy is a necessary but not sufficient condition for the long-term health of capitalism. Whereas many progressives since about 1972 have favored the socialist methods of analysis and prescription favored by Latin American liberation theologians, the neoconservatives have opposed socialism as a step toward decline. As a more fruitful way to protect the human rights of the poor and to produce economic progress that will raise the poor out of poverty, the neoconservatives make a pragmatic case for the threefold combination of capitalism, democracy, and pluralism, usually citing in this respect Peter L. Berger's *Capitalist Revolution* (1986).

Among other ideas that the neoconservatives have placed on the agenda are the following: that democracy is necessary for the securing of human rights; that democracy does not mean only majority vote but also those constitutional checks and balances against the tyranny of majorities that are intended by the classic name "republic"; that religious liberty is the first among human rights; that wealth creation is prior to distribution and that the chief cause of new wealth is invention and enterprise, which represent in humankind the image of the Creator; that enterprise (like prudence) is a moral and intellectual virtue and a fundamental human right; that peace is the fruit of order and, therefore, primarily a political achievement, as distinct from a weapons agreement; that pluralism does not mean the reduction of public discourse either to the lowest common denominator or to merely secular speech but, on the contrary, the civic conversation in which all parties speak from conscience fully, openly, and in a reasoned way.

The neoconservatives have been much criticized both by the Right and by the Left. They have been sharply denounced by self-described "paleo-conservatives" such as Patrick Buchanan, Paul Gottfried, and Claes Ryn for their belief that democracy and human rights have universal and transcultural validity. They have been stingingly attacked by the dean of American conservatives, Russell Kirk, for entertaining a progressive vision of the future ("ideology") rather than holding to the true conservative's commitment to history, experience, and tradition. The Americans around the traditionalist journal *Communio* have attacked Neuhaus and Weigel (and Murray, Maritain, and Niebuhr, for that matter) for their "ontology" and their concepts of "grace," "nature," and "secular, and have expressed hostility toward Novak's view of "democratic capitalism."

From the Left, the neoconservatives are criticized for not accepting the obviousness of the socialist hypothesis about the "oppression" of the poor; for presenting arguments that are sometimes used by conservative rather than by radical sectors of society; for showing excessive "enthusiasm" for capitalism (Novak) and democracy (Weigel) and the urgency of a classic Catholic witness in public discourse (Neuhaus).

Since the "neoconservatives" fit easily neither into the categories of the traditionalists or conservatives of the Right nor into the categories of the Left, perhaps a self-description by Neuhaus may stand for all: "religiously orthodox, culturally conservative, politically liberal, and economically pragmatic." The effort of many, Right and Left, to define them outside the mainstream evokes a doubt: it may not do justice to the older current of thought that the neoconservatives have reintroduced into the public dialogue, both within and outside Catholic circles.

See also CHRISTIAN DEMOCRACY; DEMOCRACY; ECONOMIC ORDER; HUMAN RIGHTS; MARITAIN, JACQUES; MURRAY, JOHN COURTNEY; PLURALISM; SUBSIDIARITY, PRINCIPLE OF.

Bibliography: P. Berger and R. Neuhaus, *To Empower People: The Role of Mediating Structures in Public Policy* (Washington: American Enterprise Institute, 1977). J. Cooper, *The Theology of Freedom: The Legacy of Jacques Maritain and Reinhold Niebuhr* (Macon, Ga.: Mercer Univ. Press, 1985). W. Herberg, *From Marxism to Judaism: The Collected Essays of Will Herberg,* ed. D. Dalin (New York: M. Wiener, 1989); *Protestant, Catholic, Jew: An Essay in American Religious Sociology* (Garden City, N.Y.: Doubleday, 1955). I. Kristol, *Reflections of a Neoconservative* (New York: Basic Books, 1983). J. Maritain, *Christianity and Democracy,* trans. B. Anson (New York: Scribner's Sons, 1944); *Man and the State* (Chicago: Univ. of Chicago Press, 1951); *Reflections on America* (New York: Scribner's Sons, 1958). J. Murray, *We Hold These Truths: Catholic Reflections on the American Proposition* (New York: Sheed & Ward, 1960). R. Neuhaus, *The Catholic Moment* (New York: Harper & Row, 1987); *The Naked Public Square* (Grand Rapids: Eerdmans, 1984). R. Niebuhr, *Christian Realism and Political Problems* (New York: Scribner's Sons, 1953); *Christianity and Power Politics* (New York: Scribner's Sons, 1940); *Moral Man and Immoral Society: A Study in Ethics and Politics* (New York: Scribner's Sons, 1932); *Nature and Destiny of Man,* 2 vols. (New York: Scribner's Sons, 1941–43); *The Children of Light and the Children of Darkness: A Vindication of Democracy and a Critique of Its Traditional Defense* (New York: Scribner's Sons, 1944); *The Irony of American History* (New York: Scribner's Sons, 1952). M. Novak, *A Theology for Radical Politics* (New York: Herder & Herder, 1969); *Free Persons and the Common Good* (Lanham, Md.: Madison Books, 1989); *Freedom with Justice:*

Catholic Social Thought and Liberal Institutions (New York: Harper & Row, 1984), second ed. published with new introduction and concluding chapter as *Catholic Social Thought and Liberal Institutions* (New Brunswick, N.J.: Transaction, 1989); *The Rise of the Unmeltable Ethnics* (New York: Macmillan, 1972); *The Spirit of Democratic Capitalism* (New York: Simon & Schuster, 1982); second ed. with new afterword by the author (Lanham, Md.: Univ. Press of America, 1990); *Will It Liberate? Questions for Liberation Theology* (Mahwah, N.J.: Paulist, 1986); *The Catholic Ethic and the Spirit of Capitalism.* P. Steinfels, *The Neoconservatives: The Men Who Are Changing America's Politics* (New York: Simon & Schuster, 1979). G. Weigel, *Catholicism and the Renewal of American Democracy* (Mahwah, N.J.: 1989); *Tranquillitas Ordinis: The Present Failure and Future Promise of American Catholic Thought on War and Peace* (New York: Oxford, 1987).

Articles: R. Kirk, "The Neoconservatives: An Endangered Species," *The Heritage Lectures, #178* (Washington: Heritage Foundation, 1988). "Reinhold Niebuhr: Two Divergent Views": R. Brown, "Reinhold Niebuhr: His Theology in the 1980s"; M. Novak, "Reinhold Niebuhr: Model for Neoconservatives," *The Christian Century* (January 22, 1986) 66–71. D. McCann, "Reinhold Niebuhr and Jacques Maritain on Marxism: A Comparison of Two Traditional Models of Practical Theology," *Journal of Religion* 58 (April 1978) 140–68. C. Ryn, "The Democracy Boosters," *National Review* (March 24, 1989) 30–32, 52.

MICHAEL NOVAK

O

OCTOGESIMA ADVENIENS

On May 14, 1971, Pope Paul VI sent an apostolic letter to Maurice Cardinal Roy of Quebec, chair of the Pontifical Commission Justice and Peace. Entitled *A Call to Action* (*Octogesima adveniens*), the letter commemorated the 80th anniversary of Pope Leo XIII's landmark encyclical, *On the Condition of Workers* (*Rerum novarum*). Paul VI's letter, however, was much more than an anniversary document. While addressing critical social issues of the day, *A Call to Action* advanced Catholic social thought in several thematic areas—the preferential respect due to the poor, the demand for equality and participation, the movement from economics to politics, and the call to all Christians to become active in social justice efforts.

This letter was the second of three major social documents to be published during the pontificate of Paul VI. *On the Development of Peoples* (*Populorum progressio*) appeared in 1967. In November of 1971 the Holy Father approved *Justice in the World* (*Justitia in mundo*), a document prepared by the Second General Assembly of the synod of bishops. Though not an encyclical, the public and urgent manner in which *A Call to Action* addressed all Catholics quickly made it one of the most important Catholic social documents of the past century.

In the following pages we will examine this letter and its place in Catholic social thought. Four topics provide the framework for this reflection: the style and methodology employed in the document; the new social problems it addresses; its continuity with earlier social documents; and the new developments that *A Call to Action* brings to Catholic social teachings. The latter topic constitutes the major part of this reflection.

Methodology and Style

The Second Vatican Council (1963–65) inaugurated a major methodological shift in Catholic social documents (Curran, pp. 298–306). Abandoning the natural-law methodology of earlier teachings, the council turned to the Gospels and human experience as primary sources for ethical reflection. This shift in methodology is particularly evident in the council's final document, the Pastoral Constitution on the Church in the Modern World (*Gaudium et spes*). In *A Call to Action,* this new methodology is completely in place. More influenced by the events of current history, the methodology carries greater possibility for developments and even changes within the papal social teachings. Less certain of the wisdom represented in the hierarchical teachings, this historically conscious approach exhibits a pedogogical caution not always detected in earlier documents within the tradition.

Early in this letter Pope Paul VI referred to his recent journeys where he went into the crowds and heard from the people "their appeals, cries of distress and at the same time cries of hope" (OA 2). From these experiences the pontiff was able to see the problems of his day "in a new perspective." These experiences also enabled the pope to appreciate the wide diversity of situations confronting Christians "according to regions, socio-political systems and cultures" (3). In the face of such diversity, he noted, it would be difficult for the papacy to offer a unified message or a solution to social, economic, or political problems that would have universal validity (4). That is the task of the Christian communities—to analyze their own country's situation and to discern the best options for urgently needed changes. That is the action to which this letter calls all Christians.

Pope Paul VI's reluctance to offer authoritative pronouncements on social issues stands in sharp contrast to earlier papal claims. Pius XI, for example, stated in *On Reconstructing the Social Order* (*Quadragesimo anno*) that the papacy had the "right and duty to pronounce with supreme authority upon social and economic matters" (QA 41). Even the church's social teachings are presented here in a more dynamic light than was characteristic of earlier documents. Pope Pius XII regarded the social teaching as definitely and uniquely fixed in its fundamental nature and enjoying immutable and permanent principles (Pius XII, 1945). In *A Call to Action,* however, Paul VI candidly acknowledged that this social teaching develops. Three factors guide this development: gospel-based reflection upon changing situations; the church's commitment to serve the poor; and the long experience of the church, which enables it "to undertake daring and creative innovations" called for by current global conditions (42).

We might question how daring or creative have been the papacy's responses to social questions, particularly during the period of Catholic social thought preceding the Second Vatican Council. It is far more important, however, to recognize the innovative character of those teachings that have been set forth since the council, including this apostolic letter. These developments occurred largely because of the methodological shift toward the gospel and human experience.

New Social Problems

Each historical period and every decade within the modern era seems to generate its own economic crises and political movements. These in turn generate new social problems, many of which become the subject matter of Catholic social teaching. Pope Paul VI addressed many of these new social problems in the first major section of *A Call to Action.* Urbanization, referred to as a major phenomenon in both industrialized and developing countries, is the first of these problems to be considered. The weakening of agrarian civilization, the rapid and uncontrolled industrial and technological developments, the threat to neighborhood and family, the new loneliness in the crowd—all are consequences of this new major phenomenon called "urbanization." *A Call to Action* avoids any romantic suggestions that people should return to the countryside. At this time, in 1971, Paul VI recognized that urbanization was "undoubtedly an irreversible stage in the development of human societies" (10).

The pope, however, does warn against the new dangers that inevitably seem present in urban life: increase in poverty, discrimination, and indifference and new forms of exploitation and domination that guarantee that the weakest members of society will continue to remain "victims of dehumanizing living conditions." Thus there is "an urgent need to remake at the level of the street, of the neighborhood or of the great agglomerative dwellings the social fabric" whereby persons are able to develop the needs of their personality (11). In unusually specific and concrete terms, this papal document states that centers of special interest must be created at the community or parish levels to provide for recreational, spiritual, and community gathering needs. Christians are called to join in building up the city as a place where community exists, where relationships are possible, where social justice is the norm (12).

Regarding workers, *A Call to Action* reiterates past social teachings in support of labor union rights. It notes that while most democratic societies accept this principle (labor union rights), they are not always open to the exercise of such rights. Since the publication of this letter the labor movement in the United States, and in many other countries, has struggled to maintain a strong presence in the workplace. It is ironic that some Catholic hospitals and schools have obstructed unionizing efforts in contradiction to the church's social teaching on this topic.

A Call to Action demands an end to discrimination against women. At the same time it appears to retain the traditional stance that woman's proper role is at the heart of the family (13), a position that continues in some of the most recent Catholic social documents, for example, in John Paul II's encyclical *On Human Work* (*Laborem exercens* 19). Nevertheless, *A Call to Action* calls for legislation recognizing woman's independence as a person and "her equal rights to participate in cultural, economic, social and political life" (13).

Among the many other new social problems discussed, *A Call to Action* includes a brief mention of the environment. It is one of the first Catholic social documents to do so. Echoing thoughts from an earlier discussion of the dangers in industrialization, Paul VI cautioned that the exploitation and destruction of nature will make human beings victims of their own actions. His concerns about the environment reflect a mainline Catholic communitarian ethic in which the human person tends to be the principal reason for protecting creation.

Continuity with the Tradition

A Call to Action exhibits a clear continuity with earlier Catholic social documents. That link with the past appears in many of the social problems identified and discussed. Workers' rights, for example, have been a pressing concern since the beginning of modern Catholic social thought. It was this issue that the first major social encyclical, *On the Condition of Workers,* addressed eighty years ago. Various problems related to the family appear in this letter as they do throughout the tradition—urbanization's threat to neighborhood and family, the growing tension between women's increasing presence in political and economic life and their more traditional role in the family. In this letter as in all Catholic social documents, the poor and the more vulnerable members of society receive special consideration.

Other themes appearing in *A Call to Action* represent a continuation of discussions begun in earlier papal and conciliar social teachings. Pope Paul VI's analysis of ideologies (26–36), particularly socialism and Marxism, was not a new concern among the documents. Pope Leo XIII had already presented the evils of socialism in his encyclicals *On Socialism* (*Quod Apostolici muneris,* 1878) and *On the Condition of Workers* (RN, 1891). In 1931 Pius XI insisted that "no one can be at the same time a good Catholic and a true socialist" (QA 120). However, *A Call to Action* expands the discussion by offering a more sophisticated appreciation of Marxism. Even John XXIII's distinction in *Peace on Earth* (*Pacem in terris*) between false philosophical teachings and historical movements (PT 159) is further nuanced by Paul VI, as will be noted in the next section. Socialism appears in *A Call to Action* as an old topic but one with new understandings and changing pastoral implications.

Another familiar theme appearing in *A Call to Action* is the Christian's calling to build up this world. The letter quotes directly from *Gaudium et spes*: "The expectation of a new earth must not weaken but rather stimulate our concern for cultivating this one" (GS 39). What we do in this world, especially our efforts to build a more just social order, should not be viewed as action peripheral to our eschatological hopes. Even now the new human community which we struggle to form is a foreshadowing of the new age (GS 39). It is to this action that Pope Paul VI issues his call to all Christians.

At the same time, the apostolic letter cautions that the nature of progress is ambiguous—a theme often present in the radio messages and various allocutions of Pope Pius XII. Pius frequently spoke of the rapid developments in the area of technology, of the growth of massive technological systems, and of the danger such developments pose to freedom of action and human initiative. Continuing that theme, Paul VI here wrote that scientific, quantitative growth alone is inadequate. *A Call to Action* asserts that genuine progress is found in the development of a moral consciousness that leads people to greater openness to God and a wider solidarity with others. The production and consumption of material goods is important to society. More important, however, is the degree of participation and responsibility allowed all members of society in building up this world. *A Call to Action* presents powerful new insights for Catholic social thought. The strength of these teachings rests on the fact that they are not entirely new. They bear a relationship to earlier teachings and are, therefore, a perfecting of seminal thoughts already present in the tradition, whose development is pressed by historical events.

New Developments

The importance of any social document is not located in the new economic problems identified, nor even in its linkages to documents that have gone before. The lasting importance of such messages emerges from the themes introduced or further developed—themes that speak to how a society, with its many and varied constituent groups, should function. On that point *A Call to Action* carves out an enduring mark upon the development of Catholic social thought. Five new themes provide the structure for our final section: the aspiration to participation, the preferential respect due to the poor, the need to move from economics to politics, the call to action, and the plurality of options.

Equality and Participation

One of the most exciting developments in Catholic social thought appears in *A Call to Action.* Pope Paul VI wrote that as people become better informed and better educated two aspirations grow stronger and persistently make themselves felt, "the aspiration to equality and the aspiration to participation, two forms of man's dignity and freedom" (22). By associating equality and participation with human dignity the pontiff declared that these are more than idle yearnings of disenfranchised people. Rather they are fundamental rights to which every member of the human community may lay claim.

This is a major step in the Catholic human rights tradition. No previous document had granted the status of a human right to this notion of participation. No teaching prior to this letter had so strongly insisted that every person has a right to be actively involved in all decision-making processes that affect their lives—economic, cultural, educational, political. *A Call to Action* recognizes this as a fundamental aspiration of people and one that must be respected along with every other human right. A practical consequence of these yearnings for equality and participation is that people "seek to promote a democratic type of society." Not only is this a legitimate desire but "the Christian has the duty to take part in this search and in the organization and life of political society" (24).

The challenge of this teaching on participation can be appreciated by recognizing that this human right remains but an unrealized aspiration for millions of people more than twenty years after its recognition in *A Call to Action.* The apartheid policies of South Africa have long stood as an international sign of the continuing denial of this fundamental human right. Other examples could be cited of authoritarian regimes that exclude the possibility of broad citizen involvement in the governance of their nation. Another form of participation is denied in the United States and other Western democracies. More than thirty million Americans live below the poverty level, prevented by that factor from fully participating in the economic and social life of their nation.

A Call to Action's teaching on this subject represents a major development for yet another reason: the right to participation and the recognition of equality among all people have not always been evident in Catholic social teaching. Indeed, a number of earlier documents were staunchly opposed to these two aspirations. In his encyclical *On Freemasonry* (*Humanum genus,* 1884) Pope Leo XIII rejected all claims that people are equal in this world. Because God had created people with unequal abilities, intelligence, and energy, it was repugnant to extend complete equality to the institutions of public life (HG 26). It was the wisdom and good sense of the church, he wrote on another occasion, that recognized this inequality among people (*Quod apostolici muneris* 9). One of Leo's successors, Pope Pius X, was even more specific about the types of inequality that should be accepted in society. It is part of God's established order that human society should have rulers and subjects, employers and workers, rich and poor, educated and ignorant, nobles and common people (Pius X, p. 341).

That these popes could accept and defend so vigorously the social inequalities of their day can be understood against the theological and political perspectives from which they wrote. Social, economic, and political inequalities were seen as rooted in nature itself. Inequality is a fact of nature, and natural inequality necessarily gives rise to social inequality. This is the way God created the world; this is how God wills the world to continue. All struggling against nature is in vain (RN 26).

This philosophical/theological basis for social inequalities coincided with Leo XIII's concern for maintaining political stability. He believed it to be one of the major evils of modern society that so many people were discontented with their status and longed to rise to a better station in life. These were the people who caused disruptions in society, tensions between social classes, and threats to stable governments (Camp, p. 31). With that concern before him, the pontiff did little to encourage equality. Rather, he stressed the importance of inequality as an essential aspect of society, which he viewed as a stable, hierarchical organism (Curran, p. 287).

But a profound sense of equality among all people is a necessary precondition for participation in any or all of society's decision-making processes. That sense of equality is not found in many of the early Catholic social documents. Hence an appreciation of the need for participation—as articulated in *A Call to Action*—could not have emerged.

Citizen involvement in the area of political affairs, so strongly endorsed by Pope Paul VI, was utterly discouraged by many of his predecessors. Even in the face of structural injustices inflicting pain and threatening the dignity of ordinary people, these victims of societal injustices were not encouraged to seek changes in the social or political systems that were causing human suffering. On the contrary, prayer was presented as an alternative to the kind of action that might change the unjust situation (Dorr, p. 33). Pope Leo reminded the poor and the victims of injustice that they should be content with their lot and should await their reward in heaven (QAM 9).

With a methodology rooted in the Scriptures and historical experiences, Pope Paul VI was less concerned about preserving social and political structures and in a better position to recognize the need for equality and participation. In *A Call to Action* he recalled how John XXIII had emphasized everyone's responsibility to take an active role in the area of economics. The letter then states that "today the field is wider." It extends to the political and social spheres, wherein a sharing in responsibility and in decisions must be assured (47). The task of regulating economic, political, and all social affairs is not the sole responsibility of elite members of society, however they may have entered into positions of power and decision making. That responsibility rests upon everyone in society. It is both a right and a responsibility of all Christians "to build up the city" and to create the social fabric that will enable everyone to develop themselves through participation in social progress (11–12).

For *A Call to Action* and the social documents that follow it, the principal evil resulting from a world abounding in various types of injustices and oppression is not the fact that countless persons are deprived of adequate food, clothing, or shelter. The primary concern of these teachings is what is seen as the chief threat to human dignity. That threat to personal dignity lies especially in the fact that large segments of the populations of many nations are excluded from active participation in shaping the social, economic, and political structures that provide the context for their lives (Hollenbach, p. 86). This lack of participation, this marginalization of persons, leads to the more visible social conditions referred to as poverty: lack of food, housing, education, jobs, transportation. Social marginalization with its manifestations of poverty and degrading dependency is to be overcome not primarily through increased public assistance or private charity but through the participation of those who are marginalized in the reshaping of the systems and structures of society.

Preferential Respect Due to the Poor

A second new development that this apostolic letter brought to Catholic social teaching is its call for a preferential respect for the poor. This theme is developed further in subsequent documents and figures prominently in the thinking of many liberation theologians. It is evident also in the United States Catholic bishops pastoral letter of 1986, *Economic Justice for All* (EJA 16).

While Pope Paul VI spoke approvingly of the current aspiration to equality, he also recognized that there is a negative side to an unqualified emphasis upon equality. Consistent with the entire tradition of Catholic social thought, he cautioned against too narrow an understanding of equality—one leading to an individualism wherein persons claim their rights without accountability for the common good. Regarding the poor, he also warned that strict equality before the law is not enough, for it can result in continued discrimination, exploitation, and contempt. Thus the pontiff reminded us that "the Gospel instructs us in the preferential respect due to the poor and the special situation they have in society: the more fortunate should renounce some of their rights so as to place their goods more generously at the service of the poor" (OA 23). What a remarkable development this statement brings to Catholic social teaching regarding people who are poor and those who are not! No longer are the poor exhorted to practice patience, or to offer earnest prayers to God, or to await their reward in heaven. No longer is it sufficient for the more affluent to give to the poor out of their surplus goods (RN 36; OA 50) or even out of their abundance (GS 69). Now much more is required.

The more fortunate in society must be prepared to give up some of their rights so that the poor may have access to those conditions of social living necessary for a life of dignity. *A Call to Action* will later call for political action, and future documents will insist on the need for institutional change. Combined with those teachings this preferential respect for the poor carries a serious challenge to those in society who enjoy a life of relative comfort. To renounce their rights means that they must be prepared to support those social, economic, and political changes in society that are especially beneficial to the poor. The challenge of *A Call to Action* is that I must be prepared to help enact changes in our institutions and public policies even when those changes may not be to my own advantage. That is the awesome significance of Pope Paul VI's call to Christians to demonstrate a preferential respect for the poor. In the practical realm of reorganizing the social order this respect must evolve into a preferential option.

From Economics to Politics

This preferential respect for the poor cannot be realized without changes in the basic systems and structures of society. Economic activity alone cannot correct the continuing imbalances and injustices that bind millions of people throughout the world in a state of destitution and excessive dependence. The necessary changes can only come about through political endeavors—*A Call to Action*'s third significant contribution to the development of Catholic social thought. In light of the structural changes that must be realized, Pope Paul VI asked if there were not a radical limitation to economics. Ultimate decisions, he noted, rest with political power. Thus "the need is felt to pass from economics to politics" (46). It is there—in political power—that the common good is to be achieved. Its aim is that of creating those conditions that enable all members of society to develop themselves and attain their complete good. To maintain such an environment over the long term requires intervention on behalf of justice where the social and economic systems do not function for the welfare of everyone, especially the poor.

This passing to the political dimension also provides the opportunity for greater participation, for a sharing in responsibility and decision making. *A Call to Action* refers to Pope John XXIII's teaching that access to responsibility is a fundamental demand of every person's nature, an exercise of freedom, and a path to one's development. That sharing in responsibility must now extend to the political sphere. To that end Paul VI stated that modern forms of democracy must be established (47).

Call to Action

The final section of this document bears an urgent call to all Christians to act on behalf of justice. To the laity in particular belongs the task of reforming the social order, of enacting political and economic changes designed to ensure human dignity for everyone. In language and meaning quite different from earlier encyclicals, *A Call to Action* exhorts all Christians to engage in this struggle: "It belongs to the laity, without waiting passively for orders and directives, to take the initiative freely and to infuse a Christian spirit into the mentality, customs, laws and structures of the community in which they live" (48). Each of us must recognize how we personally share in the injustices around us and how we benefit from current structural arrangements that often work against the poor and the powerless. Thus "it is not enough to recall principles, state intentions, point to crying injustices and utter prophetic denunciations." These words must lead to an awareness of our personal responsibility and to effective action.

Sounding a theme that would be developed in the 1971 synod of bishops' document, *Justice in the World,* Pope Paul VI warned that the gospel of Jesus Christ cannot be proclaimed and heard unless it is "accompanied by the witness of the Holy

Spirit, working within the action of Christians in the service of their brothers" (51). Our Christian faith demands "a just and consequently necessary, transformation of society." It is the responsibility of individuals and Christian organizations to work for these changes, and to do so with a preferential consideration for the poor.

Plurality of Options

A Call to Action recognizes that in this summons there resides the possibility of conflicting views, even among those who share the same faith. Earlier the document appealed to the imagination of responsible people in its reference to utopias and urged Christians to look again at the disregarded possibilities of the present situation (37). As this and other recent social documents have stated, the hierarchical church does not offer principles as certain solutions to the various social problems of our day. Within its own setting the Christian community must discern specific options and concrete commitments (Curran, p. 305). That can only occur if everyone is afforded the opportunity—as a right—to take a participatory role in every aspect of the society's structure—economic, political, social, cultural.

The problem of conflicting views, however, increases to the extent that greater numbers of people exercise their right and responsibility to participate in decision-making processes, particularly in the political realm. Here *A Call to Action* reminds us of the Second Vatican Council instruction on this matter, namely, that in concrete situations there will always be various legitimate options to pursue. Some individuals, and some groups, will choose different—perhaps even contradictory—paths to resolving particular problems or realizing social goals. "The same Christian faith can lead to different commitments" (OA 53; GS 43).

Where conflicting social-change goals and strategies exist among Christians, efforts should be made toward mutual understanding, respect, and the exercise of charity. It is worth noting that the document never suggests Christians must find agreement among themselves in their commitments to build a just society. Nor does it recognize the possibility of divisions within the community as a legitimate reason for Christians to refrain from social justice actions. Local churches and parish leadership will not find in this teaching a basis for the claim that raising disputed or controversial issues is too divisive for building community.

The point of this discussion in *A Call to Action* is that as Christians struggle to determine the best solutions to social and economic problems they must recognize, accept, and respect the plurality of existing options. That plurality of options, or the conflict that may result from Christians choosing different strategies, must never become a reason for not engaging in actions on behalf of justice.

While it is clear that Christians may disagree and choose different strategies and goals in responding to this call to action, yet another difficult question remains. Does this plurality of options permit Catholics to cooperate with movements or organizations advocating positions opposed to church teaching? An illustration of the inherent problems associated with this question is found in the church's social teachings regarding socialism. *A Call to Action*'s treatment of this issue is particularly revealing.

The early social documents, particularly those of Popes Leo XIII and Pius XI, saw virtually no possibility of Catholics joining with socialists in the common goal of establishing just social structures. The position of these early teachings regarding socialism was one of adamant opposition (QAM 1; QA 111–26). It was an opposition to socialism (as well as Marxism and communism) as a doctrine and as a historical movement pursuing its goals for social change. As such the teaching not only discouraged but in certain instances explicitly forbade Catholics from cooperating with the movements. As late as 1949 Catholics who supported Communist parties in Italian elections were refused admittance to the sacraments (Pius XII, 1949).

Throughout these documents there appears to be an unstated assumption that effectively precluded Christians' cooperating with any group of socialists, however reformed or moderate those groups might have become. That assumption held that one could not work with socialists without becoming a socialist. And, since it was anathema for Christians to become socialists, to believe that one could join with socialist groups to realize mutually shared goals for a just society was equally unthinkable. The basic differences between socialism and Catholic social teaching outweighed any area of common agreement and argued against collaboration.

The first significant development in the social documents regarding Catholics cooperating with socialists is found in Pope John XXIII's distinction between historical movements and their originating philosophical teachings (PT 159). While the original teachings remain the same, the movements evolve and change. Working from within constantly evolving historical situations and influenced by a myriad of social factors, these movements will undergo significant change from the philosophical teaching that gave them birth. Such distinctions between philosophical theories and the historical movements that developed out of the theories suggest possibilities for Christians' involvement and cooperation with the movements.

A Call to Action explores these distinctions in considerable detail (30–34). The document discusses the various meanings and attractions that Marxism holds for people. Consistent with the tradition, Pope Paul VI insists that Christians cannot adhere to any ideological systems that radically or substantially contradict their faith and their concept of the human person. In that respect he criticizes both the Marxist and liberal ideologies.

On the question of Christians cooperating with socialists in efforts to combat injustices, however, Paul VI appears a bit more cautious than his immediate predecessor. In *A Call to Action* he warns that historical movements "remain conditioned by the ideologies from which they originated" (31). As an example he notes that the Christian's longing for a more just society appears harmlessly compatable with the socialist movements. Nevertheless, this human aspiration of socialism cannot be regarded as completely separate and independent from other dimensions of the movement—its political organization and aim as well as its self-sufficient picture of the human person.

In spite of these concerns, *A Call to Action* does not argue against Catholics cooperating with socialists or with any other organizations and movements opposed to church teaching. Such insights and cautions do not eliminate the possibility of cooperation. Rather, they enable Christians to determine their own degree of commitment to join with socialists, or any other movements, in struggling for a just society (31).

One year after this letter was published, the United States Catholic bishops made an interesting application of this teaching. The Campaign for Human Development, which is the church's program to provide financial support to self-help social-change efforts among the poor in the United States, was under attack for making grants to projects whose sponsors did not always agree with church teaching. In response to these critics, the United States Catholic Conference's Administrative Board warned against those who "espouse the principle that CHD should give no money to any project, no matter how worthy, if it is sponsored by an organization which also has some involvement, however small, in other activities unacceptable to the Church. Such a principle, applied across the board, would presumably rule out the financial assistance given by the Holy See over the years to international agencies whose programs include population control activities. It would presumably rule out payment by Catholics of local, state, and federal taxes, since many local, state, and federal agencies have population-related programs. No principle of Catholic moral theology requires or supports such a course of action" (Krol). Both in its teaching documents such as *A Call to Action* and in its programmatic actions such as CHD, the hierarchical church acknowledges that the "plurality of options" means that Catholics may cooperate with movements and organizations that hold positions opposed to church teaching.

Conclusion

A Call to Action stands today as an urgent summons to all Christians. Its call is to engage—to become part of the global effort to build a world that more clearly reflects the standards of justice. No Christian is exempt from this responsibility. No Christian community can ignore this challenge for fear of the potential devisiveness that may ensue. The message in this apostolic letter is clear—Christians must engage in efforts to build a just society and world. To the poor and powerless of the world *A Call to Action* also directs a powerful summons: you have both a right and a responsibility to participate fully in every aspect of social life, to take part in all areas of decision making.

A Call to Action was published in 1971. Two years earlier the Catholic bishops of the United States passed a resolution creating the Campaign for Human Development (CHD, 1969). A unique aspect of that program, as called for in the bishops' resolution, is the participation of the poor in designing and implementing their own social-change projects.

We may wonder to what extent this program and this action by the church in the United States may have influenced *A Call to Action*'s insistence on the right to participation. We may hope that with a greater sensitivity to current experiences, future documents on Catholic social ethics will reflect the hopes and aspirations of God's people throughout the world.

See also CAMPAIGN FOR HUMAN DEVELOPMENT; CHURCH, SOCIAL MISSION OF; DEMOCRACY; HUMAN RIGHTS; LAITY, ROLE OF; MODERN CATHOLIC SOCIAL THOUGHT; POOR, PREFERENTIAL OPTION FOR; VATICAN COUNCIL II.

Bibliography: R. Camp, *The Papal Ideology of Social Reform: A Study in Historical Development (1878–1967)* (Leiden: E. J. Brill, 1969). CHD, *Resolution on the Campaign for Human Development* (November 1969). C. Curran, "The Changing Anthropological Bases of Catholic Social Ethics," *Thomist* 45 (April 2, 1981) 284–318. D. Dorr, *Option for the Poor: A Hundred Years of Vatican Social Teaching* (Maryknoll, N.Y.: Orbis, 1983). D. Hollenbach, *Claims in Conflict: Retrieving and Renewing the Catholic Human Rights Tradition* (New York: Paulist, 1979). J. Krol, "CHD Policies," USCC Administrative Board, February 1972, quoted in a letter to John Norton from Cardinal Krol, NCCB president (Philadelphia, May 9, 1972). Pius X, *Fin dalla prima* (motu proprio), AAS 36 (December 18, 1903) 341. Pius XII, "Speech to the Congress of Italian Catholic Action," *Bonne Press* 7 (April 25, 1945) 90. Pius XII, "Decree of the Holy Office," AAS 41 (July 1, 1949) 334.

BERNARD F. EVANS

OPERA DEI CONGRESSI

The main national association of Catholics in post-Risorgimento Italy from 1874 to 1904, the Opera dei Congressi (henceforth OC) was named for the annual congresses it held in one Italian city after another. It was the gathering place for all the various forces and groupings of Catholics ready to rally around behind the pope—from the annexation of the Papal States with the fall of Rome and the unification of Italy in 1870—until Pope Pius X dissolved it in 1904 because of internal problems. Like the Katholikentage in Germany, it was essentially a lay movement, aided and abetted by bishops and pope but corresponding in structure to a voluntary organization such as could be founded for any lawful purpose in a modern "liberal" state. It had a secretariat under the forceful presidency of the Venetian Giovanni Battista Paganuzzi (1841–1923) from 1889 to 1904, its most dynamic years. It was not itself a membership organization but a federation of Catholics organizations. Under its aegis more specialized groups, institutions, and movements such as the Catholic Youth kept in touch with one another at the annual congress.

In the history of social Catholicism, its "second section" plays a prominent role. The person in charge of this section (for social and economic concerns) from 1885 on was Stanislao Medolago Albani (1851–1921). A nobleman from Bergamo in a part of Italy still ruled by Austria in his boyhood, Medolago participated in the meetings of the Fribourg Union. But Paganuzzi did not allow him much room for initiatives until after *Rerum novarum* (1891) and the emergence of three new figures, who would respond more dynamically to the social needs of Italy from within the Catholic movement. These were the economist of Pisa, Giuseppe Toniolo (1845–1918); the priest and publicist, Romolo Murri (1870–1944); and the later party leader, statesman, and Catholic social theorist, the Sicilian priest Luigi Sturzo (1871–1959).

The dissolution of the OC was partly due to Murri's aggressiveness in practically staging a takeover of the secretariat through his numerous Christian Democratic followers. After the breakup in 1904 the second section continued under Medolago and Toniolo; Sturzo continued his local activities in Sicily while planning for the future political party he would head, whereas Murri and his brand of autonomous Christian democracy were repressed. Meanwhile, largely because of the stimulation Murri's ideas had provided, many young priests and laypersons had taken up the cause of the worker in all manner of parish associations, including such economic undertakings as rural credit unions.

It was the merit of the OC to have set up this network as well as to have provided the forums for Murri's ideas to be widely heard, through its congresses and the Catholic press that it promoted so efficaciously. A particularly notable case would be Giacomo Radini Tedeschi (1857–1914), the bishop of Bergamo who so impressed his young secretary, Angelo G. Roncalli, the future Pope John XXIII.

It may be noted that (as was the case in other European countries, but unlike the case in the United States) the social Catholic movement in Italy developed out of a viscerally antiliberal Catholicism in its origins and early development. It was from the right wing of Catholicism, to use this expression, that social Catholicism sprang. In Italy, the OC was the bastion of "intransigent" Catholicism. The conciliating wing, more open to modernity, which also existed, had no similar organization and much less influence among the masses.

A turning point occurred in 1898, after which a realignment took place. Some formerly intransigent Catholics (like Paganuzzi and Pius X) began to look upon secular social conservatives as possible allies (as the conciliating wing had always done), while others (like Murri and Sturzo) began to see the advantages of possible openings to democratic aspects of the modern age. The OC, in Pius X's pontificate, was not equal to the tensions thus generated.

See also ASSOCIATIONISM; CHRISTIAN DEMOCRACY; FRIBOURG UNION; LEO XIII; MODERNISM; RERUM NOVARUM.

Bibliography: S. Tramontin in DSMCI I/2:336–47; idem, "L'intransigentismo cattolico a l'Opera dei Congressi," *Storia del movimento cattolico in Italia,* 1:1–229 (Roma: Il Poligono, 1980). M. Clark, *Modern Italy, 1871–1982* (New York: Longmans, 1984). G. De Rosa, *Il movimento cattolico in Italia: Dalla Restaurazione all'età giolittiana* (Bari: Laterza, 1966). P. Misner, *Social Catholicism in Europe* (New York: Crossroad, 1991).

PAUL MISNER

OWNERSHIP

Ownership in the fullest sense represents the rights to use, possess, and dispose of the goods of the earth. Because of the social nature of human persons and God's creation of earthly goods for the good of all, the right to *use* such goods to meet the needs of persons is the most fundamental aspect of ownership. The right to *possess* objects for the individual's exclusive use (private property) is an important protection for the individual and in line with the dignity of a rational being, but the right to possess cannot supersede the primary right of use to meet human needs. The Catholic tradition has therefore argued against an absolute right to private property (*Mater et magistra* 43; *Populorum progressio* 23; *Laborem exercens* 14). The right to *dispose* of earthly goods involves rights to alter, destroy, and transfer such goods. It is necessarily limited by the fact that human persons are stewards rather than absolute sovereigns over God's creation and by the demands of justice in regard to the needs of other persons and future generations.

It is in the tension between the rights of use and of possession that the twofold character of ownership becomes apparent: the goods of the earth are meant for the good of all and for the common good (the social character of ownership), but at the same time private ownership (the individual character of ownership) can enhance the lives of the individual owners (*Quadragesimo anno* 45–46; MM 119–21; *Gaudium et spes* 71). The social aspect can never be completely superseded by the individual aspect.

There are several titles by which one may legitimately acquire ownership of goods. *Occupation* means taking possession of something that has not been previously owned by another for the purpose of keeping it as one's own (QA 52). Closely related is *finding,* by which an individual acquires property for which an owner cannot be located, which has been abandoned, or which cannot be returned. Similarly, *prescription* represents a legal acquisition through effective and undisputed possession in a manner and for a time legally specified. Ownership of property, even legitimately held for a long period, is still subject to the social aspect of ownership and the demands of distributive justice.

Labor, or work, represents the most frequently cited and the most important title for ownership (*Rerum novarum* 15; MM 43; LE 14)—the worker appropriates to himself or herself some part of the productive enterprise, which may be realized by actual ownership or by fair compensation through a just wage. Similarly, one may acquire title through *accession* or fruition, that is, the owner of the principal may lay legitimate claim to its increase.

Inheritance is a legitimate title for ownership, since private property is oriented to the good of the family and serves as an incentive for responsible care, though inheritance is also restricted by the social nature of all ownership and by the demands of distributive justice. The most frequent acquisition of goods occurs through *contract.* The justice of a transfer by contract requires that both parties are acting without undue economic or social pressures. *Dire necessity* may also represent legitimate title where superfluous goods are to be claimed by those in dire need (GS 69; *Summa theologiae* II-II, q. 66, a. 7). This would be a manifestation of the priority of the social aspect of the property over its individual aspect.

See also GOODS, ACCESS TO; GOODS, DISTRIBUTION OF; PRIVATE PROPERTY; STEWARDSHIP.

Bibliography: B. Häring, *Free and Faithful in Christ* (New York: Seabury, 1981) 3:290–96. H. Davis, *Moral and Pastoral Theology,* 6th ed. (New York: Sheed & Ward, 1949) 2:259–95.

MARK O'KEEFE, O.S.B.

OZANAM, FRÉDÉRIC

Frédéric Ozanam, founder of the St. Vincent de Paul Society, was born April 23, 1813, in Milan, Italy. He grew up and was schooled in Lyon, France, one of fifteen children, only four of whom survived to adolescence. In 1829 Ozanam suffered a severe "crisis of doubt," which he overcame through the assistance of his spiritual advisor, Abbé Noirot. His experience of doubt would result in a great, lifelong empathy toward non-Catholics and other nonbelievers that he met.

In 1831 he published his first essay, a refutation of St. Simon's style of socialism. In the same year, at the prodding of his father, Ozanam entered the Sorbonne in Paris to study law. He was distraught to find so few students practicing their Catholicism. He was also offended by the anti-Catholic bias of many of his professors. Ozanam gathered a group of Catholic students around him, who contested and answered any statement made by their professors that they deemed offensive to Catholicism. As Ozanam put it, "every time a rationalist professor raises his voice against revelation, Catholic voices are raised in response" (Dirvin, p. 18). His defense of Catholicism brought him into contact with the leading Catholic thinkers of his day—Chateaubriand, Lacordaire, Ballanche, Ampere, Montalmbert.

As part of their defense of the church, Ozanam and his friends organized conferences on history and literature in which they vigorously spoke out in defense of the Catholic faith. While impressive intellectually, Ozanam was challenged by one of the conference doubters to "show us your works." Stung by the rebuke, in May 1833 Ozanam and his friends formed a Conference of Charity, dedicated to "practical charity." The Conference stressed personal service to the poor through the visitation of the poor in their homes. With the aid of a Daughter of Charity, Ozanam and his friends began serving the poor in Paris. In 1835, the Conference was formally organized as the St. Vincent de Paul Society in honor of the great friend of the poor, St. Vincent de Paul. The Society spread rapidly. By the time of Ozanam's death in 1853, it consisted of close to fifteen hundred conferences with close to fifteen thousand members. By 1900 the St. Vincent de Paul Society had spread throughout the world.

Ozanam believed that modern society was becoming increasingly divided between rich and poor, a division that would ultimately result in a calamitous confrontation. The Conference of Charity was to mediate between rich and poor with "the force of love" (Dirvin, p. 88). The best way to demonstrate the force of love was through practical charity as made manifest in the spiritual and corporal works of mercy. Self-interest had to be replaced by sacrifice. Besides bearing witness to the love of God, personal service to the poor brought the server into direct contact with the poor, thereby broadening his vision. Both server and served benefited. Seemingly inconsequential, "routine" acts of charity would lead to the renewal of the social order. As the manual of the St. Vincent de Paul Society puts it, "a soul which raises itself, raises the whole moral and spiritual level of mankind."

In addition to overseeing the development of the St. Vincent de Paul Society, Ozanam became a noted historian and literary scholar specializing in Dante and in the history of the early church. In 1839 he received his doctorate in literature from the Sorbonne, where he assumed the chair of foreign literature in 1844, a position he would hold until his untimely death from tuberculosis September 8, 1853, in Marseilles.

See also CATHOLIC CHARITIES USA; CHARITY.

Bibliography: J. Dirvin, trans. and ed., *Frédéric Ozanam: His Life in Letters* (St. Louis: St. Vincent de Paul Society, 1986). D. McColgan, *A Century of Charity*, 2 vols. (Milwaukee: Bruce, 1951).

JEFFREY M. BURNS

P

PACEM IN TERRIS

Pacem in terris was issued on Holy Thursday, April 11, 1963, about six months after the Cuban missile crisis and two months before the death of its author, Pope John XXIII. As the first papal encyclical ever addressed to "all men of good will," it was remarkably well received by a wide and disparate audience. The full text was published in the *New York Times* accompanied by several lead editorials, and the Soviet press also gave it a positive evaluation.

The encyclical became the subject of discussion by international gatherings of diplomats and theologians in both New York and Geneva. The overall tone of the document received the most widespread approval, and individual aspects of its content were welcomed by Protestants as well as Catholics, capitalists as well as communists.

The document is the only papal encyclical ever to be put to music—by Olivier Messaien (Hebblethwaite, in Curran and McCormick, p. 269). It inspired the creation of the *Pacem in terris* Institute at Manhattan College to study the topic of peace and to offer an alternative to the ROTC for college campuses.

Pacem in terris was commemorated on its 10th year by a "Reflection" by the Archbishop of Paris, Maurice Cardinal Roy, and on its 25th year by a symposium sponsored by the journal *Seminarium.*

Author

John XXIII was born Angelo Giuseppe Roncalli on November 25, 1881. He studied at the local seminary in Bergamo as well as the national seminary near Rome. He served twice in the Italian army, in the medical corps and the chaplaincy. Benedict XV named him director of the Society for the Propagation of the Faith in 1920. After five years at this post he was sent to diplomatic assignments in Bulgaria, Greece, Turkey, and France. In 1953 he was named a cardinal and given the position of patriarch of Venice, where he served until his election to the papacy on October 28, 1958.

Throughout his career, Roncalli was influenced by progressive and socially conscious bishops, theologians, politicians, and activists in Catholic Action movements. Although traditional in his own spirituality and theology, he maintained a reputation in all his assignments as a person who was willing to engage in open dialogue.

Background

The composition and publication of this encyclical was undoubtedly motivated by a combination of influences, both remote and proximate.

John XXIII had experienced war firsthand in World War I as a soldier. During World War II, he ministered to prisoners of war in Greece, and he worked hard to reconcile a divided Catholic church in France as it suffered through the tensions of postwar reconciliation.

Without a doubt, the Cuban missile crisis of October 1962 was an immediate motivation. John XXIII had made a personal plea for peace to both President John F. Kennedy and Chairman Nikita Khrushchev during that crisis. Pietro Pavan, one of the drafters of *Pacem in terris,* revealed that this crisis convinced the pope to write the encyclical.

Developments within the Catholic church offered remote influences on the letter. For two hundred years prior to *Pacem in terris* the church had been struggling with the issue of its relationship to the world. A siege mentality predominated in papal condemnations of the world, such as the *Syllabus of Errors* issued by Pius IX and the oath against modernism promulgated by Pius X.

Pius XI's offering of a "third way" between capitalism and communism in *Quadragesimo anno* failed by virtue of the inherent impossibility of the project as well as the fact that that encyclical's proposals were co-opted and tainted by the Fascist leaders in Austria, Italy, Portugal, and Spain, all of whom claimed to be following its teachings (Gremillion, p. 11). A harsher criticism would say that the church's opportunistic and scandalous cooperation with these regimes forced it to make a judgment of principle about human rights (O'Brien and Shannon, pp. 40–41).

Theologians who tried to reconcile the church to the modern world, such as John Courtney Murray in his writings on religious freedom, were often silenced by Vatican authorities. And Catholic Action movements, suffering from the ill effects of clerical control, declined in size and influence as socially active Catholic laypeople joined ecumenical and secular efforts to reform society, such as the civil rights movement in the United States.

Meanwhile, the Protestant churches had begun to address many of the issues of the modern world by the formation of the World Council of Churches in 1948.

In the political world, the authoritarian dictatorships of the right and the totalitarian systems of the left presented threats to the dignity of the human person; hence both kinds of governments highlighted by contrast the value of human freedom.

After the war, the founding and successes of the Christian Democratic parties, especially those in Germany and Italy led by Konrad Adenauer and Alcide de Gasperi, raised questions about Christian participation in the "welfare state" that had arisen to meet the needs of a population devastated by the Second World War.

The founding of the United Nations, with its Declaration of Human Rights, was a political event whose influence on John XXIII is obvious, given his listing of human rights in the opening paragraphs of the encyclical.

Significant political developments mentioned in the encyclical itself are the demands of workers, women, and the newly emergent nations of the Third World.

Contents

The encyclical begins with the traditional greeting to the hierarchy, the clergy, and the faithful but then departs from tradition by addressing "all men of good will."

The introduction notes that peace, which everyone wants, must be based on that order which is "laid down by God" (PT 1). The five sections that follow are entitled (1) Order Among Human Persons; (2) Relations Between People and Public Authorities Within a Single State; (3) Relations Between States; (4) Relationship of People and Political Communities with the World Community; and (5) Pastoral Exhortations.

Section 1 includes "the most complete and systematic list of . . . human rights in the modern Catholic tradition" (Hollenbach, p. 66). Included are the rights to life, food, clothing, shelter, rest, medical care, social services, education, freedom of conscience, marriage, safe working conditions, private property (which has a "social duty," PT 22), association and free assembly, emigration and immigration, and participation in public affairs. Thus the rights are both economic and political.

The rights are accompanied by duties: to respect other's rights, to live becomingly, to pursue truth, and to collaborate with others to procure the rights of all. Society cannot be founded on force, but only on mutual respect and collaboration. A society is well ordered only if it is founded on truth, justice, love, and freedom.

Finally, the signs of the times show "three distinctive characteristics" of the present age (39). First, workers have gained power in public affairs (40); second, "women are now taking a part in public life" (41); and third, former colonies have gained their independence (42). John adds that the dignity of the human person requires the elimination of racial discrimination (44).

Section 2, on the relation of the individual to the state, shows a great concern that the individual's rights be respected by the civil authorities. Authority in general comes from God, but individual rulers are not necessarily chosen by God, nor following the order established by God. Authorities must appeal to the citizens' consciences rather than coerce them into obedience.

The role of authority is to inspire and organize the citizenry to work for the common good. Authority must, first of all, protect the rights of individuals. Unlike some past church pronouncements that denounced specific forms of government (such as democracy) or supported others (such as monarchy), *Pacem in terris* maintains that "it is impossible to determine, once and for all, what is the most suitable form of government" as long as it has "the legislative, judicial and executive functions of the state" (67). John XXIII notes with approval the instrument of the written constitution (76).

Section 3, on relations between nations, begins with the assertion that states, like individuals, have both rights and duties. The first duty is to acknowledge the truth, which entails the rejection of racism and the careful use of the modern media. The second duty is to regulate its activities by the norms of justice, which includes the watchful protection of the rights of minorities within the nation.

A third duty of nations is to cooperate with others. John notes that such cooperation in solidarity has achieved "laudable results in the economic, social, political, educational, health and sport spheres" (98). More needs to be done in the area of disarmament. People are terrified by the prospect of nuclear war. Reason demands the end of the arms race, the reduction of stockpiles, and the banishment of war from human relations.

The final duty of nations is to respect the freedom of others. Even aid to others must "respect the moral heritage and ethnic characteristics" of both donor and recipient (125). The concluding paragraphs on the signs of the times return to the necessity of disarmament.

Section 4, on the relationship of individuals and states to the global community, focuses on the reality of interdependence, which makes modern people aware of the truth that the nation-state is an inadequate structure for dealing with modern global realities. Some form of global authority is needed. This section notes, once again, the rights of individuals and the importance of intermediate institutions that should operate according to the principle of subsidiarity. The concluding notes on the signs of the times praise the work of the United Nations, especially its Universal Declaration of Human Rights.

Section 5 is entitled "Pastoral Exhortations." In addition to promoting education, the sciences, and the lay apostolate, this section raises one of the most controversial issues in the encyclical—the cooperation of Catholics with people of other faiths or even people of no faith. Using a distinction between ideologies and the historical movements that derive from those ideologies, John gives a cautious approval to such cooperation. With a concluding admonition against the impatience that leads to violent revolution, John extends a blessing to all.

Style

The most noticeable novelty of this encyclical to both its contemporaries and its subsequent commentators is a distinct change in style from previous papal pronouncements. In spite of its reliance on such traditional categories as the common good, the order willed by God, and the natural law, it avoided the "incredibly tortured language of papal monarchy" (O'Brien and Shannon, p. 118), the "unsophisticated moralizing" of previous teachings (Camp, p. 161), the "heavily pious and pretentious jargon that sometimes makes encyclicals difficult reading for Protestants" (Bennett and Niebuhr, p. 81), and the "jaw-breaker" style that dissuaded most people from reading papal documents (Gremillion, p. 68).

The letter's style has been identified as "personalist" (Murray, in John XXIII, p. 58), "existential" (Gremillion, p. 11), "forceful and clear" (Gumbleton, in Shannon, p. 224), "liberal" (Dorr, p. 87), and a clear attempt to take old truths and to present them with "a fresh sense of respect for history, contingency, change, adaptation to change" (Davis, in John XXIII, p. 72). The most frequently used word to describe its tone is "optimistic."

The style and the tone of the letter alerted readers to recognize a shift in Catholic thinking, even if the terminology was taken from "principles of natural law and traditional just-war concepts" (Finn, in Shannon, p. 5).

That shift in thinking involved such concepts as the relationship of the state to the society, that of the church to the world, the place of war in the modern world, the willingness of Catholics to engage in dialogue with others, the centrality of the human person in Catholic social thought, and the availability of pacifism as an option for Catholics.

Methodology

Some commentators were concerned at the time of the encyclical to assert its continuity with past teaching. In response to those who thought that John XXIII was breaking with the teachings of Pius XII, Thurston Davis points out that "thirty-two of the encyclical's 73 footnotes contain supporting references to the writings of Pius" (in John XXIII, p. 66).

More specifically, J. Bryan Hehir sees Pius XII and John XXIII as part of the same movement of the church toward acceptance of the constitutional state and of the approval of the concept of human rights as a theoretical tool for church social teaching (in Curran and McCormick, p. 250).

Donal Dorr is less sanguine about such continuities. On the level of doctrine John remains close to his predecessors, but on the level of application he sets the stage for the dramatic changes that have occurred in the Catholic church since his time. An example of the shift in application is the contrast of Pius XII's vehement rejection of any dialogue between the Christian Democrats and the Socialist parties (Camp, pp. 74–75) with John XXIII's "unprecedented" encouragement of that dialogue (Cronin, p. 20).

Charles E. Curran notes that John effected a major shift in methodology when he used an inductive approach, as evidenced by his reference in each section of the letter to the "signs of the times" (Curran, p. 17).

Peter Hebblethwaite agrees that this reliance on the "signs of the times" as a source for moral reflection calls for "a new humility before the data. It means listening carefully to what is being said, and then discerning (i.e., seeing in difficult circumstances) the hand of the Lord" (in Curran and McCormick, p. 269).

Christine Gudorf remains unsatisfied with this shift toward an inductive methodology. In order to analyze the world for the "historical project" of theological praxis, the church must make "use of the tools of social science—of sociology, economics, psychology, and political science—to analyze the world." The theology of the social teachings is still operating on an ethereal level, reaching conclusions "in the abstract, at the conceptual level" (in Curran and McCormick, pp. 446–47). The "signs of the times" appear at the end of each section of *Pacem in terris,* not at the beginning.

Pacifism and Just War

On the topic of war, *Pacem in terris* clearly takes a different attitude than its predecessors. In spite of his use of just-war concepts, John's encyclical is the only recent papal pronouncement on war that "provides no explicit endorsement of the right of self-defense for peoples and states" (Hehir, in Shannon, p. 21). In paragraph 127, John seems to remove completely any justification for war, thereby calling "into question the very rationale of the just-war teaching" (ibid.).

Ronald G. Musto agrees and claims that here, and in the admonitions to create a new world order built on dialogue, consensus, participation, and interdependence, John XXIII "explicitly rejects the theory of the just war" (p. 190). Musto goes on to say that John XXIII was teaching in *Pacem in terris* that "governments could no longer be trusted to seek peace and justice," which has now become "the work of the individual Christian" (p. 190). Musto's interpretation is stronger than the text itself will allow. John calls for slow change, respect for order, optimism about the modern world, and confidence in constitutional forms of government.

This strong condemnation of war, however, had repercussions throughout the Catholic world. Gordon Zahn sees *Pacem in terris* as "the watershed document of the modern Catholic peace movement" (in Shannon, p. 233), since its official status opened the way to pacifist thinking for ordinary Catholics.

Hehir points out that this option for pacifism is available for individual Catholics but that the teachings subsequent to *Pacem in terris* preclude that option for the Catholic church as an institution. The ecclesiological implications of a pacifist position make it unlikely that it will soon become the official stance of the Vatican (in Shannon, p. 35).

A close reading of the relevant passages reveals that John XXIII never explicitly affirms the pacifist position. The Pastoral Constitution on the Church in the Modern World from Vatican II expresses admiration for those who have adopted nonviolence as a way of life (*Gaudium et spes* 78), and the synod on justice asks for legal protections for conscientious objectors (*Justitia in mundo* 65), but John XXIII never explicitly addresses this issue.

Joseph Gremillion sees this lack as a serious lacuna in *Pacem in terris.* As papal nuncio to Paris, Roncalli had had frequent contacts with Cardinal Suhard of Brussels, whose secretary was one of the founders of Pax Christi. John XXIII also sent an advance copy of *Pacem in terris* to Italian pacifist and community organizer Lanzo del Vasto (Musto, p. 201). The failure to mention the option of nonviolence is either a sign of extreme caution or a serious oversight in the document.

An interesting theoretical question arises—can a single institution advocate two contrasting moral approaches to the same issue? Charles E. Curran argues that the Catholic church must allow a pluralism of moral methodologies, since it permits its members to hold either the pacifist position or the just-war theory, which are exclusive of each other. Hehir agrees that the

Catholic church has adopted the pluralism that Curran advocates (in Shannon, p. 35).

Human Rights

Before it is a document about war and peace, *Pacem in terris* is a testimony to human rights. It presents the concept of human dignity as the unifying element between the two philosophical traditions on which the encyclical is based.

The concept of human dignity has many implications that call for a revision of Catholic church teaching on a variety of issues. *Pacem in terris* allows for this revision, even though it "proceeds in a serene and irenic manner which conceals much of the struggle that raged during the preceding 200 years on both the philosophical-theological and the social-political fronts" (John Langan, in Curran and McCormick, p. 110).

The rights are not absolute, and should not be interpreted in ways "which would overturn such customary institutions of Western society as the family, the private ownership of property, the nation-state, and ethnic communities" (ibid., p. 113).

John Courtney Murray notices a significant shift in the recognition of "freedom" as an essential ingredient for the political and social order, in addition to the traditional values of truth, justice, and love (in John XXIII, p. 59). Curran points out that this recognition of freedom as a matter of "fundamental importance" for societal order is a late development occurring within the writings of John XXIII himself, since the topic was not mentioned in *Mater et magistra* (Curran, p. 13).

Murray notes that the topic of freedom presents "an urgent problem that continues to face us, namely, the problem of an organic development of traditional principles touching the relations of church and state in such wise that we may come into possession of what we still lack—a complete, a unitary Catholic doctrine capable of prudent application in the political and religious conditions of our own time." The Vatican Council would address this issue in its Declaration on Religious Liberty.

The recognition of human rights as the foundation of social order is an example of John XXIII's adaptation to the modern world. *Aggiornamento* is the term he used to describe this updating, an updating well illustrated by *Pacem in terris.* The optimistic attitude of the encyclical toward the world in general and toward specific developments—such as the freedom of former colonies, the increasing rights of women and workers, the scientific, technological, and economic advances—all signal an end to the successive condemnations of the world that began with the Council of Trent in the 16th century.

Murray praises this development and notes that one "of the most striking aspects of the encyclical is the generosity, the breadth and the contemporaneity of the pope's statement with regard to the rights and duties of the human person" (in John XXIII, p. 59).

Donal Dorr sees in the encyclical a new spirituality of the world, which will lead in later papal and episcopal documents to a new theology of the world and its needs (p. 89).

The enthusiastic praise from all quarters of this recognition of human rights is balanced by Gremillion's sober reminder that "it took centuries of experience *by and in the world* to awaken the Church to this dignity of man from which arises religious freedom" (p. 13). Langan agrees that the church "cannot claim for itself a significant place in either the theoretical or the practical struggle for human rights in the 18th and 19th centuries. Human-rights theory in an explicit and politically dynamic form confronted Catholicism as an alien force, and it has taken Catholicism a long time to appropriate it" (in Curran and McCormick, p. 117).

Theoretical Tensions

Even this belated recognition of human rights is not without its problems. Contained within the encyclical are theoretical tensions about rights, duties, and the common good that are unresolved and that became the subject of much discussion.

Rights versus duties. Reinhold Niebuhr points out that the rights language comes from the Stoics, whereas the duty language of the natural law derives from Aristotle. John XXIII has combined the two languages, attempting to ground the two concepts in the notion of human dignity (Bennett and Niebuhr, p. 83).

The attempt to combine two philosophies has touched off a still-unresolved discussion within Catholicism. O'Brien and Shannon see the encyclical as "an attempt to have it both ways at once." On the one hand, John affirms the traditional duties to society that derive from individuals' roles in society. This view allows the pope to maintain his position that only gradual reform is needed in the structures of society. On the other hand, he "validates the modern claim that individuals, by virtue of their personhood, have legitimate moral claims over and against a society." This view opened the way to later teachings in Paul VI, the synod on justice, and the Medellín documents that insisted on radical structural change. Paul VI even allows that violent revolution could sometimes be justified (*Populorum progressio* 31). How to reconcile these conflicting claims is not at all made clear in *Pacem in terris* (O'Brien and Shannon, p. 119).

Priorities of rights. Rights can be either immunities or entitlements. David Hollenbach says that each society or ideology gives priority to one set of rights over the other. He sees the tension here as an East/West or North/South debate. Western ideology tends to give priority to the political immunities—the protection of the freedoms of speech, assembly, the press, and religion. Eastern (Marxist) ideology emphasizes the rights to the economic entitlements of food, housing, employment, and education.

Likewise the Northern societies, in general, try to meet the economic needs "within the context of a social system based on a prior commitment to political and economic liberty," whereas in the Southern Hemisphere, "political and economic freedom are regarded as obtainable for the vast majority of the population . . . only in the context of policies aimed at meeting basic needs for food, clothing, shelter, and minimum education" (Hollenbach, in Curran and McCormick, p. 374).

The danger, for Hollenbach, is that the church's teaching on human rights might become so universal and general that it rises "above the actual conflicts of global society which generate human rights violations" (ibid., p. 375).

Michael Novak claims that this effort to "resist socialism" and to "stand outside of democratic capitalism" leaves the church neutral, but occupying "a sort of utopian ground—literally, no-place" (in Curran and McCormick, p. 335).

Priorities of duties. A third form of tension within the text of *Pacem in terris* arises from the assertion that there exists a common good for each nation as well as the universal common good for the whole world (98). Although the text acknowledges that "great care must be taken lest what helps some nations should injure others" (99), little is said about reconciling the conflicting claims of the global community, the nations, and the smaller institutions within the nations.

Despite these unresolved theoretical tensions, the encyclical does make a step forward, according to Hollenbach, by binding the conflicting claims and rights around the unifying "norm of human dignity." This unity prevents the listing of rights "from disintegrating in a jumble of *ad hoc* claims" (Hollenbach, p. 68). For this reason, *Pacem in terris* is one step on the way to a more integrated understanding of human rights, which gives the Catholic tradition an advantage over Marxist and liberal democratic systems in defending against threats to human rights (ibid.).

John XXIII's presentation of human rights, while overlooking their conflicting claims, is an example of his optimism toward the world.

Capitalism and Private Property

Included in John XXIII's optimistic embrace of the modern world is his nearly uncritical acceptance of the possibilities of capitalism. Richard L. Camp thinks that John was the "first pope fully to appreciate the possibilities of the modern economy and its institutions" and to see capitalism as a "positive blessing" (Camp, p. 159). John puts less emphasis on correcting abuses than his predecessors and warns against revolutionary change.

The evidence for this view was quite compelling in 1963. The postwar world was recovering at an unprecedented rate. The advances of technology were increasing production and development and generally raising the standard of living not only in the advanced countries but also in the emerging new nations. With medical advances as a model, many people began to speak of overcoming the problems of the world through economic development.

Curran cites this nearly uncritical acceptance of technological advances and its naive application to the thorny problems of poverty, war, and global politics as a "chronic case of collapsed eschaton" that prevailed throughout the 1960s (Curran, p. 50).

For Curran, "*Pacem in terris* well illustrates the failure of Catholic thought to give enough importance to the continuing reality of sin in the world" (Curran, p. 49). Pope John speaks of the positive virtues in the human heart, but lurking in the recesses of that same symbol of the human person are "disorder, a seeking for power, a spirit of aggressive self-aggrandizement both of individuals and of nations" (Curran, pp. 49–50).

Dorr disagrees that John's optimism led him to an uncritical acceptance of capitalism itself, although the encyclical does call for only moderate and gradual reform. John insists on the "social mortgage" attached to all property and seems to be content with the creation of the welfare states in Western Europe.

A related topic is that of private property. Predecessors had spoken of private property as a nearly absolute right. Leo XIII never challenged it. John XXIII continues to speak of private property as a permanently valid right, although he points out "that there is a social duty inherent in the right of private property" (22).

The Nation-State

John XXIII's willingness to accept the current forms of government stems from his position that it is not the church's job to decide on a particular form of government. Murray sees a significant shift in papal teaching here. Accepting the distinction between society and state, which Leo XIII had never acknowledged, John follows a line closer to that of Pius XII in recognizing a juridical rather than an ethical concept of the state. In the ethical concept of the society-state, the two are nearly coterminous, whereas the juridical state is marked by limited authority (in John XXIII, p. 58).

Two other principles of the juridical state include the freedom of its citizens and their participation in the administration of public goods. Both of these themes are present in *Pacem in terris* and become even more prominent in subsequent official Catholic social teaching.

A limited state requires dialogue among the various institutions within the society. Limitations of the nation-state are becoming more obvious. Two developments reveal its weaknesses: (1) the inability to exercise jurisdiction over global realities and (2) the development of regional groupings of nations into economic and military blocs. Continuing the awareness of Pius

XII, John recognizes that economic and military realities have become global. The nation-state is inadequate to regulate such global structures. Nations themselves have recognized these developments and have responded by organizing themselves into military alliances and economic partnerships at the regional level. John calls for a global authority to match the need for global regulation (138).

Opening to the Left

In one of the most controversial and evocative sections of the encyclical, John makes a distinction between "false philosophical teachings" and the "historical movements" that derive from those teachings. John was inviting Catholics to accept their freedom to enter into dialogue with people with whom they have ideological differences, since the historical movements of those people might well contain positive elements (157–60).

These paragraphs were perceived as a continuation of the "opening to the left" that had begun with the dialogue between Christian Democratic parties and the various Socialist parties in Europe. John's words could be applied to either the Communist parties or the more moderate Socialist parties of Western Europe that had established the welfare state of the post–World War II era. Dorr, much later, applies the distinction to capitalism, which in its ideological form is opposed to Christianity but whose historical manifestations contain some meritorious elements.

Initial reactions to John's distinction emphasized its application to dialogue with communists. Davis sees this as an effort of John XXIII to "break through the rigidities and ice jams of the Cold War" to appeal to leaders such as Khrushchev to deal with the topic of peace more honestly (in John XXIII, pp. 67–68). Davis construes this as an element of John's concern for the many Catholics behind the Iron Curtain in Eastern Europe. Davis warns that there is risk to such a dialogue, especially in Latin America, where Catholics might be "tempted to let down their guard against communism" (ibid., p. 69).

John Cronin dismisses the rhetoric of the "shift to the left" as mere semantics (Cronin, p. 45), but he takes seriously the encyclical's invitation to dialogue with the communists. Cronin reads this section as a justification of John XXIII's "unprecedented" negotiations with the communist governments in the early 1960s (ibid., p. 20). He agrees that the church can be "a mediator for peace rather than a partisan in the Cold War," but issues several warnings about the danger of dialogue with communists, and notes the "cautious and qualified approach of the encyclical to such ventures" (p. 21).

Murray says that he is not sure whom the pope has in mind but suspects that John XXIII is referring to "Continental socialism, whose primitive inspiration was largely atheist," although the reference could apply to both the "Marxist movement" and the "18th- and 19th-century movements towards political freedom" (in John XXIII, pp. 60–61).

Paul VI will later make an explicit application in his interpretation of four levels of Marxism in *Octogesima adveniens* (OA 37).

Dorr sees *Pacem in terris* not so much a shift to the left as a shift "away from the right" (p. 114). The rather innocuous texts of paragraphs 62 and 65 about not interfering with the rights of others had explosive potential in Latin America, where the rich and powerful clearly were interfering with the rights of the majority of the population (p. 112).

Dorr contends that the encyclical's invitation to dialogue led to fragmentation at the practical level, since there was no longer a univocal interpretation of Catholic social doctrine (p. 115).

Democracy

Despite the contention in paragraph 67 that the church does not choose a specific form of government, some commentators perceive here an explicit approval of democracy. Cronin contends that one of the "major contributions" of John XXIII was "his placing of the Catholic Church unequivocally on the side of democracy," laying to rest any "ambiguities stemming from papal reaction to the new democracies in the confused circumstances of the nineteenth century." Cronin goes on to say that John's acceptance of democracy was "specific, precise, and unreserved" (Cronin, p. 43).

John XXIII's approval of the rights to food, shelter, medical care, and education, however, are not, for Cronin, a specific, precise, and unreserved approval of the welfare state but merely a recognition that "the complexity of modern society involves necessarily a greater degree of social control than was required in the nineteenth century" (ibid., p. 45).

James V. Schall agrees with Cronin that *Pacem in terris* has recognized democracy as "the best form of government as such" in a "descriptive response to the classical problem of the best form of government" that does not necessarily deny "the older christian belief that Christianity was indifferent to all political forms of government as such" as long as they protected minimal rights, especially freedom of religion (in Curran and McCormick, p. 314).

Michael Novak disagrees. Recasting the discussion in terms of democratic capitalism, Novak maintains that although Catholic social teaching has gradually dropped its opposition to the positive aspects of democracy, its rejection of capitalism continues. For Novak, the "intellectual model for peace and justice offered by Catholic social teaching is at present closer to a mild form of socialism than to democratic capitalism" (in Curran and McCormick, p. 337).

John Coleman prefers to take paragraph 67 at face value. He perceives this stance as a return to the position of Leo XIII in *Sapientiae Christianae,* which "held that the church was not competent to adjudicate between the various forms of the state, provided only that 'religion and morality are protected'" (in Curran and McCormick, p. 172). Pius XI had attempted to provide a universal structure for all societies, but that effort failed and has never been resurrected.

Order and Natural Law

Maurice Cardinal Roy, archbishop of Paris, gives an assessment of *Pacem in terris* ten years after its publication. He addresses in particular the notions of authority, nature, order, history, and the signs of the times.

Roy acknowledges that critics of the encyclical see it as too static, too essentialist, and too content with the status quo, but he counters with the contention that although the terminology of order and natural law might seem static, actually they are understood by John to include growth and development. For Roy, the pope's understanding of natural law, for example, is illustrated by "modern synonyms" that substitute for natural law in *Pacem in terris* such as "man, human being, human person, dignity, the rights of man or the rights of peoples, conscience, humaneness (in conduct), the struggle for justice and more recently 'the duty of being,' the 'quality of life.'" All of these are contained in the notion of "values" (in Gremillion, p. 557).

Roy's interpretation is quite benign, given the realization that these terms are not synonymous with natural law, nor even with one another. What Roy is highlighting, however, is the struggle between static and dynamic concepts of natural law, which is still being waged within the Catholic church.

Curran is more critical of the use of natural law in *Pacem in terris.* He notes that the concept is not biblically based in that it appeals "exclusively to the Father and the Creator. Jesus and redemption are never mentioned" (p. 46). *Shalom,* the biblical notion of peace, is central to Christian understanding, but it never appears in *Pacem in terris,* which uses a natural-law analysis that employs biblical references as proof texts (ibid.).

Given its foundation on natural law, *Pacem in terris* takes the traditional Catholic approach to ethics, which maintains that Christianity has nothing specific to add to ethical reflection. Ethical truths are available to all people. There is no specifically Christian ethics in social matters (Curran, p. 64).

For Curran, the lack of Christian specificity of content to social ethics is an acceptable reality. For James V. Schall, it is a loss. The reentry into politics without a specific Christian value system will create a situation in which "Christians will too easily end up saying things little different from what is said by others" (Schall, in Curran and McCormick, p. 326).

John Cronin reads the encyclical in a very different light. For him, the letter "reflects nothing but pure Christian principles developed in the context of world problems" (Cronin, p. 54). But despite his positive assessment of the encyclical, he expresses a sadness about the loss of interest in social teachings among Catholics themselves. Postwar economic development gave the illusion that the problems were solved. Courses on the encyclicals were dropped from college and seminary curricula. In a summary assessment, Cronin laments: "prediction is hazardous, but it seems that the golden era of Catholic social thought beginning in 1891, has ended by 1971" (in Curran and McCormick, p. 76).

Prediction was indeed hazardous—1971 was the year of both the synod on justice and the publication of *Octogesima adveniens,* which J. Bryan Hehir calls "the most creative" of the social teachings (ibid., p. 249).

Conclusion

Pacem in terris is a transitional document. It marks the official change of attitude of the Catholic church toward the modern world. It utilized the traditional analytical categories of natural law, common good, and the order willed by God. In many ways it retained the positions of its predecessors. At the same time, the encyclical opened the way to a reinterpretation of the traditional categories and made an effort to unify them around an integrating concept of the dignity of the human person. It also contained the seeds of change on such issues as religious freedom, conscientious objection, liberation theology (at least in its openness to dialogue with Marxists, but not in its use of the Bible, which John employs as a proof text), development of doctrine, and the awareness of the obsolescence of the nation-state.

See also ARMS RACE; AUTHORITY, POLITICAL; COMMON GOOD; HUMAN RIGHTS; NATURAL LAW; PEACE; PERSON, DIGNITY OF; "SIGNS OF THE TIMES."

Bibliography: J. Bennett and R. Niebuhr, "*Pacem in Terris*: Two Views," *Christianity and Crisis,* vol. 23, no. 8 (May 13, 1963). R. Camp, *The Papal Ideology of Social Reform: A Study in Historical Development, 1878–1967* (Leiden: E. J. Brill, 1969). J. Cronin, *The Social Teaching of Pope John XXIII* (Milwaukee: Bruce, 1963). C. Curran, *Directions in Catholic Social Ethics* (Notre Dame: Univ. of Notre Dame Press, 1985). C. Curran and R. McCormick, *Readings in Moral Theology No. 5: Official Catholic Social Teaching* (Mahwah, N.J.: Paulist, 1986). D. Dorr, *Option for the Poor: A Hundred Years of Vatican Social Teaching* (Maryknoll, N.Y.: Orbis, 1983). J. Gremillion, *The Gospel of Peace and Justice* (Maryknoll, N.Y.: Orbis, 1975). D. Hollenbach, *Claims in Conflict: Retrieving and Renewing the Catholic Human Rights Tradition* (Ramsey, N.J.: Paulist, 1979). John XXIII, *Pacem in Terris, Peace on Earth* (Chicago: Claretian Publications, 1963). R. Musto, *The Catholic Peace Tradition* (Maryknoll, N.Y.: Orbis, 1986). D. O'Brien and T. Shannon, eds., *Renewing the Earth: Catholic Documents on Peace, Justice, and Liberation* (Garden City, N.Y.: Doubleday, 1977). T. Shannon, *War or Peace? The Search for New Answers* (Maryknoll, N.Y.: Orbis, 1982).

KENNETH P. J. HALLAHAN

PACIFISM

The very term "pacifism" causes confusion, since it is used to cover a wide array of positions regarding the morality of armed force. In some circles pacifism is equated with nonviolence, but others argue that the term should be restricted to the narrower stance of opposition to war. This latter usage seems to be the original sense of the term. In such a case violent acts by a domestic police force or violence in cases of individual self-defense are not necessarily proscribed by pacifism.

It is not enough that a person oppose war to be pacifist. Objection to war must be on the ground of moral principle, not inconvenience, cowardice, distaste for bloodshed, political opportunism, or utility. Pacifism entails a view that war is to be opposed because of the immoral nature of armed conflict between nations.

The most noteworthy aspect of Catholic teaching regarding pacifism is the development that has taken place in modern times. As recently as 1956 Pope Pius XII stated that a Catholic could not cite conscientious disagreement with the legitimate leaders of a state as a reason to refuse participation in war. In this he echoed the views of his predecessors.

In 1965, however, the bishops at the Second Vatican Council wrote in the Pastoral Constitution on the Church in the Modern World (*Gaudium et spes*): "We cannot fail to praise those who renounce the use of violence in the vindication of their rights and who resort to methods of defense which are otherwise available to weaker parties too, provided that this can be done without injury to the rights and duties of others or of the community itself (GS 78).

In Part 1 of the Pastoral Constitution on the Church in the Modern World there is a profound concern for the dignity of individual conscience both in the religious and civil realms. Approval of pacifism fit with the council's emphasis on the dignity of personal conscience (16). With the rise of the limited constitutional state in the West and the sad experience of abusive state power in fascism, nazism, and communism, the bishops were sensitive to the freedom of individual conscience before the state.

What the bishops affirmed was the right of the individual to refuse participation in war on the basis of conscience. At the same time, the bishops maintained that there is a right to use armed force in national self-defense. Thus the approval of pacifism was more in deference to the dignity of the person than a result of a conciliar preference for pacifism instead of just-war theory.

Pacifism within the Roman Catholic tradition must be placed in a context of concern for justice and human rights. A pacifist cannot be indifferent to the "rights and duties of others or of the community itself." Thus pacifism in the Catholic perspective cannot be equated with nonresistance. All believers must defend the cause of justice, must protect human rights, must resist evil. Individuals may differ on the matter of how that is to be done, and the pacifist may seek methods other than war in order to resist evil.

At Vatican II the bishops also declared, "It seems right that laws make humane provisions for the case of those who for reasons of conscience refuse to bear arms, provided that they accept some other form of service to the human community (GS 79). The conciliar text was addressed to those who make public policy. The council proposed that laws be passed that allow for conscientious objection to military service but stated that the duty of the individual to serve the common good remains and ought be fulfilled in some other way.

Alternative service would appear to be a duty correlative with the right of the conscientious objector to dissent from the nation's decision to engage in war. The requirement of alternative service demonstrates that pacifism, within Roman Catholic social teaching, is not a higher or purer calling. Rather it is a right of individual conscience that necessitates an expression of good faith on the part of the individual, a willingness to contribute to the nation's struggle against injustice in another way. The presumption is that the nation is just in resisting the evil of aggression and that all citizens have an obligation to contribute to that effort even if some are not required to bear arms.

In Catholic teaching both pacifism and just war are treated as having the same end—the preservation of a just social order, which is the foundation for true peace. The order that peace embodies is not the quietude accompanying tyranny but a social state achieved through justice when life is well ordered and oriented to the dignity of persons and the common good.

True peace must be served by both pacifists and just-war advocates. Where the two groups diverge is on the question of means to the proper end. Pacifism, like just war, must engage in resistance against aggression, but pacifists refuse to accept war as a valid means of resistance. The teaching of the council allows pluralism to exist at the level of individual choice as to the means but requires of all believers a devotion to the end.

Perhaps the most important gloss on the thought of the council concerning pacifism is the pastoral letter *The Challenge of Peace,* issued in 1983 by the American episcopacy. Pacifism in the American bishops' letter is viewed as a moral choice for persons committed to a genuine peace but who cannot accept that violent means may restore the peace. Pacifism cannot be a sectarian withdrawal nor can it be a dismissal of the valid claims of the state for self-preservation.

When discussing pacifism the United States bishops are explicit in their repetition of the conciliar teaching that pacifism is a choice for the individual believer. Thus those believers who maintain that pacifism is an essential aspect of the Christian moral life and therefore a duty rather than an option do not find support in Catholic social teaching.

Modern Catholic social teaching on pacifism may be summarized as follows: (*a*) Pacifism is an option that individuals may choose. Both conscientious objection and selective conscientious objection are supported by Catholic teaching. The latter is premised on just-war theory, while the former is derived from the legitimacy of pacifism. (*b*) Pacifism requires a clear commitment to resist injustice and a desire to promote human rights and the common good. (*c*) The pacifism approved by Catholic social teaching is based on the freedom of the person and the rights of individual conscience. It is not a duty for all but an option for those who discern a moral call to oppose all war.

See also CATHOLIC WORKER, THE; CONSCIENTIOUS OBJECTION; FORCE; KILLING; PACEM IN TERRIS; PAX CHRISTI; PEACE; WAR.

Bibliography: R. Bainton, *Christian Attitudes Toward War and Peace* (Nashville: Abingdon, 1960). R. Coste, "Commentary on Part II, Chapter V," in H. Vorgrimler, ed., *Commentary on the Documents of Vatican II,* vol. 5 (New York: Herder & Herder, 1969). National Conference of Catholic Bishops, *The Challenge of Peace* (Washington: United States Catholic Conference, 1983). R. Musto, *The Catholic Peace Tradition* (Maryknoll, N.Y.: Orbis, 1986). T. Shannon, ed., *War or Peace?* (Maryknoll, N.Y.: Orbis, 1980). J. Teichman, *Pacifism and the Just War* (New York: Basil Blackwell, 1986).

KENNETH R. HIMES, O.F.M.

PARTNERSHIP

The proposal of partnership (or copartnership) represents an effort to reduce unnecessary conflict between workers and employers through such practices as co-ownership, co-management, and profit sharing by workers. Such partnership may offer the further practical benefits of increased efficiency generated by ideas from the practical experience of the workers and enhanced productivity—and thus profits—through increased worker dedication, satisfaction, and job security (*Economic Justice for All* 300).

Quadragesimo anno (64–65) was the first social encyclical to suggest the benefits of a partnership contract in addition to the wage contract. The proposal of partnership was further enhanced by later discussion of greater participation of workers in the economic enterprise as a manifestation of the workers' fundamental dignity (*Mater et magistra* 91–103; *Gaudium et spes* 68; *Laborem exercens* 14). As early as 1919 the United States bishops were suggesting partnership through co-ownership and co-management (*Social Reconstruction* 36), although such ideas were later deemphasized as suggesting support for socialism or for more radical elements of the labor movement. The U.S. bishops' economic pastoral, *Economic Justice for All* (chap. 4), however, places great emphasis on a broad appeal to partnership in the economic sphere to parallel the American experiment in political democracy. This includes cooperation among government, business, and other institutions in service of the common good as well as forms of partnership between workers and employers.

See also COPARTNERSHIP.

MARK O'KEEFE, O.S.B.

PASTORAL CARE

Pastoral care embraces the broad range of ministries, services, and attentions provided by pastor and staff to the members of an ecclesial community. The parish is the usual territorial and membership unit of the local church under leadership of a pastor; the term "congregation" is often used as a synonym for "parish." Both key words derive from Latin: *pastor* means "shepherd," and *congregatio* is "flock." There are about 200,000 Catholic parishes worldwide, which compose over 2,500 dioceses, each presided usually by a bishop, "shepherding" around one billion Catholic faithful.

Pastoral Units and Agents

In the United States there are 180 dioceses formed by over 18,000 parishes, which extend pastoral care to some 60 million affiliated Catholics. Besides pastors, about half of American parishes have assistant or associate pastors, most of whom are priests. Almost all parishes have additional staff, of whom about 7,000 are deacons and over 100,000 are religious women and laity. This addition of deacons, sisters, and laypersons as permanent staff for pastoral care has occurred largely since Vatican Council II. (These figures exclude teachers in parochial schools, both lay and religious.)

Furthermore, since the 1960s thousands of lay volunteers have become pastoral agents, devoting half days of four or five hours, often several times a week and even daily, to pastoral care under supervision of professional paid staff. Many of these volunteers are retirees in their sixties; they number from at least a dozen in most congregations, to scores and hundreds in larger, more active parishes. The multiplication of these lay ministers, their training, and their acceptance by clergy and people during the generation since Vatican II marks an ecclesial development of historic dimension as to the policy, theology, and self-understanding of the Catholic church of North America. During these same three decades the number of priests and religious in Canada and the United States has declined at a serious rate.

Meanwhile, our sister regional church of Latin America has increased pastoral reliance on laity even more, as numbers of their clergy have declined proportionally for almost two centuries—since the church-state conflicts that have perdured since the French Revolution and its aftermath. In 1990 there were about 50 thousand priests in Latin America to serve some 350 million Catholics, a ratio of 7,000 Catholics to each priest. This compares with the North American situation of some 70 thousand priests serving only 70 million Catholics in Canada and the United States, a ratio of only 1,000 Catholics to each priest.

The African church has an exceptionally high number of lay ministers, over 180,000 full-time and well-trained catechists among some 100 million Catholics and 20,000 priests. This gives a ratio of one priest for 5,000 Catholics, with 9 lay ministers (catechists) on his full-time staff. Many lay staff are also Eucharistic ministers and preachers, making them in fact quasi pastors, especially when they live amidst a local community several miles from the resident priest-pastor.

Through this pastoral method of multiplying lay evangelizers and teachers, the Catholic church in black Africa has increased in three generations by a multiple of fifty, from two million in 1900 to a hundred million in 1990, only nine decades later. This rate of evangelization probably equals that of any previous mission enterprise in Christian history, certainly as to numbers, because fifteen hundred years ago Ireland and the valleys of Rhine, Rhone, and Danube were sparsely populated as compared with today's Africa. Protestant evangelicals have increased in Africa at about the same rate as Catholics since the 1960s. They offer the attraction of early access to the prestigious role of pastor without long theological studies, plus the opportunity of marriage and children, so highly valued still in the African culture.

Types and Degrees of Outreach

In addition to pastoral care within American parishes, which are almost all territorial and residential, adapted ministries are also provided among numerous institutions such as hospitals, prisons, and colleges, also through the network of military chaplaincies for service persons and their families, embracing over a million Catholics in United States forces alone.

These multiple ministries, local and specialized, and the great variety of pastoral care they offer are coordinated and supervised by bishops and their appropriate staffs of the 140 dioceses of Canada and the United States. Among their 240 million people these two countries have about 72 million affiliated Catholics in some 23,000 parishes. Another 10 to 15 million North Americans are inactive Catholics who are not inscribed on membership rolls of a parish due to indifference or other motives but who have not formally forsaken their faith heritage.

Many types of ministry are now offered in North American parishes because of the various ages and talents, lifestyles and needs, of the hundreds of households and members. These varieties of pastoral care have greatly multiplied since the 1960s, due in part to secular events and culture and still more in response to the fresh vision of the church and its relation to the world, opened for all members by Vatican Council II. For present purposes pastoral activity may be placed in three broad categories: (1) intra-parish, (2) in-church extra-parish, and (3) church-in-the-world.

Among these three degrees of outreach, the focus of pastoral care remains mainly within the range of parish territory and membership. Such parish-level ministry does of course derive from and collaborate with the wider ecclesial activity of category 2, that is, with the deanery and diocese of which the parish is a component. Through these churchly bodies parishes participate in regional and national programs and with the whole Catholic world church chaired by the pope as Peter's successor.

Pastoral activity therefore includes urging and enabling parishioners personally and/or communally to address broad concerns of the church-in-the-world, to promote national, regional, and global justice, development and peace, both as individuals and through their respective professions and positions at work and as citizens.

Pastoral Concerns Intra-Parish

With due deference to these wider activities among diocesan and national bodies of the universal church, pastoral care focuses on local, family, and personal concerns, which are best addressed at the parochial level. Even within such restricted geographic and sociological settings, most parishes generate a rich complex of multiple elements within the ministry of each local Catholic community. These are classified here in five groups, with a score of pastoral-care categories among them:

1. *Worship and Word, prayer, spiritual life*
   Liturgy: Eucharist, sacraments, funerals
   Prayer services, novenas, rosary, way of the cross
   Preaching: Sunday, daily, special occasions
   Television, radio
   Spiritual life, meditation, retreats, counseling
2. *Adults and the family*
   Marriage and family life
   Continuing education for adults, Bible study, library
   Young adults, singles, collegians, military service
   Aging and sick, dying and eternal life
   Counseling the troubled
   Recent challenge of addiction
   Welcoming and incorporating newcomers
3. *The young*
   Christian education at all levels
   Parish and other schools, supervision and support
   Nurseries for working mothers
   Recreation, sports, scouts, plays, contests
4. *Facilities, finances, staff, management*
   Terrain, buildings, equipment
   Finances, collections, debt funding drives
   Personnel selection, formation, animation, supervision
   Volunteers: inspiration, training
5. *Outreach and community witness*
   Seeking out inactive Catholics
   Initiating and integrating unchurched and converts
   Ecumenical and inter-faith relations locally
   Lay leader formation: parish, community, diocesan
   Promoting evangelization, in area, nation, world
   Social ministry: justice and peace in area, nation, world

Social Ministry via Parishes and Dioceses

This outreach to promote justice, development, and peace in and through the parish and neighborhood groups, last-listed in the above schema, signals a fresh form of pastoral ministry by the local faith community. This ecclesial initiative "in-the-world" was generated by the "signs of the times" theology of John XXIII and Vatican II, then deepened and spread through the 1971 synod of bishops, the Medellín and Puebla assemblies of the Latin American bishops in 1968 and 1979, and by the series of social encyclicals from Paul VI's *On the Development of Peoples* (1967) to John Paul II's *On Social Concern* (1988).

These planet-level documents spurred regional and national apostolates by episcopal conferences, religious orders, and lay organizations—which led in turn to Justice and Peace departments and staff in most dioceses and provinces and which reenergized local lay movements launched a generation earlier.

Into the 1980s parish and neighborhood social ministry kept multiplying, nourished in the United States by two exceptional pastoral letters of the National Conference of Catholic Bishops: *The Challenge of Peace* (1983) and *Economic Justice for All* (1986). Local application was promoted notably by the Catholic Committee on Urban Ministry (CCUM), led nationwide by Harry Fagan, Marge Tuite, David O'Brien, and John Egan.

Among diocesan programs those of Rochester, Louisville, and Chicago have been outstanding since the 1970s. The multiplication of parish councils has provided the organizational linkup and status for animating social ministry at pastoral levels throughout the church with full lay participation.

See also CATHOLIC COMMITTEE ON URBAN MINISTRY; CHRISTIAN FAMILY MOVEMENT; ECONOMIC ORDER; FAMILY; LAITY, ROLE OF; LITURGICAL MOVEMENTS, SOCIAL INFLUENCE OF; MARRIAGE; WORK, THEOLOGY OF.

Bibliography: J. Lund and M. Heidkamp, *Moving Faith into Action: Guide for Creating Parish Social Ministry* (New York/Mahwah, N.J.: Paulist, 1990). J. Gremillion and J. Castelli, *The Emerging Parish: Notre Dame Study of Catholic Life Since Vatican II* (New York: Harper & Row, 1987). J. Dolan, ed., *The American Catholic Parish: A History from 1850 to the Present,* 2 vols.: vol. 1, by J. Casino et al., *The Northeast, Southeast, and South Central States;* vol. 2., by J. Burns et al., *The Pacific, Intermountain West, and Midwest States* (New York/Mahwah, N.J.: Paulist, 1987).

JOSEPH GREMILLION

PATERNALISM

Paternalism is not so prominent a theme in social ethics as in, say, medical ethics. It is not even clear just what should count here as paternalism. Should one limit it to *benevolent* decisions over the heads of those concerned, with VanDeVeer? Or should the concept include acts for which the motivation of acting for the subordinate's own good is merely a pretext? Is the governing concept the exercise of *patriarchal* authority in circumstances in which it is not warranted, as over women and adult children? Or should one conceive the key issue to be the exercise of *parental* responsibility/authority over those who should be treated as adults? In the latter case, patriarchalism would be paternalism further specified and aggravated by sexism. In church circles it can take the form of, or be reinforced by, clericalism. In scholarly circles special expertise provides many an opportunity for paternalistic behavior. Paternalism can soften or disguise racism.

A tentative definition of paternalism in social ethics may be hazarded all the same. Paternalism is the practice of making decisions for persons who are of age and otherwise *de jure* capable of speaking for themselves, decisions, that is, that could well be left to the groups or individuals directly concerned, or at least to negotiations with them. In certain circumstances, themselves to be regretted, it may be a necessity or a duty in charity for an authority to act paternalistically ("benign paternalism"). But it is also a duty not to prolong the circumstances that require paternalism. "Pernicious paternalism" occurs when an authority extends or maintains the ambit of decision making over subordinates in such a way that their dependence and lack of autonomy is unduly prolonged or unnecessarily intensified.

Historically, the great age of paternalism in Catholic social practice was the 19th century, when the distinction of modern socioeconomic relations from "feudal" ones was not yet realized, or was consciously rejected as illegitimate. Members of an economic enterprise, just as, for example, members of a religious house, were thought to be the moral equivalent of a family, wherein the paternal authority would distribute tasks and benefits justly and wisely. Apart from "Christian Democrats," Catholics, along with most members of 19th-century *classes dirigeantes,* looked upon workers as in the main incapable of coming to well-founded judgments as to what would be in their own best interests. Many voiced the parallel with children openly. And in fact the *imperitum vulgus* (Leo XIII) was not well enough educated to take full charge of their own affairs, much less of public and economic affairs important for the common weal.

Therefore it is no reproach merely to note that social action was conceived in terms of conferring benefits upon the working people from above (see Leo XIII's encyclical *Graves de communi*). What merits reproach in conservative social Catholics of the era (cf. e.g., the *Oeuvre des cercles catholiques d'ouvriers*) was their resistance to signs of willingness and ability on the part of workers to take responsibility, to exercise leadership, and hence to emancipate themselves and their class from the prevailing relationships of subordination and dependence. It was in the obtuse opposition to such strivings that blameworthy or "pernicious" paternalism first presented itself as a difficulty to social Catholics of the "Christian democratic" tendency.

In general terms, the antipaternalists had recourse to the insistence on the dignity of the human person that runs through Catholic social teaching from its beginnings. If the dignity of the poor working-class person at an earlier juncture gave rise to duties in charity to confer benefits on him or her, now it dictated duties in justice to recognize his or her legitimate interests. In a capitalist economy, these could not simply coincide with the interests of their "betters." Among these interests was the need to have a say in the conditions of labor and to organize in order to have that say.

The controversy over the right of workers to organize independently of upper-class tutelage was one major case of paternalism. The turn to political democracy that Pope Pius XII executed and Vatican II sanctioned was another.

See also AUTHORITY, POLITICAL; CHARITY; CHRISTIAN DEMOCRACY; CHURCH, SOCIAL MISSION OF; LEO XIII; MAGISTERIUM; MODERN CATHOLIC SOCIAL THOUGHT; MODERNISM; PERSON, DIGNITY OF.

Bibliography: DTC, *Tables générales* 3:3457–58. J. Bennett, "Paternalism," in *International Encyclopedia of the Social Sciences* 11:472–77. D. Reid, "Industrial Paternalism: Discourse and Practice in 19th Century French Mining and Metallurgy," *Comparative Studies in Society and History* 27 (1985) 579–607. R. Rezsohazy, *Origines et formation du catholicisme social en Belgique, 1842–1909* (Louvain: Publications universitaires, 1958). D. VanDeVeer, *Paternalistic Intervention: The Moral Bounds of Benevolence* (Princeton, N.J.: Princeton Univ. Press, 1986).

PAUL MISNER

PAUL VI

Pope Paul VI expanded the horizon of papal social teachings by moving beyond the presumption of a European context. He drew attention to the pressing problems of the peoples of the world occasioned by the newly emerging nations of the Third World who had been gaining independence and were seeking to become economically self-sufficient. Unfortunately many of these countries suffered from extreme poverty and hunger, illiteracy, and oppressive social, economic, and political structures. To speak to their plight, Paul VI made the matters of development and liberation a part of the papal proclamation of Catholic social teaching, with its goal of justice and peace.

Historical Context

Understanding the unique context of the social teachings of Pope Paul VI is crucial for understanding the teachings themselves. Giovanni Battista Montini, then cardinal of Milan, was elected pope on June 18, 1963, succeeding John XXIII. The Second Vatican Council was Paul VI's first order of business. Under his leadership Vatican II carried on the process of *aggiornamento,* of opening the Catholic church to a new relationship with the modern world, and of reforming the church. Most significantly for Catholic social teaching, that new relationship was spelled out in *Gaudium et spes.* Paul VI's social thought consciously continued the direction set by Vatican II.

A second aspect of the historical context concerned the expansion of the Catholic church in the Third World, where great numbers of Catholics were found. Pope Paul VI gave these people greater prominence in the church by appointing cardinals for many of those countries, such as Korea and Sri Lanka. Moreover, revealing his sensitivities for the social nature of the church, Paul VI encouraged regional synods of bishops to meet and discuss specific situations. One noteworthy meeting, that of the Latin American bishops held from August 24 to September 6, 1968, in Medellín, Colombia, issued important documents on justice, peace, and the need for liberation.

A third aspect was the willingness of Paul VI to undertake foreign travel. As the first world-traveling pope, Paul VI made ten major trips to visit the people of such places as the Holy Land, India, Turkey, Bogota, Kampala, the Philippines, Australia, Hong Kong, and Singapore. He also addressed the General Assembly of the United Nations in New York City and called for the end of war and the arms race.

Paul VI's Social Teachings

Among the major sources of the social teachings of Pope Paul VI, three documents are crucial. They are the encyclical *Populorum progressio;* the apostolic letter addressed to Maurice Cardinal Roy, *Octogesima adveniens;* and the apostolic exhortation *Evangelii nuntiandi.* Each will be discussed in historical order.

Populorum Progressio

In this encyclical, issued March 26, 1967, Paul VI placed at the center of Catholic social teaching the concept of the development of all peoples around the world. Development was not to be limited to industrialization and economic development. For Paul VI it included the enhancement of the full range of human attributes across all countries, peoples, groups, and persons (PP 14–18). The gifts and abilities of each person are to be realized, especially in relation to God; furthermore, people have the right to act as the chief architects for their own development. However, the social nature of humanity requires that personal achievements be incorporated into the development of one's group and nation. Each person contributes to the development of the common good. Thus Paul VI noted that we owe much to the achievements of our ancestors and likewise we contribute to the well-being of our descendants.

Reflecting on Gen 1:28, "Fill the earth and subdue it," Paul VI taught that "the whole of creation is for man" (22). God made the created world to provide the necessities for supporting human life and to be fashioned by people into tools for progress. "Organized programs designed to increase productivity should have but one aim: to serve human nature. They should reduce inequities, eliminate discrimination, free men from the bonds of servitude, and thus give them the capacity, in the sphere of temporal realities, to improve their lot, to further their moral growth and to develop their spiritual endowments" (34).

In accord with this line of thought, Paul VI noted the issue of population growth. As it is a matter of the common good, public authorities can provide information to their citizens about this subject and adopt appropriate measures. Paul VI warned, however, that governmental activities must conform to the dictates of the moral law and the rights of married couples. "When the inalienable right of marriage and of procreation is taken away, so is human dignity" (37). Paul VI developed these and related issues in his encyclical on birth regulation, *Humanae vitae*.

According to Pope Paul VI, the mistake too often made in conceiving of development and self-fulfillment is to limit them to "soul-stifling *materialism*" (18). Avarice then rules the day and hardens people's hearts. On this basis, Paul VI criticized the dominant ideologies of Marxism and capitalism, continuing the papal practice of not identifying Catholic teaching with any particular economic system.

Industrialization and free trade are necessary for development. However, the developing nations frequently suffer from a crushing poverty that makes them an unequal partner in world markets. They must trade for the necessary manufactured goods that they are unable to produce, and they frequently have little to offer in exchange but their own mineral resources or particular foodstuffs (e.g., bananas or coffee), prices of which are often set at unjustly low levels. The result is that the rich countries expand their wealth and well-being at remarkable rates while the peoples of the poorer nations become poorer, increase their debt, and suffer the loss of their dignity and of future opportunities for an elusive development.

Paul VI urged that the advantaged nations not accept this situation as merely an economic fact of life or as the problem of the poor of the world. He called upon the wealthier countries to act in accord with obligations imposed by mutual solidarity, social justice, and universal charity (44). Specific policies recommended by Pope Paul VI included the establishing of an international monetary fund, which would provide loans and monetary assistance to developing countries, and the sending of volunteers to provide health and technical assistance, much like the Peace Corps. These policies were not meant to enhance the prestige of the wealthy countries but rather were meant to increase the capacity of the less developed countries to guide their own development. Overall, the goal of economic progress is to build a human community in which all peoples have the opportunity for development.

Octogesima Adveniens

In this apostolic letter issued May 14, 1971, Paul VI noted the difficulty of offering a solution claiming universal validity to pressing social problems faced by particular groups or nations (OA 4). His aim, instead, was to offer general guidelines from which local communities could develop their own solutions for their particular problems.

One major issue that Paul VI addressed was urbanization. Due to the weakening of agrarian culture throughout the world, urban areas were growing at an astonishing rate. Most cities possessed large populations in extreme poverty. Urbanization entailed the erosion of families, neighborhoods, and church communities together with the concomitant social ills of delinquency, criminality, drug abuse, and discrimination. Pope Paul VI had seen these problems when he served as the archbishop of Milan in 1954. He was convinced that Christian leaders must respond to these ills and support the people in overcoming them.

Once more, Paul VI warned against identifying Christianity with any particular ideology, such as Marxism or liberalism, or any concrete system, be it bureaucratic socialism, technocratic capitalism, or authoritarian democracy. Any true Christian solution, he said, must follow the guidance of the Scriptures and serve the poorest of peoples (42). It must also adhere to general social principles such as the common good and the legitimate liberties of individuals, families, and groups.

Evangelii Nuntiandi

This apostolic exhortation, issued December 8, 1975, on the topic of evangelization, deserves mention in a discussion of social teachings because it contains Paul VI's final word on the relation of the gospel proclamation to liberation. The gospel message of salvation is one of liberation from sin; what then has the gospel to do with liberation from political, social, and economic oppression? Paul VI's answer was that the gospel is linked to the concrete lives of people who are subject to injustice. The church's proclamation has included matters of human rights, of family life, of social justice, of "international life, peace, justice, and development—a message especially energetic today about liberation" (EN 29). Application of these principles is made by particular Christians as they engage in conscientious actions for the welfare of their neighbors. The mistake to be avoided, Paul VI concluded, is to reduce the gospel message of salvation to matters of temporal well-being and thus lose the importance of the human relation to God.

See also BIRTH CONTROL; COMMON GOOD; EVANGELII NUNTIANDI; GAUDIUM ET SPES; MEDELLÍN; OCTOGESIMA ADVENIENS; POPULORUM PROGRESSIO; DEVELOPMENT.

Bibliography: M. Walsh and B. Davies, eds., *Proclaiming Justice and Peace: Documents from John XXIII–John Paul II* (Mystic, Conn.: Twenty-Third Publications, 1985). C. Curran and R. McCormick, eds., *Readings in Moral Theology No. 5: Official Catholic Social Teaching* (New York: Paulist, 1986). J. Schall, ed., *Liberation Theology in Latin America: With Selected Essays and Documents* (San Francisco: Ignatius, 1982). P. Hebblewaite, *Paul VI: The First Modern Pope* (Mahwah, N.J.: Paulist, 1993).

JOHN R. POPIDEN

PAX CHRISTI

Pax Christi is an international Catholic peace movement, founded in France near the end of the Second World War. It takes as its mission to work for peace as the fruit of justice for all people, always witnessing to the peace of Christ. While Pax Christi is not structurally an official organization of the Roman Catholic church, it consciously adheres to the social teaching of the church on peace, justice, and human rights. Its headquarters presently are in Antwerp, Belgium, with chapters in over thirty countries. Its decision-making body is the International Council, which consists of delegations from all the national sections. An international secretariat runs the day-to-day operations implementing the policies of the International Council.

Pax Christi began in 1945 as a prayer movement for peace, stimulated by a French laywoman, Mme. Dortel-Claudot. Bishop Theas of Lourdes, France, a former prisoner of war known for preaching forgiveness of enemies, agreed to become president of the movement. Taking root first in France, then in Germany, the movement encouraged reconciliation between the French and German peoples after the ravages and bitterness of World War II. It quickly spread to the other countries of Western Europe and in 1952 was given recognition by Pius XII. Cardinal Feltin of France was the movement's first international president. Other presidents who followed have been Bernard Cardinal Alfrink of the Netherlands, Archbishop Luigi Bettazzi of Italy, Franz Cardinal Koenig of Austria, and Godfried Cardinal Danneels of Belgium.

In the 1960s the movement, having grown in size and in the number of sections, developed an organized international structure with a full-time secretariat. In 1963 Pax Christi International adoped John XXIII's encyclical *Pacem in terris* as its charter. In the 1970s the movement spread to the United States, Canada, and Puerto Rico, this time in a new context, namely, that of the Vietnam War. During the intense antinuclear period of the 1980s Pax Christi experienced its deepest growth both in members and in the foundation of new sections in the various countries.

Pax Christi constitutionally has never required of its members total adherence to a pacifist posture. But it has constantly emphasized that war must not be the means of resolving conflicts. Thus it has fostered the study and practice of nonviolent alternatives and has encouraged the spread of a spirituality of nonviolence. Pax Christi International has divided its program areas into (1) security and disarmament, (2) human rights, (3) East-West contacts, (4) North-South relations, (5) peace education, and (6) peace spirituality.

Pax Christi USA, a section of Pax Christi International, was organized in the early 1970s and opened its national office in 1979. Bishops Carroll Dozier, Thomas Gumbleton, and Walter Sullivan have been its national presidents. By the late 1980s membership included 6,000 people, 270 local groups, 82 bishops, with its national headquarters located in Erie, Pennsylvania. In its official statement of purpose Pax Christi USA "invites concerned Catholics to respond to the Church's call to evaluate war with an entirely new attitude and to take an active role in making secure a peace based on justice and love." From its beginnings, Pax Christi USA chose five program priorities: disarmament, nonviolent alternatives, peace education, just world order, and primacy of conscience. In its work on primacy of conscience, Pax Christi has mirrored recent teachings of the Catholic church regarding the validity of conscientious objection not only for those opposed to all war but also for those who apply the criteria of the just-war teaching (selective conscientious objection). Although the national Pax Christi sections try to establish common priorities, each section is autonomous. Individuals or groups can become members of Pax Christi International by joining the movement's section in their own country. While Pax Christi considers itself a Catholic organization following the church's social teachings on justice and peace, it strives for dialogue with all Christians, Jews, and Muslims as well as with other peace movements and all people of good will.

See also ARMS RACE; DETERRENCE; CONSCIENCE; DISARMAMENT; PACIFISM; PEACE.

Bibliography: G. Vanderhaar, *Pax Christi USA: The Early Years, 1972–78* (Erie, Pa.: Pax Christi, 1990). M. Jegen, *Pax Christi International: What It Is, What It Does* (Antwerpen, Belgium: Pax Christi International, 1989).

FRANCIS X. MEEHAN

PEACE

This last one hundred years of church history has been a rich one for reflection about peace. Work on peace in Catholic social thought began in earnest after the Second World War. One way of viewing the last hundred years would be to claim that the issues raised by the popes during the First and Second World Wars were finally addressed by episcopates and theologians after the Second World War.

There are a number of factors inside and outside the church that are important for any account of Catholic reflection about peace during the past century. The most important events in world history were the two World Wars, the "cold war" following the end of the Second World War, the technological developments during and after that war that opened up the specter of the destruction of humanity, and the movements toward freedom around the globe.

These events obviously had an impact upon the discussions within the Roman Catholic community. At the same time, there were changes within the church that were important. These changes include the renewed emphasis upon Scripture study, the effect Scripture study had upon theology, Vatican II and the theological ferment unleashed by it, and, especially in the American context, a willingness to take a more critical look at some of the practices of government.

One cannot point to a single social location as a source for new reflection about peace. A full treatment of the subject would have to distinguish the contributions of the papacy, different national episcopates, theologians, and, in some cases, local communities. One outcome of all this ferment has been the opening of a genuine pluralism of perspectives within the Catholic community on discussions of peace. For example, pacifism is recognized to be a genuine possibility for Catholics, a possibility that was not envisioned even at the end of the Second World War.

Even with the pluralism, one can identify some definite features of recent Roman Catholic reflection on peace. In what follows, those features will be developed through a description of the central events of the past hundred years; the important emphases in biblical and theological study; and papal, conciliar, and episcopal statements on this topic. It should be said at the outset that one of the most important features of contemporary Catholic reflection upon peace is the joining of peace and justice concerns once again. In this sense, Catholic thought has recaptured its previous breadth of vision on the question of peace, a breadth that has been lacking since the 16th century.

Events of the 20th Century

World War I made clear how modern war consumes both material resources and human lives. Pope Benedict XV condemned the barbarity of that war and worked to bring about a solution so that the killing could stop. In addition, the pope continued the Catholic tradition's criticism of compulsory military service. World War II was important because in addition to the destruction of human and material resources, it showed how previously uncritiqued attitudes toward Jews and others when combined with the use of a number of modern technologies could lead to unspeakable evils. The Holocaust raised the question of complicity in evil, including the complicity of Catholics. One of the responses of the church has been to forthrightly condemn such behavior and raise the possibility of resistance to those who would order such deeds (*Gaudium et spes* 79).

At the same time, the Second World War raised the question once again of how much one could do to resist evil and bring about a peace with justice. This became especially important in postwar analyses of the bombing campaigns directed against cities and their occupants, especially the attacks upon Hiroshima and Nagasaki.

With the dominance of nuclear weapons and the cold war, deterrence became a central issue in Catholic reflections upon peace in the post–World War II era. Those reflections had to confront the paradox of deterrence, that by threatening to do what all agree would be immoral, a peace of a sort occurs. Yet that resulting peace has not led to a consensus within the Catholic community about the correctness of deterrence as a way of maintaining peace.

These recent events provided the context for much of the reflection about peace. Just as important were developments in biblical and theological studies within the Catholic church.

Biblical Materials

There are many perspectives on peace in the Bible. Given that the various books were written in different historical circumstances, this is not surprising. What comes through in reading the biblical materials is a challenge to our ordinary use of the term. Peace is not just the absence of conflict but a state of well-being, both of the individual and of the community.

In the OT, peace is the perfection of a thing. It is the result of the community's being in covenant communion with God, while the lack of peace grows out of a lack of harmony in that relationship (Ezek 13). Peace includes not only union with God but righteousness. Thus there is no peace for the evildoer (Isa 48).

Peace was not always established without conflict. Indeed, in the OT, Yahweh was a warrior God who defended his people. This image was gradually modified after the exile. What becomes clear is the communitarian nature of peace. Israel looked forward to the messianic age in which peace would be established and where righteousness would prevail. It was a sign of God's fidelity to Israel that one day there would be a peace that would encompass all of creation. Until that time, the people were called upon to repent and await that fullness of time when peace and justice would be established.

In the NT, Jesus is seen as establishing the messianic kingdom. He is the presence of God, which brings the peace we cannot bring to ourselves. Again, peace does not come without conflict. There is no warrior God but there will be division, especially when the reign of God in all its fullness will be brought into being. Jesus called for conversion to enter God's reign; this was not only a time of peace but of righteousness.

Also characteristic were forgiveness and love.

That love was manifested in Jesus' crucifixion and death, and God's response of resurrection is a sign that God does reign. The gift of peace, which is part of that reign, showed itself first in the relationship of the risen Christ to the community and second in the behavior of the members of that community toward one another. Because of their relationship with Christ, Christians were to experience an inner peace; because of that same relationship, harmony was to exist within the Christian community. In addition, Christians were asked not only to be at peace with their friends but with their enemies as well.

It is clear that the biblical materials do not provide ready-made answers to the questions of war and peace today. What they do provide is a context, one where Christians acknowledge the gifts they have received and look forward in hope to the fullness of peace yet to come.

Theological Reflection

Catholic reflection upon peace has constantly attempted to reach out to persons of good will everywhere and not limit itself to members of the Catholic community (*Pacem in terris* 172). This emphasis marks papal writing, the letters of a number of episcopates (*The Challenge of Peace* 4), and the work of individual theologians. Further, it has been a constant of Catholic thought in the last hundred years to support whatever efforts the international community can make toward establishing peace (GS 84), while all the while trying to expand the conception of peace held within that community. One result has been that the statements on peace by the popes and by different episcopal conferences often receive a great deal of attention from the larger world.

How that peace is to be realized is imaged in a variety of ways within the Catholic community. In *Peace on Earth,* peace exists when human beings and their societies fulfill their respective duties and recognize the rights of other persons and societies (PT 30). In the Pastoral Constitution on the Church in the Modern World, peace is one of the results of working for justice. There must be justice within human communities as well as between communities in order for peace to be possible. However, peace is also an activity that goes beyond strict justice and requires love. The love that makes peace possible enters the picture when human beings share not only of their goods but of themselves (GS 78).

War and Deterrence

Unfortunately, war is still part of human affairs. Given that war continues to be a possibility, many theologians and bishops still use just-war theory as a framework for reflection. The use of that theory is now done with an awareness of how the members of the church failed to use this theory in the recent past, with the consequence that evil was done and opportunities for peace were lost. Many see no alternative to using just-war theory, or something like it, to help Christians decide what to do when peace and justice are threatened.

One of the reasons why war is still a part of human affairs is that there is a structural defect in the international community, with no body having the jurisdiction to authoritatively settle disputes. In the absence of such a body, Catholic thought preserves the right of war for nation-states to defend their peoples, but it limits the right of war to defense and no longer thinks of war as an apt means for restoring rights now lost (GS 79; PT 127). This means that one is constrained more in achieving justice because of the horrors of war precisely at a time when there is a growing realization that peace without justice is not the fullness of peace for Christians. This leads to the situation where many Catholic thinkers in First World countries worry about threats to peace and justice that arise out of the threat of thermonuclear war; thinkers in the Second and Third Worlds are not insensitive to these issues, but they are also concerned about threats to justice and peace that come about because of political and economic exploitation.

Once one recognizes that one can make war to protect peace and justice, it is important to recognize that one is constrained more and more in what legitimately may be done in war. Not only are international conventions and agreements binding; some specific actions made possible by modern weaponry are outlawed. Any action that aims at the destruction of entire cities, for example, is condemned. The effect of these limitations is to call into question the legitimacy of possessing certain kinds of weapons. Certain large thermonuclear weapons as well as chemical and biological weapons fall into this category.

The conclusion of much of this reflection is that deterrence, which many see as necessary to preserve some peace and justice, is also the source of many difficulties. Those who would deter by thermonuclear war threaten grave evils, and no long-term peace will grow from these threats. Even thinkers who support deterrence agree with this conclusion. After that, there is disagreement. To give just one example, the German bishops saw deterrence as a lesser evil than either war or domination by communist powers (*Out of Justice, Peace* 153), while the American bishops were concerned about the continuation of deterrence as a structural feature of international life (CP 188).

At the time of this writing, the future of nuclear deterrence is unclear. Recent events in Eastern Europe may make some forms of deterrence unnecessary; they are unlikely to still the arguments about either its effectiveness in preventing a variety of evils or whether its moral cost is too high.

New Developments: Pacifism and Liberation

One of the more remarkable changes in recent history has been the growth of a genuine pacifist alternative within Catholicism, an alternative recognized as a genuine form of service to the Christian community (CP 118). At its best, this alternative wishes to find nonviolent ways of resolving differences between nations and seeking justice both in and between nations. Very often, this pacifism begins with a concrete judgment about *modern* war; in the view of Catholic pacifists this form of war can bring neither peace nor justice and thus it is to be rejected based upon a faithful reading of Scripture. Although not the dominant perspective in Catholic social thought, pacifism has had a significant impact upon Catholic social thought. There has been renewed attention to nonviolence (GS 78) and the need for the church to become involved in an exploration of nonviolent conflict resolution (CP 221–30).

In contrast to Catholic pacifists, theologians of liberation focus more upon the current structures of injustice that prevent the possibility of peace and human fulfillment. In contrast to just-war thinkers, who aim their remarks first at persons in power, theologians of liberation speak first to those persons who have been marginalized by the powers of this world. At the same time, most liberation theologians are willing to entertain the possibility of using force to overcome "institutionalized violence." Liberation theologians also are usually far more interested in the relationships between First and Third World nations that always leave Third World nations in a dependent situation—an unjust situation in their view and one that cannot be the basis of any lasting peace.

Disarmament

Disarmament is a place where peace and justice concerns in Catholic social thought meet. Given the enormous expenditures for armaments that are morally problematic at best, given that the very existence of these arms is itself a source of international tension (GS 81), given that the expense of these armaments helps to ensure that Third World nations will not receive the necessary aid to become self-sufficient, it is not surprising that there is increasing attention to disarmament in Catholic statements on peace. Indeed, disarmament is seen as a necessary precondition to any sort of peace with justice. One of the consequences of this is that disarmament is seen as a key feature of any just deterrence policy. Any form of deterrence that would make disarmament less likely should be rejected (*Out of Justice, Peace* 148). Disarmament is imperative to slow the arms race, to establish trust between nations, and to do justice to the poorer nations of the world.

Continuing Issues

One area that has not been thought through very well is how the church's conversation on peace, if and when it reaches a consensus on a particular issue, leads to action for peace at the local level. For example, American Catholics are used to the practice of lobbying at the state and national level, but there are problems associated with the church being perceived as just one more lobbying group.

The issue here is how little reflection there has been on how the Catholic community might display its beliefs about peace, whatever these beliefs might be. What one has are a number of examples of peacemaking activity that one can use as exemplars, but there is very little systematic reflection upon them. For example, very few persons know about the movements toward conscientious objection that took place in Europe in the 1960s and 1970s, movements often led and supported by the Catholic laity. Yet without some examination of these forms of peacemaking, the usual forms of making peace and achieving justice will continue to be sought through resort to arms.

There is the continuing tension between those Catholics who argue that some use of force is still justifiable in a world marked by sin and those Catholics who argue that it is not possible to establish peace with justice through violent means. Both groups struggle with identifying what might be distinctive about the Christian message of peace, different from the message of secular peace movements and different from politics as usual. Here, most Catholic thinkers still are trying to work out a politics that is faithful to their understanding of peace as a human achievement and a gift from God.

Conclusion

Catholic social thought has shown a capacity for development through its reflection on peace. This has happened in an era of unprecedented technological and social change outside the church. Catholic social thought will have the continuing task of making clear to a world that wishes for peace that the peace the world seeks is both a gift and a task. As task, it is something for which we are to work unceasingly; as gift, it is something that our earthly peace only dimly anticipates.

See also ARMS RACE; CONSCIENTIOUS OBJECTION; DETERRENCE; DISARMAMENT; KILLING; PACIFISM; PEACE AND JUSTICE COMMISSIONS; WAR.

Bibliography: R. Musto, *The Catholic Peace Tradition* (Maryknoll, N.Y.: Orbis, 1986). J. Gremillion, ed., *The Gospel of Peace and Justice: Catholic Social Teaching since Pope John* (Maryknoll, N.Y.: Orbis, 1976). National Conference of Catholic Bishops, *The Challenge of Peace: God's Promise and Our Response* (Washington: United States Catholic Conference, 1983). J. Schall, ed., *Out of Justice, Peace* (West German bishops) and *Winning the Peace* (French bishops) (San Francisco: Ignatius, 1984). J. Johnson, *The Quest for Peace: Three Moral Traditions in Western Cultural History* (Princeton, N.J.: Princeton Univ. Press, 1987). S. Lammers, "Roman Catholic Social Ethics and Pacifism," in T. Shannon, ed., *War or Peace? The Search for New Answers* (Maryknoll, N.Y.: Orbis).

STEPHEN E. LAMMERS

PEACE AND JUSTICE COMMISSIONS

Peace and justice commissions and offices, which have been established at all levels from the Vatican to the parish, are a principal institutional reflection of and means to ensure the new place of social ministry in the life of the postconciliar church. As their name suggests, the function of these commissions is the evangelical task of promoting justice and peace in the world (*Populorum progressio* 5). This article will briefly examine the history of these commissions, their structure and function, and some challenges they face in their pastoral mission.

History

Peace and justice commissions and offices (or their equivalents) are official or quasi-official church bodies charged with addressing structural issues of justice, development, and peace. Their roots may be found in a long and rich tradition of Catholic social teaching and social action, but their institutional development and growth are directly attributable to the Second Vatican Council. The council's Pastoral Constitution on the Church in the Modern World, Dogmatic Constitution on the Church, and Decree on the Church's Missionary Activity together elaborated the theological, moral, and perhaps most importantly, ecclesiological basis for understanding peace and justice work as central to the salvific mission of the church. In the words of the pastoral constitution (*Gaudium et spes*), the church is "a sign and safeguard of the transcendence of the human person" (GS 76). These and subsequent documents reflected and helped create a growing sense among Catholics of the importance of the social ministry of the church. Moreover, they encouraged greater attention by the church and individual Christians to the fact that "the social question has become world-wide" (PP 3), and hence, the church had to establish structures that would enable it to be more active in addressing the international dimensions of development, justice, and peace (GS 90).

In response to this call for a more visible presence on the international level, Paul VI formed the Pontifical Commission Iustitia et Pax in 1967. The commission, in turn, encouraged episcopal conferences to establish similar commissions. In the United States, a comparable structure—the Social Action Department of the National Catholic Welfare Conference (NCWC)—had played an important and visible role since its inception in 1919, but its focus was primarily on domestic issues. International programs of the NCWC such as the Latin American Bureau and independent organizations with close ties to the NCWC, especially the Catholic Association for International Peace, had also done important work in this area. As part of the restructuring of the bishops' conference after the Second Vatican Council, the bishops established a new bishops' committee and office (the Division of World Justice and Peace, currently, the Office of International Justice and Peace) to serve as a counterpart to the pontifical commission that would complement and significantly expand upon these existing international efforts. This office and committee helped catalyze and direct a much more visible presence on the part of the bishops in foreign-policy debates in the 1970s and 1980s.

Perhaps the most significant impact of the council, however, was at the diocesan and parish levels. In the United States the growing sense of the church's social mission—and the need to establish church bodies specifically mandated to carry this out—was given a new urgency and focus as the church increasingly became involved in civil rights, the Vietnam War, nuclear weapons, Central America, and poverty issues, all of which were defined in large part in moral terms. Until the early 1970s diocesan social action was largely the purview of a fairly small number of priests heading small offices in large, urban dioceses, with a focus primarily on domestic issues. By 1990 about three-fourths of the dioceses in the United States had social-concerns commissions and/or offices, with anywhere from a part-time to a dozen full-time staff—mostly lay—and a vastly expanded agenda that covered the spectrum of domestic and international issues. In addition, many diocesan Catholic Charities agencies have developed a significant advocacy and social-ministry dimension, and many independent justice and peace groups have developed a structured or financial relationship with the diocese. The number of parishes with social-concerns committees has also mushroomed.

Structure and Activities

These bodies have an essentially pastoral function: to promote justice and peace and to penetrate all spheres of human society with the light and leaven of the gospel. It is a task of evangelization to stimulate the whole church to fulfill its social mission. Given this broad mandate, it is natural that the structure and activities of particular commissions vary widely, reflecting the divergent social, political, and institutional contexts in which they operate.

Two basic models predominate. One model, represented by the French and Irish national commissions, has a commission—composed of priests (including at least one bishop designated by the episcopal conference), religious, and laypersons—that works in collaboration and retains some formal ties with the episcopal conference or diocese but is a quasi-independent body that oftentimes can more readily address controversial and contingent issues. This model gives the staff and the commission considerable autonomy, which provides a certain freedom of action but which limits their ability to speak and act with the authority of the institutional church. The second model, represented by the United States Catholic Conference's Department of Social Development and World Peace and its oversight committees, places the commission strictly within the episcopal conference, diocesan, or parish structure. While more bureaucratic in nature and less free to act on controversial questions, this model has the advantage of infusing the commission's activity with the authority and credibility of the parish, diocese, or episcopal conference and makes it more likely that these activities will be integrated into the institutional life of the church. The trend at the diocesan level in the United States is toward this second model, with the commission and office incorporated into the diocesan administrative structure.

The activities of these bodies are as diverse as their structures. In general, they cover a range of domestic and international issues, from abortion and arms control to social security and Central America. The United States bishops' pastoral letters on war and peace and the economy, and Joseph Cardinal Bernardin's consistent life-ethic have provided the most systematic and comprehensive elaboration of the theological rationale and the policy agenda of these groups.

The means of addressing these issues is equally varied. They generally fall into one of four broad categories: education, policy analysis and advocacy, community organizing, and prophetic witness (e.g., demonstrations, civil disobedience). The clear trend is toward a focus on education and advocacy. The Campaign for Human Development has largely supplanted the commissions in the community-organizing field, and witness activities are increasingly the domain of groups not affiliated with the institutional church.

Challenges

The function of these commissions as instruments of the church's public ministry—entities that help define the church's relationship to the world—raise several ongoing challenges. One is theological and pastoral. How can faith and justice be better integrated so as to avoid the twin dangers of social activism without spiritual and theological rootedness (justice without faith) and indifference to the justice dimension of preaching the gospel (faith without justice)? From a moral perspective, how do these bodies raise the moral dimensions of public policy issues and work effectively for peace and justice in concrete situations without suggesting that Catholic social teaching provides an economic and political blueprint for society or falling into a partisanship that fails to respect legitimate pluralism in contingent matters? Finally, there are ecclesiological concerns. First, a principal characteristic and innovation of peace and justice commissions—best exemplified by the process used for the U.S. bishops' economic and peace pastorals—is broad-based dialogue and consultation. How can this more democratic process be used to engage a greater part of the church and the wider public in debate over these issues and still retain unity on fundamental principles of Catholic social teaching? Second, how can these commissions better define how their work can respect and reinforce the proper autonomy of the secular world and the leading role of the laity in addressing the contingent questions on their agenda? How these commissions respond to these and other challenges will have a significant impact on the nature and style of the church's public ministry in coming years.

See also CALL TO ACTION CONFERENCE; CAMPAIGN FOR HUMAN DEVELOPMENT; CATHOLIC CHARITIES USA; CHURCH, SOCIAL MISSION OF; COMMUNITY ORGANIZATION; LAITY, ROLE OF; PONTIFICAL COUNCIL FOR JUSTICE AND PEACE.

Bibliography: H. Fagan, "Ten Points for Effective Diocesan Social Action Offices," *Origins* 12, no. 42, (March 31, 1983) 672–76. J. Malone, "Questions for Social Action Ministers," *Origins* 18, no. 40 (March 16, 1989) 674–76. D. O'Brien, *Public Catholicism* (New York: Macmillan, 1989).

GERARD POWERS

PERSON, DIGNITY OF

When the human being is referred to as a "person," contemporary usage seems to have three things in mind: first, the word refers to the distinct selfhood of the individual, something that is unique and incommunicable. Second, the person is one who is the subject of rights and duties and who is therefore an end and never a means. Third, the person is one who can meaningfully experience and influence the environment—abilities that are consequent on consciousness and moral sense. All three of these elements are important for understanding human dignity.

To speak of the dignity of the human person is to speak of the worth or value of the concrete existing human being. Those who use the phrase imply that human beings have a value or a worth qualitatively different from that of anything else in the world, that this dignity is inalienable in the sense that it can never be lost, and that it is never permissible to merely *use* a human being to attain some end or purpose.

Ambiguity of the Word "Person"

The problem with speaking about the dignity of the person is that modern reflection on human personhood draws on two different sources. One of them is the Judeo-Christian tradition, based on and expressed in the Bible; the other is of more recent provenance and is discussed in the next paragraph. Although there is no single biblical word either in Hebrew or in Greek that translates all the nuances of the word in the modern languages, the concept of the person as one capable of knowledge and love and of functioning as a responsible moral agent is omnipresent in the OT and NT. However, the biblical concept is theocentric—that is, it sees human dignity as flowing from the person's relationship with God and not as the result of some quality that human beings possess independently; the person is the woman or man created by God, addressed by God, called by God, accepted by God; for both the OT and NT the dignity of the person is rooted in the fact that the human being is made in the image and likeness of God (Gen 1:26-27) and is therefore capable of being God's partner in dialogue. The biblical concept of "person" is not only relational but also dynamic. The person is both an essential structure and an ongoing task.

However, in modern discussions of human rights and of the dignity on which they are based, the concept of "person" is anthropocentric: the human being is understood as the independent, autonomous subject whose independence must be safeguarded from the incursions of society or community in all cases in which similar rights of others to noninterference are not demonstrably violated. (This statement applies to the concept of "person" current in the Western democracies. Marxism is also anthropocentric; however, its normative value is not existing human beings but an idealized abstraction—the proletariat.) This modern concept of the person had its origins in the breakdown of medieval unity with its strong sense of community—a breakdown that ushered in the individualism that has remained the trademark of the modern world, at least in the West. The rationalism of the Enlightenment placed this autonomous subject at the center of a world that had been stripped of mystery and in which God was at best a somewhat benign if distant observer of the human scene. This "God" was, of course, threatened by the growing competence of the human race, particularly in the technological realm, which has been a second hallmark of modernity, and was effectively driven from the scene by the end of the 19th century, leaving the human being supreme on earth but without a transcendent destiny to give ultimate meaning to his or her earthly striving. This "God" was quite different from the real God, of whom John Paul II could say in his encyclical *Laborem exercens* (*On Human Work*): "Christians are convinced that the triumphs of the human race are signs of God's greatness" (LE 25).

Catholic Teaching in Modern Times

It is a sad paradox that Catholic teaching on human rights, which in virtue of its access to the sources (the OT and NT, and a tradition that had, at least at times, led to striking advances in respect for human dignity) was uniquely placed to articulate a powerful statement on the dignity of the human person, discovered this value at so late a date, and did so only after more than a century and a half of rejecting the modern world's affirmation of human rights. (Pius VI condemned the French Revolution's *Declaration of the Rights of Man* in 1790, and Rome was generally hostile to the ideas of freedom of conscience and freedom of religion practically up to the time of the Second Vatican Council.) But although a late starter, Catholic social thought since the papacy of Leo XIII (1878–1903) has developed rapidly.

Leo XIII's 1891 encyclical *Rerum novarum* (*On the Condition of Workers*) saw in human dignity the norm and standard by which the political, social, and economic structures of society are to be judged. The human being is never a means, only an end, and it was because the management sector of industry in an increasingly industrialized Europe often made the worker into a mere means for accruing wealth that Leo so eloquently defended the economic rights of the working class. He defended the rights of workers to organize and to form unions because he saw that such unions were necessary if workers were to enjoy the minimal conditions demanded by human dignity. Leo still viewed society and its institutions in static and even patriarchal terms, and for this reason he saw such things as the just wage as *conditions* necessary for the attainment of human dignity and not as inherent elements. Political and economic self-determination in a democratic state was certainly not on Leo's agenda as a value demanded by human dignity.

In his 1931 encyclical *Quadragesimo anno* (*On Reconstructing the Social Order*) Pius XI reaffirmed Leo XIII's conviction of the normative role of human dignity in judging the institutions of society, but the world of 1931 was already more complex, and the worldwide depression was making it clear that threats to human dignity could not be confined by political borders. Pius XI elaborated a concept of social justice—that type of justice that demands from each individual what is necessary for the common good (*Mediator Dei* 52)—that implied that human dignity might demand structural change in society itself, and in this he broke with the static framework of Leo XIII.

By the time of Pius XII (1939–58) problems caused by the growing complexity of modern society and by the threats an increasingly intrusive technology posed to human dignity had become acute, and Pius seemed at times quite pessimistic about the future. For this reason, concern for human dignity was more conscious and explicit in his writings than had been the case for his predecessors. In his Christmas address of 1944 he initiated a new development in papal thinking by arguing that the power to participate in the political process and thus to shape one's own future was essential to the preservation and development of human dignity.

John XXIII developed this theme in his 1961 encyclical *Mater et magistra* (*On Christianity and Social Progress*). He felt that because of the sheer size and power of political and economic organizations in our day people were losing confidence in their power to shape their own futures and that this represented an assault on human dignity. At the same time, he was aware that both inside the church and outside of it the modern world is deeply concerned with affirming and defending the concrete dignity of the human person. In his 1963 encyclical *Pacem in terris* (*Peace on Earth*) there is even more emphasis on life in community as the context in which human dignity can be protected and expanded.

The Second Vatican Council met from 1962 to 1965, and in two respects its teaching (embodied in *Gaudium et spes,* the 1965 Pastoral Constitution on the Church in the Modern World) represented a significant advance. First, it affirmed that human dignity can be defended only if we recognize that human institutions *and human persons* are not static but themselves develop and change in history. However, this seems to subject reflection on human dignity to all the arbitrariness of the historical process, and the council dealt with this problem in a second and quite innovative way; it opted for an explicitly theological point of view in identifying human dignity with the task of existing as finite beings who are called to absolute transcendence. In doing this, it applied a biblical concept of freedom (freedom as the power to fashion something worthwhile out of the limited and limiting conditions of life) to the problems created by the growing complexity and interdependence of modern life, and it saw these factors as possibilities of achieving human dignity. This document defended human dignity less in negative and individualistic terms (freedom from interference with personal autonomy) and more in terms of the right to share in the decisions that structure political, social, and economic life.

After the council the encyclical *Populorum progressio* (*On the Development of Peoples*) of Paul VI, pope from 1963 to 1978, marked the next advance in Catholic social thought. As with all of its predecessors, the letter was occasioned by developments of the time, above all, the widening gap between rich nations and poor nations. The innovative element in the letter is the concept of "integral development"—the notion that human dignity is protected only by promoting the development of the whole human being, by realizing his or her potential for knowledge, responsibility, and freedom in every area of life—political, social, and economic—in such a way that these areas are not merely instrumental in attaining human dignity but become an integral part of the process.

In 1971 Paul VI celebrated the 80th anniversary of *Rerum novarum* by issuing the apostolic letter *Octogesima adveniens* (*A Call to Action*). This letter continued the turn toward a more theological point of departure in social thought by suggesting that Christian faith, in virtue of its conviction that absolute value and truth had taken historical form in Jesus, was in a unique position to reconcile the claims of the absolute and the relative, of historicity and transcendence, in the quest for practical means of promoting human dignity.

The 1971 document of the synod of bishops, *Justitia in mundo* (*Justice in the World*), moved further, arguing that the right to development and participation, personal and communal, is the foundation of all other rights and that the greatest threat to human dignity today is marginalization—denying to human beings the power to shape their own destiny in the political, social, and economic realms of life. This view implies that both the individual political rights favored in the Western democracies as well as the "social" rights favored in the various socialist and Marxist states are based on the right to participate in the decisions that shape society.

Ten years later (in 1981), on the 90th anniversary of *Rerum novarum,* John Paul II issued the encyclical *Laborem exercens* (*On Human Work*). The letter deals specifically with human dignity as manifest in and enhanced by work, and it continues the emphasis on theology by asserting that the source of the church's convictions about the dignity of human work is the revealed word of God and the transcendent destiny given by the living God. New to this letter is the view that part of human dignity consists in the fact that the human being is the "subject" of work, that for this reason work must always be a form of self-realization, and that through work we become more fully human. Because work is a "personal action," it is only through faith, hope, and charity that it can be given the meaning that it has in the eyes of God. (A book that the pope had written while still archbishop of Kraków is important for understanding the language and philosophical position of this encyclical. See K. Wojtyla, *The Acting Person.*)

On December 30, 1987, John Paul II published his encyclical *Sollicitudo rei socialis* (*On Social Concern*). The encyclical continues the emphasis on historical change as the setting of human life, and it moves still further from the deductive-logic, natural-law approach that characterized Catholic social thinking almost until Vatican II. The encyclical's particular contribution to reflection on human dignity lies in its development of the concept of solidarity.

Biblical Foundations

One factor in the church's long delay in articulating the concern for human dignity was the official philosophy of the church—Scholasticism—which like the classical Greek philosophy on which it was based was primarily concerned with the principles in virtue of which things exist, with the result that its categories were objective and not relational. The biblical concept of person is very different; it does not see the individual as definable in terms of substantial reality but rather in terms of word and response—a response empowered by the fact that the human being is made in the image and likeness of God. In the second creation narrative (the work of the J source) in Genesis, the man does not see the animals simply as products to be consumed or as means to an end; rather, he is called to give them names, and in so doing he welcomes them into the human world and they are forever changed. The human being is a speaker of the word and a hearer of the word, and this is the case because we ourselves are addressed by God and endowed in virtue of this address with inalienable dignity.

The OT often deals with the question of human dignity in stressing the need to respect the rights of the widow and the orphan. Because widows and orphans had no one to defend their rights, they were obvious victims of oppression (Job 22:9; 24:1; Isa 1:23). Jewish law extended protection to widows (Deut 24:3), indicating that although they had no one to defend them in court or before the powerful, they possessed an inviolable dignity.

As in the OT, so also in the NT, the dignity of the human person is not based on the autonomous and inviolable selfhood of the individual but on his or her relationship with God. In the earliest writings to find entry into the NT (Paul's letters) the human being is one who is unconditionally accepted, affirmed, sustained, and supported by God; and human dignity is given, through this, a foundation that human hands cannot create. It is important to note that of all NT writers it is Paul who talks most bluntly about human depravity; however, he does this not in an assault on human dignity but rather in the attempt to understand the greatness of the gift that God has given. For Paul the fact that we are claimed by God as God's own is the root of our freedom—something Paul understands as our power to accept existence as a gift, the power to hearken to a call that comes from beyond this world and that summons us to exist in a new and creative way. In the Synoptic tradition, and above all in Mark, Jesus invites into his company those very people who were regarded as sinners and who were therefore thought to be devoid of dignity: the public sinners (prostitutes) and the tax collectors (collaborators with the brutal occupying authorities and themselves oppressors of the poor), and he seems to have assumed that this invitation would transform their lives if they only accepted it. The text of Mk 2:13-17 is one of the most important in the NT. The invitation to sinners is the ultimate affirmation of inalienable dignity, which sin itself is unable to eradicate.

Paul never developed a concept of human dignity that could serve as the basis for a theory of political or economic rights because he was convinced that the present world and its structures were passing away and that the second coming of Jesus would occur, if not during his own lifetime, then very soon after. At most, Paul gives us an interim ethic, some general guidance for the brief period of history that remains; and although his conviction that God claims us as God's own despite the fact that we are sinners implies a deep understanding of the basis of human dignity, his belief that history would come to an end in his own time prevented any application of this understanding to the social and political conditions of his day. (Although Paul's writings do not deal expressly with human dignity *as the basis of rights in the secular realm,* the dialectical definitions of freedom and slavery that he worked out in his Letter to Philemon offer material for a very deep understanding of human dignity.)

With Jesus, the case is very different. He defined our relationship with God in terms of our relationship with other human beings. He never called for structural changes in society, and many today are troubled by that fact. But he brought a liberation of the mind and heart that was not blunted by any eschatological perspective—that is, not relativized by the conviction that what happened in the political, social, and economic dimensions of our earthly lives was unimportant because the world would end in the near future. The historical Jesus was probably the only person connected with the Christian movement who did not think the world was coming to an end in the near future, and texts in which he claims no knowledge of the "day and the hour" (Mk 13:32 and parr.) undoubtedly go back to him. But so intense was the conviction among early Christians that the world would end in the near future that they projected this conviction onto Jesus himself, whom they could not imagine as not sharing their certitude. Mark 13 and the parallel texts in Matthew and Luke give evidence of this. The liberty that Jesus brought empowers the engagement of the Christian in political and social concerns, not on the false pretext that Jesus counseled specific forms of involvement but because the liberation that he offers puts an end to our insecurity and makes it possible for us to use our heads to devise practical and efficient ways of loving the neighbor.

A Systematic Approach

The dignity of the human person is not abstract, not distinct from the concrete existing human being. (The *existing* human being is not abstract and cannot be reduced to any single dimension. It is this that forbids discrimination that would be based on any partial aspect of human life, whether national, sexual, or racial.) Consequently, human dignity is inseparable from the person, and it does not depend for its reality on being acknowledged by others, whether by individuals or by the state; rather, it *demands* such recognition and acknowledgment. Human dignity is simply the existence of the individual man or woman, viewed from a certain perspective—viewed, that is, as constituting a task and a challenge for the existing person and as imposing certain obligations on other individuals and communities. For our purposes the question of the dignity of the person is simply the question of what is *constitutive* of the person. Taking the popular understanding of the person (see the introduction above) as a starting point, we can list several elements that both reveal the person and point to deeper levels of human personhood.

Person and Human Rights

First, to be a person is to be someone worthy of respect and protection of a unique kind, qualitatively different from the real respect that is owed to the natural world and to the varied forms of life that populate it. Traditionally, the concept of rights in the strict sense has been used to speak of this phenomenon. A right is a title or a claim to certain things or "goods" (material and spiritual) in themselves or the title to access such goods. To describe them as "titles" or "claims" implies that these rights must be acknowledged and respected by individuals and by the state. The concept of personal dignity as the basis of real rights lies at the very center of modern Catholic social thought.

The person has rights that are to be respected and protected because of his or her personal dignity, and all rights aim at the protection and preservation of this dignity (and for precisely this reason, human rights cannot be *identified* with human dignity). However, because there is something absolute about the claims made in the name of human rights, because some, at least, are inviolable and inalienable; they do point to something deeper in the human person, on which they are based.

Person and Moral Responsibility

There is a second element in human dignity: to be a person is to be one who is morally responsible, to be one who experiences an *absolute* demand in the sense that the demand is not conditioned on our desire to obtain some particular goal or other and is therefore not under our control or disposition. The moral demand is one we must acknowledge and can ignore only at the risk of rejecting our very humanity.

Morality and moral responsibility deal with the question, What must I do to act rightly and well? and this question is related to human dignity in two distinct but closely related ways. First, the human person is one who *should* act in a morally good way. To be a person is to be claimed by values that impose an obligation. And second, moral obligation is the summons to acknowledge the concrete dignity of human persons, and in this sense human dignity is the criterion and norm of all moral activity.

Dignity and Freedom

Only one who is free can be morally responsible. Moral responsibility therefore implies at least the possibility of moral irresponsibility, and both are possible because an *answer* (the Latin etymology of "response") has to be given to a claim or a demand that has been made on us. The third element in human dignity is freedom, and this points to a still deeper level of the mystery of human dignity.

The discussion of freedom and its meaning has often led into blind alleys because the modern concept of freedom is derived from two sources, both of them quite inadequate—the Greek, and later, Scholastic notion of freedom as *indifference,* and the modern liberal and democratic notion of freedom as the absence of external interference or coercion.

The Greek and Scholastic notion emphasizes the absence of internal factors that would force us to choose one way rather than another and defines freedom as the ability to act or not to act, and if we do act, to act in one way or another. (Although Thomas Aquinas' discussion of the problems of divine and human freedom is profound, unfortunately his definition of freedom in terms of indifference [found in his *De veritate,* q. xxii, a. 6] is the one that passed into the Scholastic tradition. This is doubly unfortunate in view of the fact that in that same article he cites with approval Augustine's statement: "To choose evil is not identified with freedom, nor is it a part of freedom, although it is, in a certain sense, a sign of freedom," *De natura boni* 3.) The problem with the traditional Scholastic definition is that it does not adequately distinguish free choices from arbitrary choices, and this makes it difficult to see freedom as a value, much less an absolute value.

The liberal democratic notion of freedom is problematic because although it insists on the removal of external coercive factors, it shows little interest in the value of the act or choice in itself, usually on the grounds that it has no noncoercive way of determining which actions are valuable in themselves apart from the consensus of society, and on the grounds that no individual or group can safely be given the authority to determine which ones are valuable and which are not.

This liberal democratic notion of freedom is regarded by contemporary Catholic social thought as, at best, inadequate (although, surprisingly, a biblical concept of freedom, so essential to the defense of human dignity, has developed only in the most recent documents of this tradition). It is probable that at least some of the 19th-century papacy's opposition to what the popes of the time referred to as "liberalism" stemmed from the insight that human dignity is a transcendent value, not created by human choice, and that liberal democracy, in the absence of some way of identifying and committing itself to objective value, constantly runs the risk of becoming the tyranny of the majority. More recent papal, conciliar, and synodal (particularly the document produced by the 1971 bishops synod, *Justice in the World*) texts are far less suspicious of freedom because they refuse to define it in negative and individualistic terms. Instead, they see freedom as the power and the act of exercising responsibility.

The biblical concept of freedom and its role in human dignity. The understanding and the defense of human dignity must be based on an understanding of freedom, and it is surprising and unfortunate that Western thought has drawn so little on those biblical sources that stand at the origins of so much in Western culture—namely, the OT and NT. Although the word "freedom" appears only in the NT (that is, freedom in our sense; the Hebrew root *hphsh* refers only to the state of the free man or woman, as opposed to the slave), the concept and the reality are constantly acknowledged and presupposed in both Testaments. Human beings are addressed by God, and they are called to respond in a way that accords with God's will and with human dignity. Both Testaments assume that in our decisions we respond to God's offer and demand, and that in them we either create the selves we are called to be or lose our way. Our decisions are not merely choices of how to act; they are choices of who to be. The person is not a changeless being who makes decisions about objects or things; rather, we ourselves change profoundly in the decisions we make.

This aspect of our decision making is at the very heart of the mystery of our human dignity. Each of us is confronted with the challenge and the task of becoming human, and a truly human existence is worthy of our best efforts. We are summoned to real existence, and this is a call to advance beyond the partial and fragmentary achievement of personhood that characterizes our lives at any given moment. To be human is to have the power to create the selves we are called to be. Freedom is not the absence of limiting and constraining factors in our lives; it is the ability and the power to make use of them. The very factors commonly regarded as limiting freedom are nothing other than the raw material we are summoned to use in becoming free. Our freedom is not an abstract quality; it is accepted and exercised in the presence of very concrete limitations in life. We do not choose these limiting factors, and we usually do not have the option of rejecting them. But what we can decide is whether to let ourselves be determined by them or to take responsibility and become self-determining by incorporating them into our self-creative choices.

Central to the NT is the conception that freedom is not a natural power or propensity but rather a gift of God—a gift that is a consequence of God's unconditional offer and claim and of our saying yes to both. (This aspect of freedom is implied in the Gospels, but it is spelled out most rigorously in Paul's Epistle to the Romans, chaps. 3, 7.) This is important because it shows that the real question for the human being, and the essential way in which human dignity is manifest, does not consist in using freedom rightly rather than wrongly. The real question is whether we will accept the gift of freedom or reject it. The acceptance of freedom is the essential act of human dignity, and it *is* this because the acceptance or rejection of freedom is the act of standing in the presence of God and of taking one or another of these two stances before God.

When freedom is not defined negatively (either as indifference or as the absence of external coercive factors) but rather as the expression of something essential to the person, its character as an absolute value becomes clear. (Much of the Christian tradition has shown an unbecoming suspicion of freedom, seeming to fear that too much freedom will degenerate into license. The problem is not with freedom itself but with faulty definitions of freedom, which have been perpetuated all too often within the Christian tradition itself.) It is important to recognize freedom as an absolute value and to understand that genuine freedom does not constitute some kind of "golden mean" between tyranny and license. This absolute character of freedom is rooted in the fact that human personhood is constituted by a relationship to the infinite and unconditioned—that is, to God. It seems clear that it is this perception that accounts for the interesting turn in Catholic social thought, which began with the document *Gaudium et spes* of the Second Vatican Council and which seems to be gaining momentum: the insight that reflection on human rights cannot rest on reason alone but needs a theological basis.

The biblical concept of freedom sees much more in freedom than the indifference in which classical Greek philosophy as well as the Scholastic tradition located the mystery of free choice, and it cannot limit freedom to noninterference in the individual's political self-determination, as is common in the Western democratic tradition. The return to the biblical concept is closely connected with an important shift in Catholic social thought since the Second Vatican Council. Since freedom is the power to create the selves that we are called to be, and since we are called to a life in community with others, freedom is by definition the power to act in concert with others in order to achieve the common good. In other words, it is the power to participate in shaping the political, social, and economic order in a way that is appropriate to those who have been called to transcendence while in the world, and called to express this transcendence by transforming the world and creating a more human society.

The Drive for Transcendence

The different characteristics of personhood and the different manifestations of human dignity we have seen all point to the root of the human mystery: to the fact that we are created and called to transcend ourselves and our world, and the fact that there is a restlessness in the human heart that can be stilled by nothing in the created world. We are persons because we are called to know and love ourselves, the world, other human beings, and God. A brief reflection on the kind of knowledge and love that is distinctively human offers a good approach to transcendence. (It was in the work of Karl Rahner and Bernard Lonergan that this aspect of knowledge has been developed in a form that linked it with contemporary philosophical concerns, but both were quite consciously developing a theme that was central to the thought of Thomas Aquinas: the notion that human intelligence is simply *capax entis,* open toward everything because open on being as such.)

This knowledge does not consist in merely registering the presence of data or in fashioning ideas or mental images. It is the act of holding concrete experience up in the light of our hunger for a reality that is not conditioned, not limited. It is the act that grasps the mystery of finite being because it respects the implicit demand of limited being to affirm itself as embraced and supported by infinite being. To be a person is to experience infinity; to be a human person is to experience infinity as gift. The type of knowledge described here is not simply a condition for love; it already includes love. Real knowledge is always the act of allowing the other (person or thing) to share in one's own conscious openness toward the infinite ground of being.

However, the transcendence to which we are called and which is constitutive of our personhood is a transcendence proper to those who are in the world, living in space, time, and history and who are called to the paradoxical task of transcending this world while remaining in it and accepting responsibility for it. (In GS 10, the council picked up, in modern language, the biblical theme of cosmic redemption. Jesus frees us from the "powers." He is the savior who heals our estrangement from the world and empowers us to be responsible for the world. In mythical terms, he overcomes the alienation that is spoken of in the story of creation and the Fall. We have been exiled from Eden and alienated from our world; unaided, we do not have the power to return.) Flight from the world is not an option for those who seek to be authentically human, and in this respect the quest for self-transcendence, which is a component of Western thought (whether in consciously religious form, as in the Judeo-Christian tradition, or in apparent reaction against this in Marxism), is very different from the transcendence sought in the world of late Greek philosophy or in the religious philosophies of the Orient. Our drive for transcendence has content only when it remains anchored in history.

The fact that we who seek transcendence are subject to all of the limitations and conditions of human history was a somewhat late discovery in Catholic social thought (as in Catholic philosophy and exegesis), but since the Second Vatican Council, it has been extremely important in moving reflection on human dignity away from its earlier basis in natural law and toward the more theological view of the concrete conditions and limitations of individual and social life as the field in which transcendence is to be attained.

Origin of Our Drive for Transcendence

But where does this drive for transcendence come from? Almost by definition, this drive cannot originate *in* the individual, or in society, or in any part of the world. The desire for transcendence, whether clearly articulated or unreflectively experienced, is the desire to go beyond the confines of our earthly lives, and unless it is a cruel hoax, it must originate beyond the boundaries of the world and must find its source in no one other than God. To be a person is to be one who can hearken to a call—the call to know and love God as a partner in dialogue, as one who wants to share God's very own life with us.

In biblical terms, this call is rooted in the fact that we are made in the image and likeness of God, and in virtue of this fact, God finds in the human being a kind of counterpart who, like God, can know and love, be known and loved. This theme recurs constantly in the encyclical tradition, but it has undergone some important changes since the Second Vatican Council. Up to the time of the council (and therefore as late as the pontificate of John XXIII and *Pacem in terris*) the image of God was felt to consist in *reason* as the power to know the natural law. (Perhaps a better translation than "reason" would be "technical [or practical] *intelligence*"—the power to devise effective ways of attaining the ends and goals of human existence. The very fact that reason is thought of as a way of knowing the natural law was an unfortunate legacy of natural-law theory of the 16th to the 18th century and is very far from Thomas Aquinas' approach, which saw natural law as human intelligence itself, insofar as it has the power to perceive the ends and goals of human existence and to devise practical and effective means of attaining those goals.) But with the publication of *Gaudium et spes* in 1965, the accent shifted away from nature as an objective quantity and toward the human person as one constituted by the divine summons and call. The person is nothing other than the response to this call, and that drive for transcendence that reveals the human person and is constitutive of human dignity has its ground and basis in God's call.

Person and Community

The summons and call that is constitutive of the human person is not a call to live in isolation; it is a call to communion and community, to find ourselves in existing with and for others. (Of course, to point out that the person exists fully only in community is by no means to say that the person exists only *for* the community and that the interests of the person therefore can and must be subordinated to those of the community or the collective. Communities exist for the persons who are their members, and their purpose is the protection and promotion of human dignity.) We become persons in the act of responding to God and to other human beings and to the world, which is God's creation and which is the context in which we are called to live out our lives as persons—a context that is taken up into our personhood and can no longer be completely distinguished from it. This call to "personalize" nature is the basis of a theology of stewardship, of responsibility for the natural world. The world calls for a response, and we are responsible for the world, called to be spokespersons for the world. We are called to welcome the world into our own selves and to offer the world transcendence, to offer it a share in our knowledge, love, and freedom. The person is called to creative engagement and shared responsibility in the world, with and on behalf of other human beings. The person is called to participate in shaping society in such a way as to promote the well-being of its members, and it is in this act of participation that the essential dignity of the person is both achieved and revealed.

This emphasis on participation as a right and a duty, as creative and revealing of human dignity, is the most distinctive turn that Catholic social thought has taken since the Second Vatican Council, and it has made it possible to link the concern for individual political freedom, which has been traditional in the Western democracies, with the concern for what may be called "social" freedom in socialist states of many hues, ranging from those that favor democratic socialism to those committed to doctrinaire Marxism. Human rights discussions have often gridlocked because of the very different concepts of human dignity that underlie the concrete rights of men and women in society.

To put it simply, is human dignity protected and promoted by a "bill of rights" that guarantees political rights such as freedom of speech, freedom of assembly, freedom of religion, freedom from self-incrimination, and that limits the impact of the state on the individual to cases where concrete rights of third parties are actually being violated? Or is human dignity protected and promoted when the state guarantees certain economic and social rights such as the right to work, the right to medical care, the right to financial security in old age, so that freedom from want, freedom from economic oppression, freedom from the uncertainties and anxieties of a market economy, would take precedence?

In theory, these two kinds of rights are not mutually exclusive, and the Western democracies have in varying degrees achieved an acceptable balance of economic security and political freedom for many, and sometimes most, of their citizens. Socialist and Marxist states have not done well in securing and defending the basic political liberties for their citizens, and the events of 1990 demonstrated that the economic systems of these states were incapable of providing the degree of security and comfort that in the eyes of some could justify the subordination of political freedom. The development of the idea of participation in Catholic social thought since the end of the Second Vatican Council, together with a biblically based understanding of human freedom, can provide an effective way of reconciling both kinds of rights.

A Theological Perspective on Human Dignity

However, the concept of participation, and the biblical notion of freedom that stands behind it, while capable in the abstract of resolving the conflict between political and social rights seems to fail in the concrete by not specifying what it means for the individual to create the "authentic self," or what it means for society to create the "common good." It is this need for concreteness that has led to the final shift in Catholic social thought since the Second Vatican Council—the shift away from a natural-law ethic and toward a concept of human dignity that is overtly based on revelation and is therefore frankly theological. This is a very paradoxical shift, because it has occurred at the precise moment in history when the church has made clear its desire to engage in dialogue with non-Christians and with nonbelievers, and it would seem that the decision to ground the dignity of the person on events that are accessible only through revelation and that can therefore be possessed only in faith runs the risk of making such dialogue impossible. (This will be far less a problem in Christian-Jewish dialogue because of the common possession of what Christians refer to as the OT—a document that embodies at its highest point in the prophetic tradition a concern for justice and a concept of human dignity virtually unique in history.) How great a problem this is and what can be done to come to terms with it are questions we can raise only after a brief examination of what revelation has to say about the constitutive elements of human dignity.

The call to self-transcendence, which is constitutive of the human person and of human dignity, is a call to accept God's unconditional love and to be empowered in virtue of that love for love of others and for solidarity with them. (It is Paul who is most uncompromising in his assertion that God accepts us unconditionally and that we are saved by faith alone, who makes the strongest plea for human solidarity. See Rom 14 on not making the brother stumble and on appropriate conduct for the "strong" and the "weak.") According to the gospel tradition Jesus offered his Father's unconditional acceptance to those who had no right and no title to it on the basis of their obedience to religious law, and no hope of receiving it on the basis of their good works. It is a pure gift, an unconditioned offer, and Jesus defines faith in him as the act of letting him reveal this kind of God, of "letting God be this way," and of willingly accepting the new definition of ourselves and our task, which is consequent on such a redefinition of the word "God."

It is because God's offer of love and acceptance is absolute and unconditioned that the demand that we love one another has these same qualities. God's love is a gift of God's own self, and it is a gift in which we find our true selves and in which we experience the most fundamental mystery of life: that to exist is to exist for another. The demand to love one another is not an obligation consequent on God's love of us. It is a course of action for which we are liberated and empowered by God's love; it is an effect of that love, and it is not adequately distinguishable from that love.

To accept this love is to affirm our solidarity with others. It is to understand that we only possess ourselves in the act of being there for the other, and it is to live by the biblical dialectic of gaining and losing life in Mk 8:34-38. If we make ourselves the center of our world and use others as means to achieve (an illusory) security, then we will lose our real selves. But if we are willing to "lose" life by refusing to jealously safeguard it and instead put it on the line for others, then we will "gain" it, not holding it as a private possession but receiving it as a gift that we possess more fully in the act of giving. The call to this kind of solidarity is the deepest foundation of the dignity of the human person, and it transcends ideology by giving concreteness to human dignity.

What problems does this radically theological approach create for dialogue with non-Christians and nonbelievers? Perhaps fewer than would seem to be the case. Even after this turn to theology, Catholic social thought does not claim to find *answers* to the political, social, and economic problems of the day. It claims to find the ultimate ground and basis of human dignity in sources that are theological in the strict sense, but it is just as insistent that the concrete demands of dignity can be known, and the practical defense of dignity can be undertaken only by those who have the needed expertise in political science, economics, and the human sciences. But precisely for this reason the church cannot allow its message to be reduced to religious observances or counsels of individual piety. If the church believes, as it must, that it has been entrusted with a message that contains the uniquely valid solution to the problem of existence, then all who engage in dialogue with the church from outside of it have the right to hear this message proclaimed humbly but clearly, without arrogance but also without being muted in the interests of a false tolerance that would be nothing more than a veiled form of contempt for the partner in dialogue.

Dignity, Alienation, Estrangement

The idealism of Catholic social thought is obvious, but is this an idealism that can reasonably seek embodiment in the real world or an idealism divorced from life as we know it? Despite the very evident turn to the world signaled by the pontificate of John XXIII and the council he called into being, and despite the rejection of that hostility to the modern world that characterized most of the popes of the 19th century until (but not including) Leo XIII, the encyclical and conciliar traditions since *Rerum novarum* remain fully aware that human life is lived in a situation of alienation and estrangement and that we live in a world where sin has gotten a foothold and has stamped its destructive mark on individuals as well as on political, economic, and social structures.

Catholic social thought has not forgotten original sin, although this is a technical term that can be safely used only when demythologized. Adam and Eve were not two persons; they and their destiny are mythical symbols for factors that are universally true in the human situation—a situation characterized by estrangement from God, from the world, from other human beings, and from our own selves—an estrangement we ratify by our own choices.

There are structures in society that lead to neglect of and contempt for human rights and that are destructive of human dignity, and we find some of them singled out for mention at every stage of the encyclical tradition. Christian tradition has recognized that these structures are there and that they are the product of sin, which conspires to implicate new persons in the web of guilt; and the tradition was aware of this long before the rise of social consciousness in the church. (These structures were usually referred to as "occasions of sin," and it is true that the emphasis was generally individual and not social and that it often involved things as trivial as the violation of dietary laws.) But the fact that there are serious obstacles in the way of attaining human dignity does not mean that the Christian message should not be preached in its integrity, and it does not mean that it is futile to preach a message of hope, and this is the case for two reasons. First, the message in its integrity has not been preached that often, and we might ask if it has ever been given a chance; and second, Christian hope is eminently realistic and always aware of two things: that we need healing ("salvation," in the etymological sense of the word) in order to act rightly and well, and that such healing is always offered, always available.

In the final analysis, the social teaching of the church can never be *merely* a contribution to dialogue among men and women of good will. While being such a contribution it is also a call for faith, which is the acceptance of this healing, this salvation that touches not only the future but the present. The concrete demands of human dignity in the historical situation of the moment cannot be seen clearly without the commitment to love, which faith makes possible. (This faith may be implicit, and may be unable to make use of the words "God" or "Jesus Christ." It may, in other words, be the faith of the "anonymous Christian, who knows God only under one or another pseudonym, and who knows Jesus only in the absolute and unconditioned commitment to human values. Karl Rahner's essay "Anonymous Christians" in *Theological Investigations* 6 is excellent.) The basis of human dignity and the courses of action necessary to protect and promote that dignity can never be derived simply from the rational analysis of human nature in the abstract. We are historical animals;

we live in a world where estrangement is our destiny and our own doing; and we are called to a kind of love that is, in the strict sense, beyond our own power. Human dignity is of God and from God, and although many of its dimensions are accessible to the inquiring mind, its foundations are mysterious and therefore accessible only to faith, because it is in faith that the human person is fulfilled. Church teaching in the period since Vatican II has come to see this more clearly, and it is paradoxical but true that for this very reason the church is making a more significant contribution to dialogue on the question of human rights and human dignity than in the days when it restricted itself to the realm of natural law and philosophy.

See also DIGNITATIS HUMANAE; HUMAN RIGHTS; PERSONALISM; RIGHTS AND DUTIES; TOLERATION, PRINCIPLE OF; WORK, THEOLOGY OF.

Bibliography: Among the papal documents the most important for the concept of human dignity are Leo XIII's *Rerum novarum;* Pius XI's *Quadragesimo anno, Divini Redemptoris, Non abbiamo bisogno,* and *Mit brennender Sorge;* John XXIII's *Mater et magistra* and *Pacem in terris;* Paul VI's *Populorum progressio* and *Octogesima adveniens;* and John Paul II's *Laborem exercens* and *Sollicitudo rei socialis.* See also Pius XII's Christmas addresses of 1942 and 1944; the Vatican II documents *Gaudium et spes* and *Dignitatis humanae;* and the statement of the 1971 bishops synod, *Justitia in mundo* (*Justice in the World*); see also the U.S. bishops pastoral letter *Economic Justice for All: Catholic Social Teaching and the U.S. Economy.* (The pastoral message that precedes the letter is almost a summary of modern papal teaching on human dignity.) *Further secondary sources:* D. von Hildebrand, *Christian Ethics,* especially part 3, "Fundamental Aspects of the Sphere of Values" (New York: David McKay, 1953). J.-Y. Calvez and J. Perrin, *The Church and Social Justice,* especially chap. 5, "Person and Society" (Chicago: Henry Regnery, 1961). K. Rahner, *Theological Investigations:* vol. 2, "The Dignity and Freedom of Man" (1963); vol. 6, "Theology of Freedom" (1969); vol. 9, "Christian Humanism" (1972) (Baltimore: Helicon). W. Abbott, ed., *The Documents of Vatican II* (New York: Herder & Herder, 1966). D. Hollenbach, *Claims in Conflict* (New York: Paulist, 1979). K. Wojtyla, *The Acting Person* (Dordrecht, Holland: D. Reidel, 1979). J. Fuchs, *Christian Morality: The Word Becomes Flesh* (Washington: Georgetown Univ. Press, 1987). A. Carr, *Transforming Grace* (Harper & Row, 1990).

JOHN C. DWYER

PERSONALISM

Personalism is a social and philosophical movement that arose in the 19th century that placed great emphasis on the value of the person as the key notion that gives meaning to all of reality. Personalism should not be equated with all philosophical outlooks that affirm the dignity of the human person. Rather, it represents a movement made up of many thinkers who shared a common concern that the value of the human person was being overshadowed by the massive systems of technological society.

Personalists held that the modern world placed more emphasis on material development than on the spiritual man or woman. They sought to affirm the freedom and authentic spiritual nature of human life before the "mass society" of contemporary life. One of the best-known leaders of this movement was Emmanuel Mournier. In 1930 he began the review *Espirit,* which was dedicated to the publication of personalist ideals. These ideals were articulated as a reaction against the individualism of liberal capitalism and the collectivism of communism after the First World War. Contributors to this French review sought out new political, social, and ideological frameworks for grappling with the major social and economic problems of the depression in France.

This movement in its Catholic wing followed the breakaway from traditional monarchist leanings initiated by Leo XIII in *Rerum novarum* (1891) and Pius XI in *Quadragesimo anno* (1931). Its intellectualist circle also had a political wing in the *Troisieme Force,* organized to provide a radical alternative to capitalism and communism. Personalism can be linked to the revival of Thomism through thinkers such as Maritain and Gilson and to existentialism through the Russian intellectual and political philosopher Berdyayev. A non-Thomist movement in France, *Ordre nouveau* (1933), also was significant in the spread of personalism. Members sought to build an original philosophy that could integrate the interests of both communists and monarchists. These thinkers drew from many sources, such as Bergson and the German phenomenological writers Max Scheler and Martin Heidegger.

As an ideology personalism shared a set of values held more or less consciously by a broad spectrum of adherents. The strength of and interest in personalism did not rest primarily on its intellectual coherence but on its success as a cultural and political ideology.

See also EXISTENTIALISM; MARITAIN, JACQUES; PERSON, DIGNITY OF; QUADRAGESIMO ANNO; RERUM NOVARUM; SOCIALIZATION.

Bibliography: E. Mournier, *Personalism* (Notre Dame, Ind.: Univ. of Notre Dame Press, 1952). J. Maritain, *The Person and the Common Good,* trans. J. Fitzgerald (Notre Dame, Ind.: Univ. of Notre Dame Press, 1966).

JUDITH A. MERKLE, S.N.D.deN.

PESCH, HEINRICH

Heinrich Pesch, S.J., social philosopher and economist, was born September 17, 1854, in Köln (Cologne), Germany, and died April 1, 1926, in Valkenburg, the Netherlands. His father, an independent tailor, moved the family to the nearby university city of Bonn, where business and educational opportunities seem to have been more promising. Heinrich's brother, Tilmann (1836–99), had entered the Jesuit order and had become a recognized neo-Scholastic philosopher and theologian. After graduating from the Royal Gymnasium (classical high school) in Bonn, which provided him with a first class liberal arts education, Heinrich matriculated in the fall of 1872 at the Catholic theological faculty of the Royal Prussian Rhenish University of Bonn. After the first semester, however, he had his name removed from the register of the school of theology and entered the university's school of law, which included the "political" (social) sciences, in particular, economics. The real reason for this change, however, was evidently the fact that most of the faculty members of the school of theology had left the Roman Catholic church and had not only apostatized but were taking part in the creation of a schismatic sect, the so-called Old Catholics, in opposition to the newly declared dogma of papal infallibility. There was, in fact, no longer a Roman Catholic school of theology in Bonn.

Heinrich Pesch had a special liking for the science of law and the academic training of lawyers, especially in Roman law. It was here in the classrooms of the professors of law that Pesch became acquainted with the logical approach of jurisprudence, which conformed more-or-less rapidly to fact or reason. It was here that Pesch made his first contact with the social science of economics through able and recognized representatives of it. But shortly before he was to take the exams for admission to the practice of law or officeholder, Pesch decided to follow in the footsteps of his brother and applied for admission to the Society of Jesus.

Instead of reviewing the numerous stations of Pesch's vita—as a social thinker in the making, as a pioneer in a new phase of the development of Catholic social thought, especially in his emphasis on personhood and as a lodestar in this movement—we will restrict ourselves to some turning points, some sheet lightnings, if you will, that illuminate his basic social philosophy—his solidarism.

Pesch has never been known as one looking for errors, as one who enjoyed criticism for its own sake. But the Catholic literature on social questions left much to be desired: pamphlets, apologetic treatises—much was borrowed from the writers of the classical school, others were decidedly backward oriented, pleading for a return to the "good old times," particularly the precapitalistic, medieval era. They were lacking an objective, scholarly approach to social and economic problems of the time. For example, there were good and well-meaning authors who believed that the charging of interest was the root-evil of the modern competitive economic system. It is remarkable that Pesch, even before he had a chance to analyze in depth the present-day function of interest as a price for the use of potential capital, showed an amazing quasi-diagnostic instinct for what was to become an important issue in the confrontation between capitalism and Catholicism.

Pesch wrote a long essay in 1888 for the *Zeitschrift für Katholische Theologie* even before he was ordained. But more important is his two-volume *Liberalismus, Sozialismus, und christliche Gesellschaftsordnung* (liberalism, socialism, and Christian social order), which appeared in 1901. These two volumes are actually a prolegomenon, or prologue, to Pesch's magnum opus that was to come, his five-volume *Lehrbuch* of political economy, which is a comprehensive work summarizing the field of economics. It includes what Pesch considered typically missing in the existing standard works of what was called "principles of political economy"—its very fundamentals, its underlying axioms, postulates, and propositions. From then on, Pesch's life was one of research, looking for the missing link, the philosopher's stone, that which seemed to be lacking in the economic literature of the time. To examine all the steps he took, the summits from which he looked backward and forward, would go beyond the scope of this entry. To do so one would have to look up the appropriate literature, some of which is listed in the bibliography.

See also ECONOMIC ORDER; MATER ET MAGISTRA; NELL-BREUNING, OSWALD VON; POLITICAL PHILOSOPHY; QUADRAGESIMO ANNO; SOLIDARISM; SOLIDARITY.

Bibliography: F. Mueller, *Heinrich Pesch and His Theory of Christian Solidarism* (St. Paul: St. Thomas College Press, 1941). "Heinrich Pesch (1854–1926): Social Philosopher and Economist," *Jahrbuch fur Christliche Sozialwissenschaften,* vol. 18 (1977). R. Mulcahy, *The Economics of Heinrich Pesch* (New York: Holt, 1952). F. Mueller, *Heinrich Pesch, Sein Leben und seine Lebre* (Köln: Bachem, 1980).

FRANZ H. MUELLER

PIUS XI

Pius XI (Ambrogio Damiano Achille Ratti) was born May 31, 1857, in Desio, near Milan, Italy, and died in Vatican City February 10, 1939. Son of a factory manager, he was ordained priest after studies in Rome on December 27, 1879, and did graduate work there before becoming a professor in the Milan seminary (1882–88). From 1888 to 1918 he was a librarian, first at the Ambrosiana in Milan and after 1911 in the Vatican library, where he became prefect in 1914. By profession he was a palaeontologist and by avocation a mountain climber who dreamed of polar exploration.

He moved easily in the liberal Milanese society and won a reputation as a scholar in local church history. He traveled widely through central Europe, attended the international scholarly congresses in Fribourg (1897) and Munich (1900), and was familiar with some of the main figures in Italian modernism. In 1918, despite Ratti's lack of pastoral or diplomatic experience, Pope Benedict XV named him apostolic visitor to Poland, and in the next year he became titular archbishop of Lepanto and papal nuncio. He was in Warsaw in 1920 when Bolshevik armies threatened the city. As papal representative on the interallied plebiscite commission for Upper Silesia, he was caught up in Polish-German conflict, from which he was rescued by appointment in 1921 as archbishop of Milan and cardinal. Less than a year later he was elected pope, on February 6, 1922, in succession to Pope Benedict.

In a break from the self-imposed papal isolation observed by his four immediate predecessors, he gave the blessing *urbi et orbi* from the outside loggia of St. Peter's. He proved to be an activist pope, inspired by the vision of a new Christendom. Taking as his motto "the peace of Christ in the kingdom of Christ," he saw the solution to world problems in a religious renewal, the restoration of all things in Christ. This theme was echoed in his suspicion of the League of Nations and the "illusory peace" on which it was based; only the church offered a "true community of nations." In the encyclical *Ubi arcano* (December 23, 1922, on Catholic Action) he called for the participation of the laity in the work of the hierarchy and under their guidance and direction. The theme of Christ's kingdom was reemphasized in the letter *Quas primas* (December 11, 1925), establishing the feast of Christ the King, and underlined in jubilee years celebrated in 1925, 1929, and 1933 as well as in biennial eucharistic congresses.

Pius XI was unabashedly authoritarian, energetic, and decisive in the face of the cultural and political disillusionment and cynicism of the 1920s and 1930s. He faced up to the ongoing world economic crisis marked by famine in Russia, the financial collapse of Germany, the stock market crash, and the worldwide depression. The old enemy of secular liberalism was joined by modern statist totalitarians and Bolshevik world revolutionaries. Pope Pius responded in word and action. The encyclical *Divini illius magistri* (December 31, 1929) extended his spiritual vision of the kingdom to education, where he asserted the rights of parents and church against tendencies to state monopoly. *Casti connubii* (December 30, 1930) laid out an Augustinian doctrine on Christian marriage and, in obvious reply to the cautious approval given to contraception at the previous summer's Lambeth Conference, condemned all forms of artificial birth control. Three encyclicals addressed socioeconomic questions: *Quadragesimo anno* (May 15, 1931); *Nova impendet* (October 2, 1931); and *Caritate Christi* (May 3, 1932). The first of these reaffirmed Leo XIII's *Rerum novarum* and urged principles such as subsidiarity and organization of society along the corporative lines of medieval guilds (but not in the state-controlled style of Fascist Italy). *Nova impendet* discussed the unemployment crisis and the arms race, while *Caritate Christi* stressed that the answer to the world crisis was a religious one and called for love, prayer and penance, and devotion to the Sacred Heart of Jesus.

Pius XI's diplomatic initiatives were of a piece with his world vision. He sought concordats with the nations, as agreements between "if not two states, most certainly two sovereignties in the fullest sense," of which the religious nature of the church gave it "absolute superiority" over the state. Relations with France, ruptured since 1904, were reestablished. The Lateran Pacts were signed with Italy in 1929, ending the vexing Roman Question. The pope recognized the existence of the kingdom of Italy and Rome as its capital; Vatican City State was created, the pope was indemnified for the loss of the Papal States, and Catholicism became the official religion of Italy. Fascist interference in Catholic Action, particularly in the education and activities of youth, provoked the encyclical *Non abbiamo bisogno* (June 29, 1931), a defense of a Catholic movement "outside and above every political party," but relative calm ensued until the fall of 1938, when anti-Semitic activity imitating that in Germany again provoked papal wrath. The pope was planning a letter on the unity of the human race and against racialism when he died.

When the church was persecuted in republican Spain and in Mexico, Pope Pius spoke out strongly, calling the Mexican action "a Diocletian persecution" (*Iniquis afflictisque,* 1926). In the case of Nazi Germany, he first sought accommodation with a concordat (July 20, 1933), which effectively killed once-powerful political Catholicism in the Reich, but after repeated violations of the agreement, he condemned the Nazis in *Mit brennender Sorge*

(March 14, 1937), an encyclical read from German pulpits on Palm Sunday. In it the pope denounced the regime, with its theories of race, people, and state, as fundamentally anti-Christian. His main ire he reserved for the Marxist regime of the Soviet Union. He dispatched a famine relief mission to Russia in the early 1920s and followed it with several efforts to establish religious jurisdictions within the former Russian Empire, but in *Divini Redemptoris* (March 19, 1937) he condemned the Soviets for their atheism, philosophical materialism, doctrine of the inevitability of class struggle, denial of the right of private property, autocratic use of state power, and state terrorism.

In interreligious matters Pius XI's stance was clear. Those of other religions must "convert" to Catholicism; other Christians must "return" to Rome. He instructed the Jesuits in 1937 to begin a widescale mission to Islam, and moved to consolidate Catholic positions among Arab Christians. A Russian College and a Ruthenian College were established in Rome, and the work of the Pontifical Oriental Institute furthered. An Ethiopian College was set up within the confines of Vatican City. Although he allowed the Anglican-Roman Catholic Malines Conversations (1921–26) to continue, his attitude toward the growing ecumenical movement was negative. Catholic participation was forbidden. "Return to the one true church of Christ" was the only way to foster Christian unity, "for from that one true church other Christians have in the past fallen away" (*Mortalium animos,* January 6, 1928).

In other areas Pius XI promoted the natural sciences, reorganized the Pontifical Academy of Sciences (1936), and moved the Vatican Observatory to new quarters at Castel Gandolfo. With Marconi's help he began Vatican Radio in 1931. Theological developments during his pontificate were few and carefully controlled. Pope Pius XI died just as Europe was entering its last year of peace before the cataclysm of World War II began.

See also ANTI-SEMITISM; BIRTH CONTROL; COMMUNISM; CORPORATISM; FASCISM; MARRIAGE; MODERN CATHOLIC SOCIAL THOUGHT; QUADRAGESIMO ANNO.

Bibliography: D. Binchy, *Church and State in Fascist Italy, 1870–1931* (Oxford Univ. Press, 1970). C. Falconi, *The Popes in the Twentieth Century* (Boston: Little Brown, 1967). P. Hughes, *Pope Pius XI* (New York: Sheed & Ward, 1937). A. Rhodes, *The Vatican in the Age of the Dictators, 1922–1945* (New York: Holt, Rinehart & Winston, 1974).

JAMES HENNESEY, S.J.

PIUS XII

Eugenio Maria Pacelli was born on March 2, 1876. His paternal grandfather had been an administrator in the Papal States under Pius IX; his father Filippo was a lawyer who practiced in the papal courts. Eugenio was ordained to the priesthood in May 1899, studied civil and ecclesiastical law, and then began work in the Congregation for Extraordinary Ecclesiastical Affairs. He assisted in the codification of canon law and in 1917 was consecrated an archbishop and sent as papal nuncio to Munich. In 1920 he was made nuncio to Germany and in 1925 took up residence in Berlin. His exposure to the side effects of the Bolshevik revolution in Weimar Germany and the rise of fascism and nazism shook him deeply and affected his social vision. In 1929 he was recalled to Rome, where he participated in the final negotiations for the Lateran Treaties. In December he became a cardinal; in February 1930 he became secretary of state. As one of Pius XI's closest associates, he had a hand in shaping the pontiff's critique of totalitarian social systems and contributed to the documents *Mit brennender Sorge, Non abbiamo bisogno, Nos es muy,* and *Divini Redemptoris.* On March 2, 1939, he was elected to succeed Pope Pius XI in the shortest conclave of modern times. He reigned as pope until his death at Castel Gandolfo on October 9, 1958.

Unlike his predecessors and successors, Pius XII never issued a major social encyclical. Perhaps this was due to his diplomatic background, which avoided strong ideological statements and preferred compromise. Moreover, the recent promulgation of *Quadragesimo anno* may have made it unnecessary. However, he contributed directly to the growing body of teaching on the social question in some of the 1,367 allocutions and addresses he delivered in his eighteen-year pontificate. In his public discourse that related to the social question he reiterated and underscored the key principles of *Rerum novarum* and *Quadragesimo anno*. Indeed, it was in these forums that the term "the social teaching of the church" was actually used for the first time by a pope.

His primary contribution to social teaching is to be found in his famous peace program, announced in a series of Christmas addresses from 1939 to 1942. Moreover, his encyclicals *Mystici Corporis Christi* (1943) and *Mediator Dei* (1947) indirectly reinforced the social agenda of his pontificate.

The challenges of Pius XII's pontificate were fascist totalitarianism, war, and communism. Naturally then, issues of economic justice and the rights of labor were subordinated to diagnosing the breakdown of world order and proposing solutions for its reconstruction. In addressing this, he drew from the wellspring of the corporatist social thinking used by Leo XIII and Pius XI but applied these principles to the international community. The horror of the war, he argued, was brought on by the collectivism of the totalitarian regimes and the excessive individualism of capitalism, especially manifested in the colonialism of the Western democracies. Both of these systems, by their neglect of natural law and the principle of human solidarity, had plunged the world into darkness. In his Christmas messages of 1939–42 the pope expressed his hope that the new world order that would emerge from the ruins of war would be built not on the shifting sands of pragmatism or power politics but on the rock of the objective norms of the natural law. In 1939 the pontiff repeated the five norms for international order that had been proclaimed by Benedict XV at the outbreak of World War I. This papal peace plan was amplified in successive Christmas addresses, culminating with the message of 1942 wherein Pius laid out "five fundamental points for the order and pacification of human society." These were the dignity and rights of the human person; defense of social unity and especially of the family in principle; the dignity and prerogatives of labor; the rehabilitation of the juridic order; and the conception of the state according to the Christian spirit.

Local hierarchies, eager to have their voices heard in postwar reconstruction plans, used these ideas as lobbying points with their respective governments. For example, imitating developments in England, the bishops of the United States established a committee in 1941 to publicize the papal peace plan. Even though Pearl Harbor plunged the United States into active participation in the World War, the bishops, under the leadership of Samuel Cardinal Stritch of Chicago, worked diligently to influence the decisions of the Roosevelt administration. It published two works (*Principles on Peace* and *A World to Reconstruct*) and lent substantial support to the Atlantic Charter and efforts to establish a United Nations organization. Pius XII favored the United Nations as a sign of international solidarity for the peace of the world, though later he modified his support in view of the Russian use of the veto on the Security Council. In the last analysis, the United Nations proved to be a disappointment because it did not insist on the juridical basis for peace and world order envisioned by Pius XII.

The postwar period gave Pius XII no respite from concerns for social justice as the threat of communist takeovers of Europe loomed large. Pius XII actively intervened in the Italian elections of 1947 to assure a communist defeat. As the forties closed and the fifties dawned, the pontiff's anticommunist rhetoric sharpened especially after the communist victory in China and the persecution of Catholicism manifest in the show trials of Cardinals Aloysius Stepinac of Belgrade, Yugoslavia; Joseph Mindszenty of Budapest, Hungary; and Josef Beran of Prague, Czechoslovakia. His efforts against communism in Italy and in Eastern Europe were warmly applauded in the United States, which was caught up in the throes of cold war fears and a "Red scare." The United States government and the American hierarchy funneled money secretly to the pontiff to aid in the defeat of the Italian Communists in 1947. The pope's visible friendship with the staunchly anticommunist Francis Cardinal Spellman seemed an affirmation of American efforts to contain communist expansion in Europe and Asia. However, the pontiff was never really a warm admirer of American capitalism, although the American church contributed greatly to Vatican causes, especially the missions.

An aligned cold-war issue, the proliferation of atomic weaponry, also drew a response from the pontiff. Soon after the destruction of Hiroshima and Nagasaki, Pius XII reiterated earlier pleas for disarmament and warned periodically of the terrible consequences of atomic warfare. He continued to apply the traditional principles of the just-war theory to the question of nuclear weapons, but he began to realize that the destructive potential of these devices might require a whole new calculation of moral principles.

Indirectly important in the work of social issues was the issuance of the encyclicals *Mystici Corporis Christi* (1943) and *Mediator Dei* (1947). *Mystici Corporis Christi* underscored the ecclesiology of the mystical body of Christ, a popular concept with Catholic social activists. In stressing the organic nature of the church, Pius enhanced the role of the laity as active agents for social reform. By describing the layperson as "minister Christi" the pope significantly expanded the notion of the lay apostolate and the necessity of lay involvement in the reconstruction of society. Lay activists in many nations could easily march under the banner of papal teaching as they worked to better social conditions in their respective countries.

Mediator Dei's call for "prudent" liturgical reform and the renewal of Holy Week ceremonies in 1955 also reinforced the corporatist worldview of Catholic social teaching and heartened some elements of the international liturgical movement that had made a linkage between liturgical reform and the reconstruction of the social order.

Pius XII was not always favorable to certain aspects of social activism. For example, although Catholic social thinkers had contributed significantly to the rise of the welfare state in many European countries, Pius XII was generally negative to these "statist" encroachments on the rights of church and family. Moreover, he expressed serious concerns about the involvement and activity of priests in social issues. This was best reflected when he was confronted with the phenomenon of the so-called worker priests of France, established from the Mission de Paris by Emmanuel Cardinal Suhard. The worker priests made efforts to reevangelize the disaffected working classes of France by sharing directly in their work and daily struggles. In 1951 the Vatican slowed the recruitment of worker priests, and the apostolic exhortation *Menti Nostrae* (1950) reflected Pius XII's suspicions of the secularizing effects this experiment was having on the priesthood. Although he would not crush the movement outright, as Pope John XXIII would do, Pius XII and his curial advisors hemmed it in by restrictions and made it difficult for the group to operate.

Like so many of Pius XII's initiatives during his eighteen-year pontificate, his social teaching bore fruit in any number of developments after his death. Pacelli's social teaching provided an important bridge between the work of Leo XIII and Pius XI and the writings of John XXIII, Paul VI, and John Paul II as well as those of Vatican II.

See also ARMS RACE; CHRISTIAN DEMOCRACY; COMMUNISM; CORPORATISM; EVIL, SOCIAL; FASCISM; GENOCIDE; HOLOCAUST, THE; HUMAN RIGHTS; LAITY, ROLE OF; LEO XIII; MARITAIN, JACQUES; PIUS XI; RERUM NOVARUM; QUADRAGESIMO ANNO; SOLIDARISM; TOTALITARIANISM; WAR; WORKER PRIESTS.

Bibliography: J. Holmes, *The Papacy in the Modern World* (New York, 1981). R. Pollock, ed., *The Mind of Pius XII* (New York, 1955). R. Camp, *The Papal Ideology of Social Reform* (Leiden, 1969). V. Yzermans, *Major Addresses of Pope Pius XII,* 2 vols. (St. Paul, 1961). G. Gonella, *A World to Reconstruct,* T. Bouscaren, trans. (Milwaukee, 1944).

STEVEN M. AVELLA

PLURALISM

The recognition of the legitimacy of philosophical and theological pluralism is of recent occurrence and still in inchoate form in Roman Catholic thought. During its neo-Scholastic period Catholic intellectual life was shaped by presuppositions of an absolute worldview and a definitive conceptual system, and pluralism was accordingly understood as relativism. Since the Second Vatican Council, however, the acknowledgment of valid pluralism has been slowly emerging in Catholic thought.

Recently some moral theologians have used the term "pluralism" to mean dissent from official Catholic teaching. But a fuller, more adequate understanding is also found in contemporary theological literature: disparate viewpoints and conceptualizations (e.g., hermeneutical and transcendental methods) that are complementary although not subsumable into some higher, all-comprehensive logical system. Thus while there have always been differences and debates within Catholic theology, pluralism has to do with differences that are irreducible and, in this sense, beyond debate. It is present, scholars recognize, in the NT itself.

As affecting morality, it is found to some extent in the U.S. bishops' recent expansion of Catholic teaching on war, placing pacifism as an alternative individual moral option alongside the traditional just-war attitude (*The Challenge of Peace* 111–21), as well as in Paul VI's refusal to attempt specific social teaching that would constitute a universally valid solution to worldwide problems (*Octogesima adveniens* 4). Ultimately pluralism is rooted in the human person's radical finiteness: the human mind is unable to construct an exhaustive, unsurpassable conceptualization of creation or of God's self-disclosure within it.

See also CHURCH, SOCIAL MISSION OF; CULTURE; GAUDIUM ET SPES; INCULTURATION; METHODOLOGY, MORAL; NATURAL LAW; OCTOGESIMA ADVENIENS.

NORBERT J. RIGALI, S.J.

POLITICAL PHILOSOPHY

Catholic social teaching has been developed during a period of intense ideological conflict both in Europe and in the Third World. It has also had to situate itself in relationship to various traditions in political philosophy. Among these are Thomism and natural-law theory, which provide its roots; liberalism and Marxist communism, which have provided its most significant intellectual challenges; and conservatism and nationalism, with which it has shared some significant values but which it has often been impelled to criticize. The literary form of papal encyclicals, conciliar decrees, and pastoral letters that has expressed Catholic social teaching favored a type of exposition that relied on general philosophical modes of argumentation, which avoided the concreteness of specific cases and historical examples and which usually formulated broad policy preferences without venturing into specific details. It also avoided the complexities and ironies of modernist and postmodernist ways of formulating the demands and perplexities of political life.

The fact that the authoritative documents of Catholic social teaching express and inform the conscience of a religious community that is also a transnational political actor and is simultaneously present in many different societies means that the documents are to be read as part of a continuing tradition that feels the responsibility to be present within many different social contexts. It is misleading to regard the documents as strictly comparable to the treatises of individual political philosophers or to the manifestos and documents of political movements. Neither political effectiveness nor theoretical consistency is the primary criterion for assessing these documents. They are not themselves works of philosophy in the strict sense, though they are more reflective and general than most examples of current political argument and comment. They draw on a variety of secular sources (usually unacknowledged) in a somewhat eclectic fashion. So they need to be interpreted as part of a dialogue with the major political philosophies and movements of the modern and contemporary periods.

The major documents have a certain family resemblance that allows for both continuity and divergence. They are best seen as efforts to articulate a balance of social values (including rights, goals, and institutions) that will be in continuity with the developing Catholic tradition and will be responsive to the needs of the faithful and of the larger society, which the church serves and evangelizes (see *Gaudium et spes* 40–45). In comparison with most forms of secular political philosophy, Catholic social teaching aims to maintain a broadly comprehensive position; thus it normally affirms values that are often felt to be in conflict. Like Aquinas and Aristotle, Catholic social teaching affirms the political and social nature of the human person (John XXIII, *Pacem in terris* 46). It understands law as the work of reason intended to lead human beings to the common good (Thomas Aquinas, *Summa theologiae* I-II 90, 4) and to the goal of eternal salvation. It thus differs fundamentally from secularist and materialist theories that deny the transcendent orientation and the religious vocation of the human person, while it also differs from liberal theories that see the state as drawing its legitimacy only from consent or a social contract and from positivistic theories of law that make law dependent on either will or force. The state is a natural institution and derives its authority from God (PT 46, 78). In the 19th century papal teaching had denied the right of the oppressed to revolt against unjust governments (Leo XIII, *Immortale Dei* 31). In the 20th century, however, Catholic social teaching has taught the responsibility of the governors to the governed and has expressed strong support for the values of a democratic polity (PT 74). It thus moved away from the traditional Scholastic view that regarded the question about the best form of government as undecidable (*Immortale Dei* 4), and it gave up the church's earlier acceptance of the alliance of throne and altar.

Catholic social teaching has relied on an anthropology that strongly affirmed the dignity of the human person on both philosophical and theological grounds but that also acknowledged human ignorance and sinfulness and therefore the human need for governmental authority and for limits in the exercise of power (GS 11–20; 37–39). It thus opposed pessimism and nihilism on the one hand and utopianism and the myth of progress on the other. In contrast to racism and extreme forms of nationalism, it has affirmed both the unity of the human race and the equal dignity of all human persons. Especially in *Pacem in terris* the church accepted a comprehensive view of human rights, which included both the civil and political rights advocated by the liberal tradition and the social and economic rights proclaimed by Marxism (Hollenbach).

At the same time, church teaching on the role of women has affirmed the view that women have a special responsibility for the rearing of children and for the stability of the family as a source of moral and religious values (GS 47–52). In this as in other areas, Catholic social teaching shows a conservative reluctance to reconstruct fundamental social institutions to fit either an abstract norm of political theory such as equality or the demands of current political and social movements such as feminism or neo-Malthusian population planning or environmentalism.

Catholic social teaching, however, during the period since Vatican II, has given more attention to assessing and responding to "the signs of the times." This reflects a methodological turn from a reliance on fixed categories taken from law and philosophy to a more biblical and historical approach (Hollenbach, pp. 69–77). This turn allows for a greater responsiveness to major social changes and to the cultural diversity that marks a world church, even though it co-exists uneasily with a more deductive approach that supports immutable affirmations of the natural character of social institutions and of the exceptionless character of moral norms. This turn also reflects the fact that Catholic social teaching originally focused on the problems and conflicts produced by the rise of industrial capitalism in Europe and North America; after John XXIII issued *Mater et magistra* in 1961, it became increasingly concerned with problems of development in the Third World and with international cooperation and conflict conceived in the broadest terms.

Catholic social teaching has been consistently universalist and internationalist (PT 130–45). This takes it beyond the preoccupation of most political philosophy with the construction and legitimacy of the nation-state. It has affirmed both the urgent need for an international political authority to protect the common good and the continued legitimacy of the just war (GS 77–84). In its more recent statements it has opposed the use of new technologies of warfare when these are directed against population centers, and it has recognized the great value of nonviolent means of conflict resolution (*The Challenge of Peace* 147–48, 71–78). It has also affirmed the right of conscientious objectors to refuse to participate in war, a move that reverses the earlier teaching of Pius XII and that protects individual conscience against state authority (GS 79). The church in this century has rejected both the theory and the practice of total war, even as it has also rejected those totalitarian ideologies and political theories that called for the radical subordination of all social institutions to the state or to the revolutionary party.

Catholic social teaching has argued against both the totalitarian repression of internal conflict within the state and the Marxist view that class conflict is both inevitable and appropriate (Leo XIII, *Rerum novarum* 19). It has insisted on the principle of subsidiarity, which mandates the determination of policies at lower and more local levels, where those affected by decisions can make their voices heard (Pius XI, *Quadragesimo anno* 79–80; John XXIII, *Mater et magistra* 53; PT 140–41). This supports efforts to resist the centralizing tendency of the unitary state without endorsing strong forms of individualism; it is particularly congenial to a federal political system and to mediating structures at levels between individual and state. Catholic social teaching has opposed the tendency in liberation theology to accept the Marxist advocacy of class struggle; on the contrary, it has insisted on the need to reshape economic institutions so that they effectively serve the common good and foster human rights. It thus attempts to maintain space for criticism of government, even while it denies the legitimacy of conflict.

In its more recent statements, particularly in those addressed to Latin America, church teaching has affirmed a special concern for the poor, the marginalized, and the oppressed—a "preferential option for the poor" (Eagleson and Scharper, eds., Final Document, part 4, chap. 1, nos. 1134–65, in *Puebla and Beyond*). This concern, which is strongly rooted in the Bible, requires that the poor be seen not as abstract individuals but as shaped by historical processes so that they face special difficulties in achieving recognition of their human dignity. They are not to be regarded as objects of compassion or charity but as subjects of a new stage of history and participants in a new kind of church community. This option for the poor is not an endorsement of Marxism, but it requires a commitment to correct systemic and structural injustices. It also exemplifies the existentialist emphasis on choice and identification in our political life and the fundamental importance of the recognition of injustice as a basic step in the beginning of our political reflection.

In opposition to Marxism and other forms of socialism, Catholic social teaching has consistently maintained the right of people to hold private property, including property used for the production and distribution of goods (RN 5–15). It has seen the institution of private property as a protection of personal freedom and security against the power of the state and as something justly earned rather than as a source of greater economic productivity. But it has also maintained that the right to private property can be overridden by the common good, and that public or national ownership of certain industries is not inherently unacceptable. The right to private property does not bring with it an absolute freedom in disposing of material goods but is held subject to certain moral obligations. Developing a position taken by the Stoics and Cicero, Catholic social teaching has held that material goods are to be used to provide for the survival and welfare of all. This common purpose of material things can authorize the taking of private property in an emergency, but it can also be used to criticize existing economic systems and distributional patterns (GS 69; Paul VI, *Populorum progressio* 22). While not explicitly pronouncing on this matter, Catholic social teaching is much closer to Rawles' concern about the justice of end-state distributions than to Nozick's reliance on a history of just transactions (Langan). It is more clear in denouncing the injustice of situations in which the basic needs of the poor are not met than it is in recommending either principles of redistribution or comprehensive economic programs, though Paul VI did urge contributions to a World Fund aimed at meeting the needs of the poorest in developing countries (PP 51).

Catholic social teaching, especially in the period since 1965, has moved away from formulations that would suggest a theocratic conception of the state. The liberty of the church to proclaim the gospel, to manage its internal affairs without state interference, and to comment publicly on moral and religious aspects of political and social life is strongly affirmed, as it has usually been since the struggle of the medieval papacy against the Holy Roman Empire. But Catholicism now also acknowledges religious liberty as a universal human right, and so it has to accept a limited place for itself in the public forum, just as it also has to lower its religious expectations for the state. Since the church believes that it is an integral part of religious liberty for it to advocate its moral teachings (the principal elements of which it believes to be obligatory for all human beings), it continues to be involved in many areas of controversy, especially where public policy affects family life and moral norms governing sexuality. In these areas the church and its teaching are more conservative, not simply in the sense of adhering to traditional values but also in the sense of rejecting liberal conceptions of privacy and autonomy.

Catholic social teaching, then, is not to be identified with any one form of political philosophy, though it has clearly learned from liberalism with regard to its teaching on human rights, religious freedom, democracy, and the limited power of the state and from Marxism with regard to work, social conflict, and the dangers of encouraging an apolitical, otherworldly passivity. At the same time it opposes significant elements in both systems. Its historical affinities are in many ways with conservatism, though it resists irrationalism, racism, totalitarianism, the neglect of the poor, military rule, and other evils that have often been associated with conservative or reactionary regimes. It is committed to the exercise of reason rather than to a particular theory, to the worth of the individual rather than to individualism, and to a serious effort to integrate human rights and the major institutions of society within the framework of the common good. More clearly than the particular political philosophies that it learns from and criticizes, Catholic social teaching, especially in the period since Vatican II, exhibits both the breadth of the moral demands within contemporary society and the constructive and revolutionary tensions that this range of demands imposes on the Western moral and religious tradition.

See also COMMON GOOD; DEMOCRACY; HUMAN RIGHTS; LIBERATION THEOLOGY; MARXISM; NATURAL LAW; PACEM IN TERRIS; POOR, PREFERENTIAL OPTION FOR; TOTALITARIANISM.

Bibliography: D. Hollenbach, *Claims in Conflict* (New York: Paulist, 1979). National Conference of Catholic Bishops, *The Challenge of Peace* (Washington: United States Catholic Conference, 1983). J. Eagleson and P. Scharper, eds., *Puebla and Beyond* (Maryknoll, N.Y.: Orbis, 1979). J. Langan, "Rawles, Nozick, and the Search for Social Justice," *Theological Studies* 38 (1977).

JOHN LANGAN, S.J.

POLITICAL THEOLOGY

If theology does not wish to conduct its discussion of God past the public and private conflicts of the present, it must get involved in social conflicts and disagreements, whether implicit or explicit. The Enlightenment is a precisely classical paradigm for the occurrence and processing of such social conflicts and disagreements. It not only contributed to the fact that the so-called modern world came about as a making possible of greater freedom and a place for realization of human rights but has also become a world of the questioning of the human future in general, and within that the threatening of the rights of freedom and human rights within different states and societies as well as in the life of the individual. Where Enlightenment is inherited or derived undialectically, it necessarily turns against its own best intentions. Theology that is critically concerned with the Enlightenment will therefore also have to transcend it. Thus the significance of communicative reason elaborated in the most recent philosophical discussion still proves to be inadequate for stemming instrumental (technical) reason: only through the power of memory (as *anamnestic* reason therefore) will communicative reason become practical in the interests of human freedom and be able to preserve the "living world" from an ever-wider extension of the "system world." The insight that Christianity is not primarily a community of argumentation but one of remembrance and recounting therefore has crucial importance for the salvation of modern reason. Only remembrance protects against an ahistorical concept of rationality and prevents the disintegration of human action into the process of evolution.

Through the divergence between religion and society, between religious and social existence, that became manifest in the Enlightenment, the Christian religion appears for the first time as particular in relation to its social environment. Its claim of universality thereby is shown to be contingent on history. The religious criticism of the Enlightenment, and later of Marxism, starts immediately from this problem by formulating religious criticism as ideological criticism; that is, it attempts to expose religion as an ideological superstructure over certain social balances of power. Theology that wishes to answer this criticism must necessarily also consider the social implications of its ideas and terms. Only if the social constitution of theological reason in theology itself (and not only in so-called "auxiliary sciences") is borne in mind can religion counter the suspicion of ideology raised against it.

Considering the recent social and philosophical developments and as a corrective to an individualistically restricted understanding of faith, a "new political theology" has been developed in the 1960s in Europe. Its creation and systematic unfolding are connected in the area of the Catholic church and theology with the name of Johann Baptist Metz and in the evangelical area with the names Dorothee Sölle and Jürgen Moltmann. Liberation theology and feminist theology must first be understood against the background of political theology. Despite varying emphases, all forms are united in understanding "history" and "society" as fundamental features of theological thinking and taking them seriously. The catastrophe of Auschwitz has outstanding significance in this, which forbids for all time to come the study of theology with our backs turned to history's suffering people.

In its joint sociocritical and theologico-critical aims, political theology is therefore above all marked by two basic insights that have not been examined either in traditional systematic theology or with the categories of previous Christian social ethics.

The first insight consists of the social constitution of theological reason. Theological concepts are not "pure" concepts (that is, not ahistorical or asocial concepts), and even theological truth is not without interests. This is not a deficiency at all, since the recognition of this insight is a necessary prerequisite for relating questions of the truth and relevance of Christian faith. The choices are not pure theology or a mixture of theological and social knowledge. Instead it must be decided whether theology conceals the social constitution of its concepts from itself or attempts to create an awareness of them. To the extent that systematic theology takes on this task, it cannot delegate reflection of actual social conditions that may possibly have to be changed to a social ethics or practical theology—and that for the sake of its own identity! It would otherwise immediately block its own access to the argumentative working out of this original insight—precisely into the social constitution of theological reason. Theological theories do not develop independently of, and unaffected by, social developments and intellectual trends. The spirit of the particular age is reflected in them, consciously or not; their concepts and statements are marked by conditions which theology does not create itself and from which it cannot remove itself at will.

The second insight lies in the essentially sociopolitical content of the Christian gospel itself: the "mortal" trial between Jesus and the social authorities of his time is a constant trial between his eschatological message from the kingdom of God and our sociopolitical public; in it the NT promises of peace, freedom, justice, reconciliation, cannot simply be privatized but authorize the critical freedom of the individual from society—in opposing all existing unjust conditions and in working for more freedom and justice. The social actions of Christians cannot be understood, however, as an "application" of their prior (outside of history and society as it were) existing and confirmed faith; rather, in the moral and social practice of Christians the truth of the faith itself—and not only its preservation—is at stake. In view of the development of Christianity and its public relevance up to the late Middle Ages, denial of these facts would be cavalier. On the contrary, a nonpolitical, privatized understanding of faith can be shown to be a creature of modern religious history or an attempt to disguise the effectiveness of a socially adapted political religion. And if today the new practice of the faith made possible by the promise of the kingdom of God, and therefore if conversion and imitation, love of neighbor and love of enemy, solidarity with the poor, helpless, and persecuted privileged by Jesus, are not principles for the formation of a really existing social order, they must still, however, be brought to bear as categories of resistance to ruling social practice or at least be pursued. Otherwise what defined and even theologically definable content would the word "faith" still have?

If traditional systematic theology and especially the new Scholastic type of Catholic social doctrine do not offer any starting points for the two insights, then the question arises for the future of whether such a form of society-related theology can still be understood in the context of current theological disciplines and its various branches. This ultimately depends on the ability of these disciplines to change. In any event, this basic starting point for a politicotheological hermeneutics, which involves all theology, is not a matter of a "replacement" or a "supplement" but of a critical corrective. The partition into a philosophically reasoning Christian social ethics (more specifically founded in natural law) and a theologically reasoning dogmatics has at least strengthened the impression as though social and Christian practice involve two different areas. But both awareness of the social constitution of theological reason and the search for impetus from faith for social dealings and for the political content of the Christian gospel itself have been systematically lost from sight.

Connected with this initial stage there is a redetermination of the relationship between theory and practice in theology, a relationship guided by the primacy of practice. All previous distinctions fundamental to Catholic social doctrine and its relationship to systematic theology are based on the two concepts of reason and faith: natural law and revelation, philosophical social ethics and social theology, worldly well-being and eternal salvation, liberation and redemption, social injustice and sin, social criticism and the church's mission. If such distinctions also have their limited justification of drawing attention to the remaining difference between the kingdom of God and every political order, and therefore opposing any attempt at impermissible identifications, they are not sufficient as an initial stage for determining Christian identity in society. Besides, reason and faith (like natural law and revelation as their sources) designate two forms of knowledge as "theoretical knowledge." In opposition to this knowledge, "practice" is taken to be a derived function; it contains of course impetus for new knowledge and is intended to follow from that knowledge as "application" of such knowledge but has no cognitive position in itself. Christian knowledge is not, however, purely theoretical knowledge; nor is it theological knowledge in the narrower sense. Political theology therefore shifts the distinction of reason and faith into the relationship between theory and practice or, more precisely, into a dialectics between theory and practice. As Christian imitation is not the subsequent practice of a preceding faith (as if the disciples of Jesus had first believed him and then imitated him) but simply faith, so too the knowledge of imitation is determined practically: "Only imitating him, Christians know whom they are dealing with and who is saving them" (J.B. Metz). Those who think they can first "only" think the faith and take a "faith activity" from it and then assign it a derived and indeed subordinate function have missed a comprehensive understanding of faith and suppressed the cognitive position of imitation.

Thus the dialectics of the theory and practice of theological knowledge is also connected to the idea of the double religious/political constitution of Christian imitation. For just as knowledge of imitation acquired by way of "pure theory" remains divided, imitation limited to individual moral practice is also divided. Moral practice is individual and social practice, and in this dual structure it is a part of the double religious/political constitution of Christian imitation. This distinction in the idea of moral practice binds individual and social actions together and also points up a remaining difference between the two: individual moral action is never fully integrated into social practice, and social practice remains ethically determined.

This division of theological knowledge and Christian imitation is now surmounted by a dialectics of theory and practice in such a way that the primacy of practice applies to both. Thus the ethical certainty of social practice is removed from a purely theoretical founding connection (which does not mean that it remains unfounded and also has nothing to do with antagonism to theory). As the term "primacy of practice" already indicates, this involves a hierarchy. And if the intelligible power (or cognitive rank) of practice is the question, this stresses the meaning and relative value of theoretical work in theology. As a theory it has its place between practice and practice. This of course breaks up a monopoly in academic (university) theology. Room is created for new subjects and areas for theological activity. For the church's social preaching, this means that it cannot be used at all in a primarily doctrinaire manner and only by its functionaries. The primary subjects of Christian practice in society as a theology under the primacy of practice are Christians themselves, and the primary area for such a theology is the social basis of Christianity. Only as a question about the basis is the unity of the subject of faith, the subject of ecclesiastical activity, and the subject of theology reached in the question of the subject.

In addition, there will always have to be social preaching taught by the church so that the ethical aims preceding experience that are acquired from the revelation as insights of faith also enter into ethical reflection, and the danger of ideologization of group interests is avoided. But as the task of the church's social preaching cannot consist in presenting or even realizing an overall model of the ideal social order, the task of social Christian ethics cannot lie in the drafting of an overall theory of social order. For Christian practice is subject to constant change, and a theory of social changes better corresponds to its sociocritical certainty. "Theory" must also be understood in an open, that is, unconcluded, sense, and for two reasons.

First, such a theory cannot formulate either constants that are ahistorical and independent of society or abstract principles of change that precede the social areas of the changes and can be placed "above" concrete postulates. It would then eliminate the dialectics of theory and practice ultimately in favor, once again, of a linear relationship of principle and concretion, theory and its practical application. Guidelines, standards, norms, for ethical postulates will only be able to be found in the fields of practice themselves, to be formulated only from concrete activity. As history shows us, no overlapping theory protects against arbitrariness and misuse, since even abstract principles of social order like change have also been claimed thus far by opposing interest groups and group interests. This can only be avoided by not having different interests made invisible by abstracting theoretical forms, but rather by their being raised into consciousness by reflecting actual social practice and fields of practice and proving themselves in the battle of activities and views.

Thus there is not only a discrepancy between the real social conditions and those targeted by changes. There is also a difference between the real conditions—stamped all along by changes—and the ideal notions of social order. These ideal notions also change in the course of history. A "theory" of social change must therefore take into account that "change" itself is already an abstract term, the meaning of which can only be determined in social differentiation. Consequently, such a theory must constantly remain open to the change—even of what it itself understands by "theory of social change." So that this does not become a metatheory, however, it continues to refer fundamentally to pertinent concrete practice.

Unlike an ethics of order that, in taking the differences cited into account, can in theory arrive at ideal notions that are thoroughly historically and socially connected, this is not possible for an ethics of change. Its ideal notions are the result of theory-directed practice. Because they lie between practice and practice, they are always provisional and can only be formulated in the context of concrete fields of practice. They are not only—like the principles of an ethics of order as well—constantly in need of change and capable of changing; their actual constant change is their only real "principle," as it were. Social changes must not be raised to an absolute principle themselves or be made an end in themselves. On closer examination, what is involved here is a primacy of change over order and a reversal of the duty of legitimation: under this primacy, each existing order is characterized as provisional; it is primarily not change but order that must prove its legitimacy under this primacy. It is finally, as an ethics of change, altogether more appropriate to the eschatological condition of the message of the kingdom of God than a primacy of order or an ethics of order.

Another advantage is that an ethics of change has ideologico-critical impetus in itself, whereas an ethics of order must always be questioned—from outside—from the ideologico-critical standpoint. Faced with the "power of the de facto" and the weight of existing order, including as they do their institutionalized forms, change finds it hard to gain acceptance anyway. Precisely because there is no state of complete justice and freedom, demands for more justice and freedom in society and state have little chance of realization among those for whom they have already gained acceptance. A theory of social order thus runs easily into the suspicion of being nothing more than an ideology of the sovereign authority for legitimizing the status quo. The church in particular has seen itself increasingly and publicly exposed to this suspicion since the Enlightenment. Neither order nor change is ideologically innocent for a social ethics under the primacy of change; but the demands for concrete changes contain within them the question of which interests are served by existing conditions and who would benefit by their being changed.

Political theology is primarily practical fundamental theology, that is, it must be understood to be a theological hermeneutics of Christianity, under the social conditions of the present, that wishes to bring Christian action to bear on the basis of an ethics of change. It does not replace such an ethics but goes beyond it and outlines its theological framework. Only memory of God vouches for the universality of the standards for the right to life of all of creation and, within that, for the general acceptance of human rights, justice and solidarity, and peace and freedom. Political theology therefore also indicates the direction in which a Christian social ethics must unfold without succumbing to the dangers of social ineffectiveness and cognitive isolation. It also offers starting points for the theological/ethical debate with different social questions. Not lastly, it pursues the aim of transcending unfruitful confrontations in the realm of systematic theology and Catholic social doctrine (including liberation theology).

See also ENLIGHTENMENT, THE (INFLUENCE OF); FAITH; MORAL LIFE, CHRISTIAN; POLITICAL PHILOSOPHY; PRAXIS; REASON, ROLE OF; SOCIETY.

WERNER KROH

POLITISÉS CHRÉTIENS

"Politisés chrétiens" was the name of a Catholic-Marxist network active in Quebec between 1974 and 1982. The rapid political modernization of Quebec, the so-called Quiet Revolution, beginning in 1960, mobilized the whole of Quebec, secularized the society, strengthened the movement toward independence, and eventually generated a spectrum of socialist movements. Many Quebecers, especially among the young, were in solidarity with the anticolonial movements in Africa, the liberation movements in Latin America, and the struggle for civil rights in the United States.

Following the spirit of Vatican II, socially engaged Catholics strongly supported the Quiet Revolution. Even the bishops decided not to weep over the secularization of society and their loss of influence; instead their pastorals became increasingly concerned with social justice issues. The 1971 assembly of Christians for Socialism in Chile, attended by Christian socialists from Quebec, set a new tone among socially engaged Catholics in many parts of the world. In Quebec Catholic Action organizations—Jeunesse ouvrière catholique (JOC), Jeunesse étudiante catholique (JEC), Jeunesse rurale catholique (JRC), and Mouvement des travailleurs chrétiens (MTC)—became increasingly radicalized. This was the time when the three major labor federations of Quebec decided to adopt Marxist principles. A growing number of Catholics, following a certain trend in their society, also moved from social democracy to Marxist socialism.

Beginning in 1971 Yves Vaillancourt appealled to radical Catholics to form a network of support, political reflection, and spiritual solidarity. He looked upon Marxism as a social movement supplying two things, a utopia that summons forth vision and passion and a scientific method for analyzing the contradictions of society. Christians, Vaillancourt argued, derive their utopia from a different source, from the divine promises revealed in Christ, but they are grateful for the Marxist scientific method that allows them to analyze society and decide upon correct practice. In 1974 le réseau des politisés chrétiens, embracing several hundred men and women spread over the whole province, was formally constituted. The network was to be a support group for Christian Marxists with a political mission in the field of culture and ideology. Since many members of the network worked as facilitators in religious, social, political, or labor organizations, they hoped to make a practical contribution to the creation of a socialist Quebec.

A coordinating committee of four or five persons was the decision-making body of the network. The assemblies of the members exercised only a consultative role. The coordinating committee made the decisions regarding the correct analysis of the historical situation and the political strategy to be pursued. The organization of the network was formal and disciplined, reflecting the Catholic institutional tradition and the "democratic centralism" of more recent origin.

A pastoral letter of 1977, *A Society to Be Transformed,* approved of Catholic participation in socialist movements yet criticized the network because of its Marxist orientation. The network was also criticized by socially engaged Catholics who worked in groups closely identified with the poor and other marginalized people and who, for this reason, distrusted the Marxist analysis that focused only on the proletariat. These Catholics wanted to promote *une église populaire.* Toward the end of the 1970s it was this sector of engaged Catholics that became more influential. The network began to lose members. In 1980 the loss of the referendum on Quebec sovereignty produced discouragement and depression among socially involved Quebecers, especially among radicals. Christians were also affected by this. Because of declining interest the coordinating committee decided in 1982 to dissolve the network.

See also MARXISM.

Bibliography: G. Baum, "Politisés Chrétiens: A Christian-Marxist Network in Quebec, 1974–1982," *Studies in Political Economy* 32 (Summer 1990) 7–28.

GREGORY BAUM

PONTIFICAL COUNCIL FOR JUSTICE AND PEACE

The promotion, deepening, and ongoing development of the social teaching of the church is the specific work of the Pontifical Council for Justice and Peace, a permanent department of the central administration of the Roman Catholic church.

At the specific request of the Second Vatican Council (*Gaudium et spes* 90), Pope Paul VI established a Pontifical Commission, Iustitia et Pax, on an experimental basis (*motu proprio Catholicam Christi Ecclesiam,* January 6, 1967). At the same time, he stated that "its name, which is its programme, is Justice and Peace" (*Populorum progressio* 5). Pope John Paul II returned to the significance of this name in his encyclical *Laborem exercens,* saying that "it indicates that the social question must be dealt with in its whole complex dimension. Commitment to justice must be closely linked with commitment to peace in the modern world" (LE 2). This integrated approach to social questions is fundamental to the work of the Pontifical Council for Justice and Peace.

In 1976 the Pontifical Commission was given its definitive place within the Roman curia and its aims and objectives more precisely defined (*motu proprio Justitiam et pacem,* December 10, 1976). These were still further specified in 1988, at which time its name became the Pontifical Council for Justice and Peace (apostolic constitution *Pastor bonus* 142–44). It has had three presidents since its foundation: Maurice Cardinal Roy (Canada), 1967–75; Bernardin Cardinal Gantin (Benin), 1976–84; and Roger Cardinal Etchegaray (France), 1984 to the present.

At the direct service of the pope and of the universal church, the council's overall aim is not only to make the people of God aware of the church's concern for problems related to justice and peace but also to help them understand their responsibility in the social field (*Justitiam et pacem,* no. 1) as "an integral part of the Christian conception of life" (*Mater et magistra,* part 4). In order to do this, the council publishes studies on the theological and moral aspects of specific issues related to the overall fields of development, peace, disarmament, environment, labor relations, and human rights (recent publications include *An Ethical Approach to the International Debt Question* [1986], *The Church and Homelessness* [1987], *The Church and Racism* [1988], *The Holy See at the Service of Peace* [1988], *The Social Doctrine of the Church Revisited* [1990], *The Right to Development* [1991], and *Social and Ethical Aspects of Economics* [1992]). It also collaborates with other departments of the Roman curia (e.g., the organization of the World Day of Prayer for Peace, October 1986, by three departments of the Roman curia) and with episcopal conferences and their national justice and peace commissions so that throughout the Roman Catholic church the social teaching of the church may not only be known but also applied in widely varying local situations. Both Pope

Paul VI and Pope John Paul II also asked the Pontifical Council for Justice and Peace to be responsible for the preparation and animation of the annual World Day of Peace, a papal initiative dating from 1968. The Pontifical Council for Justice and Peace maintains contact with a broad range of international organizations, both governmental and nongovernmental, as well as with ecumenical and multireligious bodies, thus collaborating in the common task of humanity to assure those conditions necessary for the building of a just and peaceful world.

See also CHURCH, SOCIAL MISSION OF; DEVELOPMENT; ECOLOGY; GAUDIUM ET SPES; HUMAN RIGHTS; MODERN CATHOLIC SOCIAL THOUGHT; PEACE.

MARJORIE KEENAN, R.S.H.M.

POOR, PREFERENTIAL OPTION FOR

To make an option for the poor is to commit oneself to resisting the injustice, oppression, exploitation, and marginalization of people that permeate almost every aspect of public life. It is a commitment to transforming society into a place where human rights and the dignity of all are respected. This option, or choice, can be made by individuals or by communities or even by a whole church.

When we speak of an option for the poor we usually have in mind a choice freely made by people who are not already poor. Becoming aware that they are relatively wealthy or privileged, they decide freely to relinquish their privileges (to some degree at least) and to become identified with the underprivileged. (An option for the poor can also be made by those who are already poor or disadvantaged; in their case it means a choice to be in solidarity with other underprivileged people rather than trying to take advantage of them and join the rich and powerful.)

A choice of this kind is generally a profoundly religious one inspired by a deeper understanding of the Christian faith. But inevitably there is a political dimension to it. For the choice presupposes that one has become aware that in society as a whole and in almost every organization within it, there are people "at the top" who have a lot of power and others "at the bottom" who are more or less powerless. To make an option for the poor is to choose to disengage from serving the interests of the powerful and instead to take the side of those who are relatively powerless.

It is this political aspect that has provoked so much opposition and misunderstanding of the notion of an option for the poor. A major reason for the opposition is that in the Western world there has been a widespread tendency in recent centuries to empty religious faith of its public, political dimension, reducing it largely to the sphere of personal and family morality. Those who have been nourished on such a spirituality are quite shocked at the new political emphasis of liberation theology; they accuse these new theologians of reducing faith to politics. The liberation theologians respond by saying that the Christian faith necessarily has a political aspect; those who allow it to be privatized are not really eliminating this political aspect but are making an option for the present unjust status quo; they are colluding with the rich and the powerful by failing to challenge the injustice of society.

Scriptural Basis

The notion of a preferential option for the poor is solidly rooted in the Bible. A foundational event in the history of the Jews was God's call to lead the people out of slavery and into a land of their own: "I have heard the cry of my people and I see how they are being oppressed" (Exod 3:9). "Go to Pharaoh and tell him that Yahweh says, 'Let my people go'" (Exod 8:1).

Once the people had settled in their own land, injustice and oppression became widespread again. Now the oppressor was not the Egyptian emperor but those who had emerged as rich and powerful among their own people. Through the prophets, God protested in outrage against the social injustices, the bribery, and the arrogance of the rich (e.g., Amos 2:6; 4:1; 5:12; Isa 3:14-15; 10:1-2; Jer 22:3). God demanded that the laws of the land would protect and give redress to the poor, the indebted, the widows, the resident foreigners, the animals (domestic or wild), and even the earth itself (e.g., Lev 19:33; 25:10-16; Exod 15:12-15; 22:21; 23:11; Deut 23:12; 25:4).

The NT builds on and enriches the OT teaching about the poor. Jesus grew up as one of the common people, and his ministry of good news and healing was directed mainly toward them. He presented himself as the person in whom was fulfilled God's promise to send one who would come "to bring good news to the poor, to proclaim liberty to captives" (Lk 4:18-21). Central to his teaching was the proclamation that the poor and the hungry are blessed by God (Lk 6:20-21). Jesus had special concern for the rejected and outcasts of society—the lepers and others who were sick, crippled, or disturbed in mind or spirit, and those who were classed as public sinners (prostitutes and tax collectors). He reacted strongly against the lawyers and the Pharisees whom he saw as imposing a heavy religious oppression on the common people (e.g., Mt 15:1-5, 16; 23:16-24; Mk 2:23–3:6). Instead of endorsing the idea that prosperity was a sign of God's favor he spoke out on the dangers of riches (Mt 6:19, 24; 13:22; 19:24; Lk 6:24; 12:20; 16:22-23). In the end he was rejected and put to death by the authorities because they, rightly, perceived his message and his whole approach as an undermining of their power.

History

The concept of an option for the poor is a central element in the liberation theology that emerged in Latin America during the 1960s. The Peruvian theologian Gustavo Gutiérrez is generally recognized as the father figure of liberation theology. His seminal book, *A Theology of Liberation,* devotes an important chapter to an analysis of the term "poverty." Gutiérrez and his fellow liberation theologians played a key role in the Medellín Conference of 1968, where the Latin American bishops committed themselves to being in solidarity with the poor, to giving preference to the poorest and most needy sectors of society, and to arousing the consciousness of oppressed groups and helping them become agents of their own development. This amounts to an option for the poor, though the term itself was not used in the Medellín Documents.

In the years following Medellín, large segments of the church in Latin America devoted themselves to putting this option into practice; the Brazilian church led the way. However, within some sectors of the Latin American church there was very strong resistance to the whole idea. In some countries (e.g., Nicaragua) the church has been split down the middle as a result. Despite determined opposition by some strong church leaders the commitment of the Latin American bishops to justice for the poor was reaffirmed at their 1979 conference at Puebla; one chapter of the Final Document of Puebla is entitled "A Preferential Option for the Poor."

The option made by the Latin American bishops and theologians became the most important influence in the church over the next two decades. Many leaders and theologians of other Christian churches embraced the notion of an option for the poor. The World Council of Churches is firmly committed to the principle, though the phrase itself is not widely used in its documents. Within the Catholic church the idea has been, and remains, a very controversial one, adopted enthusiastically by some and vigorously opposed by others.

The notion of an option for the poor has been particularly influential among two groups in the Catholic church: (1) church leaders in certain parts of the Third World where there has been widespread poverty or oppression, for example, Latin America, the Philippines, South Africa, and Rhodesia (before it gained independence as Zimbabwe); and (2) various religious orders, congregations, and societies—above all the Jesuits (influenced in the 1970s by their charismatic head, Pedro Arrupe).

The Vatican has slowly and cautiously accepted the phrase. There was concern in Rome that an option for the poor would be understood either as an exclusion of the rich or (worse still) as a "class option" in the Marxist sense, that is, as an invitation to class struggle. Because of this concern Pope John Paul II insists that "no one must be excluded" and that "the preferential option for the poor . . . is not an ideological option; neither is it a matter of letting oneself be trapped by a false theory of class struggle" (address to priests, religious, and laity, Mexico City, May 12, 1990, in *Osservatore Romano,* English ed., May 14, 1990, p. 3).

Solidarity

In this section I shall attempt to give a fuller account of what is involved in making an option for the poor. It must be made clear that in this context the term "the poor" refers first of all to those who are economically deprived, but it is by no means confined to them. It extends also to those who are deprived of fundamental political or cultural or religious rights. It applies to women as a whole, since they are the victims of a long history of being treated as second-class humans, and even yet they suffer discrimination as women. The term "the poor" also applies to those who are the victims of racist attitudes or systems. Within the church, to make an option for the poor is to work for the interests of the laity and of women in particular. Wherever there is structural injustice Christians are called to oppose it by making an option for the poor, that is, for the victims of that injustice.

There are two equally crucial aspects to this commitment—an experiential aspect that can be summed up under the word "solidarity" and a political aspect that has to do with action. I shall outline each of these in turn. At the heart of the experiential aspect lies a deliberate choice to enter in some degree into the world of those who are deprived—to share in a significant way in their experience of being mistreated, bypassed, or left helpless. It springs from compassion and involves a choice to deepen this compassion by sharing to some extent in the suffering of the poor. By entering the world of deprived people one begins to experience not only their pain and struggle but also their hopes and their joys.

In practice, this aspect of option for the poor has to do with lifestyle. Lifestyle includes the kind of food we eat, the clothes we wear, and the way our homes are furnished. But these are of secondary importance. Much more significant are our choices about the area in which we live, the friends we cultivate, the kinds of work we undertake, and the attitudes and style we adopt in doing all these things.

Insofar as one begins to share the life of disadvantaged people, one begins to have that sense of togetherness that frequently characterizes such groups. This is the *experience* of solidarity that provides a matrix within which the *virtue* of solidarity can be developed. Without the experience of solidarity the would-be reformer cannot help thinking about the poor as "them," the objects of my sympathy. When one thinks and feels in that way it is almost impossible to avoid being both paternalistic and manipulative—and people will sense this, no matter how well it is disguised. It is only to the extent that a person becomes part of the group and is able to think of "us"—and to be treated by the people as "one of us"—that this person has the possibility of becoming a truly effective and respectful agent of change.

Of course this is not an "all or nothing" affair. The person who is making the option has probably come from a different background and may retain a different accent or even skin color. In that sense the person may always be seen as different, but the group with whom he or she has come to live or work may choose to accept the person as "one of us," one who shares their interests. It is not in my power to be fully in solidarity with a particular group of deprived people; all I can do is *offer* to be in solidarity with them. And this offer is not made in words but in the attitude with which I come to them. In response, they may choose to offer me the gift of solidarity, of treating me as "one of us" (or, perhaps, "one *with* us"). They make that choice in their own time and in their own degree; it is not something I can presume or demand or even hasten.

I have said that the *experience* of solidarity provides the matrix within which the *virtue* of solidarity can be developed. The virtue is a habitual attitude and approach that inclines one to be sensitive to the needs and feelings of others in the group and to devote oneself generously to the common welfare. The development of the virtue of solidarity takes place within the context of the struggle against injustice. Like other virtues, solidarity has to be constantly nourished. This takes place in two ways. First, one must be open to be challenged by other members of the group and to challenge them in turn. Second, one has to strive constantly to play a part in developing common policies with the other members of the group and to act on the basis of these joint policies.

Commitment

Having looked at solidarity, which is the experiential aspect of an option for the poor, we can now go on to the second major aspect of this option, namely, a commitment to take action to overcome structural injustice. This involves a series of steps:

1. There is need first of all for a careful *analysis* of the situation to bring about an understanding of the basic sources of the injustice. Otherwise a lot of energy may be wasted in working for superficial changes without tackling the real causes of the problem.

2. This should lead to a distancing of oneself from *collusion* with the groups or forces responsible for the injustice. For instance, a church person may find it necessary to refuse favors or gifts offered by certain politicians or business interests lest acceptance be construed as approval of what they are doing.

3. Then there is need for carefully planned and concerted action at the political level to *challenge* the injustice. It is clear that there should be a certain gradation in such action. At first there might be a private protest; if this does not succeed there might be letters to the newspapers; then, perhaps, a public protest march, and so on.

4. Finally, there is need to design realistic *alternatives* to the unjust structures being challenged and to begin the process of bringing these alternatives into being. For instance: suppose a large group of poor people on the outskirts of a city find they cannot afford to buy sites for their own homes, and suppose they conclude that a major reason for this difficulty is the speculation in building land by a small number of wealthy and influential people. In challenging this injustice they should have some clear alternative to propose, for example, a government-controlled limit on the price of land, and/or a publicly owned "land bank," and/or very heavy tax on profits from the sale of land.

In all these steps it is very important that those who are coming from outside to side with the poor in a particular area do not take it on themselves to set the agenda or to provide the answers. It is not for them to play the central role in describing the situation, or in deciding what the major injustices are, or which of them are the most urgent, or how they should be challenged. The people from outside should not take it on themselves to organize protests against injustice or to be the ones to decide on alternative structures. The victimized people themselves should be allowed, and empowered, to speak and act on their own behalf. For it is only in this way that they can overcome the sense of helplessness and dependency that is a fundamental part of their situation. Those who have chosen to act in solidarity with them may have to "hold back" for quite some time. When they do intervene it should be, as far as possible, to facilitate the disadvantaged people themselves in coming to understand the causes of their problems and in planning effective action to overcome them.

An Option by the Church

An option for the poor is, first of all, a very personal choice, made by an *individual* committed Christian who desires to share in Christ's work of bringing salvation to the world. But that is not enough. There is need also for *communities* of committed Christians to make such an option on behalf of the Christian institution to which they belong. In recent years this has happened fairly widely; many religious congregations and societies of laypeople have committed themselves in this way.

But even that is not sufficient. The *institutional church* itself, at every level, faces the challenge of making an option for the poor. The way in which this can be done is to have church leaders act on behalf of the church as a whole, and in a manner that shows that they have the backing of most of the membership of their churches. The Catholic bishops of Latin America at their meetings in Medellín (1968) and Puebla (1979) committed themselves very publicly to such an option. The leaders of the World Council of Churches have made a similar, though broader, commitment in dedicating themselves to "justice, peace, and the integrity of creation." Many other church leaders have felt called to be in solidarity with the poor and the powerless and to join their struggle for dignity and justice. In most cases these leaders have endeavored to make this commitment not merely in their personal capacity as Christians but also as representing the official church—and carrying with them as many of their people as possible in the option for the poor.

It is important to note this distinction between an option for the poor made by individuals or small groups of Christians and an option for the poor made by or on behalf of a whole church at a regional, national, or international level. When the leadership of a church sets out to facilitate the church in making an option for the poor, the various steps outlined above have to be undertaken. It is of particular importance that a serious *analysis* be made of how structural injustice operates in the particular society. This will provide a basis for avoiding *collusion* in injustice and for the *challenge* the church is called to make to injustice in society; it should also give some indication of the kind of *alternatives* toward which church people are called to work.

See also CHURCH, SOCIAL MISSION OF; CLASS STRUGGLE; DEVELOPMENT; HUMAN RIGHTS; LIBERATION THEOLOGY; MEDELLÍN, MODERN CATHOLIC SOCIAL THOUGHT; PUEBLA; SOLIDARITY.

Bibliography: G. Gutiérrez, *A Theology of Liberation: History, Politics, and Salvation,* rev. ed. (Maryknoll, N.Y.: Orbis, 1988). G. Gutiérrez, *The Power of the Poor in History* (Maryknoll, N.Y.: Orbis, 1983). R. Shaull, *Heralds of a New Reformation: The Poor of South and North America* (Maryknoll, N.Y.: Orbis, 1984). A. Nolan, *God in South Africa: The Challenge of the Gospel* (Grand Rapids: Eerdmans, 1988, and London: CIIR, 1988). D. Dorr, *Option for the Poor: A Hundred Years of Vatican Social Teaching* (Maryknoll, N.Y.: Orbis, and Dublin: Gill & Macmillan, rev. ed., 1992). D. Dorr, *Spirituality and Justice* (Maryknoll, N.Y.: Orbis, 1984, and Dublin: Gill & Macmillan, 1984). C. Boff and G. Pixley, *The Bible, the Church, and the Poor* (Maryknoll, N.Y.: Orbis, 1989, and London: Burns & Oates, 1989).

DONAL DORR

POPULATION

The term "population" refers to any collection of living animal or human elements continually being modified by increases through birth or immigration and by losses through death and emigration. Any population, therefore, that is unable to control its rates of birth and mortality, or that is subject to a high mortality rate because of disease, war, or natural disaster, and whose birth rate is not extremely high will either remain relatively stable or even decrease. Throughout most of human history until the contemporary era, the total population of planet Earth remained stable or increased slightly, with occasional periods of regression in numbers due to plagues, famines, and wars.

Populations, of course, are dependent upon the natural resources of the areas they inhabit. A sufficient food supply, adequate water and shelter, and other necessities of life are factors of essential importance to any population, as well as being determinative of the maximum number of people a particular environment can sustain. In the modern era, with the rise of industrial technologies and scientific medicine, a concern has arisen for the first time in human history about the maximum population the planet is capable of sustaining. Our knowledge of the finite nature of the earth's material resources and the rapid expansion of the earth's population in the 20th century have brought the question of overpopulation to the forefront of human consciousness.

The numbers of people presently inhabiting the globe, in contrast to the past, and the projected number of people if birth and death rates continue at their present levels can be sobering statistics and certainly account for the concern about the possibility of overpopulation. The population of the earth around the year 1000 has been estimated at about 340 million people. By 1650 it had grown to only 545 million and by 1800 it had reached 907 million people. One hundred years later it had nearly doubled to over 1.6 billion. By 1950 it stood at 2.5 billion, by 1970 at over 3.5 billion, and by 1990 at around 5 billion people.

Projections for the future are always difficult, but a United Nations commission has offered projections based on a number of possibilities of high, moderate, and low expectations of population increases to the year 2050. By the year 2000 the global population is expected to number between 5.4 billion and 7 billion people. By 2050 a population of between 8.5 and 13.5 billion people is projected.

In addition to the sheer magnitude of numbers, demographic studies indicate that the largest population increases are among the less-developed nations, especially in Asia and Latin America. The less-developed nations, beneficiaries of lower infant mortality rates and longer life expectancies due to modern medicine, have been experiencing a far more rapid population increase in this century than European nations did in the 19th century. Everywhere in less-developed nations the rate of population growth is over 2 percent, and in some areas of Latin America the increase is as high as 3.5 percent. A rate of 2.5 percent means a doubling of the population in just one generation. Such increases in the number of people in particular areas obviously make the tasks of economic and social development extremely difficult.

The significance of the population question for Roman Catholic social thought begins with the church's ancient understanding of human sexuality as intended by God for procreation. The command of God to Adam and Eve in the Book of Genesis to be fruitful and multiply has been understood for the greater part of Christian history to express the divine reason for creating human beings as male and female. The purpose was to populate the earth, to produce enough people to fill the earth and subdue it, and, under God, to have dominion over it (Gen 1:28).

This conviction that sex found its primary purpose in procreation was enhanced by the recognition that the family was the primary social unit and the foundation of all social life and social order. Human beings by nature are social beings, needing one another for the full flourishing of human life and for realizing their ultimate destiny of eternal union with God. Sex, then, was ordered to marriage, marriage to the procreation of children and the establishing of family, and family to the nurture and training of new citizens for society and church. The wonder and majesty of God's creative love was reflected in every new child as well as in the number and diversity of all the peoples of the earth.

By the 4th and 5th centuries after Christ it had become something of a commonplace that the earth was sufficiently populated. Thus the commitment of many Christians to lives of consecrated celibacy or virginity was in no way considered to violate the command of God in Genesis. But there was no specific knowledge or concern with the possibility of overpopulation. Governments were more inclined to foster population growth for political and economic reasons, and disease, periodic famines, and wars kept population levels down.

Although various secular authors in Europe during the 17th and 18th centuries had begun to warn their readers about the problems of overpopulation, it was the publication in 1798 of Thomas Malthus' work *An Essay on the Principle of Population* that brought to definite and vivid association in the public mind the related issues of population growth and social improvement. While Malthus' basic theory that economic improvements would never keep pace with population growth proved to be wrong, his work started an ongoing and still unfinished debate about what constitutes an optimum population level and how best to achieve it. Most population theorists today recognize that the size of a population, environmental resources, age distributions, the labor force, technical skills, and educational systems are all complementary elements in trying to arrive at population theories and policies.

Catholic social thought in its modern form has, to date, steadfastly denied that the earth's population has reached or exceeded tolerable human limits (*Familiaris consortio* 6; *Humanae vitae* 23; Medellín Documents, *Family and Demography* 10). It has not denied the need for responsible control of population growth nor that government has a proper role in executing that responsibility (*Populorum progressio* 37). It has certainly not taught that an ever-increasing human population is a good thing in and of itself. Three major concerns seem to lie behind Catholic social teaching in regard to the population question, all of them linked to the primary affirmation of Catholic social thought, the dignity of the human person.

The first concern is the inalienable right of persons to marry and beget children, and thus their right to determine the size of their own families. This right is, of course, morally limited by the economic, social, physical, and psychological circumstances of the couple (HV 10), but it ought not to be limited by the government or any other social agency. Governments may have a proper role in influencing the circumstances in which the couple make their decision, but it would be a fundamental violation of human dignity and right for any political power to impose this decision (*Gaudium et spes* 87).

The second concern is with the methods employed to limit population growth. It has never been a part of Catholic teaching that a desirable social end justifies the means taken to achieve that end. While it is certainly true that population levels can be controlled to some degree by such practices as abortion, sterilization, infanticide, and widespread use of contraceptive devices, these and other means have been traditionally found to be morally objectionable in Catholic teaching. Since human dignity is rooted in the human capacity for moral agency (*Dignitatis humanae* 2), such immoral practices would be clear violations of the dignity of human persons (HV 23; FC 6).

The third concern in Catholic social thought in regard to the population question is with a materialism that would, in the interests of a higher standard of material well-being, reject the responsibility to bring new life into the world and nurture it. The church's teaching stresses not individual material success but human solidarity and the resultant obligation to share the material and cultural goods of the world more fairly and evenly. The present problem, as Catholic social thought sees it, is not overpopulation but unequal and unfair distribution of the world's goods (*Mater et magistra* 188–92; PP 43–55).

This materialism and the resulting contraceptive mentality (HV 17), fueled by greed and selfishness and reflected in the preference for material things over the well-being of persons (*Laborem exercens* 6–8), causes human individuals and communities to lose sight of the truly human goods of relationship with God and one's fellow human beings (PP 41–42). The human aspiration "to seek to do more, know more and have more in order to be more" (PP 6) is affirmed in Catholic social thought as a fundamental aspect of human dignity, so that increased economic production and higher standards of living are seen as legitimate human goals. But this material progress should be in the service of integral human development and carried out in a spirit of human solidarity and mutual cooperation (PP; LE; *Sollicitudo rei socialis*).

The population question in Catholic social thought, therefore, is less a matter of sheer numbers than it is a matter of recognizing the basic and equal dignity of all human beings who make up the human population. While it certainly does not teach that the human population should grow unchecked, it has been more concerned to stress that a human, dignified life is well within the reach of human effort and intelligence at present levels of population, if cooperation and solidarity mark the effort. For Catholic social thought the population question has been addressed primarily from a moral perspective rather than from a technical and political perspective, and this approach to the question is both its strength and its weakness.

See also BIRTH CONTROL; DEMOGRAPHICS; ECONOMIC PLANNING, SOCIAL IMPORTANCE OF; INDUSTRIALIZATION; NATURAL RESOURCES; SOCIALIZATION; SUBSIDIARITY, PRINCIPLE OF; TECHNOLOGY.

Bibliography: J. Gremillion, "Population, Resources, Environment," in *The Gospel of Peace and Justice: Catholic Social Teaching Since Pope John* (Maryknoll, N.Y.: Orbis, 1976, pp. 91–110). B. Ward, "Looking Back on *Populorum Progressio*," in C. Curran and R. McCormick, eds., *Readings in Moral Theology No. 5, Official Catholic Social Teaching* (New York/Mahwah: Paulist, 1986, pp. 130–49). *Theological Studies* 35, 1 (March 1974) 3–163 provides a comprehensive overview of the whole population question.

JAMES HANIGAN

POPULORUM PROGRESSIO

To situate the encyclical letter *Populorum progressio* in context, it is important to note that it was published by Pope Paul VI on March 26, 1967, slightly more than a year after the publication of the Pastoral Constitution on the Church in the Modern World (*Gaudium et spes*) at the conclusion of the Second Vatican Council on December 7, 1965. Furthermore, not too long before the closing of the council Pope John XXIII had published two groundbreaking encyclical letters, which marked a new stage in modern Catholic social thought: *On Christianity and Social Progress* (*Mater et magistra*) in 1961 and *Peace on Earth* (*Pacem in terris*) in 1963. Pope Paul makes copious references and quotes often from these three documents and sees his own work as flowing directly from them.

It will also be helpful to refer to some important documents that followed the publication of *Populorum progressio.* On July

25, 1968, slightly more than a year later, Pope Paul published *On the Regulation of Birth* (*Humanae vitae*); this unleashed a firestorm of controversy around the world, especially in the United States, where public dissent broke out at Catholic University and other places. The negative consequence of all this was that the controversy and very extensive accompanying publicity almost completely eclipsed the lively debate that had begun to take place on the many important issues raised by *Populorum progressio.*

Another document that was published in the year following *Populorum progressio* was the report of the Second General Conference of Latin American bishops, held at Medellín, Colombia, from August 24 to September 6, 1968. The encyclical, with its emphasis on the reality of the Third World, was enthusiastically received in Latin America and assiduously utilized by various clerical and lay groups in both the preparatory discussions and in the concluding documents of the conference. Finally and more recently, Pope John Paul II demonstrated the importance he attributed to *Populorum progressio* when he chose its 20th anniversary in 1987 to publish his own most comprehensive and profound social encyclical, *On Social Concern* (*Sollicitudo rei socialis*), in which he emphasized his deep indebtedness to Pope Paul and quoted extensively from his letter.

General Introduction

I now turn to an introduction to *Populorum progressio,* to be followed by a summary and commentary on the text. The letter differs from previous encyclicals in a number of ways. It eschews the stately and sometimes diffuse introductions common to this literary genre, instead plunging directly into the heart of the matter. Also, instead of taking the usual panoramic overview of many issues, it focuses completely on the single dominant issue of the suffering and poverty of the Third World; this in turn leads into a complementary stress on the crucial importance of integral human development in helping to alleviate the misery of the world's poor, a situation he refers to again and again as a great scandal, a primary threat to world peace, and an enormous challenge to the consciences of those who enjoy riches or at least relative wealth. Thus the letter is suffused with heartfelt passion and an intense feeling of urgency, since the lives of hundreds of millions of human beings are seen to be at stake.

Pope Paul accompanied this, however, with an unusually incisive and honest analysis and critique of the root causes of world poverty in the present capitalist system, which predictably led to attacks on the encyclical in the First World including the now-famous charge that it was merely "warmed-over Marxism." At the same time, the pope seemed to be wracking his mind to propose every possible path to fighting and overcoming the glaring injustices that cry out to heaven, demanding "bold transformations," "innovations that go deep," "urgent reforms" (32), while challenging Christians, adherents of other religions, and all persons of good will to a profound conversion to the cause of the poor.

Outline of Encyclical

Turning to the text of the letter, it is rather simply divided into a few preliminary remarks and two main parts. The first part is concerned with a Christian vision of development, which goes beyond mere economic growth to highlight the social, cultural, and religious dimensions that are essential for integral and fully human development. In the second and larger section, the pope develops in detail the theme that true development cannot occur without a simultaneous development of all humanity in a spirit of solidarity.

Preliminary Remarks

In the very first words of the document, Paul VI plunges immediately into his subject, which will be "those peoples who are striving to escape from hunger, misery, endemic diseases and ignorance." In his introductory remarks he also presents a dramatic summary of the entire letter, depicting the church recoiling in horror at the cry of the poor: "Today the peoples in hunger are making a dramatic appeal to the peoples blessed with abundance. The Church shudders at this cry of anguish and calls each one to give a loving response of charity to this brother's cry for help" (3).

Part 1: Complete Human Development

The pope then proceeds in his first main section to present a brief but succinct social analysis of the situation of development. He points out that the many nations who have achieved political independence in recent decades now aspire to freedom from misery, that is, to move to the level of socioeconomic freedom (6). Thwarting these desires, however, loom a number of obstacles such as the enduring impact of colonialism, which bequeathed a legacy of single-crop and otherwise distorted economies to the colonies, so that at present there exists a systematic inequality of wealth: ". . . rich peoples enjoy rapid growth, whereas the poor develop slowly" (8). Other impediments to development are the social conflicts that spring up as the poor become increasingly more aware of these "glaring inequalities," the severe tensions that are created in the transition from traditional to modern societies, and the instability caused by temptation to rebellion and the lure of totalitarian ideologies (9–11).

Although he will continue to analyze the causes of underdevelopment throughout the document, the pope appears to be far ahead of his time in presenting a thumbnail sketch of what are now referred to as "structures of sin" (Pope John Paul II) or "social sin" (contemporary theology). Thus he has provided the necessary background and context to understand the proper role of the *church* in the struggle for the cause of the poor.

Pope Paul begins this discussion by acknowledging both the many achievements as well as the shortcomings of the church's missionary activities in the developing nations. He emphasizes, however, that such local and individual activities as these no longer suffice: "The present situation of the world demands concerted action based on a clear vision of all economic, social, cultural, and spiritual aspects," and thus the church's role in development is to proclaim "what she possesses as her characteristic attribute: a global vision of man and of the human race" (13). In the following paragraphs, he goes on to clarify and expand this Christian vision of development.

Moving quickly beyond a merely economic understanding of development, Pope Paul emphasizes that every person has a vocation to self-fulfillment, which will be developed through a continuous dialectic of both a personal as well as a communal responsibility. Thus he carefully avoids the various reductionisms of either an individualist or a merely communitarian spirituality that are so frequent in the contemporary world. I would, however, hesitate to endorse the statement that "by the unaided effort of his own intelligence and will each man can grow in humanity, can enhance his personal worth, can become more a person" (15), since it appears to minimize the enormous impact of socioeconomic and cultural influences on the human person today.

The major obstacle to personal-communal development, according to the pontiff, is clearly avarice fed by a stifling materialism: "Both for nations and for individual men, avarice is the most evident form of moral underdevelopment" (19). To overcome this, he accentuates the necessity of more profound reflection, aided by wise individuals, of prayer and contemplation, and of the search for higher values such as love and friendship. And he adds an extremely important articulation of authentic development, namely, "a development which is for each and all a transition from less human conditions to those which are more human" (20).

Although this may appear very general, Pope Paul continues by devoting an entire paragraph (22) to articulating numerous descriptions and examples of precisely what is meant by the transition from less human situations to those that are more human. In my reading of the literature, this paragraph has been one of the most praised and quoted, especially by authors speaking from the Third World. Although there is not space to quote it here, it should be read carefully as one of the high points of the letter. Not the least of its strengths is its ecumenical breadth and depth, applying to absolutely everyone in the human family, as well as its strong emphasis on the supreme value for more human conditions and on God's call to all women and men to share in the life of God.

The Need for Action

Having clarified the Christian vision of development, the pope moves from theory to practice and concentrates on a major preoccupation of his throughout the encyclical: the pressing, urgent need for action to achieve integral development. Consequently, Paul in this section (22–42) carefully considers and evaluates the key concepts and concrete proposals that he believes can lead to his goal of real and long-lasting progress toward true development. He reflects on the purpose of all created goods, the ethical use of property, agrarian reform, industrialization, the drawbacks of capitalism, the meaning of work, and the issue of violent revolution. With that background, he next considers plans and programs that will be at the service of human beings; these include concern for literacy, strengthening the family, appropriate regulation of birth, the role of social agencies, the promotion of each nation's values and culture, and an openness to spiritual values and God. A further consideration of concepts and plans for development will also be taken up later, in the second part of the letter, regarding the need for Christian solidarity.

The above litany of topics makes it obvious that I can only touch on some of the major issues the pontiff raises. The traditional teaching of the church both on the social nature of earthly goods as well as the right of private property is repeated (22–23), but very forceful emphasis is given to the destination of all material goods to the common good. As Pope Paul succinctly phrases it, "Private property does not constitute for anyone an absolute and unconditional right" (23). As an example of this principle, he points to large estates in some nations that are hardly or poorly utilized, so that the common good could demand that they be expropriated by the authorities and given over to those who will work the land and bring forth its fruits; from another point of view, he boldly condemns the practice that has become endemic in many countries of wealthy persons transferring much of their income abroad for selfish reasons and thus contributing nothing to the welfare and development of their own nation and of their own compatriots.

This brings the discussion to the most controversial paragraph in the entire encyclical, as the pope takes up the issues of industrialization and the present system of capitalism. While realistically accepting the need for a measured industrialization, he launches into a stern denunciation of capitalism, because it "considers profit as the key motive for economic progress, competition as the supreme law of economics, and private ownership of the means of production as an absolute right that has no limits and carries no corresponding social obligation" (26). The consequence, he says, utilizing the words of Pope Pius XI in *Quadragesimo anno,* is that the present system is really "the international imperialism of money."

Clearly, the alternative the pope envisions must be a form of moderate or democratic socialism, since capitalism is not self-regulating and clearly not even self-critical, despite the incantations of Ronald Reagan and recent governments to "the magic of the marketplace." Rather than criticism, the system invests many billions of dollars in trumpeting its own products and accomplishments, while vilifying anyone who even suggests reforms as a Communist or (since that charge is so ridiculous) as a dupe of the Communists. Surely, then, the only path for self-criticism and reform is the constant struggle for social legislation and consistently vigilant government regulation, controls, and severe penalties for failure to comply. A truly horrendous and glaring example of what happens when the government abdicates its responsibility in these matters occurred recently in the United States, when for all practical purposes unregulated savings and loan associations managed to "get government off their backs" and plundered the nation for hundreds of billions of dollars, by far the most enormous crime of grand larceny in the history of the republic. And literally generations of American workers will be called upon for higher taxes to pay for the theft. At any rate, it is clear why the *Wall Street Journal,* financial circles, and the rich attacked the letter and this particular paragraph so fiercely.

Despite his criticisms of the system, the pope moves on to a discussion of work itself and adopts a very positive, even lyrical attitude toward it: ". . . everyone who works is a creator . . . it brings together and firmly unites the wills, minds, and hearts of men: in its accomplishment, men find themselves to be brothers" (27). While it can become dehumanizing and selfish, work "also develops professional awareness, a sense of duty, and charity to one's neighbor" (28). One cannot fail here to be reminded of how many of these ideas have been taken up and developed with great depth and comprehensiveness by Pope John Paul II in his encylical letter *On Human Work* (*Laborem exercens*).

Since he is intent on profound social change in order to achieve development, Pope Paul faces squarely the issues of violence and revolution. As often happens in this area, mere discussion of these problems led some superficial critics to accuse him of stirring up revolutions. He is, however, merely continuing traditional Catholic (also in the United States Declaration of Independence) just-war teaching. Consequently, he acknowledges that there are "certain situations whose injustice cries to heaven," and that a violent revolution may be justified "where there is manifest long-standing tyranny which would do great damage to fundamental human rights and dangerous harm to the common good of the country" (31). However, he insists that such revolutions often produce new injustices and bring on new disasters; also, the entire letter is proof that Paul believes that development will ordinarily be a difficult and long-range process and not the tempting "shortcut" of violent revolution. Indeed, even after a successful revolution the struggle for development may prove to be far more difficult, costly, and long lasting, as may be seen in recent years in the experience of the nation of Nicaragua.

At this point Pope Paul leaves the subject of violent revolution and turns to the path of reform, which certainly could be referred to as a peaceful revolution, although he does not use the term. There can be little doubt that the changes and reforms he advocates are meant to be profound and radical—radical in its original sense of going to the roots of the problem—as can be seen in his assertions: "Development demands bold transformation, innovations that go deep. Urgent reforms should be undertaken without delay" (32). As an example of this, he refers to the actions of a number of bishops in Latin America, especially Manuel Larrain of Talca, Chile, who led the way in turning over church property to be given to the poor in a program of land reform.

For the remainder of Part 1 of the encyclical, Pope Paul concentrates on the careful planning and the vigorous enactment of programs that will be necessary in order to bring about his peaceful Christian revolution. It is evident that his basic strategy will involve a "mixed economy," for he insists that not only "public authority" but also "private initiative and intermediary bodies" are necessary for developmental planning and programs (33). Thus he sails cautiously between the Scylla of complete collectivization and the Charybdis of an arbitrary planning that would deny freedom and political participation.

Regarding the programs, special attention is given to literacy and basic education whether publicly or privately organized, since "hunger for education is no less debasing than hunger for food: An illiterate is a person with an undernourished mind" (35). He also emphasizes the fundamental importance of the family and observes that in some nations family influence has been excessive and in clear violation of fundamental human rights. Here the pope is not referring to Western family structures but rather to the tribal family structures in some parts of Asia and Africa, which often give rise to strife, disunity, and even war. In his view the Christian family must become and remain "the place where 'the various generations come together and help one another to grow wiser and to harmonize personal rights with the other requirements of social life'" (26, quoting GS 52).

Intimately connected with the family is the issue of demographics and the losing battle between bursting populations and a shortage of resources that complicates and increases drastically all the other problem areas in the struggle for development. Recalling that this encyclical was published more than a year before *Humanae vitae,* the following statement can only be considered startling: "*It is certain* that public authorities can intervene, within the limit of their competence, by favoring the availability of appropriate information and by adopting suitable measures, provided that these be in conformity with the moral law and that they respect the rightful freedom of married couples" (37, italics added). To my knowledge, this must be the first time that any papal document has recognized that governments have the right to distribute information on birth control to their citizens. Obviously, too, this "certain" statement of Pope Paul is not certain at the present time, at least in official documents if not in the *sensus fidelium* (the understanding of laypersons), especially women.

Next the pope proceeds to praise professional organizations (by which he refers to social agencies and institutions of all kinds) for their many devoted contributions to human development (38), and he welcomes a pluralism of outlooks in these organizations as long as they respect human life and freedom (39). And in addition to these organizations he also stresses the immense value of cultural, intellectual, and artistic persons and institutions that preserve, develop, and pass on the heritage, values, and vision of each nation, which is an essential if often ignored element of human development (40).

This first part of the encyclical closes with some stern cautions against the temptation of materialism and against the exclusion of God and religious values from the project of human development. Paul pays special attention to warning the developing nations against a slavish and uncritical acceptance of the values and exaggerated materialism of the developed countries: "Developing nations must know how to discriminate among those things that are held out to them. They must be able to assess critically, and eliminate those deceptive goods which would only bring about a lowering of the human ideal, and to accept those values that are sound and beneficial, in order to develop them alongside their own, in accordance with their own genius" (41).

Part 2: Development and Solidarity

The key idea that informs this second part is expressed by the pope in his usual succinct and blunt style: "There can be no progress toward the complete development of man without the simultaneous development of all humanity in the spirit of solidarity" (43). This assertion may well be the most important in the whole encyclical, and yet the secular media and much of the religious media in the United States overlooked it entirely, absorbed as they were in debates about economics.

Perhaps this neglect is at least partially due to the fact that the pope goes on to insist that this development in solidarity must be the special concern of the wealthy nations. For them, he continues, this is not an option but a triple duty: the duty of human solidarity, referring to aid to poor nations; the duty of social justice, referring to more equitable trade relations; and the duty of charity, referring to making the world more human *for all.* Lest these duties be seen as works of supererogation, he continues in a deadly serious vein: "This question is urgent, for on it depends the future of the civilization of the world" (44).

Focusing next on the question of hunger, the daily scourge of hundreds of millions of people, Pope Paul commends the work of the Food and Agriculture Organization, Caritas International, and other groups but then goes on to insist that even eliminating hunger or poverty is not a satisfactory solution to the problem. Rather, it is a question of "building a world where every man, no matter what his race, religion, or nationality, can live a fully human life" (47). Stressing that this will demand not only generosity but real sacrifice, he once again becomes very concrete and practical as he confronts and boldly challenges Western Christians. Will they be ready to give aid out of pocket to poor countries, to pay higher taxes, to pay higher prices for imports, to leave their country and go personally to assist the poor nations? The pope urgently poses these questions, for he knows quite well that today for the first time in history the world has the resources and the technology to eliminate poverty from every nation, that we in the rich world therefore have the means—but *we do not have the will.*

The identical failure of will applies not only to individuals but also to entire nations. Speaking in a somewhat visionary mode, Paul describes a future where "it should be considered quite normal for an advanced country to devote a part of its production to meet their needs, and to train teachers, engineers, technicians, and scholars prepared to put their knowledge and their skill at the disposal of the less fortunate peoples" (48). Again, lest this appear to be merely an option, the pope states in no uncertain terms that failure by nations to do this "will certainly call down upon them the judgment of God and the wrath of the poor, with consequences no one can foretell" (49).

Once again, however, at this point Pope Paul moves from a hortatory approach to a very concrete and pragmatic one. Earlier, during a trip to India, the pope had presented a plan for a great World Fund, which was partially to be funded by a tax on arms to aid the most destitute (51). To avoid domination of the poor countries, even bilateral and multilateral agreements could be incorporated into this framework of world collaboration. Finally, Paul argues that the World Fund would aid in preventing waste incurred by various arms races and the ostentatious squandering of wealth (53).

It is also interesting to note that the pontiff was clearly aware more than two decades ago of the terrible dangers involved in foreign debts, which today is one of the most powerful and widespread sources of domination and dependency in the Third World. To combat this, Paul makes a number of suggestions such as low-interest or interest-free loans, extension of the periods of time for repayment, and other means of avoiding excessive burdens of debt. Today, however, his words sound both prescient and poignant, for his goal was not achieved: "Developing countries will no longer risk being overwhelmed by debts whose repayment swallows up the greater part of their gains" (54).

Equity in Trade Relations

At this point, Pope Paul concentrates his attention in some detail on what constitutes the crux in North-South economic relations and the key to long-term progress toward development: the international system of trade between rich and poor countries that continues on an unchanging course to the detriment of the latter. The pope is frank in acknowledging that all the aid to developing nations that he had been advocating throughout the letter would be to no avail if they lose far more than these gains in unfair trading practices. He is realistic enough to accept some advantages in so-called free trade, but only *if* the trading partners are relatively equal. If, however, the partners are clearly unequal, then "freedom of trade is fair only if it is subject to the demands of social justice" (59).

The pope, therefore, has no hesitation in endorsing the same norms in international economics that nations use in their domestic economies, since that is essential in order to establish more equal and thus just relations between the trading partners. His proposals are radical from a purely business point of view but are certainly essential if a decent measure of justice is to be achieved. Granted that achieving such equality is a long-term process, now is the time to initiate the discussions and negotiations that will be needed to achieve it. Consequently, he proposes international agreements on a rather broad spectrum: "They would establish general norms for regulating certain prices, for guaranteeing certain types of production, for supporting certain new industries. Who is there who does not see that such a common effort aimed at increased justice in business relations among peoples would bestow on developing nations positive assistance, the effects of which would be not only immediate but lasting?" (61).

Such boldness in moving out of accustomed routine and supposedly "natural" ways of acting must win for the pope the accolade as a pioneer in the development of international economic justice, which in my view is *the* most important issue in Christian social ethics for the foreseeable future. It should be added that in the contemporary situation Pope Paul would surely have given much space and energy to the enormous burden of debt that staggers the developing world today, advancing programs and policies for the restructuring, alleviation, and even forgiveness of this mountain of debt—not only out of charity but out of basic economic justice and self-interested concern for the stability and prosperity of the world financial system. Without these or other programs that may be more effective, the Third World will be eternally relegated to the role of Sisyphus on the world scene, straining every resource and laboring assiduously with no hope of ever escaping the enormous stone of debt.

Progress along these lines toward a more just and unified world, the pope concedes, faces many obstacles, not the least of which are the twin specters of nationalism and racism (62–63). Although he honestly recognizes the deep roots and the continuing menace of these attitudes, he remains hopeful that "a more deeply felt need for collaboration, a heightened sense of unity, will finally triumph over misunderstandings and selfishness" (64) and that a day will dawn "when international relations will be marked with the stamp of mutual respect and friendship, of interdependence in collaboration, the betterment of all seen as the responsibility of each individual" (65).

Universal Charity

As the encyclical draws to a close, Pope Paul once again turns to the lack of brotherhood in the world and points to a number of areas that a more universal charity should reach. These include the duty of hospitality for strangers, pastoral care for young students and emigrant workers, the need for social security, and the importance of educating true experts in development (66–72) while also lauding the efforts of young people and advocating a regimen of deep prayer plus resolute commitment (73–75). After stressing the need for a more effective world authority (78), Pope Paul concludes the letter by appealing to the support of all Christians, men and women of good will, government authorities, and men of learning (81–86).

But the phrase that continues to echo down through the corridors of time and that has come to be praised and quoted more than any part of the encyclical is—*development is the new name for peace.* Thus, the question Pope Paul raises at the end of the letter is also a very apt ending for this essay: "For, if the new name for peace is development, who would not wish to labor for it with all his powers?"

See also COLONIALISM; DEVELOPMENT; HUMAN RIGHTS; HUMANISM; MARRIAGE; POOR, PREFERENTIAL OPTION FOR; POVERTY.

ALFRED T. HENNELLY, S.J.

POVERTY

The Situation

Today over 1 billion people live in grinding poverty. As even the World Bank has belatedly recognized, the policies of three "development decades" have only served to widen the gap between rich and poor. To take one statistic, the gross national product of the whole of sub-Saharan Africa is roughly equal to that of Belgium, but its population is forty-five times greater. The actions of notoriously corrupt local elites often result in even these meager resources being yet more inequitably distributed, and even below this, women and children are a further impoverished underclass. In addition to the traditional dependencies of many poor countries, governments and financial institutions, mostly Western, have over the past fifteen years foisted upon the poor of the world a debt of 1.4 trillion British pounds. The notion of aid, which often has political strings attached, loses much of its real significance when the World Bank estimates that in 1988 there was a net flow of 43 billion pounds from Third World countries to creditors in the industrial world. Behind these statistics lies a truly catastrophic vista of human suffering.

Poverty is also an issue in the developed world, where a minority of the population—12.4 percent in the United States—while not living in absolute deprivation, consistently fail to share in the minimal patterns of sociocultural life and survive in extreme alienation. In all cases, prolonged poverty produces in the oppressed a pattern of internalized oppression manifested in a fatalism that intensifies the cycle of poverty.

Many partial solutions are proposed, each with a major flaw. Industrialization and technological development have so far mirrored the investment needs of the donors and not the social goals of the poor. Schooling alone produces masses of overeducated unemployed. Population control overlooks the fact that children are often the only hope of the poor as well as the fact that the parents of the next generation have already been born. The way forward seems to lie in reforming the terms of trade and the policies of the financial institutions and above all, as P. Freire has argued, in conscientizing and mobilizing the poor themselves.

Scripture

According to Scripture the poor are God's chosen ones. The revelation of God to the oppressed in Exodus is the principal hermeneutical key to the OT. The sign of the observance of the covenant is an engaged care for the poor and the weak. The code of the covenant (Exod 20:22f.) stipulates the liberation of slaves and the giving of the produce of fallow ground to the poor in the Sabbatical Year. No law may be enacted to oppress the poor or to pervert justice against them. Land may not be sold in perpetuity (Lev 25:23). In the Jubilee Year alienated property must be restored even if the price cannot be found (v. 28). The rise of the monarchy, originally contrary to the will of Yahweh, produces the class difference and rural poverty denounced, for example, by Amos (2:7; 4:1). In this context we can see the poor person of the Psalms who, helpless before the injustices of society, turns humbly to God as the only hope. Deuteronomy is at once a return to the covenant as well as a socioeconomic reform whose goal is that "there shall be no poor among you" (15:4). The prophets railed against the injustice that causes poverty and announced the word of God from the perspective of the poor.

The life of Jesus is one of self-chosen poverty, and in his preaching and praxis he identifies himself with the marginalized. The "poor" he proclaims blessed, and the valid spiritual dimension of this term cannot, as J. Dupont has demonstrated, be abstracted from material conditions. The poor are not blessed because of some interior disposition. Their privilege lies in the justice of God, who is not neutral in the face of oppression, and in the manner God wishes to establish God's reign. The messianic kingdom announced and fulfilled by Jesus is defined in relation to the disinherited of the world and comes through them. Radical discipleship means leaving all things. There is a fundamental option to be made for God or Mammon (Lk 17:7-10).

Acts lays great stress on the community of goods (2:44-45; 4:36-37). Paul goes to great pains to organize a collection for the poor of Jerusalem and tells the Corinthians that it is the measure of the genuineness of their love (2 Cor 8:8). His overall attitude to poverty is evident from the radical equality he demands in the agape (1 Cor 10). For James, the poor are the chosen ones; and the rich, whether in church or public life, are attacked (2:5-6). For Revelation, the differences made between rich and poor indicates how little the churches live according to the mind of the Lord (2:9; 3:17).

Magisterium

Before Vatican II. Modern magisterial teaching on the question of poverty begins with Leo XIII's *Rerum novarum* (1891). Deeply moved by the condition of the urban proletariat, he demanded that "some opportune remedy must be found quickly for the misery and wretchedness pressing so urgently on the majority of the working-class" (RN 2). While the encyclical remained largely at the level of exhorting the rich to justice, it was groundbreaking in the manner in which it upheld the principle of the just wage. It declared that when market forces oblige the worker to accept less than what is due, "he is made the victim of force and injustice" (34). Leo rejected a fundamental argument of economic liberalism by teaching that if the contracting parties are too unequal, consent alone does not suffice to guarantee the justice of their agreement.

Pius XI in *Quadragesimo anno* communicates a similar sense of moral outrage at the suffering of the poor (QA 59, 112) as well as a recognition that the structures of economic liberalism have caused this suffering (10, 88). He went beyond moral exhortation, demanding both "a reform of social institutions and the improvement of conduct" (77, 97–98, 127). Pius XI knew he was dealing with "an unjust economic system" whose influence was ruinous (*Divini Redemptoris* 50). He rejected not only the abuses of capitalism but also its ideological basis: "the proper ordering of economic life cannot be left to free competition" (QA 88). While regarding corporatism with a degree of "benevolent attention" (*Acta apostolicae sedis* 31 [May 31, 1931] 231), his own vision was of a vocationalism traversing class barriers (QA 82–85), wages being determined with a view to maximizing employment and not to profit (74). He strongly defended labor unions and saw them as defenders of the poor (30–35, 87).

Though preoccupied with political rather than socioeconomic issues, Pius XII went further than his predecessors in subordinating the rights of private property to the common good (AAS 36 [August 1, 1944] 252–53) and often insisted on the equitable distribution of goods (June 1, 1941). Later he seemed to give the impression that in the West at least, he considered the problem of poverty solved (AAS 44 [August 14, 1952] 791–92).

Initially John XXIII felt that "anyone who is diligent and capable has the opportunity to rise to higher levels in society" (*Ad Petri Cathedram*). Although he movingly outlines the poverty of the working classes of various lands, he seems to point to industrial development as the solution (*Mater et magistra* 68, 154, 163). Yet he clearly wanted a wider distribution of property (MM 115) and saw the arms race and prestige projects in various lands as hindering the elimination of poverty (MM 69, 198, 204; *Pacem in terris* 109). At the theoretical level he made two most important contributions to the church's understanding of overcoming poverty: first, his nuanced yet positive evaluation of the increased "socialization" of contemporary life with the consequent need for increased state intervention (MM 59–60; PT 62) demanded by the common good (MM 116–17); and second, his distinction between "false philosophical theories" and "the historical movements" deriving from them (PT 159), which opened up the dialogue with the Left.

Despite the famous intervention by Cardinal Lercaro, "We shall not be fulfilling our task properly, if we do not make the center and the soul . . . of this Council, the mystery of Christ in the poor . . . not just as one problem among others but as the central problem of the Council," Vatican II did not deal in any depth with the issue. *Gaudium et spes* recognized the needs of the Third World (GS 69, 71, 86) and reiterated the right of all to share in the goods of the earth as well as the right of the poor to take from the rich in cases of necessity (69). It questioned the terms of trade and called for a new economic order (63, 85–86). It justified under certain circumstances the expropriation and redistribution of large landed estates (71). In its insistence on the duty to help the poor "not merely out of superfluous goods" (69), the council was consciously clarifying the meaning of *Rerum novarum* 19, which was open to a different interpretation on this point.

After Vatican II. Paul VI in *Populorum progressio* recognized that the problem of poverty is worldwide (PP 3) and caused first by the imbalance of power (58–60) and the dominance of neocolonialism (passim, cf. 52), especially in the form of chronic dependence on single-crop export (7) and the terms of trade that operate to make the poor nations poorer (57). He rejects the "baseless theory . . . which considers material gain the key motive for economic progress, competition as the supreme law of economics, and private ownership of the means of production as an absolute right" (26). The text argues for a mixed economy (33). It understands how easily the poor may be tempted to violence but, while leaving open the case of "a flagrant and long-standing tyranny," counsels that it leads to a greater misery (30–31). A concerted international plan, financed by a World Fund is proposed (48–51) as well as a limitation on naked competition (61), the establishment of an effective world authority (78) and arms limitation (53). The model of social change proposed involves consensus and the mobilization of the poor themselves (15, 25, 27).

The Latin American Episcopal Council (CELAM) conference at Medellín concluded that poverty arises "from a situation of injustice that can be called institutionalized violence" (Medellín 2.16). The heart of its response is that "the Church itself has to become poor, assuming voluntarily and lovingly, the condition of the needy to bear witness to the evil it represents" (14.4). The "preference for the poorest," "means that we make ours their problems and their struggles" (14.10). Medellín leaves behind "top-down" approaches and insists that the way forward is "by means of a dynamic action of conscientization and organization of the popular sectors" (2.18). The conference sought not just a notional understanding of poverty but the actual "transformation of Latin America" (cf. Medellín Documents' general title, *The Church in the Present-Day Transformation of Latin America in the Light of the Council*).

In *Octogesima adveniens,* Paul VI addressed himself to the political problems involved in the creation of a just society. He questioned the myth of progress (OA 41), the dominant model of economic growth (42), and the political power of the transnational corporations (44). This text contains an important methodological development in Catholic social thought on poverty in its move from an exhortatory approach to an inductive one, from "social doctrine" to social analysis. "It is up to Christian communities to analyze with objectivity the situation which is proper to their own country, to shed on it the light of the Gospel's unalterable words and to draw . . . directives for action" (4). Accepting the wide variety of situations, this text rejects ready-made solutions. There can be many approaches, but each will be characterized by "a preferential respect for the poor" and "a permanent education in solidarity" (23).

The synodal document *Justitia in mundo* sees the poor as the "voiceless victims of injustice" (JM 20). This injustice is institutionalized in "the objective obstacles which social structures place in the way of conversion of hearts" (16). Poverty is the result of oppression and cannot be tackled by the trickle-down theory of development (10). The problem is the concentration of wealth, power, and decision making in the hands of small groups (9). The poor should form "new political groupings" (17), and there needs to be an educational process awakening a critical sense of injustice (52). The poor themselves have a privileged role in bringing about liberation (77), and this should influence the "modes of acting, of possessions, and life-style found within the Church herself" (40). A passage from the introduction to this text, "Action on behalf of justice . . . fully appear[s] to us as a constitutive dimension of the preaching of the Gospel," has had an enormous influence in mobilizing the people of God on the poverty issue.

Evangelii nuntiandi contributed to the theological context of the discussion on poverty by reminding the church that "only the Kingdom therefore is absolute and it makes everything else relative" (EN 8). This text introduced in a systematic way the concept of liberation into magisterial documents, giving it real theological depth not only by incorporating socioeconomic liberation but by going beyond it (9, 35).

At Puebla, CELAM reiterated the commitments of Medellín. "We affirm the need for conversion on the part of the whole Church to a preferential option for the poor, an option aimed at their integral liberation" (Puebla 1134). It devoted a whole chapter to the implications of this option. Inviting the whole church to see the face of Christ in a variety of oppressed individuals and groups, it committed the church to understand and denounce the mechanisms that generate poverty. It was anxious to go beyond a merely individual concern devoid of sociopolitical options. "Christians must commit themselves to the elaboration of historical projects that meet the needs of a given moment" (553).

John Paul II endorsed these options on many occasions especially during his 1980 visit to Brazil (*Osservatore Romano* [July 4, 1980] 1; OR [July 12, 1980] 2). In his address to the Roman curia in 1984 he spoke of "the preferential option for the poor," stating, "I have made and continue to make this 'option' my own. I identify with it. . . . It is an option which is unwavering and irreversible."

According to *Laborem exercens,* "we must first of all recall a principle that has always been taught by the Church: 'the principle of the priority of labor over capital'" (LE 12). The text seeks to describe structural injustice using the concept of the "indirect employer," for example, interstate links, transnational corporations, and lobbies (17). These "exercise a determining influence on the shaping both of the work contract and consequently of just or unjust relationships" (16). The thrust of the biblical teaching on property is succinctly stated: "The right to private property is inconceivable without responsibilities to the common good. It is subordinated to the higher principle which states that goods are meant for all" (19). It is clear that justice for the poor is achieved through struggle, which, while essentially "struggle for" justice as distinct from "struggle against" a social class, is nonetheless characterized by conflict (chap. 3) and is a reaction against something unjustified (9). The key concept here is "solidarity" (8).

At the Service of the Human Community is an ethical approach to the international debt crisis stressing the values of interdependence, co-responsibility, and trust. It will be the responsibility of the better-off to assume the larger share of the burden (SHC 1.4). It notes the perception of the International Monetary Fund as technocratic and authoritarian (2) and asks it, as well as the World Bank, to increase the representation of the poorer countries on their bodies (3.4). Industrialized nations may not act without regard to the effects of their policies on the poorer nations (3.1) and should especially avoid erratic currency fluctuations (3.1.3). Leaders of developing countries should be transparently free of corruption and adopt a lifestyle consistent with the conditions of their countries (3.2). Creditor states should find reimbursement conditions compatible with a debtor state's ability to pay and, in some cases, convert loans to grants (3.3.1). Defaulting is not advocated (2; 3.3.2).

Solicitudo rei socialis sketches with penetrating accuracy the contemporary phenomenon of poverty. Noting that the hopes of *Populorum progressio* are far from realized (SRS 12; cf. 8, 33–35), it indicates how this "intolerable burden of poverty" (13) is felt in the areas of shelter, unemployment, and debt (17–18). It argues that the problem is exacerbated by distorted media presentation of the underlying problem and an "unacceptably exaggerated concern for security" (22). It stresses the moral character of the political will needed to combat the all-consuming desire for profit and power (37). On the positive side it notes a reawakening of ecological concern (26) as well as growth in solidarity among the poor themselves where the church too must take its stand (39). It offers less a technical solution than an ethical framework characterized by a preferential love of the poor and the reiteration that private property always has a social mortgage (42; cf. LE 19).

Economic Justice for All applies the principles of Catholic social teaching to United State's economic life, stressing the human nature of work over sheer economism. Consistently reiterating the teaching that market forces alone cannot determine the common economic good, it speaks of the threefold bond of creation, covenant, and community, which establishes the moral framework of economic life (EJA 30).

Stressing that economic objectives cannot be pursued without reference to all sectors of society and to poorer countries, it confesses the failure of trade and financial policies to promote justice (264).

Following on this, *Relieving Third World Debt* acknowledges that the source of the debt problem is "injudicious lending of oil money" "for often ill-conceived projects" (RTWD 8) and asks why the poor "who have received little or no benefit from it have to bear the greater burden of its payment" (11). Since in the aggregate commentators consider the debt to be unjust (28), it argues that repaying it would in many cases "violate the minimal standards of social justice" (34). The debt is a manifestation of an unworkable and inequitable system (45), and the obligation to pay should be overridden or modified (41), especially in the case of Africa (52). It asks the U.S. government to help modify the policies of the World Bank and the International Money Fund.

Theology

The core insight of contemporary Catholic theological method is that solidarity with the poor and participation in their struggle against the structures that cause poverty is a privileged hermeneutical perspective for a truly Christian theology.

As J. B. Metz has demonstrated, much "liberal" or "progressive" theology serves as a legitimation mechanism for the concerns of the bourgeois subject. He seeks to deprivatize theology and articulate it as a praxis of solidarity with the poor and suffering, its starting point being a reading of history and social reality from the "underside."

G. Gutiérrez argues that without a rootedness in the praxis of the liberation of the poor, theology will be deaf to essential nuances of the word of God, an insight implicitly endorsed by *Libertatis conscientia* (74). This rootedness is obligatory for the theologian and is even a condition of scientific work. The poor are the architects of their own liberation and also that of their oppressors. This process becomes a *locus theologicus* in which the poor themselves are no longer passive recipients. For traditional theologians this involves a conversion to the poor person and to the exploited social class. It also implies a breaking of links with certain institutions of privilege and power.

Stressing the essential poverty of all creatures before God, L. Boff calls for a conversion experience whereby there is an irruption of the reality of poverty into the consciousness of the church. This in turn needs to be focused by social analysis. The Christian community's option for the poor is not reducible to the moral condemnation of the international imperialism of money but is a matter of overcoming it historically. The poor possess a sacramental function: in them we meet the Lord in a privileged way. Christ has identified himself with them, and his kingdom comes through them and their struggle. Consequently the very identity of the church is bound up with the poor.

For J. Sobrino the otherness of God is revealed in the otherness of the poor. Thus the task of the church is not merely to help the poor nor even just to give them a greater role in its institutions. Rather it is a question of actually structuring the church on the basis of their aspirations and struggles, since it is through them that the kingdom of God comes. The transcendental correlation between the essence of the gospel and the emancipation of the poor means that neither can be understood except in terms of the other.

The present writer has sought to demonstrate the theoretical and methodological rigor of these theological approaches.

Conclusion

Within this vast body of wisdom and experience that is the Catholic tradition on the issue of poverty there are a number of developments. Among these the following stand out: the realization that (1) poverty is basically the result of structural injustice; (2) the way forward lies in a retrieval of the scriptural praxis of liberation; (3) the church's contribution is not only exhortative and didactic but a matter of freely chosen simplicity of life coupled with an insertion into the struggle of the poor for justice; (4) the poor themselves are the principal architects of a renewed humanity.

Today this tradition has recaptured the biblical urgency of justice and liberation, is equal to the nuances of contemporary socioeconomic life, and is increasingly rooted in the poor themselves.

See also AFFIRMATIVE ACTION; ALMSGIVING; HUNGER; LIBERATION THEOLOGY; PAUL VI; POOR, PREFERENTIAL OPTION FOR; WORKER PRIESTS.

Bibliography: L. Boff, *A Fè na Periferia do Mondo* (Petropolis: Vozes, 1978). D. Dorr, *Option for the Poor* (Dublin: Gill & Macmillan, 1983). P. Freire, *Pedagogy of the Oppressed* (London: Penguin, 1968). G. Gutiérrez, *The Power of the Poor in History* (New York: Orbis, 1983). J. B. Metz, *Glaube in Geschichte und Gesellshaft* (Mainz, 1977). J. O'Brien, *Theology and the Option for the Poor* (Collegeville, Minn.: The Liturgical Press, 1992). J. Sobrino, *The True Church of the Poor* (London: SCM, 1983).

JOHN O'BRIEN, C.S.Sp.

PRAXIS

The English word "praxis" means "doing" or "action"; it often refers to a customary practice. Although it is sometimes used unreflectively simply to refer to practice, it has emerged as a major category in theology over the past thirty years because it contains within itself intricate tensions of meaning. For example, the Greek form of the word is often used in dialectical relationship with *theoria.* Since *praxis* is a form of human activity, it cannot be separated from human thinking, as in the phrase "blind action." Praxis implies theoretical understanding (*theoria*) and more directly is guided by practical reasoning. In Aristotle *praxis* is further distinguished from the activity of making or constructing (*poiesis*) that is ruled by technical skill.

Praxis is not merely manipulative action, suggesting a crude utilitarianism, but is governed by wisdom and moral reasoning. The category of praxis, moreover, contains a tension between its individual and social dimensions. Beyond personal action praxis refers as well to common patterns of behavior, human action that is supported by a set or system of meanings and values that are related to public reasoning. The importance of the category lies in the dialectical co-determination of thinking and doing in the personal and social spheres. With this category theologians are in the process of binding together inextricably faith with its doctrines and Christian life, theology and ethics, and the inseparable social and personal dimensions of these four areas.

The fruitfulness of the category of praxis can be illustrated by enumerating some of its critical functions. First, both the philosophy of language and the sociology of knowledge have shown that the meaning of language is conditioned by praxis, by "forms of life" (Wittgenstein) and more generally socially accepted behavior. Thus praxis is an area of investigation for opening up both the meaning of texts from the past and the received meaning they have today. Second, praxis is the criterion for the authenticity of knowledge; one can only be said to really know or believe something important in the measure that it bears fruit in action. On the social level, then, corporate praxis becomes the criterion of authentic witness; because authority lies in praxis, witness without praxis is not credible. Third, although thinking and doing are mutually co-determinative, still praxis is often prior to thought in the sense that more spontaneous praxis generates reflective theory. This is especially true on the social level, where many doctrines of faith and morals have emerged out of reflection on praxis that was already in place. On this basis the very method of theology and ethics has taken a turn toward "reflection on the praxis of faith." Fourth, in the current situation of historical consciousness human freedom and its creativity have taken on a new central importance. Within this context reflection on the reciprocally enveloping operations of knowing, willing, and doing leads to the conclusion that thinking and deciding are *for* action and life. This yields an area that must be investigated for verifying claims to truth; what kind of action does any truth entail? The frequently heard slogan of the priority of orthopraxis to orthodoxy is based on these last two points. Fifth, it is sometimes said that praxis is the final criterion of truth, but this cannot be held undialectically. Often erroneous theory-laden praxis is itself a false consciousness that authenticates itself. It is only when such praxis is resisted by segments of society and by reality itself, thus engendering a new and coherent theory and praxis, that such false consciousness is overcome.

See also DISCIPLESHIP; FREEDOM; MARXISM; MORAL LIFE, CHRISTIAN; POLITICAL THEOLOGY; POOR, PREFERENTIAL OPTION FOR; REASON, ROLE OF.

ROGER HAIGHT, S.J.

PREACHING, ROLE OF

The creative OT scholar Walter Brueggemann recently wrote: "The theological scandal of biblical faith, especially when rendered into political, economic issues, is indeed upsetting. How is a pastor to give voice to this scandal in a society that is hostile to it, in a church that is often unwilling to host the scandal, and when we ourselves as teachers and pastors of the church are somewhat queasy about the scandal as it touches our own lives? How can the radical dimension of the Bible as it touches public reality be heard in the church?" ("The Preacher, the Text, and the People," *Theology Today* 47, no. 3 [October 1990] 237).

First, a word on two words: social justice. Preachers of the Word must recognize that Scripture is "social" from beginning to end. Deciding to share divine love with creatures shaped to intelligence and love, God had in mind not an endless succession of atoms, of monads, individual human beings that might agree by contract to band together in community so as to live more congenially, more economically, more securely. God had in mind a human family, a community wherein no one could say to any other, "I have no need of you." Such was our origin, our identity, our vocation, our destiny. From the beginning God had in view a community in the likeness of the triune God, whose very personhood is constituted by relatedness—a "being toward" one another. As Vatican II phrased it in the Decree on the Church's Missionary Activity, "According to [God's] plan, the whole human race is to form one people of God. . . . The plan of the Creator, who formed man and woman to [God's] own image and likeness, will be realized when all who share one human nature . . . will be able to say 'Our Father'" (*Ad gentes* 7). Scripture in its totality is the story of that plan's unfolding. Preaching on social issues, therefore, is not a desperate search for a handful of pertinent passages; the social dimension pervades God's Word.

Moreover, Scripture does not limit "justice" to an ethical construct: give to each what is due to each, what the other deserves, because he or she has rights that have been written into law or can be proven from philosophy. This is indeed important. But the justice Catholic social thought has extracted from Scripture includes that and rises above it. What was the justice God wanted to "roll down like waters" (Amos 5:24)? In the prophetic tradition of the OT, justice was a web of relationships that stemmed from Israel's covenant with God. The Israelites were to father the fatherless and feed the stranger, not because the orphan and the outsider deserved it but because this was the way *God* had acted with *them.* A text in Deuteronomy is telling: "You shall also love the stranger, for you were strangers in the land of Egypt" (Deut 10:19). In freeing the oppressed, they were mirroring the loving God who had delivered *them* from oppression, had freed them from Pharaoh. Their justice was to image the justice not of man and woman but of God. For Israel, the practice of justice was an expression of steadfast love. Not to execute justice was not to worship God.

Such was the justice Jesus inherited and commanded: "fidelity to the demands of a relationship" (J. Donahue, "Biblical Perspectives on Justice," in J. Haughey, ed., *The Faith That Does Justice* [New York: Paulist, 1977] 69). It is the second great commandment of the law and the gospel: "You shall love your neighbor as yourself" (Lev 19:18; Mt 22:39). This is the justice Jesus proclaimed in his programmatic message in Nazareth's synagogue: "The Spirit of the Lord is upon me, because he has anointed me to preach good news to the poor. He has sent me to proclaim release to the captives, . . . to set at liberty those who are oppressed" (Lk 4:18). This is the justice the church has inherited as a task it may not refuse. For, as the 1971 synod of bishops declared in its message *On Justice in the World,* the vindication of justice and participation in the process of transforming the world is "a constitutive element of the preaching of the gospel" (*De iustitia in mundo* [Vatican Press, 1971] introduction, p. 5). As the 1974 synod realized, the church "believes firmly that the promotion of human rights is required by the gospel and is central to her ministry" (*Origins* 4 [1974] 318). In 1976 the International Theological Commission, an advisory body serving the pope, spoke of "a new consciousness" within the church, the realization that Christians have a moral responsibility to reform "even situations and structures that are unjust" (*Origins* 7, no. 20 [November 3, 1977] 311). The "option for the poor" is a choice for the gospel.

But granted that the church must proclaim justice as part and parcel of its gospel, is the pulpit, specifically the liturgy, an appropriate locus for such proclamation? French theologian Yves Congar put it pointedly. The specific function of the homily is not simply to explain the liturgical mystery but "to bring the faithful into the mystery by throwing light on their life so that they can unite it to this mystery" ("Sacramental Worship and Preaching," in *The Renewal of Preaching: Theory and Practice* [Concilium 33; New York: Paulist, 1968] 60). The liturgy's insights are rarely obvious; liturgical texts and forms tend to get fixed and rigid, are not much different in Buenos Aires than in Boise, Idaho. What the homily does is extend the immemorial symbols to a particular time and place, to a particular people. And so the preacher must preach to this people's needs, this people's hungers, this people's Christian obligations.

But how concrete dare the preacher get? As some Catholics see it, the preacher should propound general principles, preach the unadorned Word, leave to the people the right decisions in the moral order. Two objections challenge such an approach. (1) It betrays a consistent tradition, from Jesus of Nazareth through fathers of the church like Ambrose and Chrysostom to John Paul II in Santo Domingo specifying a more just world: "no more children without sufficient nutrition, education, instruction; no more poor peasants without land; no more workers mistreated; no more who have too much while others lack everything; no inequality in administering justice" (*Origins* 8, no. 34 [February 8, 1979] 543). (2) Homilies that avoid concrete applications risk saying nothing. If I limit my preaching to the broad biblical imperatives—"No one lives on bread alone," "My peace I give to you," "Love your neighbor as you love yourself," "Seek first the kingdom of God," "Wives, be subject to your husbands"—hungry stomachs will stay bloated, the arms race will escalate, dissidents will rot in political prisons, blacks will return to their slavery, and women will continue to be second-class citizens in much of the world.

The institutional church, Karl Rahner insisted, need not, should not, and does not regard itself "solely as the doctrinaire guardian and teacher of abstract principles which . . . are liable to carry within themselves the danger of a terrifying sterility." It has and should have the courage of concrete imperatives, concrete directives, "even in regard to socio-political action by Christians in the world" (*The Shape of the Church to Come* [London: SPCK, 1974] 77, 76). This same courage the preacher must carry into the pulpit.

But, how concrete? There is no simple solution. Rarely is the issue as clear-cut as, say, the Civil Rights Act of 1964. Most political and socioeconomic issues call for discernment; some call for blood, sweat, and tears. Here a handful of suggestions:

1. We dare not bar the controversial from the pulpit simply because it is controversial. The gospel must be moved to this age, this people, but the meaning and demands of the gospel today are chock-full of complexity. And the more complex an issue, the more open to controversy.

2. The pulpit is not the place to *solve* complex issues—ecology or the economy, business ethics or health-care insurance, capital punishment or a reversal of *Roe* v. *Wade,* military intervention in the Persian Gulf. It *is* the place to *raise* the issues, to raise awareness, to raise consciousness. I may even tell the congregation where I stand. Not to impose my convictions but to spur the faithful to personal reflection in the light of the gospel. Precisely here is the preacher's key role in Catholic social action. For despite the widespread involvement of U.S. Catholicism in relieving the plight of the poor and powerless, Catholic social thought remains the church's best-kept secret.

3. Lest I take unfair advantage of a captive audience, I should provide another forum where controversial issues may be properly discussed, even debated. For I must guard against a persistent priestly peril, where I see the ordained minister as alone bearing the burden of Christian guidance. Here Vatican II was compelling: "Let the laity not imagine that their pastors are always such experts that to every problem which arises, however complicated, they can readily give a concrete solution, or even that such is their mission" (Constitution on the Church in the Modern World 43).

4. Effective preaching on social justice is a task of persuasion. It calls for competence and compassion; I must know whereof I speak and I must love the people to whom I speak. Scripture's just word and today's injustice must be the air I breathe. Yet I dare not cut a wide and savage swath across a congregation; rather, I see before me a believing community that, like the Israelites of old, needs to be led rather than driven on its tortuous pilgrimage to the Promised Land. To inflame the hearts of the faithful, the preacher must love this paradoxical people, this struggling, sinning, saintly people of God's special selecting—love them with a crucifying passion. Only if preachers love dare they address to them the word that sears as it heals, dare to proclaim, "Hear, O new Israel! The word of the Lord has come unto me."

5. To move a believing congregation to corporate action—for children hungry and the aged alone, for men homeless and women abused, for the drug-addicted and the AIDS-afflicted, for the deathly sick and the inhumanly imprisoned, for the very earth we rape—the preacher must have "fire in the belly." To be effective, therefore, a preacher of the just word must undergo a personal conversion, become a new man or woman, be turned on by the crucified, perhaps even walk in the shoes of the unfortunate.

6. Today's prophet can learn much from the Hebrew prophets. For they were extraordinarily sensitive to evil and injustice, felt fiercely for the silent agony of the

plundered poor, challenged sacred institutions and beliefs and persons, were often lonely and frustrated; their words were charged with divine power because they had experienced God as "living care" (see A. Heschel, *The Prophets* [New York: Harper & Row, 1962] 3–26). Today's prophet can learn perhaps even more from the prophet Christ, who not only preached compassion as preferable to sacrifice but preferred the company of the despised and downtrodden and sealed his just word with an unjust death.

See also CHURCH, SOCIAL MISSION OF; EVANGELII NUNTIANDI; JUSTICE IN THE WORLD; MODERN CATHOLIC SOCIAL THOUGHT; POOR, PREFERENTIAL OPTION FOR; SCRIPTURE, USE OF IN CATHOLIC SOCIAL ETHICS; SOLLICITUDO REI SOCIALIS.

Bibliography: W. Burghardt, *Preaching: The Art and the Craft* (New York: Paulist, 1987). J. Donahue, *The Gospel in Parable: Metaphor, Narrative, and Theology in the Synoptic Gospels* (Philadelphia: Fortress, 1988). F. Kammer, *Doing Faithjustice: An Introduction to Catholic Social Thought* (New York: Paulist, 1991).

WALTER J. BURGHARDT, S.J.

PRISON

A prison, generally speaking, is any institution that confines persons involuntarily either prior to trial or following a sentence. It includes city and county jails, workhouses, penal colonies, reformatories, and penitentiaries. In the strict sense, a prison is a state or federal facility that incarcerates persons only after they are convicted of serious crimes. While the prison in the general sense has existed from the beginning of human society, prison as a punitive instrument where one serves time for offenses committed is a relatively new invention. It emerged in the United States as the penitentiary in the 18th century and expanded into England, continental Europe, and Canada after 1850.

Before 1775 imprisonment was rarely used as punishment for a serious crime or felony. England or France, for example, would punish lawbreakers either by fine, corporal punishment, deportation, or execution. The accused were detained in county and borough jails (gaols) not in order to punish but to ensure their presence at the trial. British institutions of short-term confinement included the debtors' prison and the house of correction that imprisoned vagrants and put them to work.

An important issue is the variety of ways church and society have used to justify the confinement of alleged or convicted offenders through the centuries: as guaranty for their appearance at trial, as retribution, as deterrence, as rehabilitation, and as protection of citizens. A brief historical sketch reveals how these different justifications arose.

The Christian church from its inception became deeply involved in prisons and prisoners both because Jesus proclaimed liberty to captives (Lk 4:18), even identifying himself with "the least," including prisoners (Mt 25:36), and because Christians were persecuted and imprisoned until the Edict of Milan (A.D. 313). The church sought various means to free and to protect prisoners. When the church became a tolerated religion under Emperor Constantine in 324, it gained the right of asylum for those seeking refuge from civil authorities. Bishops possessed the right to seek pardon from the state for prisoners sentenced to death. The Council of Nicaea in 325 designated certain officials to visit the imprisoned and care for their spiritual needs.

While the church in the spirit of the gospel sought to temper justice with mercy, it developed during medieval times a doctrine of expiation that called for atonement for sins and crimes through temporal punishment. The church viewed immoral behavior as a violation against the divine order as well as against society. Atonement required in some cases restitution, in other cases physical punishment, and for capital crimes execution. Besides calling for punishment as expiation or retribution for crimes, the church also justified punitive measures as a deterrent, even within the monastery where it imprisoned monks who violated the Holy Rule. It would issue public penances that would serve as an example for all to see.

St. Thomas Aquinas defended punishment (including capital punishment) on the basis of retributive justice, which obliges one to render good or evil to one for having done something good or evil to another (*Summa theologiae* I-II, q. 21, art. 3). Inasmuch as an evil action injures society as well as the individual, a double retribution is owed: restitution to the victim and restoration of tranquillity to the commonwealth. Punishment carried out by the state satisfied the latter goal. St. Thomas also underscored the medicinal or rehabilitative goal of punishment.

In justifying the right to kill those threatening the common good, St. Thomas said capital punishment should be carried out by the laity and not by the clergy because the latter is entrusted with the ministry of the new law, "wherein no punishment of death or of bodily maiming is appointed" (ST II-II, q. 64, art. 4). His reasoning implies a tension if not a contradiction between the new law of love, expressed through forgiveness, and harsh corporal punishment and execution. Many others, like the contemporary U.S. Catholic bishops, have struggled with this same tension: whether cruel, vengeful punishment and execution fit with the gospel of love. The U.S. bishops said in 1980 that the teaching and example of Jesus regarding the forgiveness of enemies opposes the torturing, maiming, and exercise of vindictiveness toward prisoners. Jesus' forgiving injustices and giving up his life for the ransom of many, according to the bishops, would support the abolition of the death penalty (U.S. bishops, "Statement on Capital Punishment," *Origins* [November 27, 1980] 375–76).

This tension between cruel punishment and forgiveness reached a crisis in the 18th and 19th centuries over the inhumane floggings, torture, and maiming of offenders. Corporal punishment carried out in England and North America included flogging, stocks and pillory, mutilation, branding, and chain-gang labor (H. Barnes and N. Teeters, *New Horizons in Criminology,* Foreword by F. Tannenbaum [New York: Prentice-Hall, 1945] 405–13). The state would also execute offenders for capital crimes and would deport felons, for lesser crimes like theft, to a penal colony in America or Norfolk Island (J. Barry, *Alexander Maconochie of Norfolk Island: A Study of a Pioneer in Penal Reform* [London: Oxford Univ. Press, 1958]). England, for example, exiled annually approximately one thousand offenders to the American colonies and, following the American Revolution in 1776, transported its serious offenders to Australia until about the mid-19th century (M. Sherman and G. Hawkins, *Imprisonment in America* [Chicago: Univ. of Chicago Press, 1981] 53).

Brutal corporal punishment and public executions became intolerable. As Michel Foucault observed, "This need for punishment without torture was first formulated as a cry from the heart or from an outraged nature" (M. Foucault, *Discipline and Punish: The Birth of the Prison,* trans. A. Sheridan [New York: Vintage, 1979] 6). It questioned the justice of this type of retribution: When does state-authorized punishment become more barbarous than the original crime? Ideas from the Enlightenment combined with innovative institutional changes by religious leaders gradually shifted the emphasis from retribution-deterrence to rehabilitation.

The Enlightenment challenged the Calvinist doctrine of sin that regarded human nature as corrupt, that accepted crime as inevitable, and that insisted upon retributive measures executed severely, even cruelly, for violators of the law (D. Rothman, *The Discovery of the Asylum* [Boston: Little, Brown, 1971] 17–18, 57–58). In sharp contrast, the Deists viewed human beings as the supreme achievement of God's creation. Rationalists of the Enlightenment saw unbounded potential for improvement, especially in reforming social institutions. Prison reformer Cesare Beccaria argued that inhumane punishment provoked further criminal behavior in order to avoid punishment for the initial crime (C. Beccaria, *On Crimes and Punishment,* trans. H. Paolucci [Indianapolis, 1963] 43–44).

The monastic cloister within the Roman Catholic tradition contributed significantly to the new emphasis on rehabilitation. French Benedictine Dom Jean Mabillon observed toward the end of the 17th century that monastic cells, adjoined by a little garden, would afford the wayward the opportunity to live in quiet solitude and to work, pray, and do penance (F. Wines, *Punishment and Reformation* [Crowell, 1895] 143). The monastic idea influenced Pope Clement XI, who in 1704 founded the Hospice of San Michele for delinquent boys. The boys worked during the day and lived in private cells at night. In 1735, Pope Clement XII built a similar kind of institution for young women. Clement XI's emphasis on rehabilitation over deterrence was engraved in an inscription over the entrance to the hospice: "It is insufficient to restrain the wicked by punishment, unless you render them virtuous by corrective discipline."

Flemish magistrate Jean Vilain incorporated ideas of monastic discipline in his Octagon prison at Ghent. Built in 1773, it aimed to reform inmates by means of hard work and by teaching them a trade that would enable them to make a living upon their release. John Howard, a sheriff of Bedfordshire, England, and perhaps the greatest of prison reformers in modern times, visited San Michele and the Octagon and other European prisons. Based on his research, he wrote a classic called *The State of Prisons,* in which he conceived the ideal penitentiary, where inmates, housed in cells, could undergo penitence through religious instruction, silence, work, and education. His work exerted an important influence on the penitentiary system in the United States and Canada.

The Quakers of Pennsylvania established in 1776 a Prisoners' Aid Society, which contributed significantly to the penitentiary system. Following Howard's method, they persuaded the state of Pennsylvania that silence, isolation, and hard work were necessary ingredients for religious conversion. The Pennsylvania system built its penitentiary based on this philosophy. The prison assigned offenders to single cells and enforced this solitary confinement even during manual labor and exercise. Charles Dickens, who visited the Cherry Hill Prison in 1842, denounced it as "a slow and daily tampering with the mysteries of the brain to be immeasurably worse than any torture of the body" (C. Dickens, *American Notes for General Circulation* [London: Chapman & Hall, 1842] 120). Indeed, the solitude and silence drove some to madness and a few to suicide. Nonetheless, many European nations adopted the Pennsylvania penitentiary system. The Auburn system in New York, which became the model for state penitentiaries in the United States and Canada, modified the Pennsylvania system by allowing inmates to work in groups, but always in strict silence brutally enforced by flogging (M. Jackson, *Prisoners of Isolation: Solitary Confinement in Canada* [Toronto: Univ. of Toronto Press, 1983]. See chap. 2: "The Evolution of Penitentiary Discipline in Canada").

Imposing solitary confinement was intended to rehabilitate the prisoner and stop corporal punishment. In fact, however, it failed to achieve either goal. Nearly every form of punishment in the prepenitentiary days was brought back into the penitentiary to enforce discipline (Barnes and Teeters, *New Horizons,* 583).

Since 1925 a new concept called "corrections" followed a medical model that first diagnosed, classified, and then treated offenders. Using the behavioral sciences, skilled professionals worked to rehabilitate men and women so that they could return to the community. Prisons adopted the indeterminate sentence that allowed the professionals (who served on the parole board) to determine the release date. The community played no role in this operation.

Close observers of prisons in the United States and Canada have often pointed out that the modern prison, however progressive, continues to punish in a cruel and unusual mode. It also fails in its efforts to rehabilitate. Prisons are primarily punitive because they deprive inmates of their freedom, deny them many fundamental rights, and separate them from family and friends. In order to achieve rehabilitation, criminal-justice systems must address these issues of freedom, rights, and community. Prison chaplains and criminologists today offer a number of constructive proposals toward rehabilitating the offender and helping the community. They suggest the following: preventative methods such as community boards to resolve neighborhood grievances; programs of victim-offender reconciliation; better diagnostic and treatment centers and smaller facilities, like cottages, near the community of the offender; work-release programs; and returning more offenders to the community under strict but understanding supervision (*Who Is the Prisoner? A Project of the Conference of Jesuit Prison Personnel,* ed. G. Anderson et al. [New Orleans: The Institute of Human Relations, 1985]). Because many fewer women than men are imprisoned, correctional institutions for women are even more remote from family, friends, lawyers, and community resources. Moreover, female prison populations are more heterogenous and therefore offer a smaller range of treatment and vocational programs (N. Rafter, "Gender and Justice: The Equal Protection Issue," in *The American Prison: Issues in Research and Policy,* ed. L. Goodstein and D. MacKenzie [New York: Plenum, 1989] 94–95).

Important socioeconomic problems and issues of social justice underlie the prison and criminal-justice system today. Those who go to prison today are predominately young urban males, disproportionately black and Hispanic, unemployed, poorly educated, and often products of unstable homes. As the U.S. bishops pointed out in their 1986 pastoral letter on the U.S. economy, "the costs to society are also evident in the rise in crime associated with joblessness." Increases in unemployment give rise to increases in the prison population (National Conference of Catholic Bishops, *Economic Justice for All: Pastoral Letter on Catholic Social Teaching and the U.S. Economy* [Washington: United States Catholic Conference, 1986] 142).

See also CAPITAL PUNISHMENT; DETERRENCE; HUMAN RIGHTS; MARGINAL PERSONS; THOMAS AQUINAS, CONTRIBUTION OF; TORTURE.

THOMAS L. SCHUBECK, S.J.

PRIVACY, RIGHT TO

Historical. Though some claim the roots of the right to privacy can be found in the writings of Montesquieu, and though the right is found in Vatican II (*Dignitatis humanae; Gaudium et spes* 26) as well as the United Nation's International Covenant on Civil and Political Rights (1966; art. 17), still, the right has incomparable significance in the juridical history of the United States.

In 1886 in *Boyd* v. *United States* a victim of a crime refused to turn over certain private papers. The Fourth Amendment's protection from illegal search and the Fifth's protection against self-incrimination defended the victim against any invasion of "the privacies of life." In 1890 Samuel Warren and Louis Brandeis coauthored an article defending privacy by declaring it a general principle that protects one from defamation of character, breach of confidentiality, and invasion of property. In 1891 a citizen refused a medical examination, and in *Union Pacific Railway Co.* v. *Botsford* the Court ruled in favor of the citizen claiming that "no right is held more sacred . . . than the right of every individual to the possession and control of his own person." Later, in 1928, Brandeis declared in *Olmstead* v. *United States* that privacy is "the right to be let alone—the most comprehensive of rights and the right most valued by civilized men."

Three later uses define the right. First the right protected marriage and the raising of children from state intrusions. In *Meyer* v. *Nebraska* (1923) the Court invoked the Fourteenth Amendment on due process to protect families who wanted their children to study a modern language other than English, a choice that a Nebraska ordinance denied. The decision recognized an individual's rights to marry, establish a home, and bring up children. Privacy again appeared in the background of *Pierce* v. *Society of Sisters* (1925) when an Oregon statute required eight- to sixteen-year-old children to attend only public school. The Court ruled against Oregon on the grounds that it "unreasonably interferes with the liberty of parents and guardians to direct the upbringing and education of children under their control." More recently privacy protected marriage rights in *Loving* v. *Virginia* (1967), which struck down an antimiscegenation law, again invoking the Fourteenth Amendment.

The second use concerns "propertied privacy." Here privacy protected property owners and was used against both business investigations and many New Deal initiatives. Eventually this use of privacy was replaced, and the restricted understanding of privacy as protection from personal invasions was again the norm.

The third use is first found in 1965 in *Griswold* v. *Connecticut,* which ruled against the state's right to ban the use of or information about contraceptives. The Court ruled that procreation prevention was a fundamental right of married couples. Justice Douglas' opinion expounded on "various guarantees" found in the "penumbras" of the first, fourth, fifth, and ninth amendments, which "create zones of privacy." The majority of justices, however, saw the most solid support for privacy again in the Fourteenth Amendment. In 1972 in *Skinner* v. *Oklahoma* the Court struck down a state law that allowed a state to sterilize a felon three times convicted. The right to procreate was considered a fundamental right. In the same year *Eisenstadt* v. *Baird* argued on the basis of the Fourteenth Amendment that the right found in *Griswold* belonged to all individuals. In this decision, Justice Brennan, writing the majority opinion, stated: "If the right of privacy means anything, it is the right of the *individual,* married or single, to be free from unwarranted governmental intrusion into matters so fundamentally affecting a person as the decision whether to bear or beget a child." These decisions led to *Roe* v. *Wade* (1973), wherein invoking the Fourteenth Amendment the Court expanded the concept: "This right of privacy . . . is broad enough to encompass a woman's decision whether or not to terminate her pregnancy." This use then marks a shift from protecting the individual from social intrusions to granting several rights that had not yet been defined.

Seemingly this process of using privacy to justify further rights of self-determination was initiated in the issue concerning the withdrawal or withholding of extraordinary means of life support. In *In re Quinlan* the New Jersey Supreme Court ruled both that privacy could justify the decision to withdraw certain life support systems and that a patient's privacy could be asserted by family members when the patient is incompetent. Recently, however, as in the *Cruzan* case, the Supreme Court refuses to invoke privacy in granting more rights for self-determination. Understanding the right in its original restricted context, the justices refuse to give it the expansive and subsidiary right-begetting function it held from *Griswold* on.

The importance of context. Privacy functions according to the ethos that advocates its use. In a liberal context, the right becomes an ever-expanding concept endowing the individual with greater freedoms from any claims by the state on behalf of the common good. In a communitarian ethos, since the collective in the name of the common good already enjoys considerable access to decision making in the life of the individual, the right becomes a defensive instrument to protect individuals from further intrusion and to safeguard to some extent any possible self-determination. In the former it legitimates greater prerogatives; in the latter it prevents the ethos from becoming oppressive. Thus the more liberal a society is, the greater the right endorses individualistic behavior; the more communitarian a society is, the greater the need for the right to protect a member's self-determination. No society, however, is purely liberal or communitarian, and so differing grounds prompt the use of the right.

Theological literature. Generally privacy is linked here with self-determination but in a context that tries to capture the strengths of both the communitarian and liberal views. Johnstone, for instance, proposes privacy as the protected zone wherein a person can exercise self-determination, pursuing ends in a shared moral climate wherein the individual and society respect the claims of each other, that is, the personal good of the individual and the common good of society. This captures the more moderate use of the right as found in the initial and the very recent court decisions on the matter.

See also PLURALISM; PUBLIC AND PRIVATE, RELATIONSHIP OF.

Bibliography: B. Johnstone, "The Right to Privacy: The Ethical Perspective," *The American Journal of Jurisprudence* 29 (1984) 73–94. R. McCormick, "The Moral Right to Privacy," in *How Brave a New World* (Garden City, N.Y.: Doubleday, 1981) 352–61. P. Riga, "Privacy and the Right to Die," *The Catholic Lawyer* 26 (1981) 89–126. P. Smith, "The Right of Privacy: Roe v. Wade Revisited," *The Jurist* 43/2 (1983) 289–317. A. Westin, *Privacy and Freedom* (New York: Athenum, 1967).

JAMES F. KEENAN, S.J.

PRIVATE PROPERTY

Private property refers to the relationship of ownership obtaining between persons (individual or "juristic persons") and tangible objects (e.g., land and chattels) or intangibles (e.g., stocks and shares, or profits and rents). In both common and civil law systems, legal title to property generates property rights that confer direct and immediate authority over the disposition of property and determine the conditions of its legitimate possession, use, and enjoyment. Legal systems distinguish the original and derivative acquisition of property rights, movable and immovable property, personal and real property (realty), and goods of consumption and goods of production.

Private Property in Scripture

In the OT, Israel is itself described as God's "private possession," a divine patrimony preserved in covenantal fidelity (Deut 7:6-8). Israel's possession of the land and its fruits is contingent upon faithful observance of the Torah (Gen 24:35; 30:30; Deut 4:1-5; 8:7-20; 11:8; 28:11-14): in Psalm 37 those who possess the land are described as the "meek" who "wait for the Lord" and "the righteous" (Ps 37:9-11, 29).

In recognition of the land as a divine inheritance, the Torah forbids the irrevocable transfer of land ownership, though disposal of movable property is permitted. Traditional tribal and familial holdings were to be preserved in perpetuity so that no Israelite is denied the blessings of land (Lev 25:23-34; Deut 4:40; Josh 14:9; 1 Kgs 21:3). The Torah recognizes the right of redemption of patrimonial land (Lev 25:25-28); the general remission of debts in the Sabbath or fallow year (Exod 23:10-11; Lev 25:1-7; Deut 15:1ff., 12ff.); and the restoration of the land to its original owners or their heirs in the Jubilee Year, the culmination of seven Sabbatical Year periods (Lev 25:8ff.). Complementing the personal duty of charity to the poor and dispossessed (Lev 25:35; Deut 15:7; Eccl 5:1) were the legally established institutions of the "second tithe" (Deut 14:29ff.; 26:12) and prohibitions against interest (Exod 22:24; Lev 25:36; Deut 23:20) and harvesting the borders of fields or the gleanings (Lev 19:9ff.; Deut 14:29; 24:19ff.).

In the prophetic literature, property rights were subordinated to the covenantal obligation to defend the claims of the *anawim* so that none are deprived of earthly blessing (Isa 1:11ff.; 3:14ff.; Jer 6:18-21; 7:4-7; 22:13-17; Ezek 16:49; 22:29; 45:9ff.; Hos 4:1-3; 6:6; Amos 5:21-27; Mic 6:6-8). Amos denounced those "who trample upon the needy, and bring the poor of the land to an end" (Amos 8:4-8), while Isaiah condemned those who "turn aside the needy from justice and rob the poor of my people of their right" (Isa 10:1-3). In the Wisdom literature, Ben Sira extolled the prosperity of the just, yet decried the state of "the poor" who are but "pastures for the rich" (Sir 13:19ff.; 34:22; cf. Prov 21:3).

In the NT, Jesus announces the eschatological Jubilee Year in his messianic proclamation that "the Lord has anointed me to bring good tidings to the poor" (Lk 4:16ff.; 7:22; Isa 61:1ff.). The imminence of the "day of the Lord's favor" requires the renunciation of "unrighteous mammon," for in the reign of God inaugurated in Jesus, it is the "meek" who "shall inherit the land" (Lk 16:9; Mt 5:4). "Precious to God," the heirs of the kingdom are "a people to be God's personal possession" (1 Pet 2:4-10).

While the Gospel narratives presume customary forms of acquisition, possession, and disposal of goods, Jesus bids his disciples renounce their mundane cares and trust in the loving providence of God, their "heavenly Father" (Mt 6:25-34; Lk 12:22-32). The parables of Jesus condemn the "deceit of riches" and the idolatry of covetousness (Mt 6:24; 13:18-23; 19:16-26; Mk 4:13-20; 10:17-31; 12:41-44; Lk 8:11-15; 12:16-21; 16:13; 19-31; 18:18-30; 21:1-4). The disciples are to imitate the divine munificence of their Master, who though "rich in faithful love" (Eph 2:4-5) "became poor, so that by his poverty you might become rich" (2 Cor 8:9; cf. Mt 6:2-4; 20-21; Lk 6:30; 11:37-44; 12:33-34; Acts 9:36-43; 10:2-4, 31; 24:17).

In faith, "costing not less than everything," Jesus' disciples leave all to follow him (Mt 4:18-22; Mk 1:16-20; Lk 5:1-11; T. S. Eliot, "Four Quartets"). Their way is arduous, yet their treasure is stored in heaven (Mt 19:27-30; Mk 10:28-30; Lk 18:28-31). For those who "set their hearts" on God's "kingdom first, and on God's saving justice" shall feast at the messianic banquet (Mt 6:33; 25:31-46; Lk 10:30-37).

The primacy of the great command of love (*agape*) inspired the primitive, voluntary "communism" of the early Jerusalem church (Acts 2:44-45; 4:34-35; 5:1-11), even as it is invoked in Paul's later appeals for almsgiving on the church's behalf (Acts 11:29-30; 24:17; Rom 15:26-28; 1 Cor 16:1-4; 2 Cor 8-9; Gal 2:10). Paul praises the churches of Macedonia whose "unfailing joy and intense poverty have overflowed in a wealth of generosity" for "God's holy people" at Jerusalem (1 Cor 16:1-4; 2 Cor 8:1-6).

Property in the Church's Tradition

With the waning of the imminent expectation of the parousia, the Gospel's admonition to detachment from wealth in the fellowship of love gave rise to charitable institutions, unique in antiquity (*Didache* 4:8; *Hebrews* 13:2; *1 Clement* 10-12; in his *Letter to the Romans,* proem., Ignatius describes the Roman church as "leading in love" in its care for the needy). The *imitatio Christi* inspired the asceticism of early Christian monasticism in Egypt and the emulation of divine generosity in the bestowal of riches (*The Shepherd of Hermas,* Similitudes 1, 6ff., 2, 5-10; cf. 1 Tim 6:10ff., 1 *Clement* 38.1f.).

The theme of faithful stewardship of the earth's riches, adumbrated in the NT (Mt 25:14-30; Lk 16:1-15; 19:12-27; 1 Cor 4:7), is elaborated by the later Fathers (see Basil, *Hom.* 1 in Ps 14.5; John Chrysostom, *Hom.* in 1 Tim 11, *De Lazaro* 2.4, 6ff., *Hom.* in Rom 11.5; Ambrose, *In Psalm.* 118.8.22; Augustine, *In Joann. Ev.* 50.6, *Enarratio* in Ps 147, 12; Gregory the Great, *Regulae pastoralis liber,* par. 3, chap. 21). In the words of Clement of Alexandria, the "poor in spirit" regard property as a divine gift administered "for the sake of the brethren" (*Quis dives salvetur* 16:3). Clement condemned the unbridled avarice of those who arrogate to themselves what God has given as "common to all," for "it is monstrous for one to live in luxury, while many are in want" (*Paedagogus* 2, 119, 2–120, 5).

Imitators of "God the Father," writes Cyprian, must be "common and just in gratuitous bounties" (*De unit. ecc.* 25). For those who hoard their treasures are but "robbers and thieves": in Basil's words, "the bread which [they] withhold belongs to the poor" (*Hom. in illud Luc.*: "Destruam . . ." 1). Chrysostom lamented the "strife and contention" bred when the common patrimony bestowed by God is divided by "those cold words 'mine and thine'" (*Hom.* 12 on 1 Tim 4). In a similar vein, Gregory Nazianzen attributed the origin of private property to the "envy and quarrelsomeness" wrought by the Fall, a motif recurring in Franciscan theology and the writings of Zwingli and Melancthon (*Hom.* 14, 25). In Ambrose's words, nature's "common right" was usurped by greed into "a right for a few" (*De off.* 1.18.132; cf. *De Nabuthe Jez.,* 53ff.).

Augustine's view of private property as an institution of positive rather than divine law receives systematic exposition in the writings of Thomas Aquinas (*In Joann. Ev.* 6.25–26, *Ep.* 93.12.50). While the natural law decrees the common finality of external goods and the "right" (*dominium*) over their use, the legitimacy of private property rests on a positive specification "added to natural law" for our benefit and perfection by "the inventiveness of human reason": with respect to the "care and disposition" of external goods, the institution of private property is "legitimate," and "indeed necessary for human life" inasmuch as (*a*) persons are more likely to care for what they possess themselves, (*b*) "human affairs are more efficiently organized if the proper care of each thing is an individual responsibility," and (*c*) "peace is better preserved" if persons are content with their own property (*Summa theologiae* II-II, q. 66, arts. 1, 2, 6; cf. q. 57, art. 3).

With respect to the "use" of property, Thomas contends that one "should not possess external things as one's own alone, but for the community, so that one is ready to share them with others in cases of necessity" (ST II-II, q. 66, art. 2; cf. ST I-II, q. 94, art. 5; ST II-II, q. 32, art. 5; *De regimine principum,* bk. 1, chaps. 15, 17). The right to private property, incorporated in the *jus gentium* (law of nations), presumes the obligation of securing the "common good" of the community; indeed, Thomas concedes that "in cases of necessity everything is common property" (ST II-II, q. 66, art. 7).

In their treatises on the *jus gentium,* the Spanish Scholastics Francisco de Vitoria and Francisco Suárez adapted the Thomistic understanding of property rights to the emerging nation-states. The communal distribution of property is, in Suárez' words, a "permissive" rather than "preceptive" requirement of the natural law, so that "all property would be held in common by the force of this law" had not "a different system" of private property been introduced in the *jus gentium* (*Defensio fidei Catholicae et apostolicae adversus Anglicanae sectae errores* 1, p. 129).

The eclipse of classical and medieval notions of the common good heralded the rise of the new, contractual school of natural law in the 17th and 18th centuries. Though deferring to the "judicious Hooker's" Thomism, Locke's theory of the social contract rests less on the precepts of natural law than the preservation of the natural right to property, the "great and chief end . . . of men's uniting into commonwealths" (*An Essay Concerning the True Original Extent and End of Civil Government,* chap. 9).

Modern Church Teaching on Property

In the modern era, Roman Catholic social teaching developed as a via media between the "liberalistic individualism" of capitalism and the revolutionary criticism of Karl Marx (*Divini Redemptoris* 29). While condemning the socialization of the means of production, Leo XIII's *Rerum novarum* recognized the natural right of the industrial proletariate to just remuneration and retention of the fruits of labor (RN 43–47; cf. 3, 5–10, 20, 32–33, 40). Class divisions culminating in "the utter poverty of the masses" were to be ameliorated through a broad dissemination of the natural right to (consumptive and productive) property (RN 1, 22, 33, 47). Yet in exhorting the rich "to give of their superfluity," Leo remained beholden to an organically stratified conception of society inimical to militant labor reform (*Quod apostolici muneris* 5, 36–38; cf. RN 8, 22–23).

In *Quadragesimo anno,* Pius XI defended the institution of private property as a bulwark against undue restrictions of personal liberty and as an effective social means of fulfilling basic human needs (QA 45–51). A just wage is determined not only by an ostensibly fair contract but by a determinate social outcome: workers "must be paid a wage sufficient to support [themselves] and [their] families" consistent with the "public good" so that "the greatest possible number" are offered "the opportunity of getting work and obtaining suitable means of livelihood" (QA 71–75). For Pius XI as for his successor, Pius XII, the state must ensure that the accumulation of wealth and property subserves the commonweal in accordance with the principle of subsidiarity (QA 49, 78–80, 114–15; cf. Pius XII, *La Solennità* 31–33). Yet while concurring with Leo that "the natural order . . . demands private property," Pius XII insists that the right to property "remains subordinated to the natural scope of material goods and cannot emancipate itself from the first and fundamental right which concedes their use to all" (*Acta apostolicae sedis* 33, 198–99; cf. QA 57–58, 61).

The motifs of the Leonine tradition receive their characteristically modern inflection in the pontificate of John XXIII. As Leo, John grounds the right to private property in "the fruitfulness of labor," while affirming with Pius XI and Pius XII the common finality of material goods (MM 112, 119). In his encyclical *Mater et magistra,* John XXIII defends the right of private property as "a safeguard" and "stimulus" for "the exercise of liberty" and "the rights of the human person" (MM 109–12). Yet the *personal* right to property presumes the correlative *social* duty of ensuring not only a broader but a more equitable extension of property rights (MM 73, 113–15). In words reminiscent of Pius XII, John asserts that "the economic prosperity of any people is to be assessed not so much from the sum total of goods and wealth possessed as from the distribution of goods according to norms of justice" so that all "in the community can develop and perfect [themselves]" (MM 74).

In his encyclical *Pacem in terris,* John insists upon the "social duty essentially inherent in the right of private property" (PT 21–22). Yet John's legitimation of private property no longer presupposes a "natural" social hierarchy: the right to private property is but one of a set of interdependent, universal human rights deriving from the inherent "dignity of the human person" (MM 112–14; PT 9). John commends forms of economic partnership of capital and labor and acknowledges the enhanced role of the state, which "must have as its fundamental objective the recognition, respect, safeguarding and promotion of human rights" (PT 139, cf. 60, 63, 84; MM 65, 75, 77, 92–93, 97, 104, 120).

The Pastoral Constitution on the Church in the Modern World reaffirms the central tenets of John's teaching: private ownership, as an "expression of personality," represents "an extension of human freedom" and furnishes an "incentive" for persons to fulfill their "function and duty" in "society and in the economy" (*Gaudium et spes* 71). Yet property's "social quality," deriving "from the law of the communal purpose of earthly goods," demands that property rights be subordinated to the global common good (GS 69–70): the richer nations "are obliged to come to the relief of the poor, and to do so not merely out of their superfluous goods" (GS 69).

In accordance with the patristic tradition, private possessions must finally be regarded as "common property," which accrues "to the benefit of not only [oneself] but of others" (GS 69). In cases of "extreme necessity," the Thomistic proviso that one is entitled "to take from the riches of others what [one oneself] needs" requires that not only "individuals" but "nations" be provided with the "means for helping and developing themselves" (GS 69; cf. Thomas Aquinas, ST II-II, q. 32, art. 5, q. 66, arts. 2, 7). The council fathers thus recognize the exigency of agrarian reform and the legitimacy of expropriating private property for the sake of the common good (GS 71; cf. MM 123–49).

In his encyclical *Populorum progressio* Paul VI treats of property rights in light of the prerequisites of "integral" development: ownership must foster the good "of the whole [person]" and of "every [person]" (PP 14, 48–49). Decrying "oppressive social structures" originating in the "abuses of ownership" and "power," Paul denies that private property constitutes "an absolute and unconditioned right" (PP 23; cf. *Octogesima adveniens* 43–44). For the "primary finality" of "created goods" rests in the fulfillment of the "common good" of all peoples to which the right to private property is necessarily subordinate (PP 21–24, 26). The moral primacy of the common good enjoins a universal respect for human rights, which admit of diverse cultural and historical realization (OA 4; cf. GS 69; *Justice in the World* 43).

In his recent encyclicals John Paul II offers a rich, phenomenological interpretation of the nature, scope, and limits of property rights: in *Laborem exercens* John Paul argues that "the only legitimate title" to capital "whether in the form of private ownership or in the form of public or collective ownership" is that it "should serve labor," promoting the "solidarity" of laborers and of the poor (*Laborem exercens* 32–37, 63–69; *Sollicitudo rei socialis* 28–31, 39). In the words of *Sollicitudo rei socialis*, the right to property bears a "social mortgage" attesting the priority of the "subjectivity of human labor" over capital (LE 52–58; SRS 42). John Paul thus recognizes the legitimacy of labor unions; of workers' participation in policy formation, management, and ownership; and of socializing certain means of production (LE 64–69, 94–100, 102). In his commemorative encyclical, *Centesimus annus*, John Paul insists that the right to private property "must be circumscribed within a strong juridical framework that places it at the service of human freedom in its totality" (CA 42, 30–43). For only when socioeconomic systems respect the "just rights of workers" will the biblical promise of the land as a divine inheritance be redeemed (LE 77, 80, 85, 99; SRS 26; *Economic Justice for All* 80, 91, 110–18).

See relevant encyclicals. *Also see* GOODS, ACCESS TO; GOODS, DISTRIBUTION OF; HUMAN RIGHTS; LABOR AND CAPITAL IN CATHOLIC SOCIAL THOUGHT; MODERN CATHOLIC SOCIAL THOUGHT; OWNERSHIP; STEWARDSHIP.

Bibliography: R. Antoncich, *Christians in the Face of Injustice,* trans. M. O'Connell (New York: Orbis, 1987). W. Brueggemann, *The Land* (Philadelphia: Fortress, 1977). M. Hengel, *Property and Riches in the Early Church,* trans. J. Bowden (Philadelphia: Fortress, 1974). J. González, *Faith and Wealth* (San Francisco: Harper & Row, 1990). D. Hollenbach, *Claims in Conflict* (New York: Paulist, 1979). D. Dorr, *Option for the Poor,* rev. ed. (New York: Orbis, 1992). J. Waldron, *The Right to Private Property* (Oxford: Clarendon, 1988).

WILLIAM O'NEILL, S.J.

PROFIT

The church's teaching on the legitimacy of profit in economic activity is guided by an overarching concern with the common good of society. The legitimacy or illegitimacy of profit should neither be assessed abstractly nor in individualistic terms but rather in light of the consequences the generation of profit has for society as a whole. To the extent that profit from economic activity leads to greater collective well-being, it may be deemed legitimate and ethical. If, however, the generation of profit causes harm to other members of society, which it can easily do, it must be deemed illegitimate and unethical. In other words, profit is good or bad depending on its impact on all the members of a given society, not just its immediate beneficiaries. Those who handle wealth are not merely involved in discrete personal transactions. They are, rather, engaged in activities that affect other people. Their actions, then, are subject to collective scrutiny and assessment.

To better understand the church's position on profit in economic activity, we must attempt to define how profit is produced in the capitalist system that prevails throughout most of the world. In technical terms profit is the surplus value that accrues from the production and sale of a particular commodity. That commodity, be it a refrigerator or an automobile, is the product of complex human activity made possible by various subjects. The monetary means to extract natural resources and change them into finished products is made possible by individuals known as capitalists. They provide the funds, or capital, necessary to finance the production of goods. Capitalists, however, are not the only agents involved in the process of production. Another group of people, known as workers, extracts the raw materials or assembles the goods that will later be sold on the open market in order to create a profit. Both capitalists and workers are necessary participants in the productive process. Both are equally important. Workers receive compensation for their labor in the form of wages while capitalists receive compensation in the form of profits derived from the sale of manufactured goods.

To realize a profit on the commodity in question, the capitalist must charge a higher rate for the finished product than the cost of the raw materials and the wages paid to the laborers involved in the productive process. This difference between the cost of producing an article in terms of materials and labor and its final market price is known as surplus value, which is essentially synonymous with profit. Obviously, the greater the surplus value of an item, the greater the amount of profit. In the capitalist system the surplus value of an item is, at least in theory, determined by the laws of supply and demand. The greater the need for a particular item, the higher its price and potential margin of profit for the individuals who sell it on the market.

The church's position on profit in economic activity is generally positive to the extent that profits are ultimately shared and benefit all who generate them. Catholic social teaching even accepts the legitimacy of the capitalist mode of generating profit, but it does so with warnings about the potential for abuse inherent in such a system. These warnings are reflected in a long history of church teaching dating to the 19th century, and reiterated in contemporary episcopal and papal documents, especially *Mater et magistra* (John XXIII, 1961), *Populorum progressio* (Paul VI, 1967), and *Laborem exercens* and *Sollicitudo rei socialis* (John Paul II, 1981 and 1988). What that church teaching recognizes is that the potential for abusing the common good in the name of profit is a persistent temptation in a profit-based economic system. On occasion, the common good is sacrificed for short-term individual or class-related profits, as is evident in the history of many industrial countries. We must keep in mind that the finality of economic activity is collective human betterment, not the acquisition of individual or group wealth. Profit must be understood as a means to an end rather than an end unto itself. Unfortunately, generating profit rather than striving for human betterment often becomes the driving force for individuals and entire social classes. The result is a distorted social system in which profit takes precedence over human life. This is what Pope Pius XI meant in *Quadragesimo anno* (1931) when he alluded to the "imperialism of money."

Since surplus value, or profit, is directly related to the differential between the cost of a product and the product's market price, there is a constant temptation to maximize profit by minimizing the price paid for the resources necessary for production and the wages paid to workers who extract these materials and later create finished products. In the name of maximum profits, the owners of capital have often paid unjust prices for natural materials, particularly in developing countries whose metals, petroleum, and agricultural products have sometimes been extracted and exported by capitalists in a ruthless and unjust manner. At the same time, the laborers who transform these materials into finished goods have often been offered less than just compensation for their work. Such situations can quickly lead to resentment and violence as society, on a national and international level, is divided into distinct classes with antithetical values and roles in the productive process.

This danger was alluded to as early as 1891 in Pope Leo XIII's *Rerum novarum,* which stressed the need for a just and equitable relationship between those who possess capital and those involved in the production of goods. It is imperative to keep in mind that the productive process is a basic human activity central to our self-understanding and sense of worth. Those who provide capital and those who engage in work are equal partners in a collective endeavor. As Pope John Paul II has pointed out in *Laborem exercens,* it is through economic activity that we express our deepest aspirations and create societies that embody them. By transforming the world around us by means of work, we come to understand who we are and how we must relate to the natural world and each other.

A central point in the church's teaching on economic activity is the notion that economic systems are collective phenomena that affect every member of a society. Economic processes are not meant to benefit a few, or even a majority, but rather all the members of a given population. The purpose of economic life is to create the greatest degree of well-being for the greatest number of citizens. Capitalists and workers are united in a common endeavor—the creation of a more humane and just society. The American bishops make this point in very clear terms in their 1986 pastoral letter on the U.S. economy, *Economic Justice for All.* "We judge any economic system by what it does *for* and *to* people and by how it permits all to *participate* in it. The economy should serve the people, not the other way around." Capital is not the exclusive property of capitalists. It is, rather, a common trust that they must utilize in the most responsible and just way. As Pope John Paul II pointed out in *Sollicitudo rei socialis,* it is a "social mortgage" on capital that must be accounted for.

Likewise, labor is not a discrete activity that one engages in solely for the sake of monetary compensation. Labor must be understood as a crucial creative process. The centrality of labor has often been stressed by Pope John Paul II, particularly in sections nine and ten of *Laborem exercens.* Work fulfills us as human beings, makes family life possible, and so creates the foundational structures of society. Thus the worker has a special place in the creative process that merits respect. The pope's message is especially important in economic systems where generating profit is erroneously considered more important than labor.

The profit that flows from economic activity is a type of common property that must be shared equitably between all the people who produce it. Those who provide the materials for production, the workers who transform these materials into finished goods, and those who finance the overall processes of production have a fundamental right to be compensated for their efforts from the profits they collectively produce. This compensation must reflect the true nature of their work. No group can be denied its rightful place in the productive process or remuneration for materials or work in the name of another group or nation's interests or profits. To do so is to divide society along class and national lines and use profits, which are ultimately collective wealth, in a destructive way. This leads to the exploitation of workers and entire countries in the name of profit, a danger pointed out in *Sollicitudo rei socialis* 43.

Over the last century the question of economic systems and the values that underlie them have been a central concern in church teaching. Multiple documents written by popes and episcopal bodies offer a rich legacy to contemporary Christians trying to understand and assess the significance of economic life. Although papal and episcopal teaching on economic issues is nuanced and varies from one decade and context to another, there is a consistent concern for the welfare of all people. This concern provides criteria with which we can assess economic processes, including the generation of profit. Papal encyclicals and episcopal documents stress that economic systems must be understood as complex networks that link people together. Christians, then, must take the economic realm seriously, since it has such a pervasive impact on people's lives. Precisely for this reason, the church offers guidelines on economic issues. It sees a legitimate place for profits in economic life, but never at the expense of the common good.

See also CAPITALISM; COMMON GOOD; ECONOMIC ORDER; GOODS, DISTRIBUTION OF; JUST WAGE; LABOR AND CAPITAL IN CATHOLIC SOCIAL THOUGHT.

CURT CADORETTE, M.M.

PROSTITUTION

Prostitution is the practice of engaging in illicit and licentious sexual activity for an economic or emotional price with indiscriminately chosen partners. Practiced by both men and women, prostitution most often engages women in trade with men; however, young male prostitutes (hustlers) serve the homosexual community, males (gigolos) sell sexual services to older women, and women are available to female homosexuals (Childress and Macquarrie, p. 512). Most enter prostitution between the ages of 14 and 16 years. Studies show that 70 to 80 percent are victims of incest and come from unstable families (Hahn, pp. 415–16). Many have low self-esteem, little self-confidence, no job skills, and minimal education; significant numbers become substance addicts who live in abusive relationships with pimps. For a female prostitute, the pimp is a prostitute's security; he bales her out of jail, protects her on the streets, and occasionally makes love to her if she follows his rules.

People involved in prostitution seek a transient erotic experience primarily, rather than a relationship that is interpersonal, faithful, and that involves the whole person. The sexual nature of the interaction between prostitute and client exploits and dehumanizes both the practitioners and the participants, consequently raising issues of moral concern.

Prostitution is a moral and legal problem; its history indicates it is one of the oldest sexual offenses. Prostitution and the sacred harlots of the fertility cults were condemned by Israel as signs of infidelity and apostasy committed for strange gods. Fornication and prostitution were especially evil for the chosen people because fertility was a mission and a blessing effected only in marriage, itself a symbol of the relationship between God and the chosen people (Hos 2; Jer 3:6ff.; Exod 16:23; Isa 54). Circumcision was a symbol of Israel's covenant with the Lord; the desecration of that symbol through the harlotry of women in the service of Baal was considered blasphemy.

Although both prostitution and polygamy were practiced in the OT, prostitution was considered a moral evil and people engaged in it received harsh treatment. In the narration of Dinah, Shechem used her like a harlot; later Dinah's brothers slew all the males in Shechem's family out of revenge for Shechem's misdeed. A girl who lost her virginity before marriage was stoned if her parents could not produce proof to the contrary in the form of a bloodied bed sheet from the wedding night (Deut 22:13-21). Money paid to a harlot was abomination in the Lord's eye and was not to be used for a votive offering.

The NT writers speak of the adulteress brought to Jesus. Knowing she deserved death under Jewish law, Jesus set aside the penalty by forgiving the guilty woman when she repented and after he had warned her about future moral lapses. Jesus' response of compassion, understanding, and the love that allows another to grow in conversion is the basis for the church's response to prostitutes. Harlots were condemned in the NT because they opposed the righteousness of the kingdom (Mt 21:31ff.; Lk 15:30). The church was seen as a pure and spotless bride of Christ that struggles against unchristian forces, who like a whore misled the nations and their kings (Rev 17:1-2). Paul condemned prostitution as representative of every form of depersonalized sexual activity. In using the term *porneia* Paul denounced premarital intercourse and promiscuity typified by intercourse with prostitutes. Moreover, Paul states that men who patronize harlots are excluded from the kingdom (Eph 5:5; 1 Tm 1:10; Heb 13:4).

Hellenistic philosophy influenced the patristic theologians' views on sexuality. Premarital intercourse was gravely contrary to natural law, and pleasure connected with sexual intercourse was morally reprehensible. Sex was opposed to holiness because it was seen in terms of lust, not love. The evil of sexual relations was "excused" because of the benefits of procreation, sex was oriented toward children, and all nonprocreative sex was considered sinful. In addressing the problem of prostitution, Augustine in *De Ordinis,* book 2, states that the real problem rests with males who seek out prostitutes. Revealing a moral double standard for males, Augustine suggests that prostitution should perhaps be legally tolerated because without it male lust would only emerge in worse forms, such as rape.

The Middle Ages likewise meted out harsh punishment for prostitution. A female prostitute was excommunicated for explicitly living in sin, although she could keep the money she earned. The prevalence of the double standard acknowledged that her sexual activity was morally wrong, but she could earn from the activity. Indeed, the church and the state benefited from taxes levied on brothels.

Thomas Aquinas in *Summa theologiae* q 10, art. 11, quoting Augustine, says, "Do away with the prostitutes and you will throw everything into confusion with lusts." Thomas believed that God permits certain evils, for without them a greater good would be threatened. The consequence of doing away with prostitution would be the greater evils of unbridled lust, rape, adultery, and homosexual practices. Prostitutes were encouraged to enter a convent or marry; to one who married a prostitute, many indulgences were granted for saving her soul. This same reasoning was reflected by Napoleon Bonaparte: "Prostitutes are a necessity. Without them, men would attack respectable women on the streets." During the Victorian Age the question of prostitution was largely ignored, but its practice thrived illegally and was generally considered to be a "despicable vice."

Following the tradition of moral approbation by the churches and society, prostitution is today considered an objective moral evil and is judged in the light of church teachings on sexuality, the dignity of the person, and marriage. All sexual activity is to be within the context of the stable and faithful relationship that is marriage. In mature relationships the partners reveal themselves in a process of communication that considers and respects the whole person and all aspects of personality, not simply the sexual dimensions and possibilities of the individual. Women are to be treated as equals who deserve respect: they are not subordinate partners in a relationship. All relationships are to be characterized by mutuality, reciprocity, and love; prostitution by its nature inhibits this understanding of relationship. It does not foster communication, respect for the persons involved, personal freedom of the prostitute, a holistic relationship, or the development of a faithful and loving relationship.

Moral issues surrounding prostitution are both social and individual in nature. Frequently prostitutes are victims of social injustice; some experience themselves as having no choice other than to become prostitutes. On a social level, prostitution exposes society's dualistic attitude toward sexual ethics as found in body-spirit dualism. By separating bodily (sexual) activity from the relational-spiritual nature of the person, the client enjoys sexual excitement and arousal that is temporarily reassuring to sexual identity but alienating in terms of an intimate relationship. Since it is predominately males who traffic with prostitutes, one readily sees the effects of the double standard of morality in the unequal treatment of men and women involved in prostitution. Feminists decry the fact that men are not defamed by their promiscuous activity, while women practicing prostitution incur society's censure: he is an anonymous client, she is a slut and a whore performing immoral and illegal actions. Socially the attitude persists that it is less offensive for a man to have sexual relations outside of marriage than for a woman.

Because prostitution makes its major appeal to men, the socialization process of males must be examined and critiqued. In the growth process males more often than females are subject to sexual alienation because of contrasting experiences in their development. They experience sexual arousal through accepted forms of media but receive antisex training in the home; they are taught sexual inhibition toward ordinary women, such as mother and wife, but society allows sexual fulfillment through "extraordinary" women; they may feel sexual urges but know the restrictions of society regarding sexual expression. In the socialization of males the normal route of satisfying human needs is stifled due to sexual alienation and society's ambivalence toward sex. Social responsibility must address socialization, the double standard, and structures of social injustice.

Most recently, the double standard has beleaguered the homosexual community. Many homosexuals believe religious and social standards, or norms, on sexuality are applicable to the heterosexual population but not to them. Given this attitude, many do not find social support for faithful and committed relationships either within or outside the homosexual community. Prejudice, promiscuity, and sexually transmitted diseases plague homosexuals and create an atmosphere of fear and despair among those who would wish to form stable and healthy relationships.

On an individual level prostitution is dehumanizing, depersonalizing, and oppressive, as seen in the pimp relationship. In addition to the hedonist attitude of the clients, the prostitute also finds the commodity mentality dehumanizing—it promotes low self-esteem, lack of freedom, and introduces the prostitute to a seemingly inescapable cycle of dependency, violence, and poverty. Women, particularly, tend to engage in prostitution because of poverty and their perceived inability to obtain an income through respectable means. Women lose dignity, for they are viewed as the property of the pimp and exist only for serving and pleasuring the male. Their relationship is depersonalized: the promiscuous lifestyle prevents growth in sexual maturity and the integration of sexual desires within a faithful relationship. By entering a depersonalizing relationship, both prostitute and client are dehumanized.

Prostitution is legalized in most European countries but not in the United States except for the state of Nevada. Here prostitutes are protected by required weekly physicals and frequent police checks. Arguments in favor of legalizing brothels find that women are safer and men avoid disease and publicity; women prefer working in legalized brothels because of the protection they receive, although they are required to forgo half their earnings to the owners of these establishments.

Moral issues of prostitution can be resolved only when the church and society accept complicity in fostering prostitution. Together they must address the related issues of family violence, incest, availability of day-care centers for children, treatment for addictions, and the poverty cycle. Educational programs and job-skill training would do much to prevent the emotional victimization that hinders the prostitute's ability to learn. Moreover, education would help to eradicate aberrant views on sexuality. Women who must support a family need help in job training and finding day-care centers for their children lest they resort to prostitution as a means of income. Many female prostitutes have children, some being "trick" children fathered by a client. The woman may give the child up for adoption, or she may choose to keep the child. If she is from an abusive family, as often happens, and chooses to rear the child, there is danger the child will be abused as she herself was, thereby continuing the cycle of violence. In addition, society must reexamine the ways women are viewed. Attitudes that suggest women are not equal, can be dominated by men, and are for the sexual use of men contribute significantly to the evil of prostitution. The Christian church has a teaching and healing role regarding the equal treatment of women and an accepting, forgiving, and loving manner of dealing with prostitutes. By challenging the structures and sexual attitudes contrary to justice and love the church can bring about the kingdom that excludes no one and invites all.

See also EMPLOYMENT AND UNEMPLOYMENT; EVIL, SOCIAL; EXPLOITATION; FEMINISM AND CATHOLIC SOCIAL THOUGHT; PERSON, DIGNITY OF; SEXISM; WOMEN.

Bibliography: J. Childress and J. Macquarrie, *The Westminster Dictionary of Christian Ethics* (Philadelphia: Westminster, 1986). J. Hahn, "Loving a Prostitute," *Christian Century* 106 (April 19, 1989).

ELIZABETH WILLEMS, S.S.N.D.

PUBLIC AND PRIVATE, RELATIONSHIP OF

"Public" and "private" are terms of ordinary discourse, but there is widespread disagreement over their respective meaning and application. The content and range of public and private vary within competing modes of social thought and ways of life. Public and private are defined and understood in a relationship to each other that is often construed as oppositional. Private, meaning "not open to the public," and public, meaning "of or pertaining to the whole, done or made in behalf of the community as a whole," shape all historic philosophies and continue to reverberate in contemporary theoretical and political debates.

The dominant understandings of the relationship between public and private against which Catholic social thought emerged and interposed itself are liberalism and Marxism. Liberalism poses sharp distinctions between public and private, insisting on a zone of privacy within which the individual is inviolable. The private sphere is expanded to include property relationships. Conversely, Marxism seeks to eliminate any distinction between public and private, insisting that the world of "bourgeois right" is a charade and that all social existence should be brought under one uniform public standard. The rights-bearing private individual cherished by liberalism is absorbed by Marxism into a generic "species being."

By contrast, Catholic social thought, indebted to Thomism's insistence on the essential interrelationship of public and private such that private property rights are not inviolable, preserves a distinction between public and private but insists on the essentially social nature of all human activities and of human identity itself. This means that property is held as a social trust and that rights are not exclusive and absolute to the solitary self. But neither is the individual and such human institutions as the family absorbed within a collective enterprise that negates the dignity of the human person by denying the spiritual needs and dimensions of the person. The innate freedom of individuals is preserved but given a distinctly social cast. Rights pertain to social bodies and not to individuals alone. All activities, private and public, are to conform to the requirements of the gospel and the teachings of the common mother, the church. No moral line between private and public conduct is accepted; each is similarly subject to moral scrutiny and reproof.

Thus Leo XIII in *Rerum novarum,* drawing on St. Thomas, argues that it is lawful to own private property but that all ownership must be "according to nature's law" (Gibbons, ed., p. 4). Moreover, the "State must not absorb the individual or the family; both should be allowed free and untrammeled action as far as is consistent with the common good and the interests of others" (Gibbons, ed., p. 17). All "lesser societies" are part of civil society. Civil society "exists for the common good, and, therefore, is concerned with the interests of all in general, and with the individual interests in their due place and proportion. Hence, it is called *public* society, because by its means, as St. Thomas of Aquin says, 'Men communicate with one another in the setting up of a commonwealth.' Private societies are those formed to carry out 'private business,' always within the frame of moral law" (Gibbons, ed., p. 24).

Pius XI in *Quadragesimo anno,* John XXIII in *Mater et magistra,* and Paul VI in *Populorum progressio,* elaborating on and partially amending Leo, emphasize ever more strongly that the common good and human needs take precedence over private property rights and claims. Those rights are not to be construed as absolute. With John Paul II's *Redemptor hominis* and, most importantly, *Laborem exercens,* a "social mortgage" on all property is adumbrated and the "priority of human labor over what in the course of time we have grown accustomed to calling capital," is stressed (John Paul II, in *Origins,* p. 234). Additionally, John Paul has been insistent in all his public documents and statements that the one privileged sphere of privacy is religious liberty, or liberty of conscience, the basic human right. This right can be neither reduced nor negated by the political community and its claims.

John Paul has taken on and criticized the concepts of private and public held by individualistic and collectivistic philosophies, insisting that individualism isolates the self and opposes the self to all others; thus it precludes movement toward a genuine "we," an authentic form of group identity. Collectivism, by contrast, poses an alienated and false version of "we" by denying human dignity and responsibility. The concept of community best expresses the reality of the human person in communion with others, according to John Paul. Thus, from its official inception in modernity with *Rerum novarum,* through the encyclicals and homilies of John Paul II, Catholic social thought presents a consistent yet evolving theory of the relationship between private and public that preserves the essential sociality of that relationship in all its aspects.

See relevant encyclicals. *Also see* COMMUNITY; FAMILY; JOHN XXIII; LABOR AND CAPITAL IN CATHOLIC SOCIAL THOUGHT; MODERN CATHOLIC SOCIAL THOUGHT; PAUL VI; PIUS XI; PRIVACY, RIGHT TO; PRIVATE PROPERTY.

Bibliography: W. Gibbons, *Great Encyclicals* (New York: Paulist, 1963). John Paul II, "*Laborem exercens* (On Human Work)," *Origins,* vol. 2, no. 15 (September 24, 1981) 226–44). A. Bloch and G. Czuczka, eds., John Paul II, *Toward a Philosophy of Praxis* (New York: Crossroad, 1981). J. Elshtain, *Public Man, Private Woman: Women in Social and Political Thought* (Princeton: Princeton Univ. Press, 1981).

JEAN BETHKE ELSHTAIN

PUEBLA

From January 27, 1979, until February 13 of that year several hundred Latin American bishops, religious superiors, and lay delegates met in the Mexican city of Puebla. There they participated in the Third General Conference of the Latin American bishops or, as it came to be known, the Puebla Conference. The conference was formally opened by the newly elected pope, John Paul II, who came to Latin America to express his solidarity with the church there and to set a tone for the meetings that would follow.

The bishops of Latin America had gathered to discuss the issues facing their churches. Their first meeting, held in 1955, had done little more than create a coordinating organization that came to be known by its Spanish acronym, CELAM (Conferencia Episcopal Latinoamericana). The second conference, however, was a qualitatively different phenomenon. When the Latin American bishops met in Medellín, Colombia, in 1968 they had fresh memories of the Second Vatican Council and were anxious to implement its teachings in a coordinated way. They were also living during a painful but challenging moment in their continent's history. The traditional social paradigm in Latin America—an oligarchic political system in which the church served as chaplain to the powerful while pacifying the poor—was rapidly disintegrating. The gap and tension between rich and poor, uncontrolled urbanization, and the rise of political violence in the continent had altered Latin American society and the church's position within it. With a fair degree of courage, the bishops of Latin America opted for the new and unknown at Medellín. They did so by declaring their solidarity with Latin America's largest group of people, the poor. They allied themselves with their hopes and aspirations. Speaking of the need to remake the church and society in a more just way, they declared their "preferential option for the poor."

The primary purpose of the Puebla Conference was to reflect on the various events that had taken place in the ten tumultuous years since Medellín and assess the impact of the decisions made in 1968. The delegates at Puebla had also gathered to chart a course for the church that would guide it through the future. One decisive event that had had a tremendous impact on the church throughout the continent and the world at large was the rise of liberation theology. Prior to Vatican II the church in Latin America had looked to Europe for theological ideas and models. After the 1960s, however, that pattern changed abruptly. Latin American theologians like Gustavo Gutiérrez, Juan Luis Segundo, Leonardo Boff, and Jon Sobrino melded together academic theology, critical social thought, and the lived experience of the poor to produce what came to be called liberation theology. They spoke in convincing terms of the church's task in the struggle for justice and the Christian's duty to transform society. Suddenly the church in Latin America found itself on the forefront of theological innovation.

Wary conservatives, both political and ecclesiastical, were confronted with a new mode of theological discourse that they distrusted and disdained. Conservative politicians quickly branded liberation theology as a thinly veiled type of Marxism disguised as Christianity and used every means at their disposal to impede its growth. Conservative members of the hierarchy, both in Latin America and Rome, questioned the doctrinal soundness of some ideas proposed by certain liberation theologians. When the bishops assembled at Puebla they were immersed in a theological controversy that was going on both within and outside of the church itself. Those who favored liberation theology wanted the conference to affirm its basic insights. Those who opposed it wanted it condemned, or at least sanctioned. Perhaps more prudent than forthright, the bishops did neither. Reading the Puebla Documents, one finds many words and concepts drawn directly from liberation theology. It is clear that this new way of doing theology had penetrated the thought and language of the entire church by the late 1970s. There is, however, neither a ringing endorsement nor sharp criticism of liberation theology's principal concepts. Rather, the bishops warn against theological extremism of any sort, conservative or progressive. The fact that none of the significant liberation theologians can be interpreted as extremists has led some observers to believe that the Puebla Documents point to a tacit acceptance of liberation theology by most Latin American bishops. In the 1990s, however, this seems less the case, with many bishops favoring a more conservative theology and advocating a cautious approach to questions of social change.

Another issue that the bishops at Puebla faced was the startling transformation of the church's inner structures mandated by the Second Vatican Council and the Medellín Conference. When the bishops made their "preferential option for the poor" in 1968, they irrevocably altered the institutions in their charge. In the past the poor had often been the recipients of the paternal concern and remedial charity provided them by the hierarchical church. After Medellín, however, this pattern of one-sided assistance began to shift.

In 1968 the bishops suggested new ecclesial structures that would be more responsive to ordinary people's needs and consonant with their daily experience. In response, religious sisters and priests who worked with the poor began creating base or ecclesial communities. Unlike large parishes with hundreds or thousands of members, most unknown to each other, base communities were small groups made up of fifty or fewer people. More like families than church institutions, they afforded participants a chance to pray, study the Gospel, analyze their political environment, and think about their responsibilities in society as Christians. The leadership of these communities was drawn from the local laity, who acted as internal facilitators and external liaisons with the neighboring parish and diocese in which they lived.

In some countries, especially Brazil, base communities grew at a phenomenal rate. By the late 1970s the Brazilian church counted nearly 100,000 small communities in urban and rural areas. Although a few of these groups were made up of middle-class Christians, the vast majority represented the urban and rural poor. As a result of the base communities, the poor became progressively more vocal and articulate in their struggle to reshape the Christian community and the sociopolitical environment around them. Prior to the Second Vatican Council and Medellín the church in Latin America reflected the culture and values of a wealthy elite. By and large, it was still a colonial church far removed from the day-to-day struggles of ordinary people. It was a symbol of the past, not the present. In the post-Medellín period, however, that image began to shift. The institutional church became an ally of the poor. It began to use their language, song, and dance in its rituals. The church had found a new source of energy and a convincing reason for existence. Dioceses, parishes, and base communities became dynamic centers for prayer, thought, and action.

The rise of base communities also provoked the suspicion of conservatives. Some politicians saw the communities as seedbeds of subversion cultivated by liberation theologians, while certain members of the ecclesiastical hierarchy feared a challenge to their heretofore autocratic control of the institutional church. When the bishops gathered at Puebla, they faced many questions about the structure of the church and base communities in particular. While they affirmed the hierarchical nature of the church, they nonetheless expressed their support for base communities, which they called "causes for hope and joy" (96). It was clear to participants at the conference that base communities had become the chief and best means of evangelization in many sections of the continent.

A fundamental question behind all the deliberations at Puebla, including the issues of liberation theology and base communities, was the thorny matter of the church's relationship to the political order. Prior to Medellín the institutional church had accepted the traditional "two kingdom" schema, whereby church and state were separate but related institutions. The church generally would only intervene in political affairs that challenged the centrality of its teachings or position in society as the ultimate ethical arbiter. Outside of these circumstances, however, the church was not expected to engage in political activity. This was the responsibility of the laity, who worked in the so-called secular realm. Their task, informed by church teaching, was to exercise political power in the everyday world of government.

This system, however, rarely functioned in accord with its theoretical design. In most Latin American countries church and state related symbiotically rather than dialectically. This happened because most members of the church hierarchy were either from the oligarchy itself or they identified with its political agenda. Challenging the state was rarely in the hierarchy's interests. Likewise, few politicians wanted to contest the church's hegemony given its enormous power in an overwhelmingly Catholic continent. The church was actually a powerful political actor whose moves were disguised but nonetheless consequential. Most members of the hierarchy wanted to maintain the established order in its existing form, and most politicians were quite willing to oblige. What undid this traditional arrangement was the decline of oligarchic power that began in the 1950s and 1960s. With their power beginning to wane, social elites became more reactionary and repressive. When the bishops gathered in Medellín in 1968 they realized they had to change their role in the social order of their continent or face the possibility of abetting injustice and becoming a social anachronism.

Compounding the difficulties the bishops faced at Puebla regarding the church's sociopolitical role were two extreme and erroneous interpretations of the Medellín

Documents. On the one hand, certain members of the social elite reacted to Medellín with outrage. Convinced that the institutional church was no longer a reliable ally, they decided to attack it as an enemy. In the post-Medellín period this led to overt persecution of the church by certain states. Bishops, priests, religious women, and large numbers of laypersons were intimidated, imprisoned, tortured, and even assassinated. On the other hand, some small groups of Christians interpreted the Medellín Documents as an open invitation to engage uncritically in political activity. Often basing their viewpoint on a fallacious reading of liberation theology, they conflated Christianity and political action into an undifferentiated whole. Thus, the bishops at Puebla were forced to respond to both right- and left-wing extremism that threatened the real meaning of Medellín and the integrity of the institutional church.

At Puebla the bishops decided to steer a middle course between capitalism and Marxism, the Scylla and Charybdis of Latin American political and economic systems in the late 1970s. Quoting from the Medellín Documents to shape their argument, they assert that "the system of liberal capitalism and the temptation of the Marxist system would appear to exhaust the possibilities of transforming the economic structures of our continent. . . . We must denounce the fact that Latin America finds itself caught between these two options and remains dependent on one or the other of the centers of power that control its economy" (550).

As the quote indicates, such political ideologies had often been imported from outside Latin America. Rather than being indigenous ideas, these ideologies had been imposed by neocolonial powers such as the United States and Soviet Union that saw Latin America as a playing field for their competing visions of the world order. Tragically, capitalism and Marxism had become identity badges used to label people as good or bad. The danger the bishops point to is the confusing of an economic or political ideology, right or left, with the gospel itself. When this happens political programs assume an unwarranted importance. Misconstrued as transcendent projects, they quickly degenerate into aberrant, idolatrous belief systems that require total allegiance. Those who believe in such systems will breach no criticism of their creeds nor take stock of the price they exact from other human beings. What the bishops at Puebla advise, therefore, is political prudence and collective discernment on the part of a Christian community confronted with political choices. Nonetheless, Puebla recognizes the importance of politics and urges Christians to participate in the political process with the utmost seriousness. Political action is understood to be an integral part of every believing person's life. Politics is a special forum in which we are called to collaborate with one another and God's plan for creation.

One issue discussed at Puebla that received little attention at Medellín is the question of non-European and indigenous cultures in Latin America. Ignored for centuries, the bishops at Puebla finally recognized the existence and importance of millions of black and indigenous peoples who have maintained their cultures and languages despite centuries of pressure to assimilate into the Spanish and Portuguese speaking mainstream. In many instances these peoples have developed their own types of popular religiosity, related to but ultimately independent of the institutional church. In the words of the Puebla Documents, popular religiosity "is a storehouse of values that offers the answers of Christian wisdom to the great questions of life" (448). Nevertheless, the bishops recognize that popular religiosity has its limitations. In some cases it is mixed with superstition and fatalism. Consequently, they call on pastoral agents to approach popular religiosity with respect and caution—to affirm its positive content and reshape its deficient qualities without negating its role in the lives of millions of Latin American people.

Another area treated by Puebla that received inadequate attention at Medellín is the question of women in Latin American society. As the bishops make clear, "women have been pushed to the margins of society as the result of cultural atavisms—male predominance, unequal wages, deficient education, etc. This is manifest in their almost total absence from political, economic, and social life" (834). The principal "atavism" that they single out for condemnation is the Latin American phenomenon of *machismo,* which they explicitly mention and criticize in several sections of the text. The bishops speak of "the equality and dignity of the woman" (841) as a self-evident fact that all Christians must recognize. They speak of the need to include women in the social and economic decisions that will reshape Latin America, although they stress that the fundamental role of women is that of "mother, the defender of life and home educator" (846). Unfortunately, they make few if any suggestions about the role of women within the institutional church, presumably because they consider official ministry in the church to be reserved for males.

In the years following Puebla there has been a great deal of debate about the overall significance of the conference and its implications for the church in Latin America. Some commentators see Puebla as a retreat from the progressive social stance of Medellín. This opinion is credible given the fact that some of the conservative delegates to the conference were consciously intent on undoing the spirit and letter of Medellín. Certain of these delegates were influential in writing the official text at Puebla. Other analysts, however, see Puebla as a basic affirmation of Medellín, providing added clarity and vigor to its message. In fact, many of the delegates at Puebla arrived with the express purpose of strengthening and deepening the ideas set out in 1968. Many were articulate speakers and writers whose ideas can be found in the Final Document.

A close reading of the text reveals something of a patchwork quilt sewn together by conservative and progressive factions. Clearly, Puebla was not a harmonious meeting. There were serious differences of opinion among the participants. Nevertheless, Puebla never steps back from Medellín in any substantive way. The bishops' teaching on the centrality of social reform and the church's preferential option for the poor remain central to the Final Document despite some caveats and added nuances. It is difficult to characterize Puebla as a bold step forward in church teaching in Latin America, yet it surely cannot be characterized as regressive. There can be no doubt that Puebla pointed to deep-seated tensions between progressive and conservative forces in the Latin American church. In the post-Puebla period, these theological and political differences would lead to divisiveness among bishops and members of the church at large. In the 1990s this tension remains, as the meaning of Vatican II, Medellín, and Puebla is still contested in Latin America and the church throughout the world.

See also BASE COMMUNITIES; CULTURE; DEVELOPMENT; LIBERATION THEOLOGY; MARXISM; MEDELLÍN; POVERTY; POOR, PREFERENTIAL OPTION FOR.

Bibliography: The best and most convenient translation of the Puebla Documents can be found in *Puebla and Beyond: Documentation and Commentary,* trans. J. Drury, ed. J. Eagleson and P. Sharper (Maryknoll, N.Y.: Orbis, 1979). This volume contains the entire text of the conference and includes commentaries from diverse perspectives.

CURT CADORETTE, M.M.

Q

QUADRAGESIMO ANNO

Quadragesimo anno (*On Reconstructing the Social Order*) was issued on May 15, 1931, by Pius XI. This encyclical has sometimes been called "Forty Years After" from its first few Latin words, which refer to the time that had elapsed since Leo XIII released his important social encyclical, *Rerum novarum* (*On the Condition of Workers*), in 1891. Its purpose was to honor the anniversary of *Rerum novarum* and to reconsider the same issues in the context of the 1930s.

Background

Quadragesimo anno was written in a very turbulent time of worldwide economic depression when millions were unemployed. Germany was doubly stressed because of its war debt. In the face of the financial collapse brought about by the depression, the leftist parties in Europe were increasing their numbers among the working classes, while the extreme Right was gaining among the middle class. In parts of Europe it was a time of disillusionment as democracy's promises seemed to have been reduced to ineffective parliamentary wrangling. It was also a time of religious persecution in the Soviet Union, an anticlerical war against the church in Mexico, and the beginnings of anticlerical violence in Spain.

More immediately, it was a time of heightened tension between the Vatican and the Italian Fascist regime. The Lateran Pacts of 1929 and a concordat had finally ended the seventy-year-long dispute between the Italian government and the Vatican over the Papal States. Despite these agreements, Mussolini was determined to have a Fascist monopoly control over education, youth, and labor, something that Pope Pius XI would not concede. The struggle was primarily over Italian Catholic Action groups. Pius XI was known as "the pope of Catholic Action." His conception of Catholic Action was, as he said in his 1922 encyclical *Ubi arcano Dei,* "the participation of the laity in the apostolate of the hierarchy." The groups were intended to be the means for the defense of religious and moral principles and for the Christian reconquest of secularized society. According to Pius, they were nonpolitical and had their influence in society through training individuals in Catholic social principles.

In 1930 Italian Catholic Action groups were growing rapidly, despite being harassed and held under surveillance. In March 1931, two months before *Quadragesimo anno* was published, a Fascist trade-union newspaper called the plans for the *Rerum novarum* anniversary celebrations a cover for the expansion of Catholic Action. The newspaper also alleged that the professional Catholic Action groups were being used to gain influence in the labor field so as to convert workers from a Fascist to a Catholic allegiance. In April

Mussolini protested that Catholic Action in Italy was showing signs of becoming a political party and should stop trade-union activities. The Vatican refused to discuss the issue and defended Catholic Action's interest in social morality and justice. The press continued the accusations, however, saying that an attempt was being made to turn Catholic Action into a political party that would organize Italian youth "behind the washed-up remains" of the Partito Popolare Italiano (Catholic Popular party, forced out of existence in 1927). Historian John F. Pollard has asserted that in fact Pius had underestimated the influence and number of the *popolari* within Catholic Action. The pope was convinced that his reforms of Catholic Action in the 1920s had put it firmly in the control of bishops and clergy. The organization's anti-Fascist enthusiasm and activities could not be entirely suppressed by the pope, however, despite the fact that this was Mussolini's expectation as a result of the Lateran Pacts.

At the end of May, following the *Rerum novarum* celebrations in Rome and the release of *Quadragesimo anno,* a rash of violent anti–Catholic Action incidents took place. On May 30 Mussolini dissolved the Catholic youth groups; relations between the Vatican and the Italian government plummeted. On June 29 Pius issued an encyclical on Catholic Action, *Non abbiamo bisogno,* which condemned the persecution and violence against the organization and defended it as "outside and above all party politics." The pope went on: "In everything that We have said up to the present, We have not said that We wished to condemn the [Fascist] party as such. Our aim has been to point out and to condemn all those things in the programme and in the activities of the party which have been found to be contrary to Catholic doctrine and Catholic practice, and therefore irreconcilable with the Catholic name and profession" (62).

Relations were restored with the September Accords that same year. This required compromise on both sides, and as a result the pope never again repeated the criticisms of Fascist trade unionism that he made in *Quadragesimo anno.* After the Accords Catholic Action was allowed to continue in Italy, but its activities became more timid, prudent, and discreet. To avoid conflict, ecclesiastical authorities imposed restrictions that produced more concentration on religious exercises and less on the study of Catholic social teaching—the price paid for the maintenance of the Lateran Pacts, which disappointed those who hoped the crisis would lead to a firm anti-Fascist stand by the Vatican.

Quadragesimo anno was drafted by Oswald von Nell-Breuning, a German Jesuit who was given the assignment in strict secrecy by the superior general of the Jesuits. The latter acted as liaison between Pius XI and Nell-Breuning throughout the process. The Jesuit scholar—who had earned his doctorate in 1928 with a dissertation on the morality of the stock exchange—was not allowed to consult others. According to Nell-Breuning, he was most influenced by the social philosophy of solidarism and especially by his brother priest, the solidarist Gustav Gundlach, who later was the drafter of Pius XII's social allocutions.

German economist Heinrich Pesch, S.J. (1854–1926), was the originator of the system of economic thought known as solidarism, which was based on Catholic philosophical principles (especially the principle of solidarity) and which advocated a middle way between socialism and individualism. It proposed organizations according to industries or professions that would be neither labor unions nor political parties. Instead, vocational groupings would include both workers and employers and would operate as self-governing authorities for the various industries and professions.

Nell-Breuning was a participant in the Konigswinter Group of Catholic economists, which gave him the opportunity to bring up certain questions without hinting at the use he would make of the discussions. He met with Pius XI only once at the beginning of the project, and he reported that near the end of the drafting he received from the pope the controversial section on Italian fascism (written in Pius XI's own hand in Italian), which became paragraphs 91–96 of the encyclical. (More will be said about these paragraphs below.) In the following commentary I shall refer to Pius XI as the author of *Quadragesimo anno,* since the document was issued with his approval and in his name.

Quadragesimo anno can be considered to have three parts: (1) recollection of *Rerum novarum* and its impact (1–40); (2) vindication and further development of the social and economic doctrine of *Rerum novarum* (41–98); and (3) consideration of changes in capitalism and socialism since the time of Leo XIII and proposal of general remedies (99–148).

Recalling Rerum Novarum

In the first portion of *Quadragesimo anno* Pius XI recalled that *Rerum novarum* was written at the close of the 19th century, when industrialization and new economic methods had divided Europe into two classes, the very small class of the wealthy and the enormous class of workers, who were oppressed by dire poverty. Pius pointed out that the wealthy thought that the division was caused by inevitable and natural economic laws and were willing to leave to charity the care of the unfortunate. The working classes meanwhile were more and more unwilling to bear their harsh conditions. Some wanted reform, others sought to disrupt the whole social fabric. Many came to Pope Leo XIII for advice. *Rerum novarum* was his response.

Quadragesimo anno then outlined the impact of *Rerum novarum.* In the church, Pius XI wrote, *Rerum novarum* provoked the development of a Catholic social science that was made available to ordinary people through courses, study circles, publications, and the like. Catholic priests increased their ministries among workers. Catholic principles regarding the rights of labor had influence on civil power, legislative assemblies, courts of justice, and the development of labor law.

Pius considered the greatest impact of *Rerum novarum* to be in the area of overcoming liberalism's (meaning here liberal capitalism's) resistance to labor unions. Following *Rerum novarum,* clergy and laity assisted in the formation of Catholic unions. In some circumstances (e.g., in parts of Germany) Catholics were permitted by their bishops to join neutral trade unions; however, Catholic associations were expected to give moral and religious training to Catholic workers so they could bring the correct spirit to their unions. Meanwhile, associations of employers and heads of industry had met with less success.

Quadragesimo anno referred to *Rerum novarum* as the *Magna Charta* of Christian activities in social matters. While heralding the achievements resulting from Leo's encyclical, Pius pointed out that controversies about the interpretation of *Rerum novarum,* new needs, and changed conditions made necessary a more precise application and amplification of its teachings.

Vindication and Further Development of Rerum Novarum

In the second section, the pope provided his own perspective on three of those teachings: private property, capital and labor, and just wages. Then he presented certain proposals for what he referred to as the reconstruction of the social order. This last section included his remarks about Italian Fascist labor organization.

Property

Pius emphasized the social character of ownership over Leo's stress on the right to property as an individual's natural right. Nevertheless, for Pius the question of the proper use of property was an issue of virtues other than justice, while the right to property itself was a matter of commutative justice, so that the misuse—or nonuse—of property was seen as not destroying or forfeiting the right to ownership. Rather, according to Pius, it was the role of the state to define what was licit and illicit in the use of possessions. This definition would not be arbitrary but would follow natural and divine law. Civil authority could adjust ownership to meet the needs of the common good, and in so doing would prevent the creation of intolerable burdens on some. In taking such measures the state would actually be strengthening private ownership.

Quadragesimo anno warned against the twin dangers of individualism, which would result from minimizing the social aspect of ownership, and collectivism, which would result from minimizing the individual aspect. Nevertheless, the right to private property was strongly emphasized.

This emphasis has diminished in Catholic social teaching since Vatican II. Moral theology has once again brought to the fore the teachings on property of the early church fathers and Thomas Aquinas that emphasized social responsibility. John XXIII and Paul VI both stressed human needs over the right to private property. John Paul II in *Laborem exercens* (*On Human Work*), written for the 90th anniversary of *Rerum novarum,* continued this development: "The right to private property is subordinated to the right to common use, to the fact that goods are meant for everyone" (LE 14).

Fearing communism and socialism, both Leo XIII and Pius XI wanted all people to be able to own land and to pass on an inheritance to their children. This ideal was that of an agrarian society and was becoming increasingly unrealistic in the midst of the development of capitalist property relations of the time.

Capital and Labor

Here Pius reiterated Leo's claim: "Capital cannot do without labor, nor labor without capital." *Quadragesimo anno* rejected the conflicting views discussed at the time: (1) that by economic law the accumulation of riches belonged to the wealthy while the workers must remain in indigence or at a subsistence level; and (2) that all products and profits beyond those required to replace invested capital belonged to the workers. According to *Quadragesimo anno,* neither class should be permitted to exclude the other class from a share in the profits. Each class should receive its "due share," and the distribution must accord with the demands of the common good and social justice. From other writings of Pius XI it is clear that his teaching assumed hierarchical ranks within society, which will influence this "due share." Nevertheless, the vast differences in wealth between rich and poor were pointed out in this encyclical as clearly a grave evil of modern society. This issue naturally carries over to the concern in both *Rerum novarum* and *Quadragesimo anno* about the question of a just wage.

Pius XI used the term "social justice," which did not occur in Leo XIII. The term designated the objective norm of all social and economic activities, relations, and institutions. The concept of the common good is intimately part of the notion of social justice. The term "social justice" was used by the solidarists and was "theologically canonized" (as Nell-Breuning put it) by its usage in *Quadragesimo anno.* By using the term, Pius avoided the confusion that was present even among scholars over the subtleties of the different categories of justice. A fuller definition of social justice appears in Pius XI's encyclical *Divini Redemptoris* (51).

Pius XI made note in *Quadragesimo anno* that the conditions of workers had improved in some of the larger states since the time of Leo XIII. But he also pointed out that the conditions of the laboring masses in the newly colonized countries and in the Far East had worsened with the spread of modern machinery and industry. He called attention to the plight of hired rural laborers "who have no hope of ever obtaining a share in the land" (59). The pope thus spread his concern to workers and the poor beyond the West. After Vatican II this worldwide concern was to become prominent in papal social teaching. It was already well stated in *Quadragesimo anno:* "The immense number of propertyless wage-earners on the one hand, and the superabundant riches of the fortunate few on the other, is an unanswerable argument that the earthly goods so abundantly produced in this age of industrialism are far from rightly distributed and equitably shared among the various classes of human beings" (60).

Just Wage

Quadragesimo anno recalls that *Rerum novarum* accepted the wage contract, but Pius added that it would be advisable to modify this with some contract of partnership when possible so that wage-earners could share in some way in the ownership, or the management, or the profits. He rejected, however, the idea that an equitable return for labor should equal the worth of its net result or that labor is the only thing that gives a right to profits.

The wage should be determined with these factors in mind: (1) the wage must be sufficient to meet ordinary domestic needs (so that the father's wage would enable the mother to attend to the children and the home); (2) the condition of the business and its owner are to be taken into consideration (a just wage may become an impossibility if the business is compelled to sell its products at an unjustly low price); (3) the wage scale must be designed for the economic welfare of the whole people. To lower or raise wages without regard for the common good is depicted as contrary to social justice, which demands that wages be set so that the greatest number of opportunities for employment be provided.

It should be noted that with regard to women's role in the home, papal teaching at least through John Paul II's encyclical *Laborem exercens* has changed little. John Paul II, like Pius XI, holds that women's role as mothers is irreplaceable. In his 1937 encyclical *Divini Redemptoris* (*On Atheistic Communism*), Pius XI characterized communism as rejecting any link that binds women to the family and the home. He saw women's emancipation as a basic principle in communism. His concern about the care of children falling to the collectivity and his hierarchical view of the family with the father in authority help to explain his strong fear of communism and socialism.

Pius related wages and prices, so *Quadragesimo anno* also touched upon the question of the relationship between the prices of agrarian products and industrial products. In the years since *Quadragesimo anno,* this question has grown in importance. Papal social teaching, especially since Paul VI's 1967 encyclical, *Populorum progressio* (*On the Development of Peoples*), has highlighted the difficulties experienced by those countries that are forced to sell their unprocessed commodity exports cheaply and pay high prices for manufactured and technical imports. *Quadragesimo anno* stated that where a just proportion between prices is maintained economic activities function like a single organism and form a common body of mutual help and service.

This image of society as a united organism despite its inequalities was used both by Pius XI and Leo XIII. It expressed their nostalgia for a simpler kind of interdependent society akin to feudalism, in which people accepted their standing in a hierarchical order and conflict was minimized through paternal benevolence. The hierarchy in this model originated in God and worked downward, through church authorities and traditional rulers to the family, where the father represented God. Democracy was suspect because of its possibility of undermining this hierarchy. The organic model positively expressed the popes' hope for harmony, cooperation, and commitment to the common good—in contrast to what they perceived as the competitiveness of capitalism and the class conflict stressed by Communists and Socialists.

Reconstruction of the Social Order

After the issue of wages and prices, *Quadragesimo anno* moved on to proposals concerning the reconstruction of the social order. Two things, Pius said, are necessary: reform of the social order and correction of morals. By the social order Pius particularly meant the state. He was concerned about the loss in society of intermediate groups so that the state had become encumbered with burdens that formerly were borne by local groups. It was his conviction that the state should not step in when smaller bodies could accomplish the task. This is known in Catholic social teaching as the "principle of subsidiarity" and is also drawn from the vision of an organic society. At the time the principle was meant as a barrier against the centralizing tendencies of socialism and Fascism. It was later complemented by the notion of "socialization"—referring to the multiplication of social relations in modern society, which gives rise to the need for their coordination. This notion was developed in John XXIII's 1961 encyclical, *Mater et magistra* (*On Christianity and Social Progress*). Socialization may include state intervention for the common good. As Gregory Baum has put it, since the time of John XXIII "small is beautiful" has been counterbalanced in the teaching by "big when necessary."

Quadragesimo anno said that the primary duty of the state is "to abolish conflict between classes with divergent interests, and thus foster and promote harmony between the various ranks in society" (81). To do this Pius proposed social legislation to reestablish vocational groups that would organize workers and employers according to their function in society (somewhat like the guilds of the Middle Ages) rather than separately as workers and owners/employers who are set against each other like two armies in combat. When interests within the vocational groups were opposing, Pius proposed that separate deliberations and separate votes be taken. People would be free to choose the form the groups would take and be free to join or not. It is clear that Pius saw these groups as a higher ideal than trade unions and the goal that already-formed associations should strive for.

Italian Fascist Labor Organization

Paragraphs 91–96 are those that Nell-Breuning said were given to him as Pius XI's own contribution to the encyclical. In these paragraphs Pius called attention to a special type of union and corporative organization—the kind of vocational groupings the Italian Fascist government was introducing. Pius described how legal recognition by the state gave this type of association a monopoly status, since it alone was allowed to conclude contracts and labor agreements. These "corporations" were composed of representatives of unions of workers and employers of the same trade or profession. Strikes and lockouts had been forbidden; public authority intervened if agreement could not be reached. Pius pointed to certain advantages that could be gained from these arrangements: "peaceful collaboration of the classes, repression of socialist organizations and efforts, the moderating influence of a special ministry" (95). However, Pius felt bound to raise the objection that there was fear the state was substituting itself for private initiative and that the new institution was excessively bureaucratic and risked serving particular political aims rather than an improved social order. The latter end would be better attained indirectly by the contribution of those who were imbued with Catholic principles, such as those who had been trained by Catholic Action.

Nell-Breuning at first had a favorable impression of these paragraphs, but it did not last. He became convinced by remarks made by Pius XI after *Quadragesimo anno* was issued that the pope neither understood Fascism nor its social and political character. In his commentary on the encyclical, which was published in English in 1936, Nell-Breuning had interpreted the paragraphs as diplomatic irony. Much later, in an article written in 1971, he said he believed paragraphs 91–96 were the cause of the misunderstanding of the outline of the social order of vocational groupings presented in *Quadragesimo anno,* a social order he saw as progressive.

The paragraphs before paragraphs 91–96 stress that the proposed corporative order should be free, voluntary, and not state directed. Having stated this, the pope may have been using paragraphs 91–96 as a conciliatory gesture to Mussolini in the midst of the buildup of pressure over Catholic Action. The pope did not see any near end to fascism, and this may have been an attempt to reduce tension.

Nell-Breuning reported that the pope complained about Mussolini's reaction to his "benevolent nod" in *Quadragesimo anno* when Mussolini struck at Catholic Action at the end of May. Without doubt the ambiguity of the paragraphs in question and the papacy's failure to disavow claims by later rightist regimes that they were embodiments of the encyclical's idea of a corporate order (Seipel and Dollfuss in Austria; Franco in Spain; Salazar in Portugal; Vargas in Brazil) provide reason for what Nell-Breuning called a misreading of the encyclical. Vocational groupings quietly dropped out of papal teaching after Pius XII; however, the importance of labor unions in securing the rights of workers has remained.

It is clear that Pius XI was looking for a third way that was neither liberal capitalist nor socialist. Fascism proposed itself as an alternative to both. There were elements in fascism that appealed to those in the church who held an organic view of society and had doubts about the effectiveness and/or implications of democracy. Yet the totalitarianism and violence of fascism were already amply clear enough to prevent the pope from being totally drawn in.

Changes in Capitalism and Socialism

The final section of *Quadragesimo anno* considered changes in capitalism and socialism since the time of Leo XIII and proposed some general remedies.

Capitalism

Pius noted that Leo wanted to adjust the capitalist economic system, and hence the system was not to be condemned. Pius added that "surely it is not vicious of its very nature" (101). This is somewhat surprising given the harshness of the description that follows. Pius asserted that not only had wealth been accumulated but immense power and economic domination had become concentrated in the hands of the few. These may not have been owners but trustees and directors of invested funds who controlled money and credit and had become so powerful in the economy that "no one dare breathe against their will" (105–6).

His description sounds like a condemnation of the system rather than its abuses: "This accumulation of power, the characteristic note of the modern economic order, is a natural result of limitless free competition which permits the survival of those only who are the strongest, which often means those who fight most relentlessly, who pay least heed to the dictates of conscience" (107). The struggle for domination was described as threefold: in the economic sphere itself, for control of the state, and in clashes between states. The result is, according to the encyclical, that free competition is dead; economic dictatorship has taken its place. Confusion between civil authority and the economy has led to the state becoming the slave of human passion and greed rather than the supreme arbiter intent on justice and the common good. International relations are marred on the one hand by economic nationalism and imperialism and on the other by an international imperialism whose country is wherever profit is.

Despite this description Pius ended this segment by recommending that Christian principles be brought to bear on these issues so that the dangers of both individualism and collectivism could be avoided. Commutative justice and Christian charity must become operative in the relations between labor and capital. Free competition and economic domination must be kept within just and definite limits and brought under the control of public authority.

It appears that here the pope was afraid of the conclusion to which his own analysis led. Pius was saying that the system produces this domination, due to the consequences of competition. The domination has even taken control of the state and turned it into an instrument to serve greed. Yet Pius' response was not to condemn the system but to assume that through "effective public authority" all of this could be brought back to "the standard of social justice" (110).

These contradictions can be better understood if we consider the analysis of economic theory in Catholic social teaching offered by Mary Hobgood. Hobgood proposes that within papal teaching three economic paradigms are often in conflict. The first is the paradigm of society and the economy as *organic,* in which members of a hierarchically ordered society are seen as interdependent and, through mutual respect, capable of working together for the common good. This paradigm stresses the community over the individual and hence is in conflict with the second paradigm, that of *liberal* social theory, which stresses the need for economic autonomy of individuals who must be free to pursue their own self-interest. Western capitalism is based on this second paradigm, which includes the notion that economics and politics are separate and autonomous realms. A third paradigm, that of *radical* social theory, rejects this assumption and assumes instead that social, economic, and political structures in Western capitalism form an interlocking system that serves private capital accumulation. Radical theory affirms the reality of a common good and in this way affirms the organic model, but it critiques organic theory's acceptance of hierarchical social arrangements and instead highlights principles of democratic participation.

Elements of these three perspectives are simultaneously present in modern papal economic teaching. This can help us to understand some of the conflicts within *Quadragesimo anno.* In paragraphs 105–10 economic-political reality is looked at in a structural (radical) way that in effect precludes the workability of its own liberal policy prescriptions. Pius noted in particular this change in capitalism: that the state had become a slave of economic powers. He was critiquing the notion that politics and the economy are autonomous. The pope grasped how economic power was abusing political power and using it for private gain of the very few. This was a structural critique. The remedy suggested was to have public authority (the state) limit economic domination—falling back, then, into the liberal model, which assumes that politics and economics are separate entities. To be consistent with his analysis of the linkage of economics and politics might have led Pius to condemn capitalism. That was perhaps too frightening in the face of the alternatives of socialism, which Pius linked with atheism, and fascism, which while holding certain attractions was also in profound disagreement with Catholic principles.

Socialism

In *Quadragesimo anno*'s consideration of socialism, Pius explained how socialism was a single system at the time of Leo XIII but by 1931 could be described as having two opposing camps within it, although both, in his estimation, still opposed the Christian faith. Communism made up one camp, which aimed at class warfare and complete abolition of private property. Communism's hostility to God and the church was so well known, said the pope, that it was not necessary to elaborate on it. The pope was critical of those who allowed the propagation of communism's doctrines, but even more to be condemned were those who neglected to remove or to modify the conditions that exasperated people and prepared the way for the overthrow of the social order.

Pius described the second camp, socialism, as condemning violence and being more moderate regarding class warfare and the abolition of private property. Often its positions approached those of Christian social reformers, and if changes continued, wrote the pope, the tenets of mitigated socialism would no longer be very different from the program of those who sought reform according to Christian principles. Here the pope made an admission of agreement with Socialists over the possible need to limit private property: "For it is rightly contended that certain forms of property must be reserved to the State, since they carry with them an opportunity of domination too great to be left to private individuals without injury to the community at large" (114).

Regarding the question of whether the church could approach moderated socialism with moderated Christian principles so as to meet halfway, the pope replied that Christian truth must be preached whole and entire. To those who asked if socialism had retracted its false doctrines enough to be accepted by the church, Pius answered: "We pronounce as follows: whether socialism be considered as a doctrine, or as a historical fact, or as a movement, if it really remain socialism, it cannot be brought into harmony with the dogmas of the Catholic church, even after it has yielded to truth and justice in the points we have mentioned; the reason being that it conceives human society in a way utterly alien to Christian truth" (117).

The pope then summarized the Christian view of persons as placed on earth with a social nature under an authority ordained by God and with duties to fulfill in accord with each one's station (again the organic model of society); the fulfillment of these duties would lead to temporal and eternal happiness. In contrast, the pope depicted socialism as ignorant of the sublime destiny of humans and society and as viewing community as being instituted simply for the advantages it brings. Pius described socialism as requiring collective production and demanding total submission of people to society in the interest of production of wealth. Possession of material goods is esteemed so highly in socialism that liberty and human dignity may be sacrificed. Compulsion is seen as necessary; at the same time a false liberty is fostered, since social authority descending from God has no place in the Socialist scheme.

Socialism contains some elements of truth, but "religious socialism" and "Christian socialism" imply a contradiction in terms. "No one can be at the same time a sincere Catholic and a true socialist" (120).

This portion of the encyclical has received much comment, and more recent papal teaching has developed in a considerably different direction. John XXIII in his 1963 encyclical, *Pacem in terris* (*Peace on Earth*), made a distinction between philosophical teachings and the social movements that have arisen from them: "Neither can false philosophical teachings regarding the nature, origin, and destiny of the universe and of humanity be identified with historical movements that have economic, social, cultural and political ends, not even when these movements have originated from those teachings and have drawn and still draw inspiration from them" (PT 159).

John continued to explain why the original false teaching should not be identified with the social movements: "This is so because the teachings, once they are drawn up and defined, remain always the same, while the movements, working in constantly evolving historical situations, cannot but be influenced by these latter and cannot avoid, therefore, being subject to changes, even of a profound nature" (PT 159). Thus John moved away from Pius' ahistorical and essentialist definition of socialism. With prudence and through conversation and association, Christians will be able to judge whether particular Socialist movements are in basic theoretical and practical agreement with Catholic principles.

Paul VI continued this line of development in his 1971 apostolic letter *Octogesima adveniens* (*On the Eightieth Anniversary of* Rerum Novarum). Paul also made distinctions between movements and philosophical teaching. He dealt with Marxism as the practice of class struggle, as single-party politics, as socialist ideology based on historical materialism, and as an analytical tool for examining society. Paul saw the latter form as particularly attractive to the modern mind. He warned Catholics only that it would be illusionary and dangerous to forget that the different forms are linked.

Pius XI was not interested in such distinctions with regard to socialism. Socialism was seen as monolithic; capitalism was not. Despite his harsh criticism of capitalism and its inherent dynamic of competition, Pius did not condemn it but believed that reforms could change it. He took a quite different position with regard to socialism, even though he acknowledged how close some Socialists were coming to Catholic positions on social reform. Pius was very fearful of socialism, and *Quadragesimo anno* served to foster this fear thoughout the Catholic world.

John Coleman has suggested that the encyclical's section on socialism was aimed at a small group of religious Socialists in Germany and Austria who were urging collaboration between Catholics and Socialists. It was feared that they were breaking Catholic unity and that they might detract from the Center party, a Catholic party in Germany. Both Baum and Coleman agree that *Quadragesimo anno* had a negative social impact. In 1928 Stalin had forbidden collaboration of Communists with Socialists unless they were under Moscow's direction. So the Socialists had been cut off. *Quadragesimo anno* blocked collaboration of Catholics with Social-Democratic parties in Europe, which were resisting fascism. In Germany *Quadragesimo anno* put a brake on collaboration between the Center party and the Socialists, which might have offered more resistance to Hitler. The encyclical also kept Canadian Catholics from supporting a non-Marxist, democratic Canadian Socialist party. The English hierarchy, however, followed the arguments of *Quadragesimo anno* and came to a different conclusion—that the encyclical did not prevent Catholics from joining the Labour party.

General Remedies

It appears that Pius XI had no interest in political parties and felt that Christians should be above them. This may well have been due to his diagnosis of the root of social problems and his prescription of remedies. Pius presented these at the end of the encyclical in paragraphs 127–48.

Social reconstruction, he said, must be preceded by a profound renewal of the Christian spirit. Christianity alone can remedy "the excessive solicitude for transitory things, which is the origin of all vices"

(129) and a consequence of original sin. Yet social and economic conditions are such for vast multitudes that they have difficulty paying attention to eternal salvation. The uncertainty of economic conditions demands an unceasing straining of energy, and many have become hardened to conscience. Legal regulations for corporations are grossly abused. A stern insistence on the moral law enforced by civil authority could have averted these evils, but rationalism and an economic science alien to the true moral law has already given free rein to avarice. Workers sank into the same moral morass because of the perils that modern workplaces offered (especially to youth) and the way employers treated workers as tools, without concern for the welfare of souls.

The problem was analyzed by Pius XI as essentially a moral one; hence the remedy was not to be found in social movements or political parties but in a return to Christian principles of moderation and especially to the law of charity. Charity could not take the place of justice withheld, wrote Pius, but it was necessary to bring stability and union to humanity. In this concluding portion the pope again raised his vision of an organic society. Christian moderation would enable the rich to increase their fortunes justly. Charity would cause the rich to listen with kindly regard to workers' just complaints and would enable workers to lay aside feelings of envy and cease to be weary of the position assigned them by God in society. A new diffusion of the gospel spirit in the world would make social renewal possible.

Pope Pius XI expected Catholics to implement his teaching, and he especially favored Catholic Action as an educational program from which Christian leaders would emerge. Unfortunately, as we saw earlier, his conflict with Mussolini over Catholic Action in Italy led to the September Accords, which had the effect of restricting the organization more closely to religious matters.

In Europe and Latin America, Catholic parties used *Quadragesimo anno* to advocate a more restricted capitalism and protection of workers. In the United States some Catholics used it to support the New Deal. The encyclical was looked upon as a vindication of John A. Ryan, a professor of moral theology at Catholic University who had been working for years on such issues as distributive justice and a living wage. The encyclical, although printed in full in the *New York Times,* failed to generate wide reaction among U.S. Catholics. Nevertheless, the document played a role in the bishops' decision to fund the Social Action Department of the National Catholic Welfare Conference.

Overall, *Quadragesimo anno* strengthened Catholic teaching in defense of labor and in its critique of liberal capitalism. Its insistence on social justice and the common good held up a norm with which to evaluate economic relations and institutions. *Quadragesimo anno* began a tradition for the pope to reconsider the condition of workers periodically, a tradition that continues to the present. Perhaps most importantly, for an important minority in the church who were involved in labor and social justice issues, *Quadragesimo anno* justified their work and kept alive their hope in a church that cared for justice and for the poor.

See also CAPITALISM; CORPORATISM; FASCISM; LABOR AND CAPITAL IN CATHOLIC SOCIAL THOUGHT; NELL-BREUNING, OSWALD VON; RERUM NOVARUM; SOLIDARISM; SUBSIDIARITY, PRINCIPLE OF.

Bibliography: G. Baum, *Catholics and Canadian Socialism* (New York: Paulist, 1980). J.-Y. Calvez and J. Perrin, *The Church and Social Justice* (Chicago: Henry Regnery, 1961). R. Camp, *The Papal Ideology of Social Reform* (Leiden: Brill, 1969). J. Coleman, "Development of Catholic Social Teaching," in *Readings in Moral Theology No. 5: Official Catholic Social Teaching,* ed. C. Curran and R. McCormick (New York: Paulist, 1986). J. Cronin, "Forty Years Later: Reflections and Reminiscences," in *Readings in Moral Theology No. 5.* D. Dorr, *Option for the Poor: A Hundred Years of Vatican Social Teaching* (Maryknoll, N.Y.: Orbis, 1983). M. Hobgood, *Catholic Social Teaching and Economic Theory* (Philadelphia: Temple Univ.

Press, 1991). A. Jemolo, *Church and State in Italy, 1850–1950* (Oxford: Basil Blackwell, 1960). O. von Nell-Breuning, "The Drafting of Quadragesimo Anno," in *Readings in Moral Theology No. 5*. O. von Nell-Breuning, *Reorganization of Social Economy* (New York: Bruce, 1936). J. Pollard, *The Vatican and Italian Fascism, 1929–32* (New York: Cambridge Univ. Press, 1985).

MARIE J. GIBLIN

R

REASON, ROLE OF

In the church's vocabulary, reason is understood without further distinctions (unlike, e.g., the vocabulary of Kant) as the human person's intellectual capacity for knowledge. As theoretical reason, it is capable in principle of understanding in some way everything that exists. As practical reason, it understands what the human person in his/her freedom *ought* (from an ethical and legal perspective) to do or refrain from doing. Nothing is outside the sphere of this task of reason (*Summa theologiae* I-II 94, 2 ad 3). Thus the (practical) reason is the all-embracing regulator of human behavior. It permits the human person to understand, at first in a nonthematic way but subsequently also in a thematic way, that he/she is a moral being, that is, one not abandoned to arbitrariness. Accordingly it instructs the human person *absolutely* and in every case to behave rationally, that is, in a human manner, and consequently to do what is recognized as good (for the human person) and to avoid what is recognized as bad or evil.

Apart from these fundamental principles, which can be recognized and have been recognized in total certainty and infallibility, further principles are clear to the human person through his/her self-understanding: for example, that the personal human being is an end in himself/herself and thus may never be used *only* as a means to an end, and that all human persons have equal dignity in this. However, it is not laid down in advance for the human person in concrete terms what is the general norm of behavior or what is good or bad or evil in the individual situation for the human person. One must discover this through one's reason *in a creative process of finding,* whether this is intuitive or carried out in explicit intellectual discourse. It follows that what is good in a concrete case, as that which is to be done, is a construct that must be investigated by the human person himself or herself.

The task of discovering what is to be done from an ethical or legal perspective belongs not to reason as such but to the personal human being—although this is something done by means of reason. But the human person is not *only* reason but a totality of previously formed interpretations and evaluations of already existing realities, of options that have already been accepted, of good and less good tendencies, of the effects of the "sin of the world" (Jn 1:29), of the effects of the grace of the Holy Spirit as the "new law of Christ," and ultimately of the prospect of potential consequences of particular modes of conduct. In this total reality, it is not the human person's task to look for God's will as this has somehow or other been revealed but, as his/her own providence, to discover what ultimately serves his/her own good. This is the will of God (cf. Thomas Aquinas, *Summa contra Gentiles* 3, 122).

The Apostle Paul distinguishes between the old and the new human person (2 Cor 5). The old human person is the one who stands under the power of sin; the new human person is the one who has been withdrawn from the power of sin thanks to grace. In parallel to this statement, the distinction has recently begun to be made between the old and the new reason. Which reason do we mean when we speak of reason as the regulator of correct ethical and legal behavior: the old reason or the new? And what would be the old and the new reason? While it is not reason that thinks and comes to know but the human person as subject, the human person does this by means of the reason. Since one always stands under the power of sin or of grace (or of both), and since these powers share in determining one's personal options and attitudes, the mode of one's use of reason also will depend on these factors. *Pure* reason does not exist. The important point is how the old or the new human person makes use of reason in freedom. But alongside the oldness or newness of reason, there are many other realities in the knowing subject that determine the subject's options and attitudes. The honest profession of theism, for example, or of atheism, is not exclusively the outcome of pure thinking but also of a varied (historical) conditioned free option of the subject that makes use of his/her reason.

Without a logical prior self-understanding by means of reason there exists no ethical or legal reason, nor any path leading to the acceptance of the Christian faith. However, the Christian faith, as the "light of the gospel" (*Gaudium et spes* 46), helps to avoid a mistaken ethical or legal human conduct or deed. Since the help given by faith is only a help it does not absolutely exclude either error or a pluralism of ethical opinions (cf. GS 43). The chief reason for this is that the ethical and legal judgments of reason do not only attempt—by looking backward—a reality that already exists (creation and development) but must understand this with a view to the future. Nevertheless and despite all limitations, reason makes possible ethics and law as the highest cultural creation of the human person.

See also MAGISTERIUM; NATURAL LAW.

JOSEF FUCHS, S.J.

RECESSION

Catholic social teaching, articulated in papal encyclicals and the documents of national episcopal conferences, does not treat the question of recession in a direct way. Nonetheless, one can extrapolate certain guidelines from these documents, since they indicate the church's overall position on economic and social phenomena.

Church teaching on economic questions is shaped by a concern for the well-being of all members of society. In church teaching the purpose of economic activity is to allow every member of society the chance to become a responsible and productive person actively involved in shaping his or her sociopolitical context. The church understands economic systems and related phenomena, then, as means to an end, not ends in themselves. That end is the realization of human fullness mandated by God's creative plan, not the creation of wealth for its own sake. This principle has been clearly enunciated for over a century, from the time of Leo XIII, whose encyclical *Rerum novarum* was one of the first papal documents to discuss socioeconomic issues, to the writings of John Paul II, who follows the perspective of his predecessors. In *Laborem exercens,* an encyclical written by Pope John Paul II in 1981, economic life and human labor are defined as crucial activities that Christians must understand and try to shape in the most beneficial way possible. The American Catholic bishops reiterated this same point of view in an important document published in 1986 called *Economic Justice for All.* In their own words, "all human beings, therefore, are ends to be served by the institutions that make up the economy, not means to be exploited for more narrowly defined goals" (EJA 28). Consequently, economic phenomena must be assessed in terms of their concrete impact on human beings. When we examine a concept like recession we must remember that we are dealing with more than an abstract issue or mere statistics. We are talking about a complex social, political, and economic event that has concrete implications for every member of society.

In succinct terms, a recession is a downturn in economic activity. It is a phase of limited, zero, or even negative growth, as opposed to economic expansion. In a recession those who own the means of production, a socioeconomic class known as capitalists, realize less profit from the raw materials or finished products they sell on the open market. Simultaneously, workers, who sell their labor power to capitalists in return for wages, often receive less remuneration for their work or even find themselves unemployed. Because recessions are associated with diminished surplus value, or profit, those who own the means of production will often try to maximize their gain by minimizing the wages and the number of workers who produce marketed goods. If such strategies fail, they will cease production rather than suffer a loss of capital.

The common result of a recession is decreased wealth and well-being for all members of society. Workers, however, are the most directly affected since they have fewer socioeconomic buffers and less political power than those who own the means of production. Severe economic downturns or recessions are often classified as depressions. A recession differs from a depression in terms of its severity and the length of time it lasts. The infamous Great Depression of 1929 wiped out years of economic gain and produced intense social problems directly related to the rise of Fascism in Western Europe. Most nations now have stringent monetary and banking regulations aimed at preventing recessions from becoming depressions. These monetary control mechanisms have generally worked, although many recessions have occurred in capitalist countries and some have been serious enough to warrant classification as depressions, albeit less severe than that of 1929.

Economists tend to explain and define a recession in ways that reflect their socioeconomic loyalties. Conservative, procapitalist economists understand recessions differently from radical economists who accept certain of Marx's ideas and are consequently critical of the basic presuppositions and workings of the capitalist system. All economists, however, recognize that recessions happen, despite disagreement as to why and how they come about and what can be done to mitigate their impact. The precise chronology of the "business cycle," as it is sometimes called, varies from one national economy to another, but there is irrefutable proof that economies expand and shrink on a continuing and often predictable basis. Historians of economy can point to numerous recessionary periods in the industrial world that followed periods of growth.

It is important to keep in mind that the causes of a recession are not entirely economic. Public opinion, political decisions, national and international events, all shape economies in a positive or negative way. For example, in industrialized countries that require imported oil, a rise in petroleum prices on the world market may lead to inflation, decreased profits for capitalists, and a concomitant drop in production, workers' wages, and levels of employment. Especially in the late 20th century, when national economies are so interconnected, an economic downturn in one part of the world or even in one region of a single country often has serious consequences for members of the larger community. When developed countries enter into recessions, developing countries generally do as well. Often the havoc wrought by a recession is far more acute in the fragile and disjointed economies of developing countries than it is in North America or Europe.

To some degree the effects of a recession can be controlled and even mitigated by the fiscal policies of a central government. State controlled banks can stimulate or constrain an economy by making capital, in the form of loans, more or less expensive. This is done by manipulating the rate of interest for the loans capitalists require to finance production. This is a standard tactic, among others, used to avoid a recession or diminish its effects.

Government agencies try to maintain levels of profit at an acceptable rate. Excessive profits can overheat an economy and cause inflation. If, however, profits are too low, capitalists will refuse to finance production. This will lead to a recession. In most industrial nations, government agencies usually control the economy in ways that favor the already affluent. Such policies are based on the assumption that wealth will eventually trickle down to every social stratum. Capital, then, takes precedence over labor. Such policies, however, can have negative effects on ordinary people who do not own the means of production. Inflation can wipe out savings, while high interest rates can make it impossible for working-class people to obtain the mortgages or loans they need from banks. The result can be socioeconomic misery for millions of people, evident in homelessness, hunger, and inadequate health care.

At least on a hypothetical level, most modern societies claim to be structured democratically. In such a context it is incumbent upon the believing Christian to make his or her voice heard and strive for socioeconomic policies that benefit the largest number of people possible, especially workers and the poor, who suffer disproportionately in recessionary periods. This is the clear position of the American Catholic bishops in *Economic Justice for All.*

Recessions in modern capitalism appear to be inevitable. Their human impact, nonetheless, can be softened by remembering that the purpose of economic life is to secure the common good, not the interests of one socioeconomic group at the expense of another.

See also BANKS AND BANKING; CAPITALISM; CORPORATIONS; EMPLOYMENT AND UNEMPLOYMENT; INVESTMENT; PROFIT.

CURT CADORETTE, M.M.

REDEMPTOR HOMINIS

Redemptor hominis (*The Redeemer of Humankind*), the inaugural encyclical of John Paul II (*Acta apostolicae sedis* 71 [1979] 257–324), was originally authored in Polish, with the English translation issued by Liberia Editrice Vaticana.

Part 1: Inheritance (1–6)

The letter opens with expressions of hope and joy in anticipation of the year 2000, a year of jubilee. The theme of the letter, Advent, anticipates the continual preparation and contribution of the church and humankind to the coming of God. John Paul II describes his acceptance of the papacy as grounded in an incarnational faith and a desire to continue in the tradition of John XXIII and Paul VI and the profound legacy of John Paul I. The latter's choice of name focused the church's future on the implementation of Vatican II.

Relying on Paul VI's *Ecclesiam suam* (AAS 56, 1974), John Paul II argues for continued inter and intra church dialogue. Admittedly our church is not free from internal difficulties and tension; however, criticism from within must have limits. In spite of all appearances, our church is more united today in its service to humankind because of Vatican II's assertion of the need for collegiality. The worldwide episcopal conferences, the increased number of diocesan and provincial synods, are all structural evidence of a new surge of life in the church. The continuing collaboration between clerics, those consecrated to the evangelical counsels, and the laity also marks this deepening of collegiality. The church must trust in the directives of Vatican II regarding the unity of the Christian churches and not fear advances in this arena. All have much to teach us, yet in all dialogue "the treasures of divine truth that the church has constantly taught and confessed" must be retained (6).

Part II: The Mystery of Redemption (7–12)

The thematic question for this section of the letter is, How shall we proceed into the future so that this advent will bring us closer to God? Our movement must be toward Jesus Christ, our well-being rests in no one else. For this reason the church attempts to listen to Christ's words and reconstruct every detail of Christ's life. Christ's life, Christ's humanity, Christ's fidelity to truth, Christ's embracing love—these mysteries are unceasingly celebrated in the Eucharist and lived in the church's liturgical cycle; these mysteries are the fountain of life and holiness.

In Christ, the world recovers its original link with God, broken in Adam. In Christ, humankind is redeemed. Yet our world "groans in travail, waiting with eager longing." Our progress reveals pollution, the arms race, a lack of responsibility for the unborn, in short, futility, and this despite our space flights and other previously unattained conquests in science and technology. Humans only understand their role in the world through Christ; in Christ each one is fully revealed to himself or herself. Christ, through the Incarnation, is revealed to each one. Christ satisfied God's love, and in Christ's love creation is renewed and the fullness of justice revealed. Christ's love did not withdraw from any demand of justice.

Humans cannot live without love. If love is not revealed to us, our lives are senseless. By drawing near to Christ, in whom love is fully expressed, we understand ourselves. If we appropriate Christ's love, our understanding yields deep amazement and wonder at the worth and dignity of the human person. The church's fundamental function, then, is to direct our gaze toward the mystery of God and the depth of our redemption taking place in Christ. This redemption involves the sphere of our deepest selves: our hearts, our consciences, our events.

Various religions reveal the primacy of the spiritual in human history. The deepest aspiration of the human spirit, expressed in its quest for God, is the desire for the full meaning of human life. Organized atheism, as a secular faith of temporal liberation, competes with theism. All believers must work together toward truth. All Christians must unite around Christ to reveal the divine and human dimensions of redemption, thus struggling to restore the dignity each human has reached and can continually reach in Christ. This missionary and apostolic unity, a unity grounded in a deep esteem for the human person, is applauded by the church. The mission is the freedom of every person, a freedom only fully understood by meditating on Jesus' words, "You will know the truth and the truth will set you free." Our role as Christians is to seek an honest relationship to the truth as a condition for authentic freedom. This requirement must guide the apostolic efforts of Christians and the church's search for further interfaith unity.

Part III: Redeemed Humanity and the Human Situation in the Modern World (13–17)

Jesus Christ is redemptively present to all of human life, to each person, to men and women in their concrete historical situation. Therefore each human life is constituted through a dialogue in which God is continually present, restoring the fullness of life. Thus, the object of the church's care is each human in his/her unique, unrepeatable reality. "The church cannot remain insensible to whatever serves humanity's true welfare any more than she can remain indifferent to what threatens it" (13.2). It is the dignity of the human person that determines the way of the church; therefore, the church must always be aware of the human situation in its possibilities and threats. The church's primary endeavor is to make human life ever more human.

Humans seem ever more threatened by what they produce. Increasingly, fear holds sway because our progress often leads to further possibilities of self-destruction. The exploitation of the earth for industrial and military purposes and the uncontrolled development of technology give rise to human disquiet because our morals and ethics have failed to develop proportionately. We must question ourselves. "Do all the conquests attained until now and those projected for the future for technology accord with human moral and spiritual progress? In this context are humans, as humans, developing and progressing or are they regressing and being degraded in their humanity? In humans and in the human world . . . does good prevail over evil? In humans and among humanity is there a growth of social love, of respect for the rights of others—for every human, nation and people—or on the contrary is there an increase of various degrees of selfishness, exaggerated nationalism instead of authentic love of country . . . the propensity to dominate others beyond the limits of one's legitimate rights . . . the propensity to exploit the whole of material progress . . . ?" (15.5).

The church considers essential to its mission a solicitude for the future of humanity on earth. Our approach toward the second millennium is undoubtedly a time of great progress but also a time of great threat. To minimize the threat we must respond to the objective demands of justice and social love. Ethics must take priority over technology, persons over things, and spirit over matter. We must commit ourselves to examining all progress in the light of the advancement of persons, not just the multiplication of things persons can use. Humans cannot allow themselves to become slaves of things, of economic systems, or of production. This concern is integral to the dynamism of life and civilization.

We now have rich, highly developed societies while others are suffering from hunger. This disparity arises from an abuse of freedom, a consumer attitude uncontrolled by ethics. This picture, representative of the parable of Lazarus begging at the table of the rich banqueter, calls into question the financial, monetary, production, and commercial mechanisms that, resting on various political pressures, support the world's economy. No one can remain indifferent to this situation, for both the one who draws the maximum profit and the one who is paying the price in damage and injury are human persons. Daring and creative initiatives are needed to restore a moral order in keeping with human dignity. Our solidarity with all that is human must inspire us to redistribute wealth and control over wealth. This demands a true conversion of mind, heart, and will. No truly human economy is possible unless our instincts for individual and collective interest, for combat and domination, are taken up and dominated by our sense of moral responsibility.

Our century has been a century of great moral and material deprivation, and injustice cries out. The United Nations is to be applauded for its efforts to establish the objective and inviolable rights of humans. The establishment of human rights is closely linked with the church's mission in the modern world. The welfare of the human person is the essential criterion for peace and fundamental to all programs, systems, and regimes. If this criterion is violated, humankind is condemned to suffer, and such suffering is evident today in various forms of domination, totalitarianism, neocolonialism, and imperialism.

Part IV: The Church's Mission and the Destiny of Humankind (18–22)

Through participation in God's people, each person receives the breath of life that comes from Christ. The church also receives her life from Christ and for this reason turns to human hopes and sufferings as her mission. Precisely because Christ is united to the church, the church must be united to every human person. The fullness of life in Christ is the fulfillment of human destiny, of the human vocation; and despite all the enigmas and unsolved problems of the world, this divine destiny goes forward. That which is most deeply human, the search for truth, the insatiable need for the good, hunger for freedom, nostalgia for the beautiful, the voice of conscience, pulsate within us. These are signs that the Spirit continues to hover and breathe life into us. By invoking the Spirit, who inspires in us the sentiments of Christ, we insert ourselves into the mystery of Christ united with God and with every human.

As we become more aware of Christ's triple mission as priest, prophet, and king, we further understand the shape of the church's service. Following Christ as prophet, the church is responsible for the truth of God's word. Theologians, pastors, and catechists must take great care in their study of and transmission of the truth so that all might apprehend the depths of our mission as followers of Christ. Following Christ as priest, the church celebrates Eucharist, allowing all to share in the unique and irreversible restoration of humankind and the world carried out by Christ. The Christ who calls us to the Eucharistic banquet calls us to an ever renewed conversion in the interest of the unity of humankind. Following Christ as king, the church is ready to serve, that the world might enter into that fullness of life for which it was created.

Sources

Of the 205 citations, the most numerous are scriptural. John XXIII is cited twice and Paul VI twelve times. Twenty-eight citations refer to the documents of Vatican II, four to those of Vatican I. Pius XI is quoted once, Pius XII thrice, patristic and Scholastic sources four times. Clearly, John Paul II is most interested in the strengthening of those impulses in the church set forth by the Second Vatican Council.

Main Ideas

1. Redemption is the main theme. This restoration of humanity to that state intended before the fall is accomplished by the Incarnation. In the Incarnation, the at-one-ment of the Son of God with humanity in the person Jesus Christ satisfies not the outraged honor of God (Anselm of Canterbury) but God's eternal love, the love that finds expression in the creation of the world and humanity.

2. Christ is not only a revelation of God and God's salvific will for humankind, but Christ is also a revelation of humanity and what humanity was intended to be at creation and is by reason of the incarnation, crucifixion, resurrection, and ascension of the God-man (*Gaudium et spes* 10, 22, 29).

3. Jesus Christ is proclaimed as the protector of men and women in their history; Jesus is the promoter of truly human life in concrete, actual history; Jesus is an advocate for justice. Although the word "liberator" is not employed in this context by the pope, the concept of Jesus as liberator is implied throughout.

4. The Christian is required to see in the other and in all others the likeness of God, because every person without exception has been redeemed by Christ. It is not the abstract human of the philosophers, but the concrete human in all his or her

unrepeatable reality that is to be honored and revered.

5. Because of God's act of redemption through Jesus Christ, the essential mission of the church in following Christ is to continue to be an agent of redemption in time. The church must respect the dignity of persons and defend their rights. The church's care for the human is essential to its supernatural mission (see the title of no. 14, "For the Church all ways lead to humanity," see also no. 15.6).

6. The way to peace is respect for human rights. The United Nations Declaration is applauded.

7. The use of the word "advent" in the encyclical indicates Christ's second advent to each person in the impending third millennium. In this context the word is freed from any eschatological/judicial association with the Last Judgment. The task ahead of us, the respect for humanity and the structural change necessary for this respect, is not impossible. Our eschatological faith demands a belief in the future of the human. Comprehensively, Christ's "second advent" will be to an enlarged portion of humanity, constituting the church of the individually, experientially redeemed.

8. In the human struggle to respond to one's purpose (vocation) and the struggle for the fullness of human life, against every enslavement and oppression Christ is revealed. Therefore God's grace has a concrete, historical dimension.

9. The Holy Spirit acts to empower humans to contribute to a more just, human world. The action of the Spirit is always enfleshed, always redemptive, in the concrete human situation.

10. The neglect of the Spirit manifests itself in human self-seeking, as found in both capitalist and socialist economic power. Solidarity, an identification with the impoverished and the underclasses, an opening of the heart, is the route to a redistribution of wealth. Planning for economic change to support human rights, including political and religious liberty, must replace planning for technological change, which only advances consumerism and thus only enslaves the human. The pope movingly speaks of the fear that humans will continue as slaves to what they produce, slaves to economic systems, slaves to production (16).

11. The biblical parable of Lazarus and the rich one illustrates God's and the church's concern for the growing numbers of impoverished people in our world.

Contribution to the Tradition

1. With the publication of *Pacem in terris* John XXIII addressed not only world bishops, the clergy, and Catholic faithful but all "men of good will." John Paul II amends the greeting to include "all men and women of good will."

2. The following statement in no. 15.6 appears to vindicate the argument of the 1971 synod of bishops in *Justitia in mundo* (*Justice in the World*) that "justice and participation in the transformation of the world fully appear . . . as a constitutive dimension of the preaching of the Gospel" (JM, introduction). *Redemptor hominis* states: "Inspired by eschatological faith, the Church considers an essential, unbreakably united element of her mission this solicitude for man, for his humanity, for the future of men on earth and therefore also for the course set for the whole of development and progress. She finds the principle for this solicitude in Jesus Christ."

3. Following upon the above, the church's primary concern is for the spiritual, but John Paul II's understanding of the spiritual, the religious, is anything but a concern for the "other world." To be spiritual, to be religious, is to direct one's concern primarily and precisely toward the human person, human society, and our world. The transformation of the human is the primary route of the church and of the follower of Christ; indeed, this path is the very way traced out by Christ himself (14).

See also ANTHROPOLOGY; CHURCH, SOCIAL MISSION OF; SOLIDARITY; POLITICAL THEOLOGY.

Bibliography: G. Baum, "The First Papal Encyclical," *The Ecumenist* (May–June 1979) 55–59. R. Lawler, *The Christian Personalism of John Paul II* (Chicago: Franciscan Herald Press, 1982). G. Williams, *The Mind of John Paul II: Origins of His Thought and Action* (New York: Seabury, 1981). A. Woznicki, *The Dignity of Man As a Person: Essays on the Christian Humanism of His Holiness, John Paul II* (San Francisco: Society of Christ, 1987).

MARYANNE STEVENS, R.S.M.

RELIGIOUS FREEDOM

Depending on the context, the believing Christian appeals to two distinct aspects of religious freedom. These two aspects are normally kept separate and are often thought to be mutually incompatible or contradictory.

First, if asked in a prayer setting to portray the saving power of Christ most Western Christians would describe a relationship with God that reconstructs certain aspects of their lives. Echoing the language of the earliest Christian community, they witness to a freedom that has as its starting point God's reaching out to humanity. Foundationally this freedom is understood to be empowering or active (a "freedom for")—a movement from a condition of impotence or impoverishment to an actual living within and an ability to act according to the spirit of the risen Lord. This empowerment is undeserved, the result of God's gracious election. Often Christians have identified a specific, identifiable religious community as the foundational recipient of theological freedom within which individuals find freedom. Still, the notion of God's initiating, personalized, and enabling election remains core to both individualistic and communitarian notions of theological freedom.

Second, the same believing Christian defines religious freedom differently when questioned on the public street or outside a voting booth. Here the freedom described is social, political, or civic. In the public forum religious freedom connotes immediately a personal immunity from state-directed coercion and secondarily an immunity from those more subtle forms of coercion that result in economic or educational disadvantage. Both internal commitments to religious beliefs and external actions that are judged by the believer to flow necessarily from those beliefs are thought immune. Belief is not to be forced or constrained; actions resulting from belief are not to be restrained. The language here is not that of the early Christian community. Religious freedom as a personal immunity continues to be defined against the background of early modern attempts to limit alleged omnicompetent states, of Enlightenment affirmations of a personal dignity that persists in the face of all social relationships, and of 20th-century experiences with authoritarian and atheistic governments. Social religious freedom usually connotes a passive freedom (a "freedom from") and is thought to be a right based on individual worth. Although many theoretical arguments for social religious freedom are individualistic, communities are generally included under those immunities as necessary social expressions of the individual.

That the same person defines religious freedom so differently at prayer and at political rallies finds an echo in many Protestant and Catholic scholarly attempts to keep the two realms discrete to the point of absolute isolation. One confesses empowerment in church; one demands immunity in public. However, more adequate ways of understanding the depth and breadth of the salvation to which Jesus witnessed now permit us to reach beyond these isolated languages to more integrated ways of speaking about theological and social religious freedoms.

Witnessing to the Kingdom

Contemporary biblical scholarship suggests that Jesus understood the nearness of the kingdom to be an empowering event, enabling one to act with an extravagant mercy that participates in God's own way of dealing with the world. The pattern for this action is disclosed by Jesus' parables and his perfectionistic imperatives, such as the commands to "turn the other cheek" (Mt 5:39) and "be perfect/merciful as your heavenly Father is perfect/merciful" (Mt 5:48; Lk 6:36). Jesus' practice of gathering around a common table with the high and the low, with Pharisees, publicans, and sinners, prefigured the eschatological banquet where all destructive class and social divisions are overcome. Here a relationship to the Father as mediated through the imminent arrival of the kingdom empowers interpersonal actions, with social effects extending beyond the interpersonal. Elsewhere the gospel claims that God enables verbal as well as practical witness to the kingdom. In proclaiming the good news, the Spirit will strengthen and direct the witness even in the face of persecution (Mt 10:19-20). Nature itself will not inhibit that witness (Mk 18:16). The community gathered in Jesus' name is empowered to proclaim the good news to the ends of the earth.

Jesus' rejection of force in his living-of-the-kingdom ethics left Christianity with a permanent conviction that the gift of the kingdom must be received in freedom, in the sense of an immunity. The kingdom remains God's gift, to be offered in act and word as gift. A rejection of Jesus' kingdom ethics resulted in his death. Yet even when facing death Jesus refused to curtail his preaching or his acting out of those ethics.

While the first proclamation of the kingdom in act and word was most likely restricted to religious Jews, the outbreak of the Spirit among non-Jews challenged and erased earlier restrictions on who were considered proper recipients of the gospel (Acts 8, 10). Free confession of Jesus as Lord indicated freedom in the Spirit. Such allowed an understanding of Christ as the heart of creation as well as redemption, toward whom the entire human community and nature itself are drawn (Jn 1; Rev 1:4-8).

Facing Limits

The Christian inclusion of all peoples and the entire cosmos within the Christological promise was challenged by the pluralistic composition of the growing community, by negative encounters with nature, and by the hostility of larger societies.

Although the community attempted to understand itself ideally as united, diverse concerns, allegiances, and talents led to conflicts within and between communities. Early encounters with internal pluralism evoked from Paul a reaffirmation that only a common relationship with Christ can ground the community (1 Cor 3) and that diverse concerns and talents are equally gifts unleashed by the enabling Spirit (1 Cor 12). Actions claimed as Spirit inspired were measured for their consistency with the life of Jesus and the example of the saints, with the requirements of group solidarity, and with their usefulness in witnessing to the salvation attained in Christ Jesus. While asserting a common freedom in Christ across racial, economic, and sexual lines (Gal 3:28), Paul nonetheless sanctioned continued social discrimination for the sake of community calm and receptiveness to the gospel. Even a legitimate freedom from Mosaic Law was limited by the needs of the "weaker" members of the community (1 Cor 10:23–11:1). When pluralism hindered reception of redemption, it ceased to be a sign of richness. It became a sign of a sinful turning from the Lord. These early concerns with solidarity and universal witnessing served as precursors for later Christian adoption and adaptation of common good languages.

Christians faced the ongoing destructive effects of natural processes first in the encounter with personal death. The delayed second coming of Christ and subsequent death of some who were baptized deepened the affirmation that "nothing can separate us from the love of God in Christ Jesus our Lord" (Rom 8:36-39), focusing Christian hope for salvation on life beyond even personal death. Death as an ongoing personal reality could not itself negate the promised salvation brought in Christ Jesus.

Similarly, coerced removal from the synagogue and state-sponsored persecution could not nullify the full redemption of human society, though now gradually visualized in the eschatological terms of the old Jerusalem replaced by a New Jerusalem descending from the heavens (Rev 20). As reformulated in the apocalyptic tradition, active human participation in the ethics of that final kingdom receded into the background. Crushing force localized the this-world presence of enabling grace in the integrity and consistency of the believer and believing community more than in any actions that transform, even incrementally, the social world through their practice.

Restraining Actions

With the Roman legalizing of Christianity, newly perceived responsibilities for an empire that stubbornly refused to succumb fully to kingdom ethics challenged a Christologically based inclination against coercion. After initial hesitation Christians generally accepted the use of the sword for the sake of public peace. Pragmatically the reasons for assuming control of political coercion were obvious.

Coercion received its theoretical justification in a tradition that derived from Jesus' "Render to Caesar what is Caesar's and to God what is God's" (Lk 20:25). The saying suggested that there exists a realm in which human possibilities remain less than the perfectionistic kingdom ethics, yet a realm that is blessed by God and necessary for human existence. Paul in Rom 13 had recommended obedience to legitimate, non-Christian civil authority. This side of the indefinite Second Coming, the community could still confess God as providentially caring for the imperfect social order (through the state), while advancing the kingdom through the partial embodiment of its ethics by means of the church. The Christian lives in dual realms, both of which could be claimed as under God's direction and care.

All forms of Christian social dualism maintain that the secular order does not directly involve matters of salvation. Whether that civil order is viewed through the appreciative eyes of Origin or Tertullian's skepticism or Augustine's dismay at the collapse of the Roman Empire, the goal of civic action has been consistently viewed as outside the immediate realm of empowering grace. Later Scholasticism labeled the state's proper activity as "natural" or "temporal" and understood that activity to be the preserve of lay Christians. The proper realm of the church was the "supernatural," and its leadership dealt with eternal goods. Further, most Christian dualists understood theological freedom to have only an indirect, perhaps motivating, impact on temporal action, while they considered any insight or virtue that arose outside the church as pre-evangelical and therefore not to be expressions of redeeming grace. Up to the Second Vatican Council, and despite various Catholic and non-Catholic attempts to eliminate or ignore either the church or the state, Catholic teaching on the proper restraint of human acts remained within the dualist tradition. Coercion against moral acts or religious expressions that disturbed the public order was acceptable.

Constraining Belief

Christians also attempted to force or constrain religious belief itself. For a time Augustine resisted sanctioning Roman imperial compulsion brought against heretical belief. Only socially destructive actions were open to restraint. But the ongoing intractability and unity of the North African Donatist civil and religious rebellion led Augustine to endorse the use of coercion for the restoration of religious, not just civil, unity. In what has been called a "fatal decision," Augustine suggested that coercion might sociologically and psychologically aid heretics to reclaim their faith (*Letter* 185, chaps. 13f., 21f.). Although Augustine refused to endorse capital penalties against the heretic, subsequent Christian rulers and clergy authorized capital punishment based on a severe exegesis of Augustine's claim that "nothing can cause more complete death to the soul than freedom to disseminate error" (*Letter* 105, chap. 10).

Thomas Aquinas gave the use of capital force against the free act of faith a broader theoretical justification. He did deny the right of any Christian ruler to constrain the conversion of pagans and Jews while still allowing curtailment of non-Christian public expression (*Summa theologiae* II-II, q. 10, art. 9). Further, recognizing the natural right of pagans and, most likely, heretics to raise their children according to their beliefs, Aquinas similarly denied the right of any Christian ruler to remove children from non-Catholic families (II-II, q. 10, art. 12). Yet he strongly endorsed the persecution, including execution, of those who were once within the Christian community (II-II, q. 11, art. 3). Besides the medicinal effect of death threats, he justified this constraint by the claim that the knowing heretic had broken a promise to God and to the human community, thereby meriting capital punishment (II-II, q. 10, art. 8, rep. 3). Full exposure to a Christian society was presumed to present Christian doctrine in such a compelling manner that any turning away from the church indicates bad will, not simply ignorance or a valid moral reaction against the behavior of orthodox Christians.

Reclaiming Social Hope

Through the 19th century Catholic social teaching retreated from the claim that any humans can justly or effectively constrain belief. The magisterium, however, was not willing to abandon the hope that the redemption brought by Jesus could be socially beneficial. For the sake of the common good, Catholics should as much as possible shape public policy. Full adherence to Catholic belief was thought to be the only enabling grounds for approximating a Christian society. The church also was not willing to forgo legal restraint. States should restrain as much non-Catholic religious expression beyond the natural family as they could get away with, short of public anarchy. The truths that non-Catholics hold are less socially empowering than are those held by believing Catholics. If theological freedom was to come to fruition, it must be aided by coercion.

The Second Vatican Council's Declaration on Religious Liberty (*Dignitatis humanae*) reversed this ironic conclusion of a socially concerned Catholicism. It limited restraint of religious expression to the same narrow criterion by which destructive moral acts are restrained. To do so the council had to sharpen the autonomy of the secular and the religious orders, situate coercion entirely within the secular, and prescribe that religious witness must forgo even "the hint of coercion" (DH 4). *Dignitatis* embraced a secular notion of political religious immunity as a social and religious good, not simply as a lesser of two evils. Simultaneously, however, documents such as the Pastoral Constitution on the Church in the Modern World questioned the sharp social dualism that supported *Dignitatis'* conclusion.

Since the council the church has begun to explore in word and act the potential impact of a kingdom ethics on the full scope of God's creation. Although they differ on the legitimacy and limits of political violence, John Paul II, bishops' conferences, and various Third, First, and Second World liberation movements are focusing again on socially empowering notions of religious freedom. Postconciliar affirmations that the practice of social justice is integral to the gospel are part of these explorations. From one angle these affirmations are based in a reconceived hope that the promise of redemption extends to all human societies and all creation. From another, they are rooted in the claim that God's redeeming presence can emerge throughout human society, thus grounding a refusal to ignore or restrain preemptively any sector of human society. These hopes have not only motivated increased social concern; they have further encouraged exploration of Christian sources, including Jesus' notion of the kingdom, for hints of the form that social transformation should take.

Can theological languages of empowerment co-exist in the same public, pluralistic forum with the languages of immunity? Can both work toward social betterment? Such was the hope of the framers of *Dignitatis.* However, the believer's continuing reluctance to bring religious languages of empowerment into the public forum and the languages of immunity into the life of the church suggest that past theory and practice continue to weigh heavily. Secularists still fear religious languages that turn totalitarian, while religious leaders fear immunities based on claims of independence from the church. Yet for a church that professes the full lordship of Jesus, finding ways to overcome the believer's hesitance would itself be a sign of an enabling theological freedom. We have yet to find ways to speak about God's social hopes that foreclose "any hint of coercion." Deeper exploration of the kingdom Jesus lived and proclaimed might serve as a key to that needed new language. And new ways of approaching the public forum must be found. Like Jesus' kingdom ethics, practice here will have a priority over theory. Fear of theological and social religious freedom will fade only in the presence of teaching and actions that better reflect Jesus' kingdom ethics.

See also AUTHORITY, POLITICAL; COMMON GOOD; CONSCIENCE; DIGNITATIS HUMANAE; HUMAN RIGHTS; TOLERATION, PRINCIPLE OF.

Bibliography: J. Lecler, *Toleration and the Reformation,* 2 vols., trans. L. Westow (New York: Association Press, 1960). T. Aquinas, *Summa theologiae* II-II, q. 10 ("On Unbelief in General"), q. 11 ("On Heresy"). Augustine, *Letters* 93, 105, 185. M. Bates, *Religious Liberty: An Inquiry* (New York: International Missionary Council, 1945). A. Carrillo de Albornoz, *Roman Catholicism and Religious Liberty* (Geneva: World Council of Churches, 1959). A. Nolan, *Jesus Before Christianity* (Maryknoll, N.Y.: Orbis, 1978).

J. LEON HOOPER, S.J.

REPRODUCTIVE TECHNOLOGIES, SOCIAL ASPECTS OF

The reproductive technologies of artificial contraception, artificial insemination, in vitro fertilization (IVF), and surrogate motherhood have had a significant impact on the concept of the family, the definition and role of parent, and society. Although all these practices have been prohibited by the magisterium (*Humanae vitae* and *Donum vitae*), nonetheless Catholics utilize these technologies, and many of these practices are supported by theologians.

Of critical importance is the reality of choice in becoming a parent. Until the advent of the effective oral contraceptive in the 1950s, such a reality was not a possibility. Additionally, the oral contraceptive effectively separated sexuality from reproduction, thus giving sexuality in itself a new dimension and significance. The major impact of effective contraceptives has been a decrease in the number of children couples have, and this has had profound and unforeseen demographic effects with their own economic implications.

Artificial insemination by donor raises the significant problem of the introduction of a third party into the marriage, although this is done artificially. Many argue that the use of donor semen violates the commitment of sexual fidelity with one's partner, though others see the desire to have a child with a genetic relation to one of the partners as the more critical value. This procedure could constitute a family secret that could be the source of friction both within and without the marriage. This problem is not presented when the husband's semen is used, though many object to the procedure because masturbation is typically used to obtain semen. Given the reality of AIDS, the issues of semen screening and donor anonymity become quite critical.

In addition to continuing the separation of reproduction from sexuality, IVF also separates sexuality from reproduction. These are now two totally distinct acts. IVF also makes the human embryo available externally for a period of about four days. This allows access to it not only for reproductive purposes but also as a subject of research. Additionally, the zygote can be frozen, which has raised new problems about access to it or its ultimate disposition in the event of divorce or death. Finally, freezing the zygote poses a significant philosophical challenge to the theory of immediate animation.

As a technology IVF is indifferent to the source of the gamete or the disposition of the zygote. Thus the zygote implanted into a woman could be genetically related to neither her nor her partner. Also, the technology can be used by gay and lesbian couples who want a child. And embryo donation as well as sperm and egg donation are now possible.

Such technical possibilities permit the role of parent to be radically redefined. There are seven possibilities for the role of mother: the genetic mother, who produces the egg; carrying, in whose uterus the fetus develops; nurturing, who cares for the child after its birth; genetic-carrying, who supplies egg and uterus but does not raise the baby; genetic-nurturing, who supplies the egg and raises the baby but does not carry it; carrying-nurturing, who carries and raises the baby but does not supply the egg; and the complete mother, who does it all. The father has only three possibilities: the genetic, the nurturing, and the complete. Keeping track of one's ancestors has become slightly more complicated.

Although the magisterium argues that IVF is immoral because it makes conception the product of technology and not of love, nonetheless many theologians and a vast majority of Catholic laity see IVF as a way for an infertile married couple to have a child who comes from their marriage and their love, though not from a discrete act of sexual intercourse. Thus although technology is involved, the procedure is morally understood as assisting a couple to achieve their desire.

Individuals using the procedure should realize that IVF does not cure infertility but rather resolves childlessness. If infertility is the cause of psychological problems, those problems may remain after the birth. The reality of a child may also be a constant reminder of infertility, and this may cause problems also. Additionally, the procedure is still only about 15 percent successful, and lack of success may cause further strain on the couple.

Surrogate motherhood separates sexuality from reproduction, reproduction from sexuality, and both of these from the traditional concept of the family. Although some justify the procedure with biblical references to Abraham and Jacob, the way surrogacy is practiced in our culture is radically different. However, many of our practices seem to entail at least as many problems as Abraham and Jacob had (see Gen 16:1-6; 30:1-24).

The practice of surrogacy raises several significant questions. First, does a woman's autonomy include the right to provide herself to individuals who wish for a child? Or is such provision more analogous to prostitution? Second, does surrogacy involve baby selling? Or can a case be made that the money exchanged is a fee for a service? Third, is the analogy of surrogacy with adoption valid? Or does the fact that the child is intentionally conceived to be given away (or sold) disqualify such an analogy? Fourth, can the quest by the genetic-nurturing father to have a child genetically related to himself cause such an alienation of affection from his spouse as to constitute moral adultery even though sexual intercourse has not occurred with the surrogate? Fifth, what of the impact of pregnancy on the spouse of the surrogate and their children? Neither pregnancy nor the relinquishment of a child is a neutral experience, and both can have profound effects on ongoing relationships.

The reality is that the family is a fluid structure and has changed radically over the centuries. In our time the nuclear family is in a process of significant transition. The reality of divorce has made the single-parent family or blended or reconstituted family almost normative. The reproductive technologies give additional possibilities for constituting families. While providing a child for individuals or families, the technologies raise questions about genealogy and identity. They raise questions about our bodies and their use. They pose challenges to the understanding of marriage and reproduction. And they force us to consider how we value children and how we take into account their interests in relation to ours. Finally, the reproductive technologies challenge us to develop a reproductive ethic and an ethic of marriage that looks beyond the biological finality of individual acts to the nature of the person and his or her acts.

See also BIRTH CONTROL; FAMILY; MARRIAGE; POPULATION; PRIVACY, RIGHT TO; WOMEN.

Bibliography: T. Shannon and L. Cahill, *Religion and Artificial Reproduction* (New York: Crossroad, 1988). T. Shannon, *Surrogate Motherhood: The Ethics of Using Human Beings* (New York: Crossroad, 1988). O. O'Donovan, *Begotten or Made?* (Oxford: Clarendon, 1984).

THOMAS A. SHANNON

RERUM NOVARUM

Leo XIII's (1878–1903) landmark encyclical, *Rerum novarum* (*On the Condition of Labor;* see Gilson, ed.), issued May 15, 1891, was the first major constructive statement issued by the Vatican regarding what at that time was called the "social question." Roman Catholic social concern did not of course begin with Leo but rather has roots deep in the Scriptures and Christian tradition. Social Catholicism in the 19th century had a number of powerful exponents that preceded Leo. Frédéric Ozanam (1813–53) founded the St. Vincent de Paul Society in 1833, and Abbé Félicité de Lamennais (1782–1854) had vociferously condemned the misery caused by industrial capitalism almost seventy years before *Rerum novarum* was published (and about twenty-five years before the *Communist Manifesto*).

Influential Catholic social thinkers in this period include Baron Karl von Vogelsang of Austria (1819–91) and René de la Tour du Pin (1834–1925) of France, both of whom completely rejected capitalism as inherently unjust and proposed in its stead a social system entitled "corporatism" based on a coordination of cooperative associations of workers and owners similar to the medieval guilds. Bishop Wilhelm Emmanuel von Ketteler of Mainz (1811–77) was a powerful critic of the wage slavery inflicted on the workers and endorsed a full legislative agenda in order to achieve significant social reform. Ketteler, to whom Leo XIII himself referred as "my precursor," was the first and most powerful official Catholic voice to speak in favor of the rights of workers, democratic freedoms, and labor legislation in 19th-century Germany.

In France, corporatist Count Albert de Mun (1841–1914), a disciple of Karl von Vogelsang, worked for legislation to raise the pay and shorten the hours for workers. Henry Edward Cardinal Manning of Westminster (1808–92), a powerful advocate for union rights in England, and James Cardinal Gibbons of Baltimore (1834–1921), along with Archbishop John Ireland of St. Paul (1838–1918) and Bishop John Lancaster Spalding of Peoria (1840–1916), labored to persuade Leo not to condemn Catholic participation in the religiously neutral Knights of Labor (the predecessor of the American Federation of Labor). Most important, the results of the annual conferences of the corporatist Fribourg Union (1884–91) under the patronage of Archbishop Caspar Mermillod (1885–91) were regularly reported to Leo and played a significant role in the content of *Rerum novarum.*

Despite the innovations of some Catholic social thinkers, however, Leo's immediate predecessors in the chair of Peter were noted for their profound institutional conservativism and their unequivocal denunciation of the modern ideals of liberty and social progress. A series of thundering papal rejections of Enlightenment political doctrines (including freedom of religion, freedom of the press, universal suffrage, and the separation of church and state) reflected the profoundly negative reaction of the Holy See to the radical (and sometimes explicitly anti-Christian) challenges to traditional authority that were brought in by the French Revolution (1789), the revolutions of 1848 (in which Pius IX himself had to flee from Rome), the Paris Commune (1878), and, the final indignity, the forcible seizure of the Papal States and the elimination of the temporal sovereignty of the papacy (1860–70). Pius IX's *Syllabus of Errors* (1864) denounced what were conceived to be intellectual agents of these destructive movements: naturalism, rationalism, socialism, Gallicanism, and political liberalism. It concluded with the well-known dictum: "If anyone thinks that the Roman Pontiff can and should reconcile himself and come to terms with progress, with liberalism, and with modern civilization, let him be anathema" (*Syllabus* 80).

Unlike Pius IX, Leo believed that modernity despite its distortions held some possibilities for good. His encyclical letter *Libertas* (*On the Nature of Human Liberty* [1888]) rejected liberalism with its defiant refusal to recognize either the authority of the church or the divine law (15), but it also endorsed true liberty, in contrast to wanton license, in all domains of life (1). Similarly, while *Immortale Dei* (*On the Christian Constitution of States* [1888]) repudiated the separation of church and state and the indifferentism he believed it presupposed, it also recognized the genuine political value of freedom, acknowledged democracy as one of several legitimate forms of government, and endorsed religious toleration in some circumstances (36).

Addressing the "Social Question"

As papal nuncio in Brussels and then archbishop of Perugia, the future Pope Leo (Vincent Joachim Pecci) had become aware of the impact of industrial capitalism on the urban proletariat. Before his election to the papacy he had been familiar with the writings of Ketteler and others. More proximate stimuli for the pronouncement of *Rerum novarum* come from various quarters, including regular communication with members of the Fribourg Union (including a personal audience in 1888); the intervention of the American bishops regarding neutral labor unions in 1887–88; direct contact with workers on pilgrimages led by reforming industrialist Léon Harmel (1829–1915) beginning in 1885 (in 1888 Harmel brought ten thousand workers to Rome); Manning's public support for striking London dockworkers in 1889; and increasingly sharp disagreements between those who maintained with Ketteler and the Fribourg Union the necessity of some degree of state intervention in economic matters and their opponents from the school of Angers. These factors were all weighed in light of the pervasive struggle between socialist and liberal accounts of economic justice, both of which were unacceptable to Leo.

Given the urgency of the issue, it is appropriate that *Rerum novarum* begins not with an abstract definition of universal moral principles but with an impassioned description of what we have come to call the "signs of the times." Adapting the social denunciations of the corporatists, Leo highlights the intense conflict between the classes, the "prevailing moral degeneracy" of the times, the ironic disparity between "the enormous fortunes of some few individuals, and the utter poverty of the masses" (1), and the "misery and wretchedness pressing so unjustly on the majority of the working class" (3).

The horrors of present-day modern industrial society are typically contrasted with what Leo took to be the ordered harmony and security of the medieval period, which can be observed in the standard agricultural understanding of labor found in *Rerum novarum* 8–9. In contrast to the merciless degradation and exploitation of the modern era, the human race in the Middle Ages "was lifted up to better things . . . to so excellent a life that nothing more perfect had been known before or will come to pass in the ages that are yet to be" (27). After the French Revolution, the workers have been deprived of both the traditional guidance offered by the church and the protection provided by the medieval guilds, and as a result, they have become the victims of "hardhearted employers" and "the greed of unchecked competition" (3). They have been treated, in short, as "commodities"—mere "things" only useful for profit and production (42).

From the corporatists Leo accepted the view that in industrial capitalism, "the hiring of labor and the conduct of trade are concentrated in the hands of the comparatively few," and "a small number of very rich men have been able to lay upon the teeming masses of the laboring poor a yoke little better than that of slavery itself" (3). The ultimate danger of this situation is that "crafty agitators" will attempt "to pervert men's judgments and to stir up the people to revolt" (2); the religious and human toll attending the extremism, disorder, and social strife unleashed by revolution is one of the main targets of this letter (20, 25, 38, 55). In offering the outlines of a solution to the misery of the urban proletariat, *Rerum novarum* rejects both the economic liberalism of the "Manchester school," which claims that the social progress can only be achieved through the unfettered workings of the free market—which in Christian circles would be supplemented by the individual exercise of charity—and socialism, which strives to find a solution in the abolition of private property and state collectivism.

The Natural Right of Private Property

The first section of the encyclical emphatically rejects socialist proposals for the abolition of private property (4–15), which Leo claims is counterproductive, since the working class would be the first to suffer, unjust, since it involves robbery from property owners and overextends the activity of the state, and socially disruptive. Leo advances the following three arguments for his position:

1. The abolition of private property would undermine the ability of workers to attain security and better the condition of their lives through frugal consumption, patient saving, and modest investment (5).

2. More important, the abolition of private property violates the natural right to private property (6). Three primary arguments are given to prove the existence of this right. First, the right to private property is implied in the fact that human beings attain their natural ends not only by using whatever goods are immediately at hand, as if they were only guided by animal instincts, but also by holding external goods in "stable and permanent possession" (6). This argument basically replicates the justification of the dominion of human beings over the use of creatures found in Thomas Aquinas' *Summa theologiae* (II-II, 66, 1).

Second, Leo argues that when a person "turns the activity of his mind and the strength of his body toward procuring the fruits of nature, by such act he makes his own that portion of nature's field which he cultivates—that portion on which he leaves, as it were, the impress of his personality; and it cannot but be just that he should possess that portion as his very own, and have a right to hold it without any one being justified in violating that right" (9). This argument will be examined in more detail below.

Third, the natural right of private property flows from natural parental responsibility: private property is implied in the fact that the only way that a father can fulfill his sacred duties to meet the needs of his family is through the ownership of private property (13). Countervening the individualistic implications of the previous argument, the logic of this proof moves not from autonomous rights to duties but from natural duties to rights: because a father has a *duty* to provide his family with the basic necessities of life he also naturally has a *right* to acquire and hold the latter.

Leo adds three subsidiary arguments to these. First, the practice of the ages has "consecrated" private ownership as in conformity with human nature and as conducive to social tranquillity. Second, civil laws confirm and enforce this principle. Third, the authority of the divine law adds its support, as in the sanction of the commandment that forbids us to "covet that which is another's" (11).

A rejection of excessive government intervention is one corollary of this strong assertion of the natural right to private property. Since the family is prior to the community and the state (13), the latter have no sovereign control over the former. Against the strident noninterventionism of the liberals and the Catholic social thinkers of the school of Angers, Leo insists that public authorities as a last resort have a moral duty to protect families suffering from extreme need (14). The primary intent of the argument, however, is to protect the family from the excessive state intervention that Leo associates with socialism (and later popes, like Pius XII, would identify with fascism and communism).

3. Finally, Leo argues that by banishing private property the socialist "community of goods" would create envy and bickering, undermine the incentive to work, and reduce everyone to poverty rather than raise up the poor to the level of the middle class.

Given the centrality of the natural law in *Rerum novarum,* it comes as a surprise that Leo omits significant elements of the traditional Thomistic defense of property ownership. Though not directly influenced by Locke, Leo's second argument for the natural right to private property strongly resembles that found in the *Second Treatise on Government* (bk. 2, chap. 27). Though it is the subject of debate among historians, there is reason to believe that the basic argument of Locke, that private property has its origin in labor, was incorporated into neo-Scholasticism by the Jesuit theologian Luigi Taparelli d'Azeglio (1793–1862), who seems to be the first Catholic to employ the phrase "social justice" and who in turn influenced Leo (Camp, pp. 55, 56).

In contrast, Aquinas believed that private property was *added* to the natural law by human reason after the sin of Adam because of its relative efficiency when compared with other alternatives. External things are not subject to the dominion of human beings by their nature, since only God has such authority; but human beings do have a natural dominion "as regards *use,*" because the lower is always made to serve the good of the higher (ST II-II, 66, 1; see Aristotle, *Politics* I, 3). Aquinas explicitly claims that "the division of possessions is not according to the natural law, but rather arose from *human agreement* which belongs to positive law" (ST II-II, 66, 2 ad 1). According to Aquinas, the use of property is rooted in the natural law and ownership is an instrumental supplement to the natural law; the authority to use the goods of the earth for human benefit is not justified by a natural right of ownership entailed in the private nature of individual labor, as it is by Locke and in Leo's second argument (Calvez and Perrin, pp. 259–68).

Aquinas argues that personal possessions are necessary to human life for three reasons: first, because a person tends to be more careful to care for what is his or her own than what is owned communally; second, because human affairs are more orderly when each person is clearly assigned responsibility for certain particular things; and third, because society is more peaceful when each person is content with his or her own possessions (ST II-II, 66, 2). The second argument is used when *Rerum novarum* speaks of the virtues of extending property throughout the working class (47), but the other two are not found anywhere in *Rerum novarum.*

Practical experience of the benefits of private possessions rather than an abstract theory about a hypothetical "state of nature" led Aquinas to affirm, within limits, the moral legitimacy of private property. Leo, apparently without thought of the conceptual implications of doing so, adopted a form of the liberal argument that justifies the absoluteness of private property. This argument certainly provided him with a strong basis for rejecting socialism—only the laborer, and no one else, has a right to the fruits of his or her own labor. This argument, however, entailed a cost as well, in that it implicitly accepted elements of an individualistic social vision that, contrary to Leo's stated beliefs, excluded the traditional notions of the common use of the goods of creation and the social obligation of private property found in both Aquinas and the writings of the Fribourg Union.

Leo also departs from Aquinas' theological relativization of the dominion of personal possessions. Whereas *Rerum novarum* holds private property to be rooted in human nature from its origins, Aquinas views private property as essentially an accommodation to our fallen state, wherein a "community of possessions is a source of strife" (ST I, 98, 1 ad 3). If we had not departed from God's original plan for human nature private property would not have been necessary, as "the will of men would have been so ordered that without any danger of strife they would have used in common, according to each one's need, those things of which they were masters" (ST I, 98, 1 ad 3).

The Mutual Duties and Rights of Capital and Labor

The central constructive message of *Rerum novarum* is that the true answer to the miseries of the working class lies in the mutual recognition of the duties of capital and labor. Leo displays the assumptions of his tradition in stating that "unequal fortune is a necessary result of unequal condition" and that "each man, as a rule, chooses the part which suits his own peculiar domestic condition" (17). He opposes not only what he takes to be the unnatural egalitarian strain of socialism, which "would reduce civil society to one dead level" (17, 34), but also its romantic and utopian denial of the hard facts of life: "To suffer and to endure . . . is the lot of humanity; let them [the socialists] strive as they may, no strength and no artifice will ever succeed in banishing from human life the ills and troubles which beset it" (17). Leo argues from a "futurized" eschatology that the eternal destiny of the human person provides the final perspective from which to view the trials of the temporal world: "Nothing is more useful than to look upon the world as it really is, and at the same time to seek elsewhere . . . for the solace to its troubles" (18).

Leo argues that as the guardian of the natural law and the interpreter of true religion (19) the church has a unique ability to address the deepest roots of the social problem. Whereas the dialectical social model of socialism holds that class is naturally antagonistic to class, Leo offers an organic model of society inspired by an image of medieval unity within which classes live in mutually interdependent order and harmony: "Each needs the other: capital cannot do without labor, nor labor without capital" (19; cf. *Laborem exercens* 12). This social ontology leads to the primacy of the *duties* each class has toward the other rather than the rights each class claims over and against the other.

Rerum novarum first enumerates the duties of workers: to perform the labor he or she agreed upon in justice, not to injure the property or "to outrage the person" of the employer, never to use violence to gain his or her ends, and not to associate with "men of evil principles" (20).

Articulating what would become an axiomatic principle undergirding the social encyclical tradition, Leo argues that employers in turn are bound first of all "not to look upon their work people as their bondsmen, but to respect in every man his dignity as a person ennobled by Christian character" (20). Earning an honest living through business is honorable, but misusing human beings as mere "things" valued only for their physical powers is "truly shameful and inhuman" (20).

A series of specific duties of employers are derived from this primary duty to recognize the humanity of the worker. These include duties to see that workers are given time to exercise their religious duties not exposed to corruption and danger, not led to neglect home and family or to squander their earnings (20), not given work that is beyond their strength or age, paid a just wage, and not, one way or another, deprived of these earnings "by force, by fraud, or by usurious dealings" (20; Camp points out that this is the first reference to the sin of usury, the unjust taking of interest, since 1745 [p. 82, n. 3]). Leo does not simply preach kindness to the rich and patience to the poor; justice, motivated by the inner spirit of love, is to govern the actions of the rich as well as the poor. Conversely, charity is the motive moving the workers toward their employers as well as guiding employers to love and have mercy on their workers.

The duty of the employer to pay a just wage is the most famous contribution of the encyclical to the subsequent debate over socioeconomic rights (for the major treatment in the United States, see John A. Ryan, *A Living Wage,* 1906) and is singled out by Leo for particular emphasis: "To defraud any one of wages that are his due is a great crime which cries to the avenging anger of Heaven" (20). While workers and employers are free to make contractual agreements, these must be within the bounds of what is naturally just. According to Leo, "there underlies a dictate of natural justice more imperious and ancient than any bargain between man and man, namely, that wages ought not to be insufficient to support a frugal and well-behaved wage-earner" (45). If a worker agrees to less, "because an employer or contractor will afford him no better, he is made the victim of force and injustice" (45).

Leo's treatment of the just wage emphatically rejects the liberal doctrine of "freedom of contract" and also stands as a repudiation from the highest authority of the church of the then-current view that the payment of wages over and above the current market rate (even if below the requirements of bare subsistence) constitutes an act of charity but not justice. Endorsement of the just wage and protective labor legislation, moreover, implies at least nascent recognition of the fact that some of the deepest problems of the Industrial Revolution were structural and institutional as well as religious and moral in nature.

Though observation of these precepts of justice would be sufficient to control social strife, Leo argues, Christianity goes further in its claim that rich and poor should be bound to each other in "friendship and good feeling" (21) and even in "brotherly love" (25). Property, wealth, and possessions must be understood in terms of the Christian's progress toward eternal life.

While Leo unequivocally affirms the right to private property against socialism, he promotes the traditional Christian virtues of benevolence, mercy, and generosity as antidotes to the callous indifference toward the poor displayed by wealthy capitalists.

Though the principle is stated more forcefully in post-Leonine papal documents, Leo acknowledges the social function of property ownership (22; see *Sollicitudo rei socialis* no. 42). In this regard Leo cites Aquinas' famous claim that "man should not consider his material possessions as his own, but as common to all, so as to share them without hesitation when others are in need" (22, from ST II-II, 66, 2). Leo, however, does not also refer to Aquinas' claim that the poor have a right to take from the rich in order to meet their urgent needs (ST II-II, 66, 7 ad 3), a position that he probably would have considered too incendiary (in contrast with *Gaudium et spes* 69; LE 14).

Stewardship is balanced with the order of charity, according to which one's resources must first be directed to satisfying the needs of oneself and one's dependents and to meeting the requirements of one's social "station." This concession having been made, Leo reminds his readers of the words of Jesus according to the Gospel of Luke (Lk 11:41), that it is a solemn duty of charity to "give to the indigent out of what remains" (22). In support of stewardship, Leo refers in the same paragraph to both Gregory the Great's homily on the parable of the talents (a source frequently cited by Christian political conservatives) and to the words of the parable of the Last Judgment, "As long as you did it to one of My least brethren you did it to Me" (Mt 25:44) (a passage favored by social progressives, including Latin American liberation theologians). Leo's emphasis is important: he does not superficially concede the value of stewardship within the general context of a staunch defense of the traditional order of charity but rather recognizes the importance of natural moral obligations within the larger context of a doctrine of stewardship and the call to benefit others, especially the most needy.

Leo also reminds the poor that neither poverty nor labor is disgraceful, and that virtue—the true source of moral worth and the sole achievement meriting eternal reward—is accessible to all persons, poor as well as rich (23). Leo also mentions in passing a theme that has been extensively developed in our own time, that "God Himself seems to incline rather to those who suffer misfortune" (23). Rather than generating a "preferential option for the poor," however, this special divine solicitude is simply taken to imply a religious and moral corrective to the pride of the rich on the one hand and an encouragement to the poor on the other: "to move the former to be generous and the latter to be moderate in their desires" and to bring the classes together in "friendly concord" (24).

The Social Role of the Church

Rerum novarum clearly recognizes the church's indispensable role in addressing the problems of the poor. Leo typically appeals to the golden age of medieval Christendom as historical verification of the power of the church to transform society today (27). In strong contrast to Jean-Jacques Rousseau's almost exclusive focus on reordering external social structures, Leo insists again and again that religion alone addresses the heart of the problem in its appeal to the conscience and moral duty of each individual. Against forms of verticalism and angelism, however, Leo argues that the primarily spiritual concern of the church by no means entails a neglect or minimization of the temporal and earthly suffering of the workers: "Her desire is that the poor . . . should rise above poverty and wretchedness, and better their condition in life" (28).

Leo is quick to remind us that the church's primary assistance to the poor is through its distinctive, divinely established mission to preach the gospel and promote Christian virtue. At the same time, he does not ignore the importance of the material and external conditions of living the virtuous life (34). Christian morality of itself is said to lead to temporal prosperity in that it both merits God's blessing and inculcates self-restraint, frugality, and patience (28), an argument that, as we know, can cut both ways. Moreover, the direct charitable activities of the church have attempted to provide those temporal necessities that the poor have not been able to attain through their own efforts. The historical record of charitable institutions is a witness of love and speaks against those who would completely secularize and laicize poor relief: "No human expedients will ever make up for the devotedness and self-sacrifice of Christian charity" (30).

The Social Role of the State

Rerum novarum also insists on a recognition of the proper role of the state in dealing with the problems of the working class. Leo follows Aquinas in claiming that the primary responsibility of the ruler is to promote the common good (32). In stark contrast to the minimal state of social contract theory, Leo argues that "the end of society is to make men better" and that the government has a responsibility to promote religion and morality (32). By virtue of office the ruler has a special responsibility "to promote to the utmost the interests of the poor" (32). Two warrants are given for this duty: first, because the ruler is charged with promoting the common good, and members of the working class are "parts" of the larger social "whole" (33, 51), and second, because the more that is done for the benefit of the working classes by the laws of the society, "the less need will there be to seek for special means to relieve them" (32).

In stark contrast to Emile Durkheim's accusation that the church would substitute individual acts of charity for just social institutions, Leo in fact argues that the laws of society should be structured in such a way as to minimize the necessity of charitable poor-relief. Durkheim's accusation is, however, applicable to proponents of the school of Angers. The protection and promotion of the basic welfare of the working class is not a matter of almsgiving but of distributive justice, the virtue by which the "ruler" properly assigns the benefits and burdens to the various sectors of society (33). Since "it is only by the labor of working men that states grow rich," justice demands that the workers proportionately share in the goods that they have helped to create—"that being housed, clothed, and bodily fit, they may find their life less hard and more endurable" (34).

As will become typical of later social encyclicals, *Rerum novarum* attempts to take a balanced position regarding state intervention in the social and economic orders. Leo always insists on the freedom of the church—a principle that is used against Bismarck's unsuccessful attempt to subordinate the Catholic church to the interests of the German state in the Kulturkampf. Against socialism Leo argues that the individual and the family ought to be allowed as much liberty as possible, "so far as is consistent with the common good and the interests of others" (35).

Yet while Leo is concerned with superceding undue interference from the state, he also unequivocally rejects the laissez faire doctrine of noninterference. Anticipating the "principle of subsidiarity" (*Quadragesimo anno* 79–80), Leo lays down the general principle that the state must intervene whenever the common good, including the good of any single class, is threatened with harm and no other solution is forthcoming (36). The government may need to intervene, for example, in cases in which a strike disturbs public safety, or if laborers are degraded "with conditions repugnant to their dignity as human beings" (36); yet it would be better if these matters were resolved by internal dialogue. In general, "the law must not undertake more, nor proceed further, than is required for the remedy of the evil or the removal of the mischief" (36).

Leo clearly maintains that labor grievances should be addressed and resolved by peaceful, legal means. Although they are to be treated with strict impartiality in the courts (33), because of their vulnerability workers are entitled to special protection from the government (37, 32). The legal system must be employed to enforce the duties of justice incumbent on the classes mentioned above. The law must protect the following: private property from wanton destruction as well as to "keep the populace within the line of duty" (38); society against harm to the public good caused by strikes and the working conditions that lead to strikes (39); the worker's right to exercise his or her religious duties (40) including the duty to worship God on Sundays and certain holy days (41); and in general, workers from the "cruelty of men of greed, who use human beings as mere instruments for money-making" (42). The last sphere concerns the whole realm of "material and external" goods, which are to be governed by laws requiring the reasonable limitation of hours of work; the assignment of the tasks of labor in a way suitable to the age and sex of the worker; and the payment of just wages, that is, wages sufficient "to support a frugal and well-behaved wage-earner" (45).

Several features of Leo's proposals for labor reform stand out. First, the particular proposals stand on the foundation of Aquinas' view of human beings as "social animals" (see 50–51) and as interdependent "parts" of the larger social "whole" (see 33). In fundamental rejection of the "social atomism" of economic liberalism, Leo sees the individual as called to a life with other people rather than as standing over and against them. This form of what moral philosophers have come to call "social holism" provides the framework for Leo's claim that duties precede and form the moral justification for the recognition of individual rights.

Second, Leo's doctrine of the just wage is explicitly intended as an alternative to the reigning liberal model of wages set by free consent of the worker and employer. According to Leo, economic liberals recognize that an individual's labor is "the exclusive property of him who acts," but they ignore the equally important fact that the laborer must work in order to live. The precedence of duty is seen again: the laborer works in order to meet his or her duty to live, and therefore he or she has a right to a living wage (44). Payment of a just wage is a matter of strict justice rather than charity alone.

Leo intends here what Camp calls the "deproletarization" of the working class (p. 84). By the incremental redistribution of property by means of the just wage, private ownership could thus be extended to as many members of the working class as possible. Thus "the gulf between vast wealth and sheer poverty will be bridged over, and the respective classes will be brought nearer to one another" (47). (Note that Leo refers to ownership of land rather than to co-ownership in industry through profit sharing or participation in employees' stockholding associations [on these, see *Mater et magistra* 91–103; GS 68].) Given a decent wage, the worker "will find it easy, if he be a sensible man, to practice thrift, and he will not fail, by cutting down expenses, to put some little savings and thus secure a modest source of income" (46). Elimination of the extremes of wretched poverty and vast wealth by rejecting the liberal ideology that attempts to legitimate their existence serves the two-fold purpose of eradicating the tremendous suffering of the working class and taking the wind out of the sails of socialism.

Workers' Associations

Workers and employers can also help themselves through participation in labor unions and other intermediate associations, especially those with a religious foundation (48–61). Leo did not accept the view held by some that unions were necessarily hotbeds of radicalism. As social beings, workers have a natural desire to associate with one another and have a natural right to enter into "private societies" in order to promote their own particular good within the context of an affirmation of the common good of the larger society. Though its exercise requires prudence and at times should be restrained for the common good, in general this right deserves the legal protection of the government (52)—a claim that is understood in light of Leo's complaint that some rulers have at times hampered, abused, and even violently attacked Catholic associations despite their substantial contributions to social welfare (53).

Like most church authorities at the time, Leo also is suspicious that some unions "are in the hands of secret leaders, and are managed on principles ill-becoming with Christianity and the public well-being" (54). In these cases Catholic workers ought to form their own associations rather than submit to this kind of oppression (54; contrast with Pius XI [QA 81–87]). Members of Catholic unions have the benefit of spiritual support from the clergy and are often blessed with material assistance from wealthy benefactors (55). These unions should be strongly supported by the state, as they contribute to the material well-being of the workers, inculcate Christian charity and the observance of duty, and promote harmony between the classes (59).

Religion as the Key to the "Social Question"

Early in *Rerum novarum* Leo writes that "nothing is more useful than to look upon the world as it really is, and at the same time to seek elsewhere . . . for the solace to its troubles" (18). Christian doctrine is skeptical about what Leo took to be socialist designs for the perfect realization of love on earth, but it is also critical of the heartless indifference toward human suffering found in liberalism. As Leo repeats with great insistence, since ultimately "religion alone . . . can avail to destroy the evil at its root, all men should rest persuaded that the main thing needed is to reestablish Christian morals, apart from which all the plans and devices of the wisest will prove of little avail" (82). Yet Christianity does not counsel passivity and acquiescence. On the contrary, it charges the working class, to "make every lawful and proper effort" to remedy its situation (62).

Though order is strongly valued by Leo, he by no means preaches blind obedience to positive law. Following Aquinas' famous principle, he argues that "laws only bind when they are in accordance with right reason, and, hence, with the eternal law of God" (52). Though their primary mission is directly religious, priests are not to remain aloof from the plight of the workers: "Every minister of holy religion must bring to the struggle the full energy of his mind and all his power of endurance" (83). The grand hope expressed in *Rerum novarum* is that by the cooperative and mutually reinforcing work of the state, unions and intermediate associations, and the church, the working class can be elevated out of poverty, the tensions between the classes can be resolved, and society can be returned to a state of order, harmony, and justice inspired by Christian love and safeguarded by fidelity to the church.

Limitations and Criticisms

Rerum novarum has been criticized in a multitude of ways, several of which will be mentioned here. From our perspective Leo's social vision of course has its limitations. In many ways, *Rerum novarum* reflects the mind of a 19th-century aristocrat, an inheritor of a triumphal, highly Eurocentric view of the church and a monarchical view of the papacy. Several criticisms of *Rerum novarum* will be reviewed here.

First, the organically conceived model of the social order found in *Rerum novarum* has been criticized for its paternalism, its uncritical acceptance of inherited privilege, and its legitimation of social stratification and gross inequalities. "Complementarity" of social roles is criticized for being a mask for oppressive social relations, for example, between the sexes, since for Leo women are "by nature fitted for home-work" (42). He reminds those enamored of social equality that "there naturally exist among mankind manifold differences of the most important kind; people differ in capacity, skill, health, strength; and unequal fortune is a necessary result of unequal condition" and that "all striving against nature is in vain" (17). In Leo's paternalistic view, the "rulers" hold responsibility for the common good of the entire society, and their fatherly guidance is needed by those whom Leo regarded as the ignorant and undisciplined masses (contrast with *Dignitatis humanae* 1).

Arguing against the doctrine of class warfare, Leo states: "Just as the symmetry of the human frame is the result of the suitable arrangement of the different parts of the body, so in a state is it ordained by nature that these two classes should dwell in harmony and agreement, so as to maintain the balance of the body politic" (19). Each person is assumed to have a "station in life" (22), and "as a rule, each man chooses the part [in society] which suits his own peculiar domestic condition" (17).

The conclusion Leo draws from natural hierarchies is that "unequal fortune is a necessary result of unequal condition" (17). When taken with other passages this can even suggest a kind of otherworldly pessimism or even fatalism: the "pains and hardships of life will have no end or cessation on earth; for the consequences of sin are bitter and hard to bear, and they must accompany man so long as life lasts. To suffer and endure, therefore, is the lot of humanity" (18).

The message of *Rerum novarum,* of course, is precisely the opposite. The church desires that the poor "should rise above poverty and wretchedness, and better their condition in life" (28), and that protective labor legislation and worker organizations can and ought to effect change—although not to excess, Leo would counsel. The proposals of *Rerum novarum* represent a desire to abolish the massive poverty of industrial capitalism without forgetting that the fundamental processes of economic life entail of their very nature a class structure comprising employers and employees. More radical proposals for social reconstruction, it is implied, would not provide the immediate practical assistance needed to move the workers out of the dismal poverty to which they have been subjected.

Second, from the Left (socialists and anarchists) and the Right (the monarchists and strict corporatists), the proposals of *Rerum novarum* were criticized for being too timid and, moreover, for being issued after the worse excesses of industrial capitalism had run their course and had already been subjected to severe criticism.

Regarding the question of its timeliness, social philosopher Franz H. Mueller points out that *Rerum novarum* was issued at the beginning of the rapid growth of industry brought by the "second industrial revolution." According to Mueller, "it was exactly on the eve of that new machine age, founded on electricity [rather than steam], and marked by a gigantic acceleration of physical production, that RN appeared." Mueller concludes that "any student of social and economic history, therefore, cannot but admit that instead of belated, the encyclical was in reality unusually timely" (p. 69).

It should also be recalled that while the just wage and the right to organize in unions are taken for granted today, their universal protection by European governments and acceptance within liberal economics was not. The forty-eight hour week, union rights, and collective bargaining were not attained by workers in France, Germany, England, and Italy until 1922. The right of workers to organize in the United States was not legally protected until the National Labor Relations Act was passed in 1935.

Assertion of the rights of workers was, of course, subjecting Leo to the criticism of reactionaries that he was stirring up class antagonisms and inciting the working class to socially disruptive behavior. For all his evident attachment to order, stability, and authority, Leo made the bold move of approving of unions composed exclusively of workers in direct opposition to those who mistrusted workers' organizations as subversive and wanted instead joint associations of workers and owners. The latter were in fact more to his liking, and even more strongly to the liking of Pius XI (QA 84). Despite the possibility that reactionaries would charge him with inciting class hatred by allowing separate associations for workers, Leo deliberately amended one of the final drafts of *Rerum novarum* explicitly to approve of associations composed exclusively of workers. By endorsing these "unmixed" unions and their autonomous leadership, Leo broke with the paternalistic corporatist claim that the working class should be led by the "ruling class," and he promoted the development of initiative, internal leadership, and effective organization on the part of the workers. Had Leo's position been followed by Pius XI, fascist Italy and Austria would not have been able to employ Catholic corporatism so effectively.

Leo's cautious temperament, desire for order, and commitment to justice led him to call for a reform of present institutions rather than for their complete reconstruction (contrast with QA). It is clear that while he recognized its profound defects, Leo's approach to the current economic system was ultimately constructive and incremental rather than either reactionary or revolutionary. Staunch defenders of laissez faire capitalism, of course, accused Leo of attacking the basic constitution of the free market economy. Leo's position regarding the market economy was not based on the conviction that the virtues of capitalism made it the economic arrangement most in keeping with the natural law—there is no evidence in the text of *Rerum novarum* for such a claim—but rather simply because it happened to be the predominant economic pattern of his day.

Third, *Rerum novarum* has been criticized for being excessively vague and abstract. For example, Leo maintains that the rich must give of their superfluous wealth to those who are needy but does not provide any precise guidelines for determining what is superfluous. In a similar manner, *Rerum novarum* endorses the existence of unions but does not take up the legitimacy of strikes, a particularly important issue at the time (39; see QA 94, which forbids strikes; GS 68 gives conditional moral approval). For that matter, Leo is never sufficiently clear as to whether the "just wage" mandates the "family wage" (suggested in 46), as Ryan later argued in *A Living Wage* (see also QA 71). Leo's ambivalence on this matter is understandable given that the family wage would penalize the worker with more children, since he would require higher wages than a single worker and therefore be less likely to be given employment in conditions of labor surplus.

The abstract nature of the principles given in *Rerum novarum* can in part be explained by the pastoral rather than academic nature of the document and the wide character of its intended audience. Also important is the fact that Leo was temperamentally inclined not to make pronouncements on issues on which the church was divided and to avoid inciting unnecessary division within the church (Camp, p. 28).

Moreover, the general nature of Leo's proposals may also reflect a Thomistic insight into the danger of overly precise principles and the need for situational prudence in the judging of contingent singulars. Speaking of the various forms of worker association, Leo comments: "We do not judge it possible to enter into minute particulars touching the subject of organization; this must depend on national character, on practice and experience, on the nature and aim of the work to be done, on the scope of the various trades and employments, and on other circumstances of fact and of time—all of which should be carefully considered" (57; see *Octogesima adveniens* 4).

Fourth, Leo has also been criticized for employing abstract essentialistic caricatures of socialism and liberalism, and for not attending with sufficient care either to the theoretical variations or to the concrete empirical complexities of their historical development. For example, Leo seems oblivious to the basic difference in socialist theory between ownership of personal possessions and private ownership of the means of production. He does not grasp the real differences between the utopian socialism of Robert Owen (1771–1858); the Christian socialism of Saint-Simon (1760–1825), F. D. Maurice (1805–72), and Charles Kingsley (1819–75); or the state socialism of Ferdinand Lassalle (1825–64). Neither does Leo recognize the differences between these and the more radical form of socialism found in the Bakuninists, who advocated terrorism and violent revolution. This kind of ahistorical typological simplification of socialism is not unique to Leo, and it is in fact found with disappointing frequency throughout official church writings up to the present time (though with the notable exception found in OA 31).

Leo has been criticized on the one hand from the Left for not providing an account of the actual historical development of capitalism or a specific analysis of the present condition of capitalism. Liberals, on the other hand, have criticized Leo's ignorance of the empirical variations within the expanding market economies of his day as well as his exclusive and moralistic focus on the distribution of wealth and his concomitant inattention to economic efficiency and the empirical factors governing the creation of wealth, in particular the processes of capital accumulation and investment. Leo does not recognize that by 1891 the standard of living of the working classes in some parts of Europe, notably England and Germany, were well ahead of that found in the early decades of the 19th century. At the time *Rerum novarum* was published Italy lagged behind other industrialized nations regarding real wages, unemployment, illiteracy, working conditions, and length of the working day.

Finally, the criticism of philosophical incoherence was mentioned in the previous discussion of Leo's defense of natural property rights. Leo's appropriation of modern "rights language" is judged by some to entail an uncritical absorption of distinctively modern antiteleological implications that do not cohere with Leo's classically Thomistic teleological metaphysical assumptions. The strain, and critics will add, confusion, traced in Leo's treatment of property rights is found elsewhere in *Rerum novarum,* for example, in the mixed claims that the family exists prior to the community (13) on the one hand and that the person is inherently social (50–51) on the other. The first view is fundamental to modern social-contract views of society that recognize only voluntary responsibilities; the second to classical organic views of society that affirm natural social responsibilities. The former perspective focuses on public interest as an aggregate of the private interests of all its autonomous individuals; the latter concentrates on the common good of society as the temporal fulfillment of the good of its individual constituents (51). The mixed nature of Leo's moral discourse leads some to question the coherence of *Rerum novarum* and to call for a more self-critical and differentiated method of appropriating the insights of modernity into Roman Catholic social ethics.

Rerum Novarum and Later Catholic Social Teachings

Rerum novarum has been known as the *Magna Charta* of the social encyclicals, but this is not to suggest that later papal social thought was not to revise the teaching of *Rerum novarum* on some important matters. While Leo explicitly acknowledges the social dimension of property ownership, his statement is more timid than one would find in later papal documents (cf. QA 48; MM 119–20; *Populorum progressio* 23; LE 14; SRS 42). Recent popes have also become more critical of the "naturalness" of class distinctions and the exclusion of certain groups from active participation in society and have placed moral limits on what are considered to be justifiable inequalities (see OA 2). (These are important developments given that Leo's positions regarding property rights and social hierarchy were later taken out of context and used to legitimate authoritarianism in Latin America and elsewhere.)

Recent social teachings have obviously moved beyond the purely protective nature of Leo's proposals for such labor legislation as defending workers against unsafe working conditions in factories, unfair wages, excessive hours, child labor, and the like, into more comprehensive social-insurance legislation covering illness, disability, unemployment, and retirement (see *Economic Justice for All,* chap. 3), which Leo preferred be covered by nongovernmental "insurance and benefit societies" (58).

Most important, the static and deductive natural-law method employed by Leo was to be substantially revised in the more "historically minded" method of more recent texts. While it is an overstatement to say that the deductive and heavily philosophical method of *Rerum novarum* left *no* room for input from the social sciences as some critics charge, later social teachings beginning with the Second Vatican Council deliberately adopted a more inductive and historically conscious method that places experiential and social scientific data and insights as well as biblical and theological themes in positions of greater prominence.

Several advances beyond *Rerum novarum* can be related to this methodological shift. Later social teachings have been more attentive to the possibilities of innovation and institutional change than was Leo, who placed strong emphasis on individual charity, benevolent associations, and charitable organizations in alleviating the misery of the poor. Charity as the grace-inspired love of neighbor is seen by Leo to be an indispensable Christian alternative to the acquisitive self-interestedness of predatory capitalism.

It is clearly an overstatement to argue that Leo simply moralized about the problems of the working class and ignored institutional justice (Chenu, p. 25). In this Leo differs from Charles Périn, professor of economics from Louvain, who argued that moral reform and the exercise of individual charity within the existing capitalist system would provide sufficient means for the rectification of the conditions of labor. *Rerum novarum* clearly states that "the main thing needed is to reestablish Christian morals" (82), but it by no means assumes that this is the *only* remedy needed. Though Leo believes that bettering the conditions of labor must involve a renewed commitment to religion and virtue on the part of individuals (21), he also holds that the state has a significant role to play in attaining distributive justice for workers, and he demands protective labor legislation to enforce their natural rights (16).

The solution to the social question is obviously not taken by Leo to be solely dependent on the good will, voluntary generosity, and noblesse oblige of the ruling class. *Rerum novarum* declares not only that the principal moral obligation of the employer is to give a just wage but also that the workers' right to fair pay be defended by labor laws and, if necessary, enforced by the coercive power of the state (5, 36, 45). Leo's endorsement of labor unions acknowledges, at least in a preliminary way, the significance of organized, collective activity for social gains. Later social teachings accept these claims and even go beyond *Rerum novarum* in their clearer recognition of the possibilities of social transformation, of the occasionally conflictual nature of social change, and of the need to exert collective power in order to attain genuine justice (*Justitia in mundo* 5–6; LE 1; Medellin Documents, "Justice," 3–5).

Significance of the Encyclical

First, *Rerum novarum* represents an effort to bring the church out of the primarily defensive mentality typified by the denunciations of Pius IX and into a more positive and even transformative relationship to the world. Leo's use of the language of rights, though a departure from pure Thomism, displays an attempt to adapt what are perceived to be the best insights of modern social ethics to serve the Christian cause of human dignity. Thus even though Leo has doubts about the ethos of modernity and its liberties, *Rerum novarum* represents an attempt to bring a Christian influence to bear on the social problems of the age that his predecessors had ignored—sometimes even to the detriment of the church, as in the mass defection of the French working class in the 19th century.

Reflecting the Thomistic view that social arrangements devised by human reason must accord with the dictates of justice grounded in the natural law (ST I-II, 95, 2), Leo unequivocally rejects the dominant assumption of liberal individualism that economic practices and theories simply reflect natural laws of supply and demand and should not be disturbed by religious or moral considerations. *Rerum novarum* rejects both the otherworldly "verticalism" that is indifferent to the material welfare of workers and the poor, and the modern privatization of religion and the reduction of Christian morality to individual acts of charity. If Pius IX illustrates what H. Richard Niebuhr calls a Christ-against-culture model of church-society relations, Leo represents a first turn to the Christ-transforming-culture model that finds its full expression over seventy years later in Vatican II's Pastoral Constitution on the Church in the Modern World.

Second, *Rerum novarum* provided hierarchical support to the Catholic social conscience and a fairly coherent and ecclesially authorized body of moral and social teaching to guide social activism. It allowed and even encouraged working-class and socially committed Catholics to join independent trade unions along with associations that included workers and employers, which were preferred by the corporatists, and to work with secular organizations, so long as they were not religiously or morally dangerous. Trade unionism could no longer be dismissed as revolutionary or socialist.

A plethora of mutual-aid societies, credit associations, Catholic labor unions, cooperatives, professional organizations, and other organizations were fostered by the church in Western Europe and elsewhere as a result of Leo's teaching. After initial indifference, implementation of the tenets of *Rerum novarum* in the United States came to take the form of a significant Catholic social movement, marked by the writings of Msgr. John A. Ryan, the social activism of the German Catholic Central Verein and Fr. Peter E. Dietz' Militia of Christ for Social Service, and the work of the Department of Social Action of the U.S. bishops' National Catholic Welfare Council.

Third, *Rerum novarum* constituted for the Catholic church an important step in the direction of seeking popular support rather than relying exclusively on close alignment with the ruling class and defenders of the status quo. Some have claimed that fear of Catholic defections to socialism was one of the motivating factors behind the writing of the encyclical. There can be little doubt that the assurance to working-class Catholics that the church supported their aspirations for fair wages, humane working conditions, and a decent way of life helped to reinforce ecclesial loyalty. Cardinal Gibbons understood this well when he observed, "To lose the heart of the people would be a misfortune for which the friendship of the few rich and powerful would be no compensation."

Fourth, as the *Magna Charta* of Catholic social teachings (QA 39), the message of *Rerum novarum,* as Richard McCormick puts it, has to be "written on an ongoing basis." While it was originally addressed to an immediate social and economic situation, *Rerum novarum* has been taken to provide a body of substantive moral principles that would be extended, refined, and developed by the subsequent tradition of Catholic social teachings, although this is not to deny that some positions were reversed and others outright abandoned.

Major themes include the dignity of the person, the dignity of work and its religious significance, the just wage, the right of workers to participate in unions, the priority of peaceful and legal means in resolving social and economic disputes, the moral purpose of the state (rather than the "night watchman" view of the state found in liberalism), the social mission of the church, the promotion of the common good as the goal of the state, the centrality of justice within economic and, specifically, industrial relations, the special claims of the poor by reason of their vulnerability, and the sustained critical stance toward both liberalism and socialism (see SRS 21).

Finally, all commentators regard *Rerum novarum* as critically important for moving the papacy away from the ecclesial entrenchment and social detachment and negligence that had extended from the French Revolution (1789) until the death of Pius IX (1878). Leo was the first pope to communicate a genuine recognition of the suffering poor on the part of the official church and to register a sense of the urgency of the "social question."

Social Catholicism had flourished in the 19th century, while the highest echelon of the church was recruited from the aristocracy and identified with the forces of reaction, inherited privilege, and the ancien régime. Leo was the first pope to show some grasp of the intolerable suffering of the urban proletariat and to act on this by making the natural rights of the worker official church doctrine. *Rerum novarum* provided a doctrinal challenge to the apathy and indifference of middle-class and affluent Catholics, including the clergy, in the face of the widespread misery of the working classes. In issuing this document Leo displayed a degree of human sensitivity, courage, and social imagination absent not only in his 19th-century predecessors but unfortunately also in his immediate successor, Pius X (1903–14), as well.

The significance of *Rerum novarum* thus lies not only in what it said about the "social question" in the closing decade of the 19th century but also in the precedent it set for authoritative magisterial reflection on and practical commitment to the cause of the poor and oppressed of this world. Leo's reputation as the "champion of labor" and the "pope of the workers" is justly deserved and has provided a source of hope and inspiration for socially committed Christians up to the present day.

See also COMMON GOOD; CORPORATISM; FRIBOURG UNION; LABOR AND CAPITAL IN CATHOLIC SOCIAL THOUGHT; LEO XIII; MODERN CATHOLIC SOCIAL THOUGHT; PRIVATE PROPERTY; STRIKE, RIGHT TO.

Bibliography: A. Abell, "The Reception of Leo XIII's Labor Encyclical in America, 1891–1919," *The Review of Politics* 7 (October 1945) 464–95. J.-Y. Calvez, and J. Perrin, *The Church and Social Justice: The Social Teaching of the Popes from Leo XIII to Pius XII* (Chicago: Henry Regnery, 1961). R. Camp, *The Papal Ideology of Social Reform: A Study in Historical Development, 1878–1967* (Leiden: E. J. Brill, 1969). M.-D. Chenu, *La 'Doctrine Sociale' de l'Eglise comme Idéologie* (Paris: Cerf, 1979). E. Gilson, ed., *The Church Speaks to the Modern World: The Social Teachings of Leo XIII* (this text of RN provides the paragraph enumeration used in this article) (Garden City, N.Y.: Doubleday, 1954). J. Moody, ed., *Church and Society: Catholic Social and Political Thought and Movements, 1789–1950* (New York: Arts, Inc., 1953). F. Mueller, "The Church and the Social Question," in *The Challenge of Mater et Magistra,* ed. J. Moody and J. Lawler, (New York: Herder & Herder, 1963). J. Murray, "Leo XIII: Two Concepts of Government," *Theological Studies* 14 (1953) 551–67. N. Paulhus, *The Theological and Political Ideals of the Fribourg Union* (Ph.D. diss., Boston College–Andover Newton Theological Seminary, 1983). J. Ryan, *A Living Wage: Its Ethical and Economical Aspects* (New York: Macmillan, 1906, rev. ed., 1920). A. Vidler, *A Century of Social Catholicism, 1820–1920* (London: S.P.C.K., 1964). L. Wallace, *Leo XIII and the Rise of Socialism* (Chapel Hill, N.C.: Univ. of North Carolina Press, 1966). P. Misner, *Social Catholicism in Europe: From the Onset of Industrialization to the First World War* (New York: Crossroad, 1991).

STEPHEN J. POPE

REVELATION

Of the many controversial doctrines in contemporary theology, none is more so than that of revelation. Revelation implies a specific intervention of God in human affairs and a disclosure of hidden truths. Intrinsic to the concept is that barriers to certain truths or types of truth exist and that these barriers are impenetrable to our normal or "natural" way of knowing, so that revelation demands faith. Furthermore, in the Christian perspective all salvific knowledge of God is mediated through Jesus Christ: "All things have been delivered to me by my father; and no one knows the son except the father, and no one knows the father except the son and any one to whom the son chooses to reveal him" (Mt 11:27). Jesus is claimed to be the definitive revelation of the ultimate mystery of God and universe.

While Christians have not always expressed their understanding of revelation in the same way, there has always been a common assumption: what is necessary for salvation is divinely given and as such is reliable because guaranteed by supernatural authority. Implicit in this common understanding is a two-level understanding of the world, an empirical world of phenomena behind which lies a second world of ultimate or spiritual reality. Because of our finitude, or sinfulness, we are as human barred from knowing such a spiritual world. Such a knowledge must be graciously given to us by God. The idea of an initiative on the part of God is central to the concept of revelation and also the fact that divinely given knowledge will be substantially different from knowledge arrived at through human resources alone. This approach to revelation led to the perception of the Scriptures as basically sacred Scripture, that is, the very word of God and, within Roman Catholicism, its authoritative interpretation of Scripture as dogma.

Many aspects of this concept of revelation have disappeared in current Christian writings, while emphasis has been given to faith. Following Vatican II theologians have emphasized the interpersonal nature of revelation and faith and have applied to revelation the basic metaphor of personal encounter. Revelation in its fundamental aspect is to be understood as the self-communication of God and the personal appropriation of faith. Revelation at its deepest level is a personal encounter with God in faith. Far from being reduced to a form of knowledge, it is a transformative response to the self-communication of God.

As personal encounter with God, revelation is necessarily social and historical. So whatever knowledge of God and of human selves emerge in the revelatory encounter will be mediated historically. Revelation in all of its dimensions is subject to the limitations of history and cannot be understood as the insertion of "supernatural truths" in the historical continuum.

Ultimate and revealed truths are historically and socially located and must be situated historically prior to their analysis and evaluation. The insights of the social sciences render questionable that revelation is a socially disembodied process dealing with "eternal truths." Revelation is therefore tradition-constituted and cannot be separated from specific religious communities.

Contemporary thought has emphasized the importance of tradition in the structuring of communal and personal identities (cf. Rom 10:13-15). Revelation reaches each generation through tradition. So the Liturgy, creeds, the use of the Bible and of the sacraments, anchor the religious community both in the founding events of its past and within the overall framework of its ongoing life.

"Revealed truth" is closely related to the social context in which it arises and is not immune to the ideologizing influence of this context. A specific revelation tends to be embodied in the social circumstances and conditions of its time. To the extent that the Christian revelation is historical, it is subject to change. Jesus' message contained elements that would be developed long after him, while other elements would no longer be accepted, for Jesus himself was bound by the cultural limitations of his time. Revelation in its concrete, historical nature is always in need of some reinterpretation.

The reinterpretation of the revelation as ultimate metaphor will have to reemphasize that all truth is an "uncovering," a "discovery" attained not by conquest but as a donation, as a gift. Revelation is ultimately a way of being in relation, for the revelation of God in Jesus Christ is not a message concerned with theoretical speculation but a praxis of salvation.

See also AGNOSTICISM; ATHEISM; ENLIGHTENMENT, THE (INFLUENCE OF); MAGISTERIUM; MODERNISM; RELIGIOUS FREEDOM; SCRIPTURE, USE OF IN CATHOLIC SOCIAL ETHICS.

Bibliography: E. Brunner, *Revelation and Reason* (Philadelphia: Westminster, 1946). H. Niebuhr, *The Meaning of Revelation* (New York: Macmillan, 1960). A. Dulles, *Models of Revelation* (New York: Doubleday, 1983). E. Schillebeeckx, *Revelation and Theology* (New York: Sheed & Ward, 1967). R. Thiemann, *Revelation and Theology: The Gospel as Narrated Promise* (Notre Dame, Ind.: Univ. of Notre Dame Press, 1985).

LUCIEN RICHARD, O.M.I.

RIGHT-TO-LIFE GROUPS

The right-to-life movement emerged in the mid–1960s in reaction to proposed changes in the states' abortion laws. Before the early 1960s there was little discussion about or opposition to state laws that by the turn of the century prohibited all nonmedically indicated abortions. The first changes proposed by the American Law Institute in 1959, and by the late 1960s adopted by nineteen states, recommended legal therapeutic abortions within a specified period of time. By 1965 modifications of the abortion laws received support from influential professional and cultural groups such as the American Medical Association, the American College of Obstetrics and Gynecologists, and the American Public Health Association, and from various committees of the Episcopal, Presbyterian, Methodist, and American Baptist churches and branches of Judaism. But a limited right to abortion for predefined, serious causes did not remain the goal of abortion reformers, who soon pressed for elective abortion. Especially significant were the 1967 decision by the newly formed National Organization for Women to define elective abortion as necessary for women's equality and the formation in 1969 of the National Association for the Repeal of Abortion Laws. In 1972 the Presidential Commission on Population Control and The American Future broke still another link with traditional views of abortion when it recommended that abortion be defined as birth control.

Professional and cultural elites are not nearly as represented among opponents to legal abortion. The earliest antiabortion activists were largely legal and health professionals who were disproportionately Roman Catholic but who formed explicitly ecumenical and interfaith groups. By 1967 thousands of local right-to-life groups had formed. In 1966 the director of the Family Life Bureau, Msgr. (now Bishop) James McHugh, gathered a small number of advisors whom he called the "National Right to Life Committee" to monitor state developments and serve as a central information network. By 1967 most activists were no longer professionals but religiously affiliated women with young children, who described themselves for the most part as self-recruits averaging ten hours a week in lobbying, recruitment, letter-writing campaigns, and other movement activity. There was successful recruitment of Protestant and Jewish activists, though the limited changes sought by the first abortion reformers impeded Protestant antiabortion mobilization until the mid–1970s. Most grass-roots groups held no formal elections, raised their own funds, and met around kitchen tables. Many found little local clerical support but were able to use parish facilities and networks for recruitment. Early activists report few political mentors and no clear movement strategy, save that of opposing changes in their states' abortion laws. During the fragmented and localized pre-*Roe* phase of the movement, activists could claim at least as much success as pro-choice activists, since only nineteen of the fifty states modified their laws.

From the start opposition to abortion exhibited the usual characteristics of social movements: jealousy about group autonomy, disputes about principles and compromises, disagreements over strategies and tactics, organizational divisions. The editors of the 1989 edition of the *Encyclopedia of Associations* were able to obtain information from sixty-one distinct antiabortion groups. Given this diversity one could legitimately refer to the antiabortion movements.

The dominant organization remains the National Right to Life Committee (NRLC), legally incorporated in the summer of 1973 and claiming seven million members in chapters in every state. NRLC has successfully sought an "umbrella" status in the movement and limits its educational and political lobbying entirely to the issues of abortion, infanticide, and euthanasia. "Left" and "right" dissident groups that separated from NRLC included American Citizens for Life, which explicitly supports family planning, sex education, and social legislation aimed at reducing the number of abortions, and the much larger American Life League, which explicitly opposes government involvement in birth control and which serves as the rallying point for those in the movement who accuse the NRLC and the American bishops of compromising principles when they support measures that do not explicitly prohibit all abortions.

Important autonomous groups formed in the 1970s include Americans United for Life, the most significant legal resource of the movement, Evangelical Protestant groups such as the Christian Action Council and Evangelicals for Social Action, and pro-life groups within mainstream Protestantism such as The National Organization of Episcopalians for Life, Presbyterians for Life, Lutherans for Life, Friends of Life (United Church of Christ), and Baptists for Life. By the 1980s every major Protestant denomination was reexamining its initial appraisal of *Roe* in the light of the annual abortion rate of more than 1.5 million, signaling the frequent use of abortion as birth control.

Any list of fiercely independent antiabortion groups should include Human Life International, United States Coalition for Life, Libertarians for Life, the Ad Hoc Committee in Defense of Life, the Long Island–based Families for Life, the New

York Right to Life party, and the March on Washington Committee.

The year 1975 marked the explicit entrance of right-to-life groups into electoral politics. To protest the unwillingness of the Democratic party (at that time thought by most pro-lifers more likely to support them than the Republican party) to endorse a human life amendment, Ellen McCormack, a Long Island housewife and co-founder of Women for the Unborn, ran for the Democratic nomination for president in about a dozen state primaries. Her campaign commercials consisted of slides showing fetal life and a short message by Mildred Jefferson, a Harvard-educated doctor who was then president of NRLC. Later McCormack helped found the New York State Right to Life party. In 1978 Charles Fiore started the first political action committee (National Pro-Life Political Action Committee), and similar PACs were quickly formed by rival groups such as the National Right to Life Committee and the American Life Lobby. Individual American bishops financially support the Committee for a Human Life Amendment, which has its own lobbyist. While many of the early political-action committees are now defunct, James McFadden's Ad Hoc Committee for the Defense of Life and his newsletter, *LifeLetter,* continue their autonomous political campaign against *Roe,* criticizing any rival anti-abortion legal initiative that does not preclude all abortions.

Groups devoted to direct action and political action (besides lobbying) also began in the mid–1970s. While direct-action groups began when it seemed that no political party would endorse their efforts to reverse *Roe,* these forms of "street" politics have continued, even during both terms of President Reagan and the first term of President Bush, when the Republican party platform included support for a human life amendment. The first systematic nonviolent protests were coordinated by the Pro-Life Non-Violent Action Committee, which was made up of veterans from the civil-rights and peace movements and whose tone was left-pacifist and whose chief goal was "witness."

In the early 1980s Joe Scheidler's National Pro-Life Action Council followed a Saul Alinsky confrontational style. Hospital pickets by Protestant pastors organized by the Christian Action Council and the street counseling practiced by Catholics United for Life and others more quietly gave local voice to antiabortion sentiment throughout the 1980s. In the late 1980s Randall Terry's Operation Rescue brought many religious fundamentalists and a mass confrontational style to direct-action antiabortion protest. While there were approximately 3,200 arrests for antiabortion civil disobedience from 1975 to 1988, in 1988 there were approximately 10,000 people arrested among the estimated 46,000 "rescuers" during the hundreds of Operation Rescue campaigns held in dozens of major American cities.

Deep divisions remain in the right-to-life movement and have included disputes about the appropriate pro-life strategy—whether to seek a constitutional convention (generally favored by locally based groups) or an amendment to the Constitution, favored by NRLC. Disputes remain over how an amendment should be worded—whether it should ban all non-lifesaving abortions or permit restricted abortion; whether an amendment should ban abortions or simply permit the states to again legislate their own abortion laws; whether opposition to legal abortion must also in consistency include support for legislation against capital punishment, poverty, military spending, and the like.

A large and generally overlooked part of the pro-life movement are the "service" groups that help women with unwanted pregnancies choose birth rather than abortion. Birthright was formed in 1970, and Alternatives to Abortion International the next year. Many of these volunteer groups provide far more than pregnancy counseling, emergency funds, and immediate help. More than a fifth provide housing, low-cost or free medical services, and employment help. Later in the decade the Christian Action Council started several hundred emergency pregnancy centers, and as recently as 1988 Mary Cunningham Agee began "The Nurturing Network," which aids college and professional women to bring their child to term without endangering their education or their careers. In the United States there are more than three thousand emergency pregnancy centers. In this context it should be noted that many Roman Catholic dioceses have publicly announced that they will provide either referral services or medical and financial assistance to any women who without them would feel forced to abort.

An important development in the pro-life movement has been an explicit linking of women's rights and the rights of the unborn. Polls have consistently shown that elective abortion is more likely to be approved by affluent males than by women, the poor, and minorities. When the National Organization for Women defined elective abortion as essential to gender equality, some dissidents formed pro-life groups such as Liberated Women's Coalition Against Abortion, Life and Equality, Women's Association for Human Rights, and Women for Universal Human Rights. In 1972 they merged to form Feminists for Life, which now has more than two thousand members and chapters in almost every state. Members support all the mainstream feminist positions except legal abortion, arguing as 19th-century feminists did that abortion requires women to adapt themselves to essentially masculine conceptions of work, sexuality, and politics. In 1976 women whose experience of abortion convinced them that abortion harms women psychologically and sometimes physically formed Women Exploited, and shortly thereafter, others started American Victims of Abortion.

The role of the Catholic church in the pro-life movement is also complex. Catholicism's moral disapproval of all directly intended abortions and its suspicion that the principle justifying legal abortion would in time expand beyond the "hard" cases of rape, incest, and maternal health to include, first, abortion on demand, and then a lessened regard for handicapped neonates and an increased acceptance of euthanasia, provided a major ideological resource for abortion opponents. The institutional networks linking local parishes, state chapters, and the United States Catholic Conference were indispensable for laying the groundwork for the quick post-*Roe* nationalization of state antiabortion efforts. But the Catholic reaction to legal abortion was never as a single issue and from the start included voluntary and government support for alternatives to abortion. Cardinal Bernardin's 1983 address "A Consistent Ethic of Life" explicitly linked opposition to abortion with other life issues and the causes of abortion. In November 1985 the National Conference of Catholic Bishops officially adopted the phrase "consistent ethic of life" in its revised plan for pro-life activities.

Many antiabortion groups argued that this "seamless garment" approach diluted their political impact. Groups that have explicitly embraced the notion of a consistent ethic that links abortion to issues of poverty, military spending, and gender justice—Feminists for Life, JustLife, American Citizens for Life, Evangelicals for Social Action, the Seamless Garment Network, Pax Christi, Sojourners—are not as widely known either within or outside the right-to-life movement as are those right-to-life groups focused solely on abortion and euthanasia. They rarely receive media attention. During the post-*Webster* phase of the abortion controversy the long-term task of activists will be to contest the tendency of the media to describe them as "antiabortion" rather than as "pro-life."

The long-term cultural significance of the pro-life movement probably depends on its ability to keep vital the theme of a consistent ethic and to extend it explicitly to questions of gender justice and equality. Given the tactical alliances with conservative Republicans made by dominant sectors of the movement during the 1980s, the linkage between justice for women and the unborn remains fragile. The June 29, 1992, Supreme Court ruling *Planned Parenthood of Southeastern Pennsylvania* v. *Casey*, which narrowly upheld (5–4) *Roe* but permitted (7–2) state regulations that do not pose an "undue burden" (such as a brief waiting period during which a woman reviews information about abortion and community-assisted alternatives, and parental notification of unemancipated minors), indicates that for some time any constitutionally successful state abortion regulations will focus on ensuring that abortions are knowledgeably and freely chosen. With the advent of state abortion laws withholding additional benefits from poor women, some abortion-rights activists have found common ground with abortion opponents in protesting abortions that do not reflect "choice."

Probably the majority of church leaders and laity have yet to find the appropriate tone and position on legal abortion that would conjoin the teaching that human life is a continuum that warrants community protection at every stage of development *with* the public acknowledgment that there is not likely to be a consensus strong enough to support laws entirely congruent with this conviction. The effort to apply moral principles wisely to political realities always causes inner-movement conflict. Some have lately suggested that European laws that decriminalize all previable abortions but describe fetal life as human come closer than *Roe* to expressing in secular societies the traditional moral abhorrence of abortion.

See also ABORTION, SOCIAL IMPLICATIONS OF; BIRTH CONTROL; CHILDREN, RIGHTS OF; CIVIL LAW, FUNCTION OF; EUTHANASIA, SOCIAL IMPLICATIONS OF; FEMINISM AND CATHOLIC SOCIAL THOUGHT; KILLING; PLURALISM; POPULATION; PRIVACY, RIGHT TO; PUBLIC AND PRIVATE, RELATIONSHIP OF; TOLERATION, PRINCIPLE OF.

Bibliography: M. Glendon, *Divorce and Abortion in Western Law* (Harvard, 1988). J. Kelly, "Toward Complexity: The Right-to-Life Movement," in *Research in the Social Scientific Study of Religion*, vol. 1 (JAI Press, 1989). K. Luker, *Abortion and the Politics of Motherhood* (Univ. of California, 1984). J. Noonan, Jr., *A Private Choice* (The Free Press, 1979).

JAMES R. KELLY

RIGHTS AND DUTIES

The municipal law of the state grants rights to and imposes duties on its citizens. A citizen granted a right can seek redress through instruments of the state if the right is being infringed by other citizens or even by the state itself. A citizen failing to perform duties can be punished by the law and forced to comply with the requirements of the obligation.

Some rights are said to be so fundamental that they are not granted by the state but rather are simply recognized by the law, or ought to be. A legal regime that failed to recognize such rights would be defective, perhaps inviting conscientious refusal to comply with its laws, civil disobedience, and even revolution. Some duties are to be performed by the individual even if they are not imposed by the state.

The inherent dignity of the human person is the starting point for any consideration of rights and duties that are said to exist independently from the municipal law of the state or from international law expressed in agreements between nations. No longer do we derive these rights only from the characteristics of human nature; rather we reflect on the needs of the human person as an individual living in relationship with other individuals in a cultural context as part of the environment and with God. There is a growing interdependence of each to the other. Wants and needs of the individual do not automatically translate into rights. Priority must be given to equality or liberty. The assertion of a right does not necessarily establish a duty for the other to provide.

The liberal capitalist takes seriously the freedom of the individual whose wants and needs are not determined by others. Being able to transcend enlightened self-interest and class interest, the individual is able to seek the good for self and others, contributing to the common good, which is the sum of requirements for all individuals in community to achieve their human flourishing. The right of economic initiative is important. Individual political rights are emphasized over social and cultural rights and over livelihood. The right to vote, freedom of association, and free enterprise are espoused as the way to justice and peace for all. Liberty is more prized than equality. Liberty is restricted only for the sake of liberty. Social and economic inequalities are tolerated because the trickle-down effect ensures that there is benefit for all, even the poorest, in allowing the rich and powerful to produce more, which can then be distributed in unequal portions.

For the collectivist there is no magic and little scope in personal choice. The market and advertisers determine many of the individual's wants, needs, and aspirations. Freedom or license for the rich and powerful renders optional the pursuit of cultural and economic rights for the poor. Rights are not the stuff of opportunity and freedom from constraint but of the provision and equal distribution of the basic material and cultural elements needed for the survival and fulfillment of all.

Since the Second Vatican Council, many church documents have catalogued not the legal rights of citizens but the human rights of all persons, often without any extensive correlative list of duties but always with the rider that the common good is to be promoted. John XXIII developed this approach in *Pacem in terris,* giving priority to social rights and stating that every person "has the right to life, to bodily integrity and to the means which are necessary and suitable for the proper development of life" (PT 11). He catalogued many natural rights, which he derived from the natural law. Much of the catalogue echoes the United Nations' Universal Declaration of Human Rights (1948), which recognizes that the inherent dignity and the equal and inalienable rights of all members of the human family is the foundation of freedom, justice, and peace in the world. John XXIII asserted that the natural rights of a person were inseparably connected "in the very person who is their subject, with just as many respective duties" (PT 28).

In *Gaudium et spes* (Pastoral Constitution on the Church in the Modern World), the Second Vatican Council gave priority to the basic equality of all "since all persons possess a rational soul and are created in God's likeness, since they have the same nature and origin, have been redeemed by Christ and enjoy the same divine calling and destiny." Without an exhaustive catalogue of the fundamental personal rights, the council insisted that these rights be recognized and that "every type of discrimination, whether social or cultural, whether based on sex, race, color, social condition, language or religion" be overcome and eradicated (GS 29). If they are to develop, human beings need their individual dignity, community, culture, family, socioeconomic life, participation in the political community, and the assurance of peace in the community of nations.

Seeking a balance between equality and liberty, John Paul II in *Sollicitudo rei socialis* emphasized the right of economic initiative because the limitation of this right "in the name of an alleged 'equality' of everyone in society, diminishes or in practice absolutely destroys the spirit of initiative, that is to say the creative subjectivity of the citizen" (SRS 15). Equality is not the same as leveling down each person to the same plane of mediocrity. Acknowledging nations' and individuals' underdevelopment and our growing interdependence in the world, he espoused the rights of participation in social, cultural, economic, and political aspects of life. Advocating the virtue of solidarity, he underlined the duty of all persons to be committed to the common good "because we are all really responsible for all" (SRS 38). The individual may have a right to private property, but all private property is under a social mortgage. Development is a duty as well as a right, encumbent on nations as well as individuals.

The catalogue of rights and duties in modern church documents is now so extensive that it is often difficult to determine the priority of different classes of rights and duties, the content of which are now more relative and culture-determined. This catalogue is deduced from a combination of philosophical inquiry, scriptural exegesis, and theological reflection. Rights talk is becoming inflated and more rhetorical, while outside church circles the grounding and content of rights claims is disputed. Only if love be accepted as the supreme law, God being the Father of all calling all into relationship as brothers and sisters in Christ, does it make sense to speak of "each people's equal right 'to be seated at the table of the common banquet' instead of lying outside the door like Lazarus, while 'the dogs come and lick his sores' (cf. Lk 16:21)" (SRS 33).

Having accepted the primacy of the law of love, whereby we do to others as we would have them do to us, and as Christians, aspiring to love others as Christ loved us, we must still establish normative ethical standards for right relationships with one another, each having been called into right relationship with God. When rights or duties conflict in any social arrangement there is a need for further reflection on doing the right. For the Christian no discharge of duties can guarantee salvation; no enjoyment of rights can be equated with the kingdom. Morality of duty must lead to morality of aspiration and vice versa. The tensions between freedom and equality, private property and the social mortgage, the common good and the preferential option for the poor, ought be creative and graced urgings for individuals and communities to discern what God is asking of us. The poor, the powerless, and the marginalized are like the stranger, the widow, and the orphan who were the concern of the prophets. Their rights are the only universal rights. The benefits that others enjoy are not universal rights but liberties or privileges. These universal rights are realizable only to the extent that there is a morally binding duty on all to provide, especially for the least. Rights are exercised only to the extent that the correlative duties are performed under coercion from the state under encouragement from others or, most suitably, under the guidance of conscience inspired by the Spirit.

See also CAPITALISM; CENTESIMUS ANNUS; CIVIL LAW, FUNCTION OF; COLLECTIVISM; COMMON GOOD; FREEDOM; HUMAN RIGHTS; SOLIDARITY.

Bibliography: J. Gremillion, *The Gospel of Justice and Peace* (New York: Orbis, 1976). D. Hollenbach, *Claims in Conflict* (New York: Paulist, 1979).

FRANK BRENNAN, S.J.

RYAN, JOHN AUGUSTINE

John A. Ryan was the foremost American Catholic social theorist for the first four decades of the 20th century. He developed a social reform agenda grounded in natural-law theory that was compatible with both the Catholic moral tradition and the American progressive reform tradition. Ryan insisted that the social and economic problems that confronted the modern era were essentially moral problems, and as such, the Catholic church as the ultimate arbiter of morality had an important role to play in the reconstruction of the social order. Economic welfare should not be left to impersonal market forces. Nor could Catholics allow the triumph of socialism. Ryan attempted to articulate a middle way between individualistic capitalism and socialism. In an era in which the church's social teaching and policy were too often simply a reaction against socialism, he offered a positive, practical program of social reform that was both Catholic and American.

Biographical Data

Ryan was born May 25, 1865, the eldest son of eleven children, in the rural farming community of Vermillion, Minnesota. His parents, William and Mary, had immigrated to the United States from Ireland in the 1850s to escape the potato famine. John was influenced early on by the populist thought of Patrick Ford, editor of the *Irish World,* and Ignatius Donnelly as well as by the forthright stands of his archbishop, John Ireland. In 1887 Ryan entered St. Thomas Seminary in St. Paul, where he was ordained to the priesthood June 4, 1898. While in the seminary he was introduced to Pope Leo XIII's social encyclical, *Rerum novarum,* on the condition of the working class. He would take as his life's work the explanation and adaptation of *Rerum novarum* to the American situation.

In 1898 Ryan was sent to the Catholic University of America (CUA) in Washington, D.C., for graduate study in moral theology, where he studied under the great Catholic "scientific" social reformers Thomas Bouquillon and William Kerby, who insisted that questions of social morality had to be grounded in precise observations of social reality and not just considered in abstract terms. Ryan began work on a dissertation that would not be completed until 1906. It was published the same year as *A Living Wage: Its Ethical and Economic Aspects,* in which he argued that each worker had a natural right to a wage that would allow him to live in a manner in accord with his dignity as a human being. In 1902 Ryan returned to St. Paul's seminary, where he taught moral theology and economics until 1915.

In 1911 Ryan helped draft minimum-wage legislation for the state of Minnesota as part of the Minnesota Committee on Social Legislation, and he worked hard lobbying for the bill. While the minimum wage did not ensure a living wage, it was a step on the way to attaining a living wage. State enforcement of a minimum wage would also assist workers not protected by unions.

In 1913 Ryan engaged noted socialist Morris Hillquit in a series of debates, published in *Everybody's Magazine,* over the relative merits of socialism. Ryan used the debate in part to deflect the constant criticism accusing him of being a socialist or "too socialistic." The essays were published in book form in 1914 as *Socialism: Promise or Menace?*

In 1915 Ryan returned to CUA as a professor in the school of sacred theology, where he remained until 1940 (though he spent his last three years as a professor in the school of social sciences). He also taught at Trinity College for women and later at the National Catholic School of Social Service after it was begun in the 1920s.

In 1916 he published his second and last major economic treatise, *Distributive Justice: The Right and Wrong of Our Present Distribution of Wealth,* in which he argued that present economic maladies were the result of an improper distribution of wealth. Ryan considered this his "most important work" (Ryan, p. 136). It was his last major scholarly work. From 1916 on he would concentrate on popularizing the concepts he developed in *Living Wage* and *Distributive Justice.*

From 1917 to 1921 Ryan served as the first editor of the *Catholic Charities Review.* While he supported charities, he believed that charity did not supersede the demand for justice. "Charity is a poison when taken in substitute for justice" (Broderick, p. 23). Like William Kerby, Ryan believed that real charity called for changes in the root causes of poverty and not in mere relief of the symptoms.

In 1919 at the urging of Father John O'Grady, Ryan reworked a speech he had intended to deliver to the Knights of Columbus of Louisville into a program of social reconstruction for the post–World War I world. Ryan's program was adopted with few revisions and published by the Administrative Board of the National Catholic Welfare Council as the Bishops' Program of Social Reconstruction in 1920. Ryan and the Bishops' Program called for the retention of the National War Labor Board and the United States Employment Service as well as a number of practical reforms such as minimum wage laws, social security insurance, and public housing projects. In addition it advocated such long-term reforms as the abolition and control of monopolies and called for greater participation of workers in industrial management. The document gave authority to Ryan's prescription for reconstruction and represented a bold step by the American hierarchy. No longer content with the "masterly inactivity" of the Gibbons era, the Bishops' Program announced that the American Catholic church would henceforth be actively involved in determining the direction of American society and culture. The document was met with a good deal of surprise; Upton Sinclair referred to the Bishops' Program as the "Catholic miracle" (Broderick, p. 107).

In 1919 Ryan was appointed director of the newly created Social Action Department (SAD) of the National Catholic Welfare Council. With the able assistance of Fr. Raymond McGowan, Ryan would serve as director until 1944. The SAD served as a platform from which Ryan could publicize his notions of social reform. In addition, it sought to educate the general American Catholic populace in the basic tenets of Catholic social teaching. To further this end, the Catholic Conference on Industrial Problems was created in 1923 as a forum to discuss and disseminate information.

Ryan's long and hard fight for an amendment to the United States Constitution prohibiting child labor was the occasion for his most bitter intramural dispute. In the early 1920s William Cardinal O'Connell of Boston vigorously (and viciously) opposed the amendment (and Ryan), dubbing the amendment "Soviet legislation" that allowed the government to usurp the rights of parents. This pernicious precedent would ultimately lead to government interference in Catholic schools. Ryan contended the greater danger was the continued abuse of the child in the workplace. The amendment was defeated and the controversy between Ryan and O'Connell subsided.

During the 1920s Ryan became an advocate of international peace through disarmament. In 1927 he assisted in the creation of the Catholic Association for International Peace. The association steered clear of pacifism, opting to propagate the Catholic theory of the just war. Ryan also belonged to the National Council for the Prevention of War but resigned when the council became too pacifist and because of its sympathy with the antichurch forces in the Mexican disputes of the 1920s.

Ryan belonged to numerous non-Catholic or secular organizations over the course of his lifetime: the National Popular Government League, the Public Ownership League, the National Conference of Charities and Corrections, the National Consumers League, the National Child Labor Committee, and a variety of others. Most controversial was Ryan's position on the board of the American Civil Liberties Union. Ryan believed that Catholic isolation was self-defeating. Catholics needed to serve in these organizations to ensure that the Catholic viewpoint would be heard. The Catholic viewpoint would serve as a brake on the radical tendencies of these groups. Finally, Catholics could not achieve social reform alone—they had to work with other groups to attain their goals.

Ryan became involved in a sideshow during the 1928 presidential campaign that featured the first Catholic presidential candidate, Al Smith. Critics argued that Smith would be unable to preserve the constitutionally guaranteed separation of church and state, using as evidence a textbook written in 1922 by Ryan with M. F. X. Millar entitled *The State and the Church.* In it Ryan argued that in ideal terms the church and the state should be united, with Catholicism as the established religion. Ryan argued, however, that in real terms no such state had ever existed and would never exist, so it offered no threat to the American notion of separation of church and state. Such distinctions were lost in the political rhetoric of the 1928 election.

During the first years of the Depression, Ryan attacked the Hoover administration's lack of action in combating the Depression. Ryan argued that the Depression was brought on by underconsumption, which was created by a maldistribution of wealth. Purchasing power had to be restored to the many if the Depression was to be curtailed. Ryan urged federal and state governments to become more active, advocating minimum-wage laws and public-works programs.

In 1931 Pope Pius XI promulgated his encyclical *Quadragesimo anno,* "On Reconstructing the Social Order." *Quadragesimo anno* was heralded in America as an endorsement of John Ryan's social agenda. CUA rector Fr. Thomas Shahan reportedly said, "Well, this is a great vindication for John Ryan" (Broderick, p. 196). Papal approval of Ryan was further suggested in 1933, with Ryan's designation as a domestic prelate.

Though initially lukewarm to Franklin D. Roosevelt, Ryan became an ardent supporter of the New Deal, which he regarded as a close approximation of the papal reform program as well as of his own. The New Deal, he believed, was a via media between socialism and individualism. Ryan served on several government panels, most notably the Industrial Appeals Board of the National Recovery Administration. In 1936, in response to mounting attacks on FDR by Fr. Charles Coughlin, Ryan defended FDR and the New Deal in a nationally broadcast radio speech. Coughlin, somewhat caustically, dubbed Ryan "Right Reverend New Dealer." In 1937 Ryan became the first Catholic priest to provide the benediction at a president's inauguration. For the remainder of his life he supported FDR, including FDR's controversial court-packing plan.

In 1940 Ryan retired from CUA but continued as director of the SAD until 1944. Ryan died on September 16, 1945.

Economic Thought

Ryan's basic economic thought, as articulated in *A Living Wage* and *Distributive Justice* and popularized in countless journal articles and speeches, centered around three basic concepts: the worker's right to a living wage, the need for a better distribution of the world's material goods, and the right of the state to promote the common good through social legislation.

Each worker had a natural right to a wage that would allow the worker to live a life in accord with his or her dignity as a human being. This was a minimum of justice. The living wage had to enable the worker to provide for basic needs—food, shelter, and clothing—as well as for insurance against sickness, disability, and old age. In light of the requirements of human nature the living wage also had to provide for the religious, educational, and recreational needs of the worker. Further, the living wage was to be a "familial" living wage, as marriage was an essential part of a decent life. The living wage was a fundamental right; while Ryan acknowledged the right to private property and the right to a profitable return on an investment, these were not absolute rights. Both rights were subordinate to the worker's right to a living wage, which was grounded in a more fundamental right—the right to life. Ryan endorsed unions and collective bargaining as a means of securing the living wage, but when these failed it was the duty of the state to step in and secure that right. Some objected that Ryan's program violated the right of "free contract" between employer and employee. Ryan did not see free contract as a right or a reality. No worker would freely consent to less than a living wage unless forced to do so by a superior economic force. Ryan wrote, "The name free contract is a misnomer. There can be no freedom of contract [for] laborers who must work or starve" (Ryan, p. 71). The worker's right to a living wage supersedes all other rights in the industrial world. It is the keystone of Ryan's program of social reform.

Equally important was the proper distribution of wealth and goods. Adopting economist John A. Hobson's theory that depressions result from underconsumption and oversaving, Ryan argued that the central economic problem was one of distribution, not production. America had the capability of producing enough to supply all its people with an adequate standard of living. Depressions resulted when supply exceeded demand, but the lack of demand was the result of a lack of purchasing power created by a maldistribution of wealth, or as Ryan put it, "speaking generally we may say that capital receives too much purchasing power and labor too little" (Ryan, p. 68).

To achieve a more equitable distribution workers had to become more involved in what Ryan called "industrial management." While he affirmed the usefulness of unions, unions did not go far enough. Workers had to become involved in "the control of processes and machinery, nature of product" and other fundamental concerns of the industry in which they worked. ("Bishops' Program," p. 342). He asserted that the majority of workers must "become owners, or at least in part, of the instruments of production" ("Bishops Program," p. 345), though he acknowledged that this was a long-term goal. After *Quadragesimo anno,* Ryan adopted Pius XI's call for a "vocational group system" similar to the medieval guild system in which labor and management would work together cooperatively in directing their industry. The vocational group system would give the worker greater control over the industrial process but would maintain the right of individuals to private property.

While this remained a long-term goal, Ryan insisted on the right of the state to ensure immediate economic justice and order by guaranteeing the natural rights of the workers. The state was to provide for the common good by protecting the weak (the poor laborer), from the strong (the rich capitalist). He was fond of quoting the following passage from *Rerum novarum:* "Whenever the general interest or any particular class suffers, or is threatened with evils which can in no other way be met, the public authority must step in to meet them" (Ryan, p. 44). Whenever Ryan might be accused of being too socialistic because of his heavy reliance on the state, he would refer people to this passage from *Rerum novarum.*

Ryan not only argued the right of state intervention in abstract terms, he presented a detailed plan of social legislation. The ultimate test of any economic theory for Ryan was its social utility. Did it contribute to "human welfare" (Curran, p. 32)? Ryan believed in gradual, not radical, reform. While upholding the ideal as the ultimate goal, he worked for short-term gains.

In 1909 he clearly articulated his short-term goals in an article for the *Catholic World* entitled "A Program of Social Reform by Legislation." His program included a legal minimum wage, the eight-hour work day, protective legislation for women and children, the right to boycott and picket, unemployment insurance and employment bureaus, social security against sickness, accidents, and poverty in old age, public housing, public ownership of public utilities and of mines and forests, control of monopolies, land taxes, and prohibition of speculation in the stock market (Broderick, pp. 58–59). These proposals would dictate Ryan's social agenda over the course of the next three decades. He would reiterate much of his program in the Bishops' Program of Social Reconstruction, and he would see many of his proposals become law during the New Deal in the 1930s.

Conclusion

Ryan's great contribution was that in a time when American Catholic social thought was negative, primarily antisocialist, hesitant, and isolated, he presented a positive, practical agenda for social reform. More importantly, he presented a theoretical framework for his agenda that could be understood in both Catholic and American terms. He succeeded in making the church more relevant to America and in making America more responsive to the church.

See also BISHOPS' PROGRAM OF SOCIAL RECONSTRUCTION OF 1919; ECONOMIC ORDER; GOODS, DISTRIBUTION OF; JUST WAGE; LABOR AND CAPITAL IN CATHOLIC SOCIAL THOUGHT; NATURAL LAW; QUADRAGESIMO ANNO; SUBSIDIARITY, PRINCIPLE OF.

Bibliography: J. McShane, *"Sufficiently Radical": Catholicism, Progressivism, and the Bishops' Program of 1919* (Washington: CUA Press, 1986). F. Broderick, *Right Reverend New Dealer: John A. Ryan* (New York: Macmillan, 1963). J. Ryan, *Social Doctrine in Action: A Personal History* (New York: Harper, 1941). C. Curran, *American Catholic Social Ethics: Twentieth Century Approaches* (Notre Dame: Univ. of Notre Dame Press, 1982). D. O'Brien, *American Catholics and Social Reform: The New Deal Years* (New York: Oxford, 1968). P. Gearty, *The Economic Thought of Monsignor John A. Ryan* (Washington: CUA Press, 1953). "The Bishops' Program of Social Reconstruction," in A. Abell, ed., *American Catholic Thought on Social Questions* (New York: Bobbs-Merrill, 1968).

JEFFREY M. BURNS

S

SACRED AND SECULAR, RELATIONSHIP OF

The relationship of the sacred and secular has taken manifold expressions depending on the era as well as the issue. This article will outline the parameters of the discussion, the scriptural foundation for the issue, the church's teaching on the matter, and a contemporary understanding of the interpenetration of the two spheres, especially as related to action on behalf of justice.

Parameters

The inner-outer, yin-yang dynamics have been articulated in terms of cult and culture, Word and world, religion and society, salvation and history, spiritual and material, heaven and earth, spirit and flesh, spirituality and secularization, church and state, theology and sociology, self and other, piety and politics, creed and creation, and faith and justice, among many others.

The "two kingdoms" notion has been the focus of much debate throughout history. H. Richard Niebuhr was convinced that the enigma connected to the relationship between Christianity and society represented the "enduring problem" of Christian history. This has been compounded in the United States because of the First Amendment to the Constitution. Reacting against the pattern that linked various denominations with state interests, the framers of the rationale for the nation insisted that no specific denomination or religion would be singled out for preferences and that all would be able to function without interference from the state. The disestablishment clause states: "Congress shall make no law respecting an establishment of religion, or prohibiting the free exercise thereof." While the theory of legal disestablishmentarianism holds, in actual practice there is a symbiotic relationship, even in the United States, between Christianity and the culture despite the large presence of Jews, the increasing numbers of Moslems, and other religious persuasions.

The sacred and secular, religious and political, faith and justice dimensions of life are not opposite poles; rather they represent alternative dimensions of reality that interrelate and actually interpenetrate in varying degrees of sophistication and complexity. However, this approach has not always been predominant; in fact it seems to be the third alternative to two other approaches that have dominated thinking in the past centuries.

The first approach can be considered the *withdrawal* tactic. The world was seen as evil, outside God's reign. The role of the Christian thus demands that the disciple become a pilgrim buttressed by the church, which serves as a bastion against the world and its allurements. Society is corrupt, lost, and of little or no value except as a place of pilgrimage and purification for the sojourner. Sects such as Jehovah's Witnesses often articulate elements of the withdrawal approach in their philosophies. This approach fails to recognize the lordship of Jesus Christ and the discipleship demands that are inherent in the Incarnation.

The second approach can be considered the *accommodationist* tactic. The world is seen as having intrinsic value in itself; its cultural patterns are uncritically accepted as morally correct. The role of the Christian thus demands that a true believer become a good citizen, unquestionably accepting the norms and patterns of society. Society, or the nation, becomes the ultimate definer of religion. A classic case of this has been shown in the silence of the Catholic church as well as in the confessing church in Hitler's Nazi Germany. The "accommodationist" approach fails to recognize the prophetic dimension of the Scriptures and how the state, or mammon-forms, becomes the controlling ideology for the life of faith.

A third approach has been the *Christendom* model. The church (Catholic or Protestant) is seen as the ultimate arbitrator of social values and institutional life. While the leader is free in the political sphere, ultimate obedience is rendered by the leader to the religious leaders, who have the power to bind and loose. Religion, or "the church," becomes the ultimate determinant of civic values. The period of the Middle Ages under Pope Innocent III represents this model, which is based more on the notion of religious power than Christian service.

A fourth approach finds sacred and secular, faith and justice, in varying degrees of tension, a tension inherent in the notion of incarnation itself.

Biblical Foundations

In the first words in the OT the world is perceived as the locus of God's involvement, especially when conditions in the world reflect darkness, chaos, and dynamics alien to the plan of God. Into the midst of such conditions God "created humankind in his image, in the image of God he created them; male and female he created them. God blessed them, and God said to them, 'Be fruitful and multiply, and fill the earth and subdue it, and have dominion over the fish of the sea and over the birds of the air and over every living thing that moves upon the earth'" (Gen 1:27-28). The last words of the Book of Revelation speak of God's new heaven and new earth (Rev 21-22).

Despite this vision of creation as good, a large part of history in Christianity has been influenced by an interpretation of the Pauline theology that makes a strong dichotomy between the spiritual and material, the spirit and the flesh, God's Word and "this world." In the early Pauline letters, Christians were to live in the world as though they were not of it, since it was passing away (1 Cor 7:31). Indeed, Paul's First Letter to the Corinthians—which contains almost as many references to the "world" as the rest of the Pauline corpus together—offers a vision of worldly wisdom that contrasts with the vision of those who are weak in the eyes of the world but wise in the eyes of God.

In reference to the relationship between faith and justice as the way God's Word is to relate to the world, Paul's Letter to the Romans declares that Christians should "not be conformed to this world, but be transformed by the renewing of [their] minds" (Rom 12:2), as well as that in the gospel is revealed the justice of God, which begins and ends in faith, noting that those who are just live by faith (Rom 1:16-17).

While maintaining some of the dichotomy between the world and the Word, John's Gospel and letters reveal more of the notion of interpenetration because of the notions of the Incarnation and God's Word entering the world to dwell in it and among its inhabitants. God's relationship to the world is best summarized in the classic statement that even today is used at secular gatherings to proclaim God's concern for humankind: "For God so loved the world that he gave his only Son, so that everyone who believes in him may not perish but may have eternal life" (Jn 3:16). In virtue of the redemptive incarnation, it is no longer possible to determine where God "ends" and humans "begin"; incarnation, in light of Christ's passover from all forms of death to life, means interpenetration of Word and world.

Church Teaching

The interpenetration of God with humanity and the vision of grace and nature intertwined at all levels of life has been best summarized in the opening statement of the Second Vatican Council's Pastoral Constitution on the Church in the Modern World (*Gaudium et spes*): "The joy and hope, the grief and anguish of the people of our time, especially of those who are poor or afflicted in any way, are the joy and hope, the grief and anguish of the followers of Christ as well. Nothing that is genuinely human fails to find an echo in their hearts" (GS 1). If there are tensions in the world, it is because these same tensions exist within each human being. Asking What can humans contribute to society? and What can humans expect from society? the document outlines an approach motivated by faith that engages men and women in active participation to help build on this earth relations that reflect God's plan for the world. This plan envisages people whose dignity as images of God is ensured through freedom, whose right to the resources of the earth is realized through equality, and who can live in community with one another through deeper forms of participation and solidarity.

The council perceived the church sharing in the same lot as humans themselves; thus the need for an incarnational approach is necessary: "That the earthly and the heavenly city penetrate one another is a fact open only to the eyes of faith; moreover, it will remain the mystery of human history, which will be harassed by sin until the perfect revelation of the splendor of the [children] of God. . . . The Church, then, believes it can contribute much to humanizing the human family and its history through each of its members and its community as a whole" (GS 40).

Probably the most groundbreaking document of the council relating to the sacred-secular sphere and to the fact that there are different religions (i.e., the "sacred") in the secular world is the council's Declaration on Religious Liberty (*Dignitatis humanae*). In the eyes of the council, all people have the freedom to determine their own religion, and no religion has the right to act in a coercive way to force the obedience of others. One of the purposes and aims of such religious liberty is to enable people "to act with greater responsibility in fulfilling their own obligations in society" (DH 8).

As a result of the 1971 synod of bishops statement, *Justice in the World* (*Justitia in mundo*), the bishops noted that they had "listened to the Word" that they might be led to understand how they might be converted to bring the gospel of justice into the world. The relationship of Word and world led them to realize that faith demands action on behalf of justice in the world to make it reflect the original vision of God (JM, introduction).

Contemporary Understanding

Perhaps the classic study probing the possible ways religion and society issues have been and can be discussed is H. Richard Niebuhr's *Christ and Culture.* The possible dynamics can be organized around parallels of (1) Christ against culture (typified by Tertullian), wherein every phase of culture falls under the indictment of the gospel; (2) Christ accommodating to culture (as in Gnosticism), wherein a kind of civil religion dominates; (3) Christ above culture (in a synthetical, dualistic, or conversionistic approach) but whose interpenetration is found in the conciliar documents; (4) Christ and culture in paradox (as in the dualism of Paul's letters, Augustine, and Luther); and finally, (5) Christ the transformer of culture (as held by Niebuhr himself).

The Christ-culture relationship receives further need for clarification when considering the actual dynamics between the sacred and secular and the faith and justice spheres. This has been necessary in a special way in the West where increased secularization and technological progress has challenged basic assumptions regarding the notion of the sacred and where many people of "faith" are threatened by the demands of biblical justice.

Given the rise of secular progress, social critics such as Auguste Comte and Karl Marx envisaged religion replaced by science. Even Max Weber, who believed that the prophetic and charismatic dimensions of religion could transform society, ultimately believed that technology would gradually make religion meaningless.

While the overwhelming majority of people in the United States profess faith in a personal God, the translation of that faith in the form of lay support for positions held by church leaders on justice issues (especially related to race and economics, war and peace) indicates the present way secularization has come to dominate the sacred. Furthermore, with contemporary atheism effectively expressed in religious indifference even among professed believers, whether or not the sacred has not been brought under the domination of the secular is open to question.

See also ATHEISM; CREATION; DISCIPLESHIP; JUSTICE IN THE WORLD; KINGDOM OF GOD; POLITICAL THEOLOGY; POLITISÉS CHRÉTIENS; SPIRITUALITY.

Bibliography: H. Niebuhr, *Christ and Culture* (New York: Harper Torchbooks, 1951).

MICHAEL H. CROSBY, O.F.M. CAP.

SANGNIER, MARC (AND SILLON)

Marc Sangnier was a radical social Catholic leader, and Sillon was the movement he created in France (1894). The man himself (1873–1950) was a pious and mystical Catholic from the prosperous French middle class. Well educated within the privileged French school system, he was destined to a life of comfort and success. Instead he experienced a mystical call within a group of young men at the Collège Stanislaus, the school he was attending before becoming a privileged *polytechnicien.* Out of this tiny handful of young men was born the Sillon movement, which Sangnier led into the world in the name of social transformation. He called for "the reconciliation of Christ and the people, of Catholicism and the suffering of the revolutionary masses" (quoted in George Hoog, *Histoire du Catholicisme Social en France,* 1946). At the time France was divided deeply in its social and political life between the anticlerical Third French Republic and a monarchically inclined Catholic church conservatively defensive of its former privileges and resolutely against the democratic traditions of the French Revolution.

It was Sangnier's vision and the genius of Sillon to break from this church-state impasse and face religious and social issues from a radically different perspective. Rather than serve Christ in a battle between two elites, he led his movement into a grass-roots approach that challenged both the ecclesiastical and republican establishment. "We must reconquer French public opinion for Christ," he affirmed, over against the church's notion that France was a Christian nation stolen by a band of ruthless Republican politicians. Though he was devoted to Republican democracy, he was critical, nonetheless, of a government that he felt was elitist and did not "allow the workers to . . . defend their interests by favoring the development of unions" (*Eveil Démocratique,* November 1, 1908).

Sangnier was as good as his word. He plunged the Sillon movement into a number of activities that threatened his more conservative Catholic colleagues, even those involved in social Catholic projects. The monthly review *Le Sillon* and especially the weekly newspaper *L'Eveil Démocratique* advocated Christian solidarity with the working class along the lines of what later generations would call democratic socialism. In contrast to other Catholic progressives in France, Sangnier and his Sillon promoted independent trade-union movements of a nonconfessional and radical nature. Sillonists tended to avoid Catholic unions because of their class collaborationism and social paternalism. Instead they joined the more militant Confédération Générale du Travail. Sillon's popular universities, dialogue with Marxists, cooperatives, and increasingly leftist political activities enhanced its reputation of Catholic radicalism.

These advanced positions were costly to both the organization and its charismatic leader. Attacks by right-wing Catholics and the anti-Semitic Action Française soon bore fruit in Rome. After the passage of the church-state separation bill in 1905, an increasing number of French bishops turned against Sillon. On August 25, 1910, Pius X promulgated a decree condemning the organization. Loyal to his church, Sangnier closed down Sillon, but like a phoenix from the ashes, both Sangnier and his views took wing. He continued his social-democratic and peace work in France until his death in 1950. The ideas that inspired his life bore fruit within French Christian Democratic parties and in the specialized Catholic Action movements of the interwar years. Sillonist values once condemned would become common wisdom in Catholic social teaching after World War II and the Second Vatican Council.

See also CATHOLIC WORKER, THE; CHRISTIAN DEMOCRACY; CLASS STRUGGLE; LABOR AND CAPITAL IN CATHOLIC SOCIAL THOUGHT.

Bibliography: J. Caron, *Le Sillon et la démocratie chrétienne, 1894–1900* (Paris: Plon, 1967). M. Barthélemy-Madaule, *Marc Sangnier* (Paris: Seuil, 1973). O. Arnal, *Ambivalent Alliance,* (Pittsburgh: Univ. Press, 1985). C. Breunig, "The Condemnation of the Sillon," *Church History* 26, (September 1957) 227–44.

OSCAR COLE ARNAL

SCRIPTURE, USE OF IN CATHOLIC SOCIAL ETHICS

Critical reliance on biblical materials marks a fundamental change in the method of Roman Catholic moral theology. No longer the most neglected source of moral theology, Scripture increasingly grounds discussions of moral questions in the gospel and person of Jesus Christ. While this renewal began in the 1940s in the work of Fritz Tillmann and Bernard Häring, the Second Vatican Council mandated this change from the philosophical argumentation of traditional moral theology. The 1970s and 1980s saw the emergence of theologies of liberation and narrative theology that make extensive appeals to biblical symbols and stories. "Proof-texting" that used Scripture as a garnish for arguments entirely derived from natural law and tradition is less common, even in magisterial documents. Finally, a more biblical moral theology has opened up greater collaboration with Protestant Christian ethics.

These developments raise particular problems for incorporating Scripture in moral reflection. Accordingly, we will examine the question of sources, the problems of interpreting an ancient text authoritatively for today's world (hermeneutics), the challenge of narrative and liberation theologies, and the difficulties these developments pose for a universal rational ethics. Then we will examine different models for analyzing how theologians use Scripture. In all of these dimensions we will investigate the role of Scripture in ethics rather than the moral teachings in the biblical text. (For the latter, see Schrage.)

Sources of Moral Theology

Theological reflection on moral questions, whether personal or social, arises from four sources: Scripture, tradition, philosophical ethics, and the empirical data relevant to the issue. All four are indispensable. *Scripture* portrays Christian identity in the community's foundational document and testifies to the divine reality to which it responds. In order for Scripture to be morally authoritative, we must normally presume a community of faith loyal to its ethos (Kelsey). *Tradition* represents the accumulated wisdom of the community in living the gospel. It includes major theologians, saints, and prophetic voices, along with official church teaching. *Philosophical ethics* incorporates the best rational accounts of human value and obligation. Although natural law had dominated Catholic moral theology from the Council of Trent, personalism, responsibility ethics, and Kantian universalism have become more common since Vatican II. It is difficult to point to a well-defined method in recent Catholic social ethics; even papal documents blend social analysis, prophetic critique, natural-law principles, and personalist argumentation. *Empirical data* from the social, biological, and personality sciences provide the descriptive foundation for normative reflection guided by the other three sources. As part of its descriptive task moral theology must gauge the ordinary experience of people affected by the moral issue under consideration.

There is no fixed formula for combining these ingredients into a balanced moral argument. On some questions one source will be more illuminating or determinative than another; nevertheless, a complete moral argument will ignore none of the sources. Unlike the theology of the Reformation that proclaimed *sola Scriptura,* Catholic theology's conviction that God's intentions structure the natural order enables moral theologians to place confidence in nonbiblical ethics and empirical data. Its ecclesiology allows it to appeal readily to church tradition. Indeed, natural law and tradition have so monopolized Catholic moral reflection since medieval times that it has virtually ignored Scripture. A highly rational system divorced from history that deduced courses of action from universal moral principles left little room for biblical symbols and stories. The early papal social encyclicals moved quickly from a doctrine of creation and hierarchical order into natural-law prescriptions; in contrast, Protestant Christian ethics found moral guidance in Scripture and personal experience while playing down both tradition and ethics. The great challenge for moral theology today is how to combine the renewed interest of Catholics in the authority of Scripture, empirical data, and experience with philosophical ethics and tradition. Protestant Christian ethics, which is rediscovering the normative function of tradition and ethical thought, becomes a necessary conversation partner for a revised moral theology.

Ideally, the sources of moral reflection should complement one another and mutually correct one another's limitations. Scripture can exercise authority without being the exclusive repository of moral wisdom; it is unique but not absolute. When moral theology incorporates the full range of sources, it no longer confines itself to the application of norms to cases; it must expand its scope to include the development of the Christian person in community and the transformation of social institutions in light of the Gospel. This broader method will discover that every type of biblical literature has a moral function, not only its prescriptive texts. Even though the metaphor of law has dominated Western moral theology since Augustine (the divine lawgiver, eternal laws, obedience, exceptions, etc.), Scripture provides many other images of moral response that should nullify the temptation to legalism.

Hermeneutical Challenge

How should we move from a text composed in several cultures at great distance from our own to address the moral questions of our time and place? While historical-critical studies can determine what the biblical text meant, they cannot tell us what it should mean for us. For this conversation with the text we turn to hermeneutics, that is, critical interpretation of authoritative texts. This turn forces us to acknowledge that we bring presuppositions and specific interests that inevitably shape our reading of Scripture. Since "there is no innocent eye" we cannot achieve a neutral or exhaustive reading of the text. The concerns we bring to the text serve as lenses that highlight certain dimensions and obscure others (Ogletree, pp. 15–45).

Self-critical awareness of our own perspective (confessional commitments, social location, class, gender, race, nationality, etc.) can prevent this "hermeneutical circle" from becoming a vicious one. If the reader merely seeks to find biblical support for moral positions arrived at on other grounds, Scripture no longer functions as an authoritative source. Often the concerns that prompt the recourse to Scripture, such as a commitment to liberating the oppressed, arise from a biblically informed perspective. Even in these cases, Scripture should always be a two-edged sword that can challenge the reader's presuppositions. (Some liberation theologians dispute this point, as we shall see.) The "fusion of horizons" between reader and the way of life embodied in the text does not always occur smoothly (Ogletree, pp. 3–4, 147–48). For instance, does the eschatological framework of the NT make the Gospel's urgent demands an "interim ethic," applicable only for the short period before the Lord would come again? Or should Paul and Mark's eschatological urgency still speak to us today?

Vatican II endorsed the priority of the original meaning of Scripture over other ways in which it can be interpreted. It validated historical-critical methods for establishing the original meaning, that is, what it meant to the original audience. That meaning, however, does not exhaust the text's potential. When new questions are posed to the text, it yields insights that were latent in the original setting. For example, a feminist theological reading discovers that Gen 1 and 2 portray male and female as created equal in dignity. This inference is grounded in the literary presentation, whether the original author-redactor realized it or not. The egalitarian conclusion follows the trajectory of meaning set by the Genesis account.

When we begin to interpret biblical texts as products of specific communities, we cannot take them as advice to individuals. The text mediates between four principals in the hermeneutical conversation. At one pole stands the faith community that produced the text and the world represented in the text (the social, economic, political forms of the time); at the other stands the contemporary faith community and its own "world."

Recent studies of the social setting of the NT insist that more careful attention be paid to the economic and sociological character of the various communities that produced the canonical traditions. Lisa Sowle Cahill describes the "hermeneutics of social embodiment" favored by Wayne E. Meeks: "It investigates the patterns of interaction between biblical narratives and their generating environment, then seeks appropriate recapitulations of such patterns in the contemporary church" (Cahill, p. 40). Faced with today's moral tensions, a given faith community should investigate how NT communities fashioned a Christian approach to the particular economic and social world they inhabited. Their strategies are not timeless archetypes for replication but historical prototypes that serve as imaginative models for future generations (Schüssler Fiorenza, 1984, p. 14).

Today's communities move by analogy to novel but faithful practices that respond to the social institutions of this world. They must choose which biblical patterns to emulate according to normative reflection based upon the other moral sources. Social structures that deprive people of dignity and the means of survival pose a perennial challenge to Christian communities. In this fourfold conversation of social ethics the locus of moral discernment is always communal. The connection between what the text meant morally and what it means today must be the community. NT mandates to achieve justice by almsgiving or to practice nonviolence must become enacted in "coherent social embodiments of a community formed by Scripture" (Cahill, p. 43).

This historical approach argues that NT commands that have been taken to be general Christian mandates were often addressed to more specific audiences. Luise Schottroff holds that the command of Mt 5:44ff. to love the enemy was addressed to Christians under persecution: "For in a case like this the love of enemy is an attitude adopted by groups which have no legal means of redress as the rest of society does. . . . The strong can show love and compassion for the weak and *vice versa,* but love of the enemy is practiced by the weak toward the strong. Only those who are involved in resistance can teach this or demand it" (Schottroff, p. 13). Matthew's command, therefore, provides no basis for those in power to recommend nonviolence to the oppressed. One can argue that love for the enemy is a general mandate for Christians, but on other grounds than Mt 5.

The OT with its concerns for social and economic order, justice, and relations between the powerful and the weak forms a necessary background to the ministry of Jesus and the moral stance of the earliest Christian communities. Often it pays more detailed attention to social strategies, from the case law of the Holiness Code (Exod 20–22) to the cancellation of debts in the Jubilee Year (Lev 25:8–55). The predominant emphasis differs, as Stephen Charles Mott explains: "In Old Testament social ethics economic deprivation is the central concern; in the New Testament status is the key to social ethics" (Mott, p. 234).

Liberation Theologies and Narrative Theology

The most creative challenges to mainstream moral theology during the past two decades have been liberation and narrative theologies. Beginning with Gustavo Gutiérrez's seminal *Theology of Liberation* in 1971, this movement has given expression to the aspirations of Third World peoples, African-Americans, and First World feminists. It advocates an explicitly partisan reading of Scripture. Only those committed to the liberation of oppressed peoples can correctly hear the Word of God because God's cause is human liberation. Genuine faith is pragmatic and performative, since only those who do the Word of God can comprehend it. Consequently, theology does not consist of revealed truths but critical reflection upon praxis. The truth of a theological position is found in its practical transformative potential. Third World liberation theologians usually focus on the Exodus event and the ministry of Jesus to the poor and outcast as the paradigms for Christian practice. Unlike the advocates of the social gospel in the early 20th century, these theologians are generally less willing to identify the transformation of social structures with the advent of the kingdom of God.

Feminist liberation theologians apply the hermeneutics of suspicion to the biblical text itself and discover considerable material that oppresses women. The male-centered perspective of biblical authors ignored women's experience, and sexist institutional arrangements endorsed in

Scripture contributed to their oppression. Some feminists reject the canonical Scriptures as hopelessly biased; others concentrate on the stories of women in the text; others cite larger doctrinal themes to support the struggle for justice.

Elisabeth Schüssler Fiorenza rejects these approaches. She does not select a "canon within the canon," that is, certain portions of the text to function authoritatively. Instead, she holds that women's struggle against patriarchal oppression is itself the norm for interpreting Scripture. "The personally and politically reflected experience of oppression and liberation must become the criterion of appropriateness for biblical interpretation and evaluation of biblical authority claims" (Schüssler Fiorenza, 1983, p. 32). It is not immediately clear whether "experience" means a perspective, a criterion, or an ideology here. Does it mean that Scripture, tradition, and moral philosophy have no authority for Christian ethics or that any appeal to them that furthers the oppression of women is invalid? Even on the latter account, women's human dignity serves as an absolute value that cannot be compromised. No combination of the other moral sources should negate a fundamental human value. However, if feminist theologians dispense with whatever fails to advance the movement, they may jettison material that would challenge present strategies or prove helpful at a later date. Witness how some Third World liberation theologians are turning from Exodus to Exile as a more instructive paradigm for enduring under systems of oppression that remain entrenched.

Richard B. Hays replies to Schüssler Fiorenza, "The Bible's perspective is privileged, not ours." Since it forms the fundamental source for Christian identity, Scripture has a hermeneutical priority that "by no means excludes exceedingly serious consideration of other sources of wisdom, but it assigns them an explicitly subordinate role in normative judgments" (Hays, p. 51). A liberationist might reply that the commitment to the perspective of the poor brings us into line with the original perspective of Scripture. A feminist might respond that the locus of moral reflection is the community of "Woman Church," hence the common struggle against oppression forms its identity more than Exodus or other biblical symbols. The question of sources then remains: are tradition and moral philosophy so patriarchal that they too lose normative status?

Narrative theologians challenge the prevailing emphasis in moral philosophy on universal obligations and their application to individual behavior. Many ethicists accept Immanuel Kant's requirement that for an obligation to be *moral* it must bind any rational agent who faces a similar problem. This paradigm produces an "ethics of doing" that focuses on specific actions and relevant rules while it ignores an "ethics of being" that concentrates on character and motivation (Birch and Rasmussen). It treats covenant ethics, the way of Christian discipleship, and the example of Jesus as too particular to ground a rational, "universalizable" ethics. At best they are examples of more general principles and values.

Stanley Hauerwas attacks the Kantian paradigm by insisting that all virtues are "narrative-dependent," that is, they draw their meaning from the fundamental stories of specific communities. Universal rules set outer limits on moral action but cannot instruct us on what to do within the limits. They cannot form the moral vision and character of moral agents. (The "universalist" would reply that rational accountability does connote a moral vision.) For character formation to occur, according to Hauerwas, there must be communities that exemplify a way of life and conform their members to behavior faithful to that way. The key to this formation of community is story: "The narrative of scripture not only 'renders a character' but renders a community capable of ordering its existence appropriate to such stories. Jews and Christians believe this narrative does nothing less than render the character of God and in so doing renders us to be the kind of people appropriate to that character" (Hauerwas, in Curran and McCormick, 1984, p. 260). The Christian community inculcates a particular "ethics of being" that often conflicts with the various secular stories that surround it. As Matthew's Sermon on the Mount shows, the Christian story insists that *how* we act (motivation, intention) is even more important than *what* we do.

Some narrative theologians follow the lead of H. Richard Niebuhr in *The Meaning of Revelation* and hold that personal identity requires a story; to be an integral self one needs a coherent historical image of the evolving self. Christian conversion occurs when we take the Gospel story as the pattern for our lives and begin to interpret our histories on its terms. The memory of Jesus then becomes "the Rosetta stone" that helps us decipher our experience to discern God's action within it and respond appropriately.

Critics of narrative theology reply that rules and principles play an indispensable role in moral reasoning. James F. Childress points out that biblical stories may alert us to recognize moral obligations but they do not constitute them. Fairness obliges human beings whether or not they read Scripture. Moral justification requires that we be able to give publicly intelligible reasons for our actions by referring to consequences and common moral standards. When appeals to biblical narratives do not make sense to those outside the Judeo-Christian tradition, ethical discourse fails in its role of justification. Furthermore, an aversion to legalism may blind narrative theologians to the considerable body of rules and principles found in the Scriptures (Childress, in Curran and McCormick, 1984, 276–88).

Paul Nelson argues that narrative is necessary but not sufficient for Christian ethics. Necessary because it captures a specific way of life and forms personal identity. Insufficient because some appeal to more general human moral standards and values is indispensable for addressing problems not envisioned in the text and for keeping believers accountable to a larger public than their own circle. Second, Scripture contains narratives that cannot be harmonized, and selection must be made among them on grounds other than narrative. Finally, even stories that are central to Scripture can be interpreted in different ways and used to back diverse moral strategies of action (Nelson, pp. 149, 128).

A Distinctive Christian Ethics?

These new approaches to Scripture and ethics raise the most widely debated question in fundamental moral theology since the council: Is there a distinctive Christian ethics? Traditional moral theology did not need to refer to Scripture for moral insight. Natural-law theologians echoed Thomas Aquinas: The new law of Christ does not add any new values or obligations to the human morality inscribed in the human person through God's creation. Because sin disorders our desires and clouds our judgment, Scripture and tradition remind us of what we are called to as human beings.

Recently, most Catholic moralists have interpreted human standards as autonomously valid and not dependent on religious warrants. Scripture provides motivation for moral living through its paraenesis, or exhortative appeals, but it adds no new content to natural rules or principles (Bruno Schuller, in Curran and McCormick, 1980, pp. 208–21). A fundamental Christian intentionality orients the moral act to God without altering common human structures of obligation. Even the hard sayings of the Sermon on the Mount do not impose any additional obligations on Christians (Josef Fuchs, in Curran and McCormick, 1980, pp. 5–16, and Daly, pp. 68–73, 90–97). This "autonomy school" rests on the conviction that ethics must be universal and consequently not dependent upon any particular revelation. Its proponents insist that reliance on Scripture for moral argument runs the risk of cutting Christians off from dialogue and practical cooperation with people of good will in secular society.

It appears that a definition of moral philosophy on strictly universal lines minimizes the testimony of the other sources of moral theology. It is one thing to argue that Jesus' command to "take up your cross" exhorts Christians to accept the self-renunciation that a committed life requires. However, does the rest of the sentence, "and follow me," not add a specifically Christian definition to that self-renunciation? Vincent MacNamara argues that motivation and content cannot be neatly distinguished because *why* we act enters into the meaning of *what* we do (MacNamara, pp. 104–7). Even at the level of moral rules Christians are obliged to do actions that may not be compelling or even intelligible to reasonable nonbelievers. He cites Gospel imperatives to practice nonviolence, detachment from worldly security, voluntary poverty, and renouncing one's legitimate claims in deference to others as distinctively Christian moral obligations (MacNamara, pp. 120–45). Others may agree with Christians on a moral practice but on different grounds. While both Mohandas Gandhi and Dorothy Day practiced similar strategies of nonviolence, the background beliefs and distinctive motivations from their respective religious traditions were so intertwined with the practices that they make them different forms of nonviolence.

A basic disagreement over the definition of truth underlies this dispute. The autonomy school holds that a statement must be logically necessary and universally valid (within the limits of moral knowing) to be true. Proponents of a distinctive Christian ethics define truth as that which discloses meaning and can transform the situation of action. They reject the Enlightenment quest for universally valid truths in favor of a sense of meaning based in a particular community. Living the Gospel proves its validity: "No secondary process of abstraction is required in order to make the ethical 'content' of these stories accessible to the community; rather, the stories themselves become the framework in which we understand and measure our lives" (Hays, p. 50). The challenge faced by such communities is how to live faithfully without ignoring other sources of wisdom such as scientific truth and historical experience. They cannot forget that Jesus in the Gospels taught in parables drawn from common worldly experience.

On the other hand, the autonomy school needs to attend to the basic pattern of biblical moral reasoning, which usually moves from the *indicative* (what God has done) to the *imperative* (how we ought to respond). "If we live by the Spirit, let us walk by the Spirit" (Gal 5:25). The moral imperative, therefore, cannot be detached easily from the indicative of faith. Believers do not deduce moral claims from narratives and doctrines by strict logic; the process is usually more imaginative and prudential. They discern actions and dispositions that are coherent with God's self-disclosure in Scripture by using imagination and analogical reasoning. The common biblical command "Go and do likewise" mandates just such discernment. Believers who have experienced the reality of God expressed in the "indicatives" should recognize the authority of biblical imperatives. Because the gift defines and motivates the call, content and motivation are inseparable.

James Gustafson describes the formal pattern of this ethics of imitation and response to God that runs through Scripture: "God has done *a, b,* and *c* for the well-being of the human community and the whole creation; those who have experienced the reality of God's *a, b,* and *c* are moved and required to do similar things for others"

(Gustafson, p. 115). An ethics faithful to Scripture must maintain the priority of the revealed reality (the indicative, the gift) to morality (the imperative, call, and response).

Philosophical approaches that reduce moral reflection to the rational justification of specific acts minimize the illuminative role of Scripture. For example, "turn the other cheek" (Mt 5:39) is not a primitive attempt at a concept of nonretaliation but a vivid picture-ideal. Neither a direct action guide nor a universal principle, it functions, through the imagination, as a firebreak for angry reactions. It urges Christians to seek acts harmonious with its image. This picture-ideal gains authority for the believing community from its coherence with key elements of the larger story (the Servant Songs of Deutero-Isaiah and the nonretaliation of Jesus in the passion accounts) as well as from personal recollection of God's forbearance and forgiveness.

Christian moral discernment seeks actions that fit and harmonize with a particular worldview. Curiously, the universality or generalizability of Scripture may depend more on images that cross cultural barriers than on abstractions that attempt to transcend them. James Fischer states a basic conviction for applying biblical images to decision making: "It is presumed that most decision-making arises out of images more than out of abstract reasoning. . . . It proceeds from a nondiscursive awareness, decision, commitment" (Daly, p. 289). When we examine how Scripture actually functions in moral reflection we must expand the scope of ethics to include convictions, dispositions, and imaginative models as well as norms and principles. An ethics of universal principles and rules artificially restricts the contribution that biblical materials can make to the moral life.

Although the discovery process of discernment comes first, justification of one's decisions is still necessary. Even those who favor a distinctive Christian ethics must be willing to show that their conclusions are valid and consistent. The larger Christian community and tradition are the context for a "public" testing of one's moral judgments. The reflective Christian should be able to explain to the rest of the community the stories, beliefs, symbols, and the like that were ingredients in the decision. In addition, it should usually be possible to offer a plausible if not always persuasive rationale to those outside the community.

Constructive Proposals

We will now examine some recent proposals for using Scripture in moral argumentation. James M. Gustafson made two major proposals in the 1970s. In the first he analyzed the debate over the morality of the U.S. invasion of Cambodia in 1970 and showed how Scripture could have a bearing on each of the components of the discussion. Not only do theologians turn to Scripture for moral rules, principles, and ideals, they also use it to determine broader issues: the structure and meaning of historical processes, the motives and intentions of agents, the circumstances and consequences of action. He concludes that "Scripture *alone* is not the final court of appeal for Christian ethics. Its understanding of God and his purposes, of man's condition and needs, of precepts, events, human relationships, however, do provide the basic *orientation* toward particular judgments" (Gustafson, in Curran and McCormick, 1984, p. 176). The community is called to discern what God enables and requires; Scripture informs and guides this discernment without dictating its outcome.

Later, in *Can Ethics Be Christian?* Gustafson continues to focus on the formation in community of "the sort of person" the Christian moral agent should be. He describes three main ways in which Scripture functions:

1. It provides the reasoning heart with *convictions about God that shape distinc-*

tive moral dispositions. Christian faith has particular "reasons of mind and heart for being moral" based on the attributes of God's character that emerge in biblical traditions. Each major aspect under which God was experienced (creator, the one who led the people out of slavery, sovereign Lord, the one who exhibits steadfast love and mercy, etc.) informs and shapes a correlative disposition (dependence, gratitude, obedience, loyalty, hope, repentance, etc.). Insofar as Christians today find that those images are compelling because they illuminate their experience of God, they will continue to shape their moral dispositions. Because these senses renew and direct moral seriousness, they give believers distinctive reasons for being moral.

2. The believer who seeks to interpret the significance of present opportunities and problems turns to Scripture for *symbols and concepts that will illumine the situation.* Biblical symbols such as Exodus, Exile, Cross, and Resurrection provide lenses through which believers examine the flow of events to discover how to respond to God. "Some symbols and concepts that are used are decisive in highlighting the moral significance, and thus determine, at least in part, what values are at stake, what attitudes are fitting, what principles ought to govern action in particular occasions, and what means of action are appropriate" (Gustafson, p. 118). Here Scripture plays a more illuminative than prescriptive role. The events and symbols are paradigms for responding to God's actions, not universal principles.

Gustafson discusses H. Richard Niebuhr's use of the symbols of divine judgment and the cross to interpret what God was doing in World War II, especially in the sufferings of the innocent. He does not agree with Niebuhr that we can detect God's action and respond to it directly. Instead, the appropriate question to ask is, What is God enabling and requiring us to be and to do in these circumstances? Recent Catholic social teaching that encourages believers to examine the signs of the times "in light of the Gospel" seems to have this illuminative discernment in view but fails to explain it with the clarity of Niebuhr or Gustafson.

A problem of control arises from the polyvalent character of symbols. The same symbol can point in different directions. Does Exodus and its portrayal of God as liberator indicate that the oppressed should revolt or simply pack up and depart from their own Egypt as the Israelites did? Other theological doctrines, moral principles, and factual considerations need to be weighed as reasonable controls on the guidance offered by symbols. Is the symbol chosen only as rhetorical support for a course of action derived entirely from other sources? Is it central or peripheral to the canon? Is it consonant with the story of Jesus Christ? Does it measure up to ordinary human moral standards? Does it illuminate the actual circumstances of action?

3. Finally, Scripture grounds *religious beliefs from which practical reflection infers norms of conduct.* Members of a community that experiences "with compelling clarity" the love of God manifest in the self-giving of Jesus in the crucifixion should reasonably infer a special obligation to service. Those convictions form the premises of a principle of Paul's ethics that goes beyond ordinary human obligation: "Let no one seek his own good, but the good of his neighbor" (1 Cor 10:24). What may be moral ideals for some people become obligations for Christians "to be engaged in costly actions of resistance to unjust and repressive social institutions, to costly participation in struggles to achieve greater distributive justice in society" (Gustafson, p. 165).

Having examined the dialectic between experience and theological reflection that appeals to Scripture, we will now propose a way to analyze ethical texts that use Scripture. The process of moving from any classic text, including Scripture, to the world of the reader necessarily involves three distinct but related moments. These moments provide a framework for analyzing how a theologian uses Scripture. First, *what* classic is selected, or what portions of the text are focused upon? Second, *why* has this literature been chosen? Some justification should be offered for the way in which the text is read. The author should explicate the horizon of meaning in which the text is being interpreted. Finally, *how* will the conversation with the text make a difference for the reader? We move from the classic text to action only by passing through some form of ethics. Will the reading yield moral principles, rules, ideals, values, community practices, or paradigms for dispositions? The Christian ethicist who appeals to Scripture should be forthcoming about each of these moments.

Selection. What material does the author include and what is left out? Do some genres, authors, or periods have more authority than others? Turning to Scripture as moral source is akin to consulting a library of texts spread over thirteen hundred years and several cultures. Selection is unavoidable but too often unacknowledged. Theologians need not apologize for having "a canon within the canon," but they should provide some rationale for their choices.

Biblical revelation occurs in distinctive ways through the different literary genres, as Paul Ricoeur and other literary critics point out. Prophetic discourse addresses the reader as divine self-disclosure; narrative emphasizes the foundational events as the imprint of God's action; prescriptive discourse symbolically expresses God's call and requirement for holiness; wisdom literature locates community *ethos* in the regular patterns of the *cosmos;* and hymnic discourse voices and forms sentiments responsive to the divine reality (Ricoeur, pp. 1–19). Apocalyptic, instructional discourse, myth, parable, metaphor, and gospel have been added to the list of literary forms.

In the past twenty years scholars have attempted to chart the ways in which each of these forms of discourse shapes moral consciousness. Dominic Crossan, Sallie McFague, Dan O. Via, and John R. Donahue have focused particularly on parable as the key to NT ethical vision. Parables subvert our familiar world and challenge our presuppositions about morality. Is metaphor, however, more fundamental than parable? Is the central vehicle of moral formation narrative or prophecy? Even though the different genres mutually affect one another (would narrative be complete without lyric celebration?), biblical theologians often select one genre as most authoritative.

Different *eras* within the canon may also be selected. For a classic Anabaptist the "New Law of Christ" renders the Hebrew Scriptures obsolete. Some redaction critics grant authority only to the most primitive stratum of the Synoptics. By contrast, a theologian of hope finds the center of NT morality in eschatological promise or apocalyptic vision (Ogletree, pp. 87–134). Often the post-Pauline epistles are devalued as dilutions of gospel freedom under the impetus of institutionalization.

Particular *authors* also hold primacy for some theologians. Martin Luther found the key to Christian moral life in what Paul taught in Romans and Galatians about law and gospel, while Paul is largely overlooked by liberation theologians, who prefer the prophets and Synoptic accounts of Jesus' public ministry. The high Christology and symbolic universe of John's Gospel appeal more to Roman Catholic than to Protestant ethicists.

What an author does not treat can also be instructive. For example, in Pope John Paul II's encyclical *Laborem exercens* the argument about the meaning of work flows from three verses of the first creation account in Genesis (1:26-28). The newly created male and female are instructed to multiply and subdue the earth and so to image forth God (LE 4, 25–26). No reason is given for ignoring the second account of creation in Genesis. That version describes the Sabbath rest and pictures the humans as naming the rest of creation. These two features would at least temper the vocation to "dominate" nature. According to many ecologists, that mandate has skewed Western culture's approach to the ecosystem.

The attempt to avoid selection by harmonizing divergent passages is also suspect. As Richard B. Hays writes, "Romans 13 and Revelation 13 are *not* two complementary expressions of a single New Testament understanding of the state; rather they represent radically different assessments of the relation of the Christian community to the empire" (Hays, p. 46). The theologian must choose between them for a theology of secular power or reject them both.

Finally, passages that explicitly treat a moral problem rarely exhaust the biblical testimony on the subject. One must inquire whether broader moral themes in the Hebrew Scriptures and the NT augment, qualify, or correct the specific norms that bear on the problem. While the Jesus of the Gospels has little to say about sexuality beyond an unqualified opposition to adultery, the larger themes of covenant love, service, God's fidelity to promises, forgiveness, and the redemption of the individual in community help to supplement and give a theological context to the more explicit material.

Interpretation. The *what?* question yields to the *why?* question. Why are these materials morally authoritative? Fundamental theological themes and methodological commitments now move to center stage. Basic images of God, human experience, and the world, the relation of sin and grace (or grace and nature), provide warrants for using Scripture in a certain way. David Kelsey has shown how hermeneutics at this stage depends upon use of the imagination to integrate different methods in theology. Rudolf Bultmann's view of self-constituting freedom is a different imaginative *discrimen* from Karl Barth's sovereign divine commander. Where Barth warns against evading the specific commands of the text, Bultmann suspects that literal obedience is a pretext for avoiding authentic freedom that cannot hide behind the rules.

Selection usually flows from the conceptual and doctrinal priorities that the author brings. Basic methodological options are key: Is Incarnation central to Christology, or is the Cross and Resurrection? Does the grace of Christ heal natural human inclinations or radically transform them? What image of God is central: creator, lawgiver, merciful parent, predestinating sovereign, liberator? Is the Christian community primarily a haven for the broken or an exemplary light to the world?

Recent Catholic moralists have been careful to spell out their ordering principles. In *Natural Law: A Theological Investigation* Josef Fuchs uses Jn 1, Eph 1, and Col 1 to ground natural law in Christology through the motif of incarnation. The centrality of incarnation relies in turn on Karl Rahner's distinctive configuration of nature and grace. Rahner's model of the human subject as self-defining freedom open to transcendent mystery underlies the subject-centered approach of most contemporary Catholic moral theology. Political theologian J.-B. Metz and liberation theologians question whether Rahner's transcendental subjectivity appreciates the impact that social structures have on individual consciousness or supports the moral obligation to transform dehumanizing institutions.

A more promising interpretation of Scripture's social teachings is found in the American Catholic bishops' *Economic Justice for All.* Along with the proponents of the social gospel and current liberation theologians, the bishops interpret Scripture through a social anthropology. Human dignity is realized through social solidarity; hence economic institutions are morally accountable because they set the material conditions for solidarity and human dignity (EJA 29). The bishops find in Scripture a perspective and vision of life that supports "the fundamental moral criterion for all economic decisions. . . . They must be at the service of *all people, especially the poor*" (24). This Christian vision relies on specific "focal points" drawn from the faith of Israel "—creation, covenant and community—[that] provide a foundation for reflection on issues of economic and social justice" (30). For Walter Rauschenbusch, the foremost theologian of the social gospel, human solidarity was rooted in the kingdom of God and the values that cluster around it: "the inclusion of all people, democracy, justice, brotherhood, solidarity, the law of service" (Haight and Langan, p. 110). Liberation theologians view oppression in solidarity with the poor, adopting "the perspective from below."

The bishops combine the three OT symbols with NT themes of discipleship, God's justice and kingdom, and the love command. Roger Haight and John Langan describe these themes' hermeneutical function in the pastoral letter: "These symbols and themes are shown to be intrinsic to the Christian imagination. They provide a language that helps define the Christian tradition from its origins and they serve to constitute the perspective from which it views reality" (Haight and Langan, p. 109). Material from Genesis and Exodus, the Prophets, and Luke mandate a fundamental option for the poor. "The obligation to evaluate social and economic activity from the viewpoint of the poor and powerless arises from the radical command to love one's neighbor as oneself" (EJA 87). This biblical vision of social life is joined with principles of social justice derived from tradition to yield moral prescriptions. The bishops' approach, therefore, differs from the social gospellers and liberationists in the application phase of reflection as well as in other basic principles of theological interpretation.

Application. The *why?* question in turn yields to the *how?* query. How are these texts, so interpreted, to be applied practically? Some particular form of ethics must provide the conduit from theory to practice: Scripture provides rules and principles, or values and ideals, or community practices. (Obviously, these are not mutually exclusive moral categories.) What should be the main vehicle for moral application, the graced imagination, prayerful intuition, inferential reason, or calculation of consequences? If all are employed, how do they work together?

At this juncture exegetes and theologians often take a great deal of moral philosophy for granted. Sometimes they assume that ethics is simply about norms and principles, or self-evidently about character formation, or limited to social transformation. Not infrequently the type of ethics assumed in the application determines the selection. Martin Luther's deep suspicion of legalism minimized the role of law for those who have gospel faith; accordingly, he reinterpreted the Decalogue and Sermon on the Mount as "disposition ethics." The fifth commandment is not primarily about killing but about meekness and respect for the welfare of others. If the model of ethics follows Kant's categorical imperative, biblical exhortations based on reward or afterlife are considered embarrassing concessions to prudence that are not worthy of true morality.

The Catholic bishops' statement on the U.S. economy moves through general moral principles when it applies the biblical vision to social policy. "Biblical justice is the goal we strive for. This rich biblical understanding portrays a just society as one marked by the fullness of love, compassion, holiness and peace." Historically, we require the more specific guidance "contained in the norms of basic or minimal justice. These norms state the *minimum* levels of mutual care and respect that all persons owe to each other in an imperfect world" (68). They then distinguish three forms of justice (commutative, distributive, and social) that provide the moral principles to address issues of unequal distribution of wealth, lack of participation by the powerless, and other social problems.

By contrast, the social gospellers and many liberationists often move directly from their vision of biblical justice to practical strategies. They bypass the "middle axioms" that the Catholic social teaching draws from tradition and social philosophy (Haight and Langan, p. 110). This makes their analysis less accessible to those who do not share a biblical perspective. The bishops work from the explicit assumption that believers and nonbelievers share a common humanity and appreciation of human dignity that can ground a public moral vision. Christians can legitimately use the language of human rights to spell out social obligations because the doctrine of creation gives theological warrant for this postbiblical tradition. "These rights are bestowed on human beings by God and grounded in the nature and dignity of human persons. They are not created by society" (EJA 79).

Sophisticated historical criticism has made many theologians hesitant to cite specific biblical action-guides. The broader outlines of biblical story and symbol, the paradoxical challenge of parable and metaphor, seem to travel better across the historical gulf. Universalist methods of ethics abstract a relatively timeless moral core from time-bound biblical mandates (e.g., the rational moral core of NT *agape* is "mutual regard"). Others insist that specific NT prescriptions should not be translated into common moral terms. Hays urges that NT texts should be granted authority in the mode in which they speak or be ruled to be invalid: "The interpreter should not turn narratives into law (for instance, arguing that Acts 2:44-45 requires Christians to own all things in common) or rules into principles (e.g., by suggesting that the commandment to sell possessions and give alms [Luke 12:33] is not meant literally but that it points to the principle of inner detachment from our wealth)" (Hays, p. 50). John Howard Yoder's influential book *The Politics of Jesus* derives specific strategies for Christian ethics from narrative and prescriptions in Luke as well as consideration of the household codes. This prescriptive material is interpreted through a vision of the church as resistant that is derived from imagery of the principalities and powers (Ephesians and Colossians) and "the lamb who was slain" but is victorious (Revelations).

In each of these moments we should respect the diversity of moral material in Scripture by appreciating a plurality of methods for selecting, interpreting, and applying the Word of God. Catholic social ethics still has much to learn from the ways that Protestants have integrated Scripture into the moral life. Whether the turn to Scripture and a hermeneutics based on community meaning and practice will qualify moral theology's traditional confidence about a common natural-law ethics remains to be seen.

See also COMMUNITY; CREATION; FEMINISM AND CATHOLIC SOCIAL THOUGHT; IMAGINATION, ROLE OF; LABOREM EXERCENS; METHODOLOGY, MORAL; NATURAL LAW; POOR, PREFERENTIAL OPTION FOR.

Bibliography: B. Birch and L. Rasmussen, *Bible and Ethics in the Christian Life* (1989). L. Cahill, "The New Testament and Ethics: Communities of Social Change," *Interpretation* (December 1990). R. Daly et al., *Christian Biblical Ethics* (1984). E. Schüssler Fiorenza, *In Memory of Her* (1983); *Bread Not Stone* (1984). J. Gustafson, *Can Ethics Be Christian?* (1975). R. Haight and J. Langan, "Recent Catholic Social and Ethical Teaching in the Light of the Social Gospel, *Journal of Religious Ethics* (Spring 1990). R. Hays, "Scripture-Shaped Community: The Problem of Method in New Testament Ethics," *Interpretation* (July 1990). John Paul II, *Laborem Exercens* (1981). D. Kelsey, *The Uses of Scripture in Recent Theology* (1975). V. MacNamara, *Faith and Ethics* (1985). S. Mott, "The Use of the New Testament for Social Ethics," *Journal of Religious Ethics* (Fall 1987). P. Nelson, *Narrative and Theology* (1989). T. Ogletree, *The Use of the Bible in Christian Ethics* (1985). C. Curran and R. McCormick, eds., *Readings in Moral Theology No. 2: The Distinctiveness of Christian Ethics* (1980) and *Readings in Moral Theology No. 4: The Use of Scripture in Moral Theology* (1984). P. Ricoeur, "Toward a Hermeneutic of the Idea of Revelation," *Harvard Theological Review* (January–April 1971). W. Schrage, *The Ethics of the New Testament* (1988). L. Schottroff,

"Non-Violence and the Love of One's Enemies" in L. Schottroff et al., eds., *Essays on the Love Commandment* (1978). W. Spohn, *What Are They Saying About Scripture and Ethics?* (1984). National Conference of Catholic Bishops, *Economic Justice for All* (1986).

WILLIAM C. SPOHN, S.J.

SECULARISM

Rather than a theory or ideology, secularism is a vague, profane anthropology that the U.S. hierarchy on November 14, 1947, described as "a view of life that limits itself not to the material in exclusion of the spiritual, but to the human here and now in exclusion of man's relation to God here and hereafter" (*Statement on Secularism* 2).

The source of this anthropology may be traced to the scientific discoveries of the Renaissance and Enlightenment together with the philosophical speculations they gave rise to. This new knowledge sometimes conflicted with principles related to the faith, such as the earth as the center of the universe or Moses as the author of the Pentateuch. Many theologians held that such discoveries cast doubt upon the whole of Christianity. The world of Christian faith, essentially transcultural, had become confused with the cultural values of Latin Christendom.

More important than the actual scientific discoveries was the recognition that the analytico-causal explanation of physical and social phenomena was possible. The ever-increasing growth in the understanding of nature placed the human person in an active role and led to a fundamental change in the understanding of our total environment, of ourselves as persons and as members of humankind.

The enthusiastic application to production of the new technologies made possible by scientific advances gave rise to the formal theory of secularism. In 1859 G. J. Holyoake published in London *Principles of Secularism.* To foster social and political progress Holyoake proposed a theory of natural morality without reference to a deity or future life. The resulting protest movement had a short life. The secularist mind-set persisted.

Holyoake produced his theory partly as a result of the failure of the European socialist revolutions of 1848. In that same year Karl Marx proposed another theory to realize the secularist social dream while overcoming the evil social consequences of the prevailing capitalist mode of production. In 1891 Leo XIII addressed the issue in *Rerum novarum,* which initiated the development of modern Catholic social doctrine.

The 1989 political events in China, the Soviet Union, and Eastern Europe herald the rejection from within of the most explicitly secularist movement of the modern era. A new paradigm concerning our understanding of reality is struggling to come to birth. The converging insights of physics, biology, and ecology are leading to a profound shift away from the mechanistic understanding of space and time, cause and effect, and most revealing of all, matter itself. Nature is beginning to be seen as an interconnected process of dynamic relations. A new process-philosophy is building bridges between a more subtle science and a deeper religion.

Nevertheless, the consumerist mentality and practice interacting with the dominance of technical production dulls people's sensitivity to nuclear danger, pollution of ecosystems, and massive structural poverty. Hence it leaves unquestioned for too many the prevailing secularist assumption that humanity is the master of its own destiny.

The church as community, aware that it is truly and intimately linked with humankind and its history (*Gaudium et spes* 1), is challenged to help modern humanity to discover and realize the limits of immanence and the necessity of transcendence.

See also CENTESIMUS ANNUS; ENLIGHTENMENT, THE (INFLUENCE OF); HUMANISM; MARXISM; MODERNISM; POLITICAL THEOLOGY; REASON, ROLE OF; VATICAN COUNCIL II.

Bibliography: E. Dussel, "From Secularization to Secularism: Science from the Renaissance to the Enlightenment," Concilium 7, no. 5 (1969) 45. D. Lane, *Foundations for a Social Theology* (Paulist, 1984).

CYRIL T. HALLY, S.S.C.

SECULARIZATION

The concept of secularization has been developed by sociologists in an effort to understand the interaction between specifically religious changes and general sociocultural changes that have accompanied the emerging of modern Western culture. The concept is the subject of controversy. Most definitions of secularization refer to a process by which sectors of society and culture are removed from the domination of religious institutions and symbols.

It is generally recognized that secularization is a part of the wider process of modernization, the transformation of the world as a result of knowledge dynamically translated into technology. Much of the attempt to understand change has been concerned with the replacement of communally based societies by societies dominated by formal organizations. Now there is discussion of a postindustrial, technetronic society, one shaped culturally, psychologically, socially, and economically by the impact of technology and electronics, particularly in the area of computers and information/communication.

Corresponding to secularization is the concept of sacralization, by which is understood the incarnation of the transcendent, the linking of the visible everyday world with transcendent being and order. The present theological understanding of the process of sacralization has been conceptualized as inculturation, that is, the dynamic relationship between the Christian message and cultures, the insertion of Christian life into a culture, and the ongoing process of reciprocal and critical interaction and assimilation between them.

There is little doubt that secularization stories have attained the status of public knowledge, a significant part of contemporary cultural reality. Like other myths, secularization has the capacity to become a self-fulfilling prophecy. Indeed, for some in both academia and the lay world, it has attained the status of an ideology (secularism). Some pastoral agents aggressively question the truth of the myth. Others, it renders apathetic.

In its crudest form the story of unidimensional, irreversible secularization says that industrial society produces rational persons and that rational persons reject religion. However, most sociologists recognize that secularization is a multidimensional phenomenon at both the religious and sociocultural levels. At the cognitive, or cultural and symbolic level there has been a decline of religious content in the arts, literature, and philosophy, while science has become autonomous. At the experiential level of individual consciousness, many persons understand the world and live out their lives without reference to religious interpretations in which they no longer believe. The former dominant and transcendent Christian religious system is being reduced in the process of secularization to a subsystem of society alongside other subsystems such as the educational, commercial, and legal institutions.

How is this social phenomenon to be interpreted theologically? What is the correct role of religion with regard to the functioning of society and its culture? In the OT God is totally other, intervening but apart from the world. The religion of Israel removed whole spheres of human endeavor from dominion by the institutions and symbols of an invisible order while at the same time asserting a higher transcendence. At the center of the NT is the Incarnation. God in Christ, remaining other, takes on human nature. In addition, the church established sacraments, rituals, and institutions that connect the mundane to the transcendent. There is therefore a genuinely human sociocultural autonomy that constantly demands a response to the command of Christ to render to Caesar what is Caesar's and to God what is God's.

Was there once a golden age when religion had a positive influence on human life simultaneously at the institutional, cognitive, and normative levels? Has sacralization declined? The historical record indicates that there has been a dialectic between secularization and sacralization due to the multidimensional nature of both. For example, when the church ceased to provide legitimation for the political institution it was freer to carry out its prophetic role. Persecution by the civil power has led to increased impact at the experiential level. At one time the church was in the position of maintaining external conformity of all citizens by employing coercive means. Today in most states legislation is no longer linked to a transcendental order. Hence people have to choose to live by Christian norms through a personal internalization of kingdom values. Secularization, focused on one dimension of religion, has been associated with a freedom to achieve sacralization through other dimensions of religion.

While there has never been a golden age of sacralization, neither has secularization been linear or inevitable. Nevertheless, there are no indications that religious institutions and the Catholic church specifically will ever again exercise the institutional and symbolic dominance over the mundane order, as it once did in Europe.

The modern world is characterized by ecological, economic, and communications interdependence together with philosophical, ideological, and religious pluralism. On the one hand there is remarkable numerical increase in Catholicism in the Third World and on the other an even more remarkable increase, mostly in the West, of those who claim to have no religion. The former, who are the majority, are poor; the latter, rich and powerful. One may argue that poverty is the result of lack of modernization. As a consequence the initiatives and creativity, both pastoral and theological—at present coming from the periphery and from below—will not survive, and so millions more will be removed from linkage with the transcendent. The Christian movement began at the periphery and from below. Reading the signs of the times is not easy.

In the sociology of knowledge it is taken for granted that the plausibility of views of reality—what people find credible—depends upon the social support they receive. The Christian framework in Western civilization on the eve of modern times was the all-embracing plausibility structure of Christian faith. Modern societies are characterized by unstable, incohesive, and unreliable plausibility structures, resulting in competition among worldviews and giving rise to a crisis of faith. Such relativism renders claims of universal truth implausible.

By contrast, the technetronic era of multidimensional modernity has been analyzed as a set of processes composed of contradictory but interacting tendencies. It leads to a dialectic between trends toward centralized, bureaucratically managed growth and decentralized, communally organized development. Modernity viewed thus as a dialectical process calls for new explanations and predictions regarding secularization and sacralization. New movements challenging modern culture such as the ecological, feminist, and peace movements can now be seen as protests not outside the public and bureaucratized spheres but as integral to modern societies. They are able to move them despite having originated at the margin or bottom of society. There are free spaces in modern culture for creative, persuasive sacralization.

The fundamental pastoral challenge to the membership of the church is how to shape the institution in such a way that it can be a transparent milieu for the constant action of God on humanity. The goal is not to secularize theology but to enable it to introduce the transcendent God to the secular mind of humanity. That is only possible if theological reflection refrains from the attempt to sacralize the whole of human life and recognizes that humanity can provide itself with many answers that were formerly sought from religion. The awareness of secularization is one means of attempting to shape new and acceptable plausibility structures for our contemporaries. A precondition for a real inculturation of the message is attainment by the church of internal freedom in relationship to its own historical development in premodern Western civilization. Neither defense against, nor accommodation to, but a critical and honest facing up to modernity is the challenge the secularization-sacralization phenomenon presents to the membership of the global church.

See also COMPUTERIZATION; ENLIGHTENMENT, THE (INFLUENCE OF); INCULTURATION; INDUSTRIALIZATION; OCTOGESIMA ADVENIENS; PLURALISM; SACRED AND SECULAR, RELATIONSHIP OF; TECHNOLOGY.

Bibliography: M. Azevedo, *Inculturation and the Challenges of Modernity* (Rome: Gregorian University, 1982). P. Berger, *Facing up to Modernity* (New York: Basic Books, 1977). R. Ireland, *The Challenge of Secularisation* (Melbourne: Collins Dove, 1988).

CYRIL T. HALLY, S.S.C.

SETTLEMENT HOUSES

The urban social reform movement known as the settlement house movement was begun in London with the establishment of Toynbee Hall by Anglican minister Samuel A. Barrett. Barrett intended to give students an experience of living with the poor. The movement soon spread to America. The first American settlement house was established in 1886 in New York City. Three years later the most famous settlement, Hull House, was founded in Chicago by Jane Addams and Ellen Gates Starr. By 1891 there were six settlement houses and by 1910, four hundred. The settlement houses in America were established for the most part in poor, immigrant neighborhoods and were staffed primarily by young, white, middle-class, college-educated females. The houses became educational and social centers in the neighborhoods, offering courses in English, hygiene, home economics, and the like. The settlement workers also pushed hard for social legislation such as tenement-house reform, labor reform, and legislation for the protection of women and children workers.

Settlement-house work was carried on primarily by Protestants, however non-Catholic settlement houses established in Catholic immigrant neighborhoods prompted Catholics to develop their own houses to counteract Protestant "proselytizing." Catholic houses offered instruction in the Catholic faith as well as other services. Houses were founded by women religious and by laywomen. The first Catholic settlement house, the Sancta Maria Institute, was established in Cincinnati in 1887 in an Italian neighborhood. Catholic settlement houses soon developed in most major urban centers, most notably St. Rose in New York City (1898), Brownson House in Los Angeles (1901), and Madonna Center in Chicago (1912).

See also AID; CULTURE; EDUCATION, ROLE OF; EVANGELIZATION; HOPE.

JEFFREY M. BURNS

SEXISM

Though recent 20th-century Catholic social teaching contains a number of condemnations of discrimination based on sex, those condemnations are best understood as opposing inappropriate discrimination based on sex, for social teaching has consistently demanded some social discrimination between human persons based on sex. With the exception of the U.S. bishop's pastoral letter, "Partners in the Mystery of Redemption," the term "sexism" is seldom found in Catholic social teaching, probably because it derived from the women's movement, which recognizes few, if any, legitimate social distinctions between the sexes. The direction of social teaching has been to preserve traditional understandings of the different but complementary natures of men and women, while gradually insisting that difference between the sexes need not imply superiority/inferiority, and to justify increasingly less discrimination between the sexes.

The most obvious shift in Catholic social teaching began with Pius XII. Until Pius XII (1939–58) Catholic social teaching rather consistently denied not only the sameness but also the equality of men and women and condemned those who advocated it, especially socialists and communists ("Divini illius Magistri," p. 72; "Divini Redemptoris," p. 71; "Casti connubii," pp. 549–50, 567–68). The first distinction on gender equality in social teaching was that of Pius XII between equality of dignity and worth between the sexes in the eyes of God, which he approved, and equality of power and role: "But they [men and women] are not equal in every respect. Certain natural gifts, inclinations and dispositions, are proper only to the man, or only to the woman, according to the distinct fields of activity assigned them by nature" ("Address to Girls of Catholic Action," p. 134). For Pius XII, women were meant to be mothers, were gifted with compassion and intuition but not with the discretion or discernment given to men, who were assigned the headship of the family and overall responsibility for the public realm ("Address to Italian Women," p. 285; "Le vingteinquirme," pp. 41–42). One area where Pius XII insisted on same treatment of men and women was equal pay for equal work, though in general he disapproved of women working except when necessary and taught that men and women should not be doing the same work because of the differences in their natures ("Address to Italian Women," pp. 291–92).

With John XXIII little changed. The sexes were equal in dignity but not in function; differential social treatment was necessary ("Convenuti a Roma," p. 611). John continued to stress the authority of husbands in the home and to advise discretion in assigning work to women but was more open to women working ("Ad petri cathedram," pp. 509–10; "Ci e gradito"). This is the framework for interpreting the section of *Pacem in terris* (no. 41) where John wrote with approval that women were becoming less passive in both domestic and public life and more conscious of their natural dignity. For John women's natural dignity, involvement in social life, and subordination to men's authority all fit together nicely in a complementary pattern.

"Gaudium et spes" (Gremillion, ed., p. 1081) carried forth the trend of increased approval of women's employment and involvement in cultural life and condemned discrimination against cultural participation on the basis of sex. Paul VI continued to defend women's equal right to participate in cultural, economic, social, and political life at the same time he emphasized women's and men's differences, false secular equality, and women's primary vocation to motherhood and family. His call for "prudent realism" in "the ascension of women to positions of policymaking decisions" ("Apres plus") must be interpreted in light of his understanding of women's "qualities of intuition, creativity, and a profound capacity for understanding and love" ("A tutti")—the very qualities that his predecessors felt complemented men's qualities of discernment, realism, prudence, and responsible decision making. Yet Paul also wrote, "Let us willingly vote for: 1) the recognition of the civil rights of women as full equals of men, wherever these rights have not yet been acknowledged; 2) laws that will make it really possible for women to fulfill the same professional, social and political roles as men, according to the individual capacities of the person . . . ("Ricordi antichi").

There is a clear contradiction within Paul's documents regarding women's roles (Gudorf, pp. 318–22). "Prudent realism" in allowing women social decision-making power is a far cry from women's legal access to "the same professional, social and political roles as men." The obvious reason for "prudent realism" is Paul's concern for women's role in the family.

"The Declaration on the Question of the Admission of Women to the Ministerial Priesthood" (p. 98), issued under Paul, refused to consider ordaining women but interestingly enough did not use the nature of women as a reason, instead constructing a series of historically and theologically controversial arguments from the tradition of the church.

John Paul II's teaching on sexism follows the same general pattern as Paul's. Though John Paul condemns discrimination against women, he sees woman's purpose as motherhood and calls for providing incomes for mothers at home because of children's need for the full-time presence of mothers ("Familiaris consortio," pp. 107–09; "Considerando che" 10; "Laborem exercens" 19; "I Am Pleased," p. 250; "E'guinto al termine," p. 182). John Paul understands procreation as one of, if not the, primary purpose(s) of marriage, and the primary bond within marriage as between mother and child: "What is happening in the stable, in the cave hewn from rock, is something very intimate, something that goes on 'between' mother and child. No one from outside has access to it. Even Joseph, the carpenter from Nazareth, is but a silent witness" ("Chi troviamo," p. 166).

"We should devote special care to mothers and to the great event that is peculiarly theirs: the conception and birth of a human being. This event is the foundation on which the education of a human being builds. Education depends upon trust in her who has given life.

"Motherhood is a woman's vocation. It is a vocation for all times; it is a vocation today. The words of a song popular among young people in Poland comes to mind at this moment: 'The mother who understands everything and in her heart embraces each of us.' The song goes on to say that the world has a special 'hunger and thirst' for this motherhood which is women's 'physical' and 'spiritual' vocation, as it is Mary's" ("All 'indirizzo," pp. 181–82).

This mystique and romantization of conception, childbirth, and motherhood heightens the central danger of understanding the Nativity as paradigmatic for motherhood and families. The role of Joseph as outsider in a virgin birth projects a role for husbands and fathers as protectors and material providers for a primary relation between mother and child. This is not easily reconciled with traditional teaching on the marital relationship as the central bond within families, still affirmed by John Paul in "Familiaris consortio" (FC 19, 21). For John Paul one role of the church is to urge men to remain loyal to their wives and children—"Do not abandon her!" ("Family Stability and Respect for Life," pp. 174–79)—despite their peripheral status in the familial circle of intimacy. The family they support offers them warmth and humanization not available in the public realm.

The writings of John Paul and his predecessors are open to feminist charges of sexism against women as well as reverse discrimination against men. For while the restriction of mothers to the home and exclusive care of children may be regarded as discrimination against women, the portrait of men that emerges from the writings of 20th-century popes, despite its depiction of men as rational and competent, is one devoid of capacity for nurture, intuition, compassion, and bonding (except with their mothers). The public world of men, as opposed to the domestic sphere of women, is characterized by harshness, toil, suffering, and inhumanity.

In terms of episcopal social teaching on sexism, perhaps two of the most relevant documents are the U.S. bishops' pastoral letter, "Partners in the Mystery of Redemption" (*Origins* 17:45) and the Quebec Assembly of Catholic Bishops' pastoral letter, *Violence en hèritage? Rèflexion pastorale sur la violence conjugale.* An episcopal letter on women and sexism seemed advisable in the United States after the confusion over the bishops' stance on the Equal Rights Amendment. After congressional ERA passage in 1972, the amendment required ratification by three-fourths of the states. The U.S. Catholic Conference's 1972 response was initially neutral; the bishops said that they supported justice for women but that the ERA could have far-reaching effects on such collateral issues as abortion funding and the tax-exempt status of church institutions. Since the wording of the ERA merely banned discrimination based on sex, the same language found in social teaching for over a decade, the bishops' neutrality was construed by some as evidence that earlier church statements lacked sincerity. After the ERA had failed and was reintroduced into Congress in early 1984, the United States Catholic Conference issued a report saying that unless approval of abortion and abortion funding were explicitly severed from the amendment, the bishops would oppose the ERA (May, p. 29).

"Partners in the Mystery of Redemption" not only uses the term "sexism" frequently (unlike most social teaching), but also refers to it explicitly as a sin, a much stronger stance than any since John XXIII, who tended to treat discrimination against women, like colonialism, as a modern anachronism. The series of national hearings preceding the drafting led the bishops to consider the implications of a group of celibate male church authorities drafting a teaching document on women and to incorporate many quotations of women from the hearings, arranged into two categories, "Voices of Affirmation" and "Voices of Alienation." Because the bishops attempted to speak to both those women who more-or-less affirm the status quo and those women who feel alienated by church and society's treatment of women, they were constricted in their treatment of the sin of sexism.

The November 1989 Quebec bishops' draft letter *Violence en hèritage?* focuses on domestic violence and accepts on behalf of the church partial responsibility for violence against women; the bishops assert that the church has tended to value the permanency of the marital bond above the welfare and even lives of women, so that abused wives have been counseled not to end marriages or to take action that could lead men to end marriages. The bishops also suggested that the exclusion of women from posts such as ordained priesthood has contributed to a patriarchal mentality that abets domestic violence against women. This is not only the most comprehensive church treatment of domestic violence, it is a complete reversal of the traditional claim in Catholic social teaching that the church has been the constant protector and defender of women through its teaching on marriage ("Arcanum," p. 390; "Dilette figlie," p. 367; "Address to Catholic Women's Organizations" pp. 224–25).

See also AFFIRMATIVE ACTION; FAMILY; GAUDIUM ET SPES; LABOREM EXERCENS; NATIONAL CONFERENCE OF CATHOLIC BISHOPS, CANADA; NATIONAL CONFERENCE OF CATHOLIC BISHOPS, UNITED STATES; WOMEN.

Bibliography: C. Gudorf, *Catholic Social Teaching on Liberation Themes* (Washington: University Press of America, 1980). John XXIII, "Convenuti a Roma," *Acta apostolicae sedis* 53 (1961), trans.: *The Pope Speaks* 7:345; "Ad petri cathedram," AAS 51 (1959), trans.: *The Pope Speaks* 5:368; "Ci e gradito," *Osservatore Romano* (December 8, 1960) trans.: *The Pope Speaks* 7:171. John Paul II, "All'indirizzo," *The Pope Speaks* 24; "Chi tioviamo," *The Pope Speaks* 24; "Considerando che (The Charter of Rights of the Family)," *The Pope Speaks* 29; "E'guinto al termine," *The Pope Speaks* 24; "Familiaris consortio," AAS 74 (1982) trans.: *Origins* 11:28, 29 (December 24, 1981); "Family Stability and Respect for Life," *The Pope Speaks* 26; "I Am Pleased," *The Pope Speaks* 29;

"Laborem exercens," AAS 73 (1981), trans.: *Origins* 11:15 (September 24, 1981). Leo XIII, "Arcanum," AAS 12, *Papal Teaching: Matrimony,* trans. M. Byrnes (Boston: Daughters of St. Paul, 1963) 132–34. J. May, "The Bishops and the Equal Rights Amendment," *Origins* 14:29 (January 3, 1985). Paul VI, "A tutti," *The Pope Speaks* 19; "Apres plus," *The Pope Speaks* 21; "Ricordi antichi," *The Pope Speaks* 19. Pius XI, "Casti connubii," AAS 22 (1930), trans.: W. Gibbon, ed., in *Seven Great Encyclicals* (New York: Paulist, 1963); "Divini illius Magistri," AAS 22 (1930), trans.: W. Gibbon, ed., in *Seven Great Encyclicals* (New York: Paulist, 1963); "Divini Redemptoris," AAS 29 (1937), trans.: W. Gibbon, ed., in *Seven Great Encyclicals* (New York: Paulist, 1963). Pius XII, "Address to Girls of Catholic Action, April 24, 1943," AAS 35 (1943), trans.: *Papal Teaching: The Woman in the Modern World* (Boston: Daughters of St. Paul, 1959) p. 109; "Address to Italian Women," October 21, 1945, AAS 37 (1945), trans.: *Papal Teaching: Woman in the Modern World* (Boston: Daughters of St. Paul, 1959) pp. 128–29; "Address (1957) to Catholic Women's Organizations," *Atti e discoursi di Pio XII* 3 (Rome: Instituto Missionaria, 1939–45) trans.: *Papal Teaching: Woman in the Modern World* (Boston: Daughters of St. Paul, 1959) pp. 63–64; "Dilette figlie," *The Pope Speaks* 3; "Le vingteinquieme," *Atti e discoursi di Pio XII* 4 (Rome: Instituto Missionaria, 1939–45) trans.: *Papal Teaching: Woman in the Modern World,* pp. 82–83. Quebec Assembly of Catholic Bishops, *Violence en héritage? Réflexion sur la violence conjugale* (November 1989). F. Seper, "Declaration on the Question of the Admission of Women to the Ministerial Priesthood," AAS 69 (1977), trans.: L. Swidler and A. Swidler, eds., in *Women Priests: A Catholic Commentary on the Vatican Declaration* (New York: Paulist, 1977). United States Conference of Bishops, "Partners in the Mystery of Redemption," *Origins* 17:45. Vatican Council II, "Gaudium et spes," AAS 58 (1966) trans.: J. Gremillion, ed., in *The Gospel of Peace and Justice* (Maryknoll, N.Y.: Orbis, 1976).

CHRISTINE E. GUDORF

"SIGNS OF THE TIMES"

Gaudium et spes, the aptly named Pastoral Constitution on the Church in the Modern World, promulgated by Vatican II (1963–65), begins its introductory statement with the following observation: "To carry out such a task [i.e., 'to serve the world' as Christ did, 'and not to be served' by it], the Church has always had the duty of scrutinizing the signs of the times and of interpreting them in light of the Gospel" (GS 4). The signs of the times to be scrutinized, as the rest of the introductory statement makes clear, are the main features of the modern world as characterized by profound changes in society, politics, and the moral and religious dimensions of cultural values. This broad usage of the term is consistent with Pope John XXIII's reference to such signs in his celebrated encyclical, *Pacem in terris* (1963), by which he attempts to position Catholic social teaching's traditional perspective on international relations closer to the world's own emerging aspirations toward general disarmament and economic development (PT 126–29).

To scrutinize the signs of the times in this manner was controversial at the time of the council and has remained so ever since, but for different reasons. The conciliar debates over this phrase concerned its eschatological significance in the Bible. When Jesus is quoted, for example, in Mt 16:4 as saying to the Pharisees and Sadducees, "You know how to read the face of the sky, but you cannot read the signs of the times," the signs seem to be those marking the boundary between the present age and the messianic era. Though the signs mentioned by Pope John included the threat of nuclear holocaust, there is no hint that he meant to add a sense of apocalyptic urgency or adopt a rhetoric of impending doom with reference to the problems of the modern world. Some of the council fathers, therefore, found his broad use of the term confusing and would have preferred to avoid it.

At the same time, at least one of the rejected preparatory drafts of *Gaudium et spes* took Pope John's broad understanding of the signs of the times as an endorsement of a distinctive program of theological reflection, namely, *kairos* theology. Best known to American Catholics through the early writings of the Protestant theologian Paul Tillich, this theology strongly emphasizes the revelatory significance of human history, not only in general but in the societal challenges specific to each historical epoch. To scrutinize the signs of the times, the rejected draft thus speculated, is to "hear the voice of God in the voice of Time, so that in the light of faith the vicissitudes of the present might reveal to the conscience of humanity the concrete mandate of charity." In light of later developments in theological method such an acknowledgment of the historicity of Christian faithfulness might not seem so startling. But at the time it marked a step the council fathers apparently were not prepared to take.

The final draft of *Gaudium et spes* thus opts for a reassuring though possibly incoherent equilibrium of modern and traditional themes: "Thus, in language intelligible to each generation, [the church] can respond to the perennial questions . . ." (4). The purpose of scrutinizing the signs of the times, in the final draft, is to enter into more effective dialogue with our contemporaries concerning the perennial questions of living the faith. Like so many other expressions of the council's desire to achieve consensus, this one proved to be unstable. Discerning "the signs of the times" soon came to be regarded as the point of departure for programs of critical reflection on praxis, particularly in various political and liberation theologies. Gustavo Gutiérrez's groundbreaking work, *A Theology of Liberation* (1971), explicitly links his theological method with the conciliar text and pointedly insists that *Gaudium et spes* invites "the entire People of God, especially pastors and theologians" to the church's work of scrutinizing the signs of the times (GS 44). Presumably this is why the pastoral strategy of Latin American Catholicism, and particularly the church's social ministries, can and ought to be shaped by the critical discernment of the people gathered locally in base communities.

In the immediate aftermath of the council Pope Paul VI (1963–78) seemed to accept this notion of shared responsibility for scrutinizing the signs of the times. For his commemorative letter to Maurice Cardinal Roy, *Octogesima adveniens* (1971), acknowledges that with reference to questions of Catholic social teaching, "it is difficult for us to utter a unified message and to put forward a solution which has universal validity" (OA 4). Instead, "it is up to these Christian communities, with the help of the Holy Spirit, in communion with the bishops who hold responsibility and in dialogue with other Christian brethren and all men of good will, to discern the options and commitments which are called for in order to bring about the social, political and economic changes seen in many cases to be urgently needed." Nevertheless, the Vatican's more recent but oft repeated skepticism about the *mandatum docendi* exercised by various national and regional episcopal conferences in the development of Catholic social teaching, through pastoral letters and other authoritative forms of instruction, suggests that only the Holy See is fully authorized to scrutinize the signs of the times.

Though it remains to be seen which of these perspectives will be vindicated as the appropriate interpretation of the church's new posture toward the world opened up by Vatican II, clearly Pope John XXIII's perspective has already had a profound impact on the development of Catholic social teaching. Over and above the optimism about the world that it originally meant to convey, the attempt to scrutinize the signs of the times has provoked an unprecedented inquiry into the methodology of Catholic social action, particularly at the intersection of faith and history, ethics and politics. Contextual questions that today are prominent in all postconciliar theologies of social praxis could not have been formulated, let alone answered, apart from Vatican II's heady appeal to the signs of the times.

See also ARMS RACE; CLASS STRUGGLE; DEMOCRACY; DEVELOPMENT; DISARMAMENT; EPISCOPAL CONFERENCES, CONCEPT OF; GAUDIUM ET SPES; GENOCIDE; HUMAN RIGHTS; INDUSTRIALIZATION; JOHN XXIII; LIBERATION THEOLOGY; METHODOLOGY, MORAL; OCTOGESIMA ADVENIENS; PLURALISM; POOR, PREFERENTIAL OPTION FOR; RELIGIOUS FREEDOM; TECHNOLOGY; VATICAN COUNCIL II.

Bibliography: W. Abbott, ed., *The Documents of Vatican II,* trans. J. Gallagher (London: Geoffrey Chapman, 1967). C. Curran, *Directions in Catholic Social Ethics* (Notre Dame, Ind.: Univ. of Notre Dame Press, 1985). A. Dulles, "Episcopal Conferences: Their Teaching Authority," *America,* vol. 162, no. 1 (January 6–13, 1990) 7–9. G. Gutiérrez, *A Theology of Liberation: 15th Anniversary Edition* (Maryknoll, N.Y.: Orbis, 1988). R. McBrien, *Catholicism* (San Francisco: Harper & Row, 1981). Paul VI, "The Coming Eightieth (*Octogesima adveniens*)" (Boston: Daughters of St. Paul, 1971). H. Vorgrimler, ed., *Commentary on the Documents of Vatican II, Volume 5: Pastoral Constitution on the Church in the Modern World* (New York: Herder & Herder, 1969).

DENNIS P. McCANN

SIN

This article is concerned with sin as it is treated in Catholic social thought. The key concept to be addressed is the relationship between personal and social sin and the theological problems that arise when sin is considered in this way.

Foundations

Biblical Teaching

The general sense of sin in the OT is reflected in the words *het', hatta't,* which mean "to miss the mark." Sin is a failure to fulfill an obligation. The heart of sin in the OT is the failure to live a covenantal relationship with Yahweh. This relationship is made clear in the laws of the covenant (Exod 19:4-5).

The essence of sin is not the breaking of some external code of conduct. It is a free decision of the heart in which one rejects God. Men and women express this inner rejection in sinful actions. Hence sin involves the inward decision to evil, evil with regard to God and others.

Sin offends God because it is a refusal to know God, to accept God, and to recognize God's reality and the right relationships it directs (Isa 58:6-7). Sin also harms the sinner. Since the right relationships that covenant with Yahweh directs are for the good of the person and the community, sin is an act of self-destruction. To sin is to choose to be twisted, to pretend to be something other than what one is. It is a rebellion, a denial of reality.

Sin eventually leads to a breakdown of community and society. Society breaks down because of the failure of its members. This dimension of the mystery of sin is reflected in the story of Babel (Gen 11:1-9). The NT also stresses this element of the reality of sin. In John, sin is more than a single act of the heart, a turning away from God and the truth of reality. Sin is a state or condition induced by an evil act (1 Jn 3:4). This state of alienation from God is reflected in one's alienation from one's neighbor.

For Paul sin is not only a state or condition, it is the human condition. Paul presents a world where sin reigns as a power. The individual person cannot escape this (Rom 5–8). All people are sinners through this situatedness in the world. They are sinners even though they have not sinned personally. While the Bible does not describe personal and social sin in terms of categories of contemporary philosophy, it lays the foundation for their integration in the ongoing reflection of the church.

Development of Doctrine

The development of the doctrine of sin in its personal and social dimensions is uneven in the history of the church. The earliest penitential tradition involved public penance, which stressed the social or communal aspect of the individual act of sin. The early fathers of the church taught the social responsibilities that the Christian life imposed on the believer. These sins usually involved decisions of participation or nonparticipation in various forms of pagan culture. The social responsibility of the Christian to create the "City of God" centered primarily on making personal, licit choices in the midst of a situation hostile to his or her faith (*City of God* 19.17, 21).

From the 6th century on the communal sense of sin in the liturgical tradition was less evident. Private confession put more stress on the sinful acts of the individual, the primary paradigm for sin in the theology of the church. Moral theology in subsequent centuries shifted its full attention to sin as an individual act and tended to place more responsibility for the social dimension of sin, or actions that harmed the society and community, on those who held authority (ST II-II, q. 60, 1 ad 4, II-II, q. 60). Obedience to authority was required of all others. The ongoing theological reflection on the nature of sin focused for the most part on the individual and the needs of the confessor in the sacrament of penance. It assisted him to make accurate judgments as to the degree and kind of sin of the penitent.

The Scholastic view of the human person held in the church until Vatican II also focused theological attention on the act of sin of the individual. The person was seen as a substance, a being that exists in itself, who had a rational nature. The person was understood as one who could think and make choices. Sin was defined as a deliberate act against the law of reason, which was inherent to one's own rational nature (Rigali, p. 322). Moral evil was created through free will, the ability to act or not to act and to act in one way or another. This approach to the person emphasized an act-centered rather than a relational and more biblical concept of sin. Furthermore, sin as "in the world," as influencing personal choice and creating a climate of sin affecting the community, was less visible in this moral tradition.

Social teaching from Leo XIII to Vatican II followed this Scholastic tradition. Social evil in capitalist societies was understood as created primarily by a failure of charity, the refusal of the wealthy class to have concern for the worker and the poor or to afford them their rights through a personal sense of justice (*Rerum novarum*).

By the time of Vatican II the church had begun to shift its attention from moral acts that created injustice to attention to the moral actor and the situation of sin in the world. The social dimension of sin was given new attention in the church's liturgy and its view of the redemptive mystery as it confronted new international problems (*Justitia in mundo*). At Vatican II personal sin remained the primary paradigm through which the church addressed sin in the social arena. The fact that evil structures are built up and sustained by individual choice was affirmed; however, a new recognition was given to social sin.

Ongoing reflection on sin since Vatican II involves a basic tension. Social sin is defined as (1) the social ramifications of every personal sin and (2) acts done by an individual or community that have as their object the harm of the neighbor. This includes acts of individuals, communities, and nations, the understanding being that collective sins are at root an aggregate of personal sins. This recognition is juxtaposed to an acknowledgment that social sin, after being initiated by individual choice, appears to virtually take on an independent existence in the social world, unavoidably becoming part of the individual's experience of sin (*Reconciliation* 16). How is this latter sense of sin truly sin? Is it sin by analogy? How does it share in the mysterious communion of sin in which all humanity is united? This latter question reflects a return to the tradition of John and Paul.

As the church confronts massive poverty, torture, marginalization of cultures, ecological and nuclear threat, it struggles to link these dehumanizing agents to its traditional language of sin. In the next section we will explore two aspects of this theological development: new theological currents in the language of sin and key theological problems involved in linking personal and social sin.

Toward a Language of Personal and Social Sin

Evil

The discussion of evil sets the stage for an integration of the personal and social dimensions of sin. Contemporary theology considers evil (1) as ontological reality (fact) rather than only as moral evil (evil done to another) and (2) as mystery. The mystery of evil is reflected in the fact that even though evil, or lack of what is good, is continually brought about in the world through human choice, it retains its identity as ontological evil or mystery. It is a force against which one always struggles through the grace of the redemption of Jesus Christ (*Reconciliation* 20). This struggle is never collapsed through a moral victory alone. Hence the moral struggle against sin includes but transcends the struggle between good and bad acts. It is a struggle against evil itself (*Gaudium et spes* 22, 37). While social sin is the social effect of personal sin, it shares in the mystery that evil is itself, and appears to take on a life of its own after being initiated by human choice. Baum refers to this as an experience of the demonic in the social sphere (pp. 118–26).

Original Sin

The church has traditionally claimed that the reality of original sin is made evident in the social question. No society however perfectly planned will be without the need for social reform. This is due to the nature of the human condition as described by the reality of sin. Original sin is the primordial situation of guilt in which our freedom and its history are situated and embedded. Human nature exists in a state of sin and grace prior to human choice. This fact of sin has been an essential element in the church's rejection of (1) any social philosophy that posits a utopian communal existence that can occur through a mechanical or automatic process (*Octogesima adveniens* 26) and (2) the belief that institutional and structure change without a change of heart in individuals will be effective (*Reconciliation* 16).

The situation of humanity is seen as the result of two historical events deriving from two liberties, Adam's sin and Christ's redemption (GS 22). These liberties are symbolic of the moral struggle of each person—the movement from the slavery of Adam's sin to a historical existence imbued with the grace of Christ. These events, however, are not static realities. They form the principle of each human life and society and that of the entire evolution of the universe (Segundo, p. 28ff.).

The meaning of original sin is not fully illumined by opposing it to individual avoidance of sin. It is more than an individual condition that each person tries to overcome with the help of grace. Inherent to the nature of this sin is "an unfailing situation of sin" (Segundo, p. 20). We do not confront this sin per se. All we encounter is our tendency to sin, but even this tendency is revealed to us only through the grace of redemption. Inherent to the effect of sin is blindness to its presence. In the social sphere this is manifested in communal blindness (Häring), ideological rigidity (Segundo), bias (Lonergan), and relativism (*Sollicitudo rei socialis*).

Sin of the World

This refers to the entrance into the world of the rejection of God's initiative of grace through free choice. Sin of the world is more than a sinful free act. It refers to the state of enslavement that characterizes the sinful dimension of human existence. As a structure of human existence, the sin of the world affects all human actions in a manner that is prior to human decisions.

People cannot decide whether they will or will not encounter the sin of the world. It is a given of human existence. Some manifestations of sin of the world are (1) blindness toward human actions as to their real import, (2) a system of personal or communal desires that is satisfied with less-than-human conditions in the world, and (3) a satisfaction with the lack of change in the human spirit.

This aspect of sin influences human freedom in spite of the call and gift of grace. It is the objective condition of men and women insofar as they are beings conditioned by sin (Schoonenberg, p. 20ff.). A contemporary attempt to capture this dimension of sin in its social manifestations is the notion of sin as "addiction." It is the cyclic and dead-end approach to human problem solving, which is handed on to successive generations, groups, political parties, and governments (McCormick).

Concupiscence

If sin can be understood as "missing the mark," concupiscence is the experience of the tendency to sin. As an internal human constituent it conditions every act of freedom. It is essentially the tendency to egotism. While it is a dimension of human existence, it does not define the human person. The redemptive relationship of grace always remains the stronger force in human life.

Concupiscence can function both from within and from without the human person. As a power from within, it accounts for the experience of the split in the human person between the desire to love and egotism. It is the tendency of human beings to ignore God's law of love and, alienated from God, to follow their own law, the law of their members (Rom 7:23). Coupled with this primary moral situation in which all persons share are the tendencies, defects, and habits linked with the personal condition of each human being (*Reconciliation* 16).

Concupiscence can also be seen as a force of sin that influences human behavior from without through social structures and cultural trends. Social structures are institutionalized sets of interdependent human relationships that influence social behavior and regulate the life-chances of people at a given time and place (O'Keefe, p. 34). The influence of social structures on the person was noted by John XXIII and Vatican II (*Mater et magistra* 59–67; GS 25): "When the structures of affairs is flawed by the consequences of sin, the human person, already born with a bent toward evil, finds there new inducements to sin, which cannot be overcome without strenuous efforts and the assistance of grace" (GS 25).

The Latin American bishops at Medellín recognized the sinful influence of structures as situations of "institutionalized violence" against the poor in their country. Here structures not only induce individuals to sin but discourage and seek to defeat the human spirit from seeking its full humanity. Those who are dependent on a structure for life sustenance or cultural support experience instead, through the very way the structure organizes and distributes goods and services, an affront to their basic human rights.

A sinful human structure as an anonymous social entity does not sin in itself. Rather it reflects and incarnates the sinful condition of humanity and the sinful choices of individuals. No structure can force an individual to sin, but it can make it easier to sin than to be just (*Reconciliation* 16). Hence a social structure is sinful insofar as by the way it organizes the distribution of goods, services, or power it violates human dignity in a manner that could be avoided or it facilitates and supports individual acts of selfishness.

Social structures, however, are also internalized as an individual becomes socialized (Berger and Luckmann, pp. 53–67). When the dehumanizing aspects of a culture are accepted by an individual or even unconsciously adopted as part of his or her moral horizon, social sin as a false consciousness promotes the complicity or silent acquiescence of persons in injustice and reinforces a sense of irresponsibility for the quality of social life. Lonergan refers to this as a bias, an obstruction of authentic self-transcendence that can only be overcome through conversion (O'Keefe, p. 80).

The relationship of these social and psychological dynamisms to concupiscence is reflected by an attitude of disregard of God (or ultimate matters) prior to human performance. This is translated into a system of thought and behavior that justifies injustice in human actions. These actions in turn become part of the actual condition in which all human freedom must function.

Culture can foster the human tendency to idolatrous and unjust living. More than an internal force, the tendency to resist grace can also be experienced as a social dynamism or consensus, such as is the case of racism or chauvinism. Culture can be critiqued as sharing in the moral reality represented by concupiscence to the degree its own dynamisms support egotism rather than love (*Reconciliation* 16).

Personal Sin

Personal sin is free cooperation with the forces of the sin of the world and concupiscence. It is a rejection of the inward summons by God through conscience to follow the moral call written on the heart and to live a life of love. Personal sin is always expressed in a concrete way to a person—an aspect of reality—and to the living God (Rigali, p. 326). For believers this call is also mediated through the revealed truth proclaimed by the church. Personal sin involves knowledge, freedom, and responsibility for actions one performs or fails to perform. It is precisely in rethinking the categories traditionally associated with personal sin that the theological tensions in a concept of sin that embraces both its personal and social dimensions become apparent. These tensions are around three areas: knowledge and freedom, responsibility for sin, and institutions as moral agents.

Knowledge and freedom. The moral tradition has always allowed for mitigated responsibility for sin due to ignorance. While this tradition has served well the area of personal sin, the catechesis surrounding it has also fostered a type of indifference toward social sin (Henriot, p. 42). It becomes very easy to claim ignorance of social injustice in a cultural climate that actually promotes social unconsciousness (Bellah). The theological question arises as to what degree one is responsible to become aware of social injustice as an aspect of forming one's conscience.

The question of responsibility also arises in another fashion. People can attribute all sin to social or environmental factors, thus shifting responsibility for sin to some collectivity such as the situation, the system, society, structures, or institutions (*Reconciliation* 18). This ignores the reality that people can cause or support evil in a situation, exploit it, avoid it, and even limit it. There is still a great deal of unclarity around the degree to which a social situation can or cannot be seen as an impediment, or that which lessens the guilt of personal sin.

Responsibility for sin. There is currently some debate as how to realistically appraise the nature of a sin of an individual in the creation of an evil outcome over which he or she has a limited effect. The traditional teaching on material cooperation recognized that it is impossible in a complex world to avoid all involvement with evil. Sin was assessed by whether one intended evil and by the immediacy of one's contribution to the evil outcome.

However, with greater emphasis in the Christian life on the call not just to avoid evil but to transform it, it becomes more difficult to assess sins of omission in failing to address a social situation or sins of commission in participating in an unjust action. Two main areas are involved, assessing responsibility to change a situation and assessing the power of a group over individual behavior.

One question that arises is the degree of freedom the moral agent has to have in order to be held responsible to change the situation or overcome injustice. Fuchs suggests that it may not be immediately feasible for an isolated individual to change an unjust situation. In this situation it may be necessary to cooperate further with unjust situations in order to avoid a greater evil. "In this case, such action is just, even though it includes inevitably a partial furthering of the 'sin of the world' and its evil consequences" (*Gregorianum* 61 [November 1980] 61).

Another question is to what extent the power of the group over the individual can be a mitigating factor in assessing an individual's responsibility for sin in an unjust action. A group or society can be thought of as having spiritual authority over its members. Himes argues that evil can become part of the standards of morality sanctioned by the authority of the society. A group can limit responsibility in three ways: by limiting a person's alternatives, by depriving a person of the necessary critical distance to evaluate the action, and by placing heavy internal or external pressure upon the person (p. 205ff.). Schoonenberg sees a group (1) giving bad example, (2) creating an absence of good example, or (3) being responsible for an absence of grace, which should be mediated through other persons (O'Keefe, p. 63). However, the teaching of the church holds firm to the principle that a sinful situation in itself is not a cause of sin; only individual free choice creates sin (*Reconciliation* 16). Some authors see this only as "institutionalized temptation" (Häring).

Institutions or groups as moral agents. The social teaching of the church has addressed moral guidelines to groups. It recognizes that people enter into association in order to attain objectives that each one desires but that exceed the capacity of single individuals. The question arises, can a group sin? Church teaching affirms that a situation or an institution, structure, or society is not in itself a subject of moral acts (*Reconciliation* 16).

Further inquiry regarding this matter centers around the nature of groups. If a group has no corporate identity upheld by some customary rules or a way of life that characterizes them, then it has little moral responsibility beyond that of a random collective to observe the common law. Discussion of the responsibilities of groups that do have a corporate identity fall into three areas: (1) whether its values are coherent with its tasks, (2) whether its goals are adequate to direct decisions, and (3) whether its rationality uses appropriate means for its ends (Himes, p. 210ff.).

As these questions are resolved in the future it is undeniable that further integration of sociology and theology will further illumine the limits and responsibilities of groups as moral actors and link their actions to the church's traditional language of sin.

See also ALIENATION; BLACK THEOLOGY; CONSCIENCE; EVIL, SOCIAL; FEMINISM AND CATHOLIC SOCIAL THOUGHT; FREEDOM; MORAL LIFE, CHRISTIAN; WOMEN.

Bibliography: G. Baum, *Man Becoming* (New York: Herder & Herder, 1970). R. Bellah et al., *Habits of the Heart* (Berkeley: Univ. of California Press, 1985). P. Berger and T. Luckman, *The Social Construction of Reality* (New York: Doubleday, 1966). P. Henriot, "The Concept of Social Sin," *Catholic Mind* 71 (October 1973) 38–53. John Paul II, apostolic exortation *Reconciliation and Penance* (Washington: United States Catholic Conference, 1984). K. Himes, "Social Sin and the Role of the Individual," in *Annual of the Society of Christian Ethics* (1986) 183–218. P. McCormick, *Sin as Addiction* (New York: Paulist, 1989). J. McKenzie, *Dictionary of the Bible* (Milwaukee: Bruce, 1965). M. O'Keefe, *What Are They Saying About Social Sin?* (New York: Paulist, 1990). N. Rigali, "Sin in a Relational World," *Chicago Studies* 23, no. 3 (November 1984) 321–32. J. Segundo, *Evolution and Guilt,* trans. J. Drury (New York: Orbis, 1974). P. Schoonenberg, *Man and Sin* (Notre Dame, Ind.: Univ. of Notre Dame Press, 1965).

JUDITH A. MERKLE, S.N.D.deN.

SOCIAL SECURITY

Social security refers to a society's systematic efforts to provide for those of its members who are in need. Construed narrowly, social security entails specific programs designed to insure persons against income loss, either on the job or off. For example, Americans conceive of social security as the federal, contributory, old-age insurance plan in which they are required to participate. Construed broadly, social security encompasses all of society's efforts to secure its citizens against the contingencies of a modern economy by insuring some level of income flow throughout life. In this sense, it carries the broader meaning of economic security.

The concern for social security originated with the insecurity that a wage-oriented, industrial, capitalist economy created for workers and the poor. The primary system of income distribution in this economy rested on incentive and efficient participation in the labor force. Yet this placed individuals in a precarious position. There are many contingencies associated with modern capitalist economies. Through no fault of their own, people dependent on wages for their livelihood found themselves insecure during the ups and downs of the business cycle. "Any interruption of income-flow reduced or destroyed entirely [their] ability to command goods or services" (Lubove, p. 24). The situation was worse for those unattached to the labor market such as the chronically ill, single mothers with small children, and workers with no skills. Social security began as society's attempt to rationalize the income-maintenance system. Through its social security programs society assumed some responsibility for insuring its citizens against hard times by establishing a secondary income-distribution system geared to need.

Techniques of Income Maintenance

Social security programs consist of three types: contributory, means-tested, and noncontributory non-means-tested. Contributory programs require some compulsory contribution on the part of workers, employers, government, or some combination of the three. These programs fundamentally link benefits to labor-force participation. Ideally the first program needed to provide security for the able-bodied is one that fosters maximum productive employment, preferably through stimulating the private market but also through public employment when necessary. However, when these efforts fail, and they have never been totally successful, some preventive income-maintenance programs are needed. Their purpose is to put aside income during times when work and economic opportunities are plentiful to insure against times when they are not. These programs include all social insurance schemes. Workmen's compensation insures against loss of income due to injury on the job. Unemployment insurance protects workers against the peaks and troughs of the business cycle. Health insurance pays for prohibitive medical-care costs. Old-age insurance provides for times when one is too old to work.

Social insurance programs protect those with labor-market experience. A society moves from a narrow view of social security as social insurance to a broader view of social security as economic security when it implements guaranteed-income programs for all citizens. These guarantees extend to those who participate minimally or not at all in the labor market, such as the chronically sick and disabled, single parents with small children, and the able-bodied with no skills or unneeded skills. These guaranteed-income programs include means-tested programs: people are eligible for these programs if they can demonstrate need; the guarantees stay in effect until their need no longer exists. In the United States these programs fall under the heading of public assistance, or welfare.

Unfortunately, benefits from means-tested programs have a certain stigma attached to them. Unlike social insurance benefits, which recipients consider a contractual right because of prior contribution, people view public assistance benefits pejoratively as a handout, or dole. Recipients have no right to receive them. Because of this attitude, most means-tested programs do not guarantee anything beyond a subsistence level of income. For example, while Social Security (old-age insurance) benefits in the United States have had cost-of-living increases, public assistance programs such as Aid to Families with Dependent Children (AFDC) seldom keep pace with inflation.

In light of this, many persons advocate an expansion of noncontributory, non-means-tested programs to provide a basic level of income to all families. Receiving benefits from these programs does not require prior contribution or demonstration of need but membership in a particular group or category. The clearest example of this type of program is children's allowances, which many European countries have adopted. For every child a family receives a specified income out of general revenues. Many believe that for the sake of justice some of the social insurance programs ought to fall under this heading. For example, in the United States, Social Security payments reflect one's contributions during one's working life. Those who earn less contribute less and, thus, receive less in benefits. The result is that Social Security maintains the inequality in income distribution in retirement that exists during working life. However, if society paid everyone who became elderly a set income, society would become more egalitarian.

Catholic Social Thought

Since Leo XIII issued *Rerum novarum,* Catholic social thought has focused on the negative effects that a wage-centered money economy has on the human person, especially workers and the poor. Since God has endowed all human beings with dignity, every person has the right and the duty to develop his or her life in a manner that promotes that dignity. This requires basic resources of food, clothing, shelter, health care, and the like (*Pacem in terris* 11). Ideally people should procure these resources through gainful employment at living wages "sufficient to lead a life worthy of man and to fulfill family responsibilities properly" (*Mater et magistra* 71). However, wage-centered capitalist economies have never provided all able-bodied adults the opportunity to meet their needs through work. Moreover, many people are unable to work. In these cases other individuals and institutions in society must secure the basic right to "a share of earthly goods sufficient to oneself and one's family" (*Gaudium et spes* 69).

The claim against individuals rests on the Catholic understanding of the social function of property. Those who have goods beyond what they require for their own fulfillment must share their excess with those in need (RN 19; MM 119; GS 71). The claim against institutions finds justification in the belief that promoting the dignity of the human person is "the foundation, cause, and end of all social institutions" (MM 219). If economic institutions cannot or will not provide the resources sufficient for human dignity, other institutions, including the state, must assume part of that responsibility.

Catholic social thought recognizes the potential of social security provisions for bringing about basic justice in society. According to the Second Vatican Council, "a body of social institutions dealing with insurance and security can, for its part, make the common purpose of earthly goods effective" (GS 69). Pope John XXIII felt that systems of social insurance and social security can have an egalitarian effect and "be instrumental in reducing imbalances between the different classes of citizens" (MM 136). How extensive should these provisions be? Catholic teaching understands social security in its broadest sense of economic security. Therefore, social security provisions should guarantee basic minimums in those goods and services that enable people to have a standard of living that befits human dignity.

For the security of the able-bodied, society must first "build and sustain a healthy economy that provides employment opportunities at just wages" (*Economic Justice for All* 196). Whether these opportunities are in the private sector or include some public employment, they reduce the need for other programs and allow the able-bodied to contribute to the needs of the incapacitated. In addition, society must establish social insurance programs that protect workers from deprivation due to the contingencies endemic to the labor market, such as disability, unemployment, and old age (PT 11). For the security of those unable to work, Catholic social thought calls for public assistance and other programs designed to guarantee these citizens a level of income sufficient to sustain themselves and their families in dignity and without stigma.

Finally, in answer to the question of which social agent should provide social security, Catholic social thought contends that it is the role of every individual and institution in society to attend to the basic security of each citizen in his, her, or its economic decisions (GS 70). Undoubtedly the state plays an important part in this. It is a part of the state's moral function to guarantee basic economic and social rights to all citizens (EJA 122). However, the principle of subsidiarity guarantees room for all social agents to play a role: citizens, employers, intermediate institutions, and the state.

See also COMMON GOOD; ECONOMIC ORDER; GOODS, DISTRIBUTION OF; INCOME; JUST WAGE; POVERTY; WELFARE/WELFARE STATE.

Bibliography: N. Furniss and T. Tilton, *The Case for the Welfare State* (Bloomington, Ind.: Indiana Univ. Press, 1977). R. Lubove, *The Struggle for Social Security, 1900–1935* (Pittsburgh: Univ. of Pittsburgh Press, 1986). T. Skocpol and J. Ikenberry, "Political Formations of the American Welfare State," *Comparative Social Research* 6 (1983) 87–148.

FRED GLENNON

SOCIALISM

See FASCISM; KETTELER, WILHELM EMMANUEL VON; LABOR AND CAPITAL IN CATHOLIC SOCIAL THOUGHT; MARXISM; POLITICAL PHILOSOPHY; QUADRAGESIMO ANNO; RERUM NOVARUM; SOCIALIZATION.

SOCIALIZATION

The word "socialization" has many meanings, but we can distinguish broadly between its use in political economy and its use in psychology, sociology, and developmental studies. Even within each of these circles the word is widely interpreted. Generally, for the political economist socialization is the integration of resources—industry, for example, or land or property—into a social unit. For the psychologist or sociologist it is the process by which people, especially the young, become integrated in themselves and into the family and community in which they live. The word "socialization" in any sense was rarely used in magisterium documents before the publication of *Mater et magistra*, and when it was used it was roundly condemned (Campbell-Johnston, p. 380ff.). However, even though references to socialization are comparatively recent in the documents of the magisterium, the reality behind the word has been discussed frequently since the publication of the social encyclicals of Leo XIII.

Socialization and Political Economy

Karl Marx foresaw a progressive socialization, or social ownership, of the processes of industry and manufacture through various stages, leading eventually to a classless society and the complete socialization of the productive system. This was socialization in an extreme and wide-ranging form. Usually, however, it has had a narrower meaning. It may be a nationalization of resources with or without compensation to their owners, or a form of public or semipublic ownership other than direct ownership by the state, or ownership of industry and services by public boards or corporations established and regulated by the state. The organization of a welfare state may also be considered a form of socialization. Because of this wide range of meaning as well as the fact that socialism can take many forms, one has to look carefully at the context of a reference to socialization or its equivalent in order to understand it fully. This context has changed from Leo XIII to John Paul II.

The form of socialism Leo XIII had in mind in *Rerum novarum* was Marxist. For several reasons he rejected the abolition, or socialization, of private property. Forty years later, however, Pius XI remarked that "since the time of Leo XIII important changes have taken place both in the economic regime and in socialism" (*Quadragesimo anno* 99). On the economic side, power and wealth had become concentrated in the hands of a few "who for the most part are not the owners, but only the trustees and directors of invested funds which they administer at their own good pleasure" (QA 105). Socialism, too, had changed with the emergence, alongside communism, of a more moderate form of socialism. Pius XI said that "it may well come about that gradually these tenets of mitigated socialism will no longer be different from the program of those who seek to reform human society according to Christian principles." He continued, "It is rightly contended that certain forms of property must be reserved to the state, since they carry with them a power too great to be left to private individuals without injury to the community at large" (114). A little over two decades later, Pius XII had harsh words about socialization: "The person and the family must be saved from falling into the abyss into which an all-embracing socialization tends to lead them, a socialization at the end of which the terrifying image of the Leviathan would become a horrible reality" (radio broadcast to the Congress of Austrian Catholics in Vienna, September 14, 1952, *Acta apostolicae sedis* [1952] 792).

In *Mater et magistra* (1961) John XXIII took a more open view of state intervention in society. "In the economic order," he said, "first place must be given to the personal initiative of private citizens, working either as individuals or in association with each other in various ways for the furtherance of common interests" (MM 51), but "the civil power must also have a hand in the economy" (52). He saw that there had been an increase in "social relationships" and in "mutual ties," of which a symptom and a cause are "the growing intervention of the state even in matters of such intimate concern to the individual as health and education, the choice of a career, and the care and rehabilitation of the physically and mentally handicapped. . . . This sort of development in social relationships . . . makes it possible for the individual to exercise many of his personal rights, especially . . . those which pertain to the necessities of life, health care, education on a more extensive and improved basis, a more thorough professional training, housing, work, and suitable leisure and recreation" (60, 61).

A good summary of the position of John XXIII is given by Michael Campbell-Johnston: "The few paragraphs of *Mater et Magistra* (MM 59–67) which deal specifically with socialization can be summarized briefly. After stressing that this development in society is characteristic of our times—elsewhere in the encyclical he speaks more precisely of 'the last twenty years' (MM 46)—John XXIII emphasizes that he is not describing a politico-juridical process, such as nationalization, but a more far-reaching social and cultural change which is 'the result and the expression of a natural and well-nigh irresistible urge in man to combine spontaneously with his fellows for the attainment of aims and objectives which are far beyond the means or the capabilities of single individuals' (MM 60). This tendency obviously carries with it certain dangers in the form of restrictive laws and regulations. . . . But it also brings many advantages in its train and the Pope places a strong emphasis on these, claiming that they make it possible for 'the individual to exercise many of his personal rights, especially in the economic and social spheres' (MM 61). Consequently when he arrives at the crucial question so often asked of Catholics: 'Must we conclude that an ever-increasing socialization will necessarily reduce men to the condition of being mere automatons?' he is able to reply with a firm antideterministic 'By no means' (MM 62). . . . Socialization is neither good nor evil. Its moral note depends on the particular forms which it assumes and the uses to which these are put. . . . The Pope affirms . . . man in society remains a free agent. . . . The present trend towards socialization 'is not a product of natural forces, working by some blind instinct. It is . . . the work of man who is free by nature and responsible for his action' (MM 63)" (Campbell-Johnston, p. 384).

John XXIII well understood "the insistent demands on those in authority, since they are responsible for the common good, to increase the degree and scope of their activities in the economic sphere, and to devise ways and means and set the necessary machinery in motion for the attainment of this end" (MM 54). For John XXIII the acceptable level of economic and political socialization lay midway between two extremes: the political tyranny that comes from the destruction of personal initiative and the refusal of the state to intervene when the weak need protection (57, 58). It has been suggested that Pope John's teaching in *Mater et magistra* "made a major contribution towards putting the Church on the side of the poor" (Dorr, p. 102). (For a note on the reaction to John XXIII's use of the term "socialization," see Campbell-Johnston, p. 382ff., and Dorr, p. 102ff.).

Gaudium et spes (1965), the Second Vatican Council's Pastoral Constitution on the Church in the Modern World, accepts that it is inevitable in the complexity of modern times for public authority to intervene more often in "social, cultural and economic matters" to bring about the circumstances people need in order to live well (GS 75). It goes further and acknowledges "the good to be found in the social dynamism of today, particularly progress towards unity, healthy socialization, and civil and economic co-operation" (42); and although "socialization, as it is called, is not without its dangers . . . it brings with it many advantages for the strengthening and betterment of human qualities and for the protection of human rights" (25). The degree of socialization may vary from place to place depending on a community's economic and social development (75), but in all cases intervention should be for the common good, restrictions should be minimal, and "totalitarian methods or dictatorship" can never be justified.

Later, in *Laborem exercens* (1981), John Paul II said that "one cannot exclude the socialization, in suitable conditions, of certain means of production" (LE 14.3). It may be necessary in order to ensure that the goods of the earth are available for all. However, it is not sufficient simply to convert the means of production into state property in a collectivist system. This is not a real "socializing" of property: "We can speak of socializing only when the subject character of society is ensured, that is to say, when on the basis of his work each person is entitled to consider himself a part-owner of the great workbench at which he is working with everybody else" (14.6). One way of making a worker a part owner of the workbench is by associating labor as far as possible with the ownership of capital and by producing a wide range of intermediary bodies—economic, social, and cultural—with genuine autonomy. In cooperation with each other they would pursue specific aims for the good of all, and they would be "living communities both in form and in substance" in that the members would be treated as persons and encouraged to take an active part in the life of the group (14.6).

Central to an understanding of the church's attitude to socialization is its teaching on the right to private property and the accompanying social obligations. The position of the Second Vatican Council is clear: "The right of private property is no obstacle to the right inherent in various forms of public ownership. The transference of wealth to public ownership cannot be made except by competent authority, and within the limits of the common good, as well as with fair compensation. Moreover it is the business of the public authority to see that no one abuses private ownership against the common interest. Private ownership has naturally a certain social character, founded in the law that goods are destined for all in common. If this social aspect is neglected, property often becomes the occasion of greed and serious disturbance and its opponents are given excuse to call the right itself into question. In many underdeveloped regions, there are large, even vast country estates poorly cultivated for reasons of gain or left uncultivated while the majority of people have no land and only small plots—all this when an increase in productivity is evidently urgent. . . . Whenever the common good requires confiscation, compensation should be fairly estimated according to all the circumstances" (GS 71.3, 4, 5). (Aquinas discusses private property and its social obligations in *Summa theologiae* II-II, q. 66, aa. 2, 6; *De regimine principum,* bk. 1, cc. 15, 17; ST II-II, q. 134, aa. 1, 2).

In a commentary on the above extract from *Gaudium et spes* Rodger Charles has written: "The question a christian should be asking first of all, if a new proposal for nationalization or public ownership comes up is, is it justified in terms of the common good? Similarly, concerning the workings of a particular nationalized industry we should be asking whether it is truly working to the public advantage. To treat all public ownership, all nationalized industries, with derision is as bad as treating them all as beyond criticism. In principle, they are a socially necessary institution in a free society, and they must be assessed on their record, not dismissed out of hand or accepted uncritically" (Charles and Maclaren, p. 311).

In summary, therefore: The goods of the world are for the benefit of all, and if individuals or families or groups are being deprived of their use, a higher political body may intervene to protect them; the level of this intervention will vary from time to time or from place to place depending on the circumstances. The purpose of all socialization in political-economic areas must be the common good; but the state, or any organization between individuals and the state, should not do for the individual or for lower groups what they can do for themselves provided, of course, they are in a genuine position to meet their just needs. Here the function of the state is subsidiary. Because of its special responsibility for the common good, the state should be alert to ensure justice for individuals, families, and groups and, if necessary, intervene to remove injustices. Finally, although private citizens, families, and groups should be alert to any encroachment by the state, they need to remember the benefits that can come from a socialization inspired by a full acceptance of what John Paul II called the "social mortgage" on the goods of the world (*Sollicitudo rei socialis* 42), that is, that they are meant by God to be used for the benefit of all.

Socialization, Psychology, and Developmental Studies

Educational studies refer frequently to socialization, not in the sense in which the word is used in political economy but as the process by which people, especially the young, become integrated in themselves and into the various communities in which they live. Much has also been written about the individuals and groups who influence this integration. A typical definition of socialization as used in anthropology, psychology, and developmental studies (education) is "the process by which the individual becomes a participating member of a society of human adults" (Danziger, p. 17). Danziger suggests that the use of the term in this modern sense originated in the late 1930s and early 1940s, and then socialization emerged as a field of study in several disciplines, a reflection of what he calls "a powerful undercurrent of ideas" (p. 13). The actual term "socialization" in this sense is not explicitly used in the social documents of the church, but the magisterium has made significant comments on what students of psychology, sociology, and education call "socialization."

The main influences on the socialization of children are their parents and family, the attitudes of people with whom they are in contact including peer groups, and the school, through teachers and the curriculum in its widest sense. In modern times, the development of easier and attractive forms of international communication has brought children under influences far beyond their family and local communities. Finally, in a category of its own is the church, a unique community into which children and adults need to be integrated.

Education is a frequent theme in the documents of the church and is discussed comprehensively in Pius XI's encyclical *Divini illius magistri* (1929) and in *Gravissimum educationis* (1965), the Second Vatican Council's Declaration on Christian Education. *Gravissimum educationis,* for example, refers to the almost irreplaceable role of parents in education and describes the family as the principal school of the social virtues necessary in every society. The family is the first and most important influence in the socialization of children. There they will have their "first experience of a well-balanced human society and of the Church. . . . It is through the family that they are gradually initiated into association with their fellow-men in civil life and as members of the people of God. Parents should, therefore, appreciate how important a role the truly Christian family plays in the life and progress of the whole people of God" (GE 3). Even though the task of imparting education belongs primarily to the family, it requires the help of society. Help is given in various ways, but among the agents of education the school is of outstanding importance. *Gravissimum educationis* refers to the socialization function of the school: "In nurturing the intellectual faculties which is its special mission, it develops a capacity for sound judgment and introduces the pupils to the cultural heritage bequeathed to them by former generations. It fosters a sense of values and prepares them for professional life. By providing for friendly contacts between pupils of different characters and backgrounds it encourages mutual understanding. Furthermore it constitutes a center in whose activity and growth not only the families and teachers but also the various associations for the promotion of cultural, civil and religious life, civic society, and the entire community should take part" (GE 5). In non-Catholic schools Catholic children may need special help. This can be given "by the living example of those who teach and have charge of these children and by the apostolic action of their fellow students, but especially by the efforts of those priests and laypeople who teach them Christian doctrine in a manner suited to their age and background and who provide them with spiritual help by means of various activities adapted to the requirements of time and circumstance" (GE 6). The main agent in the socialization of children, in preparing them to be stable people and integrated members of the community, is the family. The modern family requires considerable support from society, but the core relationship of father-mother-child within the family remains the center for the emotional development needed for maturity as an adult.

Just as the state has a concern that its citizens are prepared for mature membership in society, the church has a role in a socialization of a very different kind, with a special responsibility for religious formation and for helping people to a fullness of life in a spiritual society of which Christ is the head. The Second Vatican Council's Declaration on Christian Education says: "Education is in a very special way the concern of the Church, not only because the Church must be recognized as a human society capable of imparting education, but especially because it has the duty of proclaiming the way of salvation to all people, of revealing the life of Christ to those who believe, and of assisting them with unremitting care so that they may be able attain to the fullness of that life" (GE 3).

This point is developed in several documents from the magisterium of the church. *Evangelii nuntiandi,* for example, says: "It is absolutely necessary for us to take into account a heritage of faith that the Church has the duty of preserving in its untouchable purity, and of presenting it to the people of our time, in a way that is as understandable and persuasive as possible" (EN 3). This apostolic exhortation of Paul VI, On Evangelization in the Modern World, notes also that through the power of the Gospel, evangelization should affect people's judgment and values, their interests and way of life (19). It has a personal and social dimension involving an explicit message about human rights, peace, justice, development, and liberation (29). As for the question of how to evangelize, methods vary according to the different circumstances of time, place, and culture. They include preaching, the witness of one's life, the mass media, personal contact, the Liturgy, and popular devotions (41–48). Evangelization has a "limitless universality" (49) based on Jesus' last words in Mark's Gospel: "Go out to the whole world; proclaim the good news to all creation." Contained within that universality, however, is the reality of socialization: the process of assisting people to become full, living members of a community, the spiritual community founded by Christ, a process in which all members of his mystical body are invited to share.

In summary: The concept of socialization in education is different from its use in politico-economic studies. For the educator it is the process by which people, especially the young, become integrated in themselves and into the communities of which they are members. However, the first agent of socialization is the family. A particularly important agent is the school—through teachers, the curriculum, and the influence of other children. The community in which a child lives and the experiences it provides are also agents, while the state, because it is a society into which people must be integrated and because of its subsidiary functions in education, has an important role in socialization. Finally, the church is involved, through its promotion of the basic virtues and values of human living and particularly through its mission of helping all to become full, living members of the community of the people of God.

See also COMMUNISM; EDUCATION, ROLE OF; EVANGELIZATION; FAMILY; MARXISM; PRIVATE PROPERTY.

Bibliography: M. Campbell-Johnston, "The Social Teaching of the Church," *Thought* (Autumn 1964) 380–410. R. Charles and D. Maclaren, *The Social Teaching of Vatican II* (Oxford/San Francisco: Ignatius-Plater, 1988). K. Danziger, *Socialization* (Penguin, 1971). D. Dorr, *Option for the Poor: A Hundred Years of Vatican Social Teaching* (Dublin: Gill & Macmillan, 1983).

EUSTÁS Ó HÉIDEÁIN, O.P.

SOCIETY

In the century since the publication of *Rerum novarum,* documents issued by the magisterium of the church have referred to many kinds of society. Although they may differ significantly from one another, they share a basic definition: the union of several people for a common good not within reach of the members as individuals in isolation. Ideally they share also a basic structure: their members, directed by some form of a serving leadership in which they participate, cooperate in providing a common good to benefit all, especially the weaker members; and the group is characterized by love, justice, and a solidarity to which reference is frequently made in the later documents. Because love is important in society, Leo XIII emphasized it in the final paragraph of *Rerum novarum,* and he concludes with a quotation from St. Paul: "Love is patient, is kind, . . . seeks not her own, . . . suffers all things, . . . endures all things" (1 Cor 13:4-7).

People, Social by Nature

Although each person is a unique individual, all people are by nature social beings. Aristotle expressed this in a vivid way: "He who is unable to live in society, or who has no need because he is sufficient for himself, must be either a beast or a god" (*Politics* 1.2.14). Leo XIII referred to the fundamental reason people live in the society of others: "The consciousness of his own weakness urges man to call in aid from without" (RN 37). Aquinas expressed this in another way in his commentary on the *Ethics* of Aristotle: "Man is by nature a social animal in that he needs many things for his life which alone he cannot provide; it follows that he is naturally part of some multitude which helps him to live well" (In Eth 1 lect 1 n 4).

Both Aristotle and Aquinas would have completely rejected the position of Thomas Hobbes (1588–1679), who said that in a state of nature people are like beasts in a jungle, motivated by self-interest and at war with everybody else. Leo XIII turns to Sacred Scripture: "It is better that two should be together than one; for they have the advantage of their society. If one fail he shall be supported by the other. Woe to him that is alone, for when he falls he has none to lift him up" (Eccl 4:9-10). "A brother that is helped by his brother is like a strong city" (Prov 18:19). And he concludes, "It is this natural impulse which binds men together in civil society; and it is likewise this which leads them to join together in associations which are, it is true, lesser and not independent societies, but, nevertheless, real societies" (RN 37). This natural need of people to come together in groups of one kind or another has been referred to frequently in magisterium documents since the publication of *Rerum novarum.*

Societies Classified

Societies, depending on what basis one selects, may be classified in different ways. Leo XIII, for example, distinguishes between "public" and "private" societies (RN 37). Civil society is "public" because it is concerned with the interests of all in general, although it must also consider individual interests. Other societies within the state are "private" because their immediate purpose is the private advantage of the members.

A distinction may also be made between "natural" or "necessary" societies (the family and the state) and "voluntary" societies (those devoted to freely chosen purposes). Membership in a voluntary society is open and free, but membership in a family or in civil society is different. Birth makes us members of a family and, through the family, members immediately of a civil society that gives us a share in the common good.

It is possible also to distinguish between "perfect" and "imperfect" societies. Natural-law writers have described the state as a "perfect" society because "it is the abiding function of the state, by initiating, fostering and directing all-round social cooperation, to create the full development of human nature" (Messner, p. 542). In modern times individual political communities depend on international cooperation to carry out this function, but the basic responsibility still remains with the individual state. And so inevitably we are led to a consideration of world society. These three "natural" societies—family, state, and world community—have been discussed frequently and in depth in papal and church documents during the past century.

Finally, in a category of its own is the church, which "constituted and organized as a society in the present world, subsists in the Catholic Church, which is governed by the successor of Peter and by the bishops in communion with him" (*Lumen gentium* 8).

Changing Emphasis

While society in one form or another figures prominently in the wide range of social documents issued between 1891 and the present, inevitably there have been changes in the aspects of society emphasized. The reasons for this change of emphasis are clear. Society itself has changed. The social issues of concern to people and to the church today are different from those of a century ago, and points made in earlier papal documents have been developed and honed, sometimes considerably, in later documents, especially in those issued by the Second Vatican Council and by John Paul II. In the time of Leo XIII, for example, power was based on property and land. In today's industrial and political society it is based on other things, in some cases on knowledge, on a control of technology or finance, on weapons. *Rerum novarum* critically examined society and the individual's place in it. It may be indeed that it underemphasized the needs and claims of the common good, a balance that was restored in later documents.

There have been other changes. In recent decades, for example, the interdependence of the peoples of the world has become increasingly evident, and this has sharpened the concern of the church about world society, the relationship between developed and developing countries, and the need for all to have a fair share in the goods of the world. International cooperation has therefore become increasingly important, a cooperation encouraged particularly by Pius XII in a series of Christmas messages during the years of the Second World War.

Where societies are concerned, there has therefore been a changing emphasis in magisterium documents since *Rerum novarum,* a development referred to by John Paul II in *Laborem exercens:* "If one studies the development of the question of social justice, one cannot fail to note that, whereas during the period between *Rerum novarum* and Pius XI's *Quadragesimo anno* the Church's teaching concentrates on the 'labor question' within individual nations, in the next period the church's teaching widens its horizon to take in the whole world. The disproportionate distribution of wealth and poverty and the existence of some countries and continents that are developed and of others that are not call for a leveling out and a search for ways to ensure just development for all. This is the direction of the teaching in John XXIII's encyclical *Mater et magistra,* in the pastoral constitution *Gaudium et spes* of the Second Vatican Council, and in Paul VI's encyclical *Populorum progressio.* This trend of development of the Church's teaching and commitment in the social question exactly corresponds to the objective recognition of the state of affairs. While in the past the 'class' question was especially highlighted as the center of this issue, in modern times it is the 'world' question that is emphasized" (LE 2.2-2.3).

In any study of what the magisterium of the church has said about society during the past century, the three "natural" societies—family, civil society, and world community—must get special consideration. The church, a society in a category of its own, must also be included.

The Family as a Society

References to the family not surprisingly occur very frequently in the period from Leo XIII to John Paul II. A good summary of what has been written about the family as a society is contained in the *Charter of the Rights of the Family,* compiled at the request of the synod of bishops in 1980 and presented by the Holy See in 1983 to all who are concerned with the mission of the family in today's world. Some may regard the charter as legalistic, but behind the apparent legalisms are profound philosophical considerations. The introduction says that it aims at "presenting to all our contemporaries, be they Christian or not, a formulation—as complete and ordered as possible—of the fundamental rights that are inherent in that natural and universal society which is the family."

Some basic principles about the family as a society are summarized in the preamble to the charter. The family is based on marriage, "that intimate union of life in complementarity between a man and a woman which is constituted in the freely contracted and publicly expressed indissoluble bond of matrimony, and is open to the transmission of life" (*Charter,* Preamble B). It is a natural society, existing prior to the state or any other community, with inherent rights that are inalienable; it is a community of love and solidarity, a place where different generations come together to help one another grow in human wisdom; it is a community that must be protected by the state and international organizations "through measures of a political, economic, social and juridical character, which aim at consolidating the unity and stability of the family" (*Charter,* Preamble D-I).

Having outlined these basic principles in the preamble, the charter, in twelve articles, considers the aspects of the family that should be given special attention by the larger civil society. For example: "those who wish to marry and establish a family have the right to expect from society the moral, educational, social and economic conditions which will enable them to exercise their right to marry in all maturity and responsibility" (art. 1); "the spouses have the inalienable right to found a family and to decide on the spacing of births and the number of children to be born, taking into full consideration their duties towards themselves, their children already born, the family and society, in a just hierarchy of values and in accordance with the objective moral order which excludes recourse to contraception, sterilization and abortion" (art. 3); "since they have conferred life on their children, parents have the original, primary and inalienable right to educate them; hence they must be acknowledged as the first and foremost educators of their children" (art. 5).

Moving from the spouses who are responsible for the existence of the family, the charter considers a number of points centering on the family as a unit. The family has the right to exist and progress as a family, the right to live freely its own domestic religious life under the guidance of the parents, the right to exercise its social and political function in the construction of society, the right to be able to rely on an adequate family policy on the part of public authorities, a right to a social and economic order in which the organization of work permits the members to live together, the right to decent housing (arts. 6–11). The final article refers to the right of migrants' families to the same protection as that accorded to other families. Their culture must be respected, they must be helped to integrate into the community to which they contribute, and public authorities and international organizations should help in the reunion of the families of emigrant workers (art. 12).

The *Charter of the Rights of the Family* was written, as the title page notes, for the attention of "all . . . concerned with the mission of the family in to-day's world." Its reasoning is philosophical, not theological, with arguments the Holy See hoped would be acceptable to all. The Catholic view of the family as a society includes everything contained in the charter; the principles and conclusions summarized there are developed in other magisterium documents on the family and marriage.

In other documents, also, a theology of the family as a society is formulated. *Evangelii nuntiandi,* for example, refers to the family as the "domestic church": "At different moments in the Church's history and also in the Second Vatican Council, the family has well deserved the beautiful name of 'domestic Church.' This means that there should be found in every Christian family the various aspects of the entire Church. Furthermore, the family, like the Church, ought to be a place where the gospel is transmitted and from which the gospel radiates. In a family which is conscious of this mission, all the members evangelize and are evangelized. . . . And such a family becomes the evangelizer of many other families, and of the neighborhood of which it forms part" (EN 71).

Civil Society

The civil society most often discussed in magisterium documents is the state. The purpose of the state is to provide for the general welfare or common good of its citizens. It meets a basic human need: "Individuals, families, and the various groups which make up the civil community, are aware of their inability to achieve a truly human life by their own unaided efforts; they see the need for a wider community where each one will make a specific contribution to an even broader implementation of the common good. For this reason they set up various forms of political communities. The political community, then, exists for the common good: this is its full justification and meaning and the source of its basic right to exist" (GS 74). Political communities are among the instruments planned by God for the welfare of people.

As in all societies, a center of authority is needed to coordinate the activity of its members and take whatever initiatives are necessary for their general welfare. A typical magisterium comment is: "Human society can neither be well ordered nor prosperous without the presence of those who, invested with legal authority, preserve its institutions and do all that is necessary to sponsor actively the interests of all its members. And they derive their authority from God" (*Pacem in terris* 46). Pope John quotes the words of Paul, written as a caution for some Christians who felt that they were not bound to obey pagan authorities: "There is no power but from God" (Rom 13:1-6), and he then refers to St. John Chrysostom's commentary on Paul's Epistle to the Romans (c. 13, vv. 1–2, homily 23): "What are you saying? Is every ruler appointed by God? No, that is not what I mean, he says, for I am not talking about individual rulers, but about authority as such. My contention is that the existence of a ruling authority—the fact that some should command and others obey, and that all things should not come about as result of blind chance—this is a provision of divine wisdom."

After quoting from Chrysostom, John XXIII goes on to argue that since the social nature of people comes from God, and since a society cannot hold together unless someone is in command, it follows that God is the author both of society and of political authority within it (PT 46). This clear statement on the divine origin of authority is important not simply because it encourages respect for government but also because it helps define the exercise and the limits of authority.

The nature of political authority, the authority of state government, is best seen perhaps by a consideration of what is meant by the common good. When John XXIII said that "the attainment of the common good is the sole reason for the existence of civil authorities" (PT 54), he was simply restating a principle that has been very much a part of Catholic social teaching. In modern times Leo XIII emphasized it in *Immortale Dei,* an encyclical preceding *Rerum novarum* that again takes up the theme and summarizes what he had previously said: "The foremost duty of the rulers of the State should be to make sure that the laws and institutions, the general character and administration of the commonwealth, shall be such as of themselves to realize public well-being and private prosperity. This is the proper scope of wise statesmanship and is the work of the heads of the State" (RN 26). The state, therefore, ought to care for the common good.

Much later, John XXIII defined the common good as "all those social conditions which favor the full development of human personality" (MM 65). A somewhat wider definition is given in *Gaudium et spes:* "The common good embraces the sum total of all those conditions of social life which enables individuals, families, and organizations to achieve complete and efficacious fulfillment" (GS 74). Everybody must be able to benefit from the common good, with no group excluded. Government has to be impartial, not giving preferential treatment to any group except perhaps to those in need of special help or protection; it has to be balanced, not allowing some to exercise their rights at the expense of the rights of others; it has to be comprehensive, defending spiritual as well as material rights, the right to practice one's religion as well as the right to be able to walk the roads in safety and peace; it has to be positive as well as negative, promoting employment and giving financial help to those unemployed as well as restraining any one group from harming another; it has to walk the difficult line between interfering too much or too little in the life of the nation.

Magisterium documents since *Rerum novarum* frequently refer to the need for individual citizens to participate in the government of their political society. *Gaudium et spes,* for example, speaks of "participation by all in public life," including the use of one's vote in elections and on issues affecting the life of the community, and it praises those who "take upon themselves the burdens of office" (GS 75). It has always been implicit in Catholic teaching that the functions of political society are mainly "subsidiary," that is, in helping its members to lead a full life without however arrogating to itself all initiative and responsibility.

One of the first to make this principle clearly explicit in magisterium documents was Pius XI in *Quadragesimo anno:* "Just as it is wrong to withdraw from the individual and commit to a community what private enterprise and industry can accomplish, so too it is an injustice, a grave evil and a disturbance of right order, for a larger and higher association to arrogate to itself functions which can be performed efficiently by smaller and lower societies. Of its very nature the true aim of all social activity should be to help members of the social body, but never to destroy or absorb them" (QA 79). John XXIII reaffirms this principle in *Mater et magistra* (MM 53). Dennis Chiles gives a good gloss on this principle of subsidiarity: "The principle means that there are some responsibilities which we can discharge for ourselves; some which we can achieve more effectively by voluntary association with others; and some which need action at national or international level. . . . The principle requires that responsibility should rest at the lowest level where it can be adequately discharged. If people are denied the opportunity to do for themselves things they are perfectly capable of doing, they will become, in the literal meaning of the word, irresponsible" (Chiles, p. 34).

There are occasions when the state must intervene, and *Gaudium et spes* suggests that "the growing complexity of modern situations makes it necessary for public authority to intervene more often in social, cultural and economic matters in order to bring about more favorable conditions to enable citizens and groups to pursue freely and effectively the achievement of man's well-being in its totality" (GS 75). If restrictions have to be imposed, they must be lifted as soon as possible and they should not be used by public authority to justify totalitarian methods or dictatorship (ibid.). The "subsidiary" character of political society implies, therefore, that the state will not intervene unnecessarily in our lives and that we will accept those responsibilities that we can adequately discharge.

World Society

Peace and justice are frequent themes in magisterium documents during the past century, but the context in which they are discussed has changed. One of the most notable changes has been the increasing emphasis on world society. In *Laborem exercens,* planned for publication in May 1981 but delayed until September by the attempted assassination of the pope, John Paul II comments on this change: "The key position, as regards the question of world peace, is that of John XXIII's encyclical *Pacem in Terris.* However if one studies the question of social justice, one cannot fail to note that, whereas during the period between *Rerum Novarum* and Pius XI's *Quadragesimo Anno* the Church's teaching concentrates mainly on the just solution of the 'labor question' within individual nations, in the next period the Church's teaching widens its horizon to take in the whole world" (LE 2.2).

This world dimension of the social problem is referred to in *Mater et magistra* (1961) and in the pastoral constitution *Gaudium et spes* (1965) of the Second Vatican Council. In *Sollicitudo rei socialis* (1987) John Paul II suggests, however, that at the time of the publication of these two earlier documents "the social teaching of the Church had not yet reached the point of affirming with such clarity that the social question had acquired a worldwide dimension, nor had this affirmation and the accompanying analysis yet been made into a 'directive for action'" (SRS 9). This was done in Paul VI's encyclical *Populorum progressio* (1967) and again more fully twenty years later by John Paul II in *Sollicitudo rei socialis.*

Even though the emphasis on a world society is comparatively recent, it has always been an essential element in Catholic social teaching that the goods of the world are meant for all. In *Sollicitudo rei socialis,* for example, John Paul II refers to several magisterium documents and to the writings of Aquinas where this point is developed, and he describes private property as being subject to a "social mortgage" in that it has an intrinsically social function, based upon and justified by the principle that the goods of the earth belong to all (SRS 42).

While this right of access by all to the goods of the world has always been recognized by the church, only in recent decades have we become more conscious that we live in a world society. It was inevitable, perhaps, that the teaching and thinking of the Second Vatican Council, the first council to reflect a truly world church, would soon be applied to a world society and its problems.

Several developments explain why we are more conscious now than we formerly were that we live in a world society. "Never before," said the synod of bishops in 1971, "have the forces working for bringing about a unified world society appeared so powerful and dynamic. . . . Since men are members of the same human family, they are indissolubly linked with one another in the one destiny of the whole world, in the responsibility in which they all share" (*Justitia in mundo* 7). The synod lists some of these forces: the unity of science, easy communication between all parts of the world, their economic interdependence, and a realization that the physical resources of the world—including air and water without which there cannot be life—and "the small delicate biosphere of the whole complex of all life on earth" are not infinite but have to be "saved and protected as a unique patrimony belonging to all mankind" (JM 8). John Paul II suggests a reason why we must now consider the world dimension of the "social question," which has been a main concern of the church during the past century: "If the social question has acquired a worldwide dimension, this is because *the demand for justice* can only be satisfied on that level. To ignore this demand could encourage the temptation among the victims of injustice to respond with violence, as happens at the origin of many wars" (SRS 10).

Yet in spite of these pushes toward a world society, forces encouraging division and antagonism seem now to be getting stronger. Old enemies—nations, races, classes—have new instruments of destruction; the poor are becoming poorer, the rich richer; there are new divisions, with a concentration of wealth, power, and decision making in the hands of a small public or private controlling group; there has been a rapid growth of population in some areas, rural stagnation, lack of agrarian reform, migration to cities where industry cannot provide jobs for all, the rise of a great number of marginal people, "ill fed, inhumanly housed, illiterate and deprived of political power as well as of the suitable means of acquiring responsibility and moral dignity" (JM 9, 10). It seems that the colonialism of the old world society is being replaced by "a new form of colonialism in which the developing nations will be the victims of the interplay of international economic forces" (JM 16).

The world society behind these comments of the 1971 synod of bishops was considered again by John Paul II in *Sollicitudo rei socialis* (1987): "As we observe the various parts of the world separated by this widening gap, and note that each of these parts seems to follow its own path with its own achievements, we can understand the current usage which speaks of different worlds within our *one world:* the First World, the Second World, the Third World and at times the Fourth World" (SRS 14). A footnote comments: "The expression 'Fourth World' is used not just occasionally for the so-called *less advanced* countries, but also and especially for the bands of great or extreme poverty in countries of medium and high income." And the text continues: "Such expressions, which obviously do not claim to classify exhaustively all countries, are significant: they are a sign of a widespread sense that the *unity of the world,* that is, the *unity of the human race,* is seriously compromised" (ibid.).

John Paul II, like several of his predecessors, has said that the church does not have "technical solutions" for the problems of society (SRS 41). It is, however, "expert in humanity" (ibid.) and very sensitive to human problems. He speaks particularly about the poor of the world, "the immense multitudes of the hungry, the needy, the homeless, those without medical care and, above all, those without hope of a better future. It is impossible not to take account of these realities. To ignore them would mean becoming like the 'rich man' who pretended not to know the beggar Lazarus lying at his gate" (SRS 42). Concern for the poor—"the Lord's poor"—must be translated into concrete action at both national and international levels: "Each local situation will show what reforms are most urgent and how they can be achieved. But those demanded by the situation of international imbalance, as already described, must not be forgotten" (SRS 43). John Paul II then considers a number of reforms needed at an international level, including a fairer system of international trade, monetary reform, greater generosity in promoting new technologies in developing countries, and a review of international organizations (SRS 44). He stresses the need for national, regional, and global cooperation, a "solidarity which includes everybody, beginning with the most neglected," and "a readiness to accept the sacrifices necessary for the good of the whole world community" (SRS 45). (Donal Dorr in *Option for the Poor* has examined the social teaching of the church over the past hundred years in order to find out what church leaders have to say about poverty and social injustice. He shows that an "option for the poor," called for by the church in Latin America, has a solid traditional basis.)

Sollicitudo rei socialis ends on a note of optimism that must encourage those concerned with difficulties faced by societies at all levels. In spite of sad experiences, past and present, "the Church must strongly affirm the possibility of overcoming the obstacles which, by excess or by defect, stand in the way of development" (SRS 47). Why be so optimistic? Ultimately the reason is the church's awareness of "the divine promise guaranteeing that our present history does not remain closed in on itself but is open to the Kingdom of God" (ibid.).

The church also believes in people, in their basic goodness, and in the effective action of the Holy Spirit, which "fills the earth" (Wis 1:7). And so: "There is no justification for despair or pessimism or inertia. . . . We are all called, indeed obliged, to face the tremendous challenge of the last decade of the second millennium, also because the present dangers threaten everyone: a world economic crisis, a war without frontiers, without winners or losers. In the face of such a threat, the distinction between rich individuals and countries and poor individuals and countries will have little value, except that a greater responsibility rests on those who have more and can do more" (SRS 47).

John Paul II asks Mary to place before her Son the problems faced by individuals as well as "social situations and the international crisis itself, in their worrying aspects of poverty, unemployment, shortage of food, the arms race, contempt for human rights, and situations or dangers of conflict, partial or total" (SRS 49). He concludes his encyclical with the prayer from the Mass for the Development of Peoples: "Father, you have given all peoples one common origin, and your will is to gather them as one family in yourself. Fill the hearts of all with the fire of your love, and the desire to ensure justice for all their brothers and sisters. By sharing the good things you give us may we secure justice and equality for every human being, an end to all division, and a human society built on love and peace." The thoughts in that prayer summarize much of what has been said about human societies in the social documents of the church magisterium during the past century.

The Church: A Society

Aquinas, with the *Politics* of Aristotle as his starting point, proposed a theory of political society based on human nature and its social needs. This Thomist and Aristotelian idea of the state inspired theologians of his school, beginning with John of Paris, to formulate a theory of political society that separated church and state and protected political autonomy.

It was in this tradition that Leo XIII in *Immortale Dei* spoke of the "two great societies," civil society and religious society, each sovereign but differing in origin and purpose: "The only-begotten Son of God established on earth a society which is called the Church, and to it he handed over the exalted and divine office which he had received from his Father, to be continued through the ages to come. . . . As Jesus Christ came into the world that people 'might have life and have it more abundantly' (Jn 10:10), so also has the Church for its aim and end the eternal salvation of souls, and hence it is so constituted as to open wide its arms to all mankind, unhampered by any limit of either time or place. . . . Over this mighty multitude God has himself set rulers with power to govern; and he has willed that one should be the head of all, and the chief and unerring teacher of truth, to whom he has given 'the keys of the kingdom of heaven' (Mt 16:19). 'Feed my lambs, feed my sheep' (Jn 21:16-17). 'I have prayed for you that your faith will not fail' (Lk 22:32). . . . This society is made up of people, just as civil society is, and yet it is supernatural and spiritual, on account of the end for which it was founded, and of the means by which it aims at attaining that end. Hence it is distinguished and differs from civil society; and, what is of the highest moment, it is a society chartered as of divine right, perfect in its nature and in its title, to possess in itself and by itself, through the will and loving kindness of its founder, all needful provision for its maintenance and action" (*Immortale Dei,* CTS ed., *The Pope and the People,* pp. 49, 50).

The encyclical *Immortale Dei* was published in 1885. Eighty years later, in 1965, the Second Vatican Council approved *Gaudium et spes,* the Pastoral Constitution on the Church in the Modern World. *Lumen gentium,* the Dogmatic Constitution on the Church, had been published a year earlier, in 1964. Together these two modern documents are a substantial statement on "the people of God." *Gaudium et spes,* for example, reaffirms Leo XIII's teaching on the unique origin and mission of the church as a society: "Coming forth from the eternal father's love, founded in time by Christ the redeemer and made one in the Holy Spirit, the Church has a saving and an eschatological purpose which can be fully attained only in the future world" (GS 40.1). The children of this "family of God" are, "during the present history of the human race" also members of civil society, but "constituted and structured as a society" by Christ, at once "a visible association and a spiritual community," meant by God to serve "as a leaven and as a kind of soul for human society" (ibid.).

Christ did not give the church as a society any specific program in the political, economic, or social order. When circumstances produce the need, however, "she can and indeed should initiate activities on behalf of all" (GS 42.1), and there are few areas in which, either as a society or through individual members, the church cannot act as a "leaven." These areas are indicated throughout the documents of the Second Vatican Council and in the papal encyclicals of recent decades. *Gaudium et spes,* for example, lists some of the areas of special concern today: marriage and the family, culture, economic and social life, politics, the solidarity of peoples, and peace (GS 47ff.). John XXIII made it clear that the solution of social problems must be the concern of all people, and his encyclical *Pacem in terris* was the first papal encyclical to be addressed officially to "all men of good will." In *Mater et magistra,* however, he described the church as the "mother and teacher of all nations" whose mission is "to hold the world in an embrace of love, that people, in every age, should find in her their own completeness in a higher order of living, and their ultimate salvation" (MM 1).

Summary

Society can take many forms, but they all share a common element—a group of people, few or many, under an authority appropriate for the group and its aims, cooperating to achieve a good not possible for them individually. In the century since the publication of *Rerum novarum,* the magisterium of the church has emphasized different aspects of society or widened its commentary to meet changing circumstances.

The family, the "domestic Church," is a basic, natural society, a community of love and solidarity with rights that are inalienable but needing the assistance of civil society to meet fully its responsibilities.

The civil society most often discussed in magisterium documents is the state, a political community that exists for the common good, which is its full justification and meaning and the source of its specific and basic right to exist. The common good is the sum total of all those conditions of social life that enable individuals, families, and organizations to achieve complete human fulfillment. Political communities have their origin in the awareness of individuals and families that they cannot fulfill their human needs simply by their own unaided efforts. Political community and political authority are therefore founded in human nature and belong to an order established by God, although the choice of regime and rulers are left to the people themselves, subject to the basic condition that they serve the common good.

In recent decades, for a number of reasons the magisterium has spoken more than previously about world society and the need for international cooperation.

Finally, the church is a society, like civil society made up of people, but supernatural and spiritual because of the purpose for which it was founded and the means it uses to achieve that purpose. The members of this "family of God's children," a visible association and a spiritual community, are also members of civil society, and it is God's wish that they should serve "as a leaven and as a kind of soul for human society."

See also AUTHORITY, POLITICAL; COMMON GOOD; COMMUNITY; FAMILY; HUMAN RIGHTS; NATURAL LAW; SOLIDARITY; SUBSIDIARITY, PRINCIPLE OF.

Bibliography: M. Campbell-Johnston, "The Social Teaching of the Church," *Thought* (Autumn 1964) 380–410. R. Charles, with D. Maclaren, *The Social Teaching of Vatican II: Its Origin and Development* (Oxford: Plater, and San Francisco: Ignatius Press, 1982). D. Chiles, *Christianity And Politics* (CTS: London, 1989). D. Dorr, *Option for the Poor: A Hundred Years of Vatican Social Teaching* (Dublin: Gill & Macmillan, 1983). T. Gilby, *Between Community and Society: A Philosophy and Theology of the State* (London: Longmans, 1957). J. Maritain, *Man and the State* (Chicago, 1963). J. Messner, *Social Ethics* (London: Herder, 1965). H. Vorgrimler, *Commentary on the Documents of Vatican II* (London, 1968). E. Welty, *A Handbook of Christian Social Ethics* (New York, 1960).

EUSTÁS Ó. HÉIDEÁIN, O.P.

SOLIDARISM

The term "solidarism" is not an invention of Heinrich Pesch, who was aware that solidarism was the leading motive of a school of thought in France. Pesch had been looking for a name for the Scholastic philosophy of society that could best serve in a comparison with the social philosophies of individualism on the one hand and collectivism on the other. It seems important to point out, right at the beginning, that solidarity and solidarism are not exactly synonymous. Solidarity is primarily an attitude of mind, perhaps a principle. Solidarism is a philosophy, teleologically oriented, rooted in the personhood and the social nature of the human person. The idea that solidarism is a "third way," equally removed from the extremes of individualism and collectivism, may and often does give the notion of a practical via media that selects what is good in each of the two approaches, simply rejecting their extremes, combining their virtuous means. This approach, however, reverses the sequence of action and being (*agere sequitur esse*).

The human person is a society-oriented person, society a person-oriented accidence. It is important to realize that one's social orientation is by no means rooted in any insufficiency of one's nature but, on the contrary, on the metaphysical plenitude of one's personhood, which enables a human person to share one's truth, one's goodness, and one's beauty creatively with fellow human beings, with fellow children of God. Solidarity is more than mutual assistance. As individuals we are indeed limited in our humanity, but as persons we are blessed by our very ability to make up for one another's insufficiencies.

Pesch's solidarism, which he himself considered an anthropocentric-teleological system, may be confidently called quasi-personalistic, yet this falls somewhat short of an adequate appreciation of the personhood of the human being. One may wonder whether Pesch was aware of the philosophical anthropology of Thomas Aquinas, or whether those who taught him neo-Scholastic philosophy did justice to what they somewhat inadequately called "psychology," which is no less than the human person's likeness to the Divine Persons and which tremendous insight has led Romano Guardini to speak of human society as image of the Blessed Trinity (pp. 86–94). There is, in what might be called a sociotheological foundation of society, the supernatural root of solidarism. Pesch deserves the special acknowledgment of Catholic social science for his emphasis on the role of the so-called *causae secundae,* the secondary, created causes in the area of the empirical sciences, such as sociology and economics.

Pesch carefully avoided the error of integralism, whose disregard of the secondary causes amounts to a disesteem of the First Cause, the very creator of their own quasi-autonomous causality. But Pesch gives unstinted credit to the theological progenitors of Christian solidarism, Donoso Cortes (1809–53) and Charles Perin (1815–44). Pesch reminds his readers that the idea of solidarity of the entire human family was strengthened through the Christian doctrine of original sin. Beyond this, the principle of solidarity (like that of subsidiarity) may be looked upon as a principle of the natural law, embedded in the core of human society and representing itself as a norm: French jurisprudence early adopted from Roman law the concept of joint and several liability.

The term "solidarism," of course, derives from the Latin *solidus,* firm, whole, and—in an altered and metaphorical sense—the whole sum, that is, the entire amount owed by each and all members of the group that borrowed it and not just an individual, corresponding share of it. *Webster's Collegiate Dictionary* defines "solidarity" very well as unity of a social group, producing and based upon a community of interests, objectives, and standards; and "solidarism" as a social concept maintaining that the interdependence of the members of a society offers a basis for a social organization grounded upon solidarity of interests. What we cannot expect of a dictionary is that it stress the decisive role of the kind of interest, the purpose involved, whether human-made or nature-made, inborn or affected, personhood-motivated or ego-centered, serving the common good or being merely a servant of the collectivity. But given the human-oriented nature of *genuine* solidarism, it follows that social action, which is the implementation of solidarism, is not primarily a question of feelings and pragmatism but one of following the true being and nature of the human person, anthropocentric both in origin and in aim.

Solidarism is a philosophy, not a program. As an economist Pesch was particularly interested in determining and demonstrating the socioeconomic conclusions of that philosophy. He called the economic "practice" of solidarism a *soziales Arbeitssystem* (as did Hermann Roesler before him; see Pesch, vol. 2, p. 213ff.), a social system of industry, as distinguished from Adam Smith's individualistic system. But he shared with Smith the conviction that the wealth, or better, the welfare, of any nation is primarily the fruit of its "industry." By "industry" neither Pesch nor Smith meant merely the world of factories or power-driven machinery—the mechanical way of production—but industry in the Latin sense of *industria* or in the sense that one might speak of an industrious student, of diligence in the employment and pursuit of productive, value-creating activity. The Germans speak of *Gewerbefleiss.* Not just the work of the farmer, of the artisan, the merchant, the writer, the worker, the inventor, the manager, the entrepreneur, but everybody's diligence lifts the income of the nation. What saved the nations that lost World War II and faced the ruins that resulted? It is certainly not by chance that Pesch called his economic system an "industrial" one, that is, one of diligence. Oil wells will eventually dry up, but where there are human persons, there is hope, there is a chance. Labor, both physical and mental, is a function, *the* function of personhood, not punishment for sin. The burden is *not* the action, which is life—creative and at least potentially a latent power in the society if allowed to be dispersed, to seed, to fructify, to prime the pump.

There is not and never will be *one* economic system for all times and places. Unfortunately there is one way for humans to destroy all opportunities, namely, by promising everyone effortless security, by replacing contributive justice with a merely distributive one. One cannot distribute what has not been produced in the first place!

There can be no enduring economic welfare unless no one is permitted to enrich himself or herself without effort at the expense of his or her fellow human beings. That could be done by a negative, selfish solidarity such as consumer-hostile abuse of "united" market power: there is "solidarity" even in the drug cartels! As Messner rightly states, the expression "solidarism" emphasizes the coordination of person and society demanded by natural-law principles. The old saying "one for all and all for one" expresses well the underlying metaphysical principle of being, which precedes all doing, and is the basis of all moral and political application.

Bibliography: R. Guardini, *Auf dem Wege* (Mainz: Versuche, 1923). D. von Hildebrand, *Metaphysik der Gemeinschaft* (Augsburg, 1930). H. Pesch, *Lehrbuch der Nationalökonomie,* vol. 1 (Freiburg, 1924). K. Rahner and H. Vorgrimler, *Theological Dictionary* (New York, 1965) p. 440.

FRANZ H. MUELLER

SOLIDARITY

Only in the last century did the term "solidarity," denoting common interests uniting a group or nation, appear in English from the French. Along with a modern German term, *Solidarismus,* "solidarity" was adopted from labor-union movements by Catholic social theorists (e.g., H. Pesch, G. Gundlach, O. v. Nell-Breuning). They used "solidarity" to differentiate Catholic social theory from the modern theories of liberalism and communism. Liberal capitalism stressed individualism so strongly that it dehumanized individuals, exalting individual choice and interests over our common humanity with responsibility for others. The individual becomes a monad, in which all intersubjective relations of birth and family are downgraded in comparison with individual preferences. Communities are no more than associations of like-minded individuals. Instead of solidarity and solidarism, liberalist theory promotes a pluralism or pluriformity open to moral relativism and cultural nihilism.

Eighteenth-century capitalist individualism provoked 19th-century communist collectivism. If excessive individualism tended to dehumanize, collectivism tended to depersonalize by completely subordinating individuals to "the collective will" as represented by the Communist party. Communist collectivism assured that any organic understanding of solidarity would be replaced with an extrinsic authoritarianism unable to promote both personal freedom and social order. Instead of pluriformity, collectivism promoted a drab and dominative uniformity.

The theories of liberalism and collectivism view the state as an extrinsic aggregate constructed by the conventions of "social contracts." Morality is subordinated to conventional legality. An ethics of friendship and virtue is replaced by an ethics of stern duty and law. Catholic solidarism aimed at transposing pre-modern understandings of natural law, of human being as essentially social, and of society itself as organic and cooperative, into the modern contexts of industrialized societies with complex exchange economies.

These efforts largely coincided with the development of Catholic social teaching in the 20th century. Building upon the critique of liberalism and socialism in Leo XIII's *Rerum novarum,* the principles of Christian solidarity made explicit entrance in Pius XI's *Quadragesimo anno,* written by Nell-Breuning. Where modern liberalism and collectivism viewed social reality as ultimately competitive and conflictive, Catholic social teaching emphasized society and economy as ontologically and ethically oriented toward cooperation and harmony. Against liberalism, "Catholic social science," as Pius XI called it, would spell out the mutually cooperative responsibilities of owners, managers, and workers, along with the responsibilities of the state, for the common welfare. Against socialism, it emphasized the God-gifted dignity of the human person, the importance of subsidiarity to encourage individual and communal initiatives, and the orientation of governmental and economic orders toward the service of the transcendent values of persons. Solidarity cannot be limited only to a group or a class or a time. Solidarity is as concrete and universal as the entire human species created and redeemed by God.

Pius XI was also able to invoke Christian solidarity against the 20th-century nationalist reactions to capitalist international finance and Communist world revolution. This nationalism in fascism and nazism combined both pluriformity and uniformity by exalting particular peoples or nations to dominate and impose their superior "form" or race upon others. The catholic or universal character of solidarity was denied not only theoretically but apocalyptically in the horror of the Holocaust.

Solidarity was expanded from workers within nations to global solidarity in any just and humane development in the social encyclicals of John XXIII, especially *Mater et magistra* and *Pacem in terris.* The theories of liberalism and collectivism were differentiated from the concrete liberal and socialist movements, which, the pope pointed out, were changing as the errors and shortcomings of the theories became evident in practice. Profound changes can occur without violence. Vatican II's *Gaudium et spes* as well as its decree on the apostolate of the laity articulated the need for cooperation and solidarity both ecclesially and politically. Two years after the council Paul VI's *Populorum progressio* centered more than any previous encyclical on "the spirit of solidarity" needed for integral human development. With this encyclical Catholic social teaching put its reflections on social justice within a heuristic framework. It no longer simply criticized the sins and shortcomings of liberalism and collectivism. Rather, solidarity and social justice are heuristically explicated within larger cultural, ethical, and theological developments.

The growing importance of solidarity in the church's social teaching found particularly fertile ground in Poland during the subsequent decade, where it provided a fuller intelligibility and cohesion to the worker's union solidarity over against an authoritarian Communist party. In *Laborem exercens* John Paul II acknowledged the importance of the historical movements that had promoted worker solidarity; he also advanced the teaching on solidarity by making a "turn to the subject": solidarity is both ontological and historical. As ontological, human solidarity is gifted by God in creating and redeeming the human species; as historical, solidarity is also a challenge, an imperative calling workers to appropriate their own labor, and all human beings to appropriate their own activity for the common good. In *Sollicitudo rei socialis* this is further advanced by calling attention to the "virtue" of solidarity, which is not just a vague feeling of compassion but "a firm and persevering determination to commit oneself to the common good." Solidarity must be practiced between individuals, professions, classes, communities, and nations, as all must be committed to the common good and to overcoming the alienation and injustice oppressing so many. Solidarity among and with the poor is seen as both a human and a gospel imperative. The encyclical also stresses the need for an ecological solidarity, since modern industrialism poses so many threats to the natural environment.

Catholic teaching on solidarity has been primarily pastoral. There are still few systematic analyses of the scientific, philosophical, and theological implications of this very important pastoral teaching. Modern notions of solidarity as only "common interests" tend to be extrinsic and voluntarist: solidarity is a tool for survival in the conflictive struggles of existence. Solidarity is thereby linked to violence and domination. This is evident in Hegel's very influential dialectic of master and slave. There are two fundamental presuppositions on which most modern philosophers agree, whether they are of conservative, liberal, or radical bent. The first views natural and historical realities as ultimately conflictive, as though reality were made up of fields of contradictory forces contending for dominance. The second common presupposition casts knowledge as power to control, a learning of secrets in order to enforce order and secure dominance. Neither Judaism nor Catholicism can accept these presuppositions. This has several important consequences relating to solidarity.

The ontology of solidarity is the fact of the human species. The human species is constituted by spiritual, intellectual, cultural anthropological, sociological, psychological, zoological, biological, ecological, chemical, and physical processes. Any *metaphysics of human solidarity* has to relate its heuristic metaphysical analysis to the natural sciences, the life sciences, and the human sciences. The excessive individualism of modern cultures makes it difficult for Catholicism to transpose into modern contexts its very enlightening memories of the species being of humankind and the redemption of our species in the body of Christ. This is especially so in that realm that deeply relates each and every individual to the species: sexuality. Individualist theories inattentive to a metaphysics of human solidarity can minimize the responsibility for the species intrinsic to any genuine understanding of human sexuality. Another area is the ongoing debates between nature and nurture in the human sciences; they indicate the need to analyze "nature" and "human nature" in the context of solidarity as both ontological and historical.

A metaphysics of solidarity would also require a dialectics capable of differentiating the normative advances in the sciences from the scientistic and ideological constructions of those advances. It is often such ideological constructions that promote unjust public policies. Such a dialectical discernment would be a great assistance in mediating human solidarity in the pressing questions of biomedical research and bioethics. Variations on social and cultural Darwinism continue to misconstrue genuine advances in the life sciences in terms of struggle, conflict, and violence. A metaphysics of human solidarity also needs a cognitional theory or epistemology to advance an understanding of human intelligence as not just a Cartesian thinking ego but as intrinsically acts of understanding and knowing in solidarity with all intelligence. Mind is public and communicative by nature. The privatization and collectivization of mind in modern cultures is at the root of much alienation. Wisdom is divorced from science as knowledge is engendered more by fear than by a love of understanding and wisdom.

A metaphysics leads also to an *ethics of human solidarity.* The common good in Catholic social teaching is not a Kantian regulative idea. The universality of human solidarity in the common good is concrete. It is not an abstract or ideal universality, to be imposed "from the top down" by idealists with little or no understanding of the concrete diversity of life. An ethics of solidarity is not a Kantian ethics of uniform duty under a categorical imperative. The "common" or "universal" is as concrete as the "good." The human race is not an abstract idea. It concretely exists in each human being who ever has, does, or will exist. Each individual exists in the universal and vice versa. In this sense an ethics of solidarity overcomes the legacy of nominalism in contemporary ethical discourse. Universals are not just nouns or ideas, nor do only individuals exist. Ontological solidarity is real as the concrete universality of the human race. An ethics of solidarity is also not a situation ethics, which treats historical diversity as if it were so unique as to be unrelated to others, as if the good could not be common. Historical solidarity in the practice of peace and justice is an orientation avoiding the false alternatives of either a totalitarian uniformity or an aimless relativism and nihilism in mere pluriformity. The rich cultural diversity of the human species is nurtured in a human solidarity manifested in the ever-renewed efforts at communication and mutual understanding. The universality of solidarity is a universality mediated in and through particularity and diversity.

An ethics of solidarity also develops systematically the context in which pastoral teachings support and promote human rights. These rights are rooted in the dignity of each human person, which dignity is itself grounded in the concrete universality of each person's ontological solidarity with the human race. Where modern theories of rights (e.g., Hobbes, Locke, Kant) project the rights as individualistic defenses within inevitably conflictive natural and/or civil environments, an ethics of solidarity defends human rights as required by any just and cooperative common good. Rights are grounded not in acts of willful self-assertion in the struggle of existence but in the responsibilities of promoting intelligent and reasonable cooperation in the common good.

An ethics of solidarity respects human intelligence and love by avoiding moral imperatives that lack serious intellectual content. The "virtue" of solidarity requires the development of both intellectual and moral virtues within contexts of friendship. Intellectual discoveries and moral achievements are not the private property of the scientific, the wise, or the good. There is a moral and intellectual solidarity that points to the unity of human intellectual and moral achievements. The dichotomy between wisdom and science is paralleled by dichotomies between human reason, morality, and religious faith. Recognizing the intrinsic relations between morality and rationality means that the common good is not promoted by well-intentioned but unintelligent calls to action. Massive poverty demands a cooperative solidarity in the corporal and spiritual works of mercy. It also demands more creatively intelligent analyses of contemporary exchange economies. An ethics of solidarity must collaborate with economic theorists in order to develop moral and economic precepts that have a basis in the economic process and so can effectively direct it toward the common good.

Finally, a *theology of solidarity* indicates how the ontological unity of the human species is redeemed as a "new creation" in Christ. Political and liberation theologians insist on the theological truth and reality of the identification of God with the least of the human species in Christ Jesus (Mt 25:31-46). The mystery of the body of Christ, of our membership one with the other, is a reality embracing the concrete totality of those graced with God's love and compassion. The importance of theology for the tasks of peace and justice are decisive. Modern secular cultures, having rejected theology, have read into human nature what is not natural but sinful. Warfare, violence, and the vices that wreak so much havoc on human history do not arise from our created natures. They result from human sinfulness. The ontological gift of human solidarity was shattered by human sinfulness and redeemed by God becoming one with us in Jesus Christ. An interdisciplinary collaboration between theology and the human sciences would promote a more critically realist and hopeful understanding of both human nature and how solidarity in peace and justice are concretely possible.

Given the massive injustices that sin causes and the myriad victims of injustice in history, a human justice is inadequate. How can we render justice to the murdered and dead? Human solidarity breaks down in the cycles of violence and counterviolence, as one grievance evokes another, as one war is followed by another. A theology of solidarity insists that the depths of human suffering in history can only be redeemed by God's loving solidarity with us in Christ. The practice of the theological virtue of agapic love continually makes present the Spirit of Christ redeeming human solidarity. We humans are enabled to forgive as God has forgiven, loving not only our friends but also our enemies, that is, being as universal in our solidarity as God. Such love can end the cycles of violence, not by muting the cries of the victims but by transforming, as only God can, those sufferings into new life. The church, communicating the missions of the Word and Spirit, is the sacramental presence of human solidarity in the crucified and risen Christ. Human solidarity becomes communion. As incarnating the presence of agapic love, the church proclaims the coming fullness of human solidarity with all the just, who are enfolded in the eternal life of the triune God.

See also CAPITALISM; COLLECTIVISM; COMMUNISM; COMMUNITY; LABOREM EXERCENS; MODERNISM; SOLIDARISM; SOLLICITUDO REI SOCIALIS.

Bibliography: T. Ash, *The Polish Revolution: Solidarity* (New York: Scribners, 1984). G. Baum, *Compassion and Solidarity: The Church for Others* (Toronto: CBC Enterprises, 1987). G. Baum and R. Ellsberg, eds., *The Logic of Solidarity: Commentaries on Pope John Paul II's Encyclical "On Social Concerns"* (Maryknoll: Orbis, 1989). D. Dorr, *Option for the Poor: A Hundred Years of Vatican Social Teaching* (Maryknoll: Orbis, 1983). Y. Durand, *Les solidarités dans les sociétés humaines* (Paris: Presses Universitaires de France, 1987). J. Gremillion, ed., *The Gospel of Peace and Justice* (Maryknoll: Orbis, 1976). D. Hollenbach, *Claims in Conflict: Retrieving and Renewing the Catholic Human Rights Tradition* (New York: Paulist, 1979). M. Lamb, *Solidarity with Victims: Toward a Theology of Social Transformation* (New York: Crossroad, 1982). B. Lonergan, *The Metaphysics of Human Solidarity: An Early Manuscript,* to be published in vol. 14 of his *Collected Works* (Toronto: Univ. of Toronto Press). A. MacIntyre, *Whose Justice? Which Rationality?* (Notre Dame: Univ. of Notre Dame Press, 1988). B. Misztal, ed., *Poland After Solidarity: Social Movements Versus the State* (Oxford: Transaction Books, 1985). J. Segundo, *The Humanist Christology of Paul* (Maryknoll: Orbis, 1986). J. Sobrino and J. Pico, *Theology of Christian Solidarity* (Maryknoll: Orbis, 1985). J. Tischner, *The Spirit of Solidarity* (New York: Harper & Row, 1984). K. Wojtyla, *Toward a Philosophy of Praxis* (New York: Crossroad, 1981). K. Wojtyla, *The Acting Person* (Boston: D. Reidel, 1979). P. Misner, *Social Catholicism in Europe: From the Onset of Industrialization ot the First World War* (New York: Crossroad, 1991). O. Jackson, *Dignity and Solidarity: An Introduction to Peace and Justice Education* (Chicago: Loyola Univ. Press, 1992). E. Loewy, *Freedom and Community: The Ethics of Interdependence* (Albany: SUNY, 1993).

MATTHEW L. LAMB

SOLLICITUDO REI SOCIALIS

Dated December 31, 1987, published in February 1988, the encyclical *Sollicitudo rei socialis* commemorates the 20th anniversary of *Populorum progressio,* Paul VI's encyclical on development (1967). Its purpose is to reexamine the "question of development" as that issue had been raised throughout the 1960s, indeed has not been settled; in a sense, it has become more pressing.

But *Sollicitudo rei socialis* goes markedly beyond this perspective. Other issues prominently studied include views on global international politics, a critical examination of Western economic civilization, even an attempt at redefining the social teaching of the church in general. The idea of development is furthermore situated in the context of a concept that is strictly theological, even more clearly than was the case as viewed by Paul VI: the encyclical is more theological than ethical, just as it is more political than social.

Diagnosis of the State of Development

John Paul II is aware that some progress has been made. Furthermore, he is aware of the magnitude of the efforts involved. But he considers it his responsibility to conclude that they have failed or that they have at least suffered a serious setback. This diagnosis will be contested by some as too general. It will also be contested insofar as it is linked, as we will see, to a concept of the world divided into (two) blocs, which will soon collapse, and which as early as 1987 has lost something of its pertinence.

Recommendations

Sollicitudo rei socialis hardly makes any innovations over the recommendations of *Populorum progressio* (necessary industrialization, indispensible international solidarity, the obligation to restrain and even to restrict the liberalism that characterizes dealings between rich countries and developing countries) except in the cultural and political sectors. First, it appears more and more clearly, according to the encyclical, that development is a matter of culture, and of a culture that promotes initiative. One of the best-known passages of the encyclical is a protest against obstacles hindering initiative in several social systems (here one must think of both Eastern communist systems and authoritarian but ineffective regimes that exist in a good part of the Third World).

Education and easy access to information are among the most positive means of achieving development. But John Paul II thinks that the problems will not be resolved without radical political reforms. The Catholic church had already insisted on this point in the document issued in the beginning of 1987 by the Pontifical Justice and Peace Commission regarding the international debt of the Third World. But rarely had the idea of democracy, in the current sense of the term, been treated so extensively in a pontifical document. The word "democracy" had not been used so naturally; in Vatican II the issue of "participation" had prevailed. The less developed nations, says John Paul II, "need to reform certain unjust structures, and in particular their political institutions, in order to replace corrupt dictatorial and authoritarian forms of government by democratic and participatory ones. . . . The health of a political community—as expressed in the free and responsible participation of all citizens in public affairs, in the rule of law and in respect for and promotion of human rights—is the necessary condition and sure guarantee of the development of 'the whole individual and of all people'" (SRS 44).

In *Sollicitudo rei socialis,* John Paul II's analysis of international politics was striking. Due to this analysis, the accusation was made (by T. Saphire, M. Buckley, M. Novak) that John Paul supported the idea of a "moral equivalence" between the Western social system and the communist social system, or between the United States and the USSR. It is only indirectly that John Paul had given cause for this accusation. Above all, he had intended to emphasize that the conflict between East and West over the past forty years had been and still was harmful for the Third World: not only had resources that could have improved development been used for armament and even the excessive armament brought about by this conflict, but the blocs had also had a tendency to associate the developing countries with their own causes. The conflict between the blocs had thus often come to involve the Third World. With all the focus on the great quarrel between the East and the West, it had not been possible to devote enough attention and consideration to the problems of development.

John Paul II came to this judgment (on a whole era): "The present division of the world is a direct obstacle to the real transformation of the conditions of underdevelopment in the developing and less advanced countries." He explained: "Each of the two blocs harbors in its own way a tendency toward imperialism, as it is usually called, or toward forms of neocolonialism: an easy temptation to which they frequently succumb, as history, including recent history, teaches. It is this abnormal situation, the result of a war and of an exaggerated concern for security, which deadens the impulse toward united cooperation by all for the common good of the human race, to the detriment especially of peaceful peoples who are impeded from their rightful access to the goods meant for all" (22).

Probably no prior encyclical had carried out such a precise judgment on the actions of the major partners in international politics. At the same time, it must be noted that John Paul II sensed that the situation was in the process of changing (the Washington Treaty had just been signed): "Peoples do not always resign themselves to their fate. Furthermore, the very needs of an economy stifled by military expenditure and by bureaucracy and intrinsic inefficiency now seem to favor processes which might mitigate the existing opposition and make it easier to begin a fruitful dialogue and genuine collaboration for peace" (22).

Worldwide Development

A distinguishing feature of *Sollicitudo rei socialis* is the very broad range of meaning it gives to the concept of development. Development is, of course, economic and social in its modalities, manifestations, and results, but it is above all a process within the human being; it is the expression of a moral dynamic. The moral concept of development occupies a privileged position within the thinking of John Paul II, so much so that some have concluded that by giving greater importance to the consideration of attitudes from which he expects so much, he gives less attention—compared to his predecessors, Paul VI, for example—to structures and to their necessary reform. (We have seen before, however, that he pays close attention to the reform of both political institutions and political mores.)

In the moral perspective with which he is concerned, the pope generalizes the consideration of development: the problem of development exists not only in economically underdeveloped or developing countries but in rich or economically developed countries as well. One could almost say, in countries that are apparently developed. John Paul II explains his point (in terms which seemed to some, particularly in the United States, to pass too severe a moral judgment on the attitudes of people in Western economic civilizations): "Side-by-side with the miseries of underdevelopment, themselves unacceptable, we find ourselves up against a form of superdevelopment, equally inadmissible, because like the former it is contrary to what is good and to true happiness. This superdevelopment, which consists in an excessive availability of every kind of material goods for the benefit of certain social groups, easily makes people slaves of "possession" and of immediate gratification, with no other horizon than the multiplication or continual replacement of the things already owned with others still better. This is the so-called civilization of 'consumption' or 'consumerism,' which involves so much 'throwing-away' and 'waste'. An object already owned but now superseded by something better is discarded, with no thought of its possible lasting value in itself nor of some other human being who is poorer. All of us experience firsthand the sad effects of this blind submission to pure consumerism: in the first place a crass materialism, and at the same time a radical dissatisfaction, because one quickly learns—unless one is shielded from the flood of publicity and ceaseless and tempting offers of products—that the more one possesses the more one wants, while deeper aspirations remain unsatisfied and perhaps even stifled" (28).

Theological Scope

If the concept of development as applied by John Paul II in *Sollicitudo rei socialis* has this moral scope—and results in an ethical criticism aimed at developing civilizations, whatever their level of development—it is because it has first and foremost a theological scope. To justify the undertaking of development and the great effort it requires, not only of developing countries but also of all the others who should share their concern, Paul VI had already resorted to the notion of vocation: the human person is a being who is called upon or driven forward, constantly pulled beyond self or beyond present achievement; eventually this is how God calls each human person. To develop oneself is no less than to answer this call. Moreover, we know the meaning that, in *Gaudium et spes,* Vatican II found in the activity of humans in the universe—in the historical undertaking or adventure of humankind—to the point of seeing in it the premises of the final and everlasting kingdom of God.

John Paul II in turn takes up this view (relying on, among other things, Greek patristic; this view thus is not a modern invention of Vatican II but the most traditional tenet of the church): "A part of this divine plan, which begins from eternity in Christ, the perfect 'image' of the Father, and which culminates in him, 'the firstborn from the dead' is our own history, marked by our personal and collective effort to raise up the human condition and to overcome the obstacles which are continually arising along our way. It thus prepares us to share in the fullness which 'dwells in the Lord' and which he communicates 'to his body, which is the Church.' At the same time sin, which is always attempting to trap us and which jeopardizes our human achievements, is conquered and redeemed by the 'reconciliation' accomplished by Christ. Here the perspectives widen. The dream of 'unlimited progress' reappears, radically transformed by the new outlook created by Christian faith, assuring us that progress is possible only because God the Father has decided from the beginning to make man sharer of his glory in Jesus Christ risen from the dead, in whom 'we have redemption through his blood, the forgiveness of our trespasses.' In him God wished to conquer sin and make it serve our greater good, which infinitely surpasses what progress could achieve. We can say therefore—as we struggle amid the obscurities and deficiencies of underdevelopment and superdevelopment—that one day this corruptible body will put on incorruptibility, this mortal body immortality, when the Lord 'delivers the Kingdom to God the Father' and all the works and actions that are worthy of man will be redeemed" (31).

It is possible, John Paul II points out, to find in the teaching of the Fathers "an optimistic vision of history and work, that is to say, of the perennial value of authentic human achievements, inasmuch as they are redeemed by Christ and destined for the promised Kingdom" (31). Thus John Paul II and Paul VI are both concerned with justifying theologically the hard effort asked of humankind.

The Concept of Solidarity

Much is also asked of men and women in developed countries. John Paul II returns here to the concept of solidarity and to some of its consequences in order to highlight its radical aspects. Solidarity, which goes beyond interdependence, "helps us to see the 'other'—whether a person, people or nation—not just as some kind of instrument, with a work capacity and physical strength to be exploited at low cost and then discarded when no longer useful, but as our 'neighbor,' a 'helper,' to be made a sharer on a par with ourselves, in the banquet of life to which all are equally invited by God" (39).

The concept of solidarity is thus not far from that of charity. There is, in addition, a special dimension of solidarity seen in the light of charity, which can be presented as follows: "One's neighbor is then not only a human being with his or her own rights and a fundamental equality with everyone else, but becomes the living image of God the Father, redeemed by the blood of Jesus Christ and placed under the permanent action of the Holy Spirit. One's neighbor must therefore be loved, even if an enemy, with the same love with which the Lord loves him or her; and for that person's sake one must be ready for sacrifice, even the ultimate one: to lay one's life for one's brethren. At this point, awareness of the common fatherhood of God, of the brotherhood of all in Christ—'children in the Son'—and of the presence and life giving action of the Holy Spirit will bring to our vision of the world a new criterion for interpreting it. Beyond the human and natural bonds, already so close and strong, there is discerned in the light of faith a new model of the unity of the Human race, which must ultimately inspire our solidarity. The supreme model of unity, which is a reflection of the intimate life of God, one God and three Persons, is what we Christians mean by the word 'communion'" (40).

Solidarity implies that the goods of the earth are destined for all. This must be taken in a broad sense: it is not limited to natural resources, that is, everything that is not produced by human industry (insofar as one can say today that anything exists without human industry when almost everything depends, if only in its accessibility, on humanmade infrastructures). Equally destined for all are the riches produced or processed by our work: "That which human industry produces through the processing of raw materials, with the contribution of work, must serve equally for the good of all" (39).

In the past, Paul VI had spoken of the obligation of rich countries to prepare and educate competent specialists both for their own development and for that of needier countries. Problems of translating the universal destination of the goods of the earth into legal and political action certainly arise beyond the wording of these moral concepts. Obviously, ethical reflection connected with the social teaching of the church will still have to be devoted to this matter in the future.

In *Sollicitudo rei socialis* John Paul II finally tries to formulate a new definition of the very teaching of the church regarding these social matters. The highlighting of the church's concern for social matters in the very first words of the encyclical, which serve as the title, *Sollicitudo rei socialis* (the concern about social matters), is already significant in this regard.

John Paul II gives an interesting definition of the social teaching of the church at the very beginning of the encyclical: "An updated doctrinal corpus builds up gradually as the church, in the fullness of the Word revealed by Christ Jesus and with the assistance of the Holy Spirit, reads events as they unfold in the course of history. She thus seeks to lead people to respond, with the support also of rational reflection and of the human sciences, to their vocation as responsible builders of earthly society." One will notice that there is room left here for concrete personal judgment beyond the general doctrine.

John Paul II returns to this issue at the end. He insists on emphasizing the fact that the social teaching of the church does not consist in political or even complete socioeconomic programs, nor does it consist in any kind of set system. He shows that the church is somewhat indifferent to systems. The church in no way suggests that there is a "moral equivalence" among all the concrete political or social positions, but it does not make a radical choice among those global institutional frameworks for which the systems stand (defined by only a few parameters such as free ownership or the absence of free ownership of the goods of production). It is not satisfied with any of them in their concrete configurations (see SRS 20–22). At the same time, it does not exclude any of them in its general definition. It tries to provide the criteria needed to correct, compensate for, or balance any system—or at least to try to correct it.

In *Sollicitudo rei socialis* 41 John Paul II brings social teaching or social doctrine, which at times has been somewhat isolated, back to "moral theology." This expression also points to the clearly theological tone the encyclical takes when it deals with development.

John Paul II also stresses the importance of this social teaching—by no means optional or secondary but (in the face of much indifference within the church) an essential part of the pastoral ministry of the church: "The teaching and spreading of her social doctrine are part of the Church's evangelizing mission. And since it is a doctrine aimed at guiding people's behavior, it consequently gives rise to a 'commitment to justice,' according to each individual's role, vocation and circumstances" (41).

In another part of the encyclical John Paul declares: "Thus, part of the teaching and most ancient practice of the Church is her conviction that she is obliged by her vocation—she herself, her ministers and each of her members—to relieve the misery of the suffering, both far and near, not only out of her 'abundance' but also out of her 'necessities'" (31). With those remarks, one can say, *Sollicitudo rei socialis* is not so much a specific and precise social encyclical, applying general principles to new individual cases (except when it comes to cultural and political aspects of development), but as its title suggests, it deals with the social concern of the church, the extent of this concern and the reason for it. It thus extends the comments made in the second instruction (1986) on liberation theologies (*Christian Freedom and Liberation*), in particular this thought: "By restoring man's true freedom, the radical liberation brought about by Christ assigns to him a task: Christian practice which is the putting into practice of the great commandment of love. The latter is the supreme principle of Christian social morality, founded upon the Gospel and the whole of tradition since apostolic times and the age of the Fathers of the Church up to and including the recent statements of the Magisterium" (*Christian Freedom and Liberation* 71).

Sollicitudo rei socialis contributes in this way, along with several other postconciliar texts, to combining ethics and spirituality, or "social doctrine" and a fundamentally religious theory on how Christians should act (the theory of a "Christian practice"). One must hope that this brings about no weakening of the strict obligations stated in the social code of ethics of the church but that it strengthens what it has already accomplished through a richer and deeper motivation.

See also CULTURE; DEVELOPMENT; INDUSTRIALIZATION; MODERN CATHOLIC SOCIAL THOUGHT; OWNERSHIP; PONTIFICAL COUNCIL FOR JUSTICE AND PEACE; POPULORUM PROGRESSIO; SOLIDARITY.

JEAN-YVES CALVEZ, S.J.

SPIRITUALITY

"Spirituality" as a word rarely appears in Catholic social teaching, especially in those documents that have emanated from Rome. However, it is used—infrequently —in statements from the United States Catholic bishops. In their letter on the U.S. economy the bishops wrote: "We need a spirituality which calls forth and supports lay initiative and witness not just in our churches but also in business, in the labor movement, in the professions, in education and in public life. Our faith is not just a weekend obligation, a mystery to be celebrated around the altar on Sunday. It is a pervasive reality to be practiced every day in homes, offices, factories, schools and businesses across our land. We cannot separate what we believe from how we act in the marketplace and the broader community, for this is where we make our primary contribution to the pursuit of economic justice" (*Economic Justice for All* 25).

While the word "spirituality" may not be dominant in Catholic social thought, its assumptions are woven throughout. The spirituality assumed in Catholic social thought revolves around the understanding of God's involvement in the world through humans as well as the human response to the divine initiative. Given this understanding, this article examines the notion of spirituality in general, the evidence of spirituality in Catholic social thought, and the notion of the "option for the poor" as inherent in a spirituality of discipleship.

The Notion of Spirituality

Every religious tradition or group claiming to be religious has its unique spirituality. Consequently we can speak of the spirituality of Catholic social thought. Although there has been a tendency to identify the notion of spirituality with the interior life or the inner dimension of the person, called "the spiritual," a holistic approach to spirituality considers not only the inner religious experience of the "Other" but also one's expression of or search for that experience in one's relationships with God, self, others, and the world. From this perspective spirituality can be defined as the experience of the transcendent that is expressed in one's world. While conditioned by various cultures and ages, these two dimensions of spirituality—experience and expression—are essential for all kinds of spirituality whether they are monotheistic, Christian, or "Catholic" (i.e., Franciscan, Jesuit, Carmelite, Josephite). This holds true for the "spirituality" of Catholic social teaching.

The spirituality of the NT, which grounds any spirituality implicit in Catholic social thought, centers around the notion of "a spirituality that sees the signs of true discipleship in our sharing of goods and working for justice" (EJA 331). In the Gospels, especially the Synoptic Gospels, the experiential dimension of discipleship involves *sharing* in the life of the Master (through baptism and grace) and the expressive manifestation of that experience by *walking* in the Master's footsteps (through understanding and putting into practice his teachings).

If justice be constitutive of the Gospels (*Justitia in mundo* 6), only Matthew develops what can be considered a "justice spirituality." His unique sevenfold use of the word for justice (*dikaiosyne*) presents Jesus coming to "fulfill all justice" (Mt 3:15), prefigured by John's message (Mt 21:32). Human beings are blessed for hungering and thirsting for the reign of God's justice in their lives (Mt 5:6) and are invited to seek first that reign and its justice (6:32). Experiencing this justice, the disciples are called to express it in a way that exceeds the "justice" of the scribes and Pharisees (Mt 5:20) through specific acts of justice (Mt 6:1): almsgiving, prayer, fasting. The consequence of this justice-discipleship will be persecution (Mt 5:10-12).

Spirituality from another perspective can be considered as a special field of academic interest separate from moral or ascetical theology or even spiritual theology. Spirituality has a definite foundation in theology and cannot be divorced from it, especially if it is practical or pastoral theology. Since 1980 increasing numbers of people involved in theology and religious studies have concluded that spirituality has enough of its own identity and characteristics to suffice for a distinct and separate discipline. Thus it can be predicted that future courses in spirituality will have offerings in the spirituality of Catholic social teaching.

Given the above reflection, spirituality assumes for its object two distinct realities: the experience of God and God's will for the world, which is expressed in that world, and the reflection upon the concrete manifestations of that experience and its expression in various social settings (*Octogesima adveniens* 4). The former meaning deals with the experience of God's work in one's life and world as expressed in one's relationship with others and society at large; the latter notion represents the formal, more academic reflection on the notions of and interrelations among God, humans, and society as articulated in the corpus of church social teaching.

Spirituality in Catholic Social Thought

Behind the spirituality of Catholic social thought is the notion of the Holy Spirit as described by St. Paul: "If we live by the Spirit, let us also be guided by the Spirit" (Gal 5:25). The same Spirit that led Jesus into the desert to experience God (Lk 4:1) led him into the synagogue (Lk 4:14). There he declared that his spirituality was identified with the fulfillment of the text from Isaiah: "The Spirit of the Lord is upon me, because he has anointed me to bring good news to the poor. He has sent me to proclaim release to the captives and recovery of sight to the blind, to let the oppressed go free, to proclaim the year of the Lord's favor" (Lk 4:18-19; see Isa 61:1f. [*Evangelii nuntiandi* 6]). Those who share in the same Spirit are "the sons and daughters of the Church," who are called to be committed to live "in conformity with the program announced by Jesus himself in the synagogue at Nazareth, to 'preach good news to the poor.' . . . It is their task to animate temporal realities with Christian commitment, by which they show that they are witnesses and agents of peace and justice" (*Sollicitudo rei socialis* 47).

In considering the "pattern of Christian life" for U.S. Christians claiming to be discipled to Jesus, the bishops find special relevance for spirituality in the model of the Master: "In her Magnificat, Mary rejoices in a God who scatters the proud, brings down the mighty and raises up the poor and lowly (Lk 1:51-53). The first public utterance of Jesus is 'The Spirit of the Lord is upon me, because he has anointed me to preach the good news to the poor' (Lk 4:18; cf. Isa 61:1-2). Jesus adds to the blessing on the poor a warning: 'Woe to you who are rich, for you have received your consolation' (Lk 6:24). He warns his followers against greed and reliance on abundant possessions and underscores this by the parable of the man whose life is snatched away at the very moment he tries to secure his wealth (Lk 12:13-21). In Luke alone Jesus tells the parable of the rich man who does not see the poor and suffering Lazarus at his gate (Lk 16:19-31). When the rich man finally 'sees' Lazarus, it is from the place of torment, and the opportunity to conversion has passed. Pope John Paul II has often recalled this parable to warn the prosperous not to be blind to the great poverty that exists beside great wealth" (EJA 48).

Spirituality and the Option for the Poor

In Luke, as in the other Synoptics, the issue is not so much "the option for the poor" as the decision to follow Jesus. *If* discipleship is embraced, one must follow the example of the Master, who lived in solidarity with the poor. The only difference will be that today temporal realities have conditioned not the "experience" dimension of spirituality so much as the "expressive" dimension. The notion of God's grace and presence in humans made in God's image has remained quite constant. However, given changes that have taken place in society, a contemporary understanding of the "poor" and the way Catholic social thought understands how disciples of Jesus express his pattern of presence and ministry among the poor reveal a clear change in Catholic social thought as well.

Given the hierarchical and static interpretation of the world of Leo XIII and Pius X, theirs might be called a "status quo" spirituality, wherein the poor were at the bottom of the economic ladder in a world ordained by God to remain classist. In the thought of Pius XI the poor were poor not because of unjust structures but because of personal sin and selfishness that refused to extend right order to the dispossessed. Pius XII maintained the basically classist ideology of his predecessors, as did John XXIII, though in less absolutist terms. For these popes, spirituality did not challenge the underlying hierarchical structures and the place of the poor within those systems.

With Paul VI and John Paul II, as well as the documents of the Latin American and North American bishops, a definite shift from seeing the "plight of the poor" as part of reality and demanding charity to the "misery of the poor" as part of disordered systems, demanding justice came to be expressed in a "spirituality as solidarity" approach. Hearing the "cry of the poor," for Paul VI demands "no compromise whatsoever with any form of social injustice" (EN 18). For John Paul II the spirituality of solidarity with the poor "does not exclude the attitude of opposition" to those dynamics that are fundamentally opposed to solidarity (Dorr, p. 246).

In virtue of the Incarnation, God participates in the human community, whose members are made to image God. They are invited to the banquet of life free of political and economic barriers. Sharing in this redemptive incarnation through the Holy Spirit, disciples of Jesus live in solidarity with those who demand and work for a more just world. To them, God's reign is promised. Participation in the process that will remove obstacles to the poor demands a spirituality that recognizes that change must take place not only in the hearts of individuals but in attitudes and structures as well (EJA 327–28).

See also ALMSGIVING; BEATITUDES; CULTURE; KINGDOM OF GOD; PEACE; POOR, PREFERENTIAL OPTION FOR; SACRED AND SECULAR, RELATIONSHIP OF; SOLIDARITY.

Bibliography: D. Dorr, *Option for the Poor: A Hundred Years of Vatican Social Teaching* (Maryknoll, N.Y.: Orbis, 1983). C. Gudorf, *Catholic Social Teaching on Liberation Themes* (Washington: University Press of America, 1981).

MICHAEL H. CROSBY, O.F.M. CAP.

STEWARDSHIP

The 1979 edition of the *New Catholic Encyclopedia* says that in the past the concept of stewardship applied almost exclusively to managerial skills relating to property and income; today, however, there is a "revival" of the notion of stewardship that has clear social implications related to ecological and environmental concerns (Byron, p. 625). This revised concept has come to be defined as a responsibility to care for and to share the goods we hold in trust (Byron, *Toward Stewardship,* p. 8).

Originally, in Anglo-Saxon terminology, "stewardship" referred to the person in charge of feeding the people of the manor. The steward (styweard) was the central figure in the sustenance of a household. The steward, like the biblical deacon, was one who maintained the *oikos* (Everett, p. 6). The word "stewardship" has come down to us as describing one who was responsible to the lord of the manor for managing essential resources and functions (the *oikonomia*). In terms of the church, the household (*oikos*) of God, stewards are those entrusted with the responsible management of all God has given to humanity, including God's plan of salvation, the "divine economy" (Rogers, p. 11; McKenzie, p. 847).

Clearly, stewardship has come to mean more a way of life than a single, particular action. Stewardship is a Christian lifestyle: "The life of stewardship is an ongoing process of integration whereby we relate our whole person to the whole action of God. . . . By acknowledging our dependence upon God for all life, we are called to regard both material things and human capacities not as private possessions or as the property of limited groups, but as God's" (Dietterich, p. 10). Scriptural and ecclesiological data support the fact that our model for a life of stewardship is Jesus, who is the authentic steward because he is the faithful, obedient servant who gives his life to bring humanity into wholeness and communion with God. This modeling should be envisioned as an exercise of Christian faith and responsibility, understood to emerge gradually in the course of religious development (Whiteheads, pp. 135–50). The maturing of a Christian steward may be envisioned as involving three movements: the experience of self as child of God, as disciple of the Lord, and as steward in the church.

From a Christian point of view, stewardship is based on three principles: responsibility for all others in the world, based on Christ's commandment of love; forming a critical judgment to inculcate Christian values into our society; and assuming the courage to be prophetic by speaking out regarding both justice and injustice (Smutko, pp. 37–39). Thus there may be no more meaningful scriptural text for the Christian steward than the one from Paul's First Letter to the Corinthians: "People must think of us as Christ's servants, stewards entrusted with the mysteries of God" (1 Cor 4:1).

To be a steward presupposes one has a deep personal spirituality. Being responsible for the "mysteries of God" is an awesome task that requires a continual personal prayer life and faith experience (Flaherty, p. 604). If we are to complete the *imago Dei,* we must grow into the *likeness* of God. The steward realizes that one's existence, and that of others, is not a possession to be grasped. The steward is neither a vitalist nor a pessimist, but always a person of hope (Maestri, p. 169). From an ethical point of view, then, there can be no human being to whom we do not owe what Paul Ramsey calls "canons of loyalty" (Ramsey, p. xii).

Rootedness in prayer and spirituality necessarily leads to stewardship, alerting us to be sensitive to life and to the needs of others. An attribute of an authentic steward is generativity—the willingness to move beyond self into involvement with the larger world, to mentor others in life-giving ways, to use power responsibly, to engage in wise and future-oriented decision making, and to have the courage to "let go and let God" (Rogers, p. 14; May).

Authentic stewardship necessarily leads one to reverence and awe: an attitude of profound respect before life itself. Christian stewardship presupposes a belief in an all-encompassing presence of God in all of life and the totality of creation, with an openness to sharing the gifts of God and to receiving God's gifts from others and through others. Reverence and awe connote seeing God in all and all in God (Hogan, p. 7). Stewardship calls us to recapture something of the wonder, awe, and ecstatic joy that flows from the contemplation of the created world. The well-known *Benedicite* calls upon all creation—angels, humanity, birds, animals, fish, sky, land, sea, and all the forces of nature—to "bless the Lord; praise and exalt God above all forever" (Dan 3:52-90). Today we need to recall those forgotten aspects of creation theology that call upon all of us to respect nature and to live in harmony with it (Snell, p. 2181). A "theology" of stewardship de facto reaffirms the concept of the sacramentality of nature.

Such reverence for all creation implies that stewards do not function on some island, making decisions and plans in isolation. Stewards are collaborators, responsible for each other and for all of creation. When God said to Cain, "Where is your brother, Abel?" and Cain replied, "Am I my brother's keeper?" the implication seemed to be Yes, you are responsible for your brother. Indeed, at the Last Judgment God will say to the condemned, "Whatever you have done to the least of my brothers and sisters you have done to me." A clear example of such collaboration may be found in such organizations as Bread for the World, Pax Christi, Network, and the Coalition for Responsible Investment.

The classic biblical texts are the first three chapters of Genesis. Here humankind is called to be stewards of creation *under* God; all greed, abuse of creatures, and insensitivity are against the Creator's will. God desires and commands a harmony within the creation (a will reflected in many of the psalms as well as in Jewish harvest customs and the counsels to moderation in the Wisdom literature). God's first command to us is that of responsibility: "Let them have dominion over the fish of the sea, the birds of the air, and the cattle and over all the wild animals and all the creatures that crawl on the ground" (Gen 1:26). This dominion is not license to exploit creation but the mandate to be conscious that all of creation has been entrusted to us to care for. Genesis thus defines stewardship: The responsibility to recognize and reverence the interconnection and interdependence of the entire created world. It clarifies our relationships—with God, with one another, with the whole cosmic environment—and indicates that we must give of ourselves in order to fulfill our covenant relationships with God.

Jesus' proclamation of the kingdom of God is an announcement of a world transformation. This is referred to in Revelation as the advent of a "new heavens" and a "new earth" (Rev 21:1). Since Jesus has declared that he has come not to destroy but to fulfill (Mt 5:17), we believe that the material universe *will* achieve the end for which it was created. To be a steward means to believe in the advent of Christ's kingdom, the ultimate triumph of good over evil, and with it the restoration of harmony in this broken universe. St. Paul tells us of his vision of creation in which all things are subject to a loving God and Christ's liberating power. All of creation is to be respected (see especially Rom 8:12-14; 1 Cor 8-11).

As "stewards of the mysteries of God," Christians are responsible for the gift of the gospel and the gifts of the church, the sacraments, and ministry. The gospel should be considered the greatest of all responsibilities for Christians, not to be "hidden under a bushel" but proclaimed and witnessed. The parable of the three servants (Mt 25:14-30) calls us to be stewards of the gospel by preserving, sharing, and witnessing our faith in the risen Jesus and by becoming *communio* with other communities in service to the world (Sider, p. 220). Biblical parables of both testaments stress that God's concern for the poor is boundless. At pivotal points of revelation history (e.g., Exod 3-6) God was at work liberating the oppressed. Jesus' identification with the poor is astonishing. Consequently, an authentic steward clearly follows in the footsteps of the God of the poor. As stewards of the poor we are especially called to be stewards of values: for example, the gift of healing. Luke 10:8-9 tells us that Jesus said to his disciples, "Into whatever city you go, after they welcome you . . . cure the sick that are there. . . . Say to them, 'the reign of God is at hand.' " Healing, then, is a respected value in and for the church (Malone; Curley).

Stewards are aware of the biblical concept that all evil in the world stems from sin, when we deviate from God's designs reflected in creation. Throughout the biblical narrative we find that fidelity to the covenant and obedience to God's laws always evoke a promise of fruitfulness (e.g., Isa 11:6-8). The biblical implication that our lives are inextricably bound up with creation ought not to be lightly dismissed. Everything we possess we hold in trust, and an ethic of stewardship concerns itself with fidelity to and violations of that trust (1 Jn 4:8-10, 19). The unethical steward is the one who violates that trust: by neglecting to care for that which has been entrusted, by destroying without adequate reason the substance of that which has been entrusted, by appropriating or assigning to oneself the exclusive use of that which has been entrusted and doing so in a way that denies the legitimate claims of others. The unethical steward is characterized by insensitivity, pride, avarice, and greed (Byron, "Ethics" 231).

Church fathers such as Basil the Great and Augustine dealt with the concepts of ownership and the redistribution of resources. In these patristic writings there is clear moral insistence that possessions and land are intended for the benefit of all. More recently, numerous church documents have dealt with the concept of stewardship. *Gaudium et spes* teaches: "In the face of this immense enterprise now involving the whole human race, men and women are troubled by many questionings. How ought all of these things be used? To what goal is all this individual and collective enterprise heading?" (GS 33). The document continues with an essential principle: "Redeemed by Christ and made a new creature by the Holy Spirit, humanity can, indeed must, love the things of God's creation. . . . Humanity thanks the divine benefactor for all these things, uses them and enjoys them in a spirit of poverty and freedom; thus they are brought to a true possession of the world, as having nothing, yet possessing everything" (37).

The 1986 U.S. bishops' pastoral *Economic Justice for All* raises the consciousness of Christians that we "are obliged to come to the relief of the poor and to do so not merely out of . . . superfluous goods" (69). The statement of the 1971 synod of bishops, *Justice in the World* (*Justitia in mundo*), indicates that the gospel and the ongoing teaching of the church make radical demands, calling us as Christian stewards to fulfill basic obligations of justice, and beyond that, to the fullness of love, for "justice attains its inner fullness only in love" (JM, part 2, no. 8). Moreover, the bishops insist that working for justice is an integral part of evangelization. This is repeated and elaborated in *Evangelii nuntiandi* (1975).

In *Laborem exercens* John Paul II calls for a spirituality of stewardship, a theology of work that encompasses the broad range of "secular" endeavors. The pope describes the world as a workbench where all are contributing to a master design. One remembers the medieval view of Thomas à Kempis, who testified that each time he went into the world he came back less a man. Certainly this attitude is shattered in a revised concept of stewardship. Stewardship calls us to hold in trust numerous values: natural resources (Weber, p. 337; Fox), care for the poor and those who are sick, the sanctity of life (Kelly, p. 40), and conservation of the world's goods (Mische; Land; Jones; Pignone).

Stewardship demands that we adopt an ethic of responsibility toward the earth as well as toward all human persons. Stewardship demands that we reverse the effects of exploitation as we strive to feed the hungry, house the homeless, seek ethical means of population control, terminate pollution, and cease the rape of the world's resources. As stewards we must also be sensitive to the *quality* needed for a life to be fully human. We must make both urban and rural areas habitable places that can nurture a life that is fully human. And we must care for our wilderness areas so that their beauty will be preserved and even enhanced (Snell, p. 2184).

See also CREATION; ECOLOGY; GOODS, DISTRIBUTION OF; JUSTICE IN THE WORLD; LABOREM EXERCENS; LAND RIGHTS; NATURAL RESOURCES; POPULATION.

Bibliography: W. Byron, "The Ethics of Stewardship," *New Catholic World* 220 (1977) 230–37; *Toward Stewardship* (New York: Paulist, 1975); "Stewardship," *New Catholic Encyclopedia* 17:625. J. Curley, "Stewardship: Service, Management, Advocacy," *Hospital Progress* 64 (1983) 32–35. P. Dietterich, *New Prospectives on Christian Stewardship* (Chicago: Center for Parish Development, 1984). W. Everett, *Stewardship, Talented Trust* (Oikos Project, 1984). H. Flaherty, "Fiscal Management and Christian Stewardship," *Sisters Today* 56 (1985) 599–604. M. Fox, *A Spirituality Named Compassion* (San Francisco:

Harper & Row, 1990). W. Hogan, "Stewardship, Reverence and Prayer," *The Priest* 10 (1983) 7–8. B. Jones, "World Grain Reserve," *New Catholic World* 220 (1977) 250–53. M. Kelly, "A Stewardship Challenge: Reconciling Faith and Finances," *Health Progress* 65 (1984) 36–54. P. Mische, "Parenting in a Hungry World," *New Catholic World* 220 (1977) 238–43. W. Maestri, "The Stewardship of Life," *Linacre Quarterly* 47 (1980) 166–70. J. Malone, "Church as Steward: Our Healing Heritage," *Hospital Progress* 64 (1983) 28–31. G. May, *Addiction and Grace* (San Francisco: Harper & Row, 1988). J. McKenzie, "Stewardship," *Dictionary of the Bible* (Milwaukee: Bruce, 1965). M. Pignone, "Concentrated Ownership of Land: A Problem of Stewardship and World Hunger," *New Catholic World* 220 (1977) 254–59. P. Ramsey, *Ethics on the Edge of Life* (New Haven: Yale Univ. Press, 1978). M. Rogers, "Stewardship," *Church* 2 (1986) 11–17. R. Sider, "A Biblical Prospective on Stewardship," *New Catholic World* 220 (1977) 212–21. G. Smutko, "Toward a Spirituality of Stewardship," *The Priest* 35 (1979) 37–39. P. Snell, "The Bible of Ecology," *The Bible Today* 104 (1979) 2180–85. L. Weber, "Practical, Utopian, or Poor—Just Stewards," *Spirituality Today* 33 (1981) 329–39. E. Whitehead and J. Whitehead, "The Evolution of Stewardship," *Spirituality Today* 36 (1984) 135–50.

GERALD COLEMAN, S.S.

STRIKE, RIGHT TO

A growing understanding of social sin has led to the church's appreciation for the importance of withdrawal of participation from industrial or civic processes as a bargaining tool to secure other rights. Initially Catholic social teaching was marked by an understanding of society as an organic whole; obedience to authority and acceptance of one's lot in life were cherished as the underpinnings of harmony and good order. Lack of attention to the rights of workers was acknowledged as the cause for worker strikes, but the results (idleness, unavailability of goods, threats to trade and commerce, precipitation of violence and rioting) withheld the magisterium from a completely positive judgment on work stoppage. The hope was for a legitimate authority, namely, the state, to intervene on behalf of the worker when the employer was not moved by exhortations of justice and charity to honor the rights of workers. As the church has recognized the need for various sectors of society to collaborate on a planned world economy supportive of both labor and capital, the strike (which presumes the right to work, to a just wage, to associate and organize) has become the mainstay in the list of rights afforded workers in Catholic social teaching. However, concerns about violence, class polarization, overt class warfare, and the politicization of trade unions make it a right carefully circumscribed by the church.

Papal and Conciliar Thought

In Leo XIII's 1891 encyclical *On The Condition of Workers* (*Rerum novarum*) vital importance is attached to peace and good order (RN 53). Harmony among the classes was natural, conflict unnatural. Therefore what might make a strike wrong rather than what might justify a strike is emphasized. Although Leo notes the condition of workers as a subject of bitter controversy (81), he calls for workers to press their claims with reason (82) and cautions them "not . . . to injure the property or to harm the person of employers; in protecting their own interest, to refrain from violence and never to engage in rioting" (31). Although work stoppages may be caused by "labor which is too long and too hard and the belief that pay is inadequate," strikes themselves are named as "this evil, which is frequent and serious" (56). The state is called on as the most effective source of authority to anticipate and completely prevent a strike that "interrupts work, injures trade and commerce and the general interests of the State" (56). Leo does not hesitate to give the church's blessing to those activities and organizations that seemed best fitted to protect and further the legitimate interest of the worker. Yet his fears of socialism and strife between the classes motivated a parallel concern that the worker understand what was considered the natural order, the order in which all do not occupy an equal place in the community.

The fear of precipitating class struggle and the challenge of Marxism is the context for the proscription of strikes by Pius X and Benedict XV. Pius X's *motu proprio* of 1903 affirms inequality in society as "innate," the "work of God who wanted a diversity of conditions." Exhorting all to charity, he condemns strikes throughout his papacy, declaring that they are against the well-being of the workers and the quiet life of the citizen. Benedict XV's 1914 *Ad beatissimi apostolorum* places strikes in the same context. The poor should not strive against the rich as though the rich had taken part of the goods of others. Such class strife is considered "irrational," particularly because the poor themselves by honest industry can improve their fortunes if they choose. Benedict deplores the frequency of strikes, "which suddenly interrupt the course of city and of national life. . . . We see hostile gatherings and tumultuous crowds and it not unfrequently happens that weapons are used and human blood is spilled" (12).

In the 1931 *On Reconstructing the Social Order* (*Quadragesimo anno*) Pius XI argues again for the state, whose authority comes from God, to intervene in matters of employer-employee dispute: "Strikes and lockouts are forbidden; if the parties cannot settle their dispute, public authority intervenes" (QA 94). However, in later encyclicals written at the height of Nazi power, Pius XI develops an understanding of when it might be appropriate to withdraw one's allegiance from civic authorities. The church, he asserts in *Firmissimam,* "condemns every unjust rebellion or act of violence against the properly constituted civil power. On the other hand . . . if the case arose where the civil power should so trample on justice and truth so as to destroy even the very foundations of authority, there would be no reason to condemn citizens for uniting to defend the nation and themselves by lawful and appropriate means" (35). This statement represents a breakthrough in Catholic social teaching regarding the necessity to obey those who present themselves with authority. From 1937 to the present both the economic and the political strike are no longer presented as forbidden actions but rather as extreme actions necessitating thoughtful discernment.

By 1961, when John XXIII's *On Christianity and Social Progress* (*Mater et magistra*) affirms labor unions for "no longer recruiting workers for the purpose of strife but rather for the purpose of pursuing a common aim" (MM 97), collective bargaining and the legitimacy of the strike are recognized and affirmed. Vatican II's Pastoral Constitution on the Church in the Modern World (*Gaudium et spes*) refers to the strike as "a necessary though ultimate means for the defense of the workers' own rights and the fulfillment of their just demands" (GS 168). Paul VI's *Call to Action* (*Octogesima adveniens*) in 1971 simply regards the strike as a legitimate measure if used under appropriate conditions and within the just limits of last resort and proportionality. "Union activity is not without its difficulties. Here and there the temptation can arise of profiting from a position of force to impose, particularly by strikes—the right to which as a final means of defense remains certainly recognized—conditions which are too burdensome for the overall economy and for the social body, or to desire to obtain in this way demands of a directly political nature" (OA 14). The distinction between the political and the economic spheres of society is probably motivated by a desire to maintain societal stability and a recognition that economic and social divisions do not always reflect political divisions. Strikes are not to be of a political nature, that is, they are not to be inspired by the attempt to undermine the operation of an existing society. More recent papal social teaching remains unsympathetic toward strikes of a general nature designed to bring about the downfall of an unjust political system. In *On the Development of Peoples* (*Populorum progressio*) workers who try to undermine the operation of the existing society are cautioned against fighting a real evil at the cost of greater misery (PP 31).

Other potential abuses of the strike weapon are noted by Paul VI and are reiterated in John Paul II's works. First, workers and unions may be so affected by the spirit of the market system that a strike is used to obtain the most they can get rather than to combat oppression. Second, work stoppages, especially those affecting public services, affect the life of an entire nation, and discernment must prevail to assess when the harm becomes inadmissible. And finally, workers inspired by resentment toward oppression are warned not to place false hopes in class warfare.

John Paul II's 1981 *On Human Work* (*Laborem exercens*) does not regard human society as a complex social system in equilibrium that must be protected even if the lower sector lives in poverty. Rather, the latest encyclicals, aware of world economic systems and the potential for a sharp political polarization along economic lines, encourage dialogue, collaboration, and solidarity between all participants in the economic processes. John Paul II identifies the primary value of human work in the fact that the one who is doing it is a person, and he urges both capital and labor to share a mutual interest in economic change. If labor is alienated, capital is alienated. Capital and labor are to collaborate together to provide for worker participation in industry and to shape the kind of state and social systems that will lead to a just economy. To call on people to consider systems, in addition to worker-employer relations, as forces behind injustice is to expose structural or systemic sin. Unions are considered a mouthpiece for the struggle for social justice, a struggle that is the "normal endeavor for the just good" (LE 20). Unions are not to "play politics," but John Paul II acknowledges union activity as undoubtedly entering the field of politics. The strike is called "a kind of ultimatum to the competent bodies, especially the employers. This method [of pursuing just rights] is recognized by Catholic social teaching as legitimate in the proper conditions and within just limits. . . . We must at the same time emphasize that a strike remains . . . an extreme means" (20).

United States Tradition

Examination of the right to strike in the Catholic tradition of one country further illustrates the development of Catholic social teaching in this area. In the late 19th century little U.S. Catholic support was available for trade unions because of their association with violence, Protestants, nonbelievers, socialists, and other radicals. Prior to Leo XIII's 1891 encyclical Bishops Gibbons, Ireland, and Spaulding upheld the right of workers to unionize and acknowledged in theory the right to strike. However, the 1919 Bishops' Program of Social Reconstruction issued by the U.S. hierarchy claimed that "the great number of unnecessary strikes . . . is evidence that justice has been widely violated as regards the rights and needs of the public" (SR 149) and called for industry to be carried on "as a cooperative enterprise for the common good, not as a contest between two parties for a restricted product" (SR 156).

By 1920 John A. Ryan had become a foremost spokesperson for progressive social reform. In his work *Social Reconstruction* he argued that the strike, the most powerful instrument a union had, could be justified by three principles: (1) if what is sought by the strike is just, (2) if all peaceful and less harmful means of bargaining have been exhausted, and (3) if the good to be attained outweighs the evil that will occur. Ryan's appeal was not only to theology but also to common sense, a theme reiterated in a 1933 letter, *The Present Crisis,* issued with the authorization of the hierarchy in response to the depression. This document called for unions to seek "competent and disinterested advisers, that their organizations may ever be characterized by sanity" (71). In addition to Ryan, the study of Dorothy Day, Peter Maurin, Paul Hanley Furfey, and labor priests Peter Yorke, Edward McGlynn, Peter E. Dietz, Raymond A. McGowan, Francis J. Haas, John O'Grady, and the early Charles E. Coughlin provides insight into the controversial participation of Catholics in unions and strikes through the depression era.

Before the Second Vatican Council the publications of the U.S. episcopacy remained ambivalent about strikes. However, in the early 1970s the United States Catholic Conference openly supported striking farm and migrant laborers. A strike and boycott of lettuce in addition to the leadership of Cesar Chavez and the negotiating skill of Fr. George Higgins, a member of the bishops' Ad Hoc Committee on Farm Labor, proved successful in negotiating a series of labor contracts for United Farm Workers. Again, in 1973 the Bishop's Committee on Social Development and World Peace issued a statement supporting the strike of the Amalgamated Clothing Workers of America against the Farah Manufacturing Company for resisting the formation of a union. And in 1980, several southern bishops endorsed a union boycott of J. P. Stevens, a textile company, helping to resolve a dispute between the company and the union. In addition, the United States Catholic Conference has continuously been involved in lobbying Congress on behalf of labor and the right to strike, and the 1986 pastoral letter, *Economic Justice for All,* asks workers to reject calls for less adversarial relations with employers when "they are a smokescreen for demands that labor make all the concessions" (EJA 302).

Many works can be studied for a reflection of the varied U.S. Catholic lay and clerical responses to union organization and strikes throughout the 20th century. *The Central-Blatt and Social Justice,* a periodical published from 1910 (continuing today as *The Social Justice Review*) by the Federation of German American Catholics, and *The Catholic Worker,* published from 1933 by Dorothy Day and Peter Maurin's Catholic Worker movement, are especially notable.

See also ASSOCIATION OF CATHOLIC TRADE UNIONISTS; CATHOLIC WORKER, THE; DIETZ, PETER E.; LABOR AND CAPITAL IN CATHOLIC SOCIAL THOUGHT; LABOREM EXERCENS; RERUM NOVARUM; RYAN, JOHN AUGUSTINE; WORK, THEOLOGY OF.

Bibliography: O. v. Nell-Breuning, "Streik," *Lexikon für Theologie und Kirche* 9 (Freiburg, 1957–68). S. Agócs, *The Troubled Origins of the Italian Catholic Labor Movement, 1878–1914* (Detroit, Wayne State Univ. Press, 1988). G. Baum, *The Priority of Labor* (Paulist, 1982). P. Sullivan, *Blue Collar—Roman Collar—White Collar: U.S. Involvement in Labor Management Controversies, 1960–1980* (Univ. of Notre Dame Press, 1987).

MARYANNE STEVENS, R.S.M.

SUBSIDIARITY, PRINCIPLE OF

A central norm of 20th-century Roman Catholic social theory, the principle of subsidiarity was initially used to protect individuals and groups, but more recently it has been employed to define the relationship between individual nation-states and worldwide public authorities.

The principle of subsidiarity assumes the natural right to associate and to organize. More essentially and contrary to Hobbesian political theory, it presupposes the central tenets of Catholic social thought: the individual and the family precede the state; that is, individuals do not exist for the state but rather the state exists for the well-being of individuals and families entrusted to its care; individual rights including that of ownership are prior to the state. The principle also affirms that there is nothing done by a higher or larger organization that cannot be done as well by a lower or smaller one; intervention, therefore, should occur only as a last resort to make up for deficiencies.

The principle of subsidiarity is not stated in *Rerum novarum,* nor does it play a prominent role in the political writings of

John A. Ryan or Joseph Husslein. It holds a central place, however, in Pius XI's *Quadragesimo anno,* in John XXIII's *Mater et magistra* and *Pacem in terris,* in Vatican II's *Gaudium et spes*, and it also appears in the writings of Paul VI and John Paul II.

In order to appreciate the growing importance of this principle in 20th-century papal thought, one must recall the political context of late 19th-century Europe and its prevailing social theories, the milieu in which Leo XIII wrote *Rerum novarum.*

As Etienne Gilson has observed, Leo's encyclical deals not so much with improving the social conditions of the working class as with the rights and duties that bind rich and poor in the body politic. Although Leo is careful throughout *Rerum novarum* to uphold the natural rights to property and work as well as the rights of parents and families, he nevertheless openly supports the authority of the state to participate actively in welfare, labor, and economic programs. The state, therefore, may set minimum wages, restrict work for women and children, and regulate working conditions and the working day.

The encyclical's support for the intervention of civil authority can best be seen in a frequently misunderstood statement about strikes. Leo holds that it is correct and valid to invoke the aid and authority of the law to intervene in a strike if there is an imminent danger of disturbance to the public peace. However, the pope does caution that the state should not undertake more nor proceed further than is required to remedy the evil or remove the mischief (RN 53–56).

However, Leo's strong endorsement for state intervention poses several problems: What are the limits concerning state control in education, health, and labor? What place should small unions and associations have in the community? Nowhere does *Rerum novarum* provide a specific principle that sets safe limits to government intervention and at the same time specifies the reasonable autonomy and independence of groups within political communities. Such a task fell to Pius XI in *Quadragesimo anno.*

In *Quadragesimo anno* Pius XI explicitly makes the principle of subsidiarity the guiding norm upon which the social order is to be restored: "That most weighty principle, which cannot be set aside or changed, remains fixed and unshaken in social philosophy. Just as it is gravely wrong to take from individuals what they can accomplish by their own initiative and industry and give it to the community, so also it is an injustice and at the same time a grave evil and disturbance of right order to assign to a greater or higher association what lesser and subordinate organizations can do. For every social activity ought of its very nature to furnish help to the members of the body social, and never destroy and absorb them" (QA 79). Pius XI, embracing the principle of subsidiarity, seeks to establish the proper role of government in the social and economic life of the community and to rebuild the correct relationships that ought to exist between large and small associations of citizens and workers. He employs the principle of subsidiarity to indicate how conflicts between classes can be removed and how harmony between the state, trades, professions, labor, and capital can be restored. Contrary to Leo XIII's desire to encourage state action against the resistance of liberal capitalism, Pius XI uses the principle of subsidiarity to curb excessive involvement of the state in the affairs of labor, economics, and welfare. More positively, subsidiarity helps to establish the autonomy of groups and to specify the correct relationships that ought to exist between different organizations and associations within society (QA 49).

In both *Mater et magistra* and *Pacem in terris* John XXIII employs the principle of subsidiarity to teach that the individual is the foundation, cause, and end of all social functions. *Mater et magistra* affirms the notion that labor is both a duty and a right of every human being. "Consequently, it is in the first place the responsibility of men themselves to regulate mutual labor relations. Only in the event that the interested parties are unwilling or unable to fulfill their functions, does it devolve upon the state to intervene and to assign labor equitably, safeguarding the standards and aims that the common good properly understood demands" (MM 44). John recognizes, however, that recent developments of science and technology provide additional reasons for greater intervention by public authorities. The purpose of such intervention is clear: the reduction of economic imbalances or political tensions on the regional, national, or international levels (MM 54).

In *Pacem in terris* John XXIII explicitly applies the principle of subsidiarity to the international situation and appeals for the establishment of an international public authority to address the vast, complex, and urgent economic, social, political, and cultural problems of the day. While not intending to limit the sphere of action of public authority within the individual political community, the pope nevertheless argues that individual states are currently not in a position to address pressing international problems with any hope of a positive solution. His ultimate goal is an international authority that can protect a universal common good and thereby create an environment in which the public authorities of each political community, its citizens, and its intermediate associations can carry out their tasks, fulfill their duties, and exercise their rights with greater security (PT 140–41).

Finally, Paul VI in *Populorum progressio* and *Octogesimo adveniens* draws on the principle of subidiarity when he reiterates the need for international authority to coordinate the establishment of just political and economic spheres (e.g., PP 78), as does John Paul II's *Sollicitudo rei socialis* when it examines international structures and movements that attempt to foster authentic development throughout countries unable to do so on their own (e.g., SRS 21, 26).

See also AUTHORITY, POLITICAL; COMMUNITY ORGANIZATION; COOPERATIVE ASSOCIATIONS; ECONOMIC ORDER; FREEDOM; MODERN CATHOLIC SOCIAL THOUGHT; POLITICAL PHILOSOPHY; QUADRAGESIMO ANNO.

Bibliography: J.-Y. Calvez, and J. Perrin, *Eglise et societe economique: L'enseignement social des Papes de Leon XIII a Pie XII, 1878–1958,* 2nd ed. (Paris: Aubier, 1959); *The Social Thought of John XXIII: Mater et Magistra* (Chicago: Henry Regnery, 1964). J. Beyer, "Le principe de subsidiarite: Son application en Eglise," *Gregorianum* 69:3 (1988) 435–59.

MICHAEL E. ALLSOPP

SUFFRAGE MOVEMENT

The Catholic church did not officially oppose the suffrage movement of the late 19th and early 20th centuries. American Catholic sentiment in the movement's early stages, however, was predominantly one of opposition. Attacks on women's suffrage were made by James Cardinal Gibbons of Baltimore and Archbishops Henry Moeller of Cincinnati, Sebastian B. Messmer of Milwaukee, and John H. Williams of Boston. Political activity by Catholic leadership to prevent suffrage was especially intense in Massachusetts, buttressing forces that were able to delay the enfranchisement of Massachusetts women until 1920. The opposition of Catholic clergy reflected the sentiment of Catholic journals. The *Catholic Encyclopedia* described antisuffrage groups as "the voice of common sense," since "the female sex is in some respects inferior to the male sex as regards body and soul" (Kenneally, p. 47). In 1900 the National American Woman Suffrage Association listed only six Catholic clergy as supporters of woman suffrage. Lucy Burns was the only nationally prominent Catholic suffrage leader in the early stages of the movement.

Reasons cited for Catholic opposition to extension of the franchise to women included (1) natural-law arguments that claimed distinct spheres for the sexes and the fear that usurpation by women of political activites belonging to the male sphere would upset the natural order; (2) an equation by many Catholics of suffrage with birth control; and (3) reaction to the development of a social climate hostile to Catholicism due to anti-Catholic sentiments of the 19th-century suffrage movement.

Although many Catholics feared woman suffrage in the early stages of the movement, the Catholic church never officially opposed woman suffrage. A compilation of letters and addresses by Catholic clergy in 1915 sought to correct the impression held by many Americans that the Catholic church officially opposed woman suffrage. An editorial in the official organ of the Archdiocese of Chicago stated that the church "has never taken any stand either for or against the proposal. True, individual members of the Church . . . have expressed opinions pro and con in regard to it, but these are but individual opinions" (Rorke, pp. 9–10). Officially, the Catholic church left the issue of woman suffrage alone.

Catholic sentiment slowly began to change in the latter part of the suffrage movement. Catholic union members began to believe suffrage could be a means of improving working conditions. Catholic women in New York, Philadelphia, and Boston began to organize statewide suffrage organizations with the help of Margaret Foley, an active Catholic suffragette in the later stages of the movement. In 1895 Thomas Scully of St. Mary's in Cambridge became the first Massachusetts priest to support women's suffrage publicly. Other priests began to support the movement, including Patrick W. Riordan, archbishop of San Francisco, who expressed support in a letter read in all archdiocesan churches on August 11, 1912; Paul P. Rhode, auxiliary bishop of Chicago; and Jones Corrigan, S.J., chair of the department of philosophy at Boston College. Corrigan claimed that in a democracy women have a moral right to vote.

Following ratification of the Nineteenth Amendment Catholic leadership abandoned opposition to woman suffrage. The reform was accepted, and voting was seen as a duty that Catholic women should exercise with wisdom.

See also FEMINISM AND CATHOLIC SOCIAL THOUGHT; WOMEN.

Bibliography: J. Kenneally, "Catholicism and Woman Suffrage in Massachusetts," *Catholic Historical Review* 53:1 (1967) 143–57. J. McKee, "Shall Women Vote?" *Catholic World* 102 (October 1915) 45–54. M. Rorke, *Letters and Addresses on Woman Suffrage by Catholic Ecclesiastics* (New York: Devin-Adair, 1915).

LOIS ANN LORENTZEN

SYNOD OF BISHOPS

According to the revised Code of Canon Law, "the synod of bishops is that group of bishops who have been chosen from different regions of the world and who meet at stated times to foster a closer unity between the Roman Pontiff and the bishops, to assist the Roman Pontiff with their counsel in safeguarding and increasing faith and morals and in preserving and strengthening ecclesiastical discipline, and to consider questions concerning the Church's activity in the world" (can. 342).

Responding to a variety of proposals made by the Fathers during the debates at Vatican Council II, Pope Paul VI announced the establishment of the synod by his *motu proprio* entitled *Apostolica sollicitudo* of September 5, 1965. The council itself then described the synod in its Decree on the Pastoral Office of Bishops in the Church (*Christus Dominus* 5).

Although the synod meets only when called to do so by the pope, it is a permanent institution with a general secretary named by the pope, a standing secretariat, and a council of the secretariat whose members are periodically elected by synod assemblies.

The synod can meet in three types of assembly: ordinary, extraordinary, and special. The ordinary or general assemblies consist of members who serve *ex officio,* by election, and by appointment. Among the *ex officio* members are certain dignitaries of the Eastern Catholic churches and heads of dicasteries of the Roman curia. The elected members include one to four members sent by each episcopal conference, depending on its size, and ten religious men chosen by the Union of Superiors General of Clerical Institutes. The pope may appoint additional members up to 15 percent of the total membership.

At extraordinary sessions the episcopal conferences are represented by the presidents alone, and the representatives of religious superiors of men are reduced to three. At special sessions, which deal with problems specific to a particular region, the representatives of the episcopal conferences and religious institutes are limited to those from the region involved.

Since the first meeting in 1967, which dealt with a variety of questions growing out of Vatican II, ordinary sessions have been held approximately every three years. These assemblies have been in 1971 (on faith and justice and on the ministerial priesthood); 1974 (on evangelization); 1977 (on catechetics); 1980 (on the family); 1983 (on penance and reconciliation); 1987 (on the laity); and 1990 (on priestly formation). The 1994 meeting is to deal with the consecrated life.

The synod of 1971 produced the documents *Justice in the World* and *The Ministerial Priesthood.* All the ordinary assemblies since then have been followed up by apostolic exhortations issued by the pope in his own name on the subject treated by the synod.

Extraordinary assemblies have been held twice, the first in 1969 dealing with papal primacy and episcopal collegiality; the second in 1985 to discuss the fruits of Vatican Council II. The synod of 1985 issued *Message to the People of God* and a final report.

There have been three special assemblies, each concerned with a particular region, and all held in Rome. The first (1980) dealt with the Dutch church; the second (also in 1980) dealt with the Ukrainian church. The third (1991) dealt with the role of the church in a changing Europe. A special assembly on the church in Africa is to open in April 1994.

The pope convokes the meetings of the synod, determines the agenda, and presides in person or through others. The primary purpose of the synod is to assist the pope in his care for the universal church. Since it is advisory in nature, the synod does not normally have power to issue binding decrees, although the pope could give it such power in a particular case.

Besides advising the pope, the synod is intended to promote the collegial union of all the bishops. Pope John Paul II, in a speech on April 30, 1983, spoke of the synod as "a particularly fruitful expression and an effective instrument of episcopal collegiality, i.e., of the particular responsibility of the bishops surrounding the bishop of Rome" (*Acta apostolicae sedis* 75 [1983] 650). Some theologians hold that the synod, inasmuch as it is described as "representing the entire Catholic episcopate" (*Apostolica sollicitudo* 1.1; CD 5), can perform strictly collegial acts. Others maintain that its acts, while not strictly collegial, are expressions of the collegial spirit.

The structures and procedures of the synod of bishops are still in the process of development. Some have proposed that it should have statutory power to issue binding decrees in its own name, but others respond that the sessions are too short for such decrees to be carefully prepared and that lengthier sessions would keep the bishops away from their dioceses too long. Another proposal is that the synod should be in permanent session, but this would turn the synod into a double of the Roman curia and would prevent it from reflecting the current perspectives of the various regions from which the bishops come. Among other proposed reforms are that the synod should sometimes meet in different continents, that the preliminary reports and speeches should not be kept secret, and that more nonbishops, including women, should be invited to attend, at least as nonvoting members. There is nothing in the Vatican II documents or the present Code of Canon Law that would prevent the implementation of these last three suggestions.

See also EVANGELII NUNTIANDI; JUSTICE IN THE WORLD; PAUL VI; VATICAN COUNCIL II.

Bibliography: J. Coriden et al., eds., *The Code of Canon Law: A Text and Commentary* (New York: Paulist, 1985). P. Granfield, *The Limits of the Papacy* (New York: Crossroad, 1987) 90–97. J. Ratzinger, "The Structure and Tasks of the Synod of Bishops," in *Church, Ecumenism, and Politics* (New York: Crossroad, 1988) 46–62. J. Tomko, ed., *Il sinodo dei Vescovi: Natura, Metodo, Prospettive* (Vatican City: Libreria Editrice Vaticana, 1985).

AVERY DULLES, S.J.

T

TARIFFS

To understand the nature and role of tariffs in the contemporary economic and political world, one must first grasp how profit is generated in the capitalist system. In condensed terms, profit is the differential between the cost of producing an item and its selling price on the open market. To produce a finished commodity, a capitalist must buy the requisite raw materials, finance the purchase of machinery and tools, and purchase the labor power of workers who manufacture the item in return for wages. Raw materials, machinery, and labor, therefore, represent costs incurred by the capitalist. These expenses must be surpassed by the market price of the commodity to produce a profit. Profit, then, is surplus value above and beyond the various costs of an item and the labor invested in its production. Since the free-market system is theoretically driven by open competition, capitalists who can minimize costs and manufacture items in large volume can quickly surpass and eliminate competitors whose mode of production is more costly or less efficient.

In a global economy like that of the late 20th century, national industries are constantly threatened by international competitors who can produce the same or better goods in a more efficient and profitable manner. An influx of foreign-produced items can lead to the decline and even collapse of national industries. For example, automobile manufacturers in the United States have been directly threatened since the 1970s by foreign competitors. Asian and European manufacturers have taken over a large share of the American market by selling vehicles of equal or superior quality at lower prices than comparable American automobiles. The result has been a marked erosion of the American automotive industry with a concomitant rise in unemployment in many industrial areas of the United States.

To counteract the effects of foreign competition, many nations resort to tariffs. In essence, a tariff is a surtax added to the market price of foreign-made goods. When a tariff is imposed on imported items, nationally produced goods retain a competitive edge, since their cheaper price makes them more appealing to consumers. This guarantees adequate levels of sales and profit for national manufacturers and provides continued work for laborers who might otherwise face unemployment. Almost all nations use tariffs to protect their industries and workers, albeit in varying degrees.

The ostensive rationale for a tariff, then, is to protect a nation's economic foundations. In some instances, however, tariffs are used as a political weapon to defend the class-related interests of a certain social strata. Since the wealthy generally own the means of production and often wield disproportionate political power, they may attempt to force their government to shape its economic and political policies in accord with their needs. As a result, tariffs may be enforced to protect inefficient or moribund industries that cannot tolerate international competition. Shielded from competitors, local manufacturers can fix the price of their goods and reap disproportionate profits. In essence, they have a captive clientele who has no choice but to accept nationally produced commodities that may be of inferior quality or unjustly priced. In such instances tariffs are not only a surtax on foreign products. They are also a surtax on every member of society, including the poor, who are forced to pay inflated prices for their material needs. Under such circumstances, the poor end up obliquely subsidizing the already affluent.

Catholic social teaching in the past century has constantly stressed that economic systems must be free and open. The purpose of economic activity is collective well-being, not individual or class-specific wealth. To the extent that tariffs protect local production from unfair competition, they fall within the realm of ethical economic policy. If, however, the purpose of a tariff is the protection of inefficient industries or the interests of a limited segment of the population, it cannot be considered an acceptable instrument of economic or political policy.

The question of just economic relationships between nations and among social classes has been articulated most recently by Pope John Paul II in *Sollicitudo rei socialis* (1988). The pope calls for a more just and open world economy, thus calling into question tariffs whose ends are short-sighted and ultimately unjust.

See also COMPETITION; CONGLOMERATES; DEVELOPMENT; ECONOMIC ORDER; EMPLOYMENT AND UNEMPLOYMENT; INDUSTRIALIZATION; PROFIT; TAXES.

CURT CADORETTE, M.M.

TAXES

There are three ethical questions dealing with taxation: what constitutes a just tax system? how should tax money be justly distributed? and what is the obligation to pay taxes? The second question concerns the broader question of distributive justice within society and will not be treated here as a separate topic. Catholic hierarchical social teaching and Catholic social ethics in general have addressed these questions but not to the degree that one might have expected.

The general outline of the Catholic approach to a just tax structure is clear and generally agreed upon. In the words of *Economic Justice for All: Pastoral Letter on Catholic Social Teaching and the U.S. Economy*: "The tax system should be structured according to the principle of progressivity so that those with relatively greater financial resources pay a higher rate of taxation. . . . Action should be taken to reduce or offset the fact that most sales taxes and payroll taxes place a disproportionate burden on those with lower incomes" (EJA 202).

A progressive tax system means that those who have more should not only pay more arithmetically but should pay a greater percentage of their income and wealth in taxes. The justice of a progressive tax structure is based on an understanding of the social nature of human beings, the social destiny of the goods of creation, and distributive justice.

The Catholic tradition insists that human beings are by nature social and called to live with one another in political community to achieve the common good. The Catholic tradition insists that the goods of creation exist to serve the needs of all God's people. While recognizing the right to private property, the Catholic tradition and contemporary hierarchical teaching stress that such a right is both limited and grounded in the communal destiny of the goods of creation to serve the needs of all God's people.

Distributive justice talks about the relationship between society, or the state, and the individual. How should the goods and burdens of the society be distributed? Burdens should be distributed with a heavy emphasis on one's capacity to contribute. Those who have more must contribute more. Whereas commutative justice (that which involves the relationship of one individual to another individual) is blind, no respecter of persons, and deals with arithmetic equality, distributive justice is not blind, does respect persons, and involves proportional equality. A too individualistic anthropology and perspective sees everything in terms of commutative justice and insists on arithmetic equality. The understanding that human beings are by nature social and called to live in political communities grounds a communitarian ethic that recognizes the role of distributive justice. For the sake of the common good, those who have more have an obligation to contribute more not only arithmetically but also proportionately. The care for the poor and concern in overcoming unjust gaps between the rich and the poor are part of the common good and also part of the purpose of just taxation.

A progressive tax system, as the American bishops point out, argues against regressive forms of taxation, such as the sales tax or the social security levy as it exists in this country, since they are not based on proportional justice. In today's world Catholic hierarchical teaching and social ethics in general could learn a lesson from John A. Ryan, who in the early 1900s insisted on a very heavy tax on increased land value. The increase in land value comes not from what the individual owner does but from the value given to the land by society. Hence not only a social view of the human person but also the very source of the increased value here indicates that much of such profit should go to society and not to the individual.

On the second issue of the obligation to pay taxes, most contemporary Catholic thinkers maintain there is a moral obligation to pay just taxes based on social or legal justice, which governs the relationship of individuals to society and the state. The Catholic tradition, perhaps because moral theology was primarily directed toward the confession of sins, has dealt more extensively with this question than with the just distribution of the tax burden.

The most surprising aspect in the tradition was the contention that tax laws were purely penal laws that involved no moral obligation to pay taxes but only a moral obligation to accept the penalty for not paying taxes. A purely penal-law theory of taxation goes back in some form to the 15th century. In retrospect, it seems that such a theory was devised as a way to protect people against unfair taxes that were often proposed by the rulers of the day. To this day a few Catholic theologians still defend the purely penal-law theory of taxes, but the vast majority insist that just tax laws oblige in conscience. There is a moral obligation for the individual to contribute to the needs of the common good of society.

Also, in the historical tradition many held that tax laws oblige in commutative justice based on a presumed contract between the individual and the ruler or the state. Taxes are paid for the service rendered by the ruler or the state. With the development of hierarchical Catholic social teaching under Pope Leo XIII in the 19th century and the simultaneous importance given to Thomistic thought, most Catholic commentators grounded the obligation to pay just taxes in legal or social justice, which governs the individual's relationship to society and the state.

See also CIVIL LAW, FUNCTION OF; COMMON GOOD; GOODS, DISTRIBUTION OF; LAND; OWNERSHIP; PRIVATE PROPERTY; SOCIAL SECURITY; STEWARDSHIP.

Bibliography: M. Crowe, *The Moral Obligation of Paying Just Taxes* (Washington: Catholic Univ. of America Press, 1944). C. Curran, *Toward an American Catholic Moral Theology* (Notre Dame, Ind.: Univ. of Notre Dame Press, 1987) 93–118. R. Pasquariello, *Tax Justice: Social and Moral Aspects of American Tax Policy* (Lanham, Md.: Univ. Press of America, 1985).

CHARLES E. CURRAN

TECHNOLOGY

The word "technology" has acquired a highly charged, even quasi-religious meaning in 20th-century United States society. Because of the peculiar nature of the West's love affair with progress and its identification of progress with science and technology, the question of who gets to define the meaning and tell the story of technology continues to be hotly contested by an ideologically diverse array of individuals and institutions.

Most important among these various tellers of technological stories, more than textbook authors, technological museums, or academic historians of technology, are representatives of corporate America. Firms such as General Motors and Exxon devote very considerable resources toward teaching what they consider an acceptable version of the history of their technology. Their efforts merit attention because they represent the best-funded and most effectively disseminated definition of what "technology" has come to mean within United States society.

Although corporations frequently use print and electronic media advertisements to propagate their technological ideologies, the most complete current example of corporate technological history can be found in the major pavilions at the Walt Disney World's EPCOT Center. EPCOT (Experimental Prototype City of Tomorrow) attracts an astonishing fifteen to twenty million patrons every year, each willing to endure long lines for high priced indoctrination in a relentlessly smiling contempt for the past together with the invocation of a sanitized and inexorably beneficial technological future. EPCOT's message is based on and imitates the vision that took shape in the corporate pavilions of the United State's three major 20th-century World's Fairs (Chicago, 1933; New York, 1939; New York, 1964), in brief, (1) that earlier human attempts to solve life's problems resulted in laughably primitive technologies; (2) that the coming of Western science and technology produced the present-day set of technologies, which benefit all society while generating no serious liabilities; (3) that the present array of technologies and their managers can be trusted to lead ordinary citizens, such as those visiting the exhibit hall, to a bright, trouble-free future.

For EPCOT-style ideologues, there exists an entity called "technology," a single force, godlike and autonomous, that advances inevitably through the power of the scientific method applied through research and development (R&D). Nonexperts should never involve themselves in the debates by which specific technological investments are decided. These decisions must be taken by experts precisely because, according to the ideology, the only question to be determined is how to discover the next best step in "progress's" gradual shaping of the future world, wherein science and technology control more and more of natural reality.

The ideology of an inevitably benign technological progress rests, therefore, on a foundation of contempt for the often turbulent political processes by which technologies come into existence. Because it masks the politics of technological decision making, the corporate technological vision is important for those who are seriously concerned with Catholic social thought. When granted uncritical acquiescence, the ideology of autonomous technological progress fosters self-contempt and passivity in adult citizens in what must be considered one of the most important areas of contemporary life, that is, how the body politic allocates its scarce resources when creating and modifying technological systems.

Over the past three decades a new branch of history, the history of technology, has begun to articulate an alternative language for understanding how technological change occurs and how technologies, particularly those that become very successful within their host societies, operate as an integral part of the larger societal order. Historians of technology begin by refusing to study technology as the singular, inevitable, and progressive force of the corporate ideology. A careful study of the past reveals instead many specific technologies, each with its unique circumstances. This approach (the contextual history of technology) attempts to achieve the sort of understanding of technology-society relationships that serves what has always been history's primary purpose: to liberate human beings through the demythologizing of false and absolutizing oversimplifications and by restoring people to an awareness of the inherently messy and unpredictable character of their heritage.

Successful technologies, say the historians of technology, happen by cultural and political choice more than by fate. Human beings, with their tangled motives, decide which designs are attended to, which are ignored, and why the technologies found worthy of inventive and fiscal attention take the final shape they do. This maxim, the central tenet of contextual history of technology, provides a basis for understanding what has been called the "technological style" of some given body politic, and it offers a method for interpreting the specific values that a society deems worth a major investment of its resources.

Because a technical design reflects the motives of those who designed it, historians of technology look to the values, biases, motives, and worldview of the designers when asking why a given technology turned out as it did. Every technology, then, embodies some distinct set of values. Then, too, to the extent that a given technology becomes successful within its society, it fosters some values while it inhibits others. Trade-offs abound. There is no technological free lunch. The set of values that are favored by a technology, especially when these are seen against the backdrop of other values that "lose" because of the technology's success, represents that technology's "style." For example, think of the triumph of individualistic over communal values in a nation that chooses to invest much more of its tax money in automobile-oriented highways than it does in electric-rail, mass-transit systems.

To take the matter one step further, we might note that the men and women with access to the venture capital that every successful technology requires while being designed tend to be the same people who hold cultural hegemony in their society. "Holding cultural hegemony" means belonging to that group of people who shape the dominant values and symbols of their society. While they never form a single, historically tidy group—as a technological conspiracy theory might suggest—they do tend to view the world from the same perspective. Consequently we can look for a *set* of successful technologies that, in any relatively stable era of history, embody the same technological style.

Thus, beginning in the late 19th century we find a set of technologies that achieve societal dominance in the United States (rail networks, electric light and power systems, and automotive production systems dominate the list for a half century) and embody a commitment to centralized, authoritarian systems that define conformity to pre-set standards as their primary human virtue, displacing an earlier style that depended more on the messier processes of negotiation among a diverse array of actors to solve technical problems (e.g., the earlier American shop-floor, where management and highly skilled master artisans openly debated the pace and method of production). Such a pattern can lead the historian of technology to ask whether 20th-century American society has been marked by an effort on the part of its elite members to foster conformity and a set of standardized habits in the less powerful members of society.

It would be an oversimplification to say that technological style operates as the sole cause of prevailing cultural values. The values embedded in successful technologies originate in the worldview of those who design and maintain them. Designers at the Ford Motor Company doubtless brought prior attitudes about the desirability of social control over "non-American" immigrants with them to their explicit task of planning the company's 1914 moving assembly line. Still, it would be equally oversimple to say that technologies exert no influence on the values of their host society. If technological designs are not value-neutral, and this is the central premise of the approach taken here, then their very success, the many ways their host society comes to depend on them and adapt to their constraints, operates as an amplification of their inherent values. Thus to follow the example of standardization used above, one could argue that certain styles of consumerist advertising, which matured just after World War I, simultaneously represent a societal response to earlier standardized systems (in particular, to the need of mass producers of automobiles and electrical appliances to motivate ordinary United States citizens to higher levels of consumption), while at the same time they constitute a new mechanism for generating standardized behavior in a new area of societal life (i.e., not only the prior standardization of worker behavior on the moving assembly line but, it is hoped by advertisers, standardization of consumer motivation through the mediation of advertisements).

Even this brief and overly simple sketch of the contextual approach to technological history demonstrates that when the discussion of technological change has been rescued from the abstract ahistoricity of progress talk, technological decisions stand revealed in terms of their inherent power relationships. Every technical choice—to invest inventive or entrepreneurial attention in any given design, to bring venture capital to bear on the endeavor—allocates scarce resources. Which citizens have access to the design process? Whose values are embodied and whose ignored in the systems that become economically and politically successful? Questions such as these, political as they must be, lie at the heart of any historically valid understanding of technology.

It follows, then, that how we think and talk about technology influences our political as well as our intellectual stance. Insofar as we retain the linguistic habits of Disney-style progress talk we define ourselves as passive drifters on the technological tide. By doing so we choose a schizoid life, understanding ourselves as responsible adults within some narrowly defined arena of family and close friends, but abdicating responsibility for the many decisions by which investments come to shape technologies. Belief in one's personal ineptitude, when it comes to deciding technological priorities, means belief in our culture's most popular form of idolatry, the worship of progress and technology as apolitical and ahistorical forces. It appears, then, that the commitment of faith together with the basic requirements of adult citizenship require attention to the debates that must go on whenever human beings create or continue to maintain the specific technical systems that give shape to their culture.

See also ADVERTISING; CAPITALISM; COMPUTERIZATION; CORPORATIONS; DEMOCRACY; INDUSTRIALIZATION; PLURALISM; PUBLIC AND PRIVATE, RELATIONSHIP OF.

Bibliography: W. Bijker et al., eds., *The Social Construction of Technological Systems* (Cambridge, Mass.: MIT Press, 1987). S. Goldman, ed., *Science, Technology, and Social Progress* (Bethlehem, Pa.: Lehigh Univ. Press, 1989). J. Staudenmaier, *Technology's Storytellers: Reweaving the Human Fabric* (Cambridge, Mass., MIT Press, 1985). L. Winner, *Autonomous Technol-*

ogy: Technics-Out-of-Control as a Theme in Political Thought (Cambridge, Mass., MIT Press, 1977).

JOHN M. STAUDENMAIER, S.J.

TERRORISM

A broad spectrum of means of armed coercion is available to states, political movements, activist groups, and individuals. These means range from nuclear deterrence and defense to conventional war to various types of revolutionary war and counterinsurgency, often in the form of guerrilla and counterguerrilla warfare. All of these means of armed coercion may be potentially justified if their aim is "counterforce," not "countervalue." That is, if they are used primarily to attack enemy armed forces and military targets, not noncombatants and nonmilitary targets. If counterforce means do destroy or damage noncombatants and nonmilitary targets we treat these results as "collateral damage." We then judge whether the efforts to limit collateral damage and the results of those efforts have been such as to make that damage proportionate to the military necessity to engage in the primarily counterforce actions. If, however, it appears that collateral damage was not seriously limited or even that it was deliberately maximized, we call the attacks countervalue.

Beyond the spectrum of means of armed coercion that are at least potentially consonant with legitimate military necessity, law, and morality, there is terrorism. Despite the ubiquitous shadow that terrorism has cast on contemporary life and the enormous literature on the subject, there is little agreement on definitions of terrorism. An adequate definition is provided in Charles W. Kegley Jr.'s useful collection of essays. Kegley, emphasizing that terrorism is "international in scope, origin and effects," cites a definition of terrorism as "a form of political violence, directed at governments but often involving ordinary citizens, whose aim is to create a climate of fear in which the [demands] of the terrorists will be granted by the government in question [but] extended to apply to acts perpetrated by governments themselves in order to instill a sense of fear" (Kegley, p. 6).

Seen in contrast to the possibly permissible counterforce means of armed coercion, terrorism is an extreme form of deliberate, usually exclusively, countervalue violence that has no justification in legitimate military necessity, international law, or morality. Maximization of collateral damage and the threat of more is the essence of terrorism. Viewed from the perspectives of accepted forms of military counterforce coercion, the definition of terrorism is the intentional use of disproportionate and indiscriminate means of violence to obtain political ends. By definition, then, terror is illegal and immoral—unless one adopts an extreme position that any means is justified by particular ends. Neither international law nor modern just-war doctrine accepts such a position. There is no legal terror, no just terror.

Some religious and ideological perspectives in the world today do, however, justify terror on the basis of the supposed ultimate goals of those who employ it. Terror has many advantages. Since it only requires a small number of active terrorists, often employing simple means, it is economical. It offers ways for movements that could not possibly engage incumbent governments by conventional or even guerrilla means to challenge them. Terror brings international publicity to terrorist causes and spreads fear and confusion, weakening target governments and societies.

Because of its apparent utility, terrorism is often condoned or even supported and encouraged by states such as Libya or Syria that see this form of violence as advancing their own political and ideological ends. On the whole, however, states condemn terrorism in principle. Still, the problem of suppressing terrorist activity remains. Suppression requires serious international cooperation through sharing of intelligence, cooperation of law-enforcement agencies, and extradition of suspected terrorists. Progress along these lines has been modest. Underlying the problem of terrorism has been the difficulty of obtaining consistent commitment by states of all kinds to the proposition that no political, religious, or ideological end justifies terrorist activity.

See also FORCE; KILLING; TOTALITARIANISM; WAR.

Bibliography: B. Jenkins, *International Terrorism* (Santa Monica, Calif.: RAND Project Air Force, November 1985). C. Kegley, Jr., *International Terrorism: Characteristics, Causes, Controls* (New York: St. Martin's Press, 1990). W. Laqueur, *The Age of Terrorism* (Boston: Little Brown, 1987). W. O'Brien, "Counterterror Deterrence/Defense and Just War Doctrine," *Theological Studies* 48 (1987) 647–75.

WILLIAM V. O'BRIEN

THOMAS AQUINAS, CONTRIBUTION OF

It is not difficult to describe the contribution of Aquinas to the social teaching of the Catholic church. Better than anyone else, Aquinas defines the moral categories that govern Catholic moral teachings. He gives better expression to the moderate Catholic position on political, economic, and social ethics than did anyone before him, and his account has become the moral basis of Catholic teachings on these issues up to the Second Vatican Council. Aquinas bases many of his ethical doctrines on the teachings of Aristotle, which entered the West at his time and which were more secular and positive than were the prevailing Augustinian doctrines. In the late Middle Ages, in early modern times, and both before and after the reign of Leo XIII (1878–1903) his moral thought on social issues shaped the growth and development of Catholic teaching. Aquinas' social teachings are a cohesive whole, for he believes that the same moral norms that govern individual human actions and choices should also regulate social, economic, and political activities.

Aquinas' social ethical thought was invoked by the modern popes to resolve what they called the "social problem," the set of economic-social-political problems that emerged from the collapse of the medieval guild system under the weight of nationalism, capitalism, and the Industrial Revolution in the mid-19th century. These forces exacerbated the exploitation of the worker and farmer with the consequent threat to family life, the social order, and political stability. From the 18th century until the Second Vatican Council the church found in Aquinas' social ethical teachings a formidable means to deal with these problems. Modern popes spoke of the root of the "social problem" as fundamentally spiritual, which reflects Aquinas' view that the root of social, economic, and political problems are failures of faith, charity, and ethics.

In what follows, I will first summarize Aquinas' social ethics and then briefly recount the impact of these doctrines on Catholic social teaching.

Aquinas' Social Thought

Natural law. Aquinas' greatest contribution to Catholic social thought is his account of the natural law, for he developed what most regard as its fullest and most complete formal expression. His formulation is far in advance of anything previously enunciated, and no Catholic moralist since him has expressed this doctrine in its theological, philosophical, and moral dimensions with his clarity and coherence.

Traditionally, Aquinas has been understood primarily as a natural-law ethicist, and more recently he has been seen as a virtue moralist or rationalist moralist, but none of these adequately capture the scope and depth of his thought. It is true that he teaches that nature obliges all to perfect their nature by means of actions that promote self-development and fulfillment. But all find their happiness and fulfillment by acting in accord with not just nature but also reason, grace, and the virtues, and this is why it is not entirely accurate to classify him purely as a natural-law moralist (*Summa theologiae* 1-2 94, 3; 1-2 109, 2; 1-2 63, 2).

The natural law is grounded in the eternally established order of God, the eternal law, and it enables us to develop our uniquely human qualities (ST 1-2 94, 1). It is known by reason and our natural inclinations, and its moral requirements stem not only from reason and the human will but also from the reality of our human nature itself. Our abiding and stable nature is rational, free, spiritual, and intelligent, and actions are good or bad to the extent they promote these natural qualities (ST 1 18, 2 ad 2; 1 18, 3; 1 19, 10; 1 59, 3; 1 75, 3; 1 76, 1; 1 76, 4; 1 77, 5; 1 78, 1; 1 83, 1; 1 86, 4 ad 3; 1-2 50, 3 ad 2). Nature itself is the remote moral norm governing human action, and on occasion it will proximately determine the moral character of some acts (ST 1-2 94, 2), even though the sinful is ordinarily defined by its opposition to the virtues (ST 1-2 72, 1; 55, 3).

Virtue theory. Following Aristotle, Aquinas teaches that the virtues are habits that perfect human rational powers and orient them toward ends that fulfill and perfect human nature (ST 1-2 55, 1). They are differentiated according to their generative principles and the powers they specifically perfect (ST 1-2 62, 1). The intellectual virtues of wisdom, science, and understanding perfect the intellect (ST 1-2, 57, 2). The cardinal virtues of prudence, justice, temperance, and fortitude dispose our emotions toward their proper objectives and form our nature according to its natural principles (ST 1-2 58, 2). Justice and charity give a proper and legitimate orientation to the will (ST 1-2 57, 1). Prudence is a distinctive virtue because it perfects our reason as well as our passions in their orientation toward operations (ST 1-2, 61, 1). All of the virtues support one another and are interdependent, and the virtue of prudence is necessary for them to realize the good (ST 1-2 65, 3). While prudence perfects reason and surpasses temperance and fortitude, justice is the greatest of the moral virtues because it is closest to reason and establishes proper relationships with others (ST 1-2 66, 4). Fortitude controls anger, while justice and charity perfect the will (ST 1-2 57, 1). And temperance regulates and perfects our drives for sexual pleasure, food, and drink (ST 1-2 60, 4).

The cardinal virtues perfect us according to natural principles, while the theological virtues do so from supernatural grounds (ST 1-2 62, 2 ad 1). The theological virtues of faith, hope, and charity are from grace, and they direct us to God and supernatural happiness (ST 1-2 62, 1). True charity is defined by Aquinas as friendship coupled with benevolence (ST 2-2 23, 1), and it is a virtue because it is in accord with right reason (ST 2-2 23, 3). Charity is the greatest of the theological virtues because it has God as its object (ST 1-2 66, 1), draws closer to God than do any of the other virtues that only lead to reason (ST 1-2 66, 5), and makes all of the other virtues to be true virtues by binding them together (ST 1-2 66, 6). One begins a charitable relationship with goodwill, which is wishing another well and is the beginning of friendship (ST 2-2 27, 2).

The order of charity demands that those closest be the first beneficiaries of our generosity (ST 2-2 26, 7), but Thomas gives such emphasis to love of neighbor that one should love others more than one's body and be willing to sacrifice for their sake (ST 2-2 26, 5). It is better to love one's friends than one's enemies (ST 2-2, 27, 7), but even enemies should be loved and be the objects of charity. We should be ready to come to the assistance of our enemies in situations of urgency and care for their basic necessities (ST 2-2 25, 9). Those who act beneficently toward others love them more than they are loved by their beneficiaries (ST 2-2 26, 12).

Theory of justice. Aquinas was not blind to issues of social justice in his time, and his writings on justice, society, politics, and economics can only be adequately understood if they are seen in the context of his concern for these issues. He gives much consideration to the social aspects of justice, and he considers respect of persons (unfairly favoring one over another) to be the fundamental violation of distributive justice and one of the most grave sins against justice (ST 2-2 63, 2). Following Aristotle, he holds that the common good takes precedence over private goods (ST 1-2 90, 2), and he regards justice as the highest moral virtue because it resides in the highest part of the soul, our reason, and orients us toward the common good (ST 2-2 58, 1).

The object of justice is right (*jus*), which does not mean that justice is absurdly oriented toward the just but rather toward what is equal, fair, and balanced in relationships (ST 2-2 57, 1). Rendering to each person what is properly theirs is the proper act of justice (ST 2-2 58, 7), and justice serves right (*jus*) because it is the enduring will to render another what is commensurate, balanced, and fair in a relationship (ST 2-2 58, 1). The object of the right is that which is naturally, relatively, or absolutely commensurate between two individuals or groups (ST 2-2 57, 3). Thomas holds that there are two kinds of rights, (1) natural rights, which are based on an equality deriving from nature, and (2) positive rights, which are based on an equality or balance deriving from common consent or an agreement (ST 2-2 57, 2). This applies to not only commutative justice but also distributive justice (ST 2-2 63, 1).

In different situations different virtues define what is morally good and morally evil, but in general the virtue of justice dominates Aquinas' thought on social, economic, and political issues. Justice is primarily concerned with external actions rather than the interior emotions or passions and with rendering to others what is properly theirs in order to establish a proportionality, balance, equality, and fairness in the relationship (ST 2-2 58, 9).

Legal justice is the preeminent form of justice, directs all of the virtues to the common good, and is the closest concept in Aquinas' thought to what we call social justice today (ST 2-2 58, 5). Its two proper forms are commutative justice, which governs relations between two persons, and distributive justice, which governs the relation of the part to the whole (ST 2-2 61, 1). The mean of justice is the real and rational mean, and what Aquinas calls the arithmetical mean governs exchanges or commutations (ST 2-2 58, 10). Commutative justice demands that a strict equality prevail in exchanges between individuals (ST 2-2 61, 2). A different standard governs distributions because they are based on the importance of the person to the entire community (ST 2-2 61, 2).

Social theory. Aquinas devotes much attention to the acts and attitudes that cause conflict and strife in society, and he believes that charity in all of its dimensions is the key to establishing and protecting social peace and prosperity (ST 2-2 37, 1). Peace is tranquillity resulting from order (ST 2-2 29, 1 ad 1), and it is only possible where the appetites are directed at what is truly good (ST 2-2 29, 1 ad 2). He argues that true peace cannot take place among those who are evil, but only among the virtuous (ST 2-2 29, 1). Authentic peace is the result of charity, because this causes one to fulfill the others' will as one would one's own (ST 2-2 29, 3). The unity of peace is not based on unity of opinions, which are primarily intellectual in nature, but on a unity of desire and appetite (ST 2-2 29, 3 ad 2). Peace is a work of justice because justice removes the obstacles to peace, but it is primarily a work of charity, which causes peace by its very nature (ST 2-2 29, 3 ad 2). The sin of discord, which is the result of vanity, is against charity, and it is different from strife, which results from anger because discord results from a divergence of wills (ST 2-2 37, 1, 2).

Aquinas devotes much attention to the virtues of beneficence, magnanimity, liberality, and almsgiving because they are acts of friendship that foster the common good and society's unity (ST 2-2 31, 1). They promote common aspects of the good, which society needs because they build the bonds of community and promote peace (ST 2-2 31, 1). Friendliness is necessary to promote social peace, and generosity from one's excess to the poor is necessary to foster bonds of friendship between the rich and the poor, but it is not simply required of justice because no debt is paid by friendliness (ST 2-2 114, 2).

Almsgiving is obligatory because it is demanded by right reason and is necessary for the virtuous life (ST 2-2 32, 5). Justice only obliges to give from one's surplus but not from one's necessity, and to refuse to give to the needy from one's excess when the need is urgent and clear is a mortal sin. He does hold, however, that it is not necessary to give alms if this would reduce one's station or put one's family in jeopardy (ST 2-2 32, 6). One should give to those who are personally closer and holier than others and to promote the common good (ST 2-2 32, 9). Alms should be given that are sufficient to relieve another's need but not more, so that one can give to others who are in need (ST 2-2 32, 11).

Human beings are social animals by nature (ST 1-2 61, 5; *De regimine principum* 12), and society, family, and the state are natural, as is their hierarchical ordering (ST 1-2 105, 4; *De reg. prin.* 1). The family, too, is natural, and it cannot be deterred from its natural ends for other purposes (ST 3 41, 1). The family and society are necessary to achieve their proper and legitimate ends, and they are to be granted the necessary freedom to accomplish these ends (ST 3 41, 1).

In Aquinas' view, the proper grounding and end of law is reason, nature, and the common good (ST 1-2 90, 2). Law is a rule or measure that prescribes the virtues useful for the common good (ST 1-2 96, 3), and an unjust law or one that does not foster the common good is not true law (ST 1-2 95, 2). The law allows some vices and only oppresses the most serious ones, not quickly or suddenly, but gradually and through time (ST 1-2 96, 1). Laws that are just and promote the common good and are not promulgated beyond the lawgiver's power are binding in conscience and must be obeyed.

Aquinas holds that marriage is natural because it provides the best protection for children (ST 3 67, 1) and nature allows spouses to separate, (ST 3 67, 1), but it prohibits remarriage (ST 3 67, 3). Aquinas separates himself from Aristotle on the issue of slavery and claims that it is not only just but also beneficial, because it spares the life of the slave and provides needed services for the former (Pol. 1, 4, n. 75, 79).

Economic theory. With Aristotle, Aquinas contends that ownership of private property is morally legitimate because it was both natural and served utilitarian purposes (ST 2-2 66, 1, 2). Private property also promotes peace and maintains greater order because it promotes responsibility toward material things (ST 2-2 66, 2). But while allowing private property, he requires owners to use goods for the common good (ST 2-2 66, 2).

Aquinas devotes an entire article to condemn cheating and using deceit to sell things for more than they are worth (ST 2-2 77). For justice to prevail in commercial transactions, one must maintain an equality and balance between what a commodity or service is worth and the price paid (ST 2-2, 77, 1). Contrary to what many believe today, Aquinas believes that the seller has to state known defects in items offered for sale (ST 2-2, 77, 3). Theft is a mortal sin except when this is necessary because of the stress of dire need (ST 2-2 66, 7). Usury is seriously immoral because it is selling money twice, first to consume it and second to use it (ST 2-2 78, 1). But Aquinas allows lenders and borrowers to enter into agreements to compensate for a lender's losses greater than those incurred by the borrower (ST 2-2 78, 2). And he allows borrowers to repay lenders for the favor of granting them a loan and to express a debt of friendship (ST 2-2 78, 2 ad 2).

Aquinas emphasizes the virtue of liberality, which enables one to use well the things given for one's life (ST 2-2 117, 1). The liberal person gives to another in need from one's excess, and Aquinas gives it such emphasis because this virtue is critical to promoting the common good and social justice. He holds that excess riches are given to some to use for the benefit of others, and the rich man should spend more on others than on himself (ST 2-2 117, 1). The virtue of liberality is determined by the means available to one, and one has this virtue more because of one's habits than because of the amount one donates to the needs of others (ST 2-2 117, 1, ad 3).

Liberality is not the greatest virtue, even though it is one of the most gratifying, but it is one of the most important for creating bonds of friendship between the rich and poor (ST 1 18, 6). Motivating this virtue is mercy, which is sorrow at another's misfortune and is a sign of friendship (ST 2-2 30, 1). Mercy is a virtue if it protects justice (ST 2-2 30, 3), and cruelty (*cruditas*) is a vice because it is an excess in exacting punishment because of the pleasure it gives (ST 2-2 159, 1). One who is angry without being hurt is cruel, and Aquinas notes that the term points to a similarity with wild beasts (ST 1 59, 2).

While extolling liberality he condemns covetousness, the undue love of material things (ST 1 19, 1). Covetousness is a form of theft and is not primarily a sin of the flesh but a spiritual sin resulting from spiritual and religious failures rather than from the weakness of the flesh (ST 1 18, 7). The covetous are without mercy, which is the first effect of greed, are excessively restless and anxious, and are given to violence, fraud, and deceit (ST 1 18, 8). Riches give the false and empty impression of self-sufficiency, and greed generates treachery, fraud, falsehood, perjury, restlessness, violence, and insensibility, all of which are serious social sins (ST 1 18, 8). He claims that avarice is more commonly found among the elderly (ST 1 18, 2) and is a capital sin that causes many other sins (ST 1 18, 8). Prodigality is contrary to covetousness and involves loving material goods less than one should, and it is a less serious vice for Aquinas than covetousness because the prodigal person is good to others while the covetous person is of no good to anyone (ST 2-2 119, 3). Prodigality is cured by old age because the prodigal are usually reduced to want in their later years, and it is less serious a fault than covetousness because it easily turns into liberality.

One of the most important virtues that fosters social harmony for Aquinas is *epikeia,* which enables one to set aside the requirements of positive law to promote justice and the common good (ST 2-2 120, 1). The virtue of *epikeia* does not set aside justice itself but strives to realize it more perfectly and is thus a kind of general justice (ST 2-2 120, 1).

Political theory. Aquinas holds that the state is a natural society based on the rational and social nature of the person and is necessary for full human development. It is public, natural, permanent, perfect, and its immediate end is to assist citizens in finding happiness. It is from nature, and its relationship to society is organic, and its purpose is to promote the virtue of the community (*De reg. prin.* 1, 1). Because the state has the responsibility to promote the happiness of its citizens, it can legitimately assume more functions than can a state that is only responsible for preventing harm to its citizens.

In his letter *De regimine principum* to the King of Sicily, Aquinas outlines the responsibilities of a ruler, and he argues in behalf of monarchy because he believes it expresses the unity of a people, which should prevail (*De reg. prin.* 1, 1). This is the ideal form of government, but he acknowledges that the next best form that should prevail where unity is fragile is the democratic form (*De reg. prin.* 1, 3). Under most circumstances rule by the many is bad because it is rule by the mob to oppress the wealthy. This is the worst form of rule, but polity, rule of the many in justice, is the best form of government when unity is difficult or impossible (*De reg. prin.* 1, 1). And he believes the ruler should give sufficient freedom to subjects to permit and promote their political well-being and integration.

Aquinas is no pacifist, and he claims that Jesus did not forbid soldiering (ST 2-2 40, 1). War could be just if done under proper authority, undertaken for just cause, have right intention, and if those who are attacked have done something to deserve attack (ST 2-2 40, 1). The only legitimate intention for engaging in war is to establish peace (ST 2-2 40, 1). Strife is always sinful because it is a conflict between private persons (ST 2-2 41, 1). It proceeds from private feelings of hatred and anger, and for Aquinas only the public authority is allowed to use force in society (ST 2-2 41, 1 ad 3). Public authorities can use force not to take property but to enforce justice (ST 2-2 66, 8).

Sedition is a preparation for strife and war between people, and it destroys the unity of people (ST 2-2 42, 1). Sedition is opposition to the unity created by authentic law and realization of the common good (ST 2-2 42, 2). It is a mortal sin to act seditiously because it is against the common good, and it is morally legitimate to defend the common good against sedition (ST 2-2 42, 2). It is not sedition to disturb the rule of a tyranny when directed at the private good of the ruler who does not seek the common good, for the ruler has disturbed the common good (ST 2-2 42, 2, ad 3).

Aquinas and Catholic Social Thought

Aquinas' social-ethical doctrines gave the church powerful instruments after the French Revolution to challenge socialism, liberalism, totalitarianism, capitalism, and atheism. His moral principles established the prevailing moral standards for Catholic social teachings, and they clearly retained this position up to the Second Vatican Council. These teachings required that all economic, social, and political decisions be governed by the moral norms of the virtues as enunciated by Aquinas.

Aquinas has been frequently understood as making the common good the sole norm of social ethics, but in fact he subordinated it to the more universal and specific moral norm of the virtues. He gave little material and concrete expression to his doctrine of the common good, and when confronted with claims that capitalism served the common good better than did medieval economies, the church developed precise material content in its social teachings, and this only in the reign of Leo XIII. The principle of the common good acquired new importance in the hands of the church, which used it as guiding principle for society, economics, and politics for what was just, charitable, and virtuous. It united his doctrine of the common good with an expanded version of his theory of rights to create an imposing moral edifice that demanded that all political, social, and economic policies be oriented toward fostering and promoting justice and the life of the virtues.

Aquinas' theory of rights is not as well developed as is ours, and he believes that there are correlative duties to all rights, which many today would doubt. In its primitive form, his theory regards rights as guaranteeing a balance in relationships, and the social encyclicals and teachings of the church elaborated on this notion to govern and regulate all relations in society (ST 2-2 57, 2). And Catholic social teachings condemned governmental policies and social practices primarily because they are violations of the virtues of charity, justice, and fairness, among others.

I wish to trace here the influence of Aquinas' thought on the social teachings of the church on industrial development, economics, society, and the political thought, and by "social teachings of the church," I mean the encyclicals and the mainstream social and theological doctrines developed in the medieval and modern eras.

Industrial development. The Industrial Revolution of the 18th and 19th centuries shattered the ossified guild system of the late Middle Ages, destroyed what little security the serfs and guild members had, and brought terrible sufferings to workers in both Europe and America. Rather than bringing greater wealth, prosperity, and security to medieval serfs and artisans, this revolution created the class of the impoverished and exploited proletariat, which was virtually at the mercy of capitalists, mercantilists, and industrialists (*Rerum novarum* 6). They imposed extraordinarily harsh conditions and created untold misery for workers in their drive to increase profits. In England the workers' shantytowns were matched in their squalor only by the Roman slave quarters of antiquity. Women and children there frequently worked seventeen-hour days for six days a week, and women hauled coal cars up mine shafts that were too small for animals (Cronin, 1959, p. 15). In America children worked twelve hours a day on average, and in 1870 there were more than a quarter of a million children working in industrial jobs.

Many early capitalists saw labor as merely another factor in the profit equation, and popes during the Industrial Revolution were quite correct in saying that most capitalists thought the only noticeable difference between laborers and machines was that the former were less docile than the latter. These capitalists believed that poverty was primarily the result of indolence and lack of initiative, but early Catholic social teachings stressed that social and economic forces often were responsible for destitution and impoverishment (*Quadragesimo anno* 59-62). These early Catholic social teachings argued that not all of the misery of the impoverished was the consequence of their own personal moral failures but that their economic and social circumstances often contributed significantly to their plight.

Catholic social teachings invoked Aquinas' moral doctrines repeatedly to argue for improved social, political, and economic conditions, and in the 19th and 20th centuries they expanded his doctrines to exert moral pressure on the greed and oppression of the early capitalists and industrialists. Following Aquinas, these teachings asserted that wealth was not solely the product of individual effort and initiative but was the consequence of many factors and forces that required the rich to be socially responsible to society in the use of their wealth (RN 36, 65). Catholic social teachings demanded that workers be given a "living wage" that was adequate not only for their basic needs but for them to live with dignity (RN 51, 61–63). This wage was to be sufficient to provide for clean and decent housing, adequate rest, and a secure environment for the rearing of children (*Casti connubii* 126–27). Workers were also to be accorded the right to strike and provided with safe working conditions in their places of employment (RN 56, 59–60). And both before and after the Second Vatican Council, these were all demanded in the social teachings of the church as matters of justice and right. In particular, improvements in the working conditions of women and children were called for because these were exceedingly harsh and posed more dangers to their moral and physical well-being than to that of men (RN 60).

Leonine and pre–Vatican II teachings gave greater emphasis to the role of the common good and less importance to the role of rights in setting social policy (*Immortale Dei* 22; QA 25, 49, 57, 71, 74, 85, 88, 101, 110; RN 14, 48, 50, 52). Post–Vatican II social teachings, however, gave greater emphasis to human dignity as the moral grounds of these claims rather than to the virtues or the common good (*Gaudium et spes,* part 1). Ultimately this shift may not benefit the church because of its ambiguity, formality, and abstractness, and justice and fairness in society might be served better by restoring the social virtues and common good to their former prominence.

Economics. Catholic teachings on economic issues in the early capitalist era fused Aquinas' doctrine of the common good with his theory of moral rights. His doctrine of the common good together with his principles of justice and fairness were employed to criticize the modern economic notions of the profit motive driving all economic activity.

Some of the most serious economic abuses in early capitalism occurred because, in accord with laissez-faire dogma, the state did not intervene to protect workers and their families. Against the laissez-faire social theorists, the church's social teachings invoked Aquinas' claim that the state is not being fully responsible if it only seeks to curb the most severe forms of harm (QA 25, 133). The state has a positive obligation not only to intervene in order to protect the common good and prevent serious injustices but also to create the social, economic, and political conditions that promote the life of virtue among its citizens (RN 48). Aquinas' principle of distributive justice was invoked to compel the state to distribute wealth and resources from the wealthy to the poor (Ryan, 1916, p. 356ff.).

Aquinas' views about private property were invoked by Catholic social teaching to bolster its claims that it was morally legitimate to own property if used responsibly for the common good and not merely to promote personal gain (RN 10–17, 36, 65; QA 45–49, 57, 60, 63). And even further, it was ethical for the state to take positive measures to guarantee that private property was used for the common good (RN 65). These teachings also emphasized Aquinas' doctrine of the just price not only because it was good ethics but good economics as well, because it preserved economic stability and consumer capabilities (Cronin, 1939).

While not condemning the pursuit of limited profits, Catholic social teachings again appealed to Aquinas' doctrines and sought to balance the right to profits with the needs of the common good (QA 53, 60). Leonine social teachings not only called on employers to promote justice and fairness in economic matters, but it also reminded workers of their obligation to be fair, honest, and responsible to their employers (RN 30). Thus, in the official social teachings of the church, capitalists not only had a right to a just and fair profit for their efforts but laborers had a similar right to enjoy adequate compensation for their labors (RN 31). Catholic social teachings did not denounce capitalism so harshly that it was forced into espousing socialist expropriation of private property but appealed to Aquinas' assertions about the right to private property.

Aquinas was most concerned with promoting fairness in economic relationships, which was achieved by maintaining a balance in commercial exchanges. Because he denied that interest taking promoted fairness, he repeated the ancient and scriptural condemnation of usury. Many of the early capitalists accumulated a good portion of their wealth from usurious practices, and the church launched strong protests grounded on Aquinas' censure of usury (Wouters, L, *Man. Theo. Mor.* I, 887). But over time the social teachings of the church only allowed lenders to be compensated for their risks and for the temporary loss of their funds and not solely for the use of the money they lent.

Aquinas' condemnation of usury was so forceful that it retarded the process of reconciling the church with industrial society and modern finance, and the church had to define more precisely than did Aquinas the sorts of charges on lending that could be ethically imposed in order to finally achieve some accommodation with the world of modern finance. His views of economic stability rendered the church ill suited for the dynamic and growth-oriented economies that are more typical of modern times. After World War I little was said in official church pronouncements about the immorality of usury, and in its place emphasis has been given to promoting social justice and protecting the poor (RN 6; Cronin, 1959, VIII). Giving less emphasis to this teaching, however, may ultimately be detrimental to the church, because a great deal of harm is still done through usury and speculation and they remain at the root of many modern social problems and injustices.

Like the teachings on social issues, post–Vatican II teachings on economic matters continued to invoke Aquinas' doctrine of the common good, but this doctrine also has lost its priority to teachings invoking rights claims and the principle of human dignity (GS, part 1). This, too, may not be to the benefit of the church, ultimately because of the lack of clarity about the limits of rights and the ambiguity of the principle of human dignity. The use of rights language might create more confusion than did the older doctrine of the common good.

Social theory. The French and Industrial Revolutions shattered medieval agrarian communities, thrust thousands of people into terrible social conditions in the new industrial cities, and broke the communal bonds of agrarian society that had previously supported and protected them. Many in the church were sympathetic to the social and political changes of the early French Revolution, and hostility only emerged when the more radical elements gained control and revolutionaries began to attack the church itself. Aquinas' doctrines supported the teachings of the church seeking to protect the rights of individuals and the integrity of society, but they inhibited the church's acceptance of modern liberal society because this was alien to Catholic hierarchical and organic understanding of the social order.

In reaction to the French Revolution, papal teachings consistently condemned liberal social proposals, especially those calling for universal suffrage, freedom of religion, association, and press (*Syllabus of Errors* 15, 47, 79). One reason for this was the belief that these freedoms would be inimical not only to political and social stability but also to the legitimate prerogatives of the church. Even a strong advocate of the rights of workers such as Leo XIII in *Immortale Dei* rejected freedom of the press because it would be of no benefit to society, and freedom of religion would harm the church, a view that can be traced to Aquinas (ST 2-2 93, 1). He rejected separation of church and state because the church was needed to train youth and regulate family life, even though it was becoming evident that this new church-state relationship was becoming the wave of the future (*Immortale Dei*). But in the 20th century, when it was discovered that these social policies were not necessarily inimical to the church, objections weakened, and few 20th-century teachings endorsed these teachings.

Catholic social teachings also offered positive proposals to liberal society with a number of different models of society, and virtually all who argued for these theories claimed they were grounded in Aquinas' doctrines of society, the common good, justice, or charity (RN; QA 4, 88, 137). More liberal proposals for social reform, like that of John A. Ryan, stressed Aquinas' doctrine of distributive justice (Ryan, 1916, p. xiii), and more conservative reformers such as William Engelen emphasized his teachings on the hierarchical nature of society (*The Central-Blatt and Social Justice* 12). And solidarism, advanced by Henry Pesch, emphasized the Thomistic theme that society was to be marked by cooperation (*Central-Blatt*

19). This program, too, was grounded on Aquinas' doctrine of charity, and it played down the role of conflict, which emphasized so much in communist and capitalist models of society.

The most commonly advocated reforming proposal was corporatism, which espoused Aquinas' view of society as an organic, hierarchically ordered unity of social and vocational organizations related to one another by the principle of subsidiarity (*Code of Social Principles* 82–86, 161; QA 79–82, 86–87). Corporatist teachings criticized the excessive emphasis of modern individualism on the rights and protection of individuals at the expense of society and family as well as the dominating power of the modern socialist state at the expense of society. Catholic social teachings believed that this model, grounded in Aquinas' thought, provided the stability and protection sought by modern workers that capitalists denied them. Because it conceived of society organically and hierarchically, this form of society would respect lower social orders and would not usurp their freedom or authority, but corporatism was discredited by Fascist endorsement in the 20th century, and it has been all but repudiated in post–Vatican II Catholic social teachings.

Prior to the Second Vatican Council, Catholic social teachings developed the notion of "social charity," which was based on Aquinas' teachings about charity, as a means of resolving social conflicts and creating harmony in society (QA 4, 88, 137; *Divini Redemptoris* 46–49; *To Italian Workers*) These teachings called for social charity not only to prevent harm, but also to promote justice, heal wounds, end divisions, and foster unity within a community. Social charity demanded a much more active role for both the state and citizens than what laissez-faire theorists demanded (*Graves de communi re* 11; RN 83).

At the beginning of the 16th century church teaching condemned modern slavery but was generally uncritical of major revisions in the social order, and this too was based on Aquinas' view of slavery (Gregory XVI, *Supremo*; Paul III, *Sublimis Deus*). Perhaps wrongly, the church did not condemn serfdom because it believed the common good of the community could be served by it in some instances, but it did not take this view of slavery, which it condemned repeatedly. Church teaching recognized that different peoples would find greater benefit from different social arrangements and did not dictate a single social order for all people.

Against conservative objections the church supported legislation that required more dignified living conditions for even the most impoverished and least profitable. Most of the teachings dealing with social issues were based on a concept of dignity that cannot be located in Aquinas' thought. Since Vatican II Catholic social teachings have stopped appealing to social charity as a means to promote harmony and community, probably because of the presumption that social harmony and community will result from mutual respect for rights rather than from the practice of social charity. This is not an optimal situation, however, for the discrediting of corporatism and abandonment of the doctrine of "social charity" as the basis of community effectively leaves the Catholic community without serious proposals for remedying social conflicts and disharmony.

Political thought. Aquinas' theory of the state had not only beneficial but also harmful influences on Catholic social teachings. Aquinas taught that the most perfect political order achieved stability and fostered the life of virtue in citizens because this would enable them to fulfill their human nature more perfectly. But his belief that monarchy grounded on divine authority was the only truly ethical form of government impaired the church's ability to be reconciled with 19th-and 20th-century liberalism.

Leo XIII revived Thomistic studies in 1879, a short six years before his encyclical *Immortale Dei,* which articulated his theory of society and state and repeated many of Pius IX's charges against the modern liberal state (*Aeterni Patris*). The hostility of early Catholic social teachings to modern democracy cannot be accounted for merely by politics or papal personality but must take into account the long-standing Catholic belief (based on Aquinas' views) that modern democracies were morally defective. Modern liberal democracy was regarded as inferior to divinely authorized monarchy because it neither promoted the common good nor actively fostered the life of virtue (*Syllabus of Errors* 41–44, 49–50, 55; *Quanta cura*). During the era of liberalism the papacy did not regard modern liberal democracy as a Thomistic "polity" but as a rule of the mob, primarily because the liberals and democrats attacked the church and did not protect its interests.

During the liberal era, papal teachings claimed that the sovereignty was not to be based on the popular will but on divine authority (*Diuturnum* 5; *Immortale Dei; Quanta cura*). The common good could be secured not by the consent of the governed but by the submission of wise rulers to the will of God, and it called for subordination of the state to the church (*Immortale Dei*). Popular sovereignty was rejected as little more than mob rule, which left rulers as its delegates and subordinated the church to the power of the state. It was unfortunate that the church could not accommodate modern democracy more readily, for its resistance to popular sovereignty made efforts to promote better conditions for workers look disingenuous.

No other Christian thinker has contributed as much to the doctrine of just-war theory as Aquinas. His basic teachings on *jus in bello* and *jus ad bellum* were preserved and developed by the great just-war theorists in the modern era, and the preeminence of his thought on this issue is beyond dispute (Vitoria, *De Jure Bel;* Ryan & Boland, Cath. Princ. of Pol., XX). And particularly in the era of nuclear deterrence his doctrines became the basis for Catholic attempts to guide society in the use of nuclear deterrence (*The Challenge of Peace,* chaps. 2–3). But probably because modern nationalist, industrial, and scientific warfare has become so much more destructive than medieval warfare ever could have been, Catholic social teachings, particularly in the 20th century, have become much more open to the moral validity of pacifism than was Aquinas (CP 4). While he would hold pacifism to be an abandonment and betrayal of justice, modern Catholic teachings wonder if "turning the other cheek" might not be more damaging to the common good than fighting for it.

The collapse of European communism should be of concern because it leaves the church very much alone to face moral and social challenges of contemporary capitalism, nationalism, and industrialism. With its collapse, Catholicism alone possesses in its Thomistic heritage the only credible and comprehensive moral, social, economic, and political program. With the liberal, individualistic, capitalist model of the social and political order in disrepute, a revived Thomistic moral, social, and political theory could provide needed guidance for this era.

Contemporary liberation theology lacks the comprehensive moral and philosophical framework of classical Thomism, and the church would be better off by giving greater prominence to Thomistic concepts of society, ethics, politics, and economics than by reconciling its traditional social, economic, and political theory with this late 20th-century Marxist Leninism. Post-communist Thomism should emphasize the prominence of the common good and the necessity of virtue in both the public and private forum as the basis for a sound social, political, and economic policy. Many of Aquinas' teachings, such as his claim that harmony and stability are to be the objective of the social order, are by no means obsolete, and in light of this, other teachings should also be reconsidered.

See also AUTHORITY, POLITICAL; BUSINESS ETHICS; GOODS, DISTRIBUTION OF; JUST WAGE; MODERN CATHOLIC SOCIAL THOUGHT; NATURAL LAW; SOCIETY; WAR.

Bibliography: T. Aquinas, *Summa Theologica* (New York: Benzinger, 1947); *De Regimine Principum* (London: Sheed & Ward, 1938). C. Barry, ed., *Readings in Church History* (Westminster, Md., 1985). C. Carlen, ed., *The Papal Encyclicals,* 5 vols. (Wilmington, N.C.: McGrath, 1981). D. Cronin, *Social Principles and Economic Life* (Milwaukee: Bruce, 1959); *Economics and Society* (New York: American Book, 1939). C. Curran, "American Catholic Social Ethics: 1880–1965," in *Transition and Tradition in Moral Theology* (Notre Dame: Univ. of Notre Dame Press, 1979) pp. 83–117. J. Ryan, *Distributive Justice* (New York: Macmillan, 1916); *A Living Wage* (New York: Macmillan, 1906). E. Welty, *A Handbook of Christian Social Ethics,* 2 vols. (New York: Herder & Herder, 1965). National Conference of Catholic Bishops, *The Challenge of Peace* (Washington: United States Catholic Conference, 1983).

ROBERT BARRY, O.P

TOLERATION, PRINCIPLE OF

Unlike the principles of cooperation and double effect, the principle of toleration represents not a calculus for moral decision making but rather a particular attitude. As such it does not belong necessarily to a classical theological context such as Scholasticism. Rather the attitude can be invoked by proponents of either classical or historical theologies.

In any context, the attitude first considers another's activity as threatening certain values, then disagrees with the activity, and refuses to approve or recommend the activity, but to prevent greater harm it permits the activity with which it disagrees. Unlike the other two principles, which concern particular courses of action, toleration is not a positive action. On the contrary, toleration is the decision not to act, not to obstruct, not to coerce. Nonetheless, like the other principles the decision itself represents a form of controversy or possible scandal because the decision presumes that action to prevent the activity could have been taken. Furthermore, like the other principles toleration is invoked to prevent greater harm from occurring.

Examples in the classical school of theology are found in Augustine's decision regarding the houses of prostitution (*De ordine* 2.4.12) and more recently in the United States Catholic Conference's positions on nuclear deterrence (*The Challenge of Peace*) and AIDS educational programs (*The Many Faces of AIDS*). In each of these cases the decision is made because an intolerant stance could prompt those who are presently the source of dangerous activity to endanger the common good.

In the classical school, which characterizes behavior as right or wrong with great clarity and incision, the attitude of toleration includes not only the presumption that the tolerant person, institution, or society refuses to approve or recommend the activity but also the determination that the activity is wrong. Vermeersch writes, "Strictly speaking, tolerance has always some evil for its object, such as physical defect, an intellectual error, or a moral deformity" (Vermeersch, p. 5).

The classicists warn against several considerable abuses that can result from adopting an appropriately tolerant posture. On the one hand, indifferentism holds that the social conduct of others does not need to be morally evaluated. Relativism holds that the social conduct of each has equal merits and claims. Privatism claims that one's own social conduct is not subject to any other's evaluation. On the other hand, absolute intolerance poses other threats, in particular, avoidable harm and grave scandal.

The historical school tends to emphasize the tentativeness of moral formulations without endorsing indifferentism, relativism, or privatism. This school believes that human insight advances and matures. For instance, the earlier teaching that masturbation was murder was changed when the discovery of the ovum and the subsequent discovery of human fertilization brought the realization of the difference between an individual sperm and a fertilized egg. Thus in the interest of moral objectivity, the historical school maintains the somewhat provisional nature of expressions of moral insight.

This assertion does not deny that in the present historical situation certain particular expressions of moral insight demand protection. Such positions as the indissolubility of marriage, the normativity of heterosexual union, and religious *obsequium* for the ordinary magisterium are insights the church safeguards. For this reason the church does not approve or recommend any activity that is presently recognized as incompatible with these insights.

In the historical context, the tolerant position considers that questionable behavior is apparently threatening or undermining a particularly important value. Nonetheless, this tolerant position does not require the additional step of judging that the questionable behavior is wrong, evil, or sinful. Rather it simply holds that at present the behavior is not evidently compatible with the value that needs to be protected. Instead of concluding that the behavior is unacceptable, it continually challenges those who accept or endorse the behavior to demonstrate that they are not by their conduct undermining the merit of the value apparently being threatened. Here the tolerant are looking for either moral truth (if the challenge is still outstanding) or moral conversion (if the conduct is eventually understood as nothing more than an assault on moral value).

Inasmuch as moral and religious truth are based on the believing community's ever-emerging self-understanding as it stands awaiting the kingdom, the historical school looks to avoid unnecessary suppressions and rather seeks to allow the data of human experience to express itself. By the same token, the historical school recognizes the church's obligation to protect certain moral values and abiding insights. Thus, different from the classicist context, this school adopts tolerance not as a form of patience nor as a form of disapproval but rather as an admission that in the present limited situation, the obligation to protect certain values overrides the ability to recognize as right or acceptable others' decisions in conscience to live or act as they do. Thus the tolerant attitude is one of hope that one day greater understanding will resolve the present incompatibility or threat and lead somehow to the reconciliation of which Paul calls us all to be ministers (2 Cor 5:11–6:13).

An obvious example of this concerns divorced and remarried Catholics. Since the church witnesses to and safeguards the indissolubility of marriage, the church does not bless, recommend, or approve the marriages of divorced Catholics. Nonetheless, proponents of the historical school would recommend not that these Catholics have a right to Communion or other services but rather that the church not invoke punitive or exclusionary measures. The school recommends to these Catholics that they make their decision to take Communion through a decision made in conscience. At the same time they are engaged to demonstrate how the divorced and remarried state does not undermine the indissolubility of marriage.

The *Declaration on Religious Liberty* (*Dignitatis humanae*) is the fruit of a passage of the church from intolerance, to a classical expression of tolerance, to a historical expression of it, to finally an approval of the position that recognizes the claims of all believers. It is also an expression of the words of John XXIII in his speech opening the Second Vatican Council: "The Church has always opposed these errors. Frequently she has condemned them with the greatest severity. Nowadays, however, the Spouse of Christ prefers to make use of the medicine of mercy rather than that of severity. She considers that she meets the needs of the present day by demonstrating the validity of her teaching rather than by condemnations."

See also AUGUSTINE, INFLUENCE OF; CHURCH-STATE RELATIONS IN THE UNITED STATES; COOPERATION, PRINCIPLE OF; DIVORCE; DOUBLE EFFECT, PRINCIPLE OF; MURRAY, JOHN COURTNEY; PLURALISM.

Bibliography: K. Demmer, "Der Anspruch der Toleranz," *Gregorianum* 63 (1982) 701–20. K. Rahner, "Dialog und Toleranz als Grundlage einer humanen Gesellschaft," *Stimmen der Zeit* 201 (1983) 579–89. A. Vermeersch, *Tolerance* (New York: Benziger, 1912).

JAMES F. KEENAN, S.J.

TORTURE

The practice of torture is as old as humanity: the deliberate inflictions of physical or mental pain upon one person by another—for fun, for spite, to coerce, to subdue—has been practiced since time began, and now in the "civilized" 20th century it is still widely practiced. In Amnesty International's comprehensive report *Torture in the Eighties* evidence is presented of the practice of torture in ninety-eight countries. This document makes disturbing reading, for it is difficult to believe that human beings are capable of such deliberate cruelty. The evidence, however, is there: we can either face it or ignore it. But do we have the right to ignore torture any more than we have the right to ignore hunger, poverty, cancer, drug addiction, AIDS, or any other distressing fact of life? Does not our humanity lay upon us the burden of facing up to the reality of our world, learning the facts about injustice, struggling to understand why things are as they are, and then asking ourselves what we can do both individually and collectively to right what is wrong?

The Facts

On December 9, 1975, the United Nations defined torture as "any act by which severe pain or suffering whether physical or mental, is intentionally inflicted by or at the instigation of a public official on a person for such purposes as obtaining from him or a third person information or confession, punishing him for an act he has committed, or intimidating him or other persons." This authoritative international text highlights essential aspects of torture: the physical or mental pain is severe; it is deliberately inflicted; it is done for a purpose by agents of the state. The methods of torture employed will vary from age to age and from country to country depending upon the ingenuity and whim of the torturer and the equipment available.

Works published by the International Rehabilitation and Research Center for Torture Victims in Copenhagen suggest that modern torture methods fall into two broad categories: techniques designed to weaken the victim and those designed to invade, undermine, and destroy personality. Depending upon the intention of the torturer, the same techniques can be used to either end and may be classified as follows:

1. *Deprivation:* This includes solitary confinement; sleep deprivation, starvation, and deprivation of adequate facilities for toileting; deprivation of light and sight by blindfolding, hooding, or other means; confinement in inadequate space, for example, a cage.

2. *Constraint techniques:* This includes all forms of physical and psychological compulsion including mock executions; actual and threatened death threats of associates, family, and friends; imposition of impossible choices.

3. *Communication techniques:* Victims are exposed to ambiguous situations and contradictory messages that induce confusion.

4. *Abuse of pharmacology and psychiatric institutions:* Victims are confined in psychiatric institutions with psychotic patients. They may be forcibly given disorientating drugs; a particularly cruel practice is the use of curare-like drugs that paralyze and induce panic of suffocation.

5. *Physical methods:* (*a*) *Electric shock.* The victim is subjected to electric shocks, with the electrodes being applied to sensi-

tive areas of the body such as mouth, nose, breasts, and genitals. (*b*) *Hanging.* Victims are suspended by hands or feet for varying periods of time. (*c*) *Immersion.* The victim's head is immersed to near drowning in water that frequently is contaminated by excrement. (*d*) *Beating of the soles of the feet.* (*e*) *Hitting of the sides of head* simultaneously so as to rupture the ear drums. (*f*) *General physical abuse.* This includes beating, whipping, burning with cigarettes. (*g*) *Genital abuse* or mutilation by insects, animals, or instruments. (*h*) *Sexual abuse and rape,* often in the presence of the victim's partner or child.

This sad inventory of human cruelty could be continued almost indefinitely. Why, why is it done!

Reason for Torture

It is important to understand that while individual torturers may be sadistic and may delight in their craft, torture is deliberately used by agents of the state for a particular purpose. Torture is most commonly employed in the context of war or terrorism (*a*) to "persuade" the victim to reveal specific information, (*b*) to "extract" a confession, (*c*) to intimidate the victim and potential dissidents from further political activity, (*d*) to intimidate whole populations so they do not resist the state or support guerrillas.

Morality of Torture

The question must be asked, is torture *ever* justified? For example, a terrorist has planted a bomb timed to explode and kill a group of innocent people. May the police torture him in order to save the others? It is important to face this question because it is in principle the very question posed to security forces dealing with terrorists. Briefly, the answer is no. The deliberate infliction of pain to force a suspect to confess is never permissible. Even here, the end does not justify the means.

Effects of Torture

1. *The immediate effect* on the victim is to cause profound terror and anguish and disorientation. Severe physical abuse may result in brain damage, heart or lung problems, wounds, fractures, death. It is thought that many people die under torture.

2. *The long-term effects of torture* upon the victim are both physical and psychological. Depression, anxiety, nightmares, and phobias may last for many years if not indefinitely, and a significant proportion of victims commit suicide. The psychological effects of torture are not confined to the victim. Not only are family and friends profoundly affected but the whole society is affected by the fear of repression—and often a sense of guilt—at not having had the courage to speak out. Torture is like a spider's web that traps not only victim and torturer but all who come in contact with it. Victims of torture require skilled and patient help from medical and other caregivers if they are to regain equilibrium and function in ordinary settings. Their rehabilitation is frequently bedeviled by the fact that the torture experience is in the intimacy of its relationship a perversion of the normal healing relationship between patient and doctor or client and therapist. Establishing trust in a healing relationship is thus more than ordinarily difficult.

What Can Be Done?

The past two decades have seen a growing concern over the problem of torture, with the foundation of a number of organizations dedicated to its abolition. Amnesty International, formed in 1961 to campaign on behalf of prisoners of conscience, has been a forerunner in this field. Work continues in these areas: (*a*) monitoring situations in which torture is likely, and collecting and publishing data; (*b*) campaigning for individuals at risk; (*c*) treating victims of torture; (*d*) lobbying governments to impose sanctions on states implicated in torture; (*e*) developing international standards of care for prisoners and international law against torture.

Conclusion

It has not been easy to write this essay, not least because to read and think about torture inevitably opens old wounds. As a doctor working with men and women hurt, mutilated, and killed through natural causes, I am filled with cold fury that the world's natural burden of pain should be added to by deliberate cruelty.

My heart is a always torn between a terrible pragmatism that says things never really change and the hope of a young man who said to his therapist, "Yours is the hand of humanity that reaches out to save me from drowning in my sorrow." Then, reaching out his hand to a fellow victim, he said, "This is one chain. One link, then another, and then we will make another link and another. It will be a great chain, and when eventually we shake this great chain, the world will stop to listen and then there will be no more torture."

See also AGGRESSION; EVIL, SOCIAL; HUMAN RIGHTS; PEACE AND JUSTICE COMMISSIONS; PRISON.

Bibliography: *Torture in the '80s* (New York: Amnesty International, 1984). J. Schlapobersky, *Torture: The Perversion of a Healing Relationship* (London).

SHEILA CASSIDY

TOTALITARIANISM

The term "totalitarianism" was first used in the late 1930s to designate all authoritarian systems of government and movements that had sprung up in the preceding decade, such as German national socialism, Soviet communism, and different kinds of fascism. Since 1945 "totalitarian" has become a common word referring to states, ideologies, and parties; however, insofar as its usage has become commonplace and its field of application widened, the term has lost its precision. It has been subject to various and contrasting interpretations by science and political philosophies, which are, nevertheless, in agreement in ascribing to totalitarianism some specific characteristics:

1. Its link with an ideology that, as Hannah Arendt (p. 469) puts it, "is quite literally what its name indicates: it is the logic of an idea. . . . The ideology treats the course of events as though it followed the same 'law' as the logical exposition of its 'idea.' Ideologies pretend to know the mysteries of the whole historical process—the secrets of the past, the intricacies of the present, the uncertainties of the future—because of the logic inherent in their respective ideas."

2. A one-party system that uses ideology to legitimate its power and actions and strives at the same time to fulfill the vision of the world and history that its ideology commands.

3. The one who holds complete sway over the state apparatus rules without public constitutional checks and balances; this one relies on a sizeable and efficient secret police and tries to ensure full control of all groups, associations, and organizations that are part of the civil society.

4. The novelty of regimes that are unprecedented because of the extensive means they have at their disposal to assert their absolute domination. These regimes can be distinguished from autocratic and despotic regimes of the past and contrasted with pluralistic and constitutional models of modern democracies.

The Catholic church seldom uses the word "totalitarianism" in the official documents but has nonetheless denounced since the 1930s the aims and means of totalitarian regimes. Two encyclical letters, published within the same week, are fundamental. On March 19, 1937, Pope Pius XI published *Divini Redemptoris* (*On Atheistic Communism*); on Palm Sunday, March 21, 1937, *Mit brennender Sorge* (*On the Place of the Catholic Church in the German Reich*) was read in almost all the parishes of Nazi Germany. This last encyclical, which was immediately understood as a firm and public condemnation of the totalitarian state, had been written at the request of the German episcopate: it came after the publication on July 20, 1935, of a report by German bishops listing the violations of the 1933 concordat and within a context of discriminatory and coercive measures of the Third Reich against the Catholic church, its pastors, and its faithful. It was followed by a pastoral letter of the German bishops read on August 28, 1938, denouncing the Nazi project of destroying the faith and its actual realization by the Hitlerian regime. *Mit brennender Sorge* and *Divini Redemptoris* are texts that, beyond the particular circumstances of their publication, still appeal strongly to the modern conscience and deserve to remain a point of reference.

These two encyclicals do not provide us with an analysis of the political nature of totalitarian regimes; rather, they denounce the ideologies these regimes embody. It is not totalitarianism as such that is qualified as "intrinsically perverse" but atheistic communism (DR 58); it is not the political structure of the national socialist state nor even its corrupt practices that are denounced but the risk of alluring people's consciences through ideological falsehood and contempt of human beings and laws or whatever the cult of power. The abuses and atrocities of communism in Russia and Spain are seen as "natural fruits of an unbridled system" (DR 21) that wants to wipe out all signs of religious worship; concentration camps are mentioned (MbS 46) only as places where fidelity to truth can lead priests and religious. Thus the papal writings do not take up the question of totalitarianism in its strict political aspect: Pope Pius XI makes it clear in his encyclical of 1931 on Fascism, *Non abbiamo bisogno,* in which he writes that "the battle which is going on today is not political: it is moral and religious." Such an approach to totalitarianism underrates two important dimensions: (1) the novelty of totalitarian systems, which, through the organization of mass movements and the role of terror, the function of ideology and the one-party machinery forces us to consider anew the question of the nature of the state and the finality of political actions; and (2) the practical contradictions of a situation where German Catholics are doomed to be torn between antagonistic duties, as they have to live out their loyalty as citizens toward the legal state, at the same time objecting as Christians to its illegal methods and its anti-Christian doctrine (MbS 40–51).

The two encyclicals are concerned above all with the denunciation of the idolatrous ideology of totalitarian regimes: by definition, the totalitarian state negates the idea of and the authority of God, for it cannot stand that God has any significance on the social and political scene. God would be a competing power that puts into question the totalitarian claim to absolute power. Thus the communist state is a godless state; communist society wishes to inaugurate the era of a "godless humanity" (DR 12); what communism lays before our eyes is "a deliberate, cleverly prepared and cold-blooded human struggle against 'all that is divine'" (DR 22). In a different way but with no less vigor the Nazi regime denies all dependence on God: the race, the people, the state, the leader, are deified by an idolatrous cult (MbS 12). By being itself its own origin and foundation, by claiming authority and rights so absolute as to be properly divine, totalitarian power becomes an absolute and supreme entity, boundless and with no responsibility toward anyone. Power becomes God. That is why the ideologies of totalitarian regimes appear as a substitute for religion, offering a pseudoideal or a fake mysticism: thus Pius XI affirms that communism contains an idea of "false redemption" (DR 8) and that the Nazi regime makes an abuse of the vocabulary of the Christian faith to formulate its own doctrinal themes (MbS 9–15). *Mit brennender Sorge* denounces the pantheistic confusion between God and the universe, the identification of a personal God with destiny, the will to make of God the Creator the God of only one race and one people.

The argumentation of both encyclicals aims at showing that a political system without God or against God or one that makes itself God cannot respect human dignity and freedom: the fundamental rights of the human person cannot be respected by the one who ignores the true origin, nature, and end of the state (DR 14). It is by appealing to natural law that one can draw a link between refusal of God and contempt for the human person. The question of natural law is at the core of *Mit brennender Sorge* (35–39), for morals and law rest on "the divine foundation of Revelation." By refusing all reference to the will of the eternal and creator God, totalitarian regimes give away morals to people's subjective opinions and leave to positive law the care of stating what is right, with no other law or point of reference outside itself to judge its capacity to bind human consciences.

In his confrontation with totalitarianism Pius XI brings to the fore two important issues that are at the core of present-day political philosophy: (1) A society that refuses to be totalitarian must preserve in its center a space free from power, preserved from constraint. This is the place where the individual and social relationship to God can be lived and expressed; it is the place of symbols that transcend the power of the state and all other powers. (2) Since the Second World War the question of natural law has been raised again because the juridical positivism under totalitarian regimes had shown the limits of any kind of legal justice and its powerlessness to prevent unjust and monstrous statutes.

Thus the starting point of the unequivocal denunciation of ideas and practices opposed to Christian faith is the conception of human society these encyclicals hold to be true: civil society and the human person have God as their origin and are naturally ordered to each other; the role of the state is a service, and its end must be the common good. Persons have rights they hold from God and not from society, and these must be kept untouched; the social doctrine of the church is a middle way between extremes and preserves the legitimate and necessary diversity of society. Consequently *Mit brennender Sorge* and *Divini Redemptoris* call for resistance to the falsehood of pseudoideals as well as to the coercive practices of the totalitarian state. What is actually at stake is faith in God, in Christ, and in the church (MbS 18–26). With no choice but to follow the path of "heroic courage" there is nothing higher for the believer than to object to the establishment of a national church separated from the universal church; to oppose seizure by the state of social organizations, youth movements, and education programs; and to refuse any collaboration with the schemings of a power denying freedom of faith.

Whether praised, questioned, or rejected, *Mit brennender Sorge* and *Divini Redemptoris* are texts that have marked modern times by their rejection of the idolatry of power and state inherent to totalitarianism. From this point of view they are basic documents, but since 1937 the church has never stopped dealing with the manifold reality of totalitarianism. This old and new experience has shaped the present-day church approach to totalitarianism, which seems to be informed by three ideas: (1) the conception of the church-state relationship, (2) a constant reference to the human rights and (3) to this fundamental right that is religious freedom.

The church-state relationship. The conciliar documents *Gaudium et spes* and *Dignitatis humanae* provide us with the framework within which the church understands any relationship with the state. The church does not want to be tied down by one political system in particular and rejects totalitarianism in refusing "any kind of government which blocks civil or religious liberty . . . and wrenches the exercise of authority from pursuing the common good to serving the advantage of a certain faction or of the rulers themselves" (GS 73). The church is not afraid of denouncing "these totalitarian and dictatorial forms" (GS 75), labeling them as inhuman because they infringe seriously on the rights of persons or of groups. Although the term "democracy" does not appear in the conciliar documents, one can find statements of the demands for the constitutional state, the political system that is the very opposite of totalitarian regimes: its powers and functions are limited by law, and its secular character is now acknowledged by the church (GS 73–76). Although the church does not want to formulate a political opinion on systems of government that peoples adopt or are subject to, the council wanted to raise the moral and religious significance of political questions. Thus the church has the fundamental right and duty to denounce the nature and practices of a political system; it is the proper task of God's people to protect and promote the transcendent dignity of the human person throughout the whole of history. Therefore the church sees political issues through the prism of the dignity of the person. The defense of the human person is at the very center of post–Vatican II Catholic ecclesiology.

The reference to human rights. Within the memory of humankind, the death camp of Auschwitz-Birkenhau is the symbol of totalitarian horror. There, on March 7, 1979, Pope John Paul II in a moving speech said: "I come to kneel down on the Golgotha of the contemporary world. . . . If this great plea of Auschwitz, the cry of martyred people is to bear fruits for Europe (and also for the world), we must draw all consequences from the Decaration of human rights as Pope John XXIII urged us to do in the encyclical letter *Pacem in Terris.*" There could not be a more meaningful place from which this pope, hailing from a country that Nazi and Stalinian totalitarianism had wounded in its flesh, could say to the world how much the church embraces as her own these human rights, which modern moral conscience acknowledges as fundamental. The duty to respect human dignity and rights—a leitmotif in the conciliar documents and the teaching of John Paul II—is the most radical and permanent criticism of regimes that politically, economically, and socially develop this basic form of totalitarianism, which refuses to grant people what is vital to lead a life that is human. In *Dignitatis humanae* the Second Vatican Council expresses the wish "to develop the doctrine of recent Popes on the inviolable rights of the human person and on the constitutional order of society" (DH 1), thus setting forth the first and ultimate criterion by which the church can judge matters pertaining to the exercise of public authority.

The right to religious freedom. Referring both to *Pacem in terris* and *Mit brennender Sorge,* the Second Vatican Council declares that "the right to religious freedom has its foundation in the very dignity of the human person, as this dignity is known through the revealed word of God and by reason itself. This right of the human person to religious freedom is to be recognized in the constitutional law whereby society is governed. Thus it is to become a civil right" (DH 2). If the church recognizes religious pluralism as the very condition necessary to fulfill any ministry, then the freedom of the believer must be recognized, guaranteed, and respected as a fundamental human right. The right to religious freedom is not merely one right among others. It has a special place among the other rights because it concerns what is most intimate and personal to the human being. The recognition of religious freedom as the complete freedom to live the life of faith is an essential criterion by which to judge the limits that any power or any state sets to their hold on free consciences and the juridical means they implement to ensure the fundamental rights of the human person. It is through the prism of religious freedom that the church looks at the recognition of and respect for human rights, envisions the question of church-state relationships, and denounces in the slightest violation of the right to religious freedom an act where looms the shadow of totalitarianism.

The church is, as Pope Paul VI puts it, "expert in humanity." Because of its age-old experience, the church has a particular expertise in political affairs: conflicts and persecutions, heroic figures like Rupert Mayer and Maximilian Kolbe, have taught all believers how power could be the object of idolatry and lead to madness and death camps. Holding the promise of eternal life, Christ's disciples can always yield to the temptation proper to all human groups of asserting in various areas of life an ascendancy over people and consciences, but the church is very much aware that Christ is the Crucified, that the history of the Christian community unfolds at the foot of the cross, and that the very call of Christians is to be servants to their brothers and sisters (Jn 13). Enriched by this historical and spiritual experience, the church is well prepared to be tomorrow, as was often the case in the past and continues to the present day, the heart of resistance and the defender of liberty against the assaults of the reviving hydra of totalitarianism.

See also ANTI-SEMITISM; COMMUNISM; DEMOCRACY; GOD, IMAGES OF; HUMAN RIGHTS; PIUS XI; POLITICAL THEOLOGY; RELIGIOUS FREEDOM.

Bibliography: H. Arendt, *The Origins of Totalitarianism* (New York/London: Harcourt Brace Jovanovich, 1973). J. Gremillion, ed., *The Gospel of Peace and Justice: Catholic Social Teaching since Pope John* (Maryknoll, N.Y.: Orbis, 1975). D. Hollenbach, *Claims in Conflict: Retrieving and Renewing the Catholic Human Rights Tradition* (New York: Paulist, 1979).

FRANÇOIS-XAVIER DUMORTIER, S.J.

TRANSNATIONAL CORPORATIONS

To understand the nature and role of transnational corporations in the contemporary world one must first grasp how profit is generated in the capitalist system. In condensed terms, profit is the differential between the cost of producing an item and its selling price on the open market. A social and economic class known as capitalists provides money to finance the extraction of natural resources and their conversion into finished products by laborers, who receive compensation for their work in the form of wages. Materials and labor represent costs incurred by the capitalist. These costs, however, are recaptured by means of the market price of the commodity that surpasses both the cost of the material and the labor value invested in its production. The positive differential between production cost and market price is known as profit. It is the motor force of capitalism.

Prior to the Second World War most capitalist manufacturing and marketing was done within the confines of a nation's borders. Money for production came from a nation's capitalist class, while national workers provided labor. Profits and wages generally remained within the confines of a state. This pattern began to shift drmatically in the postwar period with the rise of the United States as the world's preeminent military and economic power. Immediately after 1945 U.S. industries began to reach beyond their borders in search of cheap raw materials, more economical labor, new markets, and higher profits. Given the economic and political disarray of the postwar world, U.S. industries encountered little resistance.

In order to minimize costs, U.S. corporations began to buy and control raw materials at their source in other countries rather than purchasing them on the open market. They also began to employ workers outside the United States in countries where wage scales were lower and labor laws less stringent. Finished goods were then marketed in countries where there was high demand and large profits. In effect, these firms had nearly total control over the production process, from initial extraction of raw materials to the marketing and pricing of finished goods. Precisely because of these characteristics, such industries became known as transnational or multinational corporations. Freed from nearly all political and geographic restraints, they achieved prodigious levels of profit and power. After recuperating from the Second World War many European and Asian countries followed the United States model of transnational capitalist expansion. Today transnational corporations also operate out of Germany, Great Britain, France, Holland, and Japan.

The rise of transnational corporations marks a qualitative change in the evolution of modern capitalism. Many transnational corporations—all of which operate out of the developed world—wield economic resources that surpass the total national wealth of many developing countries. Such power can quickly lead to abuses. It is a well-documented fact that many multinational corporations have exploited developing countries by paying too little for natural resources as well as inadequate wages to workers.

Given their power and visibility, transnational corporations have become a central concern in Catholic social teaching and have been analyzed at length in recent papal encyclicals and national episcopal documents. The question of transnational corporations occupies a key place in Pope John Paul II's encyclicals on economic issues, especially *Laborem exercens* (1981) and *Sollicitudo rei socialis* (1988). They are also discussed in *Economic Justice for All,* the pastoral letter of the U.S. bishops issued in 1986. In these letters the hierarchy of the church calls on the leaders of transnational corporations to respect the independence and national needs of developing countries and to pay laborers wages that reflect the true value of their work. Church leaders point to the undeniable fact that transnational corporations are exacerbating the economic gap between wealthy and poor nations, thus obstructing development rather than fostering it. The church does not condemn multinational corporations as such but rather their record of political and economic abuse. What the church calls for is a world economic order grounded on justice. In the climate of transnational capitalism, however, a profound conversion is required in order to reorient economic life toward its real purpose—the creation of a true global community.

See also CAPITALISM; COMMON GOOD; CORPORATIONS; ENTERPRISE; GOODS, DISTRIBUTION OF; INDUSTRY; LABOREM EXERCENS; PROFIT.

CURT CADORETTE, M.M.

TRUSTS

"Trust" is a 19th-century term for monopoly. It is derived from an early form of corporate ownership that allowed a large accumulation of capital in one firm. Thus in 19th-century America, people referred to the oil trusts, tobacco trusts, steel trusts. Their size enabled them to control the supply in their markets, which in turn allowed them to raise prices above a competitive level. These trusts were seen as engaging in unfair competitive practices that destroyed rival firms and attempts by workers to organize into trade unions.

See also COMPETITION; CONGLOMERATES; CORPORATIONS; MONOPOLY.

CHARLES K. WILBER

V

VALUES

Values can exist only in relation to intelligent and free beings. They are "good things" that contribute to the development of persons (Örsy, p. 472). All beings are unfinished, incomplete and imperfect. All beings are historical. All human beings progress by appropriating good things for themselves or by creating good things within themselves. Intelligent and free beings appropriate good things on various levels: on a biological level (nourishment), on a psychological level (one's emotional environment), on an intellectual level (instructions), on a spiritual level (grace). In all these processes the pattern is the same—intelligent and free persons appropriate good things, and when a symbiosis between persons and good things takes place, the persons are enriched; they become more perfect.

Consequently a value is a good thing not in itself alone but in its relationship to human persons. The concept of value always includes two elements: it signifies a thing *and* its capacity to contribute to the perfection of human beings (when we speak of value judgments, we mean precisely a judgment about the suitability of an object to perfect human beings) (Tumulty, pp. 53–63). Laws, then, must be seen as subservient to values in order to be instrumental in promoting the appropriation of important needed values. When law moves away from the world of values, distortions occur, for example, legalism (the law reigns supreme) and the neglect of values (anarchy). These types of distortions see law as the ultimate value and exalt obedience as the highest of the virtues. In this mentality an inquiring mind is judged a disloyal mind.

The philosophy of value has a long and divergent history. Attempts to describe a philosophy of value can be traced from about 1890 and are associated mainly with Austrian philosophers such as Brentano, Meinong, and Ehrensels, and with Americans such as Perry and Dewey. Although human values have always been a concern of philosophers, the rise of modern science and mathematics occasioned a renewal of interest in the notion of value and in theories of value (Kline, p. 527). The contribution of science and mathematics was essentially negative and resulted in a neutrality with respect to values. Descartes is the model of this unconcern, and Kant also expelled values from what he considered his scientific work, that is, from his speculative studies. In order to make life possible, however, he allowed "practical reality" to values. The gap between science and values continued into the 20th century, with philosophers taking sides for either science or values. Contemporary philosophy of value is said to have begun most properly with Lotze and Nietzsche.

Despite differences and various approaches, philosophers of value begin with the human experience of wanting something or other, that is, with the fact of desiring (*appetitus*). In this regard, Thomas Aquinas suggests that "the ultimate end of any agent (*faciens*), insofar as he is an agent, is the agent himself, for we use for ourselves things made by us; and if a man at any time makes anything for any other end, the thing is referred to his own good, either as useful or pleasurable or simply good. And God, as maker-cause of all things . . . is, himself, the end of all" (*Summa contra gentiles* 3.17). This notion of the agent really seeking himself or herself is also claimed by Whitehead (p. 100). Rahner has pointed to several tendencies distinguishable in the philosophy of values: idealist, psychological, sociological, phenomenologist, and spiritualist (pp. 332–33).

Some worry about the relativization of values, which permits large scale manipulation of conscience-consciousness (Sullivan, pp. 217–18; Harrington, pp. 407–22). In this connection, the thesis of Alasdair MacIntyre is important and provocative (MacIntyre).

In Scripture Qoheleth is an important critiquer of values: "Vanity of vanities! All things are vanity" (Eccl 1:2). Nowhere in Scripture is the criticism of meaning and value as thoroughgoing. Qoheleth outlines the positive values of life: knowledge, wisdom, personal excellence, self-worth, social equity. Like Job before him, Qoheleth advocates a positive acceptance of life, for it is a divine gift to be fully lived even if it cannot be completely grasped and understood. Qoheleth's skepticism is testimony that God is God and that the created universe, human wisdom, and human activities are finite, limited, and incomplete. (Scheide, p. 248).

Consequently, whereas formerly values consisted in the perfection of the earthly image reflecting an external Logos in a world of fixed natures, values are now determined by the sensitivity of humans in responding to the creative urgencies of a developing world. The transforming sequence is in the direction of an increasing differentiation, a deepening subjectivity, and a more comprehensive communion with the total order of the real (Berry, p. 194; Frankena, pp. 229–32).

See also ANTHROPOLOGY; BUSINESS ETHICS; CAPITALISM; COMMON GOOD; CONSCIENCE; HUMAN RIGHTS; POOR, PREFERENTIAL OPTION FOR; RIGHTS AND DUTIES.

Bibliography: T. Berry, "The New Story: Comments on the Origin, Identification, and Transmission of Values," *Cross Currents* 37 (1987) 187–99. W. Frankena, "Value and Valuation," *Encyclopedia of Philosophy* (New York: Macmillan, 1967) 229–32. M. Harrington, "The Search for Transcendental Common Values," *Cross Currents* 31 (1981–82) 407–22. R. Kline, "Philosophy of Value," *New Catholic Encyclopedia* (New York: McGraw-Hill, 1967) 527–31. A. MacIntyre, *After Virtue: A Study in Moral Theory* (Notre Dame: Univ. of Notre Dame Press, 1981). L. Örsy, "The Relationship Between Values and Laws," *The Jurist* 47 (1987) 471–83. K. Rahner, "Value," *Sacramentum Mundi: An Encyclopedia of Theology* (New York: Herder & Herder, 1970) 331–33. E. Scheide, "Qoheleth: Criticism of Values," *The Bible Today* 25 (1987) 244–51. T. Sullivan, "Conscience in the Value Wilderness," *Philosophical Studies* 29 (1982–83) 210–18. P. Tumulty, "A Contemporary Bridge from Facts to Values: But Will Natural Law Theorists Pay the Toll?" *International Philosophical Quarterly* 28 (1988) 53–63. A. Whitehead, *Religion in the Making* (New York: New American Library, 1926, rpt. 1960).

GERALD COLEMAN, S.S.

VATICAN COUNCIL II

The Second Vatican Council (1962–65) is arguably one of the most significant expressions ever of the teaching authority of the Roman Catholic church. The intent of the council, especially as focused by Paul VI at the beginning of the second session, supports such an assessment. The council, Paul VI said, was to concern itself with the church's teaching about itself, the church's renewal and its unity with other Christians, and the church's relation to the contemporary world. Vatican II, though, cannot be seen apart from developments in the church prior to the council, especially those of the previous hundred years. Nor will Vatican II be adequately appreciated apart from a consideration of its reception by the church and its influence in subsequent church life and thought.

What is said of the council as a whole might also be said of the council's place in the development of Catholic social thought. Vatican II represents a major contribution to Catholic social teaching. The social teaching of the council, however, must be seen as part of a continuum that begins with the magisterial teaching of Leo XIII (1878–1903), though the social teaching associated with him had its beginnings in developments prior to his pontificate. Vatican II develops and at times significantly modifies the social teachings of Pius XI (1922–39), Pius XII (1939–58), and John XXIII (1958–63). Vatican II makes its distinctive contribution to Catholic social thought not only in those texts that directly address social concerns but indirectly in many of its other documents.

The conciliar teaching inspired further efforts and is itself developed in subsequent papal and episcopal teaching. These later developments come in the teaching of Paul VI (1963–78) and John Paul II (1978–) and in the statements of the synods of bishops. The teaching of episcopal conferences from various countries and groups of countries stands in the same tradition. Examples of such teaching are numerous: the documents of the General Conference of Latin American Bishops at Medellín (1968), Puebla (1979), and Santo Domingo (1992), the pastoral letters and statements of conferences of bishops from Africa, Asia, and the nations of the Pacific, from Europe, and from Canada and the United States. As implied above, this article assumes that the teaching of the council itself and the council's contribution to the development of Catholic social thought is best understood in a historical perspective that looks both to what preceded the council and to the developments that have taken place since.

The Pastoral Constitution on the Church in the Modern World (*Gaudium et spes*) and the Declaration on Religious Liberty (*Dignitatis humanae*) are the principal conciliar statements on Catholic social thought. Separate articles dealing with these two texts are found elsewhere in this volume. The present article will look to a more general overview of the social teaching of the council, drawing upon the pastoral constitution and the declaration just mentioned but on the other conciliar documents as well.

The Agenda of the Council

That the council would make a major contribution to the development of Catholic social thought was not immediately obvious at the time it opened. None of the preparatory commissions was charged with preparing a text on the topic of the church in the world, and of the seventy preparatory schemata of the council only one dealt with social issues. Further, while John XXIII's 1961 encyclical *Mater et magistra,* marking the 70th anniversary of *Rerum novarum,* dealt with social concerns, it did so without any reference to the work of the council. John XXIII's final encyclical, *Pacem in terris,* issued after the first session, seemed to anticipate the work of the council on the topic of peace. Some participants wondered what role the council might take on a matter so recently dealt with in a papal encyclical.

Other factors, however, prepared the way for the inclusion of social thought on the council's agenda. In a speech a month before the council's opening John XXIII spoke of the church's interior structure and vitality but also of the church's concern for the problems of the world, especially the poor, and of the world's search for peace. In that speech he addressed many of the issues that would become the topics of the Pastoral Constitution on the Church in the Modern World. In his address at the opening session, two of the three purposes that John put forward touch upon our theme: the council was called to foster a spiritual renewal of the church in the light of the gospel and, more specifically, to promote an updating (*aggiornamento*) of the church to respond to the needs of modern times.

The bishops, for their part, evidenced their interest in social issues in their *Message to the World* issued nine days after the opening of the council. They expressed their concern for the two great problems facing humankind: peace and social justice. In the final days of the first session, several speakers called for the council to address not only issues touching the inner life of the church but also questions concerning the church's role in the modern world. Before the end of the first session a decision was made to develop a conciliar document on that specific issue.

God's Redeeming Work in the World

As significant, perhaps, as any specific conciliar teaching in the area of Catholic social thought are several general considerations that form the groundwork for that teaching and for much of its subsequent development. The first of these foundational themes is the understanding of God's universal redemptive plan, which is the context for understanding the church and its responsibilities in the world. In the Dogmatic Constitution on the Church (*Lumen gentium*) the council opens its statement about the church by invoking the theme of God's redemptive work and speaking of the church as "a sacrament or instrumental sign of intimate union with God and of the unity of all humanity" (LG 1). The church is seen to be situated in the design of God that begins with creation and will be fulfilled when all will be restored to God in Christ (LG 2–3). This breadth of vision and integral understanding of salvation stand behind the council's social teaching.

Related to its emphasis on the universal character of God's redeeming work is the council's attempt to overcome a tendency, at times, to so stress the distinction between the world and the realm of the divine that there appears to be a dichotomy between the concerns of the world and matters of salvation and grace. In such a perspective one might see concern for social issues as not belonging directly to the specific and religious concerns of the church. By attempting to give a more holistic view of the relationship between God and the world the council prepared the way for a changed view of the relation of the church to the world. This leads to a second foundational consideration.

The Church in the World

Among the draft documents distributed for discussion at the first session of the council was a proposed constitution on the church. The ninth chapter of the proposed text dealt with the relationship between church and state and the matter of religious tolerance. There was no chapter dedicated to a consideration of the role of the church in the world. During the course of the council the approach represented by the proposed constitution on the church was radically transformed. In place of that original ninth chapter there would emerge the two separate documents that deal most directly with the social teaching of the council, the Pastoral Constitution on the Church in the Modern World and the Declaration on Religious Liberty. The pastoral constitution says in effect that the church is constituted as church, in part, by its relationship to the world. And the declaration affirms not only that religious freedom is a personal and collective human right to be respected and guaranteed by civil government but that the freedom of the church is the fundamental principle guiding the relations between the church and the social, political, and economic orders.

The council's move in these areas reflects its decision to see the church's relationship to the world as more fundamental than the relation between itself and the state. Further, its teaching in the Declaration on Religious Liberty concerning the limits of civil government and its willingness to forego political privilege for itself (GS 76) dispose the church to address, in freedom, its responsibilities in the world. The stance of the council as regards the church's relationship to the world and the church's relationship to the state is fundamental to the social thought of Vatican II.

A Change in Method

Prior to Vatican II the dominant approach to Catholic social thought and to magisterial teaching on the topic was one based on a consideration of natural law. Leo XIII made this quite explicit in *Rerum novarum,* as did Pius XI and Pius XII in their social teaching. It may have been a desire to stem an apparent lessening of regard for the natural-law approach that led John XXIII in *Mater et magistra* and, even more pointedly, in *Pacem in terris* to insist that the social teaching of those two encyclicals was based on principles of natural law.

Two aspects of natural law enter into discussion of its place in social ethics. A philosophical aspect concerns the understanding, through the exercise of reason, of what it means to be human. A theological aspect of natural law asks whether the Christian has access to a source of ethical wisdom distinct from divine revelation in Christ and the Scriptures. While many in the Protestant tradition for various reasons have denied the presence of such an extrabiblical source, the Roman Catholic tradition has affirmed the existence of such a source. Catholic tradition has located that source in human nature, created by God and understood by human reason.

Much of Catholic social thought before Vatican II, especially that of the papal magisterium, based itself on human reason and natural law as the principal sources of moral wisdom. John XXIII, in part 1 of *Mater et magistra,* described previous social teaching from Leo XIII to his day as based upon the order inscribed by God in human nature. Revelation was invoked, but generally as corroborating what is known by human reason reflecting on human nature. In the conclusion of *Pacem in terris* John XXIII reminded his readers that the doctrinal principles put forth in that document were, for the most part, derived from or suggested by requirements inherent in human nature itself.

While Vatican II, in the first part of the Pastoral Constitution on the Church in the Modern World, does not explicitly advert to it, the council in fact adopts a different method in the development of its social teaching. The council says that we cannot understand human dignity, human community, or human activity in the world apart from a consideration of creation, the presence of sin, and the mysteries of incarnation and redemption. The third chapter of part 2 adds a consideration of eschatology as another factor in its consideration of the meaning of human activity in the world. The teaching of the pastoral constitution, then, is based upon reason and nature and biblical revelation.

The significance of this modification is twofold. By explicitly grounding its social thought in the symbols of biblical revelation, the council encourages believers to see social concerns as fundamentally related to religious self-understanding. Yet the use of specifically religious symbols renders more complex the church's efforts to promote a public mode of discourse in promoting human dignity and human rights.

Historical Consciousness

Besides its making use of biblical revelation as a basis of its social teaching, Vatican II is noteworthy for the adjustment of its approach to the philosophical aspect of natural law. It does this in its recognition of the historical character of human and social life and of its readiness to make that historical sensitivity an element of its social reflection.

Social thought prior to the council, especially in Leo XIII though perhaps less so in Pius XI, used a natural-law method in a classical manner that emphasized the universal and the unchanging. Principles of natural law were used as a basis from which to deduce applications to address questions in new circumstances. The presuppositions of this method did not allow for a thorough appreciation of the fundamentally historical character of human existence, of social change and development, and of the need to incorporate a historical consciousness in reflection on social issues. John XXIII in *Pacem in terris* did signal a shift of direction and so anticipated the historical sensitivity characteristic of much of the social thought of Vatican II. In the concluding paragraphs of each section of his encyclical, John XXIII made a statement of the characteristics of the day that were to enter a consideration of the various topics on which he wrote.

Vatican II picks up on that historical sensitivity in the introduction to the Pastoral Constitution on the Church in the Modern World. Here the council describes what it sees as the more important features of the modern world that must be part of any effort to look to the role of the church in the world. In a significant summary statement the council observes: "The human race is moving from a more static view of things to one which is more dynamic and evolutionary, giving rise to new combinations of problems which call for new analyses and syntheses" (GS 5). A similar awareness of the contemporary situation is seen at the outset of the various chapters dealing with specific issues in the second section of the constitution.

This historical consciousness became an important factor in the council's method of moral reasoning and is related to the shift in method described above. The council's sensitivity to contemporary changes and, to some extent, to the variety of situations in different parts of the world led the council to take a more inductive approach in its moral reflection.

Vatican II and Previous Church Teaching

This heightened sense of historical consciousness is also a factor in the council's appreciation of its teaching vis-à-vis earlier statements of the magisterium. This awareness is most evident in the council's introduction to its treatment of religious liberty (DH 1). But there are other instances as well. In its treatment of atheism in the Pastoral Constitution on the Church in the Modern World the council cites past occasions when the official teaching of the church deplored the teachings of atheism (GS 21). But the council omits reference to the July 1, 1949, condemnation of the Holy Office and takes note of statements of John XXIII and Paul VI that indicate changes of attitude toward atheistic communism because of historical developments within that system.

Concerning yet another issue, the council takes a more positive stance toward the phenomenon of "socialization" than was the case in the writings of Pius XI. The council (GS 25) refers to the teaching of *Quadragesimo anno* but with it cites the passages in *Mater et magistra* that indicate a rethinking on this issue. The direction of Vatican II would be taken further still by Paul VI in *Octogesimo adveniens.* Where John XXIII and Vatican II took the first steps toward an openness to some features of socialism, Paul VI teaches that, with qualifications, a Christian may embrace certain socialist currents as a way of implementing Christian values.

The Epistemological Reserve of Vatican II

If Vatican II recognizes that there has been development in Christian social thought, it also recognizes limitations to church teaching in the complex area of social obligation.

At the very outset of the pastoral constitution a footnote alerts the reader that while some of the constitution's teaching contains permanent principles, other elements are, because of changing circumstances, to be regarded as contingent (GS, n. 1). That distinction has been widely recognized in subsequent official teaching on social matters.

In at least two instances the council specifically asserts that church officials do not have ready answers to all the varied and complex questions that might arise in the area of social teaching. An example of this admission is found in the Pastoral Constitution on the Church in the Modern World where the council initiates its reflection on human activity in the world (GS 33). In the same chapter, the council states that while the laity may expect guidance from the clergy, they should know that their pastors do not always have the expertise to speak on every issue, even some of those that are most serious (GS 43). Paul VI some years later showed the same reserve when speaking of the church's evaluation of models of society (OA 40).

Akin to the above, the council also teaches that people holding the same Christian worldview may take quite different approaches to the same question. The council calls for honest dialogue in such instances and counsels against too easy an assumption that one's position coincides with the demands of the gospel or the authority of the church (GS 43).

Social Concerns and the Mission of the Church

As the concern to relate Catholic social thought to the basic mysteries of the Christian faith is one of the major contributions of the council, so too is the council's effort to provide an ecclesiological grounding to the church's social mission. Vatican II does that in several places and in different ways.

A first statement concerning the role of the church in the world comes in the first article of the Dogmatic Constitution on the Church. Here the church is spoken of as, in Christ, "a sacrament or instrumental sign of intimate union with God and of the unity of all humanity" (LG 1). While this first use of the expression does not relate explicitly to the concerns associated with social justice, references to this same image in the Pastoral Constitution on the Church in the Modern World (GS 42, 45) indicate that the image came to include such considerations.

A second manner of presenting the role of the church comes in the council's relating the church to the reign of God. In the Dogmatic Constitution on the Church, the church is said to have received "the mission of announcing the kingdom of Christ and of God and of inaugurating it among all peoples." The church, the text continues, "has formed the seed and the beginning of the kingdom on earth" (LG 5). The relation of church, the kingdom of God, and the social mission of the church is made explicit in sections of the Pastoral Constitution on the Church in the Modern World (GS 39, 45, 72).

Yet another way in which the Dogmatic Constitution on the Church speaks of the social dimension of the church's mission comes in its description of the laity in the church as those who by baptism share in Christ's priestly, prophetic, and royal office in the church and in the world (LG 31). It is in treating the third part of this threefold office that social concerns figure most prominently. The laity of the church have a principal role in working for a more equitable distribution of the goods of the earth, progress in human and Christian freedom, and improving "those secular structures and conditions which constitute an inducement to sin" (LG 36).

Two of the conciliar decrees provide ways of relating the church to social concerns. In the Decree on the Apostolate of the Laity (*Apostolicam actuositatem*) the laity are said to have a twofold role: to work for the evangelization and sanctification of people (AA 6) and to renew the temporal order as a part of God's plan (AA 5, 7). These roles are based on an understanding of Christ's work of redemption, which, while "primarily" concerning the salvation of human beings, "also embraces the renewal of the whole temporal order" (AA 5).

The Decree on the Church's Missionary Activity (*Ad gentes*) stresses the call to work for the growth of the mystical body of Christ but includes also a call to work "for the right ordering of social and economic affairs" (AG 12). Christian faithful are to join with others who work to overcome famine, ignorance, and disease, to improve people's living conditions, and to establish peace in the world (AG 12).

The most sustained effort to describe the social dimension of the church's mission comes in the Pastoral Constitution on the Church in the Modern World. The constitution focuses on three areas in which the church understands its social responsibility in the world: in promoting human dignity and human rights, in encouraging and fostering human community, and in offering guidance and direction as to the meaning and value of human activity. In a summarizing statement Vatican II asserts that the mission Christ gave to the church is in the religious order and not in the political, economic, or social order. Yet "this mission of a religious nature produces a function, enlightenment and resources which can be of service in constructing and strengthening the human community in accordance with the divine law" (GS 42).

In these various attempts to show the ecclesiological grounding of the church's social mission, Vatican II marks a new stage in the long process of the church's efforts to understand its relationship to the world. Not ten years earlier in a 1956 speech of Pius XII, which the council cites as a resource in its attempt to articulate the social mission of the church, the pope taught: "Its divine founder, Jesus Christ, gave to the church no mandate or fixed purpose in the cultural order. The end given to it by Christ is strictly religious. . . . The church ought to lead men and women to God, so that they may unreservedly surrender themselves to him. . . . The church can never lose sight of this strictly religious and supernatural end. The purpose of all its activities, down to the last canon of its law, can only be to converge directly or indirectly upon this end" (GS 42, n. 11). Vatican II clearly goes well beyond the strictures outlined by Pius XII in its efforts to describe the mission of the church in the world. From the perspective of later developments, one sees that the council is charting a new course and proceeding with caution.

Efforts to understand the place for a concern for justice in human relations and in human structures in the mission of the church would receive further attention in papal and episcopal teaching after the council. If one notes a marked difference between the teaching of Pius XII and Vatican II, one notes a marked difference again between the teachings of Vatican II and the statement of the synod of bishops in 1971: "Action on behalf of justice and participation in the transformation of the world fully appear to us as a constitutive dimension of the preaching of the Gospel, or, in other words, of the church's mission for the redemption of the human race and its liberation from every oppressive situation" (*Justitia in mundo,* introduction). Vatican II has been a stimulus to continued reflection on this topic. The same theme would be taken up again in the synod of 1974 on the topic of evangelization and in Paul VI's response to the synod, his 1975 statement *Evangelii nuntiandi.*

The Dignity of the Human Person

A basic principle of Vatican II's social thought is its teaching on human dignity and human rights.

Related to the change in the council's approach to natural law by its acceptance of historical consciousness is its shift from an emphasis on human nature to an emphasis on the human person. This shift and the personalist approach to moral responsibility that it supports is found especially in the first part of the Pastoral Constitution on the Church in the Modern World but also in the chapter on marriage and the family in the second part of the constitution. The council's considerations on the human person in these chapters also continue the methodological change that not only uses reason's reflection on human reality but that also draws upon divine revelation.

The human person, the council teaches, is created to the image of God and finds his or her fullness of meaning in Christ "the last Adam, who fully discloses humankind to itself and unfolds its noble calling by revealing the mystery of the Father and the Father's love" (GS 22). The human person is essentially a relational being, open to God and to other human beings. Embodied beings, human persons are distinguished by a dignity of intellect and a secret core, the human conscience, where the voice of God speaks from within. Human persons are gifted with freedom, an especially important manifestation of the image of God in human reality. While affected by the presence of sin in themselves and in their social relationships and facing the mystery of death, all human persons are united to God by the mystery of the Incarnation and, by the power of God's Spirit and in a way known to God, are made partners in the paschal mystery (GS, part 1, chap. 1).

It is on the basis of their distinctively human characteristics and the fact that all persons have a common origin, are redeemed by Christ, and share a common destiny in being called to communion with God, the council teaches, that one understands the fundamental dignity and the basic equality of all human persons.

Human Rights

The Catholic Church had struggled with the notion of human rights as thinking on this topic developed in the late 18th and throughout the 19th centuries. Leo XIII, in his writings on the nature and role of civil authority, had little tolerance for the political freedoms advocated by liberal social thought. Yet his writings on social concerns lay the foundations for the developments of 20th-century Catholic thought on human rights. Leo did argue for the existence of certain basic economic rights and insisted that the state had the obligation to safeguard the rights of the poor and those who did not have the means to defend themselves.

Catholic thinking on human rights received further attention in the writings of Pius XI, both in his enumeration of human rights in *Divini Redemptoris* and in his focus upon the institutional dimensions of human relationships. Pius XII, for his part, made the dignity of the person an explicit and central place in his moral teaching. Influenced, though, by the political situation of the time, he tended to give greater emphasis to political rights than to those in the economic order. John XXIII, both in *Mater et magistra* and even more so in *Pacem in terris,* gave a strong emphasis to human dignity and to human rights. In the second of these two encyclicals John XXIII recognized the many areas of human rights, personal and religious, social, political, and economic. And the protection and integration of human rights, he taught, is a concern that belongs to all aspects of organized society.

Vatican II, in its treatment of human dignity and human rights draws upon previous Catholic tradition, especially as articulated by John XXIII, and makes its own contribution. Perhaps that contribution is most evident in the council's recognition that the claims based on human dignity and the structures that serve to promote and protect human rights are historically conditioned (GS 25). That recognition entails the challenge to protect and defend human dignity and human rights in the midst of changing situations and varying circumstances. A single social, political, and economic structure cannot be presented as the final word.

One of the most basic of human rights is the civil right of religious freedom. Where previous papal teaching viewed the claim to religious liberty from within the framework of secular and liberal political thought, Vatican II, in its Declaration on Religious Liberty, recognizes the changed circumstances in which this right has come to be understood. The human and civil right to religious liberty, the council declares, is one of the fundamental demands of human dignity and is known as such from reason itself and from revelation.

Human Participation and Social Responsibility

Integral to the teaching of Vatican II on human dignity and human freedom is the council's teaching on the right and responsibility of human persons to participate in shaping the structures of human society for the common good. Repeatedly the Pastoral Constitution on the Church in the Modern World emphasizes the social nature of the human person (GS 12, 24, 25, 32). Not only does the council pronounce a negative judgment on a merely individualist morality (GS 30), it insists that the advancement of the human person and the growth of society are mutually dependent (GS 25). Human activity directed to the improvement of society is integral to human perfection (GS 35). Individual and collective human activity to improve the conditions of life are said to correspond in principle to God's design (GS 34). Education is to be directed to help people accept social responsibility, and nations are commended whose structures are such as to allow and promote personal responsibility and participation in public affairs (GS 31). In the chapter on the development of culture in the second part of the pastoral constitution the council notes with approval that a "new humanism" is being born "in which the human is defined above all in terms of our responsibility to our sisters and brothers and to history" (GS 55).

The emphasis on personal responsibility in social concerns receives support in several other documents of the council. The laity, and among them young people in particular, are encouraged to accept their social responsibilities (AA 7, 12; AG 12). Bishops, priests, and candidates for ordained ministry are each encouraged to see their responsibilities in areas of social concern (*Christus Dominus* 12; *Presbyterorum ordinis* 3; *Optatam totius* 11). And, while the connection between liturgy and social concerns is not mentioned in either The Constitution on the Sacred Liturgy (*Sacrosanctum concilium*) or in the Pastoral Constitution on the Church in the Modern World, the call for all the faithful to full and active participation in the liturgy can, when the connection between liturgy and justice is made, indirectly support the latter.

Postconciliar development of the themes of social responsibility and participation would come in Paul VI's *Populorum progressio* and *Octogesima adveniens* and in John Paul II's *Laborem exercens.*

Sin and Structures Corrupted by Sin

There are four other topics that deserve to be included in this overview of Vatican II and its place in Catholic social thought. The first of these concerns the council's attentiveness to the reality of sin as it affects the human person and human structures.

The topic of sin is introduced as one of the factors that enters a correct understanding of human reality. The whole of human life, personal and social, is said to be engaged in a struggle between good and evil (GS 13). Yet the council's presentation on the human person and the human community is, overall, rather optimistic in outlook (GS, part 1, chaps. 1 and 2). The council participants sought to correct that optimism in their treatment of human activity. To a greater emphasis on the impact of sin there was added a more explicit treatment of the theme, from biblical eschatology, that the struggle with sin will continue until the end of human history when God's plan in Christ will be brought to completion (GS 37–39).

There is an important observation in the Pastoral Constitution on the Church in the Modern World that recognizes that social structures can also be affected by the consequences of sin (GS 25), though we do not see in Vatican II so specific a recognition of the reality of "social sin" as is found in later magisterial documents. Further hints in the direction toward an idea of social sin are found in both the Dogmatic Constitution on the Church and the Decree on the Apostolate of the Laity. The former speaks of "secular structures and conditions which constitute an inducement to sin" (LG 36) and which the laity are urged to bring into harmony with the norms of justice. The Decree on the Apostolate of the Laity gives its own hint of the notion of social sin in its reference to "human institutions" that have become corrupted because of the influence of sin (AA 7). The understanding of social sin, only broached in Vatican II, would receive greater clarity in later official documents, in the statement *Justice in the World* of the synod of 1971, and in the exhortation *Reconciliatio et paenitentia* and the encyclical *Solicitudo rei socialis* of John Paul II.

Concern for Structural Change

Related to its recognition of the influence of sin on social structures and its strong emphasis on human responsibility to shape structures for the common good, Vatican II also addresses the need for change in economic and political structures.

The social thought of Leo XIII, influenced as it was by his approach to civil authority and public order in the context of the late 19th century, did not include a call for social restructuring. Pius XI, by contrast, writing at a time of worldwide depression, looked to a restructuring of the social order through the distribution of just wages and even some form of worker partnership in ownership or profits. The focus on economic change in Pius XI shifted with Pius XII. Concerned during so much of his pontificate with political questions, Pius XII gave correspondingly less attention to social and economic issues. In the cold war situation following World War II, the pope was very critical of totalitarian regimes and supportive, by contrast, to democratic forms of government. And while he was critical of abuses in capitalism, his attitude toward change in social and economic structures was more like that of Leo XIII than that of Pius XI.

John XXIII generally took up the approach of Pius XI in his emphasis on a just distribution of wealth and, keeping in mind the common good, allowed that government might have a role to play toward that end. Toward the end of *Pacem in terris,* though, John XXIII criticized those whose zeal for justice leads to revolutionary-type tactics. He called instead for a gradual renovation of human institutions working from within.

Vatican II generally follows the approach taken by John XXIII, even if it tempers the pope's optimism toward structural change and offers a theological grounding to its call for more equitable structures. The council addresses the question of social change in several sections of the Pastoral Constitution on the Church in the Modern World: in its reflection on human community (GS, part 1, chap. 2); on the proper development of culture (GS, part 2, chap. 2); on economic and social life (GS, part 2, chap. 3); and in the chapter on promoting peace and encouraging the community of nations (GS, part 2, chap. 5). The council repeatedly criticizes excessive social and economic imbalances (GS 29, 63, 66, 88) and calls for an economic and social development that overcomes glaring disparities (GS 26, 60, 66, 85, 86). The council's attitude toward social change is also seen in its teaching on the potential good to be had from healthy forms of socialization (GS 25, 42), to which reference was made above.

In its treatment of economic questions the council notes its desire to relate a respect for the methods and laws of economic activity with a concern that that activity be undertaken within the limits of moral order (GS 64). How those two concerns are related in practice will probably remain one of the abiding elements of discussion in this area of social reflection.

The issues of social and economic change, the principles for promoting such change, and the agents responsible for such change would continue to be addressed in later magisterial statements.

Private Property

Related to what Vatican II says about economic structures is its teaching about private property.

Leo XIII insisted on the right to private property as a counter to the socialist denial of that right. Leo's teaching, however, tended to overlook the classical distinction between the generic dominion by which all human beings have a right to use the goods of the earth and private property in the strict sense by which property belongs to an individual. Pius XI put more emphasis on the social function of property. Property owned by an individual to provide for his or her own security should be seen in light of the general divine provision that the goods of the earth serve the entire human family. Pius XII and John XXIII continued the tradition of Pius XI, though John XXIII made more explicit the teaching that private property is secondary to the right of all people to the goods of the earth.

Vatican II continues in the tradition of John XXIII on this issue. The council teaches that any disposition of property adapted to the legitimate institutions of people in differing and changing situations must attend to the prior claim of the universal destiny of the goods of creation for all people (GS 69, 71). The council teaches, too, that the common good may in certain circumstances require the disposition of insufficiently cultivated lands (GS 71). The council also reaffirms the ancient principle that persons in extreme need have the right to secure from others what is needed for sustenance (GS 69). In its treatment of property, as in its treatment of social change, Vatican II is generally content to urge the wealthy and powerful to make changes to benefit the poor rather than to engage in social analysis or offer support or guidance to the poor to work for their own betterment. This approach is consistent with the gradualist approach taken by the council.

Vatican II provides an impetus, though, for further development. A couple of years after the council *Populorum progressio* would reinforce the teaching of the council and affirm that private property and the right of free commerce are both subordinate to the principle of the universal destiny of the goods of creation (PP 22).

In its deliberations on the economic order Vatican II recognizes the benefits and liabilities of both capitalist and socialist forms of economic policy. The council's openness is a pragmatic one that, not surprisingly, has generated various responses and continued probing.

Peace and the Community of Nations

Another area of social thought of Vatican II, related to its treatment of economic issues but also standing on its own, is the council's teaching on promoting peace and fostering the community of nations. This teaching occurs in the final chapter of part 2 of the Pastoral Constitution on the Church in the Modern World. Presupposing the "just-war tradition," the council recognizes the need for and legitimacy of military defense. At the same time the council calls for "an entirely fresh scrutiny" of war because of the production of modern scientific weapons, and it endorses condemnations of total war issued previously by Pius XII, John XXIII, and by Paul VI just two months earlier at the United Nations (GS 80). The council issues its own condemnation of actions undertaken to exterminate an entire people, nation, or ethnic minority (GS 79) and those that look to the destruction of whole cities or of widespread areas with their inhabitants (GS 79, 80). The council, however, does not condemn nuclear weapons, even though an earlier draft of the text did tend in that direction.

The council recognizes the existence of policies of deterrence and, briefly, argues for the inherent limitations in such policies. The council also calls for efforts to put an end to the arms race, regarded as a "virulent plague affecting humanity" and doing "intolerable harm" to the poor (GS 81). The council urges a mutually agreed-upon disarmament protected by effective safeguards (GS 82). While the council sees that those in military service who perform their duties in a right manner are contributing to the establishment of peace (GS 79), it also calls for legal provision for conscientious objectors who are willing to accept alternate forms of community service (GS 79) and praises those who renounce violent means in claiming rights, provided they do this "without harm to the rights and obligations of others or of the community" (GS 78). The council's position on conscientious objection reverses a position taken by Pius XII in 1956.

The teaching of the council on war and peace is complemented by a call for "the establishment of a universal public authority, recognized by all, which will possess the effective means on behalf of all to safeguard security, the observance of justice and respect for rights" (GS 82). The entire second part of the last chapter of the pastoral constitution is given to a reflection on this issue.

Vatican II's teaching on war and peace invites further discussion, as, for example, on the issues surrounding the matter of nuclear deterrence. But its contribution may be measured not only by what it says but by the stimulus it has given to national conferences of bishops to engage in further reflection on the complex issues involved in this area. It should be noted that the explicit condemnations found in the treatment of issues of war are the only explicit condemnations of the council, even though in other texts there is strong rejection of abortion and infanticide (GS 51) and a reprobation of atheism (GS 21) and of all persecutions against any people, and specifically, of hatred, persecutions, and demonstrations directed against the Jews (*Nostra aetate* 4).

Omissions in the Council's Teaching

The council addresses many issues and makes a significant contribution to several areas of Catholic social thought. There are, to be sure, many statements that invite further reflection. Some of those have been taken up in subsequent theological exploration and in official teaching.

There are omissions, too, in the council's teaching. While Vatican II is notable for its use of biblical and theological symbols in its effort to ground its social teaching and its understanding of social responsibility, its failure to relate the concerns of the Constitution on the Sacred Liturgy and the concerns of the Pastoral Constitution on the Church in the Modern World is an important one. The synod of 1971 did address, if briefly, the relation between liturgy and education for justice.

Vatican II makes a major contribution in its ecclesiological grounding of the church's social ministry. The council's ecclesiology also gives prominence to the notion of the universal church as a communion of local churches and has contributed to a development of the theology of the local church. But nowhere does the council deal explicitly with the local church and its role in social reflection and social ministry. That omission would be corrected by Paul VI in *Octogesima adveniens.* There the pope calls for Christian communities in different countries to develop their own theological insights and practical applications (OA 4).

In *Pacem in terris* John XXIII mentioned the changing understanding of the role and rights of women among the characteristics of the present day (PT 1). While Vatican II makes several references to this theme (AA 9; GS 8, 29, 60), the council documents do not give it an extended treatment. The most sustained attention to the role of women in church and society comes in the *Message to Women* read at the final session of the council.

While later social teaching, notably John Paul II's *Sollicitudo rei socialis* (SRS 34), gives attention to the limitations of natural resources and the pollution of the environment, there is little attention to these concerns in the conciliar texts.

Vatican II makes references to the need for continual reformation in the church (*Unitatis redintegratio* 6) and admits the failings of the church in several instances (GS 19; DH 12), but we do not find in Vatican II the call, present in the synod of 1971, that the demands of justice be carried out in the church itself.

The council gives repeated emphasis to the role and responsibility of the laity in concerns of social justice, even deliberately urging them to take their "full part" in the development of the church's social doctrine (AA 31). By contrast, the council's Decree on the Up-to-Date Renewal of Religious Life (*Perfectae caritatis*) shows less interest in developing the relationship between religious life and social concerns. There is an opening for such reflection in the principles for the renewal of religious life (PC 2) and in the council's awareness of the connection between religious poverty and the needs of the poor (PC 13). Vatican II's teaching on the fundamental role of baptism, the universal call to holiness, and the church's relationship to the world would have a profound impact on efforts at renewal of religious life after the council. An official recognition of the relationship between consecrated poverty and the plight of the poor and the demands of justice on their behalf came in the 1971 exhortation issued by the Congregation for Religious and Secular Institutes (*Evangelica testificatio* 17–18).

Omissions in the social teaching of Vatican II and the need for clarification and development in various areas of its thought are reminders that the council is itself a stage, albeit a very important one, in the church's life and thought. In its teaching on the relationship of the church to the world and of the church to the state, in its providing a theological grounding to the church's social thought, an ecclesiological basis for the social dimension of the church's mission, and a stimulus to the church's reflection and praxis, Vatican II makes its most significant contribution.

See also CHURCH, SOCIAL MISSION OF; DIGNITATIS HUMANAE; GAUDIUM ET SPES; HUMAN RIGHTS; NATURAL LAW; PERSON, DIGNITY OF.

Bibliography: N. Tanner, ed., *Decrees of the Ecumenical Councils,* vol. 2 (Washington: Georgetown Univ. Press, 1990). J.-Y. Calvez and J. Perrin, *The Church and Social Justice: The Social Teaching of the Popes from Leo XIII to Pius XII (1878–1958)* (Chicago: Henry Regnery, 1961). C. Curran, *Directions in Catholic Social Ethics* (Notre Dame: Univ. of Notre Dame Press, 1985); *Tensions in Moral Theology* (Notre Dame: Univ. of Notre Dame Press, 1988). C. Curran and R. McCormick, eds., *Readings in Moral Theology No. 5: Official Catholic Social Teaching* (New York: Paulist, 1986). D. Dorr, *Option for the Poor: A Hundred Years of Vatican Social Teaching* (Maryknoll: Orbis, 1983). J. Dwyer, *"Questions of Special Urgency": The Church in the Modern World Two Decades After Vatican II* (Washington: Georgetown Univ. Press, 1986). J. Gremillion, *The Gospel of Peace and Justice: Catholic Social Teaching Since Pope John* (Maryknoll: Orbis, 1976). J. Hehir, "Church-State and Church-World: The Ecclesiological Implications," *Catholic Theological Society of America Proceedings* 41 (1986) 54–74. D. Hollenbach, *Claims in Conflict: Retrieving and Renewing the Catholic Human Rights Tradition* (New York: Paulist, 1979). L. Richard, ed., *Vatican II: The Unfinished Agenda: A Look to the Future* (New York: Paulist, 1987). H. Vorgrimler, ed., *Commentary on the Documents of Vatican II,* 5 vols. (New York: Herder & Herder, 1967–69).

FREDERICK J. CWIEKOWSKI, S.S.

VOLKSVEREIN

Founded in 1890 at the instigation of the German Center party leader, Ludwig Windthorst (1812–91), the Volksverein (People's Association for Catholic Germany) was taken in hand by Franz Brandts (1834–1914), a Rhenish textile manufacturer, and Franz Hitze (1851–1928), a priest and politician who distinguished himself in social policy questions. It grew into a mass organization for the schooling of Catholics in view of the participation in civic and social affairs to which they could again aspire after the settling of the Kulturkampf. By the eve of the First World War it counted 800,000 members. No wonder that the Milanese archbishop, Andrea Cardinal Ferrari, when he addressed the 1903 Katholikentag in Cologne, could say, "Germania doceat!" German Catholicism, with its myriad organizations closely bound to the church yet without canonical ties to the hierarchical structure, served as a model and exemplar to Catholics in other nations.

Through extension courses and publications the Volksverein staff trained a body of activists and enlightened them about ethical values in social and economic life. They in turn developed a welcome educational and organizational activity at the local level. The Volksverein took root and grew during the same period in which labor unionism in Germany spread and split into a socialist, a Christian, and a liberal wing, with the liberal unions sinking into virtual insignificance and the Christian ones claiming about one-sixth of organized labor; in some regions they constituted a much greater proportion. The headquarters of the Volksverein in Mönchengladbach became a center of Christian trade-union planning and training, with a number of labor leaders relying on its services in one form or another. The so-called Mönchengladbach or "Cologne tendency" favored the development of autonomous unions, "Christian" only because the socialist unions were avowedly anti-religious; the "Berlin tendency," by contrast, frowned on assertive unionism and insisted upon the subordination of all labor activity to religious authorities in the church. This polarization led to no end of trouble in the years 1900–14 and called forth the encyclical *Singulari quadam* of 1912; what was in question from the point of view of church teaching was the bearing of different parts of *Rerum novarum* on the question of trade unionism.

The Volksverein and even the German Center party were sucked into this controversy, indeed made responsible for it in the eyes of their Catholic critics. But with the support of the archbishop of Cologne they were able to hold their own and even, in the case of the Volksverein, flourish. The leading spirit was now August Pieper (1866–1942), a priest of the archdiocese of Paderborn. He assembled a highly qualified staff around him as general secretary in Mönchengladbach. His efforts to keep the Volksverein free of doctrinal quicksand so as to pursue its practical work unhindered were only partly successful.

A first sign of change, requiring a new formula, came in the form of the need to address the women's question. The socialists and the Protestants in Germany had already started organizations of women; in 1903 a convert, Elisabeth Gnauck-Kühne, founded the German Catholic Women's League. The Volksverein considered itself *the* general association of German Catholics and started to enroll women members and respond to women's issues. The women's organization, however, was able to persuade it to restrict its activities, in the main, to men. This was the start of a trend to more specialized and yet open membership organizations of Catholics. After World War I this trend continued and ate into the Volksverein's size and its importance in the Catholic organizational scheme of things in Germany. Despite valiant efforts to regear for the new challenges of civic education in the Weimar Republic, the Volksverein declined and was finished off by the Nazis in 1933. (Other thriving Catholic organizations were also shut down or harassed after the Nazi takeover, despite the 1933 concordat.)

In the United States, Peter E. Dietz organized social-studies institutes inspired by the Volksverein model under the auspices of the Central Verein (*New Catholic Encyclopedia* 4:865).

See also ASSOCIATIONISM; CHRISTIAN DEMOCRACY; CHURCH, SOCIAL MISSION OF; DIETZ, PETER E.; EDUCATION, ROLE OF; MAGISTERIUM; MODERNISM; RERUM NOVARUM; WOMEN.

Bibliography: E. Brose, *Christian Labor and the Politics of Frustration in Imperial Germany* (Washington: The Catholic Univ. of America Press, 1985). H. Hurten in *Der soziale und politische Katholizismus: Entwicklungslinien in Deutschland, 1803–1963* 2:248–61, A. Rauscher, ed. (Munich: Olzog, 1982). P. Misner, *Social Catholicism in Europe* (New York: Crossroad, 1991).

PAUL MISNER

W

WAR

Roman Catholicism has a guardedly optimistic attitude toward war. Within the tradition one finds the conviction that war is not inevitable or a necessity of the human condition. Thus there is the hope that war can be abolished. This is tempered by the conviction that conflict is inevitable in a sinful world. Without serious effort to avert it, conflict can evolve into the armed violence of war.

Another element of the Roman Catholic attitude is that even in the midst of war the moral dimension of human existence cannot be ignored, and restraints must be placed upon both the reasons for initiating war and the manner whereby war is waged.

These two elements of Roman Catholic thought—that conflict, but not war is inevitable and that the violence of war is subject to moral restraint—reflect the guarded optimism of the tradition on war.

History

The history of church teaching has largely been shaped by attention to the experience of war in specific circumstances. Opposition to warfare certainly was part of the ethos of the early church. Whether this was due solely to a committed pacifist stance is not easy to determine. During the NT and postapostolic period the social position of many Christian converts in the Roman Empire as well as the nature of the Roman military created a barrier to Christian involvement in warfare. Nevertheless, there is a strong sense that shedding blood was at odds with the gospel.

By the later decades of the 2nd century this was changing, and in the 4th-century writing of Augustine there are arguments for taking up arms as a duty. Using domestic analogies of police and criminals, Augustine saw war as punishment against evildoers and as a requirement of neighbor love. War and the harm it causes might be tragic, but it could be just. The context for Augustine's analysis was the place of the church within a political order that was officially Christian. In this new setting, so different from the NT era, there was concern about the church's responsibility for preserving public order and defending the empire against Germanic invaders.

Later commentators tended to adopt Augustine's approach of defending Christian participation in war. There were dissenters from this position as a number of individuals and groups continued to practice pacifism. As the relationship of church and state grew closer from the time of Constantine there was an accompanying separation within the church between the great mass of believers and those who sought a higher or more perfect form of discipleship. This distinction within the Christian community accomodated those who found moral teachings such as the just war too much of a compromise with the sinful world. A vocational pacifism developed that made refusal to participate in war a part of certain vocational choices, for example, of most religious orders.

It was during the medieval period that the idea of a crusade, or holy war, was revived. Based on themes in the OT of Yahweh as warrior and tales of the conquest (Joshua, Judges) as well as select passages in the NT (Jn 2:15; Mt 10:34; Lk 22:35-38), the idea arose that combat with Islam was divinely sanctioned. In the crusade, the Augustinian view of the sense of war's tragic nature was suppressed. Thus the historical circumstance, the presence of militant Islamism, was a major factor in the teaching on war.

More commonly cited than the crusade arguments, however, was the practice of canonists who sought to develop clear criteria for determining a just war when princes engaged in armed conflict. In order to regulate and minimize the harm of warfare a number of policies were urged such as the Truce of God (which restricted the times for war) and the Peace of God (which established categories of people exempt from war).

This canonical literature was later systematized by Thomas Aquinas in his treatment of war. For Thomas there were three central concerns in establishing a just war: just cause, legitimate authority, and right intention. Similar to Augustine, Thomas held that war might be an obligation derived from the virtue of charity. Protecting the well-being of innocent persons from aggression was a requirement of the common good.

Medieval developments in just-war theory illustrate how ecclesial teaching took note of the rivalries arising within a feudal political system and the need for critieria to adjudicate disputes. Also, the code of chivalry governing the behavior of a military class was integrated with just-war ideas. This concern to establish criteria for how justice governed medieval warfare testifies to the ongoing desire of the church to practice gospel imperatives in a complex and sinful world.

Subsequent church teaching as formulated by Scholastic theologians like Francisco de Vitoria and Francisco Suarez had to deal with a political and cultural context far different than the medievalists. The emergence of independent nation-states and the decline of a united Christendom after the Reformation meant the end of any universally recognized authority. This, in turn, meant that it would be difficult to establish the justice of any one side's cause in war. Consequently attention shifted to justice in the manner war was waged.

With the development of the modern industrial state the church was once more confronted with a new context for war. Large conscript armies, modern weaponry, and the economic burdens of large-scale war all conspired to make warfare more destructive than previous ages imagined. Vatican I expressed horror at modern warfare, and the sense of immediacy the council fathers brought to the issue was embodied in the efforts of the papacy in the late 19th and early 20th centuries. Benedict XV in particular was widely regarded as an opponent of the destruction caused by the First World War.

It was Pius XII with his experience of the Second World War who sharpened the tension between the church's just-war teaching and the experience of war. World War II led Pius to enunciate two basic convictions: that all wars of aggression were to be prohibited and that defensive war to repel aggression was reluctantly necessary.

Pius redefined the meaning of just cause in Catholic just-war theory. Traditionally, the church had acknowledged three appeals for just cause: to vindicate rights, to repel unjust attack, to avenge injury. Pius restricted the just-war theory's appeal to one cause—defense against aggression. Even this appeal to self-defense might not justify war. For Pius the risks of war could outweigh the injustice done by the aggressor. If so, then a nation would have to endure the injustice rather than resort to war.

War might be worse than a measure of injustice in the existing social order.

Pius taught that nations must seek peaceful means of settling disputes, yet he did not abandon the right to national self-defense, believing that "there can be verified in a nation the situation wherein, every effort to avoid war being expended in vain, war—for effective defense and with the hope of a favorable outcome against unjust attack—could not be considered unlawful" (*Christmas Message,* 1956). Pius' conviction regarding national self-defense was so firm that in the same message he declared a Roman Catholic could not in good conscience refuse to participate in a war declared by legitimate authority. While Pius may have narrowed the category of just cause in church teaching on the just war, it is clear that the theory remained dominant in Roman Catholic discussion on the morality of war.

With John XXIII a new era began in Catholic reflection on war. His papacy is characterized by a more searching challenge to the just-war tradition's viability in the modern age. For John the emerging international order placed new demands upon all people to contribute to a global common good. Just as individuals must regulate their activity so as to support and contribute to the common good of their society, so too, nation-states must regulate themselves in order not to violate the requirements of the universal common good. In the papal view there is a genuine international order that must be respected.

John never explicitly denied the just-war theory in *Pacem in terris,* but his silence about the right of national self-defense coupled with his opposition to nuclear war created a mood of questioning on the topic of warfare. With his death it was left for Vatican II to treat the question of war. The context for the episcopal discussion, however, was a growing papal disenchantment with modern war.

When discussing war the bishops called for "an evaluation of war with an entirely new attitude" (*Gaudium et spes* 80). In the text of the document the major reason cited for this new attitude is the manner whereby the "horror and perversity of war are immensely magnified by the multiplication of scientific weapons" (GS 80). The onset of a new generation of weapons, especially nuclear arms, pushed the church to look at war in a new way. The scale of devastation likely in any modern war required reconsideration of the moral problematic of armed confict. The historical context within which the analysis took place was one marked by anxiety over whether modern war had ceased to be a politically rational enterprise.

All the same, the bishops did not remove Roman Catholicism from the just-war tradition. And yet the church was moving in a new direction as the council declared that individual Catholics could refuse to take up arms on the basis of moral principle (GS 78). Since 1965, then, the Catholic church has officially accepted that a believer may subscribe to either the just-war or pacifist tradition of moral evaluation. During the space of nine short years church teaching had undergone a dramatic change from Pius XII's opposition to conscientious objection to Vatican II's statement endorsing the idea.

During the papacy of Paul VI there was a marked increase in Catholic interest in pacifism. It has been suggested that "the legitimization of a pacifist perspective" is the "principal development" within Catholic teaching on war over the last three decades (Hehir, in Shannon, pp. 19–20). By his writing on development Paul promoted serious reflection on the conditions for peace in the world. Further, by initiating the annual celebration of the World Day of Peace in 1968 as well as by his landmark speech at the United Nations in 1964, he kept the church focused on issues of war and peace.

On numerous occasions during his papacy John Paul II has spoken on the reality of armed conflict. The pope distinguishes between recourse to arms in the name of social change, which he has consistently opposed, and armed force as a last resort in the defense of a nation. In speeches in Ireland, Latin America, and South Africa John Paul has opposed the use of violence even as he condemns the injustice that leads some to consider armed resistance.

When discussing conflict between states, however, the papal position is the traditional one of support for self-defense by proportionate means (*World Day of Peace Message,* 1982). It would appear from comments made on several occasions that the pope does not think nuclear arms pass the test of proportionality when considering self-defense (*Address at United Nations' University in Hiroshima, Appeal for Peace at the Hiroshima Peace Memorial*).

During the pontificate of John Paul there have been significant writings on the topic of war by various episcopal bodies. In part, this has been in response to the tensions of the nuclear powers during the 1980s as well as the sense that the arms race was proceeding undeterred. In most of these episcopal texts one finds respect and approval for the pacifist tradition, an acceptance of the right of national self-defense, and a questioning of the moral legitimacy of nuclear war.

Three Approaches

Catholic teaching has supported three different traditions of thought regarding war. The crusades are a part of Catholic history as is the theory that supported them. As war sanctioned for a holy purpose, the crusade was not seen as differing in a significant way from the just war, since the stated aim was the safe passage of pilgrims to the shrines of the Holy Land. Wars are waged for a variety of reasons, however, and eventually the essentially religious tone of the crusades became clear. Centuries later the cause of "true religion" also was cited in the religious wars of Europe.

Both in age and influence the more important treatments of war in Catholic teaching are the just war and pacifism. Despite the early church's pacifism the predominant tradition on war has been the just war. While no single theory of just war has been taught consistently, the body of material within Catholicism in support of the just war tradition is impressive.

Understood properly, the just war tradition recognizes the horror of war and believes that violence must be justified since there is a presumption in favor of nonviolence. Adherents of the just-war tradition hold that in some cases the justification for armed force can be made and the presumption against war overridden.

In the course of history the criteria for when and how force may be employed have been refined and extended. Traditionally these criteria are commonly grouped under two headings, the *jus ad bellum* and the *jus in bello.* According to the 1983 pastoral letter of the U.S. Catholic bishops, the *jus ad bellum* criteria governing why and when it is permissible to go to war are (1) just cause, (2) competent authority, (3) comparative justice, (4) right intention, (5) last resort, (6) probability of success, (7) proportionality (*The Challenge of Peace* 85–99). The *jus in bello* criteria of how war ought to be waged are (1) proportionality and (2) discrimination (CP 101–110).

Paramount in its impact on the experience of modern war has been the development of nuclear weapons. Nuclear arms have altered the way many people think about the usefulness of armed conflict. Recent years have seen the emergence of nuclear pacifism and selective conscientious objection in the Catholic community. Both stances flow from the just-war tradition, for the argument is that some wars, principally nuclear ones, cannot satisfy the criteria of the just-war tradition.

Another framework for assessing war, pacifism, has had varying acceptance within Roman Catholicism. In every age individual believers have been pacifist either as a matter of moral principle or because of a vocational choice. But formal church approval of pacifism has been lacking in many cases. Vatican II's Pastoral Constitution on the Church in the Modern World changed that situation. Yet the pacifism approved by the council did not make opposition to all war a duty of either the nation or the individual. Instead pacifism was accepted as a valid moral choice for the individual.

A proper understanding of peace is important to understand the way Catholicism thinks about war. The discussion of war within Catholic social teaching takes place within the context of the broader idea of peace. The teaching of Vatican II demonstrates the Catholic conviction that "peace is not merely the absence of war." At the council the bishops stated that peace is "an enterprise of justice" and "the fruit of love" (GS 78). The social order that peace embodies is achieved when life is well ordered and oriented to the dignity of persons and the common good of all.

Because peace is not simply the absence of war but entails a measure of justice and order, the council had to consider the duties of both pacifists and just-war theorists to serve true peace. Catholic teaching presumes that the pacifist is dedicated to the cause of justice as it also presumes that the just-war proponent is dedicated to the cause of peace. With these twin presumptions Catholicism permits pluralism as to how the individual believer may live out the commitment to a just and peaceful order.

To be opposed are versions of either just war or pacifism that are inconsistent with the Catholic dedication to building a peaceful order founded on human dignity and human rights. Therefore what is not permitted is a pacifism of indifference to the common good and the basic rights of others. Such a stance is no more acceptable than that of a just-war supporter who is motivated by nationalistic fervor or the spoils of war rather than the establishment of true peace.

The Future of Catholic Teaching

Just as every age has brought with it new questions that Catholic social thought must address, the present age is no exception. Several issues surrounding the contemporary experience of warfare will require increased attention.

In their pastoral letter *The Challenge of Peace* the U.S. Catholic bishops sought to describe the relationship between just war and pacifism. Because both traditions of moral evaluation of war can be understood as serving the cause of true peace, "Catholic teaching sees these two distinct moral responses as having a complementary relationship" (CP 74). It can be expected that future development of Catholic teaching on war will explore further the meaning and nature of this complementary relationship.

No doubt the strong presence of the Catholic church in many Third World nations has heightened interest in what can be called wars of liberation or revolution. Closely linked to this phenomenon is the strategy employed in guerrilla war. Defenders of such wars and/or strategy have sometimes tried to explain their position in categories of the just war. It is not always easy, however, to determine in a revolutionary situation how the criteria of competent authority, last resort, or probability of success are to be assessed. In addition, guerrilla war purposely obscures easy determination of the principle of discrimination. At present, it appears that Catholic social teaching generally opposes recourse to violence on behalf of societal change but does not rule out revolutionary violence in principle.

A final issue that has become more common in the experience of war today is the claim that humanitarian reasons justify armed intervention. Wars waged in the name of protecting the human rights of others can be interpreted as fitting within the just cause of defending innocents against aggression. But the topic of intervening in the internal affairs of another nation, even when the government is oppressive, raises problems of state sovereignty and national self-determination.

In the future Catholic social teaching will be called on to address such questions as these, since the tradition of thought on war is an ongoing effort to relate the moral wisdom of the church to conflicts rooted in the historical conditions of human life.

See also AGGRESSION; ARMS RACE; DETERRENCE; FORCE; KILLING; PACEM IN TERRIS; PACIFISM; PEACE.

Bibliography: R. Bainton, *Christian Attitudes Toward War and Peace* (Nashville: Abingdon, 1960). J. Hehir, "Catholic Teaching on War and Peace: The Decade 1979–1989," in C. Curran, *Moral Theology: Challenges for the Future* (New York: Paulist, 1990). J. Langan, "Violence and Injustice in Society: Recent Catholic Teaching," *Theological Studies* 46 (1985) 685–99. T. Shannon, ed., *War or Peace?* (Maryknoll: Orbis, 1980). L. Walters, Jr., *Five Classic Just War Theories* (Ph.D. diss., Yale Univ., 1971).

KENNETH R. HIMES, O.F.M.

WELFARE/WELFARE STATE

The word "welfare" refers fundamentally to well-being. Of course, human well-being has many dimensions. It includes at least physical and mental health, personal assets, and material prosperity. Yet the word "welfare" does not relate to human well-being in its totality but to its "basic requisites" (Rescher, p. 3). A person's welfare hinges on striking a basic healthy balance in each of these dimensions over time. For instance, literate, healthy people who live comfortably enjoy good welfare even though they may not possess all of the good life that they desire. Illiterate, ill, or indigent people experience poor welfare.

Welfare, however, is not individualistic. Humans are social beings whose welfare is intricately interrelated. Personally, individual well-being often depends on the welfare of significant others. Inquiring into a person's welfare often elicits a response concerning the well-being of a family member or close friend. Materially, the measurement of an individual's welfare considers his or her standing relative to the prosperity of others in society. The First World poor may be better off than their Third World counterparts, but in their own societies they suffer deprivation and exclusion. Socially, the welfare of one individual or group often results in diswelfare for others. For example, many of the industrial, technological, and demographic changes that have taken place in modern society have had social costs borne disproportionately by the poor (Titmuss, p. 258).

Finally, phrases like "social welfare" and "public welfare" suggest that the welfare of society transcends the individuals who make it up. Yet individual and social welfare are interrelated. As Nicholas Rescher contends, "Social welfare relates in general to the social order as an instrumentality for promoting the common, shared individual-welfare needs of the members of society" (Rescher, p. 6). The well-being of a society rests on its ability to empower its members to develop a healthy balance in each of these dimensions. These shared individual-welfare needs require some capacity for interacting meaningfully with other members of society.

Welfare State

This understanding of welfare as the basic condition for well-being in community with others underlies the emergence of the modern welfare state. Harry Girvetz defines the welfare state as "the institutional outcome of the assumption by a society of legal and therefore formal and explicit responsibility for the basic well-being of all of its members" (Girvetz, p. 512). Any society that assumes some responsibility for the welfare of its citizens through its state apparatus is a welfare state.

Modern forms of the welfare state emerged with the transition into an urban, industrialized, capitalistic society that created serious problems for individual and social welfare. The philosophy of the welfare state assumes that these problems are not the fault of the individual but a by-product of failures in the free market. In addition, it assumes that society has a responsibility to solve these problems through state involvement in the procurement of basic requisites for individual and social well-being. And this involvement is a matter of social justice, not charity.

What should be the extent of that responsibility? A brief survey of Western welfare states reveals many answers to this question. Various countries assume different levels of responsibility for the well-being of their respective citizens. Moreover, differences of opinion exist *within* each state as well. The key to understanding those differences is to distinguish between the multiple value commitments that dominate public policy debate. Within Western society, these value commitments give rise to at least three models of the welfare state that compete to shape social welfare policy.

The first model stresses the values of personal freedom and responsibility. In this view, the individual or family is the primary unit of society and ought to assume responsibility for basic welfare needs. Such independence and self-reliance provide the foundation for self-respect and personal dignity. A strong welfare state places too many constraints on individual freedom and responsibility. Redistributive tax and transfer programs coerce participation from everyone and discourage individual initiative, economic efficiency, and voluntary charity. Paternalistic social welfare programs promote dependency and irresponsibility among recipients and cut off the possibility for self-respect that self-reliance provides. To avoid these problems the welfare state should intervene only in times of economic or social crisis and assume responsibility primarily for those incapable of providing for themselves.

Although the welfare programs associated with this model of the welfare state include some frugal relief programs for the incapacitated, social insurance programs are the norm. The latter, using insurance principles rather than need as the basis for benefits, "are designed to even out income over a person's life-cycle and to spread the risk of unemployment and illness from the individual to the general population" (Furniss and Tilton, pp. 15–16). Social insurance programs maintain the current means of income distribution, linking income to efficient labor-force participation. Since an individual must contribute periodically to receive benefits, social insurance becomes a form of compulsory savings rather than a guarantee of individual welfare out of general revenues. One's economic security continues to depend on one's personal achievement and production in the labor market, not on government largess. As a result, social insurance promotes individual over social responsibility for basic well-being.

The second model promotes the value of equality, understood as the equal moral worth of each citizen's life-chances. All humans have the same basic needs for their well-being—good health, material prosperity, freedom. If society guarantees political and social rights to enhance the life and welfare of its members, it must do so for all. This is the only way to protect the underlying equality of all citizens. Social conditions and the accidents of birth do not justify unequal treatment in the distribution of these essential social goods. Rather, society must justify any departure from the norm of equality with relevant reasons.

This model calls for an expanded welfare state whose primary purpose is to redistribute resources in such a way as to make it possible for individuals of different social and economic backgrounds to compete on an equal footing. These redistributive schemes go beyond social insurance to economic security. Social insurance programs, with their emphasis on individual and employer contributions, do not provide adequately for the basic needs of citizens unable to achieve steady labor-market participation. This group's needs require guaranteed minimums in income and other resources such as health care and education below which no citizen can fall. These guarantees provide basic security from cradle to grave for every citizen. Undoubtedly, these programs mandate greater redistribution of economic resources than the previous model. In a world of scarcity, providing greater access to and distribution of resources to the disadvantaged requires that the advantaged give something up. However, redistributive schemes extend only to the provision of basic welfare needs. Beyond these, advocates of this model consider inequalities in the distribution of resources efficient and just.

The third model tries to inculcate the values of solidarity and democracy. This model recognizes that human society is a shared environment that nurtures, shapes, and relates every individual within it. The well-being of both the individual and the society requires not only freedom and equality of opportunity but also meaningful participation from each member of society. Realizing this end means redistributing resources in a way that both raises minimum standards and attacks the problem of inequality. Glaring inequities in income and wealth divide members from one another. Moreover, meaningful participation mandates that people have some control over the decisions that affect them individually and socially. Thus achieving social solidarity rests upon the removal of extreme inequalities and the extension of democracy to every institution in society, including the workplace.

This model of the welfare state assumes the most responsibility for the well-being of its members because, in addition to guaranteeing certain minimums for its citizens, it seeks to create more equality in living conditions. It does this not through social insurance or public assistance programs; rather, this model expands the state's public or universal social services to include such services as child care, health care, and legal assistance. Providing these services to everyone requires extremely progressive tax policies. However, advocates argue that the benefits outweigh the costs. By meeting basic needs that citizens share in common through communal provision, society removes the stigma attached to meeting individual needs, reduces extreme inequalities, and lays the foundation for social solidarity.

Catholic Social Thought

Since Leo XIII issued the first great social encyclical, *Rerum novarum,* in 1891, Catholic social thought has concerned itself with the problems that an urbanized, industrialized, capitalistic society has created for human welfare, especially the poor and the working class. Yet it has wavered on the question of which social agents should assume responsibility for remedying those problems. Before John XXIII, papal teaching looked suspiciously upon state involvement in the economy and social welfare as a threat to personal freedom and a prelude to socialism. However, in his encyclicals *Mater et magistra* and *Pacem in terris* Pope John eliminates that suspicion. He argues that the state has a fundamental responsibility to secure the basic well-being of its citizens against the fluctuations of a capitalist society (MM 54). With this precedent the welfare state has found some legitimation in Catholic social thought.

The basis for affirming the state's welfare function is the belief that the state is an order of creation and, therefore, has a "divinely foreordained" role to play in bringing about the common good—"the sum of those conditions of social life which allow social groups and their individual members relatively thorough and ready access to their own fulfillment" (*Gaudium et spes* 26, 74). This understanding of the common good is clearly pluralistic, not collectivistic. It respects the rights of individuals and other social groups to determine freely and creatively the path to their fulfillment.

What is the extent of the responsibility of the state for basic human well-being? Catholic social thought holds up the dignity of the human person as "the foundation, cause, and end of all social institutions" (MM 219). The values of freedom, responsibility, equality, and solidarity are essential to human dignity. Respecting the dignity of the human person means respecting the individual's freedom to decide and direct the path her or his fulfillment will take (PT 15). It also means ensuring that each person has equal access to the resources required for human development (PT 11). However, humans are also social beings. The "bonds of community and solidarity . . . are essential to the dignity of persons" (*Economic Justice for All* 28). Individual fulfillment and social progress are interrelated. Individuals must use their freedom responsibly so they contribute not only to their own fulfillment but also to the common good (EJA 36). The responsibility of the state is to guarantee the basic conditions through which individuals and groups within a society can realize the dignity of the human person in community with others. It is a part of the state's moral function (EJA 122).

The programs of the welfare state advocated by Catholic social thought demonstrate concern for the dignity of workers, their families, and the poor. On behalf of workers, Catholic teaching calls for social insurance programs and safety laws to protect workers from unemployment, sickness, impoverished old age, and unsafe working environments. It also advocates a living wage—"payment for labor must be such as to furnish a man with the means to cultivate his own material, social, cultural, and spiritual life worthily, and that of his dependents" (GS 67). The state facilitates living wages through minimum wage legislation, public employment, wage subsidies, and other structural changes that allow employers to pay decent wages without fear of bankruptcy (*Laborem exercens* 16, 17).

On behalf of the poor and marginalized, Catholic social thought contends that justice requires that the state guarantee the rights of the poor to minimums in income, health care, education, and other essential services below which no individual or family can fall regardless of labor-market status (PT 13). In addition, the state must empower the poor to take responsibility for their lives by guaranteeing rights to work, property ownership, and other means. The egalitarian effect of guaranteeing these resources and rights to the poor opens the door not simply to economic security but also to more meaningful participation in society (EJA 77).

Welfare State vs. Welfare Society

What is the future of state involvement in welfare? Conservative critics of the welfare state have long argued that the state has no role in the welfare business. This is the function of intermediate, voluntary, or charitable organizations. When the state gets involved in welfare, private philanthropy dies. Studies have shown there is some cause for concern here. Yet other critics recommend that although there is certainly room for the state to enhance the welfare of its citizens, we must move beyond the welfare state toward the welfare society. Chastened by the statism of totalitarian societies, these critics contend that the achievement of a more just, participatory society mandates the dispersal of responsibility for basic well-being to every level of social life. Not only will this socialization of welfare countervail the negative tendencies of welfare statism, it will also promote community and solidarity (Walzer).

Recent Catholic social thought clearly supports the latter position. Affirming the positive welfare function of the state does not mean that the state arrogates all welfare functions to itself. On the contrary, the principle of subsidiarity prohibits larger associations from usurping those tasks that "lesser and subordinate organizations can do" (*Quadragesimo anno* 79). On the one hand, by rejecting purely statist solutions to basic well-being, this principle guarantees room for other social agents to contribute to individual and social welfare. Vital mediating structures enable individuals to participate more fully and more meaningfully in society than state institutions (MM 61). On the other hand, this principle requires that other groups make such a contribution. The common good is not the responsibility of the state alone; it is the vocation of all (EJA 100).

Finally, it is important to note that the welfare society envisioned here is not a return to a premodern, corporatist community in which guilds and intermediate forms of association dominate social life. There is no turning back from the differentiation and rationalization of modern Western society. Rather, welfare-society advocates recognize the need for continued state involvement in individual and social welfare. What they envision is a society in which each individual and social group works together to ensure the basic welfare of all, and a state that works with and empowers others to realize this end.

See also COMMON GOOD; ECONOMIC ORDER; GOODS, DISTRIBUTION OF; INCOME; JUST WAGE; POVERTY; SOCIAL SECURITY; SUBSIDIARITY, PRINCIPLE OF.

Bibliography: D. Dorr, *Option for the Poor: A Hundred Years of Vatican Social Teaching* (Maryknoll, N.Y.: Orbis, 1983). N. Furniss and T. Tilton, *The Case for the Welfare State* (Bloomington, Ind.: Indiana Univ. Press, 1977). N. Rescher, *Welfare: The Social Issues in Philosophical Perspective* (Pittsburgh: Univ. of Pittsburgh Press, 1972). H. Girvetz, "Welfare State," in *Encyclopedia of the Social Sciences,* D. Sills, ed. (New York: Macmillan/Free Press, 1968). T. Skocpol, "The Limits of the New Deal System and the Roots of Contemporary Welfare Dilemmas," in *The Politics of Social Policy in the United States,* M. Weir et al., eds. (Princeton: Princeton Univ. Press, 1988). R. Titmuss, "Developing Social Policy in Conditions of Rapid Change: The Role of Social Welfare," in *The Philosophy of Welfare: Selected Writings of Richard M. Titmuss,* B. Abel-Smith and K. Titmuss, eds. (London: Allen & Unwin, 1987). M. Walzer, "Socializing the Welfare State," in *Democracy and the Welfare State,* A. Gutmann, ed. (Princeton: Princeton Univ. Press, 1988).

FRED GLENNON

WOMEN

Before the encyclicals of Pope John XXIII, women are seldom mentioned in papal documents except implicitly under generic statements regarding the dignity of "man" (i.e., the human person) and under the category of family.

In the first social encyclical, Leo XIII's *On the Condition of Workers* (*Rerum novarum*), 1891, two themes concerning women are introduced: women, like children, are dependent and in need of special protection, and women are "by nature" bound to the home. These themes remain more or less constant throughout the body of Catholic social teaching. Leo writes: "Finally, it is not right to demand of a woman or a child what a strong adult man is capable of doing or would be willing to do. . . . Certain occupations likewise are less fitted for women, who are intended by nature for work of the home—work indeed which especially protects modesty in women and accords by nature with the education of children and the well-being of the family" (RN 60).

Leo XIII's worldview was authoritarian and paternalistic, with clearly defined roles for everyone (Curran, p. 176). For Leo XIII a woman's place and role were clear, divinely ordained according to her nature and therefore in no need of elaboration. It was the worker and the family that occupied his concern. Workers are men. If women or children did work outside the home, Leo considered it an aberration. Justice for workers meant that the rights of their families would be protected and that they, as heads of families, would receive just wages. Women as wives and mothers would be economically dependent on this just wage of the working father/husband.

In *On Reconstructing the Social Order* (*Quadragesimo anno*), 1931, Pius XI repeats the same themes in the section "Support of the Worker and His Family." Women and children are again mentioned in the same sentence: "But to abuse the years of childhood and the limited strength of women is grossly wrong. Mothers, concentrating on household duties, should work primarily in the home or in its immediate vicinity. It is an intolerable abuse, and to be abolished at all cost, for mothers on account of the father's low wage to be forced to engage in gainful occupations outside the home to the neglect of their proper cares and duties, especially the training of children" (QA 71). Women are not seen as autonomous adults. This habit of identifying women with children and other dependent persons has been the accepted norm in most Catholic writing, particular in canon law (Morrisey, p. 2).

Women enter Catholic social thought in their own right in John XXIII's encyclical *Peace on Earth* (*Pacem in terris*), 1963. He identifies three "distinctive characteristics" of our age—signs of our times: the rise of the working class, the participation of women in public life, and the emergence of new nations. John writes: "It is obvious to everyone that women are now taking a part in public life. This is happening more rapidly perhaps in nations with a Christian tradition, and more slowly, but broadly, among peoples who have inherited other traditions or cultures. Since women are becoming ever more conscious of their human dignity, they will not tolerate being treated as inanimate objects or mere instruments, but claim, both in domestic and in public life, the rights and duties that befit a human person" (PT 41).

Moreover, in this encyclical John declares that every person is endowed with intelligence and free will and has universal and inviolable rights and duties. He identifies these rights as political, economic, social, cultural, and moral. By including women specifically in this document he is explicitly declaring that women have the same rights and duties as men.

However, the double vision with which churchmen view women is also evident: women and men have the same human rights, but women's rights are consistently circumscribed by their nature. John writes: "Human beings have, in addition, the right to choose freely the state of life which they prefer. They therefore have the right to set up a family, with equal rights and duties for man and woman, and also the right to follow a vocation to the priesthood or the religious life" (PT 15). Yet women are denied the right to follow a vocation to the priesthood.

Several paragraphs later John writes: "Indissolubly linked with those rights is the right to working conditions in which physical health is not endangered, morals are safeguarded, and young people's normal development is not impaired. Women have the right to working conditions in accordance with their requirements and their duties as wives and mothers" (PT 19). The "equal rights and duties of man and woman" in a family are predetermined by roles and duties, according to "woman's nature," as wife and mother. No predetermined roles and duties are man's nature as husband and father.

With the writings of John XXIII and the opening of the Second Vatican Council in 1962, the worldview of Catholic social thought had altered significantly. The static, hierarchical, authoritarian, and paternalistic world of Leo XIII had shifted to a view shaped by historical consciousness, a recognition of the radical freedom of the human person, and the autonomy of the world from religion's control. However, this view does not apply equally to women and men.

The Pastoral Constitution on the Church in the Modern World (*Gaudium et spes*) was the centerpiece of social teaching that emerged from Vatican Council II. The document rings with affirmation of the fundamental dignity of the human person.

Moreover, it states that "with respect to the fundamental rights of the person, every type of discrimination, whether social or cultural, whether based on sex, race, color, social condition, language, or religion, is to be overcome and eradicated as contrary to God's intent" (GS 29). The reader is tempted to accept the generic *man* and *mankind* as including women until the language of the document slips and reveals that the fathers of the council are really talking about men. Such words as "brotherly dialogue" and brotherhood" (GS 23) exclude women.

It is interesting to note that the first time women are specifically mentioned is in relation to a perceived problem. The first such reference comes in a section entitled "Imbalances in the Modern World": "As for the family, discord results from demographic, economic, and social pressures, or from difficulties which arise between succeeding generations, or from new social relationships between men and women" (GS 8). Setting the "new social relationships" under the heading "Imbalances in the Modern World" reflects a patriarchal interpretation of the changes related to women's rising consciousness.

In the section entitled "Dignity of the Human Person," the document reads: "But God did not create man as a solitary. For from the beginning 'male and female he created them' (Gen 1:27)." The discussion of marriage and family succeeds in talking about women and men, spouses and parents, evenhandedly.

However, in the section on culture, the traditional ambiguity concerning women's rights appears. Recognizing that humans are the authors of culture, the document states, "In every group or nation, there is an ever-increasing number of men and women who are conscious that they themselves are the artisans and the authors of the culture of their community" (GS 55). Several sections beyond this statement of mutual responsibility and participation the document qualifies itself: "Women are now employed in almost every area of life. It is appropriate that they should be able to assume their full *proper role in accordance with their own nature.* Everyone should acknowledge and favor the *proper* and necessary participation of women in cultural life" (GS 60, emphasis mine). We are confronted here with a statement that women's nature, and therefore presumably their rights contingent upon that nature, are different from men's nature and rights. We are confronted with a concept of a dual human nature: there is human nature, which is equated with men's nature, and then there is women's nature.

Women as women next appear in Paul VI's *Call to Action* (*Octogesima adveniens*), 1971. He continues the concept of a dual human nature: "Similarly, in many countries a charter for women which would put an end to an actual discrimination and would establish relationships of equality in rights and of respect for their dignity is the object of study and at times of lively demands. We do not have in mind that false equality which would deny the distinctions laid down by the Creator himself and which would be in contradiction with woman's *proper role,* which is of such capital importance, at the heart of the family as well as within society. Development in legislation should on the contrary be directed to *protecting* her *proper vocation* and at the same time recognizing her independence as a person, and her equal rights to participate in cultural, economic, social and political life" (OA 13, emphasis mine). Can a person having a proper role and vocation, predetermined by her nature and needing special protection, still be independent and have equal rights with a person who has no such qualifying and limiting definitions predetermined by his nature?

Justice in the World (*Justitia in mundo*), the statement of the 1971 synod of bishops, introduces the question of justice in the church regarding women. The document declares that anyone who ventures to preach justice must first be perceived as being just. It states: "Within the church rights must be preserved. No one should be deprived of his ordinary rights because he is associated with the church in one way or another. Those who serve the Church by their labor, including priests and religious, should receive a sufficient livelihood and enjoy that social security which is customary in their region. Lay people should be given fair wages and a system for promotion. We reiterate the recommendations that lay people should exercise more important functions with regard to Church property and should share in its administration" (JM 41). The reader is again lulled into believing that women are included under the generic *he* or *lay people* only to read in the following paragraph, "We also urge that women should have their own share of responsibility and participation in the community life of society and likewise of the church" (JM 42). The words, "their own share" raise the questions, is women's share different from men's? If so, why?

Justice in the World also speaks of the social movements among peoples as "a new awareness which shakes them out of any fatalistic resignation and which spurs them on to liberate themselves and to be responsible for their own destiny" (JM 4). Furthermore, it introduces the need to change social structures if justice is to become a reality in people's lives: "This desire [for human rights], however, will not satisfy the expectations of our time if it ignores the objective obstacles which social structures place in the way of conversion of hearts, or even of the realization of ideal charity" (JM 16).

This document brings together several powerful themes that support women's struggle for justice in the church and in the world. In calling for justice in the church, especially for women, and in affirming social movements whereby people assume responsibility for their own lives to change oppressive structures, *Justice in the World* affirms women's struggle for liberation.

In *On Human Work* (*Laborem exercens*), 1981, John Paul II makes explicit his views on the proper role and vocation of women. The encyclical, while recognizing that women do work outside the home, continues the tradition that the primary role of women is to be responsible for the family and the primary role of men is to be responsible for economic support of the family. John Paul continues the position that the man, as head of the family, is entitled to a family wage. In reality, he is reasserting the patriarchal model of the family. He calls for a "social re-evaluation of the mother's role," calling for a society to support a woman in this role, not inhibiting her freedom or in any other way penalizing her as compared with other women. He speaks of women "having to abandon" their tasks as mothers as being wrong from the point of view of society and the family. Finally, he insists that "true advancement of women requires that labor should be structured in such a way that women do not have to pay for their advancement by abandoning what is specific to them and at the expense of the family, in which women as mothers have an irreplaceable role" (LE 19). John Paul does not call for a concomitant social reevaluation of fatherhood.

Two church documents introduce gender into their analysis of the contemporary world: The Puebla Document, published after the 1979 meeting of the Latin American bishops in Puebla, Mexico, and the U.S. bishops' 1986 pastoral on the economy, *Economic Justice for All: Catholic Social Teaching and the U.S. Economy.* The Puebla Document identifies the marginalization of women from political, economic, and social life as the result of "cultural atavisms—male predominance, unequal wages, deficient education" (Puebla 834). It further identifies some specifics of that marginalization: prostitution as a result of stifling economic situations, exploitation of women in the workplace, the overburdening of women in the family, and the church's undervaluing of women. The document speaks of being encouraged by women's initiatives and growing consciousness.

The document also calls the church to "consider" the equality and dignity of women and to recognize the mission of women in the church and in the world. It recognizes women's aspirations for liberation as an "authentic sign of the times" while specifically underlining "the fundamental role of the woman as mother, the defender of life and the home educator" (Puebla 835–40). This document marks a significant advance in Catholic social teaching's recognition of the complex reality that shapes women's lives.

Economic Justice for All treats the complexity of the economic issues faced by women with some depth. Women's economic issues are treated integrally throughout the whole document rather than in just one section, thereby avoiding the implicit statement that these are only "women's issues" rather than problems of the economic system. For the first time in a church document, the language is clearly gender specific in order to illumine the different economic issues faced by women and men. The causes of the "feminization of poverty" are examined and condemned. The document calls for greater economic justice for women in the workplace, and it recognizes the changing patterns in family life with mutual responsibilities for both fathers and mothers.

The various drafts of the pastoral addressed the mutual responsibilities of both parents in family life, but for the first time in the final document the position of John Paul II emphasizing the special role of mothers in families was introduced: "We affirm the principle enunciated by John Paul II that society's institutions and policies should be structured so that mothers of young children are not forced by economic necessity to leave their children for jobs outside the home" (EJA 207).

The purpose of raising these issues is not to deny or denigrate the social role and value of women who choose childrearing and homemaking as their primary work. Rather it is to bring into perspective the multiple roles and potential of women. Furthermore, to so emphasize that women are primarily responsible for the quality of family life diminishes the social role and value of fatherhood. It disenfranchises men from the full potential of their fatherhood while it disenfranchises women from the full potential of their personhood. Until the church is able to recognize the mutuality of women and men in all dimensions of life, its reflection and teaching will remain inadequate to contemporary realities.

On Social Concern (*Sollicitudo rei socialis*), 1987, John Paul II's encyclical on international development, was written to celebrate the 20th anniversary of Paul VI's *On the Development of Peoples.* Both these documents lack a gender perspective; women are included under the generic terms of man, humanity, human family. In several instances John Paul II does name women as women, specifically when he is outlining the failure of the development process. For example, "looking at all the various sectors—the production and distribution of foodstuffs, hygiene, health and housing, availability of drinking water, working conditions (especially for women), life expectancy and other economic and social indicators . . ." (SRS 14).

It is worth noting that in the section on the "demographic problem," John Paul II develops his argument about population and the birthrate without alluding to women's specific role and need. The encyclical does not add any new insights concerning women to Catholic social thought. Nor does it contain any of the insights of current feminist critiques of the development processes.

The church's social teaching continues to be caught on the horns of the dilemma of its dual anthropology: it insists women have full and equal human rights and responsibilities—politically, economically, socially, culturally, and ecclesially—as befits a human person. However, in continuing to insist upon women's proper nature and role as something distinct from human nature, it restricts women's potential for realizing these rights.

See relevant encyclicals. *Also see* FAMILY; FEMINISM AND CATHOLIC SOCIAL THOUGHT; HUMAN RIGHTS; JUSTICE IN THE WORLD; MARRIAGE; SEXISM; "SIGNS OF THE TIMES"; VATICAN COUNCIL II.

Bibliography: C. Curran, *Moral Theology: A Continuing Journey* (Notre Dame, Ind.: Notre Dame Univ. Press, 1982). F. Morrisey, "The Juridical Status of Women in Contemporary Ecclesial Law," in *Sexism and Church Law*, J. Coridan, ed. (New York: Paulist, 1977). M. Riley, *Transforming Feminism* (Kansas City, Mo.: Sheed & Ward. 1989).

MARIA RILEY, O.P.

WORK, THEOLOGY OF

An initial difficulty in developing a theology of work lies in the fluidity of the term "work," which can be applied to a wide range of human activities. In its widest sense "work" can mean "*any* human activity, whether manual or intellectual, whatever its nature or circumstances" (John Paul II, *Laborem exercens*, preface). In this sense it includes everything human beings do as free and responsible subjects. Some, seeking to distinguish work from play, limit it to human activity in which one engages not for its own sake but rather for the contribution it makes to human living (Kaiser, 1965, p. 1015). But this is too limiting, since work is frequently humanly fulfilling in itself. There are simply many different kinds of human activity that can be considered work. It is an analogous, not a univocal concept, applicable to an indefinite range of human activities.

Many languages commonly distinguish two broad types of work, namely "work" taken in a narrower sense and "labor." The difference between the two is strikingly brought out by John Locke, who wrote of "the labor of our body and the work of our hands" (*Second Treatise on Government*, sec. 26). Labor is human activity that implies pain and anguish, sweat and toil, whereas the "work of our hands" (perhaps better, the work of our hands and minds) connotes a more creative kind of human activity. Labor is the toil required to serve the biological necessities of life, a tiring activity that needs to be done over and over again, for example, cultivating the fields, cleaning toilets and dishes. Labor is essentially a bodily activity and a reminder of our condition as bodied persons. The work of our hands and minds is more enduring, resulting in "products" that last, at least for a time, including works of art, of philosophy, of culture. Indeed, as Hannah Arendt has noted, the distinction between laboring bodies and working hands is reminiscent of the "ancient Greek distinction between the *cheirotechnēs*, the craftsman . . . and those who, like 'slaves and tame animals with their bodies minister to the necessities of life'" (Arendt, p. 80; citation from Aristotle's *Politics*, 1254b25). This distinction is also relevant to what John Paul II refers to as the "objective" sense of work, that is, the bringing about of products (the work of our hands and minds) and the rendering of service to the needs of human life (LE 5). Historically, the work of our hands and minds has been and is valued more highly (and correspondingly rewarded more richly) than the labor of our bodies. But an adequate theology of work, which must center, as John Paul II rightly insists, on the "subjective" sense of work as a free, self-determining activity, must manifest a deeper appreciation for and evaluation of the "labor of our hands" (LE 6).

A theology of work must examine the reality of work in the light of the great themes of creation, sin, incarnation, redemption, and eschatology. We are only beginning to develop a true theology of work. The very term "theology of work" is of recent vintage, appearing in theological literature only about the middle of this century (Chenu, 1963, p. 4). Although earlier theologians had, of course, taken some account of work into consideration, their reflections on this reality were more or less tangential in character. But stimulated no doubt by the tremendous advances in technology that this century has witnessed, theologians today are forced to recognize that work is a reality central to human existence and of profound theological significance.

Biblical Teaching on Work

The Old Testament. It is worth noting that in the OT two principal words are used to refer to work, corresponding to the distinction, already made, between the labor of our bodies and the work of our hands and minds. These are *melakha,* which denotes God's creative work and includes his presence within human history in carrying out his divine plan, and *avoda,* used to designate the work of slaves. But as Chenu observes, "the words overlap; and work has the paradoxical connotations of inexorable constraint and joyful expressiveness, unremitting compulsion and liberating self-fulfillment" (Chenu, 1970, p. 369).

It is most important to note that unlike the Greeks, who viewed work, especially the labor of slaves, as opposed to the *necotium* and *a-skolia* that should characterize the truly free person, the chosen people valued all forms of work as good and worthy of human persons, including the labor of our bodies. This approving attitude toward work is rooted in the teaching of Genesis, which portrays God as "working" in bringing the universe and humankind into existence and which places the creation of the human person, male and female, at a determined moment in the process of forming the universe. "The Lord God then took the man and settled him in the garden of Eden, to cultivate and care for it" (Gen 2:15). Shortly before, the Yahwist author had said, "As yet there was no field shrub on earth and no grass in the field had sprouted, for . . . there was no man to till the soil" (Gen 2:5). Human work is thus inserted into the framework of God's activity as something ordered to the perfection of the universe. Indeed, in the Priestly account of creation we are told that human persons, made in the image and likeness of God, are to fill the earth and subdue it and have dominion over "the fish of the sea, the birds of the air, and all the living things that move on the earth" (Gen 1:27-28). Work is indeed an activity proper to human beings: *homo nascitur ad laborem, et avis ad volatum* (Job 5:7; Vulgate text).

The Wisdom literature stresses the obligation to work, linking the duty to work to the condemnation of laziness and the human ills to which this gives rise (Pss 65; 127; 128; Prov 24:30-34; Sir 33:25-32; Wis 14:5). Work is something that serves the common good, and kings as well as slaves are obliged to work.

Yet the OT recognizes that pain and suffering are inevitably associated with work. As a result of the Fall human work is made burdensome. "Cursed be the ground because of you! In toil shall you eat its yield. . . . By the sweat of your face shall you get bread to eat" (Gen 3:17, 19; see Gen 4:12). Nonetheless, as Illanes rightly notes, "it is worth noting that God's curse falls directly not on man nor on his work, but on the earth, which brings forth thorns and thistles. It is only indirectly that the curse affects human work, insofar as, being exercised over a hostile earth, it is made difficult and harsh" (Illanes, 1975, p. 655).

The OT, moreover, emphasizes the foolishness of those who neglect God and look on themselves and their own work as autonomous. The products of human work, as Genesis notes, frequently occasion enormous pride and folly (Gen 4:17-24). Humans have a propensity to worship the work of their hands, forgetting God and ordering their lives independently of him (see Isa 2:20; 31:7; 44:9-20; Pss 112:12-16; 114:8; 134:15-18). Like all human activity, work is ambivalent: if it leads human persons to become self-centered, it is idolatrous; but if it is realized in accordance with God's plan, it forms part of the goods proper to God's kingdom (see Isa 2:2-4).

The New Testament. Two major themes permeate the NT, the *soteriological* and the *eschatological.* The good news, the gospel, is that God has personally visited God's people in the person of Jesus Christ, God's eternal word become man, to save them from sin—the soteriological theme. Furthermore, God's kingdom or reign has begun and is present in the midst of this world, although it will be finally and fully realized only when the Lord Jesus returns in glory to judge the living and the dead—the eschatological theme. All human existence, including the reality of human work, is to be seen in the light of these themes.

Redemption is won for us because God has become incarnate. The Incarnation presupposes that God, in becoming human, assumed all the conditions of human life, including work. Thus Jesus was himself, prior to his public ministry, an "artisan" or "carpenter" (Mk 6:3). This fact, as Illanes has noted, has transcendent significance; it "pertains to the very heart of the historicity of the Incarnation and shows the existence of a profound link between creation and redemption" (1975, p. 655). While it is true that Jesus called his apostles to abandon their worldly professions, he did so not to devalue the ordinary life and work of human persons and societies but only because these specific persons were divinely commissioned for a new task, that of preaching the gospel.

The great message of the NT is that the whole of human existence is now transformed because of Christ and our union with him. The Christian is a "new creature" (Gal 6:15), defined by life in and for Christ (Rom 14:7-9). The whole of human existence now has a saving significance, and this applies in principle to each and every type of life. The specific "work" now entrusted to each Christian is to believe in Christ and to live in accordance with this faith, to be "co-workers with God" (1 Cor 3:9; 2 Cor 8:1; Mk 16:20) and to participate in Christ's redemptive work, making up in their own lives what is lacking in Christ's afflictions so that his body, the church, can be built up (Col 1:24). However, Christians are to do this "work" in the midst of their ordinary workaday lives: "Everyone ought to continue as he was when he was called" (1 Cor 7:20; see 1 Cor 10:31). The Christian's earthly vocation, including the work proper to it, does not, as such, define the Christian's being *as a Christian,* but it must be integrated into the whole existence of the Christian by being inwardly shaped by Christ's spirit. Ordinary work thus has a soteriological significance, for it can and ought to be integrated into the being of Christians as they seek, in, with, and through Christ to be a holy people and to share in Christ's redemptive work.

In addition, the entire life of the Christian is to be a preparation for the parousia, when Jesus will return in glory to bring to final completion his saving mission. Paul's prayer is that "the God of peace himself may sanctify [us] wholly," so that our whole being, "spirit, soul, and body, may be kept sound and blameless for the coming of our Lord Jesus Christ" (1 Thess 5:23-24). The ordinary, day-to-day work of the Christian thus has an eschatological significance, for through this work Christians prove themselves worthy of their vocation, give glory to God and to Christ, and prepare the way for his coming in glory (see 2 Thess 1:11-12). In fact, through their everyday work Christians can and ought to contribute to the redemption of the cosmos, to the "making new" of all things in Christ (see 1 Cor 12; Rom 12:1-8; Eph 4:7-16; Col 1:15-23).

The NT likewise, in union with the OT, stresses the duty to work and the dangers of idleness and laziness (1 Thess 4:10-11; 2 Thess 3:6-15); indeed, "whoever does not wish to work, let him not eat" (2 Thess 3:10). Work contributes to the community and allows persons not only to care for themselves but also to come to the aid of those in need—it has clearly a social significance (see Eph 4:23-28). Moreover, it enables persons to develop the talents entrusted to them (Mt 25:14-30; Lk 19:11-26).

Finally, in the perspective of the NT all human work, whether that of artisans or of lowly slaves, has a dignity because it is *human* work, the activity of persons called to union with Christ, in whom all, whether slave or free, are one (Col 3:11; Gal 6:15).

Work in the Catholic Theological Tradition

The patristic period. In the writings of many Fathers there are passages inviting Christians to sanctify their lives and their own earthly vocations, at the same time noting that some kinds of work, because of their immoral or idolatrous nature, were incompatible with Christian life. In addition, several Greek Fathers, particularly Gregory of Nyssa and Maximus the Confessor, at times offered a cosmic vision, stressing the role that human work could play in the redemption of all things in Christ—a vision that could have been developed in articulating an authentic theology of work, as could some of the sweeping themes set forth by Augustine in the theology of history found in his *City of God.* Unfortunately, however, these themes were not pursued vigorously during the patristic period. Several factors account for this. For one thing, the burning questions demanding attention at that time were the great Trinitarian and Christological issues. For another, particularly in the West, the rise of the monastic movement and an attitude that sought to flee the world inhibited the development of a theology of work.

In some ways this is paradoxical. After all, the Benedictine motto is *ora et labora.* And work was central to the monastic life. But the work carried out in the monastery, although *materially* similar to work carried out in the world, had a completely different significance. Its principal function was ascetic, a means of fighting idleness. This is poignantly illustrated by the story, told by Cassian, of Paul the Hermit. Paul devoted himself to making baskets, although there was no need for him to do so since he could maintain himself and provide alms for the poor by working a small plot of land. At the end of each year he would burn the baskets he had made (Cassian, *De institutis coenobiorum,* bk. 10, 24). In other words, work was regarded as a pure means to something else, as a way of acquiring virtues, not as an activity worthwhile in itself.

The major purposes that work could serve, as developed by theologians of the first millennium, have been well summed up by Vacek (1987, p. 1100): "Through work persons 1) become self-sufficient, and thus are no burden to others; 2) avoid idleness, the devil's workshop; 3) imitate Christ and Paul; 4) chastise the flesh; 5) gain humility and simplicity; 6) practice obedience and submission; 7) earn enough to help the needy; 8) exercise self-discipline; 9) do penance; 10) experience a leveling equality."

In short, work was esteemed by theologians at this time for the role it played in the cultivation of virtues and ministering to justice and charity; but there was no sustained effort to explore its deeper theological significance.

From the Middle Ages to the modern period. Certain developments, both sociological and theological, in the Middle Ages offered the opportunity to enrich the theological appreciation of work, but unfortunately such enrichment did not take place. Sociologically, the rise of the guilds and of military orders, which frequently had their own insurance programs, etc., posed in a fresh way the reality of human work and its significance for human life. Theologically, there was a widespread concern for justice and the common good. In addition, theologians, preeminently Thomas Aquinas, came to appreciate quite fully that human persons are called to share in God's governance of the universe (cf. in particular

Summa contra Gentes 3.21). In fact, as Thomas stressed in his initial "lectio" on Aristotle's *Nicomachean Ethics,* one of the four major "orders" within which human intelligence is exercised is the order of human culture, the order brought into being by human work. The virtue enabling human persons to make things well—one of the principal forms of work—is the virtue of art (*Summa theologiae* 1-2, 57). Thus the groundwork for a more comprehensive theology of work was present. Nonetheless, such a theology did not emerge chiefly because of the widespread attitude, derived largely from the monastic tradition, that life in the world and "worldly" work inhibited and did not contribute to the "spiritual life" of the Christian.

An even more negative attitude toward work was reflected in the highly popular *Imitation of Christ,* written on the eve of the Renaissance. In it we read: "He [man] must eat and drink, sleep and wake, labor and rest—all these natural needs have their claim on him, and it makes a devout soul feel wretched and harassed; why can't he be clear of it all, beyond the reach of sin" (bk. 1, chap. 22; similar phrases are found in bk. 1, chap. 25; bk. 3, chap. 26). The times were simply not ripe for the development of a rich theology of work.

During the Renaissance persons like Thomas More and Erasmus sought to inculcate a more positive attitude toward "worldly" activities, including work. But nothing of significance for a theology of work was articulated by theologians of the period. Luther and Calvin spoke of professions and work (which Luther described as "service to the Lord"), and they related human work to the continuation of God's creation. Nonetheless, as Illanes notes, they saw work as a service to man but as having no value of itself in God's sight; "this dualism led to a severe dichotomy between an individualistic pietism on the one hand and a humanism without theological roots on the other" (1980, p. 29).

During the 17th century efforts were made to correct the flee-the-world mentality and the highly negative attitude, reflected in works such as the *Imitation of Christ,* toward involvement with the world and with work. Francis de Sales, for example, sought to "instruct those who live in towns, in families, or at court"—those leading ordinary lives as workers in the world—in the spiritual life (*Introduction to a Devout Life,* introduction). But although his writings and that of others who followed in his steps did much good for ordinary Christians, they did not serve to stimulate renewed and deepened inquiry into the theological meaning of work. They wrote for Christians who were, indeed, "in the world," but they did not seek to show how being in the world of itself could contribute to the Christian's spiritual life. As Illanes observes, "they speak of living *like* others, of acting *in the same way as* ordinary citizens, of *joining* those who work, etc. [But] the center of their spiritual life is placed away from that world; the interior life is nourished from the cloister. Saint Jerome's celebrated phrase, 'the city is for me a prison; the wilderness a paradise' (*Epistle* 125, n. 8), is still the rule of religious spirituality, which seeks in the solitude of the cloister the strength to give content to its presence in apostolic work" (1980, p. 32). A true theology of work was yet to develop.

Contemporary developments. Several factors have helped in stimulating 20th-century theologians to initiate a true theology of work. First, the vast sociological changes, including those affecting the structure of work itself, resulting from the tremendous scientific and technological advances of our era, have made theologians aware that work is a reality that profoundly affects our existence as human persons. Theologians have been forced to take seriously the intrinsic worth of secular, worldly realities, including work. Second, various movements endeavoring to develop a lay spirituality, one profoundly in accord with the needs and real-life situations of laymen and laywomen, have played an important role in compelling theologians to consider more seriously the meaning of work in the lives of Christians. Of significance here has been, for example, the spirituality proposed by Josemaria Escriva, founder of Opus Dei, who stressed that we must love the world and ordinary, everyday work, for it is not only something that can and ought to be sanctified but is also something that of itself contributes to the ordinary Christian's growth in holiness.

No contemporary theologian holds a "penitential" view of work, that work is a punishment imposed upon humankind as a result of the Fall—although as shall be seen, an adequate theology of work must recognize that there is in a significant sense a penitential aspect to human work, which is, particularly as the labor of our bodies, quite frequently burdensome and accompanied by pain. What contemporary theologians have done is focus attention on the significance of work from the perspective of creation (better, of incarnation) and of eschatology.

Those theologians who have developed what can be called a "creationist" or "incarnationalist" theology of work (Chenu, Schoonenberg, Thomas et al.) focus on work in the sense of the "work of our hands" (and minds). Thus Chenu describes work as the activity whereby human persons share in God's creative activity: "Man fulfills himself by dominating, through his discoveries, reason, strength, and virtue that Nature which is his kingdom and out of which he creates a new world, a human world. God appointed him lord of creation" (1963, p. 10). And again: "In the encounter of man with nature, work is his proper activity, the original condition of man, the embodiment of his being" (1970, p. 371). Through work human beings "humanize the world," making it their "home" (ibid.). On this understanding of work, as Schoonenberg stresses, human persons develop themselves and in this way complete God's creative work (Schoonenberg, p. 138). Work, understood as participation in God's creative work and as fulfilling human persons, "means to make the earth subservient but also, through it, to liberate ourselves from nature, to give to ourselves the freedom to be ourselves, to have dominion" (ibid., p. 140).

In other words, for these theologians work must be viewed within the context of a creationist or incarnational theology. These theologians take their inspiration from the texts of Genesis that describe the human as the lord of all living things, as the image of God who has the power to name the animals, to till the soil and make it bear fruit. Work is considered chiefly as the work of the hands and mind, as the making of a product. Thus Chenu, for example, says that work is "first of all the making of a product. . . . It is precisely by creating a product, by accommodating himself to it, and by accepting the laws which govern its manufacture, that the worker achieves his completion as a man" (1963, pp. 26–27).

It is certainly true that human persons, through their work, order nature and construct a "new" world. It is likewise true that through the work of their hands and minds human persons "humanize" the world and make of it their "home." Indeed, today, as a result of enormous technological achievements, the human person has become, as Schoonenberg says, "a technologically equipped nomad, roaming a megapolis and even entire continents" (p. 139). Human work *is* creative, that is, productive, and there is surely a sense in which human persons "fulfill" themselves through work and participate, in a certain sense, in the "creative" work of God.

Yet it seems to me that Chenu, Schoonenberg, and others who have focused on a creationist or incarnational understanding of work have one-sidededly considered work only in as a productive kind of reality, ignoring the "labor of our bodies" and the painful, at times dehumanizing aspects of work. In addition, they have not adequately considered the possibility, clearly understood in the OT, that the very products of human creative and inventive genius, precisely because of their objectivity, can become idols, captivating human intelligence and leading humankind to forget its status as creatures who need to stand in awe before the *mysterium tremens et fascinans. Homo faber* today has, through advances in genetics, the potential to remake himself. But the potentially *dehumanizing* effects of this kind of human work have not, unfortunately, been given serious consideration by those who have developed what can be called a creationist or incarnationalist theology of work. In short, those theologians who have sought to understand work within the perspective of creation and incarnation have indeed recognized that work must be understood as an activity whereby human persons fulfill themselves and in this way complete the creative work of God. They have clearly understood the incarnational significance of human work as a way of embodying God's creative and redemptive work. But, so it seems to me, they have neglected to integrate into their theology of work an appreciation of the "labor of our bodies" and have failed to recognize the potentially dehumanizing and indeed idolatrous possibilities of human productive work.

Yet it should be noted that these creationist or incarnationalist theologies of work have rightly stressed the social significance of human work. Thus Chenu has insisted that one of the principal purposes of work is to create a "kind of social energy at the immediate service of humanity as a whole" (1963, pp. 13–14).

The eschatological meaning of work has likewise been a matter of central importance to such contemporary authors as Chenu, Schoonenberg, Savary, Thomas, and others. Work is seen as intimately related to the task of preparing for Christ's glorious coming and for ushering in the day when the whole cosmos is made new in Christ.

In addition, several writers today, for example, McCabe, seek to show that work has a sacramental meaning, precisely insofar as it plays a part in the Christian's sacramental life insofar as it can be seen as an exercise of the Christian's baptismal priesthood and a means of furthering the unity among humankind, rooted in our unity in the body of Christ that is realized most deeply in the Eucharist (McCabe, pp. 220–21).

The Magisterium and Work

Here I will first summarize briefly some major themes relevant to a theology of work found in papal social teaching from Leo XIII through Paul VI. I will then center attention on the teaching of Vatican Council II and of John Paul II insofar as these sources provide a synthesis and development of prior magisterial teaching.

Papal social teaching from Leo XIII through Paul VI emphasized the great human significance of work. In particular this teaching affirmed that human work is humanly and theologically meaningful insofar as it (1) contributes to the development or fulfillment of human persons; (2) enables human beings to exercise their dominion over the created universe and in this way participate in God's creative work; (3) allows them to provide for human needs and (4) give service to God and neighbor; (5) contributes to the glory of God and the preparation for our Lord's glorious coming; and (6) plays a role in the expiation of sin. (For a development of these themes and references to pertinent documents see Rodriguez, 1975, pp. 653–54.)

But it is important to note that these popes likewise warned against an overevaluation of work and of the dangers to human dignity posed by the development of technology and a "technological spirit." Their principal concerns were to stress the dignity of the worker and of work as a free activity of human persons; to secure the rights of workers, particularly to a living and, indeed, to a family wage; to instill in all a love for the common good not only of individual nations but of the whole human race; and to help everyone recognize that the material goods of the universe are intended to serve the needs of all human persons, in particular the weak and the poor. In addition, there was clear recognition of the dignity of all human work, including the "labor of our bodies," precisely because of the priceless dignity of the human persons who are the subjects of work.

It is in the teaching of Vatican Council II and of John Paul II that we find a rich synthesis and development of previous papal and theological reflection on the significance of human work. Thus Vatican Council II recognizes fully the creationist (or incarnationalist), redemptive, and eschatological meaning of human work. Thus in *Gaudium et spes* we read: "Human work . . . proceeds from the human person, who as it were impresses his seal on the things of nature and reduces them to his will. By his work, a man ordinarily provides for himself and his family, associates with others as his brothers, and renders them service; he can exercise genuine charity and be a partner in the work of bringing divine creation to perfection. Moreover, we believe by faith that through the homage of work offered to God man is associated in the redemptive work of Jesus Christ" (GS 67). This passage clearly stresses the significance of work as a participation in the creative and redemptive work of God.

The eschatological meaning of work is well brought out in another passage from *Gaudium et spes* in which the council teaches that the Lord's command is to "spread on earth the fruits of our nature and our enterprise (*industriae*)—human dignity, brotherly communion, and freedom," that is, the goods that "we will find again . . . transfigured" in the completed kingdom of "truth and life, holiness and grace, justice, love, and peace" (GS 39).

In addition, by focusing attention on the distinctive and indispensable role that laypeople, precisely by reason of their worldly or secular character, have to play in continuing Christ's redemptive work, the council clearly indicated that human work is not only a reality that can and ought to be sanctified but also one in and through which human persons grow in Christ and holiness (see *Lumen gentium,* chaps. 4 and 5; *Apostolicam actuositatem*). This theme, highly important to a theology of work, was developed at the synod of 1987 and by John Paul II in his apostolic exhortation *Christifideles laici* (1989). A passage from Vatican II's *Lumen gentium* is of special relevance here: "The Lord desires that his kingdom be spread by the lay faithful . . . [who] must recognize the inner nature, the value and ordering of the whole of creation to the praise of God. By their secular activity they must aid one another to a greater holiness of life, so that the world may be filled with the spirit of Christ and may the more effectively attain its destiny in justice, love, and peace. . . . By their competence in secular disciplines and by their activity, interiorly raised by grace, let them work earnestly in order that created goods may, through human labor, technical skill, and civil culture, serve the good of all men according to the plan of our creator and the light of his Word" (LG 36; AA 7).

In his encyclical *Laborem exercens,* John Paul II developed and deepened many of these conciliar themes with respect to work. He sharply distinguished between the objective sense of work, i.e., the results of work, and its subjective sense as the free and self-determining activity of human persons (LE 5–6), and he emphasized the intrinsic value of work in its subjective sense. For this reason work, including the "labor of our bodies," has an inherent dignity: "The basis for determining the value of human work is not primarily the kind of work being done but the fact that the one doing it is a person" (LE 6). For him work is good not only in the sense that it is useful but also in the sense of being something worthy, corresponding to human dignity and capable of expressing this dignity precisely because through work the human person not only transforms nature (the creative aspect of work) but also and more importantly achieves fulfillment as a human being and "in a sense, becomes more of a human being" (LE 9).

With previous popes John Paul recognizes that human persons can be exploited and degraded because of the conditions under which they are at times made to work. But he teaches that the principal factor contributing to the degradation of human workers is caused when all personal satisfaction and incentives to creativity and responsibility are denied to workers and, above all, when they are made unable to recognize that they are, in a true sense, working for themselves as free and responsible persons (LE 5).

John Paul II devotes much of his encyclical to a "spirituality of work" (LE 24–27). Here, following Vatican Council II, he centers attention on the creative, redemptive, and eschatological significance of human work. In addition, he emphasizes that it is only in the light of the cross that the full meaning of human work can be understood. He recognizes that at times work is painful and burdensome, but "by enduring the toil of work in union with Christ crucified for us, man in a way collaborates with the Son of God for the redemption of humanity" (LE 27). Then turning to the eschatological meaning of work, he concludes the encyclical by affirming that we can, by viewing work from the perspective of Christ's resurrection, find a glimmer of new life, "an announcement of 'the new heavens and the new earth' in which man and the world participate precisely through the toil of work. . . . Is not this new good—the fruit of human work—already a small part of that 'new earth' where justice dwells?" (LE 27).

Elements of a Theology of Work

From the foregoing it seems reasonable to conclude with Illanes (1975, pp. 657–58; 1980, pp. 89–93) that the major elements in a theology of work are the following: (1) work and the building up of the universe; (2) work and our personal vocation to share in Christ's redemptive work; (3) work and eschatology; and (4) work and suffering.

Work and the building of the universe. Here the themes of creation and incarnation are central. The starting point is provided by the Genesis texts already noted (1:27-28; 2:15). Human persons are utterly unique in the universe precisely because, as beings made in the image and likeness of God, they are persons, that is, beings of moral worth or dignity. They have the radical capacity to know the truth and to determine their own lives by free choices, which ought to be made in accordance with the truth they come to know.

As persons, they share in God's providence, for God has entrusted to them the task not only of providing for themselves but also for the entire universe. Thomas Aquinas distinguished four distinct "orders" to which human intelligence is related: (1) the order it discovers and does not invent—the order of nature investigated by the natural sciences and speculative philosophy; (2) the order that the intellect imposes on its own activities and products—the order of logic and mathematics; (3) the order that it brings into human choices and actions—the order of morality and ethics; and (4) the order that it brings about through human enterprise—the order of culture, the order to which "work" pertains (*In decem libros ethicorum Aristotelis expositio* 1.1.2). Through work human persons bring this order into existence and in this way contribute to the unity of the universe, which is a unity of actions based on the inner connection of causalities (*Summa theologiae,* 1, 104, 2, ad 1). In fact, the development of contemporary technology, which has so profoundly transformed the world of human work, was made possible by the discovery of the laws of nature and the organizing of the world of work in such a way as to cooperate with these laws in structuring the world brought into being through human endeavors.

Yet human persons, as workers, must never forget that they are not, properly, creators. Rather they are creatures wholly dependent upon God. The created universe has been entrusted to them so that they can care for it, not destroy it. The failure to recognize this has in large measure contributed to the dangers facing our environment today. In order properly to fulfill their mission of building up the universe and in this way participating in God's creative and providential plan, human persons must see their work as an activity in which they render glory to God by respecting God's dominion over all of creation and by respecting the intrinsic finalities of created things.

An incarnational motif is also present here. The God of Christian faith is the God who is revealed through created realities; indeed, this God has taken flesh in order to disclose God's love more fully to humankind. And the response of human persons to this call of God's love must itself be incarnated in actions, in work carried out in union with God and God's incarnate Son.

Work and our personal vocation to share in Christ's redemptive work. Our common vocation as Christians is to seek holiness, for we are called to sanctity, to perfection (see Mt 5:48; 1 Thess 4:3; Eph 1:4; 1 Pet 1:14-16). We are to participate in Christ's redemptive work, making up in our lives, our own bodies, what is lacking to Christ's and in this way redeeming the universe (see Col 1:24; Phil 3:21). But in addition, as Vatican II (GS 43), and John Paul II (*Redemptor hominis* 71) have insisted, each one of us has a unique, personal vocation, an indispensable role to play in redeeming all things in Christ.

Laypersons, in particular, "follow" Christ *in the world*, because they are distinguished by their secular character. Consequently, "by reason of their special vocation it belongs to the laity to seek the kingdom of God by engaging in temporal affairs and directing them according to God's will. They live in the world, i.e., they are engaged in each and every work and business of the earth and in the ordinary circumstances of social and familial life which, as it were, constitute their very existence. There they are called by God that, being led by the spirit of the Gospel, they may contribute to the sanctification of the world, as from within like leaven, by fulfilling their particular duties" (GS 31; see GS 36 and AA 7). But this common vocation of the laity can be fulfilled only if each layman and laywoman discovers his or her own personal vocation, developing his or her special gifts in the service of God and neighbor (see GS 43; Grisez, pp. 559–62).

What this means is that the inner, spiritual life of the Christian cannot be merely juxtaposed in extrinsic fashion to his or her professional life as a worker, whatever the work may be. Rather, one's everyday work must be integrated into one's whole existence so that one's daily work is not only in harmony with the great truths of Christian faith but is inwardly shaped and transformed by these truths.

Work and eschatology. Here the key idea is that set forth at Vatican Council II and noted already (GS 39), namely that there is a real continuity between God's kingdom or reign as already present in our midst and the fullness of this kingdom that will be realized in the eschaton. Human work, properly undertaken, is not a mere means, instrumental in character, to an end utterly extrinsic to it, like mowing a lawn in order to gain some money. Rather it is itself a meaningful participation in those precious goods and fruits of human existence that will continue, now transformed, in the new heavens and the new earth. Human activity rightly undertaken is fulfilled in the paschal mystery. For "when we have spread on earth the fruits of our nature and enterprise—human dignity, brotherly communion, and freedom—according to the command of the Lord and in his Spirit, we will find them once again, cleansed this time from the stain of sin, illuminated and transfigured, when Christ presents to his Father an eternal and universal kingdom, a 'kingdom of truth and life, a kingdom of holiness and grace, a kingdom of justice, love, and peace.' Here on earth the kingdom is mysteriously present; when the Lord comes it will enter into its perfection" (GS 39). In short, what will be transfigured in the eschaton is not *any* world but *this* world, that is, the world shaped by human work and effort.

Work and suffering. Although it is wrong to look upon work primarily as a penance for sin, it is most important to keep in mind that human persons are sinners and that there is indeed an expiatory element in work, particularly in the "labor of our bodies." Work in the world does in fact entail toil and sweat, suffering and pain. Here we must keep in mind that redemption implies the cross, and that each one of us in participating in Christ's redemptive work is likewise called to take up our own cross each day and bear it patiently and in union with Christ. No theology of work can forget this.

Christ saved us by becoming flesh and suffering in the flesh. By doing so he shows us that the "labor of our bodies," so demeaned by the pagans, is, like the work of our hands and minds, worthy of human persons and has a role to play in building the universe, fulfilling our vocation, and preparing for the eschaton. One of the reasons why many throughout history, including our present times, look upon the "labor of our bodies" as intrinsically demeaning—servile—is that they hold the body in low esteem. They are infected with the Gnostic and Manichean view that the human body is a thing or instrument *of* the person. But Christians believe that the human body is integral to the person and is indeed the sacrament of the person. Human labor, painful as it frequently is as a result of sin, is itself something inherently full of dignity and value, for it is the act of a person (the subjective aspect of work). Through labor we can and do serve God and neighbor; in and through the labor of our bodies we can and do participate in the sufferings of Christ and, through them, in the redemption that he accomplishes and wills to bring to completion by making us his co-workers. No adequate theology of work can neglect this dimension of the reality of human work.

See also CREATION; CULTURE; ESCHATOLOGY; GAUDIUM ET SPES; LABOREM EXERCENS; LAITY, ROLE OF; SPIRITUALITY; VATICAN COUNCIL II.

Bibliography: H. Arendt, *The Human Condition* (Chicago: Univ. of Chicago Press, 1958). J. Bauer, "Work," in *Sacramentum Verbi* (New York: Herder & Herder, 1970) 3:995–1001. G. Bertram, "ergon," in *Theological Dictionary of the New Testament,* G. Kittel and G. Friedrich, eds., G. Bromiley, trans. (Grand Rapids: Eerdmans, 1964) 2:635–55. Braun, "poieo," in *Theological Dictionary of the New Testament,* 6:458–83. M.-D. Chenu, *The Theology of Work,* L. Soiron, trans. (Chicago: Regnery, 1963). M.-D. Chenu, "Work," in *Sacramentum Mundi* (New York: Herder & Herder, 1970) 6:368–72. J. Finnis, "The Fundamental Themes of Laborem Exercens," in *Catholic Social Thought and the Teaching of John Paul II: Proceedings of the Fifth Convention (1982) of the Fellowship of Catholic Scholars* (Scranton Pa.: Northeast Books, 1983) pp. 19–31. G. Goesen, *The Theology of Work* (Dublin: Mercier, 1974). G. Grisez, *Christian Moral Principles* (Chicago: Franciscan Herald Press, 1983). J. Illanes Maestre, "Trabajo, humano. VII. Teologia," *Gran Enciclopedia Rialp* (Madrid, 1975) 22:654–59. J. Illanes Maestre, *On the Theology of Work: Aspects of the Teaching of the Founder of Opus Dei* (New Rochelle, N.Y.: Scepter, 1980). E. Kaiser, *Theology of Work* (Westminster, Md.: Newman, 1963). E. Kaiser, "Work," in *New Catholic Encyclopedia* (New York: McGraw-Hill, 1965) 15:1015–17. W. May, "Animal Laborans and Homo Faber: Reflections on a Theology of Work," *Thomist* 36 (1972) 626–44. A. Rodriguez, "Trabajo, humano. VI. Doctrina Social Cristiana," *Gran Enciclopedia Rialp* (Madrid, 1975) 22:653–54. L. Savary, ed., *Man: His World and His Work,* articles by L. Savary, J. Thomas et al. (New York: Paulist, 1967). P. Schoonenberg, *God's World in the Making* (Pittsburgh: Duquesne Univ. Press, 1964). J. Todd, ed., *Work: Christian Thought and Practice,* especially H. McCabe, "Theology and Work—A Thomist Perspective," pp. 212–25 (Baltimore: Helicon, 1960). E. Vacek, "Work," in J. Komanchak et al., *The New Dic-*

tionary of Theology (Wilmington, Del.: Glazier, 1987) pp. 1099–1105.

WILLIAM E. MAY

WORKER PRIESTS

"Worker priests" is that term given to Christian clergy, mostly Catholic, who are sent by their church officially to enter the full-time work force, there to exercise an apostolic vocation. Although the term has been applied loosely to any member of the clergy or religious (there are worker nuns and lay brothers as well) who work outside of traditional religious vocations, this broader definition is a distortion. More precisely, the nature of work defined by the title "worker priest" is oppressive toil among the urban and rural proletariat. The purpose of this clergy is incarnational—to identify fully with the marginalized and exploited toilers by adopting their lifestyle in toto.

Although the movement had its forerunners, it began in earnest in Belgium and France during the Second World War. The growing realization that the industrial work force was outside of, even against, the church led some visionaries to call for more radical means to reach this sector of the population. Two Catholic Action chaplains, Henri Godin and Yvan Daniel, wrote a manifesto *France pays de mission?* which challenged the status quo and called for special nonparish missions in the midst of the working class. Seminarians, clandestine chaplains, and prisoner-of-war priests returned from German imprisonment advocating a priesthood that would toil to earn its bread. Emmanuel Cardinal Suhard, archbishop of Paris, took up their cause. His support of the various radical missions to the proletariat in the 1940s was essential to their creation and survival. In spite of Vatican suspicion and right-wing Catholic hostility, the ailing cardinal defended the worker priests and their colleagues.

At first the worker priests lived in the proletarian ghettos of Paris, Lyon, Marseille, Lille, and other cities without gainful employment, but gradually they convinced their bishops that factory toil was essential to a full incarnation. Soon they became union militants and active partisans of the peace movement. They worked for substantive social change, led strikes, were arrested in peace marches, and were elected to important trade-union posts. Their brothers and sisters in solidarity were often grass-roots Communists, and most of these working priests joined Communist-led unions instead of the more timid reformist unions linked to the Catholic federation. Traditional Catholics were scandalized, and pressure was put on the French and Vatican hierarchy to close down the movement. Pius XII, caught up in the anticommunist cold war crusade and concerned lest the church lose control of its priests, ordered France's three leading cardinals to circumscribe the experiment. In spite of a massive outcry of protest in France, the worker priests were ordered to lay down their tools and turn in their union cards by March 1, 1954. Approximately half obeyed, half did not.

The story, however, did not end with this tragedy. Worker priests were restored by decree at the Second Vatican Council, and today they are found in countries throughout the world among Catholic, Protestant, and Eastern Orthodox clergy. The vision of their incarnation, vowed so poignantly by one of their pioneers, remains constant to the present day: "I commit my life and offer all that I am . . . to become and to be a true worker while, at the same time, a priest among the workers, just as you have been a man, God among men (*sic*). To take up and carry in my priestly heart their entire life, work, poverty, struggles, sufferings and hopes, the humiliations of their most base conditions. . . . To place my destiny with their destiny and my life with their life and to be in communion with all their aspirations" (Henri Barreau papers).

See also CAPITALISM; CATHOLIC WORKER, THE; CLASS STRUGGLE; COMMUNISM; MANUAL LABOR; WORK, THEOLOGY OF.

Bibliography: O. Arnal, *Priests in Working-Class Blue* (New York: Paulist, 1986). E. Poulat, *Naissance des prêtres-ouvriers* (Paris: Casterman, 1965). J. Petrie, ed., *The Worker-Priests* (London: Routledge & Kegan Paul, 1956). H. Perrin, *Itinéraire d'Henri Perrin* (Paris: Seuil, 1958).

OSCAR COLE ARNAL

INDEX

Pax Christi, 716–17. *See also* arms race; deterrence; conscience; disarmament; pacifism; peace